D1436166

# ERRATA

In the following cases the 1992 turnout percentage had mistakenly been given in place of the winning party's percentage. The figures should be:

**Page 55**
Aberavon: 53.2%
Aberdeen Central: 14.3%
Aberdeen North: 11.3%

**Page 56**
Aberdeen South: 10.7%

**Page 57**
Aldershot: 31.7%
Aldridge-Brownhills: 21.1%
Altrincham & Sale West: 28.1%

**Page 58**
Alyn & Deeside: 14.0%
Amber Valley: 2.1%
Angus: 1.1%

**Page 59**
Antrim East: 18.5%
Antrim North: 32.8%

**Page 60**
Argyll & Bute: 7.2%
Arundel & South Downs: 37.7%
Ashfield: 22.2%

**Page 61**
Ashford: 30.5%
Ashton under Lyme: 28.3%
Aylesbury: 29.5%

**Page 63**
Barnsley Central: 52.2%

**Page 64**
Barnsley West & Penistone: 30.2%
Barrow & Furness: 6.4%

**Page 65**
Bath: 3.5%

**Page 66**
Beaconsfield: 44.3%

**Page 67**
Bedford: 9.0%
Bedfordshire Mid: 41.2%

**Page 68**
Bedfordshire SW: 30.3%

**Page 69**
Belfast North: 33.5%

**Page 70**
Berwick-Upon-Tweed: 11.6%
Beverley & Holderness: 29.2%

**Page 71**
Bexleyheath & Crayford: 22.9%
Billericay: 35.3%

**Page 72**
Birmingham Edgbaston: 10.0%
Birmingham Erdington: 16.8%

**Page 73**
Birmingham Hodge Hill: 17.3%
Birmingham Ladywood: 51.0%

**Page 74**
Birmingham Northfield: 3.4%

**Page 75**
Bishop Auckland: 14.8%

**Page 76**
Blackburn: 10.9%

**Page 77**
Blackpool South: 0.7%
Blaenau Gwent: 69.2%
Blaydon: 26.0%

**Page 78**
Blyth Valley: 16.4%
Bognor Regis & Littlehampton: 30.2%
Bolsover: 39.2%

**Page 79**
Bolton North East: 5.4%
Bolton South East: 25.6%
Bolton West: 8.2%

**Page 80**
Bootle: 62.4%
Boston & Skegness: 22.6%
Bosworth: 25.2%

**Page 81**
Bournemouth East: 24.4%

**Page 82**
Bradford North: 15.6%
Bradford West: 19.4%

**Page 83**
Braintree: 23.1%
Brent East: 16.2%

**Page 84**
Brent North: 27.1%
Brent South: 26.5%
Brentford & Isleworth: 2.8%

**Page 85**
Brentwood & Ongar: 27.2%
Bridgend: 15.6%
Bridgwater: 17.1%

**Page 86**
Brigg & Goole: 14.2%
Brighton Kemptown: 20.2%

**Page 87**
Bristol East: 9.7%
Bristol North West: 6.4%
Bristol South: 14.1%

**Page 88**
Bromley & Chislehurst: 44.2%
Bromsgrove: 23.4%

**Page 89**
Broxtowe: 16.2%
Buckingham: 41.4%

**Page 90**
Burnley: 22.4%
Burton: 7.0%
Bury North: 8.1%

**Page 91**
Bury South: 1.4%
Bury St Edmunds: 19.0%

**Page 92**
Caerphilly: 45.6%
Caithness, Sutherland & Easter Ross: 22.8%
Calder Valley: 8.0%

**Page 93**
Camberwell & Peckham: 36.6%
Cambridge: 1.2%
Cambridgeshire North East: 22.6%

**Page 94**
Cambridgeshire North West: 36.5%
Cambridgeshire South East: 36.3%

**Page 95**
Cannock Chase: 10.8%
Canterbury: 17.8%
Cardiff Central: 8.1%

**Page 97**
Carmarthen East & Dinefwr: 12.4%
Carmarthen West & Pembrokeshire South: 3.0%

**Page 98**
Carrick, Cumnock & Doon Valley: 28.4%
Carshalton & Wallington: 18.8%

**Page 99**
Ceredigion: 4.5%

**Page 100**
Cheadle: 28.1%
Chelmsford West: 25.9%
Cheltenham: 2.9%

**Page 101**
Chesham & Amersham: 38.9%
Chester, City of: 4.1%
Chesterfield: 11.5%

**Page 102**
Chichester: 32.7%
Chipping Barnet: 30.4%

**Page 103**
Chorley: 4.2%
Cities of London & Westminster: 35.2%

**Page 104**
Cleethorpes: 12.1%
Clwyd West: 17.6%

**Page 105**
Clydebank & Milngavie: 28.8%

**Page 107**
Conwy: 2.3%
Copeland: 5.3%
Corby: 0.6%

**Page 108**
Cornwall South East: 12.9%
Cotswold: 21.0%

**Page 109**
Coventry North West: 14.2%
Coventry South: 5.1%

**Page 110**
Crawley: 3.7%
Crewe & Nantwich: 8.7%
Crosby: 20.0%

**Page 111**
Croydon Central: 24.0%
Croydon North: 0.3%
Croydon South: 40.1%

**Page 112**
Cumbernauld & Kilsyth: 25.1%
Cunninghame North: 6.9%
Cunninghame South: 28.7%

**Page 113**
Cynon Valley: 56.2%
Darlington: 5.1%

**Page 114**
Dartford: 14.7%
Daventry: 33.9%
Delyn: 7.3%

**Page 115**
Denton & Reddish: 19.1%
Derby North: 7.5%
Derby South: 7.4%

**Page 116**
Derbyshire North East: 10.6%
Derbyshire South: 3.1%
Derbyshire West: 30.7%

**Page 117**
Devizes: 20.6%
Devon North: 1.4%

**Page 118**
Devon South West: 32.0%
Devon West & Torridge: 5.4%
Dewsbury: 7.3%

**Page 119**
Don Valley: 13.8%
Doncaster Central: 20.8%
Doncaster North: 42.1%

**Page 120**
Dorset North: 19.1%
Dorset South: 24.3%

**Page 121**
Dorset West: 14.7%
Dover: 1.5%

**Page 122**
Dudley North: 1.7%

**Page 123**
Dulwich & West Norwood: 3.5%
Dumbarton: 13.9%

**Page 124**
Dundee East: 12.2%
Dundee West: 23.1%
Dunfermline East: 46.6%

**Page 125**
Dunfermline West: 18.5%
Durham North: 35.0%
Durham North West: 30.7%

**Page 126**
Durham, City of: 29.6%
Ealing North: 15.6%

**Page 127**
Ealing Southall: 9.0%

**Page 128**
East Kilbride: 23.8%

**Pages 13, 249 & 347**
The MP for Totnes is Anthony Steen (not Sir Anthony)

**Page 296**
Labour seats won in Glamorgan Mid should read 7, Conservatives 0

# THE TIMES
## Guide to
# THE HOUSE OF COMMONS
## MAY 1997

## Edited by Tim Austin

ASSOCIATE EDITOR
### Ruth Winstone

PARLIAMENTARY CONSULTANT
### Alan H. Wood

**TIMES BOOKS**
**London**

Published by Times Books
77-85 Fulham Palace Road
London W6 8JB

Compiled by Clive Cardy, William Cater, Steve Gibbs, Robert Hands, Rachel Jenkinson, Robert Morgan, David Segrove and Wendy Showell

Additional research by James Ashton and Angus Hampel

Cartoons by Richard Willson

Pictures by Flying Colours

Map by Times Graphics Department

Printed and bound in Great Britain by
Caledonian International Book Manufacturers

British Library Cataloguing in Publication Data.
A catalogue record for this book is available from
the British Library.

ISBN 0-7230-0956-2

# CONTENTS

# THE GENERAL ELECTION 1997

**T**HE GENERAL ELECTION on May 1, 1997, swept the Labour Party led by Tony Blair into power with a massive overall majority of 178 seats in a House of Commons of 659 MPs, eight more than in 1992 because of boundary changes. The Conservatives were wiped out in Scotland and Wales and suffered severe losses in all parts of England. The Liberal Democrats made inroads into the Tories, ending with 46 seats compared with 26 at the dissolution of the last Parliament.

Within a few days the entire ministerial team was in place, the Cabinet making history with its five women occupants reflecting the fact that 101 members of the 418-strong Parliamentary Labour Party were women, yet another record. And Mr Blair had six new life peers in government appointments in the House of Lords, including two of the four law officers. John Prescott, deputy Labour leader, became Deputy Prime Minister and Secretary of State for the huge Department of Environment and Transport. As expected, Gordon Brown became Chancellor of the Exchequer and Robin Cook Foreign Secretary. The women Cabinet members were Margaret Beckett, President of the Board of Trade and Trade and Industry Secretary; Ann Taylor, Leader of the Commons; Harriet Harman, Social Security Secretary; Marjorie Mowlam, Northern Ireland Secretary, and Clare Short, International Development Secretary.

John Major, Prime Minister from November 1990, immediately announced his resignation as Conservative Party leader, setting off a Tory leadership campaign involving five ministers from his last Cabinet — Kenneth Clarke, Michael Howard, Peter Lilley, Stephen Dorrell and William Hague — plus the former Welsh Secretary John Redwood. In the election, seven Tory Cabinet ministers lost their seats.

Seven days after election day, the Conservative MP for Uxbridge, Sir Michael Shersby, died from a heart attack, precipitating the first by-election of the new Parliament.

The state of the parties in the Commons after this election compared with dissolution and the outcome of the 1992 election is:

|  | 1997 | Dissolution | April 1992 |
|---|---|---|---|
| Labour | 418 | 273 | 271 |
| Conservative | 165 | 324 | 336 |
| Liberal Democrat | 46 | 26 | 20 |
| Ulster Unionist | 10 | 9 | 9 |
| Scottish National | 6 | 4 | 3 |
| Plaid Cymru | 4 | 4 | 4 |
| Social Democratic and Labour | 3 | 4 | 4 |
| Democratic Unionist | 2 | 3 | 3 |
| Sinn Fein | 2 | — | — |
| Ulster Popular Unionist | — | — | 1 |
| UK Unionist | 1 | 1 | — |
| Independent | 1 | — | — |
| The Speaker | 1 | 1 | — |
| Vacant seats | — | 2 | — |
| **Totals** | **659** | **651** | **651** |

Because of the huge boundary changes, gains and losses are more easily identified by area. For instance, in Greater London the Tories ended up with only 11 seats compared with 41 in 1992; the South East region 73 (112 in 1992); East Anglia 14 (19); East Midlands 14 (29); the North West 7 (25); Northern 3 (6); South West 22 (39); West Midlands 14 (31); Yorks and Humberside 7 (22).

In by-elections during the 1992-97 Parliament, the Conservatives lost eight seats: Newbury, Christchurch, and Eastleigh to the Liberal Democrats; Dudley West (to Labour); Perth & Kinross (to the Scottish National Party); Littleborough & Saddleworth (to the Liberal Democrats); Staffordshire South East, and Wirral South, to Labour. In the only Ulster by-election, at Down North, the UK Unionists gained the seat from the Ulster Popular Unionists. The Conservatives also lost three seats by defections — Alan Howarth (Stratford-on-Avon) was the first Conservative MP to cross the floor of the House and join the Labour Party, becoming MP for Newport East at the election; and Emma Nicholson (Devon West & Torridge) and Peter Thurnham (Bolton North East) joined the Liberal Democrats but failed to find seats.

# HER MAJESTY'S GOVERNMENT

## THE CABINET

**Prime Minister, First Lord of the Treasury and Minister for the Civil Service**
Tony Blair

**Deputy Prime Minister and Secretary of State for Environment, Transport and the Regions**
John Prescott

**Lord Chancellor**
Lord Irvine of Lairg

**Secretary of State for Foreign and Commonwealth Affairs**
Robin Cook

**Chancellor of the Exchequer**
Gordon Brown

**Secretary of State for the Home Department**
Jack Straw

**President of the Board of Trade and Secretary of State for Trade and Industry**
Margaret Beckett

**Secretary of State for Defence**
George Robertson

**Lord Privy Seal and Leader of the House of Lords**
Lord Richard

**President of the Council and Leader of the House of Commons**
Ann Taylor

**Secretary of State for National Heritage**
Chris Smith

**Secretary of State for Education and Employment**
David Blunkett

**Secretary of State for Social Security and Minister for Women**
Harriet Harman

**Chancellor of the Duchy of Lancaster**
David Clark

**Secretary of State for Scotland**
Donald Dewar

**Secretary of State for Northern Ireland**
Marjorie (Mo) Mowlam

**Secretary of State for Health**
Frank Dobson

**Minister of Agriculture, Fisheries and Food**
Jack Cunningham

**Chief Secretary to the Treasury**
Alistair Darling

**Secretary of State for Wales**
Ron Davies

**Secretary of State for International Development**
Clare Short

**Minister for Transport**
Gavin Strang

## DEPARTMENTS OF STATE AND MINISTERS

### AGRICULTURE, FISHERIES AND FOOD

**Minister**
Jack Cunningham

**Minister of State:**

**Minister for Food Safety and Animal Health**
Jeff Rooker

**Parliamentary Secretaries:**

**Minister for Fisheries and Countryside**
Elliot Morley

**Minister for Farming and Food Industry**
Lord Donoughue

### CABINET OFFICE

**Deputy Prime Minister and Secretary of State for Environment, Transport and the Regions**
John Prescott

**Chancellor of the Duchy of Lancaster**
David Clark

**Minister without Portfolio**
Peter Mandelson

**Under Secretary of State, Office of Public Service**
Peter Kilfoyle

### DEFENCE

**Secretary of State**
George Robertson

**Ministers of State:**

**Minister for Defence Procurement**
Lord Gilbert

**Minister for Armed Forces**
John Reid

**Under Secretary of State:**
John Spellar (Service personnel, environmental protection)

### EDUCATION AND EMPLOYMENT

**Secretary of State**
David Blunkett

**Ministers of State:**

**Minister for Employment and Disability Rights**
Andrew Smith

**Minister for School Standards**
Stephen Byers

**Minister for Higher Education**
Baroness Blackstone

**Under Secretaries of State:**

**Minister for Schools Standards**
Estelle Morris

**Minister for Lifelong Learning**
Kim Howells

**Minister for Employment and Equal Opportunities**
Alan Howarth

### ENVIRONMENT & TRANSPORT

**Deputy Prime Minister and Secretary of State**
John Prescott

**Minister for Transport**
Gavin Strang

**Ministers of State:**

**Minister for the Environment**
Michael Meacher

**Minister for Local Government and Housing**
Hilary Armstrong

**Minister for the Regions, Regeneration and Planning**
Richard Caborn

**Under Secretaries of State:**

**Minister for London and Construction**
Nick Raynsford

**Minister for Transport in London**
Glenda Jackson

**Minister for Roads**
Baroness Hayman

**Junior Minister for Environment and Regions**
Angela Eagle

### FOREIGN AND COMMONWEALTH AFFAIRS

**Secretary of State**
Robin Cook

**Ministers of State:**
Doug Henderson (Minister for Europe)
Derek Fatchett (Far East, South East Asia, Pacific and Middle East)
Tony Lloyd (Latin America, Africa)

**Under Secretary of State:**
Baroness Symons
of Vernham Dean (North America, Caribbean)

### HEALTH

**Secretary of State**
Frank Dobson

**Ministers of State:**
Alan Milburn (NHS structure and resources)

**Minister for Public Health**
Tessa Jowell

Baroness Jay of Paddington
Deputy Leader of House of Lords
(NHS services, scientific and pharmaceutical issues)

# HER MAJESTY'S GOVERNMENT

**Under Secretary of State:**
Paul Boateng (social care and mental health)

## HOME OFFICE
**Secretary of State**
Jack Straw (security issues, terrorism, royal matters and public spending)
**Ministers of State:**
**Minister for Crime and Police**
Alun Michael
**Minister for Prisons and Immigration**
Joyce Quin
**Under Secretaries of State:**
George Howarth (prisons, gambling and drugs)
Mike O'Brien (immigration and nationality; community relations)
Lord Williams of Mostyn (constitution)

## INTERNATIONAL DEVELOPMENT
**Secretary of State (overseas development, aid and pensions)**
Clare Short
**Under Secretary of State**
George Foulkes

## LAW OFFICERS
**Attorney-General**
John Morris
**Solicitor-General**
Lord Falconer of Thoroton
**Lord Advocate**
Lord Hardie
**Solicitor-General for Scotland**
Colin Boyd

## LORD CHANCELLOR'S DEPARTMENT
**Lord Chancellor**
Lord Irvine of Lairg
**Parliamentary Secretary**
Geoffrey Hoon

## NATIONAL HERITAGE
**Secretary of State**
Chris Smith
**Minister of State:**
**Minister for Film and Tourism**
Tom Clarke
**Under Secretaries of State:**
**Minister for Sport**
Tony Banks
**Minister for the Arts**
Mark Fisher

## NORTHERN IRELAND OFFICE
**Secretary of State**
Marjorie (Mo) Mowlam
**Ministers of State:**
**Minister for Security and Economic Development**
Adam Ingram
**Minister for Stormont Talks, Finance and Personnel**
Paul Murphy

**Under Secretary of State:**
**Minister for Education, Employment and Health**
Tony Worthington
**Minister for Environment and Agriculture**
Lord Dubs

## PRIVY COUNCIL OFFICE
**President of the Council and Leader of the Commons**
Ann Taylor
**Lord Privy Seal and Leader of the House of Lords**
Lord Richard

## SCOTTISH OFFICE
**Secretary of State**
Donald Dewar
**Ministers of State:**
**Minister for Home Affairs and Devolution**
Henry McLeish
**Minister for Education and Industry**
Brian Wilson
**Under Secretaries of State:**
**Minister for Local Government and Transport**
Malcolm Chisholm
**Minister for Health and the Arts**
Sam Galbraith
**Minister for Agriculture, Fisheries and Food**
Lord Sewel

## SOCIAL SECURITY
**Secretary of State and Minister for Women**
Harriet Harman
**Minister of State:**
**Minister for Welfare Reform**
Frank Field
**Under Secretaries of State:**
Keith Bradley (jobseeker's allowance, family credit, housing benefit and income support)
John Denham (fraud, pensions, NI contributions, long-term care)
Baroness Hollis of Heigham (child benefit, one-parent benefit, Child Support Agency)

## TRADE AND INDUSTRY
**President of the Board of Trade and Secretary of State for Trade and Industry**
Margaret Beckett
**Ministers of State:**
**Minister for Trade and Competitiveness in Europe**
Lord Simon of Highbury
**Minister for Trade and Exports**
Lord Clinton-Davis
**Minister for Labour Market, Company Law and Corporate Affairs**
Ian McCartney
**Minister for Manufacturing and Services, Energy, Science and Technology**
John Battle

**Under Secretaries of State:**
**Minister for Consumer Affairs**
Nigel Griffiths
**Minister for Small Firms**
Barbara Roche

## TREASURY
**Prime Minister, First Lord of the Treasury and Minister for the Civil Service**
Tony Blair
**Chancellor of the Exchequer**
Gordon Brown
**Chief Secretary (control of spending)**
Alistair Darling
**Financial Secretary (Customs revenues and taxes)**
Dawn Primarolo
**Paymaster General (Private Finance Initiative and privatisation issues)**
Geoffrey Robinson
**Economic Secretary (financial services and City regulation)**
Helen Liddell

## WELSH OFFICE
**Secretary of State**
Ron Davies
**Under Secretaries of State:**
Peter Hain (economic development and industry, education, Europe)
Win Griffiths (children and countryside, agriculture, health)

## GOVERNMENT WHIPS
**House of Commons**
**Parliamentary Secretary to the Treasury (Government Chief Whip)**
Nick Brown
**Treasurer of HM Household (Deputy Chief Whip)**
George Mudie
**Comptroller of HM Household**
Thomas McAvoy
**Vice-Chamberlain of HM Household**
Janet Anderson
**Lords Commissioners**
Robert Ainsworth; Graham Allen; James Dowd; John McFall; Jon Owen Jones
**Assistant Whips**
Clive Betts; David Clelland; Kevin Hughes; David Jamieson; Jane Kennedy; Greg Pope; Bridget Prentice
**House of Lords**
**Captain, Gentlemen-at-Arms (Government Chief Whip)**
Lord Carter
**Captain, Yeomen of the Guard (Deputy Chief Whip)**
Lord McIntosh of Haringey
**Lords and Baronesses in Waiting (Whips)**
Lord Haskel; Baroness Farrington of Ribbleton; Lord Whitty; Baroness Gould of Potternewton; Lord Hoyle

# THE HOUSE OF COMMONS

The following have been elected Members of the House of Commons in the 1997 general election:

Abbreviations to designate political parties:

**Lab** – Labour
**Lab and Co-op** – Labour and Co-operative
**C** – Conservative
**LD** – Liberal Democrat
**SNP** – Scottish National Party
**PC** – Plaid Cymru
**UU** – Ulster Unionist
**SDLP** – Social Democratic and Labour Party
**DUP** – Democratic Unionst Party
**UKU** – United Kingdom Unionist
**SF** – Sinn Fein
**Ind** – Independent

## A

**Abbott,** Diane; Hackney North & Stoke Newington   Lab
**Adams,** Gerry; Belfast West   SF
**Adams,** Irene; Paisley North   Lab
**Ainger,** Nick; Carmarthen West & Pembrokeshire South   Lab
**Ainsworth,** Bob; Coventry North East   Lab
**Ainsworth,** Peter; Surrey East   C
**Allan,** Richard; Sheffield Hallam   LD
**Allen,** Graham; Nottingham North   Lab
**Amess,** David; Southend West   C
**Ancram,** Michael; Devizes   C
**Anderson,** Donald; Swansea East   Lab
**Anderson,** Janet; Rossendale & Darwen   Lab
**Arbuthnot,** James; Hampshire North East   C
**Armstrong,** Hilary; Durham North West   Lab
**Ashdown,** Paddy; Yeovil   LD
**Ashton,** Joe; Bassetlaw   Lab
**Atherton,** Candy; Falmouth & Camborne   Lab

**Atkins,** Charlotte; Staffordshire Moorlands   Lab
**Atkinson,** David; Bournemouth East   C
**Atkinson,** Peter; Hexham   C
**Austin-Walker,** John; Erith & Thamesmead   Lab

## B

**Baker,** Norman; Lewes   LD
**Baldry,** Antony; Banbury   C
**Ballard,** Jackie; Taunton   LD
**Banks,** Tony; West Ham   Lab
**Barnes,** Harry; Derbyshire North East   Lab
**Barron,** Kevin; Rother Valley   Lab
**Battle,** John; Leeds West   Lab
**Bayley,** Hugh; York, City of   Lab
**Beard,** Nigel; Bexleyheath & Crayford   Lab
**Beckett,** Margaret; Derby South   Lab
**Begg,** Anne; Aberdeen South   Lab
**Beggs,** Roy; Antrim East   UUP
**Beith,** Alan; Berwick-upon-Tweed   LD
**Bell,** Martin; Tatton   Ind
**Bell,** Stuart; Middlesbrough   Lab
**Benn,** Tony; Chesterfield   Lab
**Bennett,** Andrew; Denton & Reddish   Lab
**Benton,** Joe; Bootle   Lab
**Bercow,** John; Buckingham   C
**Beresford,** Sir Paul; Mole Valley   C
**Bermingham,** Gerry; St Helens South   Lab
**Berry,** Dr Roger; Kingswood   Lab
**Best,** Harold; Leeds North West   Lab
**Betts,** Clive; Sheffield Attercliffe   Lab

**Blackman,** Elizabeth; Erewash   Lab
**Blair,** Tony; Sedgefield   Lab
**Blears,** Hazel; Salford   Lab
**Blizzard,** Robert; Waveney   Lab
**Blunkett,** David; Sheffield Brightside   Lab
**Blunt,** Crispin; Reigate   C
**Boateng,** Paul; Brent South   Lab
**Body,** Sir Richard; Boston & Skegness   C
**Boothroyd,** Betty; West Bromwich West   Speaker
**Borrow,** David; Ribble South   Lab
**Boswell,** Tim; Daventry   C
**Bottomley,** Peter; Worthing West   C
**Bottomley,** Virginia; Surrey South West   C
**Bradley,** Keith; Manchester Withington   Lab
**Bradley,** Peter; Wrekin, The   Lab
**Bradshaw,** Ben; Exeter   Lab
**Brady,** Graham; Altrincham & Sale West   C
**Brake,** Thomas; Carshalton & Wallington   LD
**Brand,** Dr Peter; Isle of Wight   LD
**Brazier,** Julian; Canterbury   C
**Breed,** Colin; Cornwall South East   LD
**Brinton,** Helen; Peterborough   Lab
**Brooke,** Peter; Cities of London & Westminster   C
**Brown,** Gordon; Dunfermline East   Lab
**Brown,** Nick; Newcastle upon Tyne East & Wallsend   Lab
**Brown,** Russell; Dumfries   Lab
**Browne,** Desmond; Kilmarnock & Loudoun   Lab
**Browning,** Angela; Tiverton & Honiton   C
**Bruce,** Ian; Dorset South   C
**Bruce,** Malcolm; Gordon   LD

**Buck, Karen**; Regent's Park
& Kensington North   Lab
**Burden, Richard**;
Birmingham Northfield
Lab
**Burgon, Colin**; Elmet   Lab
**Burnett, John**; Devon West
& Torridge   LD
**Burns, Simon**; Chelmsford
West   C
**Burstow, Paul**; Sutton &
Cheam   LD
**Butler, Christine**; Castle
Point   Lab
**Butterfill, John**;
Bournemouth West   C
**Byers, Stephen**; Tyneside
North   Lab

## C

**Cable, Dr Vincent**;
Twickenham   LD
**Caborn, Richard**; Sheffield
Central   Lab
**Campbell, Alan**;
Tynemouth   Lab
**Campbell, Anne**;
Cambridge   Lab
**Campbell, Menzies**; Fife
North East   LD
**Campbell, Ronald**; Blyth
Valley   Lab
**Campbell-Savours,
Dale**; Workington   Lab
**Canavan, Dennis**; Falkirk
West   Lab
**Cann, Jamie**; Ipswich   Lab
**Caplin, Ivor**; Hove   Lab
**Casale, Roger**; Wimbledon
Lab
**Cash, William**; Stone   C
**Caton, Martin**; Gower   Lab
**Cawsey, Ian**; Brigg &
Goole   Lab
**Chapman, Ben**; Wirral
South   Lab
**Chapman, Sir Sydney**;
Chipping Barnet   C
**Chaytor, David**; Bury
North   Lab
**Chidgey, David**; Eastleigh
LD
**Chisholm, Malcolm**;
Edinburgh North & Leith
Lab
**Chope, Christopher**;
Christchurch   C
**Church, Judith**; Dagenham
Lab

**Clapham, Michael**;
Barnsley West &
Penistone   Lab
**Clappison, James**;
Hertsmere   C
**Clark, Alan**; Kensington &
Chelsea   C
**Clark, David**; South Shields
Lab
**Clark, Linda**; Edinburgh
Pentlands   Lab
**Clark, Dr Michael**;
Rayleigh   C
**Clark, Paul**; Gillingham
Lab
**Clarke, Charles**; Norwich
South   Lab
**Clarke, Eric**; Midlothian
Lab
**Clarke, Kenneth**;
Rushcliffe   C
**Clarke, Tom**; Coatbridge &
Chryston   Lab
**Clarke, Tony**;
Northampton South   Lab
**Clelland, David**; Tyne
Bridge   Lab
**Clifton-Brown,
Geoffrey**; Cotswold   C
**Clwyd, Ann**; Cynon Valley
Lab
**Coaker, Vernon**; Gedling
Lab
**Coffey, Ann**; Stockport
Lab
**Cohen, Harry**; Leyton &
Wanstead   Lab
**Coleman, Iain**;
Hammersmith & Fulham
Lab
**Collins, Tim**; Westmorland
& Lonsdale   C
**Colman, Anthony**; Putney
Lab
**Colvin, Michael**; Romsey
C
**Connarty, Michael**;
Falkirk East   Lab
**Cook, Frank**; Stockton
North   Lab
**Cook, Robin**; Livingston
Lab
**Cooper, Yvette**; Pontefract
& Castleford   Lab
**Corbett, Robin**;
Birmingham Erdington
Lab
**Corbyn, Jeremy**; Islington
North   Lab
**Cormack, Sir Patrick**;
Staffordshire South   C

**Corston, Jean**; Bristol East
Lab
**Cotter, Brian**; Weston-
super-Mare   LD
**Cousins, Jim**; Newcastle
upon Tyne Central   Lab
**Cox, Tom**; Tooting   Lab
**Cran, James**; Beverley &
Holderness   C
**Cranston, Ross**; Dudley
North   Lab
**Crausby, David**; Bolton
North East   Lab
**Cryer, Ann**; Keighley   Lab
**Cryer, John**; Hornchurch
Lab
**Cummings, John**;
Easington   Lab
**Cunliffe, Lawrence**; Leigh
Lab
**Cunningham, Jack**;
Copeland   Lab
**Cunningham, Jim**;
Coventry South   Lab
**Cunningham, Roseanna**;
Perth   SNP
**Curry, David**; Skipton &
Ripon   C
**Curtis-Tansley, Clare**;
Crosby   Lab

## D

**Dafis, Cynog**; Ceredigion
PC
**Dalyell, Tam**; Linlithgow
Lab
**Darling, Alistair**;
Edinburgh Central   Lab
**Darvill, Keith**; Upminster
Lab
**Davey, Edward**; Kingston
& Surbiton   LD
**Davey, Valerie**; Bristol
West   Lab
**Davidson, Ian**; Glasgow
Pollok   Lab Co-op
**Davies, Denzil**; Llanelli
Lab
**Davies, Geraint**; Croydon
Central   Lab
**Davies, Quentin**;
Grantham & Stamford   C
**Davies, Ron**; Caerphilly
Lab
**Davis, David**; Haltemprice
& Howden   C
**Davis, Terry**; Birmingham
Hodge Hill   Lab
**Dawson, Hilton**; Lancaster
& Wyre   Lab

**Day,** Stephen; Cheadle    C
**Dean,** Janet; Burton    Lab
**Denham,** John;
   Southampton Itchen   Lab
**Dewar,** Donald; Glasgow
   Anniesland    Lab
**Dismore,** Andrew;
   Hendon    Lab
**Dobbin,** Jim; Heywood &
   Middleton    Lab Co-op
**Dobson,** Frank; Holborn &
   St Pancras    Lab
**Donaldson,** Jeffrey; Lagan
   Valley    UUP
**Donohoe,** Brian;
   Cunninghame South   Lab
**Doran,** Frank; Aberdeen
   Central    Lab
**Dorrell,** Stephen;
   Charnwood    C
**Dowd,** Jim; Lewisham West
   Lab
**Drew,** David; Stroud
   Lab Co-op
**Drown,** Julia; Swindon
   South    Lab
**Duncan,** Alan; Rutland &
   Melton    C
**Duncan** Smith, Iain;
   Chingford & Woodford
   Green    C
**Dunwoody,** Gwyneth;
   Crewe & Nantwich   Lab

## E

**Eagle,** Angela; Wallasey
   Lab
**Eagle,** Maria; Liverpool
   Garston    Lab
**Edwards,** Huw;
   Monmouth    Lab
**Efford,** Clive; Eltham   Lab
**Ellman,** Louise; Liverpool
   Riverside    Lab Co-op
**Emery,** Sir Peter; Devon
   East    C
**Ennis,** Jeff; Barnsley East &
   Mexborough    Lab
**Etherington,** William;
   Sunderland North   Lab
**Evans,** Nigel; Ribble Valley
   C
**Ewing,** Margaret; Moray
   SNP

## F

**Faber,** David; Westbury   C

**Fabricant,** Michael;
   Lichfield    C
**Fallon,** Michael; Sevenoaks
   C
**Fatchett,** Derek; Leeds
   Central    Lab
**Fearn,** Ronnie; Southport
   LD
**Field,** Frank; Birkenhead
   Lab
**Fisher,** Mark; Stoke-on-
   Trent Central    Lab
**Fitzpatrick,** Jim; Poplar &
   Canning Town    Lab
**Fitzsimons,** Lorna;
   Rochdale    Lab
**Flight,** Howard; Arundel &
   South Downs    C
**Flint,** Caroline; Don Valley
   Lab
**Flynn,** Paul; Newport West
   Lab
**Follett,** Barbara; Stevenage
   Lab
**Forsythe,** Clifford; Antrim
   South    UUP
**Forth,** Eric; Bromley &
   Chislehurst    C
**Foster,** Derek; Bishop
   Auckland    Lab
**Foster,** Donald; Bath   LD
**Foster,** Michael; Hastings
   & Rye    Lab
**Foster,** Michael; Worcester
   Lab
**Foulkes,** George; Carrick,
   Cumnock & Doon Valley
   Lab Co-op
**Fowler,** Sir Norman;
   Sutton Coldfield    C
**Fox,** Dr Liam; Woodspring
   C
**Fraser,** Christopher;
   Dorset Mid & Poole North
   C
**Fyfe,** Maria; Glasgow
   Maryhill    Lab

## G

**Galbraith,** Sam;
   Strathkelvin & Bearsden
   Lab
**Gale,** Roger; Thanet North
   C
**Galloway,** George;
   Glasgow Kelvin    Lab
**Gapes,** Mike; Ilford South
   Lab Co-op
**Gardiner,** Barry; Brent
   North    Lab

**Garnier,** Edward;
   Harborough    C
**George,** Andrew; St Ives
   LD
**George,** Bruce; Walsall
   South    Lab
**Gerrard,** Neil;
   Walthamstow    Lab
**Gibb,** Nick; Bognor Regis &
   Littlehampton    C
**Gibson,** Dr Ian; Norwich
   North    Lab
**Gill,** Christopher; Ludlow
   C
**Gillan,** Cheryl; Chesham &
   Amersham    C
**Gilroy,** Linda; Plymouth
   Sutton    Lab Co-op
**Godman,** Dr Norman;
   Greenock & Inverclyde
   Lab
**Godsiff,** Roger;
   Birmingham Sparkbrook
   & Small Heath    Lab
**Goggins,** Paul;
   Wythenshawe & Sale East
   Lab
**Golding,** Llin; Newcastle-
   under-Lyme    Lab
**Goodlad,** Alastair;
   Eddisbury    C
**Gordon,** Eileen; Romford
   Lab
**Gorman,** Teresa;
   Billericay    C
**Gorrie,** Donald;
   Edinburgh West    LD
**Graham,** Thomas;
   Renfrewshire West   Lab
**Grant,** Bernie; Tottenham
   Lab
**Gray,** James; Wiltshire
   North    C
**Green,** Damian; Ashford   C
**Greenway,** John; Ryedale
   C
**Grieve,** Dominic;
   Beaconsfield    C
**Griffiths,** Jane; Reading
   East    Lab
**Griffiths,** Nigel;
   Edinburgh South   Lab
**Griffiths,** Win; Bridgend
   Lab
**Grocott,** Bruce; Telford
   Lab
**Grogan,** John; Selby   Lab
**Gummer,** John; Suffolk
   Coastal    C
**Gunnell,** John; Morley &
   Rothwell    Lab

## H

**Hague,** William; Richmond (Yorks) C
**Hain,** Peter; Neath Lab
**Hall,** Mike; Weaver Vale Lab
**Hall,** Patrick; Bedford Lab
**Hamilton,** Sir Archibald; Epsom & Ewell C
**Hamilton,** Fabian; Leeds North East Lab
**Hammond,** Philip; Runnymede & Weybridge C
**Hancock,** Mike; Portsmouth South LD
**Hanson,** David; Delyn Lab
**Harman,** Harriet; Camberwell & Peckham Lab
**Harris,** Dr Evan; Oxford West & Abingdon LD
**Harvey,** Nick; Devon North LD
**Haselhurst,** Sir Alan; Saffron Walden C
**Hawkins,** Nick; Surrey Heath C
**Hayes,** John; South Holland & The Deepings C
**Heal,** Sylvia; Halesowen & Rowley Regis Lab
**Heald,** Oliver; Hertfordshire North East C
**Healey,** John; Wentworth Lab
**Heath,** David; Somerton & Frome LD
**Heath,** Sir Edward; Old Bexley & Sidcup C
**Heathcoat-Amory,** David; Wells C
**Henderson,** Doug; Newcastle upon Tyne North Lab
**Henderson,** Ivan; Harwich Lab
**Hepburn,** Stephen; Jarrow Lab
**Heppell,** John; Nottingham East Lab
**Heseltine,** Michael; Henley C
**Hesford,** Stephen; Wirral West Lab
**Hewitt,** Patricia; Leicester West Lab

**Hill,** Keith; Streatham Lab
**Hinchliffe,** David; Wakefield Lab
**Hodge,** Margaret; Barking Lab
**Hoey,** Kate; Vauxhall Lab
**Hogg,** Douglas; Sleaford & North Hykeham C
**Home Robertson,** John; East Lothian Lab
**Hood,** Jimmy; Clydesdale Lab
**Hoon,** Geoff; Ashfield Lab
**Hope,** Phil; Corby Lab Co-op
**Hopkins,** Kelvin; Luton North Lab
**Horam,** John; Orpington C
**Howard,** Michael; Folkestone & Hythe C
**Howarth,** Alan; Newport East Lab
**Howarth,** George; Knowsley North & Sefton East Lab
**Howarth,** Gerald; Aldershot C
**Howells,** Dr Kim; Pontypridd Lab
**Hoyle,** Lindsay; Chorley Lab
**Hughes,** Beverley; Stretford & Urmston Lab
**Hughes,** Kevin; Doncaster North Lab
**Hughes,** Simon; Southwark North & Bermondsey LD
**Humble,** Joan; Blackpool North & Fleetwood Lab
**Hume,** John; Foyle SDLP
**Hunter,** Andrew; Basingstoke C
**Hurst,** Alan; Braintree Lab
**Hutton,** John; Barrow & Furness Lab

## I

**Iddon,** Brian; Bolton South East Lab
**Illsley,** Eric; Barnsley Central Lab
**Ingram,** Adam; East Kilbride Lab

## J

**Jack,** Michael; Fylde C

**Jackson,** Glenda; Hampstead & Highgate Lab
**Jackson,** Helen; Sheffield Hillsborough Lab
**Jackson,** Robert; Wantage C
**Jamieson,** David; Plymouth Devonport Lab
**Jenkin,** Bernard; Essex North C
**Jenkins,** Brian; Tamworth Lab
**Johnson,** Alan; Hull West & Hessle Lab
**Johnson,** Melanie; Welwyn Hatfield Lab
**Johnson Smith,** Sir Geoffrey; Wealden C
**Jones,** Barry; Alyn & Deeside Lab
**Jones,** Fiona; Newark Lab
**Jones,** Helen; Warrington North Lab
**Jones,** Jenny; Wolverhampton South West Lab
**Jones,** Ieuan Wyn; Ynys Mon PC
**Jones,** Lynne; Birmingham Selly Oak Lab
**Jones,** Martyn; Clwyd South Lab
**Jones,** Nigel; Cheltenham LD
**Jowell,** Tessa; Dulwich and West Norwood Lab

## K

**Kaufman,** Gerald; Manchester Gorton Lab
**Keeble,** Sally; Northampton North Lab
**Keen,** Alan; Feltham & Heston Lab Co-op
**Keen,** Ann; Brentford & Isleworth Lab
**Keetch,** Paul; Hereford LD
**Kelly,** Ruth; Bolton West Lab
**Kemp,** Fraser; Houghton & Washington East Lab
**Kennedy,** Charles; Ross, Skye & Inverness West LD
**Kennedy,** Jane; Liverpool Wavertree Lab
**Key,** Robert; Salisbury C

**Khabra,** Piara; Ealing
Southall — Lab
**Kidney,** David; Stafford — Lab
**Kilfoyle,** Peter; Liverpool
Walton — Lab
**King,** Andy; Rugby &
Kenilworth — Lab
**King,** Oona; Bethnal Green
& Bow — Lab
**King,** Tom; Bridgwater — C
**Kingham,** Tess;
Gloucester — Lab
**Kirkbride,** Julie;
Bromsgrove — C
**Kirkwood,** Archy;
Roxburgh & Berwickshire — LD
**Kumar,** Ashok;
Middlesbrough South &
Cleveland East — Lab

## L

**Ladyman,** Stephen;
Thanet South — Lab
**Laing,** Eleanor; Epping
Forest — C
**Lansley,** Andrew;
Cambridgeshire South — C
**Lawrence,** Jackie; Preseli
Pembrokeshire — Lab
**Laxton,** Bob; Derby North — Lab
**Leigh,** Edward;
Gainsborough — C
**Lepper,** David; Brighton
Pavilion — Lab Co-op
**Leslie,** Christopher;
Shipley — Lab
**Letwin,** Oliver; Dorset
West — C
**Levitt,** Tom; High Peak — Lab
**Lewis,** Ivan; Bury South — Lab
**Lewis,** Julian; New Forest
East — C
**Lewis,** Terry; Worsley — Lab
**Liddell,** Helen; Airdrie and
Shotts — Lab
**Lidington,** David;
Aylesbury — C
**Lilley,** Peter; Hitchen &
Harpenden — C
**Linton,** Martin; Battersea — Lab
**Livingstone,** Ken; Brent
East — Lab
**Livsey,** Richard; Brecon &
Radnorshire — LD

**Lloyd,** Tony; Manchester
Central — Lab
**Lloyd,** Sir Peter; Fareham — C
**Llwyd,** Elfyn; Meirionnydd
Nant Conwy — PC
**Lock,** David; Wyre Forest — Lab
**Lord,** Michael; Suffolk
Central & Ipswich North — C
**Loughton,** Tim; Worthing
East & Shoreham — C
**Love,** Andy; Edmonton — Lab Co-op
**Luff,** Peter; Worcestershire
Mid — C
**Lyell,** Sir Nicholas;
Bedfordshire North East — C

## M

**MacGregor,** John; Norfolk
South — C
**MacKay,** Andrew;
Bracknell — C
**MacShane,** Denis;
Rotherham — Lab
**MacTaggart,** Fiona;
Slough — Lab
**Macdonald,** Calum;
Western Isles — Lab
**Mackinlay,** Andrew;
Thurrock — Lab
**Maclean,** David; Penrith &
The Border — C
**Maclennan,** Robert;
Caithness, Sunderland &
Easter Ross — LD
**McAllion,** John; Dundee
East — Lab
**McAvoy,** Thomas;
Glasgow Rutherglen — Lab Co-op
**McCabe,** Stephen;
Birmingham Hall Green — Lab
**McCafferty,** Christine;
Calder Valley — Lab
**McCartney,** Ian;
Makerfield — Lab
**McCartney,** Robert;
Down North — UKU
**McDonagh,** Siobhain;
Mitcham & Morden — Lab
**McDonnell,** John; Hayes
& Harlington — Lab
**McFall,** John; Dumbarton — Lab Co-op

**McGrady,** Edward; Down
South — SDLP
**McGuinness,** Martin;
Ulster Mid — SF
**McGuire,** Anne; Stirling — Lab
**McIntosh,** Anne; Vale of
York — C
**McIsaac,** Shona;
Cleethorpes — Lab
**McKenna,** Rosemary;
Cumbernauld & Kilsyth — Lab
**McLeish,** Henry; Fife
Central — Lab
**McLoughlin,** Patrick;
Derbyshire West — C
**McMaster,** Gordon;
Paisley South — Lab Co-op
**McNamara,** Kevin; Hull
North — Lab
**McNulty,** Tony; Harrow
East — Lab
**McWalter,** Tony; Hemel
Hempstead — Lab Co-op
**McWilliam,** John; Blaydon — Lab
**Madel,** Sir David;
Bedfordshire South West — C
**Maginnis,** Ken;
Fermanagh & South
Tyrone — UUP
**Mahon,** Alice; Halifax — Lab
**Major,** John; Huntingdon — C
**Malins,** Humfrey; Woking — C
**Mallaber,** Judy; Amber
Valley — Lab
**Mallon,** Seamus; Newry &
Armagh — SDLP
**Mandelson,** Peter;
Hartlepool — Lab
**Maples,** John; Stratford-on-
Avon — C
**Marek,** John; Wrexham — Lab
**Marsden,** Paul;
Shrewsbury & Atcham — Lab
**Marsden,** Gordon;
Blackpool South — Lab
**Marshall,** David; Glasgow
Shettleston — Lab
**Marshall,** Jim; Leicester
South — Lab
**Marshall-Andrews,**
Robert; Medway — Lab
**Martin,** Michael; Glasgow
Springburn — Lab

**Martlew,** Eric; Carlisle  Lab
**Mates,** Michael; Hampshire
East  C
**Maude,** Francis; Horsham  C
**Mawhinney,** Dr Brian;
Cambridgeshire North
West  C
**Maxton,** John; Glasgow
Cathcart  Lab
**May,** Theresa; Maidenhead  C
**Meacher,** Michael;
Oldham West & Royton  Lab
**Meale,** Alan; Mansfield  Lab
**Merchant,** Piers;
Beckenham  C
**Merron,** Gillian; Lincoln  Lab
**Michael,** Alun; Cardiff
South & Penarth  Lab Co-op
**Michie,** Bill; Sheffield
Heeley  Lab
**Michie,** Ray; Argyll & Bute  LD
**Milburn,** Alan; Darlington  Lab
**Miller,** Andrew; Ellesmere
Port & Neston  Lab
**Mitchell,** Austin; Great
Grimsby  Lab
**Moffatt,** Laura; Crawley  Lab
**Moonie,** Lewis; Kirkcaldy  Lab Co-op
**Moore,** Michael;
Tweeddale, Ettrick &
Lauderdale  LD
**Moran,** Margaret; Luton
South  Lab
**Morgan,** Alasdair;
Galloway & Upper
Nithsdale  SNP
**Morgan,** Julie; Cardiff
North  Lab
**Morgan,** Rhodri; Cardiff
West  Lab
**Morley,** Elliot; Scunthorpe  Lab
**Morris,** Estelle;
Birmingham Yardley  Lab
**Morris,** John; Aberavon  Lab
**Moss,** Malcolm;
Cambridgeshire North
East  C
**Mountford,** Kali; Colne
Valley  Lab

**Mowlam,** Dr Marjorie;
Redcar  Lab
**Mudie,** George; Leeds East  Lab
**Mullin,** Chris; Sunderland
South  Lab
**Murphy,** Denis; Wansbeck  Lab
**Murphy,** Jim; Eastwood  Lab
**Murphy,** Paul; Torfaen  Lab

# N

**Naysmith,** Doug; Bristol
North West  Lab Co-op
**Nicholls,** Patrick;
Teignbridge  C
**Norman,** Archie;
Tunbridge Wells  C
**Norris,** Dan; Wansdyke  Lab

# O

**O'Brien,** William;
Normanton  Lab
**O'Brien,** Michael;
Warwickshire North  Lab
**O'Hara,** Eddie; Knowsley
South  Lab
**O'Neill,** Martin; Ochil  Lab
**Oaten,** Mark; Winchester  LD
**Olner,** Bill; Nuneaton  Lab
**Opik,** Lembit;
Montgomeryshire  LD
**Organ,** Diana; Forest of
Dean  Lab
**Osborne,** Sandra; Ayr  Lab
**Ottaway,** Richard;
Croydon South  C
**Owen Jones,** Jon; Cardiff
Central  Lab Co-op

# P

**Page,** Richard;
Hertfordshire South West  C
**Paice,** James;
Cambridgeshire South
East  C
**Paisley,** Rev Ian; Antrim
North  DUP
**Palmer,** Nick; Broxtowe  Lab
**Paterson,** Owen;
Shropshire North  C

**Pearson,** Ian; Dudley
South  Lab
**Pendry,** Tom; Stalybridge
& Hyde  Lab
**Perham,** Linda; Ilford
North  Lab
**Pickles,** Eric; Brentwood &
Ongar  C
**Pickthall,** Colin;
Lancashire West  Lab
**Pike,** Peter; Burnley  Lab
**Plaskitt,** James; Warwick
& Leamington  Lab
**Pollard,** Kerry; St Albans  Lab
**Pond,** Chris; Gravesham  Lab
**Pope,** Greg; Hyndburn  Lab
**Pound,** Stephen; Ealing
North  Lab
**Powell,** Sir Raymond;
Ogmore  Lab
**Prentice,** Bridget;
Lewisham East  Lab
**Prentice,** Gordon; Pendle  Lab
**Prescott,** John; Hull East  Lab
**Primarolo,** Dawn; Bristol
South  Lab
**Prior,** David; Norfolk
North  C
**Prosser,** Gwyn; Dover  Lab
**Purchase,** Ken;
Wolverhampton North
East  Lab Co-op

# Q

**Quin,** Joyce; Gateshead
East & Washington West  Lab
**Quinn,** Lawrence;
Scarborough & Whitby  Lab

# R

**Radice,** Giles; Durham
North  Lab
**Rammell,** Bill; Harlow  Lab
**Rapson,** Syd; Portsmouth
North  Lab
**Raynsford,** Nick;
Greenwich & Woolwich  Lab
**Redwood,** John;
Wokingham  C
**Reed,** Andrew;
Loughborough  Lab Co-op

**Reid,** John; Hamilton North & Bellshill — Lab
**Rendel,** David; Newbury — LD
**Robathan,** Andrew; Blaby — C
**Robertson,** George; Hamilton South — Lab
**Robertson,** Laurence; Tewkesbury — C
**Robinson,** Geoffrey; Coventry North West — Lab
**Robinson,** Peter; Belfast East — DUP
**Roche,** Barbara; Hornsey & Wood Green — Lab
**Roe,** Marion; Broxbourne — C
**Rogers,** Allan; Rhondda — Lab
**Rooker,** Jeff; Birmingham Perry Barr — Lab
**Rooney,** Terry; Bradford North — Lab
**Ross,** Ernie; Dundee West — Lab
**Ross,** William; Londonderry East — UUP
**Rowe,** Andrew; Faversham & Kent Mid — C
**Rowlands,** Ted; Merthyr Tydfil & Rhymney — Lab
**Roy,** Frank; Motherwell & Wishaw — Lab
**Ruane,** Chris; Vale of Clwyd — Lab
**Ruddock,** Joan; Lewisham Deptford — Lab
**Ruffley,** David; Bury St Edmunds — C
**Russell,** Christine; Chester, City of — Lab
**Russell,** Bob; Colchester — LD
**Ryan,** Joan; Enfield North — Lab

## S

**Salmond,** Alex; Banff & Buchan — SNP
**Salter,** Martin; Reading West — Lab
**Sanders,** Adrian; Torbay — LD
**Sarwar,** Mohammad; Glasgow Govan — Lab
**Savidge,** Malcolm; Aberdeen North — Lab
**Sawford,** Philip; Kettering — Lab

**Sayeed,** Jonathan; Bedfordshire Mid — C
**Sedgemore,** Brian; Hackney South & Shoreditch — Lab
**Shaw,** Jonathon; Chatham & Aylesford — Lab
**Sheerman,** Barry; Huddersfield — Lab Co-op
**Sheldon,** Robert; Ashton-under-Lyne — Lab
**Shephard,** Gillian; Norfolk South West — C
**Shepherd,** Richard; Aldridge-Brownhills — C
**Shersby,** Sir Michael; Uxbridge — C
**Shipley,** Debra; Stourbridge — Lab
**Short,** Clare; Birmingham Ladywood — Lab
**Simpson,** Alan; Nottingham South — Lab
**Simpson,** Keith; Norfolk Mid — C
**Singh,** Marsha; Bradford West — Lab
**Skinner,** Dennis; Bolsover — Lab
**Smith,** Andrew; Oxford East — Lab
**Smith,** Angela; Basildon — Lab Co-op
**Smith,** Chris; Islington South & Finsbury — Lab
**Smith,** Geraldine; Morecambe & Lunesdale — Lab
**Smith,** Jacqui; Redditch — Lab
**Smith,** John; Vale of Glamorgan — Lab
**Smith,** Llewellyn; Blaenau Gwent — Lab
**Smith,** Sir Robert; Aberdeenshire West & Kincardine — LD
**Smyth,** Rev Martin; Belfast South — UUP
**Snape,** Peter; West Bromwich East — Lab
**Soames,** Nicholas; Sussex Mid — C
**Soley,** Clive; Ealing Acton & Shepherd's Bush — Lab
**Southworth,** Helen; Warrington South — Lab
**Spellar,** John; Warley — Lab
**Spelman,** Caroline; Meriden — C

**Spicer,** Sir Michael; Worcestershire West — C
**Spring,** Richard; Suffolk West — C
**Squire,** Rachel; Dunfermline West — Lab
**St Aubyn,** Nick; Guildford — C
**Stanley,** Sir John; Tonbridge & Malling — C
**Starkey,** Phyllis; Milton Keynes South West — Lab
**Steen,** Sir Anthony; Totnes — C
**Steinberg,** Gerry; Durham, City of — Lab
**Stevenson,** George; Stoke-on-Trent South — Lab
**Stewart,** David; Inverness East, Nairn & Lochaber — Lab
**Stewart,** Ian; Eccles — Lab
**Stinchcombe,** Paul; Wellingborough — Lab
**Stoate,** Howard; Dartford — Lab
**Stott,** Roger; Wigan — Lab
**Strang,** Gavin; Edinburgh East & Mussleburgh — Lab
**Straw,** Jack; Blackburn — Lab
**Streeter,** Gary; Devon South West — C
**Stringer,** Graham; Manchester Blackley — Lab
**Stuart,** Gisela; Birmingham Edgbaston — Lab
**Stunell,** Andrew; Hazel Grove — LD
**Sutcliffe,** Gerry; Bradford South — Lab
**Swayne,** Desmond; New Forest West — C
**Swinney,** John; Tayside North — SNP
**Syms,** Robert; Poole — C

## T

**Tapsell,** Sir Peter; Louth & Horncastle — C
**Taylor,** Ann; Dewsbury — Lab
**Taylor,** Dari; Stockton South — Lab
**Taylor,** David; Leicestershire North West — Lab Co-op
**Taylor,** Ian; Esher & Walton — C
**Taylor,** John D; Strangford — UUP

Taylor, John M; Solihull   C
Taylor, Matthew; Truro & St Austell   LD
Taylor, Sir Teddy; Rochford & Southend East   C
Temple-Morris, Peter; Leominster   C
Thomas, Gareth; Clwyd West   Lab
Thomas, Gareth R; Harrow West   Lab
Thompson, William; Tyrone West   UUP
Timms, Stephen; East Ham   Lab
Tipping, Paddy; Sherwood   Lab
Todd, Mark; Derbyshire South   Lab
Tonge, Dr Jenny; Richmond Park   LD
Touhig, Don; Islwyn   Lab Co-op
Townend, John; Yorkshire East   C
Tredinnick, David; Bosworth   C
Trend, Michael; Windsor   C
Trickett, Jon; Hemsworth   Lab
Trimble, David; Upper Bann   UUP
Truswell, Paul; Pudsey   Lab
Turner, Desmond; Brighton Kemptown   Lab
Turner, Dennis; Wolverhampton South East   Lab Co-op
Turner, George; Norfolk North West   Lab
Twigg, Derek; Halton   Lab
Twigg, Stephen; Enfield Southgate   Lab
Tyler, Paul; Cornwall North   LD
Tyrie, Andrew; Chichester   C

## V

Vaz, Keith; Leicester East   Lab
Viggers, Peter; Gosport   C
Vis, Rudolph; Finchley & Golders Green   Lab

## W

Walker, Cecil; Belfast North   UUP
Wallace, Jim; Orkney & Shetland   LD
Walley, Joan; Stoke-on-Trent North   Lab
Walter, Robert; Dorset North   C
Ward, Claire; Watford   Lab
Wardle, Charles; Bexhill & Battle   C
Wareing, Robert; Liverpool West Derby   Lab
Waterson, Nigel; Eastbourne   C
Watts, Dave; St Helens North   Lab
Webb, Prof Steven; Northavon   LD
Wells, Bowen; Hertford & Stortford   C
Welsh, Andrew; Angus   SNP
White, Brian; Milton Keynes North East   Lab
Whitehead, Alan; Southampton Test   Lab
Whitney, Sir Ray; Wycombe   C
Whittingdale, John; Maldon & Chelmsford East   C
Wicks, Malcolm; Croydon North   Lab
Widdecombe, Ann; Maidstone & The Weald   C
Wigley, Dafydd; Caernarfon   PC
Wilkinson, John; Ruislip Northwood   C
Willetts, David; Havant   C
Williams, Alan; Swansea West   Lab
Williams, Alan Wynne; Carmarthen East & Dinefwr   Lab
Williams, Betty; Conwy   Lab
Willis, Phil; Harrogate & Knaresborough   LD
Wills, Michael; Swindon North   Lab
Wilshire, David; Spelthorne   C
Wilson, Brian; Cunninghame North   Lab
Winnick, David; Walsall North   Lab

Winterton, Ann; Congleton   C
Winterton, Nicholas; Macclesfield   C
Winterton, Rosa; Doncaster Central   Lab
Wise, Audrey; Preston   Lab
Wood, Mike; Batley & Spen   Lab
Woodward, Shaun; Witney   C
Woolas, Phil; Oldham East & Saddleworth   Lab
Worthington, Tony; Clydebank & Milngavie   Lab
Wray, James; Glasgow Bailliestown   Lab
Wright, Tony; Cannock Chase   Lab
Wright, Tony; Great Yarmouth   Lab
Wyatt, Derek; Sittingbourne & Sheppey   Lab

## Y

Yeo, Tim; Suffolk South   C
Young, Sir George; Hampshire North West   C

# ANALYSIS
# AND COMMENT

# TORY UNITY COLLAPSES
# AS LABOUR IS REBORN

## *By Peter Riddell, Political Columnist of The Times*

**T**HE 1992-97 Parliament was a period of transition − from the certainties and big majorities of the Thatcher era to the slow rebirth of Labour as a governing party. The unexpected triumph that John Major enjoyed on April 9, 1992, in confounding expectations − and the pollsters − by winning an overall Commons majority of 21 was short-lived. For most of the Parliament he was struggling to hold his Government and his party together.

The story of the Parliament was dominated by Europe and by the Conservative Party's inability to unite around an agreed line. Within a few weeks of the election, the Government had obtained a majority of 244 votes for the second reading of the Bill implementing the Maastricht treaty on European Union. Just 22 Tory MPs voted against. But only a few days later, on June 2, 1992, everything was thrown into doubt by the narrow rejection of the treaty by the Danish public in a referendum. This triggered a revolt by the Tory Eurosceptics and forced the Government to delay the committee stage of the Bill until the situation was clarified.

The promised end to the recession did not occur and pressure developed against sterling within the European exchange-rate mechanism during the summer. Both a devaluation and a realignment within the ERM were ruled out. But in September this turned into an acute financial crisis, particularly ahead of a French referendum on Maastricht. Attempts by Norman Lamont, the Chancellor, to persuade the Bundesbank to reduce German interest rates failed and on Wednesday, September 16, the fate of sterling − and in the

*Major: embattled*

long term of the Major Government − was determined in a flurry of speculative activity. Interest rates were raised in two stages by five percentage points in a fruitless attempt to stem the pressure. But in the evening of that gloomy Wednesday, Mr Lamont announced that Britain had pulled out of the system. Whatever the longer-term economic impact in permitting a reduction in interest rates and therefore fuelling recovery, the political effects of such a dramatic reversal were direct and humiliating.

The Cabinet looked shaken and unsteady for a time. Tory morale had not been helped by the sudden resignation of David Mellor, the flamboyant National Heritage Secretary, after press stories about an affair with a young actress and his links with a prominent Palestinian. Mr Major was badly bruised by John Smith, the new Labour leader, in an emergency Commons debate over the ERM debacle, and the subsequent Conservative conference in Brighton was the most bad-tempered and divided in recent memory.

To make matters worse, Michael Heseltine, usually the most sure-footed of politicians, triggered a big row when he announced the closure of 31 pits with the loss of 30,000 jobs in the mining industry. There were widespread public protests and a threatened Tory revolt forced Mr Heseltine to back down temporarily and order a review. After lengthy consultations − and a report by the Commons Trade and Industry Committee − the closures eventually went ahead and the rump of the coal industry was privatised.

The weakened Government just about managed to revive the Maastricht Bill, though it survived a key procedural vote in the Commons on November 4, 1993, by only three votes after undignified arm-twisting. Skilful diplomacy by Mr Major and by Douglas Hurd, the Foreign Secretary, did manage to produce a deal for Denmark at the Edinburgh summit in December 1992, and in the following spring the Danes voted to accept the treaty. During that winter and spring, the Maastricht Bill meandered slowly through the Commons in the face of opposition from a vocal and effective minority of Tory Eurosceptics. It eventually became law in July 1993, but the Government lost a key vote on acceptance of the social chapter and was forced the next day to table a motion of confidence which it then won.

Mr Major was widely criticised for failing to sack Mr Lamont immediately after the ERM debacle. Mr Lamont carried on – increasingly a lame duck – until May 1993 when he was finally sacked as Chancellor. He declined another post and remained a vigorous critic of Mr Major from the back benches.

The Government was also dogged by scandals, including a bizarre one involving Michael Mates, the Northern Ireland Minister, after his too-overt support for Asil Nadir, the fugitive businessman. It was a trivial matter but was followed by many similar episodes involving the private lives of ministers and MPs, particularly after Mr Major unwisely launched a so-called "back to basics" initiative at the Conservative conference in October 1993. This was intended to be about school standards, discipline and the like, but was widely, and wrongly, seen as being about personal morality, so ministers were accused of being hypocrites when sexual and other misdemeanours were publicised. More serious, however, were allegations of financial impropriety – the so-called "cash for questions" affair over allegations about MPs accepting money for raising matters in Parliament. These led directly to the formation in October 1994 of the Committee on Standards of Conduct in Public Life, under Lord Nolan. Its report the following May provoked fierce controversy, but led to a wide-ranging system of new rules limiting MPs' outside business interests and the creation of the Parliamentary Commissioner for Standards.

**T**HROUGHOUT this period, the Government's popularity continued to decline and it suffered a series of reverses at by-elections and in local council elections. It still implemented most of its legislative programme, including privatisation of the coal and rail industries and big changes in schools. But Labour made big advances – starting under John Smith, who had been elected party leader in July 1992 after Neil Kinnock's resignation. Mr Smith, from Labour's old Right, was instinctively a unifier, not someone to confront his party with the implications of its four election defeats. He did, however, carry forward one key element of the Kinnock agenda in narrowly winning approval in October 1994 for the selection of parliamentary candidates on the basis of one member, one vote – in part thanks to a rallying speech by John Prescott.

Mr Smith's death in May 1994 after a heart attack at his Barbican flat transformed the political scene. Tony Blair rapidly emerged as the favourite to carry forward the modernisation of Labour. After lengthy agonising, Gordon Brown deferred to Mr Blair's better prospects. Mr Blair convincingly defeated Mr Prescott, who became his deputy, and Margaret Beckett, who had been Mr Smith's deputy. He signalled his intention to change Labour by his surprise announcement at the Labour conference in October 1994 of a proposal to rewrite Clause Four of the party constitution – particularly the section on its aims which talked of the common ownership of the means of production, distribution and exchange. While Labour leaders had only paid lip-service to this clause for many years, they feared that removing it would provoke bitter battles.

However, Mr Blair believed Clause Four was a symbol of Labour's socialist past and should be rewritten. He lined up an initially wary Mr Prescott and, after a hesitant start, he mobilised support among the growing band of Labour members to secure overwhelming support for the change at a special conference in April 1995. In the process, he brushed aside the opposition of leading trade unionists. His victory demonstrated not only his ascendancy over his party but also his determination to create what he described as new Labour. While Mr Blair and his party enjoyed sky-high ratings, Mr Major and the Tories remained in the doldrums, suffering continued divisions over Europe, low poll ratings and recurrent electoral setbacks. This was despite growing evidence of economic recovery, low inflation and sharp falls in unemployment. There was a mild sense of relief in June 1994 when the Tories were not entirely wiped out in the elections for the European Parliament, as some polls had been suggesting. Mr Major's bold initiative to break through the stalemate on Northern Ireland via the Downing Street declaration in December 1993 won him respect, but few votes. These hopes were undermined in early 1996 when the 18-month IRA ceasefire ended.

European arguments exploded again in late 1994 when the Government turned a vote on the second reading of a Bill to expand the European budget into a confidence issue. Eight Tory MPs rebelled and duly lost the whip, with another joining the whipless band. They took their vengeance a week later when they voted with Labour not to implement the second stage of the imposition of VAT on domestic fuel. The defeat mattered more in political than financial terms. The malaise continued into the first half of 1995, with bad local election results that May and rumblings of dissent.

Mr Major contemplated resignation but decided to confront his critics in the most dramatic fashion on June 22, 1995, when he summoned reporters to the Rose Garden of 10 Downing Street and announced he would be resigning the leadership of the Conservative Party and seeking re-election. The challenge came not from a sceptic backbencher, but from one of his own Cabinet, John Redwood — who, after a weekend's reflection, resigned in order to stand. After more than a week of in-fighting, Mr Major won comfortably on July 4, by 218 votes to 89 for Mr Redwood. This showed the extent of dissatisfaction with Mr Major, but the win was enough to establish his leadership for the rest of the Parliament. A key factor was the support for Mr Major from Mr Heseltine, then President of the Board of Trade. That was later explained when it was disclosed that Mr Major had offered him the post of Deputy Prime Minister before the ballot.

**H**OWEVER, the Tories lost by-elections and, from October 1995 onwards, a series of defectors — Alan Howarth to Labour, then Emma Nicholson and Peter Thurnham to the Liberal Democrats. The repercussions of the Nolan report and the row over the Scott report in February 1996 into the sale of arms-related equipment to Iraq did not help the Government's standing. The cash for questions affair resurfaced in the autumn of 1996 when a libel case brought against *The Guardian* by Neil Hamilton, a former minister, and by Ian Greer, the lobbyist, was dropped at the last minute. That led to a series of other damaging allegations and, two months later, the resignation of David Willetts, a rising star of the Government, over his role as a whip during an earlier inquiry into the affair.

But Europe remained to curse the Government. In spring 1996, the European Union imposed a ban on British beef exports after the discovery that "mad cow" disease could be passed to human beings. Britain then inaugurated a policy of non-cooperation within the EU, blocking new decisions. This lasted a few weeks before being dropped in return for promises to review the ban in the light of actions taken by Britain to eradicate the disease. By the time of the election, the ban on beef exports remained fully in force.

Throughout this period, there were pressures for a more sceptical line over the single currency. Kenneth Clarke, the Chancellor and leading pro-European in the Cabinet, reluctantly agreed in spring 1996 to the promise of a referendum during the next Parliament if a Conservative Cabinet recommended entry. Labour continued its smooth transformation, as Mr Brown announced that it would also hold a referendum over entry into a single currency, while it would not raise the basic and higher rates of income tax for five years. Despite the steady erosion — and, in February 1997, final disappearance — of his Commons majority, Mr Major succeeded in keeping his Government in place for its whole five-year term and enacting almost all its 1992 manifesto pledges, before announcing on Monday, March 17, 1997, that the election would be on May 1.

# MAJOR'S SIX-WEEK HAUL
# TO POLITICAL DISASTER

### By Philip Webster, Political Editor of The Times

TONY BLAIR strode triumphantly into Downing Street on May 2, 1997, with the highest majority ever won by the Labour Party at a general election. Eighteen long and painful years in the wilderness had ended in the most dramatic manner.

The opinion polls had suggested it for months, if not years. The Wirral by-election in February, with its 17 per cent swing to Labour, had given another firm pointer.

But the massive scale of Labour's election landslide — leaving Mr Blair with an overall majority of 178 seats — took the country by surprise, most of all the politicians. He was not the only joyful leader. Paddy Ashdown's Liberal Democrats took full advantage of the anti-Tory mood to double their 1992 tally. Their 46 seats were the most for any third party since 1929. The Conservatives won 336 seats in 1992. Five years later that figure fell to 165. It was a political earthquake of a kind not seen since 1906, when the Conservatives collapsed from 402 to 157 seats.

**Blair: triumphant**

When he went to bed on the night before polling, Mr Blair would happily have settled for a majority of between 30 and 40. Late that evening he was telling friends who telephoned him in his Sedgefield constituency that he did not believe the polls — he hoped to win but there would be no landslide and the important thing was to get out the Labour vote the next day.

He need not have worried. Britain was ready to change. Maybe it had been for five years. In the wider sweep of political history the 1992 election may have been an accident. Many senior Conservatives admitted after that result that they had expected, even deserved, to lose.

John Major, however, the unlikely winner in 1992, always believed that he could turn it round again. He had huge self-belief when it came to elections. He believed as he approached his date with destiny in 1997 that he could once more convince the electorate that, in spite of all the difficulties of the intervening years, it was better off with the devil it knew, the Conservatives. He believed, too, that the discipline that had been the hallmark of Mr Blair's "new" Labour would crack under the pressure of an election campaign and that Mr Blair himself might not stand up to the rigours it would impose.

The story of the 1997 campaign, one of the longest in political history, was that none of those things happened and that Labour itself caught the imagination and mood of the nation, consigning the defeated Mr Major swiftly to the history books.

When 1997 began there were three possible dates for the election: March 20, April 10 and May 1. Although Mr Major flirted with the first, the big poll deficit always made the last the most likely. He was always going to need the maximum amount of time to start eating into the lead. But once the April 10 option had gone, Mr Major decided to make the most of the time available and to go for a campaign lasting 6½ weeks. On March 17 he went to the Palace to seek a dissolution of Parliament. Forty-five days later, after one of the most miserable campaigns in the annals of the Tory party, he was going back there to resign.

Day one was unpromising for the Tories. *The Sun* newspaper, fierce opponent of Labour in previous elections, announced that it would back Mr Blair, a big psychological boost.

What Mr Major needed least in these early days was what he was about to get. The issue of parliamentary sleaze, the row about MPs allegedly taking cash for tabling questions, resurfaced. Sir Gordon Downey, the Parliamentary Commissioner for Standards, who had been asked to investigate the affair, had been unable to publish his report before Parliament rose. Labour and the Liberal Democrats said they smelt a rat and accused Mr Major of trying to evade the findings.

Sir Gordon then rushed out an interim report to exonerate some of those under investigation, but one of those he was unable to clear, Tim Smith, came under pressure in his Beaconsfield constituency and stood down as a candidate. The attention of the media then swung to Neil Hamilton, the Tatton candidate, who had been at the centre of the allegations. Despite tough pressure from Central Office, Mr Hamilton was in no mood to follow Mr Smith's lead. In the midst of all this Allan Stewart, then MP for Eastwood, the Tories' safest seat in Scotland, resigned on health grounds amid allegations about his private life; another MP, Piers Merchant, was accused of having an affair with a nightclub hostess, denied it and survived; and then the chairman of the Conservative Party in Scotland resigned after allegations of a homosexual affair.

Mr Hamilton's rivals in Tatton announced they were standing down to make way for an anti-sleaze candidate. The BBC broadcaster Martin Bell emerged from the ether to fill the vacancy. Two weeks into the battle — and the Government had never managed to get out of the sleaze mire. Mr Major was furious but helpless.

The manifestos duly appeared, with the Conservatives unexpectedly promising a £1.2 billion package of tax concessions designed to help married couples in which one of the partners stays at home to look after children. Sleaze at last faded from the scene. A slightly nervous Mr Blair formally launched Labour's programme for government with a warning that it would "blow its place in history" if it betrayed the trust of the people. It sounded suspiciously as if he was setting out his stall for two terms, rather than one.

IRONICALLY, in view of what was to occur later, the first wobbles in the post-manifesto campaign proper came from Labour. Mr Blair got himself into hot water by apparently comparing his proposed Scottish parliament to a parish council. Then Labour's briefers, faced with Tory claims of a big hole in their spending plans, put out the word that Mr Blair would if necessary privatise remaining state industries, including air traffic control, to fill the gap. The Tories claimed it was proof he would do anything to win. And when a MORI poll showed a big cut in the Labour lead, there was a flutter down at Millbank Tower, in Labour's Clinton-style headquarters. It was decided firmly that there should be no more policymaking on the hoof and that the campaign should be dominated more than ever by Mr Blair. If there were any more wobbles, they were well hidden.

Mr Major was now to become embroiled yet again, and this time probably fatally, in the issue that had dogged him throughout the Parliament — Europe. A millionaire businessman from Yorkshire, Paul Sykes, had made the astonishing offer to assist financially with the campaigns of Tory candidates who opposed the single currency. He had scores of takers.

Mr Major's line remained to wait-and-see. Then two ministers were found to have breached the line in their election addresses. Euro-chaos had enveloped the Tories at the time they could least afford it. The memory of past divisions, the image of a leader being stabbed in the back by his own colleagues, returned with a terrible vividness.

The Prime Minister's response was typical. He was in a corner and he came out fighting. In one of the most dramatic moments of the campaign he strode into Central Office, tore up the script for the day and decided to make Europe the central issue of the campaign. He passionately defended his own line on the single currency but turned the attack on to Mr Blair, saying that he would sell out at the forthcoming Amsterdam summit. The next day he offered his party a free vote on any future decision to go into the single currency.

He then authorised the most notorious advert of the campaign, a picture of a tiny Mr Blair sitting on the knee of the German Chancellor, Helmut Kohl. The Tory pro-Europeans were outraged, and allowed their unhappiness to become known. Jacques Santer, President of the European Commission, then obliged by attacking British Euroscepticism. The Tory strategists claimed that Europe was turning the corner for them, but they were probably whistling in the wind.

Then, in a pre-election coup that Labour parties of old would not have swallowed, Gordon Brown first said that he would accept the spending programmes already budgeted for by the Tories, and secondly that there would be no rises in the top or basic rate of tax for the five years of a Parliament. Astonishingly, Labour was able to fight the campaign attacking the Tories on tax — reminding the country of the 22 tax rises that had taken place in the previous Parliament. Try as they did, the Conservatives seemed hardly to lay a glove on Labour over the subject that had sunk it in the past.

**M**R BLAIR was well ahead, but Labour had one more card to play. Before the election the Tories had unveiled their "big idea", a drastic revision of pensions which by the year 2040 would have privatised the state system, although leaving everyone with a guarantee of the basic state figure. The Conservative policymakers had been proud of their plan, but it did not go down well on the doorsteps. Labour picked up the feeling and went on the attack, accusing the Tories of "abolishing" the state pension.

It provoked the fiercest clashes of the election, with ministers lashing out at Mr Blair and accusing him of "bare-faced lies". They were later ruefully to admit that any last hope of recovery disappeared at that moment.

As the campaign drew to its conclusion, Conservative strains began to show. Mr Major let it be known that he was assuming overall control for the final push; there were recriminations among the image gurus about adverts being turned down; the supporters of future Tory leadership contenders began to circle ominously; and the polls steadfastly refused to move in Mr Major's favour.

Over at Millbank, on the open-plan floor where Peter Mandelson and Mr Brown directed operations, confidence was sky-high. But after the experience of 1992, when the pollsters got it wrong, no one was allowed to take anything for granted. The caution was palpable. With memories of the disastrous Sheffield rally of the last campaign still fresh, triumphalism was banned.

The Labour campaign had been a triumph for control. The divisions and gaffes that characterised past elections were absent. Candidates were told by pager, computer and fax the line to be taken on the emerging issues. The political broadcasts were of high quality. One showing Mr Blair at home with his children talking about the driving forces of his politics was said later to have made a big impact on the electorate. Mr Major resorted to hyperbole, warning voters on the final Monday that there were only 72 hours left to save the United Kingdom. The regular refrain from Mr Blair was that Britain is not a landslide country. From his own standpoint he was soon to be proved blissfully wrong.

Politicians of all parties later observed that on the morning of May 1, as the voters went about their business, there was an air of particular excitement that occurs only at watershed elections. A political shift was occurring and the Tory candidates knew they would be the ones to suffer. Regardless of their stance on specific issues, all the Conservatives in marginal and semi-marginal seats, and some in constituencies which had been regarded as safe, were rejected. They were wiped out in Scotland and Wales; now their only strongholds are in the English countryside and suburbs.

The Liberal Democrats ruthlessly targeted the Tory marginals; their doubled tally came despite a slight drop in their share of the vote from 1992.

The supreme victor, however, was Mr Blair. New Labour, conceived by Mr Blair, Mr Brown and Mr Mandelson, had arrived in government. As the new Prime Minister remarked as he arrived back from the Palace: "Enough of talking. It is time now to do."

# Voting patterns analysed
# BIGGEST SHAKE-UP FOR 50 YEARS

## *By Peter Riddell*

**T**HE **1997** general election produced the biggest electoral and parliamentary upheaval since 1945. Labour achieved its highest ever number of MPs and biggest majority, while the Conservatives suffered their worst result since 1906, and, on some measures, since 1832 or 1859.

After the general election, Labour had 418 MPs, exactly double its total in 1983, and 25 more than its previous record in 1945. So Labour's overall Commons majority is now 178 (after deducting the Speaker), against 146 in 1945. By contrast, the Conservative rump of 165 MPs compares with its peak of 397 in 1983 and its previous low of 213 in 1945. After May 1, the Tories had less than half the number of MPs elected five years earlier, losing seven Cabinet ministers and nearly half the Government front bench when Parliament was dissolved.

The bare arithmetic is startling enough. Labour, which had edged steadily upwards from the disaster of 1983, saw its share of the vote leap from 34.4 to 43.2 per cent – higher than the Conservatives achieved at any point during the Thatcher era but lower than Labour's postwar peaks of over 48 per cent in 1945 and 1951. By contrast, the Tory share fell from 41.9 to 30.7 per cent. This was admittedly nearly four percentage points higher than Labour's low point in 1983, but was five points less than October 1974, previously the Tories' worst performance this century and lower than at any time since 1832. The resulting swing of 10 per cent from Conservatives to Labour is less than the switch of more than 12 per cent in 1945.

The Liberal Democrats also had a good day, more than doubling their number of MPs to 46, compared with the 20 elected in 1992. This is the highest number of Liberal MPs since 1929 during Lloyd George's "Indian Summer". However, the party's share of the total vote was just 16.8 per cent. This compared with 17.8 per cent five years earlier and a postwar peak of 25.4 per cent for the old SDP-Liberal Alliance in 1983, when the linked parties won just 23 MPs.

**T**HE **ELECTION** was primarily a massive rejection of the Tories. Their vote fell from a record for any party of 14.1 million in 1992 down to 9.60 million. Labour's vote rose from 11.56 million to 13.52 million. But overall turnout was well down, from 77.7 per cent to 71.5 per cent, the lowest since the 1930s. This suggests that many former Tory voters stayed at home.

What these figures show is that the Tories suffered a twin squeeze from both main opposition parties. Labour organised effectively and achieved larger swings in its target seats, and even in some which it had never dared hope to win, than in its safe seats. For instance, Labour won Hastings, Harrow West and East, Hove and Ilford North, Finchley and Golders Green, Enfield North and Southgate on swings of more than 15 per cent, compared with under 5 per cent in its heartlands in Glasgow or in the South Wales Valleys. In Wales, the seat with the lowest turnout was Merthyr Tydfil and Rhymney, at just 65.1 per cent, but this also had the largest Labour majority in the Principality.

The much-discussed phenomenon of tactical voting occurred with a vengeance. In Labour target seats, the Liberal Democrat vote fell more sharply than nationally, allowing Labour to capture such unlikely previous Tory bastions as Hastings, Hove and Wimbledon. But the Labour vote rose less than the national average in Tory-held seats targeted by the Liberal Democrats. The latter, as a result, captured constituencies such as Lewes and Thames-side seats such as Richmond Park and Twickenham.

As advocates of proportional representation were quick to point out, the result was to exaggerate the number of seats won by Labour. It scooped up a massive 65.2 per cent of the seats for 43.2 per cent of the votes. The Liberal Democrats still managed only 7.2 per cent of the seats for 16.8 per cent of the vote, but this was their best return per vote for decades. For once, the Tories were the victims of the first-past-the-post electoral system, winning only 25.7 per cent of the seats for 30.7 per cent of the overall vote. The vulnerability of the Tories is shown by the fact that they now hold only nine seats with an absolute majority, their safest seat being John Major's in Huntingdon.

Of the minority parties, the Scottish Nationalists had one of their more successful campaigns, moving into second place in share of the vote in Scotland, ahead of the Tories and the Liberal Democrats, but only boosting their number of MPs from three to six. Plaid Cymru consolidated its position with four MPs. The Tories were completely wiped out for the first time in Scotland and Wales, making it much harder for the party to fight Labour's devolution proposals. The Tories' decline in Scotland has been one of the most startling electoral trends of recent years – back in 1955 they had 36 seats, or just over half the total, north of the border.

S IR JAMES GOLDSMITH'S Referendum Party managed 812,000 votes in total, an average share of the vote of 2.7 per cent. Sir James himself won only 1,518 votes in Putney, just 3.4 per cent of the vote. Its best performances were in Harwich, where it won 4,923 votes, or 9.2 per cent, and in Reigate where the former Tory MP Sir George Gardiner recorded 3,352 votes, or 6.9 per cent. The intervention of the party could have cost several Tory candidates their seats. It is impossible to be precise since the party will have attracted votes from across the spectrum, but the Referendum Party vote was larger than the amount by which 17 Tories were defeated.

The exit poll conducted by NOP for the BBC underlines Tony Blair's success in reassuring and winning over the middle classes. There was a swing to Labour of 13 per cent among this group. A Tory lead of 32 per cent over Labour among professionals and managers in 1992 narrowed to 7 per cent in 1997. There was a dramatic shift among white-collar workers, where Tory support dropped from nearly a half to just over a quarter, with Labour support rising nearly as much. Another striking change was the elimination of the previous gender gap favouring the Tories among women. There was equal support for Labour among both sexes following a larger swing to the party among women than men.

Labour made its biggest gains among young people, winning well over half the support of first-time voters and those aged under 30. It made steadily smaller gains the further up the age range you go. The biggest shift was among the middle-aged. Labour lost support compared with 1992 among pensioners, winning a third of their votes. By contrast, the Tories won just over one fifth of the votes of those aged under 30 but more than two fifths of the votes of those aged more than 65.

# YOUTHFUL BLAIR THROWS OUT HIS PARTY'S OLD BAGGAGE

*By Anthony Howard, an Assistant Editor of The Times*

IT IS given to few politicians to transform the nature and character of the parties that they lead. By successfully repealing the Corn Laws, Sir Robert Peel certainly did that in the 19th century — but at the price of keeping the Tories out of power for the next twenty years. It has been the singular achievement of Tony Blair, only the fifth Labour Party leader to become Prime Minister, to achieve the same result without sacrifice or suffering — and, what is more, to bring it off in face of the numbed gaze of his opponents within the space of three short years.

Of course, when the nation's youngest 20th-century Prime Minister first took his place on the Treasury bench on May 7, 1997 (the day of the Speaker's re-election), he was only too aware that he owed various debts. The principal one undoubtedly was to his predecessor-bar-one, Neil Kinnock. Without his essential spadework in the task of trying to bring old Labour up to date, the whole concept of new Labour could never have been packaged and merchandised. (Nor, for that matter, could it ever have been manufactured had Mr Blair's immediate predecessor, John Smith, not successfully put his leadership on the line over the crucial issue of one member, one vote at the party conference of 1993 — but that is another, and rather more edgy, story.)

Yet, slightly less conveniently, Tony Blair is also recognisably the heir of the former Social Democratic Party, that band of nearly thirty former Labour MPs who broke away from the party then under the leadership of Michael Foot to — as they hoped — "break the mould" of British politics in 1981. They did, in fact, no such thing: in the general election of 1983 they were rewarded with six parliamentary seats and, four years later just before the SDP imploded, with merely five.

Mr Blair, however, has never been slow to acknowledge the debt he owes, if not to the Gang of Four, then at least to the Gang of Three (for some reason — perhaps because he endorsed the Tories in 1992 — David Owen has long since been written out of this particular script). But the Prime Minister has always gone out of his way to emphasise that with people like Roy Jenkins, Shirley Williams and Bill Rodgers (to say nothing of his own economic adviser Derek Scott, a former SDP candidate) it was not so much a case of their leaving the Labour Party as of the Labour Party leaving them.

Nevertheless, it was his own personal decision to hold fast to the faith — at just about the lowest point in his party's fortunes — that eventually made everything else possible. Politicians can seldom exactly foresee the logical and probable consequences of their own actions. That was certainly true of Neil Kinnock's bold refusal to vote for Tony Benn in the deputy leadership election of 1981, the first such contest to be settled under the recorded vote rules of the new electoral college. But, just as Michael Foot's eventual successor as party leader then took a bet on the likely future shape of the politics of the Left in Britain — and got it right — so, in a much more minor way, did Tony Blair a few months later. The determining point in his own political history lay in his decision in the spring of 1982 to seek the Labour nomination at a by-election then pending in the rock-ribbed Conservative seat of Beaconsfield.

The 28-year-old rising young barrister with a mop of unruly fair hair did not do well. He came third with fewer than 4,000 votes, well behind the Liberal/Alliance candidate and even managed to lose his deposit (under the old rules, in existence until 1985, you had to get one eighth of the total vote in order to save your £150). But the important point was that he had put down his marker and provided a genuine token of his party allegiance.

In politics, as elsewhere, it is all too easy to be wise after the event; but it is at least possible to argue that, but for that forlorn electoral excursion into the Home Counties 15 years ago, the new Prime Minister would never have been able to carry through the political revolution that he has. Beaconsfield did not merely provide him with his battle honours, scarred though he may have been: it also offered him a breastplate and shield against any allegations that he was merely a Johnnie-come-lately who had sidled his way into a safe Labour seat.

Of course, when one year later he did snatch the Labour nomination in the Sedgefield division of Durham from under the nose of the then prominent left-winger Les Huckfield, it *was* held against him. But what enabled him to carry that selection conference – and he won it fair and square, leading on each of the five ballots – was precisely his lack of ideological baggage, the very quality that he was subsequently to bring to bear in getting the Labour Party to "think the unthinkable".

There has never been a Labour leader with fewer roots in "the movement", as it was always traditionally known, than the Scottish public schoolboy and Oxford law graduate who now leads it. Clement Attlee had his years at Toynbee Hall in the East End, Hugh Gaitskell his evenings of regular WEA lecturing in the Nottinghamshire coalfield – but Tony Blair (unless middle-class infiltration of the Queensbridge ward of the Hackney South constituency party is considered to count) originally had nothing by way of even adoptive working-class credentials to offer. At the outset there were those who saw this as confronting him with a challenge; in retrospect it is perfectly clear that it supplied him with an opportunity.

*Kinnock: the trailblazer*

It is precisely because Mr Blair is recognisably not a product of the Labour movement that he has so brilliantly been able to cut the painter with the party's past. In the United States in 1992 President Clinton conducted his presidential election campaign on the basis of himself and his running-mate, Al Gore, representing "a new generation of Democrats"; in Britain five years later Mr Blair and (however reluctantly) his deputy leader John Prescott went one better, claiming that they represented not so much "a new generation" as "a new party". And all the evidence suggests that in the eyes of the electorate – particularly in the South East – they brought it off, new Labour being perceived as an entirely novel (and thus smart and fashionable) political product.

Will it, though, prove to be more than a one-off trick? Harold Wilson, after all, tried his hardest to turn Labour into "the natural party of government" but, however promising the prospects for that once looked, he subsequently lived long enough as an ex-Prime Minister into the Thatcher and Major eras to sense his original aspiration turning to ashes in his mouth. Are there any reasons for thinking that the new Labour Government, which – whatever its vast parliamentary majority – got only 43.2 per cent of the national aggregate vote, will prove any more durable and lasting?

The answer has to be that this time things do at least *seem* different. There has, for one thing, been no performance with mirrors – Mr Blair has actually changed his party and done it in the most permanent manner possible by altering its entire power structure. Gone are the days when the annual Labour Party conference still struck terror into the hearts of the party's parliamentary wing. Today, with all important issues put straight to a vote of the party's mass membership, it survives only as a mere shadow of its former self — with its wings due to be further clipped by the growth over the next few years of "policy forums".

Or take again the trade unions. The original Labour Party may have sprung from their loins, but no one in Mr Blair's new model party emphasises that form of direct descent any more. The unions will, one is assured, enjoy the same rights as any legitimate pressure group — neither less nor more. And, if things should get tense in any of their discussions with the Government, it will be no good their invoking any of the sacred texts about "workers by hand or brain" or "the means of distribution, production and exchange". Such phrases, along with the rest of the once-revered Clause Four of the party's constitution, have gone straight into the lumber room of Labour history — and nobody, one suspects, will be moving them out from there at least for as long as the modernisers retain control of all the party's levers of power. They believe they have seen the future, and they are sure they know how to make it work.

# REVOLUTION THAT CHANGED
# THE FACE OF POLITICS

## By Simon Jenkins

**A REVOLUTION DIVIDES** the politics of 1997 from those of 1979. That revolution is greater than any since the conversion of a war economy into the welfare state in 1945. In retrospect, the 18 years of Conservative Government seem a Bunyanesque pilgrimage from national despair, through agony, to a new self-confidence. The old political economy had settled a pox on the face of post-imperial Britain, immune to cure by Tories and Socialists alike. In 1974 a Conservative Government protested that the nation was ungovernable, and was sent packing. In 1979 a Labour Government had the same experience. Yet by 1997 the voters could gaze out over a revitalised economy and restored international standing. They could turn to the Tories and, almost casually, said "Thanks but no thanks". They accepted the revolution but knew it was time for a change.

The years associated with Margaret Thatcher's ascendancy should properly embrace those of her "children" under John Major. Though Mr Major's governing style could hardly have been more different, he sustained Mrs Thatcher's continuity of policy both at home and abroad, a continuity mostly hidden in the noise of the Westminster bear garden. There was no noticeable break in the Thatcherite agenda with her fall in November 1990. Nor were the pitfalls that afflicted Mr Major's Cabinet — notably Black Wednesday and the split over Europe — ones that Mrs Thatcher could have avoided. She suffered the same pitfalls. History will treat the Thatcher-Major years as a political unity.

That said, the era was no monolith. The Tory party that took power in 1979 was divided and hesitant. Mrs Thatcher was regarded by most of her colleagues as gauche and probably temporary. Her manifesto was timid. On taking office, her one obsession was to cut taxes, which clashed with her spending concessions to party supporters in the Armed Forces, the police and public services. The clash wrecked public finances for the first three years of her Government. Apart from the sale of council houses, she opposed the radicalism of colleagues such as Geoffrey Howe and Nigel Lawson. She refused to fight the miners in 1981. Divisions between "wets" and "dries" led to a 1981 party conference that was alive with threats to her leadership. Observers doubted if Mrs Thatcher could survive the winter.

**T HIS HELPS** to explain the great turning point, the Falklands War of early summer 1982. The Argentine invasion arose directly from a British Government error: a failure to take defensive measures against a threat to territory because relations between the Foreign Office, Defence Ministry and Downing Street had all but collapsed. The response was that of a doomed Prime Minister. She acceded to the most reckless advice, from the Royal Navy, that the islands could be recaptured. The gamble was exceptionally close. But victory was achieved and victory knows no buts. Margaret Thatcher's standing both at home and abroad was completely transformed.

The Falklands gave her a new self-confidence and mastery over her Government. Her opinion poll rating soared and opponents both within and outside the party were crushed. She had demoted or discarded such rivals as Francis Pym and James Prior. She cruised to her greatest election victory in 1983. It was not until then that the defining characteristics of Thatcherism started to emerge: a belief in market forces and private over public enterprise and a scepticism towards government. These were not new to Toryism. Many in Sir Edward Heath's Government had similar ambitions. But the 1983 mandate enabled Mrs Thatcher to practise what she had so far been mostly preaching. She now saw herself as a fighter, a survivor of wars, political battles and, in 1984, an IRA assassination attempt in Brighton. She sought new enemies.

The first two were old socialist foes in the unions and local government. The reforms to labour law of the previous Parliament now led to a confrontation with the miners' union, culminating in open war in 1985. It was a battle that tested the body politic and the Cabinet's nerve as had few peacetime encounters. The Government was frequently isolated and, as in the Falklands, the outcome was often in doubt. Eventual victory further enhanced Mrs Thatcher's self-confidence (though not her popularity). Against local government, victory was swifter. Rate-capping was introduced in 1984 and the left-wing Greater London Council abolished in 1985. But the attempt to introduce a poll tax to replace the local property tax was to prove catastrophic. Not only was the tax phenomenally unpopular, but its chief purpose, to make local councils more accountable for high spending, was vitiated by Mrs Thatcher, allowing the Treasury to cap the tax centrally. The party of the shires and local democracy was made to seem the party of "Whitehall knows best". The Government was blamed.

But that was to come. The mid-Eighties saw Thatcherism girding itself for what were to be its golden years. The Prime Minister had Nigel Lawson as Chancellor, strongly committed to privatisation. In Whitehall were men who, with varying degrees of effectiveness, were of like mind: Norman Tebbit, Kenneth Baker, Nicholas Ridley, Norman Fowler and Patrick Jenkin. Privatisation moved from fringe trading activities to core industries, to British Telecom and British Airways in 1984 and on to shipbuilding, cars, ports and airports. The pace became frenetic. If Cabinet ministers seemed to fall by the wayside — Leon Brittan, Michael Heseltine, John Moore — they could be seen as the unavoidable casualties of war. To Margaret Thatcher, the Conservative Party

*Thatcher: ever a fighter*

was a revolutionary party and the bitterest crusade always lay ahead.

Mrs Thatcher found her final endorsement in the election victory in 1987, an election won, she was convinced, by her own efforts. The outcome brought forward root and branch reform to two pillars of state provision, education in 1988 and the NHS reforms of 1990. Privatisation moved to centre stage as gas and electricity came under the hammer. The dispersal of public services to agencies and the private sector became messianic. From street cleaning to government hospitality, from prisons to royal shipyards, nothing was immune. A civil servant, Sir Terence Heiser, compared it to the Battle of Waterloo, constant noise, fog and destruction, with soldiers praying that someone somewhere had a plan. Yet this reformist turmoil gave Thatcherism a dynamism that carried it forward into the Major Governments and beyond.

Mrs Thatcher's fall was spectacular. The cause was simple. Her insistence on carrying on with the poll tax ignored and demoralised her party in the country. It convinced Tory MPs that they would lose the next election. In addition, her high-handed treatment of once close colleagues such as Sir Geoffrey Howe and Mr Lawson lost her support when she most needed it. Even as she conceded entry into a European exchange-rate mechanism at Madrid in 1989, she found herself replacing Sir Geoffrey with John Major and then Mr

Lawson with Mr Major. Both men joined Michael Heseltine on the back benches in a lethal trio of the dispossessed.

Her failure to establish a Cabinet consensus on Europe left Mrs Thatcher isolated, as it did her successor seven years later. It needed only Sir Geoffrey Howe to goad Mr Heseltine to his leadership challenge in November 1990 for the rock of Mrs Thatcher's party ascendancy to shatter. Each of her Cabinet colleagues trooped into her room, gritted their teeth and told her to stand down. They and their party had had enough. They would prefer the mild-mannered John Major or the patrician Douglas Hurd, anything but the hectoring, battling, unyielding Margaret Thatcher. She had forgotten that the Tory party, like Britain as a whole, liked to be ruled by oligarchs, not autocrats. Not since the 1945 ejection of Winston Churchill had a British political event so electrocuted the world.

**M**R MAJOR'S subsequent period in office can easily seem in retrospect a chaotic decline from the humiliation of Black Wednesday in 1992 to the disintegration of the Government five years later. That is a misconception. The early years were dominated not just by the successful Gulf War and the opt-outs of the 1991 Maastricht treaty but by a reinvigorated Thatcherism. The coalmines, water and the railways, which Mrs Thatcher had not dared privatise, were sold. The poll tax was abolished and property taxes restored. A start was made to social security reform. An abortive attempt was made to nationalise the local school system through schools opting for central funding.

Most remarkable was John Major's election victory against all odds in 1992. This deserves to rank among the most crucial incidents of the era. It averted what would have been the dismantling of much of Mrs Thatcher's work by Neil Kinnock's unreformed Labour Party. Mr Major may have lacked his predecessor's charisma. He was also cursed for most of his premiership with a single-figure parliamentary majority. But he gave his party a record-breaking term of power and without betraying any substance of the Thatcher programme. John Major entrenched Thatcherism. He convinced Labour that there was no alternative and thus made it last.

His shortcomings in power were similar to Mrs Thatcher's. Neither was prepared to attack the central pillars of the welfare state, and thus had to watch public spending remain at the same proportion of the nation's output (roughly 40 per cent) as under old Labour. If the fringes of state activity had been shorn, the core had grown. It had also become more centralised. Local government discretion had, by the mid-1990s, all but vanished. Aspirations to modest autonomy in Scotland and Wales were crushed by Mr Major's bizarrely personalised campaign against devolution.

This march of centralisation was repeated inside government. To most officials Thatcherism meant more bureaucracy not less, the result of "market testing", performance targeting, auditing and league tabling. The once relaxed style of British public administration became more efficient, but acquired a domineering corporatism. The Treasury was more powerful than ever. Subsidiary government fell under vetted quangos rather than democratic assemblies. Thatcherism was the antithesis of laisser faire – indeed the lady vigorously denied the term. It was about strong government with firm objectives. The casualties were pluralism, localism and democratic accountability. To Margaret Thatcher, they were a small price to pay for the final trouncing of socialism.

What a trouncing it was. Britain in 1997 was a magnet not just for renewal of foreign investment but for visitors eager to study Thatcherism in practice. Other nations found their industries and welfare services as bloated as Britain's once were. They realised what Tony Blair's new Labour Party had realised. The United Kingdom had pulled off a revolution in modern government. It had torn every institution and tradition up by the roots. Few corners of the British political economy escaped the era unscathed. The irony was that the agency of that revolution was a party that called itself Conservative. Small wonder that the effort was Herculean, the strain intense. Small wonder that when, in the spring of 1997, the party presented itself to the electorate, it fainted dead away.

# IMPOVERISHED LIB DEMS HIT THE JACKPOT FOR ASHDOWN

*By Polly Newton, Political Reporter of The Times*

**B**Y THEIR own standards, the election was a triumph for the Liberal Democrats. They took 46 seats compared with 20 in 1992, with the best electoral performance by a third party since 1929.

They proved that they could win in places other than their traditional South and South West strongholds, taking seats in Yorkshire (Sheffield Hallam, Harrogate and Knaresborough), Scotland (Edinburgh West, Aberdeenshire West and Kincardine) and the North West (Hazel Grove, Southport). They gained five seats in and around London and dramatically increased their representation in the West Country. Their scalps included the former Chancellor of the Exchequer, Norman Lamont, in Harrogate and Knaresborough, and the maverick Tory author of spy novels, Rupert Allason, whom they beat by just 12 votes in Torbay.

It was a significant personal achievement for the Liberal Democrat leader, Paddy Ashdown, and the result scotched talk of an early post-election contest for his job. Mr Ashdown had determined from the start to fight a positive and consistent campaign that distinguished the party's policies from those of Labour in the minds of voters.

But his party's success in 1997 was also due to a strategy of concentrating its limited resources on the seats it had a chance of winning. Essentially, the Liberal Democrats learnt for the first time how to use to their best advantage the first-past-the-post voting system to which they remain so strongly opposed. Although their overall share of the vote fell slightly, they managed to pick up support in constituencies where it could help them to victory.

The party made no secret of either the decision to target particular seats or the relative poverty that was partly the reason for it. Lord Holme of Cheltenham, the Liberal Democrats' campaign director, said from the outset that the party would have to "fight smart". What that meant, in effect — although it was never acknowledged publicly by Lord Holme or anyone else involved in the campaign — was that hundreds of seats were identified as hopeless for the Liberal Democrats and ignored almost completely by the national party machine. There might have been a Liberal Democrat candidate in every constituency, but that did not mean the party seriously believed that each and every one could win. This caused dissent in some of the party's unwinnable seats from local party activists who demanded equal support from the centre, but with the benefit of hindsight their case looks even weaker than it did at the time. Only if Britain adopts a system of proportional representation will they be able to argue convincingly for Liberal Democrat campaign resources to be spread evenly across the country.

During the campaign itself, the Liberal Democrats took no advertising space in national newspapers. What little media advertising they could afford was done in regional newspapers covering their target seats. The sorry state of their bank balance was illustrated shortly before the campaign began when they unveiled a poster in London on a billboard-carrying van hired for £2,000, which had to be back at the rental company's headquarters by the end of that day. It was driven back via a handful of key constituencies in the hope that it would be seen by as many voters as possible. Labour and the Tories, by contrast, spent millions on fixed billboard sites in the run-up to polling day.

Apart from targeting seats, the Liberal Democrats' most effective campaign tactic was to highlight their policies in the two areas they believed were of particular concern to voters: education and health. Their promise to put 1p on the basic rate of income tax to fund a £2 billion annual investment in education was, by the end of the campaign, probably the best-known policy put forward by any of the parties.

Along with their manifesto, they published a supplement explaining how they would fund policies such as the restoration of free eye and dental checks (5p on a packet of cigarettes) and the recruitment of up to 5,000 doctors (a tightening of the rules on employers' national insurance contributions). Time and again, Mr Ashdown contrasted his own party's "menu with prices" ith what he said was Labour's refusal to explain how it would pay for its promises.

As he travelled the length and breadth of Britain on a 17,000-mile tour of more than 60 key seats, Mr Ashdown rarely spoke voluntarily about electoral or constitutional reform, those staples of previous Liberal Democrat election campaigns. Strategists had recognised that these were not, by and large, the issues which would convince a floating voter to back the party.

Ironically, constitutional reform is the one issue over which the Liberal Democrats are guaranteed some influence under Tony Blair's Government. The party signed an agreement with Labour before the election setting out a joint approach to Scottish and Welsh devolution, electoral reform, reform of the House of Lords and a Freedom of Information Act.

In all other areas, the Liberal Democrats will continue to struggle to "make the difference", despite their campaign slogan which promised to do so. It was perhaps the greatest irony of the 1997 election that the tactics which brought the party such dramatic success in terms of the sheer number of MPs returned to Westminster also helped to ensure that it will remain insignificant in terms of policymaking in the House of Commons.

By their strategy of targeting winnable seats, the Liberal Democrats effectively allowed their vote to collapse in many of the

*Ashdown: personal success*

constituencies where Labour had come second to the Tories in 1992. Labour candidates in those seats scooped up anti-Tory votes by the bucketload because there was no real Liberal Democrat campaign locally. That helped to unseat Conservative candidates who had thought themselves safe, delivering Tony Blair a massive majority which put paid to any hopes that the Liberal Democrats could exert more power in the new Parliament than they had previously. In fact, the way they vote in the House will matter less. There is now no possibility, for example, that Mr Blair will have to rely on the Liberal Democrats to push through legislation on Europe which is opposed by Eurosceptics within his own party.

If there is another sour note, it is the reduced and paltry number of Liberal Democrat women MPs after the 1997 election. The party had finished the previous Parliament with 26 MPs (following four by-election victories and the defection from the Tories of Emma Nicholson in 1995 and Peter Thurnham in 1996), of whom four were women. Of the 46 Liberal Democrats elected this time, there were only three women: Jenny Tonge in Richmond Park, Jackie Ballard in Taunton and Rae Michie in Argyll and Bute. Liz Lynne, who had been returned for Rochdale in 1992, and Diana Maddock, who won the 1993 by-election in Christchurch, both lost their seats.

# LORDS OLD GUARD SWEPT AWAY

## By James Landale, Political Reporter of The Times

**THE ROUGH** bristles of Tony Blair's new broom were felt immediately in the House of Lords when the new Prime Minister appointed his ministerial team for the "other place". Most of the ermine-clad old guard who had defended Labour's flank through years of opposition were banished to the back benches. In their place came some new faces, many of whom were raised to the peerage in the past few years precisely so that they would be ready for a job in government.

Significantly, more women than before were appointed to Labour's 23-strong team in the Lords. **Baroness Jay of Paddington,** 58, daughter of the former Prime Minister, Lord Callaghan of Cardiff, is a Health Minister and Deputy Leader. **Baroness Hollis of Heigham,** 56, the jazz-loving academic, is a junior Social Security Minister. **Baroness Symons of Vernham Dean,** 48, the former head of the First Division Association (the top civil servants' union), becomes a junior Foreign Office Minister. She was raised to the peerage in 1996. **Baroness Blackstone,** 55, Master of Birkbeck College, London, is a Minister of State at the Education and Employment Department. **Baroness Hayman,** 48, the former MP for Welwyn and Hatfield who was raised to the peerage in 1995, becomes a junior Minister at the Environment and Transport Department.

As expected, **Lord Irvine of Lairg** is the new Lord Chancellor. He is a close friend of Mr Blair's and introduced him to Cherie Booth, who was to become his wife. He will be a key figure in orchestrating Labour's constitutional reforms in the Lords.

Many Labour peers who had held key frontbench posts during the long years of opposition were notable by their absence from the new team. Out went Lord Graham of Edmonton, Opposition Chief Whip between 1990 and 1997, and his deputy, Lord Morris of Castle Morris. Also gone were Lord Williams of Elvel (defence and environment), and Lord Peston (energy and trade). The chief survivor is **Lord Richard,** 65, Opposition Leader between 1992 and 1997, who becomes the new Leader of the Lords. Another veteran, the former farm worker **Lord Carter,** 65, is appointed to perhaps the most important job, that of Chief Whip, to steer through the controversial reforms.

**Lord Whitty,** the former Labour Party general secretary, joins the Whips' Office, as does **Lord Hoyle,** former chairman of the Parliamentary Labour Party. He was raised to the peerage after the dissolution of Parliament. Several others had to be created peers so that they could join the Government: **Lord Simon of Highbury**, who as Sir David Simon stood down as chairman of BP to become Minister for Trade and Competitiveness in Europe at the DTI; **Lord Falconer of Thoroton, QC,** 45, a personal friend of Mr Blair, to become Solicitor-General; **Lord Gilbert,** who as Dr John Gilbert stood down as MP for Dudley East before the election, to be Minister for Defence Procurement; and **Lord Hardie, QC,** to become Lord Advocate.

## MINISTERS IN THE HOUSE OF LORDS

**CABINET MINISTERS: Lord Irvine of Lairg,** Lord Chancellor; **Lord Richard,** Lord Privy Seal and Leader of the Lords.
**MINISTERS OF STATE: Baroness Jay of Paddington,** Health Minister and Deputy Leader of the Lords; **Lord Gilbert,** Minister for Defence Procurement – created life peer May 6, 1997; **Baroness Blackstone,** Education and Employment Minister; **Lord Clinton-Davis,** Minister for Trade and Exports; **Lord Simon of Highbury,** Minister for Trade and Competitiveness in Europe – created life peer May 7, 1997.
**UNDER SECRETARIES OF STATE: Baroness Hayman,** junior Environment and Transport Minister; **Baroness Symons of Vernham Dean,** junior Foreign Office Minister; **Lord Williams of Mostyn,** junior Home Office Minister; **Lord Donoughue,** junior Agriculture Minister; **Lord Sewel,** junior Scottish Office Minister; **Baroness Hollis of Heigham,** junior Social Security Minister; **Lord Dubs,** junior Northern Ireland Minister.
**LAW OFFICERS: Lord Falconer of Thoroton, QC,** Solicitor-General – created life peer May 6, 1997; **Lord Hardie, QC,** Lord Advocate – created life peer May 6, 1997.
**GOVERNMENT WHIPS: Lord Carter,** Chief Whip; **Lord McIntosh of Haringey,** Deputy Chief Whip; **Lord Haskel,** junior whip; **Baroness Farrington of Ribbleton,** junior whip; **Lord Whitty,** junior whip; **Baroness Gould of Potternewton,** junior whip; **Lord Hoyle,** junior whip – created life peer after dissolution of Parliament.

# NEW MEMBERS, NEW JOBS

*By Ruth Winstone, Associate Editor, House of Commons Guide*

**L**ANDMARK ELECTIONS this century have produced their distinctive Parliaments: the 1906 "cottage-bred" Liberal revival; the hard-faced men of 1919; the middle-class Labour revolution of 1945; the victory of Basildon man in 1983 and 1992. If the 1997 landslide election is epitomised by one feature, it is "Labour woman": in her mid-forties, a prison visitor or a JP, with political experience on a local council, a member of the Fabian Society, educated at grammar school and redbrick university.

"Conservative man" in the 1997 House of Commons is in his early forties, has been advising a senior minister in John Major's Government, has worked for a lobbying company or a City firm and has been educated at university, likely to be Oxbridge.

On the severely depleted Conservative benches, men and women active in banking, finance and business comprise less than 20 per cent of their total of 165 Members, a significant fall from the 1992 level. The most noticeable increase among Tory MPs has been John Betjeman's *Young Executive* – "partly a liaison man and partly PRO". Nearly 10 per cent of Conservative MPs are now from marketing, PR and journalism. Only 13 Tory women MPs were returned in 1997, just two more than in 1964.

Among the 418 Labour MPs, the socio-economic change from manufacturing to the service industries, from "proper jobs" in production towards teaching, local authority and consultancy roles, has reduced the trade union representation on the government benches to a handful of engineers, steelworkers and miners, while teachers, lecturers and academics dominate the Parliamentary Labour Party: one quarter of the total. Journalists are the next largest group, while there are 28 lawyers.

As if to reflect their appeal to both political wings, the 46 Liberal Democrats are spread evenly across the middle-class professions of teaching/academia, law and medicine, journalism and public relations.

Proximity to power or influence or the parliamentary process was grist to many a would-be MP's mill: 7½ per cent of Members in the three main parties (26 Conservatives, 20 Labour and four Liberal Democrats) had come into the House with some political kudos, whether as advisers to ministers, or researchers to MPs, or political lobbyists, or attached to think-tanks of Left or Right, or even as "aide to an MP" during a previous general election, the most humble of qualifications.

*The new intake: Labour woman and Tory man*

To judge by the Christian colours carried by MPs, the Tory party is still the Church of England's representative in Parliament, but Christian socialism is making a comeback among Labour MPs: 20 are members of the Christian Socialist Movement, Christian churches or other organisations. The Liberal Democrats have a strong Christian contingent; interestingly, religious affiliations are almost exclusive to male MPs.

# PORTILLO HEADS THE CULL
# OF DOOMED MINISTERS

*By Jill Sherman, Chief Political Correspondent of The Times*

**M**ICHAEL PORTILLO will probably be remembered as the most unlucky victim of the 1997 general election Tory rout. In the early hours of May 2, the Defence Secretary saw his political ambitions crushed as a Labour landslide swept away his 15,000 majority. The man whom many had tipped as the favourite to win the Tory leadership if John Major stepped down after the election suddenly found himself without a seat or a job. He looked devastated as his Enfield Southgate constituency rejected him by 1,400 votes.

Before and during the general election campaign 117 MPs had already declared they were standing down. By May 2 it was clear that a further 132 MPs would be joining them against their will – the biggest exodus from the House of Commons this century.

Mr Portillo joined six other Cabinet ministers who were defeated at the hands of Labour that night. At least two of them, Malcolm Rifkind, the Foreign Secretary, and Ian Lang, President of the Board of Trade, could also have been contenders for the Tory leadership. They saw their chances to further their political ambitions disappear along with all the other Tory MPs in Scotland.

The other Cabinet departures included Michael Forsyth, the Scottish Secretary whose chances of holding on to his slim majority were always in doubt; Roger Freeman, the Public Service Minister, who lost his seat by just 189 votes; William Waldegrave, Chief Secretary to the Treasury; and Tony Newton, Leader of the House.

As the political map changed from blue to red, ministers toppled by the hour. Sir Nicholas Bonsor, the Foreign Office Minister, John Bowis, the Health Minister, Alistair Burt, the Social Security Minister, Iain Sproat, the Sports Minister, Tom Sackville, the Home Office Minister, and John Watts, the Transport Minister, were all defeated as 33 ministers in total lost their seats.

The ministerial cull was the highest this century. In 1945 five Tory Cabinet ministers lost their seats but on May 1, over a third of the Government was defeated.

Other casualties included the former Trade Minister, Neil Hamilton, the MP at the centre of the "cash for questions" affair, who was defeated by Martin Bell, the former BBC foreign correspondent. Mr Bell had stepped in to fight the Tatton seat on an anti-sleaze ticket after the Labour and Liberal Democrat candidates had decided to withdraw.

David Mellor, the former Heritage Secretary who resigned after a much-publicised affair, was ousted by Labour in Putney. But when he made his speech minutes after defeat he focused on the failure of his opponent, Sir James Goldsmith, leader of the Referendum Party, even to keep his deposit.

**N**ORMAN LAMONT, the former Chancellor, was unable to win the Harrogate and Knaresborough seat where he was eventually adopted after his own Kingston constituency was eaten up in the boundary changes. Jonathan Aitken, who quit as a minister to fight a libel action over allegations about his past business interests, was another casualty, as was Edwina Currie, the controversial former Health Minister who spent much of the election campaign highlighting the divisions in her party over Europe.

Other colourful figures who will no longer grace the House of Commons green benches include Sir Marcus Fox, chairman of the Tory backbench 1922 Committee. The surprise exit of Sir Marcus left a vacancy in a post crucial for organising the leadership election.

David Evans, one of the most blunt-speaking MPs, was defeated, as were two of the MPs who had the whip withdrawn over refusing to vote with the Government on Europe,

Nicholas Budgen and Michael Carttiss. A leading pro-European, Hugh Dykes, of Harrow East, also made an unplanned exit.

Sebastian Coe, the Olympic athlete, who lost at Falmouth and Camborne, may decide to return to a sporting career after five years of relative obscurity in the Commons. Rupert Allason, who was defeated at Torbay, may find writing further spy novels more lucrative.

The casualties included several women working their way up the Tory hierarchy. Angela Knight, the Treasury Minister, Jacqui Lait, the first female Tory whip, Dame Angela Rumbold, Lady Olga Maitland and Elizabeth Peacock all failed to make it back to Westminster.

The Liberal Democrats had a good election but nevertheless lost three MPs, two of whom had come in through by-elections: Chris Davies, Oldham East and Saddleworth, and Diana Maddock at Christchurch. Liz Lynne, who clashed with her boss Paddy Ashdown over closer relations with the Labour Party, conceded defeat before the vote was completed at Rochdale.

The defeated MPs join another 72 Tory MPs, 38 Labour MPs, six Liberal Democrats and one Ulster Unionist, who have opted for retirement or more lucrative pastimes.

Long before the size of the Tory defeat was clear, the Conservatives had already decided to disappear in their droves. They left through age, disillusionment, or because they could no longer boost their incomes with outside interests. In contrast, Labour MPs, smelling victory, were anxious to reap the rewards of 18 years of Opposition by fighting another campaign.

Two Conservative Cabinet ministers – Sir Patrick Mayhew, the Northern Ireland Secretary, and Lord Mackay of Clashfern, the Lord Chancellor – stood down before the election, as did seven Tory ex-Cabinet ministers and three Labour ex-Cabinet ministers.

One of the most senior MPs to forsake the green benches was Douglas Hurd, who held three Cabinet posts over nine years – Foreign Secretary, Home Secretary and Northern Ireland Secretary – and who entered the Tory leadership election after Margaret Thatcher stepped down in 1990. He is expected to devote more time to writing political thrillers.

**O**THER senior Tories who stood down included Kenneth Baker, former Home Secretary; Paul Channon, the former Trade and Industry Secretary; David Howell, former Transport Secretary; and John Patten, former Education Secretary. Three former Chief Whips, Michael Jopling, Tim Renton and Richard Ryder, as well as John Biffen, former Leader of the House, also retired.

Prominent Labour MPs who retired included Roy Hattersley, the former deputy Labour leader, Peter Shore and Stanley Orme, all former Cabinet ministers.

The most noteworthy of the six Liberal Democrats who departed was Sir David Steel, who was leader of the Liberal Party from 1976 to 1988, when it merged with the SDP to form the Social and Liberal Democratic Party.

Weeks before the election there was a scramble to get a seat for Alan Howarth, the Tory defector – with all eyes on MPs who might suddenly decide to stand down. Mr Howarth eventually won the selection of the safe Labour seat of Newport East, on March 16, the day before the general election was called, when Roy Hughes, the sitting MP, decided to retire.

Sir Geoffrey Lofthouse, the Deputy Speaker, retired at the last minute, as did John Gilbert, John Evans, Doug Hoyle, Stewart Randall and Norman Hogg.

There was also an unexpected decision by Allan Stewart, the former Scottish Office Minister, to stand down from his Eastwood seat on health grounds, amid allegations about his private life, days after the election was called. The Conservative MP Tim Smith also stood down from his Beaconsfield seat when evidence from the Downey report on the cash for questions affair was leaked.

*Bowing out and voted out, page 302*

# GOLDSMITH HAMMERED – BUT HIS EURO FOES SUFFER TOO

### By Andrew Pierce, Political Correspondent of The Times

**S**IR JAMES GOLDSMITH'S Referendum Party, which waged a £20 million election campaign, has been written off by many politicians as an expensive irrelevance after securing less than 3 per cent of the vote.

The party attracted 810,000 votes, which was way short of its target of one million, and worked out at a cost of £24.68 per voter. Sir James, the founder and principal financial backer, suffered the added humiliation of losing his deposit in Putney where David Mellor, the former Tory Cabinet minister, lost his seat. But the businessman was in good company. Only 30 of his 547 candidates saved their £500 deposits. Most had to pay the £500 themselves.

But the dismissive initial verdict of some commentators on the Goldsmith factor is not shared by some of the Tory casualties of the rout of May 1. An analysis of the result has shown that the Referendum Party had a decisive influence on the fate of up to 20 Tory MPs who lost their seats.

Tony Newton, Leader of the House of Commons, was the biggest scalp. The Referendum Party amassed 2,165 votes in his Braintree constituency. The pro-European Mr Newton was defeated by Labour by a 1,451 margin. His Cabinet colleague Roger Freeman, Chancellor of the Duchy of Lancaster, also took a different view from the conventional one that Sir James wasted his money. Mr Freeman was a surprise loser in Kettering where he was defeated, after a recount, by 189 votes. The Referendum Party picked up 1,551 votes. Even if only half the Referendum Party votes came from traditional Tories, the damage to both Cabinet ministers would have been considerable.

*Goldsmith: out, out, out*

Few would dispute that, whatever direct effect the party had on the results, the imposing presence of Sir James was a considerable influence on the tone and conduct of the election campaign.

Europe dominated the closing stages. Almost one third of Tory candidates openly defied the leadership on the single currency in their election literature. It was an unprecedented uprising in an election campaign which even the most optimistic Tories feared they would lose. When government ministers also breached the collective responsibility rule, the Referendum Party sought to take much of the credit.

A week before the election, Europe was the third most important issue after health and education, according to MORI. At the same stage in 1992 it was ninth on the list.

But there is no firm evidence that the Referendum Party was right to claim responsibility for making it a more important issue on the doorstep. John Major always thought that by sounding more Eurosceptic than Labour he would pick up support. But Labour matched his utterances each time: whether it was on fish quotas or the Amsterdam inter-governmental conference only weeks later, all party leaders had sounded more sceptical towards a single currency.

Most inquests on the performance of the Referendum Party will record the simple fact that the £4 million spent on videos, £2 million on newspapers and £3 million on billboards failed to deliver a single seat or save most deposits. Sir James attributed this to a loss of nerve on the eve of polling day. But the opinion pollsters predicted precisely, from the beginning to the end of the campaign, the level of support for the Goldsmith party.

There were, however, many creditable performances where the Referendum Party tally was higher than the margin of defeat. Discontent among fishing communities was a big factor. Peter de Savary secured 3,534 votes in Falmouth and Camborne where Sebastian Coe, the Tory, went down by 2,688 votes. Iain Sproat, the Sports Minister, lost Harwich by 1,216, where the Referendum Party scored its biggest total, 4,923.

David Nicholson, in Taunton, was squeezed out by the Liberal Democrats, who secured a 2,443-vote majority, while the Referendum Party's vote was 2,760. Margaret Daly, a former Tory Euro MP and prominent pro-European, lost Weston-super-Mare where she had hoped to succeed Sir Jerry Wiggin. The Liberal Democrats won by a 1,274-vote majority. The Referendum Party polled 2,280.

**B** UT THE conclusion that the Referendum Party was responsible for up to 20 Tory losses contains the assumption that most or all of those who voted for the Goldsmith party would otherwise have voted for Mr Major. The claim that Michael Portillo was squeezed out by the Referendum Party in Enfield Southgate is not borne out by the figures. The Labour candidate would have won even if every Referendum Party supporter had voted Conservative. The same was true in Hastings and Rye, where Jacqui Lait, the first Tory woman whip, lost in a large protest against the Government's fishing policy. The Labour majority was 2,560; the Referendum Party polled 2,511. However, the UK Independence Party, which is committed to withdrawal from the EU, added 472 votes to the strong Tory anti-Europe vote.

While Sir James was disappointed to have polled only 1,500 votes in Putney, where Mr Mellor was unseated by a large swing to Labour, his comrade in arms John Aspinall marked one of the hgh points with 4,188 votes in Folkestone and Hythe, 8 per cent of the total. His Tory opponent was Michael Howard. Other high-profile candidates were David Bellamy, the botanist, who gathered 3,114 votes in John Major's Huntingdon constituency.

Within a week of polling day, moves had begun to wind down the Referendum Party to a pressure group. It was to be renamed the Referendum Movement and lobby against further EU integration.

It had by then already made one lasting contribution to political debate. There is continuing controversy over the allocation of the number of election broadcasts. Sir James, having put up 547 candidates, received only one broadcast, which was the same as several fringe parties who qualified because they fought the minimum 50 seats. It secured a judicial review against the decision.

At the next election the main broadcasters might seek to rewrite the rules to ensure that broadcasts are allocated not on the number of seats but only on the grounds of proven electoral support — by which time Sir James's party will have long since withdrawn from the battlefield.

# Future of the Union: Scotland
# TORY SILENCE IN THE GLENS

## By Gillian Bowditch, Scotland Correspondent of The Times

**T**HE GENERAL election of 1997 saw a complete change in the political make-up of Scotland, with the Scottish Conservatives and Unionists losing all ten of their seats. For the first time, the Tories have been left without a single MP, MEP or control of a local authority in Scotland.

Although the Conservatives were hit harder in terms of lost seats and huge swings in England than in Scotland, it is the complete lack of representation north of the border that will give them constitutional headaches, particularly in the Scottish Grand Committee, the parliamentary committee made up of all Scottish MPs which meets regularly to discuss Scottish matters.

The election was a story of Conservative weakness and Labour strength, with the Scottish National Party and the Liberal Democrats incidental beneficiaries of the power struggle between the two main players. Labour took 56 seats, a net gain of seven and 78 per cent of the total, with 45.6 per cent of the Scottish vote. Despite having 17.5 per cent of the vote, the Conservatives won nothing.

The Liberal Democrats, long advocates of proportional representation, ironically did better with the first-past-the-post system. They had only 13.0 per cent of the vote but took ten seats, a net gain of one. The Scottish National Party took six seats, a net gain of three on 1992, with 22 per cent of the vote.

Of the seven Cabinet ministers who lost seats, three were in Scotland. Michael Forsyth, the Scottish Secretary, lost Stirling to Labour's Anne McGuire with a majority of 6,411. She became the first person to unseat a sitting Secretary of State for Scotland since Winnie Ewing defeated Gordon Campbell, now Lord Campbell of Croy, in 1974.

The two other Scottish Cabinet ministers — Ian Lang, President of the Board of Trade, and Malcolm Rifkind, Foreign Secretary — also lost their seats. Mr Lang's constituency of Galloway and Upper Nithsdale went to the SNP for the first time, and Edinburgh Pentlands was taken for Labour by the Scottish advocate Linda Clark.

**S**HORTLY AFTER Mr Forsyth's demise, the Tories' two safest seats in Scotland fell. Eastwood, where the Solicitor-General for Scotland, Paul Cullen, was defending a majority of over 11,800, and Dumfries, where Struan Stevenson, a local farmer, was defending a majority of over 6,700 , both fell to Labour. The swing in both cases averaged 15 per cent. Labour also took Ayr and Aberdeen South, where Anne Begg, 41, made history by becoming the first wheelchair user to enter the House of Commons as an MP.

The Conservative seats of Edinburgh West, held by the Scottish Office Minister Lord James Douglas-Hamilton, the man who gave up the Earldom of Selkirk to prevent a by-election, and Aberdeenshire West and Kincardine fell to the Liberal Democrats. Their joy was tempered by the loss of Inverness East, Nairn and Lochaber to Labour.

The SNP held Perth, which it had taken from the Tories in a by-election in 1995 after the death of Sir Nicholas Fairbairn. It also won for the first time the neighbouring seat of Tayside North, previously held by the Conservative Bill Walker.

The election fell on the the 290th anniversary of the signing of the Act of Union, which gave the kingdoms of Scotland and England one Parliament, one flag and one Sovereign. May 1, 1997, may prove to be an equally historic date, for, by voting in a Labour Government, the people of Scotland have given tacit approval for the first Scottish parliament in almost 300 years.

Before 1997 is out, voters north of the border will be back in the polling booths for a referendum on a Scottish parliament. The Government has promised a two-question referendum in which Scots will vote on whether they want a parliament and then whether that parliament should have tax-raising powers. Labour has promised that a Scottish parliament controlled by it would not raise taxes in its first term of office.

If the new parliament is given a mandate by the people, it is likely to be housed in the old Royal High School on Edinburgh's Calton Hill. The basis for such a parliament has been set out in a document drawn up by the Scottish Constitutional Convention, a Labour-led body whose members include trade unionists, local government officials, prominent churchmen and politicians from the Labour and Liberal Democrat parties. The Conservatives and the Scottish National Party have not participated in the Convention.

Under this scheme Scots would have two votes. The first, based on 73 rather than 72 constituencies — Orkney and Shetland being split into two — would be a conventional vote with the MSP (member of a Scottish parliament) elected on a first-past-the-post system. The second vote would be cast for the party of the elector's choice. These votes would be used to top up the constituency section and would be based on the existing eight Euro-constituencies. This system would result in greater proportional representation and could favour both the Conservatives and the SNP. It could also make a coalition more likely in Scotland than in England.

*Sent packing by Scottish voters: Forsyth, Rifkind and Lang*

# Future of the Union: Wales
# RECLAIMING THE VALLEYS

## By Valerie Elliott

THE LABOUR PARTY has restored its dominance of the Welsh political landscape as Ron Davies, the new Welsh Secretary, triumphantly claimed his office in Cathays Park, Cardiff, the first Welsh MP to do so in ten years.

Since the former Tory Cabinet minister Nicholas Edwards left his Pembroke seat in 1987 — he is now Lord Crickhowell — a succession of English overlords was sent to Wales: Peter Walker, David Hunt, John Redwood and William Hague. This English formula did not satisfy the Welsh people. The Conservatives were truly routed on May 1, 1997 — not one of their six MPs, three of them ministers, survived.

Plaid Cymru, despite an energetic campaign by Dafydd Wigley, party president, was stalled in its tracks and returned the same four MPs, while there was jubilation in the Liberal Democrat camp as they asserted firm control on the rural Mid-Wales belt. Richard Livsey regained his former seat at Brecon and Radnorshire, suspending the political career of the former junior Welsh Office Minister Jonathan Evans, while in Montgomeryshire Lembit Opik, a Tyneside councillor of Estonian parentage who was brought up in Belfast, held the seat vacated by the former Welsh Lib Dems' leader Alex Carlile, QC.

But within days of the election, a new political battle was already looming in Wales. The parties began preparing their lines for the referendum campaign to create a Welsh assembly. The Tories saw this as their first opportunity to galvanise their troops. The defeated Tory ministers — Jonathan Evans, Gwilym Jones (Cardiff North) and Roger Evans (Monmouth) — started leading the fightback on the ground. They no longer had a voice at Westminster but were planning to mount a vigorous campaign against devolution. The irony in their position, however, was that Ron Davies, the Welsh Secretary, had promised proportional representation to elect the assembly. The Tories might hate the assembly but PR in Welsh politics could be their only hope of salvation.

CRITICS of an assembly claim it will be merely a talking-shop and will further divide the north and the south. Welsh Nationalists, in particular, consider the plan feeble and are indignant that Wales is not being treated on the same terms as Scotland. The Welsh assembly will not have the tax-varying powers promised to the Scottish parliament but will take over Welsh Office responsibilities such as health, education, transport, environment, agriculture, employment and inward investment.

But Mr Davies is excited about the plan and is determined to ensure that the legislation succeeds. The assembly will also take over many of the responsibilities at present carried out by the 117 quangos in Wales. Eventually he hopes that the assembly can also take over the law and order areas looked after by the Home Office. Nonetheless, there is still a difficult task bringing round dissenters on his own side. He does not want a Labour faction campaigning against the Labour Government's policies and a rerun of 1979 when leading Labour figures such as Neil Kinnock led the "no" campaign in Wales.

Plaid Cymru's hope after polling day was to ensure that it would be the main opposition party in the assembly. The original plan was to campaign with the SNP to ensure that self-government was offered as a choice to the Welsh and Scottish people in the referendum ballot. Faced with a stark "yes"/"no" choice in the referendum ballot, it was unlikely that Plaid would oppose the plan. For them it would be the first step towards self-government.

Mr Davies's task, then, is to make certain that the assembly is effective and popular, to keep Plaid Cymru at bay, and to ensure that the Conservatives as a force in Wales are consigned to history.

# Future of the Union: Northern Ireland
# ADAMS COMES IN FROM THE COLD

*By Nicholas Watt, Chief Ireland Correspondent of The Times*

S INN FEIN stamped its mark on the political map of Northern Ireland when republicans captured two seats in the party's most successful election in 40 years. After one of the Province's bitterest campaigns, Gerry Adams and Martin McGuinness, the republican movement's most senior strategists, swept aside nationalist and Unionist opponents in West Belfast and Mid Ulster to end Sinn Fein's days as a marginal electoral force.

Their victories, which contributed to a 6 per cent increase in Sinn Fein's overall vote to 16.1 per cent, unsettled the larger Social Democratic and Labour Party, which saw votes slip away to republicans. The sight of Mr Adams and Mr McGuinness being held aloft by supporters in the aftermath of their success prompted a debate within the SDLP over the merits of the extensive discussions that John Hume, the party leader, had held with Sinn Fein. Many grassroots SDLP activists, who had to bear the brunt of republican intimidation during the campaign, felt that Mr Hume legitimised an ogre at the expense of his own party.

*Adams: marginal no more*

The dismay within the SDLP was felt most strongly in West Belfast, where Dr Joe Hendron, the highly respected party veteran, was roundly defeated by Mr Adams, who won back his old seat with a majority of 7,909. Raucous Sinn Fein supporters chanted "Out, out" during the count at Belfast City Hall as boundary changes helped Mr Adams to recapture the seat which he lost to Dr Hendron in 1992 by 589 votes. Angry SDLP workers were left to reflect that Dr Hendron had faced an impossible struggle after their leader spent four years trying to persuade Northern Ireland that Mr Adams was serious about trying to secure peace. A warning from Mr Hume late in the election campaign that a vote for Sinn Fein was a vote for violence clearly fell on deaf ears in West Belfast.

Sinn Fein's success in West Belfast and Mid Ulster, combined with its 16.1 per cent overall vote, heralded the party's arrival as a potent electoral force. The days when ministers could dismiss Mr Adams as "Mr Ten Per Cent" were swept away as Sinn Fein replaced the Democratic Unionist Party as Northern Ireland's third largest party. However, Mr Adams and Mr McGuinness pledged that they would not take their seats at Westminster because they refuse to take the oath of allegiance to the Queen.

Seamus Mallon, the deputy leader of the SDLP, spoke for many in his party when he described Sinn Fein's success as "very worrying". Mr Mallon, who held on to Newry and Armagh despite a massive increase in the Sinn Fein vote, said: "People should realise that by voting for Sinn Fein they could be giving a blank cheque to the IRA and for continuing violence."

The only highlights of the election for the SDLP came in Foyle, where Mr Hume retained his seat with an increased majority over Sinn Fein of 13,664, and in South Down, where Eddie McGrady increased his majority to 9,933. The party's overall share of the vote increased from 23.5 per cent in 1992 to 24.1 per cent. However, the increase was deceptive because the SDLP contested all of Northern Ireland's 18 parliamentary seats for the first time, including the new constituency of West Tyrone, which was added under boundary changes.

On the other side of the sectarian divide David Trimble, the Ulster Unionist leader, recaptured Upper Bann and moved closer to his goal of turning the UUP into Northern Ireland's only major Unionist party. He increased the number of UUP MPs from nine to ten, winning West Tyrone after a close three-way contest with the SDLP and Sinn Fein. The Rev Ian Paisley, the DUP leader, could only look on in despair as the loss of Mid Ulster to Sinn Fein reduced his parliamentary strength to two — Mr Paisley in North Antrim and Peter Robinson, the deputy leader, in East Belfast.

Mr Trimble's success was due largely to a tough stance he took with Mr Paisley in negotiations over the distribution of seats. The two main Unionist parties, who normally do not challenge each other in marginal seats, both insisted on fielding candidates in North Belfast and West Tyrone. An intensive round of meetings failed to produce a deal until Mr Paisley suddenly withdrew his candidates from the two seats less than three weeks before polling day. Cecil Walker of the UUP then romped home in North Belfast, while his party colleague Willie Thompson narrowly won West Tyrone.

Overall, the UUP vote declined slightly from 34.5 per cent in 1992 to 32.7 per cent, while the DUP vote increased marginally from 13.1 per cent to 13.6 per cent. The eighteenth and final seat was won in North Down by Robert McCartney, the leader and founder of the United Kingdom Unionist Party.

# The Opinion Polls

# ALL RIGHT ON THE NIGHT

## *By Robert M. Worcester*

**THE HEADLINE** on the front page of *The Times* on the morning of May 1 stated "MORI points to 180-plus majority". By the time the dust had settled on the afternoon of May 2, the figure was 178 (excluding the Speaker).

Over the long election campaign, it was apparent that the Conservatives were going to lose, unless there was a comeback greater than any party had ever achieved before. It never happened. The five major polling organisations' average result over the six-week campaign for the Conservative share of the vote was 31 per cent; on the day, the Tories got 31.4 per cent. What was not apparent until the end was the size of the Labour victory. Even so, on April 30 the average forecast of the Reuters panel of "experts" was an overall Labour majority of 92 seats.

The table opposite shows the 47 national polls (down from 50 in the shorter 1992 and 54 in 1987 elections) conducted by the major polling companies, full members of APOPO, the Association of Professional Opinion Polling Organisations, during the 1997 campaign. In all, nearly 100,000 people were interviewed by Gallup, Harris, ICM, MORI and NOP during the six-week campaign.

The picture after the 1992 election was somewhat different, however. "The error in the polls at the 1992 general election said more about the British people than the polls," an American academic said then. After a run of five elections with a record of never being more than 1 per cent away from the actual result, in 1992 MORI was 4 per cent too low on the Tory share, and 5 per cent too high on Labour. With a 1 per cent Labour lead, MORI was in the middle of the five major pollsters' forecast on the outcome. All forecast a hung Parliament, and if one Tory voter in 200 had voted for the second party in his or her constituency it would have indeed been a hung Parliament. Not so this time.

All of this is not to say that nothing happened during the 1997 campaign. From panel studies it can be estimated how many people change their mind as to whether to vote or not, and if they do vote, which party they will vote for. The best measure comes from the eve-of-poll telephone recall conducted for the *Evening Standard* on people interviewed initially face-to-face in the first week of the election. This showed that 29 per cent of the electorate, nearly 13 million people, gave different answers at the end of the campaign than they did at the beginning. This may underestimate the "churn", for there will be within this sample many people who will have had their doubts during the six weeks of the election but who, on the eve of polling day, returned to their original choice.

Much was made of the public's boredom with this long campaign. There is some evidence for this. When asked in 1992 whether they were interested in news about the election, six people in ten said they were; in 1997, those interested fell to 52 per cent. In 1992, 43 per cent said they were interested in politicians' speeches; this time 40 per cent said they were interested. At the end of the last election, 40 per cent said they were interested in what the opinion polls were saying – in 1997 a third said they were; and in 1992, 36 per cent said they were interested in the party election broadcasts – in this campaign, these broadcasts were of interest to 32 per cent. As forecast, it was, at 71.4 per cent, the lowest turnout since the war.

Just over six people in ten, 63 per cent, said they were aware of any national opinion polls in this election, down sharply from 89 per cent in 1992, when there were more polls over a shorter period, with certainly more coverage on the BBC than in this election.

□ *Robert M. Worcester is Chairman of MORI, and Visiting Professor of Government at the London School of Economics and Political Science*

# 1997 ELECTION: THE CAMPAIGN POLLS

| Fieldwork dates | Agency (client) | Public'n date | Sample size | C | Lab | LD | Oth | Lead | Swing 92-97 |
|---|---|---|---|---|---|---|---|---|---|
| 19-21 Mar | Gallup (S Telegraph*) | 23 Mar | 985 | 29 | 54½ | 10½ | 6 | -25½ | -16.75 |
| 20-24 Mar | Harris (Independent) | 28 Mar | 1,096 | 30 | 54 | 11 | 6 | -24 | -16.0 |
| 21-24 Mar | MORI (Times) | 27 Mar | 1,932 | 29 | 50 | 14 | 7 | -21 | -14.5 |
| 27-31 Mar | Harris (Independent) | 4 Apr | 1,091 | 28 | 52 | 14 | 6 | -24 | -16.0 |
| 26 Mar-2 Apr | Gallup (D Telegraph*) | 4 Apr | 1,126 | 31 | 52 | 11 | 6 | -21 | -14.5 |
| 29-31 Mar | ICM (Guardian*) | 2 Apr | 1,200 | 32 | 46 | 17 | 5 | -14 | -11.0 |
| 1 Apr | MORI (Times) | 3 Apr | 1,118 | 28 | 55 | 11 | 6 | -27 | -17.5 |
| 1-3 Apr | Gallup (C4 News*) | 9 Apr | 1,035 | 30 | 54 | 11 | 5 | -24 | -16.0 |
| 2-3 Apr | MORI (Ind on S/S Mirror+) | 6 Apr | 1,069 | 30 | 55 | 9 | 6 | -25 | -16.5 |
| 2-4 Apr | ICM (Observer*+) | 6 Apr | 1,793 | 33 | 48 | 14 | 5 | -15 | -11.5 |
| 3 Apr | NOP (S Times) | 6 Apr | 1,575 | 28 | 52 | 12 | 8 | -24 | -16.0 |
| 4 Apr | NOP (Reuters) | 7 Apr | 1,088 | 30 | 51 | 11 | 8 | -21 | -14.5 |
| 4-6 Apr | Gallup (D Telegraph*) | 7 Apr | 1,026 | 32 | 53 | 10 | 5 | -21 | -14.5 |
| 4-7 Apr | Harris (Independent) | 11 Apr | 1,138 | 28 | 52 | 14 | 6 | -24 | -16.0 |
| 6-7 Apr | ICM (Guardian*) | 9 Apr | 1,022 | 34 | 46 | 15 | 5 | -12 | -10 |
| 7-9 Apr | Gallup (D Telegraph*) | 10 Apr | 1,019 | 30 | 53 | 11 | 6 | -23 | -15.5 |
| 8 Apr | MORI (Times) | 10 Apr | 1,114 | 34 | 49 | 12 | 5 | -15 | -11.5 |
| 9-11 Apr | ICM (Observer*+) | 13 Apr | 1,002 | 32 | 48 | 15 | 5 | -16 | -12.0 |
| 9-12 Apr | Gallup (S Telegraph*) | 13 Apr | 1,043 | 33 | 49 | 12 | 5 | -16 | -12.0 |
| 11 Apr | NOP (S Times) | 13 Apr | 1,595 | 28 | 48 | 17 | 7 | -20 | -14.0 |
| 11-14 Apr | MORI (Eve Standard) | 15 Apr | 1,778 | 29 | 50 | 15 | 6 | -21 | -14.5 |
| 11-14 Apr | Harris (Independent) | 18 Apr | 1,136 | 31 | 49 | 13 | 6 | -18 | -13.0 |
| 12-15 Apr | Gallup (D Telegraph*) | 16 Apr | 1,025 | 30 | 51 | 12 | 7 | -21 | -14.5 |
| 13-14 Apr | ICM (Guardian*) | 16 Apr | 1,007 | 31 | 45 | 19 | 5 | -14 | -11.0 |
| 15 Apr | MORI (Times) | 17 Apr | 1,137 | 32 | 49 | 13 | 6 | -17 | -12.5 |
| 15-18 Apr | Gallup (D Telegraph*) | 19 Apr | 1,018 | 32 | 50 | 13 | 5 | -18 | -13.0 |
| 16-18 Apr | ICM (Observer*+) | 20 Apr | 1,000 | 32 | 47 | 16 | 5 | -15 | -11.5 |
| 18 Apr | NOP (S Times) | 20 Apr | 1,595 | 31 | 45 | 17 | 7 | -14 | -11.0 |
| 17-21 Apr | Harris (Independent) | 25 Apr | 1,177 | 30 | 48 | 15 | 7 | -18 | -13.0 |
| 18-21 Apr | Gallup (D Telegraph*) | 22 Apr | 1,294 | 32 | 48 | 12 | 8 | -16 | -12.0 |
| 18-22 Apr | Gallup (C4 News*) | 23 Apr | 1,120 | 31 | 50 | 13 | 6 | -19 | -13.5 |
| 20-21 Apr | ICM (Guardian*) | 23 Apr | 1,004 | 37 | 42 | 14 | 6 | -5 | -6.5 |
| 22 Apr | MORI (Times) | 24 Apr | 1,133 | 27 | 48 | 17 | 8 | -21 | -14.5 |
| 21-23 Apr | Gallup (D Telegraph*) | 24 Apr | 1,069 | 30 | 50 | 12 | 8 | -20 | -14.0 |
| 23-24 Apr | MORI (Ind on S/S Mirror+) | 27 Apr | 941 | 29 | 53 | 12 | 6 | -24 | -16.0 |
| 23-25 Apr | Gallup (D Telegraph*) | 26 Apr | 1,012 | 32 | 48 | 14 | 6 | -16 | -12.0 |
| 23-25 Apr | ICM (Observer*+) | 27 Apr | 1,000 | 32 | 47 | 16 | 5 | -15 | -11.5 |
| 25 Apr | NOP (S Times) | 27 Apr | 1,588 | 29 | 47 | 16 | 9 | -18 | -13.0 |
| 24-28 Apr | Gallup (C4 News*) | 29 Apr | 1,466 | 31 | 49 | 14 | 6 | -18 | -13.0 |
| 25-27 Apr | Gallup (D Telegraph*) | 28 Apr | 1,028 | 30 | 49 | 14 | 6 | -19 | -13.5 |
| 27-29 Apr | Harris (Independent) | 1 May | 1,154 | 31 | 48 | 15 | 6 | -17 | -12.5 |
| 28-29 Apr | Gallup (D Telegraph*) | 30 Apr | 1,038 | 31 | 51 | 13 | 6 | -20 | -14.0 |
| 29 Apr | NOP (Reuters) | 30 Apr | 1,093 | 28 | 50 | 14 | 8 | -22 | -15.0 |
| 29-30 Apr | MORI (Times) | 1 May | 2,304 | 28 | 48 | 16 | 8 | -20 | -14.0 |
| 29-30 Apr | ICM (Guardian*) | 1 May | 1,555 | 33 | 43 | 18 | 6 | -10 | -9.0 |
| 30 Apr | Gallup (D Telegraph*) | 1 May | 1,849 | 33 | 47 | 14 | 6 | -14 | -11.0 |
| 30 Apr | MORI (E Standard+*) | 1 May | 1,501 | 29 | 47 | 19 | 5 | -18 | -13.0 |
| 1 May | MORI (ITN@) | 1 May | 15,761 | 30 | 46 | 18 | 6 | -16 | -12.0 |
| 1 May | NOP (BBC@) | 1 May | 17,073 | 29 | 47 | 18 | 6 | -18 | -13.0 |
| 1 May | **Election Result** | | | **31.4** | **44.4** | **17.2** | **7** | **-13** | **-10.5** |

*Telephone survey      +Panel survey      @Exit poll

# TORY PRESS TURNS OUT
# THE LIGHTS ON MAJOR

## By Brian MacArthur

**A**FTER THE general election of 1992, the defeated Labour leader Neil Kinnock made harsh criticisms of the manner in which both he and the Labour Party had been treated by the British press and in particular by *The Sun, Daily Mail* and *Daily Express,* the three biggest selling Tory tabloids. All three — two of their editors had been knighted by Margaret Thatcher — used the campaign to rubbish Mr Kinnock. On polling day, *The Sun* published its notorious front page: "If Kinnock wins today will the last person to leave Britain please turn out the lights." As John Major snatched his victory, the paper declared that it was *"The Sun* wot won it". It was a claim, given its readership of one in two voters in some of the most critical marginal constituencies, that was arguably true.

In 1997, television, especially the often brutal interviewing techniques of David Dimbleby and Jeremy Paxman, was more controversial than the press. That was because Tony Blair was determined that he would not suffer, at the hands of the merciless editors of the "Tory tabloids", the same fate as was suffered by Neil Kinnock in 1987 and 1992 and Michael Foot in 1983. By assiduously wooing newspaper editors and proprietors, and removing from new Labour's manifesto most of the policies so derided by Labour's Fleet Street opposition, he ensured that new Labour got its fairest treatment from the 19 national newspapers in living memory. The 1997 election was the first since the Second World War in which the press was not itself a controversial political issue.

The most significant difference in 1997 was that *The Sun,* with a daily circulation of almost four million and ten million readers — seven million of them among the C2DEs who are one in two of the nation's voters — declared for Mr Blair from Day One. Its theme was "Give Change a Chance". It promoted new Labour throughout the campaign, featuring several articles by Tony Blair himself, as well as several interviews with the Labour leader.

With the Express Group's *Daily Star* joining Labour's natural supporter, *The Mirror* (upstaged by *The Sun* and forced to declare itself as "Loyal to Labour, Loyal to You"), all three mass-market tabloids backed Mr Blair, as they also did in the Sunday market, with the *News of the World* following *The Sun,* its sister paper, in endorsing new Labour, along with the *Sunday Mirror* and *The People.*

So Fleet Street's political map was transformed, as was the content of the news pages. Studies by three organisations introducing to British elections American-style content analysis of newspaper coverage showed that the bulk of reporting was considered "neutral", with roughly equal space devoted to favourable and negative reports on the two main parties. The critical difference shown between 1992 and 1997 in the new media influence indexes was the amount of positive coverage of Labour and negative coverage of the Tories in *The Sun.* Eight in ten of its reports on Labour were neutral or favourable.

*The Mirror,* entering into the election with fewer inhibitions about boring its readers than in the recent past, was the most partisan newspaper

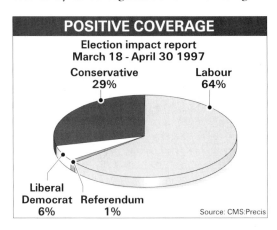

**POSITIVE COVERAGE**

Election impact report
March 18 - April 30 1997

Conservative 29%
Labour 64%
Liberal Democrat 6%
Referendum 1%

Source: CMS:Precis

| Dailies | Sun | Mirror | Star | Mail | Express | Telegraph | Guardian | Times | Independent | FT |
|---|---|---|---|---|---|---|---|---|---|---|
| C | 30 | 14 | 17 | 49 | 49 | 57 | 8 | 42 | 16 | 48 |
| Lab | 52 | 72 | 66 | 29 | 29 | 20 | 67 | 28 | 47 | 29 |
| Lib Dem | 12 | 11 | 12 | 14 | 16 | 17 | 22 | 25 | 30 | 19 |
| Sundays | | NoW | Mirror | People | Mail | Express | Times | Telegraph | Observer | IoS |
| C | | 28 | 18 | 21 | 49 | 53 | 43 | 56 | 11 | 14 |
| Lab | | 55 | 67 | 62 | 28 | 27 | 30 | 19 | 63 | 48 |
| Lib Dem | | 11 | 12 | 11 | 15 | 14 | 21 | 17 | 22 | 32 |

☐ *Source: MORI*

of all (for Labour), *The Daily Telegraph* was least negative to the Conservatives and the *Daily Mail* most critical of Labour. *The Observer,* by publishing the "biggest poll ever conducted by a newspaper during a general election" which demonstrated the vulnerability of Michael Portillo, the favourite to succeed John Major, almost certainly contributed to his defeat by prompting tactical voting against him and a Labour drive in his Enfield Southgate seat. With Lord Hollick, a Labour life peer, as chief executive of *The Express,* its coverage was even-handed: one remarkable innovation was that *The Express on Sunday* published a page by Lord Hollick on why he supported Labour alongside a page by Lord Stevens of Ludgate, the chairman, on why he supported the Conservatives.

As the newspapers delivered their endorsements at the end of the campaign, Tony Blair won more for Labour − 11 out of 19 − than at any time in living memory.

**Dailies for Blair:** *The Sun, The Mirror, Daily Star, The Guardian* and *The Independent* (both suggesting tactical voting against Tories), *Financial Times.* Total sales: 8 million.

**Sundays for Blair:** *News of the World, Sunday Mirror, The People, The Observer* and *Independent on Sunday* (both again suggesting tactical voting). Sales: 9.6 million.

**Dailies for Major:** *Daily Mail, The Express, The Daily Telegraph.* Sales: 4.5 million.

**Sundays for Major:** *The Express on Sunday, Mail on Sunday, The Sunday Times, The Sunday Telegraph.* Sales: 5.5 million.

**Eurosceptic:** *The Times* suggested voting for Eurosceptic candidates from six parties.

# TV NEWSMEN STRIKE BACK

### By Nicholas Wapshott

T HE 1997 television election differed markedly from those that went immediately before. The Thatcher years (embracing the Major postscript) had refined the art of exploiting television as a contrived picture opportunity to steal the television news headlines. This time the news broadcasters, tiring perhaps of being so obviously manipulated, made an effort to record more genuine events.

And events worked in their favour from the start as the Government proved incapable of clearing the decks of a live, damaging issue before the campaign began. Television news in the election's early days was dominated by the issue of corruption among MPs thrown up by the "cash for questions" affair. This was aggravated by the Government's decision to defer publication of the parliamentary report into the matter until after election day and the failure of Conservative Central Office to persuade a number of its candidates accused of impropriety, among them most notably Neil Hamilton, from standing.

It was ironic, too, that it was a product of television journalism, the BBC foreign reporter Martin Bell, who was chosen as the white knight to stand against Mr Hamilton. There was no better example of the way that television was obliged to follow events rather than make them than the electric pictures of the spontaneous encounter on a village green in Tatton between Mr Bell and Mr Hamilton, as always backed by his vocal wife Christine.

The Conservatives remained impotent in the face of such uncontrollable images and soon discovered that their own well-laid television plans were inadequate for the task in hand. Maurice Saatchi, the party's advertising guru, had prepared a series of election broadcasts preying on the voters' fears of what a Labour Government might mean in practice. One, shot in faux cinéma vérité style and set in the future, interviewed a number of disillusioned citizens who had voted Labour; another was an extended metaphor in which a tree without roots, symbolising new Labour, was felled by the slightest breeze.

But when dozens of Tory candidates declared themselves opposed outright to a single European currency, contradicting the government line, John Major cancelled the planned anti-Labour broadcast in favour of a straight appeal to his own party, and coincidentally to the country, to trust him on Europe. As the tenor of the election slipped daily beyond the reach of the Conservative strategists, direction of the Tory campaign switched from Central Office to Downing Street. Mr Major, who had vetoed a number of Saatchi's aggressive personal assaults on Tony Blair, cancelled his party's final two broadcasts in favour of personal appeals direct to camera. His self-portrayal as Honest John on a soapbox had worked in 1992; five years on, the image looked care-worn and impotent.

Labour, meanwhile, kept to its well-prepared schedule. As in previous elections, the party employed the talents of sympathetic commercial film-makers to spread the word. Molly Dineen, a prizewinning television documentary maker, made a film biography of Tony Blair which, until the last minutes, appeared to be more impartial than it was. And the distinguished cinema director Stephen Frears made a masterly mini-epic, borrowing freely from Frank Capra's *Miracle on 34th Street,* in which an angelic taxi driver turned the clocks back so that a young father could vote Labour.

**O**THER PARTIES failed to screen broadcasts of such distinction or originality, though the Referendum Party understood the power of television well enough and tried to buy its way onto people's sets. It opened its campaign with a costly nationwide mailshot containing a video that set out to frighten voters about the alleged drift towards a single European state. Its sole election broadcast revealed the source of the party's immense funds, Sir James Goldsmith, talking unblinking into the camera about the need for a referendum on British membership of the European Union. In their xenophobic tone, the Referendum Party's efforts were only outstripped by the British National Party's broadcast, which tested the limits of the law with its primitive racialist appeal.

The television hustings entailed the traditional circuit of television studios by the champions of each party. There was no television breakthrough in this election, no unscripted utterance or ill-considered aside which turned the direction of the campaign, but two journalists did distinguish themselves by the clarity of their approach: Jeremy Paxman on *Newsnight* and David Dimbleby on *Panorama.*

There were, as usual, a number of programmes which used audiences as a sounding-board. For the most part, the intervention of the public in such circumstances served to obstruct a more clinical grilling by the hosts, most notably Sue Lawley, with the *Granada 500,* and Jonathan Dimbleby, also on ITV. But the anger of the electorate revealed in the final *Granada 500* programme when John Major failed to appear, leaving his deputy Michael Heseltine to fill the gap, betrayed a pent-up passion and a latent hostility directed at the governing party which hinted at the landslide to come.

Election night turned out to be one of the most extraordinary nights in live television, starting at 10pm with exit polls which predicted a landslide, followed from 11pm by an avalanche of Tory defeats, ending with Prime Minister Tony Blair arriving at the Labour victory party at the Festival Hall. The cameras were present to record all the notable defeats, among them those of the Defence Secretary Michael Portillo, the Foreign Secretary Malcolm Rifkind, and the former Trade Minister Neil Hamilton. Mr Major's count was completed at 3.30am, the same moment that Labour reached 330 seats, enough for an absolute majority. When his result was announced, Mr Major told the nation, through television, that he had already spoken to Mr Blair an hour before, conceding defeat.

# WHY IS THERE ONLY ONE MONOPOLIES COMMISSION?

## By Matthew Parris, Political Sketchwriter of The Times

**W**HEN THE headlines about landslides, avalanches and seismic shifts are forgotten, and the reams of earnest commentary about polls, policies and personalities are filed beyond retrieval, one image will still leap fresh and strong into the recollections of the millions who watched the results on late-night television. At the declaration of the count in Tatton, as the Independent Martin Bell's victory over the incumbent Conservative Neil Hamilton was announced, every viewer's eye was distracted from both candidates, and from the Returning Officer himself.

Behind both, towering above them and swaying from side to side in a weird dance, writhed a 7ft being. A 6ft transvestite in 12in platform heels, wearing a birdcage on her head, her face painted with wild shapes and red and green colours, dressed in royal robes, covered with glitter and plastered in £5 notes, "Miss Moneypenny" — in reality Burnel Penhaul, 32, from Birmingham — was standing for the Miss Moneypenny's Glamorous One Party. Campaigning on the slogan "Put the tat back into Tatton" she won 128 votes. Later she also gained the Outfit of the Campaign award from the *New Statesman*.

"There are two candidates whom I wish to avoid," Mr Bell recalled in his campaign diary. "One is Hamilton. The other is Miss Moneypenny. She bears down on me and I have no escape. I knew politics would bring strange experiences, but nothing in life can prepare a man to make smalltalk to a transvestite birdcage." This was a man who, as BBC war correspondent in Bosnia, had never flinched the flying bullets and stray shrapnel of a real conflict. "When Bell and Hamilton start to talk sense," was Moneypenny's response, "I will fade away."

And she has. So have all the other joke candidates, crazy candidates, and serious fringe candidates. Of these, 1997 produced a bumper harvest.

As suddenly as they appear and as fast as they fade, fringe candidates are as reliable a crop at a British general election as are magic mushrooms in an autumn wood. The world is baffled, our continental partners are aghast, our American cousins amazed. The more high-minded Briton deplores the phenomenon. But the rest of the nation delights in this welcome distraction from the pre-packaged tedium of a modern election.

This time, even the strangest candidates found it hard to stand out from an ever-more exotic background: in 1997, 3,717 people risked their £500 deposit, an average of five per constituency and 769 more than in 1992. All the fringe candidates lost their deposits. Most of them expected to.

**T**WO FAMILIAR faces were missing from this last election. Commander Bill Boakes, a colourful feature of every by-election for decades, has died and is sorely missed. And, for the first time in years, Screaming Lord Sutch had to hang up his top hat and leopard-skin suit to tend his ailing mother, who died just after the election.

David Sutch and his Monster Raving Loony Party (which still managed to field 18 candidates, including a fellow called Freddie Zapp) have always been more than simply a joke. Sutch points out that half a dozen of his policies — including compulsory seatbelts, all-day pub opening and passports for pets — are either law, or in serious prospect as law. If he had done nothing else, Sutch would deserve immortality for one political question alone: "Why is there only one Monopolies Commission?"

In 1997, the gap left by Boakes and Sutch was filled by a rich variety on the fringe. Arthur Pendragon, who has changed his name by deed poll and dresses in Druid robes, carried his sword through Aldershot where he campaigned (as you might expect of a Druid) against cars and roads. Asked how he had found the money for his deposit, he mentioned that three orders of Druids had collected £100 each. "Many people around here know me, so I'm getting a pretty good reception," he added, falling into the classic error of the local candidate throughout history. Pendragon received 361 votes.

Elsewhere, voters had a choice, variously, of such causes as the Independently Beautiful Party, the Happiness Stan's Freedom to Party Party, and the Nirdosh Uday of the Black Haired Medium Build Caucasian Male Party — whose candidate in St Ives (his real name William Hitchens) described himself as virtually bankrupt and used his credit card to pay his deposit. Insisting throughout that victory was in sight (sadly it was not) Mr Hitchens may have found himself saddled with his unusual party as a result of a misreading of the form which would-be candidates have to complete. There is one section for personal details, another for party name. A distraught (and perfectly serious) Natural Law Party candidate for Orkney and Shetland, Christian Wharton, found her party described on the ballot papers as "artist and teacher". She had misunderstood the section-heading "description".

Other candidates were less straightforward in their intentions. In the 1994 European elections Richard Huggett won some 10,000 votes standing as a "Literal Democrat" candidate and (by general consensus) robbed a Liberal Democrat of the Devon and East Plymouth seat. The courts having failed to overturn the result, 1997 offered a platform to a scattering of "spoiler" candidates. Richard Huggett cropped up again, in 1997, and chose to stand as the Liberal Democrat — Top Choice for Parliament candidate in Winchester. What prescience! He gained 640 votes and the real Liberal Democrat, Mark Oaten, won by a nail-biting two votes. I have heard suggestions from activist friends who would prefer not to be named that if Mr Oaten had lost by two, Mr Huggett would have been in serious danger of being murdered by undercover Liberal Democrats.

But Rod Richards (Conservative) would have lost his seat of Clwyd West anyway, without the intervention of the Conservatory candidate, who tried to change his name to Rod Richard; and the former Attorney-

*Scargill: fringe, but no joke*

General, Sir Nicholas Lyell, QC, in Bedfordshire North East, gained the courts' protection against the proposed candidature of a Mr Frank Foley under the name he had assumed by deed poll, "Sir Nicholas Lyell".

Not every fringe candidature represented a flight of fancy, of eccentricity, of deception or of idealism on the candidate's part. Remember that for ten counter-signatories and a deposit of £500 (lost unless the votes gained exceed 5 per cent of the total cast) a candidate gains access to a freepost facility for contacting every voter, and a good deal of free publicity in the local media. Far be it from us to cast aspersions, but this may help to explain the unexpected birth and equally sudden disbandment, post-election, of the Mongolian Barbecue Great Place to Party Party.

If you want to know which candidatures were trivial in intent, the results are the last place to look. The Socialist Labour Party (Arthur Scargill's challenge to the new Labour Party) scored pitifully: a fringe effort if not a joke. Scargill himself gained no more than 1,951 votes. Nationally, the Green Party hardly registered. But — the conventions of British political commentary being what they are — the Socialist Labour Party is seldom included in reviews of the lunatic fringe; whereas the Natural Law Party, who in vote-gathering terms are in the same league as Mr Scargill's party, are treated as a joke.

A joke, however, may be in the eye only of the beholder. *The Times* printed a correction, at the request of Lisa Lovebucket (Rainbow Referendum Dream Ticket Connection Party), for describing her candidature in Hackney North and Stoke Newington in joking terms. Though she was to receive only 146 votes, her complaint had some justice. I met and talked with her and it is true she had some serious points to make. Perhaps we were misled by Miss Lovebucket's response, when I asked her how many votes she aimed to get. "Twenty-three," she replied. "Not 24?" I asked. "No, 23. It's the number of the Illuminati."

Among the more serious of her manifesto proposals was a plan to build an Internet facility which would enable householders to express their wishes and influence political choices over a range of local and national issues — a sort of rolling-referendum system. It struck me that, like the Monster Raving Loonies' plans for extended pub hours and passports for pets, Miss Lovebucket's proposals — dismissed as fanciful today — may become the serious politics of the next millennium.

In fact the Rainbow Referendum (etc) Party fielded scores of candidates, in part funded by a businessman, "Rainbow" George Weiss, who once tried to convince social security officers that he was seeking employment by applying for the post of manager of Newcastle United FC. Mr Weiss was reported to have heard a voice advising him to help the campaign. The deceased comedian, Peter Cook, had urged Ronnie Carroll (a pop singer who in the Sixties reached fourth place in the Eurovision Song Contest with *Ring-a-ding-girl*) to stand for Rainbow George's Party. "He told me, 'Ronald, you must stand. Promise me you will stand.' Then he went and died on me. But a promise is a promise."

STANDING IN the same constituency as Lisa Lovebucket was another candidate it would have been wrong to consider as a joker — though you might have been misled by his party name: "None of the Above." Dickon Tolson's name came last on the ballot, but his invitation to north London voters to register their support for None of the Above was not a joke. The 24-year-old actor, a philosophy and politics student and an extra in television's *Peak Practice* serial, cycled to meet me when I spent a day following the campaign in Hackney. After being interviewed by me, he took out a camcorder and requested permission to reverse roles and interview me — for a project he was undertaking as part of his politics course. In the end he scored 368 votes.

"Being frustrated and concerned at the apathy and lack of moral cohesion which makes up the current political climate," Mr Tolson's election address read, "I have decided to put my life savings into standing for election." The address included a 19-point plan for improving politics and political life in Britain, and read cogently. Mr Tolson and Miss Lovebucket joined me for a photograph, *The Times* photographer being on hand to photograph the Labour candidate, left-wing Diane Abbott, who was refusing to emerge from her office.

Ms Abbott seemed to be under some kind of injunction (self-imposed or otherwise) not to communicate with the media. Invited to comment on her party's leadership, she had refused that morning to venture beyond the thought that "Tony Blair walks on water". My visit to her constituency had come not long after a trip to Exeter, whose Conservative candidate, Dr Adrian Rogers, was stumping around the cathedral square with a soapbox denouncing homosexuality and calling his Labour opponent, Ben Bradshaw (who won), "Bent Ben".

The recollection of Dr Rogers fresh in my mind, and chatting outside Diane Abbott's office to her rather serious-minded Rainbow Referendum and None of the Above challengers, as Ms Abbott skulked within, I did wonder whether the joke candidatures in the general election of 1997 were necessarily those with the funny names.

# RESULTS BY CONSTITUENCY

# HOUSE OF COMMONS, MAY 1997

**F**ULL RESULTS for the 659 parliamentary constituencies of the United Kingdom contested at the general election are set out in alphabetical order. Constituencies in cities, boroughs or towns are listed under that city, borough or town, eg, Edgbaston will be found under Birmingham Edgbaston.

Between the elections of 1992 and 1997 the Boundary Commissions for England, Scotland, Wales and Northern Ireland redrew the boundaries of many constituencies, from very small to major changes, and created eight new constituencies. Where there was a boundary change the percentage change is shown next to the constituency name, eg, YORKSHIRE EAST 70.9% change; SAFFRON WALDEN 5.3% change.

In those seats for which there were no boundary changes, the actual 1992 voting figures are given alongside the 1997 result, which is described as a Gain or Hold; the results box is plain white.

In seats with any boundary changes, the result is described as a Win, and the 1992 results box is shaded grey, giving notional 1992 results. These notional figures and swings were calculated by Colin Rallings and Michael Thresher of Plymouth University and were adopted by all the broadcasting and press media covering the 1997 general election.

The percentage of the constituency turnout, the votes cast for candidates, the winning majority and the swings have been calculated to two decimal places and rounded up.

The electoral register on which this general election was fought came into effect on February 16, 1997. The electorate figures are of those eligible to vote when the register came into force, including the relevant proportion of those reaching 18 years of age between February 16 and May 1.

On appointment to office, ministers resign directorships and consultancies.

An asterisk (*) indicates that the candidate was an existing MP in a a non-boundary change seat. A dagger (†) indicates that the candidate was an existing MP standing in a boundary change seat or moving into a different constituency.

☐ *Full list of abbreviations used in biographies on pages 275 and 276*

# PARTY ABBREVIATIONS

**Major parties:** C - Conservative; Lab - Labour; Lab Co-op - Labour & Co-operative; LD - Liberal Democrat; PC - Plaid Cymru; SNP - Scottish National Party; Ref - Referendum Party; Green - Green; UUP - Ulster Unionist Party; DUP - Democratic Unionist Party; SDLP - Social Democratic and Labour Party; SF - Sinn Fein; Alliance - Alliance.

**Minor parties:** 21st Cent - 21st Century Independent Foresters; Albion - Albion Party; ANP - All Night Party; Alt LD - Alternative Liberal Democrat; Embryo - Anti Abortion Euthanasia Embryo Experiments; ACA - Anti Child Abuse; ACC - Anti-corruption Candidate; AS - Anti-sleaze; AS Lab - Anti-sleaze Labour; B Ind - Beaconsfield Ind, Unity Through Electoral Reform; Bert - Berties Party; BHMBCM - Black Haired Medium Build Caucasian Male; BDP - British Democratic Party; BFAIR - British Freedom and Individual Rights; Home Rule - British Home Rule; BIPF - British Isles People First Party; BNP - British National Party; Fair - Building a Fair Society; By-pass - Newbury By-pass stop Contruction Now; Care - Care in the Community; Rights - Charter For Basic Rights; Ch D - Christian Democrat; Ch Nat - Christian Nationalist; Ch P - Christian Party; Ch U - Christian Unity; CSSPP - Common Sense Sick of Politicians Party; Comm Lge - Communist League; Comm Brit - Communist Party of Britain; CRP - Community Representative Party; CASC - Conservatives Against The Single Currency; CVTY - Conservatory; Constit - Constitutionalist; CFSS - Country Field and Shooting Sports; D Nat - Democratic Nationalist; EDP - English Democratic Party; Ind Hum - English Independent Humanist Party; EUP - European Unity Party; FDP - Fancy Dress Party; Fellowship - Fellowship Party for Peace and Justice; Dynamic - First Dynamic Party; NIFT - Former Captain NI Football Team; FP - Freedom Party; FEP - Full Employment Party; Glow - Glow Bowling Party; GRLNSP - Green Referendum Lawless Naturally Street Party; Stan - Happiness Stan's Freedom To Party Party; Heart - Heart 106.2 Alien Party; Hemp - Hemp Coalition; HR - Human Rights '97; Hum - Humanist Party; Ind - Independent; Ind AFE - Independent Against a Federal Europe; IAC - Independent Anti Corruption in Government/TGWU; Anti-maj - Independent Anti-majority Democracy; Ind BB - Independent Back to Basics; Ind C Independent Conservative; Ind CRP - Independent Conservative Referendum Party; Consult - Independent Democracy Means Consulting The People; Ind Dem - Independent Democrat; Ind ECR - Independent English Conservative and Referendum; Ind F - Independent Forester; Ind Green - Independent Green; Your Children's Future; Ind Lab - Independent Labour; Ind No - Independent No to Europe; Ind OAP - Independent OAP; Ind Dean - Independent Royal Forest of Dean; Barts - Independent Save Barts Candidate; Beaut - Independently Beautiful Party; IZB - Islam Zinda Baad Platform; Ind Isl - Island Independent; Juice - Juice Party; JP - Justice Party Ind; JRP Justice and Renewal Independent Party; KBF - Keep Britain Free and Independent Party; Lab Change - Labour Time for Change Candidate; LCP - Legalise Cannabis Party; Lib - Liberal; Loc C - Local Conservative; LGR - Local Government Reform; Loc Ind - Local Independent; Logic - Logic Party Truth Only Allowed; Byro - Lord Byro versus The Scallywag Tories; LC - Loyal Conservative; Mal - Male Voice of the people Party; MRAC - Multi-racial Anti-corruption Alliance; Musician - Musician; Nat Dem - National Democrat; NF - National Front; NLP - Natural Law Party; N Lab - New Labour; New Way - New Millennium New Way Hemp Candidate; NPC - Non-party Conservative; None - None of the Above Parties; NIP - Northern Ireland Party; NI Women - Northern Ireland Women's Coalition; O Lab - Old Labour; Pacifist - Pacifist for Peace, Justice, Co-operation, Environment; PF - Pathfinders; Slough - People in Slough Shunning Useless Politician; Choice - People's Choice; PLP - People's Labour Party; PP - People's Party; Plymouth - Plymouth First Group; Shields - Pro Interests of South Shields People; ProLife - ProLife Alliance; PUP - Progressive Unionist Party; PAYR - Protecting All Your Rights Locally Effectively; R Alt - Radical Alternative; Rain Isl - Rainbow Connection Your Island Candidate; Dream - Rainbow Dream Ticket Party; Rain Ref - Rainbow Referendum; R Lab - Real Labour Party; Ren Dem - Renaissance Democrat; Rep GB - Republican Party of Great Britain; RA - Residents Association; Rizz - Rizz Party; Ronnie - Ronnie The Rhino Party; Route 66 - Route 66 Party Posse Party; SCU - Scottish Conservative Unofficial; SLI - Scottish Labour Independent; SLU - Scottish Labour Unofficial; SSA - Scottish Socialist Alliance; Scrapit - Scrapit Stop Avon Ring Road Now; SIP - Sheffield Independent Party; Soc Dem - Social Democrat Socialist; SEP - Socialist Equality Party; Soc Lab - Socialist Labour Party; Soc - Socialist Party; SPGB - Socialist Party of Great Britain; Beanus - Space Age Superhero from Planet Beanus; Spts All - Sportsman's Alliance: Anything but Mellor; SFDC - Stratford First Democratic Conservative; Ind SD - Sub-genius Party; Teddy - Teddy Bear Alliance Party; FP - The Fourth Party; Mongolian - The Mongolian Barbecue Great Place to Party; NLPC - the New Labour Party Candidate; PPP - The People's Party Party; Speaker - The Speaker; Third - Third Way; Top - Top Choice Liberal Democrat; UK Ind - UK Independence Party; UKPP - UK Pensioners Party; UKU - United Kingdom Unionist; UA - Universal Alliance; Value - Value Party; Wessex Reg - Wessex Regionalist; WCCC - West Cheshire College in Crisis Party; Whig - Whig Party; WP - Workers' Party; WRP - Workers Revolutionary Party.

| ABERAVON | | | | | Lab hold | |
|---|---|---|---|---|---|---|
| Electorate % Turnout | | 50,025 | 71.9% | **1997** | 51,650 | 77.6% | **1992** |
| *Morris, J | Lab | **25,650** | 71.3% | **+4.2%** | 26,877 | 67.1% | Lab |
| McConville, R | LD | 4,079 | 11.3% | -1.1% | 5,567 | 13.9% | C |
| Harper, P | C | 2,835 | 7.9% | -6.0% | 4,999 | 12.5% | LD |
| Cockwell, P | PC | 2,088 | 5.8% | +1.0% | 1,919 | 4.8% | PC |
| David, P | Ref | 970 | 2.7% | | 707 | 1.8% | Real Bean |
| Beany, C | Beanus | 341 | 0.9% | | | | |
| **LD to Lab swing 2.7%** | | **35,963** | Lab maj 21,571 | | 40,069 | Lab maj 21,310 | |
| | | | 60.0% | | | 77.6% | |

**JOHN MORRIS,** QC, b Nov 5, 1931. Became Attorney-General May 5, 1997. Barrister, Recorder of Crown Court, 1982- . Elected 1959. Chief Lab spokesman on legal affairs since 1983; Sec of State for Wales, 1974-79. On back benches 1981-83 after spell as spokesman on Wales and then legal affairs; defence spokesman 1970-74; Min of Defence for Equipment, 1968-70; Privy Counsellor 1970; Parly Sec, Min of Transport, 1966-68, and Min of Power, 1964-66. Member, privileges select cttee 1994-95 and previously. Ed Ardwyn, Aberystwyth; Univ Coll of Wales, Aberystwyth; Gonville and Caius Coll, Cambridge; Acad of International Law, The Hague.

**RON McCONVILLE,** b May 8, 1935. Newsagent/bookseller. Member, Friends of the Earth; ex-sec, Fed of Retail Newsagents.
**PETER HARPER,** b Aug 8, 1964. Computer consultant. Vice-chair Surrey Heath C Assoc, former chair SE Area YCs; Surrey Heath borough cllr 1994- . Ed Oxted Comp; Univ Coll of Wales, Swansea.
**PHIL COCKWELL,** b March 1, 1933. Former teacher. Past chair of party Neath Rhanbarth cttee. Member, Neath Borough Council, 1991-96, currently member of Blaenhonddan community council. Ed Neath Boys' GS; Teacher Training Coll, Worcester.

| ABERDEEN CENTRAL | | 93.5% change | | | | | Lab win |
|---|---|---|---|---|---|---|---|
| Electorate % Turnout | | 54,257 | 65.6% | **1997** | 55,882 | 67.6% | **1992** |
| Doran, F | Lab | **17,745** | 49.8% | **+6.7%** | 16,269 | 43.1% | Lab |
| Wisely, Mrs J | C | 6,944 | 19.5% | -9.3% | 10,872 | 28.8% | C |
| Topping, B | SNP | 5,767 | 16.2% | -1.4% | 6,636 | 17.6% | SNP |
| Brown, J | LD | 4,714 | 13.2% | +2.7% | 3,985 | 10.6% | LD |
| Farquharson, J | Ref | 446 | 1.3% | | | | |
| **C to Lab notional swing 8.0%** | | **35,616** | Lab maj 10,801 | | 37,762 | Lab maj 5,397 | |
| | | | 30.3% | | | 67.6% | |

**FRANK DORAN,** b April 13, 1949. Solicitor. Elected for this seat 1997; MP for Aberdeen S 1987-92; contested Scotland North East 1984 Euro elections. Lab spokesman on energy, 1988-92. Asst editor, Scottish Legal Action Group bulletin, 1975-78. Member, GMB. Ed Ainslie Park Sec; Leith Acad; Dundee Univ.
**JILL WISELY,** b May 19, 1943. Non-exec director, Grampian Health Board; chairman, Community Care Cttee, presiding magistrate 1986- . Aberdeen district cllr 1984-96, Aberdeen city cllr 1995- ; Grampian cllr 1992-96. Ed Albyn School for Girls, Aberdeen; St

Leonard's, St Andrews; Chatelard School, Switzerland; Aberdeen Univ.
**BRIAN TOPPING,** b Feb 14, 1955. Ex-chef/hotel manager. JP. Aberdeenshire County/UA cllr 1984- ; member of SNP national council, political ed officer for SNP, Fraserborough. Ed Currie HS; Telford Coll, Edinburgh.
**JOHN BROWN,** b Oct 23, 1960. Mature law student and nightclub disc jockey. Grampian cllr 1994- ; Huntingdon district cllr, 1991-92. Ed Elgin Acad; Hitchin Coll; Robert Gordon Univ.

| ABERDEEN NORTH | | 87.7% change | | | | | Lab win |
|---|---|---|---|---|---|---|---|
| Electorate % Turnout | | 54,302 | 70.7% | **1997** | 53,944 | 69.7% | **1992** |
| Savidge, M | Lab | **18,389** | 47.9% | **+12.8%** | 13,189 | 35.1% | Lab |
| Adam, B | SNP | 8,379 | 21.8% | -0.7% | 8,952 | 23.8% | LD |
| Gifford, J | C | 5,763 | 15.0% | -3.6% | 8,443 | 22.5% | SNP |
| Rumbles, M | LD | 5,421 | 14.1% | -9.7% | 7,002 | 18.6% | C |
| Mackenzie, A | Ref | 463 | 1.2% | | | | |
| **SNP to Lab notional swing 6.7%** | | **38,415** | Lab maj 10,010 | | 37,586 | Lab maj 4,237 | |
| | | | 26.1% | | | 69.7% | |

**MALCOLM SAVIDGE,** b May 9, 1946. Teacher. Contested Kincardine and Deeside 1992, and 1991 by-election; Aberdeen city cllr, 1980- (dep leader, 1992-96). Member, EIS; TGWU. Ed Wallington County GS; Aberdeen Univ; Aberdeen Coll of Ed.
**BRIAN ADAM,** b June 10, 1948. Biochemist, Aberdeen Royal Hospitals NHS Trust; Contested Gordon 1992; Aberdeen city cllr 1988- ; SNP national council; asst to SNP employment spokesman. Ed Keith GS; Aberdeen Univ.

**JAMES GIFFORD,** b Nov 5, 1956. Civil engineer/surveyor. Member, C North East area council; NE Area Euro election cttee; Scottish C and Unionist Assoc environmental policy cttee. Ed Lenzie Acad; Glasgow Coll of Tech.
**MIKE RUMBLES,** b June 10, 1956. Team leader, human resource management at Aberdeen Coll. Ex-army officer, commanding army education and training in Gibraltar. Ed Durham Univ; Univ of Wales.

| ABERDEEN SOUTH | | 90.1% change | | | | | Lab win |
|---|---|---|---|---|---|---|---|
| Electorate % Turnout | | 60,490 | 72.8% | **1997** | 60,352 | 73.1% | **1992** |
| **Begg, Ms M A** | **Lab** | **15,541** | **35.3%** | **+11.4%** | 16,487 | 37.4% | C |
| Stephen, N R | LD | 12,176 | 27.6% | +1.0% | 11,762 | 26.7% | LD |
| +Robertson, R | C | 11,621 | 26.4% | -11.0% | 10,545 | 23.9% | Lab |
| Towers, J | SNP | 4,299 | 9.8% | -2.3% | 5,336 | 12.1% | SNP |
| Wharton, R | Ref | 425 | 1.0% | | | | |
| **LD to Lab notional swing 5.2%** | | **44,062** | | **Lab maj 3,365** | **44,130** | | **C maj 4,725** |
| | | | | 7.6% | | | 73.1% |

**ANNE BEGG,** b Dec 16, 1955. Teacher. Member, Scottish General Teaching Council. Confined to wheelchair as suffers from rare blood disease; member, board of management, Scottish Physically Handicapped-Able Bodied; Disabled Scot of the Year, 1988. Ed Brechin HS; Aberdeen Univ; Aberdeen Coll of HE.

**NICOL STEPHEN,** b March 23, 1960. Solicitor and management consultant. LD MP for Kincardine and Deeside from 1991 by-election to 1992 election when defeated. LD spokesman on small business and enterprise, 1992. Grampian regional cllr 1982-92. Dir of Glassbox Ltd, Aberdeen Executive Properties Ltd. Ed Robert Gordon's Coll, Aberdeen; Aberdeen and Edinburgh Univs.

**RAYMOND ROBERTSON,** b Dec 11, 1959. Ex-teacher. Regained Aberdeen S for C 1992; contested Clydesdale 1987. Scottish Under Sec, 1995-97; previously PPS to Michael Ancram, former N Ireland Min. Member, select cttee on Scottish affairs 1992-95. Vice-chair, Scottish C Party, 1993-95. Ed Garrion Acad; Glasgow Univ; Jordanhill Coll of Ed.

**JIM TOWERS,** b June 13, 1937. Part-time OU tutor. Grampian regional cllr 1990-96, Aberdeenshire cllr 1995- . Ed Stromness Acad; Edinburgh Univ; Moray House Coll; Aberdeen Univ.

| ABERDEENSHIRE WEST & KINCARDINE | | | 63.0% change | | | | LD win |
|---|---|---|---|---|---|---|---|
| Electorate % Turnout | | 59,123 | 73.0% | **1997** | 55,093 | 76.9% | **1992** |
| **Smith, Sir Robert** | **LD** | **17,742** | **41.1%** | **+6.4%** | 19,123 | 45.1% | C |
| +Kynoch, G | C | 15,080 | 34.9% | -10.2% | 14,686 | 34.7% | LD |
| Mowatt, Ms J | SNP | 5,639 | 13.1% | +0.6% | 5,280 | 12.5% | SNP |
| Khan, Ms Q | Lab | 3,923 | 9.1% | +2.3% | 2,886 | 6.8% | Lab |
| Ball, S | Ref | 805 | 1.9% | | 381 | 0.9% | Other |
| **C to LD notional swing 8.3%** | | **43,189** | | **LD maj 2,662** | **42,356** | | **C maj 4,437** |
| | | | | 6.2% | | | 10.5% |

**SIR ROBERT SMITH,** baronet, b April 15, 1958. Manages family estate in Aberdeenshire. Contested Aberdeen N for SDP/All 1987. Aberdeenshire cllr 1995-, LD ed spokesman in Scotland. Member Electoral Reform Soc, European Movement. Ed Merchant Taylors', London; Aberdeen Univ.

**GEORGE KYNOCH,** b Oct 7, 1946. MP for Kincardine and Deeside 1992-97. Under Sec of State for Scotland 1995-97. PPS to Education Sec 1994-95, to Foreign Office Min of State 1992-94. With G&G Kynoch, subsequently Kynoch Group, 1971-92. Pres, Scottish woollen industry, 1990-91; chair, Scottish woollen publicity council, 1983-90. Ed Cargilfield School, Edinburgh; Trinity Coll, Glenalmond; Bristol Univ; Paisley Tech Coll.

**JOY MOWATT,** b Dec 20, 1946. Project co-ordinator, WRVS. Membership sec, Brechin SNP. Member, Justice of the Peace exec cttee. Ed Blairgowrie HS.

**QAISRA KHAN,** b Aug 9, 1963, in Pakistan. Community care planning officer. Newham cllr 1994- . Member, Unison. Ed St David's Univ Coll, Lampeter.

| AIRDRIE & SHOTTS | | 52.7% change | | | | | Lab win |
|---|---|---|---|---|---|---|---|
| Electorate % Turnout | | 57,673 | 71.4% | **1997** | 59,264 | 74.7% | **1992** |
| **+Liddell, Mrs H L** | **Lab** | **25,460** | **61.8%** | **-0.7%** | 27,678 | 62.5% | Lab |
| Robertson, K | SNP | 10,048 | 24.4% | +6.3% | 8,023 | 18.1% | SNP |
| Brook, Dr N | C | 3,660 | 8.9% | -6.0% | 6,588 | 14.9% | C |
| Wolseley, R | LD | 1,719 | 4.2% | -0.3% | 1,997 | 4.5% | LD |
| Semple, C | Ref | 294 | 0.7% | | | | |
| **Lab to SNP notional swing 3.5%** | | **41,181** | | **Lab maj 15,412** | **44,286** | | **Lab maj 19,655** |
| | | | | 37.4% | | | 44.4% |

**HELEN LIDDELL,** b Dec 6, 1950. Became Economic Secretary to the Treasury, May 4, 1997. Elected for this seat 1997; MP for Monklands East 1994-97, having won by-election caused by death of Lab leader, John Smith; contested Fife E Oct 1974. Lab spokesman on Scotland 1995, dealing with education and social work. Chief exec, Business Venture Programmer, 1993-94; Scottish secretary, Lab Party, 1977-88; vice-chair, all-party Scottish Opera group, 1996- . Dir, personnel and public affairs, Scottish Daily Record and Sunday Mail (1986) Ltd, 1988-92. Ed St Patrick's HS, Coatbridge; Strathclyde Univ.

**KEITH ROBERTSON,** b Nov 22, 1955. Ex-Royal Navy. Perth and Kinross cllr; convener of Auchterarder SNP branch; vice-convener Perth constituency assoc. Ed Invergowrie Sec; Perth Coll of FE.

**NICHOLAS BROOK,** b June 2, 1964. Physicist programmer at Glasgow Univ, research assoc Lancaster Univ 1988-90. Vice-chair, local C assoc. Ed Salendine Nook Secondary; Manchester Univ.

**RICHARD WOLSELEY,** b July 19, 1973. Trainee chartered accountant. Ex-press officer and treas of Scottish Young LDs. Ed Wishaw HS; Glasgow Univ.

*Details of 1994 Monklands East by-election on page 278*

| ALDERSHOT | | 8.1% change | | | | | C win |
|---|---|---|---|---|---|---|---|
| Electorate % Turnout | | 76,189 | 71.1% | **1997** | 75,321 | 78.3% | **1992** |
| **Howarth, G** | C | **23,119** | **42.7%** | **-15.4%** | **34,300** | **58.1%** | C |
| Collett, A | LD | 16,498 | 30.5% | +4.1% | 15,584 | 26.4% | LD |
| Bridgeman, T | Lab | 13,057 | 24.1% | +10.3% | 8,154 | 13.8% | Lab |
| Howe, J | UK Ind | 794 | 1.5% | | 956 | 1.6% | Lib |
| Pendragon, A | Ind | 361 | 0.7% | | | | |
| Stevens, Dr D | BNP | 322 | 0.6% | | | | |
| **C to LD notional swing 9.7%** | | **54,151** | | **C maj 6,621** | **58,994** | | **C maj 18,716** |
| | | | | 12.2% | | | 78.3% |

**GERALD HOWARTH,** b Sept 12, 1947. MP for Cannock and Burntwood 1983-92. PPS to Margaret Thatcher 1991-92; to Sir George Young, Min for Housing and Planning, 1990-91, and to Michael Spicer, Under Sec for Energy, 1987-90; member, sound broadcasting select cttee, 1987-92. Joint man dir, Taskforce Communications, since 1993. UK adviser, Sukhoi design bureau, Moscow. International banker with Richard Unwin International 1983-87; Standard Chartered Bank 1981-83; Bank of America International 1971-77; European Arab Bank 1977-81; Bank of America International 1971-77. Hounslow cllr 1982-83. Joint sec, C backbench aviation cttee, 1983-87. Holds private pilot's licence.

Dir, Freedom Under Law 1973-7; gen sec, Soc for Individual Freedom, 1969-71. Ed Bloxham School, Banbury; Southampton Univ.
**ADRIAN COLLETT,** b March 31, 1958. Ex-retail manager. Contested seat 1992. Hants county cllr 1983- ; Hart district cllr 1980- ; Yateley town cllr 1983-87. Was on Lib Party council. Ex-associate, Inst of Grocery Distribution. Ed Salesian Coll, Farnborough.
**TERENCE BRIDGEMAN,** b Feb 21, 1949. Self-employed heating engineer. Member, Co-op Party; Camra, Mensa. Ed Farnborough GS; OU.

| ALDRIDGE-BROWNHILLS | | | | | | | C hold |
|---|---|---|---|---|---|---|---|
| Electorate % Turnout | | 62,441 | 74.3% | **1997** | 63,404 | 82.6% | **1992** |
| *Shepherd, R | C | 21,856 | 47.1% | -7.2% | 28,431 | 54.3% | C |
| Toth, J | Lab | 19,330 | 41.7% | +8.4% | 17,407 | 33.3% | Lab |
| Downie, Ms C | LD | 5,184 | 11.2% | -1.2% | 6,503 | 12.4% | LD |
| **C to Lab swing 7.8%** | | **46,370** | | **C maj 2,526** | **52,341** | | **C maj 11,024** |
| | | | | 5.4% | | | 82.6% |

**RICHARD SHEPHERD,** b Dec 6, 1942. Won the seat 1979; fought Nottingham E, Feb 1974. Member, select cttees on Severn Bridges Bill, 1991, Treasury and Civil Service, 1979-83. Joint vice-chair, all-party constitutional & parly affairs group, 1996- . SE economic planning council 1970-74. Non-exec dir, Partridges of Sloane Street Ltd, food retailing, 1972- , and Shepherd Foods (London) Ltd, 1970- . Underwriting member of Lloyd's 1974-94. Ed Isleworth GS; LSE; Johns Hopkins Univ, School of Advanced International Studies.

**JANOS TOTH,** b Oct 18, 1964. Sales adviser. Former Lab Party organiser Bedfordshire and Milton Keynes; vice-chair, SW Surrey CLP; Staffordshire county cllr; Cannock Chase cllr. Member, GMB. Ed Rodborough School; Wolverhampton Poly.
**CELIA DOWNIE,** b Feb 15, 1957. Teacher. Avon county cllr. Ed St Mary Redcliffe and Temple School; University Coll, Swansea.

| ALTRINCHAM & SALE WEST | | 52.7% change | | | | | C win |
|---|---|---|---|---|---|---|---|
| Electorate % Turnout | | 70,625 | 73.3% | **1997** | 71,031 | 78.4% | **1992** |
| **Brady, G** | C | **22,348** | **43.2%** | **-11.3%** | **30,343** | **54.5%** | C |
| Baugh, Ms J | Lab | 20,843 | 40.3% | +13.8% | 14,727 | 26.4% | Lab |
| Ramsbottom, M | LD | 6,535 | 12.6% | -5.8% | 10,261 | 18.4% | LD |
| Landes, A | Ref | 1,348 | 2.6% | | 366 | 0.7% | Other |
| Stephens, J | ProLife | 313 | 0.6% | | | | |
| Mrozinski, Dr R | UK Ind | 270 | 0.5% | | | | |
| Renwick, J | NLP | 125 | 0.2% | | | | |
| **C to Lab notional swing 12.6%** | | **51,782** | | **C maj 1,505** | **55,697** | | **C maj 15,616** |
| | | | | 2.9% | | | 78.4% |

**GRAHAM BRADY,** b May 20, 1967. Chair, Northern area C students, 1987-89. Dir of Waterfront Partnership, transport and strategic consultancy; previously asst dir, Centre for Policy Studies. Ed Altrincham GS; Durham Univ (chair, univ C assoc, 1987-88).
**JANE BAUGH,** b Oct 29, 1947. Chartered physiotherapist. Trafford cllr 1990- . Member, Manchester Port HA, North West Council for

Museum and Arts. Ed Whitchurch GS, Glamorgan; Cardiff Physiotherapy School.
**MARC RAMSBOTTOM,** b Nov 27, 1963. Higher education manager. Manchester city cllr 1987-91. Member Stonewall. Dir, LSU Services Ltd. Ed Morecambe HS; Manchester Metropolitan Univ.

| ALYN & DEESIDE | | 6.0% change | | | | | Lab win |
|---|---|---|---|---|---|---|---|
| Electorate % Turnout | | 58,091 | 72.2% | **1997** | 57,815 | 78.7% | **1992** |
| +Jones, B | Lab | 25,955 | 61.9% | +11.0% | 23,157 | 50.9% | Lab |
| Roberts, T | C | 9,552 | 22.8% | -14.1% | 16,770 | 36.9% | C |
| Burnham, Mrs E | LD | 4,076 | 9.7% | -0.0% | 4,431 | 9.7% | LD |
| Jones, M | Ref | 1,627 | 3.9% | | 517 | 1.1% | PC |
| Hills, Mrs S | PC | 738 | 1.8% | +0.6% | 433 | 1.0% | Grn |
| | | | | | 200 | 0.4% | Ind |
| C to Lab notional swing 12.5% | | 41,948 | | Lab maj 16,403 | 45,508 | | Lab maj 6,387 |
| | | | | 39.1% | | | 78.7% |

**BARRY JONES,** b June 1, 1938. Teacher and ex-regional organiser. MP for E Flint 1970-83, for this seat 1983- ; contested Northwich 1966. Chief Lab spokesman on Wales 1988-92 and 1983-87; employment spokesman 1980-83. Under Sec for Wales 1974-79. Member, Commons chairmen's panel; Commons intelligence and security cttee; PAC 1979-82. Member, NUT. Ed Hawarden GS; University Coll of North Wales.
**TIMOTHY ROBERTS,** b Feb 18, 1971. Private client fund manager, previously policy analyst with Adam Smith Inst. Vice-chair Nat

Assoc C Graduates 1995- . Ed Cleeve School, Cheltenham; St Hugh's Coll, Oxford.
**ELEANOR BURNHAM,** b April 17, 1951. Business consultant. Ed Radbrook Coll, Shrewsbury; Manchester Metropolitan Univ. Soprano singer. Married to Derek Burnham, LD candidate for Ynys Mon.
**SIW HILLS,** b Oct 9, 1951. Former housing department manager. Member, Chartered Inst of Housing. Ed Nottingham and Liverpool John Moores Univs.

| AMBER VALLEY | | 2.7% change | | | | | Lab win |
|---|---|---|---|---|---|---|---|
| Electorate % Turnout | | 72,005 | 76.1% | **1997** | 72,931 | 83.7% | **1992** |
| Mallaber, Ms J | Lab | 29,943 | 54.7% | +10.3% | 28,360 | 46.5% | C |
| +Oppenheim, P | C | 18,330 | 33.5% | -13.0% | 27,077 | 44.4% | Lab |
| Shelley, R | LD | 4,219 | 7.7% | -1.4% | 5,582 | 9.1% | LD |
| McGibbon, Mrs I | Ref | 2,283 | 4.2% | | | | |
| C to Lab notional swing 11.7% | | 54,775 | | Lab maj 11,613 | 61,019 | | C maj 1,283 |
| | | | | 21.2% | | | 83.7% |

**JUDY MALLABER,** b July 10, 1951. Research Fellow, Local Government Information Unit, and its director 1987-95. Advisory council member, Northern Coll for Adult Ed, Barnsley. Research officer, Nupe, 1975-85. Member, Unison; Action for Southern Africa; Liberty; SEA; Friends of the Earth; Amnesty. Ed N London Collegiate School; St Anne's Coll, Oxford.
**PHILLIP OPPENHEIM,** b March 20, 1956. Author. Elected 1983. Appointed to new position of Exchequer Secretary at the Treasury 1996, taking over duties previously done by Paymaster General;

Under Sec for Trade and Industry 1995-96; Under Sec for Employment 1994-95. PPS to Kenneth Clarke 1988-94. Vice-pres, Videotex Industry Assoc, 1985-90. Co-editor, *What to Buy for Business* 1980-85. Ed Harrow; Oriel Coll, Oxford.
**ROGER SHELLEY,** b May 23, 1966. Museum curator. Member of Transport 2000; Charter 88; sec, Derbyshire Electoral Reform Group. Ed Raynes Park HS; Lancaster and Leicester Univs.

| ANGUS | | 22.9% change | | | | | SNP win |
|---|---|---|---|---|---|---|---|
| Electorate % Turnout | | 59,708 | 72.1% | **1997** | 58,883 | 74.9% | **1992** |
| +Welsh, A P | SNP | 20,792 | 48.3% | +9.1% | 17,274 | 39.2% | SNP |
| Leslie, S | C | 10,603 | 24.6% | -13.5% | 16,801 | 38.1% | C |
| Taylor, Ms C | Lab | 6,733 | 15.6% | +2.7% | 5,708 | 12.9% | Lab |
| Speirs, Dr R | LD | 4,065 | 9.4% | +0.6% | 3,878 | 8.8% | LD |
| Taylor, B | Ref | 883 | 2.0% | | 449 | 1.0% | Other |
| C to SNP notional swing 11.3% | | 43,076 | | SNP maj 10,189 | 44,110 | | SNP maj 473 |
| | | | | 23.7% | | | 74.9% |

**ANDREW WELSH,** b April 19, 1944. Former lecturer in business studies. Vice-Pres of SNP since 1987. Won Angus E 1987; contested it 1983; SNP MP for Angus S, Oct 74-79; contested Dunbartonshire Central Feb 1974. SNP spokesman on trade and industry; SNP whip at Westminster. Joint vice-chair, all-party Scottish housing party group. Exec vice-chair of SNP responsible for local govt 1984-87, and for administration 1979-87. Angus District Council 1984-87, and Angus cllr 1984-87; Stirling district cllr 1974. SFHEA and EIS. Ed Govan HS; Glasgow Univ.
**SEBASTIAN LESLIE,** b March 5, 1954. Accountant and management consultant. Contested Cunninghame S 1992. Former SDP

member. Cttee member Thatcher Foundation (Prague). Founder, Executive Search, accountant with Coopers & Lybrand 1975-90. Ed Ampleforth Coll; Grenoble Univ.
**CATHERINE TAYLOR,** b July 30, 1973. Postgraduate student. Member, Scottish exec of Lab Party 1993-95, Young Lab rep on NEC 1995-97. Member MSF, Co-op Party. Ed Coltness HS; St Andrews Univ (former SU president).
**RICHARD SPEIRS,** b Sept 14, 1942. General practitioner. Founder member SDP. Tayside Regional/Angus UA cllr since 1990. Ed West Kirby GS; St Andrews.

| ANTRIM EAST | | 21.8% change | | 1997 | | | UUP win |
|---|---|---|---|---|---|---|---|
| Electorate % Turnout | | 58,963 | 58.3% | **1997** | 56,732 | 62.5% | **1992** |
| +Beggs, R | UUP | 13,318 | 38.8% | -4.8% | 15,465 | 43.6% | UUP |
| Neeson, S | Alliance | 6,929 | 20.2% | -5.0% | 8,919 | 25.1% | Alliance |
| McKee, J | DUP | 6,682 | 19.5% | -3.2% | 8,046 | 22.7% | DUP |
| Dick, T | C | 2,334 | 6.8% | -1.1% | 2,788 | 7.9% | C |
| Donaldson, B | PUP | 1,757 | 5.1% | | 250 | 0.7% | NLP |
| O'Connor, D | SDLP | 1,576 | 4.6% | | | | |
| Mason, R | Ind | 1,145 | 3.3% | | | | |
| McAuley, Ms C | SF | 543 | 1.6% | | | | |
| McCann, Ms M | NLP | 69 | 0.2% | -0.5% | | | |
| **No swing calculation** | | **34,353** | **UUP maj 6,389** | | **35,468** | **UUP maj 6,546** | |
| | | | 18.6% | | | 62.5% | |

**ROY BEGGS,** b Feb 20, 1936. Ex-teacher and vice-principal. Elected 1983; resigned seat in 1985 in protest at Anglo-Irish agreement and retained it in 1986 by-election. Party spokesman on education, employment and heritage. Member, PAC 1984-86 since 1987. Member for N Antrim, N Ireland Assembly 1982-86; chair, economic development cttee 1982-84. Larne cllr 1973- ; Mayor of Larne 1978-83. Pres, NI Assoc of Ed and Library Boards

1984-85. Ed Ballyclare HS; Stranmillis Training Coll.
**SEAN NEESON,** b Feb 6, 1946. Marketing consultant; Alliance Party chief whip; negotiator at multi-party talks. Carrickfergus cllr; Mayor of Carrickfergus 1993-94. Ed St Malachy's Coll, Belfast; Queen's Univ, Belfast; St Joseph's Coll of Ed, Belfast; Ulster Univ. **JACK McKEE,** b Sept 4, 1943. Alderman on Larne Borough Council, member of N Ireland Forum. Ed Greenland Sec, Larne.

| ANTRIM NORTH | | | | 1997 | | | DUP hold |
|---|---|---|---|---|---|---|---|
| Electorate % Turnout | | 72,411 | 63.8% | **1997** | 69,124 | 65.8% | **1992** |
| *Paisley, Rev I | DUP | 21,495 | 46.5% | -4.3% | 23,152 | 50.9% | DUP |
| Leslie, J | UUP | 10,921 | 23.6% | +5.6% | 8,216 | 18.1% | UUP |
| Farren, S | SDLP | 7,333 | 15.9% | +1.6% | 6,512 | 14.3% | SDLP |
| McCarry, J | SF | 2,896 | 6.3% | +2.1% | 3,442 | 7.6% | Alliance |
| Alderdice, Dr D | Alliance | 2,845 | 6.2% | -1.4% | 2,263 | 5.0% | C |
| Hinds, Ms B | NI Women | 580 | 1.3% | | 1,916 | 4.2% | SF |
| Wright, J | NLP | 116 | 0.3% | | | | |
| **No swing calculation** | | **46,186** | **DUP maj 10,574** | | **45,501** | **DUP maj 14,936** | |
| | | | 22.9% | | | 65.8% | |

**THE REV IAN PAISLEY,** b April 6, 1926. Leader of Democratic Unionist Party. MP for Antrim N since 1970. Resigned seat in 1985 in protest at Anglo-Irish agreement and retained it in 1986 by-election. MEP, 1979- ; N Ireland Assembly, 1982-86; member Stormont 1970-72. Pres, Whitefield Coll of the Bible, 1979- . Hon dir, Voice Newspapers Ltd and Protestant Telegraph Ltd. Ed Model School, Ballymena; Ballymena Tech Coll; S Wales Bible Coll; Reformed Presbyterian Theological Hall, Belfast.

**JAMES LESLIE,** b March 1, 1958. Executive with Guinness Flight investment company. Member, Ulster Defence Regiment, 1976-78. Ed boarding school in England, Cambridge Univ (boxing Blue). **SEAN FARREN.** Senior lecturer, Ulster Univ. Party chair 1980-84. Former member, NI Assembly, 1982. **DAVID ALDERDICE,** b May 28, 1955. Leader of the Alliance Party. Dermatologist. Contested Belfast E 1992 and 1987. Ed Ballymena Acad; Queen's Univ, Belfast.

| ANTRIM SOUTH | | 4.7% change | | 1997 | | | UUP win |
|---|---|---|---|---|---|---|---|
| Electorate % Turnout | | 69,414 | 57.9% | **1997** | 67,045 | 59.5% | **1992** |
| +Forsythe, C | UUP | 23,108 | 57.5% | -13.9% | 28,447 | 71.4% | UUP |
| McClelland, D | SDLP | 6,497 | 16.2% | +2.6% | 5,397 | 13.5% | SDLP |
| Ford, D | Alliance | 4,668 | 11.6% | +0.7% | 4,362 | 10.9% | Alliance |
| Smyth, H | PUP | 3,490 | 8.7% | | 1,220 | 3.1% | SF |
| Cushinan, H | SF | 2,229 | 5.5% | +2.5% | 442 | 1.1% | Loony G |
| Briggs, Ms B | NLP | 203 | 0.5% | | | | |
| **No swing calculation** | | **40,195** | **UUP maj 16,611** | | **39,868** | **UUP maj 23,050** | |
| | | | 41.3% | | | 57.8% | |

**CLIFFORD FORSYTHE,** b Aug 24, 1929. Plumbing and heating contractor; former professional footballer. Elected 1983; resigned seat in 1985 in protest at Anglo-Irish agreement and retained it at 1986 by-election. Party spokesman on social security, transport, local gvt and communications; Chair, all-party plumbing group. Exec member, UU council, 1980-83. NI Assembly 1982-86. Ed Glengormley Public Elementary School.

**DONOVAN McCLELLAND,** b Jan 14, 1949. University lecturer. Contested this seat in 1987 and 1992. Antrim borough cllr, 1989- . SDLP delegate to government talks 1992. Elected to inter-party talks, May 1996. Ed Ballymena Acad; Queen's Univ, Belfast. **DAVID FORD,** b Feb 24, 1951. Former social worker. Gen sec of Alliance Party; local councillor. Spokesman on agriculture and rural development. Ed Dulwich Coll; Queen's Univ, Belfast.

| ARGYLL & BUTE | | | | | | LD hold |
|---|---|---|---|---|---|---|
| Electorate % Turnout | | 49,451 | 72.2% | **1997** | 47,894 | 76.2% | **1992** |
| *Michie, Mrs R | LD | 14,359 | 40.2% | +5.3% | 12,739 | 34.9% | LD |
| MacCormick, Prof N | SNP | 8,278 | 23.2% | -0.6% | 10,117 | 27.7% | C |
| Leishman, R | C | 6,774 | 19.0% | -8.8% | 8,689 | 23.8% | SNP |
| Syed, A | Lab | 5,596 | 15.7% | +2.1% | 4,946 | 13.6% | Lab |
| Stewart, M | Ref | 713 | 2.0% | | | | |
| **SNP to LD swing 3.0%** | | **35,720** | **LD maj 6,081** | | **36,491** | **LD maj 2,622** | |
| | | | 17.0% | | | 76.2% | |

**RAY MICHIE**, b Feb 4, 1934. Won this seat 1987; contested it 1983 and Argyll 1979; LD spokesman on Scottish affairs and transport; Lib spokesman on transport and rural environment 1987-88; joint vice-chair, all-party Scotch whisky industry group. Speech therapist with Argyll and Clyde Health Board 1977-87; vice-pres, Coll of Speech and Language Therapists, 1989- . Chair, Scottish LDs, 1992-93. Ed Aberdeen HS for Girls; Lansdowne House, Edinburgh; Edinburgh School of Speech Therapy.
**NEIL MacCORMICK**, b May 27, 1941. Regius Professor of Public Law, Edinburgh Univ since 1972. Contested this seat 1992; Edinburgh Pentlands 1987 and 1983; Edinburgh N 1979. Member, SNP nat council; SNP nat exec 1978-81. Ed Glasgow HS; Glasgow Univ; Balliol Coll, Oxford (pres of Union 1965); LlD Edinburgh 1982.

**RALPH LEISHMAN**, b Jan 24, 1956. Chartered accountant. Contested Cunninghame N for SDP 1983 and Eastwood for SDP/All 1987; chairman, C transport group, exec member, Scots Tory Reform Group. Principal, Leishman Management Consultants. Ed Glasgow Acad; Glasgow Coll of Tech.
**ALI SYED**, b Nov 18, 1936. Clinical scientist. at Dept of Clinical Physics and Bio-Engineering, West of Scotland Health Boards, Western Infirmary Glasgow. Member, SHA; Royal Philosophical Soc of Glasgow; Scientists for Lab. Ed All Saints' HS and Osmania Univ, Hyderabad, India; Karachi Univ; Strathclyde Univ.

| ARUNDEL & SOUTH DOWNS | | 104.7% change | | | | | C win |
|---|---|---|---|---|---|---|---|
| Electorate % Turnout | | 67,641 | 75.9% | **1997** | 65,056 | 81.7% | **1992** |
| Flight, H | C | 27,251 | 53.1% | -9.7% | 33,365 | 62.8% | C |
| Goss, J | LD | 13,216 | 25.7% | +0.6% | 13,349 | 25.1% | LD |
| Black, R | Lab | 9,376 | 18.3% | +8.9% | 4,957 | 9.3% | Lab |
| Herbert, J | UK Ind | 1,494 | 2.9% | | 1,464 | 2.8% | Other |
| **C to LD notional swing 5.2%** | | **51,337** | **C maj 14,035** | | **53,135** | **C maj 20,016** | |
| | | | 27.3% | | | 81.7% | |

**HOWARD FLIGHT**, b June 16, 1948. Managing director, Guinness Flight Global Asset Management Ltd, specialising in international cash, bond and equity management. Ex-member of Govt's tax consultative cttee. Worked for Hong Kong Bank 1977-79 in Hong Kong and India. Ed Brentwood School, Essex; Magdalene Coll, Cambridge; Univ of Michigan Business School.

**JOHN GOSS**, b Dec 26, 1933. Industrial consultant. Has worked in industry, and abroad for EU institutions. Member, European Movement; Unison. Ed King's, Rochester; LSE; Amsterdam Univ.
**RICHARD BLACK**, b Aug 10, 1964. Lecturer, Sussex Univ. Ed Oxford and London Univs.

| ASHFIELD | | 0.1% change | | | | | Lab win |
|---|---|---|---|---|---|---|---|
| Electorate % Turnout | | 72,269 | 70.0% | **1997** | 73,276 | 79.5% | **1992** |
| +Hoon, G | Lab | 32,979 | 65.2% | +10.3% | 31,978 | 54.9% | Lab |
| Simmonds, M | C | 10,251 | 20.3% | -12.4% | 19,015 | 32.6% | C |
| Smith, W | LD | 4,882 | 9.6% | -2.9% | 7,285 | 12.5% | LD |
| Betts, M | Ref | 1,896 | 3.7% | | | | |
| Belshaw, S | BNP | 595 | 1.2% | | | | |
| **C to Lab notional swing 11.3%** | | **50,603** | **Lab maj 22,728** | | **58,278** | **Lab maj 12,963** | |
| | | | 44.9% | | | 79.5% | |

**GEOFFREY HOON**, b Dec 6, 1953. Became Parly Sec, Lord Chancellor's Department, May 5, 1997. Elected for this seat 1992; MEP for Derbyshire, 1984-94. Opposition spokesman on trade and industry 1995 with responsibility for information superhighway; Lab whip 1994-95; chair, all-party Friends of Music parly group 1992- ; member, Euro Parliament legal affairs and citizens' rights cttee 1984-94, being Lab spokesman; leader, Euro Parliament delegation for relations with China, 1987-89, and with US 1989-92. Unpaid dir, Westminster Foundation for Democracy. Worked in local furniture factory before reading law at

Cambridge. Lecturer in law, Leeds Univ, 1972-82; Visiting Prof of Law, School of Law, Louisville Univ, Kentucky, 1979-80. Member, TGWU. Ed Nottingham HS; Jesus Coll, Cambridge.
**MARK SIMMONDS**, b April 12, 1964. Partner in management consultancy, Strutt & Parker. Chair of local gvt working party reporting to Sec of State, Environment, on housing; vice-chair, Putney C assoc; Wandsworth cllr 1990-94. Ed Worksop Coll; East Midlands Univ.
**BILL SMITH**, b Jan 10, 1936. Teacher. Ed Gordonstoun; Edinburgh Univ.

| ASHFORD | | | | | **C hold** | | |
|---|---|---|---|---|---|---|---|
| Electorate % Turnout | | 74,149 | 74.6% | **1997** | 71,767 | 79.2% | **1992** |
| Green, D | C | **22,899** | 41.4% | -13.2% | 31,031 | 54.6% | C |
| Ennals, J | Lab | 17,544 | 31.7% | +11.7% | 13,672 | 24.1% | LD |
| Williams, J | LD | 10,901 | 19.7% | -4.3% | 11,365 | 20.0% | Lab |
| Cruden, C | Ref | 3,201 | 5.8% | | 773 | 1.4% | Grn |
| Boden, R | Green | 660 | 1.2% | | | | |
| Tyrell, S | NLP | 89 | 0.2% | | | | |
| C to Lab swing 12.5% | | 55,294 | | C maj 5,355 9.7% | 56,841 | | C maj 17,359 79.2% |

**DAMIAN GREEN**, b Jan 17, 1956. Public affairs consultant. Contested Brent E 1992. Speech writer/researcher for John Major 1988-94, worked in Major leadership campaign team 1995. Presenter/City editor of Channel 4 business daily programme 1987-92. Business editor, *Channel 4 News*, 1985-87; news editor, *The Times* Business News, 1984-85. Vice-chair, Nat Assoc of C Graduates, 1980-82. Ed Reading School; Balliol Coll, Oxford (pres of Union 1977).

**JOHN ENNALS**, b Sept 16, 1951. Professor, Kingston Univ Business School. Chair, Twickenham Lab Party, 1991-94, W London European Lab Party 1994-95. Member NATFHE; Fabian Soc. Founder, Coalition Against Starwars, 1986. Ed King's College School, Wimbledon; Phillips Acad, US; King's Coll, Cambridge; London Univ.
**JOHN WILLIAMS**, b June 25, 1949. Medical translator. Contested 1994 Euro elections in Sussex S and Crawley. Ed King Henry VIII GS, Abergavenny.

| ASHTON UNDER LYNE | | **52.3% change** | | | | | **Lab win** |
|---|---|---|---|---|---|---|---|
| Electorate % Turnout | | 72,206 | 65.5% | **1997** | 74,551 | 73.3% | **1992** |
| +Sheldon, R | Lab | 31,919 | 67.5% | +10.5% | 31,138 | 57.0% | Lab |
| Mayson, R | C | 8,954 | 18.9% | -9.8% | 15,706 | 28.7% | C |
| Pickstone, T | LD | 4,603 | 9.7% | -2.2% | 6,519 | 11.9% | LD |
| Clapham, Mrs L | Ref | 1,346 | 2.8% | | 965 | 1.8% | Lib |
| Cymbal, P | Loony | 458 | 1.0% | | 307 | 0.6% | NLP |
| C to Lab notional swing 10.2% | | 47,280 | | Lab maj 22,965 48.6% | 54,635 | | Lab maj 15,432 73.3% |

**ROBERT SHELDON**, b Sept 13, 1923. Elected 1964; contested Manchester Withington, 1959. Chair, Commons PAC since 1983, also member 1965-70 and 1975-79. Lab spokesman on Treasury and economic affairs 1979-83; Financial Sec to the Treasury 1975-79; Min of State, Treasury, 1974-75; Min of State, Civil Service Dept, 1974. Member, Treasury and Civil Service select cttee 1979-81; public expenditure cttee 1972-74. Former dir, Manchester Chamber of Commerce. Adviser to R.E. Sheldon Ltd and Acronyl Ltd, manufacturers of household textiles. Ed elementary, GS, and tech colls; external graduate, London Univ.

**RICHARD MAYSON**, b July 8, 1961. Company director in family textile and investment firm. Writer, lecturer and consultant on wine; consultant to Portuguese Gvt Trade Office; exec cttee member, Anglo-Portuguese Soc. Campaign manager and PA to Charles Hendry, MP, 1992. Ed Beech Hall School, Macclesfield; Uppingham; Sheffield Univ.
**TIM PICKSTONE**, b Nov 11, 1968. Admin and contracts manager. Member, Charter 88; Electoral Reform Soc. Ed Bishop Rawstorne C of E HS; Manchester Metropolitan Univ.

| AYLESBURY | | **4.0% change** | | | | | **C win** |
|---|---|---|---|---|---|---|---|
| Electorate % Turnout | | 79,047 | 72.8% | **1997** | 76,093 | 80.2% | **1992** |
| +Lidington, D | C | 25,426 | 44.2% | -13.1% | 34,983 | 57.3% | C |
| Bowles, Ms S | LD | 17,007 | 29.5% | +1.8% | 16,943 | 27.8% | LD |
| Langridge, R | Lab | 12,759 | 22.2% | +8.7% | 8,205 | 13.4% | Lab |
| John, M | Ref | 2,196 | 3.8% | | 675 | 1.1% | Grn |
| Sheaff, K | NLP | 166 | 0.3% | -0.1% | 229 | 0.4% | NLP |
| C to LD notional swing 7.5% | | 57,554 | | C maj 8,419 14.6% | 61,035 | | C maj 18,040 80.2% |

**DAVID LIDINGTON**, b June 30, 1956. Elected 1992; contested Vauxhall 1987. PPS to Michael Howard when Home Secretary; former joint sec, C backbench home affairs cttee; member, education select cttee 1992-96. Special adviser to Douglas Hurd, as Home Secretary and Foreign Secretary, 1987-90. On secondment from Rio Tinto-Zinc, in charge of media relations 1986-87. Consultant, PPU Ltd, 1991-92. With BP 1983-86, in external affairs division and corporate press office. Ed Haberdashers' Aske's, Elstree; Sidney Sussex Coll, Cambridge.

**SHARON BOWLES**, b June 12, 1953. European patent attorney. Contested this seat 1992, Bucks and Oxford East in 1994 Euro elections. A founder, LD Engineers and Scientists. Ed Our Lady's Convent, Abingdon; Reading Univ; Lady Margaret Hall, Oxford.
**ROBERT LANGRIDGE**, b Oct 5, 1953. Senior lecturer in transport economics. Leader of Lab group, Oxfordshire CC. Member, NATFHE regional cttee. Ed Ruskin Coll, Oxford; Reading and Warwick Univs.

| AYR | | 16.6% change | | | | | Lab win |
|---|---|---|---|---|---|---|---|
| Electorate % Turnout | | 55,829 | 80.2% | **1997** | 55,307 | 81.9% | **1992** |
| **Osborne, Mrs S** | **Lab** | **21,679** | **48.4%** | **+5.8%** | **19,312** | **42.6%** | **Lab** |
| +Gallie, P | C | 15,136 | 33.8% | -4.6% | 17,417 | 38.4% | C |
| Blackford, I | SNP | 5,625 | 12.6% | +1.4% | 5,057 | 11.2% | SNP |
| Hamblen, Miss C | LD | 2,116 | 4.7% | -2.7% | 3,382 | 7.5% | LD |
| Enos, J | Ref | 200 | 0.4% | | 132 | 0.3% | NLP |
| **C to Lab notional swing 5.2%** | | **44,756** | | **Lab maj 6,543** | **45,300** | | **Lab maj 1,895** |
| | | | | 14.6% | | | 4.2% |

**SANDRA OSBORNE,** b Feb 23, 1956. Works for Kilmarnock Women's Aid. S Ayrshire cllr; former Kyle and Carrick cllr. Member, TGWU, Scottish Women's Cttee. Ed Campshill HS, Paisley; Anniesland Coll; Jordanhill Coll; Strathclyde Univ.

**PHIL GALLIE,** b June 3, 1939. Engineer and power stations manager in electricity supply industry. Retained seat for C 1992; contested Dunfermline W 1987 and Cunninghame S 1983. Member, select cttee on Scottish affairs, 1992-97; sec, Scottish group Tory MPs; joint vice-chair, all-party Scottish housing parly group; chair, W of Scotland area C council, 1989-90; Strathclyde W Euro council

1987-89; Bute and N Ayrshire C assoc 1978-80; Cunninghame N assoc 1985-87. Cunninghame cllr 1980-84. Member, EPEA. Ed Dunfermline HS; Kirkcaldy Tech Coll.

**IAN BLACKFORD,** b May 14, 1961. Managing dir of NatWest Securities (head of Scotland and The Netherlands); financial adviser to Netherlands Finance Min. Chair of SNP currency commission cttee; organiser of Edinburgh dist assoc. Ed Royal HS.

**CLARE HAMBLEN,** b Jan 1, 1974. Nurse. East Dunbartonshire cllr. Bearsden Acad; Glasgow Caledonian Univ.

| BANBURY | | 3.8% change | | | | | C win |
|---|---|---|---|---|---|---|---|
| Electorate % Turnout | | 77,456 | 75.5% | **1997** | 69,557 | 81.0% | **1992** |
| **+Baldry, A B** | **C** | **25,076** | **42.9%** | **-11.9%** | **30,886** | **54.9%** | **C** |
| Peperell, Ms H | Lab | 20,339 | 34.8% | +7.9% | 15,155 | 26.9% | Lab |
| Bearder, Mrs C | LD | 9,761 | 16.7% | -1.1% | 10,027 | 17.8% | LD |
| Ager, J | Ref | 2,245 | 3.8% | | 241 | 0.4% | NLP |
| Cotton, Ms B | Green | 530 | 0.9% | | | | |
| King, Mrs L | UK Ind | 364 | 0.6% | | | | |
| Pearson, I | NLP | 131 | 0.2% | -0.2% | | | |
| **C to Lab notional swing 9.9%** | | **58,446** | | **C maj 4,737** | **56,309** | | **C maj 15,731** |
| | | | | 8.1% | | | 27.9% |

**TONY BALDRY,** b July 10, 1950. Barrister, ex-publisher and company director. Elected 1983; contested Thurrock 1979. Fisheries Minister 1995-97; Under Sec for Foreign and Commonwealth Affairs 1994-95; for Environment 1990-94; for Energy Jan-Dec 1990. PPS to John Wakeham, Leader of Commons and then Energy Sec, 1987-90, and to Lynda Chalker, Min of State for Transport and then FCO, 1985-87; member, employment select cttee 1983-86. Awarded Robert Schumann Silver Medal,

1978, for contributions to European politics. Dir, Newpoint Publishing, 1983-90. Ed Leighton Park, Reading; Sussex Univ.

**HAZEL PEPERELL,** b Oct 26, 1949. Performance analyst; lecturer, Oxford Brookes Univ. Member NATFHE. Ed Welwyn Garden City GS; Hatfield Poly.

**CATHERINE BEARDER,** b Jan 14, 1949. Manager. Cherwell cllr since 1995. Member, Friends of the Earth, Charter 88. Police lay visitor. Ed St Christopher's, Letchworth.

| BANFF & BUCHAN | | 11.6% change | | | | | SNP win |
|---|---|---|---|---|---|---|---|
| Electorate % Turnout | | 58,493 | 68.7% | **1997** | 58,015 | 70.3% | **1992** |
| **+Salmond, A** | **SNP** | **22,409** | **55.8%** | **+4.9%** | **20,724** | **50.8%** | **SNP** |
| Frain-Bell, W | C | 9,564 | 23.8% | -10.9% | 14,156 | 34.7% | C |
| Harris, Ms M | Lab | 4,747 | 11.8% | +3.2% | 3,501 | 8.6% | Lab |
| Fletcher, N | LD | 2,398 | 6.0% | +0.1% | 2,387 | 5.9% | LD |
| Buchan, A | Ref | 1,060 | 2.6% | | | | |
| **C to SNP notional swing 7.9%** | | **40,178** | | **SNP maj 12,845** | **40,768** | | **SNP maj 6,568** |
| | | | | 32.0% | | | 16.1% |

**ALEX SALMOND,** b Dec 31, 1954. Won this seat 1987. Elected leader of SNP 1990. Member, select cttee on energy. SNP/PC spokesman on Treasury and economic affairs, energy, fishing, environment, 1988- . Founder, Scottish Centre for Economic and Social Research. Energy economist with Royal Bank of Scotland, 1980-87; asst economist, Dept of Agriculture and Fisheries, Scotland, 1978-80. Senior vice-convener (dep leader and former senior vice-chair) SNP 1987-90; SNP vice-chair (publicity) 1985-87; member, SNP nat exec, 1981- ; Bifu. Ed Linlithgow Acad; St Andrews Univ.

**WILLIAM FRAIN-BELL,** b May 18, 1971. Trainee solicitor. Parly researcher to Sir Hector Monro, when MP; chair, NE area YCs. Ed Loretto; St Andrews and Aberdeen Univs.

**MEGAN HARRIS,** b Dec 7, 1969. Supply teacher; office administrator for Robert Evans, MEP. Ed Ellon Acad; Bradford Univ; Northern Coll, Aberdeen.

**NEIL FLETCHER,** b July 10, 1964. Accountant. Ed Chell HS, Stoke-on-Trent.

| BARKING | | 10.6% change | | | | | Lab win |
|---|---|---|---|---|---|---|---|
| Electorate % Turnout | | 53,682 | 61.4% | **1997** | 56,574 | 69.1% | **1992** |
| +Hodge, Mrs M | Lab | **21,698** | **65.8%** | +13.6% | **20,409** | **52.2%** | Lab |
| Langford, K | C | 5,802 | 17.6% | -16.3% | 13,229 | 33.9% | C |
| Marsh, M | LD | 3,128 | 9.5% | -4.4% | 5,436 | 13.9% | LD |
| Taylor, C | Ref | 1,283 | 3.9% | | | | |
| Tolman, M | BNP | 894 | 2.7% | | | | |
| Mearns, D | ProLife | 159 | 0.5% | | | | |
| C to Lab notional swing 14.9% | | 32,964 | Lab maj 15,896 | | 39,074 | Lab maj 7,180 | |
| | | | 48.2% | | | 18.4% | |

**MARGARET HODGE**, b Sept 8, 1944. Elected 1994 by-election. Member, deregulation select cttee 1996 and also education and employment cttee. Chair, London group of Lab MPs 1995- . Islington cllr 1973-94 (leader 1982-92); chair, Assoc of London Authorities 1984-92. Member, Home Office advisory cttee on race relations 1988-92; local govt commission 1993-94; council, London Univ; Lab local govt cttee 1983-92. Visiting Fellow, Inst for Public Policy Research, 1992- ; director, London First, 1992- ; senior consultant, Price Waterhouse, 1992-94. Ed Bromley HS; LSE (governor, 1990- ).

**KEITH LANGFORD**, b Sept 25, 1959. Joint partner in property service co. Redbridge cllr. Bow Group officer 1991-95, and dep chair 1994-95. Aide to Sir Neil Thorne, MP, 1983 election and Nigel Waterson, MP, in 1992 election. Ed Westcliff-on-Sea GS.
**MARK MARSH**, b Aug 22, 1967. Teacher. Ed Rydens School, Walton-on-Thames; Lancaster Univ.

*Details of 1994 by-election on page 277*

| BARNSLEY CENTRAL | | 14.3% change | | | | | Lab win |
|---|---|---|---|---|---|---|---|
| Electorate % Turnout | | 61,133 | 59.7% | **1997** | 64,092 | 70.2% | **1992** |
| +Illsley, E | Lab | **28,090** | **77.0%** | +6.2% | **31,844** | **70.8%** | Lab |
| Gutteridge, S | C | 3,589 | 9.8% | -8.7% | 8,340 | 18.5% | C |
| Finlay, D | LD | 3,481 | 9.5% | -1.2% | 4,823 | 10.7% | LD |
| Walsh, J | Ref | 1,325 | 3.6% | | | | |
| C to Lab notional swing 7.5% | | 36,485 | Lab maj 24,501 | | 45,007 | Lab maj 23,504 | |
| | | | 67.2% | | | 70.2% | |

**ERIC ILLSLEY**, b April 9, 1955. Elected 1987. Lab spokesman on N Ireland 1995; health spokesman 1994-95; Lab whip 1991-94; member, select cttees on procedure 1991- , business 1994-95, energy 1987-91, broadcasting 1988-91; chair, all-party glass parly group, 1989- ; joint dep chair, parly and scientific cttee, 1995- . Treas, Yorkshire group of Lab MPs, 1988- . Worked for Yorkshire area NUM from 1978. Ed Barnsley Holgate GS; Leeds Univ.

**SIMON GUTTERIDGE**, b 1956. Publisher. Chair, Bexhill and Battle C assoc. Member, Waltham Forest comm health council. Ed Ealing Tech Coll.
**DARREN FINLAY**, b Aug 19, 1972. Barrister. Ed Oxford School; Keele Univ.

| BARNSLEY EAST & MEXBOROUGH | | 56.6% change | | | | | Lab win |
|---|---|---|---|---|---|---|---|
| Electorate % Turnout | | 67,840 | 63.9% | **1997** | 69,088 | 72.2% | **1992** |
| +Ennis, J | Lab | **31,699** | **73.1%** | +0.2% | **36,375** | **72.9%** | Lab |
| Ellison, Miss J | C | 4,936 | 11.4% | -6.0% | 8,654 | 17.3% | C |
| Willis, D | LD | 4,489 | 10.4% | +0.6% | 4,864 | 9.7% | LD |
| Capstick, K | Soc Lab | 1,213 | 2.8% | | | | |
| Miles, A | Ref | 797 | 1.8% | | | | |
| Hyland, Ms J | SEP | 201 | 0.5% | | | | |
| C to Lab notional swing 3.1% | | 43,335 | Lab maj 26,763 | | 49,893 | Lab maj 27,721 | |
| | | | 61.8% | | | 55.6% | |

**JEFF ENNIS**, b Nov 13, 1952. Teacher. Won Barnsley E in 1996 by-election. Barnsley metropolitan borough cllr 1980- (leader of council 1995- ). Chair, S Yorks Fire and Civil Defence Authority, 1995. Ed Hemsworth GS; Redland Coll, Bristol.
**JANE ELLISON**, b Aug 15, 1964. Customer communications manager, John Lewis Partnership. Contested Barnsley E by-

election 1996. Chair N London YCs 1990-93; Barnet cllr 1991-94. Ed St Joseph's Coll, Bradford; St Hilda's Coll, Oxford.
**DAVID WILLIS**, b Feb 5, 1971. Marketing manager. Contested Barnsley E 1996 by-election. Ed Forest School, Winnersh; East Anglia Univ.

*Details of 1996 Barnsley East by-election on page 278*

| BARNSLEY WEST & PENISTONE | | | | | Lab hold | | |
|---|---|---|---|---|---|---|---|
| Electorate % Turnout | | 64,894 | 65.0% | **1997** | 63,374 | 75.8% | **1992** |
| *Clapham, M | Lab | 25,017 | 59.3% | +1.0% | 27,965 | 58.3% | Lab |
| Watkins, P | C | 7,750 | 18.4% | -9.7% | 13,461 | 28.0% | C |
| Knight, Mrs W | LD | 7,613 | 18.0% | +6.4% | 5,610 | 11.7% | LD |
| Miles, Mrs J | Ref | 1,828 | 4.3% | | 970 | 2.0% | Grn |
| C to Lab swing 5.3% | | 42,208 | Lab maj 17,267 | | 48,006 | Lab maj 14,504 | |
| | | | 40.9% | | | 75.8% | |

**MICHAEL CLAPHAM,** b May 15, 1943. Ex-miner and ex-lecturer. Elected 1992. Member, trade and industry select cttee; chair, all-party occupational safety and health group 1996- ; joint vice-chair, PLP trade and industry cttee 1995- . National industrial relations officer of NUM 1983-92; dep head, Yorks NUM compensation dept, 1977-83. Ed Barnsley Tech Coll; Leeds Univ; Leeds Poly; Bradford Univ.

**PAUL WATKINS,** b Feb 25, 1947. Nurse. Treas, Dover and Deal C assoc; member, SE area exec cttee, C Party; ex-leader, Dover District Council, 1987-95; Kent county cllr. Ed Archers Comp, Dover; Dover Group of Hospitals.
**WINIFRED KNIGHT,** b Jan 21, 1933. Retired lecturer. East Riding cllr since 1995. Ed Burnley Girls' School; Washington Hall Training Coll.

| BARROW & FURNESS | | | | | Lab hold | | |
|---|---|---|---|---|---|---|---|
| Electorate % Turnout | | 66,960 | 72.0% | **1997** | 67,764 | 82.1% | **1992** |
| *Hutton, J | Lab | 27,630 | 57.3% | +9.5% | 26,568 | 47.7% | Lab |
| Hunt, R | C | 13,133 | 27.2% | -14.1% | 22,990 | 41.3% | C |
| Metcalfe, Mrs A | LD | 4,264 | 8.8% | -2.1% | 6,089 | 10.9% | LD |
| Hamzeian, J | PLP | 1,995 | 4.1% | | | | |
| Mitchell, D | Ref | 1,208 | 2.5% | | | | |
| C to Lab swing 11.8% | | 48,230 | Lab maj 14,497 | | 55,647 | Lab maj 3,578 | |
| | | | 30.1% | | | 82.1% | |

**JOHN HUTTON,** b May 6, 1955. Won this seat 1992; contested Penrith and the Border 1987, and Cumbria and Lancs North in 1989 Euro elections. Member, home affairs select cttee 1992- , unopposed Bills panel 1992- ; chair, PLP home affairs cttee, 1995- , all-party welfare of park homeowners parly group; ex-chair, PLP defence cttee. Senior lecturer, Newcastle Poly, 1981-92. Member, TGWU; NATFHE. Trustee, Furness Animal Rescue. Ed Westcliff HS, Essex; Magdalen Coll, Oxford.

**RICHARD HUNT,** b June 29, 1958. Financial manager. Member, Freedom Assoc; YCs. Ed St Aidan's C of E HS; Huddersfield Poly.
**ANNE METCALFE,** b April 17, 1937. Teacher. Cumbria cllr 1993- . Member, Cumbria police authority. Charity fundraiser. Ed Belvedere School; Bristol and Cambridge Univs.

| BASILDON | 68.1% change | | | | | Lab win | |
|---|---|---|---|---|---|---|---|
| Electorate % Turnout | | 73,989 | 71.7% | **1997** | 76,236 | 79.4% | **1992** |
| Smith, Ms A | Lab Co-op | 29,646 | 55.8% | | 27,291 | 45.1% | C |
| Baron, J | C | 16,366 | 30.8% | -14.3% | 24,645 | 40.7% | Lab |
| Granshaw, Ms L | LD | 4,608 | 8.7% | -5.5% | 8,599 | 14.2% | LD |
| Robinson, C | Ref | 2,462 | 4.6% | | | | |
| C to Lab notional swing 14.7% | | 53,082 | Lab Co-op maj 13,280 | | 60,535 | C maj 2,646 | |
| | | | 25.0% | | | 4.4% | |

**ANGELA SMITH,** b Jan 7, 1959. Political analyst. Contested Southend W 1987. Research officer for Alun Michael, MP. Essex cllr 1989- (Lab group chief whip, 1991-95). Member, Amnesty; League Against Cruel Sports; RSPCA; TGWU. Ed Chalvedon School, Basildon; Leicester Poly.
**JOHN BARON,** b June 21, 1959. Investment manager; dir, Henderson Private Investors Ltd. Formerly Capt, Royal Regiment of Fusiliers. Member, Foundation for Manufacturing and Industry;

Securities Inst. Ed Queen's, Taunton; Jesus Coll, Cambridge; Sandhurst.
**LINDSAY GRANSHAW,** b Aug 21, 1954. University lecturer. Contested Welwyn Hatfield 1983 and 1987. Founder member SDP; past chair, Women LDs. Member, LD Federal Executive. Ed Brighton and Hove HS; St Anne's Coll, Oxford; Bryn Mawr Coll; Pennsylvania Univ.

| BASINGSTOKE | | 9.5% change | | | | | C win |
|---|---|---|---|---|---|---|---|
| Electorate % Turnout | | 77,035 | 74.2% | **1997** | 75,307 | 83.6% | **1992** |
| +Hunter, A | C | **24,751** | **43.3%** | -10.2% | **33,695** | **53.5%** | C |
| Lickley, N | Lab | 22,354 | 39.1% | +14.0% | 15,809 | 25.1% | Lab |
| Rimmer, M | LD | 9,714 | 17.0% | -3.4% | 12,819 | 20.4% | LD |
| Selim, E | Ind | 310 | 0.5% | | 653 | 1.0% | Grn |
| C to Lab notional swing 12.1% | | **57,129** | | **C maj 2,397** | **62,976** | | **C maj 17,886** |
| | | | | 4.2% | | | 28.4% |

**ANDREW HUNTER,** b Jan 8, 1943. Elected 1983; contested Southampton Itchen, 1979. Member, N Ireland select cttee 1994- ; select cttees on environment 1986-92, agriculture 1985 and 1993-94; chair, C backbench N Ireland cttee, 1992- ; joint vice-chair, C agriculture cttee, 1987-91. Dep chair, Monday Club, 1990- . Dir, Political Planning Services; consultant to Lilly Industries, pharmaceuticals; Scott, Wilson, Kirkpatrick, consulting engineers; Timeshare Council; unpaid non-exec dir, Emission Control Systems International Ltd. Asst master, Harrow, 1971-83. Hon member, Soc of Sealed Knot, 1990- ; member, court, Southampton Univ, 1983- ; chair, falconry cttee, British Field Sports Society, 1988-92. Vice-pres, Nat Prayer Book Soc, 1987- . Major in TA 1973-

84. Ed St George's, Harpenden; Durham Univ; Jesus Coll, Cambridge.
**NIGEL LICKLEY,** b Aug 27, 1960. Barrister. Contested Christchurch July 1993 by-election. Basingstoke cllr since 1994. Member, MSF; Co-op Party; Soc of Lab Lawyers. Ed Queen Mary Sixth-Form Coll, Basingstoke; University Coll, London; Inns of Court School of Law.
**MARTIN RIMMER,** b Oct 3, 1952. Windsor and Maidenhead cllr 1987- . Founder member SDP; member, Charter 88; LD European group. Dir of Masterclass Recruitment and Training Ltd. Member of Scope. Ed Bishops Court School, Formby; Belmont, Hertford; Liverpool Univ.

| BASSETLAW | | | | | | | Lab hold |
|---|---|---|---|---|---|---|---|
| Electorate % Turnout | | 68,101 | 70.4% | **1997** | 69,415 | 78.4% | **1992** |
| +Ashton, J | Lab | **29,298** | **61.1%** | +7.8% | **29,056** | **53.4%** | Lab |
| Cleasby, M | C | 11,838 | 24.7% | -10.3% | 19,061 | 35.0% | C |
| Kerrigan, M | LD | 4,950 | 10.3% | -1.3% | 6,339 | 11.6% | LD |
| Graham, R | Ref | 1,838 | 3.8% | | | | |
| C to Lab swing 9.0% | | **47,924** | | **Lab maj 17,460** | **54,456** | | **Lab maj 9,995** |
| | | | | 36.4% | | | 18.4% |

**JOE ASHTON,** b Oct 9, 1933. Journalist and broadcaster, formerly design engineer. Elected 1968 by-election. Member, select cttees on national heritage, 1992- ; home affairs 1989-92; trade and industry 1987-92; members' interests 1979-83; members' salaries 1981-82; and nationalised industries 1974-76. Chair, all-party association football parly group 1992- . Lab spokesman on energy 1979-81. Asst govt whip 1976-77; PPS to Tony Benn 1974-76. Sheffield city cllr 1962-69. Became director (unpaid) of Sheffield

Wednesday FC 1990. Ed High Storrs GS, Sheffield; Rotherham Tech Coll.
**MARTIN CLEASBY,** b July 9, 1939. Teacher. Contested this seat 1983. Asst master, Worksop Coll; entered teaching 1973, previously export manager. Bassetlaw cllr 1976- . Ed Barnsley GS; Durham Univ.
**MIKE KERRIGAN,** b Nov 18, 1929. Management consultant. Bassetlaw cllr 1995- . Ed Belvedere Coll, Dublin; University Coll, Dublin.

| BATH | | 11.2% change | | | | | LD win |
|---|---|---|---|---|---|---|---|
| Electorate % Turnout | | 70,815 | 76.2% | **1997** | 70,277 | 82.8% | **1992** |
| +Foster, D M E | LD | **26,169** | **48.5%** | +1.6% | **27,298** | **46.9%** | LD |
| McNair, Ms A | C | 16,850 | 31.2% | -12.2% | 25,289 | 43.4% | C |
| Bush, T | Lab | 8,828 | 16.4% | +8.2% | 4,761 | 8.2% | Lab |
| Cook, A | Ref | 1,192 | 2.2% | | 475 | 0.8% | Grn |
| Scrase, R | Green | 580 | 1.1% | | 186 | 0.3% | Lib |
| Sandell, P | UK Ind | 315 | 0.6% | | 127 | 0.2% | Anti-Fed |
| Pullen, N | NLP | 55 | 0.1% | | 86 | 0.1% | Ind |
| C to LD notional swing 6.9% | | **53,989** | | **LD maj 9,319** | **58,222** | | **LD maj 2,009** |
| | | | | 17.3% | | | 82.8% |

**DON FOSTER,** b March 31, 1947. Lecturer. Won this seat 1992, contested Bristol E 1987. LD spokesman on education and employment. Avon cllr 1981-89 (Alliance group leader 1981-86). Parly and political adviser to Inst of Professional Managers and Specialists. Ed Lancaster Royal GS; Keele and Bath Univs.
**ALISON McNAIR,** b Dec 19, 1941. Financial dir of small family business, chartered accountant. Contested Greenwich 1992.

Lewisham cllr 1986-90 (dep leader of C group); North Wilts cllr 1976-79. Ed Pate's GS for Girls, Cheltenham; Manchester Univ.
**TIM BUSH,** b May 1, 1962. Chartered accountant (Coopers & Lybrand). Election campaign co-ordinator, Bath and Wilts North Euro elections. Member, Fabian Soc; Socialist Env Resources Assoc; Lab Campaign for Electoral Reform; Bath and W Wilts Co-op Soc; MSF. Ed Devizes Comp; Leeds Univ. Crew member in Europa 92 round-the-world yacht race.

| BATLEY & SPEN | | 16.3% change | | | | | Lab win |
|---|---|---|---|---|---|---|---|
| Electorate % Turnout | | 64,209 | 73.1% | **1997** | 64,754 | 78.4% | **1992** |
| **Wood, M** | **Lab** | **23,213** | **49.4%** | **+6.4%** | **22,676** | **44.7%** | **C** |
| +Peacock, Mrs E | C | 17,072 | 36.4% | -8.3% | 21,831 | 43.0% | Lab |
| Pinnock, Mrs K | LD | 4,133 | 8.8% | -2.5% | 5,757 | 11.3% | LD |
| Wood, E | Ref | 1,691 | 3.6% | | 520 | 1.0% | Grn |
| Smith, R | BNP | 472 | 1.0% | | | | |
| Lord, C | Green | 384 | 0.8% | | | | |
| C to Lab notional swing 7.4% | | **46,965** | | Lab maj 6,141 | **50,784** | | C maj 845 |
| | | | | 13.1% | | | 1.7% |

**MICHAEL WOOD,** b March 3, 1946. Social worker. Founder member of newspaper and food workers co-operatives. Ed Nantwich and Acton GS, Cheshire; Leeds Poly; Southampton Univ.
**ELIZABETH PEACOCK,** b Sept 4, 1937. Elected 1983. PPS to Angela Rumbold when Home Office Min, 1991-92, and to Nicholas Scott, Social Security Min, 1992. Member, exec, 1922 Cttee, 1987-91; Commons services cttee 1987-91; unopposed Bills panel 1987-92; select cttee on employment 1983-87. Joint vice-chair, Yorkshire group Tory MPs; joint vice-chair, 1991-92, and member, 1987-91,

exec cttee, UK branch, CPA. Former joint sec, Pro-Life group. Unpaid non-exec dir, White Rose Radio Ltd; adviser to Forests Forever campaign. Magistrate. Member, BBC general advisory council, 1987-93; N Yorks county cllr 1981-84. Ed St Monica's Convent, Skipton.
**KATH PINNOCK,** b Sept 25, 1946. Teacher. Kirklees borough cllr 1987- , LD leader. Ed City of Bath HS for Girls; Keele Univ. Mrs Pinnock's son, Richard, was LD candidate in Midlothian.

| BATTERSEA | | 0.3% change | | | | | Lab win |
|---|---|---|---|---|---|---|---|
| Electorate % Turnout | | 66,928 | 70.8% | **1997** | 67,426 | 77.8% | **1992** |
| **Linton, M** | **Lab** | **24,047** | **50.7%** | **+9.5%** | **26,411** | **50.4%** | **C** |
| +Bowis, J | C | 18,687 | 39.4% | -11.0% | 21,630 | 41.3% | Lab |
| Keaveney, Ms P | LD | 3,482 | 7.3% | +0.3% | 3,700 | 7.1% | LD |
| Slater, M | Ref | 804 | 1.7% | | 586 | 1.1% | Grn |
| Banks, R | UK Ind | 250 | 0.5% | | 100 | 0.2% | NLP |
| Marshall, J | Dream | 127 | 0.3% | | | | |
| C to Lab notional swing 10.2% | | **47,397** | | Lab maj 5,360 | **52,427** | | C maj 4,781 |
| | | | | 11.3% | | | 9.1% |

**MARTIN LINTON,** b Aug 11, 1944 (in Stockholm). *Guardian* journalist. Wandsworth cllr 1971-82. Ed Christ's Hospital, Sussex; Université de Lyon; Pembroke Coll, Oxford.
**JOHN BOWIS,** b Aug 2, 1945. Gained this seat 1987. Transport Under Sec 1996-97; Health Under Sec 1993-96. PPS to Welsh Sec 1990-93, and to Local Gvt Min 1989-92. Adviser to Assoc of Colls of Further and Higher Ed 1987-93; dir, London Actors Theatre Co,

1989-92; public affairs dir, British Insurance Brokers' Assoc, 1983-87. Vice-pres, International Soc for Human Rights, 1988- . Kingston cllr, 1982-86. Ed Tonbridge School; Brasenose Coll, Oxford.
**PAULA KEAVENEY,** b Dec 29, 1959. Press officer for charity, journalist. Ed Sydenham HS; Edinburgh Univ.

| BEACONSFIELD | | 3.3% change | | | | | C win |
|---|---|---|---|---|---|---|---|
| Electorate % Turnout | | 68,959 | 72.8% | **1997** | 68,755 | 78.3% | **1992** |
| **Grieve, D** | **C** | **24,709** | **49.2%** | **-14.5%** | **34,316** | **63.7%** | **C** |
| Mapp, P | LD | 10,722 | 21.4% | +1.9% | 10,452 | 19.4% | LD |
| Hudson, A | Lab | 10,063 | 20.0% | +6.4% | 7,371 | 13.7% | Lab |
| Lloyd, H | Ref | 2,197 | 4.4% | | 1,331 | 2.5% | Ind C |
| Story, C | CASC | 1,434 | 2.9% | | 198 | 0.4% | NLP |
| Cooke, C | UK Ind | 451 | 0.9% | | 168 | 0.3% | ERIP |
| Duval, Ms G | ProLife | 286 | 0.6% | | | | |
| Dyball, T | NLP | 193 | 0.4% | +0.0% | | | |
| Matthews, R | B Ind | 146 | 0.3% | | | | |
| C to LD notional swing 8.2% | | **50,201** | | C maj 13,987 | **53,836** | | C maj 23,864 |
| | | | | 27.9% | | | 78.3% |

**DOMINIC GRIEVE,** b May 24, 1956. Barrister. Contested Lambeth Norwood 1987. Member of PM's campaign team 1992. Hammersmith and Fulham cllr 1982-86. TGWU parly group. Chair of research cttee of Soc of C Lawyers. London Diocesan Synod of C of E, 1994- . Ed Westminster; Magdalen Coll, Oxford (pres, univ C assoc, 1977). Son of Percy Grieve, QC, ex-MP for Solihull.

**PETER MAPP,** b Jan 27, 1941. Management consultant. Contested Slough for LDs 1992. Member of SDP 1981; Campaign for Electoral Reform; Soc of American military engineers. Ed Cheam County Boys' School; Reading Univ.
**ALASTAIR HUDSON,** b Nov 6, 1968. Barrister and law lecturer. Member, TGWU; Soc of Lab Lawyers; Fabian Soc. Ed King's Coll, London.

| BECKENHAM | | 24.8% change | | | 1997 | | | C win |
|---|---|---|---|---|---|---|---|---|
| Electorate % Turnout | | 72,807 | 74.6% | | **1997** | 75,388 | 77.4% | **1992** |
| +Merchant, P | C | 23,084 | 42.5% | -17.8% | | 35,154 | 60.3% | C |
| Hughes, R | Lab | 18,131 | 33.4% | +12.2% | | 12,341 | 21.2% | Lab |
| Vetterlein, Ms R | LD | 9,858 | 18.1% | +1.4% | | 9,765 | 16.7% | LD |
| Mead, L | Ref | 1,663 | 3.1% | | | 841 | 1.4% | Lib |
| Rimmer, P | Lib | 720 | 1.3% | -0.1% | | 232 | 0.4% | NLP |
| Pratt, C | UK Ind | 506 | 0.9% | | | | | |
| Mcauley, J | NF | 388 | 0.7% | | | | | |
| C to Lab notional swing 15.0% | | 54,350 | | C maj 4,953 | | 58,333 | | C maj 22,813 |
| | | | | 9.1% | | | | 39.1% |

**PIERS MERCHANT,** b Jan 2, 1951. Elected 1992; MP for Newcastle-upon-Tyne Central 1983-87; contested seat 1979. PPS to Peter Lilley, Soc Security Sec, 1992-97. Member, procedure select cttee, 1995-97. Joint vice-chair, all-party Aids party group. Public affairs dir, Advertising Assoc, 1990-92; dir of corporate publicity, NEI plc, 1987-90; editor of *Newsline*, C Party newspaper, 1982-84; on staff of *The Journal*, Newcastle, 1973-82. Elected Fellow, Univ Coll, Durham, 1975. Dir, Tyne and Wear Wastesaver Ltd, and of Tall Ships Appeal, 1986-90; joint chair, Free Flow of Information Cttee,

International Parly Group on Human Rights 1986-91. Ed Nottingham HS; Durham Univ (chair, univ C assoc, 1970-73).
**ROBERT HUGHES,** b Jan 18, 1958. Computer projects manager, British Telecom. Member, Socialist Env Resources Assoc; Greenpeace. Ed Marple Hall Boys' GS; Birmingham Univ.
**ROSEMARY VETTERLEIN,** b Jan 19, 1972. Restaurant assistant manager. Member, Scottish exec, 1992-95; London regional exec 1996- . Ed Newstead Wood School for Girls, Orpington; Orpington Coll of FE; Dundee Univ.

| BEDFORD | | 47.4% change | | | 1997 | | | Lab win |
|---|---|---|---|---|---|---|---|---|
| Electorate % Turnout | | 66,560 | 73.5% | | **1997** | 65,764 | 76.5% | **1992** |
| Hall, P | Lab | 24,774 | 50.6% | +14.2% | | 22,863 | 45.4% | C |
| Blackman, R | C | 16,474 | 33.7% | -11.8% | | 18,318 | 36.4% | Lab |
| Noyce, C | LD | 6,044 | 12.3% | -4.1% | | 8,263 | 16.4% | LD |
| Conquest, P | Ref | 1,503 | 3.1% | | | 881 | 1.8% | Other |
| Saunders, Ms P | NLP | 149 | 0.3% | | | | | |
| C to Lab notional swing 13.0% | | 48,944 | | Lab maj 8,300 | | 50,325 | | C maj 4,545 |
| | | | | 17.0% | | | | 76.5% |

**PATRICK HALL,** b Oct 20, 1951. Planning officer and town centre co-ordinator for Bedford. Contested Bedfordshire N 1992. Bedfordshire county cllr, 1989- . Member, Chartered Inst of Public Finance and Accountancy; North Beds Community Health Council; chair, Bedfordshire Door to Door dial-a-ride; on management cttee, Hillrise Urban Nature Park. Member, Nalgo. Ed Bedford Mod School.

**ROBERT BLACKMAN,** b April 26, 1956. Sales manager with BT. Contested Brent S in 1992. Brent cllr 1986- (leader 1990-96; opposition leader 1996- ). Ed Wembley HS; Preston Manor HS; Wembley; Liverpool Univ.
**CHRISTOPHER NOYCE,** b Oct 14, 1957. Solicitor. Contested London NW 1989 Euro elections and Harrow W in 1992 election. Harrow cllr 1986- . Ed Harrow County GS; Pembroke Coll, Oxford; College of Law, Guildford.

| BEDFORDSHIRE MID | | 99.4% change | | | 1997 | | | C win |
|---|---|---|---|---|---|---|---|---|
| Electorate % Turnout | | 66,979 | 78.4% | | **1997** | 60,723 | 86.0% | **1992** |
| Sayeed, J | C | 24,176 | 46.0% | -14.4% | | 31,561 | 60.4% | C |
| Mallett, N | Lab | 17,086 | 32.5% | +13.4% | | 10,016 | 19.2% | Lab |
| Hill, T | LD | 8,823 | 16.8% | +1.5% | | 7,973 | 15.3% | LD |
| Marler, Mrs S | Ref | 2,257 | 4.3% | | | 2,302 | 4.4% | Lib |
| Lorys, M | NLP | 174 | 0.3% | -0.4% | | 398 | 0.8% | NLP |
| C to Lab notional swing 13.9% | | 52,516 | | C maj 7,090 | | 52,250 | | C maj 21,545 |
| | | | | 13.5% | | | | 86.0% |

**JONATHAN SAYEED,** b March 20, 1948. MP for Bristol E 1983-92. PPS to Lord Belstead, Paymaster General and N Ireland Min, 1991-92. Member, select cttees on defence 1987-91; environment 1987. Chair (1991-92), vice-chair (1985-91) and former sec, C backbench shipping and shipbuilding sub-cttee; joint dep chair (1987-92) and former sec, all-party maritime group. Chair of Ranelagh Ltd, public affairs co, since 1992; non-exec dir, Love Lane Investments Ltd, 1983-92. In Royal Navy 1965-72; RNR 1972-76. Dir, then chair, insurance and shipping consultancy, 1973-82.

Ed Wolverstone Hall, Suffolk; RNC, Dartmouth; Royal Naval Engineering Coll, Manadon.
**NEIL MALLETT,** b Sept 8, 1954. Management consultant. Chair, Bedfordshire Mid CLP 1995- ; Bedfordshire cllr 1993- . Member, TGWU (ACTS). Ed Icknield GS; Luton Sixth-Form Coll.
**TIM HILL,** b Dec 13, 1961. Technical officer, British Telecom. Bedford cllr 1986-96. Member, CWU; Charter 88; European Movement. Ed Pilgrim Upper School, Bedford.

| BEDFORDSHIRE NORTH EAST | | | 78.2% change | | 1997 | | | 1992 |
|---|---|---|---|---|---|---|---|---|
| Electorate % Turnout | | 64,743 | 77.8% | | 1997 | 62,068 | 84.4% | 1992 |
| +Lyell, Sir Nicholas | C | 22,311 | 44.3% | -15.0% | | 31,081 | 59.3% | C |
| Lehal, J | Lab | 16,428 | 32.6% | +12.6% | | 10,478 | 20.0% | Lab |
| Bristow, P | LD | 7,179 | 14.2% | -4.3% | | 9,706 | 18.5% | LD |
| Taylor, J | Ref | 2,490 | 4.9% | | | 1,127 | 2.2% | Other |
| Foley, L | Ind C | 1,842 | 3.7% | | | | | |
| Bence, B | NLP | 138 | 0.3% | | | | | |
| C to Lab notional swing 13.8% | | 50,388 | | C maj 5,883 | | 52,392 | | C maj 20,603 |
| | | | | 11.7% | | | | 39.3% |

SIR NICHOLAS LYELL, QC, b Dec 6, 1938. MP for Bedfordshire Mid 1983-97, and for Hemel Hempstead 1979-83; contested Lambeth Central Oct 1974. Attorney-General April 1992-97; Solicitor-General 1987-92; Under Sec for Health and Soc Security 1986-87. Privy Counsellor 1990. Member, Commons privileges cttee, 1994-95. PPS to Sir Michael Havers, Attorney-General, 1979-86; select cttee on procedure (finance) 1982-83. Chair, Bow Group; home affairs standing cttee 1979-85. Recorder. Member of Lloyd's. Vice-chair, British Field Sports Soc, 1983-86. Chair, 1985-86, exec of Soc of C Lawyers. Ed Stowe School (governor 1990- ); Christ Church, Oxford.

JOHN LEHAL, b April 1, 1973. Postgraduate student. Member, Greenpeace; Amnesty. Ed Bedford School; Greenwich and Cambridge Univs.

PHILIP BRISTOW, b March 29, 1956. BT manager. Member, Charter 88. Ed Nevin Drive Senior HS, Chingford.

| BEDFORDSHIRE SOUTH WEST | | | 13.0% change | | 1997 | | | 1992 |
|---|---|---|---|---|---|---|---|---|
| Electorate % Turnout | | 69,781 | 75.8% | | 1997 | 69,727 | 82.0% | 1992 |
| +Madel, Sir David | C | 21,534 | 40.7% | -15.2% | | 32,000 | 56.0% | C |
| Date, A | Lab | 21,402 | 40.5% | +14.8% | | 14,660 | 25.6% | Lab |
| Owen, S | LD | 7,559 | 14.3% | -2.3% | | 9,475 | 16.6% | LD |
| Hill, Ms R | Ref | 1,761 | 3.3% | | | 763 | 1.3% | Grn |
| Wise, T | UK Ind | 446 | 0.8% | | | 275 | 0.5% | NLP |
| Le Carpentier, A | NLP | 162 | 0.3% | -0.2% | | | | |
| C to Lab notional swing 15.0% | | 52,864 | | C maj 132 | | 57,173 | | C maj 17,340 |
| | | | | 0.2% | | | | 82.0% |

SIR DAVID MADEL, b Aug 6, 1938. Elected for this seat 1983; MP for Bedford S 1970-83; contested Erith and Crayford 1965 by-election and 1966. Member, select cttees on Euro legislation 1983- ; transport 1995- ; members' interests 1979-87; education, science and arts 1979-83. Chair, C backbench education cttee 1983-85, joint vice-chair 1981-83; joint vice-chair, C backbench employment cttee, 1974-81; sec, C backbench home affairs cttee, 1972-73. PPS to defence mins 1973-74. Advertising exec, Thomson Organisation, 1964-70. Ed Uppingham; Keble Coll, Oxford.

ANDREW DATE, b May 17, 1956. Teacher. South Beds cllr (leader of Lab group and council leader). Member, NUT; SEA. Founder of charity for young homeless people. Ed Dorset Inst of HE.

STEPHEN OWEN, b May 15, 1943. Management consultancy director. Mayor of Leighton Buzzard; South Beds district cllr and Beds county cllr. Ed Cedars GS, Leighton Buzzard; London Univ.

| BELFAST EAST | | | 22.3% change | | 1997 | | | 1992 |
|---|---|---|---|---|---|---|---|---|
| Electorate % Turnout | | 61,744 | 63.2% | | 1997 | 63,881 | 65.0% | 1992 |
| +Robinson, P | DUP | 16,640 | 42.6% | -11.9% | | 22,635 | 54.5% | DUP |
| Empey, R | UUP | 9,886 | 25.3% | | | 11,337 | 27.3% | Alliance |
| Hendron, J | Alliance | 9,288 | 23.8% | -3.5% | | 4,170 | 10.0% | C |
| Dines, Miss S | C | 928 | 2.4% | -7.7% | | 2,250 | 5.4% | Ind U |
| Corr, D | SF | 810 | 2.1% | +0.4% | | 686 | 1.7% | SF |
| Lewsley, Mrs P | SDLP | 629 | 1.6% | | | 323 | 0.8% | WP |
| Dougan, D | NIFT | 541 | 1.4% | | | 126 | 0.3% | NLP |
| Bell, J | WP | 237 | 0.6% | -0.2% | | | | |
| Collins, D | NLP | 70 | 0.2% | -0.1% | | | | |
| No swing calculation | | 39,029 | | DUP maj 6,754 | | 41,527 | | DUP maj 11,298 |
| | | | | 17.3% | | | | 27.2% |

PETER ROBINSON, b Dec 29, 1948. Won seat 1979, but resigned 1985 in protest at Anglo-Irish agreement and retained it in 1986 by-election. Dep leader, Democratic Unionist Party; gen sec 1975-80. Member, select cttee on N Ireland 1994- ; N Ireland Assembly 1982-86. Castlereagh cllr 1977- ; Dep Mayor 1978; Mayor 1986. Dir (unpaid), Crown Publications, Belfast; hon dir, Voice Newspapers Ltd. Ed Annadale GS; Castlereagh CFE.

REG EMPEY, b Oct 26, 1947. Independent retailer. Party vice-pres and negotiator in constitutional talks. Belfast city cllr 1985; Lord Mayor 1989-90, 1993-94; Dep Lord Mayor 1988-89. Ed Royal School, Armagh; Queen's Univ, Belfast.

JIM HENDRON, b Oct 1, 1931. Solicitor. Founder member and past pres of Alliance Party. Ed Queen's Univ, Belfast. Brother of Joe Hendron, SDLP candidate for Belfast West.

| BELFAST NORTH | | 24.4% change | | | | | UUP win |
|---|---|---|---|---|---|---|---|
| Electorate % Turnout | | 64,577 | 64.2% | **1997** | 67,989 | 63.2% | **1992** |
| **+Walker, C** | **UUP** | **21,478** | **51.8%** | **+0.0%** | **22,259** | **51.8%** | **UUP** |
| Maginness, A | SDLP | 8,454 | 20.4% | +2.1% | 7,867 | 18.3% | SDLP |
| Kelly, G | SF | 8,375 | 20.2% | +8.8% | 4,882 | 11.4% | SF |
| Campbell, T | Alliance | 2,221 | 5.4% | -2.4% | 3,321 | 7.7% | Alliance |
| Emerson, P | Green | 539 | 1.3% | | 2,678 | 6.2% | C |
| Treanor, P | WP | 297 | 0.7% | -0.2% | 1,366 | 3.2% | NA |
| Gribben, Ms A | NLP | 88 | 0.2% | -0.3% | 415 | 1.0% | WP |
| | | | | | 204 | 0.5% | NLP |
| **No swing calculation** | | **41,452** | **UUP maj 13,024** | | **42,992** | **UUP maj 14,392** | |
| | | | 31.4% | | | 63.2% | |

**CECIL WALKER,** b Dec 17, 1924. Ex-sales manager in timber business. Elected 1983; contested seat 1979; resigned 1985 in protest at Anglo-Irish agreement and re-elected at 1986 by-election. Chair, all-party denture services for the public group. Belfast cllr, 1977- . Ed Methodist Coll, Belfast.

**ALBAN MAGINNESS,** b July 9, 1950. Barrister. Contested this seat 1992. Belfast city cllr, 1985- . Elected to NI Forum 1996. Ed St Malachy's Coll, Belfast; Ulster Univ; Queen's Univ, Belfast.
**GERRY KELLY,** b April 5, 1953. As Sinn Fein negotiator, he took part in secret talks with Government between 1990 and 1993.

| BELFAST SOUTH | | 26.3% change | | | | | UUP win |
|---|---|---|---|---|---|---|---|
| Electorate % Turnout | | 63,439 | 62.2% | **1997** | 64,491 | 68.5% | **1992** |
| **+Smyth, Rev M** | **UUP** | **14,201** | **36.0%** | **-16.7%** | **23,258** | **52.7%** | **UUP** |
| McDonnell, Dr A | SDLP | 9,601 | 24.3% | +10.1% | 6,921 | 15.7% | Alliance |
| Ervine, D | PUP | 5,687 | 14.4% | | 6,266 | 14.2% | SDLP |
| McBride, S | Alliance | 5,112 | 12.9% | -2.7% | 5,154 | 11.7% | C |
| Hayes, S | SF | 2,019 | 5.1% | +2.6% | 1,116 | 2.5% | SF |
| Campbell, Ms A | NI Women | 1,204 | 3.0% | | 869 | 2.0% | LTU |
| Boal, Miss M | C | 962 | 2.4% | -9.2% | 359 | 0.8% | WP |
| Cusack, N | Ind Lab | 292 | 0.7% | | 209 | 0.5% | NLP |
| Lynn, P | WP | 286 | 0.7% | -0.1% | | | |
| Anderson, J | NLP | 120 | 0.3% | -0.2% | | | |
| **No swing calculation** | | **39,484** | **UUP maj 4,600** | | **44,152** | **UUP maj 16,337** | |
| | | | 11.7% | | | 37.0% | |

**THE REV MARTIN SMYTH,** b June 15, 1931. Grand Master, Grand Orange Lodge of Ireland, 1972- ; Grand Master, Grand Orange Council of the World, 1974-82, and pres, 1985-88. Elected in 1982 by-election; resigned 1985 in protest at Anglo-Irish agreement and held seat in 1986 by-election. Member, NI Assembly, 1982-86; Constitutional Convention 1975. Ed Methodist Coll, Belfast; Magee Univ Coll, Londonderry; Trinity Coll, Dublin; Presbyterian Coll, Belfast; San Francisco Theological Seminary.

**ALASDAIR McDONNELL,** b Sept 1949. Family doctor. Contested this seat 1992; 1986 by-election; 1983; 1982 by-election; and 1979. Belfast city cllr. Ed St McNissis Coll, Co Antrim; Univ Coll, Dublin.
**DAVID ERVINE,** b July 21, 1953. PUP chief spokesman. Elected May 1996 to NI Forum. Jailed 5½ years in 1970s for paramilitary activities. Ed Orangefield Sec, East Belfast.
**STEVE McBRIDE,** b Nov 22, 1949. Barrister. Ex-High Sheriff of Belfast. Ed Queen's Univ, Belfast; Kent Univ.

| BELFAST WEST | | 21.3% change | | | | | SF win |
|---|---|---|---|---|---|---|---|
| Electorate % Turnout | | 61,785 | 74.3% | **1997** | 62,940 | 72.0% | **1992** |
| **Adams, G** | **SF** | **25,662** | **55.9%** | **+13.9%** | **20,045** | **44.2%** | **SDLP** |
| +Hendron, Dr J | SDLP | 17,753 | 38.7% | -5.5% | 19,027 | 42.0% | SF |
| Parkinson, F | UUP | 1,556 | 3.4% | -8.2% | 5,275 | 11.6% | UUP |
| Lowry, J | WP | 721 | 1.6% | -0.1% | 759 | 1.7% | WP |
| Kennedy, L | HR | 102 | 0.2% | | 216 | 0.5% | NLP |
| Daly, Ms M | NLP | 91 | 0.2% | -0.3% | | | |
| **SDLP to SF notional swing 9.7%** | | **45,885** | **SF maj 7,909** | | **45,322** | **SDLP maj 1,018** | |
| | | | 17.2% | | | 2.3% | |

**GERRY ADAMS,** b Oct 6, 1948. Pres of Sinn Fein since 1984. Regained this seat 1997; MP for Belfast W 1983-92 but did not take seat at Westminster. Member for W Belfast of NI Assembly, 1982. Interned 1971, released 1976. Ed St Mary's GS, Belfast.
**JOE HENDRON,** b Nov 12, 1933. GP practising in Belfast. Won this seat 1992, contested it in 1987 and 1983. SDLP member, NI Convention 1975, and of NI Assembly 1982-86. Belfast city cllr 1981- . Ed St Nalachy's Coll, Belfast; Queen's Univ, Belfast.
**FREDDIE PARKINSON,** b Aug 9, 1963. Sales administrator and photographer. Ed Dunmurry HS; Lisburn Coll of FE.

## BERWICK-UPON-TWEED — LD hold

| Electorate % Turnout | | 56,428 | 74.1% | 1997 | 54,919 | 79.1% | 1992 |
|---|---|---|---|---|---|---|---|
| *Beith, A | LD | 19,007 | 45.5% | +1.1% | 19,283 | 44.4% | LD |
| Brannen, P | Lab | 10,965 | 26.2% | +3.4% | 14,240 | 32.8% | C |
| Herbert, N | C | 10,056 | 24.1% | -8.7% | 9,933 | 22.9% | Lab |
| Lambton, N | Ref | 1,423 | 3.4% | | | | |
| Dodds, I | UK Ind | 352 | 0.8% | | | | |
| LD to Lab swing 1.1% | | 41,803 | | LD maj 8,042 19.2% | 43,456 | | LD maj 5,043 79.1% |

ALAN BEITH, b April 20, 1943. Dep leader of LDs since 1992. Won this seat as Lib in 1973 by-election; contested it 1970. Responsible for election manifesto; spokesman on home and legal affairs, May 1997- ; home affairs 1992-95 and on police, prison and security 1995-97; Treasury spokesman 1987-94. Dep leader of Lib Party 1985-88; spokesman on foreign affairs 1985-87. Lib chief whip 1976-85; Lib spokesman on constitutional and parly affairs 1983-87. Member, Commons intelligence and security cttee, 1994-97; select cttee on sittings of Commons 1991-94. Joint vice-chair, all-party arts and heritage parly group; Council of Christians and Jews group; insurance and financial services group. Consultant to Magellan Medical Communications Ltd, medical public affairs co, and to Bourne Leisure Group Ltd. Methodist local preacher. Ed King's, Macclesfield; Balliol and Nuffield Colls, Oxford.
PAUL BRANNEN, b Sept 13, 1962. Area co-ordinator, Christian Aid; member, Christian Soc Movement, Amnesty. Ex-anti-apartheid campaigns officer and Lab press officer. Ed Walbottle HS, Newcastle upon Tyne; Leeds Univ.
NICK HERBERT, b April 7, 1963. Public affairs consultant and political adviser. Political adviser, British Field Sports Soc, 1992-95; adviser to Countryside Movement. Ed Haileybury; Magdalene Coll, Cambridge.

## BETHNAL GREEN & BOW — 25.9% change — Lab hold

| Electorate % Turnout | | 73,008 | 61.2% | 1997 | 65,485 | 68.1% | 1992 |
|---|---|---|---|---|---|---|---|
| King, Ms O | Lab | 20,697 | 46.3% | -7.2% | 23,863 | 53.5% | Lab |
| Choudhury, K | C | 9,412 | 21.1% | +4.7% | 11,498 | 25.8% | LD |
| Islam, S | LD | 5,361 | 12.0% | -13.8% | 7,316 | 16.4% | C |
| King, D | BNP | 3,350 | 7.5% | | 1,918 | 4.3% | Other |
| Milson, T | Lib | 2,963 | 6.6% | | | | |
| Osman, S | R Lab | 1,117 | 2.5% | | | | |
| Petter, S | Green | 812 | 1.8% | | | | |
| Abdullah, M | Ref | 557 | 1.2% | | | | |
| Hamid, A | Soc Lab | 413 | 0.9% | | | | |
| Lab to C notional swing 5.9% | | 44,682 | | Lab maj 11,285 25.3% | 44,595 | | Lab maj 12,365 27.7% |

OONA KING, b Oct 22, 1967. Regional organiser, GMB southern region; former asst to Glyn Ford, MEP, and Glenys Kinnock, MEP. Ed Haverstock Comp, London; York Univ; Berkeley Univ.
DR KABIR CHOUDHURY, b Dec 31, 1943. Director of Travel Link Worldwide Ltd; founder director-general, Bangladesh British Chamber of Commerce, 1992; project dir, new pharmaceutical plant, Kuwait, 1977-86; technical dir, Nazirs Food Ltd, Manchester, 1976-77; post-doctoral research fellow, Nottingham Univ, 1975-76; held education posts in Dhaka and Tanzania 1965-70. Ed Dhaka and Manchester Univs.
SYED NURUL ISLAM, b April 6, 1956. Council housing estate officer. Active nationally in Bangladeshi community. Ed London Guildhall Univ (current).

## BEVERLEY & HOLDERNESS — 89.5% change — C win

| Electorate % Turnout | | 71,916 | 73.6% | 1997 | 69,161 | 79.1% | 1992 |
|---|---|---|---|---|---|---|---|
| +Cran, J D | C | 21,629 | 40.9% | -13.6% | 29,800 | 54.5% | C |
| O'Neill, N | Lab | 20,818 | 39.3% | +19.2% | 13,843 | 25.3% | LD |
| Melling, J | LD | 9,689 | 18.3% | -7.0% | 10,981 | 20.1% | Lab |
| Barley, D | UK Ind | 695 | 1.3% | | 62 | 0.1% | Other |
| Withers, S | NLP | 111 | 0.2% | | | | |
| C to Lab notional swing 16.4% | | 52,942 | | C maj 811 1.5% | 54,686 | | C maj 15,957 79.1% |

JAMES CRAN, b Jan 28, 1944. MP for Beverley 1987-97; contested Gordon 1983; Glasgow, Shettleston, Oct 1974. PPS to Sir Patrick Mayhew, N Ireland Sec, 1995-96. Member, select cttees on N Ireland, 1994-95; trade and industry 1987-92. Member, pension trustee forum council, 1992- . West Mids dir of CBI 1984-87, and Northern dir 1979-84. Parly consultant to board of Lincoln National (UK) plc, life assurance, pensions and unit trusts. Ed Ruthrieston School, Aberdeen; Aberdeen Coll of Commerce; King's Coll; Aberdeen Univ; Heriot-Watt Univ.
NORMAN O'NEILL, b May 31, 1943. Lecturer, Hull Univ. Former Hull and Humberside cllr. Ed York and Hull Univs.
JOHN MELLING, b April 14, 1934. Retired dir of nursing services. Contested Hertford 1970, Edinburgh E Feb 1974. Member, European Movement; Charter 88. Ed Bootham School, York.

| BEXHILL & BATTLE | | | 0.1% change | | | | C win |
|---|---|---|---|---|---|---|---|
| Electorate % Turnout | | | 65,584 | 74.7% | **1997** | 66,158 | 78.6% | **1992** |
| +Wardle, C | C | | **23,570** | 48.1% | -12.2% | **31,347** | 60.3% | C |
| Field, Mrs K | LD | | 12,470 | 25.5% | -3.4% | 15,007 | 28.9% | LD |
| Beckwith, R | Lab | | 8,866 | 18.1% | +8.7% | 4,877 | 9.4% | Lab |
| Thompson, Mrs V | Ref | | 3,302 | 6.7% | | 594 | 1.1% | Grn |
| Pankhurst, J | UK Ind | | 786 | 1.6% | | 190 | 0.4% | CSP |
| C to LD notional swing 4.4% | | | **48,994** | | C maj 11,100 | **52,015** | | C maj 16,340 |
| | | | | | 22.7% | | | 31.4% |

**CHARLES WARDLE**, b Aug 23, 1939. Elected 1983. Industry and Energy Under Sec, 1994-95; Under Sec, Home Office, 1992-94. PPS to Ian Lang, Scottish Sec, 1990-92, and to Sir Norman Fowler, Social Services Sec, 1984-87. Member, PAC, 1996-97. Chair, C One Nation Forum, 1989-90. Chair, Benjamin Priest Group, 1977-84; Warne, Wright and Rowland, 1978-84. Dir, Ray Powell Holdings Ltd, 1990-92; Asset Special Situations Trust plc, 1982-84. Consultant on corporate strategy and development to UniChem plc and Interface Europe Ltd. Member, CBI central council and CBI W Mids regional council, 1980-84. Ed Tonbridge School; Lincoln Coll, Oxford; Harvard Business School.

**KATHRYN FIELD**, b Aug 21, 1952. Assistant Town Clerk. East Sussex county cllr 1992- . Ed Bradford Girls' School; Birmingham Univ.

**ROBERT BECKWITH**, b Oct 9, 1941. Supply teacher, scientific asst and technical sales engineer. Rother district cllr 1995- (leader of Lab group); Rye town cllr 1991- ; Mayor of Rye 1994-96. Member, NUT. Ed Elizabeth Allen School, Barnet; Cambridge Tech Coll; Puttridgebury Coll of Ed; OU.

| BEXLEYHEATH & CRAYFORD | | | 74.6% change | | | | Lab win |
|---|---|---|---|---|---|---|---|
| Electorate % Turnout | | | 63,334 | 76.1% | **1997** | 64,601 | 81.1% | **1992** |
| Beard, C N | Lab | | **21,942** | 45.5% | +14.2% | **28,380** | 54.2% | C |
| +Evennett, D A | C | | 18,527 | 38.4% | -15.8% | 16,377 | 31.3% | Lab |
| Montford, Mrs F | LD | | 5,391 | 11.2% | -3.2% | 7,515 | 14.3% | LD |
| Thomas, B | Ref | | 1,551 | 3.2% | | 115 | 0.2% | Other |
| Smith, Ms P | BNP | | 429 | 0.9% | | | | |
| Jenner, W | UK Ind | | 383 | 0.8% | | | | |
| C to Lab notional swing 15.0% | | | **48,223** | | Lab maj 3,415 | **52,387** | | C maj 12,003 |
| | | | | | 7.1% | | | 81.1% |

**NIGEL BEARD,** b Oct 10, 1936. Senior manager, new business development, ICI. Contested Erith & Crayford 1992; Portsmouth N 1983; Woking 1979. Chair, Woking CLP, 1981-82, and Surrey W Euro constituency 1984-92. Member, Southern region Lab Party exec; board, Royal Marsden Hospital, 1982- , and Inst of Cancer Research, 1981- . Chief planner for strategy, GLC, 1973-74; dir, London Docklands development team, 1974-79. FRSA. Member, GMB; Fabian Soc; Co-op Party. Ed Castleford GS, Yorkshire; University Coll, London.

**DAVID EVENNETT,** b June 3, 1949. MP for Erith and Crayford 1983-97; contested Hackney S and Shoreditch 1979. PPS to Education Sec 1996-97, to Home Office Min of State 1995-96, to Welsh Sec 1993-95, to Min of State for Ed 1992-93. Member, select cttee on ed, science and arts 1986-92. Dir of Lloyd's underwriting agency 1982-91. Ed Buckhurst Hill County HS for Boys; LSE.

**FRANÇOISE MONTFORD,** b Feb 3, 1945. Part-time interpreter. Chair, Bexley Access Group; member, Greater London Assoc of Disabled People. Ed Lycée Technique, Bordeaux.

| BILLERICAY | | | 57.9% change | | | | C win |
|---|---|---|---|---|---|---|---|
| Electorate % Turnout | | | 76,550 | 72.4% | **1997** | 73,644 | 80.7% | **1992** |
| +Gorman, Mrs T | C | | **22,033** | 39.8% | -17.9% | **34,274** | 57.6% | C |
| Richards, P | Lab | | 20,677 | 37.3% | +17.3% | 13,276 | 22.3% | LD |
| Williams, G | LD | | 8,763 | 15.8% | -6.5% | 11,914 | 20.0% | Lab |
| Hughes, B | LC | | 3,377 | 6.1% | | | | |
| Buchanan, J | ProLife | | 570 | 1.0% | | | | |
| C to Lab notional swing 17.6% | | | **55,420** | | C maj 1,356 | **59,464** | | C maj 20,998 |
| | | | | | 2.4% | | | 80.7% |

**TERESA GORMAN,** b Sept 3, 1931. Founder and manager, Banta, family business manufacturing scientific teaching aids. Elected 1987. Contested Lambeth Streatham Oct 1974 as Independent (Small Business) candidate. Deprived of party whip, 1994-95, after vote against Gvt on Euro Finance Bill. Joint sec, C backbench social security cttee, 1988-89. Member, C women's national cttee, 1983- . Westminster city cllr 1982-86. Founder and chair, ASP (Alliance of Small Firms and Self-Employed People), pressure group for small businesses. Ed Fulham County School; Brighton Coll of Ed; London Univ.

**PAUL RICHARDS,** b Oct 17, 1967. Journalist. Chair, National Organisation of Lab Students 1990-91. Researcher to Anne Taylor, MP, 1991-92. Ed Dr Challoner's GS; Salford Univ; London Guildhall Univ.

**GEOFF WILLIAMS,** b Jan 26, 1947. Modern languages lecturer. Contested Basildon 1992 and Essex South in 1994 Euro elections. Ed Fryerns School, Basildon; King's Coll, London.

| BIRKENHEAD | | | | | | Lab hold |
|---|---|---|---|---|---|---|
| Electorate % Turnout | | 59,782 | 65.8% | **1997** | 62,682 | 73.0% | **1992** |
| *Field, F | Lab | 27,825 | 70.8% | +7.1% | 29,098 | 63.6% | Lab |
| Crosby, J | C | 5,982 | 15.2% | -9.9% | 11,485 | 25.1% | C |
| Wood, R | LD | 3,548 | 9.0% | -0.6% | 4,417 | 9.7% | LD |
| Cullen, M | Soc Lab | 1,168 | 3.0% | | 543 | 1.2% | Grn |
| Evans, R | Ref | 800 | 2.0% | | 190 | 0.4% | NLP |
| **C to Lab swing 8.5%** | | **39,323** | **Lab maj 21,843** | | **45,733** | **Lab maj 17,613** | |
| | | | 55.5% | | | 9.9% | |

**FRANK FIELD,** b July 16, 1942. Became Social Security Minister for Welfare Reform, May 4, 1997. Elected 1979; contested Buckinghamshire S 1966. Chair, select cttee on social security 1991-97; on social services 1987-91; member, ecclesiastical select cttee; Lab spokesman on health and social security 1983-84; on education 1979-81. Hounslow borough cllr 1964-68. Dir, Child Poverty Action Group, 1969-79, and of Low Pay Unit 1974-80. Teacher at Southwark and Hammersmith CFEs, 1964-69. Parly

consultant (unpaid) to Civil and Public Services Assoc. Member, TGWU. Ed St Clement Danes GS; Hull Univ.
**JOHN CROSBY,** b May 22, 1963. Manager, financial analysis consultancy; formerly employed by investment bank in bond and foreign exchange markets. Vice-chair, Fulham C assoc, 1991-95. Ed Crossley and Porter School, Halifax; Girton Coll, Cambridge; University Coll, Oxford.
**ROY WOOD,** b Sept 1, 1947. Maths teacher. Member, Charter 88. Ed St Edward's Coll, Liverpool; Notre Dame Coll, Liverpool.

| BIRMINGHAM EDGBASTON | | 32.2% change | | | | | Lab win |
|---|---|---|---|---|---|---|---|
| Electorate % Turnout | | 70,204 | 69.0% | **1997** | 70,873 | 71.8% | **1992** |
| **Stuart, Mrs G** | Lab | 23,554 | 48.6% | +9.3% | 25,059 | 49.3% | C |
| Marshall, A | C | 18,712 | 38.6% | -10.7% | 20,003 | 39.3% | Lab |
| Gallagher, J | LD | 4,691 | 9.7% | -0.5% | 5,158 | 10.1% | LD |
| Oakton, J | Ref | 1,065 | 2.2% | | 643 | 1.3% | Grn |
| Campbell, D | BDP | 443 | 0.9% | | | | |
| **C to Lab notional swing 10.0%** | | **48,465** | **Lab maj 4,842** | | **50,863** | **C maj 5,056** | |
| | | | 10.0% | | | 71.8% | |

**GISELA STUART,** b Nov 26, 1955. Law lecturer, publisher. Contested Worcestershire and South Warwickshire 1994 Euro elections. Ex-dep director of London Book Fair and marketing manager in publishing. Legal adviser to parly campaign on pensions Bill; postgraduate research on occupational pensions at Birmingham Univ. Member, Charter 88; Fabian Soc. Member, police custody lay visitors' panel. Represented Britain at international fencing competition, Birmingham, 1979. Ed in Germany; Manchester Poly; London Univ.
**ANDREW MARSHALL,** b May 14, 1962. Account director. Contested Leicester in 1994 Euro elections. Camden cllr 1990-94. Working

with Hill and Knowlton UK, advising business on corporate and financial communications. International banker, Deutsche Bank, 1985-94, being seconded to Toronto 1987-88; with merchant bank Schroder Wagg 1983-85. Chair, Coningsby Club, 1990-91; Tory Reform Group, 1991-94. Ed Kirkwall GS; Atlantic Coll; Robinson Coll, Cambridge (chair, univ C assoc 1983).
**JOCK GALLAGHER,** b March 31, 1938. Journalist and broadcaster. Contested Hereford and Shropshire in 1994 Euro elections. Human rights specialist to Organisation for Co-operation and Security in Europe. Ed Greenock HS; Stone Coll, Glasgow.

| BIRMINGHAM ERDINGTON | | 39.7% change | | | | | Lab win |
|---|---|---|---|---|---|---|---|
| Electorate % Turnout | | 66,380 | 60.9% | **1997** | 74,434 | 68.1% | **1992** |
| +Corbett, R | Lab | 23,764 | 58.8% | +5.5% | 27,021 | 53.3% | Lab |
| Tompkins, A | C | 11,107 | 27.5% | -9.0% | 18,498 | 36.5% | C |
| Garrett, I | LD | 4,112 | 10.2% | -0.1% | 5,187 | 10.2% | LD |
| Cable, G | Ref | 1,424 | 3.5% | | | | |
| **C to Lab notional swing 7.3%** | | **40,407** | **Lab maj 12,657** | | **50,706** | **Lab maj 8,523** | |
| | | | 31.3% | | | 68.1% | |

**ROBIN CORBETT,** b Dec 22, 1933. Journalist. Elected for this seat 1983; MP for Hemel Hempstead Oct 1974-79, contested the seat 1966 and Feb 1974; W Derbyshire by-election 1967. Appointed to agriculture select cttee, 1995; party spokesman on disabled people's rights 1994-95; national heritage 1992-94; home affairs 1985-92.Joint vice-chair, all-party motor industry parly group, 1987- . Member, council, Save the Children Fund, 1986-90; council, Royal College of

Veterinary Surgeons, 1989-92; sponsor, Terrence Higgins Trust, 1987- . Member, NUJ. Ed Holly Lodge GS, Smethwick.
**ANTHONY TOMPKINS,** b Dec 13, 1960. Barrister and legal recruitment consultant. Ed Bishop Vesey's GS; Sutton Coldfield Coll of FE; Newcastle Univ; Inns of Court School of Law.
**IAN GARRETT,** b Nov 25, 1965. Teacher. Sandwell borough cllr. Member, CND. Ed Chislehurst and Sidcup GS; St Catherine's Coll, Oxford.

## BIRMINGHAM HALL GREEN | | | | | | Lab gain

| Electorate % Turnout | | 58,767 | 71.2% | **1997** | 60,091 | 78.2% | **1992** |
|---|---|---|---|---|---|---|---|
| McCabe, S | Lab | 22,372 | 53.5% | +15.2% | 21,649 | 46.1% | C |
| *Hargreaves, A | C | 13,952 | 33.4% | -12.7% | 17,984 | 38.3% | Lab |
| Dow, A | LD | 4,034 | 9.6% | -6.0% | 7,342 | 15.6% | LD |
| Bennett, P | Ref | 1,461 | 3.5% | | | | |
| C to Lab swing 14.0% | | 41,819 | | Lab maj 8,420 | 46,975 | | C maj 3,665 |
| | | | | 20.1% | | | 17.3% |

**STEPHEN McCABE,** b Aug 4, 1955. Adviser to Central Council for the Education and Training of Social Workers. Birmingham city cllr 1990- . Climbed Himalayan peak to raise money for Reiner Foundation. Ed Port Glasgow Senior Secondary; Moray House Coll of Ed; Bradford Univ.
**ANDREW HARGREAVES,** b May 15, 1955. Elected 1987; contested Blyth Valley 1983. PPS to Foreign Office Min of State 1996-97. Member, select cttee on Parly Commissioner for Administration, 1992-97; Commons information cttee 1992-97. Sec, C backbench

arts and heritage cttee, 1994-97; vice-chair 1994-97, and joint sec, 1987-94, C urban and inner cities cttee; vice-chair, 1994-97 C defence cttee. With J. Henry Schroder Wagg and Co Ltd, 1985-87; fine art auctioneer and valuer with Christie's, 1977-81. Consultant to Midlands Electricity plc; hon sec, European Foundation for Quality and the Environment. Ed Eton; St Edmund Hall, Oxford.
**ALASTAIR DOW,** b July 22, 1945. Financial controller. Contested E Aberdeenshire 1974; N Edinburgh 1970. Ed Perth HS; St Andrews Univ.

## BIRMINGHAM HODGE HILL | | | | | | Lab hold

| Electorate % Turnout | | 56,066 | 60.9% | **1997** | 57,651 | 70.8% | **1992** |
|---|---|---|---|---|---|---|---|
| *Davis, T | Lab | 22,398 | 65.6% | +12.0% | 21,895 | 53.6% | Lab |
| Grant, E | C | 8,198 | 24.0% | -12.3% | 14,827 | 36.3% | C |
| Thomas, H | LD | 2,891 | 8.5% | -0.7% | 3,740 | 9.2% | LD |
| Johnson, P | UK Ind | 660 | 1.9% | | 370 | 0.9% | NF |
| C to Lab swing 12.1% | | 34,147 | | Lab maj 14,200 | 40,832 | | Lab maj 7,068 |
| | | | | 41.6% | | | 70.8% |

**TERRY DAVIS,** b Jan 5, 1938. Manager in motor industry, 1974-79. Elected for this seat 1983; MP for Birmingham Stechford, 1979-83, and for Bromsgrove 1971-74; contested that seat 1970; Bromsgrove and Redditch, Feb and Oct 1974, and Birmingham Stechford, 1977 by-election. Member, PAC, 1987-94; delegation to Council of Europe and WEU, 1992- . Party spokesman on industry 1986-87; on Treasury and economic affairs, 1983-86; on health and social services, 1980-83. Parly adviser to Inland Revenue Staff Fed. Member, Advisory Council on Public Records, 1989-94. Ed

King Edward VI GS, Stourbridge; London Univ; Michigan Univ.
**ED GRANT,** b May 28, 1968. Barrister in Victoria Chambers, Birmingham, since 1993. Member, nat exec cttee, Tory Reform Group, 1990-93; nat chair, Student Tory Reform Group, 1990-91. Ed Fettes Coll, Edinburgh; Southampton Univ; Inns of Court School of Law.
**HAYDN THOMAS,** b July 12, 1927. Retired director of nurse education. Warwickshire county cllr (Mayor 1995-96). Ed Porth GS; London Univ.

## BIRMINGHAM LADYWOOD | | 95.2% change | | | | Lab win

| Electorate % Turnout | | 70,013 | 54.2% | **1997** | 71,943 | 58.5% | **1992** |
|---|---|---|---|---|---|---|---|
| +Short, Ms C | Lab | 28,134 | 74.1% | +2.7% | 30,065 | 71.4% | Lab |
| Vara, S | C | 5,052 | 13.3% | -7.1% | 8,596 | 20.4% | C |
| Marwa, S | LD | 3,020 | 8.0% | -0.2% | 3,447 | 8.2% | LD |
| Gurney, Mrs R | Ref | 1,086 | 2.9% | | | | |
| Carmichael, A | Nat Dem | 685 | 1.8% | | | | |
| C to Lab notional swing 4.9% | | 37,977 | | Lab maj 23,082 | 42,108 | | Lab maj 21,469 |
| | | | | 60.8% | | | 58.5% |

**CLARE SHORT,** b Feb 15, 1946. Became International Development Secretary May 3, 1997. Shadow Overseas Development Min 1996-97. Elected 1983; elected to Shadow Cabinet 1995; Shadow Transport Sec 1995-96; spokeswoman on women's issues 1993-95; on environmental protection 1992-93; social security 1989-91; employment 1985-88. Member, home affairs select cttee, 1983-85; chair, all-party race relations group, 1985-86. Member, Lab Party NEC, 1988- . Served in Home Office 1970-75; dir, All Faiths in One Race, Birmingham, 1976-78; Youthaid 1979-83; and the Unemployment Unit 1981-83. Ed St Paul's GS; Keele and Leeds Univs.

**SHAILESH VARA,** b Sept 4, 1960. Solicitor. Member, C Nat Union exec cttee; vice-chair, Hampstead and Highgate C assoc. Worked in Hong Kong for various multinationals 1989-90; contributed to legal publications. Ed Aylesbury GS; Brunel Univ; Guildford Coll of Law.
**SARDUL MARWA,** b May 11, 1947. Lecturer. Birmingham city cllr 1982-87. Ed Sandwell Secondary; Chance Tech Coll.

| BIRMINGHAM NORTHFIELD | | 24.0% change | | | | | Lab win |
|---|---|---|---|---|---|---|---|
| Electorate % Turnout | | 56,842 | 68.3% | **1997** | 54,594 | 74.4% | **1992** |
| +Burden, R | Lab | **22,316** | **57.4%** | +11.5% | **18,652** | **45.9%** | **Lab** |
| Blumenthal, A | C | 10,873 | 28.0% | -14.5% | 17,273 | 42.5% | C |
| Ashall, M | LD | 4,078 | 10.5% | -1.1% | 4,692 | 11.6% | LD |
| Gent, D | Ref | 1,243 | 3.2% | | | | |
| Axon, K | BNP | 337 | 0.9% | | | | |
| C to Lab notional swing 13.0% | | **38,847** | Lab maj 11,443 | | **40,617** | Lab maj 1,379 | |
| | | | 29.5% | | | 74.4% | |

RICHARD BURDEN, b Sept 1, 1954. Ex-union official. Won this seat 1992; contested Meriden 1987; joint chair, all-party advisory council for transport safety; sec, 1995- , PLP trade and industry cttee; vice-chair, 1994-95; joint sec, all-party water group; vice-chair, Lab Middle East Council, 1994- . Member, HoC Motor Club; founder and sec, Joint Action for Water Services, 1985-90. Ed Wallasey Tech GS; Bramhall Comp; St John's CFE, Manchester; York and Warwick Univs.

ALAN BLUMENTHAL, b March 23, 1959. Retail manager and shopowner. Birmingham city cllr 1983- . Ed Moseley GS; Carmel Coll; Matthew Boulton Coll.

MICHAEL ASHALL, b Jan 5, 1944. Sales engineer. Ed The Tivdale School; Dudley Coll of Tech.

| BIRMINGHAM PERRY BARR | | 56.0% change | | | | | Lab win |
|---|---|---|---|---|---|---|---|
| Electorate % Turnout | | 71,031 | 64.6% | **1997** | 72,453 | 73.4% | **1992** |
| +Rooker, J | Lab | **28,921** | **63.0%** | +11.1% | **27,596** | **51.9%** | **Lab** |
| Dunnett, A | C | 9,964 | 21.7% | -15.6% | 19,867 | 37.4% | C |
| Hassall, R | LD | 4,523 | 9.9% | -0.9% | 5,720 | 10.8% | LD |
| Mahmood, S | Ref | 843 | 1.8% | | | | |
| Baxter, A | Lib | 718 | 1.6% | | | | |
| Windridge, L | BNP | 544 | 1.2% | | | | |
| Panesar, A | FP | 374 | 0.8% | | | | |
| C to Lab notional swing 13.4% | | **45,887** | Lab maj 18,957 | | **53,183** | Lab maj 7,729 | |
| | | | 41.3% | | | 14.5% | |

JEFFREY ROOKER, b June 5, 1941. Became Min of State, Agriculture, Fisheries and Food, May 5, 1997. Chartered engineer. Elected Feb 1974. Lab spokesman on House of Commons affairs 1994; education 1992-93; health and social services 1990-92; housing and construction 1984-87; local gvt 1987-88; Treasury and economic affairs 1983-84; social security 1979-83. Chair, Lab Campaign for Electoral Reform, 1989- . Contested election for Lab chief whip 1988; campaign officer, W Midlands group of Lab MPs, 1989- . Joint vice-chair, Council against Anti-Semitism, 1991. Council member, Inst of Production Engineers, 1975-81. Ed Handsworth Tech School and Coll; Aston and Warwick Univs.

ANDREW DUNNETT, b Sept 23, 1966. Public affairs consultant. Vice-chair, Tooting Bec C assoc. Ed Bromsgrove School; Durham Univ.

ROY HASSALL, b Jan 28, 1923. Retired telecoms employee. Birmingham city cllr 1990- . Ed in Ontario.

| BIRMINGHAM SELLY OAK | | | | | | | Lab hold |
|---|---|---|---|---|---|---|---|
| Electorate % Turnout | | 72,049 | 70.2% | **1997** | 72,150 | 76.6% | **1992** |
| *Jones, Dr L | Lab | **28,121** | **55.6%** | +9.6% | **25,430** | **46.0%** | **Lab** |
| Greene, G | C | 14,033 | 27.8% | -14.5% | 23,370 | 42.3% | C |
| Osborne, D | LD | 6,121 | 12.1% | +1.8% | 5,679 | 10.3% | LD |
| Marshall, L | Ref | 1,520 | 3.0% | | 535 | 1.0% | Grn |
| Gardner, Dr G | ProLife | 417 | 0.8% | | 178 | 0.3% | NLP |
| Sherriff-Knowles, P | Loony | 253 | 0.5% | | 84 | 0.2% | Rev Comm |
| Meads, H | NLP | 85 | 0.2% | -0.2% | | | |
| C to Lab swing 12.1% | | **50,550** | Lab maj 14,088 | | **55,276** | Lab maj 2,060 | |
| | | | 27.9% | | | 3.7% | |

LYNNE JONES, b April 26, 1951. Ex-housing manager. Won the seat 1992. Member, science and technology select cttee, 1992- . Birmingham city cllr 1980-94. Former exec member, Lab housing group. Member, MSF. Ed Bartley Green Girls' GS, Birmingham; Birmingham Univ; Birmingham Poly.

GRAHAM GREENE, b April 12, 1955. Engineer. Contested Birmingham Perry Barr 1992. Birmingham city cllr 1988-96; chair, Perry Barr C assoc. Lay inspector of schools. Ed Erdington Boys Sec Mod; Queen's Univ, Belfast.

DAVID OSBORNE, b Feb 25, 1942. Lecturer. Contested Birmingham Selly Oak 1992. Birmingham city cllr 1996- . Treas, NATFHE, 1988-99. Ed Queen Elizabeth Boys GS, Mansfield; City of Worcester Training Coll.

## BIRMINGHAM SPARKBROOK & SMALL HEATH

| | | Electorate % Turnout | 73,130 | 57.1% | 1997 | 72,745 | 67.7% | 1992 |
|---|---|---|---|---|---|---|---|---|
| | | | | | **40.3% change** | | | **Lab win** |
| +Godsiff, R D | Lab | | 26,841 | 64.3% | +1.2% | 31,052 | 63.1% | Lab |
| Hardeman, K | C | | 7,315 | 17.5% | -8.1% | 12,604 | 25.6% | C |
| Harmer, R | LD | | 3,889 | 9.3% | +1.4% | 3,916 | 8.0% | LD |
| Clawley, A | Green | | 959 | 2.3% | | 1,657 | 3.4% | Other |
| Dooley, R | Ref | | 737 | 1.8% | | | | |
| Patel, P | FP | | 538 | 1.3% | | | | |
| Syed, R | PAYR | | 513 | 1.2% | | | | |
| Bi, Ms S | Ind | | 490 | 1.2% | | | | |
| Wren, C | Soc Lab | | 483 | 1.2% | | | | |
| C to Lab notional swing 4.6% | | | 41,765 | | Lab maj 19,526 | 49,229 | | Lab maj 18,448 |
| | | | | | 46.8% | | | 37.5% |

ROGER GODSIFF, b June 28, 1946. Won Birmingham Small Heath for Lab 1992; contested Birmingham Yardley 1983. Lewisham cllr 1971-90 (Mayor, 1977). Chair, all-party British-Kashmir group. Political officer, Apex, 1970-90; senior research officer, GMB, 1990-92. Bank clerk 1965-70. Ed Catford Comp.

KENNETH HARDEMAN, b Jan 21, 1936. Technical education publishing adviser. Contested Birmingham Ladywood Feb and Oct 1974, 1979 and 1980 by-election for Libs; Birmingham, Hodge Hill, 1987 for Lib/Alliance. Birmingham city cllr 1992- . chair, Ladywood police liaison cttee, 1984-86. Ed Slade Boys School; Handsworth Tech Coll.

ROGER HARMER, b Nov 17, 1965. Deputy regional dir, Business in the Community. Birmingham city cllr, 1995- . Ed Bristol GS; New College, Oxford.

## BIRMINGHAM YARDLEY

| | | Electorate % Turnout | 53,058 | 71.2% | 1997 | 54,749 | 78.0% | 1992 |
|---|---|---|---|---|---|---|---|---|
| | | | | | | | | **Lab hold** |
| *Morris, Ms E | Lab | | 17,778 | 47.0% | +12.2% | 14,884 | 34.9% | Lab |
| Hemming, J | LD | | 12,463 | 33.0% | +2.8% | 14,722 | 34.5% | C |
| Jobson, Mrs A | C | | 6,736 | 17.8% | -16.7% | 12,899 | 30.2% | LD |
| Livingston, D | Ref | | 646 | 1.7% | | 192 | 0.4% | NF |
| Ware, A | UK Ind | | 164 | 0.4% | | | | |
| LD to Lab swing 4.7% | | | 37,787 | | Lab maj 5,315 | 42,697 | | Lab maj 162 |
| | | | | | 14.1% | | | 0.4% |

ESTELLE MORRIS, b June 17, 1952. Became Under Sec of State, Education and Employment with responsibility for school standards, May 5, 1997. Ex-teacher. Gained this seat for Lab 1992. Lab spokesman on education and employment 1995-97; Lab whip 1994-95. Warwick district cllr 1979-91 (group leader 1981-89). Ed Whalley Range HS, Manchester; Coventry Coll of Ed.

JOHN HEMMING, b March 16, 1960. Scientist and businessman. Contested this seat 1992; Birmingham Small Heath 1987; Birmingham Hall Green 1983. Birmingham city cllr 1990- . Dir of own Internet banking, travel and investment companies. Ed King Edward's, Birmingham; Magdalen Coll, Oxford. Jazz pianist.

ANNE JOBSON, b Jan 12, 1952. Barrister specialising in social, family and childcare law. Joint treas, 1993- , and deputy chair, 1987-90, Greater London area Conservatives. Member, London Regional Passenger Cttee, 1995- . Ed Purbrook Park GS; City of London Poly; Inns of Court School of Law.

## BISHOP AUCKLAND

| | | Electorate % Turnout | 66,754 | 68.9% | 1997 | 68,591 | 76.0% | 1992 |
|---|---|---|---|---|---|---|---|---|
| | | | | | **47.7% change** | | | **Lab win** |
| +Foster, D | Lab | | 30,359 | 66.0% | +18.4% | 24,825 | 47.6% | Lab |
| Fergus, Mrs J | C | | 9,295 | 20.2% | -12.6% | 17,109 | 32.8% | C |
| Ashworth, L | LD | | 4,223 | 9.2% | -10.4% | 10,184 | 19.5% | LD |
| Blacker, D | Ref | | 2,104 | 4.6% | | | | |
| C to Lab notional swing 15.5% | | | 45,981 | | Lab maj 21,064 | 52,118 | | Lab maj 7,716 |
| | | | | | 45.8% | | | 76.0% |

DEREK FOSTER, b June 25, 1937. Min of State at the Office of Public Service May 4, 1997 but resigned two days later. Elected 1979. Shadow Chancellor of the Duchy of Lancaster 1995-97; Lab chief whip 1985-95; PPS to Neil Kinnock 1983-85; Northern regional whip 1981-82. Chair (1988-89) and vice-chair (1987-88), Northern group of Lab MPs. Lab spokesman on social security 1982-83; member, trade and industry select cttee, 1980-82. Asst dir of education in Sunderland 1974-79. Chair, North of England development council, 1974-76; vice-chair, Youthaid, 1979-86. Sunderland cllr 1972-74; Tyne and Wear cllr 1973-77. Member of Salvation Army. Ed Bede GS, Sunderland; St Catherine's Coll, Oxford.

JOSEPHINE FERGUS, b April 9, 1931. Businesswoman and former manager for Social and Community Planning Research, a research organisation for central and local gvt and for univs. Durham county cllr 1981- (C group leader 1994- ). Member, English advisory cttee to Telecoms, 1986-93. Ed Hiatt Ladies Coll, Shropshire.

LES ASHWORTH, b Dec 10, 1946. Retired marketing manager. Tynedale district cllr. Ed Prescot GS; Newcastle Univ.

| BLABY | | 18.3% change | | | 1997 | | | C win |
|---|---|---|---|---|---|---|---|---|
| Electorate % Turnout | | 70,471 | 76.0% | **1997** | 67,238 | 83.5% | **1992** |
| +Robathan, A | C | **24,564** | 45.8% | -11.0% | 31,882 | 56.8% | C |
| Willmott, R | Lab | 18,090 | 33.8% | +12.0% | 12,213 | 21.8% | Lab |
| Welsh, G | LD | 8,001 | 14.9% | -5.1% | 11,261 | 20.1% | LD |
| Harrison, R | Ref | 2,018 | 3.8% | | 521 | 0.9% | BNP |
| Peacock, J | BNP | 523 | 1.0% | +0.0% | 260 | 0.5% | NLP |
| Stokes, T | Ind | 397 | 0.7% | | | | |
| C to Lab notional swing 11.5% | | 53,593 | | C maj 6,474 | 56,137 | | C maj 19,669 |
| | | | | 12.1% | | | 35.0% |

ANDREW ROBATHAN, b July 17, 1951. Elected 1992. PPS to Iain Sproat, Nat Heritage Min. Chair, 1994-95, and previously joint vice-chair, C backbench defence cttee; joint vice-chair, C Northern Ireland cttee; ex-joint vice-chair, renewable and sustainable energy parly group. Hammersmith and Fulham cllr 1990-92. Officer, Coldstream Guards, 1974-89; rejoined Army Jan-April 1991 to serve in Gulf War. Fellow, Royal Geographical Soc.

Freeman, City of London. Ed Merchant Taylors', Northwood; Oriel Coll, Oxford; Sandhurst; Army Staff Coll, Camberley.
ROSS WILMOTT, b Nov 4, 1957. Trainer and consultant in voluntary sector and OU tutor in voluntary sector management. Member, CND; Co-op Party. Ed King Edward VII School, Leicester; North London Poly; Warwick Univ.
GEOFF WELSH, b July 5, 1956. Computerisation project manager. Blaby district cllr. Ed Countesthorpe Coll; Lanchester Poly.

| BLACKBURN | | | | | 1997 | | | Lab hold |
|---|---|---|---|---|---|---|---|---|
| Electorate % Turnout | | 73,058 | 65.0% | **1997** | 73,251 | 75.1% | **1992** |
| *Straw, J | Lab | **26,141** | 55.0% | +6.6% | 26,633 | 48.4% | Lab |
| Sidhu, Ms S | C | 11,690 | 24.6% | -12.9% | 20,606 | 37.5% | C |
| Fenn, S | LD | 4,990 | 10.5% | -1.0% | 6,332 | 11.5% | LD |
| Bradshaw, D | Ref | 1,892 | 4.0% | | 878 | 1.6% | Grn |
| Wingfield, Mrs T | Nat Dem | 671 | 1.4% | | 334 | 0.6% | LP |
| Drummond, Mrs H | Soc Lab | 637 | 1.3% | | 195 | 0.4% | NLP |
| Field, R | Green | 608 | 1.3% | | | | |
| Carmichael-Grimshaw, Mrs M | KBF | 506 | 1.1% | | | | |
| Batchelor, W | CSSPP | 362 | 0.8% | | | | |
| C to Lab swing 9.7% | | 47,497 | | Lab maj 14,451 | 54,978 | | Lab maj 6,027 |
| | | | | 30.4% | | | 75.1% |

JACK STRAW, b Aug 3, 1946. Became Home Secretary May 2, 1997. Shadow Home Secretary 1994-97. Elected 1979; contested Tonbridge and Malling Feb 1974. Chief Lab spokesman on local gvt 1992-94; on education 1987-92; housing and local gvt spokesman, 1983-87; spokesman on Treasury and economic affairs 1980-83. Special adviser to Barbara Castle as Social Services Sec 1974-76, and to Peter Shore, Environment Sec, 1976-77. Member, NEC, 1994-95. Non-practising barrister. Visiting Fellow, Nuffield Coll, Oxford, 1990- ; governor, Blackburn Coll,

1990- . Ed Brentwood School, Essex; Leeds Univ; Inns of Court School of Law.
SANGEETA SIDHU, b July 5, 1965. In-house lawyer for Americom; legal adviser to Malawi Gvt. Ed Buckingham Univ; Coll of Law, Guildford; LSE.
STEPHEN FENN, b Dec 23, 1954. Computer systems analyst. Contested Manchester Wythenshawe 1992. Member, Amnesty; Greenpeace. Ed Northgate School, Ipswich; Bath Univ; Edge Hill Coll; UMIST.

| BLACKPOOL NORTH & FLEETWOOD | | | | 98.8% change | 1997 | | | Lab win |
|---|---|---|---|---|---|---|---|---|
| Electorate % Turnout | | 74,989 | 71.7% | **1997** | 74,797 | 80.2% | **1992** |
| Humble, Mrs J | Lab | **28,051** | 52.2% | +14.6% | 29,838 | 49.8% | C |
| +Elletson, H D H | C | 19,105 | 35.5% | -14.2% | 22,562 | 37.6% | Lab |
| Hill, Mrs B | LD | 4,600 | 8.6% | -3.4% | 7,167 | 12.0% | LD |
| Stacey, Ms K | Ref | 1,704 | 3.2% | | 387 | 0.6% | Other |
| Ellis, J | BNP | 288 | 0.5% | | | | |
| C to Lab notional swing 14.4% | | 53,748 | | Lab maj 8,946 | 59,954 | | C maj 7,276 |
| | | | | 16.6% | | | 12.1% |

JOAN HUMBLE, b March 3, 1951. Lancashire county cllr 1985- . JP. Member, Christian Socialist Movement; Co-op Party; TGWU. Ed Greenhead GS, Keighley; Lancaster Univ.
HAROLD ELLETSON, b Dec 8, 1960. Won Blackpool N 1992; contested Burnley 1987. PPS to N Ireland Sec 1996-97; to N Ireland mins 1995-96. Member, environment select cttee, 1992-97. Director, Harold Elletson Ltd; consultant to companies seeking

to develop business in former Soviet Union and Eastern Europe; adviser to BP Exploration (FSU), Rothmans of Pall Mall International Ltd; Omega Oil and Gas; Nanoquest Defence Products Ltd. Ed Eton; Exeter Univ; Voronezh Univ, USSR; Central London Poly; Bradford Univ.
BEVERLEY HILL, b Nov 5, 1958. Blackpool district cllr. Member, League Against Cruel Sports. Ed Fleetwood GS; St Anne's Coll.

| BLACKPOOL SOUTH | | 35.0% change | | | | | Lab win |
|---|---|---|---|---|---|---|---|
| Electorate % Turnout | | 75,720 | 67.8% | **1997** | 75,009 | 78.5% | **1992** |
| **Marsden, G** | Lab | **29,282** | 57.0% | +13.6% | **25,957** | 44.1% | C |
| Booth, G R | C | 17,666 | 34.4% | -9.7% | 25,563 | 43.4% | Lab |
| Holt, Mrs D | LD | 4,392 | 8.6% | -3.6% | 7,148 | 12.1% | LD |
| | | | | | 233 | 0.4% | NLP |
| C to Lab notional swing 11.6% | | 51,340 | | Lab maj 11,616 | 58,901 | | C maj 394 |
| | | | | 22.6% | | | 78.5% |

**GORDON MARSDEN,** b Nov 28, 1953. Contested this seat 1992. Editor of *History Today* since 1985; former consultant editor *New Socialist;* OU tutor; author; former public affairs adviser to English Heritage. Vice-chair, Fabian Soc; former party office holder in Brighton, Hendon S and Hazel Grove, and chaired Young Fabians. Member, GMB; Assoc of British Editors. Ed Stockport GS; New College, Oxford; London and Harvard Univs.
**RICHARD BOOTH,** b Oct 8, 1947. Contested Leeds S and Morley 1992 and Yorkshire West in 1994 Euro elections. Electrical

engineer; in partnership with wife in manufacturing floral giftware. Scarborough borough cllr 1987-95; chair, Yorkshire CPC. Member, Scarborough Sports Council; Council for Voluntary Services. Voluntary consultant to Whitby Development Agency. Ed Elland GS, W Yorkshire; Huddersfield Tech Coll.
**DOREEN HOLT,** b Jan 20, 1938. Registered foster-mother; ex-Blackpool borough cllr. Member, school governors area council. Ed Bacup and Rossendal GS.

| BLAENAU GWENT | | | | | | | Lab hold |
|---|---|---|---|---|---|---|---|
| Electorate % Turnout | | 54,800 | 72.3% | **1997** | 55,638 | 78.1% | **1992** |
| *Smith, L | Lab | 31,493 | 79.5% | +0.5% | 34,333 | 79.0% | Lab |
| Layton, Mrs G | LD | 3,458 | 8.7% | +2.3% | 4,266 | 9.8% | C |
| Williams, Mrs M | C | 2,607 | 6.6% | -3.2% | 2,774 | 6.4% | LD |
| Criddle, J | PC | 2,072 | 5.2% | +0.4% | 2,099 | 4.8% | PC |
| Lab to LD swing 0.9% | | 39,630 | | Lab maj 28,035 | 43,472 | | Lab maj 30,067 |
| | | | | 70.7% | | | 78.1% |

**LLEWELLYN SMITH,** b April 16, 1944. Elected for this seat 1992. MEP for SE Wales 1984-94, and served on Euro Parliament cttee on energy, research and technology, and cttee on economic and monetary affairs and industrial policy. Ex-labourer with Pilkington Glass and George Wimpey; computer operator with British Steel; tutor-organiser, WEA. Former chair, Abertillery CLP and exec member, Welsh Lab Party. Ed Greenfield Sec Mod, Newbridge; Harlech Coll; Univ Coll of Wales, Cardiff.

**GERALDINE LAYTON,** b Oct 18, 1937. Smallholder and dairy goat farmer. Ed Gosport GS; Sparholt Coll.
**MARGRIT WILLIAMS,** b May 9, 1964. Global investment strategist. Wandsworth borough cllr 1990-94. Member, Soc of Financial Advisers; C London local gvt advisory cttee. Ed Southend HS for Girls; Queen's School, Rheindahlen, Germany; London Guildhall Univ.
**JIM CRIDDLE,** b Oct 16, 1947. Teacher. Islwyn borough cllr 1976- ; on nat exec of Plaid Cymru.

| BLAYDON | | | | | | | Lab hold |
|---|---|---|---|---|---|---|---|
| Electorate % Turnout | | 64,699 | 71.0% | **1997** | 66,044 | 77.7% | **1992** |
| *McWilliam, J | Lab | 27,535 | 60.0% | +7.3% | 27,028 | 52.7% | Lab |
| Maughan, P | LD | 10,930 | 23.8% | +3.1% | 13,685 | 26.7% | C |
| Watson, M | C | 6,048 | 13.2% | -13.5% | 10,602 | 20.7% | LD |
| Rook, R | Ind Lab | 1,412 | 3.1% | | | | |
| LD to Lab swing 2.1% | | 45,925 | | Lab maj 16,605 | 51,315 | | Lab maj 13,343 |
| | | | | 36.2% | | | 77.7% |

**JOHN McWILLIAM,** b May 16, 1941. Elected 1979; contested Edinburgh Pentlands, Feb 1974. Ex-Post Office engineer. Appointed to defence select cttee 1987; member, Commons chairman's panel, 1988- ; member, services cttee and chair, computer sub-cttee, 1983-87; procedure select cttee 1984-87; education, science and the arts 1980-83. Chair, PLP parly affairs cttee, 1983-87; dep Shadow Leader of Commons 1983-84. Lab whip 1984-87. Unpaid dir, EURIM, a non-profitmaking organisation concerned with information technology in Europe for MPs. Joint vice-chair, all-party IT group; space group. Member,

parly ecclesiastical cttee. Member, Edinburgh Corp, 1970-75. Ed Leith Acad; Heriot-Watt Coll; Napier Coll of Science and Tech.
**PETER MAUGHAN,** b May 16, 1954. Solicitor. Contested Newcastle upon Tyne N, 1992; Tyne and Wear 1994 Euro elections. Gateshead borough cllr 1994- . Ed Dame Allan's Boys' HS, Newcastle upon Tyne; Newcastle Poly.
**MARK WATSON,** b April 23, 1971. Office manager for Wilkinson Maughan solicitors. Hon sec, Blaydon C assoc; North area council representative 1993- . Ed Blaydon Secondary.

| BLYTH VALLEY | | | | | **1997** | | | **Lab hold** |
|---|---|---|---|---|---|---|---|---|
| Electorate % Turnout | | | 61,761 | 68.8% | **1997** | 60,913 | 80.8% | **1992** |
| *Campbell, R | Lab | | 27,276 | 64.2% | +14.3% | 24,542 | 49.9% | Lab |
| Lamb, A | LD | | 9,540 | 22.5% | -11.1% | 16,498 | 33.5% | LD |
| Musgrave, Mrs B | C | | 5,666 | 13.3% | -2.3% | 7,691 | 15.6% | C |
| | | | | | | 470 | 1.0% | Grn |
| LD to Lab swing 12.7% | | | 42,482 | | Lab maj 17,736 | 49,201 | | Lab maj 8,044 |
| | | | | | 41.7% | | | 80.8% |

**RONNIE CAMPBELL,** b Aug 14, 1943. Unemployed miner when elected for this seat 1987. Member, select cttee on Parliamentary Commissioner for Administration, 1987-97. Blyth borough cllr 1969-74; Blyth Valley district cllr 1974-88. Member, NUM; worked from age of 15 at Bates Pit, Blyth. Ed Ridley HS, Blyth.
**ANDREW LAMB,** b Aug 24, 1962. Insurance officer. Blyth Valley district cllr and opposition leader. Ed St Cuthbert's GS, Newcastle upon Tyne; Queen Mary Coll, London.

**BARBARA MUSGRAVE,** b April 28, 1948. Self-employed sculptress. Guildford borough cllr 1979-91 (Mayoress 1987-88); Surrey county cllr 1981-93. Pres and chair, Surrey Valuation Tribunal. Ed Tormead School, Guildford; Guildford Tech Coll; St Martin's School of Art; Guildford School of Art.

| BOGNOR REGIS & LITTLEHAMPTON | | | | | **17.9% change** | | | **C win** |
|---|---|---|---|---|---|---|---|---|
| Electorate % Turnout | | | 66,480 | 69.9% | **1997** | 65,567 | 76.0% | **1992** |
| Gibb, N | C | | 20,537 | 44.2% | -12.6% | 28,316 | 56.9% | C |
| Nash, R | Lab | | 13,216 | 28.5% | +15.0% | 13,309 | 26.7% | LD |
| Walsh, Dr J | LD | | 11,153 | 24.0% | -2.7% | 6,700 | 13.5% | Lab |
| Stride, G | UK Ind | | 1,537 | 3.3% | | 1,474 | 3.0% | Other |
| C to Lab notional swing 13.8% | | | 46,443 | | C maj 7,321 | 49,799 | | C maj 15,007 |
| | | | | | 15.8% | | | 76.0% |

**NICK GIBB,** b Sept 3, 1960. Tax consultant and senior manager with KPMG Peat Marwick. Contested Rotherham by-election 1994; Stoke-on-Trent Central 1992. Member, C social security manifesto policy group. Chair, Bethnal Green and Stepney C assoc, 1989-90, and treas, 1988-89. With Kibbutz Merom Golan 1983; NatWest Bank 1982-83. Ed Maidstone GS; Roundhay School, Leeds; Thornes House School, Wakefield; Durham Univ.
**ROGER NASH,** b April 14, 1948. Teacher. Contested Arundel 1992. Arun district cllr 1987- (Lab group leader 1991- ). Member, NUT;

Co-op Party; Lab Campaign for Electoral Reform. Ed William Fletcher Sec Mod; Kent, Leicester and Sussex Univs.
**JAMES WALSH,** b Jan 11, 1943. GP and ex-medical director, RNR. Contested Arundel, 1983, 1987 and 1992; Hove 1974 and 1979; South Downs in 1994 Euro elections. West Sussex county cllr and dep leader. Mayor of Littlehampton 1989-90. Ed Wimbledon Coll; Royal London Hospital.

| BOLSOVER | | | | | **0.1% change** | | | **Lab win** |
|---|---|---|---|---|---|---|---|---|
| Electorate % Turnout | | | 66,476 | 71.3% | **1997** | 67,485 | 78.1% | **1992** |
| +Skinner, D | Lab | | 35,073 | 74.0% | +9.5% | 34,018 | 64.5% | Lab |
| Harwood, R | C | | 7,924 | 16.7% | -8.6% | 13,339 | 25.3% | C |
| Cox, I | LD | | 4,417 | 9.3% | -0.9% | 5,374 | 10.2% | LD |
| C to Lab notional swing 9.0% | | | 47,414 | | Lab maj 27,149 | 52,731 | | Lab maj 20,679 |
| | | | | | 57.3% | | | 78.1% |

**DENNIS SKINNER,** b Feb 11, 1932. Ex-miner. Elected 1970. Chair, Lab Party, 1988-89, and vice-chair, 1987-88; member, NEC, 1978-93 and 1994- . Unsuccessfully contested chairmanship of PLP 1990. Chair, E Midlands group of Lab MPs; miners group of Lab MPs 1977-78. Member, Campaign Group of Lab MPs, 1981- . Pres, Derbyshire miners (NUM), 1966-70; NE Derbyshire CLP, 1968-71. Clay Cross cllr 1960-70; Derbyshire county cllr 1964-70. Miner 1949-70. Ed Tupton Hall GS; Ruskin Coll, Oxford.

**RICHARD HARWOOD,** b Aug 30, 1970. Barrister. Speech-writer for Gerry Malone, MP, and Eric Pickles, MP; ex-chair, Bolsover YCs. Ed Nottingham HS; Jesus Coll, Cambridge.
**IAN COX,** b Nov 18, 1953. Bolsover district cllr 1987-95. Chair, Derbyshire group of LDs. Ed Tibshelf School, Derbyshire.

| BOLTON NORTH EAST | | 16.3% change | | | | | Lab win |
|---|---|---|---|---|---|---|---|
| Electorate % Turnout | | 67,930 | 72.4% | **1997** | 69,722 | 80.1% | **1992** |
| **Crausby, D** | **Lab** | **27,621** | **56.1%** | **+8.7%** | 26,494 | 47.5% | Lab |
| Wilson, R | C | 14,952 | 30.4% | -11.7% | 23,477 | 42.1% | C |
| Critchley, Dr E | LD | 4,862 | 9.9% | -0.2% | 5,638 | 10.1% | LD |
| Staniforth, D | Ref | 1,096 | 2.2% | | 213 | 0.4% | NLP |
| Kelly, W | Soc Lab | 676 | 1.4% | | | | |
| C to Lab notional swing 10.2% | | 49,207 | Lab maj 12,669 | | 55,822 | Lab maj 3,017 | |
| | | | 25.7% | | | 80.1% | |

**DAVID CRAUSBY,** b June 17, 1946. Engineer. Contested this seat 1992; Bury N 1987. Bury metropolitan district cllr 1979-92. Served on Bolton N police consultative cttee. Chair, Bury North CLP, 1987. AEU convener. Ed Derby GS, Bury.
**ROBERT WILSON,** b Jan 4, 1965. Director of PR company. Reading borough cllr 1992-96 (dep leader, C group). Ed Wallingford School; Reading Univ.

**EDMUND CRITCHLEY,** b Dec 25, 1931. Consultant neurologist and professor of neurology, Central Lancashire Univ. FRCP and examiner for RCP. Ed Stowe School; Oxford Univ; King's Coll Medical School.

| BOLTON SOUTH EAST | | 0.2% change | | | | | Lab win |
|---|---|---|---|---|---|---|---|
| Electorate % Turnout | | 66,459 | 65.2% | **1997** | 66,566 | 74.3% | **1992** |
| **Iddon, B** | **Lab** | **29,856** | **68.9%** | **+14.6%** | 26,863 | 54.3% | Lab |
| Carter, P | C | 8,545 | 19.7% | -9.0% | 14,192 | 28.7% | C |
| Harasiwka, F | LD | 3,805 | 8.8% | -1.8% | 5,236 | 10.6% | LD |
| Pickering, B | Ref | 973 | 2.2% | | 2,891 | 5.8% | Ind Lab |
| Walch, L | NLP | 170 | 0.4% | -0.2% | 290 | 0.6% | NLP |
| C to Lab notional swing 11.8% | | 43,349 | Lab maj 21,311 | | 49,472 | Lab maj 12,671 | |
| | | | 49.2% | | | 74.3% | |

**BRIAN IDDON,** b July 5, 1940. Reader in chemistry, Salford Univ. Bolton borough cllr 1976- . Dir, Bolton City Challenge. FRSC. Ed Christ Church Boys' School, Southport; Southport Tech Coll; Hull Univ.
**PAUL CARTER,** b Jan 2, 1967. Senior business analyst/consultant on international politics; aide to Sir Rhodes Boyson 1990-91; private sec to Japanese gvt min 1992-94. Member, Tory Reform Group;

Bow Group; Coningsby Club. Ed Hutton GS, Lancs; Manchester and London Univs; Queens' Coll, Cambridge.
**FRANK HARASIWKA,** b April 4, 1959. Logistics manager. Contested Bolton SE 1987, and Greater Manchester West in 1994 Euro elections. Bolton metropolitan borough cllr. Ed Lords Coll, Bolton; Bolton Tech Coll.

| BOLTON WEST | | 13.4% change | | | | | Lab win |
|---|---|---|---|---|---|---|---|
| Electorate % Turnout | | 63,535 | 77.4% | **1997** | 63,070 | 82.5% | **1992** |
| **Kelly, Ms R** | **Lab** | **24,342** | **49.5%** | **+10.4%** | 24,619 | 47.3% | C |
| +Sackville, T G | C | 17,270 | 35.1% | -12.2% | 20,338 | 39.1% | Lab |
| Ronson, Mrs B | LD | 5,309 | 10.8% | -2.4% | 6,862 | 13.2% | LD |
| Kelly, Mrs D | Soc Lab | 1,374 | 2.8% | | 208 | 0.4% | NLP |
| Frankl-Slater, Mrs G | Ref | 865 | 1.8% | | | | |
| C to Lab notional swing 11.3% | | 49,160 | Lab maj 7,072 | | 52,027 | C maj 4,281 | |
| | | | 14.4% | | | 82.5% | |

**RUTH KELLY,** b May 9, 1968. Economist and dep head of inflation report division, Bank of England. Economics writer, *The Guardian,* 1990-94; established *The Guardian*'s panel of "seven wise women" economists. Publicity officer for Tower Hamlets anti-racist cttee. Ed Sutton HS; Westminster; Queen's Coll, Oxford; LSE.
**TOM SACKVILLE,** b Oct 26, 1950. Won this seat 1983; contested Pontypool 1979. Appointed Under Sec, Home Office, 1995; Under Sec for Health 1992-95; gvt whip 1989-92; asst gvt whip 1988-89. Member, broadcasting select cttee, 1990-91; Commons administration cttee 1991-92. PPS to Nicholas Scott when Min for the

Disabled and a N Ireland min, 1986-88. Sec, all-party cttee on drug misuse, 1984-88. With Deltec Banking Corp, New York, 1971-74; Grindlays Bank 1974-78; and International Bullion and Metal Brokers (London) Ltd 1978-83, being a divisional director 1981-83. Ed St Aubyn's, Rottingdean, Sussex; Eton; Lincoln Coll, Oxford.
**BARBARA RONSON,** b Dec 16, 1942. Retired librarian and lecturer. Contested Bolton W 1992. Bolton borough cllr 1986-90 and 1992- (LD group leader); Horwich town cllr 1987-. Member, LD regional exec, 1988- . Ed Bolton School; Manchester Coll of Commerce; Bolton Inst of Higher Ed.

| BOOTLE | | 13.2% change | | | | Lab win | | |
|---|---|---|---|---|---|---|---|---|
| Electorate % Turnout | | 57,284 | 66.7% | **1997** | 60,913 | 71.3% | **1992** | |
| +Benton, J | Lab | **31,668** | **82.9%** | **+6.3%** | 33,250 | 76.5% | Lab | |
| Mathews, R | C | 3,247 | 8.5% | -5.6% | 6,130 | 14.1% | C | |
| Reid, K | LD | 2,191 | 5.7% | -0.7% | 2,812 | 6.5% | LD | |
| Elliott, J | Ref | 571 | 1.5% | | 1,019 | 2.3% | Lib | |
| Glover, P | Soc | 420 | 1.1% | | 229 | 0.5% | NLP | |
| Cohen, S | NLP | 126 | 0.3% | -0.2% | | | | |
| C to Lab notional swing 6.0% | | 38,223 | Lab maj 28,421 74.4% | | 43,440 | Lab maj 27,120 71.3% | | |

**JOE BENTON,** b Sept 28, 1933. Won second by-election for this seat 1990. Appointed a Lab whip 1994. Ex-member, energy select cttee; member, Commons chairmen's panel, 1992-94. Joint sec, all-party pro-life group. Sefton borough cllr 1970-90 (Lab group leader, 1985-90). Chair, governors, Hugh Baird Coll of Tech, 1972-93. Employed by Girobank 1982-90; ex-personnel manager Pacific Steam Navigation Co. Ed St Monica's Primary and Secondary; Bootle Tech Coll.

**RUPERT MATTHEWS,** b Dec 5, 1961. Freelance writer and journalist. Vice-chair, Kingston and Surbiton C assoc, 1995- ; chair, YCs 1987-89; Kingston cllr 1990-94. Ed Esher GS.
**KIRON REID,** b May 25, 1971. Barrister and law lecturer. Contested Merseyside West in Euro by-election 1996. Member, Charter 88; CND. Ed Merchant Taylors' Boys School, Crosby; Bristol Univ.

| BOSTON & SKEGNESS | | 72.8% change | | | | C win | |
|---|---|---|---|---|---|---|---|
| Electorate % Turnout | | 67,623 | 68.9% | **1997** | 65,577 | 77.2% | **1992** |
| +Body, Sir Richard | C | **19,750** | **42.4%** | **-8.4%** | 25,721 | 50.8% | C |
| McCauley, P | Lab | 19,103 | 41.0% | +12.8% | 14,299 | 28.2% | Lab |
| Dodsworth, J | LD | 7,721 | 16.6% | -4.4% | 10,613 | 21.0% | LD |
| C to Lab notional swing 10.6% | | 46,574 | C maj 647 1.4% | | 50,633 | C maj 11,422 77.2% | |

**SIR RICHARD BODY,** b May 18, 1927. MP for Holland with Boston 1966-97, and for Billericay 1955-59; contested Leek 1951, Rotherham 1950, and Abertillery by-election 1950. Resigned C whip 1994-96 in protest at increase in UK contribution to EU budget. Joint chair, Get Britain Out (of EEC) Campaign, 1975. Chair, select cttee on agriculture, 1983-87, and member 1979-87; member, joint cttee on Consolidation Bills, 1975-91. Underwriting member of Lloyd's. Chair, trustees, Centre for European Studies, 1991- . Vice-pres, Small Farmers' Assoc, 1985- . Joint Master, Windsor Forest Bloodhounds, 1988- . Joint vice-chair, all-

party Anzac group. Chair, Open Seas Forum, 1971- . Ed Reading School.
**PHILIP McCAULEY,** b Dec 5, 1961. Managing dir, Tape Techniques Ltd and TTL Music Services Ltd. Member, British Actors Equity; Lab Finance and Industry group. Ed Christ the King School, Arnold; Sheffield Univ.
**JIM DODSWORTH,** b Nov 21, 1932. Director of farming company. Contested Lindsey E 1992. Lincolnshire county cllr 1981- . Local Methodist preacher; district vice-pres and local pres, Scouts. Ed C of E elementary school.

| BOSWORTH | | 17.7% change | | | | C win | |
|---|---|---|---|---|---|---|---|
| Electorate % Turnout | | 68,113 | 76.6% | **1997** | 66,420 | 84.1% | **1992** |
| +Tredinnick, D A S | C | **21,189** | **40.6%** | **-11.0%** | 28,863 | 51.6% | C |
| Furlong, A | Lab | 20,162 | 38.7% | +12.3% | 14,732 | 26.4% | Lab |
| Ellis, J | LD | 9,281 | 17.8% | -2.9% | 11,576 | 20.7% | LD |
| Halborg, S | Ref | 1,521 | 2.9% | | 716 | 1.3% | Grn |
| C to Lab notional swing 11.7% | | 52,153 | C maj 1,027 2.0% | | 55,887 | C maj 14,131 84.1% | |

**DAVID TREDINNICK,** b Jan 19, 1950. Elected 1987; contested Cardiff S and Penarth 1983. PPS to Sir Wyn Roberts when Welsh Office minister, 1991-94. Joint sec, C backbench defence cttee and C foreign and Commonwealth affairs cttee, 1990-91; chair, British-Atlantic group of young politicians, 1989-91; treasurer, all-party alternative and complementary medicine group, 1991- . Member of Lloyd's. Chair, Anglo-East European Trading Co Ltd, 1990- ; dir, Ukraine Business Agency, 1992- ; family business of Malden, Mitcham Properties, 1985- ; Daneswood Properties. Co-chair,

Future of Europe Trust, 1991-94. Marketing manager, Q1 Europe Ltd (small business computers), 1979-81. Ed Eton; Mons Officer Cadet School; Graduate Business School, Cape Town Univ; St John's Coll, Oxford.
**ANDREW FURLONG,** b July 3, 1961. Logistics team leader in food manufacturing. Member, Lab co-ordinating cttee. Ed Brunel Univ.
**JONATHAN ELLIS,** b May 21, 1968. NHS manager. Member, Friends of the Earth; Oxfam; Charter 88; Unison. Ed St Edmund's School, Canterbury; Danum Comp, Doncaster; Durham Univ.

## BOURNEMOUTH EAST — 16.8% change — C win

| | | Electorate % Turnout | 61,862 | 70.2% | 1997 | 63,396 | 72.7% | 1992 |
|---|---|---|---|---|---|---|---|---|
| +Atkinson, D | C | | 17,997 | 41.4% | -14.0% | 25,558 | 55.5% | C |
| Eyre, D | LD | | 13,651 | 31.4% | +0.4% | 14,315 | 31.1% | LD |
| Stevens, Mrs J | Lab | | 9,181 | 21.1% | +8.3% | 5,916 | 12.8% | Lab |
| Musgrave-Scott, A | Ref | | 1,808 | 4.2% | | 277 | 0.6% | NLP |
| Benney, K | UK Ind | | 791 | 1.8% | | | | |
| C to LD notional swing 7.2% | | | 43,428 | | C maj 4,346 | 46,066 | | C maj 11,243 |
| | | | | | 10.0% | | | 72.7% |

**DAVID ATKINSON,** b March 24, 1940. Elected 1977 by-election; contested Newham NW Feb 1974, and Basildon Oct 1974. PPS to Paul Channon in various ministerial posts 1979-87. Joint vice-chair, C backbench tourism cttee; C backbench health cttee 1988- . Treas, all-party British-USSR group; chair, Albanian and Cameroon groups. Chair, national YCs, 1970-71. Essex county cllr 1973-78; Southend cllr 1969-72. Pres, Christian Solidarity International (UK), 1983- (chair 1979-83); International Soc for Human Rights

(UK) 1985- . Ed St George's Coll, Weybridge; Southend Coll of Tech; Coll of Automobile and Aeronautical Engineering.
**DOUGLAS EYRE,** b Nov 8, 1946. Chartered accountant and director, Willis Parsons Financial Services Ltd. Bournemouth cllr since 1979 (council leader 1997- ). Ed Bournemouth School.
**JESSICA STEVENS,** b Aug 11, 1968. Charity administrator. Member, Fabian Soc; Amnesty. Ed Bournemouth Girls' School; Brunel Univ.

## BOURNEMOUTH WEST — 50.2% change — C win

| | | Electorate % Turnout | 62,028 | 66.2% | 1997 | 63,222 | 73.9% | 1992 |
|---|---|---|---|---|---|---|---|---|
| +Butterfill, J | C | | 17,115 | 41.7% | -10.8% | 24,532 | 52.5% | C |
| Dover, Ms J | LD | | 11,405 | 27.8% | +0.3% | 12,815 | 27.4% | LD |
| Gritt, D | Lab | | 10,093 | 24.6% | +5.1% | 9,110 | 19.5% | Lab |
| Mills, R | Ref | | 1,910 | 4.7% | | 257 | 0.6% | NLP |
| Tooley, Mrs L | UK Ind | | 281 | 0.7% | | | | |
| Morse, J | BNP | | 165 | 0.4% | | | | |
| Springham, A | NLP | | 103 | 0.3% | -0.3% | | | |
| C to LD notional swing 5.6% | | | 41,072 | | C maj 5,710 | 46,714 | | C maj 11,717 |
| | | | | | 13.9% | | | 25.1% |

**JOHN BUTTERFILL,** b Feb 14, 1941. Elected 1983; contested Croydon NW 1981 by-election; London South Inner in 1979 Euro elections. Elected joint-vice chair, 1922 Cttee, May 21, 1997. PPS to Brian Mawhinney when N Ireland Min; PPS to Cecil Parkinson, Energy and Transport Sec, 1988-90. Member, trade and industry select cttee, 1992-97; Commons chairmen's panel. Chair, C group for Europe, 1989-92, and vice-pres, 1992-95; chair, 1995- , C backbench Euro affairs cttee. Partner, Butterfill Associates. Dir, Conservation Investments Ltd; Conservation Properties Ltd; PYV

Ltd; Delphi Group plc; Maples Stores plc. Adviser to British Insurance and Investment Brokers Assoc, Independent Financial Advisers Assoc, British Venture Capital Assoc. Ed Caterham School; Coll of Estate Management, London.
**JANET DOVER,** b July 24, 1953. Runs childcare employment agency. Contested Bournemouth W 1992. Dorset county cllr 1993- , East Dorset district cllr 1988- . Ed GS in Herts and Dorset; OU.
**DENNIS GRITT,** b March 4, 1939. Ex-Bournemouth cllr. Vice-chair, Bournemouth CLP. Technical education in telecommunications.

## BRACKNELL — 51.5% change — C win

| | | Electorate % Turnout | 79,292 | 74.5% | 1997 | 69,433 | 85.6% | 1992 |
|---|---|---|---|---|---|---|---|---|
| +MacKay, A | C | | 27,983 | 47.4% | -13.0% | 35,916 | 60.4% | C |
| Snelgrove, Ms A | Lab | | 17,596 | 29.8% | +9.5% | 12,036 | 20.2% | Lab |
| Hilliar, A | LD | | 9,122 | 15.4% | -3.9% | 11,511 | 19.4% | LD |
| Tompkins, J | N Lab | | 1,909 | 3.2% | | | | |
| Cairns, W | Ref | | 1,636 | 2.8% | | | | |
| Boxall, L | UK Ind | | 569 | 1.0% | | | | |
| Roberts, Ms D | ProLife | | 276 | 0.5% | | | | |
| C to Lab notional swing 11.3% | | | 59,091 | | C maj 10,387 | 59,463 | | C maj 23,880 |
| | | | | | 17.6% | | | 40.2% |

**ANDREW MacKAY,** b Aug 27, 1949. MP for Berkshire E 1983-97 and for Birmingham Stechford from by-election 1977 to 1979. Gvt deputy chief whip 1996-97; senior whip and pairing whip 1995-96; pairing whip 1993-95; asst whip 1992-93. Member, finance and services select cttee; selection cttee. PPS to Tom King, N Ireland and Defence Sec, 1986-92. Member, nat exec, C Party, 1979-82. Sec, C Friends of Israel group, 1986-92. Ex-adviser to Morgan Grenfell plc, D.Y. Davies plc, and Henry Burcher and Co,

chartered surveyors; dir of Cabra Estates plc, 1989-92; former non-exec dir of Barnett Consulting Group Ltd. Ed Solihull School.
**ANNE SNELGROVE,** b Aug 7, 1957. Training consultant. Berkshire county cllr and Bracknell town cllr. Member, TGWU. Ed King Alfred's Coll, Winchester; City Univ, London.
**ALAN HILLIAR,** b Aug 27, 1950. Manager. Guildford borough cllr since 1985. Ed Sutton Manor HS, Surrey; Croydon Tech College; Slough and Farnborough Colls of Tech. Barber-shop singer.

## BRADFORD NORTH — Lab hold

| Electorate % Turnout | | | 66,228 | 63.3% | 1997 | 66,719 | 73.4% | 1992 |
|---|---|---|---|---|---|---|---|---|
| *Rooney, T | Lab | | 23,493 | 56.1% | +8.2% | 23,420 | 47.8% | Lab |
| Skinner, R | C | | 10,723 | 25.6% | -6.6% | 15,756 | 32.2% | C |
| Browne, T | LD | | 6,083 | 14.5% | -4.1% | 9,133 | 18.7% | LD |
| Wheatley, H | Ref | | 1,227 | 2.9% | | 350 | 0.7% | Loony |
| Beckett, W | Loony | | 369 | 0.9% | +0.2% | 304 | 0.6% | Islamic |
| C to Lab swing 7.4% | | | 41,895 | Lab maj 12,770 | | 48,963 | Lab maj 7,664 | |
| | | | | 30.5% | | | 73.4% | |

**TERRY ROONEY,** b Nov 11, 1950. Won 1990 by-election. Chair, PLP social security cttee, 1991. Member, broadcasting select cttee. Sec, Yorkshire group of Lab MPs. Bradford cllr 1983-90 (chair, Lab group, 1988-90; dep leader of council, 1990). Ex-welfare rights advice worker and commercial insurance broker. Ed Buttershaw Comp; Bradford Coll.

**RASJID SKINNER,** b Jan 5, 1950. Consultant clinical psychologist. Chair, Bradford Division of Psychology. Converted to Islam 1977. Ed Chingford HS; Durham Univ; Queen's Univ, Belfast; Bradford Univ.
**TERRY BROWNE,** b March 13, 1940. Chartered secretary. Bradford cllr 1995- . Ed Strand School, London.

## BRADFORD SOUTH — Lab hold

| Electorate % Turnout | | | 68,391 | 65.9% | 1997 | 69,914 | 75.6% | 1992 |
|---|---|---|---|---|---|---|---|---|
| *Sutcliffe, G | Lab | | 25,558 | 56.7% | +9.1% | 25,185 | 47.6% | Lab |
| Hawkesworth, Mrs A | C | | 12,622 | 28.0% | -10.4% | 20,283 | 38.4% | C |
| Wilson-Fletcher, A | LD | | 5,093 | 11.3% | -2.4% | 7,243 | 13.7% | LD |
| Kershaw, Mrs M | Ref | | 1,785 | 4.0% | | 156 | 0.3% | Islamic |
| C to Lab swing 9.7% | | | 45,058 | Lab maj 12,936 | | 52,867 | Lab maj 4,902 | |
| | | | | 28.7% | | | 9.3% | |

**GERRY SUTCLIFFE,** b May 13, 1953. Elected at 1994 by-election. Member, PAC 1996- . Chair, all-party South Pennines group, 1996- ; vice-chair, Yorkshire group of Lab MPs, 1995- . Bradford metropolitan district cllr 1982-88 and 1990-94 (leader, 1992-94). Deputy sec, Sogat, later the Graphical, Paper and Media Union, 1980-94. Display advertising clerk, *Bradford Telegraph and*

*Argus,* 1971-75; with Field Printers, 1975-80. Ed Cardinal Hinsley GS; Bradford Coll.
**ANNE HAWKESWORTH,** b March 27, 1948. Self-employed businesswoman. Bradford city cllr 1990- . Deputy chair, Bradford South C assoc. Ed Bellevue Girls' GS, Bradford.
**ALEX WILSON-FLETCHER,** b Jan 24, 1971. Student. Member, Charter 88. Ed Grange Upper School; Bolton Inst of HE.

*Details of 1994 by-election on page 277*

## BRADFORD WEST — Lab hold

| Electorate % Turnout | | | 71,961 | 63.3% | 1997 | 70,016 | 69.9% | 1992 |
|---|---|---|---|---|---|---|---|---|
| Singh, M | Lab | | 18,932 | 41.5% | -11.7% | 26,046 | 53.2% | Lab |
| Riaz, M | C | | 15,055 | 33.0% | -0.8% | 16,544 | 33.8% | C |
| Wright, Mrs H | LD | | 6,737 | 14.8% | +4.3% | 5,150 | 10.5% | LD |
| Khan, A | Soc Lab | | 1,551 | 3.4% | | 735 | 1.5% | Grn |
| Royston, C | Ref | | 1,348 | 3.0% | | 471 | 1.0% | Islamic |
| Robinson, J | Green | | 861 | 1.9% | | | | |
| Osborn, G | BNP | | 839 | 1.8% | | | | |
| Shah, S | Soc | | 245 | 0.5% | | | | |
| Lab to C swing 5.5% | | | 45,568 | Lab maj 3,877 | | 48,946 | Lab maj 9,502 | |
| | | | | 8.5% | | | 69.9% | |

**MARSHA SINGH,** b Oct 11, 1954. NHS senior development manager. Chair, Bradford CLP 1992- . Ed Bellevue GS, Bradford; Loughborough Univ.
**MOHAMMED RIAZ,** b Sept 19, 1951. Managing director of nursing home; non-exec dir West Yorkshire metropolitan ambulance service. Contested Bradford N 1992. Bradford city cllr 1985-90;

initiated £180m Bradford West End development project. Member, C One Nation Forum. Ed Buttershore Upper School; London and Bradford Univs.
**HELEN WRIGHT,** b Aug 20, 1956. Midwife and clinic manager. Contested Bradford S in by-election, 1994. Member, Greenpeace. Ed Newland HS, Hull.

| BRAINTREE | | 22.6% change | | | **Lab win** | | |
|---|---|---|---|---|---|---|---|
| Electorate % Turnout | | 72,772 | 76.4% | **1997** | 68,995 | 84.0% | **1992** |
| **Hurst, A** | **Lab** | **23,729** | **42.7%** | **+15.3%** | 29,278 | 50.5% | C |
| +Newton, A | C | 22,278 | 40.1% | -10.5% | 15,890 | 27.4% | Lab |
| Ellis, T | LD | 6,418 | 11.5% | -9.2% | 12,039 | 20.8% | LD |
| Westcott, N | Ref | 2,165 | 3.9% | | 724 | 1.2% | Grn |
| Abbott, J | Green | 712 | 1.3% | | | | |
| Nolan, M | New Way | 274 | 0.5% | | | | |
| C to Lab notional swing 12.9% | | 55,576 | | Lab maj 1,451 2.6% | 57,931 | | C maj 13,388 84.0% |

**ALAN HURST,** b Sept 2, 1945. Solicitor. Southend Borough cllr 1980-95 (Lab group leader 1990-95); Essex county cllr 1993- . Ed Westcliffe HS; Liverpool Univ.

**TONY NEWTON,** b Aug 29, 1937. Elected Feb 1974; contested Sheffield Brightside 1970. Economist. Appointed Lord President of the Council and Leader of Commons 1992 with responsibility for gvt's anti-drug strategy. Social security Sec 1989-92; joined Cabinet in 1988 as Chancellor of Duchy of Lancaster and chief Commons spokesman for DTI; Health Minister 1986-88; Minister for Disabled 1984-86; junior DHSS minister 1982-84. Gvt whip 1981-82; asst gvt whip 1979-81. Privy Counsellor 1988. Chair, Commons standards and privileges cttee, 1995- ; privileges cttee 1994-95; broadcasting select cttee 1992- ; member, finance and services cttee, 1992- . Asst dir, C Research Dept, 1970-74; head of economic section 1965-70. Ed Friends' School, Saffron Walden; Trinity Coll, Oxford (pres of Union 1958).

**TREVOR ELLIS,** b March 4, 1954. Welfare rights worker for national charity. Braintree district cllr 1985- . Ed Earls Colne GS.

| BRECON & RADNORSHIRE | | | | | **LD gain** | | |
|---|---|---|---|---|---|---|---|
| Electorate % Turnout | | 52,142 | 82.2% | **1997** | 51,509 | 85.9% | **1992** |
| **Livsey, R** | **LD** | **17,516** | **40.8%** | **+5.1%** | 15,977 | 36.1% | C |
| *Evans, J | C | 12,419 | 29.0% | -7.1% | 15,847 | 35.8% | LD |
| Mann, C J | Lab | 11,424 | 26.6% | +0.4% | 11,634 | 26.3% | Lab |
| Phillips, Ms L | Ref | 900 | 2.1% | | 418 | 0.9% | PC |
| Cornelius, S | PC | 622 | 1.5% | +0.5% | 393 | 0.9% | Grn |
| C to LD swing 6.1% | | 42,881 | | LD maj 5,097 11.9% | 44,269 | | C maj 130 0.3% |

**RICHARD LIVSEY,** b May 2, 1935. Retired farmer and lecturer in farm management. MP for Brecon and Radnor from 1985 by-election until defeated 1992. Contested seat 1983; Pembroke 1979; Perth and E Perthshire 1970. Ex-leader, Welsh LDs; LD spokesman on Wales, May 1997- , and 1987-92; and on water 1988-89; Alliance spokesman on countryside in 1987 election; L spokesman on Wales 1987; on agriculture 1985-87. Member, Welsh select cttee, 1987-92. Ed Bedales School; Seale-Hayne Agricultural Coll; Reading Univ.

**JONATHAN EVANS,** b June 2, 1950. Solicitor. Won Brecon and Radnor 1992, having contested it 1987; Wolverhampton NE 1979; Ebbw Vale twice in 1974. Welsh Under Sec 1996-97. Parly Sec, Lord Chancellor's Department, 1995-96; Corporate Affairs Min, 1994-95. Ed Lewis School, Pengam; Howardian HS, Cardiff; Coll of Law, Guildford and London.

**CHRIS MANN,** b Oct 1, 1950. Probation officer. Contested Brecon and Radnor 1992. Powys cllr 1985- (leader, Lab group, 1989- ). Ed Kingsbury HS; Dundee Univ.

| BRENT EAST | | 0.3% change | | | **Lab win** | | |
|---|---|---|---|---|---|---|---|
| Electorate % Turnout | | 53,548 | 65.9% | **1997** | 56,812 | 64.3% | **1992** |
| **+Livingstone, K** | **Lab** | **23,748** | **67.3%** | **+14.5%** | 19,314 | 52.8% | Lab |
| Francois, M | C | 7,866 | 22.3% | -14.3% | 13,365 | 36.6% | C |
| Hunter, I | LD | 2,751 | 7.8% | -1.1% | 3,237 | 8.9% | LD |
| Keable, S | Soc Lab | 466 | 1.3% | | 546 | 1.5% | Grn |
| Shanks, A | ProLife | 218 | 0.6% | | 96 | 0.3% | Comm GB |
| Warrilo, Ms C | Dream | 120 | 0.3% | | | | |
| Jenkins, D | NLP | 103 | 0.3% | | | | |
| C to Lab notional swing 14.4% | | 35,272 | | Lab maj 15,882 45.0% | 36,558 | | Lab maj 5,949 64.3% |

**KEN LIVINGSTONE,** b June 17, 1945. Elected for this seat 1987; contested Hampstead 1979. Leader, GLC, 1981-86, when it was abolished; GLC member for Paddington, 1981-86, and for Hackney N 1973-81. Lambeth cllr 1971-78; Camden cllr 1978-82. Member, NEC, 1987-89. Member, regional exec, London Lab Party, 1974-86. Joint editor, *Labour Herald,* 1981-85. Author; dir, Localaction Ltd; former laboratory technician; lecturer for overseas students studying politics. Fellow and unpaid member, Zoological Society council. Ed Tulse Hill Comp; Philippa Fawcett Coll of Ed.

**MARK FRANÇOIS,** b Aug 14, 1965. Defence consultant. Basildon district cllr 1991-95. Chair, Bristol Univ C assoc 1984. Ed Nicholas Comp, Basildon; Bristol Univ; King's Coll, London.

**IAN HUNTER,** b Sept 14, 1963. Management consultant; dir, Curtis-Hunter Consulting Ltd. Member Charter 88; Amnesty; Ed Farnham Coll, Surrey; Bristol, Warwick and Strathclyde Univs.

| BRENT NORTH | | 16.0% change | | | | | Lab win |
|---|---|---|---|---|---|---|---|
| Electorate % Turnout | | 54,149 | 70.5% | **1997** | 55,433 | 68.0% | **1992** |
| **Gardiner, B** | **Lab** | **19,343** | **50.7%** | **+20.4%** | **21,660** | **57.4%** | **C** |
| +Boyson, Sir Rhodes | C | 15,324 | 40.1% | -17.3% | 11,430 | 30.3% | Lab |
| Lorber, P | LD | 3,104 | 8.1% | -2.5% | 3,999 | 10.6% | LD |
| Davids, T | NLP | 204 | 0.5% | -0.2% | 331 | 0.9% | Ind |
| Clark, G | Dream | 199 | 0.5% | | 293 | 0.8% | NLP |
| **C to Lab notional swing 18.8%** | | **38,174** | | **Lab maj 4,019** | **37,713** | | **C maj 10,230** |
| | | | | 10.5% | | | 68.0% |

**BARRY GARDINER,** b March 10, 1957. Arbitrator of maritime casualties; occasional lecturer for Acad of National Economy, Moscow. Cambridge city cllr (Mayor 1992). Member, MSF/GMB; Co-op Party. Ed Glasgow HS; Haileybury; St Andrews Univ; Corpus Christi Coll, Cambridge; Harvard (Kennedy Scholar).
**SIR RHODES BOYSON,** b May 11, 1925. Ex-head teacher. Elected Feb 1974; contested Eccles 1970. Local Gvt Min 1986-87; N Ireland Min 1984-86; Social Security Min 1983-84; Under Sec for Education and Science 1979-83; Member, exec, 1922 Cttee, 1987-

97; chair, all-party Methodist group 1990-97; council of Christians and Jews group. Waltham Forest borough cllr 1968-74; Haslingden cllr 1957-61. Non-exec director, Blacks Leisure plc, 1987- ; Arc Publishing; consultant on economic affairs, ARC International, 1987- . Ed Haslingden GS; Univ Coll, Cardiff; Manchester Univ; LSE; Corpus Christi Coll, Cambridge.
**PAUL LORBER,** b Sept 3, 1955, in Bratislava. Chartered accountant, tax adviser for oil industry. Contested Brent N 1992. Brent cllr 1982- (LD group leader 1994- ). Ed Kilburn HS; Manchester Univ.

| BRENT SOUTH | | 16.0% change | | | | | Lab win |
|---|---|---|---|---|---|---|---|
| Electorate % Turnout | | 53,505 | 64.5% | **1997** | 59,070 | 63.4% | **1992** |
| **+Boateng, P** | **Lab** | **25,180** | **73.0%** | **+15.4%** | **21,568** | **57.6%** | **Lab** |
| Jackson, S | C | 5,489 | 15.9% | -15.2% | 11,651 | 31.1% | C |
| Brazil, J | LD | 2,670 | 7.7% | -1.7% | 3,551 | 9.5% | LD |
| Phythian, Ms J | Ref | 497 | 1.4% | | 486 | 1.3% | Grn |
| Edler, D | Green | 389 | 1.1% | | 169 | 0.5% | NLP |
| Howard, C | Dream | 175 | 0.5% | | | | |
| Mahaldar, Ms A | NLP | 98 | 0.3% | -0.2% | | | |
| **C to Lab notional swing 15.3%** | | **34,498** | | **Lab maj 19,691** | **37,425** | | **Lab maj 9,917** |
| | | | | 57.1% | | | 63.4% |

**PAUL BOATENG,** b June 14, 1951. Became Under Secretary for Health, May 5, 1997. Barrister. Elected 1987; contested Hertfordshire W 1983. Appointed Lab spokesman on Lord Chancellor's Department 1992; spokesman on Treasury and economic affairs 1989-92. Member, environment select cttee, 1987-89. Joint sec, all-party Council of Christians and Jews group; vice-chair, Bermuda group, 1996- ; vice-chair, race and community group. GLC 1981-86. Member, World Council of Churches Commission on programme to combat racism, 1984-91; chair, Afro-

Caribbean Education Resource Project, 1978-86. Unpaid dir, English National Opera and English Touring Opera. Ed Ghana International School; Accra Acad; Apsley GS; Bristol Univ Coll of Law.
**STEWART JACKSON,** b Jan 31, 1965. Retail banker. Ealing cllr 1990- . Member, Conservative Way Forward, Tory Green Initiative. Ed Chatham House GS, Ramsgate; Royal Holloway Coll (pres, London Univ union, 1988-89); London Nautical School.
**JULIAN BRAZIL,** b March 5, 1964. Company secretary, researcher to Matthew Taylor, MP. Ed Reading Coll of Tech; Bristol Univ.

| BRENTFORD & ISLEWORTH | | 15.2% change | | | | | Lab win |
|---|---|---|---|---|---|---|---|
| Electorate % Turnout | | 79,058 | 71.0% | **1997** | 79,763 | 74.2% | **1992** |
| **Keen, Mrs A** | **Lab** | **32,249** | **57.4%** | **+14.7%** | **26,994** | **45.6%** | **C** |
| +Deva, N | C | 17,825 | 31.8% | -13.9% | 25,319 | 42.8% | Lab |
| Hartwell, Dr G | LD | 4,613 | 8.2% | -1.9% | 5,962 | 10.1% | LD |
| Bradley, J | Green | 687 | 1.2% | | 904 | 1.5% | Grn |
| Simmerson, Mrs B | UK Ind | 614 | 1.1% | | | | |
| Ahmed, M | NLP | 147 | 0.3% | | | | |
| **C to Lab notional swing 14.3%** | | **56,135** | | **Lab maj 14,424** | **59,179** | | **C maj 1,675** |
| | | | | 25.7% | | | 74.2% |

**ANN KEEN,** b Nov 26, 1948. Contested this seat 1992 and 1987. General sec, Community and District Nursing Assoc and ex-head of faculty for advanced nursing, Queen Charlotte's Coll, Hammersmith Hospital. Member, Lab Party health advisory forum. Chair, Brentford crime prevention panel, 1992- . Ed Elfed Sec Mod, Clwyd; Surrey Univ. Her husband, Alan, is Labour & Co-op MP for Feltham and Heston, and her sister Sylvia Heal is Labour MP for Halesowen & Rowley Regis.

**NIRJ DEVA,** b May 11, 1948 (in Sri Lanka). Environmental scientist, aeronautical engineer. Won this seat 1992; contested Hammersmith 1987. PPS, Scottish Office, 1996- . Dir, Ceylon and Foreign Trades Ltd, Sri Lanka. Consultant to Rothmans International and other companies. Dep Lieut, Greater London, since 1985. Ed St Joseph's Coll, Colombo; Loughborough Univ.
**GARETH HARTWELL,** b Aug 9, 1969. Computer software consultant. Ed Cricklade Coll, Andover; Durham and London Univs.

| BRENTWOOD & ONGAR | | 0.1% change | | | | | C win |
|---|---|---|---|---|---|---|---|
| Electorate % Turnout | | 66,005 | 76.9% | **1997** | 66,767 | 83.7% | **1992** |
| +Pickles, E | C | 23,031 | 45.4% | -12.2% | 32,187 | 57.6% | C |
| Bottomley, Mrs E | LD | 13,341 | 26.3% | -4.2% | 17,012 | 30.5% | LD |
| Young, M | Lab | 11,231 | 22.1% | +11.2% | 6,102 | 10.9% | Lab |
| Kilmartin, Mrs A | Ref | 2,658 | 5.2% | | 555 | 1.0% | Grn |
| Mills, Capt D | UK Ind | 465 | 0.9% | | | | |
| C to LD notional swing 4.0% | | 50,726 | C maj 9,690 | | 55,856 | C maj 15,175 | |
| | | | 19.1% | | | 83.7% | |

**ERIC PICKLES,** b April 20, 1952. Elected for this seat 1992. A vice-chair, C Party, 1993- . Member, transport select cttee, 1995-97; environment select cttee 1992-93. Leader, Bradford council, 1988-90; member 1979-91; leader, C group, 1987-91. Local gvt editor, Conservative *Newsline*, 1990- . Member, Nat Union exec cttee, 1975-91; One Nation Forum 1987-91; nat advisory cttee on local gvt 1985- (chair, 1992-93). Lecturer at C agents examination courses, 1988- ; nat chairman, YCs, 1980-81. Co-chair, joint cttee

against racialism, representing nat union, 1982-87. Ed Greenhead GS, Keighley; Leeds Poly.
**LIZ BOTTOMLEY,** b Feb 28, 1943. Teacher. Contested this seat 1992; agent for SE area 1986-89. Brentwood district cllr 1983- . Ed Slough HS for Girls; Queen Mary Coll, London.
**MARC YOUNG,** b June 4, 1972. Advertising account executive. Member, Co-op Party; Fabian Soc; Lab Campaign for Electoral Reform; GMB. Ed Hedley Walter School; Basildon Coll; York Univ.

| BRIDGEND | | | | | | | Lab hold |
|---|---|---|---|---|---|---|---|
| Electorate % Turnout | | 59,721 | 72.4% | **1997** | 58,531 | 80.4% | **1992** |
| *Griffiths, W | Lab | 25,115 | 58.1% | +6.8% | 24,143 | 51.3% | Lab |
| Davies, D T C | C | 9,867 | 22.8% | -12.9% | 16,817 | 35.7% | C |
| McKinlay, A | LD | 4,968 | 11.5% | +1.2% | 4,827 | 10.3% | LD |
| Greaves, T | Ref | 1,662 | 3.8% | | 1,301 | 2.8% | PC |
| Watkins, D | PC | 1,649 | 3.8% | +1.0% | | | |
| C to Lab swing 9.8% | | 43,261 | Lab maj 15,248 | | 47,088 | Lab maj 7,326 | |
| | | | 35.2% | | | 80.4% | |

**WIN GRIFFITHS,** b Feb 11, 1943. Became Under Secretary Welsh Office, May 5, 1997. MEP for South Wales 1979-89; a vice-pres, European Parliament, 1984-87. Won this seat 1987. Lab spokesman on Wales 1994- ; on education 1992-94; on environmental protection 1990-92. Treas, all-party fairs and showgrounds group. Chair, PLP ed, science and arts cttee, 1988-90. Vale of Glamorgan borough cllr 1973-76; Dinas Powys community council 1974-79. Methodist lay preacher since 1966. Former teacher. Ed Brecon Boys' GS; Univ Coll, Cardiff.

**DAVID DAVIES,** b July 27, 1970. General distribution manager for Burrows Heath Ltd, forwarders and tea importers. Treas, Wales area YCs; chair, Newport West C assoc, 1995. Member, Inst of Logistics; assoc member, Inst of Transport Administration. Worked his way around the world, 1989-91, at one stage being a rickshaw driver. Ed Bassaleg School, Newport.
**ANDREW McKINLAY,** b Nov 10, 1962. Housing manager. Cheltenham borough cllr. Ed Ormonde HS, Maghull; Edge Hill Coll of HE; Salford Univ.

| BRIDGWATER | | | | | | | C hold |
|---|---|---|---|---|---|---|---|
| Electorate % Turnout | | 73,038 | 74.8% | **1997** | 71,567 | 79.5% | **1992** |
| *King, T | C | 20,174 | 36.9% | -9.8% | 26,610 | 46.8% | C |
| Hoban, M | LD | 18,378 | 33.6% | +4.0% | 16,894 | 29.7% | LD |
| Lavers, R | Lab | 13,519 | 24.8% | +3.0% | 12,365 | 21.7% | Lab |
| Evens, Ms F | Ref | 2,551 | 4.7% | | 746 | 1.3% | Grn |
| | | | | | 183 | 0.3% | Ind |
| | | | | | 112 | 0.2% | NLP |
| C to LD swing 6.9% | | 54,622 | C maj 1,796 | | 56,910 | C maj 9,716 | |
| | | | 3.3% | | | 79.5% | |

**TOM KING,** b June 13, 1933. Elected at 1970 by-election. Resigned from Gvt after 1992 election. Defence Sec 1989-92; N Ireland Sec 1985-89; Employment Sec 1983-85; Transport Sec June-Oct 1983; Environment Sec Jan-June 1983; Local Gvt and Environmental Services Min 1979-83. C spokesman on energy 1976-79, and on industry 1975-76. Appointed member of Nolan Cttee on Standards in Public Life 1994; chair, parly intelligence and security cttee, 1994- . Dir, Electra Investment Trust plc; non-exec chair, London International Exhibition Centre. Chair, English Rural Housing Assoc; Water Group of Overseas Projects Board; member, Overseas Projects Board (all unpaid). Chair, Sale, Tilney

& Co Ltd, 1971-79 (dir 1965-79); general manager, E.S. and A. Robinson, Bristol, 1964-69, joining company in 1956. Chair, Lords and Commons Ski Club. Ed Rugby; Emmanuel Coll, Cambridge.
**MICHAEL HOBAN,** b July 6, 1965. Business development consultant. Contested Feltham and Heston 1992. Founder-member of SDP. Hounslow cllr 1994-95. Ed Furness Comp; York Univ.
**ROGER LAVERS,** b Dec 8, 1943. Maintenance engineer. Somerset cllr since 1989 (Lab group leader since 1991); Sedgemoor district cllr since 1995. Member, Charter 88. Ed Plymouth secondary school.

| BRIGG & GOOLE | | 86.1% change | | | | | | Lab win |
|---|---|---|---|---|---|---|---|---|
| Electorate % Turnout | | 63,648 | 73.5% | | **1997** | 63,013 | 81.2% | **1992** |
| Cawsey, I | Lab | 23,493 | 50.2% | +14.5% | | 25,499 | 49.8% | C |
| Stewart, D M | C | 17,104 | 36.5% | -13.3% | | 18,258 | 35.7% | Lab |
| Hardy, Mrs M | LD | 4,692 | 10.0% | -4.5% | | 7,406 | 14.5% | LD |
| Rigby, D | Ref | 1,513 | 3.2% | | | | | |
| C to Lab notional swing 13.9% | | 46,802 | | Lab maj 6,389 | | 51,163 | | C maj 7,241 |
| | | | | 13.7% | | | | 81.2% |

**IAN CAWSEY,** b April 14, 1960. Contested Brigg and Cleethorpes in 1992. Research asst to Elliot Morley, MP. Humberside county cllr 1989-96; North Lincolnshire Unitary Authority 1995- (council leader 1995- ); chair, Humberside police authority 1993- . Member, Friends of the Earth. Ed Wintringham School, Grimsby. **DONALD STEWART,** b April 30, 1941. Farmer. Contested Hull W 1992, and Humberside in 1994 Euro elections. Member, North Lincs Unitary Council, 1995- (C group leader); Boothferry borough cllr 1973- (Mayor 1987-88; council leader 1992- ; dep leader 1982-92); Humberside county cllr 1973- (leader, C group, 1990-92). Ed Gilmourton School; Kerswell Agricultural Coll. **MARY-ROSE HARDY,** b April 25, 1947. Full-time cllr, East Riding Unitary Authority. Police lay visitor. Ed Chichester HS for Girls; Bath Univ of Tech.

| BRIGHTON KEMPTOWN | | 41.0% change | | | | | | Lab win |
|---|---|---|---|---|---|---|---|---|
| Electorate % Turnout | | 65,147 | 70.8% | | **1997** | 65,932 | 77.1% | **1992** |
| Turner, D | Lab | 21,479 | 46.6% | +14.0% | | 26,828 | 52.8% | C |
| +Bowden, Sir Andrew | C | 17,945 | 38.9% | -13.9% | | 16,571 | 32.6% | Lab |
| Gray, C | LD | 4,478 | 9.7% | -4.2% | | 7,056 | 13.9% | LD |
| Inman, D | Ref | 1,526 | 3.3% | | | 371 | 0.7% | NLP |
| Williams, Ms H | Soc Lab | 316 | 0.7% | | | | | |
| Bowler, J | NLP | 172 | 0.4% | -0.4% | | | | |
| Newman, Ms L | Loony | 123 | 0.3% | | | | | |
| Darlow, R | Dream | 93 | 0.2% | | | | | |
| C to Lab notional swing 13.9% | | 46,132 | | Lab maj 3,534 | | 50,826 | | C maj 10,257 |
| | | | | 7.7% | | | | 77.1% |

**DESMOND TURNER,** b March 17, 1939. Teacher and biochemist. Contested Mid-Sussex 1979. East Sussex county cllr 1985- ; Brighton borough cllr 1994- ; Brighton and Hove unitary cllr 1996- . Founder of Wage-line, campaign for a minimum wage. Ed Luton GS; Imperial Coll and University Coll, London. **SIR ANDREW BOWDEN,** b April 8, 1930. Personnel consultant. Won seat 1970; contested it 1966; Kensington N 1964; Hammersmith N 1955. Member, Commons selection cttee, 1992-97; Commons standing orders cttee, 1992-97. Member, Council of Europe, 1987-97. Parly consultant to Southern Water Services plc; American Express Travel Related Services Ltd; Wyncote Group plc, commercial property developer. Pres, Captive Animals Protection Soc. Ed Ardingly Coll, Sussex (on school council since 1982). **CLIVE GRAY,** b March 7, 1958. Removals operative. Member, United Road Transport Union. Ed Selhurst GS, Croydon; Hadlow Horticulture Coll.

| BRIGHTON PAVILION | | 13.8% change | | | | | | Lab win |
|---|---|---|---|---|---|---|---|---|
| Electorate % Turnout | | 66,431 | 73.7% | | **1997** | 66,008 | 75.7% | **1992** |
| Lepper, D | Lab Co-op | 26,737 | 54.6% | | | 22,619 | 45.3% | C |
| +Spencer, Sir Derek | C | 13,556 | 27.7% | -17.6% | | 20,089 | 40.2% | Lab |
| Blanshard, K C | LD | 4,644 | 9.5% | -2.9% | | 6,169 | 12.3% | LD |
| Stocken, P | Ref | 1,304 | 2.7% | | | 992 | 2.0% | Grn |
| West, P | Green | 1,249 | 2.6% | | | 106 | 0.2% | NLP |
| Huggett, R | Ind C | 1,098 | 2.2% | | | | | |
| Stevens, F | UK Ind | 179 | 0.4% | | | | | |
| Dobbs, B | SG | 125 | 0.3% | | | | | |
| Card, A | Dream | 59 | 0.1% | | | | | |
| C to Lab notional swing 16.0% | | 48,951 | | Lab Co-op maj 13,181 | | 49,975 | | C maj 2,530 |
| | | | | 26.9% | | | | 5.1% |

**DAVID LEPPER,** b Sept 15, 1945. Contested this seat 1992. Retired teacher. Mayor of Brighton 1993-94. Member, Brighton and Hove Unitary Authority; Lab leader of Brighton council 1986-93; elected to council 1980. Ed Wimbledon County Secondary; Kent and Sussex Univs; Central London Poly. **SIR DEREK SPENCER,** b March 31, 1936. QC. Appointed Solicitor-General and knighted on his election for this seat 1992. MP for Leicester S 1983-87. PPS to Sir Michael Havers, Attorney-General, 1986-87, and to David Mellor, Home Office Min, 1986. Joint sec, C backbench legal cttee, 1985-87. Camden cllr 1978-83 (dep C leader 1980-82). Crown Court recorder 1979-92; Bencher, Gray's Inn, 1991. Ed Clitheroe Royal GS; Keble Coll, Oxford. **KENNETH BLANSHARD,** b Aug 28, 1944. IT technical manager. Mid-Sussex district cllr 1991- (leader of council 1995- ). Ed Sir Walter St John's, Battersea; The Skinners' School, Tunbridge Wells; Sussex Univ; Brighton Coll of Tech.

| BRISTOL EAST | | 43.2% change | | | | | Lab win |
|---|---|---|---|---|---|---|---|
| Electorate % Turnout | | 68,990 | 69.9% | **1997** | 69,428 | 78.5% | **1992** |
| **+Corston, Ms J** | **Lab** | **27,418** | **56.9%** | **+9.6%** | 25,754 | 47.3% | Lab |
| Vaizey, E | C | 11,259 | 23.4% | -14.2% | 20,472 | 37.6% | C |
| Tyzack, P | LD | 7,121 | 14.8% | +0.0% | 8,025 | 14.7% | LD |
| Philp, G | Ref | 1,479 | 3.1% | | 251 | 0.5% | NF |
| Williams, P | Soc Lab | 766 | 1.6% | | | | |
| McLaggan, J | NLP | 158 | 0.3% | | | | |
| C to Lab notional swing 11.9% | | 48,201 | Lab maj 16,159 | | 54,502 | Lab maj 5,282 | |
| | | | 33.5% | | | 78.5% | |

**JEAN CORSTON,** b May 5, 1942. Non-practising barrister. Gained this seat for Lab 1992. Member, select cttee on home affairs, 1995-97; on agriculture 1992-95. Chair, all-party parenting matters group, 1996- . Worked at Lab regional office, Bristol 1976-85; at Lab Party HQ 1985-86. Unpaid dir, Tribune Publications Ltd. Ed Yeovil Girls' HS, Somerset; OU; LSE; Inns of Court School of Law.

**EDWARD VAIZEY,** b June 5, 1968. Barrister. C Research Dept 1989-91. Ed St Paul's; Merton Coll, Oxford.
**PETER TYZACK,** b Dec 7, 1946. Estate agent and former teacher. Northavon district cllr and South Gloucester Unitary Authority cllr. Ed Bablake School, Coventry; Shoreditch Coll of Ed.

| BRISTOL NORTH WEST | | 22.9% change | | | | | Lab win |
|---|---|---|---|---|---|---|---|
| Electorate % Turnout | | 75,009 | 73.7% | **1997** | 73,542 | 81.2% | **1992** |
| **Naysmith, D** | **Lab Co-op** | **27,575** | **49.9%** | **+4.7%** | 27,019 | 45.2% | Lab Co-op |
| +Stern, M | C | 16,193 | 29.3% | -9.5% | 23,148 | 38.8% | C |
| Parry, I | LD | 7,263 | 13.1% | -1.7% | 8,849 | 14.8% | LD |
| Horton, C | Ind Lab | 1,718 | 3.1% | | 703 | 1.2% | Soc Dem |
| Quintanilla, J | Ref | 1,609 | 2.9% | | | | |
| Shorter, G | Soc Lab | 482 | 0.9% | | | | |
| Parnell, S | BNP | 265 | 0.5% | | | | |
| Leighton, T | NLP | 140 | 0.3% | | | | |
| C to Lab notional swing 7.1% | | 55,245 | Lab Co-op maj 11,382 | | 59,719 | Lab Co-op maj 3,871 | |
| | | | 20.6% | | | 81.2% | |

**DOUG NAYSMITH,** b April 1, 1941. Medical scientist and lecturer. Contested this seat 1992; Cirencester and Tewkesbury 1987; Bristol in 1979 Euro elections. Nat pres, Socialist Health Assoc. Bristol city cllr, 1981- (chief whip, Lab group, 1988- ; chair, Port of Bristol, 1976- ). Past chair, Bristol district Lab party; chair, Bristol Co-op Party regional council. Ed Musselburgh Burgh School; George Heriot School, Edinburgh; Edinburgh and Yale Univs.
**MICHAEL STERN,** b Aug 3, 1942. Chartered accountant. Elected 1983; contested Derby S 1979. PPS to John Redwood, Corporate

Affairs Min 1990-91; to Peter Brooke, Treasury Min and Party Chairman, 1986-89. Member, PAC, 1992-97. Vice-chair, C Party, 1991-92; chief finance officer, C Party, 1991-92. Consultant to Cohen Arnold & Co, chartered accountants. Member, editorial board, *Taxation.* Ed Christ's Coll GS, Finchley.
**IAN PARRY,** b May 12, 1962. Chartered accountant. Bristol city cllr. Dir, Coteval Ltd. Ed Meadway School, Reading; Univ Coll of Wales, Cardiff.

| BRISTOL SOUTH | | 16.0% change | | | | | Lab win |
|---|---|---|---|---|---|---|---|
| Electorate % Turnout | | 72,393 | 68.9% | **1997** | 75,860 | 76.0% | **1992** |
| **+Primarolo, Ms D** | **Lab** | **29,890** | **59.9%** | **+12.7%** | 27,259 | 47.3% | Lab |
| Roe, M | C | 10,562 | 21.2% | -12.0% | 19,144 | 33.2% | C |
| Williams, S | LD | 6,691 | 13.4% | -4.5% | 10,361 | 18.0% | LD |
| Guy, D | Ref | 1,486 | 3.0% | | 768 | 1.3% | Grn |
| Boxall, J | Green | 722 | 1.4% | | 143 | 0.2% | NLP |
| Marshall, I | Soc | 355 | 0.7% | | | | |
| Taylor, L | Glow | 153 | 0.3% | | | | |
| C to Lab notional swing 12.3% | | 49,859 | Lab maj 19,328 | | 57,675 | Lab maj 8,115 | |
| | | | 38.8% | | | 76.0% | |

**DAWN PRIMAROLO,** b May 2, 1954. Became Financial Sec to the Treasury, May 5, 1997. Ex-researcher. Elected 1987. Party spokesman on Treasury matters 1994; spokesman on health 1992-94. Member, members' interests select cttee 1988-92. Avon county cllr 1985-87. Ex-sec, Bristol South East CLP; chair, Bristol District Lab Party; SW rep, Nat Lab Women's Cttee. Ed Thomas Bennett Comp, Crawley; Bristol Poly; Bristol Univ.

**MICHAEL ROE,** b Sept 7, 1951. Computer consultant. Vice-chair, Weston-super-Mare C assoc. Avon county cllr 1993. Ed Weston-super-Mare Coll of HE.
**STEVEN WILLIAMS,** b Oct 11, 1966. Tax consultant. Avon county cllr 1993-95; Bristol city cllr 1995- (leader of LD group and of Opposition). Ed Mountain Ash Comp, Glamorgan; Bristol Univ.

| BRISTOL WEST | | 11.8% change | | | | | Lab win |
|---|---|---|---|---|---|---|---|
| Electorate % Turnout | | 84,870 | 73.8% | **1997** | 77,906 | 76.3% | **1992** |
| **Davey, Ms V** | **Lab** | **22,068** | **35.2%** | **+11.9%** | 26,850 | 45.1% | C |
| +Waldegrave, W | C | 20,575 | 32.8% | -12.3% | 17,356 | 29.2% | LD |
| Boney, C | LD | 17,551 | 28.0% | -1.2% | 13,900 | 23.4% | Lab |
| Beauchamp, Lady | Ref | 1,304 | 2.1% | 1,002 | 1.7% | | Grn |
| Quinnell, J | Green | 852 | 1.4% | | 115 | 0.2% | NLP |
| Nurse, R | Soc Lab | 244 | 0.4% | | 103 | 0.2% | Rev Comm |
| Brierley, J | NLP | 47 | 0.1% | -0.1% | 98 | 0.2% | SOADDA |
| | | | | | 53 | 0.1% | Anti-Fed |
| **C to Lab notional swing 12.1%** | | **62,641** | | Lab maj 1,493 | **59,477** | | C maj 9,494 |
| | | | | 2.4% | | | 16.0% |

**VALERIE DAVEY,** b April 16, 1940. Teacher. Avon county cllr 1981-96 (leader, Lab group, 1992-96). Member, NUT; SEA; Amnesty; Lab Campaign for Electoral Reform. Ed Birmingham and London Univs.

**WILLIAM WALDEGRAVE,** b Aug 15, 1949. MP for Bristol W 1979-97. Chief Secretary to the Treasury 1995-97; Min of Agriculture 1994-95; Chancellor of Duchy of Lancaster and Min for Citizen's Charter 1992-94; appointed to Cabinet 1990 as Health Sec; Foreign Office Min 1988-90; Environment Min 1983-88; Education Under Sec

1981-83. Member, Central Policy Review Staff, Cabinet Office 1971-73. Ed Eton; Corpus Christi Coll, Oxford (pres of Union and of C assoc); Harvard (Kennedy Fellow in Politics). Fellow, All Souls Coll, Oxford, 1971-86.

**CHARLES BONEY,** b March 21, 1950. Teacher. Contested this seat 1992; Bristol for LDs in 1989 Euro elections, and Salisbury for LDs in 1979 general election. Bristol city cllr 1979-81 for Lab, 1981-82 for Libs, and from 1986 as Lib and LD. Ed Felsted School, Essex; Bristol Univ.

| BROMLEY & CHISLEHURST | | 82.0% change | | | | | C win |
|---|---|---|---|---|---|---|---|
| Electorate % Turnout | | 71,104 | 74.2% | **1997** | 73,653 | 79.0% | **1992** |
| **+Forth, M E** | **C** | **24,428** | **46.3%** | **-15.6%** | 36,028 | 62.0% | C |
| Yeldham, R | Lab | 13,310 | 25.2% | +8.0% | 10,370 | 17.8% | LD |
| Booth, Dr P | LD | 12,530 | 23.8% | +5.9% | 10,027 | 17.2% | Lab |
| Bryant, R | UK Ind | 1,176 | 2.2% | | 1,725 | 3.0% | Other |
| Speed, Ms F | Green | 640 | 1.2% | | | | |
| Stoneman, M | NF | 369 | 0.7% | | | | |
| Aitman, G | Lib | 285 | 0.5% | | | | |
| **C to Lab notional swing 11.8%** | | **52,738** | | C maj 11,118 | **58,150** | | C maj 25,658 |
| | | | | 21.1% | | | 79.0% |

**ERIC FORTH,** b Sept 9, 1944. MP for Mid Worcestershire 1983-97; contested Barking, Feb and Oct 1974. MEP for N Birmingham 1979-84. Education and Employment Min 1995-97; Education Min 1994-95; Education Under Sec 1992-94, and for employment 1990-92; Consumer Affairs Under Sec 1988-90. PPS to Educ and Science Min 1986-87. Chair (1987-88) and vice-chair (1983-86), C backbench European affairs cttee; member, employment select

cttee, 1983-87; sec, C backbench sports cttee, 1985-86. Ed Jordanhill Coll School, Glasgow; Glasgow Univ.

**ROB YELDHAM,** b May 9, 1967. Public relations manager/parliamentary officer. Bromley borough cllr 1994- . Member, Co-op Party; MSF. Ed Wanstead HS; Kent Univ.

**PAUL BOOTH,** b Oct 7, 1951. Charity administrator. Contested Ravensbourne 1992. Bromley borough cllr 1988- . Ed Univ Coll of Wales, Cardiff.

| BROMSGROVE | | 0.2% change | | | | | C win |
|---|---|---|---|---|---|---|---|
| Electorate % Turnout | | 67,744 | 77.1% | **1997** | 71,079 | 82.7% | **1992** |
| **Kirkbride, Miss J** | **C** | **24,620** | **47.2%** | **-6.9%** | 31,773 | 54.1% | C |
| McDonald, P | Lab | 19,725 | 37.8% | +7.1% | 18,021 | 30.7% | Lab |
| Davy, Mrs J | LD | 6,200 | 11.9% | -1.9% | 8,118 | 13.8% | LD |
| Winsor, Mrs D | Ref | 1,411 | 2.7% | | 858 | 1.5% | Grn |
| Wetton, Mrs B | UK Ind | 251 | 0.5% | | | | |
| **C to Lab notional swing 7.0%** | | **52,207** | | C maj 4,895 | **58,770** | | C maj 13,752 |
| | | | | 9.4% | | | 82.7% |

**JULIE KIRKBRIDE,** b June 5, 1960. Ex-social affairs editor, *Sunday Telegraph*; political reporter, *Daily Telegraph*. Member, Halifax YCs, 1974-78. Ed Highlands GS; Girton Coll, Cambridge (vice-pres of Union).

**PETER McDONALD,** b March 17, 1947. Lecturer in business studies, economics, law.

**JENNETTE DAVY,** b Sept 18, 1938. Community services volunteer. Contested E Staffordshire 1996 by-election. Hereford & Worcester county cllr 1985- ; Malvern Hills district cllr 1983- ; Malvern town cllr. Ed Blackpool Commercial Coll.

| BROXBOURNE | | 8.7% change | | | | | | C win |
|---|---|---|---|---|---|---|---|---|
| Electorate % Turnout | | | 66,720 | 70.4% | **1997** | 66,062 | 79.0% | **1992** |
| +Roe, Mrs M | C | | **22,952** | 48.9% | -13.4% | **32,518** | 62.3% | C |
| Coleman, B | Lab | | 16,299 | 34.7% | +13.3% | 11,168 | 21.4% | Lab |
| Davies, Mrs J | LD | | 5,310 | 11.3% | -4.7% | 8,353 | 16.0% | LD |
| Millward, D | Ref | | 1,633 | 3.5% | | 181 | 0.3% | NLP |
| Bruce, D | BNP | | 610 | 1.3% | | | | |
| Cheetham, B | Third | | 172 | 0.4% | | | | |
| C to Lab notional swing 13.4% | | | **46,976** | | **C maj 6,653** 14.2% | **52,220** | | **C maj 21,350** 40.9% |

**MARION ROE**, b July 15, 1936. Elected 1983; contested Barking 1979. Elected joint sec, 1922 Cttee, May 21, 1997. Environment Under Sec 1987-88. Chair, select cttee on health, 1992-97; member, select cttees on procedure, 1991-92; sittings of Commons 1991-94; Commons administration 1991-97; social services 1988-89. Chair, all-party hospice parly group, 1992- ; joint vice-chair, gardening group, 1995- ; sec, British Canadian group, 1991- . Chair, C backbench social security cttee, 1990- ; joint vice-chair, C environment cttee, 1990- . Member, UK cttee, Euro research group; advisory cttee on women's employment, 1989- . Substitute member, UK delegation to Council of Europe and WEU, 1989-92. Managing trustee, parlycontributory pension fund, 1990- . Vice-pres, Women's Nat Cancer Control Campaign, 1985- . Freeman, City of London; Liveryman, Gardeners Company. Ed Bromley HS; Croydon HS; English School of Languages, Vevey.

**BEN COLEMAN**, b July 5, 1962. Public affairs consultant. Member, Friends of the Earth; Amnesty; Charter 88; Foundation for Victims of Torture. Ed Hampstead School; Liverpool Univ.

**JULIA DAVIES**, b July 7, 1952. Teacher. Contested Broxbourne 1992. Member, Green Democrats. Ed Merchant Taylors' Girls' School, Crosby; Bedford Coll; London Univ.

| BROXTOWE | | 0.2% change | | | | | | Lab win |
|---|---|---|---|---|---|---|---|---|
| Electorate % Turnout | | | 74,144 | 78.4% | **1997** | 73,754 | 82.5% | **1992** |
| Palmer, N | Lab | | **27,343** | 47.0% | +12.3% | **31,033** | 51.0% | C |
| +Lester, Sir James | C | | 21,768 | 37.4% | -13.5% | 21,162 | 34.8% | Lab |
| Miller, T | LD | | 6,934 | 11.9% | -1.8% | 8,378 | 13.8% | LD |
| Tucker, R | Ref | | 2,092 | 3.6% | | 293 | 0.5% | NLP |
| C to Lab notional swing 12.9% | | | **58,137** | | **Lab maj 5,575** 9.6% | **60,866** | | **C maj 9,871** 82.5% |

**NICK PALMER**, b Feb 5, 1950. Computing manager. Contested Chelsea 1983; East Sussex and Kent South in 1994 Euro elections. Ed London Univ; Copenhagen Univ.

**SIR JAMES LESTER**, b May 23, 1932. First elected for this seat 1983; MP for Beeston 1974-83. Contested Bassetlaw, 1968 by-election and 1970. Employment Under Sec 1979-81. C whip 1975-79. Member, foreign affairs select cttee 1982-97; chair, C backbench employment cttee, 1987-89 and 1983. Notts county cllr 1967-74. Former chair, all-party parly group on overseas development; refugees group; sec, association football group; chair, British-Vietnam group; joint chair, Kenya group. Former parly consultant to Direct Selling Assoc; Assoc of First Div Civil Servants; BAT Industries; Fed of CMA/IPMS; Priory Hospital Group Ltd. Ed Nottingham HS.

**TERRY MILLER**, b Dec 13, 1946. Ex-retailer/full-time cllr. Broxtowe borough cllr 1991-95; Notts county cllr (dep whip). Member LD Christian Forum. Ed Northwood Hills Sec Mod, Middlesex.

| BUCKINGHAM | | 5.7% change | | | | | | C win |
|---|---|---|---|---|---|---|---|---|
| Electorate % Turnout | | | 62,945 | 78.5% | **1997** | 59,535 | 83.7% | **1992** |
| Bercow, J S | C | | **24,594** | 49.8% | -12.5% | **31,045** | 62.3% | C |
| Lehmann, R | Lab | | 12,208 | 24.7% | +8.7% | 10,401 | 20.9% | LD |
| Stuart, N | LD | | 12,175 | 24.6% | +3.8% | 7,999 | 16.1% | Lab |
| Clements, Dr G | NLP | | 421 | 0.9% | +0.1% | 391 | 0.8% | NLP |
| C to Lab notional swing 10.6% | | | **49,398** | | **C maj 12,386** 25.1% | **49,836** | | **C maj 20,644** 83.7% |

**JOHN BERCOW**, b Jan 19, 1963. Won this seat 1997. Contested Bristol S 1992; Motherwell S 1987. Nat chair, Fed of C Students, 1986- . Special adviser to Virginia Bottomley, Nat Heritage Sec, 1995-96, and previously to Treasury Min. Lambeth cllr 1986-90 (dep C group leader, 1987-89). Senior consultant, Westminster Strategy. Former dir of Roland Sallingbury Casey; credit analyst with Hambros Bank 1987-88. Ed Finchley Manorhill School; Essex Univ.

**ROBERT LEHMANN**, b Dec 29, 1951. Managing director, WV Publications. Aylesbury Vale district cllr (dep leader, Lab group). Member, Labour's Rural Revival. Ed Sir Henry Floyd School, Aylesbury; LSE; Kingston Poly.

**NEIL STUART**, b May 14, 1947. Computer-aided facilities manager. Leader, Aylesbury Vale District Council. Ed Slough GS.

| BURNLEY | | | | | Lab hold | | |
|---|---|---|---|---|---|---|---|
| Electorate % Turnout | | 67,582 | 66.9% | **1997** | 68,952 | 74.4% | **1992** |
| *Pike, P | Lab | 26,210 | 57.9% | +4.9% | 27,184 | 53.0% | Lab |
| Wiggin, W | C | 9,148 | 20.2% | -10.4% | 15,693 | 30.6% | C |
| Birtwistle, G | LD | 7,877 | 17.4% | +1.0% | 8,414 | 16.4% | LD |
| Oakley, R | Ref | 2,010 | 4.4% | | | | |
| C to Lab swing 7.7% | | 45,245 | Lab maj 17,062 | | 51,291 | Lab maj 11,491 | |
| | | | | 37.7% | | | 74.4% |

**PETER PIKE,** b June 26, 1937. Elected 1983. Lab spokesman on housing 1992-94; on rural affairs 1990-92. Member, select cttees on deregulation, 1995-97; procedure, 1995-97; environment, 1985-90. Merton and Morden cllr 1962-63; Burnley borough cllr 1976-84. Production worker (inspection), 1973-83. Lab Party organiser and agent 1963-73; union shop steward 1976-83. Ed Hinchley Wood Sec School; Kingston Tech Coll.

**BILL WIGGIN,** b June 4, 1966. Foreign exchange trader. Vice-chair, Hammersmith and Fulham C assoc 1996. Governor, Hammersmith and West London Coll for FE. Ed Eton; Univ Coll of North Wales.

**GORDON BIRTWISTLE,** b Sept 6, 1943. Managing director of engineering supplies company. Burnley borough cllr (LD group leader). Ed Hindburn Park Sec Mod; Accrington Coll of FE.

| BURTON | **4.9% change** | | | | | Lab win | | |
|---|---|---|---|---|---|---|---|---|
| Electorate % Turnout | | 72,601 | 75.1% | **1997** | 72,244 | 81.7% | **1992** |
| Dean, Ms J | Lab | 27,810 | 51.0% | +9.8% | 28,454 | 48.2% | C |
| +Lawrence, Sir Ivan | C | 21,480 | 39.4% | -8.8% | 24,327 | 41.2% | Lab |
| Fletcher, D | LD | 4,617 | 8.5% | -2.1% | 6,219 | 10.5% | LD |
| Sharp, K | Nat Dem | 604 | 1.1% | | | | |
| C to Lab notional swing 9.3% | | 54,511 | Lab maj 6,330 | | 59,000 | C maj 4,127 | |
| | | | | 11.6% | | | 81.7% |

**JANET DEAN,** b Jan 28, 1949. Staffordshire cllr 1981- ; East Staffordshire borough cllr 1991- (Mayor). Founder member, Uttoxeter crime prevention panel; chair, Uttoxeter CAB. Ed Winsford Verdin GS, Cheshire.

**SIR IVAN LAWRENCE,** b Dec 24, 1936. QC. Elected Feb 1974. Contested Peckham 1966 and 1970. Member, exec, 1922 Cttee, 1988-89 and 1992-97. Chair, home affairs select cttee, 1992-97; member, foreign affairs select cttee, 1983-92. Chair, all-party barristers group, 1987-97. Chair 1988-97, C backbench home affairs cttee; chair, 1987-97, C legal cttee. Hon Bencher 1991;

Crown Court recorder 1987- ; asst recorder 1983-87. Member, exec, Soc of C Lawyers, 1989- . Member, UK cttee, Euro Research Group. Member, exec cttee, UK branch, CPA, 1994- ; vice-chair, C Friends of Israel, 1994- . Chair, Burton Breweries charitable trust, 1982- . Member, Council of Justice, 1989-95; council, Statute Law Soc, 1985-95. Ed Brighton, Hove and Sussex GS; Christ Church, Oxford.

**DAVID FLETCHER,** b Nov 22, 1933. Retired railway executive. Ed Derby GS; LSE.

| BURY NORTH | | | | | Lab gain | | |
|---|---|---|---|---|---|---|---|
| Electorate % Turnout | | 70,515 | 78.1% | **1997** | 69,529 | 84.8% | **1992** |
| Chaytor, D M | Lab | 28,523 | 51.8% | +10.2% | 29,266 | 49.7% | C |
| *Burt, A | C | 20,657 | 37.5% | -12.1% | 24,502 | 41.6% | Lab |
| Kenyon, N | LD | 4,536 | 8.2% | -0.3% | 5,010 | 8.5% | LD |
| Hallewell, R | Ref | 1,337 | 2.4% | | 163 | 0.3% | NLP |
| C to Lab swing 11.2% | | 55,053 | Lab maj 7,866 | | 58,941 | C maj 4,764 | |
| | | | | 14.3% | | | 84.8% |

**DAVID CHAYTOR,** b Aug 3, 1949. Ex-senior staff tutor and head of continuing education, Manchester Coll of Arts and Tech. Contested Calder Valley 1992 and 1987. Calderdale borough cllr 1982- . Member, full employment forum; NATFHE; TGWU. Ed Bury GS; Huddersfield Poly; London and Bradford Univs.

**ALISTAIR BURT,** b May 25, 1955. Solicitor. Elected 1983. Min for Social Security and Disabled People, 1995-97; Social Security Under Sec with responsibility for the Child Support Agency 1992-

95. PPS to Kenneth Baker 1985-90. Joint vice-chair, C backbench European affairs cttee, 1991-92. Member, select cttee on sittings of Commons, 1991-92. Joint sec, C backbench energy cttee, 1983-85; Christian Fellowship group 1984-97; joint vice-chair, tertiary colleges association group, 1990-92. Haringey cllr 1982-84. Ed Bury GS; St John's Coll, Oxford.

**NEVILLE KENYON,** b May 2, 1937. Company director, Stamford Group Ltd. Ed Stand GS, Manchester.

| BURY SOUTH | | 0.4% change | | | | | Lab win |
|---|---|---|---|---|---|---|---|
| Electorate % Turnout | | 66,568 | 75.6% | **1997** | 66,391 | 81.6% | **1992** |
| **Lewis, I** | Lab | **28,658** | 56.9% | +12.3% | **24,925** | 46.0% | C |
| +Sumberg, D | C | 16,225 | 32.2% | -13.7% | 24,197 | 44.6% | Lab |
| D'Albert, V | LD | 4,227 | 8.4% | -0.6% | 4,853 | 9.0% | LD |
| Slater, B | Ref | 1,216 | 2.4% | | 229 | 0.4% | NLP |
| **C to Lab notional swing 13.0%** | | **50,326** | Lab maj 12,433 | | **54,204** | C maj 728 | |
| | | | 24.7% | | | 81.6% | |

**IVAN LEWIS,** b March 4, 1967. Chief exec, Jewish Social Services, Greater Manchester (a charity); chair, North Manchester Jewish youth project. Bury borough cllr, 1990- . Chair, Bury South CLP, 1991-96. Ed William Hulme's GS; Stand Sixth-Form Coll.

**DAVID SUMBERG,** b June 2, 1941. Solicitor. Elected 1983. Contested Manchester Wythenshawe 1979. PPS to Sir Patrick Mayhew, Solicitor-General and then Attorney-General, 1986-90. Member, select cttees on foreign affairs, 1992-97; home affairs, 1991-92. Joint vice-chair, all-party war crimes group; Inter-parly Council against Anti-Semitism; industrial safety group; British-Singapore group; sec, magic group. Manchester city cllr 1982- . Member, advisory council on public records, 1993-94. Dir, Irwell Insurance Co Ltd; consultant to Eversheds, solicitors; parly consultant to Newport Capital Ltd. Ed Tettenhall Coll, Wolverhampton; Coll of Law, London.

**VICTOR D'ALBERT,** b Feb 5, 1959. Accountant. Bury cllr (leader, LDs). Ed King's Heath Tech, Birmingham; Brooklyn Coll; Tameside Coll.

| BURY ST EDMUNDS | | 96.9% change | | | | | C win |
|---|---|---|---|---|---|---|---|
| Electorate % Turnout | | 74,017 | 75.0% | **1997** | 70,181 | 79.9% | **1992** |
| **Ruffley, D** | C | **21,290** | 38.3% | -7.6% | **25,742** | 45.9% | C |
| Ereira-Guyer, M | Lab | 20,922 | 37.7% | +11.7% | 15,097 | 26.9% | LD |
| Cooper, D A | LD | 10,102 | 18.2% | -8.7% | 14,565 | 26.0% | Lab |
| McWhirter, I | Ref | 2,939 | 5.3% | | 666 | 1.2% | NLP |
| Lillis, Mrs J | NLP | 272 | 0.5% | -0.7% | | | |
| **C to Lab notional swing 9.6%** | | **55,525** | C maj 368 | | **56,070** | C maj 10,645 | |
| | | | 0.7% | | | 79.9% | |

**DAVID RUFFLEY,** b April 18, 1962. Solicitor. Special adviser to Secretary of State for Education and Science 1991-92; Home Office 1992-93; Chancellor of the Exchequer 1993-96. Consultant, Grant Maintained Schools Foundation 1991- . Ed Bolton School; Queens' Coll, Cambridge.

**MARK EREIRA-GUYER,** b Dec 14, 1961. Charity worker; former Home Office civil servant. Member, Suffolk acre rural community council; Amnesty; Greenpeace; Lab Campaign for Electoral Reform. Ed King's, Ely; Cambridge Coll of Arts and Tech; Kent Univ.

**DAVID COOPER,** b Sept 4, 1947. Charity co-ordinator and ex-teacher. Suffolk Coastal district cllr 1995- . Member, Evangelical Alliance. Ed Christopher Wren Comp, London; Canley Teacher Training Coll, Coventry.

| CAERNARFON | | | | | | | PC hold |
|---|---|---|---|---|---|---|---|
| Electorate % Turnout | | 46,815 | 72.6% | **1997** | 46,468 | 78.2% | **1992** |
| ***Wigley, D** | PC | **17,616** | 51.8% | -7.2% | **21,439** | 59.0% | PC |
| Williams, Eifion | Lab | 10,167 | 29.5% | +14% | 6,963 | 19.2% | C |
| Williams, Elwyn | C | 4,230 | 12.4% | -6.7% | 5,641 | 15.5% | Lab |
| McQueen, Ms M | LD | 1,686 | 5.0% | -0.8% | 2,101 | 5.8% | LD |
| Collins, C | Ref | 811 | 2.4% | | 173 | 0.5% | NLP |
| **PC to Lab swing 10.6%** | | **34,510** | PC maj 7,449 | | **36,317** | PC maj 14,476 | |
| | | | 21.6% | | | 39.9% | |

**DAFYDD WIGLEY,** b April 1, 1943. Won seat Feb 1974. Contested Merioneth 1970; Wales North in 1994 Euro elections. Pres of Plaid Cymru 1991- and 1981-84; also PC parly leader. Member, Welsh select cttee, 1983-87. Vice-chair, all-party human genetics group; disablement group 1992- ; treas, all-party osteoporosis group, 1996- . Sponsored Disabled Persons Act 1981. Merthyr cllr 1972-74. Pres, Spastics Soc of Wales, 1985-90; vice-pres, Wales Council for the Disabled. Ex-industrial economist, financial controller. Member, Nat Cttee for Electoral Reform. Ed Caernarfon GS; Rydal School, Colwyn Bay; Manchester Univ. Fellow, Univ of Wales, Bangor, 1994.

**EIFION WILLIAMS,** b Sept 14, 1970. Theatre director. Researcher to Alan Williams, MP. Chair, Aberystwyth Univ Lab Club, 1992-93; Lab Wales Youth Forum. Ed Plas Coch College of FE; Aberystwyth Univ.

**ELWYN WILLIAMS,** b March 9, 1935. Sheep farmer, bank manager. Member Conservative 2000 Federation. Ed John Bright's School; Friars GS, Bangor; Bala GS.

**MARY McQUEEN,** b Feb 6, 1950. Museum consultant and antiquities conservator. Member, Unison. Ed St Elphin's Darley Dale; St Mary's, Paddington, Orthopaedic Hospital; Oswestry spinal unit; London Univ Inst of Archeology; SE London Univ.

## CAERPHILLY — Lab hold

| Electorate % Turnout | | | 64,621 | 70.1% | 1997 | 64,529 | 77.2% | 1992 |
|---|---|---|---|---|---|---|---|---|
| *Davies, R | | Lab | 30,697 | 67.8% | +4.2% | 31,713 | 63.7% | Lab |
| Harris, R | | C | 4,858 | 10.7% | -7.4% | 9,041 | 18.1% | C |
| Whittle, L | | PC | 4,383 | 9.7% | +0.0% | 4,821 | 9.7% | PC |
| Ferguson, A | | LD | 3,724 | 8.2% | -0.3% | 4,247 | 8.5% | LD |
| Morgan, M | | Ref | 1,337 | 3.0% | | | | |
| Williams, Mrs C | | ProLife | 270 | 0.6% | | | | |
| C to Lab swing 5.8% | | | 45,269 | Lab maj 25,839 | | 49,822 | Lab maj 22,672 | |
| | | | | 57.1% | | | 77.2% | |

**RONALD DAVIES,** b Aug 6, 1946. Became Welsh Secretary May 3, 1997. Shadow Welsh Sec 1993-97. Elected 1983. Elected to Shadow Cabinet 1992; Lab spokesman on food, agriculture and rural affairs 1987-93; Lab whip 1985-87. Contested election for Lab chief whip 1988. Further ed adviser, Mid Glamorgan County Council, 1974-83; tutor-organiser, WEA, 1970-74; teacher 1968-70. Bedwas and Machen cllr and Rhymney Valley cllr 1969-84. Ed Bassaleg GS; Portsmouth Poly; Univ Coll of Wales, Cardiff.

**RHODRI HARRIS,** b Jan 7, 1950. Accountant. Greenwich cllr 1992-94. Ed grammar school; Kent Univ.
**LINDSAY WHITTLE,** b March 24, 1953. Housing officer. Contested this seat 1992, 1987 and 1983. Rhymney Valley district cllr 1976-96, Caerphilly county borough cllr (group leader); Mid-Glamorgan county cllr 1977-81. Ed Caerphilly Grammar Tech School.
**TONY FERGUSON,** b Sept 12, 1961. Systems analyst. Newbury district cllr (dep leader). Ed Marlborough; Essex Univ.

## CAITHNESS, SUTHERLAND & EASTER ROSS — 32.5% change — LD win

| Electorate % Turnout | | | 41,566 | 70.2% | 1997 | 41,318 | 71.7% | 1992 |
|---|---|---|---|---|---|---|---|---|
| +Maclennan, R A R | | LD | 10,381 | 35.6% | -8.8% | 13,150 | 44.4% | LD |
| Hendry, J | | Lab | 8,122 | 27.8% | +12.2% | 6,391 | 21.6% | C |
| Harper, E | | SNP | 6,710 | 23.0% | +4.6% | 5,440 | 18.4% | SNP |
| Miers, T | | C | 3,148 | 10.8% | -10.8% | 4,629 | 15.6% | Lab |
| Ryder, Ms C | | Ref | 369 | 1.3% | | | | |
| Martin, J | | Green | 230 | 0.8% | | | | |
| Carr, M | | UK Ind | 212 | 0.7% | | | | |
| LD to Lab notional swing 10.5% | | | 29,172 | LD maj 2,259 | | 29,610 | LD maj 6,759 | |
| | | | | 7.7% | | | 71.7% | |

**ROBERT MACLENNAN,** b June 26, 1936. Won Caithness and Sutherland for Lab 1966; joined SDP 1981, retained seat 1983 and 1987, and for LD in 1992. Pres of LDs 1994- ; party spokesman, national heritage, broadcasting and constitution, 1994- , and previously on home affairs and arts, 1988-94. Leader of SDP 1987-88 until merger with Libs to form Social and Lib Dem Party; joint interim leader 1988. SDP spokesman on home and legal affairs and N Ireland 1983-88, on Scotland 1982-88, and agriculture and fisheries 1982-83; Member, PAC, 1979- .

Prices and Consumer Protection under sec 1974-79. Dir, Atlantic Tele-Network Inc. Ed Glasgow Acad; Balliol Coll, Oxford; Trinity Coll, Cambridge; Columbia Univ, New York.
**JAMES HENDRY,** b Sept 10, 1958. Solicitor. Highland regional cllr 1989- . Member, TGWU. Ed Elgin Acad; Aberdeen Univ.
**EUAN HARPER,** b Feb 7, 1969. Ex-British Rail worker. Highland regional cllr 1990- . Ed Lochaber HS.
**TOM MIERS,** b July 7, 1971. Banker. Ed Winchester; Edinburgh Univ.

## CALDER VALLEY — Lab gain

| Electorate % Turnout | | | 74,901 | 75.4% | 1997 | 74,417 | 82.1% | 1992 |
|---|---|---|---|---|---|---|---|---|
| McCafferty, Ms C | | Lab | 26,050 | 46.1% | +8.7% | 27,753 | 45.4% | C |
| *Thompson, Sir Donald | | C | 19,795 | 35.1% | -10.4% | 22,875 | 37.4% | Lab |
| Pearson, S | | LD | 8,322 | 14.7% | -1.4% | 9,842 | 16.1% | LD |
| Mellor, A | | Ref | 1,380 | 2.4% | | 622 | 1.0% | Grn |
| Smith, Ms V | | Green | 488 | 0.9% | | | | |
| Jackson, C | | BNP | 431 | 0.8% | | | | |
| C to Lab swing 9.5% | | | 56,466 | Lab maj 6,255 | | 61,092 | C maj 4,878 | |
| | | | | 11.1% | | | 82.1% | |

**CHRISTINE McCAFFERTY,** b Oct 14, 1945. Manager of well woman health centre. Calderdale district cllr; Calderdale rep on police authority, and chair, policy community forum. Lay prison visitor. Member, MSF. Chair, Calderdale Domestic Violence Forum. Ed Whalley Range GS for Girls; Footscray HS, Victoria, Australia.
**SIR DONALD THOMPSON,** b Nov 13, 1931. Elected for this seat 1983; MP for Sowerby 1979-83; contested it in both 1974 elections, and Batley and Morley 1970. Junior Agriculture Min 1986-89; gvt

whip 1983-86; asst gvt whip 1981-83. Member, exec, 1922 Cttee, 1989-97; Commons privileges cttee, 1994-95. Calderdale borough cllr 1975-79; W Yorkshire county cllr 1974-75; West Riding county cllr 1967-74. Adviser to British Agrochemicals Assoc; Nat Caravan Council. Ed Hipperholme GS.
**STEPHEN PEARSON,** b July 4, 1955. Company director. Contested this seat 1992. Leader, Calderdale Metropolitan Borough Council, 1990- . Ed Bradford Univ.

## CAMBERWELL & PECKHAM — 34.6% change — Lab win

| Electorate % Turnout | | 50,214 | 56.7% | 1997 | 64,229 | 51.3% | 1992 |
|---|---|---|---|---|---|---|---|
| +Harman, Ms H | Lab | 19,734 | 69.3% | +8.9% | 19,891 | 60.4% | Lab |
| Humphreys, K | C | 3,383 | 11.9% | -11.9% | 7,841 | 23.8% | C |
| Williams, N | LD | 3,198 | 11.2% | -3.9% | 4,974 | 15.1% | LD |
| China, N | Ref | 692 | 2.4% | | 244 | 0.7% | Other |
| Ruddock, Ms A | Soc Lab | 685 | 2.4% | | | | |
| Williams, G | Lib | 443 | 1.6% | | | | |
| Barker, Ms J | Soc | 233 | 0.8% | | | | |
| Eames, C | WRP | 106 | 0.4% | | | | |
| C to Lab notional swing 10.4% | | 28,474 | | Lab maj 16,351 | 32,950 | | Lab maj 12,050 |
| | | | | 57.4% | | | 51.3% |

**HARRIET HARMAN,** b July 30, 1950. Became Social Security Secretary, May 3, 1997. Elected for this seat 1997; MP for Peckham 1982-97. Chief Lab spokesman on social security 1996; chief spokesman on health 1995-96; on employment 1994-95. In Shadow Cabinet 1992-93 and since 1994; Shadow Chief Sec to the Treasury 1992-93, retaining post when defeated in 1993 Shadow Cabinet elections; member, NEC, 1993- . Joined Lab frontbench DHSS team in 1985, being responsible for health issues from 1987. Solicitor and civil rights campaigner. Legal officer, Nat Council for Civil Liberties, 1978-82; Brent Community Law Centre, 1975-78. Ed St Paul's Girls' School; York Univ.

**KIM HUMPHREYS,** b Aug 29, 1965. Fuji Bank executive. Southwark cllr 1994. Senior research exec, Ian Greer Associates, 1993-94. Ed Eton; Trinity Coll, Dublin.

**NIGEL WILLIAMS,** b Jan 21, 1955. Charity director. Southwark cllr 1994- . Ed Portadown Coll, Co Armagh; Downing Coll, Cambridge.

## CAMBRIDGE — Lab hold

| Electorate % Turnout | | 71,669 | 71.6% | 1997 | 69,022 | 73.2% | 1992 |
|---|---|---|---|---|---|---|---|
| *Campbell, Mrs A | Lab | 27,436 | 53.4% | +13.8% | 20,039 | 39.7% | Lab |
| Platt, D | C | 13,299 | 25.9% | -12.6% | 19,459 | 38.5% | C |
| Heathcock, G | LD | 8,287 | 16.1% | -3.7% | 10,037 | 19.9% | LD |
| Burrows, W | Ref | 1,262 | 2.5% | | 720 | 1.4% | Grn |
| Wright, Ms M | Green | 654 | 1.3% | | 175 | 0.3% | Loony |
| Johnstone, Ms A | ProLife | 191 | 0.4% | | 83 | 0.2% | NLP |
| Athow, R | WRP | 107 | 0.2% | | | | |
| Gladwin, Ms P | NLP | 103 | 0.2% | +0.0% | | | |
| C to Lab swing 13.2% | | 51,339 | | Lab maj 14,137 | 50,513 | | Lab maj 580 |
| | | | | 27.5% | | | 73.2% |

**ANNE CAMPBELL,** b April 6, 1940. Won this seat 1992. Member, select cttee on science and tech, 1992- ; joint vice-pres, 1996- , and chair, parly and scientific ctte, 1994-96. Head of statistics and data processing dept, Nat Inst of Agricultural Botany, Cambridge, 1983-92. Senior lecturer in statistics, Cambridge Coll of arts and tech, 1970-83. Cambridgeshire cllr 1985-89. Dir, Welding Institute; unpaid dir, Science Policy Support Group. Fellow, Inst of Statisticians and Royal Statistical Soc. FRSA. Ed Newnham Coll, Cambridge.

**DAVID PLATT,** b Sept 13, 1964. Barrister and broadcaster. Vice-chair, Central London YCs, 1988; exec member, CPRE, 1989-91. Ed Campbell Coll, Belfast; Trinity Hall, Cambridge.

**GEOFFREY HEATHCOCK,** b Dec 8, 1952. Administration supervisor. Cambridgeshire county cllr 1993- . Ed Liskeard County Secondary.

## CAMBRIDGESHIRE NORTH EAST — 8.3% change — C win

| Electorate % Turnout | | 76,056 | 72.9% | 1997 | 73,005 | 79.8% | 1992 |
|---|---|---|---|---|---|---|---|
| +Moss, M | C | 23,855 | 43.0% | -10.5% | 31,168 | 53.5% | C |
| Bucknor, Mrs V | Lab | 18,754 | 33.8% | +20.2% | 18,007 | 30.9% | LD |
| Nash, A | LD | 9,070 | 16.4% | -14.6% | 7,928 | 13.6% | Lab |
| Bacon, M | Ref | 2,636 | 4.8% | | 927 | 1.6% | Lib |
| Bennett, C | Soc Lab | 851 | 1.5% | | 209 | 0.4% | NLP |
| Leighton, L | NLP | 259 | 0.5% | +0.1% | | | |
| C to Lab notional swing 15.4% | | 55,425 | | C maj 5,101 | 58,239 | | C maj 13,161 |
| | | | | 9.2% | | | 79.8% |

**MALCOLM MOSS,** b March 6, 1943. Won this seat 1987. N Ireland Under Sec 1994. PPS to Tristan Garel-Jones, Foreign Office Min, 1991-94. Member, energy select cttee, 1988-91; joint vice-chair, 1989-91, and sec 1987-89, C backbench energy cttee. Wisbech town cllr 1979-87; Fenland district cllr 1983-87; Cambridgeshire county cllr 1985-87. Non-exec chair, 1986-94, and ex-managing dir, Mandrake Associates Ltd. Asst master and then head of dept, Blundell's School, 1966-70; insurance consultant 1970-72; general manager, Barwick Associates, 1972-74. Ed Audenshaw GS; St John's Coll, Cambridge.

**VIRGINIA BUCKNOR,** b June 23, 1947. Business consultant. Fenland district cllr, chair of operational services. Member, MSF.

**ANDREW NASH,** b May 13, 1953. Social worker, lecturer. Ed Haberdashers' Aske's School, Elstree; Cambridge Univ.

| CAMBRIDGESHIRE NORTH WEST | | | 88.4% change | | | C win |
|---|---|---|---|---|---|---|
| Electorate % Turnout | | 65,791 | 74.2% | **1997** | 65,640 | 78.6% | **1992** |
| +Mawhinney, Dr B S | C | 23,488 | 48.1% | -14.2% | 32,170 | 62.4% | C |
| Steptoe, L | Lab | 15,734 | 32.2% | +6.3% | 13,361 | 25.9% | Lab |
| McCoy, Mrs B | LD | 7,388 | 15.1% | +6.4% | 4,503 | 8.7% | LD |
| Watt, S | Ref | 1,939 | 4.0% | | 1,559 | 3.0% | Other |
| Wyatt, B | UK Ind | 269 | 0.6% | | | | |
| C to Lab notional swing 10.3% | | 48,818 | | C maj 7,754 | 51,593 | | C maj 18,809 |
| | | | | 15.9% | | | 78.6% |

**BRIAN MAWHINNEY**, b July 26, 1940. Appointed Minister without Portfolio and chairman of Conservative Party 1995. Won this seat 1997; MP for Peterborough, 1979-97; contested Teesside, Stockton, Oct 1974. Transport Sec 1994, Health Min 1992-94; N Ireland Min 1990-92; N Ireland Under Sec 1986-90. PPS to Treasury mins 1982-84; to Employment Sec 1984-85; and to N Ireland Sec 1985-86. Member, environment select cttee, 1979-82. Radiation biologist; senior lecturer, Royal Free Hospital School of Medicine, London, 1970-84. Member, Medical Research Council, 1980-83; nat council, Nat Soc for Cancer Relief, 1981-85. Pres, C trade unionists, 1987-90. Member, General Synod of C of E, 1985-90. Ed Royal Belfast Academical Inst; Queen's Univ, Belfast; Univ of Michigan; London Univ.

**LEE STEPTOE**, b Sept 22, 1969. Teacher. Cleethorpes cllr 1993-95. Chair, Nottingham Univ Lab Club, 1989-91; Cleethorpes CLP 1994. Ed Central School, Grantham; Grantham Coll of FE; Nottingham Univ.

**BARBARA McCOY**, b Jan 14, 1947. Further education lecturer. Ed Toothill Sec Modern, Nottingham; Salisbury Coll of Tech.

| CAMBRIDGESHIRE SOUTH | | | 49.0% change | | | C win |
|---|---|---|---|---|---|---|
| Electorate % Turnout | | 69,850 | 76.9% | **1997** | 68,550 | 82.0% | **1992** |
| Lansley, A | C | 22,572 | 42.0% | -16.5% | 32,914 | 58.5% | C |
| Quinlan, J | LD | 13,860 | 25.8% | +1.0% | 13,976 | 24.9% | LD |
| Gray, A | Lab | 13,485 | 25.1% | +9.8% | 8,624 | 15.3% | Lab |
| Page, R | Ref | 3,300 | 6.1% | | 718 | 1.3% | Other |
| Norman, D | UK Ind | 298 | 0.6% | | | | |
| Chalmers, F | NLP | 168 | 0.3% | | | | |
| C to LD notional swing 8.7% | | 53,683 | | C maj 8,712 | 56,232 | | C maj 18,938 |
| | | | | 16.2% | | | 33.7% |

**ANDREW LANSLEY**, b Dec 11, 1956. Head of research department, Conservative Central Office, 1990-95, and director, Public Policy Unit, 1995. Principal private sec, Chancellor of Duchy of Lancaster, 1985-87; private sec, to Trade and Industry Sec, 1984-85. Member, nat union exec and gen purposes cttees, C Party, 1990-95. With Assoc of British Chambers of Commerce, 1987-89, being director policy, 1987, and dep director-gen, 1989-90. Ed Brentwood School; Exeter Univ.

**JAMES QUINLAN**, b Aug 8, 1951. Chartered town planner. South Cambridgeshire district cllr. Ed West Hatch HS, Chigwell; London Univ; N London Poly.

**TONY GRAY**, b March 5, 1970. Teacher. Chair, Labour Campaign for Social Justice; chair, Labour Socialist Societies. Ed Burford Comp; Royal Holloway and Bedford New Coll, London.

| CAMBRIDGESHIRE SOUTH EAST | | | 23.3% change | | | C win |
|---|---|---|---|---|---|---|
| Electorate % Turnout | | 75,666 | 75.1% | **1997** | 71,672 | 80.3% | **1992** |
| +Paice, J E T | C | 24,397 | 42.9% | -14.5% | 33,080 | 57.5% | C |
| Collinson, R | Lab | 15,048 | 26.5% | +7.0% | 12,217 | 21.2% | LD |
| Brinton, Ms S | LD | 14,246 | 25.1% | +3.9% | 11,205 | 19.5% | Lab |
| Howlett, J | Ref | 2,838 | 5.0% | | 824 | 1.4% | Grn |
| Lam, K | Fair | 167 | 0.3% | | 226 | 0.4% | NLP |
| While, P | NLP | 111 | 0.2% | -0.2% | | | |
| C to Lab notional swing 10.8% | | 56,807 | | C maj 9,349 | 57,552 | | C maj 20,863 |
| | | | | 16.5% | | | 80.3% |

**JAMES PAICE**, b April 24, 1949. Elected 1987. Contested Caernarfon 1979. Education and Employment Under Sec 1995, Employment Under Sec 1994-95. PPS to John Gummer, Agric Min and Environment Sec, 1991-94; PPS to Agric Min, 1989-91. Chair, all-party racing and bloodstock cttee, 1992-94. Member, employment select cttee, 1987-90; joint sec, C backbench employment cttee, 1988-89. Suffolk Coastal district cllr 1976-87 (chair, 1982-83). Non-exec director, United Framlingham Farmers Ltd, 1989-94; Framlingham Management and Training Services Ltd, 1987-89. Ed Framlingham Coll, Suffolk; Writtle Agricultural Coll, Essex.

**REX COLLINSON**, b Nov 6, 1947. Teacher. South Cambridgeshire district cllr 1988 (leader, Lab group, 1991- ). Ed Dorking GS; Exeter Univ; Christ's Coll, Cambridge.

**SAL BRINTON**, b April 1, 1955. College bursar. Cambridgeshire county cllr 1993; chair, SE Cambridgeshire LDs 1990-92. Ed Benenden School, Kent; Central School of Speech and Drama; Churchill Coll, Cambridge.

| CANNOCK CHASE | | 60.0% change | | | | | **Lab win** |
|---|---|---|---|---|---|---|---|
| Electorate % Turnout | | 72,362 | 72.4% | **1997** | 70,749 | 84.4% | **1992** |
| +Wright, Dr A W | Lab | **28,705** | 54.8% | +5.8% | 29,259 | 49.0% | Lab |
| Backhouse, J | C | 14,227 | 27.2% | -11.0% | 22,790 | 38.2% | C |
| Kirby, R | LD | 4,537 | 8.7% | -3.5% | 7,283 | 12.2% | LD |
| Froggatt, P | Ref | 1,663 | 3.2% | | 383 | 0.6% | Other |
| Hurley, W | N Lab | 1,615 | 3.1% | | | | |
| Conroy, M | Soc Lab | 1,120 | 2.1% | | | | |
| Hartshorn, M | Loony | 499 | 1.0% | | | | |
| C to Lab notional swing 8.4% | | 52,366 | Lab maj **14,478** | | 59,715 | Lab maj **6,469** | |
| | | | 27.6% | | | 84.4% | |

**TONY WRIGHT,** b March 11, 1948. Became PPS to Lord Irvine of Lairg, Lord Chancellor, May 14, 1997. Univ lecturer/reader in politics. Won this seat 1997; gained Cannock and Burntwood for Lab 1992; contested Kidderminster 1979. Member, select cttees on Parly Commissioner for Administration, 1992-96; public service 1995-97. Joint editor, *Political Quarterly*, 1994- ; Ed Kettering GS; LSE; Harvard; Balliol Coll, Oxford.

**JOHN BACKHOUSE,** b April 28, 1955. Managing director of Business Risk & Corporate Management Ltd. Contested Liverpool Garston 1992 and Liverpool West Derby 1987. Liverpool cllr 1988- . Ed Merchant Taylors' School; Kirkby Coll of FE; Liverpool Poly.
**RICHARD KIRBY,** b July 18, 1973. Health service manager. Member, Electoral Reform Soc. Ed Graham Balfour HS, Stafford; Lady Margaret Hall, Oxford.

| CANTERBURY | | 4.2% change | | | | | **C win** |
|---|---|---|---|---|---|---|---|
| Electorate % Turnout | | 74,548 | 72.6% | **1997** | 72,680 | 77.2% | **1992** |
| +Brazier, J | C | **20,913** | 38.6% | -11.8% | 28,290 | 50.4% | C |
| Hall, Ms C | Lab | 16,949 | 31.3% | +15.9% | 18,293 | 32.6% | LD |
| Vye, M | LD | 12,854 | 23.8% | -8.8% | 8,635 | 15.4% | Lab |
| Osborne, J | Ref | 2,460 | 4.5% | | 719 | 1.3% | Grn |
| Meaden, G | Green | 588 | 1.1% | | 194 | 0.3% | NLP |
| Moore, J | UK Ind | 281 | 0.5% | | | | |
| Pringle, A | NLP | 64 | 0.1% | -0.2% | | | |
| C to Lab notional swing 13.8% | | 54,109 | C maj **3,964** | | 56,131 | C maj **9,997** | |
| | | | 7.3% | | | 77.2% | |

**JULIAN BRAZIER,** b July 24, 1953. Elected 1987. Contested Berwick-upon-Tweed 1983. PPS to Gillian Shephard in her ministerial posts from 1990; vice-chair, all-party council of church and associated colleges parly group, 1994- ; vice-chair, C backbench defence cttee, 1993- . Was serving officer in 5(HSF) Co, 10th Battalion, Parachute Regt. Ex-project manager with H.B. Maynard, international management consultants; former sec, exec cttee, board of Charter Consolidated plc. Member, Bow Group; Centre

for Policy Studies. Ed Wellington Coll, Berkshire; Brasenose Coll, Oxford (chair, 1974, Univ C assoc).
**CHERYL HALL,** b July 23, 1950. Actor; columnist for *Kent Today*. Kent county cllr. Member, Equity. Ed Coborn GS; Kingsway Coll.
**MARTIN VYE,** b Dec 8, 1936. Retired schoolmaster. Contested this seat 1992. Kent cllr 1989- , Canterbury cllr 1995- . Ed Kingston GS; Christ's Coll, Cambridge.

| CARDIFF CENTRAL | | | | | | | **Lab hold** |
|---|---|---|---|---|---|---|---|
| Electorate % Turnout | | 60,354 | 70.0% | **1997** | 57,716 | 74.4% | **1992** |
| *Owen Jones, J | Lab Co-op | 18,464 | 43.7% | +1.7% | 18,014 | 42.0% | Lab Co-op |
| Randerson, Mrs J | LD | 10,541 | 24.9% | +3.6% | 14,549 | 33.9% | C |
| Melding, D | C | 8,470 | 20.0% | -13.9% | 9,170 | 21.4% | LD |
| Burns, T | Soc Lab | 2,230 | 5.3% | | 748 | 1.7% | PC |
| Vernon, W | PC | 1,504 | 3.6% | +1.8% | 330 | 0.8% | Grn |
| Lloyd, N | Ref | 760 | 1.8% | | 105 | 0.2% | NLP |
| James, C | Loony | 204 | 0.5% | | | | |
| Hobbs, A | NLP | 80 | 0.2% | -0.1% | | | |
| Lab Co-op to LD swing 0.9% | | 42,253 | Lab Co-op maj **7,923** | | 42,916 | Lab Co-op maj **3,465** | |
| | | | 18.8% | | | 74.4% | |

**JON OWEN JONES,** b April 19, 1954. Became gvt whip, May 7, 1997. Ex-teacher. Won this seat 1992; contested it 1987. Lab whip 1993. Ex-Cardiff cllr. Pres, Mid Glamorgan NUT, 1986. Ed Ysgol Gyfun Rhydfelin; Univ of E Anglia; Univ Coll of Wales, Cardiff.
**JENNY RANDERSON,** b May 26, 1948. Further education lecturer. Contested Cardiff 1992, Cardiff S and Penarth 1987. Cardiff city cllr for 12 years, then unitary authority cllr (LD opposition leader

1995- ). Ed Wimbledon HS; Bedford Coll; Inst of Ed, London Univ.
**DAVID MELDING,** b Aug 28, 1962. Dep director, Welsh Centre for International Affairs. Contested Blaenau Gwent 1992. Ed Dwy-y-Felin Comp, Neath; Univ Coll of Wales, Cardiff; Coll of William and Mary, Pennsylvania.
**WAYNE VERNON,** b Dec 17, 1967. Engineer. Ed Univ Coll of Wales, Cardiff.

| CARDIFF NORTH | | | | | Lab gain | | |
|---|---|---|---|---|---|---|---|
| Electorate % Turnout | | 60,430 | 80.2% | **1997** | 56,721 | 84.2% | **1992** |
| **Morgan, Mrs J** | **Lab** | **24,460** | **50.4%** | **+11.5%** | 21,547 | 45.1% | C |
| *Jones, G | C | 16,334 | 33.7% | -11.5% | 18,578 | 38.9% | Lab |
| Rowland, R | LD | 5,294 | 10.9% | -2.7% | 6,487 | 13.6% | LD |
| Palfrey, Dr C | PC | 1,201 | 2.5% | +0.6% | 916 | 1.9% | PC |
| Litchfield, E | Ref | 1,199 | 2.5% | | 121 | 0.3% | BNP |
| | | | | | 86 | 0.2% | NLP |
| **C to Lab swing 11.5%** | | **48,488** | | **Lab maj 8,126** | **47,735** | | **C maj 2,969** |
| | | | | 16.8% | | | 6.2% |

**JULIE MORGAN,** b Nov 2, 1944. Asst director, Childcare, Barnardo's Wales. Contested this seat 1992. Ex-Cardiff and S Glamorgan cllr. Ex-principal social services officer, West Glamorgan. Member, management cttee, S Glamorgan women's workshop, computer training centre. Ed Howells School; London, Manchester and Cardiff Univs. Married to Rhodri Morgan, MP for Cardiff W.
**GWILYM JONES,** b Sept 20, 1947. Elected 1983. Welsh Under Sec, 1992-97. PPS to Roger Freeman, Transport Min, 1991-92.

Ex-insurance broker; director, Bowring Wales Ltd, 1980-92. Liveryman, Welsh Livery Guild, 1993- . Ed St Clement Dane's GS; Whitchurch HS; Caerphilly Grammar Tech; Cardiff Coll of Commerce.
**ROBYN ROWLAND,** b April 28, 1967. Postgraduate student. Contested Merthyr Tydfil and Rhymney 1992. South Glamorgan county cllr. Ed H.H. Dow HS, Michigan; British School, Brussels; City of London Poly; Univ of Wales, Cardiff.

| CARDIFF SOUTH & PENARTH | | | | | Lab hold | | |
|---|---|---|---|---|---|---|---|
| Electorate % Turnout | | 61,838 | 68.6% | **1997** | 61,484 | 77.3% | **1992** |
| *Michael, A | Lab Co-op | 22,647 | 53.4% | -2.1% | 26,383 | 55.5% | Lab Co-op |
| Roberts, Mrs C | C | 8,766 | 20.7% | -12.9% | 15,958 | 33.6% | C |
| Wakefield, Dr S | LD | 3,964 | 9.3% | +1.5% | 3,707 | 7.8% | LD |
| Foreman, J | N Lab | 3,942 | 9.3% | | 776 | 1.6% | PC |
| Haswell, D B | PC | 1,356 | 3.2% | +1.6% | 676 | 1.4% | Grn |
| Morgan, P | Ref | 1,211 | 2.9% | | | | |
| Shepherd, M | Soc | 344 | 0.8% | | | | |
| Caves, Ms B | NLP | 170 | 0.4% | | | | |
| **C to Lab Co-op swing 5.4%** | | **42,400** | | **Lab Co-op maj 13,881** | **47,500** | | **Lab Co-op maj 10,425** |
| | | | | 32.7% | | | 22.0% |

**ALUN MICHAEL,** b Aug 22, 1943. Became Home Office Min of State responsible for criminal policy, May 5, 1997. Elected 1987. Lab spokesman on home affairs 1992-97; spokesman on Wales 1988-92; political co-ordinator for Vale of Glamorgan, Neath and Monmouth 1991 by-elections. Lab whip 1987-88. Chair, Welsh group of Lab MPs, 1995- ; all-party penal affairs parly group; alcohol misuse group. Vice-chair, British-German group; ex-chair, Somalia group. Youth and community worker, Cardiff, 1972-84.Cardiff city cllr 1973-89. Member, nat exec, Co-op Party, 1988-92. Ed Colwyn Bay GS; Keele Univ.

**CAROLINE ROBERTS,** b Nov 30, 1953. Dir, public affairs, Brewers & Licensed Retailers Assoc. Chair, Battersea C assoc 1993-96; C Greater London exec since 1993. Member, Inst of Public Relations. Ed Walthamstow Hall, Sevenoaks; Manchester Univ.
**SIMON WAKEFIELD,** b Feb 10, 1954. Univ lecturer. Member, Greenpeace; Friends of the Earth; Charter 88. Ed Maidstone GS; Leeds Univ.
**DAVID HASWELL,** b Jan 6, 1962. Teacher. Contested Vale of Glamorgan 1992. Ed University Coll, Cardiff; University Coll, Swansea.

| CARDIFF WEST | | 0.8% change | | | Lab win | | |
|---|---|---|---|---|---|---|---|
| Electorate % Turnout | | 58,198 | 69.2% | **1997** | 59,470 | 76.9% | **1992** |
| +Morgan, R | Lab | 24,297 | 60.3% | +7.1% | 24,319 | 53.2% | Lab |
| Hoare, S | C | 8,669 | 21.5% | -11.4% | 15,028 | 32.9% | C |
| Gasson, Ms J | LD | 4,366 | 10.8% | -0.1% | 5,002 | 10.9% | LD |
| Carr, Ms G | PC | 1,949 | 4.8% | +2.3% | 1,178 | 2.6% | PC |
| Johns, T | Ref | 996 | 2.5% | | 184 | 0.4% | NLP |
| **C to Lab notional swing 9.2%** | | **40,277** | | **Lab maj 15,628** | **45,711** | | **Lab maj 9,291** |
| | | | | 38.8% | | | 20.3% |

**RHODRI MORGAN,** b Sept 29, 1939. Elected 1987. Industrial analyst. Lab spokesman on Wales 1992-97; on energy 1988-92. Member, select cttees on energy, 1987-89; members' interests 1987-89. Vice-chair, all-party asthma parly group; treas, Lords and Commons tennis club group. Head of bureau for press and information, EC Commission Office for Wales, 1980-87; adviser to Lab Party economic planning cttes in Wales. Ed Whitchurch GS,

Cardiff; St John's Coll, Oxford; Harvard Univ. Married to Julie Morgan, Lab MP for Cardiff N.
**SIMON HOARE,** b June 28, 1969. Media public relations manager for Environmental Services Assoc. Ed Bishop Hannon School, Cardiff; Oxford Univ.
**JACQUI GASSON,** b March 15, 1938. Contested Cardiff W 1992. Islwyn 1987. Ed Tolworth GS; Univ of Wales Coll, Cardiff.

## CARLISLE — 9.2% change — Lab win

| Electorate % Turnout | | 59,917 | 72.8% | **1997** | 61,008 | 78.5% | **1992** |
|---|---|---|---|---|---|---|---|
| +Martlew, E | Lab | **25,031** | 57.4% | +12.1% | **21,667** | 45.3% | Lab |
| Lawrence, R | C | 12,641 | 29.0% | -12.3% | 19,746 | 41.2% | C |
| Mayho, C | LD | 4,576 | 10.5% | -2.5% | 6,232 | 13.0% | LD |
| Fraser, A | Ref | 1,233 | 2.8% | | 230 | 0.5% | NLP |
| Stevens, W | NLP | 126 | 0.3% | -0.2% | | | |
| C to Lab notional swing 12.2% | | **43,607** | | Lab maj 12,390 28.4% | **47,875** | | Lab maj 1,921 4.0% |

**ERIC MARTLEW,** b Jan 3, 1949. Elected 1987. Lab whip 1995-97; spokesman on defence, 1992-95. Member, agriculture select cttee 1987-92. Ex-chair, Northern group of Lab MPs; vice-chair, PLP, agriculture cttee, 1987-92. Cumbria cllr, 1973-88 (chair 1983-85); Carlisle city cllr 1972-74. With Nestlé Co Ltd 1966-87, rising to personnel manager, Dalston factory, Carlisle. Ed Harraby Sec, Carlisle; Carlisle Tech Coll.

**RICHARD LAWRENCE,** b April 25, 1956. Marketing consultant. Chair, Morecambe C Assoc, 1993- , treas 1992-93, and press officer 1991-93. Ed King Edward School, Witley.
**CHRIS MAYHO,** b Dec 4, 1950. Chief admin officer, Finchale Coll. South Lakeland district cllr 1990- , Kendal town cllr 1990- . Ed Australia; Teesside, Sunderland and Central Lancs Univs.

## CARMARTHEN EAST & DINEFWR — 39.6% change — Lab win

| Electorate % Turnout | | 53,079 | 78.6% | **1997** | 53,256 | 82.8% | **1992** |
|---|---|---|---|---|---|---|---|
| +Williams, Dr A W | Lab | **17,907** | 42.9% | +1.4% | **18,305** | 41.5% | Lab |
| Thomas, R G | PC | 14,457 | 34.6% | +5.6% | 12,815 | 29.1% | PC |
| Hayward, E R | C | 5,022 | 12.0% | -8.3% | 8,953 | 20.3% | C |
| Hughes, Mrs J M | LD | 3,150 | 7.5% | -1.6% | 4,023 | 9.1% | LD |
| Humphreys-Evans, I | Ref | 1,196 | 2.9% | | | | |
| Lab to PC notional swing 2.1% | | **41,732** | | Lab maj 3,450 8.3% | **44,096** | | Lab maj 5,490 12.%% |

**ALAN WYNNE WILLIAMS,** b Dec 21, 1945. MP for Carmarthen 1987-97. Member, select cttees on science and tech, 1992-97; Welsh affairs 1987-92; Consolidation Bills 1987-92. Joint vice-chair, PLP environment cttee, 1990- . Senior lecturer in environmental science, Trinity Coll, Carmarthen, 1971-87. Sec, Carmarthen Lab Party, 1981-84. Member, NATFHE. Ed Carmarthen GS; Jesus Coll, Oxford.
**RHODRI GLYN THOMAS,** b April 11, 1953. Director of TV production company. Contested Carmarthen 1992. PC spokesman on education. Chair, CND Cymru 1984-88. Member, British council of NSPCC, 1995- . Ed Bodhyfryd School, Wrexham; Morgan Llwyd

School, Wrexham; Univ of Wales Colls, Aberstwyth, Bangor and Lampeter.
**EDMUND HAYWARD,** b Oct 25, 1956. Accountancy and taxation consultant, owner of removal/storage business. Dir of Radnorshire Wildlife Trust Ltd since 1992. Fellow, Royal Geographical Soc. Ed Wellington Coll, Berkshire; Exeter Univ.
**JULIANA HUGHES,** b Nov 30, 1944. Teacher and freelance broadcaster. Contested Carmarthen 1992. JP, Carmarthen S bench. Hon member, Nat Eisteddfod Bardic Gorsedd. Ed Llanelli Girls' GS; Univ Coll of Wales, Aberystwyth.

## CARMARTHEN WEST & PEMBROKESHIRE SOUTH — 84.9% change — Lab win

| Electorate % Turnout | | 55,724 | 76.5% | **1997** | 55,393 | 77.7% | **1992** |
|---|---|---|---|---|---|---|---|
| +Ainger, N R | Lab | **20,956** | 49.1% | +10.6% | **16,588** | 38.5% | Lab |
| Williams, O | C | 11,335 | 26.6% | -8.9% | 15,278 | 35.5% | C |
| Llewellyn, D J R | PC | 5,402 | 12.7% | -2.4% | 6,497 | 15.1% | PC |
| Evans, K | LD | 3,516 | 8.2% | -2.6% | 4,672 | 10.9% | LD |
| Poirrier, Mrs J | Ref | 1,432 | 3.4% | | | | |
| C to Lab notional swing 9.8% | | **42,641** | | Lab maj 9,621 22.6% | **43,035** | | Lab maj 1,310 77.7% |

**NICK AINGER,** b Oct 24, 1949. MP for Pembroke 1992-97. Member, Welsh affairs select cttee. Dyfed cllr 1981-92. Rigger, Marine and Port Services Ltd, Pembroke Dock, 1977-92. Member, TGWU (senior shop steward and branch sec 1978-92). Ed Netherthorpe GS, Staveley.
**OWEN JOHN WILLIAMS,** b May 17, 1950. Barrister. Contested Ceredigion & Pembroke N 1987, 1992; Mid & West Wales, Euro elections, 1989. Chair, family group of companies. Ed Harrow; University Coll, Oxford.

**ROY LLEWELLYN,** b June 28, 1937. Fertiliser sales rep; formerly at British Rail, where he was appointed youngest ever stationmaster at age of 23. Dyfed cllr 1989-96; Carmarthern cllr 1995- . Member, Friends of the Earth; CPR Wales. Ed Whitland GS.
**KEITH EVANS,** b April 1, 1956. Economist, researcher. Contested Bury S 1983, Llanelli 1992. Carmarthenshire county cllr (leader, LD group); Llanelli borough cllr 1991- ; Greater Manchester cllr 1981-86. Ed Coleshill School, Warwicks; Wolverhampton Poly; Univ Coll of Wales, Swansea.

## CARRICK, CUMNOCK & DOON VALLEY  19.7% change  Lab win

| | | 1997 | | | 1992 | |
|---|---|---|---|---|---|---|
| Electorate % Turnout | | 65,593 | 75.0% | **1997** | 67,001 | 77.2% | **1992** |
| +Foulkes, G | Lab Co-op | **29,398** | **59.8%** | +5.7% | 27,957 | 54.1% | Lab Co-op |
| Marshall, A | C | 8,336 | 17.0% | -8.7% | 13,271 | 25.7% | C |
| Hutchison, Mrs C | SNP | 8,190 | 16.7% | +1.6% | 7,802 | 15.1% | SNP |
| Young, D | LD | 2,613 | 5.3% | +0.1% | 2,690 | 5.2% | LD |
| Higgins, J | Ref | 634 | 1.3% | | | | |
| C to Lab notional swing 7.2% | | 49,171 | Lab Co-op maj 21,062 | | 51,720 | Lab Co-op maj 14,686 | |
| | | | 42.8% | | | 77.2% | |

**GEORGE FOULKES,** b Jan 21, 1942. Became Under Sec of State for International Development, May 5, 1997. Won this seat 1983; MP for S Ayrshire 1979-83; contested Edinburgh Pentlands Oct 1974, and Edinburgh W 1970. Lab spokesman on overseas development 1994; spokesman on defence, disarmament and arms control 1992-93; foreign affairs 1985-92; European and Community affairs 1983-85. Former chair, all-party world gvt group. Treas, Parliamentarians for Global Action, 1993- (council member since 1987). Dir, Co-op Press Ltd, 1990-97. Ed Keith GS, Banffshire; Haberdashers' Aske's; Edinburgh Univ.

**ALASDAIR MARSHALL,** b Aug 15, 1968. Tutor, politics dept, Glasgow Univ (studying for PhD). Heathfield district cllr 1992- . Ed Kyle Acad; Glasgow Univ.
**CHRISTINE HUTCHISON,** b May 27, 1954. Ex-chiropodist. Dumfries and Galloway cllr until 1996; convener, Galloway and Upper Nithsdale SNP constituency assoc. Ed Dunfermline HS; Queen Margaret Coll.
**DEREK YOUNG,** b Sept 15, 1975. Postgraduate student. Member, Charter 88. Ed Belmont Acad, Ayr; Strathclyde Univ.

## CARSHALTON & WALLINGTON  LD gain

| | | 1997 | | | 1992 | |
|---|---|---|---|---|---|---|
| Electorate % Turnout | | 66,038 | 73.3% | **1997** | 65,179 | 80.9% | **1992** |
| Brake, T | LD | **18,490** | **38.2%** | +7.3% | 26,243 | 49.7% | C |
| *Forman, N | C | 16,223 | 33.5% | -16.2% | 16,300 | 30.9% | LD |
| Theobald, A | Lab | 11,565 | 23.9% | +6.2% | 9,333 | 17.7% | Lab |
| Storey, J | Ref | 1,289 | 2.7% | | 614 | 1.2% | Grn |
| Hickson, P | Green | 377 | 0.8% | | 266 | 0.5% | Loony G |
| Ritchie, G | BNP | 261 | 0.5% | | | | |
| Povey, L | UK Ind | 218 | 0.5% | | | | |
| C to LD swing 11.8% | | 48,423 | LD maj 2,267 | | 52,756 | C maj 9,943 | |
| | | | 4.7% | | | 80.9% | |

**TOM BRAKE,** b May 6, 1962. Computer software consultant. Contested this seat 1992. Hackney cllr 1988-90, Sutton cllr 1994-. Ed Lycée International, France; Imperial Coll, London.
**NIGEL FORMAN,** b March 25, 1943. MP for Carshalton and Wallington 1983-97, and for Sutton Carshalton, 1976-83; contested Coventry NE Feb 1974. Education Under Sec 1992. Member, select cttees for Treasury 1992-97; foreign affairs 1990-92. PPS to Nigel Lawson, Chancellor, 1987-89; to Lord Privy Seal 1979-81; and to Foreign Office Min 1979-83. Member, exec, 1922

Cttee, 1990-92; foreign affairs select cttee 1990-92. Non-exec dir, HFC Bank plc; parly adviser to Inst of Chartered Accountants; political consultant to Salomon Bros International Ltd. Ed Shrewsbury School; New College, Oxford; Coll of Europe, Bruges; Harvard and Sussex Univs.
**ANDREW THEOBALD,** b March 25, 1955. Underwriting superintendent. Sutton cllr 1994- (dep leader, Lab group, 1994- ). Member, MSF. Ed St Joseph's Coll; Norwood Tech; Croydon Tech; City of London Poly.

## CASTLE POINT  Lab gain

| | | 1997 | | | 1992 | |
|---|---|---|---|---|---|---|
| Electorate % Turnout | | 67,146 | 72.3% | **1997** | 66,229 | 80.4% | **1992** |
| Butler, Ms C | Lab | **20,605** | **42.4%** | +18.4% | 29,629 | 55.6% | C |
| *Spink, Dr R | C | 19,489 | 40.1% | -15.5% | 12,799 | 24.0% | Lab |
| Baker, D | LD | 4,477 | 9.2% | -9.9% | 10,208 | 19.2% | LD |
| Maulkin, H | Ref | 2,700 | 5.6% | | 643 | 1.2% | Grn |
| Kendall, Miss L | Consult | 1,301 | 2.7% | | | | |
| C to Lab swing 16.9% | | 48,572 | Lab maj 1,116 | | 53,279 | C maj 16,830 | |
| | | | 2.3% | | | 31.6% | |

**CHRISTINE BUTLER,** b Dec 14, 1943. Ex-research assistant in pharmaceutical industry and NHS. Chair, Essex Co-op Development Agency. Member, Fabian Soc; Greenpeace. Ed state primary and grammar schools; Middlesex Poly.
**ROBERT SPINK,** b Aug 1, 1948. Industrial engineer and management consultant. Elected 1992. PPS to Home Office Min, 1996-97, to Employment Min 1994-96; member, board Parly Office of Science and Tech. Chair, all-party prisoners abroad parly

group, 1995-97; joint vice-chair, Lomé group; vice-chair, C backbench employment cttee, 1993-94. Dir, Bournemouth Airport 1989-93; dir and co-owner, Seafarer Navigation International 1980-84. Engineer with EMI Electronics Ltd 1966-77. Dorset cllr 1985-93; Dorset Police Authority 1985-93. Ed Holycroft Sec Mod, Keighley; Manchester Univ; Cranfield Univ.
**DAVID BAKER,** b April 18, 1935. Informations systems consultant. Essex county cllr. Ed Bury GS; Manchester Univ.

| CEREDIGION | | 19.6% change | | | 1997 | | | PC win |
|---|---|---|---|---|---|---|---|---|
| Electorate % Turnout | | | 54,378 | 73.9% | **1997** | 54,467 | 78.0% | **1992** |
| +Dafis, C G | PC | | **16,728** | **41.6%** | **+10.7%** | **13,144** | **31.0%** | **PC** |
| Harris, R | Lab | | 9,767 | 24.3% | +5.7% | 11,251 | 26.5% | LD |
| Davies, D | LD | | 6,616 | 16.5% | -10.0% | 10,178 | 24.0% | C |
| Aubel, Dr F F E | C | | 5,983 | 14.9% | -9.1% | 7,889 | 18.6% | Lab |
| Leaney, J | Ref | | 1,092 | 2.7% | | | | |
| **Lab to PC notional swing 2.5%** | | | 40,186 | | PC maj **6,961** | 42,462 | | PC maj **1,893** |
| | | | | | 17.3% | | | 78.0% |

**CYNOG DAFIS,** b April 1, 1938. Won Ceredigion and Pembroke N 1992; contested it 1983 and 1987. Member, Welsh affairs select cttee 1995-97; sec, all-party UK Eurosolar parly group; joint vice-chair, warm homes group; ex-joint vice-chair, all-party environment group. Researcher, Univ Coll of Wales, Swansea, 1991-92; English teacher Dyffryn Comp, Llandysul, 1984-91; Aberaeron Comp 1980-84; Newcastle Emlyn Sec Mod 1962-80. Ed Aberavon County Secondary; Neath Boys' GS; Univ Coll of Wales, Aberystwyth.
**ROBERT HARRIS,** b July 8, 1955. Shopkeeper. Welsh international orienteer; League of Wales football referee. Ed Univ of Wales.

**DAI DAVIES,** b March 9, 1943. Chartered accountant. Cardiganshire county cllr 1995- (LD leader). Mayor of Cardigan 1994-95. Ed Cardigan GS.
**FELIX AUBEL,** b Sept 21, 1960. Partner in family property business in Aberdare. Contested Caernarfon for C 1987, Cynon Valley for SDP/All 1984 by-election and 1983. Welsh Ind minister (Aberaeron); univ lecturer (Lampeter); teacher, Chislehurst and Sidcup GS 1989-92. Member, exec cttee, Cardigan Union of Welsh Independents, 1993- . Ed Rhydfelen Comp, Pontypridd; Univ Coll of Wales, Lampeter.

| CHARNWOOD | | 133.1% change | | | 1997 | | | C win |
|---|---|---|---|---|---|---|---|---|
| Electorate % Turnout | | | 72,692 | 77.3% | **1997** | 71,672 | 80.9% | **1992** |
| +Dorrell, S J | C | | **26,110** | **46.5%** | **-14.1%** | **35,126** | **60.6%** | **C** |
| Knaggs, D J | Lab | | 20,210 | 36.0% | +14.4% | 12,526 | 21.6% | Lab |
| Wilson, R | LD | | 7,224 | 12.9% | -5.0% | 10,345 | 17.8% | LD |
| Meechan, H | Ref | | 2,104 | 3.7% | | | | |
| Palmer, M | BNP | | 525 | 0.9% | | | | |
| **C to Lab notional swing 14.2%** | | | 56,173 | | C maj **5,900** | 57,997 | | C maj **22,600** |
| | | | | | 10.5% | | | 39.0% |

**STEPHEN DORRELL,** b March 25, 1952. Director of family industrial clothing company 1975-87. Elected MP for Loughborough 1979; contested Hull E Oct 1974. Health Sec 1995-97; National Heritage Sec 1994; Financial Sec to Treasury, 1992-94; Under Sec for Health 1990-92; asst gvt whip 1987-88; PPS to Energy Sec 1983-87. Member, transport select cttee, 1979-83. Member, board of Christian Aid 1985-87. Ed Uppingham; Brasenose Coll, Oxford.

**DAVID KNAGGS,** b May 6, 1942. Industrial training consultant. Contested Melton Oct 1974. Leicester cllr (Lab group dep leader); Charnwood borough cllr. Member, GMB; NUT; central regional exec cttee, Co-op Party; Amnesty. Ed Leeds Central HS; City of Birmingham Coll of Ed; Southampton Univ.
**ROGER WILSON,** b April 5, 1934. Retired bank officer. Leicestershire cllr. Member, MSF. Methodist preacher. Ed Kingswood School, Bath.

| CHATHAM & AYLESFORD | | 74.8% change | | | 1997 | | | Lab win |
|---|---|---|---|---|---|---|---|---|
| Electorate % Turnout | | | 69,172 | 71.1% | **1997** | 69,821 | 78.4% | **1992** |
| Shaw, J | Lab | | **21,191** | **43.1%** | **+16.4%** | **28,056** | **51.3%** | **C** |
| Knox-Johnston, R | C | | 18,401 | 37.4% | -13.8% | 14,633 | 26.7% | Lab |
| Murray, R | LD | | 7,389 | 15.0% | -6.2% | 11,643 | 21.3% | LD |
| Riddle, K | Ref | | 1,538 | 3.1% | | 401 | 0.7% | Other |
| Harding, A | UK Ind | | 493 | 1.0% | | | | |
| Martel, T | NLP | | 149 | 0.3% | | | | |
| **C to Lab notional swing 15.1%** | | | 49,161 | | Lab maj **2,790** | 54,733 | | C maj **13,423** |
| | | | | | 5.7% | | | 24.5% |

**JONATHAN SHAW,** b June 3, 1966. Social worker. Rochester cllr. Ex-Unison steward. Ed Vintners Boys School, Maidstone; West Kent Coll of FE; Bromley Coll of FHE.
**RICHARD KNOX-JOHNSTON,** b Sept 28, 1941. Financial actuarial consultant; ex-Army captain, served in N Ireland and with UN forces in Cyprus. Bromley cllr; Kingston upon Thames cllr. JP.

Founder, dep chair, Small Business Bureau. Ed Berkhamsted School; Sandhurst.
**ROBIN MURRAY,** b June 18, 1951. Criminal lawyer, senior partner in own firm of solicitors. Aylesford town cllr 1984-88. Member, Leybourne Environment Group. Ed Crown Woods Comp, Eltham; Guildford Coll of Law.

| CHEADLE | | 2.2% change | | | | | C win |
|---|---|---|---|---|---|---|---|
| Electorate % Turnout | | 67,627 | 77.6% | **1997** | 68,789 | 82.7% | **1992** |
| +Day, S | C | 22,944 | 43.7% | -13.9% | 32,804 | 57.7% | C |
| Calton, Mrs P | LD | 19,755 | 37.7% | +8.1% | 16,828 | 29.6% | LD |
| Diggett, P | Lab | 8,253 | 15.7% | +3.3% | 7,080 | 12.4% | Lab |
| Brook, P | Ref | 1,511 | 2.9% | | 183 | 0.3% | NLP |
| C to LD notional swing 11.0% | | 52,463 | | C maj 3,189 | 56,895 | | C maj 15,976 |
| | | | | 6.1% | | | 82.7% |

**STEPHEN DAY**, b Oct 30, 1948. Sales executive. Elected 1987; contested Bradford W 1983. Member, social security select cttee, 1990; joint sec, C backbench health cttee, 1991-94; joint chair, parly advisory council for transport safety, 1989- ; all-party West Coast main line parly group; joint vice-chair, non-profitmaking clubs group; plumbing registration group; former joint sec, all-party Northern Cyprus group; member, exec cttee, CPA 1994- . Otley town cllr 1975-76 and 1979-83; Leeds city cllr 1975-80. Ed Otley Sec Mod; Park Lane Coll, Leeds; Leeds Poly.

**PATSY CALTON**, b Sept 19, 1948. Chemistry teacher in comp school. Contested this seat 1992. Stockport metropolitan borough cllr 1994- . Member, Amnesty; Stockport cerebral palsy soc; NASUWT. Ed Wymondham Coll, Norfolk; UMIST.
**PAUL DIGGETT**, b Feb 28, 1969. IT assistant and licensed house manager. Member, TGWU; Fabian Soc; Co-op Party. Ed Univ of Wales, Bangor; OU.

| CHELMSFORD WEST | | 45.1% change | | | | | C win |
|---|---|---|---|---|---|---|---|
| Electorate % Turnout | | 76,086 | 77.0% | **1997** | 73,616 | 84.9% | **1992** |
| +Burns, S H M | C | 23,781 | 40.6% | -14.2% | 34,284 | 54.8% | C |
| Bracken, M | LD | 17,090 | 29.2% | +0.2% | 18,098 | 28.9% | LD |
| Chad, Dr R K | Lab | 15,436 | 26.4% | +11.2% | 9,443 | 15.1% | Lab |
| Smith, T | Ref | 1,536 | 2.6% | | 699 | 1.1% | Other |
| Rumens, G | Green | 411 | 0.7% | | | | |
| Levin, M | UK Ind | 323 | 0.6% | | | | |
| C to LD notional swing 7.2% | | 58,577 | | C maj 6,691 | 62,524 | | C maj 16,186 |
| | | | | 11.4% | | | 84.9% |

**SIMON BURNS**, b Sept 6, 1952. Elected for Chelmsford 1987; contested Alyn and Deeside 1983. Under Sec of State for Health 1996-97; gvt whip 1995-96; asst gvt whip 1994-95; PPS to Min of Ag 1993-94, to Min of State for Employment, Education and Science and then Energy, 1990-93. Political adviser to Sally Oppenheim 1975-81. Member, policy exec, Inst of Directors, 1983-87; dir, What to Buy Ltd. 1981-83. Ed Christ the King, Accra, Ghana; Stamford School, Lincs; Worcester Coll, Oxford.

**MARTIN BRACKEN**, b Jan 2, 1959. Senior treasury manager for a European bank. Chelmsford borough cllr 1995- . Ed Harold Hill GS.
**ROY CHAD**, b Nov 4, 1950. Consultant psychiatrist. Contested Chelmsford 1992. Chelmsford borough cllr 1995- ; vice-chair, Chelmsford CLP. Member, MPU; MFS; Soc Health Assoc; NHS Consultants Assoc. Ed Holland Park Comp; Birmingham Univ Medical School.

| CHELTENHAM | | 15.8% change | | | | | LD win |
|---|---|---|---|---|---|---|---|
| Electorate % Turnout | | 67,950 | 74.0% | **1997** | 69,121 | 81.0% | **1992** |
| +Jones, N | LD | 24,877 | 49.5% | +2.1% | 26,508 | 47.3% | LD |
| Todman, J | C | 18,232 | 36.2% | -8.2% | 24,861 | 44.4% | C |
| Leach, B | Lab | 5,100 | 10.1% | +3.4% | 3,769 | 6.7% | Lab |
| Powell, Mrs A | Ref | 1,065 | 2.1% | | 573 | 1.0% | AFE |
| Hanks, K | Loony | 375 | 0.7% | | 146 | 0.3% | NLP |
| Cook, G | UK Ind | 302 | 0.6% | | 139 | 0.2% | Ind |
| Harriss, Ms A | ProLife | 245 | 0.5% | | | | |
| Brighouse, Ms S | NLP | 107 | 0.2% | -0.0% | | | |
| C to LD notional swing 5.1% | | 50,303 | | LD maj 6,645 | 55,996 | | LD maj 1,647 |
| | | | | 13.2% | | | 81.0% |

**NIGEL JONES,** b March 30, 1948. Computer systems designer. Won this seat 1992; contested it 1979. LD spokesman on science and technology and consumer affairs; member, select cttees on standards and privileges 1995-97; broadcasting 1992-97. Joint vice-chair, all-party beer club parly group; joint sec, animal welfare group. Gloucestershire cllr 1989- . Ed Prince Henry's GS, Evesham.

**JOHN TODMAN,** b Dec 7, 1939. Solicitor. Cheltenham cllr 1988- (C group leader 1990- ). Member of task force introducing council tax 1992. Ed Shrewsbury School; St Catherine's Coll, Oxford.
**BARRY LEACH,** b Dec 28, 1947. Management consultant. Sec, Cheltenham CLP. Member, Co-op Party; Friends of the Earth; Animal Welfare Soc; Shelter. Ed Wade Deacon GS, Widnes; OU.

| CHESHAM & AMERSHAM | | 4.5% change | | | | 1997 | | | 1992 | C win |
|---|---|---|---|---|---|---|---|---|---|---|
| Electorate % Turnout | | | 69,244 | 75.4% | | **1997** | 68,602 | 81.0% | | **1992** |
| +Gillan, Mrs C | C | | 26,298 | 50.4% | -13.0% | | 35,207 | 63.4% | | C |
| Brand, M | LD | | 12,439 | 23.8% | -0.7% | | 13,606 | 24.5% | | LD |
| Farrelly, P | Lab | | 10,240 | 19.6% | +9.3% | | 5,758 | 10.4% | | Lab |
| Andrews, P | Ref | | 2,528 | 4.8% | | | 734 | 1.3% | | Grn |
| Shilson, C | UK Ind | | 618 | 1.2% | | | 248 | 0.4% | | NLP |
| Godfrey, H | NLP | | 74 | 0.1% | -0.3% | | | | | |
| C to LD notional swing 6.2% | | | 52,197 | | C maj 13,859 | | 55,553 | | C maj 21,601 | |
| | | | | | 26.6% | | | | 81.0% | |

CHERYL GILLAN, b April 21, 1952. Elected for this seat 1992; contested Greater Manchester Central 1989 Euro elections. Under Sec for Education and Employment 1995-97; PPS to Lord Cranborne, leader of House of Lords, 1994-95; member, select cttees on science and tech, 1992-95; procedure 1992-95. Former vice-chair, C backbench smaller businesses cttee; ex-joint sec, C trade and industry cttee; ex-joint vice-chair, all-party cricket parly group; ex-joint sec, space cttee; chair, Bow Group, 1987-88. Dir, Kidsons Impey, 1991-93; senior marketing consultant, Ernst and Young, 1986-91. Freeman, City of London, 1991; liveryman,

Marketors' Company, 1991. International and special events dir, British Film Year, 1984-86. Ed Cheltenham Ladies Coll; Coll of Law.

MICHAEL BRAND, b Jan 14, 1952. Music publisher/composer. Chiltern district cllr. Ed Haberdashers' Aske's, Elstree; University Coll, Oxford.

PAUL FARRELLY, b March 2, 1962. Dep business editor, *Independent on Sunday*. Member NUJ; MSF; Co-op Party; SEA; Lab Irish Soc; Greenpeace; Amnesty. Ed Wolstanton GS; Marshlands Comp, Newcastle-under-Lyme; St Edmund Hall, Oxford.

| CHESTER, CITY OF | | 7.6% change | | | | 1997 | | | 1992 | Lab win |
|---|---|---|---|---|---|---|---|---|---|---|
| Electorate % Turnout | | | 71,730 | 78.4% | | **1997** | 68,557 | 83.6% | | **1992** |
| Russell, Ms C | Lab | | 29,806 | 53.0% | +12.4% | | 25,641 | 44.7% | | C |
| +Brandreth, G | C | | 19,253 | 34.2% | -10.5% | | 23,281 | 40.6% | | Lab |
| Simpson, D | LD | | 5,353 | 9.5% | -4.1% | | 7,808 | 13.6% | | LD |
| Mullen, R | Ref | | 1,487 | 2.6% | | | 486 | 0.8% | | Grn |
| Sanderson, I | Loony | | 204 | 0.4% | | | 107 | 0.2% | | NLP |
| Gerrard, J | WCCC | | 154 | 0.3% | | | | | | |
| C to Lab notional swing 11.4% | | | 56,257 | | Lab maj 10,553 | | 57,323 | | C maj 2,360 | |
| | | | | | 18.8% | | | | 83.6% | |

CHRISTINE RUSSELL, b March 25, 1945. Chester cllr 1980- ; Sheriff of Chester 1992-93. Librarian, co-ordinator of Chester and Ellesmere Port advocacy project set up by MIND. Member, Magistrates Assoc; founder, Chester economic forum; chair, annual Chester film festival. Ed Spalding HS; NW London Poly.

GYLES BRANDRETH, b March 8, 1948. Freelance journalist, author and broadcaster. Elected 1992. Appointed asst gvt whip 1995; ex-PPS to Stephen Dorrell, Health Sec and previously National

Heritage Sec. Ex-chair, now vice-pres, Nat Playing Fields Assoc. Ed Lycée Français de Londres; Betteshanger School, Kent; Bedales; New College, Oxford (president of Union). Held world record for longest after-dinner speech lasting 12hr 30min in 1982.

DAVID SIMPSON, b June 23, 1942. Research scientist. Chester city cllr. Ed Royal Naval Children's School, Malta; Portsmouth GS; Univ of Alberta; Imperial Coll, London.

| CHESTERFIELD | | | | | | 1997 | | | 1992 | Lab hold |
|---|---|---|---|---|---|---|---|---|---|---|
| Electorate % Turnout | | | 72,472 | 70.9% | | **1997** | 71,783 | 78.0% | | **1992** |
| *Benn, A W | Lab | | 26,105 | 50.8% | +3.5% | | 26,461 | 47.3% | | Lab |
| Rogers, T | LD | | 20,330 | 39.6% | +3.8% | | 20,047 | 35.8% | | LD |
| Potter, M | C | | 4,752 | 9.2% | -7.7% | | 9,473 | 16.9% | | C |
| Scarth, N | Ind OAP | | 202 | 0.4% | | | | | | |
| Lab to LD swing 0.1% | | | 51,389 | | Lab maj 5,775 | | 55,981 | | Lab maj 6,414 | |
| | | | | | 11.2% | | | | 78.0% | |

TONY BENN, b April 3, 1925. Diarist and journalist. Elected 1984 by-election. MP for Bristol SE 1950-60 and 1963-83; Energy Sec 1975-79; Industry Sec 1974-75; trade and industry chief spokesman 1970-74; Min of Tech 1966-70; Postmaster General 1964-66. Contested party leadership 1976, 1988; dep leadership 1971, 1981. Member, select cttee on privileges 1984-87 and 1989-95; Lab Party NEC, 1959-60 and 1962-93; pres, Campaign Group of Lab MPs, 1987- , and chair 1971-72. Succeeded father, Viscount Stansgate, in Nov 1960 but refused to take Lords seat; renounced

seat under the Peerage Act 1963 and was re-elected Aug 1963. Ed Westminster; New College, Oxford.

TONY ROGERS, b April 9, 1938. Market research interviewer. Contested seat 1992 and 1987, S Hams 1983, Totnes 1979 and both 1974 general elections; Sheffield in 1989 Euro elections. Ex-Mayor of Kingsbridge. Ed Kingsbridge Sec Mod; Brackenhurst Agric Coll.

MARTIN POTTER, b June 1, 1966. Group financial analysis manager. National vice-chair, YCs, 1991-93. Member, C Christian Fellowship. Ed Trinity School, Croydon; Nottingham Univ.

| CHICHESTER | | 7.6% change | | 1997 | | | C win |
|---|---|---|---|---|---|---|---|
| Electorate % Turnout | | 74,489 | 74.9% | **1997** | 75,835 | 77.8% | **1992** |
| Tyrie, A | C | **25,895** | **46.4%** | -12.9% | **34,971** | **59.3%** | C |
| Gardiner, Prof P | LD | 16,161 | 29.0% | +2.4% | 15,690 | 26.6% | LD |
| Smith, C | Lab | 9,605 | 17.2% | +5.9% | 6,703 | 11.4% | Lab |
| Denny, D | Ref | 3,318 | 5.9% | | 810 | 1.4% | Grn |
| Rix, J | UK Ind | 800 | 1.4% | | 596 | 1.0% | Lib |
| | | | | | 219 | 0.4% | NLP |
| C to LD notional swing 7.6% | | **55,779** | | C maj **9,734** | **58,989** | | C maj **19,281** |
| | | | | 17.5% | | | 77.8% |

**ANDREW TYRIE,** b Jan 15, 1957. Senior economist, European Bank for Reconstruction and Development. Contested Houghton and Washington 1992. Adviser to Prime Minister 1990-92; special adviser to Chancellors (Nigel Lawson and John Major) 1986-90; head of economic team, C Research Dept, 1984-85. Ed Felsted School; Trinity Coll, Oxford; Wolfson Coll, Cambridge; Woodrow Wilson Scholar, Smithsonian Inst; Fellow, Nuffield Coll.

**PETER GARDINER,** b Feb 10, 1940. Contested seat 1992. Professor of Civil Engineering, Brighton Poly. Member, exec cttee, Chichester LD; does leadership training. Ed Nottingham, Liverpool and Surrey Univs.
**CHARLIE SMITH,** b April 21, 1948. Housing manager. Ed Buckingham Gate Secondary School; Westminster Coll; Southampton Inst.

| CHINGFORD & WOODFORD GREEN | | 42.3% change | | 1997 | | | C win |
|---|---|---|---|---|---|---|---|
| Electorate % Turnout | | 62,904 | 70.7% | **1997** | 63,606 | 78.5% | **1992** |
| +Duncan Smith, I | C | **21,109** | **47.5%** | -13.9% | **30,656** | **61.4%** | C |
| Hutchinson, T | Lab | 15,395 | 34.6% | +13.7% | 10,455 | 21.0% | Lab |
| Seeff, G | LD | 6,885 | 15.5% | +1.2% | 7,154 | 14.3% | LD |
| Gould, A | BNP | 1,059 | 2.4% | | 1,636 | 3.3% | Other |
| C to Lab notional swing 13.8% | | **44,448** | | C maj **5,714** | **49,901** | | C maj **20,201** |
| | | | | 12.9% | | | 40.5% |

**IAIN DUNCAN SMITH,** b April 9, 1954. Elected MP for Chingford 1992; contested Bradford W 1987. Member, select cttees on standards and privileges 1995-97; health 1992-95; Commons administration cttee; joint vice-chair, C backbench European affairs cttee, 1995-97; joint sec, C backbench foreign and Commonwealth affairs cttee, 1992-97; C defence cttee 1994-95. Vice-chair, Fulham C assoc, 1991. Dir, Janes Information Group, part of Thomson International Corp, 1989-92; Bellwinch plc property company 1988-89; GEC/Marconi 1981-88. Scots Guards officer 1975-81. Trustee, Lygon Almshouses, sheltered housing,

1985-91. Ed HMS Conway (cadet school), Anglesey; Universita di Perugia, Italy; RMA Sandhurst; Dunchurch Coll of Management.
**TOMMY HUTCHINSON,** b Aug 7, 1964. Manager, government relations, NatWest Group. Chair, Hackney N and Stoke Newington CLP, 1993-96. Member, Amnesty; Friends of the Earth; Bifu. Ed Rainey Endowed GS; Magherafelt Coll; Leeds Poly; London Guildhall Univ.
**GEOFFREY SEEFF,** b Aug 29, 1947. Chartered accountant/management consultant. Member, Charter 88. Ed Beal GS, Ilford; Birmingham Univ.

| CHIPPING BARNET | | 19.3% change | | 1997 | | | C win |
|---|---|---|---|---|---|---|---|
| Electorate % Turnout | | 69,049 | 71.8% | **1997** | 69,176 | 77.3% | **1992** |
| +Chapman, Sir Sydney | C | **21,317** | **43.0%** | -13.6% | **30,241** | **56.6%** | C |
| Cooke, G | Lab | 20,282 | 40.9% | +14.7% | 14,028 | 26.2% | Lab |
| Hooker, S | LD | 6,121 | 12.3% | -3.7% | 8,594 | 16.1% | LD |
| Ribekow, V | Ref | 1,190 | 2.4% | | 307 | 0.6% | NLP |
| Miskin, B | Loony | 253 | 0.5% | | 297 | 0.6% | Fun |
| Scallan, B | ProLife | 243 | 0.5% | | | | |
| Dirksen, Ms D | NLP | 159 | 0.3% | -0.3% | | | |
| C to Lab notional swing 14.1% | | **49,565** | | C maj **1,035** | **53,467** | | C maj **16,213** |
| | | | | 2.1% | | | 77.3% |

**SIR SYDNEY CHAPMAN,** b Oct 17, 1935. Chartered architect, town and country planning consultant. Elected for this seat 1979; MP for Birmingham Handsworth 1970-Feb 1974. Contested Stalybridge and Hyde 1964. Gvt whip 1992-95 and 1990-92; asst gvt whip 1988-90. Member, Commons accommodation and works cttee; ecclesiatical cttee; select cttees on public service 1995-97; environment 1983-87; Commons services 1983-87; advisory cttee, Commons works of art, 1988-89. Vice-pres, RIBA, 1974-75; member of council 1972-77. Fellow, Incorporated Assoc of

Architects and Surveyors; Hon Fellow, Faculty of Building; FRSA. Originator, National Tree Planting Year 1973. Pres, London Green Belt Council 1985-89; vice-chair, Wildlife Link, 1985-89. Ed Rugby; Manchester Univ.
**GEOFF COOKE,** b Jan 24, 1948. Software engineer. Contested Chichester 1979. Barnet cllr 1978-86. Ed Sandown GS; London Univ.
**SEAN HOOKER,** b March 19, 1966. Insurance underwriter. Member, Charter 88. Ed Finchley Catholic HS; Keele Univ.

| CHORLEY | 7.0% change | | | | | | Lab win |
|---|---|---|---|---|---|---|---|
| Electorate % Turnout | | 74,387 | 77.6% | **1997** | 73,536 | 82.4% | **1992** |
| **Hoyle, L** | **Lab** | **30,607** | **53.0%** | **+11.4%** | **27,752** | **45.8%** | **C** |
| +Dover, D | C | 20,737 | 35.9% | -9.9% | 25,228 | 41.6% | Lab |
| Jones, S | LD | 4,900 | 8.5% | -3.5% | 7,249 | 12.0% | LD |
| Heaton, A | Ref | 1,319 | 2.3% | | 373 | 0.6% | NLP |
| Leadbetter, P | NLP | 143 | 0.2% | -0.4% | | | |
| C to Lab notional swing 10.6% | | 57,706 | | Lab maj 9,870 | 60,602 | | C maj 2,524 |
| | | | | 17.1% | | | 82.4% |

**LINDSAY HOYLE,** b June 10, 1957. Businessman and director of printing company. Chorley borough cllr (dep council leader). Founder/dir, 1988, and chair, 1992-96, Chorley Rugby League Club.
**DEN DOVER,** b April 4, 1938. Elected 1979; contested Caerphilly Oct 1974. Member, select cttees on environment 1995-97; and transport 1979-87; chair select cttee on Severn Bridges Bill, 1991.

Joint vice-chair, C backbench trade and industry cttee, 1994-97; Barnet cllr 1968-71. Formerly civil engineer; member, Instit of Civil Engineers; dir, Cosalt plc, 1988- ; pres, CTU nat engineering group. Ed Manchester Grammar; Manchester Univ.
**SIMON JONES,** b Feb 21, 1955. In music business. Chorley borough cllr (LD group leader). Member, Friends of the Earth. Ed Beechen Cliff, Bath; Univ Coll of Wales, Cardiff.

| CHRISTCHURCH | 4.7% change | | | | | | C win |
|---|---|---|---|---|---|---|---|
| Electorate % Turnout | | 71,488 | 78.6% | **1997** | 68,353 | 80.8% | **1992** |
| **Chope, C R** | **C** | **26,095** | **46.4%** | **-17.3%** | **35,237** | **63.8%** | **C** |
| +Maddock, Mrs D | LD | 23,930 | 42.6% | +19.2% | 12,913 | 23.4% | LD |
| Mannan, C | Lab | 3,884 | 6.9% | -5.2% | 6,678 | 12.1% | Lab |
| Spencer, R | Ref | 1,684 | 3.0% | | 243 | 0.4% | NLP |
| Dickinson, R | UK Ind | 606 | 1.1% | | 175 | 0.3% | CRA |
| C to LD notional swing 18.3% | | 56,199 | | C maj 2,165 | 55,246 | | C maj 22,324 |
| | | | | 3.9% | | | 40.4% |

**CHRISTOPHER CHOPE,** b May 19, 1947. Barrister; consultant, Ernst & Young, since 1992. MP for Southampton Itchen 1983-92; Minister for Roads and Traffic 1990-92; Under Sec for Environment 1986-90; PPS to Peter Brooke, Min of State, Treasury, 1985-86. Member, Health and Safety Commission 1993- ; Local Gvt Commission for England 1994- . Wandsworth cllr 1974-83 (leader 1979-83). Ed St Andrew's School, Eastbourne; Marlborough; St Andrews Univ.

**DIANA MADDOCK,** b May 19, 1945. Gained the seat for LDs in 1993 by-election; contested Southampton Test 1992. Teacher of English as a foreign language. Southampton city cllr 1984-93. Ed Brockenhurst GS; Shenestone Training Coll; Portsmouth Poly.
**CHARLES MANNAN,** b Dec 1, 1967. Barrister. Member, Amnesty; Friends of the Earth. Ed Dulwich Coll; LSE; Central Lancs Univ.
*Details of 1993 by-election on page 277*

| CITIES OF LONDON & WESTMINSTER | | 19.8% change | | | | | C win |
|---|---|---|---|---|---|---|---|
| Electorate % Turnout | | 69,047 | 58.2% | **1997** | 65,613 | 65.5% | **1992** |
| **+Brooke, P L** | **C** | **18,981** | **47.3%** | **-12.0%** | **25,512** | **59.3%** | **C** |
| Green, Ms K | Lab | 14,100 | 35.1% | +11.0% | 10,368 | 24.1% | Lab |
| Dumigan, M | LD | 4,933 | 12.3% | -1.8% | 6,077 | 14.1% | LD |
| Walters, Sir Alan | Ref | 1,161 | 2.9% | | 1,051 | 2.4% | Other |
| Wharton, P | Barts | 266 | 0.7% | | | | |
| Merton, C | UK Ind | 215 | 0.5% | | | | |
| Johnson, R | NLP | 176 | 0.4% | | | | |
| Walsh, N | Loony | 138 | 0.3% | | | | |
| Webster, G | Hemp | 112 | 0.3% | | | | |
| Sadowitz, J | Dream | 73 | 0.2% | | | | |
| C to Lab notional swing 11.5% | | 40,155 | | C maj 4,881 | 43,008 | | C maj 15,144 |
| | | | | 12.2% | | | 65.5% |

**PETER BROOKE**, b March 3, 1934. Elected for City of London and Westminster South 1977 by-election; contested Bedwellty Oct 1974. National Heritage Sec 1992-94; N Ireland Sec 1989-92 (resigning after 1992 election and contesting Speakership); chair, C Party, 1987-89; Paymaster General 1987-89; Treasury Min 1985-87; Under Sec for Ed and Science 1983-85; gvt whip 1981-83; asst gvt whip 1979-81. Joint chair, all-party homelessness and housing needs parly group, 1996-97. Member of Lloyd's. Chair, Building Societies Ombudsman Council; pres, British Antique Dealers'

Assoc. Ed Marlborough; Balliol Coll, Oxford (pres of Union 1957); Harvard Business School (Commonwealth Fund Fellow).
**KATE GREEN**, b May 2, 1960. Campaign Strategy Co-ordinator, Labour Party. Former bank manager. Member, Bifu; Co-op Party. Board member, Inner City Regeneration Project. Ed Currie HS, Midlothian; Edinburgh Univ.
**MICHAEL DUMIGAN**, b Nov 15, 1961. Marketing consultant. Dir, Papparazi Clothing Ltd. Member, Charter 88. Ed De La Salle Boys', Belfast; Queen's Univ, Belfast.

| CLEETHORPES | | 17.3% change | | | | | Lab win |
|---|---|---|---|---|---|---|---|
| Electorate % Turnout | | 68,763 | 73.4% | **1997** | 68,355 | 78.0% | **1992** |
| McIsaac, Ms S | Lab | **26,058** | 51.6% | +15.7% | 25,582 | 48.0% | C |
| +Brown, M R | C | 16,882 | 33.4% | -14.5% | 19,169 | 35.9% | Lab |
| Melton, K | LD | 5,746 | 11.4% | -3.3% | 7,833 | 14.7% | LD |
| Berry, J | Ref | 1,787 | 3.5% | | 751 | 1.4% | Other |
| C to Lab notional swing 15.1% | | 50,473 | Lab maj 9,176 | | 53,335 | C maj 6,413 | |
| | | | 18.2% | | | 78.0% | |

**SHONA McISAAC,** b April 3, 1960. Freelance journalist. Wandsworth cllr 1990- (dep Lab group leader, 1992-95). Qualified lifeguard at Tooting pool in mid-1980s. Ed SHAPE School, Belgium; Barbe Barton Sec Mod, Plymouth; Damerel HS, Plymouth; Durham Univ.
**MICHAEL BROWN,** b July 3, 1951. Lecturer and tutor, Swinton C Coll 1974-75. Elected 1983 for Brigg and Cleethorpes; MP for Brigg and Scunthorpe 1979-83. Asst gvt whip 1993-94; member, select cttees on ed and employment; deregulation 1995-97; energy 1986-89. PPS to Sir Patrick Mayhew, N Ireland Sec, 1992-93; to Douglas Hogg, Industry Min and then at FCO 1989-92; joint vice-chair (1987-89) and joint sec (1981-87), C backbench N Ireland cttee. Ed Andrew Cairns County Sec Mod, Littlehampton; York Univ.
**KEITH MELTON,** b June 10, 1947. Senior lecturer; director, Green Business Network (Nottingham Business School). Contested Lincoln 1979, Broxtowe 1983 and 1987; Nottingham in 1984 Euro elections; Lincolnshire and Humberside S in 1994 Euro elections. Ed North Kesteven GS; UMIST.

| CLWYD SOUTH | | 67.8% change | | | | | Lab win |
|---|---|---|---|---|---|---|---|
| Electorate % Turnout | | 53,495 | 73.6% | **1997** | 53,963 | 79.0% | **1992** |
| +Jones, M | Lab | **22,901** | 58.1% | +8.4% | 21,229 | 49.8% | Lab |
| Johnson, B | C | 9,091 | 23.1% | -7.2% | 12,897 | 30.2% | C |
| Chadwick, A | LD | 3,684 | 9.4% | -1.7% | 4,727 | 11.1% | LD |
| Williams, G V | PC | 2,500 | 6.3% | -1.6% | 3,394 | 8.0% | PC |
| Lewis, A | Ref | 1,207 | 3.1% | | 390 | 0.9% | Other |
| C to Lab notional swing 7.8% | | 39,383 | Lab maj 13,810 | | 42,637 | Lab maj 8,332 | |
| | | | 35.1% | | | 19.5% | |

**MARTYN JONES,** b March 1, 1947. Microbiologist. Elected MP for Clwyd SW 1987; Lab spokesman on agric 1994-95; member, agric select cttee 1987-94 and 1995-97, chair 1987-94, and vice-chair 1995-97; PLP agric cttee. Campaign officer 1995- , and former chair, Welsh group of Lab MPs; Lab whip 1988-92. Clwyd county cllr 1981-89. Worked in brewing industry 1968-87; member, Inst of Biology. Ex-area rep TGWU. Ed Grove Park GS, Wrexham; Liverpool and Trent Polys.
**BORIS JOHNSON,** b June 19, 1964. Asst editor and political columnist of *The Daily Telegraph;* EC correspondent in Brussels 1989-94; political columnist of *Spectator* 1994-95. Ed Eton; Balliol Coll, Oxford (pres of Union).
**ANDREW CHADWICK,** b Oct 23, 1953. Charity director in Ethiopia, Bosnia. Dir, Marchad Ltd. Ed Aireborough GS, Leeds.
**GARETH WILLIAMS,** b Dec 13, 1970. Teacher; Ed Macs Garmon School, Mold; Univ of Wales Inst, Cyncoed, Cardiff.

| CLWYD WEST | | 65.5% change | | | | | Lab win |
|---|---|---|---|---|---|---|---|
| Electorate % Turnout | | 53,467 | 75.3% | **1997** | 53,827 | 77.2% | **1992** |
| Thomas, G | Lab | **14,918** | 37.1% | +6.2% | 20,132 | 48.5% | C |
| +Richards, R | C | 13,070 | 32.5% | -16.0% | 12,819 | 30.9% | Lab |
| Williams, E | PC | 5,421 | 13.5% | +8.9% | 6,526 | 15.7% | LD |
| Williams, W G | LD | 5,151 | 12.8% | -2.9% | 1,906 | 4.6% | PC |
| Collins, Ms H | Ref | 1,114 | 2.8% | | 151 | 0.4% | Other |
| Neal, D | Cvty | 583 | 1.4% | | | | |
| C to Lab notional swing 11.1% | | 40,257 | Lab maj 1,848 | | 41,534 | C maj 7,313 | |
| | | | 4.6% | | | 77.2% | |

**GARETH THOMAS,** b Sept 25, 1954. Barrister. Flintshire county cllr 1995- . Member, MSF; Fabian Soc. Ed Rock Ferry HS, Birkenhead; Univ Coll of Wales, Aberystwyth.
**ROD RICHARDS,** b March 12, 1947. MP for Clwyd NW 1992-97; contested Vale of Glamorgan 1989 by-election, Carmarthen 1987. Under Sec for Wales 1994-96; PPS to Min of State, FCO, 1993-94; member, Welsh affairs select cttee 1992-93; special adviser to David Hunt when Sec for Wales 1990. BBC TV news and current affairs presenter 1983-89; defence intelligence staff, MoD, 1976- 83; Royal Marines 1969-71. Ed Llandovery Coll; Univ Coll of Wales, Swansea.
**ERYL WILLIAMS,** b Nov 13, 1955. Farmer. Vice-pres, Young Farmers of Wales and England, since 1994; Denbigh county cllr 1995- . Former PC agric spokesman. Ed Llysafasi Agricultural Coll.
**GWYN WILLIAMS,** b Oct 30, 1960. Farmer. Contested Clwyd SW 1992. Clwyd county cllr 1986-96; Denbighshire county cllr 1985- ; member, Clwyd HA, 1989-90. Exec cttee, Welsh LDs. Member, Amnesty. Ed Ruthin School; Reading Univ.

| CLYDEBANK & MILNGAVIE | | 7.1% change | | | | | Lab win |
|---|---|---|---|---|---|---|---|
| Electorate % Turnout | | 52,092 | 75.0% | **1997** | 51,276 | 77.3% | **1992** |
| +Worthington, T | **Lab** | **21,583** | **55.2%** | **+5.0%** | **19,923** | **50.3%** | **Lab** |
| Yuill, J | SNP | 8,263 | 21.1% | +2.7% | 8,503 | 21.5% | C |
| Morgan, Ms N | C | 4,885 | 12.5% | -9.0% | 7,319 | 18.5% | SNP |
| Moody, K | LD | 4,086 | 10.5% | +0.9% | 3,778 | 9.5% | LD |
| Sanderson, I | Ref | 269 | 0.7% | | 117 | 0.3% | NLP |
| SNP to Lab notional swing 1.1% | | 39,086 | Lab maj 13,320 | | 39,640 | Lab maj 11,420 | |
| | | | 34.1% | | | 77.3% | |

**TONY WORTHINGTON**, b Oct 11, 1941. Became Under Secretary at the Northern Ireland Office, May 5, 1997. Elected for this seat 1987. Lab spokesman on N Ireland 1995-97; on foreign affairs 1993-94; overseas development 1992-93; Scotland 1989-92. Joint sec, all-party population, reproductive health and development group, 1989-97. Chair, Lab campaign for criminal justice, 1987-89. Strathclyde regional cllr 1974-87. Social policy and sociology lecturer, Jordanhill Coll of Ed, Glasgow, 1971-87; Monkwearmouth CFE, Sunderland, 1967-71; HM Borstal, Dover, 1962-66. Ed City School, Lincoln; LSE; York and Glasgow Univs.

**JIM YUILL**, b April 11, 1940. Industrial engineer. Clydebank cllr 1994-96; convener of Clydebank and Milngavie constituency assoc. Ed Clydebank HS; Clydebank Coll of FE.
**NANCY MORGAN**, b July 24, 1947. Information services and research dept, C Central Office, 1994- . Hon sec, S Wales women's cttee, 1992-96; member, Wales area council, 1993-94. Ed Hofstra Univ; Ohio State Univ.
**KEITH MOODY**, b Nov 1, 1934. Transport manager (retired). Contested Ayr 1987. East Dunbartonshire cllr (opposition leader). Ed King Edward's GS, Birmingham.

| CLYDESDALE | | | | | | | Lab hold |
|---|---|---|---|---|---|---|---|
| Electorate % Turnout | | 63,428 | 71.6% | **1997** | 61,878 | 77.6% | **1992** |
| *Hood, J | **Lab** | **23,859** | **52.5%** | **+7.9%** | **21,418** | **44.6%** | **Lab** |
| Doig, A | SNP | 10,050 | 22.1% | -0.9% | 11,231 | 23.4% | C |
| Izatt, M | C | 7,396 | 16.3% | -7.1% | 11,084 | 23.1% | SNP |
| Grieve, Mrs S | LD | 3,796 | 8.4% | +0.1% | 3,957 | 8.2% | LD |
| Smith, K | BNP | 311 | 0.7% | -0.0% | 342 | 0.7% | BNP |
| SNP to Lab swing 4.4% | | 45,412 | Lab maj 13,809 | | 48,032 | Lab maj 10,187 | |
| | | | 30.4% | | | 21.2% | |

**JIMMY HOOD**, b May 16, 1948. Miner/coalface engineer. Elected 1987. Chair, select cttee on Euro legislation, 1992- and of its sub-cttee on road safety 1994. Chair, 1995- , and former vice-chair, Scottish group of Lab MPs; chair, miners parly group, 1990-92. Newark and Sherwood district cllr 1979-87. Ed Lesmahagow Higher Grade School, Coatbridge; Motherwell Tech Coll; Nottingham Univ.
**ANDREW DOIG**, b Dec 15, 1961. Freelance journalist. Contested Glasgow Pollok 1987; sub-agent for party leader Alex Salmond in

Banff and Buchan 1992. Member, SNP nat council; SNP asst nat sec, 1992-96. Founder member, Young Scots for Independence. Ed Denny HS; Falkirk Coll of Tech.
**MARK IZATT**, b March 23, 1969. Special adviser to Scottish Office junior mins 1994-95. Ed Woodmill HS, Dunfermline; Aberdeen Univ.
**SANDRA GRIEVE**, b May 17, 1954. Training consultant. Contested East Kilbride 1992; Monklands E 1987. Ed Uddingston GS; Bell Coll, Hamilton.

| COATBRIDGE & CHRYSTON | | 25.5% change | | | | | Lab win |
|---|---|---|---|---|---|---|---|
| Electorate % Turnout | | 52,024 | 72.3% | **1997** | 52,830 | 76.1% | **1992** |
| +Clarke, T | **Lab** | **25,697** | **68.3%** | **+6.5%** | **24,843** | **61.8%** | **Lab** |
| Nugent, B | SNP | 6,402 | 17.0% | +0.3% | 6,743 | 16.8% | SNP |
| Wauchope, A | C | 3,216 | 8.6% | -7.0% | 6,241 | 15.5% | C |
| Daly, Mrs M | LD | 2,048 | 5.4% | -0.5% | 2,388 | 5.9% | LD |
| Bowsley, B | Ref | 249 | 0.7% | | | | |
| SNP to Lab notional swing 3.1% | | 37,612 | Lab maj 19,295 | | 40,215 | Lab maj 18,100 | |
| | | | 51.3% | | | 45.0% | |

**TOM CLARKE**, b Jan 10, 1941. Became National Heritage Minister responsible for film and tourism, May 5, 1997. MP for Monklands W 1983-97; for Coatbridge and Airdrie 1982-83. Lab spokesman on disabled people's rights 1994; Shadow Cabinet 1992-94 and 1995-97. Chief spokesman on overseas aid 1993-94; Shadow Scottish Sec 1992-93. Member, Lab frontbench health team 1987-90 as spokesman on personal social services; spokesman on Scottish affairs 1987. Sponsored Disabled Persons Act 1986. Coatbridge cllr 1964-74. Provost of Monklands 1964-74. Ed Columba HS, Coatbridge; Scottish Coll of Commerce.

**BRIAN NUGENT**, b Sept 1, 1952. Computing lecturer at Shetland Coll. Sec, SNP Shetland branch. Sec, Shetland EIS College Lecturers' Assoc. Ed St Patrick's HS, Coatbridge; Galashiels Textile Coll.
**ANDREW WAUCHOPE**, b 1956. Barrister, author and journalist. C assoc sec and chair. British correspondent for *Daily Gazette*, Harare, 1993-94. Member, Soc of Authors. Ed Worth School, Sussex; Manchester Univ.
**MORAG DALY**, b Feb 21, 1950. Accountant. Sec, East Dunbartonshire and Clydebank LDs. Ed Lanark GS; Glasgow Univ.

**105**

| COLCHESTER | | 80.9% change | | | | | | LD win |
|---|---|---|---|---|---|---|---|---|
| Electorate % Turnout | | 74,743 | 69.6% | **1997** | 73,347 | 76.8% | **1992** | |
| **Russell, R E** | **LD** | **17,886** | **34.4%** | **+1.7%** | 23,692 | 42.0% | C | |
| Shakespeare, S | C | 16,305 | 31.4% | -10.7% | 18,424 | 32.7% | LD | |
| Green, R | Lab | 15,891 | 30.6% | +6.5% | 13,582 | 24.1% | Lab | |
| Hazell, J | Ref | 1,776 | 3.4% | | 658 | 1.2% | Other | |
| Basker, Ms L | NLP | 148 | 0.3% | | | | | |
| **C to LD notional swing 6.2%** | | **52,006** | | **LD maj 1,581** | **56,356** | | **C maj 5,268** | |
| | | | | 3.0% | | | 9.4% | |

**BOB RUSSELL**, b March 31, 1946. Contested Sudbury and Woodbridge, Oct 1974, and this seat 1979 for Lab. Colchester borough cllr 1971- (leader 1987-91; ex-Mayor). Ex-press officer to Essex Univ and GPO telecommunications. Ed St Helena Sec, Colchester; NE Essex Tech Coll.

**STEPHAN SHAKESPEARE**, b April 9, 1957. Teacher and journalist. Exec council, Cities of London and Westminster C assoc and West Suffolk assoc. Head of special needs, Charles Edward Brooke School, Lambeth; co-owner, Kingston Natural Health Centre; newspaper commentator on education policy. Previously founding head, Landmark West Prep School, Los Angeles. Chair, Coll of Teachers. JP, City of London. Ed Christ's Hospital, Horsham; St Peter's Coll, Oxford.

**RODERICK GREEN**, b May 29, 1943. Teacher. Contested Colchester N 1987. Member, Colchester borough cllr 1978- (Lab group leader 1987- ). Member, NUT; Co-op Party; Fabian Soc. Ed Bishop Wordsworth's GS; London Univ.

| COLNE VALLEY | | | | | | | | Lab gain |
|---|---|---|---|---|---|---|---|---|
| Electorate % Turnout | | 56,411 | 76.9% | **1997** | 72,043 | 82.0% | **1992** | |
| **Mountford, Ms K** | **Lab** | **23,285** | **41.3%** | **+11.5%** | 24,804 | 42.0% | C | |
| *Riddick, G | C | 18,445 | 32.7% | -9.3% | 17,579 | 29.8% | Lab | |
| Priestley, N | LD | 12,755 | 22.6% | -4.4% | 15,953 | 27.0% | LD | |
| Brooke, A | Soc Lab | 759 | 1.3% | | 443 | 0.8% | Grn | |
| Cooper, A | Green | 493 | 0.9% | | 160 | 0.3% | Loony | |
| Nunn, J | UK Ind | 478 | 0.8% | | 73 | 0.1% | Ind | |
| Staniforth, Ms M | Loony | 196 | 0.3% | +0.1% | 44 | 0.1% | NLP | |
| **C to Lab swing 10.4%** | | **56,411** | | **Lab maj 4,840** | **59,056** | | **C maj 7,225** | |
| | | | | 8.6% | | | 12.5% | |

**KALI MOUNTFORD**, b Jan 12, 1954. Ex-civil servant, Dept of Employment and Educaton. Sheffield city cllr.

**GRAHAM RIDDICK**, b Aug 26, 1955. Won this seat 1987. PPS to John MacGregor, Transport Sec, 1992-94; to Francis Maude, Financial Sec to Treasury, 1990-92. Member, select cttees on broadcasting, 1995-97; education and employment 1996-97, and its sub-cttee; education 1992-96; deregulation 1995-97. Vice-chair, C backbench employment cttee, 1988-90; all-party South Pennines group, 1996-97; sec, C trade and industry cttee, 1990; all-party wool textile parly group, 1988-97; joint treas, beer club group, 1994-97.Pres, Yorks CPC, 1993- . Member of Lloyd's. In sales management with Procter & Gamble 1977-82, and Coca-Cola 1982-87. Member, nat council, Freedom Assoc, 1988- . Ed Stowe; Warwick Univ (chair, univ C assoc).

**NIGEL PRIESTLEY**, b Sept 22, 1952. Solicitor. Contested this seat 1992 and 1987. Ex-Meltham town cllr. Chair, Colne Valley Lib Assoc, 1984-85. Partner in local firm of solicitors specialising in personal injury and childcare. Lay reader. Ed King James GS, Huddersfield; Warwick Univ.

| CONGLETON | | 6.6% change | | | | | | C win |
|---|---|---|---|---|---|---|---|---|
| Electorate % Turnout | | 68,873 | 77.6% | **1997** | 66,069 | 84.3% | **1992** | |
| **+Winterton, Mrs A** | **C** | **22,012** | **41.2%** | **-7.3%** | 27,007 | 48.5% | C | |
| Walmsley, Mrs J | LD | 15,882 | 29.7% | -2.0% | 17,657 | 31.7% | LD | |
| Scholey, Ms H | Lab | 14,714 | 27.5% | +8.4% | 10,684 | 19.2% | Lab | |
| Lockett, J | UK Ind | 811 | 1.5% | | 373 | 0.7% | NLP | |
| **C to LD notional swing 2.7%** | | **53,419** | | **C maj 6,130** | **55,721** | | **C maj 9,350** | |
| | | | | 11.5% | | | 16.8% | |

**ANN WINTERTON**, b March 6, 1941. Elected for this seat 1983. Member, agric select cttee, 1987-97; Commons chairmen's panel, 1992- ; unopposed Bills panel. Chair, all-party parly ProLife group, 1992- ; joint chair, breast cancer group; treas, parly and scientic cttee. Member, W Midlands C women's advisory cttee, 1969-71. Joint Master, South Staffs Hunt, 1959-64. Ed Erdington GS for Girls. Wife of Nicholas Winterton, MP for Macclesfield.

**JOAN WALMSLEY**, b April 12, 1943. Public relations consultant, ex-teacher. Contested Leeds S and Morley 1992. Member, Charter 88; Amnesty. Ed Notre Dame HS, Liverpool; Liverpool and Manchester Univs. Her husband Christopher, who died in 1995, was previous LD prospective parly candidate for Congleton.

**HELEN SCHOLEY**, b June 14, 1955. Constituency political organiser to MEP. Member, GMB; Co-op Party; regional women's cttee. Ed Manchester Metropolitan Univ.

| CONWY | | | | | **1997** | | | **1992** |
|---|---|---|---|---|---|---|---|---|
| Electorate % Turnout | | | 55,092 | 75.4% | **1997** | 53,576 | 78.9% | **1992** |
| Williams, Mrs B H | Lab | | **14,561** | **35.0%** | **+9.3%** | **14,250** | **33.7%** | C |
| Roberts, R | LD | | 12,965 | 31.2% | -0.2% | 13,255 | 31.4% | LD |
| Jones, D I | C | | 10,085 | 24.3% | -9.5% | 10,883 | 25.8% | Lab |
| Davies, R | PC | | 2,844 | 6.8% | -0.5% | 3,108 | 7.4% | PC |
| Barham, A | Ref | | 760 | 1.8% | | 637 | 1.5% | Ind C |
| Bradley, R | Alt LD | | 250 | 0.6% | | 114 | 0.3% | NLP |
| Hughes, D | NLP | | 95 | 0.2% | -0.0% | | | |
| LD to Lab swing 4.7% | | | **41,560** | Lab maj 1,596 | | **42,247** | C maj 995 | |
| | | | | 3.8% | | | 78.9% | |

**BETTY WILLIAMS**, b July 31, 1944. Freelance media researcher. Contested this seat 1992 and 1987 and Caernarfon 1983. Ex-Gwynedd county cllr; Arfon borough cllr 1970-91 (Mayor 1990-91). Ed Ysgol Dyffryn Nantlle.
**THE REV ROGER ROBERTS**, b Oct 23, 1935. Broadcaster and Methodist superintendent minister. Contested this seat 1992, 1987, 1983 and 1979. LD federal vice-pres. Ex-Aberconwy borough cllr. Ed John Bright GS, Llandudno; Univ Coll of Wales, Bangor; Handsworth Coll, Birmingham.
**DAVID JONES**, b March 22, 1952. Solicitor. Ed Ruabon GS; University Coll, London; Coll of Law, Chester.
**RHODRI DAVIES**, b Nov 25, 1947. Solicitor. Contested this seat 1992 and 1987. Ed Friars GS, Bangor; Univ Coll of Wales, Aberystwyth; Coll of Law, Guildford.

| COPELAND | | | | | **1997** | | | **1992** |
|---|---|---|---|---|---|---|---|---|
| Electorate % Turnout | | | 54,263 | 76.2% | **1997** | 54,911 | 83.5% | **1992** |
| *Cunningham, Dr J | Lab | | **24,025** | **58.1%** | **+9.4%** | **22,328** | **48.7%** | Lab |
| Cumpsty, A | C | | 12,081 | 29.2% | -14.1% | 19,889 | 43.4% | C |
| Putnam, R | LD | | 3,814 | 9.2% | +1.6% | 3,508 | 7.6% | LD |
| Johnston, C | Ref | | 1,036 | 2.5% | | 148 | 0.3% | NLP |
| Hanratty, G | ProLife | | 389 | 0.9% | | | | |
| C to Lab swing 11.8% | | | **41,345** | Lab maj 11,944 | | **45,873** | Lab maj 2,439 | |
| | | | | 28.9% | | | 83.5% | |

**JACK CUNNINGHAM**, b Aug 4, 1939. Became Agriculture Minister, May 3, 1997. Shadow Heritage Sec 1995-97. MP for Copeland since 1983, for Whitehaven 1970-83. Shadow Trade and Industry Sec 1994-95; chief spokesman on foreign and Commonwealth affairs 1992-94; Shadow Leader of Commons and Lab campaigns co-ordinator 1989-92; industry spokesman 1979-83; Energy Under Sec 1976-79. PPS to James Callaghan 1974-76. Chester-le-Street district cllr 1969-74. Former adviser to Albright and Wilson (UK) Ltd, Hays Chemicals, Centurion Press Ltd. Ed Jarrow GS; Bede Coll, Durham.

**ANDREW CUMPSTY**, b Feb 16, 1963. Communications officer, McDonald's Restaurants Ltd. Freeman, City of Lancaster, 1995. On management boards, Lancaster City Centre and Lancaster CAB. Ed Lancaster RGS; Bradford Univ.
**ROGER PUTNAM**, b July 27, 1935. Guesthouse owner. Contested Copeland 1992, Cumbria and North Lancs in Euro elections 1994. Principal of Outward Bound Mountain School at Eskdale for 20 years. Lay inspector of schools. Ed Wellingborough School, Northants; St John's Coll, Oxford.

| CORBY | | | | | **1997** | | | **1992** |
|---|---|---|---|---|---|---|---|---|
| Electorate % Turnout | | | 69,252 | 77.9% | **1997** | 68,333 | 82.9% | **1992** |
| Hope, P | Lab Co-op | | **29,888** | **55.4%** | | **25,203** | **44.5%** | C |
| *Powell, W | C | | 18,028 | 33.4% | -11.1% | 24,861 | 43.9% | Lab |
| Hankinson, I | LD | | 4,045 | 7.5% | -2.7% | 5,792 | 10.2% | LD |
| Riley-Smith, S | Ref | | 1,356 | 2.5% | | 784 | 1.4% | Lib |
| Gillman, I | UK Ind | | 507 | 0.9% | | | | |
| Bence, Ms J | NLP | | 133 | 0.2% | | | | |
| No swing calculation | | | **53,957** | Lab Co-op maj 11,860 | | **56,640** | C maj 342 | |
| | | | | 22.0% | | | 82.9% | |

**PHILIP HOPE**, b April 19, 1955. Contested Kettering 1992. Kettering borough cllr 1983-87 (dep group leader 1986-87); Northants county cllr 1993- . Management and community work consultant and youth policy adviser; teacher; director of publishing co-operative. Member, Co-op Party; MSF. Ed Wandsworth Comp; St Luke's Coll, Exeter. Enjoys tap dancing and juggling burning clubs.
**WILLIAM POWELL**, b Aug 3, 1948. Barrister. Elected 1983. PPS to Sec for Environment 1990-92. Member, select cttees on science and tech, 1992-95; foreign affairs 1990-91; procedure 1987-90; joint parly ecclesiastical cttee, 1987-97. Member, board, Fed Against Software Theft. Dir, Anchorwise Ltd, 1989-91; parly and business consultant to Unquoted Companies Group; McNicholas Construction Co. Ed Lancing Coll; Emmanuel Coll, Cambridge.
**IAN HANKINSON**, b May 23, 1946. Architect. Member, Charter 88; Greenpeace; Friends of the Earth. Ed Havelock Comp, Grimsby; School of Architecture Regional Coll of Art, Leeds.

### CORNWALL NORTH — LD hold

| Electorate % Turnout | | 80,076 | 73.2% | 1997 | 76,844 | 81.5% | 1992 |
|---|---|---|---|---|---|---|---|
| *Tyler, P | LD | 31,186 | 53.2% | +5.8% | 29,696 | 47.4% | LD |
| Linacre, N | C | 17,253 | 29.5% | -14.9% | 27,775 | 44.3% | C |
| Lindo, Ms A | Lab | 5,523 | 9.4% | +2.9% | 4,103 | 6.6% | Lab |
| Odam, Ms F | Ref | 3,636 | 6.2% | | 678 | 1.1% | Lib |
| Bolitho, J | Meb Ker | 645 | 1.1% | | 276 | 0.4% | Ind |
| Winfield, R | Lib | 186 | 0.3% | -0.8% | 112 | 0.2% | NLP |
| Cresswell, N | NLP | 152 | 0.3% | +0.1% | | | |
| C to LD swing 10.4% | | 58,581 | LD maj 13,933 | | 62,640 | LD maj 1,921 | |
| | | | 23.8% | | | 3.1% | |

PAUL TYLER, b Oct 29, 1941. Became LD Chief Whip May 1997. PR and environmental campaign consultant. Won this seat for LDs in 1992. Lib MP for Bodmin, Feb to Oct 1974, contesting that seat 1979 and 1970, Beaconsfield by-election 1982, Totnes 1966, and Cornwall and Plymouth in 1989 Euro elections. LD spokesman on agric and rural affairs, 1992-97. Member, procedure select cttee, 1992-97; chair, all-party coastal group, 1993- ; vice-chair, Brake (safe commercial transport) group; joint sec, water group, 1993- ; treas, tourism cttee, 1993- . Chair, Lib Party, 1983-86. Devon county cllr 1964-70. Director and now non-exec dir, Western Approaches Public Relations Ltd, 1987- ; senior consultant, Good Relations Ltd, 1987-92. Ed Sherborne School; Exeter Coll, Oxford.
NIGEL LINACRE, b Aug 21, 1957. Contested Ealing Southall 1983. Co-founder and director, ITS group plc; dir of Interactive Telephone Services Ltd. Ed Imberhorne, East Grinstead; George Heriot's School, Edinburgh; Reading Univ.
ANNIE LINDO, b Nov 14, 1952. Wine grower. North Cornwall district cllr 1991- ; Bodmin town cllr 1991- . Ed Wycombe Abbey School; Essex Univ.

### CORNWALL SOUTH EAST — LD gain

| Electorate % Turnout | | 75,825 | 75.7% | 1997 | 73,027 | 82.1% | 1992 |
|---|---|---|---|---|---|---|---|
| Breed, C | LD | 27,044 | 47.1% | +9.0% | 30,565 | 51.0% | C |
| Lightfoot, W | C | 20,564 | 35.8% | -15.1% | 22,861 | 38.1% | LD |
| Kirk, Mrs D | Lab | 7,358 | 12.8% | +3.6% | 5,536 | 9.2% | Lab |
| Wonnacott, J | UK Ind | 1,428 | 2.5% | | 644 | 1.1% | Lib |
| Dunbar, P | Meb Ker | 573 | 1.0% | | 227 | 0.4% | Anti-Fed |
| Weights, W | Lib | 268 | 0.5% | -0.6% | 155 | 0.3% | NLP |
| Hartley, Ms M | NLP | 197 | 0.3% | +0.1% | | | |
| C to LD swing 12.1% | | 57,432 | LD maj 6,480 | | 59,988 | C maj 7,704 | |
| | | | 11.3% | | | 82.1% | |

COLIN BREED, b May 4, 1947. Company director. Saltash cllr 1982- ; Mayor of Saltash 1989-90 and 1995-96. Dir, Gemini Abrasives Ltd; Wesley Housing & Benevolent Trust Ltd. Ed Torquay GS.
WARWICK LIGHTFOOT, b 1957. Contested Liverpool Mossley Hill 1987. Economist and special adviser to Norman Lamont when Chancellor, 1989-92. Kensington and Chelsea cllr 1986- . Ed King Edward VI, Totnes; Exeter Coll, Oxford (pres of Union 1980).
DOROTHY KIRK, b April 25, 1945. Languages teacher. Contested Cornwall and Plymouth in 1989 and 1994 Euro elections. Ed Notts County HS for Girls; Reading Univ.

### COTSWOLD — 55.4% change — C win

| Electorate % Turnout | | 67,333 | 75.9% | 1997 | 63,555 | 82.4% | 1992 |
|---|---|---|---|---|---|---|---|
| +Clifton-Brown, G R | C | 23,698 | 46.4% | -8.0% | 28,496 | 54.4% | C |
| Gayler, D | LD | 11,733 | 23.0% | -10.4% | 17,479 | 33.4% | LD |
| Elwell, D | Lab | 11,608 | 22.7% | +11.8% | 5,697 | 10.9% | Lab |
| Lowe, R | Ref | 3,393 | 6.6% | | 722 | 1.4% | Other |
| Michael, Ms V | Green | 560 | 1.1% | | | | |
| Brighouse, H | NLP | 129 | 0.3% | | | | |
| LD to C notional swing 1.2% | | 51,121 | C maj 11,965 | | 52,394 | C maj 11,017 | |
| | | | 23.4% | | | 82.4% | |

GEOFFREY CLIFTON-BROWN, b March 23, 1953. Chartered surveyor and farmer. MP for Cirencester and Tewkesbury 1992-97. PPS to Douglas Hogg, Min of Ag, Fish and Food, 1995-97; sec, C backbench European affairs cttee, 1992-95; joint vice-chair, all-party Future of Europe parly group; chair, population, reproductive health and development group, 1995-97. Vice-chair, Charities Property Assoc, 1993- ; Small Business Bureau 1995- ; Euro Atlantic Group, 1996. Freeman, City of London; Liveryman, Worshipful Company of Farmers. Ed Tormore School, Kent; Eton; Royal Agricultural Coll, Cirencester. His grandfather was C MP for Bury St Edmunds 1945-50, and his great uncle was Commons Speaker 1943-51.
DAVID GAYLER, b Sept 20, 1940. Company director. Gloucestershire county cllr 1993- . Ed Hanley Castle GS, Worcs; Hull Univ.
DAVID ELWELL, b Feb 6, 1958. Univ philosophy teacher; doctor of psychiatry. Ed Univ Coll of Wales; Cambridge and Oxford Univs.

| COVENTRY NORTH EAST | | 18.7% change | | | | | Lab win |
|---|---|---|---|---|---|---|---|
| Electorate % Turnout | | 74,274 | 64.7% | **1997** | 77,680 | 72.8% | **1992** |
| +Ainsworth, R W | Lab | **31,856** | **66.2%** | **+16.6%** | 28,083 | 49.6% | Lab |
| Burnett, M | C | 9,287 | 19.3% | -8.7% | 15,854 | 28.0% | C |
| Sewards, G | LD | 3,866 | 8.0% | -2.5% | 6,696 | 11.8% | Ind Lab |
| Brown, N | Lib | 1,181 | 2.5% | | 5,948 | 10.5% | LD |
| Hurrell, R | Ref | 1,125 | 2.3% | | | | |
| Khamis, H | Soc Lab | 597 | 1.2% | | | | |
| Sidwell, C | Dream | 173 | 0.4% | | | | |
| C to Lab notional swing 12.7% | | **48,085** | Lab maj **22,569** | | **56,581** | Lab maj **12,229** | |
| | | | 46.9% | | | 21.6% | |

**ROBERT AINSWORTH**, b June 19, 1952. Became gvt whip, May 7, 1997. Ex-Jaguar worker and shop steward. Elected 1992. Lab whip 1995-97. Member, environment select cttee, 1993-95. Ex-joint vice-chair, PLP environment cttee; joint vice-chair, all-party European secure vehicle alliance parly group; vice-chair, W Midlands group of Lab MPs, 1995- ; former sec, PLP trade and industry cttee; sec, chess group. Coventry city cllr 1984-93 (dep leader 1988-90). Ed Foxford Comp, Coventry.

**MICHAEL BURNETT**, b June 3, 1954. Manager with KPMG Peat Marwick, chartered accountants. Vice-chair, Meriden C assoc, 1995- ; Midlands Central and Coventry and N Warwickshire Euro constituency council 1993- . Ed Cannock GS; Warwick Univ.
**GEOFFREY SEWARDS**, b Feb 4, 1936. Retired univ lecturer. Contested Coventry SW 1992; Coventry and North Warwickshire in 1994 Euro elections. Ed Emanuel School, London; Clare Coll, Cambridge; Nottingham Univ.

| COVENTRY NORTH WEST | | 54.9% change | | | | | Lab win |
|---|---|---|---|---|---|---|---|
| Electorate % Turnout | | 76,439 | 71.1% | **1997** | 79,194 | 76.6% | **1992** |
| +Robinson, G | Lab | **30,901** | **56.9%** | **+5.6%** | 31,083 | 51.2% | Lab |
| Bartlett, P | C | 14,300 | 26.3% | -10.6% | 22,425 | 37.0% | C |
| Penlington, Dr N | LD | 5,690 | 10.5% | -1.3% | 7,152 | 11.8% | LD |
| Butler, D | Ref | 1,269 | 2.3% | | | | |
| Spencer, D | Soc Lab | 940 | 1.7% | | | | |
| Wheway, R | Lib | 687 | 1.3% | | | | |
| Mills, P | ProLife | 359 | 0.7% | | | | |
| Francis, L | Dream | 176 | 0.3% | | | | |
| C to Lab notional swing 8.1% | | **54,322** | Lab maj **16,601** | | **60,660** | Lab maj **8,658** | |
| | | | 30.6% | | | 76.6% | |

**GEOFFREY ROBINSON**, b May 25, 1938. Became Paymaster General May 4, 1997. Won by-election 1976. Lab spokesman on trade and industry 1983-87; spokesman on science 1982-83. Proprietor, *New Statesman* 1996- . Financial controller, British Leyland, 1971-72; managing dir, Leyland Innocenti, Italy, 1972-73; chief exec, Jaguar Cars, 1973-75; chief exec Triumph Motorcycles, 1977-80. Ed Emanuel School, London; Clare Coll, Cambridge; Yale.

**PAUL BARTLETT**, b Feb 17, 1961. Public relations manager. Contested Leeds W 1992. Milton Keynes borough cllr 1988- (C group leader 1992- ). Ed Cardinal Wiseman; Solihull Coll of Tech; Hull Univ.
**NAPIER PENLINGTON**, b Dec 22, 1928. Retired consultant anaesthetist. Contested seat 1992. Ed St John's Coll, Cambridge; Middlesex Hospital.

| COVENTRY SOUTH | | 99.0% change | | | | | Lab win |
|---|---|---|---|---|---|---|---|
| Electorate % Turnout | | 71,826 | 69.8% | **1997** | 73,575 | 77.4% | **1992** |
| +Cunningham, J D | Lab | **25,511** | **50.9%** | **+16.2%** | 22,674 | 39.8% | C |
| Ivey, P | C | 14,558 | 29.0% | -10.8% | 19,770 | 34.7% | Lab |
| MacDonald, G | LD | 4,617 | 9.2% | -0.0% | 9,229 | 16.2% | Other |
| Nellist, D | Soc | 3,262 | 6.5% | | 5,260 | 9.2% | LD |
| Garratt, P | Ref | 943 | 1.9% | | | | |
| Jenking, R | Lib | 725 | 1.4% | | | | |
| Astbury, J | BNP | 328 | 0.7% | | | | |
| Bradshaw, Ms A | Dream | 180 | 0.4% | | | | |
| C to Lab notional swing 13.5% | | **50,124** | Lab maj **10,953** | | **56,933** | C maj **2,904** | |
| | | | 21.9% | | | 77.4% | |

**JIM CUNNINGHAM**, b Feb 4, 1941. Engineer and ex-senior shop steward. MP for Coventry SE 1992-97. Member, home affairs select cttee, 1992-97; joint vice-chair, all-party building societies group, 1996- ; sec, 1995- . Coventry city cllr 1972-92 (leader 1988-92). Ed St Columbia HS, Coatbridge.

**PAUL IVEY**, b Oct 24, 1955. Senior research fellow and aerospace engineer. Expert member, Cabinet Office Technology Foresight Initiative. Bedforshire county cllr 1993- . Ed Sussex Univ.
**GORDON MACDONALD**, b Feb 2, 1968. Lecturer/research student. Ed Douglas Acad, Milngavie; Strathclyde and Glasgow Univs.

| CRAWLEY | | 15.8% change | | | | | | Lab win |
|---|---|---|---|---|---|---|---|---|
| Electorate % Turnout | | 69,040 | 73.0% | **1997** | 66,707 | 77.5% | **1992** |
| **Moffatt, Mrs L** | Lab | **27,750** | **55.0%** | **+14.7%** | **22,738** | **44.0%** | **C** |
| Crabb, Miss J | C | 16,043 | 31.8% | -12.1% | 20,848 | 40.3% | Lab |
| de Souza, H | LD | 4,141 | 8.2% | -6.3% | 7,492 | 14.5% | LD |
| Walters, R | Ref | 1,931 | 3.8% | | 645 | 1.2% | Grn |
| Saunders, E | UK Ind | 322 | 0.6% | | | | |
| Kahn, A | JP | 230 | 0.5% | | | | |
| **C to Lab notional swing 13.4%** | | **50,417** | | **Lab maj 11,707** | **51,723** | | **C maj 1,890** |
| | | | | 23.2% | | | 77.5% |

**LAURA MOFFATT**, b April 9, 1954. Nurse. Contested this seat 1992. Crawley borough cllr 1984- (Mayor 1990-91). Hon vice-pres, Assoc of Port Health Authorities; pres, Crawley Access group. Ed Hazelwick Comp, Crawley; Crawley Coll.

**JOSEPHINE CRABB**, b Sept 5, 1946. Solicitor and management consultant. Contested Coventry and Warwickshire North in 1994 Euro elections. Trained as solicitor in local gvt with Poole Borough Council. Member, Judicial Commission of Euro Union of Women. Chair, Cat Assoc of Britain, 1989-95; C animal welfare group. Member, Southern Region electricity consumers cttee, 1990-93; IBA advisory cttee for local radio 1983-88; Law Soc; Inst of Management. Ed Rosa Bassett GS; Univ Coll of Wales, Aberystwyth; De Montfort Univ; Coll of Law, Guildford.

**HAROLD DE SOUZA**, b May 29, 1937. Commercial pilot/engineer; former dir of nuclear studies in Kenya; lecturer in social engineering. Founder and managing director of Sight by Wings flying doctor service in Africa. Ed Battersea Coll; London Univ; UMIST.

| CREWE & NANTWICH | | 21.2% change | | | | | | Lab win |
|---|---|---|---|---|---|---|---|---|
| Electorate % Turnout | | 68,694 | 73.7% | **1997** | 68,307 | 81.9% | **1992** |
| **+Dunwoody, Mrs G** | Lab | **29,460** | **58.2%** | **+10.6%** | **26,622** | **47.6%** | **Lab** |
| Loveridge, M | C | 13,662 | 27.0% | -11.9% | 21,751 | 38.9% | C |
| Cannon, D | LD | 5,940 | 11.7% | -0.8% | 6,991 | 12.5% | LD |
| Astbury, P | Ref | 1,543 | 3.0% | | 579 | 1.0% | Grn |
| **C to Lab notional swing 11.3%** | | **50,605** | | **Lab maj 15,798** | **55,943** | | **Lab maj 4,871** |
| | | | | 31.2% | | | 81.9% |

**GWYNETH DUNWOODY**, b Dec 12, 1930. Elected 1983; MP for Crewe Feb 1974-83; Exeter 1966-70; contested that seat 1964. MEP, 1975-79. Member, transport select cttee, 1987-97; Commons chairmen's panel 1992- ; chief Lab spokesman on transport 1984-85, and spokesman on health 1980-83. Member, Shadow Cabinet, 1983-85; Lab Party NEC, 1981-88. Parly Sec, Board of Trade, 1967-70. Parly campaign co-ordinator 1983-84. Joint chair, all-party Brake parly group (safe commercial transport). Totnes cllr 1963-66. Dir, Film Production Assoc of GB, 1970-74. Ed Fulham County Sec; Convent of Notre Dame.

**MICHAEL LOVERIDGE**, b March 3, 1961. Self-employed, running Devonshire House School, Lyndhurst House School and Axe Cliff golf club. Was dep principal and then principal, St Godric's Coll, London, which later became part of Devonshire House. Member, Independent Schools Assoc. Liveryman; Freeman, City of London. Ed Eton; Cambridge Univ.

**DAVID CANNON**, b Aug 23, 1950. Ex-computer programmer/manager. Crewe and Nantwich borough cllr (leader, LD group). Worked in BR computing division, mostly based in Crewe, for 24 years. Ed Bideford GS, Devon; Birmingham Univ.

| CROSBY | | 51.8% change | | | | | | Lab win |
|---|---|---|---|---|---|---|---|---|
| Electorate % Turnout | | 57,190 | 77.2% | **1997** | 58,877 | 81.3% | **1992** |
| **Curtis-Tansley, Ms C** | Lab | **22,549** | **51.1%** | **+22.4%** | **23,329** | **48.7%** | **C** |
| +Thornton, Sir Malcolm | C | 15,367 | 34.8% | -13.9% | 13,738 | 28.7% | Lab |
| McVey, P | LD | 5,080 | 11.5% | -8.5% | 9,558 | 20.0% | LD |
| Gauld, J | Ref | 813 | 1.8% | | 732 | 1.5% | Lib |
| Marks, J | Lib | 233 | 0.5% | -1.0% | 399 | 0.8% | Grn |
| Hite, W | NLP | 99 | 0.2% | +0.0% | 106 | 0.2% | NLP |
| **C to Lab notional swing 18.2%** | | **44,141** | | **Lab maj 7,182** | **47,862** | | **C maj 9,591** |
| | | | | 16.3% | | | 81.3% |

**CLAIRE CURTIS-TANSLEY**, b April 30, 1958. Engineering consultant; previously head of strategic planning, Birmingham City Council; head of environmental affairs, Shell Chemicals; head of Distribution UK Ltd, Shell Chemicals. Chair and founder of two educational trusts to promote science and engineering. Member, TGWU; Co-op Party; Fabian Soc; Labour Women's Network; Soroptimist International. Ed Univ Coll of Wales, Cardiff; Aston Univ.

**SIR MALCOLM THORNTON**, b April 3, 1939. Won this seat 1983; MP for Liverpool Garston 1979-83. Chair, select cttee on ed and employment 1996, and member of its sub-cttee; chair, ed and science select cttee, 1989-96. Wallasey cllr 1965-74; Wirral cllr 1973-79. Dir, Keene Public Affairs Consultants Ltd; parly adviser to United Utilities plc. Ex-River Mersey pilot 1955-79. Ed Wallasey GS; Liverpool Nautical Coll.

**PAUL McVEY**, b March 26, 1948. Full-time Sefton metropolitan borough cllr 1990- ; on Sefton council 1986-90. Vice-chair, Bootle CAB. Ed St Mary's Coll, Crosby.

| CROYDON CENTRAL | | 87.9% change | | | | | Lab win |
|---|---|---|---|---|---|---|---|
| Electorate % Turnout | | 80,152 | 69.6% | **1997** | 81,757 | 74.8% | **1992** |
| **Davies, G** | **Lab** | **25,432** | **45.6%** | **+14.1%** | **33,940** | **55.5%** | **C** |
| Congdon, D L | C | 21,535 | 38.6% | -16.9% | 19,279 | 31.5% | Lab |
| Schlich, G | LD | 6,061 | 10.9% | -2.1% | 7,934 | 13.0% | LD |
| Cook, C | Ref | 1,886 | 3.4% | | | | |
| Barnsley, M | Green | 595 | 1.1% | | | | |
| Woollcott, J | UK Ind | 290 | 0.5% | | | | |
| **C to Lab notional swing 15.5%** | | **55,799** | | **Lab maj 3,897** | **61,153** | | **C maj 14,661** |
| | | | | 7.0% | | | 74.8% |

**GERAINT DAVIES**, b May 3, 1960. Contested this seat 1992, and Croydon S 1987. Croydon cllr 1986- . Managing dir, Pure Crete (specialist travel co) and business consultant; previously marketing manager, Colgate Palmolive Ltd. Member, MSF. Ed Llanishen Comp, Cardiff; Jesus Coll, Oxford.
**DAVID CONGDON**, b Oct 16, 1949. MP for Croydon NE 1992-97. PPS to Social Security Min 1995-97. Member, health select cttee, 1992-

97; former sec, Greater London group of C MPs. Croydon cllr 1976-92 (dep leader of council 1986-92) Computer consultant 1985-92; systems analyst with Philips Electronics 1973-85. Governor, Croydon Coll, 1979-92. Ed Alleyn's School; Thames Poly.
**GEORGE SCHLICH**, b Sept 19, 1966. Patent agent. Ed RGS, Guildford; St John's Coll, Cambridge.

| CROYDON NORTH | | 45.2% change | | | | | Lab win |
|---|---|---|---|---|---|---|---|
| Electorate % Turnout | | 77,063 | 68.2% | **1997** | 80,076 | 72.3% | **1992** |
| **+Wicks, M H** | **Lab** | **32,672** | **62.2%** | **+17.8%** | **25,865** | **44.7%** | **C** |
| Martin, I | C | 14,274 | 27.2% | -17.5% | 25,702 | 44.4% | Lab |
| Morris, M | LD | 4,066 | 7.7% | -3.2% | 6,340 | 10.9% | LD |
| Billis, R | Ref | 1,155 | 2.2% | | | | |
| Feisenberger, J | UK Ind | 396 | 0.8% | | | | |
| **C to Lab notional swing 17.6%** | | **52,563** | | **Lab maj 18,398** | **57,907** | | **C maj 163** |
| | | | | 35.0% | | | 72.3% |

**MALCOLM WICKS**, b July 1, 1947. Won Croydon NW for Lab 1992; contested it 1987. Lab spokesman on social security, 1995-97; member, social security select cttee, 1992-95. Dir, Family Policy Studies Centre, 1983-92. Member, Family Policy Observatory, Euro Commission, 1987-92; chair, Winter Action on Cold Homes, 1986-92. Worked in Home Office urban deprivation unit 1974-77; research dir and sec, study commission on the family, 1978-83. Trustee, Nat Energy Foundation, 1987- . Member, TGWU. Ed Elizabeth Coll, Guernsey; NW London Poly; LSE.

**IAN MARTIN**, b Nov 16, 1958. Vice-chair, Lewes C assoc, 1982-84; dep chair, Newham South C assoc, 1985-87; CPC chair, Tonbridge & Malling C assoc, 1988-92. General manager in business development and strategic planning, Kinetica Natural Gas. Ed Midhurst GS, West Sussex; Southampton Univ.
**MARTIN MORRIS**, b June 5, 1971. Postgraduate student in chemistry. Member, Charter 88; Esperanto Assoc of GB. Ed Hayes School, Bromley; Univ Coll of Wales, Bangor.

| CROYDON SOUTH | | 16.5% change | | | | | C win |
|---|---|---|---|---|---|---|---|
| Electorate % Turnout | | 73,787 | 73.5% | **1997** | 74,777 | 78.0% | **1992** |
| **+Ottaway, R** | **C** | **25,649** | **47.3%** | **-14.3%** | **35,937** | **61.7%** | **C** |
| Burling, C | Lab | 13,719 | 25.3% | +9.0% | 12,599 | 21.6% | LD |
| Gauge, S | LD | 11,441 | 21.1% | -0.5% | 9,513 | 16.3% | Lab |
| Barber, A | Ref | 2,631 | 4.9% | | 242 | 0.4% | Choice |
| Ferguson, P | BNP | 354 | 0.7% | | | | |
| Harker, A | UK Ind | 309 | 0.6% | | | | |
| Samuel, M | Choice | 96 | 0.2% | -0.2% | | | |
| **C to Lab notional swing 11.7%** | | **54,199** | | **C maj 11,930** | **58,291** | | **C maj 23,338** |
| | | | | 22.0% | | | 78.0% |

**RICHARD OTTAWAY**, b May 24, 1945. Elected for this seat 1992; MP for Nottingham N 1983-87. Gvt whip 1996, asst gvt whip 1995-96; member, procedure select cttee, 1996-97. PPS to Michael Heseltine when Dep Prime Minister and Pres of Board of Trade, 1992-95. Chair, all-party population, reproductive health and development parly group, 1992- . PPS to Mins of State, FCO, 1985-87. Specialist in international, maritime and commercial law and partner in Wm A. Crump & Son, solicitors, 1981-87. Dir, Coastal Europe Ltd, 1990-95; ex-dir, Coastal States Holdings (UK) Ltd.

Served in RN 1961-69; RNR 1970-80. Ed Backwell Sec Mod School, Somerset; RNC Dartmouth; Bristol Univ.
**CHARLIE BURLING**, b Dec 17, 1959. Housing support worker; chair, SE London valuation tribunal. Member, board, Wandle Valley Partnership; Lab Campaign for Electoral Reform. Ed City & Guilds.
**STEVEN GAUGE**, b May 12, 1967. Documentary producer, working for the Discovery Channel; previously worked for Croydon Cable TV. Southwark cllr 1990- . Ed King's Coll School, Wimbledon; Corpus Christi Coll, Oxford.

## CUMBERNAULD & KILSYTH — Lab hold

| Electorate % Turnout | | 48,032 | 75.0% | 1997 | 46,489 | 79.1% | 1992 |
|---|---|---|---|---|---|---|---|
| McKenna, Ms R | Lab | 21,141 | 58.7% | +4.7% | 19,855 | 54.0% | Lab |
| Barrie, C | SNP | 10,013 | 27.8% | -1.2% | 10,640 | 28.9% | SNP |
| Sewell, I | C | 2,441 | 6.8% | -4.5% | 4,143 | 11.3% | C |
| Biggam, J | LD | 1,368 | 3.8% | -2.0% | 2,118 | 5.8% | LD |
| Kara, Ms J | ProLife | 609 | 1.7% | | | | |
| McEwan, K | SSA | 345 | 1.0% | | | | |
| Cook, Ms P | Ref | 107 | 0.3% | | | | |
| SNP to Lab swing 2.9% | | 36,024 | Lab maj 11,128 | | 36,756 | Lab maj 9,215 | |
| | | | 30.9% | | | 79.1% | |

ROSEMARY McKENNA, b May 8, 1941. Cumbernauld and Kilsyth district cllr 1984-96 (leader 1984-88; provost 1988-92); North Lanarkshire cllr 1995- . Chair, CLP 1979-85. Pres, Cosla, 1994-96; exec member, Scottish Constitutional Convention. Chair, Scotland Europa Brussels 1995- ; member, Cttee of the Regions of the EU. Ed St Augustine's Comp, Glasgow; Notre Dame Coll of Ed.

COLIN BARRIE, b Oct 28, 1970. Manager with horticultural company. Ex-chair, Cumbernauld and Kilsyth SNP. Ed Kilsyth Acad; West of Scotland Agricultural Coll; Stirling Univ.
IAN SEWELL, b March 27, 1966. European sales and marketing manager for US company. Ex-Wokingham district cllr. Ed Sherborne School; Robinson Coll, Cambridge. Served as special constable.

## CUNNINGHAME NORTH — Lab hold

| Electorate % Turnout | | 55,526 | 74.1% | 1997 | 54,803 | 78.2% | 1992 |
|---|---|---|---|---|---|---|---|
| *Wilson, B | Lab | 20,686 | 50.3% | +9.3% | 17,564 | 41.0% | Lab |
| Mitchell, Mrs M | C | 9,647 | 23.5% | -10.7% | 14,625 | 34.1% | C |
| Nicoll, Ms K | SNP | 7,584 | 18.4% | +0.2% | 7,813 | 18.2% | SNP |
| Freel, Ms K | LD | 2,271 | 5.5% | -1.2% | 2,864 | 6.7% | LD |
| McDaid, Ms L | Soc Lab | 501 | 1.2% | | | | |
| Winton, I | Ref | 440 | 1.1% | | | | |
| C to Lab swing 10.0% | | 41,129 | Lab maj 11,039 | | 42,866 | Lab maj 2,939 | |
| | | | 26.8% | | | 78.2% | |

BRIAN WILSON, b Dec 13, 1948. Became Minister of State, Scottish Office responsible for education and industry, May 5, 1997. Won this seat 1987; contested Western Isles 1983, Inverness 1979 and Ross and Cromarty Oct 1974. Joined election planning team 1996; spokesman on railways 1995-96; trade and industry 1994-95; transport 1992-94; Scotland 1988-92. Journalist (first winner in 1975 of Nicholas Tomalin Memorial Award for outstanding journalism). Former adviser, Scottish Professional Footballers' Assoc. Ed Dunoon GS; Dundee Univ; Univ Coll of Wales, Cardiff.

MARGARET MITCHELL, b Nov 15, 1952. Primary school teacher. Contested Hamilton 1992. Hamilton district cllr 1988-94. Non-exec director NHS trust. Ed Coatbridge HS; Hamilton Coll of Ed; OU; Strathclyde Univ.
KIM NICOLL, b July 10, 1959. East Ayrshire cllr and former Strathclyde cllr. Ed Prestwick Acad; Dunfermline Coll of Physical Ed.
KAREN FREEL, b July 18, 1969. Sec at Glasgow Caledonian Univ. Ed St Mirin's and St Martin's HS, Paisley; Clydebank Coll, Glasgow.

## CUNNINGHAME SOUTH — Lab hold

| Electorate % Turnout | | 49,543 | 71.5% | 1997 | 49,010 | 75.9% | 1992 |
|---|---|---|---|---|---|---|---|
| *Donohoe, B H | Lab | 22,233 | 62.7% | +9.8% | 19,687 | 52.9% | Lab |
| Burgess, Mrs M | SNP | 7,364 | 20.8% | -3.4% | 9,007 | 24.2% | SNP |
| Paterson, Mrs P | C | 3,571 | 10.1% | -6.2% | 6,070 | 16.3% | C |
| Watson, E | LD | 1,604 | 4.5% | -1.7% | 2,299 | 6.2% | LD |
| Edwin, K | Soc Lab | 494 | 1.4% | | 128 | 0.3% | NLP |
| Martlew, A | Ref | 178 | 0.5% | | | | |
| SNP to Lab swing 6.6% | | 35,444 | Lab maj 14,869 | | 37,191 | Lab maj 10,680 | |
| | | | 42.0% | | | 75.9% | |

BRIAN DONOHOE, b Sept 10, 1948. Elected 1992. Member, transport select cttee, 1993-97; vice-chair, Scottish group of Lab MPs, 1995- ; sec/treas, all-party gardening party group. Nalgo official 1981-92. Ex-convener to Scottish political and ed cttee, AUEW (Tass); sec, Irvine and District Trades Council, 1973-81, and ex-chair of ICI contract draughtsmen's cttee. Chair, Cunningham industrial development cttee, 1976-80; N Ayrshire and Arran local health council, 1977-79. Was apprentice fitter/turner. Ed Irvine Royal Acad; Kilmarnock Tech Coll.

MARGARET BURGESS, b Dec 7, 1949. Manager of CAB in Kilmarnock; Cunninghame district cllr (SNP group leader) 1992-96; organiser for Cunninghame South constituency. Member, TGWU. Ed Largs HS; David Dale Coll, Glasgow.
PAMELA PATERSON, b Dec 29, 1932. Teacher. Worked for Strathclyde regional council, Ayr division, 1972-94. Kyle & Carrick district cllr 1992- . Ed Ayr Acad; Craigie Coll of Ed, Ayr.
ERLAND WATSON, b Nov 6, 1963. Freelance translator. Ed Dauntsey's School; University Coll, London.

| CYNON VALLEY | | | | | | Lab hold | |
|---|---|---|---|---|---|---|---|
| Electorate % Turnout | | 48,286 | 69.2% | **1997** | 49,695 | 76.5% | **1992** |
| *Clwyd, Mrs A | Lab | 23,307 | 69.7% | +0.6% | 26,254 | 69.1% | Lab |
| Davies, A | PC | 3,552 | 10.6% | -0.4% | 4,890 | 12.9% | C |
| Price, H | LD | 3,459 | 10.3% | +3.3% | 4,186 | 11.0% | PC |
| Smith, A | C | 2,262 | 6.8% | -6.1% | 2,667 | 7.0% | LD |
| John, G | Ref | 844 | 2.5% | | | | |
| PC to Lab swing 0.5% | | 33,424 | Lab maj 19,755 | | 37,997 | Lab maj 21,364 | |
| | | | 59.1% | | | 76.5% | |

ANN CLWYD, b March 21, 1937. Broadcaster and journalist. Elected 1984 by-election; contested Gloucester Oct 1974; Denbigh 1970. MEP for Mid and West Wales 1979-84. Contested deputy leadership of Lab Party 1992. Member, Shadow Cabinet, 1989-93. Lab spokesman on foreign affairs and assistant to John Prescott, dep Lab leader, 1994-95; on employment 1993-94; nat heritage 1992-93; Wales 1992; overseas development 1989-92; education 1987-88; women's rights 1987-88. Chair, PLP health and social security cttee, 1985-87; joint vice-chair, PLP defence cttee, 1985-87. On Lab Party NEC 1983-84. Parly and political adviser to

IPMS. Member, Royal Commission on NHS, 1976-79; NUJ. Ed Holywell GS; Queen's, Chester; Univ Coll of Wales, Bangor.
ALUN DAVIES, b Feb 12, 1964. Public affairs manager for Oxfam. Contested Blaenau Gwent 1992. Ed Tredegar Comp; Univ Coll of Wales, Aberystwyth.
HUW PRICE, b Jan 13, 1969. Solicitor. Ed Aberdare Boys' Comp; Univ Coll of Wales, Aberystwyth; Coll of Law, York.
ANDREW SMITH, b July 5, 1962. Executive with Ian Greer Associates, 1982-96. Contested Cynon Valley 1992. Ex-adviser to Neil Hamilton. Ed St Columba RC School, Kent.

| DAGENHAM | | 2.9% change | | | | Lab win | |
|---|---|---|---|---|---|---|---|
| Electorate % Turnout | | 58,573 | 61.7% | **1997** | 62,395 | 69.8% | **1992** |
| +Church, Mrs J | Lab | 23,759 | 65.7% | +14.0% | 22,499 | 51.7% | Lab |
| Fairrie, J | C | 6,705 | 18.5% | -18.3% | 16,052 | 36.9% | C |
| Dobrashian, T | LD | 2,704 | 7.5% | -4.0% | 4,992 | 11.5% | LD |
| Kraft, S | Ref | 1,411 | 3.9% | | | | |
| Binding, W | BNP | 900 | 2.5% | | | | |
| Dawson, R | Ind | 349 | 1.0% | | | | |
| Hipperson, M | Nat Dem | 183 | 0.5% | | | | |
| Goble, Ms K | ProLife | 152 | 0.4% | | | | |
| C to Lab notional swing 16.2% | | 36,163 | Lab maj 17,054 | | 43,543 | Lab maj 6,447 | |
| | | | 47.2% | | | 14.8% | |

JUDITH CHURCH, b Sept 19, 1953. Elected 1994 by-election; contested Stevenage 1992 and 1989. Member, deregulation select cttee, 1995-97; vice-chair, all-party occupational safety & health group, 1996- ; sec, all-party constitutional and parly affairs group, 1996- ; all-party landmine eradication group, 1996- . Member, Lab Party NEC, 1992-94. Chair, Hornsey and Woodgreen CLP, 1989-90. National health and safety officer with MSF, 1986-94; factory inspector, Health and Safety Exec, 1980-86. Parly adviser to Assoc of First Division Civil Servants. Member of board and trustee, Inst

of Public Policy Research, 1992-95; founding director, *New Century Magazine* (both unpaid). Ed St Bernard's GS, Slough; Leeds Univ; Huddersfield Poly; Aston Univ; Thames Valley Coll.
JAMES FAIRRIE, b 1947. Contested 1994 by-election, and Newham S 1987. Wandsworth cllr 1981-86. Employed by insurance company. Ed Downside; Sandhurst; Exeter Univ.
TOM DOBRASHIAN, b Oct 30, 1963. Management consultant. Ed Bedford Modern; Manchester and Yale Univs.
*Details of 1994 by-election on page 278*

| DARLINGTON | | | | | | Lab hold | |
|---|---|---|---|---|---|---|---|
| Electorate % Turnout | | 65,140 | 74.0% | **1997** | 66,094 | 83.6% | **1992** |
| *Milburn, A | Lab | 29,658 | 61.6% | +13.5% | 26,556 | 48.1% | Lab |
| Scrope, P | C | 13,633 | 28.3% | -14.7% | 23,758 | 43.0% | C |
| Boxell, L | LD | 3,483 | 7.2% | -1.1% | 4,586 | 8.3% | LD |
| Blakey, M | Ref | 1,399 | 2.9% | | 355 | 0.6% | BNP |
| C to Lab swing 14.1% | | 48,173 | Lab maj 16,025 | | 55,255 | Lab maj 2,798 | |
| | | | 33.3% | | | 83.6% | |

ALAN MILBURN, b Jan 27, 1958. Became Minister of State for Health, May 5, 1997. Won this seat 1992. Member, Lab Treasury team 1996- ; health spokesman 1995-96. Member, Public Accounts Cttee, 1992-95; chair, PLP Treasury cttee, 1992-95; ex-chair, all-party alcohol misuse parly group. Senior business development officer, N Tyneside MBC, 1990-92; co-ordinator, trade union studies information unit, Newcastle, 1984-90. Former exec member, Northern region Lab Party; chair, Newcastle Central CLP;

NE regional pres of MSF. Ed Stokesley Comp; Lancaster Univ.
PETER SCROPE, b Jan 3, 1955. Director of telecoms companies. Left Army 1984 with rank of Major. Member, Council of St John for Cleveland. Ed Ampleforth Coll; Sandhurst; Essex Univ.
LES BOXELL, b March 29, 1937. Supply teacher. Former active Lab Party member, former C supporter. Member, Shelter. Student of Japanese. Ed Hull GS; Nottingham, Hull, London and Durham Univs; Teesside Poly.

| DARTFORD | 7.9% change | | | | | | Lab win |
|---|---|---|---|---|---|---|---|
| Electorate % Turnout | | 69,726 | 74.6% | **1997** | 68,319 | 82.9% | **1992** |
| Stoate, H | Lab | 25,278 | 48.6% | +12.4% | 28,796 | 50.9% | C |
| +Dunn, R J | C | 20,950 | 40.3% | -10.6% | 20,482 | 36.2% | Lab |
| Webb, Mrs D | LD | 4,827 | 9.3% | -2.9% | 6,873 | 12.1% | LD |
| McHale, P | BNP | 428 | 0.8% | | 244 | 0.4% | FDP |
| Homden, P | FDP | 287 | 0.6% | +0.1% | 224 | 0.4% | NLP |
| Pollitt, J | Ch D | 228 | 0.4% | | | | |
| C to Lab notional swing 11.5% | | 51,998 | | Lab maj 4,328 8.3% | 56,619 | | C maj 8,314 82.9% |

**HOWARD STOATE**, b April 14, 1954. General practitioner. Contested Dartford 1992 and Old Bexley and Sidcup 1987. Former vice-chair, Dartford CLP. Dartford borough cllr; member, nat exec cttee, Fabian Soc; chair, Dartford Fabian Soc, 1984-90. GP tutor at London Univ; chair, ethics cttee, Bexley HA. Member, South Thames Regional Graduate Medical Board; fellow and examiner, Royal Coll of GPs. Ed Kingston GS; King's Coll, London.

**ROBERT DUNN**, b July 14, 1946. Elected 1979; contested Eccles, Feb and Oct 1974. Under Sec for Education and Science 1983-88. Member, exec, 1922 Cttee, 1988-97. Chair, Commons selection cttee, 1996-97, and member 1991-97. Pres, SE Area YCs, 1989- . Southwark cllr 1974-78. Senior buyer, J. Sainsbury, 1973-79. Ed Manchester Poly; Brighton Poly; Salford Univ.
**DOROTHY WEBB**, b June 22, 1949. Sevenoaks district cllr. Ed Hornchurch GS; Univ Coll of Wales, Aberystwyth.

| DAVENTRY | 14.1% change | | | | | | C win |
|---|---|---|---|---|---|---|---|
| Electorate % Turnout | | 80,151 | 77.0% | **1997** | 75,148 | 82.5% | **1992** |
| +Boswell, T E | C | 28,615 | 46.3% | -11.4% | 35,842 | 57.8% | C |
| Ritchie, K | Lab | 21,237 | 34.4% | +10.5% | 14,831 | 23.9% | Lab |
| Gordon, J | LD | 9,233 | 15.0% | -2.7% | 10,933 | 17.6% | LD |
| Russocki, Mrs B | Ref | 2,018 | 3.3% | | 422 | 0.7% | NLP |
| Mahoney, B | UK Ind | 443 | 0.7% | | | | |
| France, R | NLP | 204 | 0.3% | -0.3% | | | |
| C to Lab notional swing 11.0% | | 61,750 | | C maj 7,378 11.9% | 62,028 | | C maj 21,011 82.5% |

**TIMOTHY BOSWELL**, b Dec 2, 1942. Farmer. Elected 1987; contested Rugby Feb 1974. Parly Sec, Min of Agriculture, Fish and Food, 1995-97; Under Sec for Education 1992-95, with responsibility for further and higher ed; gvt whip 1992; asst gvt whip 1990-92. PPS to Peter Lilley, Financial Sec to Treasury, 1989-90. Member, agric select cttee, 1987-89; joint sec, C backbench agric, fish and food cttee, 1987-89; chair, all-party charity law review panel, 1988-90. Managed family farm business 1974-87, became self-employed partner. Ed Marlborough; New College, Oxford.

**KEN RITCHIE**, b Dec 8, 1946. Contested Beckenham 1987 and 1992. Chair, Beckenham CLP, 1987-93. UK dir, Intermediate Technology; previously dep dir, British Refugee Council; exec dir, Appropriate Health Resources and Technologies Action Group. Member, Labour Middle East Council. Ed Edinburgh and Aston Univs.
**JOHN GORDON**, b July 6, 1940. Retired diplomat, now in voluntary sector. Member, Friends of the Earth; Friends of Unesco; advisory body for International Security Information. Ed Marlborough; Cambridge Univ; Yale; LSE.

| DELYN | 20.3% change | | | | | | Lab win |
|---|---|---|---|---|---|---|---|
| Electorate % Turnout | | 53,693 | 74.0% | **1997** | 54,713 | 80.4% | **1992** |
| +Hanson, D | Lab | 22,300 | 56.1% | +9.3% | 20,606 | 46.9% | Lab |
| Lumley, Mrs K E | C | 10,607 | 26.7% | -12.9% | 17,428 | 39.6% | C |
| Lloyd, P | LD | 4,160 | 10.5% | -0.5% | 4,822 | 11.0% | LD |
| Drake, A | PC | 1,558 | 3.9% | +1.4% | 1,116 | 2.5% | PC |
| Soutter, Ms E | Ref | 1,117 | 2.8% | | | | |
| C to Lab notional swing 11.1% | | 39,742 | | Lab maj 11,693 29.4% | 43,972 | | Lab maj 3,178 80.4% |

**DAVID HANSON**, b July 5, 1957. Gained this seat for Lab 1992; contested it 1987, Eddisbury 1983 and Cheshire West in 1984 Euro elections. Member, Welsh affairs select cttee, 1992-96; public service select cttee 1996-97; sec, PLP national heritage cttee, 1994- ; all-party prevention of solvent abuse parly group. Vale Royal borough cllr 1983-92 (leader, Lab group, 1990-92); Northwich town cllr 1987-91. Director of national charity, Soc for Prevention of Solvent Abuse, 1989-92. Ed Verdin Comp, Winsford, Cheshire; Hull Univ.

**KAREN LUMLEY**, b March 28, 1964. Clwyd county cllr 1993- ; Wrexham Maelor borough cllr 1991- (leader, C/Ind group, 1995- ). Company secretary, RKL Geological Services Ltd, Wrexham. Member, C women's nat cttee 1995; Welsh C policy group, 1993. Chair, managers, Wrexham pupil referral unit. Ed Rugby HS for Girls; E Warwickshire CFE.
**PHIL LLOYD**, b Nov 22, 1957. Salesman/senior vaccine specialist. Mold town cllr 1991- . Ed Welshpool HS; Univ Coll of Wales, Cardiff.

| DENTON & REDDISH | | 24.8% change | | | | | Lab win |
|---|---|---|---|---|---|---|---|
| Electorate % Turnout | | 68,866 | 66.9% | **1997** | 70,758 | 75.1% | **1992** |
| +Bennett, A | Lab | **30,137** | 65.4% | +12.4% | **28,164** | 53.0% | Lab |
| Nutt, Ms B | C | 9,826 | 21.3% | -12.5% | 18,010 | 33.9% | C |
| Donaldson, I | LD | 6,121 | 13.3% | +3.3% | 5,298 | 10.0% | LD |
| | | | | | 1,336 | 2.5% | Lib |
| | | | | | 363 | 0.7% | NLP |
| C to Lab notional swing 12.5% | | **46,084** | | Lab maj 20,311 | **53,171** | | Lab maj 10,154 |
| | | | | 44.1% | | | 75.1% |

ANDREW BENNETT, b March 9, 1939. Elected for this seat 1983; MP for Stockport N, Feb 1974-83; contested Knutsford 1970. Chair, environment select cttee, 1992-97; member, select cttees on standing orders, 1992-96; social security 1991-92; sittings of Commons 1991-94; social services 1989-91 and 1979-83; Commons information cttee, 1991- ; members' interests 1979-83; statutory instruments and joint select cttee (chairman, 1983-87 and 1992- ). Vice-chair, PLP environmental protection cttee. Lab spokesman on education 1983-88. Ex-teacher. Oldham borough cllr 1964-74. Member, NUT. Ed Hulme GS, Manchester; Birmingham Univ.

BARBARA NUTT, b 1955. Chief exec of family trust managing commercial, investment and property interests. Member, IoD. Ed Univ of Central Lancs.

IAIN DONALDSON, b June 13, 1964. Clerk at Manchester Univ. Manchester city cllr. Member, Unison. Ed Wright Robinson HS, Gorton; Openshaw Tech Coll.

| DERBY NORTH | | | | | | | Lab gain |
|---|---|---|---|---|---|---|---|
| Electorate % Turnout | | 76,116 | 73.8% | **1997** | 73,176 | 80.7% | **1992** |
| Laxton, B | Lab | **29,844** | 53.2% | +12.3% | **28,574** | 48.4% | C |
| *Knight, G | C | 19,229 | 34.3% | -14.2% | 24,121 | 40.9% | Lab |
| Charlesworth, B | LD | 5,059 | 9.0% | -0.5% | 5,638 | 9.6% | LD |
| Reynolds, P | Ref | 1,816 | 3.2% | | 383 | 0.6% | Grn |
| Waters, J | ProLife | 195 | 0.3% | | 245 | 0.4% | NF |
| | | | | | 58 | 0.1% | NLP |
| C to Lab swing 13.2% | | **56,143** | | Lab maj 10,615 | **59,019** | | C maj 4,453 |
| | | | | 18.9% | | | 80.7% |

ROBERT LAXTON, b Sept 7, 1944. Telecoms engineer with BT. Contested this seat 1992. Derby city cllr 1979- (council leader, 1986-88 and 1994- ). Chair, NCU E Midlands district council, 1984-87. Ed Allestree Woodlands Sec; Derby Coll of Art & Tech.

GREGORY KNIGHT, b April 4, 1949. Solicitor. Elected in 1983. Min for Industry 1996-97; dep govt chief whip 1993-96; gvt whip 1990-93; asst gvt whip 1989-90. PPS to David Mellor and Lord Glenarthur, when Mins of State, FCO, 1988-89, and to Mr Mellor when at Home Office 1987. Leicester city cllr 1976-79; Leics county cllr 1977-83. Compiler, 1990, of *Honourable Insults: a century of political invective*. Dir, Leicester Theatre Trust, 1979-85. Ed Alderman Newton's GS, Leicester; Coll of Law, Guildford.

ROBERT CHARLESWORTH, b June 23, 1953. Instrument mechanic. Contested this seat 1992. Organiser, Derby City LDs. Ex-EEPTU shop steward and part-time senior steward at Rolls-Royce. Ed Aldercar Comp, Heanor; Nottingham Trent Poly.

| DERBY SOUTH | | 12.5% change | | | | | Lab win |
|---|---|---|---|---|---|---|---|
| Electorate % Turnout | | 76,386 | 67.8% | **1997** | 75,664 | 75.6% | **1992** |
| +Beckett, Mrs M | Lab | **29,154** | 56.3% | +8.0% | **27,627** | 48.3% | Lab |
| Arain, J | C | 13,048 | 25.2% | -15.7% | 23,400 | 40.9% | C |
| Beckett, J W R | LD | 7,438 | 14.4% | +3.5% | 6,195 | 10.8% | LD |
| Browne, J | Ref | 1,862 | 3.6% | | | | |
| Evans, R | Nat Dem | 317 | 0.6% | | | | |
| C to Lab notional swing 11.8% | | **51,819** | | Lab maj 16,106 | **57,222** | | Lab maj 4,227 |
| | | | | 31.1% | | | 75.6% |

MARGARET BECKETT, b Jan 15, 1943. Became President of the Board of Trade, May 2, 1997. Elected for this seat 1983; MP for Lincoln, Oct 1974-79; contested the seat Feb 1974. Shadow Trade and Industry Sec 1995-97; chief Lab spokesman on health 1994-95. Dep leader of Lab Party 1992-94, being Shadow Leader of Commons and chief campaign co-ordinator; acting leader of party in 1994 following death of John Smith. First elected to Shadow Cabinet 1989, being Shadow Chief Sec to Treasury until 1992; spokesman on health and social security 1984-89; re-elected to Shadow Cabinet Oct 1994. Privy Counsellor 1993. Member, Lab Party NEC, 1980-81, 1985-86 and 1988-94, when defeated in leader and deputy leader contests. Under Sec of State for Ed and Science, 1976-79. Ed Notre Dame HS, Manchester and Norwich; Manchester Coll of Science and Tech; John Dalton Poly.

JAVED ARAIN, b March 17, 1952. Marketing and management consultant; director of design and printing business. Ed Prince of Wales public school, Nairobi; Warwick and Aston Univs. Speaks Urdu, Punjabi, Hindi, Gujarati and Kiswahili.

JEREMY BECKETT, b April 14, 1952. Special needs teacher; guest-house/restaurant proprietor. Contested Leicestershire NW 1992. Member, Greenpeace; RSPB. Ed King Edward VI GS, Bury St Edmunds; Dudley GS; St Paul's Coll, Cheltenham; Bristol Univ.

## DERBYSHIRE NORTH EAST — Lab hold

| Electorate % Turnout | | 71,653 | 72.5% | **1997** | 70,707 | 83.6% | **1992** |
|---|---|---|---|---|---|---|---|
| *Barnes, H | Lab | **31,425** | **60.5%** | **+11.6%** | 28,860 | 48.8% | Lab |
| Elliott, S | C | 13,104 | 25.2% | -13.0% | 22,590 | 38.2% | C |
| Hardy, S | LD | 7,450 | 14.3% | +1.4% | 7,675 | 13.0% | LD |
| C to Lab swing 12.3% | | 51,979 | | Lab maj 18,321 | 59,125 | | Lab maj 6,270 |
| | | | | 35.2% | | | 83.6% |

**HARRY BARNES**, b July 22, 1936. Lecturer. Elected in 1987. Member, Euro legislation select cttee, 1989-97. Chair, PLP environmental protection cttee; former joint vice-chair, PLP N Ireland cttee; campaign officer, Central Region group of Lab MPs. Joint pres, New Consensus (Britain), 1992- (chair, 1990-92). Politics and industrial relations lecturer at Sheffield Univ 1966-87; previously lectured at North Notts Further Ed Coll. Ex-railway clerk. Member, MSF. Ed Easington Colliery Sec Mod; Ryhope GS; Ruskin Coll, Oxford; Hull Univ.

**SIMON ELLIOTT**, b July 19, 1965. Senior consultant, Shandwick Consultants, 1995- . Industry editor, *Flight International*, 1990-95; naval editor, *Jane's Defence Weekly*, 1988-90. Member, C defence advisory group. Ed Bradford and Reading Univs.
**STEPHEN HARDY**, b Jan 10, 1945. Property manager, solicitor. Contested this seat 1983 and 1987. With Ibstock Building Products Ltd, brickmakers; director, Ravenhead Renaissance Ltd, Ibstock Community Enterprise Ltd, Science & Arts Centre Ltd. Ed Nottingham HS; Jesus Coll, Cambridge; Brussels Univ.

## DERBYSHIRE SOUTH — 10.2% change — Lab win

| Electorate % Turnout | | 76,672 | 78.2% | **1997** | 74,534 | 84.8% | **1992** |
|---|---|---|---|---|---|---|---|
| Todd, M | Lab | **32,709** | **54.5%** | **+10.5%** | 29,825 | 47.2% | C |
| +Currie, Mrs E | C | 18,742 | 31.3% | -15.9% | 27,878 | 44.1% | Lab |
| Renold, R | LD | 5,408 | 9.0% | +0.7% | 5,235 | 8.3% | LD |
| North, R | Ref | 2,491 | 4.2% | | 291 | 0.5% | NLP |
| Crompton, Dr I | UK Ind | 617 | 1.0% | | | | |
| C to Lab notional swing 13.2% | | 59,967 | | Lab maj 13,967 | 63,229 | | C maj 1,947 |
| | | | | 23.3% | | | 84.8% |

**MARK TODD**, b Dec 29, 1954. Businessman. Contested this seat 1992. Cambridge city cllr 1980- (leader 1987-90). Former UK operations director of international publishers. Member, Lab Campaign for Electoral Reform; Co-op Party; Greenpeace; MSF. Ed Cambridge Univ. Started Cambridge rock music competition.
**EDWINA CURRIE**, b Oct 13, 1946. Author, lecturer and broadcaster. Elected 1983; contested Bedfordshire and Milton Keynes in 1994 Euro elections. Under Sec for Health 1986-88. PPS to Sir Keith Joseph, Sec of State for Ed and Science, 1985-86. Member, social

services select cttee, 1983-86. Joint chair, all-party Future of Europe parly group; voice group. Member, C group for Europe. Vice-chair, European Movement, UK, 1995- . Birmingham city cllr 1975-84; Birmingham AHA 1975-82; chair, Central Birmingham HA, 1981-83. Dir, Tower House (Findern) Ltd, family company. Ed Liverpool Inst; St Anne's Coll, Oxford; LSE.
**ROB RENOLD**, b April 20, 1952. Management consultant. Ex-Leics county cllr. Member, Amnesty; Charter 88. Ed Gordonstoun; Birmingham and Cranfield Univs.

## DERBYSHIRE WEST — 2.6% change — C win

| Electorate % Turnout | | 72,716 | 78.2% | **1997** | 70,158 | 84.0% | **1992** |
|---|---|---|---|---|---|---|---|
| +McLoughlin, P | C | **23,945** | **42.1%** | **-12.1%** | 31,944 | 54.2% | C |
| Clamp, S | Lab | 19,060 | 33.5% | +11.2% | 13,824 | 23.5% | LD |
| Seeley, C | LD | 9,940 | 17.5% | -6.0% | 13,164 | 22.3% | Lab |
| Gouriet, J | Ref | 2,499 | 4.4% | | | | |
| Meynell, G | Ind Green | 593 | 1.0% | | | | |
| Price, H | UK Ind | 484 | 0.9% | | | | |
| Delves, N | Loony | 281 | 0.5% | | | | |
| Kyslun, M | Ind BB | 81 | 0.1% | | | | |
| C to Lab notional swing 11.6% | | 56,883 | | C maj 4,885 | 58,932 | | C maj 18,120 |
| | | | | 8.6% | | | 84.0% |

**PATRICK McLOUGHLIN**, b Nov 30, 1957. Ex-mineworker. Elected for this seat at 1986 by-election; contested Wolverhampton SE 1983. Gvt whip 1996-97; asst gvt whip 1995-96. Under Sec for Trade and Industry 1993-94; for Employment 1992-93; for Transport 1989-92. Member, select cttees on procedure, 1995-96; national heritage 1994-95; broadcasting 1994-95. PPS to Trade and Industry Sec 1988-89; Min of State for Ed and Science 1987-88. Sec, E Midlands group of C MPs, 1987-89; joint sec, C backbench environment cttee, 1986-87. Staffs county cllr 1981-97; Cannock Chase district cllr 1980-87. Nat vice-chair, YCs, 1982-84.

Ed Cardinal Griffin RC School, Cannock; Staffordshire Coll of Agriculture.
**STEPHEN CLAMP**, b June 6, 1956. Teacher. Contested this seat 1992. Wirksworth town cllr 1982- (Mayor 1984-85); Derbyshire Dales district cllr 1987- . Head of special needs at secondary school. Member, NUT. Ed Royal HS, Edinburgh; Southampton and Nottingham Univs.
**CHRISTOPHER SEELEY**, b Aug 15, 1958. Stockport metropolitan borough cllr. Formerly a teacher, sales manager, and management trainee. Ed Dulwich Coll; Birmingham and Nottingham Univs.

### DEVIZES — 71.3% change — C win

| Electorate % Turnout | 80,383 | 74.7% | 1997 | 75,555 | 84.0% | 1992 |
|---|---|---|---|---|---|---|
| +Ancram, M — C | 25,710 | 42.8% | -10.1% | 33,603 | 53.0% | C |
| Vickers, A — LD | 15,928 | 26.5% | -5.9% | 20,584 | 32.4% | LD |
| Jeffrey, F — Lab | 14,551 | 24.2% | +12.2% | 7,613 | 12.0% | Lab |
| Goldsmith, J — Ref | 3,021 | 5.0% | | 887 | 1.4% | Lib |
| Oram, S — UK Ind | 622 | 1.0% | | 753 | 1.2% | Grn |
| Haysom, S — NLP | 204 | 0.3% | | | | |
| C to LD notional swing 2.1% | 60,036 | | C maj 9,782 16.3% | 63,440 | | C maj 13,019 84.0% |

**MICHAEL ANCRAM**, b July 7, 1945. Advocate. Elected to this seat 1992; MP for Edinburgh S 1979-87; MP for Berwick and East Lothian, Feb to Oct 1974; fought W Lothian, 1970. Min of State for N Ireland 1994-97 with duties on the Ulster peace process negotiations; Under Sec for N Ireland 1993-94; Under Sec for Scotland 1983-87. Privy Counsellor 1995. Member, energy select cttee, 1979-83. Chair, Scottish C Party, 1980-83, and vice-chair 1975-80. Member, board, Scottish Homes, 1988-90. Ed Ampleforth; Christ Church, Oxford; Edinburgh Univ.

**TONY VICKERS**, b Oct 13, 1946. Chartered land surveyor and information management consultant. Newbury district cllr 1995- . Former MoD geographical adviser; retired in 1995 as Lt-Col in Royal Engineers. Ed Wellington Coll, Berkshire; Brighton Poly; Hong Kong Poly Univ.
**FRANK JEFFREY**, b Feb 21, 1945. Political campaigner; seminar speaker; company director. Devizes CLP press officer. Ed Carlisle GS; Durham Univ.

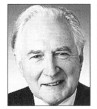

### DEVON EAST — 14.7% change — C win

| Electorate % Turnout | 69,094 | 76.1% | 1997 | 68,036 | 80.8% | 1992 |
|---|---|---|---|---|---|---|
| +Emery, Sir Peter — C | 22,797 | 43.4% | -9.2% | 28,895 | 52.5% | C |
| Trethewey, Miss R — LD | 15,308 | 29.1% | +2.0% | 14,902 | 27.1% | LD |
| Siantonas, A — Lab | 9,292 | 17.7% | +5.5% | 6,685 | 12.2% | Lab |
| Dixon, W — Ref | 3,200 | 6.1% | | 4,513 | 8.2% | Other |
| Halliwell, G — Lib | 1,363 | 2.6% | | | | |
| Giffard, C — UK Ind | 459 | 0.9% | | | | |
| Needs, G — Nat Dem | 131 | 0.2% | | | | |
| C to LD notional swing 5.6% | 52,550 | | C maj 7,489 14.3% | 54,995 | | C maj 13,993 25.4% |

**SIR PETER EMERY**, b Feb 27, 1926. MP for Honiton 1967-97, and for Reading 1959-66; contested Poplar 1951, and Lincoln 1955. Elected treas, 1922 Cttee, May 21, 1997. Chair, select cttee on procedure, since 1983 (member since 1973); member, trade and industry select cttee, 1979-87. Under Sec for Energy 1974; Under Sec for Trade and Industry 1972-74. Chair, all-party asthma group. Privy Counsellor 1993. Capt, Commons bridge team, 1984- . Chair, Winglaw Group, property developers; dir, London MoT Centre Ltd. Trustee, National Asthma Campaign. Member, advisory board, Centre for Strategic and International Studies,Washington DC, 1990- ; N Atlantic Assembly 1983- ; delegate and treas, OSCE (formerly Conference on Security and Co-operation in Europe), 1992- . Ed Scotch Plains HS, New Jersey; Oriel Coll, Oxford.

**RACHEL TRETHEWEY**, b Oct 12, 1967. Freelance journalist. Member, Charter 88. Ed Torquay Girls' GS; St Edmund Hall, Oxford.
**ANDREW SIANTONAS**, b Dec 8, 1950. Lecturer at Exeter Coll of FE; previously schoolteacher, scientific civil servant. Leeds city cllr 1984-88. Member, NATFHE. Ed Manchester and Leicester Univs.

### DEVON NORTH — 0.1% change — LD win

| Electorate % Turnout | 70,350 | 77.9% | 1997 | 70,051 | 83.0% | 1992 |
|---|---|---|---|---|---|---|
| +Harvey, N — LD | 27,824 | 50.7% | +3.6% | 27,389 | 47.1% | LD |
| Ashworth, R — C | 21,643 | 39.5% | -6.3% | 26,596 | 45.7% | C |
| Brenton, Mrs A — Lab | 5,367 | 9.8% | +3.9% | 3,406 | 5.9% | Lab |
| | | | | 659 | 1.1% | Grn |
| | | | | 107 | 0.2% | NLP |
| C to LD notional swing 5.0% | 54,834 | | LD maj 6,181 11.3% | 58,157 | | LD maj 793 83.0% |

**NICK HARVEY**, b Aug 3, 1961. Won this seat 1992; contested Enfield Southgate for L/All 1987. LD spokesman on trade and industry 1994- ; transport 1992-97; chair, LD campaigns and communications, 1994- . Member, trade and industry select cttee, 1993-95. Ex-parliamentary lobbyist. Member, Lib Party Council, 1981-82 and 1984-88. Ed Queen's, Taunton; Middlesex Poly (union pres 1981-82).

**RICHARD ASHWORTH**, b Sept 17, 1947. Company director, international dairy industrialist. Vice-chair, Hastings and Rye C assoc; East Sussex and Kent South Euro constituency. Ed King's, Canterbury; Seale-Hayne Coll; Plymouth Univ.
**ANNIE BRENTON**, b Jan 28, 1948. Supervisor for electronics company. Torridge district cllr, 1994- . Member, TGWU. Ed Ursulin Convent, Wimbledon; North Western Poly, London.

| DEVON SOUTH WEST | | 78.6% change | | | | C win | |
|---|---|---|---|---|---|---|---|
| Electorate % Turnout | | 69,293 | 76.2% | **1997** | 65,667 | 81.4% | **1992** |
| +Streeter, G N | C | **22,695** | **43.0%** | -14.7% | **30,796** | **57.6%** | C |
| Mavin, C | Lab | 15,262 | 28.9% | +13.0% | 13,666 | 25.6% | LD |
| Baldry, K | LD | 12,542 | 23.7% | -1.8% | 8,470 | 15.9% | Lab |
| Sadler, R | Ref | 1,668 | 3.2% | | 489 | 0.9% | Other |
| King, Mrs H | UK Ind | 491 | 0.9% | | | | |
| Hyde, J | NLP | 159 | 0.3% | | | | |
| C to Lab notional swing 13.9% | | 52,817 | | C maj 7,433 | 53,421 | | C maj 17,130 |
| | | | | 14.1% | | | 81.4% |

**GARY STREETER**, b Oct 2, 1955. Solicitor. MP for Plymouth Sutton 1992-97. Parly Sec, Lord Chancellor's Dept, 1996-97; asst gvt whip 1995-96; previously PPS to Sir Nicholas Lyell, Attorney-General, 1994-95, and to Sir Derek Spencer, Solicitor-General, 1993-95. Member, environment select cttee, 1992-93. Former sec, West Country group of C MPs. Plymouth city cllr 1986-92. Solicitor with Plymouth firm from 1980 and partner from 1984. Ed Tiverton GS; King's Coll, London.

**CHRIS MAVIN**, b Feb 15, 1951. Shipwright at Devonport Royal Dockyard. Plymouth city cllr (dep whip, treas of Lab group). Member, GMB. Ed Devonport Secondary.
**KEITH BALDRY**, b May 22, 1944. Retired postmaster controller, Mount Pleasant sorting office, London; previously district head postmaster, Plymouth and Cornwall. Part-time community projects adviser to Bishop of Exeter. Ex-chair, Hertford SDP. Ed Willesen County GS; Trinity Coll, Dublin.

| DEVON WEST & TORRIDGE | | 3.7% change | | | | LD win | |
|---|---|---|---|---|---|---|---|
| Electorate % Turnout | | 75,919 | 77.9% | **1997** | 74,364 | 81.2% | **1992** |
| Burnett, J | LD | **24,744** | **41.8%** | +0.1% | **28,458** | **47.1%** | C |
| Liddell-Grainger, I | C | 22,787 | 38.5% | -8.6% | 25,187 | 41.7% | LD |
| Brenton, D | Lab | 7,319 | 12.4% | +2.9% | 5,748 | 9.5% | Lab |
| Lea, R | Ref | 1,946 | 3.3% | | 868 | 1.4% | Grn |
| Jackson, M J | UK Ind | 1,841 | 3.1% | | 134 | 0.2% | NLP |
| Pithouse, M | Lib | 508 | 0.9% | | | | |
| C to LD notional swing 4.4% | | 59,145 | | LD maj 1,957 | 60,395 | | C maj 3,271 |
| | | | | 3.3% | | | 81.2% |

**JOHN BURNETT**, b Sept 19, 1945. Farmer and cattle breeder. Contested this seat 1987. Member, council of Devon Cattle Breeders Soc. Ex-officer, Royal Marine Commandos. Served for 12 years on Law Soc's revenue law cttee. Ed Ampleforth Coll; Coll of Law, London.
**IAN LIDDELL-GRAINGER**, b Feb 23, 1959. Contested Tyne and Wear in 1994 Euro elections. Adviser to chairs of defence and foreign affairs select cttees since 1992; member, Lords rural economy

group; C agricultural forum. Northern industrial rep to Euro Parliament. Tynedale district cllr 1989-95. Ed Wellesley House, Kent; Millfield School, Somerset; South of Scotland Agric Coll, Edinburgh.
**DAVID BRENTON**, b Aug 15, 1945. Basket-maker, potter and teacher. Contested this seat 1992 and 1987. Bideford town cllr (Mayor 1991-92). Member, NASUWT. Ed Barnstaple Boys GS; Bideford Art Coll; St Luke's Coll, Exeter.

| DEWSBURY | | 51.1% change | | | | Lab win | |
|---|---|---|---|---|---|---|---|
| Electorate % Turnout | | 61,523 | 70.0% | **1997** | 61,210 | 80.1% | **1992** |
| +Taylor, Mrs A | Lab | **21,286** | **49.4%** | +2.1% | **23,186** | **47.3%** | Lab |
| McCormick, Dr P | C | 12,963 | 30.1% | -9.9% | 19,637 | 40.0% | C |
| Hill, K | LD | 4,422 | 10.3% | +0.4% | 4,835 | 9.9% | LD |
| Taylor, Ms F | BNP | 2,232 | 5.2% | +3.7% | 718 | 1.5% | BNP |
| Goff, Ms W | Ref | 1,019 | 2.4% | | 511 | 1.0% | Grn |
| Daniel, D | Ind Lab | 770 | 1.8% | | 156 | 0.3% | NLP |
| McCourtie, I | Green | 383 | 0.9% | | | | |
| C to Lab notional swing 6.0% | | 43,075 | | Lab maj 8,323 | 49,043 | | Lab maj 3,549 |
| | | | | 19.3% | | | 80.1% |

**ANN TAYLOR**, b July 2, 1947. Became President of the Council and Leader of the Commons May 3, 1997. Elected 1987; MP for Bolton W, Oct 1974-83 before contesting Bolton NE; contested Bolton W, Feb 1974. Elected to Shadow Cabinet 1990; Shadow Commons Leader, 1994-97; Shadow Education Sec 1992-94; spokesman on environmental protection 1990-92; in frontbench environment team from 1988 with task of opposing water privatisation; home affairs spokesman 1987-88. Asst gvt whip 1977-79. Member, standards and privileges select cttee, 1995-97; Lab

spokesman on education 1979-81; in Lab DoE team 1981-83. Ex-teacher. Ed Bolton School; Bradford and Sheffield Univs.
**PAUL McCORMICK**, b March 17, 1955. Barrister; research Fellow, Nuffield Coll, Oxford. Contested Orkney and Shetland 1992. Specialist adviser, House of Commons, 1980-82. Havant borough cllr 1988-96. Ed Chichester HS for Boys; Balliol and Nuffield Colls, Oxford.
**KINGSLEY HILL**, b Aug 17, 1938. Consultant. Ex-engineer and teacher. Ed Leicester and Manchester Univs; Cambridge Inst; OU.

| DON VALLEY | | 44.5% change | | | | Lab win | |
|---|---|---|---|---|---|---|---|
| Electorate % Turnout | | 65,643 | 66.4% | **1997** | 65,391 | 78.7% | **1992** |
| **Flint, Ms C** | **Lab** | **25,376** | **58.3%** | **+7.7%** | **26,046** | **50.6%** | **Lab** |
| Gledhill, Mrs C H | C | 10,717 | 24.6% | -12.2% | 18,927 | 36.8% | C |
| Johnston, P | LD | 4,238 | 9.7% | -1.4% | 5,718 | 11.1% | LD |
| Davis, P | Ref | 1,379 | 3.2% | | 803 | 1.6% | Grn |
| Ball, N | Soc Lab | 1,024 | 2.4% | | | | |
| Platt, S | Green | 493 | 1.1% | | | | |
| Johnson, Ms C | ProLife | 330 | 0.8% | | | | |
| **C to Lab notional swing 9.9%** | | **43,557** | | **Lab maj 14,659** | **51,494** | | **Lab maj 7,119** |
| | | | | 33.7% | | | 78.7% |

CAROLINE FLINT, b Sept 20, 1961. Senior researcher/political officer, GMB. Member, Working for Childcare (chair 1991-95); Fabian Soc. Associate editor, *Renewal*; CWS. Ed Twickenham Girls' School; Richmond Tertiary Coll; East Anglia Univ.
CLARE GLEDHILL, b Nov 12, 1969. Architect. Adviser to John Whittingdale, MP, and Michael Fabricant, MP; chair, Assoc of C Parly Staff; vice-chair, Tewkesbury C assoc, 1993-94. Qualified and practised in architecture 1985-90; partner in practice specialising in leisure developments 1992-94. Concert flautist and music teacher. Member, Musicians Union.
PAUL JOHNSTON, b Oct 16, 1963. Managing director of Leeds-based PR consultancy. Ed Rhodesway Upper School, Bradford; Trent Poly.

| DONCASTER CENTRAL | | | | | | Lab hold | |
|---|---|---|---|---|---|---|---|
| Electorate % Turnout | | 67,965 | 63.9% | **1997** | 68,890 | 74.2% | **1992** |
| **Winterton, Ms R** | **Lab** | **26,961** | **62.1%** | **+7.7%** | **27,795** | **54.3%** | **Lab** |
| Turtle, D | C | 9,105 | 21.0% | -12.5% | 17,113 | 33.5% | C |
| Tarry, S | LD | 4,091 | 9.4% | -2.4% | 6,057 | 11.8% | LD |
| Cliff, M | Ref | 1,273 | 2.9% | | 184 | 0.4% | WRP |
| Kenny, M | Soc Lab | 854 | 2.0% | | | | |
| Redden, J | ProLife | 697 | 1.6% | | | | |
| Davies, P | UK Ind | 462 | 1.1% | | | | |
| **C to Lab swing 10.1%** | | **43,443** | | **Lab maj 17,856** | **51,149** | | **Lab maj 10,682** |
| | | | | 41.1% | | | 74.2% |

ROSIE WINTERTON, b Aug 10, 1958. Chief of staff, office of John Prescott, dep leader of Lab Party. Member, TGWU; NUJ; Co-op Party; Amnesty. Ed Doncaster GS; Hull Univ.
DAVID TURTLE, b Dec 28, 1965. Administrative officer for Metropolitan Police, New Scotland Yard. Business rating consultant and manager, Camden and Lambeth, 1994-95; business rating officer, City of Westminster, 1989-94; managing dir of own business 1995. Senior spokesman, Nat Viewers and Listeners Assoc. Ed Benton Park GS, Leeds; London Univ.
SIMON TARRY, b Oct 6, 1956. Student nurse. York city cllr 1995- . Ed Tadcaster GS; York Univ.

| DONCASTER NORTH | | 15.1% change | | | | Lab win | |
|---|---|---|---|---|---|---|---|
| Electorate % Turnout | | 63,019 | 63.3% | **1997** | 63,972 | 71.0% | **1992** |
| **+Hughes, K** | **Lab** | **27,843** | **69.8%** | **+5.4%** | **29,272** | **64.4%** | **Lab** |
| Kennerley, P | C | 5,906 | 14.8% | -7.5% | 10,131 | 22.3% | C |
| Cook, M | LD | 3,369 | 8.4% | -4.8% | 6,022 | 13.3% | LD |
| Thornton, R | Ref | 1,589 | 4.0% | | | | |
| Swan, M | AS Lab | 1,181 | 3.0% | | | | |
| **C to Lab notional swing 6.4%** | | **39,888** | | **Lab maj 21,937** | **45,425** | | **Lab maj 19,141** |
| | | | | 55.0% | | | 71.0% |

KEVIN HUGHES, b Dec 15, 1952. Became gvt asst whip, May 7, 1997. Ex-miner. Elected for this seat 1992. Lab whip 1996-97. Member, Euro legislation select cttee, 1992-96. Joint vice-chair, PLP health and personal social services cttee; sec, all-party personal social services parly group. Doncaster borough cllr 1986-92; former sec/agent, Doncaster N CLP. Miner 1970-90; member, exec cttee, Yorkshire NUM, 1983-86. Ed local state schools; Sheffield Univ on day release.
PETER KENNERLEY, b June 9, 1956. Solicitor; partner engaged in corporate and commercial law. Wandsworth cllr 1994- . Ed Collyer's School, Horsham; Sidney Sussex Coll, Cambridge; Coll of Law, Guildford.
MICHAEL COOK, b July 22, 1947. Self-employed accountant; previously in production and financial management in engineering, ship repairing, pottery and printing industries. Ed Kingston HS, Hull; Hull Coll of Commerce; Manchester Poly.

| DORSET MID & POOLE NORTH | | 120.1% change | | | C win | | |
|---|---|---|---|---|---|---|---|
| Electorate % Turnout | | 67,049 | 75.7% | 1997 | 64,833 | 77.0% | 1992 |
| Fraser, C J | C | 20,632 | 40.7% | -9.4% | 24,999 | 50.1% | C |
| Leaman, A | LD | 19,951 | 39.3% | +1.4% | 18,945 | 38.0% | LD |
| Collis, D | Lab | 8,014 | 15.8% | +3.9% | 5,959 | 11.9% | Lab |
| Nabarro, D | Ref | 2,136 | 4.2% | | | | |
| C to LD notional swing 5.4% | | 50,733 | | C maj 681 | 49,903 | | C maj 6,054 |
| | | | | 1.3% | | | 12.1% |

**CHRISTOPHER FRASER**, b Oct 25, 1962. Chairman, international communications group. Three Rivers district cllr, SW Herts, 1992-96. LEA-appointed school governor, 1992-96. Patron, Firm Link, Dorset, 1996- ; and Pramacare. Member, Chiltern open air museum advisory council, 1995-96; IoD. Freeman, City of London. Ed in Hertfordshire; Harrow Coll; Westminster Univ.
**ALAN LEAMAN**, b Jan 16, 1959. Dir of strategy and planning for LDs.

Aide to Paddy Ashdown 1988-93. Previously worked for Age Concern. Ed Tiffin Boys School, Kingston upon Thames; Bristol Univ (pres, students' union).
**DAVID COLLIS**, b Feb 4, 1948. Contracts consultant. Chair, Sandford, Wareham and Dist Lab Party. Lytchett Minster and Upton town cllr. Member, TGWU. Ed Doncaster Technical HS; Army Apprentices Coll, Harrogate.

| DORSET NORTH | | 24.2% change | | | C win | | |
|---|---|---|---|---|---|---|---|
| Electorate % Turnout | | 68,923 | 76.3% | 1997 | 64,923 | 81.4% | 1992 |
| Walter, R | C | 23,294 | 44.3% | -12.2% | 29,855 | 56.5% | C |
| Yates, Mrs P G | LD | 20,548 | 39.1% | +1.6% | 19,784 | 37.4% | LD |
| Fitzmaurice, J | Lab | 5,380 | 10.2% | +4.2% | 3,195 | 6.0% | Lab |
| Evans, Mrs M | Ref | 2,564 | 4.9% | | | | |
| Wheeler, Rev D | UK Ind | 801 | 1.5% | | | | |
| C to LD notional swing 6.9% | | 52,587 | | C maj 2,746 | 52,834 | | C maj 10,071 |
| | | | | 5.2% | | | 81.4% |

**ROBERT WALTER**, b May 3, 1948. Contested Bedwellty 1979. International banker; director and vice-pres, Aubrey G. Lanston & Co. Visiting lecturer in East-West trade, Westminster Univ. Vice-pres, C Group for Europe, chair 1992-95; ex-chair, European Democrat Forum; member, C Foreign and Commonwealth Council; founder chair, Wiltshire Europe Soc. Freeman of City of London. Ed Lord Weymouth School, Warminster; Aston Univ.

**PAULA YATES**, b Dec 27, 1947. Local gvt consultant. Contested Maidstone 1992. Maidstone borough cllr 1984-92 (leader 1987-92). Ed North London Collegiate School; Hull and London Univs.
**JOHN FITZMAURICE**, b Nov 18, 1947. Head of unit, European Commission, Brussels. Contested this seat 1992; Dorset N 1992, and Yeovil 1987. Sec, Brussels Lab group; vice-chair, Brussels Voluntary Co-op Party. Member, European public service union, 1974- . Ed Shaftesbury GS; Bristol and Oxford Univs.

| DORSET SOUTH | | 11.1% change | | | C win | | |
|---|---|---|---|---|---|---|---|
| Electorate % Turnout | | 66,318 | 74.2% | 1997 | 67,747 | 76.6% | 1992 |
| +Bruce, I | C | 17,755 | 36.1% | -14.8% | 26,405 | 50.9% | C |
| Knight, J | Lab | 17,678 | 35.9% | +15.1% | 13,788 | 26.6% | LD |
| Plummer, M | LD | 9,936 | 20.2% | -6.4% | 10,805 | 20.8% | Lab |
| McAndrew, P | Ref | 2,791 | 5.7% | | 673 | 1.3% | Ind |
| Shakesby, Capt M | UK Ind | 861 | 1.8% | | 191 | 0.4% | NLP |
| Napper, G | NLP | 161 | 0.3% | -0.0% | | | |
| C to Lab notional swing 15.0% | | 49,182 | | C maj 77 | 51,862 | | C maj 12,617 |
| | | | | 0.2% | | | 76.6% |

**IAN BRUCE**, b March 14, 1947. Elected 1987; contested Burnley 1983; Yorkshire West in 1984 Euro elections. Member, select cttees on science and technology, 1995-97; employment 1990-92. Vice-chair, 1994-95, and sec, 1990-94, C backbench social security cttee; vice-chair, C employment cttee, 1994- ; joint vice-chair, C ed cttee, 1995- . Joint chair, all-party street children parly group, 1992- ; joint sec, parly and scientific cttee. Chair and founder, Ian Bruce Associates Ltd, group of employment agencies and management consultants, 1975- . Parly adviser to Telecommunications Managers Assoc, 1989- ; to Trevor Gilbert & Associates, personal injury employment advisers, 1993- ; to Fed of

Recruitment and Employment Services. Unpaid dir, Eurim Ltd, monitoring and collating Euro informatics market. Factory manager, Sinclair Electronics, 1974-75. Ed Chelmsford Tech HS; Mid-Essex Tech Coll; Bradford Univ.
**JIM KNIGHT**, b March 6, 1965. General manager of publishing company; ex-actor and theatre manager. Frome town cllr 1995- . Member, Co-op Party; Amnesty; MSF. Ed Eltham Coll; Fitzwilliam Coll, Cambridge.
**MICHAEL PLUMMER**, b June 6, 1955. Lecturer. Poole borough cllr 1996- . Ed Teesside Poly; Wolverhampton Poly; Bournemouth Univ.

| DORSET WEST | | | | | **C hold** | |
|---|---|---|---|---|---|---|
| Electorate % Turnout | | 70,369 | 76.1% | **1997** | 67,256 | 81.2% | **1992** |
| Letwin, O | C | 22,036 | 41.1% | -9.7% | 27,766 | 50.9% | C |
| Legg, R | LD | 20,196 | 37.7% | +1.5% | 19,755 | 36.2% | LD |
| Bygraves, R | Lab | 9,491 | 17.7% | +4.8% | 7,082 | 13.0% | Lab |
| Jenkins, P | UK Ind | 1,590 | 3.0% | | | | |
| Griffiths, M | NLP | 239 | 0.4% | | | | |
| **C to LD swing 5.6%** | | 53,552 | C maj 1,840 | | 54,603 | C maj 8,011 | |
| | | | 3.4% | | | 81.2% | |

**OLIVER LETWIN,** b May 19, 1956. Merchant banker, Cambridge don, financial adviser and journalist. Contested Hampstead and Highgate 1992; Hackney N 1987. Special adviser to Prime Minister's policy unit 1983-86; special adviser to Sec of State for Ed and Science Sec 1982-88. Director and head of utilities and privatisation team and previously manager and asst director in corporate finance at N.M. Rothchild & Sons Ltd. Ed Eton; Trinity Coll, Cambridge; London Business School.

**ROBIN LEGG,** b Oct 26, 1953. Solicitor with South Somerset Council. Contested this seat 1992. Dorset county cllr 1981- ; Sherborne town cllr 1987- (Mayor of Sherborne 1995-96). Ed St Aldhelm's School and Foster's School, Sherborne; Bath Univ; Coll of Law, Guildford.
**ROBERT BYGRAVES,** b Nov 14, 1945. Teacher. Sherborne town cllr 1988- ; West Dorset district cllr 1991- . Ed Midhurst GS; Univ Coll of Wales, Swansea; Liverpool and Southampton Univs.

| DOVER | 0.2% change | | | | **Lab win** | |
|---|---|---|---|---|---|---|
| Electorate % Turnout | | 68,669 | 78.9% | **1997** | 69,646 | 82.8% | **1992** |
| Prosser, G | Lab | 29,535 | 54.5% | +11.9% | 25,443 | 44.1% | C |
| +Shaw, D | C | 17,796 | 32.8% | -11.3% | 24,583 | 42.6% | Lab |
| Corney, M | LD | 4,302 | 7.9% | -2.9% | 6,234 | 10.8% | LD |
| Anderson, Mrs S | Ref | 2,124 | 3.9% | | 638 | 1.1% | Grn |
| Hyde, C | UK Ind | 443 | 0.8% | | 407 | 0.7% | Ind |
| | | | | | 250 | 0.4% | Ind C |
| | | | | | 127 | 0.2% | NLP |
| **C to Lab notional swing 11.6%** | | 54,200 | Lab maj 11,739 | | 57,682 | C maj 860 | |
| | | | 21.7% | | | 82.8% | |

**GWYN PROSSER,** b April 27, 1943. Chartered marine engineer, ex-chief engineer on Sealink cross-Channel ferries. Contested this seat 1992. Dover district cllr 1987- ; Kent county cllr 1989- . Member, East Kent Initiative. Trustee, Kent Enterprise Office; dir, Aylesham Community Workshop Trust; trustee, Roman Painted House Trust and Crabble Cornmill Trust. Co-ordinator, local opposition groups against Channel Tunnel, 1985-87. Ed Dunvant Sec Mod School; Swansea Tech School; Swansea Coll of Tech.

**DAVID SHAW,** b Nov 14, 1950. Chartered accountant. Elected 1987; contested Leigh 1979. Member, select cttee on social security 1991-97. Chair, Bow Group, 1983-84. Founder and managing dir, Sabrelance Ltd; dir, Adscene Group plc, newspaper publishing and printing; Raptor Residential Investments plc. Ed King's Coll School, Wimbledon; City of London Poly.
**MARK CORNEY,** b May 17, 1962. Research and policy consultant. Ed Sir Harry Smith Community Coll; London Univ.

| DOWN NORTH | 31.3% change | | | | **UKU win** | |
|---|---|---|---|---|---|---|
| Electorate % Turnout | | 63,010 | 58.0% | **1997** | 61,745 | 60.9% | **1992** |
| +McCartney, R | UKU | 12,817 | 35.1% | | 15,298 | 40.7% | UPUP |
| McFarland, A | UUP | 11,368 | 31.1% | | 13,033 | 34.6% | C |
| Napier, Sir Oliver | Alliance | 7,554 | 20.7% | +5.0% | 5,894 | 15.7% | Alliance |
| Fee, L | C | 1,810 | 4.9% | -29.7% | 3,153 | 8.4% | DUP |
| Farrell, Miss M | SDLP | 1,602 | 4.4% | | 255 | 0.7% | NLP |
| Morrice, Ms J | NI Women | 1,240 | 3.4% | | | | |
| Mullins, T | NLP | 108 | 0.3% | -0.4% | | | |
| Mooney, R | NIP | 67 | 0.2% | | | | |
| **No swing calculation** | | 36,566 | UKU maj 1,449 | | 37,633 | UPUP maj 2,265 | |
| | | | 4.0% | | | 6.0% | |

**ROBERT McCARTNEY,** b April 24, 1936. QC (NI). Standing as United Kingdom Unionist, won by-election in June 1995 which followed death of Sir James Kilfedder. Admitted solicitor 1962 and called to NI Bar 1968. Ed Grosvenor GS, Belfast; Queen's Univ, Belfast.
**ALAN McFARLAND,** b Aug 9, 1949. Contested this seat in June 1995 by-election. Dir of Somme Heritage Centre in Newtownards. Former major in Royal Tank Regiment. Ed Campbell Coll, Belfast.

**SIR OLIVER NAPIER,** b July 11, 1935. Senior Partner, Napier & Sons, solicitors. Contested E Belfast 1979, 1983. Founder member Alliance Party 1970, leader 1973-84, pres 1989-92. Member, NI Assembly 1973-75 and 1982-86; Min of Legal Affairs, NI Exec, 1974; member, NI Constitutional Convention, 1975-76. Chair, Advisory Commission on Human Rights, 1988-92. Belfast city cllr 1977-89. Ed St Malachy's Coll, Belfast; Queen's Univ, Belfast.
*Details of 1995 by-election on page 278*

| DOWN SOUTH | | 16.4% change | | | | | | SDLP win |
|---|---|---|---|---|---|---|---|---|
| Electorate % Turnout | | 69,855 | 70.8% | **1997** | 67,516 | 77.6% | **1992** | |
| +McGrady, E K | SDLP | **26,181** | **52.9%** | -3.2% | **29,408** | **56.2%** | SDLP | |
| Nesbitt, D | UUP | 16,248 | 32.8% | -2.6% | 18,531 | 35.4% | UUP | |
| Murphy, M | SF | 5,127 | 10.4% | +6.8% | 1,860 | 3.6% | SF | |
| Crozier, J | Alliance | 1,711 | 3.5% | +1.0% | 1,308 | 2.5% | Alliance | |
| McKeon, Ms R | NLP | 219 | 0.4% | | 1,262 | 2.4% | C | |
| **No swing calculation** | | **49,486** | **SDLP maj 9,933** | | **52,369** | **SDLP maj 10,877** | | |
| | | | 20.1% | | | 20.8% | | |

**EDDIE McGRADY,** b June 3, 1935. Chartered accountant. Won seat 1987, defeating Enoch Powell; contested seat 1986, 1983 and 1979. Member, NI affairs select cttee, 1994-97. SDLP member for S Down of NI Assembly 1973-75, and min in NI power-sharing exec 1973-74; NI Constitutional Convention 1975-76, and NI Assembly 1982-86. First chair of SDLP 1971-73, and first chair of SDLP Assembly party. Downpatrick cllr 1961-89, chair 1964-73; chair or vice-chair, Down District Council, 1973 to 1982. Partner, M.B. McGrady and Co, chartered accountants and insurance brokers. FCA. Ed St Patrick's HS, Downpatrick; Belfast Coll of Tech.

**DERMOT NESBITT.** University lecturer in finance. Member, standing commission on human rights advising Ulster Sec. Member, N Ireland forum and chair of its economy cttee.
**MICK MURPHY,** b Feb 6, 1942. Retired publican from Rostrevor, Co Down. Involved in republican politics since civil rights campaign of 1960s.
**JULIAN CROZIER.** Retired civil servant. Ex-head of Training and Employment Agency.

| DUDLEY NORTH | | 69.2% change | | | | | | Lab win |
|---|---|---|---|---|---|---|---|---|
| Electorate % Turnout | | 68,835 | 69.5% | **1997** | 70,484 | 77.1% | **1992** | |
| Cranston, R | Lab | **24,471** | **51.2%** | +5.7% | **24,730** | **45.5%** | Lab | |
| MacNamara, C | C | 15,014 | 31.4% | -12.3% | 23,776 | 43.8% | C | |
| Lewis, G | LD | 3,939 | 8.2% | -1.5% | 5,273 | 9.7% | LD | |
| Atherton, M | Soc Lab | 2,155 | 4.5% | | 565 | 1.0% | Other | |
| Bavester, S | Ref | 1,201 | 2.5% | | | | | |
| Cartwright, G | NF | 559 | 1.2% | | | | | |
| Darby, S | Nat Dem | 469 | 1.0% | | | | | |
| **C to Lab notional swing 9.0%** | | **47,808** | **Lab maj 9,457** | | **54,344** | **Lab maj 954** | | |
| | | | 19.8% | | | 77.1% | | |

**ROSS CRANSTON,** b July 23, 1948. Professor of Law, London School of Economics. Contested Richmond (Yorks) 1992. Ex-consultant overseas for UN, World Bank and Commonwealth Secretariat. Member, AUT. Ed Harvard; Oxford.

**CHARLES MacNAMARA,** b July 14, 1958. Solicitor. Dudley cllr, 1992-96. Pres, UK American Football League, 1987-89. Ed Hall Green School, Birmingham; Birmingham Poly.
**GERRY LEWIS,** b March 17, 1926. Counsellor; contested Dudley E 1979, Dudley W 1983, 1987 and 1992. Member, Amnesty; Dudley Racial Equality Council. Ed Aberdeen, Belfast and Aston Univs.

| DUDLEY SOUTH | | 62.1% change | | | | | | Lab win |
|---|---|---|---|---|---|---|---|---|
| Electorate % Turnout | | 66,731 | 71.8% | **1997** | 66,927 | 79.5% | **1992** | |
| +Pearson, I P | Lab | **27,124** | **56.6%** | +9.6% | **25,025** | **47.0%** | Lab | |
| Simpson, M | C | 14,097 | 29.4% | -12.5% | 22,296 | 41.9% | C | |
| Burt, R | LD | 5,214 | 10.9% | -0.2% | 5,886 | 11.1% | LD | |
| Birch, C | Ref | 1,467 | 3.1% | | | | | |
| **C to Lab notional swing 11.0%** | | **47,902** | **Lab maj 13,027** | | **53,207** | **Lab maj 2,729** | | |
| | | | 27.2% | | | 5.1% | | |

**IAN PEARSON,** b April 5, 1959. Won Dudley W in 1994 by-election. Member, deregulation select cttee, 1996-97; Treasury select cttee 1996-97. Joint chief exec, W Midlands Enterprise Board, 1991-94; dep dir, Urban Trust, 1987-88. Lab Party local gvt policy research officer 1985-87. Non-exec dir (unpaid), Greater London Enterprise Ltd. Dudley cllr 1984-87. Ed Brierley Hill GS; Balliol Coll, Oxford; Warwick Univ.

**MARK SIMPSON,** b July 25, 1965. Publicity specialist. Contested Midlands West in Euro elections 1994. Chair, Wolverhampton SW C assoc, 1994-95; Wolverhampton cllr 1992-96. Ed Montrose Acad; Aberdeen Univ; Dundee Coll of FE.
**RICHARD BURT,** b May 22, 1954. Director. Dudley cllr 1996- . Ed Farnborough GS; Westhill Coll; Shrewsbury Tech Coll; OU.

*Details of 1994 Dudley West by-election on page 278*

| DULWICH & WEST NORWOOD | | 73.2% change | | | Lab win | | |
|---|---|---|---|---|---|---|---|
| Electorate % Turnout | | 69,655 | 65.5% | **1997** | 75,179 | 67.7% | **1992** |
| +Jowell, Ms T J H D | Lab | 27,807 | 61.0% | +14.6% | 23,582 | 46.3% | Lab |
| Gough, R | C | 11,038 | 24.2% | -18.6% | 21,779 | 42.8% | C |
| Kramer, Mrs S | LD | 4,916 | 10.8% | +1.0% | 4,998 | 9.8% | LD |
| Coles, B | Ref | 897 | 2.0% | | 531 | 1.0% | Other |
| Goldie, Dr A | Lib | 587 | 1.3% | | | | |
| Goodman, D | Dream | 173 | 0.4% | | | | |
| Pike, E | UK Ind | 159 | 0.3% | | | | |
| Rizz, C | Rizz | 38 | 0.1% | | | | |
| C to Lab notional swing 16.6% | | 45,615 | Lab maj 16,769 | | 50,890 | Lab maj 1,803 | |
| | | | 36.8% | | | 67.7% | |

**TESSA JOWELL,** b Sept 17, 1947. Became Minister for Public Health, May 5, 1997. Gained Dulwich for Labour 1992; contested Redbridge, Ilford N, by-election 1978 and again in 1979. Deputy to Shadow Health Sec 1996; chief Lab spokesman on women's issues 1995-96; Lab whip 1994-95. Parly adviser, Royal Coll of Nursing. Camden cllr 1971-86. Dir, community care programme, Joseph Rowntree Foundation, and Visiting Fellow, King's Fund Inst. 1990-92; dir, community care special action project, Birmingham, and senior Visiting Fellow, Policy Studies Inst, 1986-

90; asst dir, MIND, 1974-86. Ed St Margaret's, Aberdeen; Aberdeen and Edinburgh Univs.
**ROGER GOUGH,** b Aug 2, 1964. Asst dir, European banking analyst, UBS Ltd.Investment analyst with Swiss Bank Corp 1993-95; Baring Securities 1986-93. Dir, Bloomfield Centre for children with learning difficulties. Ed Dulwich Coll; Magdalen Coll, Oxford.
**SUSAN KRAMER,** b July 21, 1950. Business and finance consultant for Central and E Europe. Ed St Paul's Girls' School; St Hilda's Coll, Oxford (pres of Oxford Union); Univ of Illinois.

| DUMBARTON | | | | | Lab hold | | |
|---|---|---|---|---|---|---|---|
| Electorate % Turnout | | 56,229 | 73.4% | **1997** | 57,222 | 77.1% | **1992** |
| *McFall, J | Lab Co-op | 20,470 | 49.6% | +6.0% | 19,255 | 43.6% | Lab Co-op |
| Mackechnie, W | SNP | 9,587 | 23.2% | +4.8% | 13,126 | 29.7% | C |
| Ramsay, P | C | 7,283 | 17.6% | -12.1% | 8,127 | 18.4% | SNP |
| Reid, A | LD | 3,144 | 7.6% | -0.1% | 3,425 | 7.8% | LD |
| Robertson, L | SSA | 283 | 0.7% | | 192 | 0.4% | NLP |
| Dempster, G | Ref | 255 | 0.6% | | | | |
| Lancaster, R | UK Ind | 242 | 0.6% | | | | |
| SNP to Lab swing 0.6% | | 41,264 | Lab Co-op maj 10,883 | | 44,125 | Lab Co-op maj 6,129 | |
| | | | 26.4% | | | 77.1% | |

**JOHN McFALL,** b Oct 4, 1944. Became gvt whip, May 7, 1997. Ex-teacher. Elected 1987. Lab spokesman on Scotland 1992; Lab whip 1989-91. Member, defence select cttee, 1988-92; Commons information cttee 1990-97. Joint sec, parly and scientific cttee; treas, all-party Scotch whisky industry group. Joint vice-capt, parly golfing society. Member, EIS; GMB. Ed St Patrick's Secondary, Dumbarton; Paisley Coll; Strathclyde Univ; OU.

**BILL MACKECHNIE,** b Jan 1, 1949. Teacher. Contested seat 1992. Dumbarton cllr 1988- . Ed Perth Acad; St Andrews Univ; Moray House Coll of Ed.
**PETER RAMSAY,** b Jan 13, 1955. Bank manager.. Ed Gordonstoun; Rapid Results Coll; Clydebank Tech; Glasgow Central Coll of Ed.
**ALAN REID,** b Aug 7, 1954. Computer programmer. Contested Paisley S 1992. Ed Ayr Acad; Strathclyde Univ.

| DUMFRIES | 2.4% change | | | | Lab win | | |
|---|---|---|---|---|---|---|---|
| Electorate % Turnout | | 62,759 | 78.9% | **1997** | 63,268 | 79.2% | **1992** |
| Brown, R | Lab | 23,528 | 47.5% | +17.9% | 21,597 | 43.1% | C |
| Stevenson, S J S | C | 13,885 | 28.0% | -15.1% | 14,831 | 29.6% | Lab |
| Higgins, R | SNP | 5,977 | 12.1% | -2.7% | 7,411 | 14.8% | SNP |
| Wallace, N | LD | 5,487 | 11.1% | -0.6% | 5,854 | 11.7% | LD |
| Parker, D | Ref | 533 | 1.1% | | 312 | 0.6% | Ind Green |
| Hunter, Ms E | NLP | 117 | 0.2% | +0.0% | 107 | 0.2% | NLP |
| C to Lab notional swing 16.5% | | 49,527 | Lab maj 9,643 | | 50,112 | C maj 6,766 | |
| | | | 19.5% | | | 13.5% | |

**RUSSELL BROWN,** b Sept 17, 1951. Process operator. Dumfries and Galloway UA cllr, 1995- (leader Lab group); Dumfries and Gallowat regional cllr,1986-96. TGWU. Ed Annan Acad.
**STRUAN STEVENSON,** b April 4, 1948. Farmer and director of public affairs co. Contested Edinburgh S 1992, and Carrick, Cumnockand Doon Valley 1987. Ed Strathallan School; W of Scotland Agric Coll.

**ROBERT HIGGINS,** b June 9, 1946. Ex-policeman. Dumfries and Galloway cllr 1992- . Ed Douglas Ewart HS; Tulliallan Police Coll.
**NEIL WALLACE,** b March 10, 1957. Teacher. Contested this seat 1992; Scottish LD transport spokesman. Ed Annan Acad; Edinburgh Univ; Moray House Coll of Ed.

| DUNDEE EAST | | 11.5% change | | | | | | Lab win |
|---|---|---|---|---|---|---|---|---|
| Electorate % Turnout | | 58,388 | 69.4% | **1997** | 61,286 | 73.4% | **1992** |
| +McAllion, J | Lab | 20,718 | 51.1% | +6.8% | 19,954 | 44.3% | Lab |
| Robison, Ms S | SNP | 10,757 | 26.5% | -5.5% | 14,437 | 32.1% | SNP |
| Mackie, B | C | 6,397 | 15.8% | -2.7% | 8,297 | 18.4% | C |
| Saluja, Dr G | LD | 1,677 | 4.1% | -0.2% | 1,939 | 4.3% | LD |
| Galloway, E | Ref | 601 | 1.5% | | 295 | 0.7% | Grn |
| Duke, H | SSA | 232 | 0.6% | | 77 | 0.2% | NLP |
| MacKenzie, S | NLP | 146 | 0.4% | +0.2% | | | |
| SNP to Lab notional swing 6.2% | | 40,528 | | Lab maj 9,961 | 44,999 | | Lab maj 5,517 |
| | | | | 24.6% | | | 73.4% |

**JOHN McALLION**, b Feb 13, 1948. Ex-teacher. Won this seat 1987. Lab spokesman on Scotland 1994-96, when he resigned over decision to hold referendum on Scottish parliament. Member, Euro legislation select cttee, 1996-97; energy select cttee 1989-92; chair and campaign officer (1989-90) and vice-chair (1988-89), Scottish group of Lab MPs; chair, all-party Scottish housing parly group; sec, Scotch whisky industry group, 1987-97. Parly consultant to PTC, formerly Nat Union of Civil and Public Servants. Tayside cllr 1984-87; convener 1986-87. Ed St

Augustine's Comp, Glasgow; St Andrews Univ; Dundee Coll of Ed.
**SHONA ROBISON**, b May 26, 1966. Community worker for Glasgow City Council.Member, Unison. Ed Alva Acad; Glasgow Univ; Jordanhill Coll.
**BRUCE MACKIE**, b Nov 27, 1932. Dundee city cllr (C group leader); Tayside regional cllr 1986-96 (C group leader); Dundee cllr 1966. British Telecom worker 1953-91. Ed Morgan Acad; Dundee Inst of Art and Tech.

| DUNDEE WEST | | 9.2% change | | | | | | Lab win |
|---|---|---|---|---|---|---|---|---|
| Electorate % Turnout | | 57,346 | 67.7% | **1997** | 60,352 | 67.9% | **1992** |
| +Ross, E | Lab | 20,875 | 53.8% | +6.1% | 19,520 | 47.7% | Lab |
| Dorward, J | SNP | 9,016 | 23.2% | -1.3% | 10,056 | 24.6% | SNP |
| Powrie, N | C | 5,105 | 13.2% | -5.7% | 7,717 | 18.8% | C |
| Dick, Dr E | LD | 2,972 | 7.7% | +0.2% | 3,071 | 7.5% | LD |
| Ward, Ms M | SSA | 428 | 1.1% | | 432 | 1.1% | Grn |
| MacMillan, J | Ref | 411 | 1.1% | | 159 | 0.4% | NLP |
| SNP to Lab notional swing 3.7% | | 38,807 | | Lab maj 11,859 | 40,955 | | Lab maj 9,464 |
| | | | | 30.6% | | | 67.9% |

**ERNEST ROSS**, b July 27, 1942. Engineer. Elected 1979. Member, standards and privileges select cttee, 1996-97; education and employment select cttee 1996-97; employment select cttee 1987-96; Court of Referees 1987-97. Chair, PLP foreign affairs cttee, 1987-97; joint vice-chair, PLP trade and industry cttee, 1987-88; chair (1988-89) and vice-chair (1987-88) Scottish group of Lab MPs. Member, exec cttee, British group, IPU 1991-94. Ed St John's Junior Secondary, Dundee.

**JOHN DORWARD**, b March 21, 1942. Construction consultant. Ed King's Park Secondary, Glasgow; Stow Coll of Engineering.
**NEIL POWRIE**, b Dec 6, 1954. Ex-businessman. Dundee district cllr 1979-95 ; Tayside cllr 1994; Dundee city cllr 1995. Ed Rockwell Sec; Angus Tech Coll.
**ELIZABETH DICK**, b March 17, 1935. Medical researcher. Contested Dundee W 1992 and 1983, Falkirk E 1987. Ed St Paul's Girls' School, London; Oxford and Dundee Univs.

| DUNFERMLINE EAST | | 3.7% change | | | | | | Lab win |
|---|---|---|---|---|---|---|---|---|
| Electorate % Turnout | | 52,072 | 70.3% | **1997** | 50,674 | 75.2% | **1992** |
| +Brown, G | Lab | 24,441 | 66.8% | +3.9% | 23,966 | 62.9% | Lab |
| Ramage, J | SNP | 5,690 | 15.6% | +0.8% | 6,211 | 16.3% | C |
| Mitchell, I | C | 3,656 | 10.0% | -6.3% | 5,619 | 14.7% | SNP |
| Tolson, J | LD | 2,164 | 5.9% | -0.2% | 2,329 | 6.1% | LD |
| Dunsmore, T | Ref | 632 | 1.7% | | | | |
| SNP to Lab notional swing 1.6% | | 36,583 | | Lab maj 18,751 | 38,125 | | Lab maj 17,755 |
| | | | | 51.3% | | | 75.2% |

**GORDON BROWN**, b Feb 20, 1951. Became Chancellor of the Exchequer, May 2, 1997. Shadow Chancellor 1992-97. Elected 1983; contested Edinburgh S 1979. Chief Lab trade and industry spokesman 1989-92; elected to Shadow Cabinet 1987; Shadow Chief Sec to Treasury 1987-89; spokesman on regional affairs in Lab DTI frontbench team 1985-87. Chair, Scot Lab Party, 1983-94; member, employment select cttee, 1983-85. Privy Counsellor 1996. Columnist for *Scottish Daily Record;* journalist with, then editor, current affairs dept, Scottish Television, 1980-83; lecturer

in politics, Glasgow Coll of Tech, 1976-80; rector, Edinburgh Univ, 1972-75. Member, NUJ. Ed Kirkcaldy HS; Edinburgh Univ.
**JOHN RAMAGE**, b Oct 22, 1949. Computer consultant. Sec, SNP Kinross branch; ex-Perth and Kinross cllr, ex-Tayside cllr.
**IAIN MITCHELL**, b Nov 15, 1951. Barrister. Hon sec, Scottish C assoc; member, exec cttee, European Movement (Scottish Council). Called to the Bar 1976, appointed QC 1992. Fellow, Royal Society of Arts, 1988. Ed Perth Acad; Edinburgh Univ.
**JIM TOLSON**, b May 26, 1965. Mechanical fitter at Rosyth dockyard.

| DUNFERMLINE WEST | | 3.5% change | | | Lab win | | |
|---|---|---|---|---|---|---|---|
| Electorate % Turnout | | 52,467 | 69.4% | **1997** | 51,187 | 75.9% | **1992** |
| +Squire, Ms R | Lab | **19,338** | **53.1%** | +11.6% | 16,132 | 41.5% | Lab |
| Lloyd, J | SNP | 6,984 | 19.2% | -0.7% | 8,948 | 23.0% | C |
| Harris, Mrs E | LD | 4,963 | 13.6% | -2.0% | 7,703 | 19.8% | SNP |
| Newton, K | C | 4,606 | 12.6% | -10.4% | 6,066 | 15.6% | LD |
| Bain, J | Ref | 543 | 1.5% | | | | |
| SNP to Lab notional swing 6.1% | | 36,434 | Lab maj **12,354** | | 38,849 | Lab maj **7,184** | |
| | | | 33.9% | | | 75.9% | |

**RACHEL SQUIRE**, b July 13, 1954. Elected for this seat 1992. Member, select cttees on procedure and on Euro legislation. Chair, 1995-97, and former sec, PLP defence cttee; treas, all-party head injuries parly group. Full-time Nupe official 1981-92, having joined union in 1975; education officer with responsibility for Scotland 1985-92. Senior social worker with Birmingham social services dept 1975-81. Has served on Scottish exec of Lab Party; also Scottish Council political ed cttee. Ex-chair, Linlithgow CLP, and also political ed officer and press officer; former sec, Lothians European CLP. Ed Godolphin and Latymer Girls' School; Durham and Birmingham Univs.

**JOHN LLOYD**, b June 10, 1955. Teacher, freelance journalist and author. Contested Dunfermline E 1992. Member, SNP education cttee; PR officer, Dunfermline E. Member, EIS. Ed St Andrew's HS, Kirkcaldy; Stirling and Aberdeen Univs.
**ELIZABETH HARRIS**, b April 29, 1957. Education officer for RSPB. Contested this seat 1987 and Dunfermline E for L/All 1987. Dunfermline district cllr 1984-96; Fife cllr (dep opposition leader). EIS. Ed Beath Senior HS; Dundee Coll of Ed; OU.
**KEVIN NEWTON**, b March 26, 1973. Caravan park owner. Former part-time RSPCA asst. Ed Arnold School; Edinburgh Univ.

| DURHAM NORTH | | 9.5% change | | | Lab win | | |
|---|---|---|---|---|---|---|---|
| Electorate % Turnout | | 67,891 | 69.5% | **1997** | 66,503 | 76.3% | **1992** |
| +Radice, G | Lab | **33,142** | **70.3%** | +10.4% | 30,374 | 59.9% | Lab |
| Hardy, M | C | 6,843 | 14.5% | -10.3% | 12,610 | 24.9% | C |
| Moore, B | LD | 5,225 | 11.1% | -4.2% | 7,755 | 15.3% | LD |
| Parkin, I | Ref | 1,958 | 4.2% | | | | |
| C to Lab notional swing 10.4% | | 47,168 | Lab maj **26,299** | | 50,739 | Lab maj **17,764** | |
| | | | 55.8% | | | 76.3% | |

**GILES RADICE**, b Oct 4, 1936. Elected for this seat 1983; MP for Chester-le-Street 1973-83; contested Chippenham 1964 and 1966. Chair, public service select cttee 1995; member, Treasury and Civil Service select cttee, 1987-95; chief Lab spokesman on education 1983-87. Lab spokesman on employment 1981-83; on foreign affairs 1981. Chair, European Movement, UK, 1995- ; British Assoc for Central and Eastern Europe, 1991-. Parly Fellow, St Antony's Coll, Oxford, 1994-95. Ed Winchester; Magdalen Coll, Oxford.

**MARK HARDY**, b Oct 30, 1970. Project manager. Vice-chair, national YCs, 1994-95; chair, NW Durham C assoc, 1994. Ed Stanely Comp; New College, Durham; Sunderland Univ.
**BRIAN MOORE,** b May 14, 1960. Sales exec, former mining engineer. Contested Cleveland and Richmond in 1994 Euro elections. Newcastle city cllr. Member, Friends of the Earth. Ed Crownwoods School, south London; Wales Poly; Newcastle Poly; Northumbria Univ.

| DURHAM NORTH WEST | | 10.2% change | | | Lab win | | |
|---|---|---|---|---|---|---|---|
| Electorate % Turnout | | 67,156 | 69.0% | **1997** | 68,120 | 74.8% | **1992** |
| +Armstrong, Miss H | Lab | **31,855** | **68.8%** | +10.7% | 29,596 | 58.0% | Lab |
| St John Howe, Mrs L | C | 7,101 | 15.3% | -12.0% | 13,930 | 27.3% | C |
| Gillings, A T | LD | 4,991 | 10.8% | -3.9% | 7,458 | 14.6% | LD |
| Atkinson, R | Ref | 2,372 | 5.1% | | | | |
| C to Lab notional swing 11.4% | | 46,319 | Lab maj **24,754** | | 50,984 | Lab maj **15,666** | |
| | | | 53.4% | | | 74.8% | |

**HILARY ARMSTRONG**, b Nov 30, 1945. Became Environment and Transport Minister of State responsible for local government and housing, May 5, 1997. Elected 1987. Dep chief Lab spokeswoman on environment 1995-97; Treasury spokeswoman 1994-95. PPS to John Smith, 1992-94; in Lab education team 1988-92; member, select cttees on sittings of Commons, 1991-94; on ed, science and arts until Jan 1989. Chair, PLP ed, science and arts cttee, 1987-88; ex-member, NEC, Lab Party. Durham city cllr 1985-87. Vice-chair, British Council (unpaid). Was parly adviser to exec cttee, AUT; unpaid trustee, Project Genesis Trust, concerned with regeneration of steel works site at Consett; dir and board member

(unpaid), Childcare Enterprise Ltd. Lecturer in community and youth work, Sunderland Poly, 1975-86. Ed Monkwearmouth Comp; West Ham Coll of Tech; Birmingham Univ.
**LOUISE ST JOHN HOWE**, b June 1, 1951. Company director and restaurateur. Ed Salters Hall, Suffolk; Riddlesworth Hall, Norfolk; Bedgebury Park, Kent; Colchester Tech Coll.
**ANTHONY GILLINGS**, b June 19, 1962. Production controller; formerly in RAF. Ed Grovehill School, Hemel Hempstead; Cassio Coll, Watford.

| DURHAM, CITY OF | | | | | Lab hold | | |
|---|---|---|---|---|---|---|---|
| Electorate % Turnout | | 69,340 | 70.9% | **1997** | 68,165 | 74.6% | **1992** |
| *Steinberg, G | Lab | 31,102 | 63.3% | +10.0% | 27,095 | 53.3% | Lab |
| Chalk, R | C | 8,598 | 17.5% | -6.2% | 12,037 | 23.7% | C |
| Martin, Dr N | LD | 7,499 | 15.3% | -6.2% | 10,915 | 21.5% | LD |
| Robson, Ms M | Ref | 1,723 | 3.5% | | 812 | 1.6% | Grn |
| Kember, P | NLP | 213 | 0.4% | | | | |
| C to Lab swing 8.1% | | 49,135 | Lab maj 22,504 | | 50,859 | Lab maj 15,058 | |
| | | | 45.8% | | | 74.6% | |

**GERRY STEINBERG**, b April 20, 1945. Ex-teacher. Elected 1987. Member of education and education and employment select cttee 1987-96. Chair, PLP education cttee, 1990-96 (joint vice-chair, 1988-90). Durham city cllr 1975-87. Adviser to Educational Psychologists Assoc 1989- . Headmaster, Whitworth House Special School, 1979-87. Ed Whinney Hill Sec Mod; Johnstone GS; Sheffield Coll of Ed; Newcastle Poly.

**RICHARD CHALK**, b March 4, 1969. Investment manager with British Aerospace. Chair, C Greater London Area ed cttee. Ed Cranbrook School; St Chad's Coll, Durham.
**NIGEL MARTIN**, b April 26, 1945. Lecturer. Contested Durham City 1992 and Newcastle Central 1987; Euro elections for Co Durham 1994. Member, European Movement; AUT. Ed Clee Humberstone Foundation School, Cleethorpes; Christ's Coll, Cambridge.

| EALING ACTON & SHEPHERD'S BUSH | | | 74.8% change | | | | Lab win |
|---|---|---|---|---|---|---|---|
| Electorate % Turnout | | 72,078 | 66.7% | **1997** | 68,324 | 72.7% | **1992** |
| +Soley, C S | Lab | 28,052 | 58.4% | +12.0% | 23,024 | 46.4% | Lab |
| Yerolemou, Mrs B | C | 12,405 | 25.8% | -13.6% | 19,553 | 39.4% | C |
| Mitchell, A | LD | 5,163 | 10.7% | -1.3% | 5,998 | 12.1% | LD |
| Winn, C | Ref | 637 | 1.3% | | 1,087 | 2.2% | Other |
| Gilbert, J | Soc Lab | 635 | 1.3% | | | | |
| Gomm, J | UK Ind | 385 | 0.8% | | | | |
| Danon, P | ProLife | 265 | 0.6% | | | | |
| Beasley, C | Glow | 209 | 0.4% | | | | |
| Edwards, W | Ch P | 163 | 0.3% | | | | |
| Turner, K | NLP | 150 | 0.3% | | | | |
| C to Lab notional swing 12.8% | | 48,064 | Lab maj 15,647 | | 49,662 | Lab maj 3,471 | |
| | | | 32.6% | | | 7.0% | |

**CLIVE SOLEY**, b May 7, 1939. Ex-probation officer. Elected MP for Hammersmith 1983, MP for Hammersmith N 1979-83. Elected chair of PLP, May 20, 1997. Chair, N Ireland select cttee, 1995, member since 1994. Lab team as spokesman on housing 1987-92, on home affairs 1984-87, and on N Ireland 1981-84; chair, all-party parenting group 1994- ; vice-chair, all-party constitution and parly affairs group, 1996-97. Chair, Lab Campaign for Criminal Justice, 1983-87; and Alcohol Ed Centre, 1977-83. Fellow, Industry and Parliament Trust. Consultant (unpaid) to Talking Shop. Ed

Downshall Sec Mod, Ilford; Newbattle Abbey Adult Ed Coll; Strathclyde and Southampton Univs.
**BARBARA YEROLEMOU**, b Sept 30, 1946. PR assistant, World Wide Fund for Nature; co-founder of chain of restaurants. Ealing cllr 1990- (dep leader since 1994). Ed Dame Alice Owen's GS; West London Coll of Commerce; Inst of Ed, London.
**ANDREW MITCHELL**, b March 17, 1958. Management consultant/company director. Ealing cllr. Member, IoD; Oxfam area appeal. Ed Warwick School; Wadham Coll, Oxford.

| EALING NORTH | | | 16.1% change | | | | Lab win |
|---|---|---|---|---|---|---|---|
| Electorate % Turnout | | 78,144 | 71.3% | **1997** | 75,908 | 76.7% | **1992** |
| Pound, S | Lab | 29,904 | 53.7% | +17.9% | 29,917 | 51.4% | C |
| +Greenway, H | C | 20,744 | 37.2% | -14.2% | 20,842 | 35.8% | Lab |
| Gupta, A | LD | 3,887 | 7.0% | -3.8% | 6,266 | 10.8% | LD |
| Slysz, G | UK Ind | 689 | 1.2% | | 643 | 1.1% | Grn |
| Siebe, Ms A | Green | 502 | 0.9% | | 322 | 0.6% | NF |
| | | | | | 210 | 0.4% | CD |
| C to Lab notional swing 16.0% | | 55,726 | Lab maj 9,160 | | 58,200 | C maj 9,075 | |
| | | | 16.4% | | | 76.7% | |

**STEPHEN POUND**, b July 3, 1948. Housing association manager. Member, Fabian Soc; Co-op Party. RC church lay reader. Ed TUC postal studies course; LSE. Interests include Fulham FC and collecting comics.
**HARRY GREENWAY**, b Oct 4, 1934. Ex-deputy head teacher. Won seat 1979; contested Stepney and Poplar twice in 1974, Stepney 1970. Member, select cttees on education and employment and its

sub-cttee, 1996-97; on employment 1992-96; on ed, science and arts 1979-92. Chair Friends of Cycling group 1987-95. Member, council, OU, 1982- . Liveryman, Farriers' Co. Ed Warwick School; Coll of St Mark and St John, London; Caen Univ.
**ANJAN GUPTA**, b April 12, 1957. Investment banker/analyst. Former researcher for Peter Lilley, MP, and David Howell, ex-MP. Ed St Paul's; Imperial Coll, London.

| EALING SOUTHALL | | 13.2% change | | | Lab win | | |
|---|---|---|---|---|---|---|---|
| Electorate % Turnout | | 81,704 | 66.9% | **1997** | 75,444 | 74.3% | **1992** |
| +Khabra, P | Lab | 32,791 | 60.0% | +14.7% | 25,371 | 45.3% | Lab |
| Penrose, J | C | 11,368 | 20.8% | -15.5% | 20,340 | 36.3% | C |
| Thomson, Ms N | LD | 5,687 | 10.4% | +2.3% | 4,785 | 8.5% | True Lab |
| Brar, H | Soc Lab | 2,107 | 3.9% | | 4,567 | 8.2% | LD |
| Goodwin, N | Green | 934 | 1.7% | | 968 | 1.7% | Grn |
| Cherry, B | Ref | 854 | 1.6% | | | | |
| Klepacka, Ms K | ProLife | 473 | 0.9% | | | | |
| Mead, Dr R | UK Ind | 428 | 0.8% | | | | |
| C to Lab notional swing 15.1% | | 54,642 | | Lab maj 21,423 | 56,031 | | Lab maj 5,031 |
| | | | | 39.2% | | | 74.3% |

**PIARA KHABRA,** b Nov 20, 1924. Social and welfare voluntary worker, former teacher. Elected for this seat 1992. Member, select cttee on members' interests, 1992-95; chair, all-party advance directive parly group, 1996-97; treas, British-Uganda group. Ealing cllr 1978-82. Chair, Indian Workers' Assoc, Southall, 1979- ; Southall Community Law Centre, 1982- . Member, MSF. Ed Punjab Univ; Whitelands Coll, London.

**JOHN PENROSE,** b June 22, 1964. Publishing director. Treas, Leyton and Wanstead C assoc. Member, Bow Group. Ed Downing Coll, Cambridge; Columbia Univ, New York.
**NIKKI THOMSON,** b Dec 30, 1967. Self-employed designer. Chair, Ealing Southall LDs; Ealing community health cllr. Ed Heathfield HS, Congleton; Thames Poly.

| EASINGTON | | | | | | Lab hold | |
|---|---|---|---|---|---|---|---|
| Electorate % Turnout | | 62,518 | 67.0% | **1997** | 65,061 | 72.5% | **1992** |
| *Cummings, J | Lab | 33,600 | 80.2% | +7.5% | 34,269 | 72.7% | Lab |
| Hollands, J | C | 3,588 | 8.6% | -8.1% | 7,878 | 16.7% | C |
| Heppell, J | LD | 3,025 | 7.2% | -3.4% | 5,001 | 10.6% | LD |
| Pulfrey, R | Ref | 1,179 | 2.8% | | | | |
| Colborn, S | SPGB | 503 | 1.2% | | | | |
| C to Lab swing 7.8% | | 41,895 | | Lab maj 30,012 | 47,148 | | Lab maj 26,391 |
| | | | | 71.6% | | | 56.0% |

**JOHN CUMMINGS,** b July 6, 1943. Mining electrician. Elected 1987. Lab whip with responsibility for overseas development 1995-97; for Northern region since 1994-95. Member, Council of Europe and Western European Union, until 1997. Easington district cllr 1973-87 (leader 1979-87). Vice-chair, Coalfields Community Campaign, 1985-87. Aycliffe and Peterlee Development Corp, 1980-87; Northumbrian Water Authority 1977-83. Member, NUM. Ed Murton School; Easington Tech Coll.

**JASON HOLLANDS,** b June 6, 1969. Research director, stockbroking and investment group. Chair, National YCs, 1996- . Ed Ashcombe School, Dorking; St Hugh's Coll, Oxford.
**JIM HEPPELL,** b July 19, 1938. Town planner. Contested Shipley 1964, 1966; Gloucester City 1970; Stroud 1979; Grantham 1987, 1992; Lincolnshire 1989 Euro elections, London NE 1984, Bristol 1979. Kent county cllr 1982-96; Sleaford cllr 1995- . Ed Sleaford GS; Leeds and Wales Univs; City of London Poly.

| EAST HAM | | 19.8% change | | | Lab win | | |
|---|---|---|---|---|---|---|---|
| Electorate % Turnout | | 65,591 | 60.8% | **1997** | 69,761 | 61.7% | **1992** |
| +Timms, S C | Lab | 25,779 | 64.6% | +10.7% | 23,212 | 54.0% | Lab |
| Bray, Miss A | C | 6,421 | 16.1% | -15.9% | 13,751 | 32.0% | C |
| Khan, I | Soc Lab | 2,697 | 6.8% | | 6,049 | 14.1% | LD |
| Sole, M | LD | 2,599 | 6.5% | -7.5% | | | |
| Smith, C | BNP | 1,258 | 3.2% | | | | |
| McCann, Mrs J | Ref | 845 | 2.1% | | | | |
| Hardy, G | Nat Dem | 290 | 0.7% | | | | |
| C to Lab notional swing 13.3% | | 39,889 | | Lab maj 19,358 | 43,012 | | Lab maj 9,461 |
| | | | | 48.5% | | | 22.0% |

**STEPHEN TIMMS,** b July 29, 1955. Retained Newham NE for Labour in 1994 by-election. Member, Treasury select cttee and its sub-cttee, 1995-97; joint select cttee on Consolidation Bills, 1994-97; joint vice-chair, PLP Treasury cttee, 1995- . Newham cllr 1984- (leader 1990-94). Sec, Newham NE Lab Party, 1981-84. Hon pres, Telecommunications Users' Assoc, 1995- . Principal consultant with Ovum, 1986-94; consultant, Logica, 1978-86; manager, Telecommunications Reports, 1994. Ed Farnborough GS; Emmanuel Coll, Cambridge.

**ANGELA BRAY,** b Oct 13, 1953. Senior public affairs consultant, APCO Associates UK; previously press sec to Chris Patten, when C Party chair; also chief broadcasting officer at C Central Office and PM's press officer during leadership campaign. Ex-radio journalist, producer, presenter for LBC and British Forces Broadcasting, Gibraltar. Ed Downe House, Newbury; St Andrews Univ; LSE.
**MIKE SOLE,** b Sept 1, 1967. Accountant. Contested Dover 1992. Canterbury city cllr. Ed Sir Roger Manwood's School, Sandwich.
*Details of 1994 Newham North East by-election on page 278*

| EAST KILBRIDE | | 2.0% change | | | | | Lab win |
|---|---|---|---|---|---|---|---|
| Electorate % Turnout | | 65,229 | 74.8% | **1997** | 63,525 | 79.1% | **1992** |
| +Ingram, A | Lab | **27,584** | 56.5% | +9.2% | **23,795** | 47.4% | Lab |
| Gebbie, G | SNP | 10,200 | 20.9% | -2.7% | 11,855 | 23.6% | SNP |
| Herbertson, C | C | 5,863 | 12.0% | -6.6% | 9,365 | 18.6% | C |
| Philbrick, Mrs K | LD | 3,527 | 7.2% | -3.2% | 5,221 | 10.4% | LD |
| Deighan, J | ProLife | 1,170 | 2.4% | | | | |
| Gray, Ms J | Ref | 306 | 0.6% | | | | |
| Gilmour, E | NLP | 146 | 0.3% | | | | |
| SNP to Lab notional swing 5.9% | | **48,796** | Lab maj 17,384 | | **50,236** | Lab maj 11,940 | |
| | | | 35.6% | | | 79.1% | |

**ADAM INGRAM,** b Feb 1, 1947. Became Minister of State, Northern Ireland Office, May 5, 1997. Elected 1987; contested Strathkelvin and Bearsden 1983. Lab spokesman on trade and industry 1995-97, with responsibility for science and tech; social security spokesman 1993-95; PPS to Neil Kinnock, then Lab leader, 1988-92. Member, trade and industry select cttee, 1992-93; sec, all-party British-Singapore parly group; joint vice-chair, Japanese group, 1992-97; Lab whip 1988. Chair, E Kilbride CLP, 1981-85. E Kilbride cllr 1980-87 (council leader 1984-87). Programmer and systems analyst, S of Scotland Electricity Board, 1970-77;

programmer/analyst, Associated British Foods, 1969-70; computer programmer 1966-69. Nalgo official 1977-87. Ed Cranhill Secondary.
**GEORGE GEBBIE,** b Jan 27, 1958. Member, Faculty of Advocates; ex-solicitor and procurator fiscal depute. Ed Dalziel HS, Motherwell; Aberdeen Univ.
**CLIFFORD HERBERTSON,** b March 27, 1964. Senior manager. Ed Duncanrig Secondary; Ballerup HS; London Univ.
**KATE PHILBRICK,** b Dec 4, 1953. Barrister. Newcastle upon Tyne city cllr 1984-85. Ed St Andrews Univ.

| EAST LOTHIAN | | 16.7% change | | | | | Lab win |
|---|---|---|---|---|---|---|---|
| Electorate % Turnout | | 57,441 | 75.6% | **1997** | 56,283 | 82.6% | **1992** |
| +Home Robertson, J | Lab | **22,881** | 52.7% | +7.2% | **21,123** | 45.5% | Lab |
| Fraser, M | C | 8,660 | 19.9% | -10.2% | 14,024 | 30.2% | C |
| McCarthy, D | SNP | 6,825 | 15.7% | +2.4% | 6,171 | 13.3% | SNP |
| MacAskill, Ms A | LD | 4,575 | 10.5% | -0.5% | 5,147 | 11.1% | LD |
| Nash, N | Ref | 491 | 1.1% | | | | |
| C to Lab notional swing 8.7% | | **43,432** | Lab maj 14,221 | | **46,465** | Lab maj 7,099 | |
| | | | 32.7% | | | 15.3% | |

**JOHN HOME ROBERTSON,** b Dec 5, 1948. Farmer. Elected for this seat 1983; MP for Berwick and E Lothian 1978-83. Member, defence select cttee 1990; Scottish affairs select cttee, 1979-83; Lab spokesman on food, agriculture and rural affairs, 1988-90, previously spokesman on agric, particularly for Scotland, 1984-87; spokesman on Scotland 1987-88; Lab Scottish whip 1983-84; chair, Scottish group of Lab MPs, 1982-83. Joint chair, ASH, 1996- . Ed Ampleforth; W of Scotland Agricultural Coll.

**MURDO FRASER,** b Sept 5, 1965. Solicitor. Chair, Scottish YCs, 1989-91. Ed Inverness Royal Acad; Aberdeen Univ.
**DAVID McCARTHY,** b July 28, 1937. SNP marine resources spokesman; member, SNP nat council. Ex-managing dir, Marine Harvest (salmon farming company). Ed Oxford Univ.
**ALISON MacASKILL,** b June 9, 1968. Scottish co-ordinator of Meningitis Research Foundation. Ed Isle of Wight Tech Coll; Manchester Metropolitan Univ; Edinburgh Univ (current).

| EASTBOURNE | | 10.5% change | | | | | C win |
|---|---|---|---|---|---|---|---|
| Electorate % Turnout | | 72,347 | 72.8% | **1997** | 70,602 | 81.6% | **1992** |
| +Waterson, N | C | **22,183** | 42.1% | -10.9% | **30,548** | 53.0% | C |
| Berry, C J | LD | 20,189 | 38.3% | -2.9% | 23,739 | 41.2% | LD |
| Lines, D | Lab | 6,576 | 12.5% | +7.8% | 2,697 | 4.7% | Lab |
| Lowe, T | Ref | 2,724 | 5.2% | | 366 | 0.6% | Grn |
| Williamson, Mrs T | Lib | 741 | 1.4% | +0.9% | 277 | 0.5% | Lib |
| Dawkins, J | UK Ind | 254 | 0.5% | | | | |
| C to LD notional swing 4.0% | | **52,667** | C maj 1,994 | | **57,627** | C maj 6,809 | |
| | | | 3.8% | | | 11.8% | |

**NIGEL WATERSON,** b Oct 12, 1950. Solicitor. Regained seat for C in 1992; contested Islington S and Finsbury 1979. PPS to Gerald Malone, Ex-Health Min. Joint vice-chair, all-party daylight extra parly group 1993-97. Member, exec cttee, Soc of C Lawyers, 1993- . Chair, Bow Group, 1986-87 (hon patron 1993-95). Pres, area C ed advisory cttee, 1993- ; member, C Greater London area exec cttee, 1990-91; CPC advisory cttee, 1986-90. Ed Leeds GS; Queen's Coll, Oxford (pres, univ C assoc).

**CHRIS BERRY,** b March 19, 1948. Hotelier; former town planner; ex-development consultant for UN and World Bank. Contested Brighton Kemptown 1992 and 1987. Ed Chatham House GS, Ramsgate; Strand GS, Manchester; N London Poly; Newcastle Univ; Univ of California.
**DAVID LINES,** b Sept 2, 1961. Researcher, BBC News. Camden cllr since 1992. Ed Liverpool Univ; OU Business School.

| EASTLEIGH | 26.5% change | | | | | | LD win |
|---|---|---|---|---|---|---|---|
| Electorate % Turnout | | 72,155 | 76.9% | 1997 | 67,556 | 83.3% | 1992 |
| +Chidgey, D | LD | 19,453 | 35.1% | +5.4% | 28,620 | 50.9% | C |
| Reid, S H | C | 18,699 | 33.7% | -17.2% | 16,708 | 29.7% | LD |
| Lloyd, A | Lab | 14,883 | 26.8% | +7.4% | 10,947 | 19.5% | Lab |
| Eldridge, V | Ref | 2,013 | 3.6% | | | | |
| Robinson, P | UK Ind | 446 | 0.8% | | | | |
| C to LD notional swing 11.3% | | 55,494 | | LD maj 754 | 56,275 | | C maj 11,912 |
| | | | | 1.4% | | | 21.2% |

**DAVID CHIDGEY**, b July 9, 1942. Consulting civil engineer. Won seat for LDs at 1994 by-election; contested it 1992. Contested Hampshire Central in 1989 Euro elections and 1988 Euro by-election. LD spokesman on transport 1995- ; previously on employment and training. Sec, all-party built environment parly group. Winchester city cllr 1987-90, Alresford town cllr 1975-83. Associate partner, Brian Colquhoun and Partners, consulting engineers, responsible for Southern region from Eastleigh office, 1988-93; with Thorburn Colquhoun as assoc dir, southern England, and project dir, engineering facilities management, Hampshire, 1994. Ed Brune Park City HS, Gosport; RNC Portsmouth; Portsmouth Poly.

**STEPHEN REID**, b Aug 16, 1951. IT manager at London further ed coll. Contested 1994 by-election, and Rhondda 1987. Basingstoke and Deane borough cllr 1978-95 (council leader 1988-95); previously group leader and housing cttee chair. Chair, Wessex area YCs, 1976-78. Ed Queen Mary's GS, Basingstoke; Fitzwilliam Coll, Cambridge.
**ALAN LLOYD**, b July 13, 1952. Contested Gosport 1987 and Christchurch 1992. Hampshire county cllr 1985- (leader, Lab group); Southampton city cllr 1986- . Member TGWU; Labour Action for Peace; Fabian Soc; Campaign Group. Ed Taunton GS.

*Details of 1994 by-election on page 278*

| EASTWOOD | 2.1% change | | | | | | Lab win |
|---|---|---|---|---|---|---|---|
| Electorate % Turnout | | 66,697 | 78.3% | 1997 | 65,846 | 79.9% | 1992 |
| Murphy, J | Lab | 20,766 | 39.8% | +15.6% | 24,544 | 46.6% | C |
| Cullen, P B | C | 17,530 | 33.6% | -13.1% | 12,706 | 24.1% | Lab |
| Yates, D | SNP | 6,826 | 13.1% | +0.5% | 8,651 | 16.4% | LD |
| Mason, Dr C | LD | 6,110 | 11.7% | -4.7% | 6,589 | 12.5% | SNP |
| Miller, D | Ref | 497 | 1.0% | | 146 | 0.3% | NLP |
| Tayan, Dr M | ProLife | 393 | 0.8% | | | | |
| McPherson, D | UK Ind | 113 | 0.2% | | | | |
| C to Lab notional swing 14.3% | | 52,235 | | Lab maj 3,236 | 52,636 | | C maj 11,838 |
| | | | | 6.2% | | | 22.5% |

**JAMES MURPHY**, b Aug 23, 1967. Projects manager, Scottish Lab Party. Pres, NUS 1994-96; pres NUS (Scotland) 1992-94. Member GMB; Co-op Party. Ed Barmine Sec, Glasgow; Milnerton HS, Cape Town; Strathclyde Univ.
**PAUL CULLEN**, b March 11, 1957. QC (Scot), became Solicitor-General for Scotland 1995. Admitted to Faculty of Advocates 1982 (clerk of faculty 1986-90); advocate depute 1992-95. Ed St Augustine's HS, Edinburgh; Edinburgh Univ.

**DOUGLAS YATES**, b April 30, 1946. Police officer. Founder convener of Barrhead/Neilston SNP 1991. Ed Eastwood Senior Sec; Reid Kerr Coll, Paisley.
**CHRISTOPHER MASON**, b March 8, 1941. Retired univ lecturer. Contested Glasgow Hillhead 1992; Glasgow in 1984 Euro elections. Strathclyde regional cllr 1982-96. Chair, Scottish Lib Party 1987-88. Ed Marlborough; Magdalene Coll, Cambridge.

| ECCLES | 34.6% change | | | | | | Lab win |
|---|---|---|---|---|---|---|---|
| Electorate % Turnout | | 69,645 | 65.6% | 1997 | 72,247 | 74.4% | 1992 |
| Stewart, I | Lab | 30,468 | 66.7% | +9.1% | 30,960 | 57.6% | Lab |
| Barker, G | C | 8,552 | 18.7% | -12.4% | 16,730 | 31.1% | C |
| Boyd, R | LD | 4,905 | 10.7% | +1.1% | 5,186 | 9.6% | LD |
| de Roeck, J | Ref | 1,765 | 3.9% | | 571 | 1.1% | Grn |
| | | | | | 296 | 0.6% | NLP |
| C to Lab notional swing 10.7% | | 45,690 | | Lab maj 21,916 | 53,743 | | Lab maj 14,230 |
| | | | | 48.0% | | | 26.5% |

**IAN STEWART**, b Aug 28, 1950. Trade union regional officer (1978- ), TGWU. Dist party chair, CLP vice-chair, Euro vice-chair of Lab Party. TUC dir for Salford Compact Partnership. Ed Calder Street Sec, Blantyre; Irlam HS, Manchester; Stretford Tech Coll; Manchester Metropolitan Univ.
**GREGORY BARKER**, b March 8, 1966. Managing director, International Pacific Securities plc. Member, Hon Artillery Co (TA

active unit), 1989-94. Ed Steyning GS; Lancing Coll; Royal Holloway and Bedford New Coll, London.
**ROBERT BOYD**, b Jan 10, 1933. Senior lecturer (retired). Contested Worsley 1992. Salford cllr. Hon life member, NATFHE; Community Campaign against Toxic Waste. Ed Hymers Coll, Hull; Hull Tech Coll.

| EDDISBURY | | 47.4% change | | | | | | C win |
|---|---|---|---|---|---|---|---|---|
| Electorate % Turnout | | 65,256 | 75.8% | **1997** | 62,352 | 81.5% | **1992** | |
| +Goodlad, A R | C | 21,027 | 42.5% | -10.2% | 26,794 | 52.7% | C | |
| Hanson, Ms M | Lab | 19,842 | 40.1% | +9.1% | 15,798 | 31.1% | Lab | |
| Reaper, D | LD | 6,540 | 13.2% | -1.6% | 7,553 | 14.9% | LD | |
| Napier, Ms N | Ref | 2,041 | 4.1% | | 615 | 1.2% | Grn | |
| | | | | | 84 | 0.2% | NLP | |
| C to Lab notional swing 9.6% | | 49,450 | | C maj 1,185 | 50,844 | | C maj 10,996 | |
| | | | | 2.4% | | | 21.6% | |

**ALASTAIR GOODLAD**, b July 4, 1943. Elected for this seat 1983; MP for Northwich, Feb 1974-83; contested Crewe 1970. Gvt Chief Whip 1995-97; Min of State, Foreign Office, 1992-95; gvt dep chief whip 1990-92. Member, select cttees on broadcasting, 1987-89; Services 1989-91; agriculture 1979-81. Under Sec for Energy 1984-87. Dir, Fuel Tech Europe Ltd, 1988-89; Mersey Barrage Co Ltd 1988-89. Ed Marlborough; King's Coll, Cambridge.

**MARGARET HANSON**, b Sept 1, 1961. Research assistant. Vale Royal borough cllr 1984-94; Flintshire county cllr 1994- . Member TGWU; Co-op Party. Ed Woodford Lodge Comp, Cheshire; Brasenose Coll, Oxford.
**DAVID REAPER**, b April 14, 1947. Teacher. Contested Halton 1992. Vale Royal borough cllr 1974-83. Ed Robert Richardson GS, Ryhope; Sunderland Coll of Ed.

| EDINBURGH CENTRAL | | 38.4% change | | | | | | Lab win |
|---|---|---|---|---|---|---|---|---|
| Electorate % Turnout | | 63,695 | 67.1% | **1997** | 60,023 | 68.2% | **1992** | |
| +Darling, A | Lab | 20,125 | 47.1% | +8.6% | 15,770 | 38.5% | Lab | |
| Scott-Hayward, M D A | C | 9,055 | 21.2% | -8.2% | 12,013 | 29.4% | C | |
| Hyslop, Ms F | SNP | 6,750 | 15.8% | +0.6% | 6,232 | 15.2% | SNP | |
| Utting, Ms K | LD | 5,605 | 13.1% | -1.7% | 6,073 | 14.8% | LD | |
| Hendry, Ms L | Green | 607 | 1.4% | | 610 | 1.5% | Grn | |
| Skinner, A | Ref | 495 | 1.2% | | 227 | 0.6% | Lib | |
| Benson, M | Ind Dem | 98 | 0.2% | | | | | |
| C to Lab notional swing 8.4% | | 42,735 | | Lab maj 11,070 | 40,925 | | Lab maj 3,757 | |
| | | | | 25.9% | | | 9.2% | |

**ALISTAIR DARLING**, b Nov 28, 1953. Became Chief Secretary to the Treasury, May 3, 1997. Shadow Chief Sec to Treasury 1996-97. Won this seat 1987. In Lab Treasury and economic affairs team 1992-96, as spokesman on the City; spokesman on home affairs 1988-92; member, Lab working party on electoral systems, 1990- ; joint vice-chair, PLP transport cttee, 1987-88. Lothian regional cllr 1982-87; Lothian and Borders Police Board 1982-86. Non-practising advocate. Trustee (unpaid), Nat Library of Scotland. Governor, Napier Coll, Edinburgh, 1982-87. Member, Apex. Ed Loretto School; Aberdeen Univ.

**MICHAEL SCOTT-HAYWARD**, b Sept 7, 1947. Businessman. Contested Dunfermline W 1992. Chair, Tory Green Initiative, Scotland; Scottish C candidates assoc; NE Fife cllr 1987-92. In Royal Artillery, 1969-86 (Major). Ed Mansfield HS, Durban, S Africa.
**FIONA HYSLOP**, b Aug 1, 1964. Marketing executive. Contested Edinburgh Leith 1992. SNP environment spokeswoman; member, national exec, 1990- . Member, MSF. Ed Ayr Acad; Glasgow Univ; Scottish Coll of Textiles.
**KAREN UTTING**, b Dec 28, 1960. Ex-agent and convener, Edinburgh Central LDs. Ed Woodmill HS, Dunfermline; St Andrews Univ.

| EDINBURGH EAST & MUSSELBURGH | | 47.8% change | | | | | | Lab win |
|---|---|---|---|---|---|---|---|---|
| Electorate % Turnout | | 59,648 | 70.6% | **1997** | 59,153 | 74.4% | **1992** | |
| +Strang, Dr G S | Lab | 22,564 | 53.6% | +8.9% | 19,669 | 44.7% | Lab | |
| White, D | SNP | 8,034 | 19.1% | +1.1% | 10,568 | 24.0% | C | |
| Ward, K | C | 6,483 | 15.4% | -8.6% | 7,890 | 17.9% | SNP | |
| MacKellar, Dr C | LD | 4,511 | 10.7% | -0.8% | 5,075 | 11.5% | LD | |
| Sibbet, J | Ref | 526 | 1.2% | | 801 | 1.8% | Other | |
| SNP to Lab notional swing 3.9% | | 42,118 | | Lab maj 14,530 | 44,003 | | Lab maj 9,101 | |
| | | | | 34.5% | | | 20.7% | |

**GAVIN STRANG**, b July 10, 1943. Became Minister of Transport, May 3, 1997. MP for Edinburgh E 1970-97. Joined Shadow Cabinet 1994, becoming chief Lab spokesman on agriculture and rural affairs. Lab spokesman on employment 1987-89; on agriculture, fisheries and food 1979-82; and on trade and industry 1973-74. Parly Sec, Min of Ag, Fish and Food, 1974-79; Under Sec for Energy 1974. Chair, PLP defence cttee, 1985-87; Scottish Lab MPs 1986-87; Lab Action for Peace 1985-89. chair or sec, PLP CND group, 1982-86. Agricultural scientist. Ed Morrison's Acad; Edinburgh Univ; Churchill Coll, Cambridge.

**DERRICK WHITE**, b July 7, 1942. Self-employed training consultant. Convener and political education and training officer of SNP Haddington branch. Served in Royal Navy for 12 years after schooling in Co Dublin.
**KENNETH WARD**, b June 7, 1942. ScottishPower financial systems expert. Contested Edinburgh E 1992. Lothian regional cllr 1982-90. Ed Tynecastle Sec, Edinburgh; Stevenson Coll.
**CALLUM MacKELLAR**, b July 27, 1964. Research biochemist. Member, Democracy for Scotland. Ed Heriot-Watt Univ; EHIC, Strasbourg; Stuttgart Univ.

| EDINBURGH NORTH & LEITH | | | 43.0% change | | | | Lab win |
|---|---|---|---|---|---|---|---|
| Electorate % Turnout | | 61,617 | 66.5% | **1997** | 60,235 | 71.4% | **1992** |
| +Chisholm, M | Lab | **19,209** | 46.9% | +12.0% | 15,019 | 34.9% | Lab |
| Dana, Ms A | SNP | 8,231 | 20.1% | -0.2% | 10,685 | 24.8% | C |
| Stewart, E | C | 7,312 | 17.9% | -7.0% | 8,749 | 20.3% | SNP |
| Campbell, Ms H | LD | 5,335 | 13.0% | +1.3% | 5,038 | 11.7% | LD |
| Graham, S | Ref | 441 | 1.1% | | 3,529 | 8.2% | Other |
| Brown, G | SSA | 320 | 0.8% | | | | |
| Douglas-Reid, P | NLP | 97 | 0.2% | | | | |
| SNP to Lab notional swing 6.1% | | **40,945** | | Lab maj **10,978** | **43,020** | | Lab maj **4,334** |
| | | | | 26.8% | | | 10.1% |

**MALCOLM CHISHOLM**, b March 7, 1949. Became Under Secretary, Scottish Office responsible for local gvt and transport, May 5, 1997. MP for Edinburgh Leith 1992-97. Lab spokesman on Scotland 1996, speaking on local gvt, housing, constitutional affairs. Ed Edinburgh Univ.
**ANNE DANA,** b Nov 25, 1942. Runs architectural/design practice. Dir, Scottish Malt Whisky Soc. Ed Bellevue School, Edinburgh;

Glasgow Univ; Morro Bay Coll, California.
**EWEN STEWART,** b April 15, 1965. Fund manager. Contested Glasgow Central 1992. Ed Daniel Stewart's and Melville Coll, Edinburgh; Aberdeen Univ.
**HILARY CAMPBELL,** b July 13, 1952. Head of policy, Scottish Sports Council. Contested Leith 1992, Clackmannan 1983, Lothians in 1994 Euro elections. Ed Univ of W Ontario; Middlesex Poly.

| EDINBURGH PENTLANDS | | | 7.6% change | | | | Lab win |
|---|---|---|---|---|---|---|---|
| Electorate % Turnout | | 59,635 | 76.7% | **1997** | 59,432 | 77.3% | **1992** |
| Clark, Ms L M | Lab | **19,675** | 43.0% | +11.8% | 18,474 | 40.2% | C |
| +Rifkind, M | C | 14,813 | 32.4% | -7.8% | 14,326 | 31.2% | Lab |
| Gibb, S | SNP | 5,952 | 13.0% | -2.7% | 7,203 | 15.7% | SNP |
| Dawe, Dr J | LD | 4,575 | 10.0% | -2.7% | 5,828 | 12.7% | LD |
| McDonald, M | Ref | 422 | 0.9% | | 127 | 0.3% | NLP |
| Harper, R | Green | 224 | 0.5% | | | | |
| McConnachie, A | UK Ind | 81 | 0.2% | | | | |
| C to Lab notional swing 9.8% | | **45,742** | | Lab maj **4,862** | **45,958** | | C maj **4,148** |
| | | | | 10.6% | | | 9.0% |

**LINDA CLARK,** b Feb 26, 1949. QC (Scot), the most senior woman in practice at Scottish Bar. Contested Fife NE 1992. Appointed QC 1989; admitted advocate, Scottish Bar, 1977; called to English Bar, Inner Temple, 1988. Scottish Legal Aid Board 1991-94. Ed Lawside Acad, Dundee; St Andrews and Edinburgh Univs.
**MALCOLM RIFKIND,** b June 21, 1946. QC (Scot). MP for this seat 1974-97; contested Edinburgh Central 1970. Foreign Sec 1995-97; Defence Sec 1992-95; Transport Sec 1990-92; and Scottish Sec 1986-90. Min of State, FCO, 1983-86; Under Sec, FCO, 1982-83;

Under Sec for Scotland 1979-82. Spokesman on Scotland 1975-77 (resigned over devolution). Member, Royal Company of Archers, Queen's Bodyguard for Scotland, 1992. Ed George Watson's Coll, Edinburgh; Edinburgh Univ.
**STEWART GIBB,** b May 18, 1962. Contract software engineer. Member, SNP national organisation cttee. Ed Turiff Acad; Heriot-Watt and Glasgow Univs.
**JENNIFER DAWE,** b April 27, 1945. Senior welfare rights officer. Ed Trinity Acad, Edinburgh; Aberdeen and Edinburgh Univs.

| EDINBURGH SOUTH | | | 2.7% change | | | | Lab win |
|---|---|---|---|---|---|---|---|
| Electorate % Turnout | | 62,467 | 71.8% | **1997** | 61,638 | 72.0% | **1992** |
| +Griffiths, N | Lab | **20,993** | 46.8% | +5.3% | 18,426 | 41.5% | Lab |
| Smith, Miss E | C | 9,541 | 21.3% | -10.9% | 14,270 | 32.2% | C |
| Pringle, M S R | LD | 7,911 | 17.6% | +4.5% | 5,855 | 13.2% | LD |
| Hargreaves, Dr J | SNP | 5,791 | 12.9% | +0.0% | 5,719 | 12.9% | SNP |
| McLean, I | Ref | 504 | 1.1% | | 108 | 0.2% | NLP |
| Dunn, B | NLP | 98 | 0.2% | -0.0% | | | |
| C to Lab notional swing 8.1% | | **44,838** | | Lab maj **11,452** | **44,378** | | Lab maj **4,156** |
| | | | | 25.5% | | | 9.4% |

**NIGEL GRIFFITHS**, b May 20, 1955. Became Trade and Industry Under Secretary for Consumer Affairs, May 5, 1997. Won this seat 1987. Lab spokesman on consumer affairs 1989-97; Lab whip 1987-89. Joint chair, all-party street children parly group; treas, Interparly Council against Anti-Semitism. Exec member and convener, finance cttee, Scottish Constitutional Convention. Edinburgh district cllr 1980-87 (chair 1986-87). Ed Hawick Comp; Edinburgh Univ; Moray Coll of Ed.

**ELIZABETH SMITH,** b Feb 27, 1960. Teacher, author. Ed George Watson's Ladies Coll; Edinburgh Univ; Moray House Coll of Ed.
**MICHAEL PRINGLE,** b Dec 25, 1945. Ex-businessman. Edinburgh city cllr. Scottish LD spokesman on arts, sport and leisure. Ed Edinburgh Acad.
**JOHN HARGREAVES,** b Oct 22, 1948. Technical computer analyst. Convener, Edinburgh City SNP. Ed Accrington GS; Fitzwilliam Coll, Cambridge; Heriot-Watt Univ.

| EDINBURGH WEST | | 52.2% change | | | | | LD win |
|---|---|---|---|---|---|---|---|
| Electorate % Turnout | | 61,133 | 77.9% | **1997** | 61,995 | 83.2% | **1992** |
| **Gorrie, D** | **LD** | **20,578** | **43.2%** | **+13.3%** | **19,715** | **38.2%** | **C** |
| +Douglas-Hamilton, Lord James | C | 13,325 | 28.0% | -10.2% | 15,424 | 29.9% | LD |
| Hinds, Ms L | Lab | 8,948 | 18.8% | +1.4% | 8,961 | 17.4% | Lab |
| Sutherland, G | SNP | 4,210 | 8.8% | -3.7% | 6,471 | 12.5% | SNP |
| Elphick, Dr S | Ref | 277 | 0.6% | | 433 | 0.8% | Lib |
| Coombes, P | Lib | 263 | 0.6% | -0.3% | 384 | 0.7% | Grn |
| Jack, A | AS | 30 | 0.1% | | 210 | 0.4% | BNP |
| **C to LD notional swing 11.8%** | | **47,631** | | **LD maj 7,253** | **51,598** | | **C maj 4,291** |
| | | | | 15.2% | | | 8.3% |

**DONALD GORRIE,** b April 2, 1933. Contested this seat 1992, 1970 Feb and Oct 1974, and 1970. Full-time Edinburgh city cllr 1995- (group leader 1995- ); Edinburgh district cllr 1980-96 (group leader 1980-96); Lothian regional cllr 1974-96 (group leader 1974-96); Edinburgh town cllr 1971-75. Dir/board member of Edinburgh Festival; Lyceum Theatre; Scottish Chamber Orchestra; Edinburgh Festival Theatre. Ed Hurst Grange, Stirling; Oundle; Corpus Christi Coll, Oxford.
**LORD JAMES DOUGLAS-HAMILTON,** b July 31, 1942. Non-practising member, Faculty of Advocates; author; second son of 14th Duke of Hamilton. Elected Oct 1974; contested Hamilton, Feb 1974.

Min of State for Scotland 1995-97; Under Sec 1987-95; gvt whip 1979-81; Scottish C whip 1976-79. PPS to Malcolm Rifkind, Min of State, FCO, and then Scottish Sec, 1983-87. Ed Eton; Balliol Coll, Oxford (pres of Union, 1964; Boxing Blue). Edinburgh Univ.
**LESLEY HINDS,** b Aug 3, 1956. Leader of Edinburgh City Council. Member, Scottish LP executive . Edinburgh cllr since 1984. Ed Kirkton HS, Dundee; Dundee Coll of Ed.
**GRAHAM SUTHERLAND,** b Nov 28, 1956. Teacher. Contested this seat 1992. Member, EIS. Ed Inverness HS; Heriot-Watt Univ; Jordanhill Coll of Ed. Collector of historical vocal recordings.

| EDMONTON | | | | | | | Lab gain |
|---|---|---|---|---|---|---|---|
| Electorate % Turnout | | 63,718 | 70.4% | **1997** | 63,052 | 75.7% | **1992** |
| **Love, A** | **Lab Co-op** | **27,029** | **60.3%** | | **22,076** | **46.3%** | **C** |
| *Twinn, Dr I | C | 13,557 | 30.2% | -16.0% | 21,483 | 45.0% | Lab |
| Wiseman, A | LD | 2,847 | 6.3% | -1.9% | 3,940 | 8.3% | LD |
| Wright, J | Ref | 708 | 1.6% | | 207 | 0.4% | NLP |
| Cowd, B | BNP | 437 | 1.0% | | | | |
| Weald, Mrs P | UK Ind | 260 | 0.6% | | | | |
| **C to Lab swing 15.6%** | | **44,838** | | **Lab Co-op maj 13,472** | **47,706** | | **C maj 593** |
| | | | | 30.0% | | | 1.2% |

**ANDY LOVE,** b March 21, 1949. Contested this seat 1992. Parly officer for Co-operative Retail Soc. Haringey cllr 1980-86. Ex-board member, Greater London Enterprise; ex-member, NE Thames RHA. Trustee of fund for co-operative workers. Ex-chair, Hornsey & Wood Green CLP. Ed state schools; Strathclyde Univ.
**IAN TWINN,** b April 26, 1950. Former lecturer. Won this seat 1983. PPS to Paymaster General 1992-94; to Environment Min 1990-92; to Sir Peter Morrison 1985-90. Dep chairman, C Party, 1986-88. Former parly consultant to British Surgical Trades Assoc;

CAPITB plc, nat training and management co; ARCO (British) Ltd, oil and gas co; TNT Express (UK) Ltd; parly adviser to Chartered Soc of Physiotherapy. FRSA 1989. Ed Netherhall Sec Mod, Cambridge; Cambridge Boys GS; Univ Coll of Wales, Aberystwyth; Reading Univ.
**ANDREW WISEMAN,** b Nov 25, 1962. Solicitor. LD group leader with minority control on Harrow Council. Ed Gayton HS; Westminster Univ. Qualified football referee.

| ELLESMERE PORT & NESTON | | 6.9% change | | | | | Lab win |
|---|---|---|---|---|---|---|---|
| Electorate % Turnout | | 67,573 | 77.8% | **1997** | 67,037 | 83.7% | **1992** |
| **+Miller, A** | **Lab** | **31,310** | **59.6%** | **+11.7%** | **26,836** | **47.8%** | **Lab** |
| Turnbull, Mrs L | C | 15,274 | 29.1% | -13.0% | 23,603 | 42.1% | C |
| Pemberton, Ms J | LD | 4,673 | 8.9% | -0.0% | 5,012 | 8.9% | LD |
| Rodden, C | Ref | 1,305 | 2.5% | | 550 | 1.0% | Grn |
| | | | | | 98 | 0.2% | NLP |
| **C to Lab notional swing 12.4%** | | **52,562** | | **Lab maj 16,036** | **56,099** | | **Lab maj 3,233** |
| | | | | 30.5% | | | 5.8% |

**ANDREW MILLER,** b March 23, 1949. Won this seat 1992. Member, science and tech select cttee; Commons information cttee; board member, Parly Office of Science and Tech; vice-chair, PLP science and tech cttee, 1993-97; all-party tennis club parly group. Trade union official, member ASTMS (now MSF) from 1967 and

divisional officer 1977-92. Ed Hayling Secondary; LSE.
**LYNN TURNBULL,** b July 30, 1948. Owner and dir of complementary health clinic. Wirral cllr 1992- . Ed Minto House School, Hoylake.
**JOANNA PEMBERTON,** b May 9, 1959. Ed Hammond School, Chester; Pensby Sec School for Girls; Carlett Park Coll of FE.

| ELMET | | | | | | | Lab gain |
|---|---|---|---|---|---|---|---|
| Electorate % Turnout | | 70,423 | 76.8% | **1997** | 70,558 | 82.5% | **1992** |
| Burgon, C | Lab | **28,348** | **52.4%** | **+10.5%** | **27,677** | **47.5%** | C |
| *Batiste, S | C | 19,569 | 36.2% | -11.3% | 24,416 | 41.9% | Lab |
| Jennings, B | LD | 4,691 | 8.7% | -1.9% | 6,144 | 10.5% | LD |
| Zawadski, C | Ref | 1,487 | 2.7% | | | | |
| **C to Lab swing 10.9%** | | **54,095** | Lab maj 8,779 | | **58,237** | C maj 3,261 | |
| | | | 16.2% | | | 5.6% | |

**COLIN BURGON**, b April 22, 1948. Local gvt policy and research officer; ex-teacher. Contested this seat 1992 and 1987. Former chair and sec Elmet Lab Party; member, Yorks regional exec LP; ex-chair, Leeds Euro party; election agent at Elmet 1983 and Euro election at Leeds, 1989. Member, Nupe; MSF; NUT. Ed St Michael's Coll, Leeds; Carnegie Coll, Leeds; Huddersfield Poly.
**SPENCER BATISTE**, b June 5, 1945. Solicitor. Elected 1983; contested Sheffield in 1979 Euro elections. Member, science and tech select cttee, 1992-97; Commons information cttee 1991-97; board, Parly Office of Science and Tech. Joint vice-chair, C backbench trade and industry cttee, 1989-94, and of all-party parly space group; joint sec, Council of Christians and Jews group.

Former legal adviser to Cutlery and Silverware Assoc; law clerk, Sheffield Assay Office, 1974- ; dir and company sec, Sheffield Analytical Services Ltd and subsidiaries. Member of Lloyd's. Vice-chair, Small Business Bureau, 1983- . Consultant to Music Industries Assoc; Magellan Medical Communications Ltd, consultants on health issues; Energis Communications Ltd, telecoms business; Dibb Lupton Alsop, solicitors. Member (unpaid), British Hallmarking Council, 1988- . Nat pres, CTU, 1990. Ed Carmel Coll; Sorbonne; Cambridge Univ.
**BRIAN JENNINGS**, b Oct 29, 1960. Property consultant. Lambeth cllr 1994- . Ed Rugby; Univ Coll, Durham.

| ELTHAM | 25.6% change | o | | | | | Lab win |
|---|---|---|---|---|---|---|---|
| Electorate % Turnout | | 57,358 | 75.7% | **1997** | 60,650 | 76.5% | **1992** |
| Efford, C | Lab | **23,710** | **54.6%** | **+14.5%** | 20,384 | 43.9% | C |
| Blackwood, C | C | 13,528 | 31.2% | -12.8% | 18,604 | 40.1% | Lab |
| Taylor, Ms A | LD | 3,701 | 8.5% | -7.0% | 7,213 | 15.5% | LD |
| Clark, M | Ref | 1,414 | 3.3% | | 198 | 0.4% | Ind C |
| Middleton, H | Lib | 584 | 1.3% | | | | |
| Hitches, W | BNP | 491 | 1.1% | | | | |
| **C to Lab notional swing 13.6%** | | **43,428** | Lab maj 10,182 | | **46,399** | C maj 1,780 | |
| | | | 23.4% | | | 3.8% | |

**CLIVE EFFORD**, b July 10, 1958. London taxi driver. Contested seat 1992. Greenwich cllr 1986- (chief whip 1990-91; group sec 1986-87). Member, TGWU. Ed Walworth Comp.
**CLIVE BLACKWOOD**, b Nov 16, 1964. Barrister practising in London and Midland and Oxford Circuit, specialising in civil and commercial law. Cllr, City of London Corp; Islington cllr (C group leader). Exec member, SE Reg Assoc for the Deaf, Islington Sports

Council, and Southern Assoc for the Blind since 1992. Ed Kelvinside Acad, Glasgow; Gonville and Caius Coll, Cambridge; Inns of Court School of Law.
**AMANDA TAYLOR**, b July 3, 1962. Publishing marketing executive. Contested Peterborough 1992. Cambridge cllr. Member, Charter 88; Transport 2000; MSF. Ed Leeds Girls HS; Leeds Univ.

| ENFIELD NORTH | | | | | | | Lab gain |
|---|---|---|---|---|---|---|---|
| Electorate % Turnout | | 67,680 | 70.4% | **1997** | 67,421 | 77.9% | **1992** |
| Ryan, Ms J | Lab | **24,148** | **50.7%** | **+15.7%** | 27,789 | 52.9% | C |
| Field, M | C | 17,326 | 36.3% | -16.6% | 18,359 | 34.9% | Lab |
| Hopkins, M | LD | 4,264 | 8.9% | -2.1% | 5,817 | 11.1% | LD |
| Ellingham, R | Ref | 857 | 1.8% | | 565 | 1.1% | NLP |
| Griffin, Ms J | BNP | 590 | 1.2% | | | | |
| O'Ware, Mrs J | UK Ind | 484 | 1.0% | | | | |
| **C to Lab swing 16.1%** | | **47,669** | Lab maj 6,822 | | **52,530** | C maj 9,430 | |
| | | | 14.3% | | | 18.0% | |

**JOAN RYAN**, b Sept 8, 1955. Teacher and freelance researcher. Barnet cllr 1990- (dep council leader 1994- ). Member, NUT; MSF. Ed City of Liverpool Coll of Higher Ed; South Bank Poly.
**MARK FIELD**, b Oct 6, 1964. Solicitor, partner in recruitment firm. PA to John Patten, MP, 1984-87. Kensington and Chelsea cllr

1994- ; ward chair, Kensington and Chelsea C assoc, 1992-94. Ed Reading School; St Edmund Hall, Oxford; Coll of Law, Chester.
**MIKE HOPKINS**, b Aug 26, 1947. Police officer (retired). Member, Enfield Racial Equality Council; chair, Enfield North LDs 1995.

## ENFIELD SOUTHGATE — 0.1% change — Lab win

| Electorate % Turnout | | 65,796 | 70.7% | **1997** | 65,109 | 75.3% | **1992** |
|---|---|---|---|---|---|---|---|
| **Twigg, S** | **Lab** | **20,570** | **44.2%** | **+18.0%** | **28,390** | **57.9%** | **C** |
| +Portillo, M | C | 19,137 | 41.1% | -16.8% | 12,845 | 26.2% | Lab |
| Browne, J | LD | 4,966 | 10.7% | -3.8% | 7,072 | 14.4% | LD |
| Luard, N | Ref | 1,342 | 2.9% | | 695 | 1.4% | Grn |
| Storkey, A | Ch D | 289 | 0.6% | | | | |
| Malakouna, A | Mal | 229 | 0.5% | | | | |
| **C to Lab notional swing 17.4%** | | **46,533** | | **Lab maj 1,433** | **49,002** | | **C maj 15,545** |
| | | | | 3.1% | | | 31.7% |

**STEPHEN TWIGG,** b Dec 25, 1966. Islington cllr 1990- (dep leader until 1996). General sec, Fabian Soc. Ex-chair NUS, ex-research assistant to Margaret Hodge, MP. Member, Co-op Party; Amnesty; Lab Campaign for Electoral Reform; Stonewall. Ed Southgate Comp; Balliol Coll, Oxford.
**MICHAEL PORTILLO,** b May 26, 1953. MP for this seat 1984-97; contested Birmingham Perry Barr 1983. Defence Sec 1995-97; Employment Sec 1994-95; Chief Sec to Treasury 1992-94. Local Gvt Min 1990-92; Public Transport Min 1988-90; Under Sec for Health and Social Security 1987-88; asst gvt whip 1986-87; PPS to

Min of Transport 1986. Special adviser to David Howell, when Energy Sec, 1979-81; to Trade and Industry Sec 1983; and to Chancellor of Exchequer 1983-84. C Research Dept 1976-79. Former oil industry consultant and TV political researcher; with Kerr McGee Oil (UK) Ltd 1981-83. Ed Harrow County School; Peterhouse, Cambridge.
**JEREMY BROWNE,** b May 17, 1970. Assistant to council group; researcher to Alan Beith, MP, 1993-94. Member, Charter 88. Ed Bedales, Hampshire; Nottingham Univ (pres, student union, 1992-93).

## EPPING FOREST — 7.6% change — C win

| Electorate % Turnout | | 72,795 | 72.8% | **1997** | 71,990 | 79.1% | **1992** |
|---|---|---|---|---|---|---|---|
| **Laing, Mrs E F** | **C** | **24,117** | **45.5%** | **-14.3%** | **34,034** | **59.8%** | **C** |
| Murray, S | Lab | 18,865 | 35.6% | +13.0% | 12,851 | 22.6% | Lab |
| Robinson, S | LD | 7,074 | 13.3% | -3.4% | 9,520 | 16.7% | LD |
| Berry, J | Ref | 2,208 | 4.2% | | 544 | 1.0% | Epping |
| Henderson, P | BNP | 743 | 1.4% | | | | |
| **C to Lab notional swing 13.6%** | | **53,007** | | **C maj 5,252** | **56,949** | | **C maj 21,183** |
| | | | | 9.9% | | | 37.2% |

**ELEANOR LAING,** b Feb 1, 1958. Solicitor/business and political consultant. Contested Paisley N 1987. Adviser to John MacGregor, then Cabinet min, 1989-94. Member, IoD policy unit, 1994-95. Ed St Columba's, Kilmacolm; Edinburgh Univ (student union pres).
**STEPHEN MURRAY,** b May 8, 1959. Teacher. Contested this seat

1992, 1987, and 1988 by-election. Epping Forest cllr 1982- . Ed Bristol and London Univs.
**STEPHEN ROBINSON,** b Oct 3, 1966. Researcher. Epping Forest cllr 1990- ; Essex county cllr 1993- . Ed Central Lancashire Univ.

## EPSOM & EWELL — 24.8% change — C win

| Electorate % Turnout | | 73,222 | 74.0% | **1997** | 72,957 | 80.0% | **1992** |
|---|---|---|---|---|---|---|---|
| **+Hamilton, Sir Archibald** | **C** | **24,717** | **45.6%** | **-15.4%** | **35,621** | **61.1%** | **C** |
| Woodford, P | Lab | 13,192 | 24.3% | +9.3% | 13,561 | 23.2% | LD |
| Vincent, J | LD | 12,380 | 22.8% | -0.4% | 8,789 | 15.1% | Lab |
| Macdonald, C | Ref | 2,355 | 4.3% | | 372 | 0.6% | NLP |
| Green, L | UK Ind | 544 | 1.0% | | | | |
| Charlton, H | Green | 527 | 1.0% | | | | |
| Weeks, Ms K | ProLife | 466 | 0.9% | | | | |
| **C to Lab notional swing 12.4%** | | **54,181** | | **C maj 11,525** | **58,343** | | **C maj 22,060** |
| | | | | 21.3% | | | 37.8% |

**SIR ARCHIBALD HAMILTON,** b Dec 30, 1941. Farmer. Elected 1978 by-election; contested Dagenham, Feb and Oct 1974. Elected chairman 1922 Cttee, May 21, 1997; member exec since 1995. Min of State for Armed Forces 1988-93; PPS to Margaret Thatcher 1987-88; Under Sec for defence procurement 1986-87; gvt whip 1984-86; asst gvt whip 1982-84.Member, Commons intelligence and security cttee, 1994-97. Member of Lloyd's. Dir, Saladin Holdings Ltd, security; Woodgate Farms Dairy; Siam Selective Growth Trust plc; First Philippine Investment Trust plc; First Philippines Securities; Crownridge Industries Ltd, property

developers; Leafield Engineering Ltd.Consultant to Litton Industries Inc, US defence manufacturers; W.S. Atkins Ltd, engineering consultants; Merrill Lynch Europe Ltd, investment bankers; GenCorp Aerojet. Dir and governor (unpaid), Westminster Foundation for Democracy. Ed Eton.
**PHILIP WOODFORD,** b Nov 1, 1968. Advertising copywriter. Chair, Holborn and St Pancras CLP, 1993-95. Ed LSE.
**JOHN VINCENT,** b March 13, 1960. Aircraft safety specialist. Surrey county cllr. Member, Charter 88; Engineering Council. Ed Yeovil Coll; Coventry Poly.

| EREWASH | | 0.2% change | | | | | | Lab win |
|---|---|---|---|---|---|---|---|---|
| Electorate % Turnout | | 77,402 | 78.0% | **1997** | 76,953 | 82.5% | **1992** | |
| **Blackman, Ms E** | Lab | **31,196** | 51.7% | +13.5% | **29,970** | 47.2% | C | |
| +Knight, Mrs A | C | 22,061 | 36.6% | -10.6% | 24,247 | 38.2% | Lab | |
| Garnett, Dr M | LD | 5,181 | 8.6% | -5.0% | 8,623 | 13.6% | LD | |
| Stagg, S | Ref | 1,404 | 2.3% | | 645 | 1.0% | BNP | |
| Simmons, M | Soc Lab | 496 | 0.8% | | | | | |
| C to Lab notional swing 12.1% | | **60,338** | Lab maj 9,135 | | **63,485** | C maj 5,723 | | |
| | | | 15.1% | | | 9.0% | | |

**LIZ BLACKMAN,** b Sept 26, 1949. Head of upper school at local comp. Deputy leader, Broxtowe Borough Council. Member, Co-op Party; Fabian Soc; SEA; NASUWT. Ed Clifton Coll, Nottingham.
**ANGELA KNIGHT,** b Oct 31, 1950. Chemist and engineer, ex-adviser to engineering company. Elected for this seat 1992. Economic Secretary to the Treasury 1995-97; previously PPS to Kenneth Clarke, Chancellor of Exchequer, 1994-95 and to Min for Industry 1993-94. Held company directorships, including managing dir and chair of engineering components heat treatment company, 1977-84; chief exec, process plant company, 1984-91. Ed Penrhos Coll, N Wales; Sheffield Girls HS; Bristol Univ.
**MARTIN GARNETT,** b May 10, 1956. Cancer researcher and lecturer in pharmaceutical sciences. Ed Bentley GS, Calne; Univ Coll of Wales, Swansea.

| ERITH & THAMESMEAD | | 94.1% change | | | | | Lab win |
|---|---|---|---|---|---|---|---|
| Electorate % Turnout | | 62,887 | 66.1% | **1997** | 66,600 | 74.2% | **1992** |
| +Austin-Walker, J | Lab | **25,812** | 62.1% | +19.1% | **21,245** | 43.0% | Lab |
| Zahawi, N | C | 8,388 | 20.2% | -11.4% | 15,615 | 31.6% | C |
| Grigg, A | LD | 5,001 | 12.0% | -13.4% | 12,555 | 25.4% | LD |
| Flunder, J | Ref | 1,394 | 3.4% | | | | |
| Dooley, V | BNP | 718 | 1.7% | | | | |
| Jackson, M | UK Ind | 274 | 0.7% | | | | |
| C to Lab notional swing 15.3% | | **41,587** | Lab maj 17,424 | | **49,415** | Lab maj 5,630 | |
| | | | 41.9% | | | 11.4% | |

**JOHN AUSTIN-WALKER,** now wishes to be known as **JOHN AUSTIN,** b Aug 21, 1944. MP for Woolwich 1992-97; contested that seat 1987. Member, health select cttee, 1994-97; joint vice-chair, London group of Lab MPs, 1992-97; chair, all-party osteoporosis group, 1996-97; Campaign group of Lab MPs 1994-95; member, exec cttee, British group, IPU, 1994- ; sec, Albania group; sec, Western Sahara group, 1996-97. Former sec/agent Greenwich Lab Party. Greenwich cllr 1970-94 (Mayor 1987-88; council leader 1982-87). Vice-chair, ALA, 1983-87; London Strategic Policy Unit 1986-88. Dir, London Marathon Charitable Trust Ltd; trustee, Greenwich Mind and Adolescent and Children's Trust (all unpaid). Race equality officer 1974-92. Nat chair, Assoc of Community Health Councils; chair, London Ecology Unit, 1990-92; London Emergency Planning Information Centre 1990-92. Ed Glyn GS, Epsom; Goldsmiths' Coll, London; Bristol Univ.
**NADIM ZAHAWI,** b June 2, 1967. Wandsworth cllr since 1994. Sales director, head of marketing for Global Inc 1989-95. Ed Ibstock Place, Roehampton; King's Coll School, Wimbledon; University Coll, London.
**ALEX GRIGG,** b April 4, 1966. Marketing director of print company. Ed Westminster; St Andrews Univ. Son of John Grigg, Lloyd George's biographer and *Times* historian.

| ESHER & WALTON | | 64.7% change | | | | | C win |
|---|---|---|---|---|---|---|---|
| Electorate % Turnout | | 72,382 | 74.1% | **1997** | 71,598 | 76.5% | **1992** |
| +Taylor, I C | C | **26,747** | 49.8% | -10.9% | **33,237** | 60.7% | C |
| Reay, Ms J | Lab | 12,219 | 22.8% | +5.4% | 12,013 | 21.9% | LD |
| Miles, G | LD | 10,937 | 20.4% | -1.6% | 9,513 | 17.4% | Lab |
| Cruickshank, A | Ref | 2,904 | 5.4% | | | | |
| Collignon, B | UK Ind | 558 | 1.0% | | | | |
| Kay, Ms S | Dream | 302 | 0.6% | | | | |
| C to Lab notional swing 8.1% | | **53,667** | C maj 14,528 | | **54,763** | C maj 21,224 | |
| | | | 27.1% | | | 38.8% | |

**IAN TAYLOR,** b April 18, 1945. MP for Esher 1987-97; contested Coventry SE, Feb 1974. Under Sec for Trade and Technology at DTI 1994; PPS to William Waldegrave in his ministeral posts 1990-94. Member, foreign affairs select cttee 1987-90. Chair (1988-89) and sec (1987-88), C backbench Euro affairs cttee; chair, C Group for Europe, 1985-88; and C Foreign and Commonwealth Council 1990- ; vice-chair, assoc of C clubs, 1988-92. Ex-corporate finance adviser; former company director and economic and parly adviser. Chair, Commonwealth Youth Exchange Council, 1980-84, and vice-pres since 1984. Ed Whitley Abbey School, Coventry; Keele Univ; LSE.
**JULIE REAY,** b July 25, 1953. Part-time administrator. Contested Esher 1992. Kingston upon Thames cllr 1990- . Chair, Kingston CLP, 1990-92. Member, Unison; Greenpeace. Ed Plymouth HS.
**GARY MILES,** b April 30, 1955. Personnel and training manager. Sutton cllr 1994- . Founder member SDP, 1981; member, Charter 88; Friends of the Earth. Ed Haberdashers' Aske's, New Cross; New College, Oxford.

| ESSEX NORTH | 80.3% change | | | | | | C win |
|---|---|---|---|---|---|---|---|
| Electorate % Turnout | | | 68,008 | 75.3% | **1997** | 66,739 | 81.3% | **1992** |
| +Jenkin, B C | C | | **22,480** | 43.9% | -13.8% | 31,309 | 57.7% | C |
| Young, T | Lab | | 17,004 | 33.2% | +14.1% | 12,059 | 22.2% | LD |
| Phillips, A | LD | | 10,028 | 19.6% | -2.6% | 10,347 | 19.1% | Lab |
| Lord, R | UK Ind | | 1,202 | 2.3% | | 544 | 1.0% | Other |
| Ransome, Ms S | Green | | 495 | 1.0% | | | | |
| C to Lab notional swing 14.0% | | | 51,209 | | C maj 5,476 | 54,259 | | C maj 19,250 |
| | | | | | 10.7% | | | 35.5% |

**BERNARD JENKIN**, b April 9, 1959. MP for Colchester N 1992-97; contested Glasgow Central 1987. PPS to Michael Forsyth, Scottish Sec, 1995-97. Member, social security select cttee, 1992-97; vice-chair, C backbench small businesses cttee, 1994-95; joint sec, C foreign and Commonwealth affairs cttee, 1994-95; treas, all-party Future of Europe parly group; sec, opera group. Research asst to Sir Leon Brittan, MP, 1986-89. Adviser to Legal and General Group plc. Fund manager with Legal and General Ventures Ltd 1989-92; with Hill Samuel Bank 1988-89; with 3i, 1986-88; sales and marketing exec, Ford Motor Co, 1983-86. Governor (unpaid),

London Goodenough Trust for Overseas Graduates. Ed Highgate School; William Ellis School; Corpus Christi Coll, Cambridge (pres of Union, 1982).
**TIMOTHY YOUNG**, b Jan 30, 1961. Life assurance underwriter. Colchester borough cllr 1992- . Member, Lab Campaign for Electoral Reform. Ed Clacton County HS; Colchester Inst.
**ANDREW PHILLIPS**, b Oct 2, 1953. Management consultant. Colchester borough cllr 1995- . Member, Green Democrats; Friends of the Earth; Greenpeace. Ed Brentwood School; Salford Univ; Universita di Trieste; Université de Grenoble.

| EXETER | 0.6% change | | | | | | Lab win |
|---|---|---|---|---|---|---|---|
| Electorate % Turnout | | | 79,154 | 78.2% | **1997** | 76,587 | 81.5% | **1992** |
| Bradshaw, B | Lab | | **29,398** | 47.5% | +11.3% | 25,693 | 41.1% | C |
| Rogers, Dr A | C | | 17,693 | 28.6% | -12.5% | 22,629 | 36.2% | Lab |
| Brewer, D | LD | | 11,148 | 18.0% | -1.4% | 12,129 | 19.4% | LD |
| Morrish, D | Lib | | 2,062 | 3.3% | +1.5% | 1,125 | 1.8% | Lib |
| Edwards, P | Green | | 643 | 1.0% | | 768 | 1.2% | Grn |
| Haynes, Mrs C | UK Ind | | 638 | 1.0% | | 100 | 0.2% | NLP |
| Meakin, J | UKPP | | 282 | 0.5% | | | | |
| C to Lab notional swing 11.9% | | | 61,864 | | Lab maj 11,705 | 62,444 | | C maj 3,064 |
| | | | | | 18.9% | | | 4.9% |

**BEN BRADSHAW**, b Aug 30, 1960. BBC journalist and newspaper reporter. Won journalism awards for coverage of East German revolution, fall of Berlin Wall. Ed Thorpe St Andrew School, Norwich; Sussex Univ.
**ADRIAN ROGERS**, b Oct 29, 1947. Doctor. Exeter city cllr 1984-94.

Chair, Exeter C assoc, 1989-92; Dir, C Family Campaign. Ed Tiffin Boys GS, Kingston upon Thames; Guy's Hospital Medical School.
**DENNIS BREWER**, b June 15, 1951. Sales and management consultant. Ed Greenway Boys' School, Bristol; Bristol Poly; South Bank Poly.

| FALKIRK EAST | 29.2% change | | | | | | Lab win |
|---|---|---|---|---|---|---|---|
| Electorate % Turnout | | | 56,792 | 73.2% | **1997** | 56,737 | 76.6% | **1992** |
| +Connarty, M | Lab | | **23,344** | 56.1% | +12.0% | 19,183 | 44.2% | Lab |
| Brown, K | SNP | | 9,959 | 23.9% | -4.4% | 12,327 | 28.4% | SNP |
| Nicol, M | C | | 5,813 | 14.0% | -6.2% | 8,771 | 20.2% | C |
| Spillane, R | LD | | 2,153 | 5.2% | -2.1% | 3,159 | 7.3% | LD |
| Mowbray, S | Ref | | 326 | 0.8% | | | | |
| SNP to Lab notional swing 8.2% | | | 41,595 | | Lab maj 13,385 | 43,440 | | Lab maj 6,856 |
| | | | | | 32.2% | | | 15.8% |

**MICHAEL CONNARTY**, b Sept 3, 1947. Elected 1992; contested Stirling 1987 and 1983. Member, select cttee on Parly Commissioner for Administration, 1995-97; sec, PLP science and tech cttee, 1992- ; chair, economic industry engineering cttee, Scottish PLP group, 1994- ; co-ordinator, PLP Scottish task force, skills and training, youths and students, 1994- . Treas, all-party chemical industry parly group; skin group. Member, exec cttee, Scottish Lab Party, 1981-92; vice-chair, Lab group, Cosla, 1988-90; sec, all-party Scottish Opera group, 1996- . Stirling district cllr 1977-90 (leader 1980-90). Teacher of children with special needs 1976-92. Rector, Stirling Univ, 1983-84. Exec member, Central

Region EIS, 1978-84 and its pres 1982-83. Ed St Patrick's HS, Coatbridge; Stirling and Glasgow Univs; Jordanhill Coll of Ed.
**KEITH BROWN**, b Dec 20, 1961. Local gvt officer. Contested Dundee W 1992 and Lothian in 1994 Euro elections. Member, Nalgo. Ed Tynecastle HS, Edinburgh; Dundee Univ.
**MALCOLM NICOL**, b April 22, 1956. Site manager for clothes supplier. Falkirk district cllr 1983- . Vice-pres, Grangemouth Heritage Trust. Ed Falkirk HS; Falkirk Coll.
**RODGER SPILLANE**, b April 22, 1971. Works in customer relations. Signatory to Charter 88; member, Shelter. Ed John of Gaunt School, Wilts; Edinburgh and Exeter Univs.

### FALKIRK WEST — 14.7% change — Lab win

| Electorate % Turnout | | 38,370 | 72.6% | **1997** | 53,947 | 75.9% | **1992** |
|---|---|---|---|---|---|---|---|
| **+Canavan, D** | **Lab** | **22,772** | **59.3%** | **+7.9%** | **21,065** | **51.5%** | **Lab** |
| Alexander, D | SNP | 8,989 | 23.4% | -0.1% | 9,635 | 23.5% | SNP |
| Buchanan, Mrs C | C | 4,639 | 12.1% | -6.8% | 7,719 | 18.9% | C |
| Houston, D | LD | 1,970 | 5.1% | -1.0% | 2,522 | 6.2% | LD |
| **SNP to Lab notional swing 4.0%** | | **38,370** | Lab maj **13,783** | | **40,941** | Lab maj **11,430** | |
| | | | 35.9% | | | 27.9% | |

**DENNIS CANAVAN,** b Aug 8, 1942. Elected for this seat 1983; MP for W Stirlingshire, Oct 1974-83. Member, foreign affairs select cttee, 1982-97. Chair, all-party Scottish sports parly group, 1987- ; joint vice-chair, hospice group, 1990- . Chair, PLP N Ireland cttee, 1989- (joint vice-chair 1983-89); joint vice-chair, PLP foreign affairs cttee, 1985-91; chair, Scottish PLP group, 1980-81. Asst headmaster, Holyrood HS, Edinburgh, 1974. Chair, parly branch, EIS, 1983- . Ed St Columba's HS, Cowdenbeath; Edinburgh Univ.

**DAVID ALEXANDER,** b June 20, 1958. Falkirk cllr (leader of SNP group). Member, TGWU. Ed Falkirk HS.
**CAROL BUCHANAN,** b May 17, 1948. PA to chair of multinational company. Member, C disability group; C NHS task force; exec cttee of Scottish Tory Reform Group. Ed Edinburgh Leith Acad.
**DEREK HOUSTON,** b Nov 16, 1967. Serves on several LD cttees. Ed Mark Rutherford Upper School; St Andrews Univ (union pres).

### FALMOUTH & CAMBORNE — Lab gain

| Electorate % Turnout | | 71,383 | 75.1% | **1997** | 70,702 | 81.1% | **1992** |
|---|---|---|---|---|---|---|---|
| **Atherton, Ms C** | **Lab** | **18,151** | **33.8%** | **+4.7%** | **21,150** | **36.9%** | **C** |
| *Coe, S | C | 15,463 | 28.8% | -8.1% | 17,883 | 31.2% | LD |
| Jones, Mrs T | LD | 13,512 | 25.2% | -6.0% | 16,732 | 29.2% | Lab |
| de Savary, P | Ref | 3,534 | 6.6% | | 730 | 1.3% | Lib |
| Geach, J | Ind Lab | 1,691 | 3.2% | | 466 | 0.8% | Grn |
| Holmes, P | Lib | 527 | 1.0% | -0.3% | 327 | 0.6% | Loony |
| Smith, R | UK Ind | 355 | 0.7% | | 56 | 0.1% | NLP |
| Lewarne, Ms R | Meb Ker | 238 | 0.4% | | | | |
| Glitter, G | Loony | 161 | 0.3% | -0.3% | | | |
| **C to Lab swing 6.4%** | | **53,632** | Lab maj **2,688** | | **57,344** | C maj **3,267** | |
| | | | 5.0% | | | 5.7% | |

**CANDY ATHERTON,** b Sept 21, 1955. Journalist. Contested Chesham and Amersham 1992. Islington cllr 1986-91 (Mayor 1989-90). Co-founder of *Everywoman* magazine; ex-probation officer. Freeman, City of London, 1990. Ed Sutton HS; Midhurst GS; N London Poly. Glider pilot and ornithologist.
**SEBASTIAN COE,** b Sept 29, 1956. Ex-international athlete and Olympic gold medal-winner in 1980 and 1984. MP for this seat 1992-97. Asst gvt whip 1996. PPS to Dep Prime Minister and to Chancellor of Duchy of Lancaster in Cabinet Office 1995-96;

previously PPS to defence mins of state. Member, national heritage select cttee, 1995-96. Ed Tapton Sec Mod, Sheffield; Abbeydale Grange School; Loughborough Univ.
**TERRYE JONES,** b Nov 5, 1952. Manager/partner, Kerrier Computer Services. Contested this seat 1992. Kerrier district cllr 1987- (chair 1991-92). Ed Helston GS; Camborne Coll.
**PETER DE SAVARY,** b July 11, 1944. International entrepreneur. Former America's Cup challenger; owner of shipyard in Cornwall. Ed Charterhouse.

### FAREHAM — 19.0% change — C win

| Electorate % Turnout | | 68,787 | 75.9% | **1997** | 66,082 | 81.3% | **1992** |
|---|---|---|---|---|---|---|---|
| **+Lloyd, Sir Peter** | **C** | **24,436** | **46.8%** | **-13.8%** | **32,588** | **60.6%** | **C** |
| Pryor, M | Lab | 14,078 | 27.0% | +12.1% | 12,489 | 23.2% | LD |
| Hill, Mrs G | LD | 10,234 | 19.6% | -3.6% | 7,980 | 14.9% | Lab |
| Markham, D | Ref | 2,914 | 5.6% | | 679 | 1.3% | Grn |
| O'Brien, W | Ind No | 515 | 1.0% | | | | |
| **C to Lab notional swing 13.0%** | | **52,177** | C maj **10,358** | | **53,736** | C maj **20,099** | |
| | | | 19.9% | | | 37.4% | |

**SIR PETER LLOYD,** b Nov 12, 1937. Elected 1979; contested Nottingham W, Feb and Oct 1974. Min of State, Home Office, 1992-94; Under Sec, Home Office, 1989-92; Under Sec for Social Security 1988-89; gvt whip 1986-88; asst gvt whip 1984-86. Member, select cttees on public service, 1995- ; employment 1983-84. Privy Counsellor 1994. Chair, Bow Group, 1972-73; vice-chair, C European affairs cttee, 1980-81; sec, C employment cttee, 1979-81; PPS to Min of State for N Ireland 1982-83; to Sec of State for Ed and Science 1983-84. Joint vice-chair, exec cttee, British group,

IPU, 1994- . Ex-marketing manager of United Biscuits plc. Member of Lloyd's. Consultant to Lloyd and Associates, solicitors (marketing and legal advice). Unpaid chair, The New Bridge charity. Ed Tonbridge School; Pembroke Coll, Cambridge.
**MICHAEL PRYOR,** b March 15, 1957. Fareham borough cllr (Lab group leader). Ed Prince's School, Fareham; East Anglia Univ.
**GRACE HILL,** b Nov 20, 1940. Cllr on Town, District and Wiltshire County Council (chair). Member, Friends of the Earth. Ed Skegness Sec; Norwich Tech; Trowbridge Tech.

| FAVERSHAM & KENT MID | | 124.5% change | | | | | C win |
|---|---|---|---|---|---|---|---|
| Electorate % Turnout | | 67,490 | 73.5% | **1997** | 66,379 | 81.6% | **1992** |
| +Rowe, A J B | C | **22,016** | **44.4%** | **-14.8%** | **32,047** | **59.2%** | C |
| Stewart, A | Lab | 17,843 | 36.0% | +13.0% | 12,448 | 23.0% | Lab |
| Parmenter, B | LD | 6,138 | 12.4% | -4.7% | 9,225 | 17.0% | LD |
| Birley, R | Ref | 2,073 | 4.2% | | 456 | 0.8% | Other |
| Davidson, N | Loony | 511 | 1.0% | | | | |
| Cunningham, M | UK Ind | 431 | 0.9% | | | | |
| Currer, D | Green | 380 | 0.8% | | | | |
| Morgan, Ms C | GRLNSP | 115 | 0.2% | | | | |
| Pollard, N | NLP | 99 | 0.2% | | | | |
| C to Lab notional swing 13.9% | | **49,606** | | **C maj 4,173** | **54,176** | | **C maj 19,599** |
| | | | | 8.4% | | | 36.2% |

**ANDREW ROWE,** b Sept 11, 1935. MP for Kent Mid 1983-97. PPS to Lord Ferrers and Richard Needham, Trade and Industry Mins 1992-95. Member, PAC, 1995-97. Chair (1989-92), joint vice-chair (1987-89) and joint sec (1983-86), C backbench employment cttee; chair, all-party Christian Fellowship group; parly panel for personal social services 1986-92; joint sec, social science and policy group. Dir of Community Affairs at C Central Office 1975-79. Parly adviser to Amway plc, multilevel selling co; pres, North Downs Rail Concern; unpaid trustee and dir, Community Service

Volunteers; trustee of NSPCC; principal, Scottish Office, 1962-67. Member, Swann Cttee 1979-84. Editor, *Small Business*, 1979-90; lecturer, Edinburgh Univ, 1967-74. Ed Eton; Merton Coll, Oxford. **ALAN STEWART,** b Oct 28, 1958. Kent Univ research fellow. Faversham town cllr. Sec, Faversham and Mid-Kent CLP, 1994-95. Member, AUT. Ed Eastbourne Comp; King's Coll, Cambridge; York Univ.
**BRUCE PARMENTER,** b Aug 18, 1964. Merchant seaman/sailing instructor. Ed Meopham Secondary; National Sea Training School.

| FELTHAM & HESTON | | 11.8% change | | | | | Lab win |
|---|---|---|---|---|---|---|---|
| Electorate % Turnout | | 71,093 | 65.6% | **1997** | 73,296 | 72.8% | **1992** |
| +Keen, A | Lab Co-op | **27,836** | **59.7%** | **+14.2%** | **24,294** | **45.5%** | Lab Co-op |
| Ground, P | C | 12,563 | 26.9% | -15.9% | 22,894 | 42.9% | C |
| Penning, C | LD | 4,264 | 9.1% | -2.4% | 6,189 | 11.6% | LD |
| Stubbs, R | Ref | 1,099 | 2.4% | | | | |
| Church, R | BNP | 682 | 1.5% | | | | |
| Fawcett, D | NLP | 177 | 0.4% | | | | |
| C to Lab notional swing 15.1% | | **46,621** | | **Lab Co-op maj 15,273** | **53,377** | | **Lab Co-op maj 1,400** |
| | | | | 32.8% | | | 2.6% |

**ALAN KEEN,** b Nov 25, 1937. Systems analyst, accountant and manager. Elected for this seat 1992. Member, select cttees on education, 1995-96; deregulation 1995-96. Hounslow cllr 1986-90. Member, Co-op Party. Ed Sir William Turner's, Redcar. Former scout for Middlesbrough FC.
**PATRICK GROUND,** b Aug 9, 1932. QC. MP for Feltham and Heston 1983-92; contested Hounslow, Feltham and Heston in both 1974

elections and in 1979. PPS to Sir Nicholas Lyell, Solicitor-General, 1987-92. Member, C Group for Europe; C Action for Electoral Reform; C Christian Fellowship. Ed Beckenham & Penge County GS; Lycée Guy Lussac, Limoges; Selwyn Coll, Cambridge; Magdalen Coll, Oxford; Inner Temple.
**COLIN PENNING,** b July 24, 1973. LD Administration officer. Ed Featherstone HS, Southall; Kingston Univ; Bordeaux Univ.

| FERMANAGH & SOUTH TYRONE | | 12.7% change | | | | | UUP win |
|---|---|---|---|---|---|---|---|
| Electorate % Turnout | | 64,600 | 74.8% | **1997** | 63,090 | 75.9% | **1992** |
| +Maginnis, K | UUP | **24,862** | **51.5%** | **-0.9%** | **25,071** | **52.4%** | UUP |
| McHugh, G | SF | 11,174 | 23.1% | +4.0% | 10,982 | 22.9% | SDLP |
| Gallagher, T | SDLP | 11,060 | 22.9% | -0.0% | 9,143 | 19.1% | SF |
| Farry, S | Alliance | 977 | 2.0% | +0.3% | 1,094 | 2.3% | Prog Soc |
| Gillan, S | NLP | 217 | 0.4% | | 830 | 1.7% | Alliance |
| | | | | | 747 | 1.6% | NA |
| No swing calculation | | **48,290** | | **UUP maj 13,688** | **47,867** | | **UUP maj 14,089** |
| | | | | 28.3% | | | 29.4% |

**KEN MAGINNIS,** b Jan 21, 1938. Ex-teacher. Won seat 1983; resigned 1985 in protest at Anglo-Irish agreement and retained it at 1986 by-election; contested it in 1981 by-election. Party spokesman on internal security and defence, and on employment. Member, select cttees on N Ireland, 1994-97; defence, 1984-86. Member, N Ireland Assembly, 1982-86. Dungannon district cllr 1981-93. In UDR 1970-81 (commissioned 1972; gained rank of

Major). Ed Royal School, Dungannon, Co Tyrone; Stranmillis Teacher Training Coll, Belfast.
**GERRY McHUGH,** b Oct 9, 1952. Fermanagh district cllr. SF agriculture spokesman. Member, N Ireland Forum, May 1996- .
**TOMMY GALLAGHER,** b Aug 17, 1942. Teacher. Party spokesman on education. Fermanagh cllr, 1989- . Ed St Joseph's Coll of Ed; Queen's Univ, Belfast.

| FIFE CENTRAL | | 2.3% change | | | | | Lab win |
|---|---|---|---|---|---|---|---|
| Electorate % Turnout | | 58,315 | 69.9% | **1997** | 57,702 | 73.9% | **1992** |
| +McLeish, H | Lab | **23,912** | 58.7% | +7.9% | **21,627** | 50.7% | Lab |
| Marwick, Mrs T | SNP | 10,199 | 25.0% | +0.1% | 10,636 | 24.9% | SNP |
| Rees-Mogg, J | C | 3,669 | 9.0% | -8.4% | 7,440 | 17.4% | C |
| Laird, R | LD | 2,610 | 6.4% | -0.5% | 2,937 | 6.9% | LD |
| Scrymgeour-Wedderburn, J | Ref | 375 | 0.9% | | | | |
| SNP to Lab notional swing 3.9% | | 40,765 | | Lab maj 13,713 | 42,640 | | Lab maj 10,991 |
| | | | | 33.6% | | | 25.8% |

**HENRY McLEISH,** b June 15, 1948. Became Scottish Office Minister of State responsibile for home affairs and devolution, May 5, 1997. Ex-council officer and univ lecturer. Elected 1987; contested NE Fife 1979. Lab dep social security spokesman 1996-97; health spokesman 1995-97; transport 1994-95; Scotland 1992-94 and 1988-89; employment 1989-92. Fife regional cllr 1978-87 (council leader 1982-87). Ed Buckhaven HS; Heriot-Watt Univ, Edinburgh.

**TRICIA MARWICK,** b Nov 5, 1953. Training consultant. Contested Fife Central 1992. Convener, Fife Central SNP.
**JACOB REES-MOGG,** b May 24, 1969. Investment manager and journalist. Ed Eton; Trinity Coll, Oxford. Son of Lord Rees-Mogg, former Editor and now columnist of *The Times.*
**ROSS LAIRD,** b Nov 23, 1971. Political researcher to Ray Michie, MP. Ed Auchmuty HS, Glenrothes; Glasgow Univ; London School of Journalism.

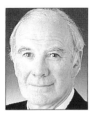

| FIFE NORTH EAST | | 0.1% change | | | | | LD win |
|---|---|---|---|---|---|---|---|
| Electorate % Turnout | | 58,794 | 71.2% | **1997** | 54,244 | 77.2% | **1992** |
| *Campbell, M | LD | **21,432** | 51.2% | +4.8% | **19,432** | 46.4% | LD |
| Bruce, A | C | 11,076 | 26.5% | -12.0% | 16,129 | 38.5% | C |
| Welsh, C | SNP | 4,545 | 10.9% | +2.3% | 3,598 | 8.6% | SNP |
| Milne, C | Lab | 4,301 | 10.3% | +4.7% | 2,337 | 5.6% | Lab |
| Stewart, W | Ref | 485 | 1.2% | | 294 | 0.7% | Grn |
| | | | | | 85 | 0.2% | Lib |
| C to LD notional swing 8.4% | | 41,839 | | LD maj 10,356 | 41,875 | | LD maj 3,303 |
| | | | | 24.8% | | | 7.9% |

**MENZIES CAMPBELL,** b May 22, 1941. Advocate, QC (Scot). Elected for this seat 1987; contested it 1983; East Fife 1979; and Greenock and Port Glasgow twice in 1974. LD spokesman on foreign and Commonwealth affairs, defence and Europe. Member, select cttees on defence, 1992-97; trade and industry 1990-92; members' interests, 1987-90. Member, advisory cttee on Commons works of art, 1988- ; UK delegation, N Atlantic Assembly, 1989- ; UK delegation, CSCE Parly Assembly, 1992- . Joint vice-chair, all-party association football parly group; sports group; Scottish sports group; aerospace group, 1994- . Broadcasting Council for Scotland

1984-87. Trustee, Scottish International Ed Trust, 1984- . International athlete and former UK 100m record holder. Ed Hillhead HS, Glasgow; Glasgow Univ; Stanford Univ, California.
**THE HON ADAM BRUCE,** b Jan 18, 1968. Solicitor, author. Ed Glenalmond Coll; Balliol Coll, Oxford (pres, Oxford Union, 1989); Edinburgh Univ.
**COLIN WELSH,** b Oct 3, 1957. Team leader, Fife Council social work dept. Ed Queen Margaret Coll.
**CHARLES MILNE,** b July 23, 1954. Solicitor, former social worker. Ed Kirkton HS, Dundee; Dundee Univ.

| FINCHLEY & GOLDERS GREEN | | 73.4% change | | | | | Lab win |
|---|---|---|---|---|---|---|---|
| Electorate % Turnout | | 72,225 | 69.7% | **1997** | 71,081 | 73.6% | **1992** |
| Vis, R | Lab | **23,180** | 46.1% | +15.2% | **28,623** | 54.7% | C |
| +Marshall, J L | C | 19,991 | 39.7% | -15.0% | 16,149 | 30.9% | Lab |
| Davies, J | LD | 5,670 | 11.3% | -1.5% | 6,690 | 12.8% | LD |
| Shaw, G | Ref | 684 | 1.4% | | 821 | 1.6% | Other |
| Gunstock, A | Green | 576 | 1.1% | | | | |
| Barraclough, D | UK Ind | 205 | 0.4% | | | | |
| C to Lab notional swing 15.1% | | 50,306 | | Lab maj 3,189 | 52,283 | | C maj 12,474 |
| | | | | 6.3% | | | 23.9% |

**RUDOLF VIS,** b April 4, 1941. Lecturer in economics. Barnet cllr 1986- . Treas, Finchley CLP, 1982-86. Member, MSF; SEA. Ed high school in The Netherlands; Univ of Maryland; Brunel Univ.
**JOHN MARSHALL,** b Aug 19, 1940. MP for Hendon S 1987-97; contested Lewisham E Feb 1974; Dundee E 1964 and 1966. MEP for London North 1979-89. PPS to Tony Newton, Social Security Sec and then Leader of the House, 1990-95; PPS to Nicholas Scott, Min for Disabled, 1989-90. Aberdeen town cllr 1968-70, and Ealing cllr 1971-86. Member, International Stock Exchange,

1979- ; analyst with MeesPierson Securities (UK) Ltd, formerly London Wall Equities, 1993- ; dir, 1986-90, and analyst, 1990-93, Kitcat & Aitken; dir, Beta Global Emerging Markets Investment Trust plc, 1990- . Parly consultant to Confed of Passenger Transport UK. Ed Harris Acad, Dundee; Glasgow Acad; St Andrews Univ.
**JONATHAN DAVIES,** b Jan 29, 1962. Solicitor. Barnet cllr 1994- . Treas, London region, LDs; chair 1993-95. Ed Gravesend GS for Boys; Christ Church, Oxford.

## FOLKESTONE & HYTHE

**C hold**

| Electorate % Turnout | | 71,153 | 73.2% | **1997** | 64,414 | 81.4% | **1992** |
|---|---|---|---|---|---|---|---|
| +Howard, M | C | **20,313** | 39.0% | -13.3% | 27,435 | 52.3% | C |
| Laws, D | LD | 13,981 | 26.9% | -8.5% | 18,527 | 35.3% | LD |
| Doherty, P | Lab | 12,939 | 24.9% | +12.8% | 6,347 | 12.1% | Lab |
| Aspinall, J | Ref | 4,188 | 8.0% | | 123 | 0.2% | NLP |
| Baker, J | UK Ind | 378 | 0.7% | | | | |
| Segal, E | Soc | 182 | 0.3% | | | | |
| Saint, R | CFSS | 69 | 0.1% | | | | |
| **C to LD notional swing 2.4%** | | **52,050** | | **C maj 6,332** | **52,432** | | **C maj 8,908** |
| | | | | 12.2% | | | 17.1% |

**MICHAEL HOWARD,** b July 7, 1941. QC. Home Secretary 1993-97. Elected 1983; contested Liverpool Edge Hill 1966 and 1970. Environment Sec 1992-93; Employment Sec 1990-92; Local Gvt Min 1987-88; Housing and Planning Min 1988-90; Corporate and Consumer Affairs Min 1985-87. Privy Counsellor 1990. Appointed Recorder 1986. Ed Llanelli GS; Peterhouse, Cambridge (pres of Union 1962).
**DAVID LAWS,** b Nov 30, 1965. Ex-managing director, Barclays Bank. LD economic adviser. Member, Inst of Fiscal Studies. Ed St

George's Coll, Weybridge; King's Coll, Cambridge.
**PETER DOHERTY,** b Nov 23, 1958. Manager, electricity industry. Contested this seat 1992. Shepway cllr 1990- . Ed Brockhill County Sec, Hythe; South Kent Coll of Tech; Seabank Tech Coll.
**JOHN ASPINALL,** b June 11, 1926. Chairman, trustees, Howletts and Port Lympne Foundation, 1984- ; founder, Howletts and Port Lympne Zoo Parks; Clermont Club 1962; Aspinall's Club 1978; Aspinall Curzon Club 1984; Aspinalls 1992- . Ed Rugby; Jesus Coll, Oxford.

## FOREST OF DEAN

**22.1% change**

**Lab win**

| Electorate % Turnout | | 63,465 | 79.1% | **1997** | 62,882 | 83.1% | **1992** |
|---|---|---|---|---|---|---|---|
| Organ, Ms D M | Lab | **24,203** | 48.2% | +5.8% | 22,176 | 42.4% | Lab |
| +Marland, P | C | 17,860 | 35.6% | -5.5% | 21,444 | 41.0% | C |
| Lynch, Dr A | LD | 6,165 | 12.3% | -3.8% | 8,422 | 16.1% | LD |
| Hopkins, J | Ref | 1,624 | 3.2% | | 204 | 0.4% | Other |
| Morgan, G | Ind Dean | 218 | 0.4% | | | | |
| Palmer, C | 21st Cent | 80 | 0.2% | | | | |
| Porter, S | Ind F | 34 | 0.1% | | | | |
| **C to Lab notional swing 5.6%** | | **50,184** | | **Lab maj 6,343** | **52,246** | | **Lab maj 732** |
| | | | | 12.6% | | | 1.4% |

**DIANA ORGAN,** b Feb 21, 1952. Special needs teacher. Contested Gloucestershire W 1992; Somerset and Dorset West in 1989 Euro elections. Former asst sec, Somerset and Frome CLP; Somerset delegate, women's cttee; member, regional exec. Former dep head of primary school; board member, TV South West. Member, Nupe. Ed Edgbaston C of E Coll for Girls; St Hugh's Coll, Oxford; Bath Univ School of Education; Bristol Poly.

**PAUL MARLAND,** b March 19, 1940. Farmer. MP for Gloucestershire W 1979-97; contested the seat Feb and Oct 1974, and Bedwellty 1970. Unpaid chair, Marland's English Table Waters Ltd; Former parly adviser to various organisations and companies. Member of Lloyd's. Ed Gordonstoun; Trinity Coll, Dublin; Grenoble Univ.
**ANTHONY LYNCH,** b Feb 12, 1935. General practitioner. Gloucestershire county cllr 1993- . Ed Marlborough GS; St John's Coll, Cambridge; Royal Free Hospital; London Univ.

## FOYLE

**16.8% change**

**SDLP win**

| Electorate % Turnout | | 67,620 | 70.7% | **1997** | 64,199 | 67.9% | **1992** |
|---|---|---|---|---|---|---|---|
| +Hume, J | SDLP | **25,109** | 52.5% | -0.9% | 23,291 | 53.4% | SDLP |
| McLaughlin, M | SF | 11,445 | 23.9% | +6.8% | 10,809 | 24.8% | DUP |
| Hay, W | DUP | 10,290 | 21.5% | -3.3% | 7,475 | 17.1% | SF |
| Bell, Mrs H | Alliance | 817 | 1.7% | -0.3% | 866 | 2.0% | Alliance |
| Brennan, D | NLP | 154 | 0.3% | -0.9% | 639 | 1.5% | WP |
| | | | | | 524 | 1.2% | NLP |
| **SDLP to SF notional swing 3.8%** | | **47,815** | | **SDLP maj 13,664** | **43,604** | | **SDLP maj 12,482** |
| | | | | 28.6% | | | 28.6% |

**JOHN HUME,** b Jan 18, 1937. Teacher. Leader, SDLP, 1979- ; dep leader 1970-79; founder member. Elected 1983; contested Londonderry Oct 1974. Member, Euro Parliament, since 1979, serving on bureau of Socialist group. MP for Foyle, N Ireland Parliament, 1969-73. Elected for Londonderry to NI Assembly 1973-75; NI Constitutional Convention 1975-76; NI Assembly 1982-86. Member, NI Forum, 1983-84. Minister for Commerce in

NI power-sharing exec, 1974. Associate Fellow, Centre for International Affairs, Harvard, 1976. Ed St Columb's Coll, Londonderry; St Patrick's Coll, Maynooth.
**MITCHEL McLAUGHLIN,** b Oct 29, 1945. Nat chair, Sinn Fein, and one of party's key strategists. Derry city cllr 1985- . NI Forum 1996- .
**WILLIAM HAY,** b April 16, 1950. Haulage contractor. Londonderry City cllr (former Mayor). Ed Faughan Valley HS, Londonderry.

| FYLDE | | 12.5% change | | | **C win** | | |
|---|---|---|---|---|---|---|---|
| Electorate % Turnout | | 71,385 | 72.9% | **1997** | 70,389 | 75.1% | **1992** |
| +Jack, M | C | **25,443** | 48.9% | -11.4% | **31,849** | 60.2% | C |
| Garrett, J | Lab | 16,480 | 31.7% | +13.1% | 10,937 | 20.7% | LD |
| Greene, W | LD | 7,609 | 14.6% | -6.1% | 9,827 | 18.6% | Lab |
| Britton, D | Ref | 2,372 | 4.6% | | 268 | 0.5% | NLP |
| Kerwin, T | NLP | 163 | 0.3% | -0.2% | | | |
| C to Lab notional swing 12.2% | | **52,067** | | C maj **8,963** | **52,881** | | C maj **20,912** |
| | | | | 17.2% | | | 39.6% |

**MICHAEL JACK**, b Sept 17, 1946. Elected 1987; contested Newcastle Central, Feb 1974. Financial Secretary to Treasury 1995-97; member, PAC; Min of state for Ag, Fish and Food 1993-95, with responsibilities for fishing; Min of State, Home Office, 1992-93; Under Sec for Social Security 1990-92. PPS to John Gummer, when Min for Local Gvt and then Agriculture Min, 1988-90. Chair, C horticulture and markets sub-cttee, 1987-88; joint sec, C transport cttee, 1987-88; sec, NW C MPs, 1988-90. Former sales director of horticultural produce. Procter & Gamble 1970-75; personal asst to Sir Derek Rayner, Marks & Spencer, 1975-80;

sales director, L.O. Jeffs Ltd, 1980-87. Ed Bradford GS; Bradford Tech Coll; Leicester Univ.
**JOHN GARRETT**, b Jan 6, 1963. Self-employed sports consultant for Cambridge Univ. Hammersmith and Fulham cllr 1994- . Rowed in three Olympic Games and Commonwealth silver medal-winner. Member, TGWU; Amnesty; Greenpeace. Ed Shrewsbury School; St John's Coll, Cambridge; Birkbeck Coll, London; LSE.
**BILL GREENE,** b Aug 25, 1946. Computer specialist (retired). Fylde borough cllr 1976-79, 1991- . Ed Bristol Central Commercial School.

| GAINSBOROUGH | | 13.3% change | | | **C win** | | |
|---|---|---|---|---|---|---|---|
| Electorate % Turnout | | 64,106 | 74.6% | **1997** | 62,796 | 80.3% | **1992** |
| +Leigh, E J E | C | **20,593** | 43.1% | -10.3% | **26,919** | 53.4% | C |
| Taylor, P | Lab | 13,767 | 28.8% | +7.9% | 12,993 | 25.8% | LD |
| Taylor, N | LD | 13,436 | 28.1% | +2.4% | 10,533 | 20.9% | Lab |
| C to Lab notional swing 9.1% | | **47,796** | | C maj **6,826** | **50,445** | | C maj **13,926** |
| | | | | 14.3% | | | 27.6% |

**EDWARD LEIGH**, b July 20, 1950. Barrister. MP for Gainsborough and Horncastle 1983-97; contested Teesside Middlesbrough Oct 1974. Under Sec of State for Trade and Industry 1990-93. Member, select cttees on social security, 1995-97; defence 1983-87. Joint sec, C backbench N Ireland cttee, 1988-90; joint vice-chair, C employment cttee, 1987-88; sec, C defence cttee, 1983-84; C agric cttee 1983-85. Member, Margaret Thatcher's private office, 1976-77. Arbitrator in trading disputes between newspaper publishers, wholesalers and retailers. Dir, Nat TeleCable; parly

and public affairs consultant to Pinnacle Insurance plc; Nat Assoc of Licensed Opencast Operators. Ed St Philip's School, Kensington; Oratory School, Berks; French Lycée, London; Durham Univ (pres of union; chair, univ C assoc).
**PAUL TAYLOR**, b Aug 7, 1957. Nacro project worker. Lincs county cllr. Ed Lafford School, Billinghay; Bishop King HS.
**NEIL TAYLOR**, b Jan 31, 1954. Teacher. Contested Gainsborough and Horncastle 1992. West Lindsey cllr 1982- (Mayor 1983-84). Ed Radcliffe School, Wolverton; Coll of All Saints, London.

| GALLOWAY & UPPER NITHSDALE | | 2.7% change | | | **SNP win** | | |
|---|---|---|---|---|---|---|---|
| Electorate % Turnout | | 52,751 | 79.7% | **1997** | 53,482 | 80.9% | **1992** |
| Morgan, A | SNP | **18,449** | 43.9% | +7.5% | **18,173** | 42.0% | C |
| +Lang, I | C | 12,825 | 30.5% | -11.5% | 15,773 | 36.4% | SNP |
| Clark, Ms K | Lab | 6,861 | 16.3% | +3.4% | 5,609 | 13.0% | Lab |
| McKerchar, J | LD | 2,700 | 6.4% | -2.2% | 3,721 | 8.6% | LD |
| Wood, R | Ind | 566 | 1.3% | | | | |
| Kennedy, A | Ref | 428 | 1.0% | | | | |
| Smith, J | UK Ind | 189 | 0.4% | | | | |
| C to SNP notional swing 9.5% | | **42,018** | | SNP maj **5,624** | **43,276** | | C maj **2,400** |
| | | | | 13.4% | | | 5.6% |

**ALASDAIR MORGAN,** b April 21, 1945. Computer systems team leader. Contested Dumfries 1992. SNP national sec 1992- (general election director 1992); sec and former nat treas and ex-senior vice-convener, SNP Scottish Cabinet. Ed Breadalbane Acad, Aberfeldy; Glasgow Univ; OU.
**IAN LANG,** b June 27, 1940. MP for this seat 1983-97; MP for Galloway 1979-83; contested Ayrshire Central 1970; Glasgow Pollok, Feb 1974. President, Board of Trade and DTI Sec, 1995-97. Scottish Sec 1990-95; Scottish Office Min 1987-90; Scottish industry and home affairs min l986-87; junior employment min

1986; gvt whip 1983-86; asst gvt whip 1981-83. Vice-chair, Scottish C Party, 1983-87. Former company director and insurance broker. Member, Queen's Body Guard for Scotland (Royal Company of Archers). Ed Rugby; Sidney Sussex Coll, Cambridge.
**KATY CLARK,** b July 3, 1967. Solicitor. Member, Scottish Council for Civil Liberties. Ed Edinburgh and Aberdeen Univs.
**JOHN McKERCHAR,** b May 11, 1947. Managing director. Contested this seat 1987 and 1992; South of Scotland in 1989 Euro elections. Ed Burnage GS, Manchester; Salford Univ.

| GATESHEAD EAST & WASHINGTON WEST | | | 68.9% change | | Lab win |
|---|---|---|---|---|---|
| Electorate % Turnout | | 64,114 | 67.2% | **1997** | 67,822 | 71.7% | **1992** |
| +Quin, Miss J G | Lab | **31,047** | 72.1% | +14.1% | **28,192** | 58.0% | Lab |
| Burns, Miss J | C | 6,097 | 14.2% | -13.6% | 13,492 | 27.7% | C |
| Ord, A | LD | 4,622 | 10.7% | -3.6% | 6,963 | 14.3% | LD |
| Daley, M | Ref | 1,315 | 3.1% | | | | |
| C to Lab notional swing 13.8% | | 43,081 | Lab maj 24,950 | | 48,647 | Lab maj 14,700 | |
| | | | 57.9% | | | 30.2% | |

**JOYCE QUIN,** b Nov 26, 1944. Became Home Office Minister of State responsible for prisons, May 5, 1997. Elected MP for Gateshead E 1987; MEP for Tyne and Wear 1979-89. Labour spokesman on Europe 1993-97; spokesman on employment 1992-93; trade and industry 1989-92. Member, Treasury and Civil Service select cttee, 1987-89. Joint vice-chair, all-party social science and policy group; European Atlantic group; treas, British-German group. Researcher, international dept, Lab Party HQ, 1969-72; lecturer in French, Bath Univ, 1972-76, and in French and politics, Durham 1977-79.

FRSA 1991. Hon Fellow, Sunderland Poly, 1986. Ed Whitley Bay GS; Newcastle Univ; LSE.
**JACQUI BURNS,** b April 6, 1960. Self-employed accountant. Newham cllr (dep group leader 1992-94; leader of opposition 1990-92). Ed Stratford GS, London.
**ALAN ORD,** b Jan 1, 1947. Claims manager. Gateshead met borough cllr 1988- ; Tyne & Wear Passenger Transport Authority 1993- . Ed South Shields Grammar-Tech School; S Tyneside Marine and Technical Coll.

| GEDLING | | | | | | | Lab gain |
|---|---|---|---|---|---|---|---|
| Electorate % Turnout | | 68,820 | 75.8% | **1997** | 68,953 | 82.3% | **1992** |
| Coaker, V | Lab | **24,390** | 46.8% | +12.3% | **30,191** | 53.2% | C |
| *Mitchell, A | C | 20,588 | 39.5% | -13.7% | 19,554 | 34.4% | Lab |
| Poynter, R | LD | 5,180 | 9.9% | -2.2% | 6,863 | 12.1% | LD |
| Connor, J | Ref | 2,006 | 3.8% | | 168 | 0.3% | NLP |
| C to Lab swing 13.0% | | 52,164 | Lab maj 3,802 | | 56,776 | C maj 10,637 | |
| | | | 7.3% | | | 18.7% | |

**VERNON COAKER,** b June 17, 1953. Teacher. Contested Rushcliffe 1983; Gedling 1987 and 1992. Rushcliffe borough cllr 1983- (council leader 1987- ). Member, NUT. Ed Drayton Manor GS; Warwick Univ; Trent Poly.
**ANDREW MITCHELL,** b March 23, 1956. Banker. Elected 1987; contested Sunderland S 1983. Appointed Under Sec for Social Security 1995; gvt whip 1994-95; asst gvt whip 1993-94. PPS to John Wakeham, Sec of State for Energy, 1990-92; and to William Waldegrave, Min of State, FCO, 1988-90. Sec, One Nation group of

C MPs, 1989-92. Chair, C collegiate forum, 1991-92; Coningsby Club 1983-84; Islington North C assoc 1983-85. Member, Islington HA, 1985-87. With Lazard Brothers & Co Ltd 1979-87; adviser to Lazards 1987-92, El Vino Co Ltd 1981-93. Ed Rugby; Jesus Coll, Cambridge (pres of Union 1978; chair, univ C assoc, 1977).
**RAY POYNTER,** b Oct 12, 1956. Market research consultant. Contested Nottingham S 1983. Nottinghamshire cllr 1985- . Ed Gedling Sec Mod; Arnold and Cralton Coll of FE; Salford and Nottingham Univs.

| GILLINGHAM | | 2.8% change | | | | | Lab win |
|---|---|---|---|---|---|---|---|
| Electorate % Turnout | | 70,389 | 72.0% | **1997** | 70,789 | 79.1% | **1992** |
| Clark, P | Lab | **20,187** | 39.8% | +16.0% | **29,092** | 52.0% | C |
| +Couchman, J | C | 18,207 | 35.9% | -16.0% | 13,332 | 23.8% | Lab |
| Sayer, R | LD | 9,649 | 19.0% | -4.4% | 13,150 | 23.5% | LD |
| Cann, G | Ref | 1,492 | 2.9% | | 240 | 0.4% | Ind |
| MacKinlay, C | UK Ind | 590 | 1.2% | | 185 | 0.3% | NLP |
| Robinson, D | Loony | 305 | 0.6% | | | | |
| Jury, C | BNP | 195 | 0.4% | | | | |
| Duguay, Ms G | NLP | 58 | 0.1% | -0.2% | | | |
| C to Lab notional swing 16.0% | | 50,683 | Lab maj 1,980 | | 55,999 | C maj 15,760 | |
| | | | 3.9% | | | 28.1% | |

**PAUL CLARK,** b April 29, 1957. Administrator, TUC. Contested Gillingham 1992. Gillingham borough cllr 1982-90 (Lab group leader 1988-90). Member, AEU. Ed Gillingham GS; Keele Univ.
**JAMES COUCHMAN,** b Feb 11, 1942. Elected 1983; contested Chester-le-Street 1979. PPS to Tony Newton, ex-Leader of Commons; formerly to Sec of State for Social Security 1989-90; to Chancellor of Duchy of Lancaster 1988-89; to Min for Health 1986-88; and to Min of State for Social Security 1984-86. Member, PAC, 1992-95; select cttee on N Ireland 1995-97; health 1990-92; social

services 1983-85. Joint vice-chair, all-party beer club parly group. Former joint vice-chair, C backbench N Ireland cttee; member, British-Irish inter-parly body. Bexley cllr 1974-82. Adviser to Gin and Vodka Assoc; Pfizer Ltd. Member, Vintners' Co. Ed Cranleigh School, Surrey; King's Coll, Newcastle upon Tyne; Durham Univ.
**ROBERT SAYER,** b Aug 12, 1939. Personnel manager, Remploy Ltd. Contested Gillingham Feb 1974. Leader, Gillingham Borough Council; former Kent county cllr. Ed Queen Elizabeth GS, Faversham; Medway Coll of Tech.

| GLASGOW ANNIESLAND | | 29.1% change | | | Lab win | | |
|---|---|---|---|---|---|---|---|
| Electorate % Turnout | | 52,955 | 64.0% | **1997** | 53,667 | 70.2% | **1992** |
| **+Dewar, D C** | **Lab** | **20,951** | **61.8%** | **+8.8%** | **20,000** | **53.1%** | **Lab** |
| Wilson, Dr W | SNP | 5,797 | 17.1% | +0.1% | 6,411 | 17.0% | SNP |
| Brocklehurst, A | C | 3,881 | 11.5% | -4.2% | 5,895 | 15.6% | C |
| McGinty, C | LD | 2,453 | 7.2% | -6.5% | 5,166 | 13.7% | LD |
| Majid, A | ProLife | 374 | 1.1% | | 213 | 0.6% | Other |
| Bonnar, W | SSA | 229 | 0.7% | | | | |
| Milligan, A | UK Ind | 86 | 0.3% | | | | |
| McKay, Ms G | Ref | 84 | 0.2% | | | | |
| Pringle, T | NLP | 24 | 0.1% | | | | |
| **SNP to Lab notional swing 4.3%** | | **33,879** | | **Lab maj 15,154** | **37,685** | | **Lab maj 13,589** |
| | | | | 44.7% | | | 36.1% |

**DONALD DEWAR**, b Aug 21, 1937. Became Scottish Secretary, May 3, 1997. Lab Chief Whip 1995-97. MP for Glasgow Garscadden 1978-97, and Aberdeen S 1966-70; contested that seat 1964 and 1970. In Shadow Cabinet 1984-97. Lab chief whip 1995-97; Chief Lab spokesman on social security 1992-95; on Scotland 1983-92. Solicitor; consultant (unpaid) to Ross Harper & Murphy (solicitors; was partner in firm). Weekly columnist for *Scottish Mirror*. Ed Glasgow Acad; Glasgow Univ (pres of union 1961-62).

**WILLIAM WILSON**, b Dec 11, 1963. Ecologist. Ed Shawlands Acad; Glasgow Univ; Aberdeen Univ; Queen's Univ, Belfast.
**ANDREW BROCKLEHURST,** b Dec 18, 1964. Business development manager. Ed Merchiston Castle School, Edinburgh; Glasgow Univ; Massachusetts Univ.
**CHRISTOPHER McGINTY,** b May 8, 1961. Investment manager. Contested Eltham 1992. Ed Bedford School; Goldsmith's Coll, London.

| GLASGOW BAILLIESTON | | 93.8% change | | | Lab win | | |
|---|---|---|---|---|---|---|---|
| Electorate % Turnout | | 51,152 | 62.3% | **1997** | 52,207 | 66.7% | **1992** |
| **+Wray, J** | **Lab** | **20,925** | **65.7%** | **+2.5%** | **22,030** | **63.2%** | **Lab** |
| Thomson, Mrs P | SNP | 6,085 | 19.1% | -3.5% | 7,865 | 22.6% | SNP |
| Kelly, M | C | 2,468 | 7.7% | -2.1% | 3,448 | 9.9% | C |
| Rainger, Ms S | LD | 1,217 | 3.8% | -0.5% | 1,505 | 4.3% | LD |
| McVicar, J | SSA | 970 | 3.0% | | | | |
| McClafferty, J | Ref | 188 | 0.6% | | | | |
| **SNP to Lab notional swing 3.0%** | | **31,853** | | **Lab maj 14,840** | **34,848** | | **Lab maj 14,165** |
| | | | | 46.6% | | | 40.7% |

**JAMES WRAY**, b April 28, 1938. Ex-heavy goods vehicle driver. MP for Glasgow Provan 1987-97. Former vice-convener, Scottish group of Lab MPs; former vice-chair, all-party anti-fluoridation cttee. Strathclyde regional cllr 1976- ; led Gorbals rent strike and anti-dampness campaign. Pres, Scottish Fed of the Blind, 1987 (vice-pres, 1986); Gorbals Utd FC; St Enoch's Drug Centre; Scottish Ex-Boxers' Assoc. Ed St Bonaventures, Glasgow.

**PATSY THOMSON**, b March 18, 1947. Asst district officer (preventative services), Glasgow social work dept. Member, Scottish CND exec; Unison. Ed Eastwood Sec; Glasgow Univ.
**MALCOLM KELLY**, b Nov 6, 1967. Accounts and clerical asst, Paisley Univ. Member, Inst of Advanced Motorists. Ed Paisley GS; Central Coll of Commerce, Glasgow.

| GLASGOW CATHCART | | 45.6% change | | | Lab win | | |
|---|---|---|---|---|---|---|---|
| Electorate % Turnout | | 49,312 | 69.2% | **1997** | 51,940 | 73.0% | **1992** |
| **+Maxton, J** | **Lab** | **19,158** | **56.2%** | **+6.8%** | **18,719** | **49.3%** | **Lab** |
| Whitehead, Ms M | SNP | 6,913 | 20.3% | +1.2% | 8,167 | 21.5% | C |
| Muir, A | C | 4,248 | 12.5% | -9.1% | 7,244 | 19.1% | SNP |
| Dick, G C | LD | 2,302 | 6.7% | -0.5% | 2,732 | 7.2% | LD |
| Indyk, Ms Z | ProLife | 687 | 2.0% | | 1,072 | 2.8% | Grn |
| Stevenson, R | SSA | 458 | 1.3% | | | | |
| Haldane, S | Ref | 344 | 1.0% | | | | |
| **SNP to Lab notional swing 2.8%** | | **34,110** | | **Lab maj 12,245** | **37,934** | | **Lab maj 10,552** |
| | | | | 35.9% | | | 27.8% |

**JOHN MAXTON**, b May 5, 1936. Lecturer. Gained seat for Lab 1979. Lab spokesman on Scotland 1985-92; Scottish and Treasury whip 1984-85. Member, national heritage select cttee, 1992- ; Scottish affairs select cttee 1979-82; Commons chairmen's panel; PAC 1983-85. Chair, PLP national heritage cttee. Dir (unpaid), Glasgow International Jazz Festival. Member, EIS; MSF. Ed Lord William's GS, Thame; University Coll, Oxford.

**MAIRE WHITEHEAD**, b Dec 15, 1940. Head teacher. Contested Hamilton 1983. Ed Notre Dame HS; St Andrews Coll of Ed.
**ALISTAIR MUIR**, b Oct 21, 1957. Broadcaster; chief exec of Clydebank Economic Development Co Ltd. Ed John Neilson School, Paisley; Paisley Univ.
**CALLAN DICK**, b Dec 21, 1957. Computer manager. Contested this seat 1992. Ed Alan Glens, Glasgow; Glasgow Univ.

| GLASGOW GOVAN | | 123.1% change | | | | | Lab win |
|---|---|---|---|---|---|---|---|
| Electorate % Turnout | | 49,836 | 64.7% | **1997** | 50,351 | 72.3% | **1992** |
| **Sarwar, M** | **Lab** | **14,216** | **44.1%** | **+1.0%** | **15,665** | **43.0%** | **Lab** |
| Sturgeon, Ms N | SNP | 11,302 | 35.1% | +7.4% | 10,056 | 27.6% | SNP |
| Thomas, W | C | 2,839 | 8.8% | -10.9% | 7,165 | 19.7% | C |
| Stewart, R | LD | 1,915 | 5.9% | +0.4% | 2,033 | 5.6% | LD |
| McCombes, A | SSA | 755 | 2.3% | | 1,475 | 4.1% | Grn |
| Paton, P | SLU | 325 | 1.0% | | | | |
| Badar, I | SLI | 319 | 1.0% | | | | |
| Abbasi, Z | SCU | 221 | 0.7% | | | | |
| MacDonald, K | Ref | 201 | 0.6% | | | | |
| White, J | BNP | 149 | 0.5% | | | | |
| **Lab to SNP notional swing 3.2%** | | **32,242** | **Lab maj 2,914** | | **36,394** | **Lab maj 5,609** | |
| | | | 9.0% | | | 15.4% | |

**MOHAMMED SARWAR,** b Aug 18, 1952. Company director. Glasgow district cllr 1992-96; Glasgow city cllr 1995- . Chair, Islamic Centre and Glasgow Central Mosque, 1985-88. Ed Faisalabad Univ, Pakistan.
**NICOLA STURGEON,** b July 19, 1970. Solicitor. Contested Glasgow Shettleston 1992. Ed Greenwood Acad, Irvine; Glasgow Univ.
**WILLIAM THOMAS,** b Feb 22, 1945. Full-time carer and fundraiser. Ed Woodside Sec, Glasgow; Barmulloch Coll.
**BOB STEWART,** b Feb 6, 1938. Market researcher. Ed Hutcheson's GS; Glasgow Univ.

| GLASGOW KELVIN | | 35.2% change | | | | | Lab win |
|---|---|---|---|---|---|---|---|
| Electorate % Turnout | | 57,438 | 56.9% | **1997** | 53,680 | 67.5% | **1992** |
| **+Galloway, G** | **Lab** | **16,643** | **51.0%** | **+4.1%** | **16,971** | **46.9%** | **Lab** |
| White, Ms S | SNP | 6,978 | 21.4% | +2.1% | 6,982 | 19.3% | SNP |
| Buchanan, Ms E | LD | 4,629 | 14.2% | -4.7% | 6,848 | 18.9% | LD |
| McPhie, D | C | 3,539 | 10.8% | -2.3% | 4,765 | 13.2% | C |
| Green, A | SSA | 386 | 1.2% | | 649 | 1.8% | Other |
| Grigor, R | Ref | 282 | 0.9% | | | | |
| Vanni, V | SPGB | 102 | 0.3% | | | | |
| Stidolph, G | NLP | 95 | 0.3% | | | | |
| **SNP to Lab notional swing 1.0%** | | **32,654** | **Lab maj 9,665** | | **36,215** | **Lab maj 9,989** | |
| | | | 29.6% | | | 27.6% | |

**GEORGE GALLOWAY,** b Aug 16, 1954. MP for Glasgow Hillhead 1987-97. Ex-joint vice-chair, PLP foreign affairs cttee. Journalist. Gen sec, War on Want 1983-87. Ed Harris Acad, Dundee.
**SANDRA WHITE,** b Aug 17, 1951. Contested Glasgow Hillhead 1992. Ed Garthamlock Sec; Cardonald Coll.
**ELSPETH BUCHANAN,** b June 18, 1927. Lecturer/curator. Contested Paisley S 1983 and Clydesdale 1992. Ed Glasgow HS for Girls; Glasgow Univ; Moray House Coll of Ed.
**DUNCAN McPHIE,** b June 7, 1969. Advocate. Ed Glasgow Acad; Glasgow Univ; LSE.

| GLASGOW MARYHILL | | 16.7% change | | | | | Lab win |
|---|---|---|---|---|---|---|---|
| Electorate % Turnout | | 52,523 | 56.6% | **1997** | 52,291 | 64.3% | **1992** |
| **+Fyfe, Ms M** | **Lab** | **19,301** | **64.9%** | **+2.3%** | **21,042** | **62.6%** | **Lab** |
| Wailes, J | SNP | 5,037 | 16.9% | -2.5% | 6,530 | 19.4% | SNP |
| Attwooll, Ms E | LD | 2,119 | 7.1% | +0.5% | 3,241 | 9.6% | C |
| Baldwin, S | C | 1,747 | 5.9% | -3.8% | 2,238 | 6.7% | LD |
| Blair, Ms L | NLP | 651 | 2.2% | +2.0% | 488 | 1.5% | Grn |
| Baker, Ms M | SSA | 409 | 1.4% | | 72 | 0.2% | NLP |
| Hanif, J | ProLife | 344 | 1.2% | | | | |
| Paterson, R | Ref | 77 | 0.3% | | | | |
| Johnstone, S | SEP | 36 | 0.1% | | | | |
| **SNP to Lab notional swing 2.4%** | | **29,721** | **Lab maj 14,264** | | **33,611** | **Lab maj 14,512** | |
| | | | 48.0% | | | 43.2% | |

**MARIA FYFE,** b Nov 25, 1938. Lecturer. Elected 1987. Spokeswoman on Scotland, 1992-95; women's issues 1988-91. Convener, Scottish group of Lab MPs, 1991-92. Ed Notre Dame HS, Glasgow; Strathclyde Univ.
**JOHN WAILES,** b March 2, 1973. Sports writer. Ed St Patrick's HS, Dumbarton; Napier and South Bank Univs.
**ELSPETH ATTWOOLL,** b Feb 1, 1943. Lecturer. Contested this seat Oct 1974, 1979, 1983.Ed Tiffin Girls' School; Queen's, Dundee.

| GLASGOW POLLOK | | 99.7% change | | | | | Lab win |
|---|---|---|---|---|---|---|---|
| Electorate % Turnout | | 49,284 | 66.6% | **1997** | 52,678 | 72.1% | **1992** |
| +Davidson, I | Lab Co-op | **19,653** | **59.9%** | +10.1% | **18,945** | **49.9%** | Lab Co-op |
| Logan, D | SNP | 5,862 | 17.9% | -7.1% | 9,492 | 25.0% | SNP |
| Sheridan, T | SSA | 3,639 | 11.1% | | 4,811 | 12.7% | SML |
| Hamilton, E | C | 1,979 | 6.0% | -2.1% | 3,107 | 8.2% | C |
| Jago, D | LD | 1,137 | 3.5% | -0.9% | 1,648 | 4.3% | LD |
| Gott, Ms M | ProLife | 380 | 1.2% | | | | |
| Haldane, D | Ref | 152 | 0.5% | | | | |
| SNP to Lab notional swing 8.6% | | 32,802 | Lab Co-op maj 13,791 | | 38,003 | Lab Co-op maj 9,453 | |
| | | | 42.0% | | | 24.9% | |

**IAN DAVIDSON,** b Sept 8, 1950. MP for Glasgow Govan 1992-97. Joint vice-chair, PLP defence cttee; all-party warm homes group. Strathclyde regional cllr 1978-92 (chair, ed cttee, 1986-92); convener, Cosla ed cttee and negotiating cttee on teachers' salaries. With community service volunteers 1985-92; PA and researcher to Janey Buchan, MEP, 1978-85. Ed Jedburgh GS; Galashiels Acad; Edinburgh Univ; Jordanhill Coll.

**DAVID LOGAN,** b July 30, 1953. Team leader, poverty alliance mobile resource team. Ed Whitehill Secondary; Langside Coll.
**TOMMY SHERIDAN,** b 1964. Anti-poll tax campaigner. Contested this seat 1992 (from prison) and Glasgow 1994 Euro elections. Scottish Militant Lab dist cllr. Ed Stirling Univ.
**EDWIN HAMILTON,** b March 9, 1961. Chartered accountant, Energy Group plc. Ed Wymondham Coll; UMIST.

| GLASGOW RUTHERGLEN | | 15.8% change | | | | | Lab win |
|---|---|---|---|---|---|---|---|
| Electorate % Turnout | | 50,646 | 70.1% | **1997** | 52,265 | 74.3% | **1992** |
| +McAvoy, T | Lab Co-op | **20,430** | **57.5%** | +4.1% | **20,742** | **53.4%** | Lab Co-op |
| Gray, I | SNP | 5,423 | 15.3% | -0.3% | 7,443 | 19.2% | C |
| Brown, R | LD | 5,167 | 14.5% | +2.9% | 6,052 | 15.6% | SNP |
| Campbell Bannerman, D | C | 3,288 | 9.3% | -9.9% | 4,529 | 11.7% | LD |
| Easton, G | Ind Lab | 812 | 2.3% | | 92 | 0.2% | Int Comm |
| Kane, Ms R | SSA | 251 | 0.7% | | | | |
| Kerr, Ms J | Ref | 150 | 0.4% | | | | |
| SNP to Lab notional swing 2.2% | | 35,521 | Lab Co-op maj 15,007 | | 38,858 | Lab Co-op maj 13,299 | |
| | | | 42.2% | | | 34.2% | |

**TOMMY McAVOY,** b Dec 14, 1943. Became gvt whip, May 7, 1997. Labour whip, 1996-97 and 1990-93. Engineering storeman. Elected 1987. Strathclyde regional cllr 1982-87. Member, AEU. Ed St Columbkilles junior secondary school.
**IAIN GRAY,** b Aug 23, 1947. Teacher. Contested Clydesdale 1992. Clydesdale district cllr 1988- . Ed Hutcheson's GS; Glasgow Univ; Jordanhill Coll of Ed.

**ROBERT BROWN,** b Dec 25, 1947. Solicitor. Contested Rutherglen Oct 1974, 1979; this seat 1983; Glasgow city cllr. Ed The Gordon Schools, Huntly; Aberdeen Univ.
**DAVID CAMPBELL BANNERMAN,** b May 28, 1960. Company director.Special adviser to Sir Patrick Mayhew, when N Ireland sec. Worked in C research dept for 1994 Euro elections campaign. Ed Bryanston School; Edinburgh Univ; Pennsylvania Univ.

| GLASGOW SHETTLESTON | | 99.9% change | | | | | Lab win |
|---|---|---|---|---|---|---|---|
| Electorate % Turnout | | 47,990 | 55.9% | **1997** | 49,358 | 64.2% | **1992** |
| +Marshall, D | Lab | **19,616** | **73.2%** | +7.7% | **20,767** | **65.5%** | Lab |
| Hanif, H | SNP | 3,748 | 14.0% | -2.2% | 5,123 | 16.2% | SNP |
| Simpson, C | C | 1,484 | 5.5% | -6.7% | 3,876 | 12.2% | C |
| Hiles, Ms K | LD | 1,061 | 4.0% | -2.2% | 1,939 | 6.1% | LD |
| McVicar, Ms C | SSA | 482 | 1.8% | | | | |
| Currie, R | BNP | 191 | 0.7% | | | | |
| Montguire, T | Ref | 151 | 0.6% | | | | |
| Graham, J | WRP | 80 | 0.3% | | | | |
| SNP to Lab notional swing 4.9% | | 26,813 | Lab maj 15,868 | | 31,705 | Lab maj 15,644 | |
| | | | 59.2% | | | 49.3% | |

**DAVID MARSHALL,** b May 7, 1941. Elected 1979. Member, transport select cttee 1985-92, chair 1987-92; Scottish affairs select cttee 1992-97 and 1981-83; unopposed Bills panel 1992- . Sec and treas, Scottish Lab MPs, 1981- ; chair (1987- ) and joint vice-chair (1983-87), PLP transport cttee. Glasgow corp member 1972-75, Strathclyde regional cllr 1974-79. Joint vice-chair (1994- ) and member (1993- ), exec cttee, British group, IPU. Ex-transport

worker and shop steward. Ed Larbert HS; Denny HS; Falkirk HS; and Woodside Sen Secondary.
**HUMAYUN HANIF,** b Jan 31, 1958. Civil engineer. Founder, Scots Asians for Independence; member, SNP nat council. Ed Woodside Secondary; Glasgow Univ; Langside Coll.
**COLIN SIMPSON,** b Aug 9, 1968. Formerly worked for Clydesdale Bank; now studying politics. Member, Hamilton C assoc exec. Ed Banff Acad; Banff & Buchan Coll of FE; City of London Poly.

| GLASGOW SPRINGBURN | | 44.3% change | | | Lab win | | |
|---|---|---|---|---|---|---|---|
| Electorate % Turnout | | 53,473 | 59.1% | 1997 | 54,822 | 65.6% | 1992 |
| +Martin, M | Lab | 22,534 | 71.4% | +6.4% | 23,347 | 64.9% | Lab |
| Brady, J | SNP | 5,208 | 16.5% | -3.4% | 7,150 | 19.9% | SNP |
| Holdsworth, M | C | 1,893 | 6.0% | -4.9% | 3,909 | 10.9% | C |
| Alexander, J | LD | 1,349 | 4.3% | -0.1% | 1,559 | 4.3% | LD |
| Lawson, J | SSA | 407 | 1.3% | | | | |
| Keating, A | Ref | 186 | 0.6% | | | | |
| SNP to Lab notional swing 4.9% | | 31,577 | Lab maj 17,326 | | 35,965 | Lab maj 16,197 | |
| | | | 54.9% | | | 45.0% | |

**MICHAEL MARTIN,** b July 3, 1945. Appointed a Dep Speaker and dep chair, Ways and Means, May 1997. Elected 1979. Former shop steward and sheet metal worker. PPS to Denis Healey, when Dep Leader of Lab Party, 1981-83. Chair, Commons admin cttee, 1992-97; member, chairmen's panel, 1987-97; Commons finance and services cttee 1992- ; services cttee 1987-91. Joint vice-chair, PLP N Ireland cttee, 1987-88. Member, Glasgow Corp, 1973-74; Glasgow district cllr 1974-79. Fellow, Industry and Parliament Trust. Ed St Patrick's School, Glasgow.

**JOHN BRADY,** b March 10, 1965. Newspaper ad sales exec. Vice-convener, SNP Kelvin West branch. Ed Craigmount HS, Edinburgh; Glasgow Univ.

**MARK HOLDSWORTH,** b April 26, 1971. Specialist in Eastern Europe equity markets. Former research assistant to Tim Rathbone, MP. Pres, Scottish YCs, 1993-94. Ed Edinburgh Univ; Pennsylvania Univ.

| GLOUCESTER | | 6.1% change | | | Lab win | | |
|---|---|---|---|---|---|---|---|
| Electorate % Turnout | | 78,682 | 73.6% | 1997 | 76,487 | 81.2% | 1992 |
| Kingham, Ms T | Lab | 28,943 | 50.0% | +13.2% | 28,274 | 45.5% | C |
| +French, D | C | 20,684 | 35.7% | -9.8% | 22,867 | 36.8% | Lab |
| Munisamy, P | LD | 6,069 | 10.5% | -7.2% | 10,961 | 17.6% | LD |
| Reid, A | Ref | 1,482 | 2.6% | | | | |
| Harris, A | UK Ind | 455 | 0.8% | | | | |
| Hamilton, Ms M | NLP | 281 | 0.5% | | | | |
| C to Lab notional swing 11.5% | | 57,914 | Lab maj 8,259 | | 62,102 | C maj 5,407 | |
| | | | 14.3% | | | 8.7% | |

**TESS KINGHAM,** b May 4, 1963. Charity official. Contested Cotswolds in 1994 Euro elections. Ed Dartford GS for Girls; Royal Holloway and Bedford New Coll, London; East Anglia Univ.

**DOUGLAS FRENCH,** b March 20, 1944. Non-practising barrister. Elected 1987; contested Sheffield Attercliffe 1979. PPS to John Gummer when Environment Sec; PPS to Lynda Chalker, Overseas Aid Min, 1988-90. Special adviser to Sir Geoffrey Howe, Chancellor of the Exchequer, 1981-83, and personal assistant to him when Shadow Chancellor, 1976-79. Dir (unpaid), P.W. Merkle Ltd; chair, Westminster and City Programmes Ltd, seminar organisers. Adviser on pensions policy to Alexander Clay and partners, consulting actuaries and pension consultants. Ed Glyn GS, Epsom; St Catharine's Coll, Cambridge; Inns of Court School of Law.

**PETER MUNISAMY,** b Dec 9, 1942. Retired nurse tutor. Cheltenham city cllr 1995- . Ed OU.

| GORDON | | 64.1% change | | | LD win | | |
|---|---|---|---|---|---|---|---|
| Electorate % Turnout | | 58,767 | 71.9% | 1997 | 56,716 | 72.0% | 1992 |
| +Bruce, M | LD | 17,999 | 42.6% | +15.4% | 19,596 | 48.0% | C |
| Porter, J | C | 11,002 | 26.0% | -21.9% | 11,110 | 27.2% | LD |
| Lochhead, R | SNP | 8,435 | 20.0% | +1.4% | 7,593 | 18.6% | SNP |
| Kirkhill, Ms L | Lab | 4,350 | 10.3% | +4.0% | 2,561 | 6.3% | Lab |
| Pidcock, F | Ref | 459 | 1.1% | | | | |
| C to LD notional swing 18.7% | | 42,245 | LD maj 6,997 | | 40,860 | C maj 8,486 | |
| | | | 16.6% | | | 20.8% | |

**MALCOLM BRUCE,** b Nov 17, 1944. Barrister. Elected for L/All 1983, becoming LD MP 1988; contested W Aberdeenshire 1979; N Angus and Mearns Oct 1974. Became party spokesman on Treasury and Civil Service in 1993. Leader, Scottish LDs, 1988-92; dep chair, Scottish Lib Party, 1975-84. Chief LD spokesman on Scotland, 1990-93; on environment; Lib and then LD spokesman on trade and industry, 1987-88; Lib spokesman on energy 1985-87; on Scotland 1983-85. Member, select cttee on Treasury and Civil Service, 1994-97; trade and industry 1992-94 and 1987-90. Ed Wrekin Coll, Shropshire; St Andrews and Strathclyde Univs.

**JOHN PORTER,** b Dec 15, 1931. Corporate finance consultant. Contested Gordon 1992. Aberdeen city cllr, Grampian regional cllr. Ed Aberdeen Central Senior School.

**RICHARD LOCHHEAD,** b May 24, 1969. SNP constituency office manager to Alex Salmond. Ed Williamwood HS, Clarkston; Stirling Univ.

**LINDSEY KIRKHILL,** b Jan 11, 1950. Lecturer in social work. Ed East London Univ; West London Inst; Dundee Univ.

| GOSPORT | | | | | **C hold** | | |
|---|---|---|---|---|---|---|---|
| Electorate % Turnout | | 68,830 | 70.3% | **1997** | 69,638 | 76.8% | **1992** |
| *Viggers, P | C | 21,085 | 43.6% | -14.5% | 31,094 | 58.1% | C |
| Gray, I | Lab | 14,827 | 30.7% | +17.1% | 14,776 | 27.6% | LD |
| Hogg, S | LD | 9,479 | 19.6% | -8.0% | 7,275 | 13.6% | Lab |
| Blowers, A | Ref | 2,538 | 5.2% | | 332 | 0.6% | Pensioners |
| Ettie, P | Ind | 426 | 0.9% | | | | |
| **C to Lab swing 15.8%** | | **48,355** | | **C maj 6,258** | **53,477** | | **C maj 16,318** |
| | | | | 12.9% | | | 30.5% |

**PETER VIGGERS,** b March 13, 1938. Solicitor and Lloyd's underwriter. Elected Feb 1974. Junior N Ireland Min 1986-89; PPS to Solicitor-General 1979-83, and to Chief Sec to Treasury 1983-86. Member, select cttees on defence, 1992-97, and members' interests 1991-93. Joint sec, C backbench defence cttee, 1991- . Chair, Tracer Petroleum Corp; chair, trustees of Corporation of Lloyd's pension fund. Delegate, North Atlantic Assembly, 1992- and 1980-86. Chair, Campaign for Defence and Multilateral Disarmament, 1984-86. Member, management cttee, RNLI. Dir, Warrior Preservation Trust. Ed Portsmouth GS; Trinity Hall, Cambridge.

**IVAN GRAY,** b Oct 26, 1953. Univ lecturer in public sector management. Ed Univ Coll, Durham; Nottingham and Portsmouth Univs.

**STEVE HOGG,** b April 20, 1946. College lecturer. Ex-Avon county cllr and Bath city cllr. Ed Apsley GS, Bath.

| GOWER | | | | | **Lab hold** | | |
|---|---|---|---|---|---|---|---|
| Electorate % Turnout | | 57,691 | 75.1% | **1997** | 57,231 | 81.9% | **1992** |
| Caton, M | Lab | 23,313 | 53.8% | +3.7% | 23,485 | 50.1% | Lab |
| Cairns, A | C | 10,306 | 23.8% | -11.3% | 16,437 | 35.1% | C |
| Evans, H | LD | 5,624 | 13.0% | +3.0% | 4,655 | 9.9% | LD |
| Williams, E | PC | 2,226 | 5.1% | +1.6% | 1,639 | 3.5% | PC |
| Lewis, R | Ref | 1,745 | 4.0% | | 448 | 1.0% | Grn |
| Popham, A | FP | 122 | 0.3% | | 114 | 0.2% | Loony G |
| | | | | | 74 | 0.2% | NLP |
| **C to Lab swing 7.5%** | | **43,336** | | **Lab maj 13,007** | **46,852** | | **Lab maj 7,048** |
| | | | | 30.0% | | | 15.0% |

**MARTIN CATON,** b June 15, 1951. Political assistant/researcher to David Morris, MEP for South Wales West; former scientific officer, Welsh Plant Breeding Station. Ex-Swansea city cllr; now Swansea UA cllr. Ed Newport GS, Essex; Norfolk School of Agriculture; Aberystwyth Coll of FE.

**ALUN CAIRNS,** b July 30, 1970. Business development consultant, Lloyds Bank. Vice-chair, Wales Area YCs, 1995- . Ed Ysgol Gyfun Ddwyieithog, Ystalyfera.

**HOWARD EVANS,** b Aug 6, 1966. Teacher. Reynoldston community cllr. Ed Ounsdale HS; Wulfrun Coll, Wolverhampton; Harper Adams Ag Coll; West of England Univ.

**ELWYN WILLIAMS.** Runs insurance company. Ex-pres, Carmarthen Young Farmers.

| GRANTHAM & STAMFORD | | 91.1% change | | | | | **C win** |
|---|---|---|---|---|---|---|---|
| Electorate % Turnout | | 72,310 | 73.3% | **1997** | 67,426 | 80.1% | **1992** |
| +Davies, J Q | C | 22,672 | 42.8% | -15.1% | 31,263 | 57.9% | C |
| Denning, P | Lab | 19,980 | 37.7% | +11.6% | 14,105 | 26.1% | Lab |
| Sellick, J | LD | 6,612 | 12.5% | -3.6% | 8,663 | 16.0% | LD |
| Swain, Ms M | Ref | 2,721 | 5.1% | | | | |
| Charlesworth, M | UK Ind | 556 | 1.0% | | | | |
| Clark, Ms R | ProLife | 314 | 0.6% | | | | |
| Harper, I | NLP | 115 | 0.2% | | | | |
| **C to Lab notional swing 13.3%** | | **52,970** | | **C maj 2,692** | **54,031** | | **C maj 17,158** |
| | | | | 5.1% | | | 31.8% |

**QUENTIN DAVIES,** b May 29, 1944. MP for Stamford and Spalding 1987-97; contested Birmingham Ladywood by-election 1977. Member, select cttees on standards and privileges, 1995-97; Treasury 1992-97. Joint sec, C trade and industry cttee, 1991- ; joint vice-chair, C trade and industry deregulation sub-cttee, 1994- . Sec, all-party British-German group, 1993- . Vice-chair, European Movement. Member of council, Action Centre for Europe. Adviser to NatWest Securities 1993- ; consultant to Chartered Inst of Taxation 1993- . Consultant to Morgan Grenfell and Co Ltd, merchant bankers, 1987-93; dir 1981-87; director-general and pres, Morgan Grenfell, France SA, 1978-81. Member, exec cttee, council for economic policy research; cttee for tax reform, Inst for Fiscal Studies. Liveryman, Goldsmiths' Co; Freeman, City of London. Diplomat 1967-74. Ed Leighton Park; Gonville and Caius Coll, Cambridge; Harvard.

**PETER DENNING,** b Feb 14, 1967. Area manager for Mencap; former electronics engineer. Ed Fairfield GS.

**JOHN SELLICK,** b Oct 28, 1943. Businessman. Contested Lindsey 1983 and 1987 and Louth 1974 and 1979. Ed Oakham School.

## GRAVESHAM — 0.9% change — Lab win

| Electorate % Turnout | | 69,234 | 76.9% | 1997 | 70,514 | 83.0% | 1992 |
|---|---|---|---|---|---|---|---|
| Pond, C | Lab | 26,460 | 49.7% | +9.3% | 29,031 | 49.6% | C |
| +Arnold, J | C | 20,681 | 38.8% | -10.8% | 23,663 | 40.4% | Lab |
| Canet, Dr M | LD | 4,128 | 7.8% | -1.1% | 5,207 | 8.9% | LD |
| Curtis, Mrs P | Ref | 1,441 | 2.7% | | 273 | 0.5% | Ind |
| Leyshon, A | Ind | 414 | 0.8% | +0.3% | 187 | 0.3% | ILP |
| Palmer, D | NLP | 129 | 0.2% | | 174 | 0.3% | Socialist |
| C to Lab notional swing 10.0% | | 53,253 | | Lab maj 5,779 10.9% | 58,535 | | C maj 5,368 9.2% |

**CHRIS POND,** b Sept 25, 1952. Director, Low Pay Unit. Contested Welwyn Hatfield 1987. Ed Michenden School, Southgate; Sussex Univ. Married to Carole Tongue, Lab MEP for London East.

**JACQUES ARNOLD,** b Aug 27, 1947. Elected 1987; contested Coventry SE 1983. PPS to Home Office Mins of State, 1993-95; to Min of State for Environment and Countryside 1992-93. Member, select cttees on Treasury, 1997; foreign and Commonwealth affairs, 1990-92. Chair, all-party Brazilian parly group, 1992-97; Portuguese group; joint vice-chair, all-party building societies group, 1996-97; sec, Latin American group, 1987-97; sec/treas, Scout Assoc group, 1987-97; joint sec, maritime group. Member,

exec cttee, British group, IPU, 1991-97. Northamptonshire county cllr 1981-85. Consultant to Norwich and Peterborough Building Society. Dir of American Express Europe Ltd, 1985-87; asst trade finance dir, Midland Bank plc, 1984-85; regional director, Thomas Cook Group, 1978-84; asst group rep, Midland Bank, São Paulo, 1976-78. Trustee, Environment Foundation, 1989- . Ed Colegio Rio Branco, São Paulo, Brazil; by correspondence, Wolsey Hall, Oxford; LSE.

**MERILYN CANET,** b April 15, 1941. Dental surgeon. Sevenoaks district cllr. Member, Charter 88; 300 Group; Amnesty. Ed Walthamstow Hall, Sevenoaks; Guy's Hospital; London Univ.

## GREAT GRIMSBY — Lab hold

| Electorate % Turnout | | 65,043 | 66.3% | 1997 | 67,427 | 75.3% | 1992 |
|---|---|---|---|---|---|---|---|
| *Mitchell, A | Lab | 25,765 | 59.8% | +8.8% | 25,897 | 51.0% | Lab |
| Godson, D | C | 9,521 | 22.1% | -14.1% | 18,391 | 36.2% | C |
| De Freitas, A | LD | 7,810 | 18.1% | +5.4% | 6,475 | 12.8% | LD |
| C to Lab swing 11.5% | | 43,096 | | Lab maj 16,244 37.7% | 50,763 | | Lab maj 7,506 14.8% |

**AUSTIN MITCHELL,** b Sept 19, 1934. Elected for this seat 1983; MP for Grimsby 1977-83. Lab spokesman on trade and industry 1987-89, when he was dismissed by Neil Kinnock after becoming co-presenter of current affairs programme, *Target,* on BSkyB. Joint vice-chair, all-party media parly group; joint sec, photography group; joint chair, British Iceland group. Vice-chair, E Midlands group of Lab MPs, 1986-90. Associate editor, *House Magazine.* Journalist, Yorkshire Television, 1969-71 and 1973-77; presenter, BBC current affairs group, 1972-73. Fellow, Ind and Parly Trust. Lecturer in history, Univ of Otago, Dunedin, New Zealand, 1959-63; senior lecturer in politics, Univ of Canterbury, Christchurch, NZ, 1963-67. Member, NUJ. Ed Woodbottom Council School; Bingley GS; Manchester Univ; Nuffield Coll, Oxford.

**DEAN GODSON,** b Aug 26, 1962. Chief leader writer/columnist, *The Daily Telegraph;* librarian to Sir James Goldsmith, 1990-92; research fellow, Inst for European Defence and Strategic Studies. Member, Bow Group; International Inst Strategic Studies; Royal Inst of International Affairs. Ed St Paul's; Gonville and Caius Coll, Cambridge.

**ANDREW DE FREITAS,** b March 6, 1945. Internal auditor in shipping industry. Contested Grimsby 1977 by-election. NE Lincs unitary authority cllr since 1995 (dep leader LD group); previously Humberside and Grimsby cllr. Member, Friends of the Earth. Ed St Mary's RC School, Georgetown, British Guyana.

## GREAT YARMOUTH — Lab gain

| Electorate % Turnout | | 68,625 | 71.2% | 1997 | 68,263 | 77.9% | 1992 |
|---|---|---|---|---|---|---|---|
| Wright, T | Lab | 26,084 | 53.4% | +15.4% | 25,505 | 47.9% | C |
| *Carttiss, M | C | 17,416 | 35.6% | -12.3% | 20,196 | 38.0% | Lab |
| Wood, D | LD | 5,381 | 11.0% | -2.6% | 7,225 | 13.6% | LD |
| | | | | | 284 | 0.5% | NLP |
| C to Lab swing 13.9% | | 48,881 | | Lab maj 8,668 17.7% | 53,210 | | C maj 5,309 10.0% |

**TONY WRIGHT,** b Aug 12, 1954. Director of Great Yarmouth tourist authority. Chair, Great Yarmouth Marketing Initiative. Great Yarmouth district cllr (leader).

**MICHAEL CARTTISS,** b March 11, 1938. Elected for this seat 1983. Norfolk county cllr 1966-85; Great Yarmouth borough cllr 1973-82 (leader 1980-82); East Anglian RHA, 1981-85. Chair, Norfolk

Museums Service, 1981-85. Ed Great Yarmouth Tech HS; Goldsmith's Coll, London; LSE.

**DEREK WOOD,** b April 11, 1937. Company director. Contested Ealing N 1964, Epping Forest Feb and Oct 1974. Norwich city cllr 1995- ; Three Rivers district cllr 1984-87. Ed Preston Manor County GS, Wembley; London Univ.

| GREENOCK & INVERCLYDE | | 54.3% change | | | | Lab win |
|---|---|---|---|---|---|---|
| Electorate % Turnout | | 48,818 | 71.1% | **1997** | 51,442 | 74.5% | **1992** |
| +Godman, Dr N A | Lab | **19,480** | 56.2% | +8.4% | 18,319 | 47.8% | Lab |
| Goodall, B | SNP | 6,440 | 18.6% | +1.3% | 8,081 | 21.1% | C |
| Ackland, R | LD | 4,791 | 13.8% | -0.1% | 6,621 | 17.3% | SNP |
| Swire, H | C | 3,976 | 11.5% | -9.6% | 5,324 | 13.9% | LD |
| SNP to Lab notional swing 3.5% | | 34,687 | Lab maj 13,040 | | 38,345 | Lab maj 10,238 | |
| | | | 37.6% | | | 26.7% | |

**NORMAN GODMAN**, b April 19, 1938. Ex-teacher and shipwright. MP for Greenock and Port Glasgow 1983-97; contested Aberdeen S 1979. Ex-Lab spokesman on agriculture and rural affairs, 1987-90. Member, N Ireland select cttee, 1996- ; Euro legislation 1990-92; Scottish affairs 1983-87. Ex-chair, Scottish group of Lab MPs; joint vice-chair, PLP foreign affairs cttee, 1991- ; chair, all-party Tibet parly group. Former teacher in Scottish further and higher education. Ed Westbourne Street Boys' School, Hull; Hull and Heriot-Watt Univs.

**BRIAN GOODALL**, b March 12, 1971. Horticultural trainer; planning convener, Pollokshields comm council. Ed Crookston Castle Secondary, Glasgow; Scottish Agricultural Coll.
**ROD ACKLAND**, b April 8, 1945. Computer analyst/lecturer. Contested Glasgow Springburn 1992, Clydebank and Milngavie 1987, Monklands W 1983. Member, Electoral Reform Soc. Ed Eastbourne Coll School; Sussex and Oxford Univs.
**HUGO SWIRE**, b Nov 30, 1959. Dep director, Sotheby's. Former Grenadier Guards officer. Ed Eton; St Andrews Univ; Sandhurst.

| GREENWICH & WOOLWICH | | 37.5% change | | | | Lab win |
|---|---|---|---|---|---|---|
| Electorate % Turnout | | 61,352 | 65.9% | **1997** | 66,051 | 71.1% | **1992** |
| +Raynsford, W R N | Lab | **25,630** | 63.4% | +18.8% | 20,951 | 44.6% | Lab |
| Mitchell, M | C | 7,502 | 18.6% | +0.3% | 16,478 | 35.1% | LD |
| Luxton, Mrs C | LD | 5,049 | 12.5% | -22.6% | 8,565 | 18.2% | C |
| Ellison, D | Ref | 1,670 | 4.1% | | 990 | 2.1% | Other |
| Mallone, R | Fellowship | 428 | 1.1% | | | | |
| Martin-Eagle, D | Constit | 124 | 0.3% | | | | |
| C to Lab notional swing 9.3% | | 40,403 | Lab maj 18,128 | | 46,984 | Lab maj 4,473 | |
| | | | 44.9% | | | 9.5% | |

**NICK RAYNSFORD**, b Jan 28, 1945. Became Under Secretary for Environment and Transport responsible for London and construction, May 5, 1997. Regained Greenwich for Lab 1992; MP for Fulham, 1986-87. Lab spokesman on housing 1994 and on London 1993. Member, select cttees on environment, 1992-93; on Channel Tunnel Bill 1986-87. Joint sec, all-party photography parly group. Hammersmith and Fulham cllr 1971-75. Consultant to Housing Assoc Consultancy and Advisory Service 1993-97; member (unpaid), advisory board, *Building* magazine; dir, Raynsford Dallison Associates, housing consultants, 1992-93;

Raynsford and Morris, housing consultants, 1990-92 (partner 1987-90). Director of SHAC, the London Housing Aid Centre, 1976-86. Gen sec, Soc for Co-op Dwellings, 1972-73. Ed Repton School; Sidney Sussex Coll, Cambridge; Chelsea School of Art.
**MICHAEL MITCHELL**, b Oct 5, 1959. Finance director. Southwark cllr 1986-90 (leader C group). Ed Wells Cathedral School; Trinity Coll, Cambridge.
**CHERRY LUXTON**, b Feb 24, 1942. Teacher, ex-pres of NUT. Hart district cllr 1994- . Ed Stella Maris, Bideford; Exmouth Teaching Coll; OU.

| GUILDFORD | | 2.2% change | | | | C win |
|---|---|---|---|---|---|---|
| Electorate % Turnout | | 75,541 | 75.4% | **1997** | 76,323 | 77.6% | **1992** |
| St Aubyn, N | C | 24,230 | 42.5% | -12.8% | 32,820 | 55.4% | C |
| Sharp, Mrs M | LD | 19,439 | 34.1% | +1.3% | 19,478 | 32.9% | LD |
| Burns, J | Lab | 9,945 | 17.5% | +6.1% | 6,732 | 11.4% | Lab |
| Gore, J | Ref | 2,650 | 4.7% | | 229 | 0.4% | NLP |
| McWhirter, R | UK Ind | 400 | 0.7% | | | | |
| Morris, J | Pacifist | 294 | 0.5% | | | | |
| C to LD notional swing 7.1% | | 56,958 | C maj 4,791 | | 59,259 | C maj 13,342 | |
| | | | 8.4% | | | 22.5% | |

**NICHOLAS ST AUBYN**, b Nov 19, 1955. Merchant banker. Contested Truro March 1987 by-election, also 1987 and 1992 general elections. Westminster cllr 1982-86. Ed Eton; Trinity Coll, Oxford.
**MARGARET SHARP**, b Nov 21, 1938. University lecturer, senior research fellow, science policy research unit, Sussex Univ. Contested this seat 1992, 1987 and 1983. Chair, LD working group on science, technology and innovation. Served on SDP

economic and industrial policy cttees and higher ed working group. Ex-member, Tawney Soc; Council for Social Democracy. Member, 300 Group; AUT. Ed Tonbridge Girls' GS; Newnham Coll, Cambridge.
**JOSEPH BURNS**, b Nov 2, 1952. Director of Office for International Policy Services. Ed Sussex Univ; East London Univ; Christ's Coll. Cambridge.

## HACKNEY NORTH & STOKE NEWINGTON · Lab hold

| Electorate % Turnout | | | 62,045 | 52.9% | 1997 | 54,655 | 63.5% | 1992 |
|---|---|---|---|---|---|---|---|---|
| *Abbott, Ms D | Lab | | 21,110 | 64.3% | +6.4% | 20,083 | 57.8% | Lab |
| Lavender, M | C | | 5,483 | 16.7% | -10.3% | 9,356 | 26.9% | C |
| Taylor, D | LD | | 3,806 | 11.6% | +0.1% | 3,996 | 11.5% | LD |
| Chong, Y | Green | | 1,395 | 4.2% | | 1,111 | 3.2% | Grn |
| Maxwell, B | Ref | | 544 | 1.7% | | 178 | 0.5% | NLP |
| Tolson, D | None | | 368 | 1.1% | | | | |
| Lovebucket, Miss L | Rain Ref | | 146 | 0.4% | | | | |
| C to Lab swing 8.3% | | | 32,852 | Lab maj 15,627 | | 34,724 | Lab maj 10,727 | |
| | | | | 47.6% | | | 30.9% | |

**DIANE ABBOTT,** b Sept 27, 1953. Elected 1987. Member, Treasury select cttee 1989- ; Lab Party NEC 1994- . Former press officer, Lambeth Borough Council; ex-civil servant and former employee of NCCL, Thames TV, Breakfast TV and ACTT. Westminster cllr 1982-86. Member, ACTT; NUJ. Ed Harrow County GS; Newnham Coll, Cambridge.

**MICHAEL LAVENDER,** b March 24, 1964. Barrister, law lecturer. Broxbourne cllr 1986- . Chair, Broxbourne constituency assoc, 1995-96. Member, Conservative Way Forward. Ed Cheshunt School, Hertfordshire; Birmingham Univ; Lincoln's Inn.
**DOUGLAS TAYLOR,** b Dec 1, 1963. Solicitor. Volunteer for Action Aid. Ed Skinners School, Tunbridge Wells; Pembroke Coll, Oxford.

## HACKNEY SOUTH & SHOREDITCH · 0.1% change · Lab win

| Electorate % Turnout | | | 61,728 | 54.7% | 1997 | 67,545 | 54.7% | 1992 |
|---|---|---|---|---|---|---|---|---|
| +Sedgemore, B | Lab | | 20,048 | 59.4% | +6.0% | 19,702 | 53.4% | Lab |
| Pantling, M | LD | | 5,068 | 15.0% | +0.1% | 10,699 | 29.0% | C |
| O'Leary, C | C | | 4,494 | 13.3% | -15.7% | 5,525 | 15.0% | LD |
| Betts, T | N Lab | | 2,436 | 7.2% | | 772 | 2.1% | Grn |
| Franklin, R | Ref | | 613 | 1.8% | | 225 | 0.6% | NLP |
| Callow, G | BNP | | 531 | 1.6% | | | | |
| Goldman, M | Comm Brit | | 298 | 0.9% | | | | |
| Goldberg, Ms M | NLP | | 145 | 0.4% | -0.2% | | | |
| Rogers, B | WRP | | 113 | 0.3% | | | | |
| LD to Lab notional swing 3.0% | | | 33,746 | Lab maj 14,980 | | 36,923 | Lab maj 9,003 | |
| | | | | 44.4% | | | 24.4% | |

**BRIAN SEDGEMORE,** b March 17, 1937. Barrister. Elected for this seat 1983; MP for Luton W Feb 1974-79. Member, Treasury select cttee, 1983- . PPS to Tony Benn 1977-78. Wandsworth cllr 1971-74. Researcher with Granada Television, 1979-83, and freelance journalist. Ed Newtown Primary; Heles School, Exeter; Corpus Christi Coll, Oxford,
**MARTIN PANTLING,** b April 13, 1969. Banker. Member, World

Development Movement; Green Democrats. Has worked for London Tourist Board. Ed in Grantham; Royal Coll of Music.
**CHRISTOPHER O'LEARY,** b July 3, 1969. University administrator, Barts School of Nursing. Hackney cllr. Member, Greater London local gvt advisory board; business liasion officer, Shoreditch crime prevention panel; adviser, Right to Buy Assoc. Ed Lings School, Northampton; Durham Univ.

## HALESOWEN & ROWLEY REGIS · 87.7% change · Lab win

| Electorate % Turnout | | | 66,245 | 73.6% | 1997 | 68,414 | 79.4% | 1992 |
|---|---|---|---|---|---|---|---|---|
| Heal, Mrs S L | Lab | | 26,366 | 54.1% | +9.6% | 24,306 | 44.7% | C |
| Kennedy, J | C | | 16,029 | 32.9% | -11.9% | 24,181 | 44.5% | Lab |
| Todd, Ms E | LD | | 4,169 | 8.5% | -1.4% | 5,384 | 9.9% | LD |
| White, P | Ref | | 1,244 | 2.6% | | 452 | 0.8% | Other |
| Meeds, Ms K | Nat Dem | | 592 | 1.2% | | | | |
| Weller, T | Green | | 361 | 0.7% | | | | |
| C to Lab notional swing 10.7% | | | 48,761 | Lab maj 10,337 | | 54,323 | C maj 125 | |
| | | | | 21.2% | | | 0.2% | |

**SYLVIA HEAL,** b July 20, 1942. MP for Staffs Mid, 1990-92. Former Lab spokeswoman on health and on women's issues 1991-92. Nat young carers officer, Carers Nat Assoc, 1992- . Advertising Standards Authority 1992- , executive council SSAFA, 1990-91. Social worker, health service and Dept of Employment, 1968-70 and 1980-90; medical records clerk, Chester Royal Infirmary, 1957-63. Ed Elfred Sec Modern, Buckley, N Wales; Coleg Harlech; Univ Coll of Wales, Swansea.

**JOHN KENNEDY,** b June 18, 1965. Public affairs consultant. Contested Barking 1992. Private Sec and Equerry to Prince Michael of Kent 1993- . Organised 1988 and 1989 Commons v Lords charity shoot in aid of The Prince's Trust; participated in Romanoff Fund for Russia 1994. Ed Royal Russell School, Addington, Surrey.
**ELAINE TODD,** b Aug 9, 1950. Teacher. Contested Warley W 1992 and 1987. Ed Northern Counties Coll; Newcastle and Keele Univs.

| HALIFAX | | | | | Lab hold | | |
|---|---|---|---|---|---|---|---|
| Electorate % Turnout | | 71,701 | 70.5% | **1997** | 73,401 | 78.7% | **1992** |
| *Mahon, Mrs A | Lab | **27,465** | **54.3%** | **+10.8%** | 25,115 | 43.5% | Lab |
| Light, R | C | 16,253 | 32.1% | -10.5% | 24,637 | 42.7% | C |
| Waller, E | LD | 6,059 | 12.0% | -0.8% | 7,364 | 12.7% | LD |
| Whitaker, Mrs C | UK Ind | 779 | 1.5% | | 649 | 1.1% | Nat |
| C to Lab swing 10.7% | | **50,556** | Lab maj **11,212** | | **57,765** | Lab maj **478** | |
| | | | 22.2% | | | 0.8% | |

ALICE MAHON, b Sept 28, 1937. Lecturer. Elected for this seat 1987. Member, health select cttee, 1991- ; joint vice-chair, PLP health and personal social services cttee, 1989- . Joint chair, all-party breast cancer parly group; sec, Brake (safe commercial transport) group. Lecturer at Bradford and Ilkley Community Coll. Calderdale borough cllr 1982-87; member, Calderdale health authority. Ed local grammar school; Bradford Univ.

ROBERT LIGHT, b Oct 12, 1964. Farmer and businessman. Contested Doncaster N 1992. Kirklees cllr 1987-95; Chair, Yorkshire Area YCs, 1988-90. Member, NFU; Country Landowners' Assoc. Ed Whitcliffe Mount HS, Cleckheaton.
ED WALLER, b July 16, 1928. Chartered engineer (retired). Three Rivers district cllr. Member, Inst of Management. Ed Shanghai (Yangchow Internment Camp); Coventry Tech Coll.

| HALTEMPRICE & HOWDEN | | 68.2% change | | | C win | | |
|---|---|---|---|---|---|---|---|
| Electorate % Turnout | | 65,602 | 75.5% | **1997** | 64,046 | 79.2% | **1992** |
| +Davis, D | C | **21,809** | **44.0%** | **-15.3%** | 30,085 | 59.3% | C |
| Wallis, Ms D | LD | 14,295 | 28.8% | +3.7% | 12,772 | 25.2% | LD |
| McManus, G | Lab | 11,701 | 23.6% | +8.3% | 7,774 | 15.3% | Lab |
| Pearson, T | Ref | 1,370 | 2.8% | | 110 | 0.2% | Other |
| Bloom, G | UK Ind | 301 | 0.6% | | | | |
| Stevens, B | NLP | 74 | 0.1% | | | | |
| C to LD notional swing 9.5% | | **49,550** | C maj **7,514** | | **50,741** | C maj **17,313** | |
| | | | 15.2% | | | 34.1% | |

DAVID DAVIS, b Dec 23, 1948. MP for Boothferry 1987-97. Foreign Office Min 1994-97. Former PPS to Francis Maude; asst gvt whip 1990-93; parly Under Sec, Office of Public Service and Science, 1993-94. Chair, Conf of C Students, 1973. Ex-dir, Tate & Lyle. Ed Bec GS; Warwick Univ; London Business School; Harvard.
DIANA WALLIS, b June 28, 1954. Solicitor. Contested Braintree 1992, and Humberside 1994 Euro elections; North Essex 1989

Euro elections. Humberside/East Riding of Yorkshire UA cllr 1994- . Ed Francis Combe School, Garston; N London Poly; Kent Univ; Chester Coll of Law.
GEORGE McMANUS, b July 28, 1955. Property manager/civil engineer. Member, TGWU; Scientists for Labour; Amnesty. Ed St Leonard's Comp, Glasgow; Glasgow Univ.

| HALTON | | 13.4% change | | | Lab win | | |
|---|---|---|---|---|---|---|---|
| Electorate % Turnout | | 64,987 | 68.4% | **1997** | 66,187 | 76.9% | **1992** |
| Twigg, J D | Lab | **31,497** | **70.9%** | **+11.3%** | 30,363 | 59.6% | Lab |
| Balmer, P | C | 7,847 | 17.7% | -12.6% | 15,426 | 30.3% | C |
| Jones, Ms J | LD | 3,263 | 7.3% | -1.5% | 4,499 | 8.8% | LD |
| Atkins, R | Ref | 1,036 | 2.3% | | 343 | 0.7% | Loony |
| Proffitt, D | Lib | 600 | 1.4% | | 294 | 0.6% | NLP |
| Alley, J | Rep GB | 196 | 0.4% | | | | |
| C to Lab notional swing 11.9% | | **44,439** | Lab maj **23,650** | | **50,925** | Lab maj **14,937** | |
| | | | 53.2% | | | 29.3% | |

DEREK TWIGG, b July 9, 1959. Political consultant, previously civil servant, Dept for Ed and Employment. Chair, Halton CLP, 1985-95; member, Labour NW regional exec cttee, 1988-92. Cheshire cllr 1981-85; Halton borough cllr 1983- . Ed Bankfield HS; Halton Coll of FE, Widnes.
PHILIP BALMER, b Oct 1, 1945. Runs own small building and design business. Treas, Halton C assoc, 1988-92. Halton borough cllr

since 1985. Ed Wade Deacon GS; Manchester Coll of Building; Salford Univ.
JANET JONES, b June 27, 1930. Head teacher (retired). Halton borough cllr. Sec, Cheshire Retired Headteachers Assoc; former chair, British Assoc of Children's Ed; co-chair, Women's Nat Commission. Member, 300 Group. Ed Hawarden GS; Froebel Ed Inst, Roehampton.

| HAMILTON NORTH & BELLSHILL | | 62.3% change | | | | Lab win |
|---|---|---|---|---|---|---|
| Electorate % Turnout | | 53,607 | 70.9% | **1997** | 52,793 | 76.1% | **1992** |
| **+Reid, Dr J** | Lab | **24,322** | **64.0%** | +5.7% | **23,422** | **58.3%** | Lab |
| Matheson, M | SNP | 7,255 | 19.1% | -0.6% | 7,932 | 19.7% | SNP |
| McIntosh, G | C | 3,944 | 10.4% | -4.8% | 6,115 | 15.2% | C |
| Legg, K | LD | 1,924 | 5.1% | -1.7% | 2,715 | 6.8% | LD |
| Conn, R | Ref | 554 | 1.5% | | | | |
| **SNP to Lab notional swing 3.2%** | | 37,999 | | Lab maj **17,067** 44.9% | 40,184 | | Lab maj **15,490** 38.6% |

**JOHN REID**, b May 8, 1947. Became Minister of State for the Armed Forces, May 5, 1997. MP for Motherwell N 1987-97. Lab spokesman on defence 1990-97; adviser to Neil Kinnock, when Leader of Opposition, 1983-85. Member, Armed Forces Parly Scheme; spokesman on children, 1989-90. Scottish organiser, Trade Unionists for Lab, 1986-87; research officer, Scottish Lab Party, 1980-83. Ed St Patrick's Senior Secondary, Coatbridge; Stirling Univ.

**MICHAEL MATHESON**, b Sept 8, 1970. Community occupational therapist. Convener, Stirling branch, SNP; nat council delegate. Member, Unison. Ed Queen Margaret Coll; OU.
**GORDON McINTOSH**, b May 1, 1954. Instrument engineer. Contested Motherwell S 1992. Lay rep to national local gvt advisory cttee 1990-93. Ed Ardrossan Acad.
**KEITH LEGG**, b July 21, 1973. Political organiser. Convener, Scottish Young LDs. Member, Charter 88. Ed Dundee Univ.

| HAMILTON SOUTH | | 24.8% change | | | | Lab win |
|---|---|---|---|---|---|---|
| Electorate % Turnout | | 46,562 | 71.1% | **1997** | 46,860 | 74.3% | **1992** |
| **+Robertson, G I M** | Lab | **21,709** | **65.6%** | +8.7% | **19,816** | **57.0%** | Lab |
| Black, I | SNP | 5,831 | 17.6% | -2.7% | 7,074 | 20.3% | SNP |
| Kilgour, R | C | 2,858 | 8.6% | -7.4% | 5,596 | 16.1% | C |
| Pitts, R | LD | 1,693 | 5.1% | -1.5% | 2,308 | 6.6% | LD |
| Gunn, C | ProLife | 684 | 2.1% | | | | |
| Brown, S | Ref | 316 | 1.0% | | | | |
| **SNP to Lab notional swing 5.7%** | | 33,091 | | Lab maj **15,878** 48.0% | 34,794 | | Lab maj **12,742** 36.6% |

**GEORGE ROBERTSON**, b April 12, 1946. Became Defence Secretary May 3, 1997. MP for Hamilton 1978-97. Elected to Shadow Cabinet 1993 and appointed chief spokesman on Scotland; spokesman on European affairs 1984-93; dep spokesman on foreign affairs, 1981-93; on defence 1980-81; on Scotland 1979-80. Member, advisory board, Know How Funds for Eastern Europe, 1990- ; council, GB/USSR Assoc, 1986- ; editorial board, *European Business Journal*, 1988- ; council, British Executive Service Overseas, 1991- . Ed Dunoon GS; Dundee Univ.

**IAN BLACK**, b May 8, 1947. Adult education officer, N Lanarkshire Council. Contested Greenock and Port Glasgow 1992. Union rep, Clydesdale SNP constituency; delegate, nat council and nat assembly. Ed Lanark GS; Hull and Glasgow Univs.
**ROBERT KILGOUR**, b May 2, 1957. Established Four Seasons Health Care, nursing homes. Member, Tory Reform Group. Ed Loretto School; Stirling Univ.
**RICHARD PITTS**, b Dec 8, 1973. Marketing exec. Ed Bearsden Acad; Glasgow and Strathclyde Univs.

| HAMMERSMITH & FULHAM | | 38.7% change | | | | Lab win |
|---|---|---|---|---|---|---|
| Electorate % Turnout | | 78,637 | 68.7% | **1997** | 72,731 | 75.9% | **1992** |
| **Coleman, I** | Lab | **25,262** | **46.8%** | +8.1% | **28,487** | **51.6%** | C |
| **+Carrington, M H M** | C | 21,420 | 39.6% | -12.0% | 21,313 | 38.6% | Lab |
| Sugden, Ms A | LD | 4,728 | 8.8% | +0.5% | 4,553 | 8.3% | LD |
| Bremner, Mrs M | Ref | 1,023 | 1.9% | | 820 | 1.5% | Other |
| Johnson-Smith, W | N Lab | 695 | 1.3% | | | | |
| Streeter, Ms E | Green | 562 | 1.0% | | | | |
| Roberts, G | UK Ind | 183 | 0.3% | | | | |
| Phillips, A | NLP | 79 | 0.1% | | | | |
| Elston, A | Care | 74 | 0.1% | | | | |
| **C to Lab notional swing 10.1%** | | 54,026 | | Lab maj **3,842** 7.1% | 55,173 | | C maj **7,174** 13.0% |

**IAIN COLEMAN**, b Jan 18, 1958. Local gvt administrator. Hammersmith and Fulham borough cllr 1991- (leader 1991- ). Vice-chair, Assoc of London Authorities, 1992.
**MATTHEW CARRINGTON**, b Oct 19, 1947. MP for Fulham 1987-97; contested Fulham by-election 1986; Haringey, Tottenham, general election in 1979. Member, Treasury and Civil Service select cttee, 1994-97; PPS to John Patten 1990-94. Joint sec, Greater London

group of C MPs, 1987-97; sec, C unpaired MPs, 1988-89. Banker with Saudi International Bank 1978-87; First Nat Bank of Chicago 1974-78. Ed French Lycée, London; Imperial Coll, London; London Graduate School of Business Studies.
**ALEXI SUGDEN**, b March 27, 1947. Company director. Hammersmith and Fulham cllr (LD group leader). Ed Bautront, Camberley; Pitman's Coll, Southampton.

| HAMPSHIRE EAST | | 109.9% change | | | C win | | |
|---|---|---|---|---|---|---|---|
| Electorate % Turnout | | 76,604 | 75.9% | **1997** | 73,748 | 80.4% | **1992** |
| +Mates, M | C | 27,927 | 48.0% | -12.6% | 35,960 | 60.6% | C |
| Booker, R | LD | 16,337 | 28.1% | +0.6% | 16,303 | 27.5% | LD |
| Hoyle, R | Lab | 9,945 | 17.1% | +7.7% | 5,605 | 9.4% | Lab |
| Hayter, J | Ref | 2,757 | 4.7% | | 1,263 | 2.1% | Grn |
| Foster, I | Green | 649 | 1.1% | | 188 | 0.3% | RCC |
| Coles, S | UK Ind | 513 | 0.9% | | | | |
| C to LD notional swing 6.6% | | 58,128 | | C maj 11,590 | 59,319 | | C maj 19,657 |
| | | | | 19.9% | | | 33.1% |

**MICHAEL MATES**, b June 9, 1934. Elected for this seat 1983; MP for Petersfield, 1974-83. Elected joint sec, 1922 Cttee, May 21, 1997. Min of State for N Ireland 1992-93. Chair, defence select cttee, 1987-92, member 1979-92; member, intelligence and security select cttee, 1992-97. Joint sec, 1922 Cttee, 1987-88. Member, British-Irish Inter-Parly Body. Dir, ABS Hovercraft Ltd, design and manufacture of hovercraft; parly consultant to Interleak (UK) Ltd, computer software co. Adviser on defence matters (no parly involvement) to ABS Aircraft AG, Swiss hovercraft maker. Army officer 1954-74. Ed Blundell's; King's Coll, Cambridge.
**BOB BOOKER**, b May 9, 1951. Solicitor advocate. Contested Hampshire E 1987. Alton cllr (ex-Mayor and LD leader). Ed Royal Masonic School, Bushey; Leeds Univ.
**BOB HOYLE**, b April 12, 1956. Trainee barrister. Oxford city cllr 1992- . Ed Merchant Taylors' School, Liverpool; Christ's Coll, Cambridge; Bristol Univ; Oxford Univ; Inner Temple.

| HAMPSHIRE NORTH EAST | | 42.5% change | | | C win | | |
|---|---|---|---|---|---|---|---|
| Electorate % Turnout | | 69,111 | 74.0% | **1997** | 65,880 | 80.1% | **1992** |
| +Arbuthnot, J N | C | 26,017 | 50.9% | -13.1% | 33,782 | 64.0% | C |
| Mann, I | LD | 11,619 | 22.7% | -2.4% | 13,242 | 25.1% | LD |
| Dare, P | Lab | 8,203 | 16.0% | +6.9% | 4,854 | 9.2% | Lab |
| Rees, D | Ref | 2,420 | 4.7% | | 907 | 1.7% | Other |
| Jessavala, K | Ind | 2,400 | 4.7% | | | | |
| Berry, C | UK Ind | 452 | 0.9% | | | | |
| C to LD notional swing 5.4% | | 51,111 | | C maj 14,398 | 52,785 | | C maj 20,540 |
| | | | | 28.2% | | | 38.9% |

**JAMES ARBUTHNOT**, b Aug 4, 1952. Non-practising barrister. MP for Wanstead and Woodford 1987-97; contested Cynon Valley 1983 and 1984 by-election. Defence Procurement Min 1995-97; Under Sec for Social Security 1994-95; asst gvt whip 1992-94; PPS to Peter Lilley, when Trade and Industry Sec, 1990-92; PPS to Archie Hamilton, Armed Forces Min, 1988-90. Kensington and Chelsea cllr 1978-87. Member of Lloyd's. Ed Wellesley House, Broadstairs; Eton; Trinity Coll, Cambridge.

**IAN MANN**, b Jan 23, 1932. Lecturer and business school administrator. Contested London North in 1994 Euro elections. Chair, Brentford and Isleworth LDs. Ed Charterhouse; Université de Poitiers.
**PETER DARE**, b Nov 17, 1947. Specialist in information security, IBM UK. Member, Fabian Soc; Lab finance and industry group; Lab Campaign for Electoral Reform. Ed London Univ.

| HAMPSHIRE NORTH WEST | | 25.7% change | | | C win | | |
|---|---|---|---|---|---|---|---|
| Electorate % Turnout | | 73,222 | 74.7% | **1997** | 7,095 | 804.6% | **1992** |
| +Young, Sir George | C | 24,730 | 45.2% | -12.8% | 33,154 | 58.1% | C |
| Fleming, C | LD | 13,179 | 24.1% | -3.9% | 15,990 | 28.0% | LD |
| Mumford, M | Lab | 12,900 | 23.6% | +11.0% | 7,175 | 12.6% | Lab |
| Callaghan, Mrs P | Ref | 1,533 | 2.8% | | 768 | 1.3% | Grn |
| Rolt, T | UK Ind | 1,383 | 2.5% | | | | |
| Baxter, B | Green | 486 | 0.9% | | | | |
| Anscomb, H | Bypass | 231 | 0.4% | | | | |
| Dodd, B | Ind | 225 | 0.4% | | | | |
| C to LD notional swing 4.5% | | 54,667 | | C maj 11,551 | 57,087 | | C maj 17,164 |
| | | | | 21.1% | | | 30.1% |

**SIR GEORGE YOUNG**, b July 16, 1941. MP for Ealing Acton, Feb 1974-97. Joined Cabinet 1995 as Transport Sec; Financial Sec to Treasury 1994-95; Min for Housing and Planning at DoE 1990-94; gvt whip 1990. Under Sec for Environment 1981-86; for Health and Social Security 1979-81; Opposition whip, 1976-79. Member, PAC, 1994-95. Pres, all-party friends of cycling parly group. Chair, C backbench social security cttee, 1989-90. Member, select cttee on violence in marriage, 1975. GLC cllr 1970-73; Lambeth cllr 1968-71. Economic adviser, Post Office, 1969-74. Economist. Non-exec dir, Lovell Partnerships Ltd, 1987-90. Trustee, Guinness Trust, 1986-90. Ed Eton; Christ Church, Oxford.
**CHARLES FLEMING**, b July 31, 1948. Defence industry worker. Rushmoor borough cllr 1985- (council leader 1996- ). Ed Fernhill School; Farnborough Coll of Tech; OU.
**MICHAEL MUMFORD**, b June 17, 1945. Retired schoolmaster. Member, NASUWT.

| HAMPSTEAD & HIGHGATE | | 7.3% change | | | 1997 | | | 1992 |
|---|---|---|---|---|---|---|---|---|
| Electorate % Turnout | | | 64,889 | 67.9% | **1997** | 62,954 | 72.4% | **1992** |
| +Jackson, Ms G | Lab | | **25,275** | **57.4%** | **+11.2%** | **21,059** | **46.2%** | Lab |
| Gibson, Miss E | C | | 11,991 | 27.2% | -13.5% | 18,582 | 40.8% | C |
| Fox, Mrs B | LD | | 5,481 | 12.4% | +1.4% | 5,028 | 11.0% | LD |
| Siddique, Ms M | Ref | | 667 | 1.5% | | 653 | 1.4% | Grn |
| Leslie, J | NLP | | 147 | 0.3% | +0.1% | 102 | 0.2% | NLP |
| Carroll, R | Dream | | 141 | 0.3% | | 52 | 0.1% | Raver |
| Prince, Miss P | UK Ind | | 123 | 0.3% | | 52 | 0.1% | Scallywag |
| Harris, R | Hum | | 105 | 0.2% | | 41 | 0.1% | Rizz |
| Rizz, C | Rizz | | 101 | 0.2% | +0.1% | | | |
| C to Lab notional swing 12.4% | | | 44,031 | | Lab maj 13,284 30.2% | 45,569 | | Lab maj 2,477 5.4% |

**GLENDA JACKSON,** b May 9, 1936. Became Under Secretary for Environment and Transport responsible for transport in London, May 5, 1997. Actress. Gained this seat for Lab 1992. Joint sec, all-party film industry parly group. Unpaid dir, Bowden Prods Ltd, film production co. Repertory company actress 1957-63; joined Royal Shakespeare Co 1963. Awarded Oscars in 1971 and 1974 for her performances in *Women in Love* and *A Touch of Class*; best film actress awards from Variety Club of GB, New York Film Critics, and US Nat Society of Film Critics. Ed West Kirby County GS for Girls; RADA.

**ELIZABETH GIBSON,** b Oct 7, 1951. Part-time teacher and dir of small business. Contested Birmingham Hodge Hill 1992. Ed St Bernard's Convent, Westcliff-on-Sea; Convent of Notre Dame, Teignmouth; Maria Assumpta Teacher Training Coll, London.

**BRIDGET FOX,** b July 14, 1964. Information manager with Sports Council. Ex-Hertford town cllr. Ed Dr Challoners HS, Amersham; Balliol Coll, Oxford.

| HARBOROUGH | | 11.5% change | | | | | | C win |
|---|---|---|---|---|---|---|---|---|
| Electorate % Turnout | | | 70,424 | 75.3% | **1997** | 68,122 | 81.5% | **1992** |
| +Garnier, E | C | | **22,170** | **41.8%** | **-10.9%** | **29,274** | **52.7%** | C |
| Cox, M | LD | | 15,646 | 29.5% | -4.9% | 19,122 | 34.4% | LD |
| Holden, N | Lab | | 13,332 | 25.2% | +12.9% | 6,828 | 12.3% | Lab |
| Wright, N | Ref | | 1,859 | 3.5% | | 290 | 0.5% | NLP |
| C to LD notional swing 3.0% | | | 53,007 | | C maj 6,524 12.3% | 55,514 | | C maj 10,152 18.3% |

**EDWARD GARNIER,** b Oct 26, 1952. Barrister. Elected 1992; contested Hemsworth 1987. Was PPS to Attorney-General and Solicitor-General and previously to FCO Mins of State. Member, home affairs select cttee, 1992-95. Sec, C backbench foreign and Commonwealth affairs cttee, 1992-94. Member, Soc of C Lawyers. Ed Wellington Coll, Berkshire; Jesus Coll, Oxford; Coll of Law, London.

**MARK COX,** b May 6, 1963. Company secretary. Contested this seat 1992. Ex-Leicestershire county cllr and ex-Harborough district cllr; Oadby and Wigston borough cllr 1991- . Ed Robert Smyth School, Market Harborough; Wigston FE Coll.

**NICK HOLDEN,** b May 22, 1969. Assistant surgery manager for GP. Ex-member, Green Party. Member, MSF; Co-op Party; NHS Federation. Ed Beauchamp Coll, Oadby.

| HARLOW | | 6.3% change | | | | | | Lab win |
|---|---|---|---|---|---|---|---|---|
| Electorate % Turnout | | | 64,072 | 74.6% | **1997** | 65,004 | 82.2% | **1992** |
| Rammell, B | Lab | | **25,861** | **54.1%** | **+11.3%** | **24,568** | **46.0%** | C |
| +Hayes, J | C | | 15,347 | 32.1% | -13.9% | 22,881 | 42.8% | Lab |
| Spenceley, Ms L | LD | | 4,523 | 9.5% | -1.8% | 6,002 | 11.2% | LD |
| Wells, M | Ref | | 1,422 | 3.0% | | | | |
| Batten, G | UK Ind | | 340 | 0.7% | | | | |
| Bowles, J | BNP | | 319 | 0.7% | | | | |
| C to Lab notional swing 12.6% | | | 47,812 | | Lab maj 10,514 22.0% | 53,451 | | C maj 1,687 3.2% |

**BILL RAMMELL,** b Oct 10, 1959. General manager of univ student services. Contested this seat 1992. Member MSF; Lab Campaign for Electoral Reform. Ed Burnt Hill Comp, Harlow; Univ Coll of Wales, Cardiff (pres, students' union, 1982-83).

**JERRY HAYES,** b April 20, 1953. Broadcaster and writer. Won the seat 1983. PPS to Environment Mins, 1994-96 and to N Ireland Min, 1992-94. Member, select cttees on national heritage, 1996-97; health 1990-91; social services 1987-90. Joint chair, all-party Action on Smoking & Health (ASH) group, 1996-97; ex-joint vice-chair, Aids group. Public affairs consultant to Hornagold and Hills, project managers; Western Provident Assoc, health insurers; Ivax Corp, pharmaceutical co. Freeman, City of London; Liveryman, Worshipful Co of Fletchers; Freeman, Co of Watermen and Lightermen. Ed Oratory School; Chelmer Inst.

**LORNA SPENCELEY,** b Dec 13, 1958. Political organiser. Contested this seat 1992. Harlow district cllr 1992- . Ed Hautlieu School, Jersey; Selwyn Coll, Cambridge.

| HARROGATE & KNARESBOROUGH | | 15.6% change | | | LD win | | |
|---|---|---|---|---|---|---|---|
| Electorate % Turnout | | 65,155 | 73.1% | **1997** | 65,257 | 76.7% | **1992** |
| **Willis, P** | **LD** | **24,558** | **51.5%** | **+18.2%** | **25,909** | **51.8%** | **C** |
| +Lamont, N S H | C | 18,322 | 38.4% | -13.3% | 16,698 | 33.4% | LD |
| Boyce, Ms B | Lab | 4,159 | 8.7% | -4.8% | 6,777 | 13.5% | Lab |
| Blackburn, J | LC | 614 | 1.3% | | 658 | 1.3% | Other |
| C to LD notional swing 15.7% | | 47,653 | | LD maj 6,236 | 50,042 | | C maj 9,211 |
| | | | | 13.1% | | | 18.4% |

**PHIL WILLIS,** b Nov 30, 1941. Head teacher. Dep leader, N Yorkshire County Council, 1993- ; Harrogate borough cllr 1988- (leader 1990- ). Ed Burnley GS; City of Leeds and Carnegie Coll; Birmingham Univ.
**NORMAN LAMONT,** b May 8, 1942. Merchant banker. MP for Kingston upon Thames 1972-97; contested Hull E 1970. Chancellor of the Exchequer 1990-93; Chief Sec to Treasury 1989; Financial Sec 1986-89; Defence Procurement Min 1985-86; Industry Min 1981-85; Energy Min 1979-81. Member, PAC, 1986-89. Opposition spokesman on industry 1976-79. Dir, First Philippine Investment Trust; Jupiter European Trust; Balli Group

plc; chair, Taiwan Investment Trust plc; E European Food Fund plc; Indonesia Fund; Archipelago Fund, investment trust; Asia Specialist Growth Fund SICAF. Consultant on non-UK business, Monsanto Co; former non-exec director, N.M. Rothschild and Sons. Occasional consultant to Jupiter Tyndall plc, financial services co. Member, UK cttee, Euro Research Group. Ed Loretto School; Fitzwilliam Coll, Cambridge (pres of Union 1964).
**BARBARA BOYCE,** b April 26, 1952. Lecturer. Rotherham metropolitan district cllr 1996- . Member, Lab Animal Welfare Soc; Lab Movement in Europe; Nalgo. Ed Mill Mount GS, York; Bradford Univ; Huddersfield Poly.

| HARROW EAST | | 2.4% change | | | Lab win | | |
|---|---|---|---|---|---|---|---|
| Electorate % Turnout | | 79,846 | 71.4% | **1997** | 77,203 | 77.4% | **1992** |
| **McNulty, T** | **Lab** | **29,927** | **52.5%** | **+18.7%** | **31,624** | **52.9%** | **C** |
| +Dykes, H | C | 20,189 | 35.4% | -17.5% | 20,219 | 33.8% | Lab |
| Sharma, B | LD | 4,697 | 8.2% | -2.6% | 6,471 | 10.8% | LD |
| Casey, B | Ref | 1,537 | 2.7% | | 1,160 | 1.9% | Lib |
| Scholefield, A | UK Ind | 464 | 0.8% | | 215 | 0.4% | NLP |
| Planton, A | NLP | 171 | 0.3% | -0.1% | 49 | 0.1% | Anti-Fed |
| C to Lab notional swing 18.1% | | 56,985 | | Lab maj 9,738 | 59,738 | | C maj 11,405 |
| | | | | 17.1% | | | 19.1% |

**TONY McNULTY,** b Nov 3, 1958. Senior poly lecturer. Contested this seat 1992. Harrow borough cllr 1986- (dep leader, Lab group). Sec, Greater London Lab exec, 1987-90. Member, NATFHE. Ed Salvatorian Coll, Harrow; Stanmore Sixth-Form Coll; Liverpool Univ; Virginia Poly Inst and State Univ.
**HUGH DYKES,** b May 17, 1939. Elected 1970; contested Tottenham 1966. MEP, 1974-76. Chair, European Movement in Britain, 1990-95 (joint hon sec, 1982-87). Member, select cttee on Euro legislation, 1979-97; chair, all-party Friends of European

Movement group; Europe group, 1988-97. Joint vice-chair, C Friends of Israel group, 1986-97. Chair, all-party Franco-British relations cttee; all-party Chinese group 1996-97. Chair, ADA Video Systems Ltd; parly adviser to British Wine Producers Cttee; Single Market Services GIE (gvt relations advisers). Member, Securities Inst and shareholder in International Stock Exchange, London. Ed Weston-super-Mare GS; Pembroke Coll, Cambridge.
**BALDEV SHARMA,** b July 19, 1934. Exec for safari operator; part-time actor. Ed AV HS, Kenya.

| HARROW WEST | | 2.4% change | | | Lab gain | | |
|---|---|---|---|---|---|---|---|
| Electorate % Turnout | | 72,005 | 72.9% | **1997** | 70,781 | 77.4% | **1992** |
| **Thomas, G R** | **Lab** | **21,811** | **41.5%** | **+19.0%** | **30,227** | **55.2%** | **C** |
| *Hughes, R G | C | 20,571 | 39.2% | -16.0% | 12,337 | 22.5% | Lab |
| Nandhra, Mrs P | LD | 8,127 | 15.5% | -4.7% | 11,045 | 20.2% | LD |
| Crossman, H | Ref | 1,997 | 3.8% | | 845 | 1.5% | Lib |
| | | | | | 306 | 0.6% | NLP |
| C to Lab notional swing 17.5% | | 52,506 | | Lab maj 1,240 | 54,760 | | C maj 17,890 |
| | | | | 2.4% | | | 32.7% |

**GARETH R. THOMAS,** b July 15, 1967. Teacher. Harrow cllr 1990- (Lab group whip); vice-chair, Assoc of Local Gvt Social Services Cttee. Member, NUT; Fabian Soc; Co-op Party; SERA. Ed Univ Coll of Wales, Aberystwyth; King's Coll, London.
**ROBERT G. HUGHES,** b July 14, 1951. Elected 1987; contested Southwark and Bermondsey twice in 1983; Stepney and Poplar 1979. Public Service and Science Min 1994-95; asst gvt whip 1992-94. PPS to Nicholas Scott, Min for Disabled, 1990-92. Member, social security select cttee, 1995-97; broadcasting select

cttee 1988-92. Joint vice-chair, 1989-90, and joint sec, 1987-89, C backbench environment cttee; joint vice-chair, C European affairs cttee, 1988-89. Member, governing body, British Film Inst, 1990-92. Former BBC news film editor. Nat chair, YCs, 1979-80. Ed Spring Grove GS; Harrow Coll of Tech and Art.
**PASH NANDHRA,** b Dec 5, 1941. Businesswoman and teacher. Contested Ealing Southall 1992. Harrow borough cllr 1986- . Member, 300 Group; Age Concern; Charter 88. Ed Coast Girls HS, Mombasa; Kenya Univ, Nairobi; London Univ Inst of Ed.

| HARTLEPOOL | | | | | **Lab hold** | | |
|---|---|---|---|---|---|---|---|
| Electorate % Turnout | | 67,712 | 65.6% | **1997** | 67,968 | 76.1% | **1992** |
| *Mandelson, P | Lab | 26,997 | 60.7% | +8.9% | 26,816 | 51.9% | Lab |
| Horsley, M | C | 9,489 | 21.3% | -13.5% | 18,034 | 34.9% | C |
| Clark, R | LD | 6,248 | 14.1% | +0.8% | 6,860 | 13.3% | LD |
| Henderson, Miss M | Ref | 1,718 | 3.9% | | | | |
| C to Lab swing 11.2% | | 44,452 | Lab maj 17,508 | 39.4% | 51,710 | Lab maj 8,782 | 17.0% |

**PETER MANDELSON,** b Oct 21, 1953. Became Minister without Portfolio in the Cabinet Office, May 4, 1997. Responsible for Labour planning in 1997 general election. Member of John Prescott's team 1995, shadowing Dep Prime Minister, Chancellor of the Duchy of Lancaster and Public Service Minister; formerly Mr Prescott's Lab campaign deputy. Lab whip 1994-95. Lab Party director of campaigns and communications 1985-90. Campaign officer, Northern group of Lab MPs. Member, international advisory cttee, Centre for European Policy Studies, 1993- . Producer, London Weekend Television, 1982-85. Chair, British Youth Council, 1978-80. Member, economics dept, TUC, 1977-88; GMB; NUJ. Ed Hendon Senior HS; St Catherine's Coll, Oxford.

**MICHAEL HORSLEY,** b Feb 14, 1971. Public affairs exec, Dixons Group. Political researcher, C research dept, 1994-96; ex-special adviser to Virgina Bottomley. Ed High Tunstall School, Hartlepool; Hartlepool Sixth-Form Coll; Durham Univ (pres, students' union).

**REGINALD CLARK,** b March 15, 1958. Finance director, Kobe Steel. Member, Charter 88; Amnesty; Securities Inst. Fellow of Royal Soc of Arts. Ed Brinkburn Comp, Hartlepool; Christ Church, Oxford.

| HARWICH | 8.1% change | | | | | | **Lab win** |
|---|---|---|---|---|---|---|---|
| Electorate % Turnout | | 75,775 | 70.6% | **1997** | 74,676 | 76.1% | **1992** |
| Henderson, I | Lab | 20,740 | 38.8% | +14.1% | 29,372 | 51.7% | C |
| +Sproat, I | C | 19,524 | 36.5% | -15.2% | 14,047 | 24.7% | Lab |
| Elvin, Mrs A | LD | 7,037 | 13.1% | -10.0% | 13,187 | 23.2% | LD |
| Titford, J | Ref | 4,923 | 9.2% | | 256 | 0.5% | NLP |
| Knight, R | CRP | 1,290 | 2.4% | | | | |
| C to Lab notional swing 14.6% | | 53,514 | Lab maj 1,216 | 2.3% | 56,862 | C maj 15,325 | 27.0% |

**IVAN HENDERSON,** b June 7, 1958. Union organiser, ex-dock operator in Harwich. Harwich district cllr 1995- . Exec officer NUR/RMT 1991-94. Ed Sir Anthony Dean Comp.

**IAIN SPROAT,** b Nov 8, 1938. National Heritage Min 1995-97 and Sports Min 1994-97. Elected for this seat 1992; MP for Aberdeen S 1970-83; contested Roxburgh and Berwickshire 1983, Rutherglen by-election and general election 1964. Under Sec for National Heritage 1993-95; junior trade min 1981-83. PPS to Scottish Sec 1973-74. Chair, Milner and Co, 1981 and 1983-93; Cricketers' Who's Who Ltd, 1980-81 and 1983-93. Trustee, African medical and research foundation (flying doctors), 1986-91; Scottish self-governing schools trust 1989- . Chair, editorial board, Oxford Univ Press history of the British Empire, 1987-92; complete works of Pushkin 1987-93. Ed St Mary's School, Melrose; Winchester; Univ of Aix-en-Provence; Magdalen Coll, Oxford.

**ANN ELVIN,** b April 22, 1940. Teacher. Tendring district cllr 1991-95. Member, CPRE. Ed St Angela's Convent, N London; London and Manchester Univs.

| HASTINGS & RYE | | | | | | | **Lab gain** |
|---|---|---|---|---|---|---|---|
| Electorate % Turnout | | 70,388 | 69.7% | **1997** | 71,838 | 74.9% | **1992** |
| Foster, M | Lab | 16,867 | 34.4% | +18.6% | 25,573 | 47.6% | C |
| *Lait, Mrs J | C | 14,307 | 29.2% | -18.4% | 18,939 | 35.2% | LD |
| Palmer, M | LD | 13,717 | 28.0% | -7.3% | 8,458 | 15.7% | Lab |
| McGovern, C | Ref | 2,511 | 5.1% | | 640 | 1.2% | Grn |
| Amstad, Ms J | Lib | 1,046 | 2.1% | | 168 | 0.3% | Loony |
| Andrews, W | UK Ind | 472 | 1.0% | | | | |
| Howell, D | Loony | 149 | 0.3% | -0.0% | | | |
| C to Lab swing 18.5% | | 49,069 | Lab maj 2,560 | 5.2% | 53,778 | C maj 6,634 | 12.3% |

**MICHAEL FOSTER,** b Feb 26, 1946. Solicitor. Contested Hastings in Feb and Oct 1974, and 1979. Ex-leader of Lab group on Hastings Council and ex-East Sussex county cllr. Dep Lieutenant of East Sussex 1993. Member, Fabian Soc; Christian Socialist Movement; Methodist Church; Soc of Lab Lawyers. Qualified FA referee. Ed Hastings Secondary; Hastings GS; Leicester Univ.

**JACQUI LAIT,** b Dec 10, 1947. Elected 1992; contested Tyne Bridge in 1985 by-election and Strathclyde West in 1984 Euro elections. Asst gvt whip 1996-97, the first woman in the C Whips' Office. PPS to William Hague, Welsh Sec, 1995-96, and formerly to social security mins. Ran Westminster and European parliamentary consultancy 1984-92. Parly adviser, Chemical Industries Assoc, 1980-84. Chair, European Union of Women (British section), and vice-chair, C women's nat cttee, 1990-92. Ed Paisley GS; Strathclyde Univ.

**MONROE PALMER,** b Nov 30, 1938. Chartered accountant. Contested this seat 1992; Hendon S 1987, 1983 and 1979. Barnet cllr 1986-94 (group leader 1986- ). Ed Orange Hill GS, Edgware.

| HAVANT | 49.5% change | | | | | | | C win |
|---|---|---|---|---|---|---|---|---|
| Electorate % Turnout | | | 68,420 | 70.6% | **1997** | 68,530 | 77.2% | **1992** |
| +Willetts, D | C | | 19,204 | 39.7% | -13.1% | 27,981 | 52.9% | C |
| Armstrong, Ms L | Lab | | 15,475 | 32.0% | +12.3% | 13,812 | 26.1% | LD |
| Kooner, M | LD | | 10,806 | 22.4% | -3.7% | 10,465 | 19.8% | Lab |
| Green, T | Ref | | 2,395 | 5.0% | | 678 | 1.3% | Grn |
| Atwal, M | BIPF | | 442 | 0.9% | | | | |
| C to Lab notional swing 12.7% | | | 48,322 | | C maj 3,729 7.7% | 52,936 | | C maj 14,169 26.8% |

**DAVID WILLETTS,** b March 9, 1956. Author. Chair, C research dept since 1996 after resigning as Paymaster General. Elected for this seat 1992. Public Service and Science Min 1995-96, in Cabinet Office. Gvt whip 1995; asst gvt whip 1994-95. PPS to chair of C Party 1993-94; research asst to Nigel Lawson 1978. Senior Treasury official 1978-84; member, PM's Downing St policy unit, 1984-86. Director of studies, Centre for Policy Studies, 1987-92; consultant director, C research dept, 1987-92. Dir, Retirement Security Ltd, 1988-94; Electra Corporate Ventures Ltd 1988-94. Ed King Edward's, Birmingham; Christ Church, Oxford.

**LYNNE ARMSTRONG,** b March 11, 1943. Freelance translator and writer. Contested South Downs in Euro elections 1994. Arun district cllr 1991-94. Member, Lab Cttee for Electoral Reform; Charter 88; TGWU. Ed The Royal School, Bath; Guildford County Tech Coll; Newnham Coll, Cambridge; Sussex Univ.
**MICHAEL KOONER,** b Aug 2, 1947. Company director and retired naval officer. Member, mine-warfare and clearance diving assoc. Ed Royal Naval Coll, Greenwich; Salford Univ.

| HAYES & HARLINGTON | 0.1% change | | | | | | | Lab win |
|---|---|---|---|---|---|---|---|---|
| Electorate % Turnout | | | 56,829 | 72.3% | **1997** | 58,665 | 74.1% | **1992** |
| McDonnell, J | Lab | | 25,458 | 62.0% | +17.2% | 19,511 | 44.9% | C |
| Retter, A | C | | 11,167 | 27.2% | -17.7% | 19,467 | 44.8% | Lab |
| Little, T | LD | | 3,049 | 7.4% | -2.9% | 4,477 | 10.3% | LD |
| Page, F | Ref | | 778 | 1.9% | | | | |
| Hutchins, J | NF | | 504 | 1.2% | | | | |
| Farrow, D | ANP | | 135 | 0.3% | | | | |
| C to Lab notional swing 17.4% | | | 41,091 | | Lab maj 14,291 34.8% | 43,455 | | C maj 44 0.1% |

**JOHN McDONNELL,** b Sept 8, 1951. Contested this seat 1992 and Hampstead and Highgate 1983. Editor, *Labour Herald*, 1985-88. Sec, Assoc of London Authorities, 1987-95; Assoc of London Government 1995- . GLC cllr 1981-86 (dep leader, Lab group). Principal policy adviser, Camden Council, 1985-87. Ed Great Yarmouth GS; Burnley Tech Coll; Brunel Univ; Birkbeck Coll, London.

**ANDREW RETTER,** b Aug 4, 1959. Accounts and logistics manager. Hillingdon borough cllr since 1990. Co-director, Hillingdon C research dept; member, C education and environment task forces; co-ordinator, Westminster Against the Rates. Ed Sir John Cass, Aldgate.
**ANTONY LITTLE,** b Jan 6, 1947. Investment manager. Contested Hayes and Harlington 1992. Hillingdon borough cllr 1982-90. Ed Gunnersbury RC GS; Reading Univ.

| HAZEL GROVE | | | | | | | | LD gain |
|---|---|---|---|---|---|---|---|---|
| Electorate % Turnout | | | 63,694 | 77.5% | **1997** | 64,302 | 84.9% | **1992** |
| Stunell, A | LD | | 26,883 | 54.5% | +11.4% | 24,479 | 44.8% | C |
| Murphy, B | C | | 15,069 | 30.5% | -14.3% | 23,550 | 43.1% | LD |
| Lewis, J | Lab | | 5,882 | 11.9% | +0.2% | 6,390 | 11.7% | Lab |
| Stanyer, J | Ref | | 1,055 | 2.1% | | 204 | 0.4% | NLP |
| Black, G | UK Ind | | 268 | 0.5% | | | | |
| Firkin-Flood, D | Ind Hum | | 183 | 0.4% | | | | |
| C to LD swing 12.8% | | | 49,340 | | LD maj 11,814 23.9% | 54,623 | | C maj 929 1.7% |

**ANDREW STUNELL,** b Nov 24, 1942. Special projects officer, ASLDC, the Lib Dem cllrs' organisation. Contested this seat 1992; City of Chester for L/All 1987 and 1983, and for Libs 1979. North West regional spokesman on international issues. Chair, LD working party on local gvt; member, English policy cttee. Chester city cllr 1979-90; Cheshire county cllr 1981-91; vice-chair, ACC, 1985-90. Member, Nalgo, 1967-81; staff side member, Whitley Council for New Towns, 1977-80. Former Baptist lay preacher. Ed Surbiton GS; Manchester Univ; Liverpool Poly.

**BRENDAN MURPHY,** b Sept 9, 1941. Businessman, marketing communications and computer graphics. Cheshire county cllr 1993- . C Party Central Office researcher 1989-91. Member RSPCA; RSPB; World Wide Fund for Nature. Ed Salesian Coll, Cheshire; St Bonaventures, London; Faculty of Law, Manchester; Henley-on-Thames Management Coll.
**JEFFREY LEWIS,** b Feb 3, 1960. Solicitor. Member, Soc of Lab Lawyers. Ed Brynteg Comp; Pembroke Coll, Cambridge; Manchester Metropolitan Univ.

| HEMEL HEMPSTEAD | | 19.0% change | | | | | Lab win |
|---|---|---|---|---|---|---|---|
| Electorate % Turnout | | 71,468 | 77.1% | **1997** | 71,471 | 82.1% | **1992** |
| McWalter, T | Lab Co-op | 25,175 | 45.7% | | **29,248** | 49.9% | C |
| +Jones, R | C | 21,539 | 39.1% | -10.8% | 19,090 | 32.5% | Lab |
| Lindsley, Mrs P | LD | 6,789 | 12.3% | -3.0% | 9,005 | 15.4% | LD |
| Such, P | Ref | 1,327 | 2.4% | | 1,313 | 2.2% | Other |
| Harding, Ms D | NLP | 262 | 0.5% | | | | |
| No swing calculation | | 55,092 | Lab Co-op maj 3,636 | | 58,656 | C maj 10,158 | |
| | | | 6.6% | | | 17.3% | |

**TONY McWALTER,** b March 20, 1945. Lecturer in philosophy and computing. Contested Luton N 1992; St Albans 1987; Bedfordshire South in 1989 Euro elections and Hertfordshire in 1984 Euro elections. St Albans dist cllr 1979-83. Ed Univ Coll of Wales, Aberystwyth; McMaster Univ, Canada; University Coll, Oxford.

**ROBERT JONES,** b Sept 26, 1950. Won this seat 1992; MP for Hertfordshire W 1983-92: contested Teesside Stockton 1979, and Kirkcaldy Oct 1974. Construction and Planning Min 1995-97; junior Environment Min 1994-95. PPS to Michael Spicer, Aviation Min, and Peter Bottomley, Roads and Traffic Min, 1986-87. Chair,

select cttee on environment, 1992-94, and member 1983-94. Sec, C employment cttee, 1985-86; chair, C organisation cttee, 1986-94. St Andrews cllr 1972-75; Fife county cllr 1973-75; Chiltern district cllr 1979-83. Vice-pres, Assoc of District Councils, 1983-94. Vice-pres, Wildlife Hospital Trust, 1985- . Freeman, City of London; Liveryman, Merchant Taylors' Co. Ed Merchant Taylors' School; St Andrews Univ.

**PATRICIA LINDSLEY,** b Sept 4, 1940. Solicitor. Chiltern district cllr and Chesham town cllr. Member, LD Lawyers; LD Greens; Ramblers' Assoc. Ed Peckham Girls' School; Oxford Brookes Univ.

| HEMSWORTH | | 21.2% change | | | | | Lab win |
|---|---|---|---|---|---|---|---|
| Electorate % Turnout | | 66,964 | 67.9% | **1997** | 68,411 | 76.1% | **1992** |
| +Trickett, J | Lab | 32,088 | 70.6% | +6.8% | 33,229 | 63.8% | Lab |
| Hazell, N | C | 8,096 | 17.8% | -8.0% | 13,428 | 25.8% | C |
| Kirby, Ms M S J | LD | 4,033 | 8.9% | -1.5% | 5,424 | 10.4% | LD |
| Irvine, D | Ref | 1,260 | 2.8% | | | | |
| C to Lab notional swing 7.4% | | 45,477 | Lab maj 23,992 | | 52,081 | Lab maj 19,801 | |
| | | | 52.8% | | | 38.0% | |

**JON TRICKETT,** b July 2, 1950. Ex-builder and plumber. Won Feb 1996 by-election and appointed to Unopposed Bills panel. Leader, Leeds City Council, 1989- ; member since 1985. Chair, Leeds City Development Co, 1989- ; board member, Leeds Development Corp, 1992- ; Leeds Health Care, 1992- . Member, West Yorkshire Passenger Transport Authority. Dir, Leeds/Bradford Airport; Leeds Playhouse; Leeds Theatre Co, all since 1988. Ed Roundhay HS; Hull and Leeds Univs.

**NORMAN HAZELL,** b April 17, 1932. Retired mechanical design engineer. Wakefield metropolitan district cllr 1975- . Chair, Normanton community police forum. Ed Thornes House GS; Wakefield Tech Coll.

**JAKI KIRBY,** b Sept 14 1956. Registered mental nurse and lecturer. Ryedale district cllr 1991-96. Ed Abbey Grange C of E, Leeds; studying at York and Huddersfield Univs.

*Details of 1996 by-election on page 278*

| HENDON | | 40.9% change | | | | | Lab win |
|---|---|---|---|---|---|---|---|
| Electorate % Turnout | | 76,195 | 65.7% | **1997** | 72,591 | 74.3% | **1992** |
| Dismore, A | Lab | 24,683 | 49.3% | +15.8% | 28,916 | 53.6% | C |
| +Gorst, Sir John | C | 18,528 | 37.0% | -16.6% | 18,068 | 33.5% | Lab |
| Casey, W | LD | 5,427 | 10.8% | -0.8% | 6,289 | 11.7% | LD |
| Rabbow, S | Ref | 978 | 2.0% | | 645 | 1.2% | Other |
| Wright, B | UK Ind | 267 | 0.5% | | | | |
| Taylor, Ms S | WRP | 153 | 0.3% | | | | |
| C to Lab notional swing 16.2% | | 50,036 | Lab maj 6,155 | | 53,918 | C maj 10,848 | |
| | | | 12.3% | | | 20.1% | |

**ANDREW DISMORE,** b Sept 2, 1954. Solicitor. Westminster city cllr 1982- (leader, Lab group, 1990- ). Member, Fabian Soc; Co-op Party; GMB. Ed Bridlington GS; Warwick Univ; LSE; Guildford Coll of Law.

**SIR JOHN GORST,** b June 28, 1928. Elected for Hendon N 1970; contested Bodmin 1966, and Chester-le-Street 1964. Member, national heritage select cttee, 1992-97; employment select cttee 1979-87. Chair (1987-90) and vice-chair (1986-87), C backbench media cttee. Chair, all-party British-Mexico group, 1996-97; joint vice-chair, all-party war crimes cttee, 1987-97; sec, C consumer

protection cttee, 1973-74. Ex-dir, John Gorst & Associates Ltd, business and public affairs consultancy; advertising and public relations manager, Pye Ltd, 1953-63. Founder (1964-80) and sec (1964-70), Telephone Users' Assoc; and Local Radio Assoc (sec, 1964-71). Political and public affairs adviser to British Amusements Caterers' Trade Assoc. Ed Ardingly Coll; Corpus Christi Coll, Cambridge.

**WAYNE CASEY,** b April 2, 1963. Internal auditor, finance and planning officer for English Heritage. Barnet cllr 1994- . Ed Kingsthorpe Upper School, Northampton; Kent Univ.

| HENLEY | | 3.2% change | | | 1997 | | | C win |
|---|---|---|---|---|---|---|---|---|
| Electorate % Turnout | | | 66,424 | 77.6% | **1997** | 66,340 | 79.6% | **1992** |
| +Heseltine, M | C | | 23,908 | 46.4% | -13.6% | 31,651 | 60.0% | C |
| Horton, T | LD | | 12,741 | 24.7% | +0.8% | 12,608 | 23.9% | LD |
| Enright, D | Lab | | 11,700 | 22.7% | +7.9% | 7,802 | 14.8% | Lab |
| Sainsbury, S | Ref | | 2,299 | 4.5% | | 438 | 0.8% | Anti H |
| Miles, Mrs S | Green | | 514 | 1.0% | | 278 | 0.5% | NLP |
| Barlow, N | NLP | | 221 | 0.4% | -0.1% | | | |
| Hibbert, T | Whig | | 160 | 0.3% | | | | |
| C to LD notional swing 7.2% | | | 51,543 | | C maj 11,167 | 52,777 | | C maj 19,043 |
| | | | | | 21.7% | | | 36.1% |

**MICHAEL HESELTINE,** b March 21, 1933. First Secretary of State and Deputy Prime Minister 1995-97; President of the Board of Trade (Trade and Industry Secretary) 1992-95. Elected for Henley, Feb 1974; MP for Tavistock 1966-74; contested Coventry N 1964, and Gower 1959. Environment Sec 1990-92, being appointed after contesting party leadership 1990. Defence Sec 1983-Jan 1986, when he resigned over future of Westland helicopter company. Environment Sec 1979-83. Aerospace and Shipping Min 1972-74; junior Min at Environment and Transport 1970-72. Formerly property developer and publisher. Chairman, Haymarket Press, 1966-70, and dir 1974-79. Member, council of Zoological Soc of London, 1987-90. Ed Shrewsbury School; Pembroke Coll, Oxford (Hon Fellow 1986; pres of Union 1954).
**TIM HORTON,** b Aug 14, 1947. Chair, South Oxfordshire District Council. Member, Friends of the Earth; CPRE. Ed Eltham Coll, London; Univ Coll of Wales, Aberystwyth; Reading Univ.
**DUNCAN ENRIGHT,** b May 25, 1964. Publisher. Contested Buckinghamshire and Oxfordshire East in 1994 Euro elections. Oxfordshire city cllr 1993- . Ed St Wilfrid's RC School, North Featherstone; Wadham Coll, Oxford.

| HEREFORD | | 1.3% change | | | 1997 | | | LD win |
|---|---|---|---|---|---|---|---|---|
| Electorate % Turnout | | | 69,864 | 75.2% | **1997** | 69,057 | 80.8% | **1992** |
| Keetch, P | LD | | 25,198 | 47.9% | +6.6% | 26,217 | 47.0% | C |
| +Shepherd, Sir Colin | C | | 18,550 | 35.3% | -11.7% | 23,063 | 41.3% | LD |
| Chappell, C | Lab | | 6,596 | 12.6% | +2.0% | 5,910 | 10.6% | Lab |
| Easton, C | Ref | | 2,209 | 4.2% | | 587 | 1.1% | Grn |
| C to LD notional swing 9.2% | | | 52,553 | | LD maj 6,648 | 55,777 | | C maj 3,154 |
| | | | | | 12.7% | | | 5.7% |

**PAUL KEETCH,** b May 21, 1961. Political consultant, specialising in Eastern European matters. Hereford city cllr 1983-87. Member, Charter 88. Ed Hereford HS; Hereford Sixth-Form Coll.
**SIR COLIN SHEPHERD,** b Jan 13, 1938. Elected Oct 1974. Chair, Commons catering cttee, 1991-97; member, Commons finance and services cttee, 1993-97. PPS to Peter Walker, Welsh Sec, 1987-90. Governor, Commonwealth Inst, 1989- . Chair, 1991-94; joint vice-chair, 1989-90, and member since 1986, exec cttee, UK branch, CPA; chair, international exec, CPA, 1993-96. Member, council, Royal Coll of Vet Surgeons, 1983- . Dir of Haigh Group Ltd, Ross-on-Wye, manufacturers of waste disposal and sewage treatment equipment. Ed Oundle; Gonville and Caius Coll, Cambridge; McGill Univ, Montreal.
**CHRIS CHAPPELL,** b Sept 19, 1948. Factory and farm worker. Contested Leominster 1987 and 1992. Hereford city cllr 1995- . Ed Down House School, Sussex; Hampshire Coll of Agriculture.

| HERTFORD & STORTFORD | | 26.3% change | | | 1997 | | | C win |
|---|---|---|---|---|---|---|---|---|
| Electorate % Turnout | | | 71,759 | 76.0% | **1997** | 70,578 | 80.1% | **1992** |
| +Wells, B | C | | 24,027 | 44.0% | -12.5% | 31,942 | 56.5% | C |
| Speller, S | Lab | | 17,142 | 31.4% | +14.6% | 14,408 | 25.5% | LD |
| Wood, M | LD | | 9,679 | 17.7% | -7.7% | 9,529 | 16.9% | Lab |
| Page Croft, H | Ref | | 2,105 | 3.9% | | 660 | 1.2% | Grn |
| Smalley, B | UK Ind | | 1,223 | 2.2% | | | | |
| Franey, M | ProLife | | 259 | 0.5% | | | | |
| Molloy, D | Logic | | 126 | 0.2% | | | | |
| C to Lab notional swing 13.5% | | | 54,561 | | C maj 6,885 | 56,539 | | C maj 17,534 |
| | | | | | 12.6% | | | 31.0% |

**BOWEN WELLS,** b Aug 4, 1935. Elected for this seat 1983; MP for Hertford and Stevenage 1979-83. Gvt whip 1995-97; asst whip 1994-95. PPS to Transport Min 1992-94. Member, select cttees on Euro legislation, 1983-92; foreign affairs 1981-92. Member exec cttee CPA; exec cttee, UK branch, CPA, 1984- . Trustee, Industry and Parliament Trust, 1985- . Governor, Inst of Development Studies, 1980-94. Ed St Paul's; Exeter Univ; Regent Street Poly School of Management.
**SIMON SPELLER,** b July 16, 1970. Senior lecturer in business and management. Member, Royal Town Planning Inst. Ed Bedford Coll, London; Oxford Poly; Birkbeck Coll, London; Middlesex Poly.
**MICHAEL WOOD,** b June 25, 1945. Theatre administrative director. Mayor of Bishop's Stortford 1991-92; Hertfordshire county cllr 1985-89 and East Hertfordshire district cllr 1991- . Ed Ashton-on-Mersey Secondary.

| HERTFORDSHIRE NORTH EAST | | 62.8% change | | | | | C win |
|---|---|---|---|---|---|---|---|
| Electorate % Turnout | | 67,161 | 77.4% | **1997** | 65,875 | 84.9% | **1992** |
| +Heald, O | C | **21,712** | 41.8% | -9.9% | **28,911** | 51.7% | C |
| Gibbons, I | Lab | 18,624 | 35.8% | +14.5% | 14,775 | 26.4% | LD |
| Jarvis, S | LD | 9,493 | 18.3% | -8.2% | 11,908 | 21.3% | Lab |
| Grose, J | Ref | 2,166 | 4.2% | | 355 | 0.6% | Other |
| C to Lab notional swing 12.2% | | 51,995 | | C maj 3,088 | 55,949 | | C maj 14,136 |
| | | | | 5.9% | | | 25.3% |

**OLIVER HEALD,** b Dec 15, 1954. Barrister. MP for Hertfordshire N 1992-97; contested Southwark and Bermondsey 1987. Junior Social Security Min 1995-97; PPS to Min of Ag, Fish and Food, 1994-95. Member, employment select cttee, 1992-94. Vice-chair, C backbench employment cttee, 1992-94. Vice-pres, Herts North C assoc, and chair 1984-86; Former member, C eastern area exec cttee. Ed Reading School; Pembroke Coll, Cambridge.

**IVAN GIBBONS,** b Aug 9, 1950. Adult education lecturer. Contested Eastbourne 1992. Hammersmith and Fulham cllr 1982- . Member, SEA; NATFHE. Ed London Oratory School; Queen's Univ, Belfast.
**STEVE JARVIS,** b June 12, 1956. Product marketing manager in telecommunications. North Herts district cllr 1992- (dep group leader 1994- ). Member, CPRE. Ed Francis Bacon School, St Albans; Hatfield Poly.

| HERTFORDSHIRE SOUTH WEST | | 38.4% change | | | | | C win |
|---|---|---|---|---|---|---|---|
| Electorate % Turnout | | 71,671 | 77.3% | **1997** | 68,566 | 84.2% | **1992** |
| +Page, R | C | **25,462** | 46.0% | -13.3% | **34,189** | 59.2% | C |
| Wilson, M | Lab | 15,441 | 27.9% | +10.4% | 13,034 | 22.6% | LD |
| Shaw, Mrs A | LD | 12,381 | 22.3% | -0.2% | 10,062 | 17.4% | Lab |
| Millward, T | Ref | 1,853 | 3.3% | | 462 | 0.8% | NLP |
| Adamson, C | NLP | 274 | 0.5% | -0.3% | | | |
| C to Lab notional swing 11.8% | | 55,411 | | C maj 10,021 | 57,747 | | C maj 21,155 |
| | | | | 18.1% | | | 36.6% |

**RICHARD PAGE,** b Feb 22, 1941. Won this seat at 1979 by-election; MP for Workington 1976-79 and contested that seat in Feb and Oct 1974. DTI junior min 1995-97. PPS to John Biffen, when Commons leader, 1982-87 and Trade Sec 1981-82. Joint vice-chair, C backbench trade and industry cttee, 1988-95. Member, PAC, 1987-95. Hon treas, Leukaemia Research Fund, 1987-95. Director of family engineering co, Page Holdings Ltd, 1964-95. Ed Hurstpierpoint Coll; Luton Tech Coll.

**MARK WILSON,** b Dec 16, 1962. Employed by John Lewis partnership, previously with BR. St Albans district cllr. Ed Emmanuel Coll, Cambridge.
**ANN SHAW.** Nursery teacher. Contested this seat 1992. Three Rivers district cllr 1971-76 and 1980- (council leader 1986-90 and 1991-92; chair, 1990-91). Ex-Lib Party researcher. Member, ALDC. Ed St Helen's School, Northwood; Lady Margaret Hall, Oxford.

| HERTSMERE | | 8.5% change | | | | | C win |
|---|---|---|---|---|---|---|---|
| Electorate % Turnout | | 68,011 | 74.0% | **1997** | 66,079 | 79.5% | **1992** |
| +Clappison, J | C | **22,305** | 44.3% | -13.7% | **30,439** | 58.0% | C |
| Kelly, Ms B | Lab | 19,230 | 38.2% | +16.5% | 11,373 | 21.7% | Lab |
| Gray, Mrs A | LD | 6,466 | 12.8% | -6.9% | 10,364 | 19.7% | LD |
| Marlow, J | Ref | 1,703 | 3.4% | | 347 | 0.7% | NLP |
| Saunders, R | UK Ind | 453 | 0.9% | | | | |
| Kahn, N | NLP | 191 | 0.4% | -0.3% | | | |
| C to Lab notional swing 15.1% | | 50,348 | | C maj 3,075 | 52,523 | | C maj 19,066 |
| | | | | 6.1% | | | 36.0% |

**JAMES CLAPPISON,** b Sept 14, 1956. Barrister and farmer. Retained this seat for C in 1992; contested both Bootle by-elections 1990; Barnsley E 1987, and Yorkshire South in 1989 Euro elections. Junior Environment Min 1995-97; ex-PPS to Lady Blatch, Home Office Min. Member, select cttee on members' interests, 1992-95. Ed St Peter's School, York; Queen's Coll, Oxford; Central London Poly; Gray's Inn.

**BETH KELLY,** b Dec 11, 1952. Senior lecturer. Hertsmere borough cllr 1992- . Member, Fabian Soc; Greenpeace; NUT; NASUWT; NATFHE. Ed local grammar school; Willfrun Coll of FE; Essex Univ; Westminster Univ.
**ANN GRAY,** b July 31, 1952. Teacher. Chiltern district cllr (group chair; dep leader). Member, Amnesty. Ed Kidbrooke Comp, London; West Midlands Coll of Ed, Staffs.

| HEXHAM | | | | | | | C hold |
|---|---|---|---|---|---|---|---|
| Electorate % Turnout | | 58,914 | 77.5% | **1997** | 57,812 | 82.4% | **1992** |
| *Atkinson, P | C | **17,701** | **38.8%** | -13.7% | **24,967** | **52.4%** | C |
| McMinn, I | Lab | 17,479 | 38.3% | +14.1% | 11,529 | 24.2% | Lab |
| Carr, Dr P | LD | 7,959 | 17.4% | -4.3% | 10,344 | 21.7% | LD |
| Waddell, R | Ref | 1,362 | 3.0% | | 781 | 1.6% | Grn |
| Lott, D | UK Ind | 1,170 | 2.6% | | | | |
| C to Lab swing 13.9% | | 45,671 | | C maj 222 | 47,621 | | C maj 13,438 |
| | | | | 0.5% | | | 28.2% |

**PETER ATKINSON,** b Jan 19, 1943. Journalist. Elected 1992. Member, select cttees on Euro legislation and Scottish affairs, 1992-97; deregulation 1995-97. PPS to Foreign Office mins 1995-96. Joint-vice-chair, 1994-95, and previously sec, C backbench ag, fish and food cttee; vice-chair, all-party forestry group. Wandsworth cllr 1978-82; Suffolk county cllr 1989-92. Journalist with London *Evening Standard* 1961-81 (news editor 1973-81). Joined S London Guardian Group and was chair, Southern Free Press Group, and on board of Deben Journal, Suffolk, 1981-87.

Dep director, British Field Sports Soc, 1987-92, becoming parly and public affairs consultant to society. Ed Cheltenham Coll.
**IAN McMINN,** b Sept 25, 1946. Self-employed sales agent. Northumberland county cllr; vice-chair (ex-chair), Haltwhistle Town Council. Ex-chair, North Tyneside community health council. Member, GMB. Ed Durham Univ; Newcastle Poly.
**PHILIP CARR,** b Sept 25, 1953. University lecturer. Tynedale district cllr 1995- . Member, Charter 88. Ed Peebles HS; Edinburgh Univ.

| HEYWOOD & MIDDLETON | | 29.6% change | | | | | Lab win |
|---|---|---|---|---|---|---|---|
| Electorate % Turnout | | 73,898 | 68.4% | **1997** | 74,759 | 74.5% | **1992** |
| Dobbin, J | Lab Co-op | **29,179** | **57.7%** | +11.2% | **25,885** | **46.5%** | Lab Co-op |
| Grigg, S | C | 11,637 | 23.0% | -8.6% | 17,591 | 31.6% | C |
| Clayton, D | LD | 7,908 | 15.6% | -4.3% | 11,119 | 20.0% | LD |
| West, Mrs C | Ref | 1,076 | 2.1% | | 922 | 1.7% | Lib |
| Burke, P | Lib | 750 | 1.5% | -0.2% | 171 | 0.3% | NLP |
| C to Lab notional swing 9.9% | | 50,550 | | Lab Co-op maj 17,542 | 55,688 | | Lab Co-op maj 8,294 |
| | | | | 34.7% | | | 14.9% |

**JIM DOBBIN,** b May 26, 1941. Contested Bury N 1992. Medical microbiologist. Dep leader, Rochdale Council; ex-chair, district Lab Party. Member, Rochdale HA; chair, Rochdale Credit Union. Fellow of Inst of Medical Laboratory Sciences. Member, MSF. Ed St Columbus HS, Cowdenbeath; St Andrews HS, Kirkcaldy.

**SEBASTIAN GRIGG,** b Dec 18, 1965. Banker with Goldman Sachs. Ed Eton; Oriel Coll, Oxford; Inseas Business School.
**DAVID CLAYTON,** b July 2, 1962. Teacher. Rochdale metropolitan borough cllr 1990-94. Ed North Chadderton Comp; St Chad's Coll, Durham. Plays guitar in a rock band.

| HIGH PEAK | | | | | | | Lab gain |
|---|---|---|---|---|---|---|---|
| Electorate % Turnout | | 72,315 | 79.0% | **1997** | 71,205 | 84.1% | **1992** |
| Levitt, T | Lab | **29,052** | **50.8%** | +12.9% | **27,538** | **46.0%** | C |
| +Hendry, C | C | 20,261 | 35.5% | -10.5% | 22,719 | 37.9% | Lab |
| Barber, Mrs S | LD | 6,420 | 11.2% | -3.6% | 8,861 | 14.8% | LD |
| Hanson-Orr, C | Ref | 1,420 | 2.5% | | 794 | 1.3% | Grn |
| C to Lab swing 3.6% | | 57,153 | | Lab maj 8,791 | 59,912 | | C maj 4,819 |
| | | | | 15.4% | | | 8.0% |

**TOM LEVITT,** b April 10, 1954. Research consultant, teacher and author. Contested this seat 1992; Cotswold in 1989 Euro elections; Stroud 1987. Derbyshire county cllr 1993- ; Stroud district cllr 1989-92; Cirencester town cllr 1983-87. Chair, county NUT. Ed Westwood HS, Leek, Staffs; Lancaster and Oxford Univs.
**CHARLES HENDRY,** b May 6, 1959. Elected 1992; contested Mansfield 1987 and Clackmannan 1983. Political adviser to Tony Newton, when Social Security Sec and DTI Min, 1988-90; political adviser to John Moore, Social Services Sec, May-Aug 1988. Member, select cttee on N Ireland affairs, 1994-97; procedure cttee, 1992-95. Former joint sec, C backbench social security cttee; ex-sec, C housing improvement sub-cttee; sec, E Midlands group of

C MPs. Former joint chair, all-party homelessness and housing need group; joint sec/treas, Lords and Commons ski club. Pres, British youth council, 1992- ; trustee, Drive for Youth, 1989- . Chair, Home Rent 16-23 plc. PR consultant to PR agency, Burson-Marsteller, and to Ogilvy & Mather, 1982-88. Ed Rugby; Edinburgh Univ (pres, univ C assoc, 1979-80).
**SUSAN BARBER,** b Dec 14, 1943. Senior biomedical scientist and former special needs teacher. Contested Bolsover 1992; Peak District in 1994 Euro elections. Mayor and chair, Tideswell Town Council, 1996, member since 1987; Derbyshire Dales district cllr 1995- . Fellow, Inst of Biomedical Science. Ed Cavendish GS, Buxton; Manchester Poly.

| HITCHIN & HARPENDEN | | 101.7% change | | | | | C win |
|---|---|---|---|---|---|---|---|
| Electorate % Turnout | | 67,219 | 78.0% | **1997** | 66,883 | 81.3% | **1992** |
| +Lilley, P B | C | 24,038 | 45.9% | -15.6% | 33,402 | 61.4% | C |
| Sanderson, Ms R | Lab | 17,367 | 33.1% | +15.3% | 10,766 | 19.8% | LD |
| White, C J | LD | 10,515 | 20.1% | +0.3% | 9,711 | 17.9% | Lab |
| Cooke, D | NLP | 290 | 0.6% | | 498 | 0.9% | Other |
| Horton, J | Soc | 217 | 0.4% | | | | |
| C to Lab notional swing 15.4% | | 52,427 | | C maj 6,671 | 54,377 | | C maj 22,636 |
| | | | | 12.7% | | | 41.6% |

**PETER LILLEY,** b Aug 23, 1943. Social Security Secretary 1992-97. MP for St Albans 1983-97; contested Haringey Tottenham Oct 1974. Trade and Industry Sec 1990-92; Financial Sec to the Treasury 1989-90; Economic Sec 1987-89. PPS to Nigel Lawson, Chancellor, 1984-87; to Lord Bellwin and William Waldegrave, Local Gvt Mins, Jan-Oct 1984. Investment adviser on N Sea oil and other energy industries 1972-84; chair, London Oil Analysts Co, 1979-80. Ed Dulwich Coll; Clare Coll, Cambridge.

**ROSEMARY SANDERSON,** b Oct 19, 1957. Company director. Hertfordshire county cllr. Member, Friends of the Earth; Greenpeace; Woodcraft Folk. Chair, St Albans CLP. Ed Leeds Univ. **CHRISTOPHER WHITE,** b June 8, 1959. Chartered accountant. Contested Hertford and Stortford 1992. Hertfordshire county cllr 1993- (LD group leader). Member, Friends of the Earth; Amnesty. Ed Merchant Taylors' School, Northwood; Corpus Christi Coll, Oxford.

| HOLBORN & ST PANCRAS | | 6.6% change | | | | | Lab win |
|---|---|---|---|---|---|---|---|
| Electorate % Turnout | | 63,037 | 60.3% | **1997** | 60,803 | 61.8% | **1992** |
| +Dobson, F | Lab | 24,707 | 65.0% | +10.8% | 20,377 | 54.3% | Lab |
| Smith, J L | C | 6,804 | 17.9% | -10.3% | 10,590 | 28.2% | C |
| McGuinness, Ms J | LD | 4,750 | 12.5% | -1.4% | 5,213 | 13.9% | LD |
| Carr, Mrs J | Ref | 790 | 2.1% | | 895 | 2.4% | Grn |
| Bedding, T | NLP | 191 | 0.5% | -0.0% | 198 | 0.5% | NLP |
| Smith, S | JP | 173 | 0.5% | | 161 | 0.4% | Socialist |
| Conway, B | WRP | 171 | 0.5% | | 126 | 0.3% | WAR |
| Rosenthal, M | Dream | 157 | 0.4% | | | | |
| Rice-Evans, P | EUP | 140 | 0.4% | | | | |
| Quintavalle, B | ProLife | 114 | 0.3% | | | | |
| C to Lab notional swing 10.5% | | 37,997 | | Lab maj 17,903 | 37,560 | | Lab maj 9,787 |
| | | | | 47.1% | | | 26.1% |

**FRANK DOBSON,** b March 15, 1940. Became Health Secretary, May 3, 1997. Elected for this seat 1983; MP for Holborn and St Pancras S 1979-83. Chief Lab spokesman on environment and London 1994-97. Elected to Shadow Cabinet 1987; chief spokesman on transport and London 1993-94; on employment 1992-93; energy 1989-92; shadow Leader of Commons and campaigns co-ordinator 1987-89; spokesman on health 1985-87; spokesman on education 1981-83. Ed Archbishop Holgate GS, York; LSE.

**JULIAN SMITH,** b Jan 17, 1965. Chartered accountant with Price Waterhouse. Brent cllr 1994- . Ed Hardenhuish Comp; Exeter Univ.
**JUSTINE McGUINNESS,** b Sept 26, 1969. Public affairs officer. Ex-member, NUS exec. Chair, Women LDs. Ed St Antony's, Leweston; Heythrop Coll, London (vice-pres, univ union 1991-92).

| HORNCHURCH | | | | | | | Lab gain |
|---|---|---|---|---|---|---|---|
| Electorate % Turnout | | 60,775 | 72.3% | **1997** | 60,522 | 79.8% | **1992** |
| Cryer, J | Lab | 22,066 | 50.2% | +15.7% | 25,817 | 53.5% | C |
| *Squire, R | C | 16,386 | 37.3% | -16.2% | 16,652 | 34.5% | Lab |
| Martins, R | LD | 3,446 | 7.8% | -3.3% | 5,366 | 11.1% | LD |
| Khilkoff-Boulding, R | Ref | 1,595 | 3.6% | | 453 | 0.9% | Soc Dem |
| Trueman, Miss J | Third | 259 | 0.6% | | | | |
| Sowerby, J | ProLife | 189 | 0.4% | | | | |
| C to Lab swing 16.0% | | 43,941 | | Lab maj 5,680 | 48,288 | | C maj 9,165 |
| | | | | 12.9% | | | 19.0% |

**JOHN CRYER,** b April 11, 1964. Journalist. Member, Euro safeguards cttee. Ed Oakbank School, Keighley; Hatfield Poly; London Coll of Printing. Son of the late Bob Cryer, Lab MP for Bradford S. His mother is Ann Cryer, Lab MP for Keighley.
**ROBIN SQUIRE,** b July 12, 1944. Chartered accountant, broadcaster. Gained this seat 1979; contested it Oct 1974. Junior Education and Employment Min 1995-97; junior Education Min 1993-95, and

junior Environment Min 1992-93. PPS to Chris Patten, party chairman, 1991-92. Dir, Link Assured Homes series of companies, 1988-92. Financial consultant to Lombard North Central plc, 1979-93. Ed Tiffin School, Kingston upon Thames.
**RABI MARTINS,** b July 5, 1945. Management consultant. Watford borough cllr. Member, London Assoc of Asian Youth Groups. Ed Dodoma Secondary, Tanzania; Royal Coll, Dublin.

## HORNSEY & WOOD GREEN — Lab hold

| Electorate % Turnout | | | 74,537 | 69.1% | 1997 | 73,491 | 75.9% | 1992 |
|---|---|---|---|---|---|---|---|---|
| *Roche, Mrs B | Lab | | 31,792 | 61.7% | +13.3% | 27,020 | 48.5% | Lab |
| Hart, Mrs H | C | | 11,293 | 21.9% | -17.2% | 21,843 | 39.2% | C |
| Featherstone, Ms L | LD | | 5,794 | 11.3% | +1.3% | 5,547 | 10.0% | LD |
| Jago, Ms H | Green | | 1,214 | 2.4% | | 1,051 | 1.9% | Grn |
| Miller, Ms R | Ref | | 808 | 1.6% | | 197 | 0.4% | NLP |
| Sikorski, P | Soc Lab | | 586 | 1.1% | | 89 | 0.2% | Rev Comm |
| C to Lab swing 15.3% | | | 51,487 | Lab maj 20,499 | | 55,747 | Lab maj 5,177 | |
| | | | | 39.8% | | | 9.3% | |

**BARBARA ROCHE,** b April 13, 1954. Became Trade and Industry Under Secretary, May 5, 1997. Non-practising barrister. Gained this seat for Lab 1992; contested it 1987, and Surrey SW by-election 1984. Lab spokeswoman on trade and industry 1995-97, with responsibility for small businesses; Lab whip 1994-95. PPS to Margaret Beckett, party deputy leader, 1993-94. Worked for local authority on crime prevention; previously with SE London law centre. Former exec cttee member, NCCL. Member, Soc of Lab Lawyers. Chair, Battersea Lab Party, 1981-85. Ed Jewish Free School Comp, Camden; Lady Margaret Hall, Oxford.

**HELENA HART,** b Aug 7, 1947. Dental practice manager (husband is dental surgeon); formerly PA in advertising, with J. Walter Thompson as PA in marketing and merchandising and PA to account exec. Barnett cllr 1990-94. Sec, Organisation for Rehabilitation through Training cttee; Sec, C Friends of Israel; C Way Forward; London area NHS task force. Ed La Sagesse Convent; Kilburn Poly; Triangle Coll, London.
**LYNNE FEATHERSTONE,** b Dec 20, 1951. Strategic design consultant. Member, LD federal exec cttee; vice-chair, Women LDs. Dir, Ryness Electrical Supplies Ltd. Ed South Hampstead HS; Oxford Brookes Univ.

## HORSHAM — 56.8% change — C win

| Electorate % Turnout | | | 75,432 | 75.8% | 1997 | 71,982 | 79.8% | 1992 |
|---|---|---|---|---|---|---|---|---|
| Maude, F A A | C | | 29,015 | 50.8% | -11.5% | 35,769 | 62.3% | C |
| Millson, Mrs M | LD | | 14,153 | 24.8% | +2.0% | 13,078 | 22.8% | LD |
| Walsh, Ms M | Lab | | 10,691 | 18.7% | +6.8% | 6,858 | 11.9% | Lab |
| Grant, R | Ref | | 2,281 | 4.0% | | 938 | 1.6% | Lib |
| Miller, H | UK Ind | | 819 | 1.4% | | 520 | 0.9% | Grn |
| Corbould, M | FEP | | 206 | 0.4% | | 246 | 0.4% | PPP |
| C to LD notional swing 6.8% | | | 57,165 | C maj 14,862 | | 57,409 | C maj 22,691 | |
| | | | | 26.0% | | | 39.5% | |

**FRANCIS MAUDE,** b July 4, 1953. Barrister. MP for Warwickshire N 1983-92. Chair, Gvt's deregulation task force, 1994-97. Financial Sec to Treasury 1990-92; Foreign Office Min for European matters, 1989-90; Corporate Affairs Min 1987-89; asst gvt whip 1985-87; PPS to Peter Morrison, Employment Min, 1984-85. Member, PAC, 1990-92. Westminster cllr 1978-84. Board member, Asda group plc, 1992- ; Morgan Stanley International Inc, 1993- ; dir, Salomon Bros, 1992-93. Ed Abingdon School; Corpus Christi Coll, Cambridge.

**MORWEN MILLSON,** b May 31, 1951. Ex-teacher. West Sussex county cllr 1989- . Member, CPRE; RSPB. Ed Ysgol Rhiwabon, Ruabon, Clwyd; Newcastle Univ.
**MAUREEN WALSH,** b Nov 12, 1955. Specialist in business admin/middle management. Member, Wandsworth community health council. Member, GMB; Co-op Retail Soc.

## HOUGHTON & WASHINGTON EAST — 41.7% change — Lab win

| Electorate % Turnout | | | 67,343 | 62.1% | 1997 | 66,678 | 69.4% | 1992 |
|---|---|---|---|---|---|---|---|---|
| Kemp, F | Lab | | 31,946 | 76.4% | +9.4% | 30,995 | 67.0% | Lab |
| Booth, P | C | | 5,391 | 12.9% | -8.8% | 10,046 | 21.7% | C |
| Miller, K | LD | | 3,209 | 7.7% | -3.6% | 5,221 | 11.3% | LD |
| Joseph, J | Ref | | 1,277 | 3.1% | | | | |
| C to Lab notional swing 9.1% | | | 41,823 | Lab maj 26,555 | | 46,262 | Lab maj 20,949 | |
| | | | | 63.5% | | | 45.3% | |

**FRASER KEMP,** b Sept 1, 1958. Full-time Lab Party official since 1981, being regional sec, W Midlands 1986-94; sec conference arrangements cttee 1993-96; national general election co-ordinator, 1994-96. Ex-civil servant. Ed Washington Comp.
**PHILIP BOOTH,** b April 14, 1964. University lecturer. Formerly

with Axa Equity & Law. Fellow of Inst of Actuaries; Fellow of Royal Statistical Soc. Ed Marist Coll, Hull; Durham Univ.
**KEITH MILLER,** b Jan 31, 1949. Senior medical rep in pharmaceutical industry. Member, MSF. Ed Newquay GS; Goldsmith's Coll, London.

## HOVE — Lab gain

| Electorate % Turnout | | 69,016 | 69.7% | **1997** | 67,450 | 74.3% | **1992** |
|---|---|---|---|---|---|---|---|
| **Caplin, I** | **Lab** | **21,458** | **44.6%** | **+20.1%** | **24,525** | **49.0%** | **C** |
| Guy, R | C | 17,499 | 36.4% | -12.6% | 12,257 | 24.5% | Lab |
| Pearce, T | LD | 4,645 | 9.7% | -9.7% | 9,709 | 19.4% | LD |
| Field, S | Ref | 1,931 | 4.0% | | 2,658 | 5.3% | Hove C |
| Furness, J | Ind C | 1,735 | 3.6% | | 814 | 1.6% | Grn |
| Mulligan, P | Green | 644 | 1.3% | | 126 | 0.3% | NLP |
| Vause, J | UK Ind | 209 | 0.4% | | | | |
| **C to Lab swing 16.4%** | | **48,121** | **Lab maj 3,959** | | **50,089** | **C maj 12,268** | |
| | | | 8.2% | | | 24.5% | |

**IVOR CAPLIN,** b Nov 8, 1958. Sales and marketing quality manager. Hove borough cllr 1991- (leader 1995- ); Brighton and Hove UA cllr 1996- . Chair, Hove CLP, 1986-92. Member, MSF; Co-op Party. Ed King Edward's School, Witley; Brighton Coll of Tech.
**ROBERT GUY,** b Dec 30, 1943. Director of merchant bank; formerly with C research dept. Contested London West in 1994 Euro elections. Assistant to Jeremy Hanley, MP, 1983, 1987 and 1992 elections. Pres, Kew C. Member, Coningsby Club. Ed Sir Joseph

Williamson's Mathematical School, Rochester; Kingswood School, Bath; Balliol Coll, Oxford.
**TOM PEARCE,** b Nov 21, 1934. Design consultant. Contested Brighton Pavilion 1992; Old Bexley and Sidcup 1987. Member, Charter 88. Trained sculptor, assistant to Dame Barbara Hepworth. Ed Porth County GS; Cardiff Coll of Art; Brentwood Coll of Ed.

## HUDDERSFIELD — Lab hold

| Electorate % Turnout | | 65,824 | 67.7% | **1997** | 67,604 | 72.3% | **1992** |
|---|---|---|---|---|---|---|---|
| ***Sheerman, B** | **Lab Co-op** | **25,171** | **56.5%** | **+7.8%** | **23,832** | **48.7%** | **Lab Co-op** |
| Forrow, W | C | 9,323 | 20.9% | -13.0% | 16,574 | 33.9% | C |
| Beever, G | LD | 7,642 | 17.2% | +1.2% | 7,777 | 15.9% | LD |
| McNulty, P | Ref | 1,480 | 3.3% | | 576 | 1.2% | Grn |
| Phillips, J | Green | 938 | 2.1% | | 135 | 0.3% | NLP |
| **C to Lab Co-op swing 10.4%** | | **44,554** | **Lab Co-op maj 15,848** | | **48,894** | **Lab Co-op maj 7,258** | |
| | | | 35.6% | | | 14.8% | |

**BARRY SHEERMAN,** b Aug 17, 1940. Elected for this seat in 1983; MP for Huddersfield E 1979-83; contested Taunton, Oct 1974. Partner in Coptech (Co-operation technology development); lecturer and academic adviser to Cornell Univ, N London Univ and Beaver Coll, Pennsylvania. Labour spokesman on disabled people's rights, 1992-94; spokesman on home affairs 1988-92; on employment and education 1983-88. Joint chair, all-party manufacturing industry group; sec, sustainable waste management group, 1995-97. Ed Hampton GS; Kingston Tech Coll; LSE.

**BILL FORROW,** b April 2, 1961. In psychiatric nursing since 1979. Teignbridge district cllr 1991- (C group leader). Ed Dawlish schools; S Devon Tech Coll; Digby School of Nursing; Tor Coll of Health Care.
**GORDON BEEVER,** b July 18, 1946. Chartered accountant; contested Batley and Spen 1992. Kirklees metropolitan borough cllr 1983- (dep group leader). Director, Kirklees Met Development Co Ltd. Ed Colne Valley GS; Pembroke Coll, Oxford.

## HULL EAST — Lab hold

| Electorate % Turnout | | 68,733 | 58.9% | **1997** | 69,036 | 69.7% | **1992** |
|---|---|---|---|---|---|---|---|
| ***Prescott, J** | **Lab** | **28,870** | **71.3%** | **+8.2%** | **30,396** | **63.1%** | **Lab** |
| West, A | C | 5,552 | 13.7% | -9.9% | 11,373 | 23.6% | C |
| Wastling, J | LD | 3,965 | 9.8% | -2.8% | 6,050 | 12.6% | LD |
| Rogers, G | Ref | 1,788 | 4.4% | | 323 | 0.7% | NLP |
| Nolan, Ms M | ProLife | 190 | 0.5% | | | | |
| Whitley, D | NLP | 121 | 0.3% | -0.4% | | | |
| **C to Lab swing 9.0%** | | **40,486** | **Lab maj 23,318** | | **48,142** | **Lab maj 19,023** | |
| | | | 57.6% | | | 39.5% | |

**JOHN PRESCOTT,** b May 31, 1938. Became Deputy Prime Minister and Secretary of State for Environm,ent, Transport and the Regions, May 2, 1997. Dep Leader of Labour Party 1994- , the office he contested in 1992 and 1988. Elected in 1970; contested Southport 1966. Elected, Lab NEC, 1989- . Joined Shadow Cabinet in 1983, being spokesman on employment 1993-94 and 1984-87; on transport 1988-93 and 1983-84; energy, 1987-88; regional affairs 1981-83; transport 1979-81. MEP 1975-79 and leader of Lab delegation 1976-79. Member, Council of Europe, 1972-75.

Officialof Nat Union of Seamen 1968-70; steward on passenger vessels, Merchant Navy, 1955-63; trainee chef 1953-55. Ed Grange Sec Mod, Ellesmere Port; Ruskin Coll, Oxford; Hull Univ.
**ANGUS WEST,** b Aug 8, 1965. Managing director, Garthwest Ltd, manufacturing company. Former vice-chair, Haltemprice and Howden C assoc; chair of Cottingham and district YCs. Ed Pocklington School; Hymers Coll; Hull Univ.
**JIM WASTLING,** b May 14, 1944. Farmer. Ex-Humberside county cllr, ex-Hull city cllr. Ed East Riding Inst of Agriculture.

164

## HULL NORTH — Lab hold

| Electorate % Turnout | | | 68,106 | 57.0% | 1997 | 71,363 | 66.7% | 1992 |
|---|---|---|---|---|---|---|---|---|
| *McNamara, K | Lab | | 25,542 | 65.8% | +9.9% | 26,619 | 55.9% | Lab |
| Lee, D | C | | 5,837 | 15.0% | -8.6% | 11,235 | 23.6% | C |
| Nolan, D | LD | | 5,667 | 14.6% | -5.4% | 9,504 | 20.0% | LD |
| Scott, A | Ref | | 1,533 | 4.0% | | 253 | 0.5% | NLP |
| Brotheridge, T | NLP | | 215 | 0.6% | +0.0% | | | |
| C to Lab swing 9.2% | | | 38,794 | Lab maj 19,705 | | 47,611 | Lab maj 15,384 | |
| | | | | 50.8% | | | 32.3% | |

KEVIN McNAMARA, b Sept 5, 1934. Elected for this seat 1983; MP for Hull Central, Feb 1974-83, and for Hull N, 1966-74; contested Bridlington 1964. Lab spokesman on Civil Service 1994-95; on N Ireland 1987-94; on defence and disarmament 1982-87. Member, foreign affairs select cttee, 1977-82. Sec, all-party Anglo-Irish group; TGWU parly group. Lecturer in law. Ed St Mary's Coll, Crosby; Hull Univ.

DAVID LEE, b Oct 28, 1963. Sales and marketing consultant. Researcher to John Whittingdale, MP. Public affairs and communications adviser 1993-95. Essex county cllr 1989-93. Ed, Rainsford School, Chelmsford; Chelmsford Coll of FE.
DAVID NOLAN, b March 5, 1959. Market research manager. East Riding of Yorkshire cllr (LD group leader); Beverley borough cllr 1991-95. Ed Windsor Boys' School, Goldsmiths Coll, London.

## HULL WEST & HESSLE — 19.4% change — Lab win

| Electorate % Turnout | | | 65,840 | 58.3% | 1997 | 66,996 | 67.1% | 1992 |
|---|---|---|---|---|---|---|---|---|
| Johnson, A A | Lab | | 22,520 | 58.7% | +7.2% | 23,151 | 51.5% | Lab |
| Tress, R D | LD | | 6,995 | 18.2% | +0.8% | 13,634 | 30.3% | C |
| Moore, C | C | | 6,933 | 18.1% | -12.3% | 7,837 | 17.4% | LD |
| Bate, R | Ref | | 1,596 | 4.2% | | 335 | 0.7% | Other |
| Franklin, B | NLP | | 310 | 0.8% | | | | |
| LD to Lab notional swing 3.2% | | | 38,354 | Lab maj 15,525 | | 44,957 | Lab maj 9,517 | |
| | | | | 40.5% | | | 21.3% | |

ALAN JOHNSON, b May 17, 1950. Ex-postman. Joint gen sec, Communications Workers' Union, 1992-97; gen sec, Union of Communication Workers, 1993-95. Postman 1968; union official since 1974. Member, TUC General Council. Dir, Unity Trust Bank plc. Governor, Ruskin Coll. Ed Sloane GS, Chelsea.
BOB TRESS, b July 22, 1941. Contested Hull W 1992. Full-time cllr; retired lecturer. Sec, Hull West LDs. East Riding of Yorkshire UA

cllr (joint leader); Beverley borough cllr 1979- (leader 1991- ); Hessle town cllr 1986- (chair, 1990-91; vice-chair, 1991- ). Dir, Starting Point (Services) Ltd, Birmingham. RSPB. Ed Manchester Grammar; Queen's Coll, Oxford.
CORMACH MOORE, b Dec 22, 1967. Ad agency marketing manager. Marketing and public relations exec. Brent cllr since 1990 (majority whip from 1993). Ed William Gladstone Comp, London.

## HUNTINGDON — 85.0% change — C win

| Electorate % Turnout | | | 76,094 | 74.9% | 1997 | 71,409 | 79.6% | 1992 |
|---|---|---|---|---|---|---|---|---|
| +Major, J | C | | 31,501 | 55.3% | -4.7% | 34,124 | 60.0% | C |
| Reece, J | Lab | | 13,361 | 23.5% | +9.0% | 12,153 | 21.4% | LD |
| Owen, M | LD | | 8,390 | 14.7% | -6.6% | 8,234 | 14.5% | Lab |
| Bellamy, D | Ref | | 3,114 | 5.5% | | 788 | 1.4% | Lib |
| Coyne, C | UK Ind | | 331 | 0.6% | | 646 | 1.1% | Grn |
| Hufford, Ms V | Ch D | | 177 | 0.3% | | 553 | 1.0% | Loony |
| Robertson, D | Ind | | 89 | 0.2% | | 181 | 0.3% | C Thatch |
| | | | | | | 82 | 0.1% | Gremloids |
| | | | | | | 66 | 0.1% | FTM |
| | | | | | | 26 | 0.0% | NLP |
| C to Lab notional swing 6.8% | | | 56,963 | C maj 18,140 | | 56,853 | C maj 21,971 | |
| | | | | 31.8% | | | 38.6% | |

JOHN MAJOR, b March 29, 1943. Prime Minister and First Lord of the Treasury Nov 1990 to May 1997. Elected Nov 1990 to succeed Margaret Thatcher as C Party leader; resigned as leader in June 1995 to force contest and defeated John Redwood. Elected for this seat 1983; MP for Huntingdonshire 1979-83; contested Camden, St Pancras N, Feb and Oct 1974. Chancellor of the Exchequer 1989-90; Foreign Secretary July to Oct 1989; Treasury Chief Sec, 1987-89; Min for Social Security and the Disabled 1986-87; Under Sec for Social Security 1985-86; gvt whip 1984-85; asst gvt whip 1983-84. Exec, Standard Chartered Bank, 1965-79; Associate of

Inst of Bankers. Chair (ex-officio), UK branch, CPA; pres, British group, IPU. Ed Rutlish GS, Merton.
JASON REECE, b Dec 28, 1968. Teacher. Peterborough city cllr 1995- . Ed Pooles Hayes School, Willenhall; Nottingham Univ.
MATTHEW OWEN, b Nov 15, 1968. Senior analyst banker. Ed Exeter School; St Catherine's Coll, Oxford.
DAVID BELLAMY, b Jan 18, 1933. Botanist, environmentalist, TV journalist. Special professor, Nottingham Univ, 1987- . Dir, David Bellamy Associates. Ed Chelsea Coll of Science and Tech; Bedford Coll, London.

| HYNDBURN | | 12.5% change○ | | | | | Lab win |
|---|---|---|---|---|---|---|---|
| Electorate % Turnout | | 66,806 | 72.3% | **1997** | 66,766 | 83.2% | **1992** |
| +Pope, G | Lab | 26,831 | 55.6% | +8.7% | 26,026 | 46.8% | Lab |
| Britcliffe, P | C | 15,383 | 31.9% | -11.3% | 23,995 | 43.2% | C |
| Jones, L | LD | 4,141 | 8.6% | -1.0% | 5,314 | 9.6% | LD |
| Congdon, P | Ref | 1,627 | 3.4% | | 219 | 0.4% | NLP |
| Brown, J | IAC | 290 | 0.6% | | | | |
| C to Lab notional swing 10.0% | | 48,272 | Lab maj 11,448 | | 55,554 | Lab maj 2,031 | |
| | | | 23.7% | | | 3.7% | |

**GREG POPE,** b Aug 29, 1960. Became gvt asst whip, May 7, 1997. Won this seat 1992; contested Ribble Valley 1987. Lab whip 1995-97. Member, education select cttee, 1992-95; former sec, PLP education committee. Local gvt officer 1987-92. Hyndburn borough cllr 1984-88; Blackburn borough cllr 1989-91. Ed St Mary's Coll, Blackburn; Hull Univ.

**PETER BRITCLIFFE,** b June 1, 1950. Teacher, special educational needs. Dir, East Lancs into Employment. Lancs county cllr (C group leader 1992- ); Hyndburn borough cllr. Ed Accrington GS; Chorley Coll of Ed.
**LES JONES,** b Dec 15, 1943. Teacher. Hyndburn district cllr. Member, Lancashire Authors' Assoc. Ed Accrington and Rossendale Coll; Lancaster Univ.

| ILFORD NORTH | | 75.5% change | | | | | Lab win |
|---|---|---|---|---|---|---|---|
| Electorate % Turnout | | 68,218 | 71.6% | **1997** | 67,904 | 74.0% | **1992** |
| Perham, Ms L | Lab | 23,135 | 47.4% | +17.5% | 29,076 | 57.8% | C |
| +Bendall, V | C | 19,911 | 40.8% | -17.1% | 15,027 | 29.9% | Lab |
| Dean, A | LD | 5,049 | 10.3% | -1.9% | 6,174 | 12.3% | LD |
| Wilson, P | BNP | 750 | 1.5% | | | | |
| C to Lab notional swing 17.3% | | 48,845 | Lab maj 3,224 | | 50,277 | C maj 14,049 | |
| | | | 6.6% | | | 27.9% | |

**LINDA PERHAM,** b June 29, 1947. Librarian. Redbridge cllr. Member, Unison; Co-op Party; SEA. Ed Mary Datchelor GS, Camberwell; Leicester Univ; Ealing Tech Coll.
**VIVIAN BENDALL,** b Dec 14, 1938. Sole principal of Bendall's, surveyors and valuers. Elected for this seat at 1978 by-election; contested Hertford and Stevenage Feb and Oct 1974. Joint vice-chair, C backbench employment cttee, 1984-87; joint sec, 1981-84; vice-chair, C backbench transport cttee, 1982-83; sec, foreign and Commonwealth affairs cttee, 1981-84. Croydon cllr 1964-78; GLC cllr 1970-74. Chair, Greater London YCs, 1967-68. Ed Coombe Hill House, Croydon; Broadgreen Coll, Croydon.
**ALAN DEAN,** b May 23, 1946. Chartered electrical engineer. Uttlesford district cllr 1987- (council leader 1995- ). Member, Charter 88; Green LDs; Soc of Telecom Executives. Ed Padiham County HS, Lancashire; Salford Univ.

| ILFORD SOUTH | | 39.3% change | | | | | Lab win |
|---|---|---|---|---|---|---|---|
| Electorate % Turnout | | 72,104 | 69.4% | **1997** | 68,665 | 76.6% | **1992** |
| +Gapes, M | Lab Co-op | 29,273 | 58.5% | | 24,677 | 46.9% | C |
| Thorne, Sir Neil | C | 15,073 | 30.1% | -16.8% | 22,147 | 42.1% | Lab |
| Khan, Ms A | LD | 3,152 | 6.3% | -4.1% | 5,493 | 10.4% | LD |
| Hodges, D | Ref | 1,073 | 2.1% | | 269 | 0.5% | NLP |
| Ramsey, B | Soc Lab | 868 | 1.7% | | | | |
| Owens, A | BNP | 580 | 1.2% | | | | |
| No swing calculation | | 50,019 | Lab Co-op maj 14,200 | | 52,586 | C maj 2,530 | |
| | | | 28.4% | | | 4.8% | |

**MIKE GAPES,** b Sept 4, 1952. Gained seat for Lab in 1992; contested Ilford N 1983. Member, foreign affairs select cttee, 1992-97. Vice-chair, PLP defence cttee, 1992- ; joint vice-chair, Inter-parliamentary council against Anti-Semitism, 1992- ; chair, PLP children and families cttee, 1994-95. Senior international officer, Lab Party, 1988-92; research officer 1980-88; nat student organiser 1977-80; chair, nat organisation of Lab students, 1976-77. Pres, Redbridge Utd Chinese Assoc. Vice-pres, Redbridge Chamber of Coimmerce. Member, Co-op Party; TGWU. Ed Buckhurst Hill HS, Essex; Fitzwilliam Coll, Cambridge; Middlesex Poly.
**SIR NEIL THORNE,** b Aug 8, 1932. Chartered surveyor and Lloyd's underwriter. MP for Ilford S, 1979-92; contested seat Oct 1974. Member, select cttee on defence, 1983-92; Court of Referees 1987-92. Joint sec, all-party group on war crimes, 1987-92. Founder and chair, Armed Forces parly scheme, 1988-97; police service parly scheme, 1994-97. Chair, Anglo-Nepalese all-party group, 1983-92; British-Korean group 1989-92; joint vice-chair, Kashmir and Pakistan groups; joint sec, Tibet group, 1989-92. Chair, Nat Council for Civil Defence, 1982-86. Dep Lieut for Greater London 1991; TA (1952-82), Lt-Col commanding London Univ Officers' Training Corps. Member, Chapter General, Order of St John, 1989- , and Almoner, 1995- . Fellow, Industry and Parliament Trust, 1980 and 1990. Ed City of London School; London Univ.
**AINA KHAN,** b June 27, 1962. Solicitor. Exec member, Ethnic Minority LDs 1990-94. Ed Ilford County HS for Girls; East London Univ; Coll of Law, Guildford.

## INVERNESS EAST, NAIRN & LOCHABER  12.1% change  Lab win

| Electorate % Turnout | | 65,701 | 72.7% | 1997 | 63,321 | 72.5% | 1992 |
|---|---|---|---|---|---|---|---|
| Stewart, D | Lab | 16,187 | 33.9% | +10.7% | 12,249 | 26.7% | LD |
| Ewing, F S | SNP | 13,848 | 29.0% | +3.9% | 11,513 | 25.1% | SNP |
| Gallagher, S H | LD | 8,364 | 17.5% | -9.2% | 10,777 | 23.5% | C |
| Scanlon, Mrs M E | C | 8,355 | 17.5% | -6.0% | 10,633 | 23.2% | Lab |
| Wall, Ms W | Ref | 436 | 0.9% | | 720 | 1.6% | Other |
| Falconer, M | Green | 354 | 0.7% | | | | |
| Hart, D | Ch U | 224 | 0.5% | | | | |
| SNP to Lab notional swing 3.4% | | 47,768 | | Lab maj 2,339 | 45,892 | | LD maj 736 |
| | | | | 4.9% | | | 1.6% |

**DAVID STEWART,** b May 5, 1956. Social work area manager, Highland Regional Council. Contested this seat 1992 and 1987. Member, Lab Party Scottish exec, 1985- ; Dumfries district cllr 1984-86; Inverness district cllr 1988- (dep leader, Lab group, 1988-96). Member, Scottish Council for Single Homeless; Nalgo; Nupe. Ed Paisley Coll; Stirling Univ.

**FERGUS EWING,** b Sept 23, 1957. Solicitor. Contested this seat 1992. Member, SNP nat exec; spokesman for small business. Ed Glasgow Univ. Husband of Margaret Ewing, MP for Moray, and son of Winnie Ewing, MEP for Highlands and Islands.

**STEPHEN GALLAGHER,** b Oct 9, 1967. Health trust manager. Contested Monklands E by-election 1994. Ed St Colomba of Iona Sec, Glasgow; Glasgow Univ (pres of union 1989-90); Gregorian Univ, Rome.

**MARY SCANLON,** b May 25, 1947. Lecturer in economics. Contested Fife NE 1992. Ed Craigo School, Montrose; Dundee Univ.

## IPSWICH  0.4% change  Lab win

| Electorate % Turnout | | 66,947 | 72.2% | 1997 | 68,148 | 79.0% | 1992 |
|---|---|---|---|---|---|---|---|
| +Cann, J | Lab | 25,484 | 52.7% | +8.8% | 23,623 | 43.9% | Lab |
| Castle, S | C | 15,045 | 31.1% | -12.2% | 23,288 | 43.3% | C |
| Roberts, N | LD | 5,881 | 12.2% | +0.8% | 6,135 | 11.4% | LD |
| Agnew, T | Ref | 1,637 | 3.4% | | 588 | 1.1% | Grn |
| Vinyard, W | UK Ind | 208 | 0.4% | | 181 | 0.3% | NLP |
| Kaplan, E | NLP | 107 | 0.2% | -0.1% | | | |
| C to Lab notional swing 10.5% | | 48,362 | | Lab maj 10,439 | 53,815 | | Lab maj 335 |
| | | | | 21.6% | | | 0.6% |

**JAMES CANN,** b June 28, 1946. Ex-teacher. Won this seat for Lab 1992. Joint sec, all-party Northern Cyprus group, 1996- . Ipswich borough cllr 1973-91 (leader, Lab group, 1976-91; council leader 1979-91). Deputy head, Handford Hall Primary School, Ipswich, 1981-92. Ex-member, Ipswich Port Authority. Ed Barton on Humber GS; Kesteven Coll of Ed.

**STEPHEN CASTLE,** b July 4, 1964. Head of marketing and managing partner of K. Castle opticians; asst dir, Sedgwick group, Lloyd's insurance brokers, 1982-93. Castlepoint district cllr 1987- . Ed Deanes School; SE Essex Sixth-Form Coll.

**NIGEL ROBERTS,** b March 1, 1958. IT chartered engineer. Dir, Ipswich Airport Assoc Ltd; Orichalk Ltd; Island Networks Ltd. Ed Prescott GS; Essex Univ.

## ISLE OF WIGHT  LD gain

| Electorate % Turnout | | 101,680 | 72.0% | 1997 | 99,838 | 79.8% | 1992 |
|---|---|---|---|---|---|---|---|
| Brand, Dr P | LD | 31,274 | 42.7% | -2.9% | 38,163 | 47.9% | C |
| Turner, A | C | 24,868 | 34.0% | -13.9% | 36,336 | 45.6% | LD |
| Gardiner, Ms D | Lab | 9,646 | 13.2% | +7.2% | 4,784 | 6.0% | Lab |
| Bristow, T | Ref | 4,734 | 6.5% | | 350 | 0.4% | NLP |
| Turner, M | UK Ind | 1,072 | 1.5% | | | | |
| Rees, H | Ind Isl | 848 | 1.2% | | | | |
| Scivier, P | Green | 544 | 0.7% | | | | |
| Daly, C | NLP | 87 | 0.1% | -0.3% | | | |
| Eveleigh, J | Rain Isl | 86 | 0.1% | | | | |
| C to LD swing 5.5% | | 73,159 | | LD maj 6,406 | 79,633 | | C maj 1,827 |
| | | | | 8.8% | | | 2.3% |

**PETER BRAND,** b May 16, 1947. Family doctor and former chair, BMA. Contested this seat 1992. Isle of Wight county and unitary authority cllr 1985- (dep group leader). Ex-chair, Isle of Wight Lib political cttee. Ed Thornbury GS, Gloucs; Birmingham Univ.

**ANDREW TURNER,** b Oct 24, 1953. Head of Grant-Maintained Schools Foundation. Contested Hackney S and Shoreditch 1992; contested Birmingham East in 1994 Euro elections. Ex-teacher and special adviser to Social Services Ministers 1986-88. Member, education manifesto groups 1987 and 1992. Oxford city cllr 1984- . Ed Rugby; Keble Coll, Oxford; Birmingham Univ.

**DEBORAH GARDINER,** b June 5, 1965. Administrator for Unison and local gvt officer. Member, Lab regional exec cttee. Member, Friends of the Earth; Greenpeace; National Childbirth Trust; League Against Cruel Sports. Ed Lancaster Univ.

| ISLINGTON NORTH | | | | | | **Lab hold** |
|---|---|---|---|---|---|---|
| Electorate % Turnout | | 57,385 | 62.5% | **1997** | 56,270 | 67.3% | **1992** |
| *Corbyn, J | Lab | **24,834** | **69.3%** | **+11.8%** | 21,742 | 57.4% | Lab |
| Kempton, J | LD | 4,879 | 13.6% | -1.5% | 8,958 | 23.7% | C |
| Fawthrop, S | C | 4,631 | 12.9% | -10.8% | 5,732 | 15.1% | LD |
| Ashby, C | Green | 1,516 | 4.2% | | 1,420 | 3.8% | Grn |
| LD to Lab swing 6.7% | | 35,860 | Lab maj **19,955** | | 37,852 | Lab maj 12,784 | |
| | | | 55.6% | | | 33.8% | |

**JEREMY CORBYN,** b May 26, 1949. Former union official. Elected 1983. Member, select cttee on social security 1990-97. Sec, Campaign Group of Lab MPs, 1987; director, Campaign Group News Ltd. Chair, London group of Lab MPs, 1993-95 (vice-chair, 1985-93). Chair, Campaign for Non-Alignment. Vice-chair, PLP health cttee, 1989-90, and PLP health and social security cttee, 1985-89. Joint vice-chair, PLP N Ireland cttee, 1988-89 and 1990- . Haringey cllr 1974-83. Member, National Trust; Unison; Cuba Solidarity. Ed Adams GS, Newport, Shropshire.

**JAMES KEMPTON,** b Sept 17, 1960. Senior manager. Sec British Paediatric Assoc. Islington cllr 1994- (chief whip). Member, Islington community health council 1995- . Member, National Trust; Stonewall. Ed Eltham Coll; York Univ.
**SIMON FAWTHROP,** b May 23, 1963. Gvt service manager, BT plc; director, Brewster's Computer Training Ltd. Lambeth cllr 1986-94. Candidate for gen sec, Nat Communications Union, in 1989. JP for Inner London. Member, National Trust. Ed Strand GS, Lambeth; Furzedown Sec, Tooting.

| ISLINGTON SOUTH & FINSBURY | | 1.6% change | | | | **Lab win** |
|---|---|---|---|---|---|---|
| Electorate % Turnout | | 55,468 | 63.7% | **1997** | 54,443 | 73.1% | **1992** |
| +Smith, C | Lab | **22,079** | **62.5%** | **+11.3%** | 20,369 | 51.2% | Lab |
| Ludford, Ms S A | LD | 7,516 | 21.3% | -1.9% | 9,818 | 24.7% | C |
| Berens, D | C | 4,587 | 13.0% | -11.7% | 9,232 | 23.2% | LD |
| Bryett, Miss J | Ref | 741 | 2.1% | | 147 | 0.4% | JBR |
| Laws, A | ACA | 171 | 0.5% | | 140 | 0.4% | Loony |
| Creese, M | NLP | 121 | 0.3% | +0.1% | 82 | 0.2% | NLP |
| Basarik, E | Ind | 101 | 0.3% | | | | |
| LD to Lab notional swing 6.6% | | 35,316 | Lab maj **14,563** | | 39,788 | Lab maj 10,551 | |
| | | | 41.2% | | | 26.5% | |

**CHRIS SMITH,** b July 24, 1951. Became National Heritage Secretary, May 3, 1997. Elected 1983; contested Epsom and Ewell 1979. Elected to Shadow Cabinet 1992, Shadow Health Sec 1996-97; Shadow Social Security Sec 1995-96; spokesman on nat heritage 1994-95; spokesman on environment 1992-94; Treasury 1987-92. Chair, Tribune Group, 1988-89; board, *Tribune*, 1990-93; board, *New Century*, 1993-96. Member, exec cttee, Fabian Soc, 1990- . Ex-governor, Sadler's Wells Theatre; ex-dir, Grand Union Orchestra. Completed ascent of all Scottish "Munro" mountains

1989. Ed George Watson's Coll, Edinburgh; Pembroke Coll, Cambridge; Harvard.
**SARAH LUDFORD,** b March 14, 1951. European affairs consultant. Contested Islington N 1992; London Central in 1994 and 1989 and Wight & Hants in 1984 Euro elections. Ed Portsmouth HS; LSE; Inns of Court School of Law.
**DAVID BERENS,** b March 16, 1962. Partner in law firm. Contested Salford E 1992. Westminster city cllr 1990-94. Ed Bury GS; Dulwich Coll; Guildford Coll of Law.

| ISLWYN | | | | | | **Lab hold** |
|---|---|---|---|---|---|---|
| Electorate % Turnout | | 50,540 | 72.0% | **1997** | 51,079 | 81.4% | **1992** |
| *Touhig, D | Lab Co-op | **26,995** | **74.2%** | **-0.2%** | 30,908 | 74.3% | Lab Co-op |
| Worker, C | LD | 3,064 | 8.4% | +2.8% | 6,180 | 14.9% | C |
| Walters, R | C | 2,864 | 7.9% | -7.0% | 2,352 | 5.7% | LD |
| Jones, D | PC | 2,272 | 6.2% | +2.4% | 1,606 | 3.9% | PC |
| Monaghan, Mrs S | Ref | 1,209 | 3.3% | | 547 | 1.3% | Loony |
| Lab Co-op to LD swing 1.5% | | 36,404 | Lab Co-op maj **23,931** | | 41,593 | Lab Co-op maj 24,728 | |
| | | | 65.7% | | | 59.5% | |

**DON TOUHIG,** b Dec 5, 1947. Journalist. Won 1995 by-election following resignation of Neil Kinnock. Sec, Welsh group of Lab MPs, 1995- ; chair, all-party alcohol misuse group, 1996- . Gen manager, Free Press Group, 1988-92; with Bailey Group 1992-93, and Bailey Print 1993-95. Parly adviser to Police Fed. Member, Co-op Party; TGWU; Mencap; Mensa. Ed St Francis School, Aberyschan; E Monmouth Coll, Pontypool.
**CHRIS WORKER,** b April 26, 1954. Theatre and concert hall house manager. Member, Railway Development Soc; National Campaign for the Arts. Ed Gasingwold Comp, Aberystwyth.

**RUSSELL WALTERS,** b July 14, 1961. Public relations director; research associate, Adam Smith Institute, 1982-83. Member, National YC advisory cttee. Chief of Staff, Scottish Central Office, 1989; dir, Campaign for Freedom in Europe. Politcal adviser, Seychelles Democratic Party, 1992-93. Treas, Holborn and St Pancras C assoc 1994- . Ed Aberdare Boys' GS; Kent Univ.
**DARREN JONES,** b June 23, 1973. Sales administrator. Delegate to Plaid Cymru nat council 1995-97. Ed Tonypandy Comp, Rhondda; Ystrad Mynach Coll.

*Details of 1995 by-election on page 278*

| JARROW | | 21.9% change | | o | | | | Lab win |
|---|---|---|---|---|---|---|---|---|
| Electorate % Turnout | | 63,828 | 68.8% | **1997** | 65,577 | 73.2% | **1992** | |
| **Hepburn, S** | Lab | **28,497** | **64.9%** | +2.4% | 29,978 | 62.5% | Lab | |
| Allatt, M | C | 6,564 | 14.9% | -8.5% | 11,243 | 23.4% | C | |
| Stone, T | LD | 4,865 | 11.1% | -3.0% | 6,749 | 14.1% | LD | |
| LeBlond, A | Ind Lab | 2,538 | 5.8% | | | | | |
| Mailer, P | Ref | 1,034 | 2.4% | | | | | |
| Bissett, J | SPGB | 444 | 1.0% | | | | | |
| **C to Lab notional swing 5.4%** | | **43,942** | | Lab maj 21,933 | **47,970** | | Lab maj 18,735 | |
| | | | | 49.9% | | | 39.1% | |

**STEPHEN HEPBURN,** b Dec 6, 1959. Won this seat 1997. Research assistant to Don Dixon, ex-Lab MP for Jarrow and party whip. South Tyneside cllr 1985- (dep council leader). Chair, Tyne and Wear Pensions. Member, Assoc of Labour Cllrs; Co-op Party. Ed Springfield Comp; Newcastle Univ.
**MARK ALLATT,** b Nov 19, 1965. Head of PR, KPMG Management Consulting. Sec, C Way Forward. Member, Central Office gen election communications team, 1992. Marketing director, A1

Steam Locomotive Trust, a charity. Ed Frederick Gough School, Bottesford; John Leggott Sixth-Form Coll, Scunthorpe; De Montfort Univ, Leicester; OU.
**TIM STONE,** b Dec 21, 1947. Private tutor and former clinical scientist. Blyth town cllr 1990-95. Chair, South Tyneside LDs. Ed Hollyhead Comp, Salford; Marple Hall GS; Liverpool Poly; Surrey Univ.

| KEIGHLEY | | | | | | | Lab gain |
|---|---|---|---|---|---|---|---|
| Electorate % Turnout | | 67,231 | 76.6% | **1997** | 66,358 | 82.6% | **1992** |
| **Cryer, Mrs A** | Lab | **26,039** | **50.6%** | +9.7% | 25,983 | 47.4% | C |
| *Waller, G | C | 18,907 | 36.7% | -10.7% | 22,387 | 40.8% | Lab |
| Doyle, M | LD | 5,064 | 9.8% | -0.7% | 5,793 | 10.6% | LD |
| Carpenter, C | Ref | 1,470 | 2.9% | | 642 | 1.2% | Grn |
| **C to Lab swing 10.2%** | | **51,480** | | Lab maj 7,132 | **54,805** | | C maj 3,596 |
| | | | | 13.9% | | | 6.6% |

**ANN CRYER,** b Dec 13, 1939. Researcher, Oral History Project, Essex Univ. Darwen borough cllr 1962-65. Member, social security appeals tribunal. Vice-pres, Keighley and Worth Valley Railway Preservation Soc. Former researcher and PA to her late husband, Bob Cryer (former Labour MP for Bradford S and MEP). Mother of John Cryer, Lab MP for Hornchurch. Ed technical coll.
**GARY WALLER,** b June 24, 1945. Won this seat 1983; MP for Brighouse and Spenborough 1979-83; contested Rother Valley Feb and Oct 1974. Joint vice-chair, all-party motor industry group;

parly food and health forum, 1985- ; vice-chair, Bangladesh group; Czech and Slovak group; Korean Republic group; sec, home safety group; cycling group; UK Eurosolar group; joint sec, rugby league group, 1989- . Vice-pres, Inst of Trading Standards Administration, 1988- . Member (unpaid), council, Consumers' Assoc, 1995- . Parly adviser to Machine Tool Technologies Assoc. Vice-chair, Friends of Settle-Carlisle Railway, 1987- . Ed Rugby; Lancaster Univ.
**MIKE DOYLE,** b April 3, 1944. Teacher, writer on IT. Craven district cllr. Ed Wyggeston Boys, Leicester; Leeds and Manchester Univs.

| KENSINGTON & CHELSEA | | 50.2% change | | | | | | C win |
|---|---|---|---|---|---|---|---|---|
| Electorate % Turnout | | 67,786 | 54.7% | **1997** | 64,046 | 66.4% | **1992** | |
| **Clark, A K M** | C | **19,887** | **53.6%** | -14.6% | 28,979 | 68.2% | C | |
| Atkinson, R | Lab | 10,368 | 28.0% | +11.3% | 7,080 | 16.7% | Lab | |
| Woodthorpe Browne, R | LD | 5,668 | 15.3% | +2.1% | 5,590 | 13.2% | LD | |
| Ellis-Jones, Ms A | UK Ind | 540 | 1.5% | | 855 | 2.0% | Other | |
| Bear, E | Teddy | 218 | 0.6% | | | | | |
| Oliver, J | UKPP | 176 | 0.5% | | | | | |
| Hamza, Ms S | NLP | 122 | 0.3% | | | | | |
| Sullivan, P | Dream | 65 | 0.2% | | | | | |
| Parliament, P | Heart | 44 | 0.1% | | | | | |
| **C to Lab notional swing 12.9%** | | **37,088** | | C maj 9,519 | **42,504** | | C maj 21,899 | |
| | | | | 25.7% | | | 51.5% | |

**ALAN CLARK,** b April 13, 1928. Historian, diarist and barrister. Elected for this seat 1997. MP for Plymouth Sutton Feb 1974-92. Min for Defence 1989-92; Min for Trade 1986-89; junior Employment Min 1983-86. Member, select cttee on broadcasting of Commons, 1979-83. Joint sec, C backbench home affairs cttee, 1982-83; vice-chair, C defence cttee, 1980-81. Ed Eton; Christ Church, Oxford.

**ROBERT ATKINSON,** b Jan 1, 1954. Director of American Inst for Foreign Study. Kensington & Chelsea cllr 1988- (leader, Lab group, 1993- ). Member, Christian Socialist Movement. Ed Carr Hill Sec Mod; Leeds Univ; John Hopkins Univ, Washington, DC.
**ROBERT WOODTHORPE BROWNE,** b May 26, 1943. Reinsurance broker. Contested Harlow 1979; London Central in 1979 Euro elections. Ed St Ignatius' Coll, Stamford Hill; Birkbeck Coll, London; Université de Poitiers; Universidad de Barcelona.

| KETTERING | | 5.3% change | | | Lab win | | |
|---|---|---|---|---|---|---|---|
| Electorate % Turnout | | 75,153 | 75.8% | **1997** | 72,383 | 80.9% | **1992** |
| Sawford, P A | Lab | **24,650** | 43.3% | +11.4% | **30,884** | 52.7% | C |
| +Freeman, R | C | 24,461 | 42.9% | -9.8% | 18,697 | 31.9% | Lab |
| Aron, R | LD | 6,098 | 10.7% | -4.7% | 9,012 | 15.4% | LD |
| Smith, A | Ref | 1,551 | 2.7% | | | | |
| le Carpentier, Mrs R | NLP | 197 | 0.3% | | | | |
| C to Lab notional swing 10.6% | | 56,957 | | Lab maj 189 | 58,593 | | C maj 12,187 |
| | | | | 0.3% | | | 20.8% |

**PHILIP SAWFORD,** b June 26, 1950. Manager of training organisation. Contested Wellingborough 1992. Desborough town cllr 1977-91; Kettering borough cllr 1979-83 and 1986-91. Ed Kettering GS; Ruskin Coll, Oxford; Leicester Univ.
**ROGER FREEMAN,** b May 27, 1942. Chartered accountant. Elected 1983; contested Don Valley 1979. Appointed to Cabinet 1995 as Chancellor of Duchy of Lancaster and Public Service Min, and supporting Michael Heseltine, Dep PM, in Cabinet Office. Defence Procurement Min 1994-95; Public Transport Min 1990-94; junior

Health Min 1988-90; junior Armed Forces Min 1986-88. General partner, Lehman Brothers, 1969-86, being exec dir, Lehman Brothers International (UK) Ltd, 1972-86, and former dir of other companies. Member, Kennel Club. Ed Whitgift School; Balliol Coll, Oxford (pres, univ C assoc, 1964).
**ROGER ARON,** b May 8, 1944. Retail jeweller. Kettering borough cllr 1991-95. Member, Friends of the Earth; Charter 88. Ed Mill Hill School.

| KILMARNOCK & LOUDOUN | | | | | Lab hold | | |
|---|---|---|---|---|---|---|---|
| Electorate % Turnout | | 61,376 | 77.2% | **1997** | 62,002 | 80.0% | **1992** |
| Browne, D | Lab | **23,621** | 49.8% | +5.0% | 22,210 | 44.8% | Lab |
| Neil, A | SNP | 16,365 | 34.5% | +3.8% | 15,231 | 30.7% | SNP |
| Taylor, D | C | 5,125 | 10.8% | -8.2% | 9,438 | 19.0% | C |
| Stewart, J | LD | 1,891 | 4.0% | -1.5% | 2,722 | 5.5% | LD |
| Sneddon, W | Ref | 284 | 0.6% | | | | |
| Gilmour, W | NLP | 123 | 0.3% | | | | |
| SNP to Lab swing 0.6% | | 47,409 | | Lab maj 7,256 | 49,601 | | Lab maj 6,979 |
| | | | | 15.3% | | | 14.1% |

**DES BROWNE,** b March 22, 1952. Advocate specialising in family law. Contested Argyll and Bute 1992. Runs own practice, McCluskey Browne. Ed St Michael's Acad, Kilwinning; Glasgow Univ.
**ALEX NEIL,** b Aug 22, 1951. Economic consultant. Contested this seat 1992, and Glasgow Central 1989 by-election. SNP vice-convener for publicity. Dir, EES Consultants Ltd; chair, Network Scotland Ltd. Ed Ayr Acad; Dundee Univ.

**DOUGLAS TAYLOR,** b Jan 31, 1970. Accountant and landlord. Chair, S Swindon YCs, 1995. Ed Dunoon GS; Jordanhill Coll School; Aberdeen Univ.
**JOHN STEWART,** b Sept 9, 1972. Agent, NE Scotland, in 1994 Euro elections. Church of Scotland Elder. Member, Stonewall. Ed Kilmarnock Acad; Aberdeen Univ.

| KINGSTON & SURBITON | | 65.0% change | | | LD win | | |
|---|---|---|---|---|---|---|---|
| Electorate % Turnout | | 73,879 | 75.3% | **1997** | 70,238 | 79.6% | **1992** |
| Davey, E | LD | **20,411** | 36.7% | +10.7% | **29,674** | 53.0% | C |
| +Tracey, R P | C | 20,355 | 36.6% | -16.5% | 14,510 | 25.9% | LD |
| Griffin, Ms S | Lab | 12,811 | 23.0% | +3.4% | 10,991 | 19.6% | Lab |
| Tchiprout, Mrs G | Ref | 1,470 | 2.6% | | 762 | 1.4% | Other |
| Burns, Ms P | UK Ind | 418 | 0.8% | | | | |
| Leighton, M | NLP | 100 | 0.2% | | | | |
| Port, C | Dream | 100 | 0.2% | | | | |
| C to LD notional swing 13.6% | | 55,665 | | LD maj 56 | 55,937 | | C maj 15,164 |
| | | | | 0.1% | | | 27.1% |

**EDWARD DAVEY,** b Dec 25, 1965. Management consultant and economics adviser to LD MPs, 1989-93. Chair, LD manifesto costings group; member, federal policy cttee. Ed Nottingham HS; Jesus Coll, Oxford; Birkbeck Coll, London.
**RICHARD TRACEY,** b Feb 8, 1943. Former TV journalist. MP for Surbiton 1983-97; contested Northampton N Oct 1974. Sports Min 1985-87. Member, PAC, 1994-97; select cttee on broadcasting 1988-92; selection cttee 1992-94. Chair, Greater London group, C

MPs, 1990-97; sec, C media cttee, 1983-84. BBC radio and television news and current affairs presenter and reporter 1966-78. Member, Economic Research Council, 1981- . Freeman, City of London. Ed King Edward VI School, Stratford-upon-Avon; Birmingham Univ.
**SHEILA GRIFFIN,** b April 13, 1939. Former teacher. Member, Lab Electoral Reform Group. Ed sec mod school; night school; Exeter Univ.

| KINGSWOOD | | 51.0% change | | | | | Lab win |
|---|---|---|---|---|---|---|---|
| Electorate % Turnout | | 77,026 | 77.7% | **1997** | 76,320 | 84.6% | **1992** |
| +Berry, Dr R | Lab | **32,181** | 53.7% | +13.1% | **29,562** | 45.8% | C |
| Howard, J | C | 17,928 | 29.9% | -15.9% | 26,222 | 40.6% | Lab |
| Pinkerton, Mrs J | LD | 7,672 | 12.8% | -0.8% | 8,771 | 13.6% | LD |
| Reather, Ms A | Ref | 1,463 | 2.4% | | | | |
| Hart, P | BNP | 290 | 0.5% | | | | |
| Harding, A | NLP | 238 | 0.4% | | | | |
| Nicolson, A | Scrapit | 115 | 0.2% | | | | |
| C to Lab notional swing 14.5% | | 59,887 | Lab maj 14,253 | | 64,555 | | C maj 3,340 |
| | | | 23.8% | | | | 5.2% |

**ROGER BERRY**, b July 4, 1948. Lecturer in economics, Bristol Univ, 1978-92. Won this seat 1992; contested it 1987; Weston-super-Mare 1983; Bristol in 1984 Euro elections. Member, select cttees on trade and industry, 1995-97; deregulation, 1995-96. Sec, all-party disablement group, 1994- . Avon county cllr 1981-93 (leader, Lab group, 1986-92). Vice-pres, Bristol Anti-Apartheid Movement. Chair, full employment forum, 1994- . Ed Huddersfield New Coll; Bristol and Sussex Univs.

**JON HOWARD,** b May 20, 1956. Solicitor. Contested South Shields 1992, and Yorkshire South in 1994 Euro elections. Chair, Leeds NW C assoc, 1990-93. Co-founded Howard group of companies which produces and exports dietary foods and pharmaceuticals. Ed Perse School, Cambridge; Downing Coll, Cambridge.
**JEANNE PINKERTON,** b March 19, 1946. Businesswoman and partner in nursery. Contested this seat 1992. Bristol city cllr 1986-88. Chair, Kingswood LDs, 1988-90 and 1994- . Ed Bishop Road and Oldland Girls School; Soundwell Tech Coll.

| KIRKCALDY | | 2.6% change | | | | | Lab win |
|---|---|---|---|---|---|---|---|
| Electorate % Turnout | | 52,186 | 67.0% | **1997** | 50,837 | 74.4% | **1992** |
| +Moonie, L | Lab Co-op | **18,730** | 53.6% | +8.0% | **17,246** | 45.6% | Lab Co-op |
| Hosie, S | SNP | 8,020 | 22.9% | +0.3% | 8,561 | 22.6% | SNP |
| Black, Miss C | C | 4,779 | 13.7% | -8.4% | 8,361 | 22.1% | C |
| Mainland, J | LD | 3,031 | 8.7% | -1.0% | 3,671 | 9.7% | LD |
| Baxter, V | Ref | 413 | 1.2% | | | | |
| SNP to Lab notional swing 3.8% | | 34,973 | Lab Co-op maj 10,710 | | 37,839 | | Lab Co-op maj 8,685 |
| | | | 30.6% | | | | 23.0% |

**LEWIS MOONIE**, b Feb 25, 1947. Elected 1987. Lab spokesman on national heritage 1995-97; Lab frontbench trade and industry team 1989-95 as spokesman on science and technology and on industry. Member, social services select cttee, 1987-89; Treasury and Civil Service select cttee, 1989. Vice-chair, PLP Treasury and Civil Service cttee, 1988-89; all-party chess parly group. Fife regional cllr 1982-86. Was community medicine specialist with Fife Health Board; previously worked as psychiatrist in Switzerland and The Netherlands. Member, ASTMS; TGWU. Ed Grove Acad, Dundee; St Andrews and Edinburgh Univs.

**STEWART HOSIE**, b Jan 3, 1963. Contested seat 1992. Information systems manager. SNP vice-convener for youth affairs. Ed Carnoustie HS; Bell St Coll of Tech, Dundee.
**CHARLOTTE BLACK,** b Jan 12, 1960. Marketing director. Dep chair, Regent's Park and Kensington North C assoc. Ed Convent of the Sacred Heart, Kilgraston; Beechlawn, Oxford; Durham Univ Business School.
**JOHN MAINLAND**, b March 29, 1972. Works for management training company. Former exec member, policy and campaigns cttee, Scottish LDs. Ed Kirkcaldy HS; Dundee Univ.

| KNOWSLEY NORTH & SEFTON EAST | | | 87.7% change | | | | Lab win |
|---|---|---|---|---|---|---|---|
| Electorate % Turnout | | 70,918 | 70.1% | **1997** | 74,154 | 75.1% | **1992** |
| +Howarth, G E | Lab | **34,747** | 69.9% | +15.5% | **30,316** | 54.4% | Lab |
| Doran, C | C | 8,600 | 17.3% | -9.5% | 14,930 | 26.8% | C |
| Bamber, D | LD | 5,499 | 11.1% | -4.5% | 8,670 | 15.6% | LD |
| Jones, C | Soc Lab | 857 | 1.7% | | 1,805 | 3.2% | Other |
| C to Lab notional swing 12.5% | | 49,703 | Lab maj 26,147 | | 55,721 | | Lab maj 15,386 |
| | | | 52.6% | | | | 27.6% |

**GEORGE HOWARTH**, b June 29, 1949. Became Home Office Under Secretary responsible for deregulation and drugs, May 5, 1997. MP for Knowsley N 1986-97. Lab spokesman on home affairs 1994 with responsibility for prisons; spokesman on environmental protection 1993-94; on environment 1990-92; member, select cttees on Parly Commissioner for Administration, 1987-90; on environment 1989-90; joint vice-chair, all-party Mersey Barrage parly group. Ex-Huyton urban district cllr; Knowsley borough cllr 1975-86 (dep leader 1982).Dir, Wales TUC Co-operative Centre

Voluntary Management Cttee, 1984-86. Ed Huyton Hey Sec; Kirkby CFE; Liverpool Poly.
**CARL DORAN,** b June 30, 1970. Asst BBC producer since 1991; freelance sports reporter on Radio Merseyside since 1986. Ed St Andrews Primary, Maghull; Deyes High Sec, Maghull; Liverpool Univ.
**DAVID BAMBER,** b July 7, 1949. Charity area manager. Contested Merseyside W in 1994 Euro elections. Sefton cllr (dep group leader). Ed Warwick Bolar CS School; Liverpool City Coll.

**171**

| KNOWSLEY SOUTH | | 14.9% change | | | | | Lab win |
|---|---|---|---|---|---|---|---|
| Electorate % Turnout | | 70,532 | 67.5% | 1997 | 72,282 | 73.8% | 1992 |
| +O'Hara, E | Lab | 36,695 | 77.1% | +7.6% | 37,071 | 69.5% | Lab |
| Robertson, G | C | 5,987 | 12.6% | -7.9% | 10,936 | 20.5% | C |
| Mainey, C | LD | 3,954 | 8.3% | -0.7% | 4,818 | 9.0% | LD |
| Wright, A | Ref | 954 | 2.0% | | 487 | 0.9% | NLP |
| C to Lab notional swing 7.8% | | 47,590 | Lab maj 30,708 | | 53,312 | Lab maj 26,135 | |
| | | | 64.5% | | | 49.0% | |

**EDDIE O'HARA,** b Oct 1, 1937. Elected at 1990 by-election. Member, education and employment select cttee, and its sub-cttee, 1996-97; education select cttee 1991-96; Commons chairmen's panel. Joint vice-chair, all-party British-Greek parly group. Knowsley cllr 1975-91. Merseyside rep on exec cttee, Regions Européennes de Tradition Industrielle, 1989-90, and member, permanent cttee, Assembly of European Regions, 1989-90. Member, management board, Royal Liverpool Philharmonic Soc, 1987-90. Head of curriculum studies, School of Ed and Community Studies, Liverpool Poly, 1983-90. Ed Liverpool Collegiate School; Magdalen Coll, Oxford; London Univ.
**GARY ROBERTSON,** b Sept 21, 1961. Bus driver, sheet metal worker, steel fabricator 1979-93. Knowsley cllr 1992-96 (C group leader 1995-96). Ed Hollin HS; Queen Elizabeth School.
**CLIFF MAINEY,** b April 24, 1946. Fire officer. Maghull town cllr (Mayor; dep group leader); Sefton metropolitan borough cllr. Member, FBU. Ed St Wilfred's RC Sec Mod, Litherland.

| LAGAN VALLEY | | 27.1% change | | | | | UUP win |
|---|---|---|---|---|---|---|---|
| Electorate % Turnout | | 71,225 | 62.2% | 1997 | 67,551 | 68.5% | 1992 |
| Donaldson, J | UUP | 24,560 | 55.4% | -11.5% | 30,957 | 66.9% | UUP |
| Close, S | Alliance | 7,635 | 17.2% | +5.4% | 5,453 | 11.8% | Alliance |
| Poots, E | DUP | 6,005 | 13.6% | | 4,192 | 9.1% | SDLP |
| Kelly, Ms D | SDLP | 3,436 | 7.8% | -1.3% | 4,170 | 9.0% | C |
| Sexton, S | C | 1,212 | 2.7% | -6.3% | 956 | 2.1% | SF |
| Ramsey, Ms S | SF | 1,110 | 2.5% | +0.4% | 542 | 1.2% | WP |
| McCarthy, F | WP | 203 | 0.5% | -0.7% | | | |
| Finlay, H | NLP | 149 | 0.3% | | | | |
| No swing calculation | | 44,310 | UUP maj 16,925 | | 46,270 | UUP maj 25,504 | |
| | | | 38.2% | | | 55.1% | |

**JEFFREY DONALDSON,** b Dec 7, 1962. Partner in financial services and estate agency. Elected 1997. Former member, NI Assembly. Member, UU negotiating team in constitutional talks on future of Province. Sec, Ulster Unionist Council, 1988- ; chair, Ulster Young Unionist Council, 1985-86. Elected to NI Assembly in 1985, aged 22, the youngest member. Former asst to Sir James Molyneaux when party leader. Former agent for Enoch Powell. Asst Grand Master, Orange Order. Ed Kilkeel HS, Co Down.
**SEAMUS CLOSE,** b Aug 17, 1947. Financial director. Contested this seat 1992, 1987, 1983 and Fermanagh and S Tyrone by-election 1981. Dep leader, Alliance Party. Lisburn district cllr 1973- . Mayor of Lisburn 1993-94. Member, NI Assembly 1982-86; NI Forum. Ed St Malachy's Coll; Belfast Coll of Business Studies.
**EDWIN POOTS,** b May 27, 1965. Farmer. Elected to NI Forum May 1996. Ed Wallace HS, Lisburn; Greenmount Agric Coll, Antrim.
**DELORES KELLY.** Occupational therapist. Craigavon borough cllr.

| LANCASHIRE WEST | | 20.6% change | | | | | Lab win |
|---|---|---|---|---|---|---|---|
| Electorate % Turnout | | 73,175 | 74.8% | 1997 | 73,013 | 81.7% | 1992 |
| +Pickthall, C | Lab | 33,022 | 60.3% | +10.9% | 29,470 | 49.4% | Lab |
| Varley, C | C | 15,903 | 29.1% | -13.3% | 25,243 | 42.3% | C |
| Wood, A | LD | 3,938 | 7.2% | +0.2% | 4,147 | 7.0% | LD |
| Carter, M | Ref | 1,025 | 1.9% | | 494 | 0.8% | Grn |
| Collins, J | NLP | 449 | 0.8% | +0.3% | 298 | 0.5% | NLP |
| Hill, D | Home Rule | 392 | 0.7% | | | | |
| C to Lab notional swing 12.1% | | 54,729 | Lab maj 17,119 | | 59,652 | Lab maj 4,227 | |
| | | | 31.3% | | | 7.1% | |

**COLIN PICKTHALL,** b Sept 13, 1944. Higher education teacher. Won this seat 1992; contested it 1987. Member, agric select cttee, 1992-97. Sec, PLP ed cttee 1995- , and of all-party group on diabetes; ex-chair, NW group of Lab MPs. Lancs county cllr 1989-93. Senior posts at Edge Hill Coll of Higher Ed 1970-92. Ex-member, NW regional advisory cttee and Lancs consultative cttee on higher ed; ex-chair of governors, Skelmersdale CFE. Member, NATFHE. Ed Ulverston GS; Wales and Lancaster Univs.
**CHRIS VARLEY,** b June 8, 1958. Computer consultant. Contested Bootle 1992, Merseyside West in 1994 Euro elections. Vice-chair, Merseyside West Euro constituency; member, One Nation Forum and C Group for Europe. Trained as engineer with British Aerospace. Ed City of London Freeman's; Kingston and City Univs.
**ARTHUR WOOD,** b June 15, 1940. Architect. Contested Manchester Openshaw Oct and Feb 1974. Vale Royal district cllr (group leader 1987-95). Ed UMIST.

| ○ LANCASTER & WYRE | | 76.3% change | | | Lab win | | |
|---|---|---|---|---|---|---|---|
| Electorate % Turnout | | 78,168 | 75.3% | **1997** | 75,314 | 78.6% | **1992** |
| **Dawson, T** | **Lab** | **25,173** | **42.8%** | **+9.7%** | **30,838** | **52.1%** | **C** |
| +Mans, K D R | C | 23,878 | 40.6% | -11.6% | 19,554 | 33.0% | Lab |
| Humberstone, J C | LD | 6,802 | 11.6% | -2.4% | 8,264 | 14.0% | LD |
| Ivell, Mrs V | Ref | 1,516 | 2.6% | | 510 | 0.9% | Other |
| Barry, J | Green | 795 | 1.4% | | | | |
| Whittaker, Dr J | UK Ind | 698 | 1.2% | | | | |
| **C to Lab notional swing 10.6%** | | **58,862** | Lab maj 1,295 | | **59,166** | C maj 11,284 | |
| | | | 2.2% | | | 19.1% | |

**THOMAS DAWSON,** b Sept 30, 1953. Social worker; manager, foster and adoption day care centre. Lancaster city cllr 1987- . Member, Unison. Ed Ashington GS; Warwick and Lancaster Univs.
**KEITH MANS,** b Feb 10, 1946. Ex-RAF pilot. MP for Wyre 1987-97; contested Stoke-on-Trent Central 1983. PPS to Virginia Bottomley, when Health Sec, 1992-95; PPS to Health Min 1990-92. Member, select cttees on defence 1995-97; environment 1987-91. Chair, C backbench defence cttee, 1995-97; joint sec, C aviation cttee, 1987-90; C environment cttee 1989-90. Chair, all-party aerospace/aviation group, 1994-97; environment group 1993-97.

Parly adviser to British Fibreboard Packaging Assoc; Inst of Waste Management. Former executive with John Lewis Partnership. RAF pilot (Flight Lt) 1964-77; pilot in RAF Reserve 1977- . Council member, Air League; member, industrial and professional advisory cttee, OU business school (both unpaid). Ed Berkhamsted School; RAF Coll, Cranwell; OU.
**JOHN HUMBERSTONE,** b Dec 9, 1943. Teacher. Contested Lancaster 1992. Member, Amnesty, Charter 88; ATL. Ed Hertford GS; Goldsmith's Coll and Birkbeck Coll, London.

| LEEDS CENTRAL | | 18.7% change | | | Lab win | | |
|---|---|---|---|---|---|---|---|
| Electorate % Turnout | | 67,664 | 54.7% | **1997** | 73,780 | 62.3% | **1992** |
| +Fatchett, D | Lab | 25,766 | 69.6% | +5.9% | 29,273 | 63.7% | Lab |
| Wild, E | C | 5,077 | 13.7% | -8.6% | 10,281 | 22.4% | C |
| Freeman, D | LD | 4,164 | 11.3% | -2.7% | 6,416 | 14.0% | LD |
| Myers, P | Ref | 1,042 | 2.8% | | | | |
| Rix, D | Soc Lab | 656 | 1.8% | | | | |
| Hill, C | Soc | 304 | 0.8% | | | | |
| C to Lab notional swing 7.3% | | 37,009 | Lab maj 20,689 | | 45,970 | Lab maj 18,992 | |
| | | | 55.9% | | | 41.3% | |

**DEREK FATCHETT,** b Aug 22, 1945. Became Minister of State, Foreign Office, May 5, 1997. Elected 1983; contested Bosworth 1979. Lab spokesman on foreign affairs 1995-97; on defence, disarmament and arms control 1994-95; trade and industry 1992-94; secondary and tertiary ed, 1988-92; dealt with youth affairs from 1988. Dep campaigns co-ordinator 1987-92; joint vice-chair, all-party parly youth affairs lobby; Lab whip 1986-87; chair, PLP ed, science and arts cttee, 1985-86. Member, Wakefield MDC 1980-84. Lecturer in industrial relations, Leeds Univ, 1971-83;

research fellow, Univ Coll of Wales, Cardiff, 1970-71; research officer, LSE, 1968-70. Dir (unpaid), Mount St Mary's Church Trust, registered charity. Ed Lincoln School; Birmingham Univ; LSE.
**EDWARD WILD,** b July 1, 1972. Religious studies teacher. Member, Nat Assoc of C Graduates. Ed St Olave's, York; Sedbergh School, Cumbria; Keble Coll, Oxford; Magdalene Coll, Cambridge.
**DAVID FREEMAN,** b Sept 26, 1970. Mature student at Leeds Univ. Member, Greenpeace, Charter 88; NUS. Ed Durham Johnston Comp; Leeds Univ.

| LEEDS EAST | | | | | Lab hold | | |
|---|---|---|---|---|---|---|---|
| Electorate % Turnout | | 56,963 | 62.8% | **1997** | 61,695 | 70.0% | **1992** |
| *Mudie, G | Lab | 24,151 | 67.5% | +9.8% | 24,929 | 57.7% | Lab |
| Emsley, J | C | 6,685 | 18.7% | -9.6% | 12,232 | 28.3% | C |
| Kirk, Mrs M | LD | 3,689 | 10.3% | -3.7% | 6,040 | 14.0% | LD |
| Parish, L | Ref | 1,267 | 3.5% | | | | |
| C to Lab swing 9.7% | | 35,792 | Lab maj 17,466 | | 43,201 | Lab maj 12,697 | |
| | | | 48.8% | | | 29.4% | |

**GEORGE MUDIE,** b Feb 6, 1945. Became gvt deputy chief whip, May 7, 1997. Elected 1992. Lab pairing whip 1995-97, previously a whip; member, Commons selection cttee, 1995-97; ex-member Commons accommodation and works cttee. Union official; joined Nupe 1968; formerly, AEU. Ex-leader, Leeds City Council. Ed local state schools.

**JOHN EMSLEY,** b April 1, 1950. Mature student, ex-mine conveyor foreman. Member, Selby District Council, 1991- (group leader 1996- ). Ed Kitson Coll; Huddersfield Univ.
**MADELEINE KIRK,** b Feb 13, 1953. Assistant finance officer; York City UA (women's working group). Member, HARP (local shelter group). Ed Loreto Convent, Manchester; St John's Coll of FE; York Coll of FE; Leeds Met Univ.

## LEEDS NORTH EAST — Lab gain

| Electorate % Turnout | | 63,185 | 72.0% | 1997 | 64,372 | 76.9% | 1992 |
|---|---|---|---|---|---|---|---|
| Hamilton, F | Lab | 22,368 | 49.2% | +12.3% | 22,462 | 45.4% | C |
| *Kirkhope, T | C | 15,409 | 33.9% | -11.5% | 18,218 | 36.8% | Lab |
| Winlow, Dr W | LD | 6,318 | 13.9% | -2.8% | 8,274 | 16.7% | LD |
| Rose, I | Ref | 946 | 2.1% | | 546 | 1.1% | Grn |
| Egan, Ms J | Soc Lab | 468 | 1.0% | | | | |
| C to Lab swing 11.9% | | 45,509 | Lab maj 6,959 | | 49,500 | C maj 4,244 | |
| | | | 15.3% | | | 8.6% | |

**FABIAN HAMILTON**, b April 12, 1955. Graphic designer, systems consultant, company dir, ex-taxi driver. Leeds cllr 1987- . Chair, Leeds W CLP 1987-88. Member, Fabian Society; Co-op Party; GPMU. Ed Brentwood School; York Univ.

**TIMOTHY KIRKHOPE**, b April 29, 1945. Solicitor and former company dir. Elected 1987; contested Darlington 1979 and Durham, Feb 1974. Under Sec, Home Office, 1995-97; Gvt whip 1992-95; asst whip, 1990-92. PPS to David Trippier, environment min, 1989-90. Northumberland County cllr 1981-85. Joint vice-

chair, C backbench legal cttee, 1988-89; joint sec, C environment cttee, 1988-89; sec, all-party solicitors' group, 1989-90. Lawyer member, Mental Health Act Commission, 1983-86. Ed Royal GS, Newcastle upon Tyne; Coll of Law, Guildford. Holder of private pilot's licence.

**BILL WINLOW**, b Feb 17, 1945. Reader in invertebrate neuroscience, Leeds Univ. Leeds MBC 1986- (group leader). Member, Greenpeace; AUT. Ed Morpeth GS, Northumberland; Newcastle and St Andrews Univs.

## LEEDS NORTH WEST — Lab gain

| Electorate % Turnout | | 69,972 | 70.6% | 1997 | 69,406 | 72.8% | 1992 |
|---|---|---|---|---|---|---|---|
| Best, H | Lab | 19,694 | 39.9% | +12.6% | 21,750 | 43.0% | C |
| *Hampson, Dr K | C | 15,850 | 32.1% | -10.9% | 14,079 | 27.8% | LD |
| Pearce, Mrs B | LD | 11,689 | 23.7% | -4.2% | 13,782 | 27.3% | Lab |
| Emmett, S | Ref | 1,325 | 2.7% | | 519 | 1.0% | Grn |
| Lamb, R | Soc Lab | 335 | 0.7% | | 427 | 0.8% | Lib |
| Toone, R | ProLife | 251 | 0.5% | | | | |
| Duffy, D | Ronnie | 232 | 0.5% | | | | |
| C to Lab swing 11.8% | | 49,376 | Lab maj 3,844 | | 50,557 | C maj 7,671 | |
| | | | 7.8% | | | 15.2% | |

**HAROLD BEST**, b Dec 18, 1939. Electrical technician. Member, Nupe; Unison; TGWU; EPIU; Liberty; Amnesty. Ed Meanwood County Secondary School.

**KEITH HAMPSON**, b Aug 14, 1943. Elected for this seat 1983; MP for Ripon Feb 1974-83, which he contested at 1973 by-election. Member, trade and industry select cttee, 1987-97; Public Accounts Commission 1992-97. PPS to Tom King as Min for Local Gvt, 1979-83, and Environment Sec, 1983, and to Michael Heseltine as Defence Sec, 1983-84. Parly adviser to NCM (Credit Insurance);

CAPITB plc, a training company; AUT; Alexander & Alexander (UK) Ltd, insurance and risk management; PowerGen. Ed King James I GS, Bishop Auckland; Bristol and Harvard Univs.

**BARBARA PEARCE**, b March 8, 1942. Dir of Leeds Univ training, research and consultancy unit. Contested this seat 1992; Richmond (Yorks) for SDP in 1989 by-election. Member, Leeds Community Health Council; British Assoc of Counselling; AUT. Ed Northumberland Heath Sec Mod; Erith GS; Nottingham and Leeds Univs.

## LEEDS WEST — Lab hold

| Electorate % Turnout | | 63,965 | 62.9% | 1997 | 67,084 | 71.1% | 1992 |
|---|---|---|---|---|---|---|---|
| *Battle, J | Lab | 26,819 | 66.7% | +11.6% | 26,310 | 55.1% | Lab |
| Whelan, J | C | 7,048 | 17.5% | -8.6% | 12,482 | 26.2% | C |
| Amor, N | LD | 3,622 | 9.0% | +0.1% | 4,252 | 8.9% | LD |
| Finley, B | Ref | 1,210 | 3.0% | | 3,980 | 8.3% | Lib |
| Blackburn, D | Green | 896 | 2.2% | | 569 | 1.2% | Grn |
| Nowosielski, N | Lib | 625 | 1.6% | -6.8% | 132 | 0.3% | NF |
| C to Lab swing 10.1% | | 40,220 | Lab maj 19,771 | | 47,725 | Lab maj 13,828 | |
| | | | 49.2% | | | 29.0% | |

**JOHN BATTLE**, b April 26, 1951. Became Trade and Industry Minister of State for Industry, Energy and Science, May 5, 1997. Won this seat 1987; contested Leeds NW 1983. Energy spokesman, 1995-97; spokesman on Commons affairs and Citizen's Charter 1994-95; on local gvt, 1992-94. Member, select cttees on environment, 1991-92; on broadcasting 1992-97. Campaign officer, Yorkshire group of Lab MPs, 1989-90. Lab whip 1988-90. Chair, all-party epilepsy parly group. National

co-ordinator, Church Action on Poverty, 1983-87. Member, MSF. Ed St Michael's Coll, Kirkby Lonsdale; Leeds Univ.

**JOHN WHELAN**, b Oct 25, 1947. Freelance journalist and broadcaster. Lambeth cllr 1990- . Ed Stonyhurst Coll, Lancs; Exeter Coll, Oxford.

**NIGEL AMOR**, b May 31, 1963. Courier and taxi driver. Ed Forest School, Horsham; Colen's Sixth-Form Coll, Horsham; Central London Poly.

| LEICESTER EAST | | | | | | Lab hold |
|---|---|---|---|---|---|---|
| Electorate % Turnout | | 64,012 | 69.4% | **1997** | 63,434 | 78.4% | **1992** |
| *Vaz, K | Lab | **29,083** | 65.5% | +9.0% | 28,123 | 56.5% | Lab |
| Milton, S | C | 10,661 | 24.0% | -9.8% | 16,807 | 33.8% | C |
| Matabudul, J | LD | 3,105 | 7.0% | -1.1% | 4,043 | 8.1% | LD |
| Iwaniw, P | Ref | 1,015 | 2.3% | | 453 | 0.9% | Grn |
| Singh Sidhu, S | Soc Lab | 436 | 1.0% | | 308 | 0.6% | Homeland |
| Slack, N | Glow | 102 | 0.2% | | | | |
| C to Lab swing 9.4% | | **44,402** | Lab maj | **18,422** | **49,734** | Lab maj | **11,316** |
| | | | | 41.5% | | | 22.8% |

**KEITH VAZ**, b Nov 26, 1956. Barrister. Won this seat 1987; contested Richmond and Barnes 1983; Surrey W in 1984 Euro elections. Former Lab spokesman on planning and regeneration. Joint vice-chair, PLP ed, science and arts cttee, 1990-91; sec, all-party Indo-British parly group, 1987- ; chair, 1990- , and sec, 1987-90, all-party footwear and leather industries parly group; sec, PLP wool and textiles group, 1988-94. Member, Clothing and Footwear Inst; nat advisory cttee, Crime Concern, 1989-93; advisory board, TV Asia, 1992- . Patron, Gingerbread,

1990-92; joint patron, UN Year of Tolerance, 1995. Ed St Joseph's Convent, Aden; Latymer HS, Hammersmith; Gonville and Caius Coll, Cambridge; Coll of Law, Lancaster Gate.
**SIMON MILTON**, b Oct 2, 1961. Managing director, APCO public affairs. Westminster city cllr 1988- . Ed, St Paul's; Gonville and Caius Coll, Cambridge; Cornell Univ, New York.
**JAY MATABUDUL**, b Sept 3, 1952. Linguist. Oadby and Wigston cllr. Voluntary worker for Multiple Sclerosis Organisation. Ed Royal Coll, Mauritius; BA Coll of Marketing.

| LEICESTER SOUTH | | | | | | Lab hold |
|---|---|---|---|---|---|---|
| Electorate % Turnout | | 71,750 | 67.1% | **1997** | 71,120 | 75.1% | **1992** |
| *Marshall, J | Lab | **27,914** | 58.0% | +5.7% | 27,934 | 52.3% | Lab |
| Heaton-Harris, C | C | 11,421 | 23.7% | -10.9% | 18,494 | 34.6% | C |
| Coles, B | LD | 6,654 | 13.8% | +2.1% | 6,271 | 11.7% | LD |
| Hancock, J | Ref | 1,184 | 2.5% | | 554 | 1.0% | Grn |
| Dooher, J | Soc Lab | 634 | 1.3% | | 154 | 0.3% | NLP |
| Sills, K | Nat Dem | 307 | 0.6% | | | | |
| C to Lab swing 8.3% | | **48,114** | Lab maj | **16,493** | **53,407** | Lab maj | **9,440** |
| | | | | 34.3% | | | 17.7% |

**JIM MARSHALL**, b March 13, 1941. Lecturer. Regained this seat 1987, being its MP Oct 1974-83; contested seat Feb 1974; Harborough, 1970. Lab spokesman on N Ireland 1987-92; on home affairs 1982-83; asst gvt whip 1977-79. Member, British-Irish inter-parly body. Leeds city cllr 1965-68; Leicester city cllr 1971-76 (leader 1974). Ed Sheffield City GS; Leeds Univ.

**CHRISTOPHER HEATON-HARRIS**, b Nov 28, 1967. Managing director of fruit and veg wholesalers. Ed Tiffin Boys, Kingston upon Thames; Wolverhampton Poly. Qualified football referee.
**BARRY COLES**, b June 15, 1934. Haberdasher. Leicester county cllr 1996- . Sec, Assoc of British Barbershop Singers guild of judges; member, Leicester Barbershop Chorus. Ed Leicester Coll of Arts & Tech. Qualified MCC youth cricket coach.

| LEICESTER WEST | | | | | | Lab hold |
|---|---|---|---|---|---|---|
| Electorate % Turnout | | 64,570 | 63.4% | **1997** | 65,510 | 73.7% | **1992** |
| Hewitt, Ms P H | Lab | **22,580** | 55.2% | +8.4% | 22,574 | 46.8% | Lab |
| Thomas, R | C | 9,716 | 23.7% | -14.8% | 18,596 | 38.5% | C |
| Jones, M | LD | 5,795 | 14.2% | +0.9% | 6,402 | 13.3% | LD |
| Shooter, W | Ref | 970 | 2.4% | | 517 | 1.1% | Grn |
| Forse, G | Green | 586 | 1.4% | | 171 | 0.4% | NLP |
| Roberts, D | Soc Lab | 452 | 1.1% | | | | |
| Nicholls, Ms J | Soc | 327 | 0.8% | | | | |
| Belshaw, A | BNP | 302 | 0.7% | | | | |
| Potter, C | Nat Dem | 186 | 0.5% | | | | |
| C to Lab swing 11.6% | | **40,914** | Lab maj | **12,864** | **48,260** | Lab maj | **3,978** |
| | | | | 31.4% | | | 8.2% |

**PATRICIA HEWITT**, b Dec 2, 1948. Contested Leicester E 1983. Gen sec, Nat Council for Civil Liberties, 1974-83; press and broadcasting sec 1983-88, and policy co-ordinator 1988-89, to Neil Kinnock. Dep dir, Inst for Public Policy Research, 1989-94. Visiting Fellow, Nuffield Coll, Oxford, 1992- . Head of research, Andersen Consulting, 1994- . FRSA 1992. Ed C of E Girls' GS, Canberra; Australian Nat Univ; Newnham Coll, Cambridge.

**RICHARD THOMAS**, b Aug 25, 1961. Senior manager, Unichem. Bracknell Forest borough cllr 1983-95. Ed Brakenhale School; Reading Coll of Tech; Kingston Univ.
**MARK JONES**, b June 12, 1964. Safety consultant. Contested Wyre Forest 1992; Leicester in 1994 Euro elections. Ed Groby Community Coll.

| LEICESTERSHIRE NORTH WEST | | 13.6% change | | | Lab win |
|---|---|---|---|---|---|
| Electorate % Turnout | | 65,069 | 80.0% | **1997** | 62,949 | 86.5% | **1992** |
| **Taylor, D** | Lab Co-op | **29,332** | **56.4%** | **+12.5%** | 24,735 | 45.4% | C |
| Goodwill, R | C | 16,113 | 31.0% | -14.5% | 23,869 | 43.8% | Lab |
| Heptinstall, S | LD | 4,492 | 8.6% | -1.7% | 5,648 | 10.4% | LD |
| Abney-Hastings, M | Ref | 2,088 | 4.0% | | 198 | 0.4% | NLP |
| **C to Lab notional swing 13.5%** | | **52,025** | Lab Co-op maj **13,219** | | 54,450 | C maj **866** | |
| | | | | 25.4% | | 1.6% | |

**DAVID TAYLOR**, b Aug 22, 1946. Freelance accountant and computer manager. Contested this seat 1992. Former chair CLP. Leicestershire district cllr 1981-87. Founder and chair, Leics NW safer communities forum. Ed Ashby-de-la-Zouch GS; Leicester Poly; Coventry Poly; OU.
**ROBERT GOODWILL**, b Dec 31, 1956. Arable and sheep farmer since 1979; company director. Contested Redcar 1992; Cleveland and Richmond in 1994 Euro elections. Member, Yorkshire waterconsumer consultative cttee, 1986-89. Chaired NFU branch 1987-89; member, Yorkshire Area C agricultural advisory cttee. Ed Bootham School, York; Newcastle Univ.
**STAN HEPTINSTALL**, b Aug 21, 1946. University professor. Broxtowe district cllr 1991- (dep group leader). Member, AUT. Ed King Edward VII School, Lytham St Annes; Newcastle Univ.

| LEIGH | | 30.9% change | | | Lab win |
|---|---|---|---|---|---|
| Electorate % Turnout | | 69,908 | 65.7% | **1997** | 70,188 | 74.9% | **1992** |
| **+Cunliffe, L** | Lab | **31,652** | **68.9%** | **+9.6%** | 31,196 | 59.3% | Lab |
| Young, E | C | 7,156 | 15.6% | -11.7% | 14,341 | 27.3% | C |
| Hough, P | LD | 5,163 | 11.2% | -1.2% | 6,539 | 12.4% | LD |
| Constable, R | Ref | 1,949 | 4.2% | | 525 | 1.0% | NLP |
| **C to Lab notional swing 10.7%** | | **45,920** | Lab maj **24,496** | | 52,601 | Lab maj **16,855** | |
| | | | | 53.3% | | 32.1% | |

**LAWRENCE CUNLIFFE**, b March 25, 1929. Elected 1979; contested Rochdale Feb and Oct 1974. Ex-joint chair, all-party minerals parly group; non-profitmaking clubs group; joint vice-chair, racing and bloodstock industries parly cttee; treas, rugby league group; cricket group. Member, exec cttee, UK branch, CPA, 1989-94. Engineer with NCB 1949-79. Farnworth borough cllr 1960-74; Bolton metropolitan district cllr 1974-79. Ed St Edmund's RC School, Worsley, Manchester.
**EDWARD YOUNG**, b Oct 24, 1966. International trade specialist with Barclays Bank International Business Operations; lecturer in international trade. Reading cllr since 1994; vice-chair, Reading East C assoc. Unpaid dir, Monkley Court Management Co; school governor and C of E reader. Ed Reading GS.
**PETER HOUGH**, b Feb 26, 1954. Freelance writer, TV consultant. Ed Lymm HS.

| LEOMINSTER | | 19.8% change | | | C win |
|---|---|---|---|---|---|
| Electorate % Turnout | | 65,993 | 76.6% | **1997** | 63,182 | 81.0% | **1992** |
| **+Temple-Morris, P** | C | **22,888** | **45.3%** | **-11.1%** | 28,837 | 56.3% | C |
| James, T | LD | 14,053 | 27.8% | -0.0% | 14,236 | 27.8% | LD |
| Westwood, R | Lab | 8,831 | 17.5% | +5.2% | 6,294 | 12.3% | Lab |
| Parkin, A | Ref | 2,815 | 5.6% | | 1,281 | 2.5% | Grn |
| Norman, Ms F | Green | 1,086 | 2.1% | | 530 | 1.0% | Anti-Fed |
| Chamings, J | UK Ind | 588 | 1.2% | | | | |
| Haycock, J | BNP | 292 | 0.6% | | | | |
| **C to LD notional swing 5.5%** | | **50,553** | C maj **8,835** | | 51,178 | C maj **14,601** | |
| | | | | 17.5% | | 28.5% | |

**PETER TEMPLE-MORRIS**, b Feb 12, 1938. Solicitor. Elected Feb 1974; contested Lambeth Norwood 1970; Newport 1964 and 1966. Joint vice-chair, C backbench Euro affairs cttee, 1991- . UK chair, British-Irish inter-parly body, 1988- ; chair, Soc of C Lawyers, 1995- (on exec cttee 1968-71 and 1990- ). Joint vice-chair (1982-90) and joint sec (1979-82), C backbench foreign affairs cttee; joint vice-chair, C Northern Ireland cttee, 1989- . Chair, Macleod group. Member, exec cttee, British group, IPU, 1977- (chair, 1982-85); exec cttee, UK branch, CPA (joint vice-chair, 1994- ). Council member, GB-USSR Assoc, 1982- . Dir, John Kendall Associates (Press Relations) Ltd, mainly agriculture and Wales. Freeman, City of London; Liveryman, Basketmakers' Co; Barbers' Co. Ed Malvern Coll (governor 1975- and council member 1978- ); St Catharine's Coll, Cambridge.
**TERRY JAMES**, b March 11, 1948. Farmer. Hereford & Worcester county cllr 1981- (group leader); Leominster district cllr 1991- . Dir, Leominster UA Ltd; Leominster Development Trust. Ed Lady Hawkins School.
**RICHARD WESTWOOD**, b June 21, 1958. Univ lecturer. Leader of Lab group on Leominster District Council; Mayor of Leominster 1995-96. Member, NATFHE. Ed The Minster School, Leominster; Leicester Univ; Worcester Coll.

| LEWES | | 32.3% change | | | | | | LD win |
|---|---|---|---|---|---|---|---|---|
| Electorate % Turnout | | 64,340 | 76.4% | **1997** | 63,412 | 81.8% | | **1992** |
| **Baker, N** | **LD** | **21,250** | **43.2%** | **+4.1%** | 26,638 | 51.3% | | C |
| +Rathbone, T | C | 19,950 | 40.6% | -10.8% | 20,301 | 39.1% | | LD |
| Patton, Dr M | Lab | 5,232 | 10.6% | +2.4% | 4,270 | 8.2% | | Lab |
| Butler, Mrs L | Ref | 2,481 | 5.0% | | 599 | 1.2% | | Grn |
| Harvey, J | UK Ind | 256 | 0.5% | | 78 | 0.2% | | NLP |
| C to LD notional swing 7.4% | | 49,169 | | LD maj 1,300 2.6% | 51,886 | | | C maj 6,337 12.2% |

**NORMAN BAKER,** b July 26, 1957. Teacher. Contested this seat 1992. Lewes district cllr 1987- (council leader); East Sussex county cllr 1989- . Dir, Brighton & Hove Enterprise Agency; Newhaven Economic Partnership. Member, Greenpeace; Amnesty. Ed Royal Liberty, Romford; Royal Holloway and Bedford New Coll, London.
**TIM RATHBONE,** b March 17, 1933. Elected Feb 1974. PPS to Min for Arts 1985; to Consumer Affairs Min 1982-83; Min of Health 1979-82. Council member, Nat Cttee for Electoral Reform. Parly and public affairs consultant to Seeboard plc and Chanel Ltd. Dir, VJT Property Ltd and VJF Property Two Ltd; unpaid dir, Business

against Drugs, registered charity; business adviser to Lexion, management consultants. Chair, advisory cttee, Inst of Management Resources, 1987- . Dir, Charles Barker Group Ltd, 1968-87. FRSA. Ed Eton; Christ Church, Oxford; Harvard Business School.
**MARK PATTON,** b Jan 7, 1965. Univ lecturer. Carmarthen town cllr 1995- . Member, regional council of NATFHE; Fabian Soc; SEA; Christian Socialist Movement. Ed Hautlieu School, Jersey; Clare Coll, Cambridge; University Coll, London; Rijksuniversiteit Te Leiden; Université de Paris.

| LEWISHAM DEPTFORD | | 1.5% change | | | | | | Lab win |
|---|---|---|---|---|---|---|---|---|
| Electorate % Turnout | | 58,141 | 57.9% | **1997** | 57,583 | 65.4% | | **1992** |
| **+Ruddock, Mrs J** | **Lab** | **23,827** | **70.8%** | **+10.2%** | 22,816 | 60.6% | | Lab |
| Kimm, Mrs I | C | 4,949 | 14.7% | -12.9% | 10,395 | 27.6% | | C |
| Appiah, K | LD | 3,004 | 8.9% | -2.8% | 4,432 | 11.8% | | LD |
| Mulrenan, J | Soc Lab | 996 | 3.0% | | | | | |
| Shepherd, Ms S | Ref | 868 | 2.6% | | | | | |
| C to Lab notional swing 11.6% | | 33,644 | | Lab maj 18,878 56.1% | 37,643 | | | Lab maj 12,421 33.0% |

**JOAN RUDDOCK,** b Dec 28, 1943. Elected 1987; contested Newbury 1979. Lab spokesman on environmental protection 1994-97; on home affairs 1992-94; on transport 1989-92. Vice-chair, PLP defence cttee, 1987-89; joint vice-chair, London group of Lab MPs, 1987- . Member, select cttee on televising Commons, 1988-91. Chair, CND, 1981-85; vice-chair 1985-86. Organiser Manpower Services Commission special programmes officer dealing with unemployed young people 1977-79; with Shelter 1968-73. Ed Pontypool GS for Girls; Imperial Coll, London.

**IRENE KIMM,** b May 15, 1949. Runs sports and leisurewear business. Southwark cllr 1986-94. Founded Dulwich Right to Buy Club 1988; founder and chair, Camberwell Traders. Ed Waverley Secondary, Southwark.
**KOFI APPIAH,** b March 24, 1943. Barrister, tenant advice and participation officer. Contested London NE in 1994 Euro elections. Tower Hamlets cllr 1982-94 (ex-Mayor). Dir, trustee, Spitalfields Market Training Initiative. Ed West London Coll of Commerce; Central London Poly; Inns of Court Coll of Law.

| LEWISHAM EAST | | 0.3% change | | | | | | Lab win |
|---|---|---|---|---|---|---|---|---|
| Electorate % Turnout | | 56,333 | 66.4% | **1997** | 58,328 | 74.2% | | **1992** |
| **+Prentice, Ms B T** | **Lab** | **21,821** | **58.3%** | **+13.0%** | 19,633 | 45.4% | | Lab |
| Hollobone, P | C | 9,694 | 25.9% | -16.9% | 18,510 | 42.8% | | C |
| Buxton, D | LD | 4,178 | 11.2% | -0.2% | 4,935 | 11.4% | | LD |
| Drury, S | Ref | 910 | 2.4% | | 196 | 0.5% | | NLP |
| Croucher, R | NF | 431 | 1.2% | | | | | |
| White, P | Lib | 277 | 0.7% | | | | | |
| Rizz, C | Dream | 97 | 0.3% | | | | | |
| C to Lab notional swing 14.9% | | 37,408 | | Lab maj 12,127 32.4% | 43,274 | | | Lab maj 1,123 2.6% |

**BRIDGET PRENTICE,** b Dec 28, 1952. Became gvt asst whip, May 7, 1997. Ex-teacher. Won this seat 1992; contested Croydon Central 1987. Lab whip 1995-97. Member, select cttee on Parly Commissioner for Administration, 1992-95; vice-chair, PLP employment cttee; PLP home affairs cttee; former joint vice-chair, London group of Lab MPs. Hammersmith and Fulham cllr 1986-92; chair, Fulham Lab Party, 1982-85. Ed Our Lady and St Francis, Glasgow; Glasgow and London Univs; South Bank Poly.

**PHILIP HOLLOBONE,** b Nov 7, 1964. Research analyst into privatised industries. Bromley cllr 1990-94. Former paratrooper, TA. Ed Dulwich Coll; Lady Margaret Hall, Oxford.
**DAVID BUXTON,** b Sept 10, 1964. Regional dir of deaf charity organisation, first born-deaf PPC in British political history. Southwark cllr 1990-94. Member, British Deaf Assoc (London area cllr); editor, *Christian Deaf Link* magazine. Ed Summerfield School, Malvern; Slough Coll of HE; South Bank Univ.

## LEWISHAM WEST — Lab hold

| Electorate % Turnout | | 58,659 | 64.0% | **1997** | 59,317 | 73.1% | **1992** |
|---|---|---|---|---|---|---|---|
| *Dowd, J | Lab | 23,273 | 62.0% | +15.0% | 20,378 | 47.0% | Lab |
| Whelan, Mrs C | C | 8,936 | 23.8% | -19.0% | 18,569 | 42.8% | C |
| McGrath, Miss K | LD | 3,672 | 9.8% | -0.1% | 4,295 | 9.9% | LD |
| Leese, A | Ref | 1,098 | 2.9% | | 125 | 0.3% | Anti-Fed |
| Long, N | Soc Lab | 398 | 1.1% | | | | |
| Oram, Ms E | Lib | 167 | 0.4% | | | | |
| **C to Lab swing 17.0%** | | **37,544** | **Lab maj 14,337** | | **43,367** | **Lab maj 1,809** | |
| | | | 38.2% | | | 4.2% | |

**JIM DOWD,** b March 5, 1951. Became gvt whip, May 7, 1997. Telecoms systems engineer. Gained this seat for Lab 1992; contested it 1987, and Beckenham 1983. Lab spokesman on N Ireland 1995-97; Lab whip 1993-95. Lewisham cllr 1974-94 (Mayor 1992). With Plessey Co, later GPT, 1973-92; senior negotiator for ASTMS, and then MSF. Ed Sedgehill Comp, London; London Nautical School.

**CLARE WHELAN,** b Sept 19, 1955. Freelance journalist. PA to Edwina Currie; Lambeth cllr 1990- . Member, Bow Group; C Group for Europe. Vice-chair of Age Concern, Lambeth, since 1992. Trustee of Brixton Dispensary Sick and Poor Fund. JP. Ed Royal Naval School, Haslemere.
**KATHY McGRATH,** b July 25, 1955. Nurse/PR manager. Dir, Galaxy Medical Advisory Service. Member, RCN. Ed More House, London; Great Ormond St, Middlesex and Brompton Hospitals.

## LEYTON & WANSTEAD — 40.8% change — Lab win

| Electorate % Turnout | | 62,176 | 63.2% | **1997** | 65,812 | 68.9% | **1992** |
|---|---|---|---|---|---|---|---|
| +Cohen, H M | Lab | 23,922 | 60.8% | +15.0% | 20,775 | 45.8% | Lab |
| Vaudry, R | C | 8,736 | 22.2% | -8.7% | 14,006 | 30.9% | C |
| Anglin, C | LD | 5,920 | 15.1% | -5.4% | 9,300 | 20.5% | LD |
| Duffy, S | ProLife | 488 | 1.2% | | 1,275 | 2.8% | Other |
| Mian, A | Ind | 256 | 0.7% | | | | |
| **C to Lab notional swing 11.8%** | | **39,322** | **Lab maj 15,186** | | **45,356** | **Lab maj 6,769** | |
| | | | 38.6% | | | 14.9% | |

**HARRY COHEN,** b Dec 10, 1949. Accountant and local gvt employee. Elected MP for Leyton 1983. Joint vice-chair and former chair, PLP defence cttee; vice-chair, PLP Treasury and Civil Service cttee, 1987-88; chair, Labour Friends of Palestine, 1987-90. Waltham Forest cllr 1972-84 (sec, Lab group). Member, Nalgo. Ed George Gascoigne Sec Mod; East Ham Further Ed Coll; Birkbeck Coll, London.
**ROBERT VAUDRY,** b May 8, 1964. Operations manager for Equity Research. Special adviser and campaign co-ordinator to Sir Edward Heath 1988-92. Chair, Croydon NE YCs. Associate,

Morgan Stanley and Co Ltd; non-exec dir constituency research. Worked for Midland Montagu 1987-88. Non-exec dir Oxleas Community Health Hospital Trust. Ed John Fisher School, Purley; Leeds Univ; London Business School.
**CHARLES ANGLIN,** b Jan 29, 1971. PR consultant. Youngest LD black PPC. Former national vice-chair, LD students; member, LD federal policy cttee and federal exec. Ed Addey and Stanhope School, Deptford; Queen Mary and Westfield Coll, London; Leeds Univ; California Univ, Berkeley.

## LICHFIELD — 103.3% change — C win

| Electorate % Turnout | | 62,720 | 77.5% | **1997** | 61,995 | 83.6% | **1992** |
|---|---|---|---|---|---|---|---|
| +Fabricant, M L D | C | 20,853 | 42.9% | -14.1% | 29,583 | 57.0% | C |
| Woodward, Ms S | Lab | 20,615 | 42.4% | +5.8% | 18,993 | 36.6% | Lab |
| Bennion, Dr P | LD | 5,473 | 11.3% | +5.5% | 2,970 | 5.7% | LD |
| Seward, G | Ref | 1,652 | 3.4% | | 312 | 0.6% | Other |
| **C to Lab notional swing 10.0%** | | **48,593** | **C maj 238** | | **51,858** | **C maj 10,590** | |
| | | | 0.5% | | | 20.4% | |

**MICHAEL FABRICANT,** b June 12, 1950. Ex-BBC current affairs broadcaster; chartered engineer. MP for Staffordshire-Mid, 1992-97, regaining that seat which C lost in 1990 by-election; contested South Shields 1987. PPS to Financial Sec to Treasury, 1996-97. Member, national heritage select cttee, 1992-96; joint vice-chair, C backbench media cttee 1992- ; sec, C ed and employment cttee, 1995- ; treas, all-party cable and satellite TV parly group, 1996- . Until 1992, senior dir and co-founder of international broadcasting and manufacturing group with clients ranging from BBC to Radio Moscow. Formerly technical, marketing and

programming consultant to BBC; ex-adviser to Home Office on broadcasting. Ed Brighton and Hove GS; Loughborough, Sussex and London Univs; Univ of Southern California, Los Angeles.
**SUSAN WOODWARD,** b Dec 8, 1952. Political assistant, teacher. Lichfield district cllr. Member, Co-op Party; GMB/Apex; Christian Socialist Movement. Ed Shire Oak GS; Leicester and Birmingham Univs.
**PHILLIP BENNION,** b Oct 7, 1954. Farmer. Staffordshire county chair, NFU. Ed Queen Elizabeth I GS, Tamworth; Aberdeen, Birmingham and Newcastle Univs.

| LINCOLN | | 17.0% change | | | **Lab win** | | |
|---|---|---|---|---|---|---|---|
| Electorate % Turnout | | 65,485 | 71.1% | **1997** | 65,087 | 79.6% | **1992** |
| **Merron, Ms G** | Lab | **25,563** | 54.9% | +8.9% | **23,869** | 46.0% | Lab |
| Brown, A | C | 14,433 | 31.0% | -13.2% | 22,905 | 44.2% | C |
| Gabriel, Ms L | LD | 5,048 | 10.8% | +2.0% | 4,561 | 8.8% | LD |
| Ivory, J | Ref | 1,329 | 2.9% | | 500 | 1.0% | Lib |
| Myers, A | NLP | 175 | 0.4% | | | | |
| C to Lab notional swing 11.0% | | 46,548 | Lab maj 11,130 | | 51,835 | Lab maj 964 | |
| | | | 23.9% | | | 1.9% | |

**GILLIAN MERRON,** b April 12, 1959. Senior Unison regional official; Unison E Midlands head of gas and electricity; former business development adviser. Member, Amnesty. Ed Wanstead HS; Lancaster Univ.

**TONY BROWN,** b Dec 11, 1956. PR partner. Contested Staffordshire W and Congleton in 1994 Euro elections. Researcher to Baroness Chalker, Andrew Bowden, ex-MP, and Stephen Dorrell, 1976-84. Ealing cllr. Partner, Chelgate PR Ltd, and member, Inst of Public Relations. Ed Haileybury; Fitzwilliam Coll, Cambridge.

**LISA GABRIEL,** b June 17, 1956. Teacher/freelance musician. Member, NASUWT. Ed Cleethorpes GS for Girls; Lindsey School; Bishop Grosseteste Coll, Lincoln.

| LINLITHGOW | | 14.5% change | | | **Lab win** | | |
|---|---|---|---|---|---|---|---|
| Electorate % Turnout | | 53,706 | 73.8% | **1997** | 53,066 | 77.1% | **1992** |
| **+Dalyell, T** | Lab | **21,469** | 54.1% | +4.9% | **20,137** | 49.2% | Lab |
| MacAskill, K | SNP | 10,631 | 26.8% | -3.3% | 12,340 | 30.1% | SNP |
| Kerr, T | C | 4,964 | 12.5% | -1.2% | 5,613 | 13.7% | C |
| Duncan, A | LD | 2,331 | 5.9% | -1.1% | 2,843 | 6.9% | LD |
| Plomer, K | Ref | 259 | 0.7% | | | | |
| SNP to Lab notional swing 4.1% | | 39,654 | Lab maj 10,838 | | 40,933 | Lab maj 7,797 | |
| | | | 27.3% | | | 19.1% | |

**TAM DALYELL,** b Aug 9, 1932. Author and former teacher. Elected for this seat 1983; MP for W Lothian 1962-83; contested Roxburgh, Selkirk and Peebles, 1959. Member, Lab Party NEC, 1986-87. MEP 1975-79. Joint vice-pres, all-party arts and heritage group; joint vice-chair, all-party Argentina group, 1996- ; sec, all-party Ecuadorean group, 1996- . Member, exec cttee, Campaign Group of Lab MPs, 1985-86; PPS to Richard Crossman 1964-70. Political columnist, *New Scientist*, 1967- . Council member, National Trust for Scotland. Ed Edinburgh Acad; Eton; King's Coll, Cambridge; Moray House Teachers' Training Coll, Edinburgh.

**KENNETH MacASKILL,** b April 28, 1958. Lawyer. Contested this seat 1992; Livingston 1987 and 1983, and Scotland Mid and Fife in 1989 Euro elections. Ed Linlithgow Acad; Edinburgh Univ.

**TOM KERR,** b July 22, 1947. Self-employed marine surveyor and consultant; former marine engineer, BP Tanker Co. Member, West Lothian District Council/UA 1992- . Ed Linlithgow Acad.

**ANDREW DUNCAN,** b Feb 6, 1958. Chartered accountant and company sec. Member. Campaign for a Scottish Parliament; Friends of the Earth. Ed Edinburgh Acad; St Andrews and Stirling Univs.

| LIVERPOOL GARSTON | | 21.0% change | | | **Lab win** | | |
|---|---|---|---|---|---|---|---|
| Electorate % Turnout | | 66,755 | 65.1% | **1997** | 69,614 | 70.9% | **1992** |
| **Eagle, Ms M** | Lab | **26,667** | 61.3% | +10.2% | **25,214** | 51.1% | Lab |
| Clucas, Ms F | LD | 8,250 | 19.0% | -2.7% | 12,340 | 25.0% | C |
| Gordon-Johnson, N | C | 6,819 | 15.7% | -9.3% | 10,680 | 21.6% | LD |
| Dunne, F | Ref | 833 | 1.9% | | 914 | 1.9% | Lib |
| Copeland, G | Lib | 666 | 1.5% | -0.3% | 190 | 0.4% | NLP |
| Parsons, J | NLP | 127 | 0.3% | -0.1% | | | |
| Nolan, S | SEP | 120 | 0.3% | | | | |
| LD to Lab notional swing 6.4% | | 43,482 | Lab maj 18,417 | | 49,338 | Lab maj 12,874 | |
| | | | 42.4% | | | 26.1% | |

**MARIA EAGLE,** b Feb 17, 1961. Solicitor specialising in housing and employment law. Contested Crosby 1992. Ex-chair, Formby Lab Party; ex-sec, Formby women's section. Ed Formby HS; Pembroke Coll, Oxford; Lancaster Gate Coll of Law. Has represented Lancashire and England in chess competitions. Twin sister of Angela Eagle, who is Lab MP for Wallasey.

**FLO CLUCAS,** b May 9, 1947. Lecturer. Contested Wirral S by-election 1997, Crosby 1992, Halton 1987, and Merseyside East in 1994 Euro elections. Liverpool city cllr (dep leader, LD group). Dir, Liverpool Institute of Performing Arts/City of Learning. Ed St Mary's, Bangor; Liverpool Inst of HE; Liverpool Univ.

**NIGEL GORDON-JOHNSON,** b Oct 18, 1967. Technical sales consultant to construction industry. Adur district cllr 1992- (leader, C group, 1993- ). Vice-chair, Shoreham C assoc. Chair, South Coast beach clearance pressure group. Ed Kelly Coll, Tavistock; Shoreham Coll.

| LIVERPOOL RIVERSIDE | | 44.5% change | | | | | Lab win |
|---|---|---|---|---|---|---|---|
| Electorate % Turnout | | 73,429 | 51.9% | **1997** | 71,118 | 59.1% | **1992** |
| Ellman, Ms L | Lab Co-op | **26,858** | **70.4%** | **+2.0%** | 28,760 | 68.4% | Lab Co-op |
| Fraenkel, Ms B | LD | 5,059 | 13.3% | -5.2% | 7,744 | 18.4% | LD |
| Sparrow, D | C | 3,635 | 9.5% | -1.3% | 4,572 | 10.9% | C |
| Wilson, Ms C | Soc | 776 | 2.0% | | 770 | 1.8% | Grn |
| Green, D | Lib | 594 | 1.6% | | 179 | 0.4% | NLP |
| Skelly, G | Ref | 586 | 1.5% | | | | |
| Neilson, Ms H | ProLife | 277 | 0.7% | | | | |
| Braid, D | MRAC | 179 | 0.5% | | | | |
| Gay, G | NLP | 171 | 0.4% | +0.0% | | | |
| **LD to Lab notional swing 3.6%** | | **38,135** | Lab Co-op maj 21,799 | | **42,025** | Lab Co-op maj 21,016 | |
| | | | 57.2% | | | 50.0% | |

**LOUISE ELLMAN,** b Nov 14, 1945. Contested Darwen 1979. Leader of Lancashire County Council since 1981 (chair 1981-85; leader, Lab group, 1977- ; member, 1970- ). Established Lancashire Enterprises as county's economic development agency in 1982 and vice-chair since then. Vice-chair, Leyland Trucks. Founder member, Co-operative Enterprises NW, 1979- . OU counsellor. Ed Manchester HS for Girls; Hull and York Univs.

**BEATRICE FRAENKEL,** b April 25, 1945. Industrial design engineer. Contested Cheshire East in 1989 Euro elections. Liverpool city cllr. Dir, Normal Properties Ltd. Member, Amnesty. Ed Huyton Coll; Leicester Poly; UMIST; Liverpool John Moores Univ.
**DAVID SPARROW,** b April 12, 1949. Solicitor, company director. Contested Manchester Wythenshawe 1987. Ed William Hulme's GS; Jesus Coll, Oxford.

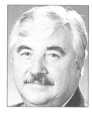

| LIVERPOOL WALTON | | | | | | | Lab hold |
|---|---|---|---|---|---|---|---|
| Electorate % Turnout | | 67,527 | 59.5% | **1997** | 70,102 | 67.4% | **1992** |
| *Kilfoyle, P | Lab | **31,516** | **78.4%** | **+6.0%** | 34,214 | 72.4% | Lab |
| Roberts, R | LD | 4,478 | 11.1% | -0.9% | 5,915 | 12.5% | C |
| Kotecha, M | C | 2,551 | 6.3% | -6.2% | 5,672 | 12.0% | LD |
| Grundy, C | Ref | 620 | 1.5% | | 963 | 2.0% | Lib |
| Mahmood, Ms L | Soc | 444 | 1.1% | | 393 | 0.8% | Prot Ref |
| Williams, Ms H | Lib | 352 | 0.9% | -1.2% | 98 | 0.2% | NLP |
| Mearns, Ms V | ProLife | 246 | 0.6% | | | | |
| **LD to Lab swing 3.4%** | | **40,207** | Lab maj 27,038 | | **47,255** | Lab maj 28,299 | |
| | | | 67.2% | | | 59.9% | |

**PETER KILFOYLE,** b June 9, 1946. Became Under Secretary of State for Public Services, May 5, 1997. Won 1991 by-election for this seat. Lab spokesman on education 1994 and on employment 1995; previously Lab whip. Party regional organiser in NW 1985-91; joined staff of Lab Party 1985; previously building labourer, teacher, youth worker. Has held many posts within party and trade union movement. Member, MSF; TGWU; Co-op Party. Ed St Edward's Coll, Liverpool; Durham Univ; Christ's Coll, Liverpool.

**RICHARD ROBERTS,** b Dec 26, 1949. Professional fundraiser. Liverpool city cllr (dep whip). Ed Liverpool Collegiate.
**MARK KOTECHA,** b Feb 1, 1964. Managing dir, Internet publishing company. Adviser to Portobello Trust on creating new businesses. Member, Bow Group. Ed Finchley Manor Hill School; Balliol Coll, Oxford; Birkbeck Coll, London.

| LIVERPOOL WAVERTREE | | 63.2% change | | | | | Lab win |
|---|---|---|---|---|---|---|---|
| Electorate % Turnout | | 73,063 | 62.8% | **1997** | 73,095 | 70.3% | **1992** |
| +Kennedy, Ms J E | Lab | **29,592** | **64.4%** | **+23.1%** | 21,237 | 41.3% | Lab |
| Kemp, R | LD | 9,891 | 21.5% | -13.2% | 17,857 | 34.7% | LD |
| Malthouse, C | C | 4,944 | 10.8% | -1.7% | 6,422 | 12.5% | C |
| Worthington, P | Ref | 576 | 1.3% | | 5,899 | 11.5% | Other |
| McCullough, K | Lib | 391 | 0.9% | | | | |
| Kingsley, Ms R | ProLife | 346 | 0.8% | | | | |
| Corkhill, Ms C | WRP | 178 | 0.4% | | | | |
| **LD to Lab notional swing 18.2%** | | **45,918** | Lab maj 19,701 | | **51,415** | Lab maj 3,380 | |
| | | | 42.9% | | | 6.6% | |

**JANE KENNEDY,** b May 4, 1958. Became gvt asst whip, May 7, 1997. MP for Liverpool Broadgreen 1992-97. Lab whip 1995-97. Chair, 1995- , and former vice-chair, NW group of Lab MPs. Nupe area organiser 1988-92; ex-childcare worker. Ed Haughton Comp; Queen Elizabeth Sixth-Form Coll; Liverpool Univ.

**RICHARD KEMP,** b Jan 8, 1953. Economic development adviser. Contested Birkenhead 1987, Runcorn 1979. Liverpool city cllr 1975-84, 1992- . Ed Leyland GS; Leeds Poly.
**CHRISTOPHER MALTHOUSE,** b Oct 27, 1966. Chartered accountant and finance director. Ed Liverpool Coll; Newcastle Univ.

| LIVERPOOL WEST DERBY | | 21.1% change | | | Lab win | | |
|---|---|---|---|---|---|---|---|
| Electorate % Turnout | | 68,682 | 61.4% | **1997** | 68,613 | 69.6% | **1992** |
| +Wareing, R N | Lab | 30,002 | 71.2% | +6.6% | 30,830 | 64.6% | Lab |
| Radford, S | Lib | 4,037 | 9.6% | +4.7% | 7,297 | 15.3% | LD |
| Hines, Ms A | LD | 3,805 | 9.0% | -6.3% | 6,975 | 14.6% | C |
| Morgan, N | C | 3,656 | 8.7% | -5.9% | 2,329 | 4.9% | Lib |
| Forrest, P | Ref | 657 | 1.6% | | 308 | 0.6% | NLP |
| Lib to Lab notional swing 0.9% | | 42,157 | | Lab maj 25,965 | 47,739 | | Lab maj 23,533 |
| | | | | 61.6% | | | 49.3% |

**ROBERT WAREING**, b Aug 20, 1930. Ex-lecturer. Elected for this seat 1983; contested Berwick-upon-Tweed 1970; Liverpool, Edge Hill, 1979 by-election and gen election. Lab whip 1987-92; member, foreign affairs select cttee, 1992- ; chair (1994- ) and vice-chair (1985-94), all-party British-Yugoslavia parly group; joint vice-chair, Russian group, 1992- . Merseyside county cllr 1981-86 (Lab group chief whip 1981-83). Vice-pres, AMA, 1984- . Ed Ranworth Square School, Liverpool; Alsop HS, Liverpool; Bolton Coll of Ed; London Univ (external student).

**STEPHEN RADFORD**, b Nov 5, 1956. Personnel manager. Liverpool cllr. Member, Gay Christian Movement. Ed George Abbot Boys Comp, Guildford; Pierrepont School, Frensham; Farnham Sixth-Form Coll; Warwick Univ.
**ANN HINES**, b Jan 17, 1953. Schoolteacher. Liverpool city cllr 1994- . Ed Notre Dame Coll of Ed; Liverpool Univ.
**NEIL MORGAN**, b June 16, 1952. Financial consultant. Dir, Instinet UK, 1992-95; Barbican Capital Management 1990-92. Ed Forest GS, Winnersh; Reading Univ.

| LIVINGSTON | | 12.6% change | | | Lab win | | |
|---|---|---|---|---|---|---|---|
| Electorate % Turnout | | 60,296 | 71.0% | **1997** | 58,068 | 73.1% | **1992** |
| +Cook, R | Lab | 23,510 | 54.9% | +9.0% | 19,461 | 45.8% | Lab |
| Johnston, P | SNP | 11,763 | 27.5% | +1.5% | 11,013 | 25.9% | SNP |
| Craigie Halkett, H | C | 4,028 | 9.4% | -8.7% | 7,689 | 18.1% | C |
| Hawthorn, E | LD | 2,876 | 6.7% | -2.4% | 3,857 | 9.1% | LD |
| Campbell, Ms H | Ref | 444 | 1.0% | | 425 | 1.0% | Grn |
| Culbert, M | SPGB | 213 | 0.5% | | | | |
| SNP to Lab notional swing 3.8% | | 42,834 | | Lab maj 11,747 | 42,445 | | Lab maj 8,448 |
| | | | | 27.4% | | | 19.9% |

**ROBIN COOK**, b Feb 28, 1946. Became Foreign Secretary, May 2, 1997. Shadow Foreign Secretary 1994-97. Elected for this seat 1983; MP for Edinburgh Central Feb 1974-83; contested Edinburgh N 1970. Chief Lab spokesman on trade and industry 1992-94; on health 1989-92; on health and social security 1987-89; member of Shadow Cabinet 1983-86 and 1987-97. Spokesman on European and Community affairs 1983-85; campaigns co-ordinator 1985-86; trade and industry spokesman 1986-87; Treasury and economic affairs spokesman 1980-83. Member, Lab Party NEC since 1988. Member, Edinburgh Corp,

1971-74. Ex-tutor and organiser in adult ed. Horse racing tipster and racing columnist. Ed Aberdeen GS; Royal HS, Edinburgh; Edinburgh Univ.
**PETER JOHNSTON**, b March 10, 1952. Teacher. Contested this seat 1992. W Lothian district cllr 1985- . Ex-convener, Livingston SNP. Member, EIS. Ed Callendar Park Coll of Ed, Falkirk.
**HUGH CRAIGIE HALKETT,** b Oct 28, 1968. Management consultant. Ed Lathallan School, Angus; Harrow.
**EWAN HAWTHORN,** b Jan 16, 1962. Investment analyst/OU tutor. Ed Jordanhill Coll School; Edinburgh Univ; OU; Heriot-Watt Univ.

| LLANELLI | | 8.5% change | | | Lab win | | |
|---|---|---|---|---|---|---|---|
| Electorate % Turnout | | 58,323 | 70.7% | **1997** | 59,729 | 77.2% | **1992** |
| +Davies, D | Lab | 23,851 | 57.9% | +3.4% | 25,122 | 54.5% | Lab |
| Phillips, M | PC | 7,812 | 19.0% | +3.2% | 7,851 | 17.0% | C |
| Hayes, A | C | 5,003 | 12.1% | -4.9% | 7,253 | 15.7% | PC |
| Burree, N | LD | 3,788 | 9.2% | -3.6% | 5,884 | 12.8% | LD |
| Willock, J | Soc Lab | 757 | 1.8% | | | | |
| PC to Lab notional swing 0.1% | | 41,211 | | Lab maj 16,039 | 46,110 | | Lab maj 17,271 |
| | | | | 38.9% | | | 37.5% |

**DENZIL DAVIES**, b Oct 9, 1938. Barrister. Elected 1970. Member, Shadow Cabinet, 1985-88. Chief Lab spokesman on defence and disarmament 1983-88, when he resigned; chief spokesman on Wales 1983; spokesman on defence 1982-83, on foreign affairs 1981-82, and on Treasury and economic affairs 1979-81; Min of State, Treasury, 1975-79. Member, select cttee on Euro legislation 1974-75; on wealth tax 1974-75. Lectured at Chicago and Leeds Univs. Ed Carmarthen GS; Pembroke Coll, Oxford.

**MARC PHILLIPS**, b Dec 8, 1953. Contested this seat 1992; Mid and West Wales in 1994 Euro elections. Chief exec of cancer charity. National chair PC; Vice-pres 1993-95. Ed Cyfarthfa HS, Merthyr Tydfil.
**ANDREW HAYES**, b Aug 13, 1963; partner with investor relations and financial PR consultancy. Founder and chair, campaign for a Referendum. Ed Hampton School; Edinburgh Univ.
**NICK BURREE**, b Feb 14, 1956. Teacher. Ed Llanelli Boys' GS; St David's Univ College, Lampeter; Univ Coll of Wales, Aberystwyth.

| LONDONDERRY EAST | | 27.1% change | | | | | UUP win |
|---|---|---|---|---|---|---|---|
| Electorate % Turnout | | 58,831 | 64.8% | **1997** | 57,023 | 63.0% | **1992** |
| **+Ross, W** | UUP | **13,558** | **35.6%** | -29.3% | **23,287** | **64.9%** | **UUP** |
| Campbell, G | DUP | 9,764 | 25.6% | | 7,134 | 19.9% | SDLP |
| Doherty, A | SDLP | 8,273 | 21.7% | +1.8% | 2,634 | 7.3% | Alliance |
| O'Kane, M | SF | 3,463 | 9.1% | +5.6% | 1,589 | 4.4% | C |
| Boyle, Ms Y | Alliance | 2,427 | 6.4% | -1.0% | 1,261 | 3.5% | SF |
| Holmes, J | C | 436 | 1.1% | -3.3% | | | |
| Gallen, Ms C | NLP | 100 | 0.3% | | | | |
| Anderson, I | Nat Dem | 81 | 0.2% | | | | |
| **No swing calculation** | | **38,102** | **UUP maj 3,794** | | **35,905** | **UUP maj 16,153** | |
| | | | 10.0% | | | 45.0% | |

**WILLIAM ROSS,** b Feb 4, 1936. Farmer. Elected for this seat 1983; MP for Londonderry Feb 1974-83. Resigned seat in 1985 in protest at Anglo-Irish agreement and was re-elected in 1986 by-election. Party spokesman on agriculture and fisheries; former spokesman on Treasury matters. Member, select cttees on deregulation. 1995-97; members' interests 1992-95; statutory instruments 1991-97; Commons administration cttee 1991-97. Member, Apprentice Boys of Derry, the Orange and Black Institutions. Limavady cllr for four years. Former sec, Mid-Londonderry Constituency Unionist Party. Ed North West Coll of Agriculture.

**GREG CAMPBELL,** b Feb 15, 1953. Self-employed businessman. Londonderry city cllr. Member, NI Forum; DUP security spokesman. Ed Londonderry Tech Coll.
**ARTHUR DOHERTY.** Former primary school principal and school head of art and design. Chair, Assoc SDLP councillors; Limavady borough cllr (Mayor 1993-94). Member, Council for Nature Conservation in the Countryside.
**MALACHY O'KANE.** Farmer. Involved in republican politics for past three decades.
**YVONNE BOYLE.** Social worker. Forum candidate for East Londonderry.

| LOUGHBOROUGH | | 39.8% change | | | | | Lab win |
|---|---|---|---|---|---|---|---|
| Electorate % Turnout | | 68,945 | 76.0% | **1997** | 65,156 | 76.8% | **1992** |
| **Reed, A** | Lab Co-op | **25,448** | **48.6%** | +8.8% | **23,412** | **46.8%** | **C** |
| Andrew, K | C | 19,736 | 37.7% | -9.1% | 19,920 | 39.8% | Lab |
| Brass, Ms D | LD | 6,190 | 11.8% | +0.6% | 5,635 | 11.3% | LD |
| Gupta, R | Ref | 991 | 1.9% | | 842 | 1.7% | Grn |
| | | | | | 239 | 0.5% | NLP |
| **C to Lab notional swing 8.9%** | | **52,365** | **Lab Co-op maj 5,712** | | **50,048** | **C maj 3,492** | |
| | | | 10.9% | | | 7.0% | |

**ANDREW REED,** b Sept 17, 1964. Contested this seat 1992; chaired CLP, 1988-91. Member, John Smith's leadership campaign team, 1992. Member, Lab Party regional exec cttee, 1992-93. European officer for Leics County Council and ex-employment initiatives officer. Charnwood borough cllr 1995- . Ed Stonehill HS; Longsade Community Coll; Leicester Poly.
**KENNETH ANDREW,** b Dec 21, 1944. Managing director and chair of small and major companies, and author. Non-exec dir, Mount

Vernon Watford NHS Hospital Trust. Council member, IMC Business; cttee member, British Refugees Homes. Chair, Herts SW C assoc. Fellow, IoD and Royal Soc of Arts. Ed Downhill School, Tottenham; Univ Coll of Wales, Cardiff; Imperial Coll, London.
**DIANA BRASS,** b Jan 10, 1939. Teacher. Contested Derbyshire S 1992; East Staffs & Derby in 1994 Euro elections. Member, AMMA. Ed Sir William Perkins School for Girls, Chertsey; Lady Margaret Hall, Oxford.

| LOUTH & HORNCASTLE | | 41.6% change | | | | | C win |
|---|---|---|---|---|---|---|---|
| Electorate % Turnout | | 68,824 | 72.6% | **1997** | 65,996 | 79.0% | **1992** |
| **+Tapsell, Sir Peter** | C | **21,699** | **43.4%** | -9.3% | **27,499** | **52.7%** | **C** |
| Hough, J | Lab | 14,799 | 29.6% | +16.0% | 16,529 | 31.7% | LD |
| Martin, Mrs F | LD | 12,207 | 24.4% | -7.2% | 7,122 | 13.7% | Lab |
| Robinson, Ms R | Green | 1,248 | 2.5% | | 1,018 | 2.0% | Other |
| **C to Lab notional swing 12.6%** | | **49,953** | **C maj 6,900** | | **52,168** | **C maj 10,970** | |
| | | | 13.8% | | | 21.0% | |

**SIR PETER TAPSELL,** b Feb 1, 1930. MP for Nottingham W 1959-64; for Horncastle 1966-83; for Lindsey E 1983-97. Contested Wednesbury by-election Feb 1957. PA to Anthony Eden, 1955 election. C spokesman on Treasury and economic affairs 1977-78 and on foreign and Commonwealth affairs 1976-77. Adviser to Japanese trading and stockbroking firms and banks. Member, council, Institute for Fiscal Studies; London Stock Exchange 1957- . Ed Tonbridge School; Merton Coll, Oxford.

**JOHN HOUGH,** b Aug 22, 1946. Member of workers' co-operative. Contested Holland and Boston, 1992 and 1987; Brigg and Cleethorpes 1983. Louth district cllr. Chair, Lab Party Rural Revival 1988- . Member, TGWU; World Development Movement; Child Poverty Action Group. Ed LSE; Massachusetts IT.
**FIONA MARTIN,** b Dec 24, 1954. Horncastle town cllr 1979- (Mayor twice); East Lindsey district cllr 1987- (group leader); Lincolnshire county cllr 1993- . Ed Queen Elizabeth GS, Horncastle.

| LUDLOW | 15.2% change | | | | | | | C win |
|---|---|---|---|---|---|---|---|---|
| Electorate % Turnout | | | 61,267 | 75.5% | **1997** | 58,316 | 81.1% | **1992** |
| +Gill, C | C | | **19,633** | 42.4% | -9.2% | 24,415 | 51.6% | C |
| Huffer, T I | LD | | 13,724 | 29.7% | +4.1% | 12,108 | 25.6% | LD |
| O'Kane, Ms N | Lab | | 11,745 | 25.4% | +4.0% | 10,134 | 21.4% | Lab |
| Andrewes, T | Green | | 798 | 1.7% | | 643 | 1.4% | Grn |
| Freeman-Keel, E | UK Ind | | 385 | 0.8% | | | | |
| C to LD notional swing 6.6% | | | 46,285 | C maj 5,909 | | 47,300 | C maj 12,307 | |
| | | | | 12.8% | | | 26.0% | |

**CHRISTOPHER GILL**, b Oct 28, 1936. Elected 1987. Member, select cttees on Welsh affairs 1995-97; agriculture 1989-95. Joint vice-chair, C backbench European affairs cttee, 1989-91 (sec 1988-89); joint vice-chair 1991-94, and sec 1990-91, C ag, fish and food backbench cttee; C food and drinks sub-cttee 1989-90; treas, all-party maritime parly group. Pres, Midlands W Euro C Council, 1984-85. Wolverhampton borough cllr 1965-72; council member, Wolverhampton Chamber of Commerce, 1984-87. Ex-chair of family business, F.A. Gill Ltd, meat processing and wholesaling;

ex-member, nat council, Bacon and Meat Manufacturers' Assoc; has served on cttee, Fed of Fresh Meat Wholesalers. Ed Shrewsbury School.
**IAN HUFFER**, b March 7, 1957. Barrister. Contested Denton & Reddish 1987. Macclesfield borough cllr 1984-88. Member Green LDs. Ed Ludlow GS; Oxford Univ.
**NUALA O'KANE**, b Feb 3, 1953. Children's charity appeals director. Wrekin district cllr 1991- . Member, MSF; Greenpeace; Amnesty. Ed Our Lady of Mercy GS, Wolverhampton.

| LUTON NORTH | 35.5% change | | | | | | | Lab win |
|---|---|---|---|---|---|---|---|---|
| Electorate % Turnout | | | 64,618 | 73.2% | **1997** | 64,559 | 81.2% | **1992** |
| Hopkins, K | Lab | | **25,860** | 54.6% | +17.4% | 26,853 | 51.2% | C |
| Senior, D | C | | 16,234 | 34.3% | -16.9% | 19,496 | 37.2% | Lab |
| Newbound, Mrs K | LD | | 4,299 | 9.1% | -1.1% | 5,311 | 10.1% | LD |
| Brown, C | UK Ind | | 689 | 1.5% | | 517 | 1.0% | Grn |
| Custance, A | NLP | | 250 | 0.5% | +0.1% | 233 | 0.4% | NLP |
| C to Lab notional swing 17.2% | | | 47,332 | Lab maj 9,626 | | 52,410 | C maj 7,357 | |
| | | | | 20.3% | | | 14.0% | |

**KELVIN HOPKINS**, b Aug 22, 1941. Economist and statistician. Hon fellow, Luton Univ; former lecturer in higher ed. Ed Queen Elizabeth GS, Barnet; Nottingham Univ.
**DAVID SENIOR**, b Feb 22, 1959. Director of ProShare. Contested Barnsley Central 1992; Cheshire West in 1994 Euro elections.

Business adviser to Prince's Youth Business Trust. Ed King's, Macclesfield; Jesus Coll, Cambridge (pres of Union, 1981).
**KATHRYN NEWBOUND**, b March 1, 1949. Teacher. Windsor and Maidenhead cllr. Ed Rochester Girls' GS; Bulmershe Coll of Ed; OU.

| LUTON SOUTH | 10.1% change | | | | | | | Lab win |
|---|---|---|---|---|---|---|---|---|
| Electorate % Turnout | | | 68,395 | 70.4% | **1997** | 66,027 | 78.4% | **1992** |
| Moran, Ms M | Lab | | **26,428** | 54.8% | +11.6% | 22,928 | 44.3% | C |
| +Bright, Sir Graham | C | | 15,109 | 31.4% | -12.9% | 22,396 | 43.2% | Lab |
| Fitchett, K | LD | | 4,610 | 9.6% | -1.6% | 5,795 | 11.2% | LD |
| Jacobs, C | Ref | | 1,205 | 2.5% | | 505 | 1.0% | Grn |
| Lawman, C | UK Ind | | 390 | 0.8% | | 171 | 0.3% | NLP |
| Scheimann, M | Green | | 356 | 0.7% | | | | |
| Perrin, Ms C | NLP | | 86 | 0.2% | -0.2% | | | |
| C to Lab notional swing 12.3% | | | 48,184 | Lab maj 11,319 | | 51,795 | C maj 532 | |
| | | | | 23.5% | | | 1.0% | |

**MARGARET MORAN**, b April 24, 1955. Director of Housing for Women, a housing assoc. Contested Carshalton and Wallington 1992. Member, Lab nat policy forum, economic policy commission and Lab NEC local gvt cttee. Lewisham cllr 1984- (was first woman council leader 1993-95). Ex-chair, London Housing Unit and ex-vice-chair, AMA housing cttee. Ed St Ursula's Convent School, Greenwich; St Mary's Coll of Ed, Twickenham; Birmingham Univ; Hackney Coll.
**SIR GRAHAM BRIGHT**, b April 2, 1942. Elected 1983; MP for Luton E 1979-83; contested Dartford Oct 1974; Thurrock 1970 and Feb 1974. Appointed vice-chair of C Party 1994; PPS to John Major, 1990-94; PPS to Earl of Caithness, Paymaster General, 1989-90; to Home Office mins, 1984-87. Chair, C cttee on smaller businesses,

1983-84 and 1987-88. Chair, 1970- , and managing dir, 1977- , Dietary Foods Ltd; dir, Mother Nature Ltd, food manufacturer. Public affairs adviser, Safeways Food Stores Ltd. Dir (unpaid), International Sweeteners Assoc; Cumberland Packing Corp Ltd; Cumberland Foods Ltd. Dir (unpaid), 1989-91, and vice-chair, 1980-89 and 1991- , Smaller Businesses Bureau. Ed Hassenbrook County School; Thurrock Tech Coll.
**KEITH FITCHETT**, b Feb 21, 1946. Information systems lecturer. Contested Hackney N 1992; Banbury 1983. Lambeth cllr 1990- . Dir, Monteverdi Choir and Orchestra. Ed Alleyn's School; New College, Oxford.

| MACCLESFIELD | | 8.1% change | | | | | C win |
|---|---|---|---|---|---|---|---|
| Electorate % Turnout | | 72,049 | 75.2% | **1997** | 70,834 | 81.5% | **1992** |
| +Winterton, N | C | **26,888** | **49.6%** | **-6.4%** | **32,332** | **56.0%** | C |
| Jackson, Ms J | Lab | 18,234 | 33.6% | +10.8% | 13,202 | 22.9% | Lab |
| Flynn, M | LD | 9,075 | 16.7% | -4.0% | 11,958 | 20.7% | LD |
| | | | | | 246 | 0.4% | NLP |
| C to Lab notional swing 8.6% | | **54,197** | | **C maj 8,654** | **57,738** | | **C maj 19,130** |
| | | | | 16.0% | | | 33.1% |

**NICHOLAS WINTERTON,** b March 31, 1938. Elected in 1971 by-election; contested Newcastle-under-Lyme 1969 by-election and 1970. Chair, health select cttee, 1991-92; member, select cttees on social services 1979-90; standing orders, 1981-97; and Commons chairmen's panel, 1987-97. Chair, all-party group for paper and board industry, 1983- ; cotton and allied textiles group; media group. Non-exec dir, Bridgwater Paper Co Ltd, 1990- ; MSB Ltd, marketing consultancy; Emerson International Inc, overseas commercial development; dir, Gvt Relations Unit. Parly adviser

to Construction Plant-hire Assoc. Freeman, City of London; Liveryman, Worshipful Co of Weavers. Ed Rugby. His wife Ann is C MP for Congleton.
**JANET JACKSON,** b April 11, 1951. Office administrator. Macclesfield borough cllr. Member, Manchester & dist branch exec of CWU, 1991-94. Ed Macclesfield HS for Girls.
**MIKE FLYNN,** b Dec 26, 1941. Retired computer systems manager. Macclesfield borough cllr 1994- . Ed St Mary's Coll, Middlesbrough; Imperial Coll, London.

| MAIDENHEAD | | 61.6% change | | | | | C win |
|---|---|---|---|---|---|---|---|
| Electorate % Turnout | | 67,302 | 75.6% | **1997** | 66,059 | 83.5% | **1992** |
| **May, Mrs T M** | **C** | **25,344** | **49.8%** | **-11.8%** | **33,958** | **61.6%** | C |
| Ketteringham, A T | LD | 13,363 | 26.3% | -3.6% | 16,462 | 29.8% | LD |
| Robson, Ms D | Lab | 9,205 | 18.1% | +9.5% | 4,741 | 8.6% | Lab |
| Taverner, C | Ref | 1,638 | 3.2% | | | | |
| Munkley, D | Lib | 896 | 1.8% | | | | |
| Spiers, N | UK Ind | 277 | 0.5% | | | | |
| Ardley, K | Glow | 166 | 0.3% | | | | |
| C to LD notional swing 4.1% | | **50,889** | | **C maj 11,981** | **55,161** | | **C maj 17,496** |
| | | | | 23.5% | | | 31.7% |

**THERESA MAY,** b Oct 1, 1956. Contested Durham NW 1992 and Barking by-election 1994. Merton cllr 1986-94 (dep leader, C group, 1992-94). Head of European affairs unit, Assoc for Payment Clearing Services; previously worked at Bank of England. Member, Merton and Sutton CHC, 1986-88; Surrey County Cricket Club. Fellow, Royal Geographical Soc. Ed Wheatley Park Comp, Oxfordshire; St Hugh's Coll, Oxford.

**ANDREW KETTERINGHAM,** b July 15, 1950. Public affairs dir for banking and insurance group. Contested Chesham and Amersham 1992 and 1987; Brent N 1979; London NW 1984 Euro elections. Chesham cllr 1982- (LD group leader; former Mayor). Ed Lascelles Sec Mod; Harrow County School; Hull Univ.
**DENISE ROBSON,** b May 16, 1955. Manager, unemployment training scheme. Ed Manning School, Nottingham; Newcastle Univ.

| MAIDSTONE & THE WEALD | | 62.9% change | | | | | C win |
|---|---|---|---|---|---|---|---|
| Electorate % Turnout | | 72,466 | 74.0% | **1997** | 71,009 | 80.2% | **1992** |
| +Widdecombe, Miss A N | C | **23,657** | **44.1%** | **-11.9%** | **31,951** | **56.1%** | C |
| Morgan, J | Lab | 14,054 | 26.2% | +13.8% | 17,237 | 30.3% | LD |
| Nelson, Mrs J | LD | 11,986 | 22.4% | -7.9% | 7,097 | 12.5% | Lab |
| Hopkins, Ms S | Ref | 1,998 | 3.7% | | 693 | 1.2% | Other |
| Cleator, Ms M | Soc Lab | 979 | 1.8% | | | | |
| Kemp, Ms P | Green | 480 | 0.9% | | | | |
| Owen, Mrs R | UK Ind | 339 | 0.6% | | | | |
| Oldbury, J | NLP | 115 | 0.2% | | | | |
| C to Lab notional swing 12.9% | | **53,608** | | **C maj 9,603** | **56,978** | | **C maj 14,714** |
| | | | | 17.9% | | | 25.8% |

**ANN WIDDECOMBE,** b Oct 4, 1947. MP for Maidstone 1987-97; contested Plymouth Devonport 1983, and Burnley 1979. Home Office Min for prisons, 1995-97; Employment Min 1994-95; Employment Under Sec 1993-94; Social Security Under Sec, 1990-93. Member, select cttee on social services, 1988-90. Sec, C backbench horticulture and markets sub-cttee, 1987-90. Former joint sec/research asst to C parly study group on disablement benefits; vice-chair, nat assoc of C graduates, 1976-78. Runnymede district cllr 1976-78. Senior administrator at London

Univ 1975-87; in marketing with Unilever 1973-75. Ed La Sainte Union Convent, Bath; Birmingham Univ; Lady Margaret Hall, Oxford.
**JOHN MORGAN,** b Jan 11, 1948. Writer, lecturer. Maidstone district cllr 1994- . Member, Writers' Guild; Co-op Party; NATFHE. Ed Hull HS for Commerce; Newcastle Poly; Durham, Hull and Kent Univs.
**JANE NELSON,** b Aug 17, 1960. IT consultant. Tandridge borough cllr 1991-96. Ed Mary Erskine School, Edinburgh; Edinburgh Univ; City Univ.

| MAKERFIELD | | 26.4% change | | | | | Lab win |
|---|---|---|---|---|---|---|---|
| Electorate % Turnout | | 67,358 | 66.8% | **1997** | 68,557 | 75.5% | **1992** |
| +McCartney, I | Lab | 33,119 | 73.6% | +10.2% | 32,787 | 63.3% | Lab |
| Winstanley, M | C | 6,942 | 15.4% | -9.0% | 12,640 | 24.4% | C |
| Hubbard, B | LD | 3,743 | 8.3% | -0.9% | 4,751 | 9.2% | LD |
| Seed, A | Ref | 1,210 | 2.7% | | 1,209 | 2.3% | Lib |
| | | | | | 373 | 0.7% | NLP |
| C to Lab notional swing 9.6% | | 45,014 | Lab maj 26,177 | | 51,760 | Lab maj 20,147 | |
| | | | 58.2% | | | 38.9% | |

IAN McCARTNEY, b April 25, 1951. Became Trade and Industry Minister of State for Corporate Affairs and Post Office, May 5, 1997. Elected 1987. Chief Lab spokesman on employment 1996, having been employment spokesman from 1994; health spokesman 1992-94. Member, select cttees on social security, 1991-92; chair (1990-92) and joint vice-chair (1989-90), PLP employment cttee; chair, all-party rugby league parly group, 1989-91; TGWU parly group. "Head Waiter", Lab MPs Supper Club. Hon parly adviser to Greater Manchester Fire and Civil Defence Authority 1987-92. Wigan borough cllr

1982-87. Ex-seaman, local gvt manual worker and chef. Ed Lenzie Acad; Langside Coll, Glasgow; Merchant Navy Sea Training Coll, Gravesend.
MICHAEL WINSTANLEY, b April 9, 1971. Hospital administrator. Sec, Makerfield C assoc 1990- ; Merseyside E and Wigan European C assoc 1992- . Member, Soc for Protection of Unborn Children. Ed St Edmund Arrowsmith RC HS, Makerfield.
BRUCE HUBBARD, b Oct 28, 1952. Teacher. Maghull town cllr (Mayor 1995-96). Member, Scouts district exec; NASUWT. Ed Brentwood School; Liverpool Univ.

| MALDON & CHELMSFORD EAST | | 80.9% change | | | | | C win |
|---|---|---|---|---|---|---|---|
| Electorate % Turnout | | 66,184 | 76.1% | **1997** | 64,712 | 79.7% | **1992** |
| +Whittingdale, J F L | C | 24,524 | 48.7% | -15.2% | 32,944 | 63.9% | C |
| Freeman, K | Lab | 14,485 | 28.7% | +16.0% | 11,359 | 22.0% | LD |
| Pooley, G | LD | 9,758 | 19.4% | -2.7% | 6,592 | 12.8% | Lab |
| Overy-Owen, L | UK Ind | 935 | 1.9% | | 696 | 1.3% | Other |
| Burgess, Ms E | Green | 685 | 1.4% | | | | |
| C to Lab notional swing 15.6% | | 50,387 | C maj 10,039 | | 51,591 | C maj 21,585 | |
| | | | 19.9% | | | 41.8% | |

JOHN WHITTINGDALE, b Oct 16, 1959. MP for Colchester S and Maldon 1992-97. PPS to Mins of State for Ed and Employment 1994-96; member, health select cttee, 1993-97; joint select cttee on Consolidation Bills 1992-97; joint sec, C backbench home affairs cttee, 1992-94. PPS to Eric Forth, Ed and Employment Min, 1994-96. Joint sec, all-party film industry parly group; treas, Friends of Music group. Political sec to Margaret Thatcher when she was PM 1988-90, then manager of her private office 1990-92; special adviser to Trade and Industry Sec 1984-87; head of political section, C research dept, 1982-84. Manager, N.M.

Rothschild & Sons, 1987. Member, Bow Group; Selsdon Group; British Mensa. Ed Winchester; University Coll, London.
KEVIN FREEMAN, b March 1, 1964. Solicitor. Member, MSF; Fabian Soc; Co-op Party. Ed state schools; Cambridge Univ.
GRAHAM POOLEY, b March 11, 1949. Management consultant. Chelmsford borough cllr. Ex-managing director and head of UK capital markets, Chase Investment Bank. Member, Friends of the Earth; Charter 88; Voting Reform Group. Ed Brentwood School; Oriel Coll, Oxford.

| MANCHESTER BLACKLEY | | 17.6% change | | | | | Lab win |
|---|---|---|---|---|---|---|---|
| Electorate % Turnout | | 62,227 | 57.5% | **1997** | 65,317 | 66.4% | **1992** |
| Stringer, G | Lab | 25,042 | 70.0% | +7.9% | 26,977 | 62.2% | Lab |
| Barclay, S | C | 5,454 | 15.3% | -10.8% | 11,285 | 26.0% | C |
| Wheale, S | LD | 3,937 | 11.0% | -0.0% | 4,786 | 11.0% | LD |
| Stanyer, P | Ref | 1,323 | 3.7% | | 342 | 0.8% | NLP |
| C to Lab notional swing 9.3% | | 35,756 | Lab maj 19,588 | | 43,390 | Lab maj 15,692 | |
| | | | 54.8% | | | 36.2% | |

GRAHAM STRINGER, b Feb 17, 1950. Analytical chemist in plastics industry. Manchester city cllr (leader of council 1984-96). Chair, Manchester Airport plc. Ed Sheffield Univ.
STEVE BARCLAY, b May 3, 1972. Trainee solicitor. Has served as Second Lt in Royal Regiment of Fusiliers and as Nato officer representing British Army. Dep chair and sec, Chester YCs. Ed Peterhouse, Cambridge; Sandhurst; Chester Coll of Law.

SIMON WHEALE, b April 6, 1962. PR consultant. Contested this seat 1992. Manchester city cllr. Member, Terrence Higgins Trust; Stonewall; LDs in PR; Business LDs. Ed Manchester Grammar; Manchester Univ.

| MANCHESTER CENTRAL | | 49.4% change | | | | | Lab win |
|---|---|---|---|---|---|---|---|
| Electorate % Turnout | | 63,815 | 52.6% | **1997** | 66,475 | 58.8% | **1992** |
| +Lloyd, A J | Lab | **23,803** | **71.0%** | **+1.8%** | **27,009** | **69.1%** | Lab |
| Firth, Ms A | LD | 4,121 | 12.3% | +1.8% | 7,581 | 19.4% | C |
| McIlwaine, S | C | 3,964 | 11.8% | -7.6% | 4,105 | 10.5% | LD |
| Rafferty, F | Soc Lab | 810 | 2.4% | | 185 | 0.5% | CL |
| Maxwell, J | Ref | 742 | 2.2% | | 185 | 0.5% | NLP |
| Rigby, T | Comm Lge | 97 | 0.3% | | | | |
| LD to Lab notional swing 0.0% | | 33,537 | Lab maj 19,682 | | 39,065 | Lab maj 19,428 | |
| | | | 58.7% | | | 49.7% | |

**TONY LLOYD**, b Feb 25, 1950. Became Minister of State, Foreign Office, May 5, 1997. MP for Stretford 1983-97. Lab spokesman on foreign affairs 1995-97; environment spokesman 1994-95; education 1992-94; employment 1988-92; transport 1987-88; previously Lab whip. Chair, PLP foreign affairs cttee, 1986-87. Member, home affairs select cttee 1985-87; social services select cttee 1983-85; joint vice-chair, PLP home affairs cttee, 1985-87.

Ed Stretford GS; Nottingham Univ; Manchester Business School.
**ALISON FIRTH**, b May 23, 1957. Teacher. Manchester city cllr 1984- . Ex-VSO worker in Malaysia. Ed York Univ.
**SIMON McILWAINE**, b March 19, 1960. Supreme Court solicitor. Dir, Edmund Burke Foundation; member, Southern African Study Circle; C Way Forward; Christian Solidarity International. Ed Belfast Royal Acad; Sidney Sussex Coll, Cambridge.

| MANCHESTER GORTON | | 0.1% change | | | | | Lab win |
|---|---|---|---|---|---|---|---|
| Electorate % Turnout | | 64,349 | 56.4% | **1997** | 62,673 | 60.6% | **1992** |
| +Kaufman, G | Lab | **23,704** | **65.3%** | **+2.9%** | **23,658** | **62.3%** | Lab |
| Pearcey, Dr J | LD | 6,362 | 17.5% | +3.5% | 7,388 | 19.5% | C |
| Senior, G | C | 4,249 | 11.7% | -7.8% | 5,324 | 14.0% | LD |
| Hartley, K | Ref | 812 | 2.2% | | 766 | 2.0% | Lib |
| Fitz-Gibbon, Dr S | Green | 683 | 1.9% | | 595 | 1.6% | Grn |
| Wongsam, T | Soc Lab | 501 | 1.4% | | 108 | 0.3% | Rev Comm |
| | | | | | 84 | 0.2% | NLP |
| | | | | | 30 | 0.1% | Int Comm |
| Lab to LD notional swing 0.3% | | 36,311 | Lab maj 17,342 | | 37,953 | Lab maj 16,270 | |
| | | | 47.8% | | | 42.9% | |

**GERALD KAUFMAN**, b June 21, 1930. Elected for this seat 1983; MP for Manchester Ardwick 1970-83; contested Gillingham 1959, Bromley 1955. Chair, national heritage select cttee, 1992-97. Chief Lab spokesman on foreign and Commonwealth affairs 1987-92; on home affairs 1983-87; in Shadow Cabinet 1980-92, being chief environment spokesman 1980-83; housing spokesman 1979-80. Min of State, Dept of Industry, 1975-79; Under Sec for Industry 1975; Under Sec for Environment 1974-75. Privy

Counsellor 1978. Member, Lab NEC, 1991-92; parly press liaison officer for Lab 1965-70. Ed Leeds GS; Queen's Coll, Oxford.
**JACKIE PEARCEY**, b Sept 23, 1963. Self-employed computer trainer. Contested Davyhulme 1992. Manchester city cllr 1991- (group whip). Ed Leeds Girls' HS; Manchester Univ; Bristol Univ.
**GUY SENIOR**, b Aug 9, 1963. Legal officer. Wandsworth cllr 1990- . Member, C Way Forward. Ed Loughborough GS; Downing Coll, Cambridge; Guildford Coll of Law.

| MANCHESTER WITHINGTON | | 0.2% change | | | | | Lab win |
|---|---|---|---|---|---|---|---|
| Electorate % Turnout | | 66,116 | 66.6% | **1997** | 63,987 | 70.9% | **1992** |
| +Bradley, K | Lab | **27,103** | **61.6%** | **+8.9%** | **23,907** | **52.7%** | Lab |
| Smith, J | C | 8,522 | 19.4% | -11.9% | 14,193 | 31.3% | C |
| Zalzala, Dr Y | LD | 6,000 | 13.6% | -0.6% | 6,442 | 14.2% | LD |
| Sheppard, M | Ref | 1,079 | 2.5% | | 724 | 1.6% | Grn |
| Caldwell, S | ProLife | 614 | 1.4% | | 127 | 0.3% | NLP |
| White, Ms J | Soc | 376 | 0.9% | | | | |
| Kingston, S | Dream | 181 | 0.4% | | | | |
| Gaskell, M | NLP | 152 | 0.3% | +0.1% | | | |
| C to Lab notional swing 10.4% | | 44,027 | Lab maj 18,581 | | 45,393 | Lab maj 9,714 | |
| | | | 42.2% | | | 21.4% | |

**KEITH BRADLEY**, b May 17, 1950. Became Under Secretary for Social Security, May 5, 1997. Elected 1987. Lab road and rail spokesman 1996-97; social security spokesman 1991-96. Member, agriculture select cttee, 1989-91. Manchester city cllr 1983-88. Dir (unpaid), Parrs Wood Rural Trust. Former health service administrator with NW RHA. Member, MSF; Cohse. Ed Bishop Vesey GS; Manchester Poly; York Univ.

**JONATHAN SMITH**, b Oct 2, 1967. Barrister. Member, Bow Group housing policy unit. Ed Oldswinford Hospital School; Liverpool Poly; Inns of Court School of Law.
**YASMEN ZALZALA**, b Nov 3, 1955. Economic development researcher. Vice-chair, police community consultation group and community health council. Member, Amnesty. Ed Baghdad Univ; Salford Univ.

| MANSFIELD | | | | | | **Lab hold** |
|---|---|---|---|---|---|---|
| Electorate % Turnout | | 67,057 | 70.7% | **1997** | 66,964 | 82.2% | **1992** |
| *Meale, A | Lab | **30,556** | **64.4%** | **+10.1%** | **29,932** | **54.4%** | Lab |
| Frost, T | C | 10,038 | 21.2% | -11.9% | 18,208 | 33.1% | C |
| Smith, P | LD | 5,244 | 11.1% | -1.5% | 6,925 | 12.6% | LD |
| Bogusz, W | Ref | 1,588 | 3.3% | | | | |
| C to Lab swing 11.0% | | 47,426 | Lab maj 20,518 | | 55,065 | Lab maj 11,724 | |
| | | | 43.3% | | | 21.3% | |

**ALAN MEALE**, b July 31, 1949. Elected 1987. Lab whip 1992-97; member, select cttees on home affairs, 1989-92; Euro legislation 1988-89. Former joint vice-chair, PLP employment and energy cttees; chair, all-party beer club parly group, 1993- ; joint sec, animal welfare group; treas, association football parly group, 1989- ; sec, greyhound group; joint vice-chair, Ukraine group. Unpaid dir, Mansfield 2010; unpaid parly spokesman and consultant to Stand By Me Club, devoted to promoting the song *Stand By Me*. Member, exec board, SSAFA; exec cttee on war pensions. Parly and political adviser to Michael Meacher, MP, 1983-87. Personal asst, gen sec, Aslef, 1980-83; nat employment

development officer, Nat Assoc for Care and Resettlement of Offenders, 1977-80. Engineering worker 1968-75; Merchant Navy seaman 1964-68. Ed St Joseph's RC School; Ruskin Coll, Oxford.
**TIM FROST**, b Jan 1, 1965. Vice-pres, J.P. Morgan, managing the international asset trading group. Former Royal Artillery officer, serving in Germany and Falklands. Hounslow cllr 1990-94. Ed Minster School, Southwell; LSE (a governor, 1986-87).
**PHIL SMITH**, b Nov 16, 1963. Senior test analyst, Midland Bank; Mansfield cllr 1992- (group leader). Member, Bifu. Ed Queen Elizabeth's US, Mansfield.

| MEDWAY | | | | | | **Lab gain** |
|---|---|---|---|---|---|---|
| Electorate % Turnout | | 61,736 | 72.5% | **1997** | 61,736 | 80.2% | **1992** |
| Marshall-Andrews, R | Lab | **21,858** | **48.9%** | **+14.3%** | 25,924 | 52.3% | C |
| *Fenner, Dame Peggy | C | 16,504 | 36.9% | -15.5% | 17,138 | 34.6% | Lab |
| Roberts, R | LD | 4,555 | 10.2% | +0.6% | 4,751 | 9.6% | LD |
| Main, J | Ref | 1,420 | 3.2% | | 1,480 | 3.0% | Lib |
| Radlett, Mrs S | UK Ind | 405 | 0.9% | | 234 | 0.5% | NLP |
| C to Lab swing 14.9% | | 44,742 | Lab maj 5,354 | | 49,527 | C maj 8,786 | |
| | | | 12.0% | | | 17.7% | |

**ROBERT MARSHALL-ANDREWS**, b April 10, 1944. QC and writer. Contested this seat 1992; Richmond upon Thames Oct 1974. Ex-chair, Richmond party. Member, Soc of Lab Lawyers. Trustee, Adamson Wildlife Trust and Geffrye Museum. Ed Mill Hill School; Bristol Univ.
**DAME PEGGY FENNER**, b Nov 12, 1922. Elected for this seat 1983; MP for Rochester and Chatham 1979-83 and 1970-Oct 1974; contested Newcastle-under-Lyme 1966; MEP 1974-75. Parly Sec, Ministry of Ag, Fish and Food, 1981-86 and 1972-73. Member, select cttee on members' interests, 1987-95; Commons

accommodation and works cttee; UK delegation, Council of Europe and WEU, 1987- . Chair, all-party retail industry parly group; sec, British fruit industry parly group, 1994-97. Sevenoaks district cllr 1957-71. Co-chair, Women's National Commission, 1983-86. Ed LCC elementary school, Brockley; Ide Hill School, Kent.
**ROGER ROBERTS**, b Sept 12, 1939. Retired BT training manager. Contested Spelthorne 1992. Sutton cllr 1986- . Member, Charter 88. Ed Cornwall Tech Coll; OU.

| MEIRIONNYDD NANT CONWY | | | | | | **PC hold** |
|---|---|---|---|---|---|---|
| Electorate % Turnout | | 32,345 | 76.0% | **1997** | 32,413 | 81.5% | **1992** |
| *Llwyd, E | PC | **12,465** | **50.7%** | **+6.8%** | **11,608** | **44.0%** | PC |
| Rees, H | Lab | 5,660 | 23.0% | +4.2% | 6,995 | 26.5% | C |
| Quin, J | C | 3,922 | 16.0% | -10.5% | 4,978 | 18.8% | Lab |
| Feeley, Mrs B | LD | 1,719 | 7.0% | -1.9% | 2,358 | 8.9% | LD |
| Hodge, P | Ref | 809 | 3.3% | | 471 | 1.8% | Grn |
| Lab to PC swing 1.3% | | 24,575 | PC maj 6,805 | | 26,410 | PC maj 4,613 | |
| | | | 27.7% | | | 17.5% | |

**ELFYN LLWYD**, b Sept 26, 1951. Solicitor. Elected for this seat 1992. Member, Welsh affairs select cttee, 1992-95; joint vice-chair, all-party head injuries parly group. Consultant to Guthrie Jones & Jones, solicitors, of Dolgellau and Bala. Ed Ysgol Dyffryn Conwy, Llanrwst; Univ Coll of Wales, Aberystwyth; Christleton Coll of Law, Chester. Pigeon breeder.
**HEFIN REES**, b June 30, 1969. Barrister. Member TGWU; Fabian Soc. Ed King David HS, Liverpool; Durham Univ; Inns of Court School of Law.

**JEREMY QUIN**, b Sept 24, 1968. Corporate stockbroker. Member, C Euro election campaign team; parly assistant and election aide to Peter Lilley 1990-93. Co-founder and chair of Millennium Group since 1993. Ed St Albans School; Hertford Coll, Oxford (pres of Union).
**BOBBY FEELEY**, b Sept 14, 1946. Retailer (clothes agency). Member, Denbighshire UA 1986- (dep group leader). Company sec, Goodman Construction Ltd. Ed Andover County Girls, Hants; Eastleigh Secretarial/Business Coll.

| MERIDEN | | | | | | | C hold |
|---|---|---|---|---|---|---|---|
| Electorate % Turnout | | 76,287 | 71.7% | **1997** | 76,994 | 78.9% | **1992** |
| Spelman, Mrs C | C | **22,997** | 42.0% | -13.1% | **33,462** | 55.1% | C |
| Seymour-Smith, B | Lab | 22,415 | 41.0% | +10.1% | 18,763 | 30.9% | Lab |
| Dupont, T | LD | 7,098 | 13.0% | -1.0% | 8,489 | 14.0% | LD |
| Gilbert, P | Ref | 2,208 | 4.0% | | | | |
| C to Lab swing 11.6% | | **54,718** | | C maj 582 | 60,714 | | C maj 14,699 |
| | | | | 1.1% | | | 24.2% |

**CAROLINE SPELMAN**, b May 4, 1958. Contested Bassetlaw 1992. Commercial negotiator specialising in purchase contracts for food and pharmaceutical industries; broker of commercial disputes. Deputy dir, International Confed of European Beetgrowers, 1984-89, and administrative sec to sugar beet cttee of NFU of England and Wales 1980-84. Research Fellow of Wye Coll, London; delegate to Gatt trade talks. Ed Herts and Essex Girls' GS; Queen Mary Coll, London.

**BRIAN SEYMOUR-SMITH**, b May 12, 1955. Freelance journalist and PR consultant; qualified teacher. Ex-press officer for Birmingham City Council and council head of media relations, environment services. Sec, Central Midlands Co-op Party. Member, TGWU; AEEU. Ed Moseley Secondary; Westhill Coll of Ed. Disc jockey.
**TONY DUPONT**, b Feb 20, 1945. Management consultant. Solihull metropolitan borough cllr; member, Solihull community health council. Ed Rayleigh Secondary; Buckingham and Aston Univs.

| MERTHYR TYDFIL & RHYMNEY | | | | | | | Lab hold |
|---|---|---|---|---|---|---|---|
| Electorate % Turnout | | 56,507 | 69.3% | **1997** | 58,430 | 75.8% | **1992** |
| *Rowlands, T | Lab | **30,012** | 76.7% | +5.1% | **31,710** | 71.6% | Lab |
| Anstey, D | LD | 2,926 | 7.5% | -3.8% | 4,997 | 11.3% | LD |
| Morgan, J | C | 2,508 | 6.4% | -4.7% | 4,904 | 11.1% | C |
| Cox, A | PC | 2,344 | 6.0% | -0.1% | 2,704 | 6.1% | PC |
| Cowdell, A | 0 Lab | 691 | 1.8% | | | | |
| Hutchings, R | Ref | 660 | 1.7% | | | | |
| LD to Lab swing 4.5% | | **39,141** | | Lab maj 27,086 | 44,315 | | Lab maj 26,713 |
| | | | | 69.2% | | | 60.3% |

**TED ROWLANDS**, b Jan 23, 1940. Lecturer in modern history and gvt. Elected for this seat 1983; MP for Merthyr Tydfil 1972-83, and for Cardiff N 1966-70. Member, foreign affairs select cttee, 1987-97. Lab spokesman on energy, 1980-87, and on foreign affairs 1979-80. Foreign Office Min, 1976-79 and Under Sec, 1975-76; Under Sec for Wales 1974-75 and 1969-70. Treas, all-party British-Kenya group; sec, UN group. Booker Prize judge 1984. Ex-member, exec cttee, British group, IPU. Member, governing body, Commonwealth Inst, 1980-92; academic council, Wilton Park, 1983-92. Chair, History of Parliament Trust, 1993- . Ed Rhondda GS; Wirral GS; King's Coll, London.

**DUNCAN ANSTEY**, b Dec 29, 1966. Marketing and development manager with disability charity. Monmouthshire county cllr (group leader); ex-Gwent county cllr. Member, Friends of Earth. Ed Monmouth Comp; Sheffield Hallam Univ. Sub-aqua diver.
**JONATHAN MORGAN**, b Nov 12, 1974. Law student. Chair, Cardiff C students, 1994-95; Wales C students 1995-96; Cardiff N YCs 1992-95. Member, S Wales Euro cl, 1993- . Ed Bishop of Llandaff Church-in-Wales HS, Cardiff; Univ Coll of Wales, Cardiff.
**ALUN COX**. Computer consultant. Member party nat exec. Ceredigion county cllr. Member, Aberystwyth ABC Choir. Ed Ysgol Gyfyn Rhydfelen.

| MIDDLESBROUGH | | 24.9% change | | | | | Lab win |
|---|---|---|---|---|---|---|---|
| Electorate % Turnout | | 70,931 | 65.0% | **1997** | 74,097 | 74.1% | **1992** |
| +Bell, S | Lab | **32,925** | 71.4% | +10.3% | **33,543** | 61.1% | Lab |
| Benham, L | C | 7,907 | 17.2% | -12.8% | 16,424 | 29.9% | C |
| Charlesworth, Miss A | LD | 3,934 | 8.5% | -0.4% | 4,925 | 9.0% | LD |
| Edwards, B | Ref | 1,331 | 2.9% | | | | |
| C to Lab notional swing 11.5% | | **46,097** | | Lab maj 25,018 | **54,892** | | Lab maj 17,119 |
| | | | | 54.3% | | | 31.2% |

**STUART BELL**, b May 16, 1938. Barrister and writer. Elected 1983; contested Hexham 1979. Lab spokesman on trade and industry 1992-97, dealing with trade and corporate affairs; spokesman on N Ireland 1984-87. Joint vice-chair, PLP Treasury and Civil Service cttee, 1990-92; former vice-chair, Northern group of Lab MPs; joint sec, all-party British-Israeli party group, 1990- . Founder member, British-Irish inter-party body, 1990, and joint vice-chair 1990-93. Joint vice-chair, 1991-94, and exec cttee member 1990-91, British group, IPU. Newcastle city cllr 1980-83. Conseil

Juridique and international lawyer, Paris, 1970-77. Member, Fabian Soc; Soc of Lab Lawyers. Ed Hookergate GS, Durham; Pitman's Coll; Council of Legal Ed, Gray's Inn.
**LIAM BENTHAM**, b March 21, 1970. Political co-ordinator, House Builders Fed. Research asst for Nick Hawkins, MP, 1992 and Michael Bates, MP, 1992-93. Ed Saltscar Comp; Sir William Turner's Sixth-Form Coll, Redcar; Bristol Univ.
**ALISON CHARLESWORTH**, b July 13, 1972. Student. Ed Manor Community Coll, Cambridge; Teesside Univ.

| MIDDLESBROUGH SOUTH & CLEVELAND EAST | | 12.9% change | | | Lab win | |
|---|---|---|---|---|---|---|
| Electorate % Turnout | | 70,481 | 76.0% | **1997** | 69,836 | 80.7% | **1992** |
| **Kumar, Dr A** | **Lab** | **29,319** | **54.7%** | **+11.4%** | 25,802 | 45.8% | C |
| +Bates, M | C | 18,712 | 34.9% | -10.9% | 24,401 | 43.3% | Lab |
| Garrett, H | LD | 4,004 | 7.5% | -3.5% | 6,163 | 10.9% | LD |
| Batchelor, R | Ref | 1,552 | 2.9% | | | | |
| C to Lab notional swing 11.1% | | 53,587 | | Lab maj 10,607 | 56,366 | | C maj 1,401 |
| | | | | 19.8% | | | 2.5% |

**ASHOK KUMAR**, b May 28, 1956. Research officer with British Steel Technical since 1992. MP for Langbaurgh when he gained seat for Lab at 1991 by-election, but defeated in 1992 general election. Middlesbrough borough cllr 1987- . Research fellow, Imperial Coll of Science and Tech, 1982-85; senior research investigator, Teesside Laboratories, British Steel, 1985-91. Ed Aston Univ, Birmingham; Imperial Coll, London.
**MICHAEL BATES**, b May 26, 1961. MP for Langbaurgh 1992-97; contested Langbaurgh by-election 1991; Tyne Bridge 1987.

Paymaster General 1996-97; gvt whip 1995-96; asst gvt whip 1994-95; PPS to Sir John Wheeler, N Ireland Min, 1994; PPS to Nicholas Scott, Social Security Min, 1992. Former asst dir, Godwins Ltd (pensions consultants and actuaries). Ed Heathfield Comp; Gateshead Coll.
**HAMISH GARRETT**, b Oct 13, 1943. Lecturer in counselling and student counsellor. Middlesbrough borough cllr (group leader) 1991-95). Ed Hereford Cathedral School; Oxford Brookes Univ.

| MIDLOTHIAN | | 21.8% change | | | | | Lab win |
|---|---|---|---|---|---|---|---|
| Electorate % Turnout | | 47,552 | 74.1% | **1997** | 47,952 | 74.1% | **1992** |
| **+Clarke, E** | **Lab** | **18,861** | **53.5%** | **+5.3%** | 17,120 | 48.2% | Lab |
| Millar, L | SNP | 8,991 | 25.5% | +2.3% | 8,256 | 23.2% | SNP |
| Harper, Miss A | C | 3,842 | 10.9% | -6.7% | 6,242 | 17.6% | C |
| Pinnock, R | LD | 3,235 | 9.2% | -0.8% | 3,552 | 10.0% | LD |
| Docking, K | Ref | 320 | 0.9% | | 377 | 1.1% | Grn |
| SNP to Lab notional swing 1.5% | | 35,249 | | Lab maj 9,870 | 35,547 | | Lab maj 8,864 |
| | | | | 28.0% | | | 24.9% |

**ERIC CLARKE**, b April 9, 1933. Ex-miner. Elected for this seat 1992; Lab whip 1994-97. Ex-member, Lab Party NEC. Trade union official 1977-89; ex-general sec of Scottish NUM and former trustee of the Mineworkers Pension Fund; member of NUM 1949- . Parly adviser to Mining Scotland Ltd. Joint treas, all-party beer club, 1994- . Ed St Cuthbert's Holy Cross Acad; W.M. Ramsay Tech Coll, Edinburgh; Esk Valley Tech Coll, Dalkeith, Midlothian.
**LAURENCE MILLAR**, b April 26, 1959. Sales and marketing director. Co-editor, *New Politics for Independence*. Ed Forrester Secondary, Edinburgh.

**ANNE HARPER**, b Sept 17, 1950. Freelance designer of training schemes for HM Inspectorate of Schools in Scotland. Ran BP corporate office in Edinburgh until 1992. Member, exec, C Group for Europe, 1996- ; Scottish C ed policy cttee; exec member, European Movement. Ed Aberdeen HS for Girls; Aberdeen Univ; University Coll, London.
**RICHARD PINNOCK**, b Nov 21, 1973. Bank registrar clerk in Edinburgh. Ed Leeds GS; Edinburgh Univ. His mother, Kath Pinnock, was LD candidate for Batley & Spen.

| MILTON KEYNES NORTH EAST | | | | | | | Lab gain |
|---|---|---|---|---|---|---|---|
| Electorate % Turnout | | 70,395 | 72.8% | **1997** | 62,748 | 81.0% | **1992** |
| **White, B** | **Lab** | **20,201** | **39.4%** | **+15.7%** | 26,212 | 51.6% | C |
| +Butler, P | C | 19,961 | 39.0% | -12.6% | 12,036 | 23.7% | Lab |
| Mabbutt, G A G | LD | 8,907 | 17.4% | -5.6% | 11,693 | 23.0% | LD |
| Phillips, M | Ref | 1,492 | 2.9% | | 529 | 1.0% | Grn |
| Francis, A | Green | 576 | 1.1% | | 249 | 0.5% | Ind C |
| Simson, M | NLP | 99 | 0.2% | +0.0% | 79 | 0.2% | NLP |
| C to Lab swing 14.2% | | 51,236 | | Lab maj 240 | 50,798 | | C maj 14,176 |
| | | | | 0.5% | | | 27.9% |

**BRIAN WHITE**, b May 5, 1957. Systems analyst for Abbey National plc; previously civil servant, HM Customs & Excise. Milton Keynes cllr (dep leader). Chair, Local Gvt Assoc planning cttee; sec, Local Gvt Assoc Lab group. Member, Southern and Central Region exec cttees. Ed Methodist Coll, Belfast.
**PETER BUTLER**, b June 10, 1951. Solicitor. Elected for this seat 1992. PPS to Kenneth Clarke when Chancellor of Exchequer, and to Gerald Malone when Health Min. Member, home affairs select cttee, 1992-96; joint select cttee and select cttee on statutory instruments, 1992-95. Dir, Oxford Business Services Ltd,

1994- ; non-exec dir, Continental Administration Co Ltd, legal trustee services, 1995- . Partner, 1981-92, and consultant, 1992- , Linnells, solicitors; solicitor, Thames Valley Police, 1978-80. Oxfordshire county cllr, 1985-89. Ed Adams GS, Newport, Shropshire; St Edmund Hall, Oxford.
**GRAHAM MABBUTT**, b Dec 20, 1941. Record industry production manager. Contested Northampton S 1992. Milton Keynes borough cllr 1994- (dep group leader). Ed Moulton Sec Mod; Ousedale Adult Ed Centre; Ruskin Coll, Oxford (correspondence course).

## MILTON KEYNES SOUTH WEST — Lab gain

| Electorate % Turnout | | 71,070 | 71.4% | **1997** | 66,422 | 77.0% | **1992** |
|---|---|---|---|---|---|---|---|
| **Starkey, Mrs P** | **Lab** | **27,298** | **53.8%** | **+16.3%** | 23,840 | 46.6% | C |
| *Legg, B | C | 17,006 | 33.5% | -13.1% | 19,153 | 37.4% | Lab |
| Jones, P | LD | 6,065 | 11.9% | -2.6% | 7,429 | 14.5% | LD |
| Kelly, H | NLP | 389 | 0.8% | +0.4% | 525 | 1.0% | Grn |
| | | | | | 202 | 0.4% | NLP |
| **C to Lab swing 14.7%** | | **50,758** | Lab maj 10,292 | | 51,149 | C maj 4,687 | |
| | | | 20.3% | | | 9.2% | |

**PHYLLIS STARKEY**, b Jan 4, 1947. Science policy administrator; ex-lecturer in obstetrics, Oxford Univ. Oxford city cllr 1983- (leader 1990-93). Assoc of Lab Cllrs rep on Lab NEC local gvt cttee. Governor, Oxford Brookes Univ. Ed Perse School for Girls, Cambridge; Lady Margaret Hall, Oxford; Clare Hall, Cambridge.
**BARRY LEGG**, b May 30, 1949. Elected for this seat 1992; contested Bishop Auckland 1983. Chair, Treasury select cttee, 1996-97, and member from 1992-97. Main board exec dir of Hillsdown Holdings plc, food manufacturers, 1978-92; with Coopers & Lybrand 1976-78; Courtaulds Ltd 1971-76. Ed Sir Thomas Rich's GS, Gloucester; Manchester Univ.
**PETER JONES**, b March 16, 1956. Salesman; director, Focus Business Forms Ltd. Chiltern district cllr 1991- . Ed Malvern Coll, Worcester; East Anglia Univ.

## MITCHAM & MORDEN — Lab gain

| Electorate % Turnout | | 65,385 | 73.3% | **1997** | 63,723 | 80.3% | **1992** |
|---|---|---|---|---|---|---|---|
| **McDonagh, Ms S** | **Lab** | **27,984** | **58.4%** | **+15.3%** | 23,789 | 46.5% | C |
| *Rumbold, Dame Angela | C | 14,243 | 29.7% | -16.8% | 22,055 | 43.1% | Lab |
| Harris, N | LD | 3,632 | 7.6% | -1.6% | 4,687 | 9.2% | LD |
| Isaacs, P | Ref | 810 | 1.7% | | 655 | 1.3% | Grn |
| Miller, L | BNP | 521 | 1.1% | | | | |
| Walsh, T | Green | 415 | 0.9% | | | | |
| Vasan, K | Ind | 144 | 0.3% | | | | |
| Barrett, J | UK Ind | 117 | 0.2% | | | | |
| Dixon, N | ACC | 80 | 0.2% | | | | |
| **C to Lab swing 16.0%** | | **47,946** | Lab maj 13,741 | | 51,186 | C maj 1,734 | |
| | | | 28.7% | | | 3.4% | |

**SIOBHAIN McDONAGH**, b Feb 20, 1960. Contested this seat 1992 and 1987. Development co-ordinator, Battersea churches housing trust. Voluntary adviser, Catholic housing advice service, Wandsworth; ex-member, Merton voluntary service council. Merton cllr 1982- . Ed Essex Univ.
**DAME ANGELA RUMBOLD**, b Aug 11, 1932. Elected at 1982 by-election. Dep chair, C Party 1992- with responsibility for candidates. Home Office Min, 1990-92; Education and Science Min 1986-90; Environment Under Sec 1985-86. Joint chair, all-party daylight extra group. Non-exec dir, Brewin & Dolphin Holdings plc, stockbrokers. Vice-chair, Grant Maintained Schools Trust (unpaid). Co-chair, Women's Nat Commission, 1986-90. Member, Doctors and Dentists Review Body, 1979-82. Kingston upon Thames borough cllr 1974-83. Freeman, City of London, 1988. Ed Notting Hill and Ealing HS; Perse School for Girls, Cambridge; King's Coll, London.
**NICK HARRIS**, b May 27, 1961. Building society manager. Merton cllr 1995- . Member, Bifu. Ed Highcliffe Comp; Birmingham Univ.

## MOLE VALLEY — 35.5% change — C win

| Electorate % Turnout | | 69,140 | 78.9% | **1997** | 70,500 | 81.6% | **1992** |
|---|---|---|---|---|---|---|---|
| **+Beresford, Sir Paul** | **C** | **26,178** | **48.0%** | **-13.3%** | 35,313 | 61.4% | C |
| Cooksey, S | LD | 15,957 | 29.3% | +0.6% | 16,486 | 28.6% | LD |
| Payne, C | Lab | 8,057 | 14.8% | +5.4% | 5,386 | 9.4% | Lab |
| Taber, N | Ref | 2,424 | 4.4% | | 373 | 0.6% | NLP |
| Burley, R | Ind CRP | 1,276 | 2.3% | | | | |
| Cameron, Capt I | UK Ind | 435 | 0.8% | | | | |
| Thomas, Ms J | NLP | 197 | 0.4% | -0.3% | | | |
| **C to LD notional swing 7.0%** | | **54,524** | C maj 10,221 | | 57,558 | C maj 18,827 | |
| | | | 18.7% | | | 32.7% | |

**SIR PAUL BERESFORD**, b April 6, 1946. Dental surgeon. Won this seat 1997; MP for Croydon Central 1992-97. Environment Under Sec 1994-97. Former vice-chair, C backbench housing improvement sub-cttee. Member, Audit Commission, 1991-92. Wandsworth cllr 1978-94 (leader 1983-92). Ed Richmond Primary and Waimea Coll, Nelson, New Zealand; Otago Univ, Dunedin, New Zealand; Eastman Dental Hospital, London.
**STEPHEN COOKSEY**, b Jan 11, 1944. Academic secretary, Roehampton Institute. Contested Skipton & Ripon 1987; Pudsey 1979, Oct and Feb 1974; Leeds S 1970; Leeds in 1984 Euro elections. Mole Valley borough cllr 1992- ; Leeds city cllr 1980-89 (group leader). Ed Middlesbrough HS for Boys; Leeds Univ.
**CHRISTOPHER PAYNE**, b July 2, 1956. Firefighter with London Fire Brigade. Ealing cllr 1994- . Ed Hitchin GS; Brunel Univ.

| MONMOUTH | | | | | | | Lab gain |
|---|---|---|---|---|---|---|---|
| Electorate % Turnout | | 60,703 | 80.8% | **1997** | 59,147 | 86.1% | **1992** |
| Edwards, H | Lab | **23,404** | **47.7%** | +6.8% | 24,059 | 47.3% | C |
| *Evans, R | C | 19,226 | 39.2% | -8.0% | 20,855 | 41.0% | Lab |
| Williams, M | LD | 4,689 | 9.6% | -1.4% | 5,562 | 10.9% | LD |
| Warry, N | Ref | 1,190 | 2.4% | | 431 | 0.8% | Green/PC |
| Cotton, A | PC | 516 | 1.1% | | | | |
| C to Lab swing 7.4% | | 49,025 | | Lab maj 4,178 | 50,907 | | C maj 3,204 |
| | | | | 8.5% | | | 6.3% |

**HUW EDWARDS**, b April 12, 1953. Lecturer. MP for Monmouth from 1991 by-election to 1992 general election. Member, Parliament for Wales campaign 1992- ; Lab Campaign for Electoral Reform 1991- . Research associate, Low Pay Unit, 1985- . Member, exec, Shelter Cymru, 1988-91. Senior lecturer in social policy, Brighton Univ 1992- and 1988-91. Lecturer in social policy, Manchester Poly, 1985-88; South Bank Poly 1984-85; Sheffield Univ 1983-84; Coventry (Lanchester) Poly 1980-81; OU tutor 1987- . Pres, Chepstow Mencap, 1992- . Member, NATFHE. Ed Eastfields HS, Mitcham, Surrey; Manchester Poly; York Univ.

**ROGER EVANS**, b March 18, 1947. Barrister. Social Security Under Sec, 1994-97. Contested 1991 by-election and regained seat for C 1992; contested Ynys Mon 1987, Warley W 1979 and Oct 1974. Member, ecclesiastical cttee of Parliament; exec cttee, Friends of Friendless Churches, 1983- ; Ecclesiastical Law Soc; exec cttee, Soc of C Lawyers. Freeman, City of London. Ed Clytha Park School, Newport; City of Norwich School; Bristol GS; Trinity Hall, Cambridge (pres of Union 1970; chair, univ C assoc, 1969).

**MARK WILLIAMS**, b March 24, 1966. Teacher. Ed Richard Hale School, Hertford; Univ Coll of Wales, Aberystwyth; Plymouth Univ.

| MONTGOMERYSHIRE | | | | | | | LD hold |
|---|---|---|---|---|---|---|---|
| Electorate % Turnout | | 42,618 | 74.9% | **1997** | 41,386 | 79.9% | **1992** |
| Opik, L | LD | **14,647** | **45.9%** | -2.6% | 16,031 | 48.5% | LD |
| Davies, G | C | 8,344 | 26.1% | -6.6% | 10,822 | 32.7% | C |
| Davies, Ms A | Lab | 6,109 | 19.1% | +6.7% | 4,115 | 12.4% | Lab |
| Jones, Ms H M | PC | 1,608 | 5.0% | +0.3% | 1,581 | 4.8% | PC |
| Bufton, J | Ref | 879 | 2.8% | | 508 | 1.5% | Grn |
| Walker, Ms S | Green | 338 | 1.1% | | | | |
| C to LD swing 2.0% | | 31,925 | | LD maj 6,303 | 33,057 | | LD maj 5,209 |
| | | | | 19.7% | | | 15.8% |

**LEMBIT OPIK**, b March 2, 1965. Training and development manager, Procter & Gamble. Contested Newcastle upon Tyne Central 1992; Northumbria 1994 Euro elections. Became LD spokesman on young people, May 1997. Newcastle upon Tyne city cllr 1992- . Member, Greenpeace; Charter 88. Ed Royal Belfast Academical Inst; Bristol Univ.

**GLYN DAVIES**, b Feb 16, 1944. Farm owner/manager. Chair, Development Board for Rural Wales, 1989-94 (member from 1986); member, Welsh Development Agency, and Welsh Tourist Board, 1989-94. Student of international law/relations, international politics dept, Univ Coll of Wales, Aberystwyth. Joint owner, with wife, of Granary Restaurants. Ed Llanfair Caereinion HS.

**ANGHARAD DAVIES**, b Oct 18, 1971. Political assistant to Eluned Morgan (MEP for Mid and West Wales). Member, Amnesty; Fawcett Soc; TGWU. Ed Lampeter Comp; Queen's Univ, Belfast; Limerick Univ.

| MORAY | 9.7% change | | | | | | SNP win |
|---|---|---|---|---|---|---|---|
| Electorate % Turnout | | 58,302 | 68.2% | **1997** | 57,743 | 71.6% | **1992** |
| +Ewing, Mrs M | SNP | **16,529** | **41.6%** | -3.0% | 18,444 | 44.6% | SNP |
| Findlay, A | C | 10,963 | 27.6% | -10.0% | 15,517 | 37.5% | C |
| Macdonald, L | Lab | 7,886 | 19.8% | +7.9% | 4,913 | 11.9% | Lab |
| Storr, Ms D | LD | 3,548 | 8.9% | +3.0% | 2,466 | 6.0% | LD |
| Mieklejohn, P | Ref | 840 | 2.1% | | | | |
| C to SNP notional swing 3.5% | | 39,766 | | SNP maj 5,566 | 41,340 | | SNP maj 2,927 |
| | | | | 14.0% | | | 7.1% |

**MARGARET EWING**, b Sept 1, 1945. Teacher, journalist and social work administrator. Gained this seat 1987, becoming leader of SNP parly group, and spokeswoman on defence, health, social security, environment and Highlands and Islands; SNP MP for Dunbartonshire E (then as Mrs Margaret Bain) from Oct 1974-79, contesting that seat Feb 1974, and Strathkelvin and Bearsden 1983. Member, select cttee on European legislation, 1990- . Joint vice-chair, all-party Scottish sports group, 1987- ; Scotch whisky industry group; chair, warm homes group. Ed Biggar HS; Glasgow and Strathclyde Univs.

**ANDREW FINDLAY**, b July 26, 1943. Marketing and product director for paper making company. Ed Balnacoul School, Moray; Aberlour House; Gordonstoun.

**LEWIS MACDONALD**, b Jan 1, 1957. Adviser to Shadow Cabinet and parliamentary researcher. Ed Inverurie Acad; Aberdeen Univ.

**DEBRA STORR**, b Feb 8, 1960. Business systems consultant and project manager. Contested Falkirk E 1992. Member, Campaign for Scottish Parliament. Ed King Edward VI HS for Girls, Birmingham; Loughborough Univ.

## MORECAMBE & LUNESDALE — 20.2% change — Lab win

| Electorate % Turnout | | | 68,013 | 72.4% | 1997 | 68,375 | 78.1% | 1992 |
|---|---|---|---|---|---|---|---|---|
| Smith, Ms G | Lab | | 24,061 | 48.9% | +19.4% | 26,292 | 49.2% | C |
| +Lennox-Boyd, Sir Mark | C | | 18,096 | 36.7% | -12.5% | 15,720 | 29.4% | Lab |
| Greenwell, Mrs J | LD | | 5,614 | 11.4% | -7.7% | 10,183 | 19.1% | LD |
| Ogilvie, I | Ref | | 1,313 | 2.7% | | 998 | 1.9% | MBI |
| Walne, D | NLP | | 165 | 0.3% | -0.1% | 225 | 0.4% | NLP |
| C to Lab notional swing 16.0% | | | 49,249 | Lab maj 5,965 | | 53,418 | C maj 10,572 | |
| | | | | 12.1% | | | 19.8% | |

GERALDINE SMITH, b Aug 29, 1961. Royal Mail clerical employee. Member, CWU. Ed Morecambe HS.

SIR MARK LENNOX-BOYD, b May 4, 1943. Barrister. Elected for this seat 1983; MP for Morecambe and Lonsdale 1979-83; contested Brent S, Oct 1974. Foreign and Commonwealth Office Under Sec 1990-94; PPS to Margaret Thatcher 1988-90; gvt whip 1986-88; an asst gvt whip 1984-86. PPS to Nigel Lawson, as Treasury Financial Sec, Energy Sec and Chancellor. Member, national heritage select cttee, 1996-97; UK cttee, Euro Research Group. Renter Warden, Fishmongers' Co, 1996-97. Ed Eton; Christ Church, Oxford.

JUNE GREENWELL, b June 8, 1939. Nurse/visiting lecturer. Contested this seat 1987. Non-exec dir, Morecambe Bay HA; Lancaster city cllr. Ed Whitehaven GS; Newcastle Univ.

## MORLEY & ROTHWELL — 44.3% change — Lab win

| Electorate % Turnout | | | 68,385 | 67.1% | 1997 | 66,804 | 75.1% | 1992 |
|---|---|---|---|---|---|---|---|---|
| +Gunnell, W J | Lab | | 26,836 | 58.5% | +9.0% | 24,843 | 49.5% | Lab |
| Barraclough, A | C | | 12,086 | 26.3% | -10.6% | 18,523 | 36.9% | C |
| Galdas, M | LD | | 5,087 | 11.1% | -1.9% | 6,506 | 13.0% | LD |
| Mitchell-Innes, D | Ref | | 1,359 | 3.0% | | 327 | 0.7% | Other |
| Wood, R | BNP | | 381 | 0.8% | | | | |
| Sammon, Ms P | ProLife | | 148 | 0.3% | | | | |
| C to Lab notional swing 9.8% | | | 45,897 | Lab maj 14,750 | | 50,199 | Lab maj 6,320 | |
| | | | | 32.1% | | | 12.6% | |

JOHN GUNNELL, b Oct 1, 1933. MP for Leeds S and Morley 1992-97; contested Leeds NE twice in 1974. Member, select cttees on broadcasting, 1992- ; deregulation 1995-96; public service 1995- . Chair, all-party personal social services parly group, 1995- ; joint chair, opera group; ex-sec, manufacturing industry group. Sec, PLP health and personal social services cttee. Leeds city cllr 1986-92; West Yorks metropolitan county cllr 1976-86. Hon president, Yorkshire and Humberside Development Assoc (chair, 1981-93) and of N of England Regional Consortium (chair 1984-92). Member, Audit Commission, 1983-90; Leeds Development Corp 1988-92; Leeds Healthcare 1990-92. Chair, Yorkshire Enterprise Ltd, 1982-90 and 1994-95; Yorkshire Fund Managers Ltd 1989-95, and now a non-exec director of the latter. Dir, Opera North Ltd; trustee, Nat Coal Mining Museum for England; hon dir, S Leeds Groundwork Trust Ltd (all unpaid). Adviser, Assembly of European Regions, 1986- . Ex-univ lecturer. Ed King Edward's, Birmingham; Leeds Univ.

ALAN BARRACLOUGH, b Feb 19, 1940. Chartered quantity surveyor. Leeds city cllr 1992-96. Member, Leeds European C constituency exec, 1990- . Hon dir, Groundwork Leeds. Ed Leeds GS.

MITCHELL GALDAS, b April 30, 1940. Sales director. Contested Normanton 1992. Pres, Lions International. Member, Amnesty. Ed Pitman's Coll.

## MOTHERWELL & WISHAW — 5.1% change — Lab win

| Electorate % Turnout | | | 52,252 | 70.1% | 1997 | 53,282 | 75.3% | 1992 |
|---|---|---|---|---|---|---|---|---|
| Roy, F | Lab | | 21,020 | 57.4% | +0.9% | 22,691 | 56.5% | Lab |
| McGuigan, J | SNP | | 8,229 | 22.5% | +1.0% | 8,601 | 21.4% | SNP |
| Dickson, S | C | | 4,024 | 11.0% | -4.6% | 6,264 | 15.6% | C |
| Mackie, A | LD | | 2,331 | 6.4% | +0.3% | 2,433 | 6.1% | LD |
| Herriot, C | Soc Lab | | 797 | 2.2% | | 146 | 0.4% | Other |
| Russell, T | Ref | | 218 | 0.6% | | | | |
| Lab to SNP notional swing 0.1% | | | 36,619 | Lab maj 12,791 | | 40,135 | Lab maj 14,090 | |
| | | | | 34.9% | | | 35.1% | |

FRANK ROY, b Aug 29, 1958. PA 1994-97 to Helen Liddell, MP; previously steelworker, Ravenscraig. Ed Our Lady's HS, Motherwell; Glasgow Caledonian Univ.

JAMES McGUIGAN, b Nov 4, 1956. Department manager, Halifax Building Soc; convener, Hamilton S constituency and Hamilton Clyde branch. Ex-chair, Halifax BS independent union. Ed Allan Glen's School, Glasgow.

SCOTT DICKSON, b Sept 22, 1972. Lawyer; formerly criminal law tutor at Glasgow Univ. Trustee and treasurer, Wishaw Development Trust. Ed Wishaw HS; Glasgow Univ; St John's Coll, Oxford.

ALEX MACKIE, b June 11, 1937. Insolvency practitioner. Contested Motherwell S 1992. East Renfrewshire UA cllr. Ex-chair, Eastwood LDs. Ed Eastwood Secondary, Clarkston, Glasgow.

| NEATH | | | | | **Lab hold** | |
|---|---|---|---|---|---|---|
| Electorate % Turnout | | 55,525 | 74.3% | **1997** | 56,392 | 80.6% | **1992** |
| *Hain, P | Lab | 30,324 | 73.5% | +5.5% | 30,903 | 68.0% | Lab |
| Evans, D | C | 3,583 | 8.7% | -6.6% | 6,928 | 15.2% | C |
| Jones, T | PC | 3,344 | 8.1% | -3.2% | 5,145 | 11.3% | PC |
| Little, F | LD | 2,597 | 6.3% | +0.9% | 2,467 | 5.4% | LD |
| Morris, P | Ref | 975 | 2.4% | | | | |
| Marks, H | LCP | 420 | 1.0% | | | | |
| C to Lab swing 6.0% | | 41,243 | Lab maj 26,741 | | 45,443 | Lab maj 23,975 | |
| | | | 64.8% | | | 52.8% | |

**PETER HAIN**, b Feb 16, 1950. Became Under Sec Welsh Office, May 5, 1997. Civil rights and anti-apartheid campaigner, and author. Elected 1991 by-election; contested Putney 1987 and 1983. Lab spokesman on employment 1996-97; Lab whip 1995-96. Sec, Tribune group of Lab MPs until 1993. Head of research, Union of Communication Workers, 1987-91; asst research officer 1976-87. Nat chair, Young Libs, 1971-73. Joined Lab Party 1977. Press officer for Anti-Nazi League 1977-80; chair, Stop the '70 (South African) Tour campaign, 1969-70. Unpaid dir, *Tribune*. Ed Pretoria Boys HS; Emanuel School, Wandsworth; Queen Mary's Coll, London; Sussex Univ.

**DAVID EVANS**, b Aug 7, 1967. Marketing exec for Business Seminars International. Campaign officer at C Central Office 1992. Ex-chair, Welsh C students. Ed Highams Park Senior School; Univ Coll of Wales, Swansea.

**TREFOR JONES**. Teacher and community cllr. Ed Ysgol Gyfun Ystalafera; Univ Colls of Wales, Cardiff and Aberystwyth.

**FRANK LITTLE**, b July 29, 1941. Freelance computer programmer/analyst. Member, RSPB. Ed Oldershaw GS, Wallasey.

| NEW FOREST EAST | | **51.2% change** | | | | | **C win** |
|---|---|---|---|---|---|---|---|
| Electorate % Turnout | | 65,717 | 74.6% | **1997** | 64,361 | 81.9% | **1992** |
| Lewis, Dr J | C | 21,053 | 42.9% | -10.1% | 27,980 | 53.1% | C |
| Dawson, G | LD | 15,838 | 32.3% | -1.1% | 17,632 | 33.4% | LD |
| Goodfellow, A | Lab | 12,161 | 24.8% | +12.1% | 6,704 | 12.7% | Lab |
| | | | | | 423 | 0.8% | Other |
| C to LD notional swing 4.5% | | 49,052 | C maj 5,215 | | 52,739 | C maj 10,348 | |
| | | | 10.6% | | | 19.6% | |

**JULIAN LEWIS**, b Sept 26, 1951. Author. Contested Swansea W 1983. Dep director, C research dept, 1990-96; dir, Policy Research Associates, 1985-90; Coalition for Peace through Security, 1981-85. Military historian until 1981. Former parly aide to MPs and peers. Ed Dynevor GS, Swansea; Balliol Coll, Oxford.

**GEORGE DAWSON**, b June 11, 1952. Chemical engineer. Contested Romsey and Waterside 1992. New Forest district cllr 1987- . Member, Greenpeace; Green LDs; CPRE; Charter 88. Ed Castleford GS; Wakefield Tech Coll; Kitson Coll, Leeds; Teesside Poly.

**ALAN GOODFELLOW**, b Jan 4, 1950. Site manager for estate maintenance. Member, GMB. Ed Marley Sec Mod, Dagenham.

| NEW FOREST WEST | | **15.8% change** | | | | | **C win** |
|---|---|---|---|---|---|---|---|
| Electorate % Turnout | | 66,522 | 74.8% | **1997** | 63,917 | 79.8% | **1992** |
| Swayne, D | C | 25,149 | 50.6% | -10.2% | 30,982 | 60.7% | C |
| Hale, R | LD | 13,817 | 27.8% | -2.8% | 15,583 | 30.5% | LD |
| Griffiths, D | Lab | 7,092 | 14.3% | +6.1% | 4,179 | 8.2% | Lab |
| Elliott, Mrs M | Ref | 2,150 | 4.3% | | 293 | 0.6% | Other |
| Holmes, M | UK Ind | 1,542 | 3.1% | | | | |
| C to LD notional swing 3.7% | | 49,750 | C maj 11,332 | | 51,037 | C maj 15,399 | |
| | | | 22.8% | | | 30.2% | |

**DESMOND SWAYNE**, b Aug 20, 1956. Manager, Royal Bank of Scotland. Contested West Bromwich W 1992, Pontypridd 1987. Ex-schoolmaster; taught economics at Charterhouse and Wrekin Coll. TA officer, Warwickshire and Worcestershire Yeomany Sqn. Prison visitor, Wormwood Scrubs and formerly Wandsworth Prison. Member, Bow Group. Ed Bedford School; St Andrews Univ (pres, univ C assoc).

**BOB HALE**, b Nov 24, 1950. Former company director in music and film industry. New Forest district cllr 1990- (LD group whip). Organiser, Britain in Europe referendum campaign, 1975. Ed Rodway Tech HS, Bristol; Bristol Poly.

**DAVID GRIFFITHS**, b July 3, 1958. Parts manager; previously office administration, printing. Sec, Romsey and District Co-op Party. Member, MSF. Ed sec modern school in Southampton; Southampton Coll of Art and Design.

| NEWARK | | ° | | | | | | Lab gain |
|---|---|---|---|---|---|---|---|---|
| Electorate % Turnout | | | 69,763 | 74.5% | **1997** | 68,801 | 82.2% | **1992** |
| Jones, Ms F | **Lab** | | **23,496** | **45.2%** | **+9.4%** | **28,494** | **50.4%** | C |
| *Alexander, R | C | | 20,480 | 39.4% | -11.0% | 20,265 | 35.8% | Lab |
| Harris, P | LD | | 5,960 | 11.5% | -1.5% | 7,342 | 13.0% | LD |
| Creedy, G | Ref | | 2,035 | 3.9% | | 435 | 0.8% | Grn |
| **C to Lab swing 10.2%** | | | **51,971** | | **Lab maj 3,016** | **56,536** | | **C maj 8,229** |
| | | | | | 5.8% | | | 14.6% |

**FIONA JONES**, b Feb 27, 1957. Journalist. Contested Gainsborough and Horncastle 1992. West Lindsey district cllr 1990-94. Chair, Lincs branch, NUJ, 1989- . Member, Rural Revival. Ed Mary Help of Christians GS, Liverpool.

**RICHARD ALEXANDER**, b June 29, 1934. Solicitor. Gained this seat for C 1979; contested Lincoln 1966 and 1970. Member, agriculture select cttee, 1988-97; statutory instruments 1979-97; environment 1983-87; unopposed Bills panel 1992-97. Chair, E Midlands C MPs, 1985-97; joint chair, all-party non-profitmaking

clubs parly group. Parly adviser to Ancient Order of Foresters Friendly Soc. Senior partner, Jones, Alexander and Co, 1964-85. Ed Eastbourne GS; Dewsbury GS; University Coll, London; Inst of Advanced Legal Studies, London.

**PETER HARRIS**, b April 6, 1955. Education authority adviser, head teacher. Contested this seat 1992. Newark and Sherwood district cllr 1991- (group leader). Ed Trinity School, Croydon; Coll of St Mark & St John, Exeter; Birkbeck Coll, London.

| NEWBURY | | 12.2% change | | | | | | LD win |
|---|---|---|---|---|---|---|---|---|
| Electorate % Turnout | | | 73,680 | 76.7% | **1997** | 71,100 | 82.8% | **1992** |
| +Rendel, D | **LD** | | **29,887** | **52.9%** | **+15.8%** | **32,898** | **55.9%** | C |
| Benyon, R | C | | 21,370 | 37.8% | -18.1% | 21,841 | 37.1% | LD |
| Hannon, P | Lab | | 3,107 | 5.5% | -0.6% | 3,584 | 6.1% | Lab |
| Snook, T | Ref | | 992 | 1.8% | | 539 | 0.9% | Grn |
| Stark, Ms R | Green | | 644 | 1.1% | | | | |
| Tubb, R | UK Ind | | 302 | 0.5% | | | | |
| Howse, Ms K | Soc Lab | | 174 | 0.3% | | | | |
| **C to LD notional swing 16.9%** | | | **56,476** | | **LD maj 8,517** | **58,862** | | **C maj 11,057** |
| | | | | | 15.1% | | | 18.8% |

**DAVID RENDEL**, b April 15, 1949. Management consultant and financial analyst. Won this seat in 1993 by-election; contested it 1992 and 1987, Fulham 1983 and 1979. LD spokesman on local gvt 1993- (also housing, May 1997- ). Joint vice-chair, all-party welfare of park home owners parly group. Newbury district cllr 1987-95. Employed by Shell International 1974-77; British Gas 1977-78; Esso Petroleum 1978-90. Ed Eton; Magdalen Coll, Oxford (rowing Blue 1974); St Cross Coll, Oxford.

**RICHARD BENYON**, b Oct 21, 1960. Farmer, chartered surveyor and company director. Officer in Royal Green Jackets 1980-84; land agent 1987-90.. Newbury district cllr 1991- (C group leader 1994-95). Ed Bradfield Coll, Reading; Royal Agric Coll, Cirencester.

**PAUL HANNON**, b Feb 5, 1952. Endangered species consultant. Berkshire county cllr; ex-leader, Newbury District Council. Ed St Joseph's Coll; Royal Veterinary Coll, London.

*Details of 1993 by-election on page 277*

| NEWCASTLE-UNDER-LYME | | | | | | | | Lab hold |
|---|---|---|---|---|---|---|---|---|
| Electorate % Turnout | | | 66,686 | 73.7% | **1997** | 66,595 | 80.3% | **1992** |
| *Golding, Mrs L | **Lab** | | **27,743** | **56.5%** | **+8.5%** | **25,652** | **47.9%** | Lab |
| Hayes, M | C | | 10,537 | 21.4% | -8.1% | 15,813 | 29.6% | C |
| Studd, Dr R | LD | | 6,858 | 14.0% | -8.0% | 11,727 | 21.9% | LD |
| Suttle, Ms K | Ref | | 1,510 | 3.1% | | 314 | 0.6% | NLP |
| Mountford, S | Lib | | 1,399 | 2.8% | | | | |
| Bell, Ms B | Soc Lab | | 1,082 | 2.2% | | | | |
| **C to Lab swing 8.3%** | | | **49,129** | | **Lab maj 17,206** | **53,506** | | **Lab maj 9,839** |
| | | | | | 35.0% | | | 18.4% |

**LLIN GOLDING**, b March 21, 1933. Won 1986 by-election for this seat. Lab spokesman on agriculture 1995-97; on children and families 1993-95; on social security 1992-95; Lab whip 1987-92. Joint chair, all-party homelessness and housing need parly group, 1989- ; vice-chair, glass group; joint vice-chair, prevention of solvent abuse, children, war crimes, and drugs misuse groups; treas, racing and bloodstock industries, diabetic and prisoners abroad groups. Member, exec cttee, British group, IPU. PLP parly affairs cttee; PLP children and family cttee, 1995- . Match sec, Lords and Commons Fly Fishing Club. Dir, Handicapped Anglers

Trust and of Foster and Angler; trustee, NSPCC and the charity Safe; member, Commonwealth War Graves Commission (all unpaid). Ed Caerphilly Girls' GS; Cardiff Royal Infirmary School of Radiography.

**MARCUS HAYES**, b Dec 17, 1964. Solicitor. Member, Bow Group; Manchester Law Soc; Inst of Credit Management. Ed Stourport-on-Severn HS; Kidderminster CFE; Sussex Univ; Chester Coll of Law.

**ROBIN STUDD**, b April 28, 1941. History lecturer. Ex-Newcastle-under-Lyme cllr. Ed King Edward VI, Stratford; Leeds and London Univs.

| NEWCASTLE UPON TYNE CENTRAL | | 14.2% change | | | Lab win | | |
|---|---|---|---|---|---|---|---|
| Electorate % Turnout | | 69,781 | 66.0% | **1997** | 69,376 | 70.5% | **1992** |
| +Cousins, J | Lab | **27,272** | **59.2%** | +7.5% | **25,281** | **51.7%** | Lab |
| Newmark, B | C | 10,792 | 23.4% | -12.2% | 17,393 | 35.6% | C |
| Berry, Ms R | LD | 6,911 | 15.0% | +2.3% | 6,208 | 12.7% | LD |
| Coxon, C | Ref | 1,113 | 2.4% | | | | |
| C to Lab notional swing 9.8% | | **46,088** | | **Lab maj 16,480** | **48,882** | | **Lab maj 7,888** |
| | | | | 35.8% | | | 16.1% |

JIM COUSINS, b Feb 23, 1944. Gained this seat 1987. Lab spokesman on foreign affairs 1994-95; spokesman on trade and industry 1992-94. Member, select cttees on public service, 1995-97, and trade and industry 1989-92. Vice-chair, Northern group of Lab MPs, 1995- . Former contract researcher and lecturer in steel, shipbuilding and inner city job markets for trade unions, Commission on Industrial Relations and Depts of Employment and Environment. Tyne and Wear county cllr 1973-86 (dep leader 1981-86); Wallsend borough cllr 1969-73. Ed New College, Oxford; LSE.

BROOKS NEWMARK, b May 8, 1958. Principal of company restructuring specialists. Chair, Southwark and Bermondsey C assoc, 1990-93; dep chair, London South Inner Euro Assoc, 1994- . Ed Bedford School; Harvard Coll; Worcester Coll, Oxford; Harvard Business School.

RUTH BERRY, b June 30, 1975. Full-time student at Newcastle Univ. Member, Friends of the Earth; 300 Group; Charter 88. Asst leader, Girl Guides. Ed Dorothy Stringer School, Brighton; Newcastle Univ.

| NEWCASTLE UPON TYNE EAST & WALLSEND | | | | | 44.6% change | Lab win | |
|---|---|---|---|---|---|---|---|
| Electorate % Turnout | | 63,272 | 65.7% | **1997** | 65,989 | 70.1% | **1992** |
| +Brown, N H | Lab | **29,607** | **71.2%** | +14.0% | **26,466** | **57.2%** | Lab |
| Middleton, J | C | 5,796 | 13.9% | -8.6% | 10,421 | 22.5% | C |
| Morgan, G | LD | 4,415 | 10.6% | -8.0% | 8,628 | 18.7% | LD |
| Cossins, P | Ref | 966 | 2.3% | | 744 | 1.6% | Other |
| Carpenter, Ms B | Soc Lab | 642 | 1.5% | | | | |
| Levy, M | Comm Brit | 163 | 0.4% | | | | |
| C to Lab notional swing 11.3% | | **41,589** | | **Lab maj 23,811** | **46,259** | | **Lab maj 16,045** |
| | | | | 57.3% | | | 34.7% |

NICK BROWN, b June 13, 1950. Became Government Chief Whip, May 3, 1997. Lab dep chief whip 1996-97. MP for Newcastle East 1983-97. Senior whip in charge of organisation 1995-96; Lab spokesman on health 1994-95; Shadow Dep Leader of House and Lab campaign co-ordinator 1992-94; spokesman on Treasury and economic affairs 1988-92; on legal affairs 1985-87. Treas, Parly and Scientific Cttee, 1991-97; Parly Office of Science and Technology 1991-97. Legal adviser, northern region of GMB,

1978-83. Newcastle upon Tyne city cllr 1980-84. Ed Swattenden Sec Mod; Tunbridge Wells Tech HS; Manchester Univ.

JEREMY MIDDLETON, b Nov 19, 1960. Management consultant. Chair, Newcastle and Wallsend C assoc. Ed Tettenhall Coll; Kent Univ.

GRAHAM MORGAN, b July 14, 1948. Unemployed. Chair, Keighley LDs, 1994-96; member, Yorkshire LD regional executive, 1993- . Ed Ipswich School; York Univ.

| NEWCASTLE UPON TYNE NORTH | | | | | | Lab hold | |
|---|---|---|---|---|---|---|---|
| Electorate % Turnout | | 65,357 | 69.2% | **1997** | 66,187 | 76.8% | **1992** |
| *Henderson, D J | Lab | **28,125** | **62.2%** | +12.8% | **25,121** | **49.4%** | Lab |
| White, G | C | 8,793 | 19.4% | -12.4% | 16,175 | 31.8% | C |
| Allen, P | LD | 6,578 | 14.5% | -4.2% | 9,542 | 18.8% | LD |
| Chipchase, Mrs D | Ref | 1,733 | 3.8% | | | | |
| C to Lab swing 12.6% | | **45,229** | | **Lab maj 19,332** | **50,838** | | **Lab maj 8,946** |
| | | | | 42.7% | | | 17.6% |

DOUG HENDERSON, b June 9, 1949. Became Minister for Europe, May 4, 1997. Elected 1987. Lab spokesman on home affairs 1995-97 and in 1996 given special brief on devolution; spokesman on public service 1994-95; local gvt 1992-94; trade and industry 1988-92. Sec, all-party British-Russia group. Chair, PLP Treasury and Civil Service cttee, 1987-88; sec, GMB parly group, 1987- . Member, exec, Scottish Council of Lab Party, 1979-87 (chair 1984-85). Regional official of GMB (small honorarium); full-time regional organiser, GMWU and then GMB, 1975-87; research officer GMWU 1973-75; clerk, British Rail, 1969; apprentice, Rolls-Royce, 1966-68. Dir, Ossian Economic Services Ltd; Premier Management International; unpaid dir, London Moscow Foundation. Consultant to Machine Tool Technologies Assoc. Ed

Waid Acad, Anstruther, Fife; Central Coll, Glasgow; Strathclyde Univ.

GREG WHITE, b Nov 17, 1964. Food and drink director of purchasing consortium; previously in sales and marketing with major brewers. Chair, York YCs, 1989-90. Ed Huntcliff Comp, Saltburn; Prior Pursflose Sixth-Form Coll, Guisborough; Loughborough Univ.

PETER ALLEN, b Oct 14, 1959. Durham Univ lecturer; previously taught at Teesside Poly; was with British Steel on Teesside. Contested Langbaurgh in 1992 and 1991 by-election. Member, ALDC; Campaign for a Northern Assembly. Ed Henry Smith School, Hartlepool; Brunel Univ; Cranfield Inst.

| NEWPORT EAST | | | | | Lab hold | | |
|---|---|---|---|---|---|---|---|
| Electorate % Turnout | | 50,997 | 73.1% | **1997** | 51,603 | 81.2% | **1992** |
| +Howarth, A | Lab | 21,481 | 57.7% | +2.7% | 23,050 | 55.0% | Lab |
| Evans, D | C | 7,958 | 21.4% | -10.0% | 13,151 | 31.4% | C |
| Cameron, A | LD | 3,880 | 10.4% | -1.5% | 4,991 | 11.9% | LD |
| Scargill, A | Soc Lab | 1,951 | 5.2% | | 716 | 1.7% | Green/PC |
| Davis, G | Ref | 1,267 | 3.4% | | | | |
| Holland, C | PC | 721 | 1.9% | | | | |
| C to Lab swing 6.3% | | 37,258 | Lab maj 13,523 | | 41,908 | Lab maj 9,899 | |
| | | | 36.3% | | | 23.6% | |

**ALAN HOWARTH**, b June 11, 1944. Became Under Secretary for Education and Employment with responsibility for welfare-to-work, May 5, 1997. Returned for this seat 1997. C MP for Stratford-on-Avon 1983 to Oct 1995, when he joined Lab Party and sat as Lab MP until 1997. Education and Science Under Sec 1989-92; gvt whip 1988-89; asst gvt whip 1987-88. Member, select cttees on social security, 1995-97; nat heritage 1992-93. Chair, all-party parly panel on charities and voluntary sector, 1992- . Vice-chair, C Party, 1980-81. Joint vice-chair, British group, IPU, 1993-94. Member of Lloyd's. Public affairs adviser to Baring Brothers and Co Ltd, 1982-87. Governor, Royal Shakespeare Theatre, 1984- ; vice-pres, British Dyslexia Assoc, 1992- . Asst master, Westminster School, 1968-74. Ed Rugby; King's Coll, Cambridge.

**DAVID EVANS**, b Aug 13, 1959. Barrister in oil and gas industry. Contested Montgomery 1987. Treas, Wycombe C assoc; chair, Swansea C assoc, 1984-86. Ed Wrekin Coll, Shropshire; Mansfield Coll, Oxford; Inns of Court School of Law.
**ALISTAIR CAMERON**, b April 8, 1960. Personnel officer with British Energy. Cheltenham borough cllr (dep council leader; dep group leader). Ed Greenhill School, Tenby; Bristol Univ; Bristol Poly.
**ARTHUR SCARGILL**, b Jan 11, 1938. Founder, Soc Lab Party, 1996. Pres, NUM, since 1981 (general sec, 1992; member, nat exec, 1972-). Member, TUC General Council, 1986-88; Lab Party 1966-95. Ed Worsbrough Dale School; White Cross Sec School; Leeds Univ.

| NEWPORT WEST | | | | | Lab hold | | |
|---|---|---|---|---|---|---|---|
| Electorate % Turnout | | 53,914 | 74.6% | **1997** | 54,871 | 82.8% | **1992** |
| *Flynn, P | Lab | 24,331 | 60.5% | +7.4% | 24,139 | 53.1% | Lab |
| Clarke, P | C | 9,794 | 24.4% | -11.6% | 16,360 | 36.0% | C |
| Wilson, S | LD | 3,907 | 9.7% | +0.3% | 4,296 | 9.5% | LD |
| Thompsett, C | Ref | 1,199 | 3.0% | | 653 | 1.4% | PC |
| Jackson, H | PC | 648 | 1.6% | +0.2% | | | |
| Moelwyn Hughes, H | UK Ind | 323 | 0.8% | | | | |
| C to Lab swing 9.5% | | 40,202 | Lab maj 14,537 | | 45,448 | Lab maj 7,779 | |
| | | | 36.2% | | | 17.1% | |

**PAUL FLYNN**, b Feb 9, 1935. Ex-steelworker. Gained this seat 1987; contested Denbigh Oct 1974. Lab spokesman on social security 1988-90; on Wales 1987. Member, transport select cttee 1992-97. Joint vice-chair, all-party daylight extra group. Research officer for Llewellyn Smith, Labour MEP for SE Wales, 1984-87; steelworker 1955-84. Ex-chair, Broadcasting Council for Wales; ex-member of South Wales Docks Board, and of council of Univ Coll of Wales, Cardiff. Gwent county cllr 1974-82; ex-Newport borough cllr. Ed St Illtyd's; Univ Coll of Wales, Cardiff.

**PETER CLARKE**, b April 1947. Journalist. Contested Fife Central 1974. Former BBC economics correspondent; writer for *Private Eye* and *The Economist*. Chair, Business Seminars International. Ex-PA to Enoch Powell, Sir Keith Joseph, Nicholas Ridley. Chair, Selsdon Group. Ed St Columbus School, Kilmacolm; Loughborough GS; Bradford Univ; Balliol Coll, Oxford.
**STANLEY WILSON**, b Nov 12, 1931. Retired teacher. Contested Caerphilly 1992. Langbaurgh district cllr 1987- . Ed Coatham GS, Redcar; King Alfred's, Winchester; OU. Cricket league umpire.

| NEWRY & ARMAGH | | 1.3% change | | | SDLP win | | |
|---|---|---|---|---|---|---|---|
| Electorate % Turnout | | 70,652 | 75.4% | **1997** | 68,656 | 76.0% | **1992** |
| +Mallon, S | SDLP | 22,904 | 43.0% | -6.3% | 25,740 | 49.3% | SDLP |
| Kennedy, D | UUP | 18,015 | 33.8% | -2.5% | 18,930 | 36.3% | UUP |
| McNamee, P | SF | 11,218 | 21.1% | +8.5% | 6,530 | 12.5% | SF |
| Whitcroft, P | Alliance | 1,015 | 1.9% | +0.0% | 972 | 1.9% | Alliance |
| Evans, D | NLP | 123 | 0.2% | | | | |
| No swing calculation | | 53,275 | SDLP maj 4,889 | | 52,172 | SDLP maj 6,810 | |
| | | | 9.2% | | | 13.1% | |

**SEAMUS MALLON**, b Aug 17, 1936. Teacher. Won this seat at by-election 1986; contested it 1983. Dep leader, SDLP 1978- . Member, Anglo-Irish inter-parly body, 1990- ; N Ireland Assembly 1973-74 and 1982; N Ireland Convention 1975-76; Irish Senate 1981-82. Ed St Mary's Coll of Ed, Belfast.

**DANNY KENNEDY,** b July 6, 1959. Employed by British Telecom. Newry and Mourne cllr since 1985 (chair 1994-95). Ed Newry HS.
**PAT McNAMEE,** b Feb 12, 1957. Estate agent. Elected to N Ireland Forum 1996. Republican activist since his teens; imprisoned in Irish Republic for six years in the 1980s.

| NORFOLK MID | | 9.9% change | | | 1997 | | | C win |
|---|---|---|---|---|---|---|---|---|
| Electorate % Turnout | | 75,311 | 76.3% | | **1997** | 71,208 | 83.6% | **1992** |
| **Simpson, K** | C | **22,739** | **39.6%** | -15.0% | | **32,481** | **54.6%** | **C** |
| Zeichner, D | Lab | 21,403 | 37.3% | +11.2% | | 15,537 | 26.1% | Lab |
| Frary, Mrs S | LD | 8,617 | 15.0% | -4.0% | | 11,316 | 19.0% | LD |
| Holder, N | Ref | 3,229 | 5.6% | | | 209 | 0.4% | NLP |
| Park, T | Green | 1,254 | 2.2% | | | | | |
| Parker, B | NLP | 215 | 0.4% | +0.0% | | | | |
| **C to Lab notional swing 13.1%** | | **57,457** | | C maj 1,336 | | **59,543** | | C maj **16,944** |
| | | | | 2.3% | | | | 28.5% |

**KEITH SIMPSON**, b March 29, 1949. Contested Plymouth Devonport 1992. Political adviser to Tom King, Defence Sec, 1988-91. Director, Cranfield Security Studies Inst, Cranfield Univ; senior lecturer in war studies and international affairs, RMA Sandhurst, 1973-86. Head, foreign affairs and defence section, C research dept, 1986-88. Vice-chair, Federation of C Students, 1972-73. Author of five books on military history. Ed Thorpe GS; Hull Univ; postgraduate research, King's Coll, London.

**DANIEL ZEICHNER**, b Nov 9, 1956. Political researcher to John Garrett, MP, and Clive Needle, MEP. Chair, South Norfolk CLP, 1987-94. Member, Lab regional exec since 1987. Ed Trinity School, Croydon; King's Coll, Cambridge.
**SUE FRARY**, b May 25, 1959. Physiotherapist and book-keeper. Member, World Wide Fund for Nature; Broads Soc. Ed Thorpe St Andrew and Thorpe GS, Oswestry; North Staffs School of Physiotherapy.

| NORFOLK NORTH | | | | | 1997 | | | C hold |
|---|---|---|---|---|---|---|---|---|
| Electorate % Turnout | | 77,113 | 76.3% | | **1997** | 73,780 | 81.0% | **1992** |
| **Prior, D** | C | **21,456** | **36.5%** | -11.7% | | **28,810** | **48.2%** | **C** |
| Lamb, N | LD | 20,163 | 34.3% | +6.9% | | 16,365 | 27.4% | LD |
| Cullingham, M | Lab | 14,736 | 25.1% | +1.9% | | 13,850 | 23.2% | Lab |
| Allen, J | Ref | 2,458 | 4.2% | | | 559 | 0.9% | Grn |
| | | | | | | 167 | 0.3% | NLP |
| **C to LD swing 9.3%** | | **58,813** | | C maj 1,293 | | **59,751** | | C maj **12,445** |
| | | | | 2.2% | | | | 20.8% |

**DAVID PRIOR**, b Dec 3, 1954. Barrister; chair, Lurmark Ltd, manufacturers of plastic and metal components for agricultural and industrial spraying; director of various companies; previously with British Steel. Member, trade and industry policy group; gvt working group on agriculture for Eastern Europe and Soviet Union. Dir, Burnbake Trust, charity which helps to rehabilitate ex-prisoners. Ed Orwell Park School; Charterhouse; Pembroke Coll, Cambridge; Inns of Court School of Law. Son of Lord Prior, former C minister.

**NORMAN LAMB**, b Sept 16, 1957. Solicitor. Contested this seat 1992. Norwich city cllr 1987-91 (group leader 1989-91); member, Cambridge CHC. Ex-chair and sec, Norwich S Lib Party. Employment lawyer and partner of East Anglian law firm, Steele & Co. Ed Wymondham Coll, Norfolk; Leicester Univ; City of London Poly.
**MICHAEL CULLINGHAM**, b Jan 26, 1946. Teacher. Contested this seat 1992. N Norfolk district cllr 1990- . Member, Norfolk Natural Trust; NASUWT. Ed Wymondham Coll, Norfolk; Sittingbourne Coll of Ed, Kent.

| NORFOLK NORTH WEST | | | | | 1997 | | | Lab gain |
|---|---|---|---|---|---|---|---|---|
| Electorate % Turnout | | 77,083 | 74.7% | | **1997** | 77,438 | 80.7% | **1992** |
| **Turner, Dr G** | Lab | **25,250** | **43.8%** | +10.2% | | **32,554** | **52.1%** | **C** |
| *Bellingham, H | C | 23,911 | 41.5% | -10.6% | | 20,990 | 33.6% | Lab |
| Knowles, Ms E | LD | 5,513 | 9.6% | -4.2% | | 8,599 | 13.8% | LD |
| Percival, R | Ref | 2,923 | 5.1% | | | 330 | 0.5% | NLP |
| **C to Lab swing 10.4%** | | **57,597** | | Lab maj 1,339 | | **62,473** | | C maj **11,564** |
| | | | | 2.3% | | | | 18.5% |

**GEORGE TURNER**, b Aug 9, 1940. Univ lecturer in electronic engineering. Contested this seat 1992. Norfolk county cllr 1977- (group leader 1985-90). Member, Norfolk police authority; AUT. Ed Laxton GS, Oundle; Imperial Coll, London; Gonville and Caius Coll, Cambridge.
**HENRY BELLINGHAM**, b March 29, 1955. Elected 1983. Barrister. PPS to Malcolm Rifkind, Foreign, Defence and Transport Sec, 1990-97. Member, environment select cttee, 1987-91; British-Irish inter-parly body. Chair, C Council on E Europe, 1989-94; joint sec, C backbench N Ireland cttee, 1983-90; joint vice-chair (1987-90)

and joint sec (1983-87), C smaller businesses cttee. Non-underwriting member of Lloyd's. Dir, Lothian plc, chemical manufacturer. Pres, British Resorts Assoc; vice-pres, Corp of Finance Brokers (both unpaid). Founder member and sponsor, W Norfolk Local Enterprise Agency, 1986-94. Ed Eton; Magdalene Coll, Cambridge; Inns of Court School of Law.
**EVELYN KNOWLES**, b April 14, 1931. Community centre director. Cambridge county cllr (dep group leader). Vice-chair, Women LDs. Ed Coborn GS for Girls, London; Ealing Coll of HE.

| NORFOLK SOUTH | | 6.6% change | | | | | C win |
|---|---|---|---|---|---|---|---|
| Electorate % Turnout | | 79,239 | 78.4% | **1997** | 76,494 | 84.1% | **1992** |
| +MacGregor, J | C | **24,935** | 40.2% | -12.2% | **33,669** | 52.4% | C |
| Hacker, Mrs B | LD | 17,557 | 28.3% | +1.4% | 17,305 | 26.9% | LD |
| Ross, Ms J | Lab | 16,188 | 26.1% | +7.7% | 11,841 | 18.4% | Lab |
| Bateson, Mrs P | Ref | 2,533 | 4.1% | | 662 | 1.0% | Grn |
| Ross-Wagenknecht, Mrs S | Grn | 484 | 0.8% | | 320 | 0.5% | Ind |
| Boddy, A | UK Ind | 400 | 0.6% | | 300 | 0.5% | NLP |
| | | | | | 213 | 0.3% | Ind C |
| C to LD notional swing 6.8% | | **62,097** | | **C maj 7,378** | **64,310** | | **C maj 16,364** |
| | | | | 11.9% | | | 25.4% |

**JOHN MacGREGOR**, b Feb 14, 1937. Elected Feb 1974. Transport Sec 1992-94; Lord President of Council and Leader of Commons 1990-92; Education Sec 1989-90; Min of Ag, Fish and Food 1987-89; joined Cabinet as Treasury Chief Sec 1985; Min of State, MAFF, 1983-85; Under Sec for Industry, 1981-83; gvt whip 1979-81. Privy Counsellor 1985. Opposition whip 1977-79. Member, standards and privilges select cttee, 1996-97. Pres, all-party magic group. Special assistant to Sir Alec Douglas-Home when PM, 1963-64, and head of Edward Heath's private office, 1965-68. Dep chair (non-exec), Hill Samuel & Co Ltd, 1994- (with them 1968-79, and a director 1973-79); non-exec dir, Associated British Foods plc,

1994- ; Slough Estates plc, 1995- ; Unigate plc, 1996- . Member, UK food and agribusiness board; Rabobank International (both unpaid). Ed Merchiston Castle School, Edinburgh; St Andrews Univ; King's Coll, London.

**BARBARA HACKER**, b Feb 3, 1946. Radiographer; worked in estates division of Norwich Union 1983-95. Norfolk county cllr 1993- (dep group leader); member, Norfolk police authority. Ed Streatham Hill HS, Clapham; St Bartholomew's Hospital, London.

**JANE ROSS**, b March 7, 1944. Nurse. Norfolk county cllr 1989- . Pres, Norwich Lab Party. Ed Croydon HS for Girls; Guy's Hospital, London.

| NORFOLK SOUTH WEST | | 1.1% change | | | | | C win |
|---|---|---|---|---|---|---|---|
| Electorate % Turnout | | 80,236 | 73.3% | **1997** | 78,711 | 79.1% | **1992** |
| +Shephard, Mrs G | C | **24,694** | 42.0% | -12.7% | **34,098** | 54.7% | C |
| Heffernan, A | Lab | 22,230 | 37.8% | +10.8% | 16,848 | 27.0% | Lab |
| Buckton, D | LD | 8,178 | 13.9% | -4.3% | 11,343 | 18.2% | LD |
| Hoare, R | Ref | 3,694 | 6.3% | | | | |
| C to Lab notional swing 11.8% | | **58,796** | | **C maj 2,464** | **62,289** | | **C maj 17,250** |
| | | | | 4.2% | | | 27.7% |

**GILLIAN SHEPHARD**, b Jan 22, 1940. Elected 1987. Education and Employment Sec 1995-97; Education Sec, 1994-95; Agriculture, Fisheries and Food Min 1993-94; joined Cabinet in 1992 as Employment Sec. Min of State, Treasury, 1990-92; Social Security Under Sec 1989-90. PPS to Peter Lilley, then Economic Sec to Treasury, 1988-89. A dep chair, C Party, 1991-92; co-chair, Women's Nat Commission, 1990-91. Norfolk county cllr 1977-89. Ex-schools inspector and Mental Health Act commissioner. Ed N Walsham Girls' HS, Norfolk; St Hilda's Coll, Oxford (Hon Fellow, 1991).

**ADRIAN HEFFERNAN**, b July 10, 1958. Postgraduate student. Former British Rail employee. Bedfordshire county cllr 1993- ; chair, Bedfordshire Police Authority. Churchill Fellowship 1977. Member, Howard League for Penal Reform; Aslef; Nacro. Ed St Joseph's RC School, Salisbury; Bedford Coll; De Montfort Univ.

**DAVID BUCKTON**, b March 28, 1934. Former TV and film producer/director; full-time Norfolk county cllr. Dir, St George's, Guildhall/King's Lynn Arts Centre and Festival; Eastern Screen and Denver Windmill Ltd. Ed Monkton Combe Senior School; St John's Coll, Cambridge.

| NORMANTON | | 41.3% change | | | | | Lab win |
|---|---|---|---|---|---|---|---|
| Electorate % Turnout | | 62,980 | 68.3% | **1997** | 61,873 | 74.8% | **1992** |
| +O'Brien, W | Lab | **26,046** | 60.6% | +9.4% | **23,659** | 51.1% | Lab |
| Bulmer, Miss F | C | 10,153 | 23.6% | -12.0% | 16,467 | 35.6% | C |
| Ridgway, D | LD | 5,347 | 12.4% | -0.9% | 6,155 | 13.3% | LD |
| Shuttleworth, K | Ref | 1,458 | 3.4% | | | | |
| C to Lab notional swing 10.7% | | **43,004** | | **Lab maj 15,893** | **46,281** | | **Lab maj 7,192** |
| | | | | 37.0% | | | 15.5% |

**WILLIAM O'BRIEN**, b Jan 25, 1929. Ex-miner. Elected 1983. Lab spokesman on N Ireland 1992-94; on local gvt 1987-92. Member, PAC, 1983-88, and energy select cttee 1986-88. Ex-chair, PLP home affairs cttee. Joint chair, all-party sustainable waste management group, 1995- ; joint sec, police group. Urban, county and metropolitan district cllr 1951-83, serving on Wakefield District Council 1973-83. Miner 1945-83. Ed St Joseph's School, Castleford; Leeds Univ (day release).

**FIONA BULMER**, b Oct 3, 1967. Part-time research asst to Ian Lang when Pres of Board of Trade; freelance consultant and researcher. Desk officer, C research dept, 1990-93. Ed Samuel Whitbread Upper School, Bedfordshire; Bristol Univ.

**DAVID RIDGWAY**, b Feb 5, 1946. Executive financial consultant. Contested Hemsworth 1996 by-election; Yorkshire South West in Euro elections 1994 and 1989. Kirklees metropolitan borough cllr. Ed Sedbergh School.

| NORTHAMPTON NORTH | | 4.5% change | | | | | Lab win |
|---|---|---|---|---|---|---|---|
| Electorate % Turnout | | 73,664 | 70.2% | 1997 | 73,395 | 77.3% | 1992 |
| Keeble, Ms S | Lab | 27,247 | 52.7% | +14.1% | 25,972 | 45.8% | C |
| +Marlow, T | C | 17,247 | 33.4% | -12.4% | 21,905 | 38.6% | Lab |
| Dunbar, Ms L | LD | 6,579 | 12.7% | -2.5% | 8,630 | 15.2% | LD |
| Torbica, D | UK Ind | 464 | 0.9% | | 232 | 0.4% | NLP |
| Spivack, B | NLP | 161 | 0.3% | -0.1% | | | |
| C to Lab notional swing 13.3% | | 51,698 | Lab maj 10,000 | | 56,739 | C maj 4,067 | |
| | | | 19.3% | | | 7.2% | |

**SALLY KEEBLE**, b Oct 13, 1951. Journalist and author. Ex-head of GMB communications 1986-90. Southwark cllr (leader 1990-93). Asst dir, external relations, ILEA 1984-86. Public affairs consultant, Public Policy Unit, 1995-97. Journalist on *Daily News*, Durban, 1974-79, and *The Birmingham Post* 1979-83. Member, Fabian Soc; Anti-Racist Alliance. Ed Cheltenham Ladies' Coll; Oxford Univ; Univ of South Africa.
**TONY MARLOW**, b June 17, 1940. Gained seat for C 1979; contested Normanton, Feb 1974, and Rugby, Oct 1974. Member, select cttee on European legislation 1983-97. Joint vice-chair (1989-90) and joint sec (1985-88), C backbench defence cttee; ex-joint sec, C trade and consumer affairs cttee. Sec, all-party Czech and Slovak group. Ex-development manager with grain shippers co. Occasional consultancy with Gulf Centre for Strategic Studies. Ed Wellington Coll, Berkshire; Sandhurst; St Catharine's Coll, Cambridge.
**LESLEY DUNBAR**, b Nov 9, 1945. Freelance TV/film writer and researcher. Member, Charter 88; 300 Group; Women LDs. Ed Blackburn Girls' HS; Nottingham Poly; RADA; OU.

| NORTHAMPTON SOUTH | | 11.6% change | | | | | Lab win |
|---|---|---|---|---|---|---|---|
| Electorate % Turnout | | 79,384 | 71.9% | 1997 | 73,499 | 80.4% | 1992 |
| Clarke, T | Lab | 24,214 | 42.4% | +12.2% | 32,898 | 55.7% | C |
| +Morris, M | C | 23,470 | 41.1% | -14.6% | 17,854 | 30.2% | Lab |
| Worgan, T | LD | 6,316 | 11.1% | -3.1% | 8,355 | 14.1% | LD |
| Petrie, C | Ref | 1,405 | 2.5% | | | | |
| Clark, D R | UK Ind | 1,159 | 2.0% | | | | |
| Woollcombe, G | NLP | 541 | 0.9% | | | | |
| C to Lab notional swing 13.4% | | 57,105 | Lab maj 744 | | 59,107 | C maj 15,044 | |
| | | | 1.3% | | | 25.5% | |

**TONY CLARKE**, b Sept 6, 1963. Social work trainer, Northants County Council. Northampton borough cllr 1991- . Manager/coach, Northampton Lab Club football team; vice-chair Northampton Town Supporters Trust. Member, GMB; Apex. Ed Lings Upper, Northampton; Inst of Training and Development; Inst of Safety and Health.
**MICHAEL MORRIS**, b Nov 25, 1936. Elected Feb 1974; contested Islington N 1966. Chairman of Ways and Means and Deputy Speaker 1992-97. Member, Commons chairman's panel, 1983-92. Member, Council of Europe and WEU, 1983-91. Privy Counsellor 1994. Capt, parly golf society, 1988-91. Islington cllr 1968-74. Non-exec director, Tunbridge Wells Equitable Friendly Society Ltd. Hon chair, Progressive Supranuclear Palsy Soc; Northants Victoria County History Trust and Bedford School governors; a Harpur Trust charity governor. Member, advisory cttee, Airey Neave Trust; trustee, M. Pierson Research Trust (both honorary). Proprietor, A.M. International, 1980-92. Ed Bedford School; St Catharine's Coll, Cambridge.
**TONY WORGAN**, b Dec 16, 1967. Railtrack operations manager. Member, TSSA. Ed St Birinus Comp, Didcot; Reading Univ.

| NORTHAVON | | 10.8% change | | | | | LD win |
|---|---|---|---|---|---|---|---|
| Electorate % Turnout | | 78,943 | 79.2% | 1997 | 74,496 | 84.7% | 1992 |
| Webb, Prof S | LD | 26,500 | 42.4% | +7.9% | 32,700 | 51.8% | C |
| +Cope, Sir John | C | 24,363 | 39.0% | -12.8% | 21,759 | 34.5% | LD |
| Stone, R E | Lab | 9,767 | 15.6% | +3.5% | 7,625 | 12.1% | Lab |
| Parfitt, J | Ref | 1,900 | 3.0% | | 709 | 1.1% | Grn |
| | | | | | 340 | 0.5% | Lib |
| C to LD notional swing 10.4% | | 62,530 | LD maj 2,137 | | 63,133 | C maj 10,941 | |
| | | | 3.4% | | | 17.3% | |

**STEVEN WEBB**, b July 18, 1965. Professor of social policy at Bath Univ since 1995; formerly worked for Inst of Fiscal Studies. Member, Amnesty; World Development Movement. Ed Dartmouth HS, Birmingham; Hertford Coll, Oxford.
**SIR JOHN COPE**, b May 13, 1937. Chartered accountant. Elected for this seat 1983; MP for S Gloucestershire Feb 1974-83; contested Woolwich E 1970. Paymaster General, Treasury, 1992-94; N Ireland Min 1989-90; Min for Small Firms 1987-89; gvt dep chief whip 1983-87; gvt whip 1981-83; asst gvt whip 1979-81. Privy Counsellor 1988. Member, select cttee on procedure, 1994-97. A dep chair of C Party 1990-92. Unpaid director, Small Business Bureau Ltd; unpaid chair, Horse and Pony taxation cttee. Hon vice-pres, Nat Chamber of Trade. Ed Oakham School, Rutland.
**RONALD STONE**, b Dec 21, 1942. Contested Woodspring 1992. Physics technician at Bristol Univ; former member, nat negotiating cttee, univ technicians. Avon county cllr 1985-96. Member, ASTMS/MSF, being shop steward at Bristol Univ. Ed Bristol Tech School; Brunel Tech Coll.

| NORWICH NORTH | | 12.2% change | | | | | Lab win |
|---|---|---|---|---|---|---|---|
| Electorate % Turnout | | 72,521 | 75.9% | **1997** | 71,785 | 80.6% | **1992** |
| Gibson, Dr I | Lab | **27,346** | **49.7%** | +9.4% | **25,558** | **44.2%** | C |
| Kinghorn, Dr R R F | C | 17,876 | 32.5% | -11.7% | 23,288 | 40.3% | Lab |
| Young, P | LD | 6,951 | 12.6% | -2.0% | 8,462 | 14.6% | LD |
| Bailey-Smith, T | Ref | 1,777 | 3.2% | | 446 | 0.8% | Grn |
| Marks, H | LCP | 512 | 0.9% | | 97 | 0.2% | NLP |
| Hood, J | Soc Lab | 495 | 0.9% | | | | |
| Mills, Mrs D | NLP | 100 | 0.2% | +0.0% | | | |
| C to Lab notional swing 10.6% | | 55,057 | | Lab maj 9,470 | 57,851 | | C maj 2,270 |
| | | | | 17.2% | | | 3.9% |

**IAN GIBSON**, b Sept 26, 1938. Contested this seat 1992. Dean of Biological Sciences, East Anglia Univ. Member, Medical Research Council and Cancer Research Campaign grants cttees. Governor, John Innes Biotechnology Centre. Former exec cttee member, ASTMS/MSF. Ed Dumfries local state schools; Edinburgh Univ. Founder and coach, Red Rose FC for 8 to 11-year-old children.
**ROGER KINGHORN**, b Aug 19, 1942. Lecturer at Imperial Coll, London, on oil and gas exploration; author of railway books.

Contested Blyth Valley 1987. Hounslow cllr 1986-96 (C group leader 1992-96); Islington cllr 1968-70. Founded C transport group, 1992. Ed Eastbourne Coll; Edinburgh and London Univs; OU. Owner of a vintage bus.
**PAUL YOUNG**, b March 1, 1964. Sales exec; ex-RAF. Member, League against Cruel Sports; Gun Control Network. Ed Sir William Borlase, Marlow.

| NORWICH SOUTH | | 8.4% change | | | | | Lab win |
|---|---|---|---|---|---|---|---|
| Electorate % Turnout | | 70,009 | 72.6% | **1997** | 69,638 | 79.8% | **1992** |
| Clarke, C | Lab | **26,267** | **51.7%** | +5.7% | **25,546** | **46.0%** | Lab |
| Khanbhai, B | C | 12,028 | 23.7% | -14.5% | 21,196 | 38.1% | C |
| Aalders-Dunthorne, A | LD | 9,457 | 18.6% | +4.5% | 7,820 | 14.1% | LD |
| Holdsworth, Dr D | Ref | 1,464 | 2.9% | | 891 | 1.6% | Grn |
| Marks, H | LCP | 765 | 1.5% | | 115 | 0.2% | NLP |
| Holmes, A | Green | 736 | 1.4% | | | | |
| Parsons, B | NLP | 84 | 0.2% | -0.0% | | | |
| C to Lab notional swing 10.1% | | 50,801 | | Lab maj 14,239 | 55,568 | | Lab maj 4,350 |
| | | | | 28.0% | | | 7.8% |

**CHARLES CLARKE**, b Sept 21, 1950. Public affairs management consultant; ex-head of Neil Kinnock's private office. Ex-pres, NUS. Ed King's Coll, Cambridge (Pres of Union, 1971-72).
**BASHIR KHANBHAI**, b Sept 22, 1945. Consultant, industrial pharmacist and economist. Exec member, Norwich South C assoc.

Ed Boys GS, Ashby-de-la-Zouch; School of Pharmacy, London; Balliol Coll, Oxford.
**ANDREW AALDERS-DUNTHORNE**, b Nov 3, 1969. Trainee teacher. Norwich county cllr 1996- . Member, NUS; Inst of Supervision & Management. Ed Bowthorpe HS; Norwich City Coll.

| NOTTINGHAM EAST | | | | | | | Lab hold |
|---|---|---|---|---|---|---|---|
| Electorate % Turnout | | 65,581 | 60.6% | **1997** | 67,939 | 70.1% | **1992** |
| *Heppell, J | Lab | **24,755** | **62.3%** | +9.7% | **25,026** | **52.6%** | Lab |
| Raca, A J | C | 9,336 | 23.5% | -12.9% | 17,346 | 36.4% | C |
| Mulloy, K | LD | 4,008 | 10.1% | +2.3% | 3,695 | 7.8% | LD |
| Brown, B | Ref | 1,645 | 4.1% | | 667 | 1.4% | Grn |
| | | | | | 598 | 1.3% | Lib |
| | | | | | 283 | 0.6% | NLP |
| C to Lab swing 11.3% | | 39,744 | | Lab maj 15,419 | 47,615 | | Lab maj 7,680 |
| | | | | 38.8% | | | 16.1% |

**JOHN HEPPELL**, b Nov 3, 1948. Regained this seat for Lab 1992. Joint vice-chair, PLP transport cttee; chair, all-party home safety group; head injuries group; treas, breast cancer group. Nottinghamshire county cllr 1981-93. Formerly workshop supervisor, British Rail. Member, Co-op Party; Nottingham Anti-Apartheid. Ed Rutherford GS; SE Northumberland Tech Coll; Ashington Tech Coll.
**ANDREW RACA**, b April 20, 1964. Senior exec with firm of corporate stockbrokers. Contested Southwark and Bermondsey

1992. Chair, Southwark and Bermondsey C assoc, 1988-90. Northampton borough cllr 1991-95; member, Northants police consultative cttee, 1993-95. Exec with Barclays de Zoete Wedd 1986-91; former export manager in family firm promoting business in E Europe. Ed Gateway Grammar Sixth-Form Coll, Leicester; Bristol Univ.
**KEVIN MULLOY**, b May 19, 1953. Projects officer/IT manager in local gvt. Ex-chair, City of Nottingham LDs; member, Transport 2000. Ed Becket School, Nottingham; OU.

| NOTTINGHAM NORTH | | | | | **Lab hold** | | |
|---|---|---|---|---|---|---|---|
| Electorate % Turnout | | | 65,698 | 63.0% | **1997** | 69,494 | 75.0% | **1992** |
| *Allen, G | Lab | 27,203 | 65.7% | +10.0% | 29,052 | 55.7% | Lab |
| Shaw, Ms G | C | 8,402 | 20.3% | -14.8% | 18,309 | 35.1% | C |
| Oliver, Ms R | LD | 3,301 | 8.0% | -0.6% | 4,477 | 8.6% | LD |
| Neal, J | Ref | 1,858 | 4.5% | | 274 | 0.5% | NLP |
| Belfield, A | Soc | 637 | 1.5% | | | | |
| C to Lab swing 12.4% | | 41,401 | Lab maj 18,801 | | 52,112 | Lab maj 10,743 | |
| | | | 45.4% | | | 20.6% | |

**GRAHAM ALLEN**, b Jan 11, 1953. Became gvt whip, May 7, 1997. Elected 1987. Lab spokesman on transport 1995-97; on national heritage 1994-95; media 1994; home affairs 1992-94; social security 1991-92. Member, select cttees on procedure, 1990-91; members' interests 1987-90; PAC 1988-91. Chair, PLP Treasury and Civil Service cttee, 1990-91. Joint vice-chair, all-party cricket group. Regional, research and ed officer, GMB, 1986-87; nat co-ordinator, political funds campaign for trades union co-ordinating cttee, 1984-86; GLC officer 1983-84; Lab Party research office, 1978-83. Ed Forest Fields GS; City of London Poly; Leeds Univ.
**GILLIAN SHAW**, b April 1, 1965. Solicitor. Member, Assoc of Women Solicitors; Solicitors Family Law Assoc. External relations adviser, Guide Assoc. Ed Parkfields Comp; Sheffield and Nottingham Trent Univs.
**RACHEL OLIVER**, b Oct 13, 1964. Press and parliamentary officer. Mid Devon district cllr. Member, Assoc of LD lawyers. Ed Cheltenham Ladies' Coll; King's Coll, London.

| NOTTINGHAM SOUTH | | | | | **Lab hold** | | |
|---|---|---|---|---|---|---|---|
| Electorate % Turnout | | | 72,418 | 67.0% | **1997** | 72,796 | 74.2% | **1992** |
| *Simpson, A | Lab | 26,825 | 55.3% | +7.6% | 25,771 | 47.7% | Lab |
| Kirsch, B | C | 13,461 | 27.7% | -14.1% | 22,590 | 41.8% | C |
| Long, G D | LD | 6,265 | 12.9% | +2.9% | 5,408 | 10.0% | LD |
| Thompson, K | Ref | 1,523 | 3.1% | | 263 | 0.5% | NLP |
| Edwards, Ms S | Nat Dem | 446 | 0.9% | | | | |
| C to Lab swing 10.8% | | 48,520 | Lab maj 13,364 | | 54,032 | Lab maj 3,181 | |
| | | | 27.5% | | | 5.9% | |

**ALAN SIMPSON**, b Sept 20, 1948. Won seat 1992; contested it 1987. Sec, Campaign Group of Lab MPs; vice-chair, Central Region group of Lab MPs. Joint vice-chair, all-party Future of Europe Trust group; sec, warm homes group. Notts county cllr 1985-93. Ex-chair, WasteNotts Ltd, a Notts County Council waste disposal co. Information officer with Nottingham Racial Equality Council, 1979-92; community worker, Nottingham areas project, 1974-78. Unpaid member, board, Tribune Newspapers. Author of books and articles on racism and on housing policies. Member, Nupe. Ed Bootle GS; Nottingham Poly.
**BRIAN KIRSCH**, b April 23, 1951. Owner of commercial insurance business; ex-marketing director of a Lloyd's broking company. Chair, Braintree C assoc, 1993-96; Eastern area CPC 1990-94; member, National Union exec cttee, 1993- ; National Union policy cttee 1995- ; CPC national cttee 1989-94. Fellow, Chartered Insurance Inst. Ed Rickmansworth GS; Sweyne GS; Nottingham Univ.
**GARY LONG**, b May 7, 1957. Contested this seat 1992. Accountant in NHS. Ex-chair, Lib Party. Nottingham county cllr 1993- . Ed Fitzwilliam Comp, Raleigh; SE Essex Sixth-Form Coll; Nottingham Univ.

| NUNEATON | | | | | **Lab hold** | | |
|---|---|---|---|---|---|---|---|
| Electorate % Turnout | | | 72,032 | 74.3% | **1997** | 70,906 | 83.7% | **1992** |
| *Olner, B | Lab | 30,080 | 56.2% | +10.5% | 27,157 | 45.8% | Lab |
| Blunt, R | C | 16,540 | 30.9% | -12.1% | 25,526 | 43.0% | C |
| Cockings, R | LD | 4,732 | 8.8% | -2.4% | 6,671 | 11.2% | LD |
| English, R | Ref | 1,533 | 2.9% | | | | |
| Bray, D | Loc Ind | 390 | 0.7% | | | | |
| Everitt, P | UK Ind | 238 | 0.4% | | | | |
| C to Lab swing 11.3% | | 53,513 | Lab maj 13,540 | | 59,354 | Lab maj 1,631 | |
| | | | 25.3% | | | 2.7% | |

**BILL OLNER**, b May 9, 1942. Engineer with Rolls-Royce and ex-shop steward. Gained seat for Labour 1992. Member, environment select cttee, 1995-97. Joint vice-chair, PLP employment cttee; chair, all-party child abduction group, 1994- ; joint vice-chair, cable and satellite TV group; engineering development group; welfare of park home owners group. Member, exec cttee, CPA, 1995- . Nuneaton and Bedworth borough cllr 1972-92 (leader 1982-87); Mayor of Nuneaton and Bedford 1986-87. Co-founder, Mary Ann Evans Hospice, Nuneaton, and chair, hospice trustees. Ed Atherstone Sec Mod; N Warwickshire Tech Coll.
**RICHARD BLUNT**, b Jan 16, 1962. Owns company involved in property restoration and letting; ex-venture capitalist. Leicestershire county cllr 1991-93. Ed Ashby GS, Leicestershire; University Coll, London.
**RON COCKINGS**, b Dec 9, 1944. Management consultant. Stratford-upon-Avon district cllr. Ed Bushmet Mears Sec Mod; Middlesex Poly; Aston Univ.

| OCHIL | | 43.5% change | | | Lab win | | |
|---|---|---|---|---|---|---|---|
| Electorate % Turnout | | 56,572 | 77.4% | **1997** | 55,483 | 77.9% | **1992** |
| +O'Neill, M J | Lab | **19,707** | 45.0% | +1.9% | 18,620 | 43.1% | Lab |
| Reid, G | SNP | 15,055 | 34.4% | +8.3% | 11,270 | 26.1% | SNP |
| Hogarth, A | C | 6,383 | 14.6% | -9.4% | 10,367 | 24.0% | C |
| Watters, Mrs A | LD | 2,262 | 5.2% | -1.7% | 2,984 | 6.9% | LD |
| White, D | Ref | 210 | 0.5% | | | | |
| McDonald, I | D Nat | 104 | 0.2% | | | | |
| Sullivan, M | NLP | 65 | 0.1% | | | | |
| Lab to SNP notional swing 3.2% | | **43,786** | | Lab maj 4,652 | 43,241 | | Lab maj 7,350 |
| | | | | 10.6% | | | 17.0% |

**MARTIN O'NEILL**, b Jan 6, 1945. Ex-teacher. MP for Clackmannan 1983-97, and for Stirlingshire E and Clackmannan 1979-83. Chair, select cttee on trade and industry 1995-97. Lab spokesman on energy 1992-95; spokesman on defence and disarmament, 1984-92; on Scotland 1980-84. Ed Trinity Acad; Heriot-Watt Univ; Moray House Coll of Ed, Edinburgh.
**GEORGE REID**, b June 4, 1939. Broadcaster and journalist. MP for Stirlingshire E and Clackmannan 1974-79, when SNP spokesman

on constitutional affairs and housing, health and social services. Ed Tullibody School; Dollar Acad; St Andrews Univ.
**ALLAN HOGARTH**, b Aug 27, 1965. Research assistant to Michael Forsyth. Contested Glasgow Central 1989 by-election. Ed Largs Acad; Fettes Coll; Stirling Univ.
**ANN WATTERS**, b Sept 23, 1926. Retired science teacher. Contested Clackmannan 1992 and 1987. Fife UA cllr (group leader). Ed St Leonards, St Andrews; London Univ; Moray House Coll of Ed.

| OGMORE | | | | | Lab hold | | |
|---|---|---|---|---|---|---|---|
| Electorate % Turnout | | 52,078 | 73.1% | **1997** | 52,195 | 80.6% | **1992** |
| *Powell, Sir Raymond | Lab | **28,163** | 74.0% | +2.2% | 30,186 | 71.7% | Lab |
| Unwin, D | C | 3,716 | 9.8% | -5.4% | 6,359 | 15.1% | C |
| Williams, Ms K | LD | 3,510 | 9.2% | +2.4% | 2,868 | 6.8% | LD |
| Rogers, J | PC | 2,679 | 7.0% | +0.7% | 2,667 | 6.3% | PC |
| C to Lab swing 3.8% | | **38,068** | | Lab maj 24,447 | 42,080 | | Lab maj 23,827 |
| | | | | 64.2% | | | 56.6% |

**SIR RAYMOND POWELL**, b June 19, 1928. Elected 1979. Chair, accommodation and works cttee, 1991-97; member, finance and services cttee, 1992-97; selection cttee 1992-95; services cttee 1987-91 (chair of new building sub-cttee 1987-91). Chair, Welsh Lab Party, 1977-78; joint chair, fairs and showgrounds group. Ex-British Rail employee; shop manager; admin officer, Welsh Water Authority. Ed Pentre GS; Nat Council of Labour Colls; LSE.

**DAVID UNWIN**, b Jan 21, 1947. Manager. Contested Bridgend in 1992. Bridgend cllr 1984-96 (Mayor 1990-91). Ed Southgate GS.
**KIRSTY WILLIAMS**, b March 19, 1971. Design consultant. Ed St Michael's School; Manchester Univ; Missouri Univ.
**JOHN ROGERS**, b Feb, 1943. Teacher. Contested Alyn and Deeside in 1992 and 1987, East Flint in 1979 and Ebbw Vale in Feb 1974. Ed Rhyl GS; St Mary's Coll, Crosby; Leeds Univ.

| OLD BEXLEY & SIDCUP | | 38.6% change | | | | C win | |
|---|---|---|---|---|---|---|---|
| Electorate % Turnout | | 68,044 | 75.5% | **1997** | 68,877 | 80.8% | **1992** |
| +Heath, Sir Edward | C | **21,608** | 42.0% | -14.2% | 31,340 | 56.3% | C |
| Justham, R | Lab | 18,039 | 35.1% | +14.0% | 11,768 | 21.1% | Lab |
| King, I | LD | 8,284 | 16.1% | -4.8% | 11,642 | 20.9% | LD |
| Reading, B | Ref | 2,457 | 4.8% | | 780 | 1.4% | Alt C |
| Bullen, C R | UK Ind | 489 | 1.0% | | 156 | 0.3% | NLP |
| Tyndall, Ms V | BNP | 415 | 0.8% | | | | |
| Stephens, R | NLP | 99 | 0.2% | -0.1% | | | |
| C to Lab notional swing 14.1% | | **51,391** | | C maj 3,569 | 55,686 | | C maj 19,572 |
| | | | | 6.9% | | | 35.2% |

**SIR EDWARD HEATH,** b July 9, 1916. Father of the House of Commons since 1992. Leader of C Party 1965-75; Prime Minister 1970-74 and Leader of Opposition 1965-70, and from Feb 1974-75. Elected for this seat 1983; MP for Bexley Sidcup 1974-83, and for Bexley 1950-74. Sec of State for Industry, Trade and Regional Development, 1963-64; Lord Privy Seal 1960-63, being chief Foreign Office spokesman in Commons; led UK team in negotiations to join EEC; Labour Min, 1959-60; gvt chief whip 1955-59; dep gvt chief whip 1952-55; gvt whip 1951-52. Privy Counsellor 1955. Musician; hon member, London Symphony Orchestra, 1974- ; vice-pres, Bach Choir, since 1970. International

yachtsman and author. Member, Brandt Commission on Third World, 1977-83. Member, board of governors, Centre for Global Energy Studies. Ed Chatham House, Ramsgate; Balliol Coll, Oxford (pres of Union, 1939).
**RICHARD JUSTHAM**, b March 23, 1966. National negotiations asst with TSSA. Bexley cllr. Member, TSSA; GMB; Fabian Soc; Co-op Wholesale Soc. Ed Parklands Secondary; Erith Coll of Tech.
**IAIN KING**, b Jan 29, 1971. LD policy and communications officer; ex-researcher to LD N Ireland spokesman. Member, Charter 88; Amnesty. Ed Katharine Lady Berkeley's Comp, Gloucester; Pembroke Coll, Oxford.

| OLDHAM EAST & SADDLEWORTH | | | 59.3% change | | | | Lab win |
|---|---|---|---|---|---|---|---|
| Electorate % Turnout | | | 73,189 | 73.9% | **1997** | 74,061 | 77.3% | **1992** |
| **Woolas, P** | **Lab** | | **22,546** | **41.7%** | **+11.5%** | 20,271 | 35.4% | C |
| +Davies, C G | LD | | 19,157 | 35.4% | +1.0% | 19,712 | 34.4% | LD |
| Hudson, J | C | | 10,666 | 19.7% | -15.7% | 17,300 | 30.2% | Lab |
| Findlay, D | Ref | | 1,116 | 2.1% | | | | |
| Smith, J | Soc Lab | | 470 | 0.9% | | | | |
| Dalling, I | NLP | | 146 | 0.3% | | | | |
| **LD to Lab notional swing 5.2%** | | | **54,101** | | **Lab maj 3,389** 6.3% | **57,283** | | **C maj 559** 1.0% |

**PHIL WOOLAS**, b Dec 11, 1959. Contested Littleborough and Saddleworth by-election 1995. Director of communications, GMB; ex-TV producer. Adviser to Friends of John McCarthy campaign. Organised "Fat Cats" campaign against high pay in privatised industries, including "Cedric the pig", 1995. Member, Lancashire CCC. Ed Nelson GS; Nelson and Colne Coll; Manchester Univ.
**CHRIS DAVIES**, b July 7, 1954. Marketing and communications consultant. Gained Littleborough and Saddleworth for LDs 1995 by-election; contested it 1992 and 1987. Liverpool city cllr 1980-84; Oldham metropolitan borough cllr 1994- . Ed Cheadle Hulme School; Gonville and Caius Coll, Cambridge; Kent Univ.
**JOHN HUDSON**, b Dec 24, 1939. Contested Littleborough and Saddleworth by-election 1995. Manager. Ed St George's C of E School, Mossley; Ashton-under-Lyne GS.
*Details of 1995 Littleborough & Saddleworth by-election on*
*page 278*

| OLDHAM WEST & ROYTON | | | 88.8% change | | | | Lab win |
|---|---|---|---|---|---|---|---|
| Electorate % Turnout | | | 69,203 | 66.1% | **1997** | 70,300 | 75.0% | **1992** |
| +Meacher, M H | **Lab** | | **26,894** | **58.8%** | **+9.7%** | 25,887 | 49.1% | Lab |
| Lord, J | C | | 10,693 | 23.4% | -14.7% | 20,093 | 38.1% | C |
| Cohen, H | LD | | 5,434 | 11.9% | +0.4% | 6,031 | 11.4% | LD |
| Choudhury, G | Soc Lab | | 1,311 | 2.9% | | 722 | 1.4% | Other |
| Etherden, P | Ref | | 1,157 | 2.5% | | | | |
| Dalling, Mrs S | NLP | | 249 | 0.5% | | | | |
| **C to Lab notional swing 12.2%** | | | **45,738** | | **Lab maj 16,201** 35.4% | **52,733** | | **Lab maj 5,794** 11.0% |

**MICHAEL MEACHER**, b Nov 4, 1939. Became Min for Environment May 3, 1997. MP for Oldham W 1970-97; contested Colchester 1966. Member of Shadow Cabinet 1983-97. Lab spokesman on environmental protection 1996-97; on employment 1995-96; transport 1994-95; Citizen's Charter 1993-94; overseas development and co-operation 1992-93; social security 1989-92; employment 1987-89; health and social security 1983-87. Contested dep leadership of Lab Party after 1983 election. Under Sec for Trade 1976-79; Health and Social Security 1975-76; Industry 1974-75. Member, Labour NEC, 1983-88. Visiting Professor, Dept of Sociology, Surrey Univ, 1980-87. Ed Berkhamsted School; New College, Oxford; LSE.
**JONATHAN LORD**, b Sept 17, 1962. Director, Lintas Worlwide. Westminster city cllr 1994- (dep chief whip). Trustee of Shrewsbury School foundation. Ed Shrewsbury School; Kent School, US; Merton Coll, Oxford.
**HOWARD COHEN**, b March 29, 1964. Travel agent. Vice-chair, British Group of Liberal International. Ed Manchester Grammar.

| ORKNEY & SHETLAND | | | | | | | LD hold |
|---|---|---|---|---|---|---|---|
| Electorate % Turnout | | | 32,291 | 64.0% | **1997** | 31,472 | 65.5% | **1992** |
| *Wallace, J | LD | | **10,743** | **52.0%** | **+5.6%** | 9,575 | 46.4% | LD |
| Paton, J | Lab | | 3,775 | 18.3% | -1.6% | 4,542 | 22.0% | C |
| Ross, W | SNP | | 2,624 | 12.7% | +1.5% | 4,093 | 19.8% | Lab |
| Vere Anderson, H | C | | 2,527 | 12.2% | -9.8% | 2,301 | 11.2% | SNP |
| Adamson, F | Ref | | 820 | 4.0% | | 115 | 0.6% | NLP |
| Wharton, Ms C | NLP | | 116 | 0.6% | +0.0% | | | |
| Robertson, A | Ind | | 60 | 0.3% | | | | |
| **Lab to LD swing 3.6%** | | | **20,665** | | **LD maj 6,968** 33.7% | **20,626** | | **LD maj 5,033** 24.4% |

**JIM WALLACE**, b Aug 25, 1954. Non-practising advocate. Elected 1983; contested Dumfries 1979; South Scotland 1979 Euro elections. Leader of Scottish LDs 1992- . LD spokesman on Scotland, May 1997- ; on energy, fisheries, maritime transport 1994-97; Scottish affairs 1992-94; employment and training and LD Chief Whip 1988-92. Parly adviser to Inst of Chartered Accountants of Scotland and to Procurators Fiscal Soc. Ed Annan Acad, Dumfriesshire; Downing Coll, Cambridge; Edinburgh Univ.
**JAMES PATON**, b April 30, 1961. Consultant. Shetland Islands cllr 1986-88. Ex-admin asst with European Lab Party in Strasbourg.
**WILLIE ROSS**, b March 28, 1955. Civil engineer. Ed Elgin Acad; Inverness Tech Coll; Robert Gordon's Coll.
**HOPE VERE ANDERSON**, b May 10, 1958. Company director.Dir of Clan Anderson Soc and chieftain of Anderson of Wyesby. Ed Uddingston GS; Hermitage Acad, Helensburgh; Middle Tennessee State Univ.

| ORPINGTON | | 41.1% change | | | | | C win |
|---|---|---|---|---|---|---|---|
| Electorate % Turnout | | 78,749 | 76.4% | 1997 | 82,032 | 81.1% | 1992 |
| +Horam, J | C | 24,417 | 40.6% | -14.7% | 36,770 | 55.3% | C |
| Maines, C | LD | 21,465 | 35.7% | +7.4% | 18,840 | 28.3% | LD |
| Polydorou, Ms S | Lab | 10,753 | 17.9% | +3.1% | 9,837 | 14.8% | Lab |
| Clark, D | Ref | 2,316 | 3.8% | | 1,085 | 1.6% | Lib |
| Carver, J B | UK Ind | 526 | 0.9% | | | | |
| Almond, R | Lib | 494 | 0.8% | -0.8% | | | |
| Wilton, N | ProLife | 191 | 0.3% | | | | |
| C to LD notional swing 11.0% | | 60,162 | | C maj 2,952 | 66,532 | | C maj 17,930 |
| | | | | 4.9% | | | 27.0% |

JOHN HORAM, b March 7, 1939. Elected as C 1992; Lab MP for Gateshead W 1970-81, SDP MP for that seat 1981-83; contested Newcastle Central 1983. Under Sec for Health 1995-97; Public Services, Science and Citizen's Charter Min 1995. Joined C Party, Feb 1987. Ed Silcoates School; St Catharine's Coll, Cambridge.

CHRIS MAINES, b Jan 11, 1958. Credit controller. Contested Orpington 1992. Bromley cllr 1986- (group leader 1990- ). Ed Ramsden Boys' School; Plymouth Poly.
SUE POLYDOROU, b March 19, 1954. Bromley cllr 1990- (Lab group leader 1994- ). Ed Greenwich Park Secondary; NE London Poly.

| OXFORD EAST | | 12.5% change | | | | | Lab win |
|---|---|---|---|---|---|---|---|
| Electorate % Turnout | | 69,339 | 69.0% | 1997 | 68,309 | 73.0% | 1992 |
| +Smith, A | Lab | 27,205 | 56.8% | +6.6% | 25,031 | 50.2% | Lab |
| Djanogly, J | C | 10,540 | 22.0% | -11.5% | 16,718 | 33.5% | C |
| Kershaw, G | LD | 7,038 | 14.7% | +0.7% | 6,971 | 14.0% | LD |
| Young, M | Ref | 1,391 | 2.9% | | 959 | 1.9% | Grn |
| Simmons, C | Green | 975 | 2.0% | | 104 | 0.2% | NLP |
| Harper-Jones, W | Embryo | 318 | 0.7% | | 49 | 0.1% | Rev Comm |
| Gardner, Dr P B | UK Ind | 234 | 0.5% | | | | |
| Thompson, J | NLP | 108 | 0.2% | +0.0% | | | |
| Mylvaganam, P | Anti-maj | 68 | 0.1% | | | | |
| C to Lab notional swing 9.1% | | 47,877 | | Lab maj 16,665 | 49,832 | | Lab maj 8,313 |
| | | | | 34.8% | | | 16.7% |

ANDREW SMITH, b Feb 1, 1951. Became Minister for Employment and Disability Rights, May 4, 1997. Won this seat 1987; contested it 1983. Shadow Transport Sec 1996-97; Shadow Treasury Chief Sec 1994-96; spokesman on Treasury and economic affairs 1992-94; on higher and continuing education 1988-92. Oxford city cllr 1976-87. Chair, board of governors, Oxford Brookes Univ, 1987-93. Ed Reading GS; St John's Coll, Oxford.

JONATHAN DJANOGLY, b June 3, 1965. Solicitor with S.J. Berwin & Co; dir, Audio Brooks Direct Ltd. Westminster city cllr 1994- . Participated in formation of Nottingham City Tech Coll. Ed Univ Coll School, Oxford; Oxford Poly; Guildford Coll of Law.
GEORGE KERSHAW, b Dec 24, 1948. Part-time lecturer in mechanical engineering at Oxford CFE; ex-member, Oxford City Council. Ed Headington Secondary; Oxford Brookes Univ.

| OXFORD WEST & ABINGDON | | 24.1% change | | | | | LD win |
|---|---|---|---|---|---|---|---|
| Electorate % Turnout | | 79,329 | 77.1% | 1997 | 77,866 | 76.7% | 1992 |
| Harris, Dr E | LD | 26,268 | 42.9% | +7.1% | 27,630 | 46.2% | C |
| Harris, L | C | 19,983 | 32.7% | -13.6% | 21,408 | 35.8% | LD |
| Brown, Ms S | Lab | 12,361 | 20.2% | +4.1% | 9,642 | 16.1% | Lab |
| Eustace, Mrs G | Ref | 1,258 | 2.1% | | 686 | 1.1% | Grn |
| Woodin, Dr M | Green | 691 | 1.1% | | 202 | 0.3% | Lib |
| Buckton, R | UK Ind | 258 | 0.4% | | 102 | 0.2% | Anti-Fed |
| Hodge, Mrs L | ProLife | 238 | 0.4% | | 79 | 0.1% | NLP |
| Wilson, Ms A | NLP | 91 | 0.1% | +0.0% | | | |
| Rose, J | LGR | 48 | 0.1% | | | | |
| C to LD notional swing 10.3% | | 61,196 | | LD maj 6,285 | 59,749 | | C maj 6,222 |
| | | | | 10.3% | | | 10.4% |

EVAN HARRIS, b Oct 21, 1965. Doctor/public health registrar. Press officer for BMA. Active trade unionist, rep on BMA Council. Member, Stonewall; ASH; Green Democrats. Ed Blue Coat School, Liverpool; Wadham Coll, Oxford.
LAURENCE HARRIS, b Sept 6, 1965. Solicitor. Contested Stoke-on-

Trent N 1992. Treas, Tory Reform Group, 1994- ; nat vice-chair, YCs, 1988-90. Associate, Chartered Inst of Arbitrators. Ed Solihull School; Downing Coll, Cambridge; Coll of Law, London.
SUSAN BROWN, b Jan 19, 1969. Press officer. Ed St Philip's and St James' C of E; Oxford HS; LSE; Univ of Texas.

| PAISLEY NORTH | | 32.3% change | | | Lab win | | |
|---|---|---|---|---|---|---|---|
| Electorate % Turnout | | 49,725 | 68.6% | 1997 | 49,702 | 73.9% | 1992 |
| +Adams, Mrs I | Lab | 20,295 | 59.5% | +7.6% | 19,043 | 51.9% | Lab |
| Mackay, I | SNP | 7,481 | 21.9% | -1.6% | 8,629 | 23.5% | SNP |
| Brookes, K | C | 3,267 | 9.6% | -6.1% | 5,757 | 15.7% | C |
| Jelfs, A | LD | 2,365 | 6.9% | -0.8% | 2,828 | 7.7% | LD |
| Graham, R | ProLife | 531 | 1.6% | | 381 | 1.0% | Grn |
| Mathew, E | Ref | 196 | 0.6% | | 75 | 0.2% | NLP |
| SNP to Lab notional swing 4.6% | | 34,135 | Lab maj 12,814 | | 36,713 | Lab maj 10,414 | |
| | | | 37.5% | | | 28.4% | |

IRENE ADAMS, b Dec 27, 1947. Won this seat in 1990 by-election, succeeding her husband, Allen Adams. Member, Commons catering cttee, 1991-95; former vice-chair, children and family backbench cttee. Sec, Scottish housing and Scottish sports parly groups. Paisley town cllr 1970-74; Renfrew district cllr 1974-78; Strathclyde regional cllr 1979-84. Became JP in 1971 aged 23. Member, GMB. Ed Stanely Green HS, Paisley.
IAN MACKAY, b Feb 1, 1949. Chartered quantity surveyor. Renfrewshire cllr 1995- ; ex-Strathclyde cllr. Member,

Renfrewshire Valuation Joint Board. Ed Glasgow Coll of Building and Printing.
KENNETH BROOKES, b Aug 29, 1949. Managing director, Keltec Petroleum Services. Contested Falkirk E 1987. Grampian cllr 1986-90. Ed St Frederick School, Aberdeen; Aberdeen Coll; North of Scotland Coll of Agriculture.
ALAN JELFS, b March 8. 1961. Information technology officer. Office holder of Paisley LDs 1993-96; member, Scottish LD policy cttee. Member, Unison. Ed Prince Henry's HS, Evesham; Reading Univ.

| PAISLEY SOUTH | | 15.0% change | | | Lab win | | |
|---|---|---|---|---|---|---|---|
| Electorate % Turnout | | 54,040 | 69.1% | 1997 | 53,800 | 74.2% | 1992 |
| +McMaster, G | Lab Co-op | 21,482 | 57.5% | +6.7% | 20,268 | 50.8% | Lab Co-op |
| Martin, W | SNP | 8,732 | 23.4% | -1.2% | 9,799 | 24.6% | SNP |
| McCartin, Ms E | LD | 3,500 | 9.4% | +0.5% | 6,129 | 15.4% | C |
| Reid, R | C | 3,237 | 8.7% | -6.7% | 3,548 | 8.9% | LD |
| Lardner, J | Ref | 254 | 0.7% | | 150 | 0.4% | NLP |
| Clerkin, S | SSA | 146 | 0.4% | | | | |
| SNP to Lab notional swing 3.9% | | 37,351 | Lab Co-op maj 12,750 | | 39,894 | Lab Co-op maj 10,469 | |
| | | | 34.1% | | | 26.2% | |

GORDON McMASTER, b Feb 13, 1960. Won this seat in 1990 by-election. Lab spokesman on disabled people's rights 1995-97. Scottish Lab whip 1992-94. Member, procedure select cttee, 1991-95; standing orders cttee 1992-97. Former joint vice-chair, all-party gardening group. Chair, Co-op group of MPs. Renfrew district cllr 1984-91. Ex-lecturer in horticulture. Ran employment training project for mentally handicapped. Member, EIS; TGWU. Ed Johnstone HS; Woodburn House FE Centre; West of Scotland Agricultural Coll; Jordanhill Coll of Ed.

WILLIAM MARTIN, b July 3, 1943. Marketing manager, Reid Kerr Coll. Renfrewshire cllr 1988- . Member, EIS. Ed Camphill Senior Secondary; Paisley Coll of Tech.
EILEEN McCARTIN, b May 6, 1952. East Renrewshire council official. Contested Paisley N 1992, 1987, 1983. Renfrewshire cllr 1975- . Member, Nalgo (Unison). Ed Notre Dame HS; Queen's Coll; Jordanhill Coll; Coll of Tech, Glasgow.
ROBIN REID, b Dec 10, 1951. Self-employed accountant. Kyle and Carrick district cllr 1992-96. S Ayrshire cllr 1995- . Ed Ayr Acad; Strathclyde Univ.

| PENDLE | | | | | Lab hold | | |
|---|---|---|---|---|---|---|---|
| Electorate % Turnout | | 63,049 | 74.6% | 1997 | 64,063 | 82.9% | 1992 |
| *Prentice, G | Lab | 25,059 | 53.3% | +9.0% | 23,497 | 44.2% | Lab |
| Midgeley, J | C | 14,235 | 30.3% | -10.0% | 21,384 | 40.3% | C |
| Greaves, T | LD | 5,460 | 11.6% | -3.4% | 7,976 | 15.0% | LD |
| Hockney, D | Ref | 2,281 | 4.8% | | 263 | 0.5% | Anti-Fed |
| C to Lab swing 9.5% | | 47,035 | Lab maj 10,824 | | 53,120 | Lab maj 2,113 | |
| | | | 23.0% | | | 4.0% | |

GORDON PRENTICE, b Jan 28, 1951. Won this seat for Lab 1992. Member, select cttees on agriculture, 1996-97; deregulation 1995-97; joint select cttee and select cttee on statutory instruments. Chair, PLP environment cttee, 1994- ; vice-chair, NW group of Lab MPs, 1995- . Lab Party's local gvt officer in policy directorate, 1982-92; local gvt officer 1978-81. Member, TGWU. Hammersmith and Fulham cllr 1986-92. Ed George Heriot's School, Edinburgh; Glasgow Univ (pres of union 1972-73).

JOHN MIDGLEY, b July 12, 1968. Solicitor. Chair, Merseyside East and Wigan Euro constituency council 1992- . Member, Society of C Lawyers. Ed St Aldred's RC HS, Newton-le-Willows; Warwick Univ; Coll of Law, Chester.
TONY GREAVES, b July 27, 1942. Book dealer. Contested Nelson and Colne Oct and Feb 1974. Lancashire county cllr 1973- ; Pendle borough cllr 1973- . Ed Clegs, Wakefield; Hertford Coll, Oxford.

| PENRITH & THE BORDER | | 25.4% change | | | | | C win |
|---|---|---|---|---|---|---|---|
| Electorate % Turnout | | 66,496 | 73.6% | **1997** | 64,311 | 79.5% | **1992** |
| +Maclean, D | C | **23,300** | **47.6%** | **-11.1%** | 30,030 | 58.7% | C |
| Walker, G | LD | 13,067 | 26.7% | -2.3% | 14,848 | 29.0% | LD |
| Meling, Mrs M | Lab | 10,576 | 21.6% | +10.6% | 5,644 | 11.0% | Lab |
| Pope, C | Ref | 2,018 | 4.1% | | 522 | 1.0% | Grn |
| | | | | | 111 | 0.2% | NLP |
| C to LD notional swing 4.4% | | **48,961** | | **C maj 10,233** | **51,155** | | **C maj 15,182** |
| | | | | 20.9% | | | 29.7% |

**DAVID MACLEAN,** b May 16, 1953. Won seat in 1983 by-election caused by elevation to peerage of William Whitelaw; contested Inverness, Nairn & Lochaber 1983. Home Office Min, 1993-97, with responsibility for police and crime prevention; Environment Min 1992-93; Parly Sec, Min of Agric, Fisheries and Food, 1989-92; gvt whip 1988-89; asst gvt whip 1987-88. Privy Counsellor 1995. Member, agriculture select cttee, 1983-86. Ed Fortrose Acad; Aberdeen Univ.

**GEYVE WALKER,** b Oct 15, 1948. Solicitor. Contested this seat 1992. Ex-chair, Penrith branch LDs; founder member, Penrith Duty Solicitor scheme. Ed Arnold School, Blackpool; St Peter's Coll, Oxford.
**MARGARET MELING,** b Nov 16, 1945. Head of peripatetic English as a Second Language schools unit. Ed St Anthony's School, Sunderland; Bede College; OU; Durham and Newcastle Univs.

| PERTH | | 20.5% change | | | | | SNP win |
|---|---|---|---|---|---|---|---|
| Electorate % Turnout | | 60,313 | 73.9% | **1997** | 58,515 | 76.7% | **1992** |
| +Cunningham, Ms R | SNP | **16,209** | **36.4%** | **+2.0%** | 18,159 | 40.5% | C |
| Godfrey, J | C | 13,068 | 29.3% | -11.1% | 15,433 | 34.4% | SNP |
| Alexander, D | Lab | 11,036 | 24.8% | +11.6% | 5,922 | 13.2% | Lab |
| Brodie, C | LD | 3,583 | 8.0% | -3.9% | 5,366 | 12.0% | LD |
| MacAuley, R | Ref | 366 | 0.8% | | | | |
| Henderson, M M | UK Ind | 289 | 0.6% | | | | |
| C to SNP notional swing 6.6% | | **44,551** | | **SNP maj 3,141** | **44,880** | | **C maj 2,726** |
| | | | | 7.1% | | | 6.1% |

**ROSEANNA CUNNINGHAM,** b July 27, 1951. Won Perth & Kinross from C in 1995 by-election; contested that seat 1992. Non-practising advocate and former local authority solicitor. Party spokesman on environment, leisure and sport. Member, SNP nat exec. Councillor with Dumbarton District Council 1983-86; Glasgow District Council 1986-89. Called as advocate in Dec 1990. Ed Univ of Western Australia; Edinburgh and Aberdeen Univs.
**JOHN GODFREY,** b March 21, 1963. Investment banker. Contested Glasgow Maryhill 1992; Perth & Kinross by-election 1995, and

Strathclyde West in 1994 Euro elections. Ed Lochaber HS; Oriel Coll, Oxford.
**DOUGLAS ALEXANDER,** b Oct 26, 1967. Solicitor. Contested 1995 Perth & Kinross by-election. Ed Park Nairns HS, Erskine; Lester B. Pearson Coll, Vancouver; Edinburgh Univ; Univ of Pennsylvania.
**CHIC BRODIE,** b May 8, 1944. Director in IT industry. Contested Glasgow Garscadden 1992, NW Surrey 1987, Ayr 1983, Dundee E 1979, Oct 1974. Ed Morgan Acad, Dundee; St Andrews Univ.

*Details of 1995 Perth & Kinross by-election on page 278*

| PETERBOROUGH | | 43.7% change | | | | | Lab win |
|---|---|---|---|---|---|---|---|
| Electorate % Turnout | | 65,926 | 73.5% | **1997** | 71,804 | 74.5% | **1992** |
| Brinton, Ms H | Lab | **24,365** | **50.3%** | **+12.5%** | 26,455 | 49.5% | C |
| Foster, Mrs J R | C | 17,042 | 35.2% | -14.3% | 20,201 | 37.8% | Lab |
| Howarth, D | LD | 5,170 | 10.7% | +1.4% | 4,973 | 9.3% | LD |
| Slater, P | Ref | 924 | 1.9% | | 1,216 | 2.3% | Lib |
| Brettell, C | NLP | 334 | 0.7% | +0.4% | 243 | 0.5% | BNP |
| Linskey, J S | UK Ind | 317 | 0.7% | | 212 | 0.4% | PP |
| Goldspink, S | ProLife | 275 | 0.6% | | 168 | 0.3% | NLP |
| C to Lab notional swing 13.4% | | **48,427** | | **Lab maj 7,323** | **53,468** | | **C maj 6,254** |
| | | | | 15.1% | | | 11.7% |

**HELEN BRINTON,** b Dec 23, 1954. Teacher; examiner/moderator. Contested Faversham 1992. Member, Lab economic strategy group; SHA; World Disarmament Campaign; Rural Revival. Political campaigns co-ordinator, Kent and Faversham CLP, 1988-94. Ed Bristol Univ.
**JACQUELINE FOSTER,** b Dec 30, 1947. Contested Newham S 1992. BA cabin crew services and operations member since 1969. Chair, BA short-haul crew in Cabin Crew '89, the union for airline crews formed that year. C Party rep on nat commission, advisory body

to Gvt, 1993- . Member, C women's nat cttee and general purposes and advisory cttees. Former vice-chair, Twickenham C assoc. Ed Prescot Girls' GS.
**DAVID HOWARTH,** b Nov 10, 1958. University lecturer. Contested Cambridge 1992. Cambridge city cllr (joint council leader 1994-96, opposition leader 1990-94, 1996- ). Member, federal policy cttee, 1989- ; ex-chair, LD economic policy working group. Ed Queen Mary's GS, Walsall; Clare Coll, Cambridge; Yale.

| PLYMOUTH DEVONPORT | | 15.3% change | | | | Lab win |
|---|---|---|---|---|---|---|
| Electorate % Turnout | | 74,483 | 69.8% | **1997** | 75,564 | 78.4% | **1992** |
| +Jamieson, D | Lab | 31,629 | 60.9% | +13.8% | 27,877 | 47.0% | Lab |
| Johnson, A | C | 12,562 | 24.2% | -11.4% | 21,111 | 35.6% | C |
| Copus, R | LD | 5,570 | 10.7% | -2.5% | 7,830 | 13.2% | LD |
| Norsworthy, C | Ref | 1,486 | 2.9% | | 2,186 | 3.7% | Soc Dem |
| Farrand, Mrs C A | UK Ind | 478 | 0.9% | | 259 | 0.4% | NLP |
| Ebbs, S | Nat Dem | 238 | 0.5% | | | | |
| C to Lab notional swing 12.6% | | 51,963 | Lab maj 19,067 | 36.7% | 59,263 | Lab maj 6,766 | 11.4% |

**DAVID JAMIESON,** b May 18, 1947. Became gvt asst whip, May 7, 1997. Won this seat 1992; contested Plymouth Drake 1987; Birmingham Hall Green, Feb 1974. Member, select cttees on education and employment, 1996-97; education 1992-96. Sec, PLP defence cttee, 1995-97; joint vice-chair, PLP ed cttee, 1995-97. Parly consultant to Natural Gas Vehicles Assoc. Vice-principal, John Kitto Community Coll, Plymouth, 1981-92. Solihull borough cllr 1970-74. Member, NUT. Ed Tudor Grange GS, Solihull; St Peter's Coll, Birmingham; OU.

**ANTHONY JOHNSON,** b Aug 15, 1959. Company sec, JDC Builders (Devon) Ltd. Officer in Royal Corps of Signals, 1979-93; staff officer logistic operations and planning, Hong Kong, 1989-91; former Squadron Commander. Vice-chair, Ermington and Holbeton branch, S Hams C assoc, 1993-94. Ed Plymouth Coll Prep School; Sandhurst.
**RICHARD COPUS,** b Feb 25, 1952. Property sales manager. Founder member, SDP. Ex-chair, South Hams LDs. Ed Reeds School, Surrey; University Coll, Buckland.

| PLYMOUTH SUTTON | | 33.8% change | | | | Lab win |
|---|---|---|---|---|---|---|
| Electorate % Turnout | | 70,666 | 67.4% | **1997** | 66,738 | 79.1% | **1992** |
| Gilroy, Mrs L | Lab Co-op | 23,881 | 50.1% | | 22,049 | 41.8% | C |
| Crisp, A | C | 14,441 | 30.3% | -11.5% | 20,989 | 39.8% | Lab |
| Melia, S | LD | 6,613 | 13.9% | -2.6% | 8,673 | 16.4% | LD |
| Hanbury, T | Ref | 1,654 | 3.5% | | 1,076 | 2.0% | NLP |
| Bullock, R P | UK Ind | 499 | 1.0% | | | | |
| Kelway, K | Plymouth | 396 | 0.8% | | | | |
| Lyons, F | NLP | 168 | 0.4% | -1.7% | | | |
| No swing calculation | | 47,652 | Lab Co-op maj 9,440 | 19.8% | 52,787 | C maj 1,060 | 2.0% |

**LINDA GILROY,** b July 19, 1949. Head of South West Office, Gas Consumers' Council, since 1979. Contested Coventry NE 1992. Chair, Cornwall Lab Party, 1990-94; sec, Plymouth Drake CLP, 1987-88. Dep director, Age Concern Scotland, 1972-79. Member, Inst of Trading Standards Administration; Nalgo; Co-op Party. Ed Edinburgh and Strathclyde Univs.

**ANDREW CRISP,** b Oct 20, 1965. Accounts director with Pauffley PRL, specialising in corporate communication and design. Nat vice-chair, YCs, 1992-93. Ed Windsor Boys' School; Leicester Univ.
**STEVE MELIA,** b May 12, 1962. Economic development officer. Member, Devon Wildlife Trust. Ed Whitby County Comp, Ellesmere Port; Liverpool Univ.

| PONTEFRACT & CASTLEFORD | | | | | | Lab hold |
|---|---|---|---|---|---|---|
| Electorate % Turnout | | 62,350 | 66.4% | **1997** | 64,648 | 74.3% | **1992** |
| Cooper, Ms Y | Lab | 31,339 | 75.7% | +5.8% | 33,546 | 69.9% | Lab |
| Flook, A | C | 5,614 | 13.6% | -7.4% | 10,051 | 20.9% | C |
| Paxton, W | LD | 3,042 | 7.3% | -1.8% | 4,410 | 9.2% | LD |
| Wood, R | Ref | 1,401 | 3.4% | | | | |
| C to Lab swing 6.6% | | 41,396 | Lab maj 25,725 | 62.1% | 48,007 | Lab maj 23,495 | 48.9% |

**YVETTE COOPER,** b March 20, 1969. Economics correspondent for *The Independent*; has worked as aide to Gordon Brown and John Smith. Worked on Bill Clinton presidential campaign 1992. Member, NUJ; GMB. Ed Eggars Comp, Alton; Alton Sixth-Form Coll; Balliol Coll, Oxford; Harvard (Kennedy Scholar); LSE.
**ADRIAN FLOOK,** b July 9, 1963. Investment banker at Société Générale; director, Julian Flook & Co Ltd. Wandsworth cllr 1994- .

Chair, City of London C Forum; dep chair, Battersea C assoc. Member, C Way Forward; English Heritage. Ed King Edward's, Bath; Mansfield Coll, Oxford.
**WESLEY PAXTON,** b June 23, 1946. Freelance writer. Contested Glanford and Scunthorpe 1992. Member, Inst of Management. Ed Bilborough GS, Nottingham; Warwick and Hull Univs.

| PONTYPRIDD | | | | | | | Lab hold |
|---|---|---|---|---|---|---|---|
| Electorate % Turnout | | 64,185 | 71.4% | **1997** | 61,685 | 79.3% | **1992** |
| *Howells, Dr K | Lab | 29,290 | 63.9% | +3.1% | 29,722 | 60.8% | Lab |
| Howells, N | LD | 6,161 | 13.4% | +4.9% | 9,925 | 20.3% | C |
| Cowen, J | C | 5,910 | 12.9% | -7.4% | 4,448 | 9.1% | PC |
| Llewelyn, O | PC | 2,977 | 6.5% | -2.6% | 4,180 | 8.5% | LD |
| Wood, J | Ref | 874 | 1.9% | | 615 | 1.3% | Grn |
| Skelly, P | Soc Lab | 380 | 0.8% | | | | |
| Griffiths, R | Comm Brit | 178 | 0.4% | | | | |
| Moore, A | NLP | 85 | 0.2% | | | | |
| Lab to LD swing 0.9% | | 45,855 | | Lab maj 23,129 | 48,890 | | Lab maj 19,797 |
| | | | | 50.4% | | | 40.5% |

**KIM HOWELLS,** b Nov 27, 1946. Became Under Secretary for Education with responsibility for lifelong learning, May 5, 1997. Elected in 1989 by-election. Lab spokesman on trade and industry 1995-97, with responsibility for competition policy; spokesman on home affairs 1994-95; spokesman on overseas development 1993-94. Former Swansea Univ research officer, lecturer, coalminer, and steelworker. Full-time official of S Wales Area NUM 1982-89. Ed Mountain Ash GS; Hornsey Coll of Art; Cambridge Coll of Advanced Tech; Warwick Univ.

**NIGEL HOWELLS,** b Aug 11, 1966. Chartered accountant. Ed Fishguard County Sec; Univ Coll of Wales, Cardiff.
**JONATHAN COWEN,** b June 25, 1954. Barrister. Hertsmere cllr 1996- . Ed Kilburn HS; Worcester Coll, Oxford; London Univ; City Univ.
**OWAIN LLEWELYN,** b Oct 3, 1953. Senior chartered surveyor. Contested South Wales Central 1994 Euro elections. Taff Ely borough cllr 1991- . Ed Ysgol Dyffryn Ogwen; Univ Coll of Wales, Aberystwyth; Chester Law Coll; Glamorgan Univ.

| POOLE | 41.5% change | | | | | | C win |
|---|---|---|---|---|---|---|---|
| Electorate % Turnout | | 66,078 | 70.8% | **1997** | 64,285 | 78.4% | **1992** |
| Syms, R A R | C | 19,726 | 42.1% | -13.0% | 27,768 | 55.1% | C |
| Tetlow, A | LD | 14,428 | 30.8% | +1.5% | 14,787 | 29.3% | LD |
| White, H | Lab | 10,100 | 21.6% | +9.9% | 5,880 | 11.7% | Lab |
| Riddington, J | Ref | 1,932 | 4.1% | | 1,643 | 3.3% | Ind C |
| Tyler, P C | UK Ind | 487 | 1.0% | | 307 | 0.6% | NLP |
| Rosta, Mrs J | NLP | 137 | 0.3% | -0.3% | | | |
| C to LD notional swing 7.2% | | 46,810 | | C maj 5,298 | 50,385 | | C maj 12,981 |
| | | | | 11.3% | | | 25.8% |

**ROBERT SYMS,** b Aug 15, 1956. Managing director of building and plant hire group. Contested Walsall N 1992. Wiltshire county cllr 1985- ; North Wiltshire district cllr 1983-87 (group leader 1984-87). Member, Wessex RHA, 1988-90. Founder director, N Wilts enterprise agency, 1986-90. Officer of N Wilts C assoc 1982-88; member, Wessex area provincial council, 1982-90. Member, Bow Group; Atlantic Council; Freedom Assoc. Ed Colston's, Bristol.

**ALAN TETLOW,** b Nov 9, 1947. Dental surgeon. Dorset county cllr (dep leader). Ed Bolton School; Dundee Univ.
**HAYDN WHITE,** b June 27, 1940. Head teacher. Contested this seat 1992; Dorset East and Hampshire West in 1989 Euro elections; Somerset N twice in 1974; Dorset N 1970. Town cllr; Mayor of Blandford Forum 1988-89. Member, NUT. Ed Maes-y-Dderwen Comp, Swansea Valley; Univ Coll of Wales, Aberystwyth.

| POPLAR & CANNING TOWN | | 66.0% change | | | | | Lab win |
|---|---|---|---|---|---|---|---|
| Electorate % Turnout | | 67,172 | 58.5% | **1997** | 62,190 | 65.7% | **1992** |
| Fitzpatrick, J | Lab | 24,807 | 63.2% | +11.9% | 20,935 | 51.2% | Lab |
| Steinberg, B | C | 5,892 | 15.0% | -10.7% | 10,517 | 25.7% | C |
| Ludlow, Ms J | LD | 4,072 | 10.4% | -9.2% | 7,986 | 19.5% | LD |
| Tyndall, J | BNP | 2,849 | 7.3% | | 1,417 | 3.5% | Other |
| Hare, I | Ref | 1,091 | 2.8% | | | | |
| Joseph, Ms J | Soc Lab | 557 | 1.4% | | | | |
| C to Lab notional swing 11.3% | | 39,268 | | Lab maj 18,915 | 40,855 | | Lab maj 10,418 |
| | | | | 48.2% | | | 25.5% |

**JIM FITZPATRICK,** b April 4, 1952. Firefighter. Chair, Greater London Lab Party, 1991- . Member, Amnesty; Greenpeace. London rep, FBU. Ed Holyrood Senior School, Glasgow.
**BENE'T STEINBERG,** b Sept 4, 1957. Senior counsellor, Chelgate Ltd. PA to David Amess, MP, and to former MPs. Founder member, Centre for a New Europe, and of Tory Green Initiative. Member, IoD. Ed Bedford School; Lancaster Univ.

**JANET LUDLOW,** b March 10, 1950. Tour guide, assessor to National Lottery Charities Board. Tower Hamlets cllr 1982- (opposition leader 1994- ; Mayor 1990-91). Ed Ensham County School for Girls; Swedish Inst Fellowship; Chelsea School of Art; Norwich School of Art; St Martin's School of Art.

| PORTSMOUTH NORTH | | 18.9% change | | | | | Lab win |
|---|---|---|---|---|---|---|---|
| Electorate % Turnout | | 64,539 | 70.1% | **1997** | 65,614 | 76.2% | **1992** |
| **Rapson, S** | Lab | **21,339** | **47.1%** | +13.9% | **25,368** | **50.7%** | C |
| +Griffiths, P | C | 17,016 | 37.6% | -13.1% | 16,610 | 33.2% | Lab |
| Sollitt, S | LD | 4,788 | 10.6% | -4.5% | 7,529 | 15.1% | LD |
| Evelegh, S | Ref | 1,757 | 3.9% | | 511 | 1.0% | Grn |
| Coe, P J | UK Ind | 298 | 0.7% | | | | |
| Bex, C | Wessex Reg | 72 | 0.2% | | | | |
| **C to Lab notional swing 13.5%** | | **45,270** | | Lab maj 4,323 | **50,018** | | C maj 8,758 |
| | | | | 9.5% | | | 17.5% |

**SYDNEY RAPSON,** b April 17, 1942. Aircraft fitter. Contested Portsmouth S 1992. Lord Mayor of Portsmouth 1990-91; Portsmouth city cllr 1971-78 and since 1979 (Lab group leader); Hampshire county cllr 1973-77. Shop steward, AEU convener since 1979. Ed Southsea Mod; Paulsgrove Mod.
**PETER GRIFFITHS,** b May 24, 1928. Elected for this seat 1979; MP for Smethwick 1964-66; contested Portsmouth N Feb 1974, and Smethwick 1959. Member, select cttee on members' interests,

1983-85. Ex-headmaster and senior lecturer in economic history. Smethwick borough cllr 1955-64 (leader, C group, 1960-64) and alderman 1964-66. Former pres, YCs. Fulbright exchange professor of economics, Pierce Coll, Los Angeles, 1968-69. Ed West Bromwich GS; City of Leeds Training Coll; London and Birmingham Univs.
**STEVE SOLLITT,** b Feb 23, 1970. Finance officer. Eastleigh district cllr 1994- . Ed Crestwood School; Barton Peveril Sixth-Form Coll.

| PORTSMOUTH SOUTH | | | | | | | LD gain |
|---|---|---|---|---|---|---|---|
| Electorate % Turnout | | 80,514 | 64.2% | **1997** | 77,645 | 69.1% | **1992** |
| **Hancock, M** | LD | **20,421** | **39.5%** | -2.5% | **22,798** | **42.5%** | C |
| *Martin, D | C | 16,094 | 31.1% | -11.4% | 22,556 | 42.0% | LD |
| Burnett, A | Lab | 13,086 | 25.3% | +10.7% | 7,857 | 14.6% | Lab |
| Trim, C | Ref | 1,629 | 3.2% | | 349 | 0.7% | Grn |
| Thompson, J | Lib | 184 | 0.4% | | 91 | 0.2% | NLP |
| Evans, Mrs J I | UK Ind | 141 | 0.3% | | | | |
| Treend, W | NLP | 140 | 0.3% | +0.1% | | | |
| **C to LD swing 4.4%** | | **51,695** | | LD maj 4,327 | **53,651** | | C maj 242 |
| | | | | 8.4% | | | 0.5% |

**MICHAEL HANCOCK,** b April 9, 1946. SDP MP for this seat from 1984 by-election to 1987; contested seat for SDP 1983 and 1987 and LD 1992; contested Wight and Hampshire South in 1994 Euro elections. Portsmouth city cllr 1970- (group leader 1989- ); Hampshire county cllr 1973- (council leader 1993- ; opposition leader 1977-81, 1989-93). District officer, Royal Soc for Mentally Handicapped Children and Adults, 1989- ; chair, Southern branch, NSPCC, 1989- . Director drug rehabilitation unit, Alpha drug clinic, Droxford, 1971- . Ed Copnor and Portsea School.

**DAVID MARTIN,** b Feb 5, 1945. Barrister and farmer. Regained this seat for C in 1987; contested Yeovil 1983. PPS to Douglas Hurd, Foreign Secretary, and to Alan Clark, Defence Min. Joint vice-capt, parly golfing soc. Teignbridge district cllr 1979-83. Ed Norwood School, Exeter; Kelly Coll, Tavistock; Fitzwilliam Coll, Cambridge.
**ALAN BURNETT,** b Sept 30, 1940. Lecturer. Contested Portsmouth N 1992; Isle of Wight and Hampshire East in 1989 Euro elections. Portsmouth city cllr 1986- . Ed Glenalmond School, Perthshire; Durham Univ; Indiana Univ; Southampton Univ.

| PRESELI PEMBROKESHIRE | | 62.7% change | | | | | Lab win |
|---|---|---|---|---|---|---|---|
| Electorate % Turnout | | 54,088 | 78.4% | **1997** | 54,295 | 80.5% | **1992** |
| **Lawrence, Mrs J** | Lab | **20,477** | **48.3%** | +10.2% | **17,270** | **39.5%** | C |
| Buckland, R J | C | 11,741 | 27.7% | -11.8% | 16,667 | 38.1% | Lab |
| Clarke, J | LD | 5,527 | 13.0% | +0.7% | 5,379 | 12.3% | LD |
| Lloyd Jones, A | PC | 2,683 | 6.3% | -2.3% | 3,773 | 8.6% | PC |
| Berry, D | Ref | 1,574 | 3.7% | | 642 | 1.5% | Other |
| Scott Cato, Ms M | Green | 401 | 0.9% | | | | |
| **C to Lab notional swing 11.0%** | | **42,403** | | Lab maj 8,736 | **43,731** | | C maj 603 |
| | | | | 20.6% | | | 1.4% |

**JACKIE LAWRENCE,** b Aug 9, 1948. Political adviser. Pembrokeshire cllr (leader, Lab group); member, police authority. Member, Christian Socialist Movement. Ed Upperthorpe School and Coll, Darlington.
**ROBERT BUCKLAND,** b Sept 22, 1968. Barrister. Dyfed county cllr 1993- . Chair, Mid and West Wales Euro council 1993- ; Wales area exec cttee member 1993- . Chair, Llanelli YCs, 1986-87; Former co-

organiser, Llanelli/Gower YC anti-drug misuse campaign. Ed St Michael's School, Bryn, Llanelli; Hatfield Coll, Durham.
**JEFFREY CLARKE,** b March 19, 1962. Barrister. Welsh LD spokesman on justice and home affairs. Ed Keele Univ.
**ALUN LLOYD JONES,** b June 4, 1946. Former pharmaceutical rep. Contested Bridgend 1992. Member, nat council, PC. Ceredigion district cllr 1991- . Ed Ardwyn GS, Aberystwyth.

| PRESTON | 30.5% change | | | | | | Lab win |
|---|---|---|---|---|---|---|---|
| Electorate % Turnout | | 72,933 | 65.9% | **1997** | 72,856 | 75.8% | **1992** |
| +Wise, Mrs A | Lab | 29,220 | 60.8% | +7.7% | 29,342 | 53.1% | Lab |
| Gray, P | C | 10,540 | 21.9% | -10.4% | 17,876 | 32.4% | C |
| Chadwick, B | LD | 7,045 | 14.7% | +0.8% | 7,644 | 13.8% | LD |
| Porter, J | Ref | 924 | 1.9% | | 376 | 0.7% | NLP |
| Ashforth, J | NLP | 345 | 0.7% | +0.0% | | | |
| C to Lab notional swing 9.0% | | 48,074 | Lab maj 18,680 | | 55,238 | Lab maj 11,466 | |
| | | | 38.9% | | | 20.8% | |

**AUDREY WISE,** b Jan 4, 1935. Elected for this seat 1987; MP for Coventry SW, Feb 1974-79; contested Woolwich 1983. Member, select cttees on health, 1991- ; social services 1987-90. Chair, PLP health and personal social services cttee, 1989- , and PLP health and social security cttee 1987-89; vice-chair, PLP social security cttee, 1989-90. Member, Lab Party NEC, 1982-87. Pres, Usdaw, 1991- . Ex-shorthand typist. Ed Rutherford HS.

**PAUL GRAY,** b April 21, 1966. New business director at marketing and PR consultancy; with David Farquar PR, Petworth, 1992, and Owen Advertising Ltd, Havant. Ed Ifield Comp, Crawley.
**BILL CHADWICK,** b July 1, 1954. Head of staff development, Equal Opportunities Commission. Contested this seat 1992. Preston borough cllr 1990- ; Lancs county cllr 1985- . Ed St Cuthbert Mayne HS; Newcastle and Manchester Metropolitan Univs.

| PUDSEY | | | | | | | Lab gain |
|---|---|---|---|---|---|---|---|
| Electorate % Turnout | | 70,922 | 74.4% | **1997** | 70,847 | 81.0% | **1992** |
| Truswell, P | Lab | 25,370 | 48.1% | +19.0% | 25,067 | 43.7% | C |
| Bone, P W | C | 19,163 | 36.3% | -7.3% | 16,695 | 29.1% | Lab |
| Brown, Dr J | LD | 7,375 | 14.0% | -12.4% | 15,153 | 26.4% | LD |
| Crabtree, D | Ref | 823 | 1.6% | | 466 | 0.8% | Grn |
| C to Lab swing 13.2% | | 52,731 | Lab maj 6,207 | | 57,381 | C maj 8,372 | |
| | | | 11.8% | | | 14.6% | |

**PAUL TRUSWELL,** b Nov 17, 1955. Local gvt officer, Wakefield Metropolitan District Council. Leeds city cllr 1982- ; member, Leeds HA, 1982-90; community health council 1990-92; family health services authority 1992-96. Ex-chair, Leeds Green Strategy group. Yorkshire regional press officer, 1992 gen election. Member, Unison; NUJ; Co-op Party; SHA; Liberty; SERA. Ed Leeds Univ.

**PETER BONE,** b Oct 19, 1952. Chartered accountant; managing director of international travel company with offices in UK and N America. Contested Islwyn 1992 and Mid and West Wales in 1994 Euro elections. Southend borough cllr 1977-86. Ex-member, All Wales C policy group. Ed Westcliff-on-Sea GS.
**JONATHAN BROWN,** b March 12, 1945. Businessman and dentist. Expert witness in dental affairs. Ed Leeds GS; Leeds Univ.

| PUTNEY | | | | | | | Lab gain |
|---|---|---|---|---|---|---|---|
| Electorate % Turnout | | 60,176 | 73.1% | **1997** | 61,914 | 77.9% | **1992** |
| Colman, A | Lab | 20,084 | 45.7% | +9.0% | 25,188 | 52.2% | C |
| *Mellor, D | C | 17,108 | 38.9% | -13.3% | 17,662 | 36.6% | Lab |
| Pyne, R D | LD | 4,739 | 10.8% | +1.2% | 4,636 | 9.6% | LD |
| Goldsmith, Sir James | Ref | 1,518 | 3.5% | | 618 | 1.3% | Grn |
| Jamieson, W B | UK Ind | 233 | 0.5% | | 139 | 0.3% | NLP |
| Beige, L | Stan | 101 | 0.2% | | | | |
| Yardley, M | Spts All | 90 | 0.2% | | | | |
| Small, J | NLP | 66 | 0.2% | -0.1% | | | |
| Poole, Ms A | Beaut | 49 | 0.1% | | | | |
| Vanbraam, D | Ren Dem | 7 | 0.0% | | | | |
| C to Lab swing 11.2% | | 43,995 | Lab maj 2,976 | | 48,243 | C maj 7,526 | |
| | | | 6.8% | | | 15.6% | |

**ANTHONY COLMAN,** b July 24, 1943. Ex-director, Burton Group plc. Leader, Merton Borough Council. Ed Paston GS, North Walsham; Magdalene Coll, Cambridge.
**DAVID MELLOR,** b March 12, 1949. QC (not practising), journalist, broadcaster and businessman. Won seat 1979; contested West Bromwich E in Oct 1974. National Heritage Sec 1992; Treasury Chief Sec 1990-92; Min for the Arts and for Civil Service 1990; Home Office Min 1989-90; Health Min 1988-89; Foreign and Commonwealth Office Min 1987-88; Home Office Min 1986-87; Under Sec, Home Office, 1983-86; Energy, 1981-83. Privy Counsellor 1990. Presenter, BBC *Six-O-Six* on Radio 5 Live.

Adviser to BAe, Racal Tacticom Ltd, Shorts and associated companies, and Vosper Thorneycroft. Has consultancies with a variety of British and overseas companies. Fellow, Zoological Soc, 1981. Ed Swanage GS; Christ's Coll, Cambridge.
**RUSSELL PYNE,** b July 11, 1967. Barrister. Member, Amnesty; Greenpeace. Ed Merchant Taylors', Northwood; Bristol Univ.
**SIR JAMES GOLDSMITH,** b Feb 26, 1933. Chief exec, Goldsmith Foundation, 1991- , and international businessman. Founder of Referendum Party. MEP for France EDN (l'autre Europe) 1994- (pres, L'Europe des Nations parly group, 1994- ). Knighted 1976; Chevalier, Légion d'Honneur, 1978. Ed Eton.

| RAYLEIGH | 18.5% change | | | | | | C win |
|---|---|---|---|---|---|---|---|
| Electorate % Turnout | | 68,737 | 74.7% | **1997** | 67,206 | 80.5% | **1992** |
| +Clark, Dr M | C | **25,516** | 49.7% | -11.4% | **33,065** | 61.1% | C |
| Ellis, R | Lab | 14,832 | 28.9% | +14.1% | 11,868 | 21.9% | LD |
| Cumberland, S | LD | 10,137 | 19.8% | -2.2% | 8,032 | 14.8% | Lab |
| Farmer, A | Lib | 829 | 1.6% | | 1,152 | 2.1% | Other |
| C to Lab notional swing 12.7% | | 51,314 | | C maj **10,684** 20.8% | 54,117 | | C maj **21,197** 39.2% |

**MICHAEL CLARK,** b Aug 8, 1935. Industrial chemist/management consultant. MP for Rochford 1983-97; contested Ilkeston 1979. Chair, energy select cttee, 1989-92; trade and industry cttee 1992-94. Member, 1987- , and chair, 1990-93, exec cttee, British group, IPU; chair, all-party British-Russia parly group, 1994- ; Venezuelan group 1995- . Parly adviser to Royal Soc of Chemistry; British Chemical Engineering Contractors Assoc; British Gas plc. Dir, MAT Group Ltd, international transport co. Trustee, the Butten Trust. Ed King Edward VI GS, East Retford; King's Coll, London; Univ of Minnesota; St John's Coll, Cambridge.

**RAYMOND ELLIS,** b March 16, 1958. National asst sec, Communication Workers' Union. Member, Full Employment Forum; Fabian Soc; Anti-Nazi League; Campaign for Electoral Reform. Ed Greensward School, Hockley; SE Essex Sixth-Form Coll, Benfleet.
**SID CUMBERLAND,** b Jan 29, 1949. Primary school teacher (deputy head). Rochford district cllr 1993- (group sec). Member, ATL. Ed Westcliffe HS, Essex; Ushaw Coll, Durham; Gregorian Univ, Rome; Keble Coll, Oxford.

| READING EAST | 66.8% change | | | | | | Lab win |
|---|---|---|---|---|---|---|---|
| Electorate % Turnout | | 71,586 | 70.2% | **1997** | 69,817 | 74.9% | **1992** |
| Griffiths, Ms J | Lab | **21,461** | 42.7% | +13.8% | **25,699** | 49.1% | C |
| +Watts, J A | C | 17,666 | 35.2% | -13.9% | 15,115 | 28.9% | Lab |
| Samuel, S | LD | 9,307 | 18.5% | -1.9% | 10,684 | 20.4% | LD |
| Harmer, D | Ref | 1,042 | 2.1% | | 814 | 1.6% | Grn |
| Buckley, J | NLP | 254 | 0.5% | | | | |
| Thornton, Miss A L | UK Ind | 252 | 0.5% | | | | |
| Packer, Ms B | BNP | 238 | 0.5% | | | | |
| C to Lab notional swing 13.9% | | 50,220 | | Lab maj **3,795** 7.6% | 52,312 | | C maj **10,584** 20.2% |

**JANE GRIFFITHS,** b April 17, 1954. BBC editor. Reading borough cllr 1989- . Member, Transport 2000; NUJ. Ed Cedars GS, Leighton Buzzard; Durham Univ.
**JOHN WATTS,** b April 19, 1947. MP for Slough 1983-97. Railways and Roads Min 1994-97. Chair, Treasury and Civil Service select cttee, 1992-94 (member 1986-94). Joint vice-chair, C backbench environment cttee, 1987-88. PPS to Ian Gow, when Housing and Construction Min, 1984-85, and Treasury Min, 1985. Hillingdon cllr 1973-86. Chartered accountant. Dir, Kenton & Middlesex Building Society, 1988-94; Global Satellite Communications plc and Global Satellite Communications (Scotland) plc, 1991-94. Ed Bishopshalt School, Hillingdon; Gonville and Caius Coll, Cambridge (chair, univ C assoc, 1968).
**SAM SAMUEL,** b April 4, 1947. Computer sales manager. Berkshire county cllr 1989- (vice-chair); member, Thames Valley police authority. Founder, Thames Valley Economic Partnership. Ed Thetford GS, Norfolk; Forres Acad, Scotland; RAF No 1 Radio School; Portsmouth Coll of Tech.

| READING WEST | 18.9% change | | | | | | Lab win |
|---|---|---|---|---|---|---|---|
| Electorate % Turnout | | 69,073 | 70.1% | **1997** | 68,848 | 77.3% | **1992** |
| Salter, M | Lab | **21,841** | 45.1% | +16.5% | **27,888** | 52.4% | C |
| Bennett, N J | C | 18,844 | 38.9% | -13.4% | 15,256 | 28.7% | Lab |
| Tomlin, Mrs D | LD | 6,153 | 12.7% | -5.1% | 9,461 | 17.8% | LD |
| Brown, S | Ref | 976 | 2.0% | | 638 | 1.2% | Grn |
| Dell, I | BNP | 320 | 0.7% | | | | |
| Black, D M | UK Ind | 255 | 0.5% | | | | |
| C to Lab notional swing 15.0% | | 48,389 | | Lab maj **2,997** 6.2% | 53,243 | | C maj **12,632** 23.7% |

**MARTIN SALTER,** b April 19, 1954. Regional manager, Co-op Services. Co-ordinator, Reading centre for unemployed. Member, Co-op Party; Greenpeace. Ed Hampton GS; Sussex Univ.
**NICHOLAS BENNETT,** b May 7, 1949. MP for Pembroke 1987-92; contested Hackney Central 1979. Welsh Under Sec 1990-92; PPS to Transport Min 1990. Public affairs adviser to Price Waterhouse 1993- ; managing partner, Sussex Associates, public affairs and education consultants, 1993- . Joint vice-chair, C backbench party organisation cttee, 1989-90; joint sec, C transport cttee, 1987-88; Lewisham cllr 1974-82; co-opted member, ILEA, 1978-81. Education officer with Havering Council 1985-87; teacher and lecturer 1976-85. Ed Sedgehill School, London; Southwark and Walbrook CFEs; N London Poly; London and Sussex Univs.
**DEE TOMLIN,** b March 13, 1962. Musician. Berkshire county cllr (group press officer). Ed Faraday HS, Acton; London Coll of Music.

| REDCAR | 16.4% change | | | | | Lab win |
|---|---|---|---|---|---|---|
| Electorate % Turnout | | 68,965 | 71.0% | **1997** | 73,753 | 79.0% | **1992** |
| +Mowlam, Dr M | Lab | 32,972 | 67.3% | +13.8% | 31,237 | 53.6% | Lab |
| Isaacs, A | C | 11,308 | 23.1% | -10.9% | 19,823 | 34.0% | C |
| Benbow, Ms J | LD | 4,679 | 9.6% | -2.9% | 7,241 | 12.4% | LD |
| C to Lab notional swing 12.3% | | 48,959 | | Lab maj 21,664 44.2% | 58,301 | | Lab maj 11,414 19.6% |

**MARJORIE (MO) MOWLAM,** b Sept 18, 1949. Became Northern Ireland Secretary, May 3, 1997. Shadow N Ireland Sec 1994-97. Elected 1987. Elected to Shadow Cabinet 1992; Shadow National Heritage Sec 1993-94; spokeswoman on Citizen's Charter and women 1992-93; on City affairs 1989-92; on N Ireland 1988-89. Elected to Labour NEC in 1995. Member, PAC, 1987-88. Administrative officer at Northern Coll, Barnsley, 1984-87. Lecturer, Florida State Univ, 1977-78; Newcastle Univ, 1979-83. Ed Coundon Court Comp, Coventry; Durham Univ; Iowa Univ.

**ANDREW ISAACS,** b 1961. Senior partner in firm of solicitors. Campaign manager in 1992 for Dr Robert Spink, ex-MP for Castle Point. Founder, women's refuge cttee for Bournemouth. Ed Doncaster GS; Nottingham Univ.
**JOYCE BENBOW,** b Sept 9, 1930. Former lecturer/charity worker (dir, Coaltham House charity); manager of fashion service for the disabled 1985-91. Redcar and Cleveland borough cllr 1996- . Ed Bromley Art School; Teesside Coll of Art; Teesside Poly.

| REDDITCH | 35.7% change | | | | | Lab win |
|---|---|---|---|---|---|---|
| Electorate % Turnout | | 60,841 | 73.5% | **1997** | 60,193 | 80.9% | **1992** |
| Smith, Ms J J | Lab | 22,280 | 49.8% | +9.4% | 22,930 | 47.1% | C |
| McIntyre, Miss A | C | 16,155 | 36.1% | -11.0% | 19,643 | 40.4% | Lab |
| Hall, M | LD | 4,935 | 11.0% | -0.7% | 5,716 | 11.7% | LD |
| Cox, R | Ref | 1,151 | 2.6% | | 384 | 0.8% | Other |
| Davis, P | NLP | 227 | 0.5% | | | | |
| C to Lab notional swing 10.2% | | 44,748 | | Lab maj 6,125 13.7% | 48,673 | | C maj 3,287 6.8% |

**JACQUI SMITH,** b Nov 3, 1962. Teacher. Contested Mid-Worcestershire 1992. Redditch borough cllr 1991- . Head of economics and business studies at local comprehensive. Board member, Redditch and Bromsgrove Business Link; chair, Redditch education forum. Member, NUT; SEA; Anti-Apartheid Movement. Ed Dyson Perrins HS, Malvern; Hertford Coll, Oxford; Worcester Coll of HE.

**ANTHEA McINTYRE,** b June 29, 1954. Management consultant specialising in business intelligence systems. Contested Warley W 1983. Member of John Major's election staff 1992. Chair, W Midlands CPC, 1994- . Chair, Hereford C assoc, 1983-85. Trustee, Community Development Foundation, 1983-85. Member, BBC Midlands Advisory Council, 1981-84. Ed Claremont, Esher.
**MALCOLM HALL,** b July 30, 1947. Leisure and tourism lecturer. Redditch borough cllr, 1994-. Ed Tinklers Farm, Northfield, Birmingham; Wolverhampton Poly.

| REGENT'S PARK & KENSINGTON NORTH | | 54.8% change | | | | Lab win |
|---|---|---|---|---|---|---|
| Electorate % Turnout | | 73,752 | 64.2% | **1997** | 69,959 | 74.9% | **1992** |
| Buck, Ms K | Lab | 28,367 | 59.9% | +11.6% | 25,317 | 48.3% | Lab |
| McGuinness, P | C | 13,710 | 29.0% | -12.1% | 21,503 | 41.1% | C |
| Gasson, Miss E | LD | 4,041 | 8.5% | +0.6% | 4,163 | 7.9% | LD |
| Dangoor, Ms S | Ref | 867 | 1.8% | | 1,385 | 2.6% | Other |
| Hinde, J | NLP | 192 | 0.4% | | | | |
| Sadowitz, Ms D | Dream | 167 | 0.4% | | | | |
| C to Lab notional swing 11.8% | | 47,344 | | Lab maj 14,657 31.0% | 52,368 | | Lab maj 3,814 7.3% |

**KAREN BUCK,** b Aug 30, 1958. Lab Party campaign strategy co-ordinator, Millbank media centre, and acting Lab director of communications 1995. Westminster city cllr 1990- . Chair, Westminster Objectors Trust. Board member, inner city regeneration project and EC urban funding project. Chair, Westminster North CLP 1988-90. Member, TGWU. Ed Chelmsford County HS; LSE.

**PAUL McGUINESS,** b Sept 23, 1964. Contracts manager; previously with John Lloyd & Co, solicitors. Deputy chair, Regent's Park and North Kensington C assoc, 1995- ; vice-chair, Westminster North C assoc, 1994. Governor, Oxford Poly, 1988. Ed St Paul's; Institut International, Montpellier; Oxford Poly (pres, students' union); Coll of Law, Guildford.
**EMILY GASSON,** b June 23, 1970. Trainee solicitor. Ed Frensham Heights; Durham Univ (president, univ LD assoc); Oxford Univ.

| REIGATE | | 29.2% change | | | | C win | |
|---|---|---|---|---|---|---|---|
| Electorate % Turnout | | 64,750 | 74.4% | **1997** | 64,307 | 78.8% | **1992** |
| **Blunt, C** | **C** | **21,123** | **43.8%** | **-13.7%** | **29,148** | **57.5%** | **C** |
| Howard, A | Lab | 13,382 | 27.8% | +10.3% | 12,208 | 24.1% | LD |
| Samuel, P | LD | 9,615 | 20.0% | -4.1% | 8,870 | 17.5% | Lab |
| +Gardiner, Sir George | Ref | 3,352 | 7.0% | | 441 | 0.9% | Soc Dem |
| Higgs, R | Ind | 412 | 0.9% | | | | |
| Smith, S P | UK Ind | 290 | 0.6% | | | | |
| **C to Lab notional swing 12.0%** | | **48,174** | | **C maj 7,741** | **50,667** | | **C maj 16,940** |
| | | | | 16.1% | | | 33.4% |

**CRISPIN BLUNT,** b July 15, 1960. Political consultant. Contested West Bromwich W 1992. Ex-adviser to Foreign Secretary, special adviser to Defence Sec, 1993-97. PI Political Consultants 1993; district agent, Forum for Private Business; former army officer. Ed Wellington Coll, Berkshire; Sandhurst; Durham Univ; Cranfield School of Management.
**ANDREW HOWARD,** b Dec 19, 1961. Lecturer, Middlesex and City Univs. Reigate and Banstead borough cllr. Ed Helsby GS, Cheshire; Leeds Univ; LSE.
**PETER SAMUEL,** b July 20, 1939. Management consultancy director.

Contested City of Chester 1966 and 1964 for Lib. Member, CBI education and training cttee; appeals authorisation cttee, Assoc of Chartered Accountants; former exec, Ford Motor Co. Ed Reigate GS; LSE.
**SIR GEORGE GARDINER,** b March 3, 1935. C MP for Reigate 1974-97 when he was de-selected and joined Referendum Party. Contested Coventry S 1970. Ex-chair, 92 Group of C backbenchers; member, exec, 1922 Cttee, 1987-93. Journalist and former political correspondent. Author of a biography of Margaret Thatcher. Ed Harvey GS, Folkestone; Balliol Coll, Oxford.

| RENFREWSHIRE WEST | | 62.7% change | | | | Lab win | |
|---|---|---|---|---|---|---|---|
| Electorate % Turnout | | 52,348 | 76.0% | **1997** | 51,833 | 77.3% | **1992** |
| +Graham, T | Lab | 18,525 | 46.6% | +3.7% | 17,174 | 42.9% | Lab |
| Campbell, C | SNP | 10,546 | 26.5% | +5.9% | 11,128 | 27.8% | C |
| Cormack, C | C | 7,387 | 18.6% | -9.2% | 8,258 | 20.6% | SNP |
| MacPherson, B | LD | 3,045 | 7.7% | -0.8% | 3,375 | 8.4% | LD |
| Lindsay, S | Ref | 283 | 0.7% | | 129 | 0.3% | Other |
| **Lab to SNP notional swing 1.1%** | | **39,786** | | **Lab maj 7,979** | **40,064** | | **Lab maj 6,046** |
| | | | | 20.1% | | | 15.1% |

**THOMAS GRAHAM,** b Dec 5, 1943. Gained Renfrew W and Inverclyde 1987. Former office manager of firm of solicitors; ex-engineer with Rolls-Royce. Strathclyde regional cllr 1978-87. Member, Usdaw. Ed Crookston Castle School, Pollok; Stow Coll of Engineering.
**COLIN CAMPBELL,** b Aug 31, 1938. Retired secondary school head. Contested this seat 1992 and 1987; Strathclyde West in 1994 and 1989 Euro elections. Chair, Renfrew W and Inverclyde SNP.

Renfrewshire cllr. Ed Paisley GS; Glasgow Univ; Jordanhill Coll of Ed.
**CHARLES CORMACK,** b July 15, 1969. Hotel manager. Ed Gordonstoun; Westminster Coll. Son of Sir Patrick Cormack, MP for Staffordshire S.
**BRUCE MacPHERSON,** b March 13, 1966. Dep director of political affairs; ex-researcher for Sir David Steel. Member, British Field Sports Soc. Ed George Watson's Coll, Edinburgh; Durham Univ.

| RHONDDA | | | | | | Lab hold | |
|---|---|---|---|---|---|---|---|
| Electorate % Turnout | | 57,105 | 71.5% | **1997** | 59,955 | 76.6% | **1992** |
| *Rogers, A | Lab | 30,381 | 74.5% | -0.1% | 34,243 | 74.5% | Lab |
| Wood, Ms L | PC | 5,450 | 13.4% | +1.5% | 5,427 | 11.8% | PC |
| Berman, Dr R | LD | 2,307 | 5.7% | +0.4% | 3,588 | 7.8% | C |
| Whiting, S | C | 1,551 | 3.8% | -4.0% | 2,431 | 5.3% | LD |
| Gardiner, S | Ref | 658 | 1.6% | | 245 | 0.5% | Comm GB |
| Jakeway, K | Green | 460 | 1.1% | | | | |
| **Lab to PC swing 0.8%** | | **40,807** | | **Lab maj 24,931** | **45,934** | | **Lab maj 28,816** |
| | | | | 61.1% | | | 62.7% |

**ALLAN ROGERS,** b Oct 24, 1932. Elected for this seat 1983; MEP for SE Wales, 1979-84 (a vice-pres, Euro Parliament, 1979-82). Lab spokesman on foreign and Commonwealth affairs 1992-94; on defence 1987-92. Member, Commons intelligence and security cttee, 1994-97. Exec cttee, British group, IPU, 1994-. Sec/treas, all-party adult ed group; sec, world govt group. Geologist and Fellow of Geological Soc. Gelligaer district cllr 1965-71; Glamorgan county cllr 1970-74; Mid Glamorgan county cllr 1973-79. Ed Bargoed Secondary; Univ Coll of Wales, Swansea.

**LEANNE WOOD,** b Dec 13, 1971. Postgraduate student in social work, Univ Coll of Wales. Cardiff city cllr and Rhondda Cynon Taff county borough cllr. Ed Glamorgan Univ; Univ Coll of Wales, Cardiff.
**RODNEY BERMAN,** b April 20, 1969. Research fellow at Coll of Medicine, Univ Coll of Wales, Cardiff. Ed Woodfarm HS, Glasgow; Glasgow Univ.
**STEPHEN WHITING,** b March 17, 1969. Teacher. Ed Chislehurst and Sidcup GS; Univ Coll of Wales, Swansea; Cardiff Inst of Higher Ed.

| RIBBLE SOUTH | | 36.3% change | | | Lab win | | |
|---|---|---|---|---|---|---|---|
| Electorate % Turnout | | 71,670 | 77.1% | **1997** | 71,002 | 83.0% | **1992** |
| **Borrow, D** | Lab | **25,856** | 46.8% | +12.0% | **29,366** | 49.8% | C |
| +Atkins, R J | C | 20,772 | 37.6% | -12.2% | 20,526 | 34.8% | Lab |
| Farron, T | LD | 5,879 | 10.6% | -4.1% | 8,695 | 14.8% | LD |
| Adams, G | Ref | 1,475 | 2.7% | | 326 | 0.6% | Other |
| Ashton, N | Lib | 1,127 | 2.0% | | | | |
| Leadbetter, Ms B | NLP | 122 | 0.2% | | | | |
| C to Lab notional swing 12.1% | | 55,231 | | Lab maj 5,084 | 58,913 | | C maj 8,840 |
| | | | | 9.2% | | | 15.0% |

**DAVID BORROW,** b Aug 2, 1952. Tribunal clerk. Member Co-op Party, Fabian Soc, Lab Campaign for Electoral Reform. Ed Mirfield GS; Manchester Poly.

**ROBERT ATKINS,** b Feb 5, 1946. Elected for S Ribble 1983; MP for Preston N 1979-83; contested Luton W, Feb and Oct 1974. Environment and Countryside Min 1994-95; N Ireland Min 1992-94; Min for Sport 1990; Roads and Traffic Min 1989-90; Trade and Industry Under Sec 1987-89. PPS to Lord Young of Graffham when a Cabinet min 1984-87. Joint vice-chair, all-party cricket group, 1996-97, and member, MCC; Middlesex and Lancashire CCCs; Lords and Commons cricket club. Parly consultant to William Hill Ltd, bookmakers, and Scottish Coal Co Ltd; employment adviser, Mawdsley Consultancy; parly adviser, ICL. Haringey cllr 1968-76. Former sales exec with Rank Xerox (UK) Ltd. Freeman, City of London. Member, Sherlock Holmes Soc of London. Ed Highgate School.

**TIM FARRON,** b May 27, 1970. University administrator, Lancaster Univ. Contested NW Durham 1992; Lancashire county cllr 1993- ; South Ribble cllr 1995- . Member, Greenpeace; Shelter. Ed Lostock Hall HS, Preston; Runshaw Tertiary Coll, Leyland; Newcastle Univ (pres, students' union).

| RIBBLE VALLEY | | 11.5% change | | | C win | | |
|---|---|---|---|---|---|---|---|
| Electorate % Turnout | | 72,664 | 78.7% | **1997** | 71,262 | 84.4% | **1992** |
| +Evans, N | C | **26,702** | 46.7% | -5.9% | **31,629** | 52.6% | C |
| Carr, M | LD | 20,062 | 35.1% | -3.2% | 23,000 | 38.2% | LD |
| Johnstone, M | Lab | 9,013 | 15.8% | +7.0% | 5,254 | 8.7% | Lab |
| Parkinson, J | Ref | 1,297 | 2.3% | | 163 | 0.3% | Loony G |
| Holmes, Miss N | NLP | 147 | 0.3% | +0.1% | 119 | 0.2% | NLP |
| C to LD notional swing 1.4% | | 57,221 | | C maj 6,640 | 60,165 | | C maj 8,629 |
| | | | | 11.6% | | | 14.3% |

**NIGEL EVANS,** b Nov 10, 1957. Newsagent and grocer in Swansea. Regained seat for C 1992; contested it in 1991 by-election; Pontypridd by-election 1989 and Swansea W 1987. PPS to Welsh Sec 1996-97; to MAFF Min of State 1995-96; to Employment Sec 1993-94; to Chancellor of Duchy of Lancaster 1994-95. Joint vice-chair, all-party European secure vehicle alliance group; Friends of Music group; treas, manufacturing industry group; Dir, Networking for Industry; Small Business Bureau (both unpaid). West Glamorgan county cllr, 1985-91. Ed Dynevor School; Univ Coll of Wales, Swansea.

**MICHAEL CARR,** b Jan 31, 1946. Ex-teacher. MP for Ribble Valley from 1991 by-election to 1992 election; contested seat 1987 and 1983. Ribble Valley borough cllr, 1979-83. Press sec, Lancs Fed NASUWT, 1984-87, and 1988-90; Rossendale NASUWT district sec 1984-87. Founder member, SDP and LD. North West Region education spokesman. Ed St Joseph's Coll, Blackpool; Catholic Coll, Preston; Margaret MacMillan Coll of Ed, Bradford.

**MARCUS JOHNSTONE,** b April 26, 1959. Lecturer. Burnley borough cllr 1986- . Chair, Burnley CLP, 1989-93. Member, NUT. Ed Bristol Univ.

| RICHMOND (YORKS) | | 22.5% change | | | C win | | |
|---|---|---|---|---|---|---|---|
| Electorate % Turnout | | 65,058 | 73.4% | **1997** | 64,287 | 78.1% | **1992** |
| +Hague, W | C | **23,326** | 48.9% | -11.6% | **30,333** | 60.4% | C |
| Merritt, S | Lab | 13,275 | 27.8% | +16.3% | 13,626 | 27.1% | LD |
| Harvey, Mrs J | LD | 8,773 | 18.4% | -8.8% | 5,797 | 11.5% | Lab |
| Bentley, A | Ref | 2,367 | 5.0% | | 445 | 0.9% | Ind |
| C to Lab notional swing 13.9% | | 47,741 | | C maj 10,051 | 50,201 | | C maj 16,707 |
| | | | | 21.1% | | | 33.3% |

**WILLIAM HAGUE,** b March 26, 1961. Welsh Secretary 1995-97. Elected at 1989 by-election; contested Wentworth 1987. Min for Social Security and the Disabled 1994-95; Under Sec for Social Security 1993-94; PPS to Norman Lamont, Chancellor, 1990-93. Management consultant, McKinsey & Co Ltd, 1983-88. Political adviser, Treasury, 1983. Sec, Yorkshire group of C MPs 1989-93. Ed Wath-upon-Dearne Comp; Magdalen Coll, Oxford (pres of Union); Institut Européen d'Administration des Affaires.

**STEVE MERRITT,** b Jan 3, 1962. Electronics engineer, GEC Telecoms; teacher of physics; IT training; local gvt officer. Ed Grange Comp, Christchurch, Dorset; City of London Poly.

**JANE HARVEY,** b Nov 12, 1951. Local gvt officer. Contested Leeds in 1994 Euro elections. Northallerton town cllr 1983- (Mayor three times); Hambleton district cllr 1991- . Member, Charter 88. Ed Mount St Mary's GS, Leeds; Avery Hill Coll of Ed, Eltham; OU.

| RICHMOND PARK | | 57.4% change | | | 1997 | | | LD win |
|---|---|---|---|---|---|---|---|---|
| Electorate % Turnout | | 71,572 | 79.4% | **1997** | 69,091 | 85.5% | **1992** | |
| Tonge, Dr J | LD | 25,393 | 44.7% | +7.0% | 30,609 | 51.8% | C | |
| +Hanley, J J | C | 22,442 | 39.5% | -12.4% | 22,225 | 37.6% | LD | |
| Jenkins, Ms S | Lab | 7,172 | 12.6% | +3.8% | 5,211 | 8.8% | Lab | |
| Pugh, J | Ref | 1,467 | 2.6% | | 1,008 | 1.7% | Other | |
| Beaupre, D | Loony | 204 | 0.4% | | | | | |
| D'Arcy, B | NLP | 102 | 0.2% | | | | | |
| Davies, P | Dream | 73 | 0.1% | | | | | |
| **C to LD notional swing 9.7%** | | **56,853** | | **LD maj 2,951** | **59,053** | | **C maj 8,384** | |
| | | | | 5.2% | | | 14.2% | |

**JENNY TONGE,** b Feb 19, 1941. Doctor and NHS manager. Contested Richmond and Barnes 1992. Richmond cllr 1981-90. Friend of Kew Gardens and of Richmond Park. Member, Friends of the Earth; Amnesty; RSPB; BMA. Ed Dudley Girls' HS; University Coll and University Coll Hospital, London.
**JEREMY HANLEY,** b Nov 17, 1945. Foreign and Commonwealth Office Min 1995-97. Elected for Richmond and Barnes 1983; contested Lambeth Central 1978 by-election and 1979. Member of Cabinet as Min without Portfolio and Chairman of C Party 1994-95; Min for Armed Forces 1993-94; N Ireland Under Sec 1990-93.

PPS to Richard Luce, Arts Min, 1987-90, and to Chris Patten when Environment Sec. Sec, all-party Europe group, 1988-90. Chartered accountant. Chair, Fraser Green Ltd, 1986-90; deputy chair, Financial Training Co Ltd, 1973-90. Parly adviser, Inst of Chartered Accountants in England and Wales, 1986-90. Freeman and Liveryman, City of London. Chartered Accountants' Co, 1993- . Member, Soc of C lawyers; Bow Group; One Nation. Ed Rugby.
**SUE JENKINS,** b Nov 7, 1963. Personnel director, Hasbro UK. Member, Amnesty; MSF. Ed Bishop Gore Comp, Swansea; Fitzwilliam Coll, Cambridge.

| ROCHDALE | | 46.8% change | | | 1997 | | | Lab win |
|---|---|---|---|---|---|---|---|---|
| Electorate % Turnout | | 68,529 | 70.2% | **1997** | 69,019 | 77.2% | **1992** | |
| Fitzsimons, Ms L | Lab | 23,758 | 49.4% | +11.7% | 20,204 | 37.9% | LD | |
| +Lynne, Miss L | LD | 19,213 | 40.0% | +2.0% | 20,076 | 37.7% | Lab | |
| Turnberg, M | C | 4,237 | 8.8% | -14.4% | 12,378 | 23.2% | C | |
| Bergin, G | BNP | 653 | 1.4% | +0.5% | 470 | 0.9% | BNP | |
| Mohammed, S | IZB | 221 | 0.5% | | 159 | 0.3% | NLP | |
| **LD to Lab notional swing 4.8%** | | **48,082** | | **Lab maj 4,545** | **53,287** | | **LD maj 128** | |
| | | | | 9.5% | | | 0.2% | |

**LORNA FITZSIMONS,** b Aug 6, 1967. Parliamentary consultant to PR firm. Member of Inst of Public Relations; Young Communicator of the Year 1995-96. Pres, NUS, 1992-94. Governor, Sheffield Hallam Univ. Member, Further Ed Funding Council quality cttee; Lab co-ordinating cttee's commission on party democracy; Lab industry forum; Fabian Soc; Co-op Party. Ed Wardle HS, Wardle; Loughborough Coll of Art and Design.
**LIZ LYNNE,** b Jan 22, 1948. Speech consultant and actress. Elected 1992; contested Harwich 1987. LD spokeswoman on social

security and disability, 1994-97; health and community care 1992-94. Joint chair, all-party breast cancer group; vice-chair, all-party osteoporosis group, 1996-97; joint vice-chair, child support group; sec, ASH. Speech consultant 1989-92; actress from 1966 in repertory and West End. Member, Green Democrats. Ed Dorking County GS.
**MERVYN TURNBERG,** b Aug 6, 1950. Marketing sales exec. Bury metropolitan borough cllr 1984-92. Member, Bow Group; Tory Green Initiative. Ed King David HS; Bury Coll of FE.

| ROCHFORD & SOUTHEND EAST | | 19.2% change | | | 1997 | | | C win |
|---|---|---|---|---|---|---|---|---|
| Electorate % Turnout | | 72,848 | 64.0% | **1997** | 67,171 | 75.9% | **1992** | |
| +Taylor, Sir Teddy | C | 22,683 | 48.7% | -10.3% | 30,096 | 59.0% | C | |
| Smith, N | Lab | 18,458 | 39.6% | +12.1% | 14,019 | 27.5% | Lab | |
| Smith, Ms P | LD | 4,387 | 9.4% | -2.4% | 6,011 | 11.8% | LD | |
| Lynch, B | Lib | 1,070 | 2.3% | | 861 | 1.7% | Other | |
| **C to Lab notional swing 11.2%** | | **46,598** | | **C maj 4,225** | **50,987** | | **C maj 16,077** | |
| | | | | 9.1% | | | 31.5% | |

**SIR TEDDY TAYLOR,** b April 18, 1937. MP for Southend E 1980-97, and for Glasgow Cathcart 1964-79; contested Glasgow Springburn 1959. Under Sec for Scotland 1974, and in 1970-71, when he resigned over gvt policy on Europe. C whip withdrawn 1994-95. Sec, C Euro reform group, 1980- . Parly adviser to Port of London Police Fed; adviser to Lawrence Building Co, Glasgow; parly consultant to Law Holdings, opencast coal mining co. Non-exec director, Shepherd Foods Ltd, 1968- , and Ansvar Insurance Co. Ed Glasgow HS; Glasgow Univ.

**NIGEL SMITH,** b Oct 9, 1947. Teacher. Contested Chichester Feb and Oct 1974; SE Essex 1979; Chipping Barnet 1983; Romford 1987. Basildon district cllr 1975-79; Southend borough cllr 1986- . Member, League Against Cruel Sports; SEA; Lab Action for Peace; NUT. Ed Chichester HS for Boys; Manchester Poly; Kent State Univ, Ohio; Oxford Univ. Husband of Angela Smith, Lab MP for Basildon.
**PAULA SMITH,** b Sept 8, 1951. Company director (aviation industry). Essex county cllr 1993- . Ed St John's School, Billericay.

| ROMFORD | | 11.6% change | | | | | Lab win |
|---|---|---|---|---|---|---|---|
| Electorate % Turnout | | 59,611 | 70.7% | **1997** | 60,903 | 77.6% | **1992** |
| Gordon, Mrs E | Lab | **18,187** | 43.2% | +14.8% | 27,462 | 58.1% | C |
| +Neubert, Sir Michael | C | 17,538 | 41.6% | -16.5% | 13,398 | 28.3% | Lab |
| Meyer, N | LD | 3,341 | 7.9% | -4.5% | 5,865 | 12.4% | LD |
| Ward, S | Ref | 1,431 | 3.4% | | 546 | 1.2% | Grn |
| Hurlstone, T | Lib | 1,100 | 2.6% | | | | |
| Carey, M | BNP | 522 | 1.2% | | | | |
| C to Lab notional swing 15.6% | | 42,119 | | Lab maj 649 | 47,271 | | C maj 14,064 |
| | | | | 1.5% | | | 29.8% |

**EILEEN GORDON,** b Oct 22, 1946. Contested Romford 1992. Constituency caseworker for Tony Banks. Member Co-op Party; League Against Cruel Sports. Ed Harold Hill GS; Shoreditch Comp; Westminster Coll of Ed.

**SIR MICHAEL NEUBERT,** b Sept 3, 1933. Elected Feb 1974; contested Romford 1970, Hammersmith N 1966. Defence Procurement Min 1989-90; Armed Forces Min 1988-89; gvt whip 1986-88 and asst gvt whip 1983-86. PPS to Lord Cockfield, Trade Sec, 1982-83, and other ministers, 1980-82. Member, exec, 1922 Cttee, 1992-97. Adviser to Fed of Master Builders and Nat Market Traders' Fed. Former travel and industrial consultant. Bromley cllr 1960-68 (alderman 1968-74; leader 1967-70; Mayor 1972-73). Ed Queen Elizabeth's School, Barnet; Bromley GS; Downing Coll, Cambridge.

**NIGEL MEYER,** b May 15, 1961. Manager and insurance broker. Ed St Edward's C of E School, Romford.

| ROMSEY | | 104.8% change | | | | | C win |
|---|---|---|---|---|---|---|---|
| Electorate % Turnout | | 67,306 | 77.0% | **1997** | 65,546 | 82.6% | **1992** |
| +Colvin, M K B | C | 23,834 | 46.0% | -17.2% | 34,218 | 63.2% | C |
| Cooper, M | LD | 15,249 | 29.4% | +6.3% | 12,496 | 23.1% | LD |
| Ford, Ms J | Lab | 9,623 | 18.6% | +5.7% | 6,982 | 12.9% | Lab |
| Sked, Dr A | UK Ind | 1,824 | 3.5% | | 420 | 0.8% | Other |
| Wigley, M | Ref | 1,291 | 2.5% | | | | |
| C to LD notional swing 11.8% | | 51,821 | | C maj 8,585 | 54,116 | | C maj 21,722 |
| | | | | 16.6% | | | 40.1% |

**MICHAEL COLVIN,** b Sept 27, 1932. Landowner, farmer and member of Lloyd's. MP for Romsey and Waterside 1983-97; Bristol NW 1979-83. Chair, defence select cttee, 1995-97. Chair, C foreign and Commonwealth affairs cttee, 1992-. Joint vice-chair exec cttee, UK branch, CPA. Pres, Palace of Westminster shooting club; capt, HoC team. Chair, Council for Country Sports, 1988-; vice-chair, British Field Sports Soc, 1987-. Qualified pilot and parachutist. Parly and public affairs consultant to Fed of Retail Licensed Trade (N Ireland); Caledonia Investments plc; Meridian Broadcasting Ltd. Ed Eton; Sandhurst; Royal Agricultural Coll, Cirencester.

**MARK COOPER,** b April 16, 1948. Teacher. Test Valley district cllr 1986-; Romsey town cllr 1986- (Mayor 1991-92). Ed St Mary's Coll, Southampton; Taunton's School, Southampton; Leeds Univ.

**JOANNE FORD,** b Nov 19, 1971. Business adviser. Ed Mountbatten School, Romsey; Barton Peveril Sixth-Form Coll, Eastleigh; Warwick Univ.

**ALAN SKED,** b Aug 22, 1947. UK Independence Party leader. Univ teacher and historian. Contested Paisley 1970 as Lib; Bath 1992 and Newbury 1993 by-election as Anti-Federalist. Ed Allen Glen's School, Glasgow; Glasgow Univ; Merton Coll, Oxford.

| ROSS, SKYE & INVERNESS WEST | | | 33.2% change | | | | LD win |
|---|---|---|---|---|---|---|---|
| Electorate % Turnout | | 55,639 | 71.8% | **1997** | 52,810 | 73.2% | **1992** |
| +Kennedy, C P | LD | 15,472 | 38.7% | +0.0% | 14,957 | 38.7% | LD |
| Munro, D | Lab | 11,453 | 28.7% | +9.8% | 8,452 | 21.9% | C |
| Paterson, Mrs M | SNP | 7,821 | 19.6% | +0.8% | 7,296 | 18.9% | Lab |
| Macleod, Miss M | C | 4,368 | 10.9% | -10.9% | 7,276 | 18.8% | SNP |
| Durance, L | Ref | 535 | 1.3% | | 688 | 1.8% | Other |
| Hopkins, A | Green | 306 | 0.8% | | | | |
| LD to Lab notional swing 4.9% | | 39,955 | | LD maj 4,019 | 38,669 | | LD maj 6,505 |
| | | | | 10.1% | | | 16.8% |

**CHARLES KENNEDY,** b Nov 25, 1959. Journalist; associate editor, *The House Magazine.* Won Ross, Cromarty & Skye 1983 for SDP/All and became LD MP in 1988. Pres of Liberal Democrats 1990-94. Chair, SDP Council for Scotland, 1986-88. LD spokesman on agriculture, fisheries, food and rural affairs, 1997-; EU 1992-97; health 1989-92; trade and industry 1988-89; social security 1987. Joint vice-chair, all-party Future of Europe group. Ed Lochaber HS, Fort William; Glasgow Univ (student union pres, 1980-81); Indiana Univ.

**DONNIE MUNRO,** b Aug 2, 1953. Art/design teacher and broadcaster; former rector of Edinburgh Univ. Founder, rector's trust for students with special needs. Ed Portree HS; Gray's School of Art; Robert Gordon Univ, Aberdeen; Moray House Coll of Ed.

**MARGARET PATERSON,** b Jan 19, 1945. Library assistant. Highland regional cllr 1990-96; Highland unitary cllr 1995-. Ed Dingwall Acad.

**MARY MacLEOD,** b Jan 4, 1969. Management consultant. Ed Dingwall Acad; Glasgow Univ.

| ROSSENDALE & DARWEN | | 9.6% change | | | | | Lab win |
|---|---|---|---|---|---|---|---|
| Electorate % Turnout | | 69,749 | 73.4% | **1997** | 70,176 | 81.9% | **1992** |
| +Anderson, Mrs J | Lab | 27,470 | 53.6% | +10.1% | 25,044 | 43.6% | Lab |
| Buzzard, Mrs P M | C | 16,521 | 32.3% | -11.2% | 24,995 | 43.5% | C |
| Dunning, B | LD | 5,435 | 10.6% | -1.2% | 6,798 | 11.8% | LD |
| Newstead, R | Ref | 1,108 | 2.2% | | 539 | 0.9% | Grn |
| Wearden, A | BNP | 674 | 1.3% | | 113 | 0.2% | NLP |
| C to Lab notional swing 10.6% | | 51,208 | | Lab maj 10,949 | 57,489 | | Lab maj 49 |
| | | | | 21.4% | | | 0.1% |

**JANET ANDERSON,** b Dec 6, 1949. Became gvt whip, May 7, 1997. Gained this seat for Lab 1992; contested it 1987. Lab spokeswoman on women's issues 1996-97; Lab whip 1995-96. PPS to Margaret Beckett, then Lab dep leader, 1992-93. Campaign organiser for PLP, 1988-89. Member, Royal Coll of Nursing parly panel. Sec, Tribune group of Lab MPs, 1993-97. Public affairs consultant, Safeway Stores plc (fees to CLP). Joint vice-chair, all-party exports group; treas, opera group. PA to Barbara Castle 1974-81, and to Jack Straw 1981-87. Member, TGWU. Ed Kingsfield Comp, Bristol; Central London Poly; Nantes Univ.

**TRICIA BUZZARD,** b Aug 4, 1945. Managing director of small design and marketing services co. Contested St Helens S 1992. Chair, Wallasey C assoc, 1992-94. Wirral borough cllr 1987-88. Manager, family hotel in Lake District, 1975-79. Ex-chair, Liverpool branch, Inst of Legal Executives. Ed Maris Stella Convent, New Brighton; Huyton Coll, Liverpool; Queen's Secretarial Coll, London.
**BRIAN DUNNING,** b Dec 6, 1938. Teacher and senior school manager. Contested Bolton NE 1992. Ed Bolton County GS; Bolton Technical Coll; Bolton Teacher Training Coll.

| ROTHER VALLEY | | | | | | | Lab hold |
|---|---|---|---|---|---|---|---|
| Electorate % Turnout | | 68,622 | 67.3% | **1997** | 68,303 | 75.0% | **1992** |
| *Barron, K | Lab | 31,184 | 67.6% | +7.1% | 30,977 | 60.5% | Lab |
| Stanbury, S | C | 7,699 | 16.7% | -10.2% | 13,755 | 26.9% | C |
| Burgess, S | LD | 5,342 | 11.6% | -1.1% | 6,483 | 12.7% | LD |
| Cook, S | Ref | 1,932 | 4.2% | | | | |
| C to Lab swing 8.6% | | 46,157 | | Lab maj 23,485 | 51,215 | | Lab maj 17,222 |
| | | | | 50.9% | | | 33.6% |

**KEVIN BARRON,** b Oct 26, 1946. Ex-miner. Elected 1983. Lab spokesman on health 1995-97; on employment 1993-95; on energy, particularly coal, 1988-92. PPS to Neil Kinnock, Opposition Leader, 1985-88. Chair, Yorkshire group of Lab MPs, 1987- . Member, select cttees on energy, 1983-85; environment 1992-93. Pres, Rotherham and District TUC, 1982-83. Coalminer 1962-83; NUM delegate for Maltby colliery. Ed Maltby Hall Sec Mod; Ruskin Coll, Oxford.

**STEVEN STANBURY,** b Oct 20, 1964. Company director; research assistant with Heritage Foundation, Washington DC, 1986. Campaign manager for Teresa Gorman, 1987. Member, exec cttee, C Way Forward, 1994-96. Ed Sackdell School, East Grinstead; Guildhall Univ, London.
**STAN BURGESS,** b June 21, 1940. Semi-retired teacher. Ed Central GS, Birmingham; St Peter's Coll, Saltley.

| ROTHERHAM | | | | | | | Lab hold |
|---|---|---|---|---|---|---|---|
| Electorate % Turnout | | 59,895 | 62.9% | **1997** | 60,937 | 71.7% | **1992** |
| *MacShane, D | Lab | 26,852 | 71.3% | +7.4% | 27,933 | 63.9% | Lab |
| Gordon, S | C | 5,383 | 14.3% | -9.4% | 10,372 | 23.7% | C |
| Wildgoose, D | LD | 3,919 | 10.4% | -1.9% | 5,375 | 12.3% | LD |
| Hollibone, R | Ref | 1,132 | 3.0% | | | | |
| Neal, A | ProLife | 364 | 1.0% | | | | |
| C to Lab swing 8.4% | | 37,650 | | Lab maj 21,469 | 43,680 | | Lab maj 17,561 |
| | | | | 57.0% | | | 40.2% |

**DENIS MacSHANE,** b May 21, 1948. Journalist. Elected 1994 by-election. Member, Commons deregulation select cttee, 1996-97. Joint vice-chair, all-party Future of Europe group. Dir, European Policy Inst, 1992-94. Associate dir, European Policy Inst; editorial board member, *Critical Quarterly* (both unpaid). Policy dir, International Metalworkers Fed, 1980-92. BBC reporter 1969-77; pres, NUJ, 1978-79. Ed Merton Coll, Oxford; Birkbeck Coll, London.

**SIMON GORDON,** b Sept 19, 1950. Public affairs manager, Electricity Assoc. Fought London North-East in 1994 Euro elections. Pres, London NE C assoc; political asst to Keith Hampson, MP, 1983-85. Ed Pitman's Coll, Birmingham; Leeds Univ.
**DAVID WILDGOOSE,** b March 13, 1965. IT contractor. Contested this seat in 1994 by-election, and 1992. Member, Greenpeace; Amnesty; Rare Breed Survival Trust; Camra. Ed Oakwood Comp; Rotherham Coll; Hull Univ.

*Details of 1994 by-election on page 277*

217

| ROXBURGH & BERWICKSHIRE | | | 7.0% change | | | LD win |
|---|---|---|---|---|---|---|
| Electorate % Turnout | | 47,259 | 73.9% | **1997** | 47,068 | 76.9% | **1992** |
| +Kirkwood, A | LD | 16,243 | 46.5% | +0.0% | 16,807 | 46.5% | LD |
| Younger, D | C | 8,337 | 23.9% | -10.3% | 12,354 | 34.2% | C |
| Eadie, Ms H S | Lab | 5,226 | 15.0% | +6.2% | 3,844 | 10.6% | SNP |
| Balfour, M | SNP | 3,959 | 11.3% | +0.7% | 3,167 | 8.8% | Lab |
| Curtis, J | Ref | 922 | 2.6% | | | | |
| Neilson, P T | UK Ind | 202 | 0.6% | | | | |
| Lucas, D | NLP | 42 | 0.1% | | | | |
| C to LD notional swing 5.2% | | 34,931 | | LD maj 7,906 | 36,172 | | LD maj 4,453 |
| | | | | 22.6% | | | 12.3% |

**ARCHY KIRKWOOD**, b April 22, 1946. Notary public; solicitor. Elected 1983, becoming LD MP 1988. LD spokesman on social security and welfare, May 1997- ; Chief Whip 1992-97; spokesman on community care 1994-97; social security 1992-94; welfare 1989-92; overseas development, and Scottish whip, 1987-89; health and social security 1983-87. Member, Commons finance and services cttee 1992- ; cttee of selection 1992-97. Treas, all-party group on Aids; joint vice-chair, wool textile group. Member, Court of Referees, 1987- . Unpaid dir, Joseph Rowntree Reform Trust; London Moscow Foundation; Family Budget Unit. Ed Cranhill Sec, Glasgow; Heriot-Watt Univ (ex-union pres).

**DOUGLAS YOUNGER**, b May 31, 1956. Ex-farm manager. Sec, local C assoc. Ed Abbey School, Melrose; Winchester; Edinburgh Univ; Edinburgh School of Agriculture; Strathclyde Univ.

**HELEN EADIE**, b March 7, 1947. Union official; full-time cllr, Fife Regional Council (dep leader and group sec). Vice-pres, North Sea Commission. GMB officer. Ed Larbert HS; Falkirk Tech Coll; LSE.

**MALCOLM BALFOUR**, b April 3, 1954. Ice-cream salesman.

| RUGBY & KENILWORTH | | | 0.3% change | | | Lab win |
|---|---|---|---|---|---|---|
| Electorate % Turnout | | 79,384 | 77.1% | **1997** | 78,639 | 83.0% | **1992** |
| King, A | Lab | 26,356 | 43.1% | +11.1% | 34,218 | 52.4% | C |
| +Pawsey, J | C | 25,861 | 42.3% | -10.2% | 20,894 | 32.0% | Lab |
| Roodhouse, J M | LD | 8,737 | 14.3% | -1.0% | 9,971 | 15.3% | LD |
| Twite, M | NLP | 251 | 0.4% | +0.1% | 202 | 0.3% | NLP |
| C to Lab notional swing 10.6% | | 61,205 | | Lab maj 495 | 65,285 | | C maj 13,324 |
| | | | | 0.8% | | | 20.4% |

**ANDY KING**, b Sept 14, 1948. Social services manager. Ed Coatbridge Tech Coll; Missionary Inst, London; Hatfield Poly.

**JAMES PAWSEY**, b Aug 21, 1933. Elected for this seat 1983; MP for Rugby 1979-83. Chair, select cttee on Parly Commissioner for Administration, 1993-97 (member 1983-97); member, select cttee on standing orders, 1987-97. Court of Referees, 1993- . Member, exec, 1922 Cttee 1989-97. Chair, C backbench ed cttee, 1985-97; chair, W Midlands group of C MPs, 1993-97. Member, exec cttee, British group, IPU. Rugby rural district and borough cllr 1964-74; Warwickshire county cllr 1974-79. Member of Lloyd's. Dir, Autobar Ltd (food, plastics, and fast food processing), 1983- ; St Martin's Hospitals, private hospital group, 1989- ; non-exec dir, Love Lane Investments, property co. Ed Coventry Tech School; Coventry Tech Coll.

**JERRY ROODHOUSE**, b June 26, 1953. Sales engineer. Contested Rugby and Kenilworth 1992. Warwickshire county cllr 1990- (dep group leader); Rugby district cllr (group leader). Member, Friends of the Earth. Ed Horres CE, Rugby; Rycatewood Coll, Thorne.

| RUISLIP NORTHWOOD | | | 9.3% change | | | C win |
|---|---|---|---|---|---|---|
| Electorate % Turnout | | 60,393 | 74.2% | **1997** | 61,393 | 78.1% | **1992** |
| +Wilkinson, J | C | 22,526 | 50.2% | -12.6% | 30,130 | 62.9% | C |
| Barker, P | Lab | 14,732 | 32.9% | +13.0% | 9,521 | 19.9% | Lab |
| Edwards, C | LD | 7,279 | 16.2% | -0.4% | 7,981 | 16.7% | LD |
| Griffin, Ms C | NLP | 296 | 0.7% | +0.0% | 294 | 0.6% | NLP |
| C to Lab notional swing 12.8% | | 44,833 | | C maj 7,794 | 47,926 | | C maj 20,609 |
| | | | | 17.4% | | | 43.0% |

**JOHN WILKINSON**, b Sept 23, 1940. Marketing consultant, lecturer and author. Elected for this seat 1979; MP for Bradford W 1970-Feb 1974; contested that seat Oct 1974. Had C whip withdrawn 1994-95 over failure to support Gvt's EU policy. Member, defence select cttee, 1987-90; chair, C backbench defence cttee, 1993-94; chair, C aviation cttee, 1983-85 and 1992-93; C space sub-cttee, 1986-90 (vice-chair, 1983-85). PPS to Industry Min 1979-80; to Defence Sec 1981-82. Vice-chair, all-party RAF group; member, Asean-British, Chilean and Philippines groups. Chair, Euro Freedom Council, 1982-90. Delegate to Council of Europe (chair, space sub-cttee, 1984-88) and WEU (chair, cttee on scientific, technology and aerospace, 1986-89), 1979-90. Ex-RAF flying instructor/inspector; French interpreter in RAF. Flying instructor/inspector, Cranwell, 1966-67, and Stansted 1974-75. Ed Eton; RAF Coll, Cranwell; Churchill Coll, Cambridge.

**PAUL BARKER,** b Jan 24, 1958. Trade union official. Hillingdon cllr 1994- . Chair, Uxbridge CLP. Member, Nalgo/Unison. Ed Walpole School, Ealing.

**CHRIS EDWARDS,** b Sept 21, 1952. Partner in printing company. Woking borough cllr (dep group leader). Ed Royal GS, High Wycombe; Sheffield and Kingston-upon-Hull Univs.

| RUNNYMEDE & WEYBRIDGE | | 68.8% change | | | | | C win |
|---|---|---|---|---|---|---|---|
| Electorate % Turnout | | 72,177 | 71.4% | **1997** | 71,478 | 79.0% | **1992** |
| **Hammond, P** | C | **25,051** | **48.6%** | -12.8% | **34,645** | **61.4%** | C |
| Peacock, I | Lab | 15,176 | 29.4% | +13.5% | 11,905 | 21.1% | LD |
| Taylor, G | LD | 8,397 | 16.3% | -4.8% | 9,004 | 16.0% | Lab |
| Rolt, P | Ref | 2,150 | 4.2% | | 878 | 1.6% | Other |
| Slater, S J | UK Ind | 625 | 1.2% | | | | |
| Sleeman, J | NLP | 162 | 0.3% | | | | |
| **C to Lab notional swing 13.1%** | | **51,561** | | **C maj 9,875** | **56,432** | | **C maj 22,740** |
| | | | | 19.2% | | | 40.3% |

**PHILIP HAMMOND,** b Dec 4, 1955. Won this seat 1997; contested Newham NE by-election 1994. Co-founder and managing director of business development consultancy with clients in oil, gas, engineering and brewing industries. Man dir, small housebuilding and development co, 1984- ; consultant economist to World Bank, Washington DC, 1986- . Ex-chair, E Lewisham C assoc. Ed Shenfield School, Brentwood; University Coll, Oxford.

**IAN PEACOCK,** b Dec 29, 1964. Barrister. Member, Lab Campaign for Electoral Reform; Amnesty; Child Povery Action Group; Fabian Soc. Ed Forest School, Walthamstow; Trinity Coll, Cambridge; City Univ.

**GEOFFREY TAYLOR,** b April 11, 1933. Chemical engineer and company dir, Kodak. Co-founder of IMMPACT (anti-age discrimination in employment campaign). Sec, Runnymede and Weybridge LDs. Ed Portsmouth GS; Birkbeck Coll, London.

| RUSHCLIFFE | | | | | | | C hold |
|---|---|---|---|---|---|---|---|
| Electorate % Turnout | | 78,735 | 78.9% | **1997** | 76,253 | 83.0% | **1992** |
| *Clarke, K | C | 27,558 | 44.4% | -10.0% | 34,448 | 54.4% | C |
| Pettit, Ms J | Lab | 22,503 | 36.2% | +13.0% | 14,682 | 23.2% | Lab |
| Boote, S | LD | 8,851 | 14.3% | -5.7% | 12,660 | 20.0% | LD |
| Chadd, Miss S | Ref | 2,682 | 4.3% | | 775 | 1.2% | Grn |
| Moore, J | UK Ind | 403 | 0.6% | | 611 | 1.0% | Ind C |
| Maszwska, Ms A | NLP | 115 | 0.2% | -0.1% | 150 | 0.2% | NLP |
| **C to Lab swing 11.5%** | | **62,112** | | **C maj 5,055** | **63,326** | | **C maj 19,766** |
| | | | | 8.1% | | | 31.2% |

**KENNETH CLARKE,** b July 2, 1940. Barrister, QC. Chancellor of the Exchequer 1993-97. Elected 1970; contested Mansfield 1966 and 1964. Home Secretary, 1992-93; Education and Science Sec 1990-92; Health Sec 1988-90; Trade and Industry Min 1987-88. Joined Cabinet 1985 as Paymaster General and was Employment Min 1985-87; Health Min 1982-85; Health Under Sec 1979-81; Transport Under Sec 1981-84. C spokesman on industry 1976-79, and social services 1974-76; gvt whip 1974; asst gvt whip 1972-74. Pres YCs, 1986-87. Hon Bencher, Gray's Inn, 1989. Ed

Nottingham HS; Gonville and Caius Coll, Cambridge (pres of Union 1963).

**JOCELYN PETTITT,** b Nov 2, 1956. Local government housing warden. Member, Amnesty; Greenpeace. Ed Eastwood Comp; Clarendon Coll of FE.

**SAM BOOTE,** b Aug 23, 1946. Systems analyst in local gvt. Member, Families Against Cuts in Education. Ed St Anselm's Coll, Birkenhead; UMIST.

| RUTLAND & MELTON | | 38.5% change | | | | | C win |
|---|---|---|---|---|---|---|---|
| Electorate % Turnout | | 70,150 | 75.0% | **1997** | 67,694 | 82.1% | **1992** |
| +Duncan, A | C | 24,107 | 45.8% | -15.6% | 34,137 | 61.4% | C |
| Meads, J | Lab | 15,271 | 29.0% | +13.3% | 11,556 | 20.8% | LD |
| Lee, K | LD | 10,112 | 19.2% | -1.6% | 8,730 | 15.7% | Lab |
| King, R | Ref | 2,317 | 4.4% | | 891 | 1.6% | Grn |
| Abbott, J S | UK Ind | 823 | 1.6% | | 245 | 0.4% | NLP |
| **C to Lab notional swing 14.5%** | | **52,630** | | **C maj 8,836** | **55,559** | | **C maj 22,581** |
| | | | | 16.8% | | | 40.6% |

**ALAN DUNCAN,** b March 31, 1957. Oil trader. Elected 1992; contested Barnsley W and Penistone 1987. PPS to Brian Mawhinney, C Party chairman, 1995-97. Member, social security select cttee, 1992-95; chair, C backbench constitutional affairs cttee, 1994-95; ex-joint sec, C backbench environment cttee; treas, all-party Anglo-Swiss parly group. Oil trader with Marc Rich and Co 1982-88; owner of Harcourt Consultants, trading as oil broker and adviser on energy matters. With Shell International Petroleum 1979-81. Freeman, City of London; Liveryman, Merchant Taylors' Co. Ed Beechwood Park School, St Albans;

Merchant Taylors' School, Northwood; St John's Coll, Oxford (pres of Union 1979); Harvard Univ (Kennedy Scholar, 1981-82).

**JOHN MEADS,** b Oct 1, 1951. Human resouces consultant. Former general secretary, British Association of Colliery Managers. Member, Co-op Party. Ed Stevenage School; Corpus Christi Coll, Cambridge.

**KIM LEE,** b April 19, 1967. Solicitor. Rutland district cllr, UA cllr 1991- . Ed Rutland Sixth-Form College, Oakham. Fitzwilliam Coll, Cambridge.

## RYEDALE — 38.4% change — C win

| Electorate % Turnout | | 65,215 | 74.8% | **1997** | 63,182 | 81.0% | **1992** |
|---|---|---|---|---|---|---|---|
| **+Greenway, J** | C | **21,351** | 43.8% | -11.6% | **28,338** | 55.4% | C |
| Orrell, J | LD | 16,293 | 33.4% | +3.4% | 15,340 | 30.0% | LD |
| Hiles, Ms A | Lab | 8,762 | 18.0% | +3.3% | 7,497 | 14.6% | Lab |
| Mackfall, J | Ref | 1,460 | 3.0% | | | | |
| Feaster, S | UK Ind | 917 | 1.9% | | | | |
| **C to LD notional swing 7.5%** | | **48,783** | | **C maj 5,058** | **51,175** | | **C maj 12,998** |
| | | | | 10.4% | | | 25.4% |

**JOHN GREENWAY**, b Feb 15, 1946. Insurance broker, former policeman and financial journalist. Regained seat for C 1987. Member, home affairs select cttee, 1987-97. PPS to Agriculture Min 1991-92. Vice-chair, C backbench agric, fisheries and food cttee, 1989- ; joint sec, C health cttee, 1988-91; member, C home affairs cttee, 1994- , and 1990-91; joint chair, all-party opera group, 1994- ; chair, all-party insurance and financial services group, 1992- . Parly adviser to Inst of Insurance Brokers; Yorkshire Tyne Tees Television plc; General Healthcare Ltd. Unpaid adviser to British Health Care Assoc. Dir, Smart and Cook

Group Ltd, insurance brokers. Member, Insurance Brokers' Registration Council. Ed Sir John Deane's GS, Northwich, Cheshire; Hendon Police Coll.
**KEITH ORRELL,** b May 22, 1944. Retired head of unit for autistic children. Contested Jarrow 1992. S Tyneside cllr 1990- (opposition leader 1991). Member, Amnesty; Electoral Reform Soc. Ed Hutton GS; Sunderland Coll of Ed; OU.
**ALISON HILES,** b Feb 7, 1945. Market research interviewer. Ryedale district cllr 1995- . Ed Colne Valley HS; Letchworth GS; Univ Coll of Wales, Aberystwyth.

## SAFFRON WALDEN — 5.3% change — C win

| Electorate % Turnout | | 74,097 | 77.0% | **1997** | 70,475 | 83.7% | **1992** |
|---|---|---|---|---|---|---|---|
| **+Haselhurst, Sir Alan** | C | **25,871** | 45.3% | -11.2% | **33,378** | 56.6% | C |
| Caton, M | LD | 15,298 | 26.8% | -1.8% | 16,885 | 28.6% | LD |
| Fincken, M | Lab | 12,275 | 21.5% | +7.2% | 8,468 | 14.4% | Lab |
| Glover, R | Ref | 2,308 | 4.0% | | 246 | 0.4% | NLP |
| Evans, I | UK Ind | 658 | 1.2% | | | | |
| Tyler, B | Ind | 486 | 0.9% | | | | |
| Edwards, C | NLP | 154 | 0.3% | -0.1% | | | |
| **C to LD notional swing 4.7%** | | **57,050** | | **C maj 10,573** | **58,977** | | **C maj 16,493** |
| | | | | 18.5% | | | 28.0% |

**SIR ALAN HASELHURST,** b June 23, 1937. Appointed Deputy Speaker and chair, Ways and Means, May 1997. Elected in 1977 by-election; MP for Middleton and Prestwich 1970-Feb 1974. Member, Commons chairman's panel; select cttees on European legislation 1982-97; on transport 1992-97. Joint vice-chair, C backbench ed cttee, 1983- ; ex-chair and vice-chair, C aviation cttee. Chair, trustees, Community Development Foundation, 1986- (trustee from 1982); chair, Rights of Way Review Cttee, 1983-93. Consultant to Albright & Wilson Ltd, chemicals manufacturer; Johnson Matthey plc,

advanced materials technology; National Power plc. Ed King Edward VI, Birmingham; Cheltenham Coll; Oriel Coll, Oxford (pres, univ C assoc, 1958).
**MELVIN CATON,** b July 7, 1951. Company director, family firm. Uttersford district cllr 1984- ; Essex county cllr 1993- . Member, Friends of the Earth; Green LDs; Charter 88. Ed Bishop's Stortford Coll; Salford and Loughborough Univs.
**MALCOLM FINCKEN,** b April 18, 1947. Teacher. Braintree district cllr 1983-87, 1995- ; Halstead town cllr 1979- (Mayor 1993-95). Ed Enfield GS; Sussex, Leicester and Cambridge Univs; OU.

## ST ALBANS — 61.8% change — Lab win

| Electorate % Turnout | | 65,560 | 77.5% | **1997** | 64,771 | 79.8% | **1992** |
|---|---|---|---|---|---|---|---|
| **Pollard, K** | Lab | **21,338** | 42.0% | +17.0% | **23,586** | 45.7% | C |
| Rutley, D | C | 16,879 | 33.2% | -12.4% | 14,452 | 28.0% | LD |
| Rowlands, A | LD | 10,692 | 21.0% | -6.9% | 12,932 | 25.0% | Lab |
| Warrilow, J | Ref | 1,619 | 3.2% | | 566 | 1.1% | Grn |
| Craigen, Ms S | Dream | 166 | 0.3% | | 124 | 0.2% | NLP |
| Docker, I | NLP | 111 | 0.2% | -0.0% | | | |
| **C to Lab notional swing 14.7%** | | **50,805** | | **Lab maj 4,459** | **51,660** | | **C maj 9,134** |
| | | | | 8.8% | | | 17.7% |

**KERRY POLLARD,** b April 27, 1944. Engineer. Contested seat 1992. St Albans district cllr 1982- ; Herts county cllr 1989- . Member, Nalgo; MSF. Ed Thornleigh Coll, Bolton.
**DAVID RUTLEY,** b March 7, 1961. Business development director

(PepsiCo Int). Member, Bow Group. Ed Lewes Priory School; LSE; Harvard Graduate School.
**ANTHONY ROWLANDS,** b Aug 11, 1952. Teacher. St Albans district cllr 1986- (dep leader); Herts county cllr 1993- . Ed Ryde School; Queen's Coll, Oxford; Cambridge and London Univs.

## ST HELENS NORTH — Lab hold

| Electorate % Turnout | | | 71,380 | 69.0% | 1997 | 71,261 | 77.4% | 1992 |
|---|---|---|---|---|---|---|---|---|
| Watts, D | Lab | | 31,953 | 64.9% | +7.0% | 31,930 | 57.9% | Lab |
| Walker, P | C | | 8,536 | 17.3% | -11.1% | 15,686 | 28.5% | C |
| Beirne, J | LD | | 6,270 | 12.7% | -0.4% | 7,224 | 13.1% | LD |
| Johnson, D | Ref | | 1,276 | 2.6% | | 287 | 0.5% | NLP |
| Waugh, R | Soc Lab | | 832 | 1.7% | | | | |
| Rudin, R D | UK Ind | | 363 | 0.7% | | | | |
| C to Lab swing 9.1% | | | 49,230 | Lab maj 23,417 | | 55,127 | Lab maj 16,244 | |
| | | | | 47.6% | | | 29.5% | |

**DAVE WATTS,** b Aug 26, 1951. Research assistant to John Evans, former Lab MP for this seat. Leader, St Helens Borough Council. NW regional organiser at 1992 election. Ed Seel Street Sec Mod.
**PELHAM WALKER,** b Feb 9, 1967. Chartered surveyor (for Unicorn Consultancy Services). Estate surveyor with Property Services Agency 1988-93. Chair, Dulwich YCs, 1990-91. Member, Tory Green Initiative. Ed Rossall School, Fleetwood; Westminster Univ.
**JOHN BEIRNE,** b May 2, 1961. Hairdresser. Contested St Helens N 1992. St Helens metropolitan borough cllr 1990- (group leader). Ed Parr HS; City & Guilds.

## ST HELENS SOUTH — 0.6% change — Lab win

| Electorate % Turnout | | | 66,526 | 66.5% | 1997 | 68,545 | 73.1% | 1992 |
|---|---|---|---|---|---|---|---|---|
| +Bermingham, G E | Lab | | 30,367 | 68.6% | +7.6% | 30,572 | 61.0% | Lab |
| Russell, Ms M | C | | 6,628 | 15.0% | -9.5% | 12,263 | 24.5% | C |
| Spencer, B | LD | | 5,919 | 13.4% | -0.5% | 6,961 | 13.9% | LD |
| Holdaway, W | Ref | | 1,165 | 2.6% | | 304 | 0.6% | NLP |
| Jump, Ms H | NLP | | 179 | 0.4% | -0.2% | | | |
| C to Lab notional swing 8.5% | | | 44,258 | Lab maj 23,739 | | 50,100 | Lab maj 18,309 | |
| | | | | 53.6% | | | 36.5% | |

**GERALD BERMINGHAM,** b Aug 20, 1940. Barrister. Elected 1983. Contested SE Derbyshire 1979. Member, home affairs cttee, 1983-97. Former chair, PLP home affairs cttee; sec, all-party industrial safety parly group; joint treas, space parly cttee; treas, magic group. Sheffield city cllr 1975-79, 1980-82. Vice-pres, League Against Cruel Sports. Ed Cotton Coll, N Staffs; Wellingborough GS; Sheffield Univ.
**MARY RUSSELL,** b Sept 1, 1954. Solicitor to Newspaper Society's gvt and legal affairs dept, and to Guild of Editors. US Peace Corps volunteer in Ecuador 1976-78. Ed Univ of North Carolina; Reading Univ; College of Law, Chancery Lane.
**BRIAN SPENCER,** b June 25, 1947. Employment services trainer, retired electrician. Contested this seat 1992. St Helens borough cllr 1980- (group leader). Ed Lowe House; St Helens Coll of Tech.

## ST IVES — LD gain

| Electorate % Turnout | | | 71,680 | 75.2% | 1997 | 71,152 | 80.3% | 1992 |
|---|---|---|---|---|---|---|---|---|
| George, A | LD | | 23,966 | 44.5% | +4.4% | 24,528 | 42.9% | C |
| Rogers, W | C | | 16,796 | 31.2% | -11.8% | 22,883 | 40.1% | LD |
| Fegan, C | Lab | | 8,184 | 15.2% | -0.8% | 9,144 | 16.0% | Lab |
| Faulkner, M | Ref | | 3,714 | 6.9% | | 577 | 1.0% | Lib |
| Garnier, Mrs P E | UK Ind | | 567 | 1.1% | | | | |
| Stephens, G | Lib | | 425 | 0.8% | -0.2% | | | |
| Lippiatt, K | R Alt | | 178 | 0.3% | | | | |
| Hitchins, W | BHMBCM | | 71 | 0.1% | | | | |
| C to LD swing 8.1% | | | 53,901 | LD maj 7,170 | | 57,132 | C maj 1,645 | |
| | | | | 13.3% | | | 2.9% | |

**ANDREW GEORGE,** b Dec 2, 1958. Charity worker. Contested St Ives 1992. Member, Friends of the Earth; World Development Movement. Ed Helston School; University Coll, Oxford; Sussex Univ. Interests include Cornish history, language and culture.
**WILLIAM ROGERS,** b Feb 23, 1960. Insurance broker and dir of broadcasting companies. Penwith cllr 1982-90 (C group leader 1984-90; council leader 1988-90). Chair, St Ives C assoc. Housing assoc chair. Ed Humphry Davy GS.
**CHRISTOPHER FEGAN,** b April 22, 1959. Postgraduate student. Cornwall county cllr; Penwith district cllr. Member, Unison. Ed St Bede's Coll, Manchester; Essex Univ.

| SALFORD | 15.4% change | | | | | | | Lab win |
|---|---|---|---|---|---|---|---|---|
| Electorate % Turnout | | 58,610 | 56.5% | **1997** | 61,048 | 65.2% | **1992** |
| **Blears, Ms H A** | **Lab** | **22,848** | **69.0%** | **+9.9%** | **23,532** | **59.1%** | **Lab** |
| Bishop, E | C | 5,779 | 17.4% | -9.0% | 10,545 | 26.5% | C |
| Owen, N | LD | 3,407 | 10.3% | -2.3% | 5,017 | 12.6% | LD |
| Cumpsty, R | Ref | 926 | 2.8% | | 711 | 1.8% | Other |
| Herman, Ms S | NLP | 162 | 0.5% | | | | |
| **C to Lab notional swing 9.5%** | | **33,122** | **Lab maj 17,069** | | **39,805** | **Lab maj 12,987** | |
| | | | 51.5% | | | 32.6% | |

**HAZEL BLEARS,** b May 14, 1956. Solicitor. Contested Bury S 1992; Tatton 1987. Salford city cllr 1984- . Chair, NW regional Lab Party. Trustee, Working Class Museum and Library. Member, Greater Manchester low pay unit. Ed Wardley GS; Eccles Sixth-Form Coll; Trent Poly; Chester Coll of Law.

**ELLIOT BISHOP,** b April 9, 1971. Trainee solicitor. Member, Bow Group; Assoc of C Lawyers. Ed King David School, Liverpool; London Univ; Coll of Law, Chester.
**NORMAN OWEN,** b April 9, 1943. Senior technician. Contested Salford E 1992. Member, Charter 88; AEEU. Ed Salford Tech.

| SALISBURY | | | | | | | C hold |
|---|---|---|---|---|---|---|---|
| Electorate % Turnout | | 78,973 | 73.7% | **1997** | 75,916 | 79.8% | **1992** |
| ***Key, R** | **C** | **25,012** | **42.9%** | **-9.1%** | **31,546** | **52.1%** | **C** |
| Emmerson-Peirce, Ms Y | LD | 18,736 | 32.2% | -5.0% | 22,513 | 37.2% | LD |
| Rogers, R | Lab | 10,242 | 17.6% | +8.5% | 5,483 | 9.0% | Lab |
| Farage, N P | UK Ind | 3,332 | 5.7% | | 609 | 1.0% | Grn |
| Soutar, H | Green | 623 | 1.1% | | 233 | 0.4% | Ind |
| Holmes, B | Ind | 184 | 0.3% | -0.1% | 117 | 0.2% | Wessex |
| Haysom, Mrs S | NLP | 110 | 0.2% | +0.0% | 93 | 0.2% | NLP |
| **C to LD swing 2.1%** | | **58,239** | **C maj 6,276** | | **60,594** | **C maj 9,033** | |
| | | | 10.8% | | | 14.9% | |

**ROBERT KEY,** b April 22, 1945. Elected 1983; contested Camden, Holborn and St Pancras S 1979. Under Sec for Transport 1993-94; National Heritage Under Sec 1992-93; Environment 1990-92. Member, select cttees on defence, 1995-97; health 1994-95; ed, science and arts, 1983-86. PPS to Chris Patten, Min for Overseas Development, and then Environment Sec, 1987-90; and to Energy Min 1985-87. Political sec to Sir Edward Heath, 1984-85. Chair, all-party parly group on Aids, 1996- , and its joint vice-chair, 1988-90; sec, C backbench cttee on arts and heritage, 1983-84. Joint parly chair, Council for Education in Commonwealth, 1985-87; member, advisory cttee on Commons works of art, 1988-90; and of C Party nat union exec 1981-83. An assistant master at Harrow 1969-83. Non-exec director Hortichem Ltd. Member, Medical

Research Council, 1989-90, and of its Aids cttee 1988-90. Chair, Inner Cities Religious Council, 1991-93. Member, chorus of Academy of St Martin-in-the-Fields, 1975-89. Ed Sherborne School; Clare Coll, Cambridge.
**YVONNE EMMERSON-PEIRCE,** b Jan 16, 1953. Non-exec director, Surrey Careers Service, Careers Enterprise Ltd. Surrey county cllr 1993- . Member, British Dyslexic Assoc. Ed St George's C of E, Gravesend.
**RICKY ROGERS,** b June 19, 1954. Construction manager, civil engineering. Salisbury district cllr 1988- ; Wiltshire county cllr 1989- . Member, TGWU. Ed St Thomas Boys' School, Salisbury; Salisbury Coll of Tech.

| SCARBOROUGH & WHITBY | | | | | | | Lab gain |
|---|---|---|---|---|---|---|---|
| Electorate % Turnout | | 75,862 | 71.6% | **1997** | 76,364 | 77.2% | **1992** |
| **Quinn, L** | **Lab** | **24,791** | **45.6%** | **+15.8%** | **29,334** | **49.8%** | **C** |
| *Sykes, J | C | 19,667 | 36.2% | -13.6% | 17,600 | 29.9% | Lab |
| Allinson, M | LD | 7,672 | 14.1% | -4.8% | 11,133 | 18.9% | LD |
| Murray, Ms S | Ref | 2,191 | 4.0% | | 876 | 1.5% | Grn |
| **C to Lab swing 14.7%** | | **54,321** | **Lab maj 5,124** | | **58,943** | **C maj 11,734** | |
| | | | 9.4% | | | 19.9% | |

**LAWRIE QUINN,** b Dec 25, 1956. Planning and development engineer, Railtrack. Member, Lab Electoral Reform Soc; Fabian Soc; Inst of Civil Engineers; Transport 2000. Ed Harraby School, Carlisle; Hatfield Poly.
**JOHN SYKES,** b Aug 24, 1956. Company director. MP for Scarborough 1992-97; contested Sheffield Hillsborough 1987. PPS to Viscount Cranborne, Leader of House of Lords, 1995-97. Member, select cttees on deregulation, 1995-97; national heritage 1992-95. Chair, C backbench trade and industry deregulation sub-cttee, 1995-97; sec, Yorkshire group of C MPs. Kirklees

metropolitan borough cllr 1987-91. Joined family company, Shaw Fuels Ltd (now Shaws Petroleum Ltd) 1974. Dir, Farnley Estates Ltd, agricultural estate; EMJ Plastics Ltd. Ed Giggleswick School, N Yorkshire.
**MARTIN ALLINSON,** b March 30, 1935. Engineering teacher; ex-locksmith, navy ganger, electronics engineer in Canada, poly lecturer in Yorkshire, Brunei and Singapore, and hill farmer. Ex-Lab cllr in Bradford, resigned 1984 and joined LDs. Ex-officer, NATFHE, ATTI, EPEA. Ed Manchester Grammar; John Bright GS, Llandudno; Univ Coll of North Wales.

| SCUNTHORPE | | 26.6% change | | | | Lab win |
|---|---|---|---|---|---|---|
| Electorate % Turnout | | 60,393 | 68.8% | **1997** | 62,268 | 78.0% | **1992** |
| +Morley, E A | Lab | 25,107 | 60.4% | +6.1% | 26,370 | 54.3% | Lab |
| Fisher, M | C | 10,934 | 26.3% | -9.6% | 17,467 | 35.9% | C |
| Smith, G | LD | 3,497 | 8.4% | +0.7% | 3,727 | 7.7% | LD |
| Smith, P | Ref | 1,637 | 3.9% | | 1,035 | 2.1% | Other |
| Hopper, B | Soc Lab | 399 | 1.0% | | | | |
| C to Lab notional swing 7.9% | | 41,574 | Lab maj 14,173 | | 48,599 | Lab maj 8,903 | |
| | | | 34.1% | | | 18.3% | |

**ELLIOT MORLEY**, b July 6, 1952. Became Under Secretary for Fisheries and Countryside, May 5, 1997. MP for Glanford and Scunthorpe 1987-97; contested Beverley 1983. Lab spokesman on agriculture, food and rural affairs 1989-97, with responsibilities for animal welfare and fisheries. Member, agric select cttee 1987-89; vice-chair, PLP ed, science and arts cttee, 1987-89. Sec, all-party British-Cyprus parly group. Hull city cllr 1979-85. Remedial teacher at Hull comprehensive, then head of individual learning centre until 1987. Ornithologist; vice-pres, Wildlife and Countryside Link, 1990- ; council member, British Trust for Ornithology, 1992-95; RSPB, 1989-93. Ed St Margaret's CE HS, Liverpool; Hull Coll of Ed.

**MARTYN FISHER**, b Nov 13, 1969. Management consultant. PA to Michael Portillo 1992. Ed Solihull School; Manchester Univ.

**GORDON SMITH**, b Aug 5, 1938. Quality manager. Voluntary adviser, Citizens Advice Bureau. Ed Brudnell Rd Sec Mod, Leeds.

| SEDGEFIELD | | 56.7% change | | | | Lab win |
|---|---|---|---|---|---|---|
| Electorate % Turnout | | 64,923 | 72.6% | **1997** | 66,143 | 76.3% | **1992** |
| +Blair, T | Lab | 33,526 | 71.2% | +8.9% | 31,391 | 62.2% | Lab |
| Pitman, Mrs E | C | 8,383 | 17.8% | -10.3% | 14,161 | 28.1% | C |
| Beadle, R | LD | 3,050 | 6.5% | -3.2% | 4,897 | 9.7% | LD |
| Hall, Miss M | Ref | 1,683 | 3.6% | | | | |
| Gibson, B | Soc Lab | 474 | 1.0% | | | | |
| C to Lab notional swing 9.6% | | 47,116 | Lab maj 25,143 | | 50,449 | Lab maj 17,230 | |
| | | | 53.4% | | | 34.2% | |

**TONY BLAIR**, b May 6, 1953. Became Prime Minister on May 2, 1997, having been elected leader of Lab Party and Leader of the Opposition in 1994. Won this seat 1983; contested Beaconsfield by-election 1982. Joined Shadow Cabinet 1988, being chief Lab spokesman on home affairs 1992-94; on employment 1989-92; on energy 1988-89; spokesman on trade and industry 1987-88; on Treasury and economic affairs 1984-87. Barrister (non-practising); called to Bar (Lincoln's Inn) 1976; hon Bencher 1994. Vice-pres, British group, IPU, and UK branch, CPA. Ed Durham Choristers School; Fettes Coll, Edinburgh; St John's Coll, Oxford.

**ELIZABETH PITMAN**, b Sept 24, 1967. Freelance writer and journalist, consultant for nationwide training co. Former vice-chair, Regent's Park and Kensington North C assoc. Ex-civil servant; worked for Prison Service at Wormwood Scrubs. Annual volunteer on holidays for disabled. Member, Polite Society; Amnesty. Ed St Mary's, Ascot; Manchester Coll, Oxford.

**RON BEADLE**, b Jan 28, 1966. Senior lecturer in human resource management. Contested Gateshead E 1992. Gateshead cllr. Ex-Lab Commons researcher. Member, European Movement; NATFHE. Ed Westminster City School; LSE (chair, students' union 1989).

| SELBY | | 6.2% change | | | | Lab win |
|---|---|---|---|---|---|---|
| Electorate % Turnout | | 75,141 | 74.9% | **1997** | 72,159 | 80.5% | **1992** |
| Grogan, J | Lab | 25,838 | 45.9% | +10.2% | 29,739 | 51.2% | C |
| Hind, K | C | 22,002 | 39.1% | -12.1% | 20,752 | 35.7% | Lab |
| Batty, T | LD | 6,778 | 12.0% | -1.0% | 7,595 | 13.1% | LD |
| Walker, D | Ref | 1,162 | 2.1% | | | | |
| Spence, P A | UK Ind | 536 | 1.0% | | | | |
| C to Lab notional swing 11.1% | | 56,316 | Lab maj 3,836 | | 58,086 | C maj 8,987 | |
| | | | 6.8% | | | 15.5% | |

**JOHN GROGAN**, b Feb 24, 1961. PA to leader of Leeds City Council. Contested this seat 1992 and 1987, and York in Euro elections 1989. Former asst to Dr Barry Seal, MEP for Yorkshire West and ex-leader of Lab group in Euro Parliament. Member, Nupe. Ed St Michael's Coll, Leeds; St John's Coll, Oxford (first Lab pres of Oxford students' union, 1982-83).

**KENNETH HIND**, b Sept 15, 1949. Barrister. MP for Lancashire W 1983-92. PPS to Peter Brooke, N Ireland Sec, 1990-92; to John Cope, Min of State for Employment and then for N Ireland, 1987-90; and to Lord Trefgarne, Min of State for Defence Procurement, 1986-87. Chair, British-Irish environment, ed and culture cttee, and member, steering cttee, British-Irish inter-parly body, 1990-92. Sec, C backbench legal cttee, 1986-90. Non-exec chair, De Keyser Europe Ltd, 1989- . Member Justice, international commission of jurists, 1983- . Hon vice-pres, Merseyside Chamber of Commerce, 1983- ; Central and W Lancs Chamber of Industry and Commerce, 1983- . Ed Woodhouse Grove School, Bradford; Leeds Univ (pres of union 1971-72); Inns of Court School of Law.

**TED BATTY**, b Feb 5, 1936. Contested this seat 1992. Arbitrator and quantity surveyor. Selby district cllr 1970-76 and 1987-92 (group leader 1987-92). Ed Cockburn GS, Leeds; London Univ. Elder, Selby United Reformed Church.

| SEVENOAKS | | 22.1% change | | | | | C win |
|---|---|---|---|---|---|---|---|
| Electorate % Turnout | | 66,474 | 75.4% | **1997** | 66,706 | 80.2% | **1992** |
| **Fallon, M** | C | **22,776** | **45.4%** | **-12.2%** | 30,847 | 57.6% | C |
| Hayes, J | Lab | 12,315 | 24.6% | +8.4% | 13,160 | 24.6% | LD |
| Walshe, R | LD | 12,086 | 24.1% | -0.5% | 8,626 | 16.1% | Lab |
| Large, N | Ref | 2,138 | 4.3% | | 700 | 1.3% | Grn |
| Lawrence, Ms M | Green | 443 | 0.9% | | 187 | 0.3% | NLP |
| Ellis, M | PF | 244 | 0.5% | | | | |
| Hankey, A | NLP | 147 | 0.3% | -0.1% | | | |
| C to Lab notional swing 10.3% | | 50,149 | | C maj 10,461 | 53,520 | | C maj 17,687 |
| | | | | 20.9% | | | 33.0% |

**MICHAEL FALLON,** b May 14, 1952. Company director. MP for Darlington 1983-92; contested Darlington by-election 1983. Education and Science Under Sec 1990-92; gvt whip 1990; asst gvt whip 1988-90; PPS to Cecil Parkinson 1987-88. Assistant to Lady Elles, MEP, 1979-83; EEC adviser, C research dept, 1977-79; sec, Lord Home's cttee on future of House of Lords, 1977-78; asst to Lord Carrington, 1974-77. Dir, Quality Care Homes plc since 1992. Joint managing dir, European Consultants Ltd, 1979-81. Ed Craigflower School, Fife; Epsom Coll; St Andrews Univ.

**JOHN HAYES,** b Dec 16, 1969. Solicitor then barrister, specialising in employment law. Treas, Young Lab Lawyers, 1995- . Member, Lab sub-cttees on employment and criminal law; Soc of Lab Lawyers; Christian Socialist Movement; Fabian Soc; Amnesty. Ed Northwood School, Middlesex; Brasenose Coll, Oxford; Inns of Court School of Law.

**ROGER WALSHE,** b April 5, 1935. Managing dir of foreign trade agency. Contested this seat 1992. Sevenoaks district cllr 1987- (leader 1995- ). Ed Whitgift School, Croydon; London Univ.

| SHEFFIELD ATTERCLIFFE | | | | | | | Lab hold |
|---|---|---|---|---|---|---|---|
| Electorate % Turnout | | 68,548 | 64.7% | **1997** | 69,177 | 71.8% | **1992** |
| ***Betts, C** | Lab | **28,937** | **65.3%** | **+7.8%** | 28,563 | 57.5% | Lab |
| Doyle, B | C | 7,119 | 16.1% | -10.3% | 13,083 | 26.3% | C |
| Smith, Mrs G | LD | 6,973 | 15.7% | +1.1% | 7,283 | 14.7% | LD |
| Brown, J | Ref | 1,289 | 2.9% | | 751 | 1.5% | Grn |
| C to Lab swing 9.0% | | 44,318 | | Lab maj 21,818 | 49,680 | | Lab maj 15,480 |
| | | | | 49.2% | | | 31.2% |

**CLIVE BETTS,** b Jan 13, 1950. Became gvt asst whip, May 7, 1997. Elected for this seat 1992; contested Louth 1979; Sheffield Hallam Oct 1974. Lab whip 1996- . Member, Treasury select cttee, 1995-96; chair 1995- , and sec 1994-95, PLP Treasury cttee; sec, Lab leader's campaign team, 1995-97. Sheffield city cllr 1976-92 (council leader 1987-92; dep leader 1986-87). Dep chair, AMA, 1988-91; chair, S Yorks pension authority, 1989-92. Was principal economist with S Yorkshire County Council; previously an

economist with TUC and Derbyshire County Council. Member, TGWU. Ed King Edward VII, Sheffield; Pembroke Coll, Cambridge.
**BRENDAN DOYLE,** b June 26, 1965. Management consultant. Ed St Joseph's RC HS, Widnes; Lancaster Univ (pres of union); Manchester Business School.
**GAIL SMITH,** b July 31, 1953. Sales manager. Ex-Sheffield city cllr. Ed Bearer Hill HS; Sheffield School of Nursing.

| SHEFFIELD BRIGHTSIDE | | | | | | | Lab hold |
|---|---|---|---|---|---|---|---|
| Electorate % Turnout | | 58,930 | 57.5% | **1997** | 63,810 | 66.3% | **1992** |
| ***Blunkett, D** | Lab | **24,901** | **73.5%** | **+3.1%** | 29,771 | 70.4% | Lab |
| Butler, F | LD | 4,947 | 14.6% | +2.1% | 7,090 | 16.8% | C |
| Buckwell, C | C | 2,850 | 8.4% | -8.4% | 5,273 | 12.5% | LD |
| Farnsworth, B | Ref | 624 | 1.8% | | 150 | 0.4% | Int Comm |
| Davidson, P | Soc Lab | 482 | 1.4% | | | | |
| Scott, R | NLP | 61 | 0.2% | | | | |
| LD to Lab swing 0.5% | | 33,865 | | Lab maj 19,954 | 42,284 | | Lab maj 22,681 |
| | | | | 58.9% | | | 53.6% |

**DAVID BLUNKETT,** b June 6, 1947. Became Education and Employment Secretary, May 2, 1997. Shadow Education Sec 1994 and for employment in 1995. Elected 1987; contested Sheffield Hallam Feb 1974. Shadow Health Sec from 1992, when elected to Shadow Cabinet, to 1994; Shadow Min for Local Gvt 1988-92. Member, Lab Party NEC, 1983- ; party chair, 1993-94. Lab leader of Sheffield City Council 1980, serving on council 1970-88; South Yorks county cllr 1973-77. Dep chair, AMA, 1984-87. Parly adviser to Chartered Soc of Physiotherapy. Former industrial relations tutor. Member, Unison. Ed Royal Nat Coll for the Blind,

Shrewsbury; Richmond CFE, Sheffield; Sheffield Univ; Huddersfield Coll of Ed (Tech).
**FRANCIS BUTLER,** b May 4, 1942. Retired lecturer. Contested this seat 1983, 1979; contested Sheffield Park Oct 1974, Feb 1974, 1970. Sheffield city cllr 1969-87, 1993- (group leader 1973-79, 1993- ); South Yorks county cllr 1987- ; Ecclesfield town cllr 1987- . Ed Owlerlan Sec Mod; Huddersfield Poly and Univ.
**CHRISTOPHER BUCKWELL,** b Feb 6, 1958. Solicitor. Rochester city cllr 1983-91, 1992-95. Ed King's, Rochester; City of Birmingham Poly.

| SHEFFIELD CENTRAL | | 24.8% change | | | | | Lab win |
|---|---|---|---|---|---|---|---|
| Electorate % Turnout | | 68,667 | 53.0% | **1997** | 71,980 | 59.3% | **1992** |
| +Caborn, R | Lab | 23,179 | 63.6% | +4.0% | 25,448 | 59.6% | Lab |
| Qadar, A | LD | 6,273 | 17.2% | -1.7% | 8,068 | 18.9% | LD |
| Hess, M | C | 4,341 | 11.9% | -6.8% | 7,983 | 18.7% | C |
| D'Agorne, A | Green | 954 | 2.6% | | 840 | 2.0% | Grn |
| Brownlow, A | Ref | 863 | 2.4% | | 238 | 0.6% | EUVJJ |
| Douglas, K | Soc | 466 | 1.3% | | 103 | 0.2% | CL |
| Aitken, Ms M | ProLife | 280 | 0.8% | | | | |
| Driver, M | WRP | 63 | 0.2% | | | | |
| LD to Lab notional swing 2.8% | | 36,419 | Lab maj 16,906 | | 42,680 | Lab maj 17,380 | |
| | | | 46.4% | | | 40.7% | |

**RICHARD CABORN**, b Oct 6, 1943. Became Environment and Transport Minister of State responsible for regions, regeneration and planning, May 5, 1997. Elected 1983; MEP for Sheffield 1979-84. Lab spokesman on Chancellor of the Duchy of Lancaster 1995-97; chair, select cttee on trade and industry, 1992-95; member, select cttee on Euro legislation, 1983-88. Sec, all-party Southern Africa parly group; vice-chair, Tribune Group, 1986-87. Non-executive dir, Sheffield United. Unpaid dir, Freedom Productions Ltd; Sheffield City Trust; Sheffield Festival. Worked as a fitter; convener of shop stewards, Firth Brown Ltd, 1967-79; vice-pres,

Sheffield Trades Council, 1968-79. Member, BBC advisory council, 1975-78; Co-op Party. Ed Hurlfield Comp, Sheffield; Granville CFE; Sheffield Poly.
**ALI QADAR**, b Aug 8, 1948. Chartered accountant. Sheffield city cllr 1996- (first Asian LD cllr in South Yorks). Ed Multan Coll, Pakistan; Punjab Univ.
**MARTIN HESS**, b Sept 19, 1959. Sales and marketing director, computer software. Deputy chair, Hove C assoc. Worked over 10 years with IBM. Ed Cardinal Newman School, Hove; LSE; London Business School.

| SHEFFIELD HALLAM | | 19.0% change | | | | | LD win |
|---|---|---|---|---|---|---|---|
| Electorate % Turnout | | 62,834 | 72.4% | **1997** | 61,133 | 73.1% | **1992** |
| Allan, R | LD | 23,345 | 51.3% | +20.6% | 22,180 | 49.6% | C |
| +Patnick, Sir Irvine | C | 15,074 | 33.1% | -16.5% | 13,740 | 30.7% | LD |
| Conquest, S | Lab | 6,147 | 13.5% | -4.9% | 8,246 | 18.4% | Lab |
| Davidson, I | Ref | 788 | 1.7% | | 384 | 0.9% | Grn |
| Booler, P | SIP | 125 | 0.3% | | 82 | 0.2% | NLP |
| | | | | | 80 | 0.2% | Rev Comm |
| C to LD notional swing 18.5% | | 45,479 | LD maj 8,271 | | 44,712 | C maj 8,440 | |
| | | | 18.2% | | | 18.9% | |

**RICHARD ALLAN**, b Feb 11, 1966. NHS computer manager. Avon county cllr 1993- ; Bath city cllr 1994- . Member, World Development Movement; Voting Reform Group; CPRE. Ed Oundle; Pembroke Coll, Cambridge; Bristol Poly.
**SIR IRVINE PATNICK**, b Oct 11, 1929. Elected 1987; contested Sheffield Hillsborough 1979 and 1970. Gvt whip 1990-94; asst gvt whip 1989-90. Member, environment select cttee, 1994-97; selection cttee, 1996-97. Joint vice-chair, C backbench environment cttee, 1988-89, joint sec 1987-88. Chair, C national

local gvt advisory cttee, 1989-90; nat exec, C Party, 1982-89. Sheffield city cllr 1967-70; Sheffield metropolitan district cllr, 1971-88; S Yorks county cllr (opposition leader 1973 to 1986, when it was abolished). Former dir, Eversure Textiles Ltd. Governor, Sports Aid Foundation, Yorkshire and Humberside, 1980-85. Ed Central Tech School; Sheffield Poly.
**STEPHEN CONQUEST**, b Aug 4, 1959. Counsellor. Merton borough cllr. Member, MSF; SHA; Fabian Soc. Ed Ernest Bailey GS; Univ of Central England.

| SHEFFIELD HEELEY | | | | | | | Lab hold |
|---|---|---|---|---|---|---|---|
| Electorate % Turnout | | 66,599 | 65.0% | **1997** | 70,953 | 70.9% | **1992** |
| *Michie, B | Lab | 26,274 | 60.7% | +5.1% | 28,005 | 55.7% | Lab |
| Davison, R | LD | 9,196 | 21.3% | +2.9% | 13,051 | 25.9% | C |
| Harthman, J | C | 6,767 | 15.6% | -10.3% | 9,247 | 18.4% | LD |
| Mawson, D | Ref | 1,029 | 2.4% | | | | |
| LD to Lab swing 1.1% | | 43,266 | Lab maj 17,078 | | 50,303 | Lab maj 14,954 | |
| | | | 39.5% | | | 29.7% | |

**BILL MICHIE**, b Nov 24, 1935. Ex-maintenance electrician and laboratory technician. Elected for this seat 1983. Member, Commons privileges cttee, 1994-95; select cttee on members' interests 1992-95. Treas, Campaign group of Lab MPs, 1987- ; vice-chair, Yorkshire group of Lab MPs, 1985-87. Sheffield city cllr 1970-84; S Yorks county cllr 1974-86. Ex-shop steward of AEEU, which he joined in 1952. Ed Abbeydale Sec, Sheffield.

**ROGER DAVISON**, b Dec 25, 1947. Teacher. Sheffield city cllr. Ex-director, Crucible Theatre. Member, NUT. Ed Gregg School, Sheffield; East Anglia Univ; Huddersfield Poly; Plater Coll, Oxford.
**JOHN HARTHMAN**, b March 8, 1957. Emergency planning officer. Sheffield city cllr 1992-94; campaign assistant to Sir Irvine Patnick, MP, 1992 election. Previously worked as hang-gliding instructor. Ed King's, Chester; Sheffield Univ; Sheffield City Poly.

## SHEFFIELD HILLSBOROUGH — Lab hold

| Electorate % Turnout | | 74,642 | 71.0% | 1997 | 77,343 | 77.2% | 1992 |
|---|---|---|---|---|---|---|---|
| *Jackson, Mrs H | Lab | 30,150 | 56.9% | +10.7% | 27,563 | 46.2% | Lab |
| Dunworth, A | LD | 13,699 | 25.8% | -8.5% | 20,500 | 34.3% | LD |
| Nuttall, D | C | 7,707 | 14.5% | -5.0% | 11,640 | 19.5% | C |
| Rusling, J | Ref | 1,468 | 2.8% | | | | |
| LD to Lab swing 9.6% | | 53,024 | Lab maj 16,451 | | 59,703 | Lab maj 7,063 | |
| | | | 31.0% | | | 11.8% | |

**HELEN JACKSON**, b May 19, 1939. Ex-teacher. Elected for this seat 1992. Member, environment select cttee, 1992-97. Chair, all-party water parly group, 1994- . Joint chair, PLP women's group, 1992- ; joint vice-chair, PLP environment cttee; sec, PLP environmental protection cttee. Sheffield city cllr 1980-91; Huyton urban district cllr 1972-74. Founder member and chair, Centre for Local Economic Strategies, 1986-91. Member, TGWU. Ed Berkhamsted Girls' School; St Hilda's Coll, Oxford.

**ARTHUR DUNWORTH,** b Dec 8, 1939. Retired sales and marketing director. Sheffield city cllr 1992- ; Bradfield cllr. Represented LDs on South Yorks joint authorities for passenger transport and pensions. Ed King Edward VII, Sheffield; Nottingham Univ.
**DAVID NUTTALL,** b March 25, 1962. Solicitor. Rotherham metropolitan borough cllr 1992- (opposition leader 1995-96). Member, nat local gvt advisory cttee; Yorkshire County Cricket Club; life member, Monday Club; Rotherham United FC. Ed Aston Comp, Rotherham; London Univ.

## SHERWOOD — Lab hold

| Electorate % Turnout | | 74,788 | 75.6% | 1997 | 73,354 | 85.5% | 1992 |
|---|---|---|---|---|---|---|---|
| *Tipping, P | Lab | 33,071 | 58.5% | +11.0% | 29,788 | 47.5% | Lab |
| Spencer, R | C | 16,259 | 28.8% | -14.1% | 26,878 | 42.9% | C |
| Moult, B | LD | 4,889 | 8.6% | -1.0% | 6,039 | 9.6% | LD |
| Slack, L | Ref | 1,882 | 3.3% | | | | |
| Ballard, P | BNP | 432 | 0.8% | | | | |
| C to Lab swing 12.5% | | 56,533 | Lab maj 16,812 | | 62,705 | Lab maj 2,910 | |
| | | | 29.7% | | | 4.6% | |

**SIMON (PADDY) TIPPING**, b Oct 24, 1949. Ex-social worker. Gained this seat for Lab 1992; contested Rushcliffe 1987. Member, select cttee on Parliamentary Commissioner for Administration, 1996-97. Joint chair, all-party minerals group, 1996- ; all-party epilepsy group, 1994- ; Armenia group; sec, PLP home affairs cttee; chair, Central Region group of Lab MPs. Notts county cllr 1981-93. Project leader, C of E Children's Soc, Nottingham, 1979-83. Dir, Notts Co-operative Development Agency, 1983-92; Nottingham

Development Enterprise 1987-93. Member, Co-op Party; Unison. Ed Hipperholme GS; Nottingham Univ.
**ROLAND SPENCER,** b Oct 22, 1947. Builder and property developer. Gedling borough cllr 1987- (Mayor 1992-93); Notts county cllr 1989-93. Vice-chair, Sherwood C assoc, 1989-95. Ed Robert Mellors Secondary.
**BRUCE MOULT,** b April 8, 1961. Business development manager. Ashfield district cllr 1987-91. Ed Chilwell Comp.

## SHIPLEY — Lab gain

| Electorate % Turnout | | 69,281 | 76.3% | 1997 | 68,816 | 82.1% | 1992 |
|---|---|---|---|---|---|---|---|
| Leslie, C | Lab | 22,962 | 43.4% | +15.0% | 28,463 | 50.4% | C |
| *Fox, Sir Marcus | C | 19,966 | 37.8% | -12.6% | 16,081 | 28.5% | Lab |
| Cole, J | LD | 7,984 | 15.1% | -4.9% | 11,288 | 20.0% | LD |
| Ellams, Dr S | Ref | 1,960 | 3.7% | | 680 | 1.2% | Grn |
| C to Lab swing 13.8% | | 52,872 | Lab maj 2,996 | | 56,512 | C maj 12,382 | |
| | | | 5.7% | | | 21.9% | |

**CHRISTOPHER LESLIE,** b June 28, 1972. Political research asst/office administrator. Bradford city cllr 1994- . Chair, Shipley constituency area panel sub-cttee. Member, TGWU; GMB. Ed Bingley GS; Leeds Univ.
**SIR MARCUS FOX,** b June 11, 1927. Elected 1970; contested Dewsbury 1959; Huddersfield W 1966. Chair, 1922 Cttee of C backbenchers, 1993-97 (joint vice-chair 1983-93); chair, Commons selection cttee, 1984-92; member, Commons privileges cttee, 1994-95. Privy Counsellor 1995. Under Sec for Environment 1979-81; gvt whip 1973-74; asst gvt whip 1972-73.

Chair, Nat Assoc of C Clubs, 1988- ; joint vice-chair, Yorkshire C MPs, 1990-92. Dir, Care Services Group; McCarthy and Stone, sheltered housing; Hartley Investment Trust; Bristol Port Co; Illingworth Morris Ltd, wool textile group; Yorkshire Food Group plc. Parly consultant to 3M (UK) Ltd; Shepherd (Construction) Ltd; Gratte Brothers, electrical engineers. Ed Eastborough Council School, Dewsbury; Wheelwright GS, Dewsbury.
**JOHN COLE,** b July 6, 1944. Teacher. Contested Shipley 1992. Member, Yorkshire Water Watch; Friends of the Earth; Charter 88; ATL. Ed Hampton GS, Middlesex; Dundee and Southampton Univs.

| SHREWSBURY & ATCHAM | | | | | Lab gain | | |
|---|---|---|---|---|---|---|---|
| Electorate % Turnout | | 73,542 | 75.3% | **1997** | 70,620 | 82.5% | **1992** |
| **Marsden, P** | **Lab** | **20,484** | **37.0%** | **+11.0%** | **26,681** | **45.8%** | **C** |
| *Conway, D | C | 18,814 | 34.0% | -11.8% | 15,716 | 27.0% | LD |
| Woolland, Mrs A | LD | 13,838 | 25.0% | -2.0% | 15,157 | 26.0% | Lab |
| Barker, D | Ref | 1,346 | 2.4% | | 677 | 1.2% | Grn |
| Rowlands, D W | UK Ind | 477 | 0.9% | | | | |
| Dignan, A | CFSS | 257 | 0.5% | | | | |
| Williams, A | PPP | 128 | 0.2% | | | | |
| **C to Lab swing 11.4%** | | **55,344** | Lab maj **1,670** | | **58,231** | C maj **10,965** | |
| | | | 3.0% | | | 18.8% | |

**PAUL MARSDEN,** b March 18, 1968. Quality assurance manager. Member, Institute of Management; American Society of Quality Control; CWU; nat exec Young Fabians, 1990. Chair, Nesscliffe branch, Shrewsbury CLP, 1995- . Ed Helsby HS; Mid-Cheshire Coll; Teesside Poly; OU.
**DEREK CONWAY,** b Feb 15, 1953. Elected 1983; contested Newcastle upon Tyne E 1979; Durham Oct 1974. Senior gvt whip 1996-97; gvt whip 1994-96; asst gvt whip 1993-94. PPS to Sir Wyn Roberts, Min of State for Wales, 1988-91. Member, select cttees on broadcasting 1995-97; transport 1987-88; agriculture 1986-87;

Commons administration cttee; Commons accommodation and works cttee. Member, nat exec, C Party, 1971-81; C nat local gvt cttee, 1979-83; Tyne and Wear metropolitan county cllr 1977-83 (leader 1979-82); Gateshead metropolitan borough cllr 1974-78. Principal organiser, nat fund for research into crippling diseases, 1974-83.. Ed Beacon Hill Boys' School; Gateshead Tech Coll; Newcastle Poly.
**ANNE WOOLLAND,** b April 20, 1946. Laboratory technician, ex-teacher. Shrewsbury and Atcham borough cllr 1992- . Ed Grove Park Girls' GS, Wrexham; Liverpool Univ.

| SHROPSHIRE NORTH | | 16.9% change | | | | | C win |
|---|---|---|---|---|---|---|---|
| Electorate % Turnout | | 70,852 | 72.7% | **1997** | 68,301 | 78.2% | **1992** |
| **Paterson, O** | **C** | **20,730** | **40.2%** | **-10.6%** | **27,159** | **50.8%** | **C** |
| Lucas, I | Lab | 18,535 | 36.0% | +13.0% | 13,978 | 26.2% | LD |
| Stevens, J | LD | 10,489 | 20.4% | -5.8% | 12,283 | 23.0% | Lab |
| Allen, D | Ref | 1,764 | 3.4% | | | | |
| **C to Lab notional swing 11.8%** | | **51,518** | C maj **2,195** | | **53,420** | C maj **13,181** | |
| | | | 4.3% | | | 24.7% | |

**OWEN PATERSON,** b June 24, 1956. Tanner. Contested Wrexham 1992. Assisted John Biffen in Shropshire N 1987 election. Managing dir, British Leather Co, Birkenhead, since 1985; UK rep to Euro Tanning Fed. Member, Ellesmere Cottage Hospital action group, 1988-89. Ed Radley; Corpus Christi Coll, Cambridge.
**IAN LUCAS,** b Sept 18, 1960. Solicitor. Chair, Wrexham CLP, Gresford community cllr. Member, Soc of Lab Lawyers. Ed

Newcastle RGS; New College, Oxford; Chester Coll of Law.
**JOHN STEVENS,** b May 17, 1943. Computer projects manager. Contested this seat 1992; Staffordshire W and Congleton in 1994 Euro elections; South Fylde for Libs in 1979, Bristol S Feb 1974 and Bristol NW 1970. Shropshire county cllr (group leader). Ed Trowbridge HS, Wilts.

| SITTINGBOURNE & SHEPPEY | | 26.5% change | | | | | Lab win |
|---|---|---|---|---|---|---|---|
| Electorate % Turnout | | 63,850 | 72.3% | **1997** | 65,141 | 77.6% | **1992** |
| **Wyatt, D M** | **Lab** | **18,723** | **40.6%** | **+16.6%** | **24,669** | **48.8%** | **C** |
| +Moate, Sir Roger | C | 16,794 | 36.4% | -12.4% | 13,541 | 26.8% | LD |
| Truelove, R | LD | 8,447 | 18.3% | -8.5% | 12,106 | 23.9% | Lab |
| Moull, P | Ref | 1,082 | 2.3% | | 236 | 0.5% | Other |
| Driver, C | Loony | 644 | 1.4% | | | | |
| Risi, N | UK Ind | 472 | 1.0% | | | | |
| **C to Lab notional swing 14.5%** | | **46,162** | Lab maj **1,929** | | **50,552** | C maj **11,128** | |
| | | | 4.2% | | | 22.0% | |

**DEREK WYATT,** b Dec 4, 1949. Works in corporate dept, BSkyB. Haringey cllr. Chair of Alexandra Palace Trust. Member, NUJ; Amnesty; Greenpeace; ANC London; Charter 88. England rugby union international (one cap), Oxford rugby union Blue. Ed OU; St Catherine's Coll, Oxford.
**SIR ROGER MOATE,** b May 12, 1938. Insurance broker, consultant and company director. MP for Faversham 1970-97; contested that seat 1966. Member, agriculture select cttee, 1995-97; Court of Referees. Chair, all-party British-Norwegian parly group; sec, paper and board industry group, 1994-97; British-American group

1974-81; treas, British fruit industry group, 1995-97; joint sec, all-party Hungarian group, 1996-97. Dir, Robinco CS, Robinco-Migert Ltd, both sale of office equipment. Parly consultant, British Paper and Board Industry Fed. Ed Latymer Upper School, Hammersmith.
**ROGER TRUELOVE,** b Dec 8, 1944. Retired teacher. Contested Faversham 1992. Swale district cllr 1987-95. Policy chair, SE region. Member, Amnesty; Friends of the Earth; CPRE. Officer, English Schools Cricket Assoc, 1974-92. Ed Abbey and Stanhope GS; Oxford and London Univs.

| SKIPTON & RIPON | | 7.5% change | | | | | C win |
|---|---|---|---|---|---|---|---|
| Electorate % Turnout | | 72,042 | 75.4% | **1997** | 70,154 | 81.2% | **1992** |
| +Curry, D | C | 25,294 | 46.5% | -11.3% | 32,944 | 57.9% | C |
| Mould, T | LD | 13,674 | 25.2% | -2.1% | 15,547 | 27.3% | LD |
| Marchant, R | Lab | 12,171 | 22.4% | +7.6% | 8,442 | 14.8% | Lab |
| Holdsworth, Mrs N | Ref | 3,212 | 5.9% | | | | |
| C to LD notional swing 4.6% | | 54,351 | | C maj 11,620 | 56,933 | | C maj 17,397 |
| | | | | 21.4% | | | 30.6% |

**DAVID CURRY**, b June 13, 1944. Freelance journalist. Elected 1987; contested Morpeth in both 1974 elections. MEP for Essex NE 1979-89. Appointed Min of Local Gvt, Housing and Urban Regeneration with rank of Min of State, DoE, 1993, and in 1996 also became Min for the West Country; Min of State, Ag, Fish and Food 1992-93; Parly Sec, Min of Ag, Fish and Food, 1989-92. Privy Counsellor 1996. Member, agriculture select cttee, 1987-89. Joint sec, C backbench ag, fish and food cttee, 1987-89. Euro democratic group and C spokesman, Euro Parliament budgets cttee, 1985-89; rapporteur-general on 1987 EEC budget; chair, Euro Parliament agric cttee, 1982-84. *Financial Times* foreign news editor, London, 1978. Ed Ripon GS; Corpus Christi Coll, Oxford; Kennedy Inst of Gvt, Harvard.

**ROBERT MARCHANT**, b March 5, 1967. Business/IT consultant to banking industry. Has worked as volunteer counsellor at Shelter. Member, MSF; Labour Finance and Industry Group; Industry Forum. Ed Ripon GS; New College, Oxford.

**THOMAS MOULD**, b Jan 13, 1948. Contractor. North Yorks county cllr; Harrogate borough cllr. Ed Bedale HS; Askham Bryant Coll, York.

| SLEAFORD & NORTH HYKEHAM | | 52.4% change | | | | | C win |
|---|---|---|---|---|---|---|---|
| Electorate % Turnout | | 71,486 | 74.4% | **1997** | 66,382 | 80.4% | **1992** |
| +Hogg, D M | C | 23,358 | 43.9% | -14.5% | 31,180 | 58.4% | C |
| Harriss, S | Lab | 18,235 | 34.3% | +12.4% | 11,698 | 21.9% | Lab |
| Marriott, J | LD | 8,063 | 15.2% | -1.5% | 8,873 | 16.6% | LD |
| Clery, P | Ref | 2,942 | 5.5% | | 1,603 | 3.0% | Other |
| Overton, R | Ind | 578 | 1.1% | | | | |
| C to Lab notional swing 13.4% | | 53,176 | | C maj 5,123 | 53,354 | | C maj 19,482 |
| | | | | 9.6% | | | 36.5% |

**DOUGLAS HOGG**, b Feb 5, 1945. Barrister (non-practising). MP for Grantham 1979-97. Joined Cabinet 1995 as Min of Agriculture, Fisheries and Food; Min of State for Foreign and Commonwealth Affairs 1990-95; Min for Industry, with rank of Min of State for Trade and Industry, 1989-90; Under Sec, Home Office, 1986-89; asst gvt whip 1983-84. Member, agric select cttee, 1979-82; PPS to Chief Secretary to Treasury 1982-83. Chair, exec cttee, Soc of C Lawyers. Ed Eton; Christ Church, Oxford (pres of Union); Lincoln's Inn. Elder son of Lord Hailsham of St Marylebone, former Lord Chancellor.

**SEAN HARRISS**, b May 12, 1968. Local gvt officer with Bolton Metropolitan Borough Council. Member, Unison. Ed Horncastle GS; Nottingham Univ.

**JOHN MARRIOTT**, b Oct 11, 1943. Teacher. North Kesteven district cllr 1987- (group leader). Ex-chair, Lincolnshire LDs. Member, Charter 88; Shelter; NASUWT. Ed Alderman Newton Boys' GS, Leicester; Selwyn Coll, Cambridge; Trent Poly.

| SLOUGH | | 7.4% change | | | | | Lab win |
|---|---|---|---|---|---|---|---|
| Electorate % Turnout | | 70,283 | 67.9% | **1997** | 69,450 | 77.0% | **1992** |
| MacTaggart, Ms F | Lab | 27,029 | 56.6% | +12.5% | 23,580 | 44.1% | Lab |
| Buscombe, Mrs P | C | 13,958 | 29.2% | -14.8% | 23,544 | 44.0% | C |
| Bushill, C | LD | 3,509 | 7.4% | +0.2% | 3,841 | 7.2% | LD |
| Bradshaw, Ms A | Lib | 1,835 | 3.8% | +1.4% | 1,319 | 2.5% | Lib |
| Sharkey, T | Ref | 1,124 | 2.4% | | 647 | 1.2% | Ind Lab |
| Whitmore, P | Slough | 277 | 0.6% | | 268 | 0.5% | NF |
| | | | | | 142 | 0.3% | NLP |
| | | | | | 124 | 0.2% | ERIP |
| C to Lab notional swing 13.7% | | 47,732 | | Lab maj 13,071 | 53,465 | | Lab maj 36 |
| | | | | 27.4% | | | 0.1% |

**FIONA MacTAGGART**, b Sept 12, 1953. Lecturer in primary education, London Univ Inst of Ed. Founder, board member and assoc editor of *Renewal* discussion journal. Dir, Fabian Education School, 1995, and author/editor of Fabian pamphlet on education. Founder, David Hodge Memorial Trust/Young Photojournalist of the Year award. Ed Cheltenham Ladies' College; King's Coll, London.

**PETA BUSCOMBE**, b March 12, 1954. Barrister. S Oxfordshire district cllr 1995- ; vice-chair, South Oxfordshire C assoc, and chair, CPC. Partner in firm exporting limited edition china pieces to US. Ed Rosebery GS, Epsom; Inns of Court School of Law; Gray's Inn; Columbia Law School, New York.

**CHRIS BUSHILL**, b June 5, 1946. Electrical engineer. Berkshire county cllr. Member, Wey and Arun canal trust; National Trust; Electrical Power Engineers' Assoc (shop steward). Ed Southall Tech School; Southall Coll of Tech.

| SOLIHULL | | 0.3% change | | | 1997 | | | C win |
|---|---|---|---|---|---|---|---|---|
| Electorate % Turnout | | 78,898 | 74.7% | | 1997 | 78,171 | 80.5% | 1992 |
| +Taylor, J M | C | 26,299 | 44.6% | -16.2% | | 38,277 | 60.8% | C |
| Southcombe, M | LD | 14,902 | 25.3% | +4.3% | | 13,202 | 21.0% | LD |
| Harris, Ms R | Lab | 14,334 | 24.3% | +7.6% | | 10,512 | 16.7% | Lab |
| Nattrass, M | Ref | 2,748 | 4.7% | | | 925 | 1.5% | Grn |
| Caffery, J | ProLife | 623 | 1.1% | | | | | |
| C to LD notional swing 10.3% | | 58,906 | | C maj 11,397 | | 62,916 | | C maj 25,075 |
| | | | | 19.3% | | | | 39.9% |

**JOHN MARK TAYLOR**, b Aug 19, 1941. Non-practising solicitor. Elected for this seat 1983; contested Dudley E Feb and Oct 1974; MEP for Midlands East 1979-84. Corporate Affairs Min at DTI 1995-97 with rank of Under Sec of State; Parly Sec, Lord Chancellor's Department, 1992-95; Vice-Chamberlain of HM Household 1990-92; gvt whip 1989-90; asst gvt whip 1988-89. As MEP was C EEC budget spokesman 1979-81, and group dep chair 1981-82. PPS to Kenneth Clarke, Trade and Industry Min, 1987-88; joint vice-chair, C backbench Euro affairs cttee, 1986-87 (joint sec, 1983-86); member, environment select cttee, 1983-87; vice-chair, C backbench sports cttee, 1985-87. Solihull county borough cllr 1971-74, and W Midlands county cllr 1973-86. Vice-pres, AMA, 1979- . Ed Bromsgrove School.

**MICHAEL SOUTHCOMBE**, b March 9, 1962. Environmental protection officer. Contested this seat 1992. Solihull borough cllr; Chard town cllr 1985-90. Member, Friends of the Earth; Unison. Ed Holyrood School, Somerset; Royal Holloway and Bedford New Coll, London.

**RACHEL HARRIS**, b Dec 4, 1957. Part-time lecturer; previously civil servant, sales manager and office supervisor. Member, Co-op Party; chair, Dudley Soc Ed Assoc. Ed Wolverhampton Univ.

| SOMERTON & FROME | | 1.1% change | | | 1997 | | | LD win |
|---|---|---|---|---|---|---|---|---|
| Electorate % Turnout | | 73,988 | 77.6% | | 1997 | 72,545 | 82.3% | 1992 |
| Heath, D | LD | 22,684 | 39.5% | -0.8% | | 28,287 | 47.4% | C |
| +Robinson, M | C | 22,554 | 39.3% | -8.1% | | 24,036 | 40.3% | LD |
| Ashford, B | Lab | 9,385 | 16.3% | +5.9% | | 6,217 | 10.4% | Lab |
| Rodwell, R | Ref | 2,449 | 4.3% | | | 744 | 1.2% | Grn |
| Gadd, R P | UK Ind | 331 | 0.6% | | | 388 | 0.7% | Lib |
| C to LD notional swing 3.7% | | 57,403 | | LD maj 130 | | 59,672 | | C maj 4,251 |
| | | | | 0.2% | | | | 7.1% |

**DAVID HEATH**, b March 16, 1954. Consultant (also non-practising optician). Contested this seat 1992. Parly consultant to World Wide Fund for Nature 1991, and to Age Concern 1991. Somerset county cllr 1985- (leader 1985-89; opposition leader 1989-91). Chair, Avon and Somerset police authority 1993-96. Vice-chair, Assoc of County Councils. Ed Millfield; St John's Coll, Oxford; City Univ.

**MARK ROBINSON**, b Dec 26, 1946. Non-practising barrister. Elected for this seat 1992; MP for Newport W 1983-87; contested South Yorkshire in 1979 Euro elections. Under Sec for Wales 1985-87; PPS to William Waldegrave, Chief Sec to Treasury, and other Treasury mins, 1995-97; to Douglas Hurd, Foreign Sec, 1994-95; to Overseas Development Min and junior FCO min 1992-94; to Welsh Sec 1984-85. Member, Winston Churchill Memorial Trust, 1993- ; Commonwealth Development Corp, 1988-92. Asst dir, Commonwealth Secretariat, Marlborough House, 1977-83; second officer, exec office, UN Secretary-General, 1974-77. Ed Harrow; Christ Church, Oxford; Middle Temple.

**BOB ASHFORD**, b July 13, 1953. Social worker. Contested Somerton and Frome 1992. Frome town cllr 1991- ; Mendip district cllr 1991- . Member, Unison; Greenpeace. Ed Henbury Comp, Bristol; Filton Tech Coll, Bristol; New Univ of Ulster; Bristol Univ.

| SOUTH HOLLAND & THE DEEPINGS | | 83.7% change | | | 1997 | | | C win |
|---|---|---|---|---|---|---|---|---|
| Electorate % Turnout | | 69,642 | 72.0% | | 1997 | 64,244 | 79.2% | 1992 |
| Hayes, J | C | 24,691 | 49.3% | -7.8% | | 29,017 | 57.0% | C |
| Lewis, J | Lab | 16,700 | 33.3% | +9.2% | | 12,254 | 24.1% | Lab |
| Millen, P | LD | 7,836 | 15.6% | -3.3% | | 9,619 | 18.9% | LD |
| Erwood, G | NPC | 902 | 1.8% | | | | | |
| C to Lab notional swing 8.5% | | 50,129 | | C maj 7,991 | | 50,890 | | C maj 16,763 |
| | | | | 15.9% | | | | 32.9% |

**JOHN HAYES**, b June 23, 1958. Sales director. Contested Derbyshire NE 1992 and 1987. Nottinghamshire county cllr 1985- . Member, nat cttee, Fed of C Students, 1982-84; chair, Aspley ward, Nottingham C, 1980-83. With The Data Base, Nottingham computer company, since 1983. Ed Colfe's GS, London; Nottingham Univ.

**JOHN LEWIS**, b June 1, 1942. Retired principal of technical college.

Member, Mersey Reg Health Authority, 1982-85; Co-op Party; SEA; SHA; Fabian Soc; Railway Development Soc; Nene Valley Railway. Life member of Camra. Ed Univ Coll of Wales, Aberystwyth; Manchester Poly.

**PETER MILLEN**, b July 19, 1948. Teacher, specialising in careers advice. Member, NUT. Ed Heathfield GS, Gateshead. Amateur cartoonist.

| SOUTH SHIELDS | | 9.6% change | | | Lab win | | |
|---|---|---|---|---|---|---|---|
| Electorate % Turnout | | 62,261 | 62.6% | **1997** | 65,863 | 69.7% | **1992** |
| +Clark, Dr D | Lab | **27,834** | 71.4% | +10.3% | **28,041** | 61.1% | Lab |
| Hoban, M | C | 5,681 | 14.6% | -12.1% | 12,220 | 26.6% | C |
| Ord, D | LD | 3,429 | 8.8% | -3.5% | 5,626 | 12.3% | LD |
| Loraine, A | Ref | 1,660 | 4.3% | | | | |
| Wilburn, I | Shields | 374 | 1.0% | | | | |
| C to Lab notional swing 11.2% | | 38,978 | Lab maj 22,153 | | 45,887 | Lab maj 15,821 | |
| | | | 56.8% | | | 34.5% | |

**DAVID CLARK,** b Oct 19, 1939. Became Chancellor of the Duchy of Lancaster, May 3, 1997. Shadow Defence Sec 1992-97. Elected for this seat 1979; MP for Colne Valley 1970 to Feb 1974; contested Manchester Withington 1966, and Colne Valley Feb and Oct 1974. Elected to Shadow Cabinet 1986; chief spokesman on food, agric and rural affairs 1987-92; spokesman on environmental protection and development 1986-87. Lab spokesman on defence 1980-81, and environment 1981-86. Forester and lecturer. Exec member, National Trust; council member, World Wildlife Fund UK. Ed Windermere GS; Manchester and Sheffield Univs.
**MARK HOBAN,** b March 31, 1964. Chartered accountant, Coopers & Lybrand. Ed St Leonards Comp, Durham; LSE.
**DAVID ORD,** b Oct 26, 1961. Computer programmer. Ed Burnside HS; Luton Coll of HE.

| SOUTHAMPTON ITCHEN | | 28.1% change | | | Lab win | | |
|---|---|---|---|---|---|---|---|
| Electorate % Turnout | | 76,869 | 70.1% | **1997** | 73,697 | 77.5% | **1992** |
| +Denham, J | Lab | **29,498** | 54.8% | +10.8% | **25,118** | 44.0% | Lab |
| Fleet, P | C | 15,289 | 28.4% | -13.8% | 24,065 | 42.1% | C |
| Harrison, D | LD | 6,289 | 11.7% | -2.2% | 7,924 | 13.9% | LD |
| Clegg, J | Ref | 1,660 | 3.1% | | | | |
| Rose, K | Soc Lab | 628 | 1.2% | | | | |
| Hoar, C R | UK Ind | 172 | 0.3% | | | | |
| Marsh, G | Soc | 113 | 0.2% | | | | |
| Barry, Ms R | NLP | 110 | 0.2% | | | | |
| McDermott, F | ProLife | 99 | 0.2% | | | | |
| C to Lab notional swing 12.3% | | 53,858 | Lab maj 14,209 | | 57,107 | Lab maj 1,053 | |
| | | | 26.4% | | | 1.8% | |

**JOHN DENHAM,** b July 15, 1953. Became Under Secretary for Social Security, May 5, 1997. Gained this seat for Lab 1992; contested it 1987 and 1983. Lab spokesman on social security 1995-97. Joint sec, all-party overseas development group; insurance and financial services group; vice-chair, refugees group. Hampshire county cllr 1981-89; Southampton city cllr 1989-93. Consultant to voluntary organisations 1988-92; nat campaigns officer, War on Want, 1984-88. Head of youth affairs, British Youth Council, 1979-82; transport campaigner for Friends of the Earth 1977-79. Ed Woodroffe Comp, Lyme Regis; Southampton Univ.
**PETER FLEET,** b April 17, 1967. Advertising manager, Ford Motor Co. PA to Christopher Chope, MP, 1992. Ed Sheredes School, Southampton; Southampton Univ.
**DAVID HARRISON,** b Oct 9, 1956. Insurance claims controller. New Forest district cllr; Totton and Eling town cllr (ex-chair). Ed Testwood; Totton Coll.

| SOUTHAMPTON TEST | | 28.6% change | | | Lab win | | |
|---|---|---|---|---|---|---|---|
| Electorate % Turnout | | 72,983 | 71.9% | **1997** | 71,957 | 75.1% | **1992** |
| Whitehead, A | Lab | **28,396** | 54.1% | +8.7% | **24,565** | 45.5% | Lab |
| +Hill, Sir James | C | 14,712 | 28.1% | -12.4% | 21,843 | 40.4% | C |
| Dowden, A | LD | 7,171 | 13.7% | +0.6% | 7,087 | 13.1% | LD |
| Day, P | Ref | 1,397 | 2.7% | | 452 | 0.8% | Grn |
| Marks, H | LCP | 388 | 0.7% | | 85 | 0.2% | NLP |
| McCabe, A M | UK Ind | 219 | 0.4% | | | | |
| Taylor, P | Glow | 81 | 0.2% | | | | |
| Sinel, J | NLP | 77 | 0.1% | -0.0% | | | |
| C to Lab notional swing 10.5% | | 52,441 | Lab maj 13,684 | | 54,032 | Lab maj 2,722 | |
| | | | 26.1% | | | 28.6% | |

**ALAN WHITEHEAD,** b Sept 15, 1950. Professor of public policy, Southampton Inst. Contested New Forest 1979, Southampton Test 1983, 1987 and 1992. Southampton city cllr 1980- (council leader 1984-92). Member, SERA; Greenpeace. Ed Isleworth GS; Southampton Univ.
**SIR JAMES HILL,** b Dec 21, 1926. Regained seat for C 1979; held seat 1970 to Oct 1974; contested it 1968. MEP 1973-75. Member, Commons chairmen's panel, 1990-97. Chair/sec, C constitutional affairs cttee, 1993-97. Ex-Southampton city cllr. Dir, Clanfield Properties Ltd. Ed Regent's Park School, Southampton; N Wales Naval Training Coll; Southampton Univ.
**ALAN DOWDEN,** b Dec 14, 1944. Independent investment analyst. Hampshire county cllr, Test Valley borough cllr. Ed Newport Gwent Tech School; Newport Tech Coll.

## SOUTHEND WEST — C hold

| Electorate % Turnout | | | 66,493 | 70.0% | **1997** | 64,198 | 77.8% | **1992** |
|---|---|---|---|---|---|---|---|---|
| **+Amess, D A** | C | | **18,029** | **38.8%** | -15.9% | **27,319** | **54.7%** | C |
| Stimson, Mrs N | LD | | 15,414 | 33.1% | +2.3% | 15,417 | 30.9% | LD |
| Harley, A | Lab | | 10,600 | 22.8% | +10.5% | 6,139 | 12.3% | Lab |
| Webster, C | Ref | | 1,734 | 3.7% | | 495 | 1.0% | Lib |
| Lee, B | UK Ind | | 636 | 1.4% | | 451 | 0.9% | Grn |
| Warburton, P | NLP | | 101 | 0.2% | -0.0% | 127 | 0.3% | NLP |
| **C to LD swing 9.1%** | | | **46,514** | | C maj 2,615 | **49,948** | | C maj 11,902 |
| | | | | | 5.6% | | | 23.8% |

**DAVID AMESS**, b March 26, 1952. MP for Basildon 1983-97; contested Newham NW 1979. PPS to Michael Portillo, as Defence Sec and previous posts, 1989-97; to Under Secs of State for Health 1987-89. Redbridge cllr 1982-86. Chair (unpaid), Accountancy Ltd, personnel consultants; senior partner, 1981-87, Employment Agency (Accountancy Aids), a specialist agency, and ex-chair of executive search and selection company. Ed St Bonaventure GS; Bournemouth Coll of Tech.

**NINA STIMSON,** b June 21, 1947. Managing editor, business manager. Contested this seat 1992. Vice-chair LD English party. Managing ed, *European Cosmetic Markets*; ex-editor, *In Focus*. Member, Charter 88; Business & Professional Women. Ed Herts and Essex HS for Girls, Bishop's Stortford.

**ALAN HARLEY,** b March 4, 1954. National organiser, Communication Workers' Union; former BT internal audit manager. Ed Eastwood HS, Southend.

## SOUTHPORT — LD gain

| Electorate % Turnout | | | 70,194 | 72.1% | **1997** | 71,443 | 77.6% | **1992** |
|---|---|---|---|---|---|---|---|---|
| **Fearn, R** | LD | | **24,346** | **48.1%** | +6.6% | **26,081** | **47.0%** | C |
| *Banks, M | C | | 18,186 | 35.9% | -11.1% | 23,018 | 41.5% | LD |
| Norman, Ms S | Lab | | 6,125 | 12.1% | +1.9% | 5,637 | 10.2% | Lab |
| Buckle, F | Ref | | 1,368 | 2.7% | | 545 | 1.0% | Grn |
| Ashton, Ms S | Lib | | 386 | 0.8% | | 159 | 0.3% | NLP |
| Lines, E | NLP | | 93 | 0.2% | -0.1% | | | |
| Middleton, M | Nat Dem | | 92 | 0.2% | | | | |
| **C to LD swing 8.8%** | | | **50,596** | | LD maj 6,160 | **55,440** | | C maj 3,063 |
| | | | | | 12.2% | | | 5.5% |

**RONNIE FEARN,** b Feb 6, 1931. Retired banker. MP for Southport 1987-92; contested this seat 1970, Feb and Oct 1974, 1979, 1987. When MP, was variously LD spokesman on health and social services, tourism, local gvt, transport, and housing. Southport town cllr; Sefton metropolitan borough cllr; Merseyside county cllr (ex-leader of councils). Ed King George V GS, Southport.

**MATTHEW BANKS,** b June 21, 1961. Gained this seat for C 1992;

contested Manchester Central 1987. PPS to Environment Mins, 1995-97. Wirral borough cllr 1984-90. FRGS. Ed Calday Grange GS, Sheffield; Sheffield City Poly; Sandhurst.

**SARAH NORMAN,** b Sept 29, 1962. Full-time cllr, Liverpool City Council, 1990- . Ed Queen Elizabeth Girls', High Barnet; Emmanuel Coll, Cambridge.

## SOUTHWARK NORTH & BERMONDSEY — 15.7% change — LD win

| Electorate % Turnout | | | 65,598 | 62.2% | **1997** | 69,011 | 62.5% | **1992** |
|---|---|---|---|---|---|---|---|---|
| **+Hughes, S H W** | LD | | **19,831** | **48.6%** | -2.8% | **22,158** | **51.4%** | LD |
| Fraser, J | Lab | | 16,444 | 40.3% | +5.8% | 14,889 | 34.5% | Lab |
| Shapps, G | C | | 2,835 | 6.9% | -5.0% | 5,170 | 12.0% | C |
| Davidson, M | BNP | | 713 | 1.7% | | 909 | 2.1% | Other |
| Newton, B | Ref | | 545 | 1.3% | | | | |
| Grant, I | Comm Lge | | 175 | 0.4% | | | | |
| Munday, J | Lib | | 157 | 0.4% | | | | |
| Yngvison, Ms I | Nat Dem | | 95 | 0.2% | | | | |
| **LD to Lab notional swing 4.3%** | | | **40,795** | | LD maj 3,387 | **43,126** | | LD maj 7,269 |
| | | | | | 8.3% | | | 16.9% |

**SIMON HUGHES**, b May 17, 1951. Non-practising barrister. Won Southwark and Bermondsey for L/All at 1983 by-election and became LD MP 1988. LD spokesman on health; also variously on urban policy, young people, education, community relations, environment, natural resources, and science; ex-LD whip. Member, joint ecclesiastical cttee; joint vice-chair, all-party Christian Fellowship group; joint treas, Council of Christians and Jews group. Dir, Rose Theatre Trust; Thames Heritage Parade Ltd;

Cambridge Univ Mission Ltd. Ed Westgate School, Cowbridge, Glamorgan; Llandaff Cathedral School, Cardiff; Christ Coll, Brecon; Selwyn Coll, Cambridge; Inns of Court School of Law; Coll of Europe, Bruges.

**JEREMY FRASER,** b Feb 10, 1958. Social worker, postman. Southwark cllr (leader 1993- ). Ed Ramsey Comp; NE London Poly.

**GRANT SHAPPS,** b Sept 14, 1968. Company director. Ed Watford Boys GS; Cassio Coll, Watford; Manchester Metropolitan Univ.

## SPELTHORNE — C hold

| Electorate % Turnout | | 70,562 | 73.6% | **1997** | 69,343 | 80.4% | **1992** |
|---|---|---|---|---|---|---|---|
| *Wilshire, D | C | 23,306 | 44.9% | -13.7% | 32,627 | 58.5% | C |
| Dibble, K | Lab | 19,833 | 38.2% | +15.3% | 12,784 | 22.9% | Lab |
| Glynn, E | LD | 6,821 | 13.1% | -3.4% | 9,202 | 16.5% | LD |
| Coleman, B | Ref | 1,495 | 2.9% | | 580 | 1.0% | Grn |
| Fowler, J D | UK Ind | 462 | 0.9% | | 338 | 0.6% | Loony |
| | | | | | 195 | 0.3% | NLP |
| C to Lab swing 14.5% | | 51,917 | C maj 3,473 | | 55,726 | C maj 19,843 | |
| | | | 6.7% | | | 35.6% | |

**DAVID WILSHIRE**, b Sept 16, 1943. Political consultant; ex-personnel officer; teacher. Elected 1987. PPS to Min of State for Defence Procurement, 1991-92, and to Home Office Min 1992-94. Member, select cttee on N Ireland, 1994-97; exec cttee, British group, IPU, 1994- . Former sec, C cttee on N Ireland; sec, C food and drinks industries sub-cttee, 1990-91; sec, all-party Methodist parly group. Wansdyke district cllr, Avon, 1976-87 (leader 1981-87); Avon county cllr 1977-81. Partner, Western Political Research Services, 1979- ; co-director, political management programme,

Brunel Univ, 1986-90. Ed Kingswood School, Bath; Fitzwilliam Coll, Cambridge.
**KEITH DIBBLE**, b July 4, 1955. Facilities manager. Contested E Berks 1992. Rushmoor borough cllr 1984- . Member, AEEU; Co-op Party; Lab Campaign for Electoral Reform; Lab Rural Revival. Ed Woomer Hill Comp, Haslemere.
**EDWARD GLYNN**, b Nov 23, 1933. Retired chemist and ex-teacher. Surrey county cllr (group spokesman). Member, Greenpeace; Charter 88. Ed Westcliffe HS; London Univ.

## STAFFORD — 50.6% change — Lab win

| Electorate % Turnout | | 67,555 | 76.6% | **1997** | 66,380 | 82.9% | **1992** |
|---|---|---|---|---|---|---|---|
| Kidney, D | Lab | 24,606 | 47.5% | +12.6% | 26,464 | 48.1% | C |
| Cameron, D | C | 20,292 | 39.2% | -8.9% | 19,229 | 34.9% | Lab |
| Hornby, Mrs P | LD | 5,480 | 10.6% | -5.9% | 9,097 | 16.5% | LD |
| Culley, S | Ref | 1,146 | 2.2% | | 129 | 0.2% | Hardcore |
| May, A | Loony | 248 | 0.5% | | 128 | 0.2% | NLP |
| C to Lab notional swing 10.7% | | 51,772 | Lab maj 4,314 | | 55,047 | C maj 7,235 | |
| | | | 8.3% | | | 13.1% | |

**DAVID KIDNEY,** b March 21, 1955. Solicitor. Contested this seat 1992. Stafford borough cllr 1987-95. Member, MSF; Soc of Lab Lawyers. Ed Longdon HS, Stoke-on-Trent; Stoke-on-Trent Sixth-Form Coll; Bristol Univ.
**DAVID CAMERON,** b Oct 9, 1966. Head of corporate affairs at Carlton Communications plc. Former special adviser to Home Secretary and Treasury Mins 1992-94. Member, 1992 general

election team. C research dept 1988-92. Ed Eton; Brasenose Coll, Oxford.
**PAM HORNBY,** b Sept 4, 1935. Retired teacher. Congleton district cllr (dep town mayor). Part-time work with National Trust. Chair, Nat Council Parent-Teacher Assoc, and Staffs and Cheshire federations. Associate member, ATL. Ed Wallington City GS; Leeds Univ. Interests include tapestry.

## STAFFORDSHIRE MOORLANDS — 59.5% change — Lab win

| Electorate % Turnout | | 66,095 | 77.3% | **1997** | 67,045 | 80.2% | **1992** |
|---|---|---|---|---|---|---|---|
| Atkins, Ms C | Lab | 26,686 | 52.2% | +11.3% | 21,972 | 40.9% | Lab |
| Ashworth, Dr A J | C | 16,637 | 32.5% | -6.1% | 20,787 | 38.7% | C |
| Jebb, Mrs C | LD | 6,191 | 12.1% | -5.3% | 9,381 | 17.4% | LD |
| Stanworth, D | Ref | 1,603 | 3.1% | | 1,451 | 2.7% | Anti-Fed |
| | | | | | 178 | 0.3% | NLP |
| C to Lab notional swing 8.7% | | 51,117 | Lab maj 10,049 | | 53,769 | Lab maj 1,185 | |
| | | | 19.7% | | | 2.2% | |

**CHARLOTTE ATKINS,** b Sept 24, 1950. Parly officer for Unison. Contested 1990 Eastbourne by-election. Member, Lab nat policy forum and nat exec women's cttee. Wandsworth cllr 1982-86 (dep leader). Ed Colchester County HS for Girls; LSE; School of American Studies, London.
**ANDREW ASHWORTH,** b Jan 22, 1956. GP. Contested Bradford W 1992. Served in Royal Navy, including Falklands task force, 1977-90, reaching rank of Surgeon Lt-Cmdr. Became medical officer to MoD. Member, BMA; Royal Coll of Gen Practitioners. Ed Greenhill School, Rochdale; Leeds Univ; RN Staff Coll. Plays euphonium.

**CHRISTINA JEBB,** b June 27, 1949. Company director and full-time cllr, ex-teacher, lecturer. Contested this seat 1992. Staffs county cllr 1989- (group leader); Staffordshire Moorlands district cllr 1991- . Member, NSPCC regional council; ALDC; Nat Women's Register; Liberty; Amnesty; National Trust; Friends of the Earth; Racial Equality Council; British Red Cross; 300 Group. Ed St Agnes Convent HS; Holte GS, Birmingham; Doncaster Coll of HE; OU; Keele Univ. Married to Henry Jebb, LD candidate for Stoke-on-Trent N.

| STAFFORDSHIRE SOUTH | | 17.2% change | | | C win | | |
|---|---|---|---|---|---|---|---|
| Electorate % Turnout | | 68,896 | 74.2% | **1997** | 68,716 | 81.1% | **1992** |
| +Cormack, Sir Patrick | C | 25,568 | 50.0% | -9.1% | 32,982 | 59.2% | C |
| LeMaistre, Ms J | Lab | 17,747 | 34.7% | +8.9% | 14,367 | 25.8% | Lab |
| Calder, Mrs J | LD | 5,797 | 11.3% | -3.7% | 8,391 | 15.1% | LD |
| Carnell, P | Ref | 2,002 | 3.9% | | | | |
| C to Lab notional swing 9.0% | | 51,114 | C maj 7,821 | | 55,740 | C maj 18,615 | |
| | | | 15.3% | | | 33.4% | |

**SIR PATRICK CORMACK**, b May 18, 1939. Journalist. Elected for this seat Feb 1974; MP for Cannock 1970-Feb 1974; contested Grimsby 1966; Bolsover 1964. Joined Commons chairmen's panel 1983. Chair, advisory cttee on Commons works of art, 1988- ; member, Commons accommodation and works cttee; joint parly ecclesiastical cttee. Chair, C Party advisory cttee on arts and heritage, 1988- ; Council for Independent Ed, 1979- . Editor, Parliament's *House Magazine*, and pres (international affairs) of *First* magazine. Programme adviser to Catholic Univ of America. Public affairs and parly adviser to Machinery Users' Assoc; Council for Awards in Children's Care and Education. Project consultant to Colebrand Ltd, high tech private co. Heritage adviser to Linford-Bridgeman, conservation and restoration co. Council member, Georgian Group, 1985- . Vice-chair, Heritage in Danger, 1974- . Member, Royal Commission on Historical Manuscripts, 1981- ; Worshipful Co of Glaziers 1979- . Fellow, Soc of Antiquaries, 1978- . Elected to General Synod of C of E 1995. Freeman, City of London; Hon Citizen of Texas. Ed St James's Choir and Havelock Schools, Grimsby; Hull Univ.

**JUDITH LeMAISTRE,** b Sept 26, 1954. Healthcare consultant. Chair, W Midlands Special Health Authority. Ed Waverley GS, Birmingham; Essex and Birmingham Univs.

**JAMIE CALDER,** b April 6, 1954. Company director. Contested Stafford 1992. Stafford borough cllr (group leader 1991-92). Ed More House, London; London Poly, Accountancy Foundation.

| STALYBRIDGE & HYDE | | 24.8% change | | | Lab win | | |
|---|---|---|---|---|---|---|---|
| Electorate % Turnout | | 65,468 | 65.8% | **1997** | 67,303 | 73.2% | **1992** |
| +Pendry, T | Lab | 25,363 | 58.9% | +7.3% | 25,435 | 51.6% | Lab |
| de Bois, N | C | 10,557 | 24.5% | -11.4% | 17,708 | 35.9% | C |
| Cross, M | LD | 5,169 | 12.0% | +3.0% | 4,443 | 9.0% | LD |
| Clapham, R | Ref | 1,992 | 4.6% | | 1,144 | 2.3% | Lib |
| | | | | | 322 | 0.7% | Loony |
| | | | | | 227 | 0.5% | NLP |
| C to Lab notional swing 9.3% | | 43,081 | Lab maj 14,806 | | 49,279 | Lab maj 7,727 | |
| | | | 34.4% | | | 15.7% | |

**TOM PENDRY**, b June 10, 1934. Elected 1970. Lab spokesman on national heritage, sport and tourism 1992-97. Member, select cttees on environment, 1987-92; MPs' interests 1987-92. Chair, all-party association football cttee, 1980-92, and PLP sports cttee, 1984-92; joint vice-chair, PLP environment cttee, 1988- ; joint chair, all-party jazz parly group, 1991- . Under Sec of State for N Ireland 1978-79; gvt whip 1974-77. Paddington cllr 1962-65. Trustee, Tameside Community Care Trust. Member, nat advisory cttee, Duke of Edinburgh's Award Scheme. Full-time official, Nupe, 1960-70. Ed St Augustine's, Ramsgate; Oxford Univ.

**NICK DE BOIS,** b Feb 23, 1959. Managing director, Rapier Assoc Ltd, marketing communications agency. Ed Culford School, nr Bury St Edmunds; Cambridge Coll of Art and Technology.

**MARTIN CROSS,** b July 29, 1945. Salesman, technical writer. Formerly ran paint supply business before moving to chemical industry. Ed Bredbury Secondary Boys; Salford Tech Coll.

| STEVENAGE | | 5.7% change | | | Lab win | | |
|---|---|---|---|---|---|---|---|
| Electorate % Turnout | | 66,889 | 76.8% | **1997** | 67,015 | 81.8% | **1992** |
| Follett, Mrs B | Lab | 28,440 | 55.3% | +16.8% | 24,078 | 43.9% | C |
| +Wood, T J R | C | 16,858 | 32.8% | -11.1% | 21,159 | 38.6% | Lab |
| Wilcock, A | LD | 4,588 | 8.9% | -8.2% | 9,379 | 17.1% | LD |
| Coburn, J | Ref | 1,194 | 2.3% | | 220 | 0.4% | NLP |
| Bundy, D | ProLife | 196 | 0.4% | | | | |
| Calcraft, A | NLP | 110 | 0.2% | -0.2% | | | |
| C to Lab notional swing 13.9% | | 51,386 | Lab maj 11,582 | | 54,836 | C maj 2,919 | |
| | | | 22.5% | | | 5.3% | |

**BARBARA FOLLETT**, b Dec 25, 1942. Lecturer and research fellow at Inst of Public Policy and Research. Contested Woking 1983, Epsom and Ewell 1987. Member, Lab national training team, 1988-92. Asst in Leader's Office during 1992 general election. Founded Emily's List 1988; co-founder, Lab Women's Network. Ed Sandford School, Addis Ababa, Ethiopia; Ellerslie Girls' HS, Cape Town; Cape Town Univ; LSE; OU. Married to Ken Follett, the novelist.

**TIMOTHY WOOD,** b Aug 13, 1940. Won this seat 1983. Gvt whip 1992-97; asst gvt whip 1990-92. PPS to Peter Brooke, N Ireland Sec, 1989-90; to Sir Ian Stewart, N Ireland Min, 1988-89; and to Sir John Stanley, when Min for Armed Forces and then for N Ireland, 1986-88. Bracknell district cllr 1975-83. Ed King James's GS, Knaresborough; Manchester Univ.

**ALEX WILCOCK,** b Oct 30, 1971. Ex-national chair, LD youth and student section. Ed Harrytown RC HS, Stockport; Essex Univ.

233

| STIRLING | | 11.8% change | | | | | Lab win |
|---|---|---|---|---|---|---|---|
| Electorate % Turnout | | 52,491 | 81.8% | **1997** | 51,902 | 81.7% | **1992** |
| **McGuire, Mrs A** | **Lab** | **20,382** | **47.4%** | **+8.8%** | 16,607 | 39.2% | C |
| +Forsyth, M | C | 13,971 | 32.5% | -6.7% | 16,371 | 38.6% | Lab |
| Dow, E G | SNP | 5,752 | 13.4% | -1.1% | 6,145 | 14.5% | SNP |
| Tough, A | LD | 2,675 | 6.2% | -0.5% | 2,854 | 6.7% | LD |
| McMurdo, W | UK Ind | 154 | 0.4% | | 342 | 0.8% | Grn |
| Olsen, E | Value | 24 | 0.1% | | 68 | 0.2% | Loony |
| **C to Lab notional swing 7.7%** | | **42,958** | | **Lab maj 6,411** | **42,387** | | **C maj 236** |
| | | | | 14.9% | | | 0.6% |

**ANNE McGUIRE,** b May 26, 1949. Chair, Lab Party Scotland, 1992-93; member, Scottish exec, 1984- ; Scottish Council of GMB; Co-op Party. Parly agent to Norman Hogg, MP, 1979-92. Dep dir, Scottish Council for Voluntary Organisations. Ed Our Lady and St Francis Secondary, Glasgow; Glasgow Univ.
**MICHAEL FORSYTH,** b Oct 16, 1954. Won this seat 1983. Became Cabinet min 1995 on being appointed Scottish Sec; Home Office Min, 1994-95; Employment Min 1992-94; Scottish Office Min 1990-92 and Under Sec 1987-90. Ex-chair, Scottish C Party. PPS to Sir Geoffrey Howe, Foreign Secretary, 1986-87. Westminster city cllr

1978-83. Member, exec cttee, Nat Union of C and Unionist Assoc, 1975-77. Ex-company director. Ed Arbroath HS; St Andrews Univ.
**EWAN DOW,** b Dec 8, 1971. Leader, Tayside Regional Council, 1994-96; Perth & Kinross Unitary Authority cllr (dep leader, 1995- ). Ed Kirkcaldy HS; Beath HS, Cowdenbeath; Aberdeen Univ.
**ALISTAIR TOUGH,** b April 27, 1953. Archivist, Glasgow Univ. Contested Clydebank & Milngavie 1992. Member, Royal African Society; AUT. Ed Robert Gordon's Coll, Aberdeen; Aberdeen Univ; University Coll, London.

| STOCKPORT | | 13.8% change | | | | | Lab win |
|---|---|---|---|---|---|---|---|
| Electorate % Turnout | | 65,232 | 71.5% | **1997** | 67,141 | 80.1% | **1992** |
| +Coffey, Ms A | **Lab** | **29,338** | **62.9%** | **+14.8%** | 25,852 | 48.0% | Lab |
| Fitzsimmons, S | C | 10,426 | 22.3% | -15.5% | 20,384 | 37.9% | C |
| Roberts, Mrs S | LD | 4,951 | 10.6% | -2.2% | 6,894 | 12.8% | LD |
| Morley-Scott, W | Ref | 1,280 | 2.7% | | 608 | 1.1% | Grn |
| Southern, G | Soc Lab | 255 | 0.5% | | 70 | 0.1% | NLP |
| Newitt, C | Loony | 213 | 0.5% | | | | |
| Dronfield, C | Ind | 206 | 0.4% | | | | |
| **C to Lab notional swing 15.2%** | | **46,669** | | **Lab maj 18,912** | **53,808** | | **Lab maj 5,468** |
| | | | | 40.5% | | | 10.2% |

**ANN COFFEY,** b Aug 31, 1946. Won this seat for Lab 1992; contested Cheadle 1987. Appointed PPS to Tony Blair, May 1997. Lab whip 1995-97. Member, trade and industry select cttee, 1992-95; joint vice-chair, PLP trade and industry cttee, 1993-95; ex-hon sec, NW group of Lab MPs; joint chair, all-party lighting parly group. Stockport borough cllr 1984-92 (Lab group leader 1988-92). Member, parly panel, Usdaw; Unison's non-affiliated parly group; local HA 1986-90; Nalgo. Social worker 1972-88; team leader,

fostering, Oldham social services dept,1988-92. Ed Nairn Acad; Bodmin GS; Bushey GS; South Bank Poly; Manchester Univ.
**STEPHEN FITZSIMMONS,** b Aug 20, 1956. General manager. Contested Liverpool Riverside 1987, Liverpool West Derby 1992. Liverpool city cllr. Ed Hillfoot Hey HS; Millbank Coll of Commerce.
**SYLVIA ROBERTS,** b July 4, 1940. Tourist guide. Macclesfield borough cllr. Member, Guild of Registered Tourist Guides. Ed Levenshulme HS for Girls, Manchester; Macclesfield Coll of FE.

| STOCKTON NORTH | | 5.0% change | | | | | Lab win |
|---|---|---|---|---|---|---|---|
| Electorate % Turnout | | 64,380 | 69.1% | **1997** | 66,795 | 75.8% | **1992** |
| +Cook, F | **Lab** | **29,726** | **66.8%** | **+12.8%** | 27,332 | 54.0% | Lab |
| Johnston, B | C | 8,369 | 18.8% | -14.1% | 16,666 | 32.9% | C |
| Fletcher, Mrs S | LD | 4,816 | 10.8% | -1.1% | 6,060 | 12.0% | LD |
| McConnell, K | Ref | 1,563 | 3.5% | | 550 | 1.1% | Ind Lab |
| **C to Lab notional swing 13.5%** | | **44,474** | | **Lab maj 21,357** | **50,608** | | **Lab maj 10,666** |
| | | | | 48.0% | | | 21.1% |

**FRANK COOK,** b Nov 3, 1935. Elected 1983. Member, select cttees on defence, 1992-97; consolidation Bills 1987-91; procedure 1988-92; employment 1983-87; Commons chairmen's panel; advisory cttee on Commons works of art 1988- . Chair (1989-90) and vice-chair (1988-89), Northern group of Lab MPs; chair, all-party parly group for renewable and sustainable energy; all-party landmine eradication group 1996- ; UK Eurosolar group; vice-chair, skin group. Ex-construction project manager, teacher, transport manager, gravedigger and Butlins Redcoat. Trustee and

dir, Faithfull Foundation, a charity. Ed Corby School, Sunderland; De La Salle Coll, Manchester; Inst of Ed, Leeds.
**BRYAN JOHNSTON,** b March 14, 1957. Solicitor and ex-army officer. Member, Tendring district cllr 1995- . Ed Guisborough GS; Prior Pursglove Sixth-Form Coll; Teesside Poly; Sandhurst; Westminster Univ; College of Law.
**SUZANNE FLETCHER,** b Feb 22, 1945. Contested this seat 1992. Full-time Stockton borough cllr 1981- (group leader). Ed Mexborough GS; Skipton Girls' HS; London Univ.

| STOCKTON SOUTH | | | **23.9% change** | | 1997 | | | **Lab win** |
|---|---|---|---|---|---|---|---|---|
| Electorate % Turnout | | | 68,470 | 76.1% | **1997** | 65,354 | 79.3% | **1992** |
| **Taylor, Ms D** | Lab | | **28,790** | **55.2%** | **+19.7%** | **23,331** | **45.0%** | **C** |
| +Devlin, T | C | | 17,205 | 33.0% | -12.0% | 18,435 | 35.6% | Lab |
| Monck, P | LD | | 4,721 | 9.1% | -10.4% | 10,080 | 19.4% | LD |
| Horner, J | Ref | | 1,400 | 2.7% | | | | |
| C to Lab notional swing 15.8% | | | 52,116 | | Lab maj 11,585 | 51,846 | | C maj 4,896 |
| | | | | | 22.2% | | | 9.4% |

**DARI TAYLOR,** b Dec 13, 1944. Union officer. Sunderland city cllr 1986- ; vice-chair, NATFHE, 1970-80; chair, Trade Union Studies and Information Unit, 1991-95. Regional education officer, GMB. Member, SEA. Ed Ynshir GS; Nottingham and Durham Univs.
**TIM DEVLIN,** b June 13, 1959. Barrister and company director. Gained seat 1987. PPS to Trade and Industry Mins 1995-97; to Attorney-General 1992-94. Member, select cttee on Scottish affairs, 1995-97; dep chair, C Foreign Affairs Forum; sec, all-party chemical industry parly group; joint vice-chair, Japan group; sec,

Tibet group; Nepal group; chair, Northern group of C MPs, 1990-91; joint vice-chair, all-party France group, 1996-97; former joint sec, C backbench smaller businesses cttee; joint sec, C arts and heritage cttee, 1988-90. Ed Dulwich Coll; LSE; City Univ, London; Inns of Court School of Law; and Financial Training Ltd. Hardwicke and Thomas More Scholar at Lincoln's Inn.
**PETER MONCK,** b Aug 28, 1949. Garage manager. Chair, Yarm Town Council, 1995- (Mayor 1995-97). Chair, Stockton South LDs. Ed St Bride's Sec Mod; Teesside Univ.

| STOKE-ON-TRENT CENTRAL | | | | | 1997 | | | **Lab hold** |
|---|---|---|---|---|---|---|---|---|
| Electorate % Turnout | | | 64,113 | 62.8% | **1997** | 65,527 | 68.1% | **1992** |
| *Fisher, M | Lab | | **26,662** | **66.2%** | **+8.2%** | **25,897** | **58.0%** | **Lab** |
| Jones, N | C | | 6,738 | 16.7% | -11.2% | 12,477 | 27.9% | C |
| Fordham, E | LD | | 4,809 | 11.9% | -1.7% | 6,073 | 13.6% | LD |
| Stanyer, P | Ref | | 1,071 | 2.7% | | 196 | 0.4% | NLP |
| Coleman, M | BNP | | 606 | 1.5% | | | | |
| Oborski, Ms F | Lib | | 359 | 0.9% | | | | |
| C to Lab swing 9.7% | | | 40,245 | | Lab maj 19,924 | 44,643 | | Lab maj 13,420 |
| | | | | | 49.5% | | | 30.1% |

**MARK FISHER,** b Oct 29, 1944. Became Minister for the Arts with rank of National Heritage Under Secretary, May 7, 1997. Elected for this seat 1983; contested Leek 1979. Lab spokesman on national heritage and the arts 1993-97; on Citizen's Charter 1992-93; on the arts 1987-92. Member, select cttee on Treasury and Civil Service, 1983-86. Joint chair, all-party Central Asia parly group. Chair, PLP ed, science and arts beckbench cttee, 1984-86; vice-chair, PLP Treasury cttee, 1983-88. Lab whip 1985-87. Staffordshire county cllr 1981-85. Member, council, Policy Studies

Inst, 1989- . Documentary film producer and script writer 1966-75; principal, Tattershall Education Centre, 1975-83. Dep Pro-Chancellor, Keele Univ, 1989- . FRCA 1993. Member, Musicians' Union; NUT. Ed Eton; Trinity Coll, Cambridge.
**NEIL JONES,** b Sept 20, 1966. Retail banking consultant. Ed Olchfa School, Swansea; York Univ.
**EDWARD FORDHAM,** b March 13, 1971. Univ administrator. Member, W Midlands regional exec cttee. Ed Spalding GS, Lincs; Nottingham Univ (pres of union).

| STOKE-ON-TRENT NORTH | | | **32.1% change** | | 1997 | | | **Lab win** |
|---|---|---|---|---|---|---|---|---|
| Electorate % Turnout | | | 59,030 | 65.5% | **1997** | 61,250 | 73.6% | **1992** |
| +Walley, Ms J | Lab | | **25,190** | **65.1%** | **+10.4%** | **24,693** | **54.8%** | **Lab** |
| Day, C | C | | 7,798 | 20.2% | -13.5% | 15,189 | 33.7% | C |
| Jebb, H | LD | | 4,141 | 10.7% | +0.2% | 4,718 | 10.5% | LD |
| Tobin, Ms J | Ref | | 1,537 | 4.0% | | 466 | 1.0% | NLP |
| C to Lab notional swing 11.9% | | | 38,666 | | Lab maj 17,392 | 45,066 | | Lab maj 9,504 |
| | | | | | 45.0% | | | 21.1% |

**JOAN WALLEY,** b Jan 23, 1949. Elected 1987. Lab spokesman on transport 1990-95; environmental protection and conservation 1988-90. Member, trade and industry select cttee, 1995-97; Commons services cttee 1987-91. Joint vice-chair, PLP environment cttee, 1987-88; joint sec, all-party lighting parly group, 1991- . Lambeth cllr 1982-86; Swansea city cllr 1974-78; Wandsworth cllr 1978-79. Vice-pres, Inst of Environmental Health Officers, 1987- ; pres, W Midlands, Home and Water Safety Council, 1990- . With Alcoholics Recovery Project 1970-73; Nat Assoc for Care and Resettlement of Offenders 1979-82. Ed Biddulph GS; Hull Univ; Univ Coll of Wales, Swansea.

**CHRISTOPHER DAY,** b May 5, 1962. Strategic projects manager, American Express 1996- ; management consultant and accountant, Price Waterhouse, 1985-93. Chair, Tunbridge Wells C assoc. Member, Bow Group. Ed St Wilfred's Comp, Crawley; Imperial Coll, London; London Business School.
**HENRY JEBB,** b July 10, 1951. Self-employed carpenter. Staffordshire Moorlands district cllr 1991-95; LD chair, Endon and Brown Edge branch. Ed Wellington Coll, Berks; Keele Univ. Married to Christina Jebb, LD candidate for Staffordshire Moorlands.

| STOKE-ON-TRENT SOUTH | | | | | | Lab hold |
|---|---|---|---|---|---|---|
| Electorate % Turnout | | 69,968 | 66.1% | **1997** | 71,316 | 74.3% | **1992** |
| *Stevenson, G | Lab | **28,645** | **62.0%** | **+12.2%** | 26,380 | 49.8% | Lab |
| Scott, Mrs S | C | 10,342 | 22.4% | -14.4% | 19,471 | 36.7% | C |
| Barnett, P | LD | 4,710 | 10.2% | -2.8% | 6,870 | 13.0% | LD |
| Adams, R | Ref | 1,103 | 2.4% | | 291 | 0.5% | NLP |
| Micklem, Mrs A | Lib | 580 | 1.3% | | | | |
| Batkin, S | BNP | 568 | 1.2% | | | | |
| Lawrence, B | Nat Dem | 288 | 0.6% | | | | |
| C to Lab swing 13.3% | | 46,236 | Lab maj 18,303 | | 53,012 | Lab maj 6,909 | |
| | | | 39.6% | | | 13.0% | |

**GEORGE STEVENSON,** b Aug 30, 1938. Elected for this seat 1992. MEP for Staffordshire East 1984-94, serving on Euro Parliament cttees on transport, budgets, and agriculture; chair, Euro Parliament delegation for relations with S Asia, 1989-92; Lab group of MEPs 1987-88. Member, Euro legislation select cttee, 1995-97; agriculture select cttee 1992-95; chair, PLP agric cttee. Member, all-party British-Tibet parly group. Stoke-on-Trent city cllr 1972-86; Staffs county cllr 1981-85. Transport driver 1966-84; miner 1957-64; pottery caster 1953-57. Ed Queensberry Rd Secondary, Stoke-on-Trent.
**SHEILA SCOTT,** b Dec 18, 1948. Chief executive, Nat Care Homes Assoc. Member, Dept of Health community care force 1992-93. Barnet cllr 1990- . Ed Wisbech HS for Girls.
**PETER BARNETT,** b June 1, 1966. Works for mineral extraction firm. Congleton borough cllr 1990- (dep leader 1992-94). Ed Keele Univ.

| STONE | 127.3% change | | | | | | C win |
|---|---|---|---|---|---|---|---|
| Electorate % Turnout | | 68,242 | 77.8% | **1997** | 66,426 | 83.8% | **1992** |
| +Cash, W N P | C | 24,859 | 46.8% | -9.2% | 31,156 | 56.0% | C |
| Wakefield, J | Lab | 21,041 | 39.6% | +10.8% | 16,077 | 28.9% | Lab |
| Stamp, B | LD | 6,392 | 12.0% | -1.5% | 7,554 | 13.6% | LD |
| Winfield, Ms A | Lib | 545 | 1.0% | | 854 | 1.5% | Other |
| Grice, Ms D | NLP | 237 | 0.4% | | | | |
| C to Lab notional swing 10.0% | | 53,074 | C maj 3,818 | | 55,641 | C maj 15,079 | |
| | | | 7.2% | | | 27.1% | |

**WILLIAM CASH,** b May 10, 1940. Solicitor. MP for Stafford 1984-97. Founder and chair, European Foundation, 1993- . Member, select cttees on Euro legislation, 1985-97; employment 1989-90; statutory instruments 1986-90; consolidation Bills 1987-90. Chair, C backbench Euro affairs cttee, 1989-91; vice-chair, C Small Business Bureau, 1984- ; joint vice-chair (1988-89) and joint sec (1985-88), C small businesses cttee; sec, C employment cttee, 1986-87; joint vice-chair (1985-87) and sec (1984-85), C constitutional affairs cttee. Chair, all-party alternative and complementary medicine group, 1989- ; joint chair, British-Kenya group; chair (1987- ) and sec (1984-87), all-party British-East Africa parly group. Legal and legislative adviser to Inst of Company Accountants; Ilex Tutorial Services Ltd; consultant to Radcliffe's & Co, solicitors. Dir, Ironbridge Gorge Museum Trust, 1980- . Ed Stonyhurst Coll; Lincoln Coll, Oxford.
**JOHN WAKEFIELD,** b Sept 26, 1950. Univ lecturer. Staffs county cllr 1989- ; Stone town cllr 1991-95. Dir, Business Link, Staffordshire. Ed St Bartholomew's GS, Newbury; London and Sheffield Univs.
**BARRY STAMP,** b March 22, 1952. Teacher adviser. Contested Stafford 1992. Stafford borough cllr (group leader). Ed King Edward VI, Stafford; West Midlands Coll of HE; St Peter's Coll, Birmingham; OU.

| STOURBRIDGE | 83.3% change | | | | | | Lab win |
|---|---|---|---|---|---|---|---|
| Electorate % Turnout | | 64,966 | 76.5% | **1997** | 65,947 | 77.3% | **1992** |
| Shipley, Ms D | Lab | 23,452 | 47.2% | +8.9% | 24,907 | 48.8% | C |
| +Hawksley, P W | C | 17,807 | 35.8% | -13.0% | 19,519 | 38.3% | Lab |
| Bramall, C | LD | 7,123 | 14.3% | +2.5% | 6,011 | 11.8% | LD |
| Quick, P | Ref | 1,319 | 2.7% | | 566 | 1.1% | Other |
| C to Lab notional swing 11.0% | | 49,701 | Lab maj 5,645 | | 51,003 | C maj 5,388 | |
| | | | 11.4% | | | 10.6% | |

**DEBRA SHIPLEY,** b June 22, 1957. Author, lecturer. Member, Nat Policy Forum; nat exec SERA; trustee and management cttee, National Alliance of Women's Organisations. GMB. Ed Kidderminster HS; Oxford Poly; London Univ.
**WARREN HAWKSLEY,** b March 10, 1943. MP for Halesowen and Stourbridge 1992-97; MP for The Wrekin 1979-87; contested Wolverhampton NE Feb and Oct 1974. Member, select cttees on home affairs, 1996-97; employment 1994-96 and 1986-87; Welsh affairs. Sec, W Midlands group of C MPs, 1992-97; joint sec, C backbench urban and new towns cttee, 1984-87. Shropshirecounty cllr 1970-81; West Mercia police authority 1977-81. Owner, with wife, of country house hotel; hon pres, Catering Industries Liaison Council, 1992- . Worked for Lloyds Bank 1960-79. Ed Mill Mead, Stourbridge; Denstone Coll, Staffs.
**CHRIS BRAMALL,** b Aug 2, 1942. Solicitor. Dudley metropolitan borough cllr 1995- (group sec). Member, National Trust; MSF. Ed Latymer Upper School, Hammersmith; Christ's Coll, Cambridge; St Mary's Coll of Ed, Twickenham.

| STRANGFORD | | 65.0% change | | | | | UUP win |
|---|---|---|---|---|---|---|---|
| Electorate % Turnout | | 69,980 | 59.5% | **1997** | 66,420 | 62.8% | **1992** |
| +Taylor, J D | UUP | **18,431** | **44.3%** | **-4.8%** | **20,473** | **49.0%** | **UUP** |
| Robinson, Mrs I | DUP | 12,579 | 30.2% | +10.4% | 8,295 | 19.9% | DUP |
| McCarthy, K | Alliance | 5,467 | 13.1% | -3.0% | 6,736 | 16.1% | Alliance |
| O'Reilly, P | SDLP | 2,775 | 6.7% | | 5,945 | 14.2% | C |
| Chalk, G | C | 1,743 | 4.2% | -10.1% | 295 | 0.7% | NLP |
| O Fachtna, G S | SF | 503 | 1.2% | | | | |
| Mullins, Mrs S | NLP | 121 | 0.3% | -0.4% | | | |
| **No swing calculation** | | **41,619** | **UUP maj 5,852** | | **41,744** | **UUP maj 12,178** | |
| | | | 14.1% | | | 29.2% | |

**JOHN D. TAYLOR,** b Dec 24, 1937. Civil engineer. Elected 1983; resigned seat in 1985 in protest at Anglo-Irish agreement and retained it at 1986 by-election. Elected MEP 1979-89. Privy Counsellor (NI) 1970. MP, Stormont, 1965-72; NI Assembly 1973-75; NI Constitutional Convention 1975-76; NI Assembly 1982-88. Cabinet Min for Home Affairs in NI Gvt, 1970-72. Castlereagh borough cllr 1989- . Dir, West Ulster Estates Ltd, 1968- ; Tontine Rooms Holding Co Ltd 1978- , publishing and printing; proprietor (unpaid) of Cerdac Business Systems in N Ireland and of Tyrone Printing Co Ltd; publisher (unpaid) of *Tyrone Courier, Ulster Gazette, Carrickfergus Advertiser, Ballyclare Gazette, Larne Gazette.* Ed Royal School, Armagh; Queen's Univ, Belfast.

**IRIS ROBINSON,** b Sept 6, 1949. Elected to N Ireland Forum 1996; Mayor of Castlereagh Borough Council. Married to Peter Robinson, who was first elected as DUP MP for Belfast E 1979 and is now DUP dep leader.

**KIERAN McCARTHY.** Draper. Alliance Party spokesman on disability. Forum member for Strangford.

**PETER O'REILLY.** Belfast City Hospital Trust employee. Belfast city cllr 1993- .

| STRATFORD-ON-AVON | | 6.7% change | | | | | C win |
|---|---|---|---|---|---|---|---|
| Electorate % Turnout | | 81,434 | 76.3% | **1997** | 77,443 | 81.8% | **1992** |
| Maples, J | C | **29,967** | **48.3%** | **-10.5%** | **37,252** | **58.8%** | **C** |
| Juned, Dr S | LD | 15,861 | 25.5% | -0.1% | 16,247 | 25.6% | LD |
| Stacey, S | Lab | 12,754 | 20.5% | +7.1% | 8,512 | 13.4% | Lab |
| Hilton, A | Ref | 2,064 | 3.3% | | 681 | 1.1% | Grn |
| Spilsbury, J | UK Ind | 556 | 0.9% | | 535 | 0.8% | Ind C |
| Brewster, J | NLP | 307 | 0.5% | +0.3% | 121 | 0.2% | NLP |
| Marcus, S | SFDC | 306 | 0.5% | | | | |
| Miller, Ms S | ProLife | 284 | 0.5% | | | | |
| **C to LD notional swing 5.2%** | | **62,099** | **C maj 14,106** | | **63,348** | **C maj 21,005** | |
| | | | 22.7% | | | 33.2% | |

**JOHN MAPLES,** b April 22, 1943. Barrister; chief executive, Saatchi & Saatchi. MP for Lewisham W 1983-92. Economic Sec to the Treasury 1990-92; PPS to Norman Lamont when Treasury Min 1987-90. Dep chairman, C Party, 1994- . Ed Marlborough Coll; Downing Coll, Cambridge; Harvard Business School.

**SUSAN JUNED,** b March 26, 1948. Scientist. Stratford-upon-Avon district cllr 1990- ; Warwickshire county cllr 1993- . Ed Swanwick Hall GS; Birmingham Univ.

**STEWART STACEY,** b March 21, 1953. Train driver. Dir, W Midlands Special Needs Transport Ltd. Ed Maidenhead GS.

| STRATHKELVIN & BEARSDEN | | 13.5% change | | | | | Lab win |
|---|---|---|---|---|---|---|---|
| Electorate % Turnout | | 62,974 | 78.9% | **1997** | 63,483 | 80.8% | **1992** |
| +Galbraith, S | Lab | **26,278** | **52.9%** | **+6.8%** | **23,658** | **46.1%** | **Lab** |
| Sharpe, D | C | 9,986 | 20.1% | -12.5% | 16,710 | 32.6% | C |
| McCormick, G | SNP | 8,111 | 16.3% | +3.4% | 6,621 | 12.9% | SNP |
| Morrison, J | LD | 4,843 | 9.7% | +1.5% | 4,252 | 8.3% | LD |
| Wilson, D | Ref | 339 | 0.7% | | 85 | 0.2% | NLP |
| Fisher, Ms J | NLP | 155 | 0.3% | +0.1% | | | |
| **C to Lab notional swing 9.6%** | | **49,712** | **Lab maj 16,292** | | **51,326** | **Lab maj 6,948** | |
| | | | 32.8% | | | 13.5% | |

**SAM GALBRAITH,** b Oct 18, 1945. Became Under Secretary, Scottish Office, responsible for health and arts, May 5, 1997. Won this seat 1987. Lab spokesman on employment 1992-93; health 1988-92; Scotland 1988-92. Former consultant neurosurgeon, Inst of Neurological Sciences, Southern General Hospital, Glasgow; consultant in neurosurgery, Greater Glasgow Health Board, 1978-87.. Ed Greenock HS; Glasgow Univ.

**DAVID SHARPE,** b March 26, 1956. Civil engineer. Contested Paisley N 1992. Ed Jordanhill Coll School, Glasgow; Glasgow Coll.

**JOHN MORRISON,** b June 14, 1962. Solicitor. Contested Dumbarton 1992; Glasgow in 1989 Euro elections; Glasgow Provan 1987. East Dunbar UA cllr 1995- . Ed North Kelvinside sec; Glasgow Univ.

**GRAEME McCORMICK,** b May 23, 1954. Solicitor. Ed Paisley GS; Edinburgh Univ.

| STREATHAM | | 27.2% change | | | | | Lab win |
|---|---|---|---|---|---|---|---|
| Electorate % Turnout | | 74,509 | 60.2% | **1997** | 71,008 | 70.1% | **1992** |
| +Hill, K | Lab | **28,181** | 62.8% | +13.4% | 24,585 | 49.4% | Lab |
| Noad, E | C | 9,758 | 21.7% | -16.7% | 19,114 | 38.4% | C |
| O'Brien, R | LD | 6,082 | 13.6% | +3.6% | 4,966 | 10.0% | LD |
| Wall, J | Ref | 864 | 1.9% | | 585 | 1.2% | Grn |
| | | | | | 203 | 0.4% | Islamic |
| | | | | | 191 | 0.4% | ADS |
| | | | | | 128 | 0.3% | NLP |
| C to Lab notional swing 15.0% | | 44,885 | | Lab maj 18,423 41.0% | 49,772 | | Lab maj 5,471 11.0% |

**KEITH HILL,** b July 28, 1943. Won this seat 1992; contested Blaby 1979. Member, transport select cttee, 1992-97; joint vice-chair, London group of Lab MPs, 1995- ; ex-sec, PLP transport cttee. Political liaison officer, RMT (formerly NUR), 1976-92; research officer, Lab Party international dept, 1974-76; lecturer in politics, Strathclyde Univ, 1969-73; Belgian Gvt scholar, Brussels, 1968-69; research asst in politics, Leicester Univ, 1966-68. Ed City of Leicester Boys' GS; Corpus Christi Coll, Oxford; Univ Coll of Wales, Aberystwyth.

**ERNEST NOAD,** b Nov 8, 1951. Financial adviser. Contested Islington N 1987, Streatham 1992. Croydon cllr 1987-90. Ed St Joseph's Coll, Norwood.
**ROGER O'BRIEN,** b Aug 1, 1964. Solicitor. Contested Battersea 1992. Ed Hull GS; Manchester Univ; Coll of Law, Chester; Chancery Lane Coll of Law.

| STRETFORD & URMSTON | | 98.1% change | | | | | Lab win |
|---|---|---|---|---|---|---|---|
| Electorate % Turnout | | 69,913 | 69.7% | **1997** | 73,507 | 74.8% | **1992** |
| Hughes, Ms B | Lab | **28,480** | 58.5% | +9.5% | 26,925 | 48.9% | Lab |
| Gregory, J | C | 14,840 | 30.5% | -10.3% | 22,443 | 40.8% | C |
| Bridges, J | LD | 3,978 | 8.2% | -1.1% | 5,084 | 9.2% | LD |
| Dore, Ms C | Ref | 1,397 | 2.9% | | 567 | 1.0% | Other |
| C to Lab notional swing 9.9% | | 48,695 | | Lab maj 13,640 28.0% | 55,019 | | Lab maj 4,482 8.2% |

**BEVERLEY HUGHES,** b March 30, 1950. Manchester univ lecturer on social work and former probation officer. Trafford borough cllr 1986- (council leader 1995- ; Lab group leader 1992- ). Ed Ellesmere Port GS; Manchester and Liverpool Univs.
**JOHN GREGORY,** b April 18, 1949. Barrister. Chair, Stretford and Urmston C assoc, 1980-82. Member, Northern Circuit Chancery

Bar Assoc. Ed St Ambrose Coll, Hale Barns; Stretford GS; Hull Univ.
**JOHN BRIDGES,** b Dec 3, 1961. Manchester city cllr. Member, exec cttee, Gorton Community Forum; Unison. Ed Monks Walk School, Welwyn Garden City; Manchester Univ.

| STROUD | | 19.2% change | | | | | Lab win |
|---|---|---|---|---|---|---|---|
| Electorate % Turnout | | 77,494 | 80.5% | **1997** | 75,249 | 83.4% | **1992** |
| Drew, D | Lab Co-op | 26,170 | 42.0% | | 29,032 | 46.2% | C |
| +Knapman, R | C | 23,260 | 37.3% | -8.9% | 18,451 | 29.4% | Lab |
| Hodgkinson, P | LD | 9,502 | 15.2% | -6.4% | 13,582 | 21.6% | LD |
| Marjoram, J | Green | 3,415 | 5.5% | | 1,718 | 2.7% | Grn |
| No swing calculation | | 62,347 | | Lab Co-op maj 2,910 4.7% | 62,783 | | C maj 10,581 16.9% |

**DAVID DREW,** b April 13, 1952. Senior lecturer, Bristol Poly. Contested this seat 1992. Treas, Gloucs Lab Party; member, exec, Stroud CLP. Stroud district cllr 1987- ; Stevenage borough cllr 1981-82. Member, NATFHE; Nupe. Ed Kingsfield School, Kingswood, Bristol; Nottingham and Birmingham Univs; Bristol Poly.
**ROGER KNAPMAN,** b Feb 20, 1944. Chartered surveyor and farmer. Elected 1987. Gvt whip 1996-97; asst gvt whip 1995-96. Member, agriculture select cttee, 1994-95. PPS to Archie Hamilton, Min for

Armed Forces, 1991-93. Joint vice-chair, C backbench European affairs cttee, 1989-90; vice-chair, 1990-91, and sec 1988-90, C forestry sub-cttee. Joint vice-chair, all-party East African parly group. Member, Agricultural and Food Research Council, 1991-94. Ex-partner, R.J. & R.M. Knapman, builders; ex-associate partner, Carters, chartered surveyors. Ed Allhallows School, Lyme Regis; Royal Agricultural Coll, Cirencester.
**PAUL HODGKINSON,** b May 10, 1962. Training manager. Gloucs county cllr 1993- . Ed Weymouth GS, Dorset; Reading Univ.

| SUFFOLK CENTRAL & IPSWICH NORTH | | | **67.7% change** | | | **C win** |
|---|---|---|---|---|---|---|
| Electorate % Turnout | | 70,222 | 75.2% | **1997** | 66,188 | 80.1% | **1992** |
| +Lord, M N | C | 22,493 | 42.6% | -13.2% | 29,610 | 55.8% | C |
| Jones, Ms C | Lab | 18,955 | 35.9% | +15.2% | 11,604 | 21.9% | LD |
| Goldspink, Dr M | LD | 10,886 | 20.6% | -1.3% | 10,980 | 20.7% | Lab |
| Bennell, Ms S | Ind | 489 | 0.9% | | | 850 | 1.6% | Other |
| C to Lab notional swing 14.2% | | 52,823 | | C maj 3,538 6.7% | 53,044 | | C maj 18,006 33.9% |

MICHAEL LORD, b Oct 17, 1938. Appointed a Dep Speaker and dep chair, Ways and Means, May 1997. MP for Suffolk Central 1983-97; contested Manchester Gorton 1979. Member, select cttee on Parliamentary Commissioner for Administration, 1990-97; on agriculture 1983-84. Member, Commons chairmen's panel; PPS to John MacGregor, Min for Agric and then Chief Sec to Treasury, 1984-87. Sec, all-party forestry parly group. Member, Council of Europe and WEU, 1987-91. Bedfordshire county cllr 1981-83. Exec cttee, CPA, 1995- . Dir, Palmer Family Trust, 1988- , commercial property co. Arboricultural consultant. Parly consultant to British Printing Industries Fed. Member, British Inst of Management. Ed William Hulme's GS, Manchester; Christ's Coll, Cambridge (rugby union Blue).

CAROLE JONES, b April 5, 1953. Head of English at comprehensive school. Mid-Suffolk district cllr 1993- . Member, Amnesty; Friends of the Earth. Ed Univ Coll of Wales.

MIONE GOLDSPINK, b April 2, 1941. GP. East Herts district cllr; Stortford town cllr (Mayor 1996). Member, Charter 88; BMA. Ed Godolphin School, Salisbury; St Mary's Hospital Med School; London Univ.

| SUFFOLK COASTAL | | | **38.4% change** | | | **C win** |
|---|---|---|---|---|---|---|
| Electorate % Turnout | | 74,219 | 75.8% | **1997** | 70,061 | 81.8% | **1992** |
| +Gummer, J | C | 21,696 | 38.6% | -13.9% | 30,030 | 52.4% | C |
| Campbell, M | Lab | 18,442 | 32.8% | +10.1% | 13,325 | 23.3% | LD |
| Jones, Ms A | LD | 12,036 | 21.4% | -1.9% | 13,008 | 22.7% | Lab |
| Caulfield, S | Ref | 3,416 | 6.1% | | 739 | 1.3% | Grn |
| Slade, T | Green | 514 | 0.9% | | 182 | 0.3% | NLP |
| Kaplan, Ms F | NLP | 152 | 0.3% | -0.0% | | | |
| C to Lab notional swing 12.0% | | 56,256 | | C maj 3,254 5.8% | 57,284 | | C maj 16,705 29.2% |

JOHN GUMMER, b Nov 26, 1939. Elected for this seat 1983; MP for Eye 1979-83, and for Lewisham W 1970-Feb 1974; contested Greenwich 1964 and 1966. Environment Secretary 1993-97; joined Cabinet 1989 as Min of Agriculture, Fish and Food. Chair of C Party 1983-85; Privy Counsellor 1985. Min for Local Gvt, 1988-89; Min for Ag, Fish and Food 1985-88; Paymaster General 1984-85; Min for Employment 1983-84; Employment Under Sec Jan-Oct 1983; gvt whip 1981-83; asst gvt whip 1981. Member, joint parly ecclesiastical cttee; General Synod, C of E, 1979-92. Writer and broadcaster. Dir, Walsingham Coll (Affiliated Schools) Ltd; guardian, Shrine of Our Lady of Walsingham; member, advice panel, Templeton Foundation; trustee, Theodore Trust, Open Churches Trust (all unpaid). Ed King's, Rochester; Selwyn Coll, Cambridge (pres of Union, 1962).

MARK CAMPBELL, b Jan 6, 1960. Manager of children's home. Suffolk county cllr 1989- . Member, Amnesty; Unison. Ed Prescot School, Prescot; Keble Coll, Oxford; Univ Coll of Wales, Cardiff.

ALEXANDRA JONES, b Jan 2, 1960. Senior exec, international development assistance. Member, Charter 88. Ed Old Palace GS for Girls, Croydon; Oxford, Harvard and London Univs.

| SUFFOLK SOUTH | | | **23.9% change** | | | **C win** |
|---|---|---|---|---|---|---|
| Electorate % Turnout | | 67,323 | 77.2% | **1997** | 65,382 | 80.6% | **1992** |
| +Yeo, T | C | 19,402 | 37.3% | -14.0% | 27,036 | 51.3% | C |
| Bishop, P | Lab | 15,227 | 29.3% | +7.5% | 13,828 | 26.2% | LD |
| Pollard, Mrs K | LD | 14,395 | 27.7% | +1.5% | 11,504 | 21.8% | Lab |
| de Chair, C | Ref | 2,740 | 5.3% | | 319 | 0.6% | NLP |
| Holland, Mrs A | NLP | 211 | 0.4% | -0.2% | | | |
| C to Lab notional swing 10.7% | | 51,975 | | C maj 4,175 8.0% | 52,687 | | C maj 13,208 25.1% |

TIMOTHY YEO, b March 20, 1945. Elected 1983; contested Bedwelty Feb 1974. Min of State for Environment 1993-94; Under Sec for Environment 1990-93; PPS to Douglas Hurd, Home Secretary and then Foreign Secretary, 1988-90. Member, select cttees on employment, 1994-96; social services 1985-88. Capt, parly golfing society, 1991-95. Freelance journalist; formerly taught agriculture in Tanzania. Dir, Univent Ltd, private nursing homes; Worcester Engineering Co Ltd, 1975-86; adviser to Greater London Enterprise Ltd. Dir, Spastics Soc, 1980-83, and on its exec council 1984-86. Treas, International Voluntary Service, 1975-78. Ed Charterhouse; Emmanuel Coll, Cambridge.

PAUL BISHOP, b Feb 17, 1963. Actor, writer, teacher. Member, Equity; MSF. Ed Fyfield Boarding School; Colchester Inst of FE; Kent Univ.

KATHY POLLARD, b Dec 15, 1951. BT human factors consultant. Contested this seat 1992. Babergh district cllr 1987-95; Suffolk county cllr 1993- (chair, 1995-96). Member, Friends of the Earth. Ed Llwyn-y-Bryn HS, Swansea; Swansea and Birmingham Univs.

| SUFFOLK WEST | | 67.7% change | | | | | C win |
|---|---|---|---|---|---|---|---|
| Electorate % Turnout | | 68,638 | 71.5% | **1997** | 67,074 | 78.8% | **1992** |
| +Spring, R J D | C | **20,081** | 40.9% | -12.9% | 28,455 | 53.8% | C |
| Jefferys, M | Lab | 18,214 | 37.1% | +13.1% | 12,692 | 24.0% | Lab |
| Graves, A | LD | 6,892 | 14.0% | -7.3% | 11,283 | 21.3% | LD |
| Carver, J | Ref | 3,724 | 7.6% | | 419 | 0.8% | Other |
| Shearer, A | NLP | 171 | 0.3% | | | | |
| C to Lab notional swing 13.0% | | **49,082** | | **C maj 1,867** | 52,849 | | **C maj 15,763** |
| | | | | 3.8% | | | 29.8% |

**RICHARD SPRING**, b Sept 24, 1946. MP for Bury St Edmunds 1992-97; contested Ashton-under-Lyne 1983. PPS to Defence Mins of State 1996-97. Member, select cttees on health, 1995-96; on N Ireland 1994-97; on employment 1992-94. PPS to N Ireland Sec until 1995. Joint vice-chair, all-party racing and bloodstock industries parly group; joint sec, drug misuse group. Joint vice-chair, C backbench arts and heritage cttee, 1992-96; sec, C cttee on N Ireland, 1994-95. Pres, arts and heritage cttee, Bow Group, 1992- . Unpaid dir, Small Business Bureau Ltd. Managing dir, Xerox Furman Selz financial services co, 1989-92. Consultant on international economic trends to Malabar Capital Ltd and Malabar Unit Trusts. Ed Rondebosch, Cape Town; Cape Town Univ; Magdalene Coll, Cambridge.

**MICHAEL JEFFERYS**, b July 22, 1952. Teacher. Forest Heath district cllr 1983-87. Member, NUT. Ed Thames Poly; Univ of London Inst of Ed; East Anglia Univ.

**ADRIAN GRAVES**, b Oct 6, 1948. Public relations consultant. Contested London South Inner in 1994 Euro elections. Member, Transport 2000; Rail Freight Group; Railway Development Soc. Ed King's, Ely; Cambridge Coll of Arts & Technology.

| SUNDERLAND NORTH | | 11.2% change | | | | | Lab win |
|---|---|---|---|---|---|---|---|
| Electorate % Turnout | | 64,711 | 59.1% | **1997** | 65,400 | 68.4% | **1992** |
| +Etherington, W | Lab | **26,067** | 68.2% | +8.6% | 26,649 | 59.6% | Lab |
| Selous, A | C | 6,370 | 16.7% | -11.1% | 12,423 | 27.8% | C |
| Pryke, G | LD | 3,973 | 10.4% | -0.6% | 4,895 | 10.9% | LD |
| Nicholson, M | Ref | 1,394 | 3.6% | | 747 | 1.7% | Lib |
| Newby, K | Loony | 409 | 1.1% | | | | |
| C to Lab notional swing 9.9% | | **38,213** | | **Lab maj 19,697** | 44,714 | | **Lab maj 14,226** |
| | | | | 51.5% | | | 31.8% |

**WILLIAM ETHERINGTON**, b July 17, 1941. Elected 1992. Member, select cttees on Parliamentary Commissioner for Administration, 1996-97; members' interests 1992-95; Commons catering ctte 1995-97. Member, NUM, 1963- ; vice-pres, NE area, 1988-92; full-time NUM official 1983-93. Fitter at Dawdon Colliery 1963-83; branch delegate of Durham mechanics branch 1973-83, also served as chair and later sec of branch. Member (unpaid), exec cttee, Durham Aged Mineworkers' Homes Assoc. Ed Monkwearmouth GS; Durham Univ.

**ANDREW SELOUS**, b April 27, 1962. Reinsurance underwriter, Great Lakes UK plc; accountant, Price Waterhouse, 1984-89; dir of family business, CNS Electronics Ltd, 1984-94. TA officer, 1981-93. Treas, Battersea C assoc. Ed LSE.

**GEOFFREY PRYKE**, b May 3, 1946. Teaches physics, maths and information technology at local comp. Wrote and published regional restaurant guide. Member, Electoral Reform Soc; ATL. Ed Chelmsford Tech HS; Bede Coll, Durham.

| SUNDERLAND SOUTH | | 25.9% change | | | | | Lab win |
|---|---|---|---|---|---|---|---|
| Electorate % Turnout | | 67,937 | 58.8% | **1997** | 72,010 | 69.7% | **1992** |
| +Mullin, C | Lab | **27,174** | 68.1% | +10.6% | 28,829 | 57.5% | Lab |
| Schofield, T | C | 7,536 | 18.9% | -10.4% | 14,706 | 29.3% | C |
| Lennox, J | LD | 4,606 | 11.5% | -0.3% | 5,933 | 11.8% | LD |
| Wilkinson, M A M | UK Ind | 609 | 1.5% | | 690 | 1.4% | Grn |
| C to Lab notional swing 10.5% | | **39,925** | | **Lab maj 19,638** | 50,158 | | **Lab maj 14,123** |
| | | | | 49.2% | | | 28.2% |

**CHRIS MULLIN,** b Dec 12, 1947. Journalist and author; editor of *Tribune* 1982-84. Elected for this seat 1987; contested Kingston upon Thames Feb 1974; Devon N 1970. Member, home affairs select cttee, 1992-97. Chair, PLP civil liberties group, 1992- ; sec, all-party Vietnam and Cambodia parly groups; chair, Cambodia group. Author of *Error of Judgement*, on Birmingham Six. Member, Campaign for Lab Party Democracy, 1975-83; Lab Co-ordinating Cttee, 1978-82; Lab NEC working party on media, 1978-82. Dir (unpaid), Friends of Hanoi Architectural Heritage International Foundation. Ed St Joseph's Coll, Birkfield, Ipswich; Hull Univ.

**TIM SCHOFIELD,** b May 9, 1960. Sales and marketing manager. Vice-chair, City of Durham C assoc, 1993-96. Ed Ashville Coll, Harrogate; Imperial Coll, London; St John's Coll, Durham.

**JOHN LENNOX,** b June 17, 1947. Senior lecturer. Contested this seat 1992; Jarrow 1983; Sunderland N 1979, Feb and Oct 1974. Sunderland city cllr 1988- (leader, minority party in opposition). Member, NATFHE. Ed St Aidan's GS; Durham Univ; De la Salle Coll, Manchester; Sidney Sussex Coll, Cambridge.

| SURREY EAST | | 26.1% change | | | | | C win |
|---|---|---|---|---|---|---|---|
| Electorate % Turnout | | 72,852 | 75.0% | **1997** | 71,659 | 81.5% | **1992** |
| +Ainsworth, P | C | 27,389 | 50.1% | -10.9% | 35,676 | 61.1% | C |
| Ford, Ms B | LD | 12,296 | 22.5% | -4.4% | 15,704 | 26.9% | LD |
| Ross, D | Lab | 11,573 | 21.2% | +10.7% | 6,135 | 10.5% | Lab |
| Sydney, M | Ref | 2,656 | 4.9% | | 919 | 1.6% | Grn |
| Stone, A B | UK Ind | 569 | 1.0% | | | | |
| Bartrum, Ms S | NLP | 173 | 0.3% | | | | |
| C to LD notional swing 3.3% | | 54,656 | | C maj 15,093 | 58,434 | | C maj 19,972 |
| | | | | 27.6% | | | 34.2% |

**PETER AINSWORTH,** b Nov 16, 1956. Elected 1992. Asst gvt whip 1996-97. PPS to Virginia Bottomley, National Heritage Sec, 1995-96; PPS to Jonathan Aitken when Chief Sec to Treasury 1994-95. Member, public service select cttee, 1995-96. Ex-joint sec. C backbench arts and heritage cttee. Former non-exec dir, JLI Group plc, food manufacturing; Gartmore Shared Equity Trust plc; S.G. Warburg Holdings Ltd; dir, S.G. Warburg Securities Corporate Finance, 1989-92 (asst dir, 1987-89); investment analyst, Laing & Cruickshank, stockbrokers, 1981-85; S.G. Warburg Securities, 1985-87.

Wandsworth cllr 1986-94. Member, council of Bow Group, 1984-86. Ed Bradfield Coll, Berkshire; Lincoln Coll, Oxford.
**BELINDA FORD,** b Aug 16, 1942. Ex-medical secretary. Tandridge district cllr. Member, East Surrey community health council, 1987- (chair 1995- ). Non-exec director, East Surrey Priority Care NHS Trust. Ed Oxted House School; Queen's Secretarial Coll, London.
**DAVID ROSS,** b March 12, 1956. Freelance journalist and writer. Middlesbrough borough cllr 1982-95. Member, NUJ. Ed Marr Coll, Troon; Kilmarnock Acad; Teesside Poly.

| SURREY HEATH | | 47.3% change | | | | | C win |
|---|---|---|---|---|---|---|---|
| Electorate % Turnout | | 73,813 | 74.1% | **1997** | 71,492 | 78.4% | **1992** |
| +Hawkins, N J | C | 28,231 | 51.6% | -12.1% | 35,731 | 63.7% | C |
| Newman, D | LD | 11,944 | 21.8% | -1.3% | 12,977 | 23.1% | LD |
| Jones, Ms S | Lab | 11,511 | 21.0% | +9.8% | 6,326 | 11.3% | Lab |
| Gale, J | Ref | 2,385 | 4.4% | | 1,035 | 1.8% | Other |
| Squire, R P F | UK Ind | 653 | 1.2% | | | | |
| C to LD notional swing 5.4% | | 54,724 | | C maj 16,287 | 56,069 | | C maj 22,754 |
| | | | | 29.8% | | | 40.6% |

**NICK HAWKINS,** b March 27, 1957. Barrister. MP for Blackpool S 1992-97; contested Huddersfield 1987. PPS to Defence Mins 1995-96. Member, transport select cttee 1992-95. Chair, C backbench sports cttee 1994- ; joint vice-chair, all-party insurance and financial services group, 1995- ; sec, railways group. Member, Bar Council, 1988-95. Parly consultant to Building Employers Confed. Research sec, Bow Group, 1990-91; Bow Group campaign director, 1991-92; elected to group council 1989 (managing dir.

Bow Publications Ltd, 1989-90). Legal adviser, Lloyds Abbey Life,1989-92. Company legal adviser to Access (Joint Credit Card Co Ltd), 1987-89. Ed Bedford Modern School; Lincoln Coll, Oxford; Middle Temple; Inns of Court School of Law.
**DAVID NEWMAN,** b June 10, 1969. Administrator. Guildford borough cllr. Ed Guildford County School.
**SUSAN JONES,** b June 1, 1968. Charity fundraiser. Ed Bristol Univ; Univ Coll of Wales; Coll of Law, London.

| SURREY SOUTH WEST | | | | | | | C hold |
|---|---|---|---|---|---|---|---|
| Electorate % Turnout | | 72,350 | 78.0% | **1997** | 72,288 | 82.8% | **1992** |
| *Bottomley, Mrs V | C | 25,165 | 44.6% | -13.9% | 35,008 | 58.5% | C |
| Sherlock, N | LD | 22,471 | 39.8% | +6.3% | 20,033 | 33.5% | LD |
| Leicester, Ms M | Lab | 5,333 | 9.4% | +3.0% | 3,840 | 6.4% | Lab |
| Clementson, Mrs J | Ref | 2,830 | 5.0% | | 710 | 1.2% | Grn |
| Kirby, J P | UK Ind | 401 | 0.7% | | 147 | 0.2% | NLP |
| Quintavalle, Ms J | ProLife | 258 | 0.5% | | 98 | 0.2% | Anglo Sax |
| C to LD swing 10.1% | | 56,458 | | C maj 2,694 | 59,836 | | C maj 14,975 |
| | | | | 4.8% | | | 25.0% |

**VIRGINIA BOTTOMLEY,** b March 12, 1948. National Heritage Secretary 1995-97. Elected 1984 by-election; contested Isle of Wight 1983. Joined Cabinet 1992 as Health Sec; Health Min 1989-92; junior Environment Min 1988-89. PPS to Foreign Sec 1987-88; and to Min for Ed and Science and Overseas Development Min, 1985-87. Gvt co-chair, Women's Nat Commission. Member, Medical Research Council, 1987-88. Vice-chair, Nat Council of Carers and their Elderly Dependants, 1982-88. Exec member, C of E Children's Soc, 1978-83. Psychiatric social worker 1973-84. Member, court of governors, LSE, 1985- ; governor, Ditchley

Foundation, 1991- . Ed Putney HS; Essex Univ; LSE. Her husband is Peter Bottomley, MP for Worthing W.
**NEIL SHERLOCK,** b Aug 13, 1963. Director of Communications, KPMG. Contested this seat 1992. Member, Charter 88; European Movement; Electoral Reform Soc. Ed Esher County GS; Esher Coll; Christ Church, Oxford (pres of Union).
**MARGARET LEICESTER,** b Sept 13, 1961. Public health physician. Vice-pres, SHA. Adviser to Tessa Jowell on health and women's issues. Ed St Bernard's Convent, Westcliff-on-Sea; Clare Coll, Cambridge; St Thomas' Hospital, London; Hong Kong Univ.

| SUSSEX MID | | 15.0% change | | | | | C win |
|---|---|---|---|---|---|---|---|
| Electorate % Turnout | | 68,784 | 77.7% | **1997** | 70,654 | 80.3% | **1992** |
| +Soames, A N W | C | **23,231** | **43.5%** | -15.5% | **33,415** | **58.9%** | C |
| Collins, Mrs M | LD | 16,377 | 30.6% | +2.4% | 16,008 | 28.2% | LD |
| Hamilton, M | Lab | 9,969 | 18.6% | +8.0% | 6,034 | 10.6% | Lab |
| Large, T | Ref | 3,146 | 5.9% | | 655 | 1.2% | Grn |
| Barnett, J V | UK Ind | 606 | 1.1% | | 332 | 0.6% | Loony |
| Tudway, E | Ind JRP | 134 | 0.3% | | 209 | 0.4% | PR |
| | | | | | 75 | 0.1% | NLP |
| C to LD notional swing 8.9% | | **53,463** | | **C maj 6,854** | **56,728** | | **C maj 17,407** |
| | | | | 12.8% | | | 30.7% |

**NICHOLAS SOAMES,** b Feb 12, 1948. MP for Crawley 1983-97; contested Central Dumbartonshire 1979. Armed Forces Min 1994-97; junior MAFF Min 1992-94. PPS to Nicholas Ridley, Environment Sec and Trade and Industry Sec; to John Gummer, Employment Min and C Party chairman. Equerry to Prince of Wales 1970-72. Former non-exec director, Robert Fraser & Partners, bankers; Tolgate Holdings plc; Abela Holdings (UK); Roche Products Ltd. Ed St Aubyn's, Sussex; Eton. Son of Lord

Soames and grandson of Sir Winston Churchill.
**MARGARET COLLINS,** b Nov 10, 1940. Teacher. Contested this seat 1992, Hove 1987. W Sussex county cllr 1985- . East Grinstead town cllr. Ed Brondesbury and Kilburn HS; Trent Park Training Coll, Herts; Sussex Univ; Goldsmith's Coll, London.
**MERVYN HAMILTON,** b Oct 4, 1949. Hotel sales manager. West Sussex county cllr (leader, Lab group); Mid Sussex district cllr; Haywards Heath town cllr. Ed Presentation Coll, Birr, Co Offley.

| SUTTON & CHEAM | | | | | | | LD gain |
|---|---|---|---|---|---|---|---|
| Electorate % Turnout | | 62,785 | 75.0% | **1997** | 60,949 | 82.4% | **1992** |
| Burstow, P | LD | **19,919** | **42.3%** | +8.5% | **27,710** | **55.2%** | C |
| *Maitland, Lady Olga | C | 17,822 | 37.8% | -17.3% | 16,954 | 33.8% | LD |
| Allison, M | Lab | 7,280 | 15.5% | +5.5% | 4,980 | 9.9% | Lab |
| Atkinson, P | Ref | 1,784 | 3.8% | | 444 | 0.9% | Grn |
| McKie, S P | UK Ind | 191 | 0.4% | | 133 | 0.3% | NLP |
| Wright, D | NLP | 96 | 0.2% | -0.1% | | | |
| C to LD swing 12.9% | | **47,092** | | **LD maj 2,097** | **50,221** | | **C maj 10,756** |
| | | | | 4.5% | | | 21.4% |

**PAUL BURSTOW,** b May 13, 1962. Director, Business Ecologic, Business Link London South. Contested this seat 1992. LD spokesman on disabled people, May 1997- . Acting political sec, Assoc of LD Cllrs. Member, London regional LD exec; fed policy cttee 1988-90. Sutton cllr 1986- (dep leader). Ed Glastonbury HS, Carshalton; South Bank Univ.
**LADY OLGA MAITLAND,** b May 23, 1944. Journalist. Elected 1992; contested Bethnal Green & Stepney 1987. Member, select cttees on health, 1996-97; education 1992-96; statutory instruments

1995-97; procedure 1992-95. Former joint sec, C backbench defence cttee; C cttee on N Ireland. Parly adviser (unpaid) to Kuwaiti cttee for missing PoWs. Columnist, *Sunday Express.* 1967-91. Pres, defence and security forum, 1992- ; founder and chair, Families for Defence, 1983- . Ed St Mary and St Anne, Abbots Bromley; Lycée Français de Londres.
**MARK ALLISON,** b May 8, 1968. Political researcher and public affairs consultant. Member, Fabian Soc. Ed York Univ; Birkbeck Coll, London.

| SUTTON COLDFIELD | | | | | | | C hold |
|---|---|---|---|---|---|---|---|
| Electorate % Turnout | | 71,864 | 72.9% | **1997** | 71,410 | 79.5% | **1992** |
| *Fowler, Sir Norman | C | **27,373** | **52.2%** | -12.9% | **37,001** | **65.2%** | C |
| York, A | Lab | 12,488 | 23.8% | +8.9% | 10,965 | 19.3% | LD |
| Whorwood, J E | LD | 10,139 | 19.3% | +0.0% | 8,490 | 15.0% | Lab |
| Hope, D | Ref | 2,401 | 4.6% | | 324 | 0.6% | NLP |
| C to Lab swing 10.9% | | **52,401** | | **C maj 14,885** | **56,780** | | **C maj 26,036** |
| | | | | 28.4% | | | 45.9% |

**SIR NORMAN FOWLER,** b Feb 2, 1938. Elected for this seat Feb 1974; MP for Nottingham S 1970-74. C Party chairman 1992-94; Employment Sec 1987-90; Social Services Sec 1981-87; Transport Sec 1981; Transport Min 1979-81. Chief Opposition spokesman on transport 1976-79; social services 1975-76. Joined Shadow Cabinet 1975. Spokesman on home affairs 1974-75; PPS to N Ireland Sec 1972-74. Chair, C backbench European affairs cttee, 1991-92. Non-exec chair, Midland Independent Newspapers, 1991- ; Nat House Building Council 1992- ; non-exec director, Express Newspapers plc; Bardon Group plc, building materials

and quarrying. Member of Lloyd's. Journalist on *The Times* 1961-70 (home affairs correspondent 1966-70). Ed King Edward VI School, Chelmsford; Trinity Hall, Cambridge.
**ALAN YORK,** b Jan 6, 1940. Retired college asst principal. Birmingham city cllr 1996- . Ed Coleshill GS; Keele Univ; OU.
**JIM WHORWOOD,** b Oct 17, 1934. Head of engineering management, Coventry Univ. Contested this seat 1992. Sutton Coldfield borough cllr 1965-74. Ed Handsworth Tech School; Aston Tech Coll; Bolton Tech Teachers Coll; Aston Univ.

## SWANSEA EAST — Lab hold

| Electorate % Turnout | | 57,373 | 67.4% | 1997 | 59,196 | 75.6% | 1992 |
|---|---|---|---|---|---|---|---|
| *Anderson, D | Lab | 29,151 | 75.4% | +5.7% | 31,179 | 69.7% | Lab |
| Dibble, Ms C | C | 3,582 | 9.3% | -7.9% | 7,697 | 17.2% | C |
| Jones, E V | LD | 3,440 | 8.9% | -0.6% | 4,248 | 9.5% | LD |
| Pooley, Ms M | PC | 1,308 | 3.4% | -0.2% | 1,607 | 3.6% | PC |
| Maggs, Ms C | Ref | 904 | 2.3% | | | | |
| Job, R | Soc | 289 | 0.7% | | | | |
| C to Lab swing 6.8% | | 38,674 | Lab maj 25,569 | | 44,731 | Lab maj 23,482 | |
| | | | 66.1% | | | 52.5% | |

**DONALD ANDERSON,** b June 17, 1939. Non-practising barrister and former diplomat. Elected for this seat Oct 1974; MP for Monmouth 1966-70. Commons chairman's panel, 1995. Lab spokesman on legal affairs 1994-95; on defence 1993-94; foreign affairs 1983-92. Member, joint parly ecclesiastical cttee. Vice-chair, all-party Methodist group; Norwegian group; joint vice-chair, Council of Christians and Jews group; Christian Fellowship group; South Africa group; dep chair, Franco-British group, 1984-96, and joint vice-chair, 1996- ; joint chair, German group; joint sec, Europe group. Treas, 1988-90 and 1992- , and vice-chair, 1985-88, exec cttee, British group, IPU. Member, 1986- , and treas 1990-93, exec cttee, UK branch, CPA. Senior vice-pres, Assoc of W European Parliamentarians for Africa (Southern), 1984- . Member, North Atlantic Assembly, 1992- . Kensington and Chelsea cllr 1971-75. Methodist local preacher. Consultant, Royal Soc of Chemistry. Ed Swansea GS; Univ Coll of Wales, Swansea (Hon Fellow).

**CATHERINE DIBBLE,** b Sept 26, 1971. Researcher; ex-assistant to Bernard Jenkin, MP and Tim Kirkhope. Ed Howell's School, Cardiff; Leeds Univ.

**ELWYN JONES,** b Sept 25, 1938. Teacher. Contested Edmonton 1992. Ed Lewis Boys, Pengam, Hull; King's Coll, London.

## SWANSEA WEST — Lab hold

| Electorate % Turnout | | 58,703 | 68.9% | 1997 | 59,785 | 73.3% | 1992 |
|---|---|---|---|---|---|---|---|
| *Williams, A | Lab | 22,748 | 56.2% | +3.2% | 23,238 | 53.0% | Lab |
| Baker, A C S | C | 8,289 | 20.5% | -10.9% | 13,760 | 31.4% | C |
| Newbury, J | LD | 5,872 | 14.5% | +4.0% | 4,620 | 10.5% | LD |
| Lloyd, D | PC | 2,675 | 6.6% | +2.8% | 1,668 | 3.8% | PC |
| Proctor, D | Soc Lab | 885 | 2.2% | | 564 | 1.3% | Grn |
| C to Lab swing 7.1% | | 40,469 | Lab maj 14,459 | | 43,850 | Lab maj 9,478 | |
| | | | 35.7% | | | 21.6% | |

**ALAN WILLIAMS,** b Oct 14, 1930. Economics lecturer. Elected 1964. Member, PAC 1990-97; privileges cttee 1994-95. Lab spokesman on Commons affairs and dep campaigns co-ordinator 1988-89; chief spokesman on Wales 1987-88; on trade and industry 1983-84; Civil Service 1980-83. Joint chair, all-party transport forum parly group. Industry Min 1976-79; Prices and Consumer Protection Min 1974-76; Parly Sec, MinTech, 1969-70; Under Sec for Economic Affairs 1967-69. Parly adviser to Inst of Plant Engineers. Ed Cardiff HS; Cardiff Coll of Tech; University Coll, Oxford.

**ANDREW BAKER,** b Nov 6, 1965. Business development consultant. Vice-pres, Wales area YCs, 1993-94. Ed Monkton House GS, Cardiff; S Glamorgan Inst of HE.

**JOHN NEWBURY,** b Jan 3, 1939. Electrician. Swansea city cllr 1987-96. Shop steward 1974-83. Member, AEEU. Ed Bishop Gore GS, Swansea; Pontardawe Tech Coll.

**DAI LLOYD,** b Dec 2, 1956. GP. Contested this seat 1992. Plaid Cymru spokesman on health 1994- . Doctor on SC4 medical programme. Member, Welsh council, Royal Coll of GPs; BMA. Ed Lampeter Comp, Dyfed; Welsh Nat School of Medicine, Cardiff.

## SWINDON NORTH — 100.2% change — Lab win

| Electorate % Turnout | | 65,535 | 73.7% | 1997 | 64,530 | 77.2% | 1992 |
|---|---|---|---|---|---|---|---|
| Wills, M | Lab | 24,029 | 49.8% | +7.1% | 21,273 | 42.7% | Lab |
| Opperman, G | C | 16,341 | 33.9% | -7.1% | 20,391 | 40.9% | C |
| Evemy, M | LD | 6,237 | 12.9% | -1.7% | 7,299 | 14.6% | LD |
| Goldsmith, Ms G | Ref | 1,533 | 3.2% | | 879 | 1.8% | Other |
| Fiskin, A | NLP | 130 | 0.3% | | | | |
| C to Lab notional swing 7.1% | | 48,270 | Lab maj 7,688 | | 49,842 | Lab maj 882 | |
| | | | 15.9% | | | 1.8% | |

**MICHAEL WILLS,** b May 20, 1952. TV producer since 1980, first with LWT. Former FO diplomat, policy adviser to Lab Treasury team over VAT on fuel and "Fat cats". Formed Juniper Communications TV co 1984, producers of economic and current affairs programmes, documentaries and period drama for BBC and Channel 4. Ed Haberdashers' Aske's School, Elstree; Clare Coll, Cambridge.

**GUY OPPERMAN,** b May 18, 1965. Barrister; journalist; univ lecturer. Member, C Political Centre; Soc of C Lawyers; C Way Forward. Ed Harrow; Lille Univ; Buckingham Univ.

**MIKE EVEMY,** b March 16, 1967. Direct marketer, Nationwide Building Society. Thamesdown district cllr (group leader 1994- , opposition leader 1996- ). Member, Amnesty. Ed St Joseph's Coll, London; York Univ.

| SWINDON SOUTH | | 46.6% change | | | | | Lab win |
|---|---|---|---|---|---|---|---|
| Electorate % Turnout | | 70,207 | 72.9% | **1997** | 68,197 | 81.8% | **1992** |
| **Drown, Ms J** | **Lab** | **23,943** | **46.8%** | **+16.0%** | **27,312** | **48.9%** | **C** |
| +Coombs, S C | C | 18,298 | 35.8% | -13.2% | 17,209 | 30.8% | Lab |
| Pajak, S | LD | 7,371 | 14.4% | -4.3% | 10,439 | 18.7% | LD |
| Mackintosh, D | Ref | 1,273 | 2.5% | | 842 | 1.5% | Other |
| Charman, R | Route 66 | 181 | 0.4% | | | | |
| Buscombe, K | NLP | 96 | 0.2% | | | | |
| C to Lab notional swing 14.6% | | 51,162 | | Lab maj 5,645 | 55,802 | | C maj 10,103 |
| | | | | 11.0% | | | 18.1% |

**JULIA DROWN,** b Aug 23, 1962. NHS accountant. Wiltshire county cllr 1989-96. Member, Unison; Friends of the Earth; Greenpeace; Co-op Party. Ed Hampstead Comp; University Coll, Oxford.
**SIMON COOMBS,** b Feb 21, 1947. MP for Swindon 1983-97. PPS to Ian Lang, President of Board of Trade, 1995-97, and Scottish Sec 1993-95. Chair, all-party cable and satellite TV group 1987-92. Joint vice-chair, manufacturing industry group, 1993-97; tourism cttee 1992-97; treas, info tech cttee, 1987-97. Parly consultant to Blick plc, AIM UK, trade assoc for automatic identification technologies. Southern Electricity consultative council 1981-84. Ed Wycliffe Coll; Reading Univ.
**STANLEY PAJAK,** b March 5, 1957. Distribution manager. Wiltshire county cllr 1985-. Thamesdown district cllr 1987-. Ed St Joseph's RC Comp; Salford Univ.

| TAMWORTH | | 7.8% change | | | | | Lab win |
|---|---|---|---|---|---|---|---|
| Electorate % Turnout | | 67,205 | 74.2% | **1997** | 65,089 | 81.6% | **1992** |
| **+Jenkins, B** | **Lab** | **25,808** | **51.8%** | **+12.6%** | **26,209** | **49.3%** | **C** |
| Lightbown, Lady | C | 18,312 | 36.7% | -12.6% | 20,804 | 39.2% | Lab |
| Pinkett, Mrs J | LD | 4,025 | 8.1% | -1.9% | 5,275 | 9.9% | LD |
| Livesey, Mrs D | Ref | 1,163 | 2.3% | | 825 | 1.6% | Other |
| Lamb, C A | UK Ind | 369 | 0.7% | | | | |
| Twelvetrees, Ms C | Lib | 177 | 0.4% | | | | |
| C to Lab notional swing 12.6% | | 49,854 | | Lab maj 7,496 | 53,113 | | C maj 5,405 |
| | | | | 15.0% | | | 10.2% |

**BRIAN JENKINS,** b Sept 19, 1942. Lecturer. Won Staffordshire SE in 1996 by-election. Joined Unopposed Bills panel. Tamworth borough cllr (ex-leader). Previously industrial engineer, instrument mechanic and labourer. Member, NATFHE. Ed Aston and Coventry Tech Colls; Coleg Harlech; LSE; Wolverhampton Poly.
**LADY LIGHTBOWN,** b July 8, 1939. Ex-primary school teacher. Widow of Sir David Lightbown, MP for Staffordshire SE 1983-96, and his personal assistant. Pres, Tamworth C assoc, 1996-. Ed Lewis School for Girls, Hengoed; Coventry Teacher Training Coll.
**JENNIFER PINKETT,** b April 23, 1945. Teacher (learning support/child abuse co-ordinator). Ed Sedgehill Comp, London; Cartrefle Coll, Wrexham; OU.
*Details of 1996 Staffordshire SE by-election on page 278*

| TATTON | | 28.6% change | | | | | Ind win |
|---|---|---|---|---|---|---|---|
| Electorate % Turnout | | 63,822 | 76.5% | **1997** | 63,700 | 81.4% | **1992** |
| **Bell, M** | **Ind** | **29,354** | **60.2%** | | **32,235** | **62.2%** | **C** |
| +Hamilton, M N | C | 18,277 | 37.5% | -24.7% | 9,870 | 19.0% | Lab |
| Hill, S | Ind | 295 | 0.6% | | 9,387 | 18.1% | LD |
| Kinsey, S | Ind | 187 | 0.4% | | 350 | 0.7% | FP |
| Penhaul, B | Miss M | 128 | 0.3% | | | | |
| Muir, J | Albion | 126 | 0.3% | | | | |
| Kennedy, M | NLP | 123 | 0.3% | | | | |
| Bishop, D | Byro | 116 | 0.2% | | | | |
| Nicholas, R | Ind | 113 | 0.2% | | | | |
| Price, J | Juice | 73 | 0.1% | | | | |
| No swing calculation | | 48,792 | | Ind maj 11,077 | 51,842 | | C maj 22,365 |
| | | | | 22.7% | | | 43.1% |

**MARTIN BELL,** b Aug 31, 1938. BBC TV reporter and correspondent 1965-96; TV Journalist of the Year 1992. Formerly East European corr 1993-94, pool TV reporter during Gulf War 1991, Berlin corr 1989-93, chief Washington corr 1978-89, diplomatic corr 1977-78, BBC reporter 1965-77. Fought 1997 election on an "anti-sleaze" ticket. Ed The Leys, Cambridge; King's Coll, Cambridge.
**NEIL HAMILTON,** b March 9, 1949. Barrister (non-practising). Elected 1983; contested Bradford N 1979; Abertillery, Feb 1974. Under Sec for Corporate Affairs, DTI, 1992-94; asst gvt whip 1990-92. Member, Treasury and Civil Service select cttee, 1987-90. Member, strategy advisory group NTL telecommunications co; legal adviser to Nat Transcommunications co. Former Euro and parly affairs director, IoD. Vice-pres, Cheshire Agricultural Soc 1986-; Small Business Bureau 1985-. Ed Amman Valley GS; Univ Coll of Wales, Aberystwyth; Corpus Christi Coll, Cambridge. *Spectator* Parliamentary Wit of the Year 1990.

| TAUNTON | | | | | | | LD gain |
|---|---|---|---|---|---|---|---|
| Electorate % Turnout | | 79,783 | 76.5% | **1997** | 78,036 | 82.3% | **1992** |
| **Ballard, Mrs J** | LD | **26,064** | **42.7%** | **+1.9%** | 29,576 | 46.0% | C |
| *Nicholson, D | C | 23,621 | 38.7% | -7.3% | 26,240 | 40.8% | LD |
| Lisgo, Ms E | Lab | 8,248 | 13.5% | +0.8% | 8,151 | 12.7% | Lab |
| Ahern, B | Ref | 2,760 | 4.5% | | 279 | 0.4% | NLP |
| Andrews, L | BNP | 318 | 0.5% | | | | |
| **C to LD swing 4.6%** | | **61,011** | | **LD maj 2,443** | 64,246 | | **C maj 3,336** |
| | | | | 4.0% | | | 5.2% |

**JACKIE BALLARD,** b Jan 4, 1953. Local gvt adviser, ex-social worker. Contested this seat 1992. Became LD spokeswoman on women, May 1997. Member, LD fed policy cttee, 1992-95. Council support officer to Assoc of LD Cllrs. Somerset county cllr 1993- (deputy leader 1993-95); ex-South Somerset district cllr (leader 1990-91). Member, Friends of the Earth; Charter 88; Amnesty. Ed Monmouth School for Girls; LSE.
**DAVID NICHOLSON,** b Aug 17, 1944. Elected 1987, contested Walsall S 1983. PPS to Min for Overseas Development 1990-92. Joint vice-

chair, all-party gardening group; treas, water group, 1993-97; sustainable waste management group 1995-97; joint sec, population and development group, 1990-94. Parly adviser to Nat Assoc of Cider Makers. Assoc of British Chambers of Commerce 1982-87, dep director-general 1986-87. Ed Queen Elizabeth's GS, Blackburn; Christ Church, Oxford.
**ELIZABETH LISGO,** b April 1, 1956. Chief exec, Age Concern Somerset. Taunton Deane cllr 1995- . Member, Lab Campaign for Electoral Reform. Ed Teesside HS; Hereford Coll of Ed; OU.

| TAYSIDE NORTH | | 21.5% change | | | | | SNP win |
|---|---|---|---|---|---|---|---|
| Electorate % Turnout | | 61,398 | 74.3% | **1997** | 59,626 | 76.1% | **1992** |
| **Swinney, J** | SNP | **20,447** | **44.8%** | **+6.1%** | 21,036 | 46.4% | C |
| +Walker, B | C | 16,287 | 35.7% | -10.6% | 17,597 | 38.8% | SNP |
| McFatridge, I | Lab | 5,141 | 11.3% | +4.3% | 3,579 | 7.9% | LD |
| Regent, P F | LD | 3,716 | 8.2% | +0.3% | 3,156 | 7.0% | Lab |
| **C to SNP notional swing 8.4%** | | **45,591** | | **SNP maj 4,160** | 45,368 | | **C maj 3,439** |
| | | | | 9.1% | | | 7.6% |

**JOHN SWINNEY,** b April 13, 1964. Strategic planning principal, Scottish Amicable. Contested this seat 1992. SNP Treasury spokesman; vice-convener for publicity 1992- ; nat sec 1986-92, asst nat sec 1984-86; dir, SNP Euro election unit 1988-89. Ed Forrester HS, Edinburgh; Edinburgh Univ.
**BILL WALKER,** b Feb 20, 1929. Elected for this seat 1983; MP for Perth and E Perthshire 1979-83; contested Dundee E, Oct 1974. Chair, C backbench aviation cttee, 1994-97. Vice-chair, Scottish C Party. Vice-pres, World Scout Parly Union. Chair, all-party Scout parly group; joint vice-chair, Scotch whisky industry

group; Scottish sports group; sec, RAF group. Chair, Walker Assocs management consultancy, 1975- ; dir, Intervision Systems Inc. Vice-pres, British Gliding Assoc; hon pres, Air Cadet Gliding. Ed Logie and Blackness Schools, Dundee; Dundee Trades Coll; Dundee Coll of Arts; Coll for Distributive Trades, London.
**IAN McFATRIDGE,** b Feb 24, 1958. Solicitor/hotelier. Ed Oban HS; Edinburgh and Leicester Univs; OU.
**PETER REGENT,** b Dec 8, 1929. Sculptor and writer. Contested this seat 1987. NE Fife rural cllr 1984-92. Ed Thetford GS; Keble Coll, Oxford.

| TEIGNBRIDGE | | 24.2% change | | | | | C win |
|---|---|---|---|---|---|---|---|
| Electorate % Turnout | | 81,667 | 77.1% | **1997** | 76,740 | 82.3% | **1992** |
| +Nicholls, P | C | **24,679** | **39.2%** | **-11.0%** | 31,740 | 50.3% | C |
| Younger-Ross, R | LD | 24,398 | 38.8% | +3.6% | 22,192 | 35.1% | LD |
| Dann, Ms S | Lab | 11,311 | 18.0% | +5.0% | 8,181 | 13.0% | Lab |
| Stokes, S A | UK Ind | 1,601 | 2.5% | | 682 | 1.1% | Loony |
| Banwell, N | Green | 817 | 1.3% | | 365 | 0.6% | NLP |
| Golding, Mrs L | Dream | 139 | 0.2% | | | | |
| **C to LD notional swing 7.3%** | | **62,945** | | **C maj 281** | 63,160 | | **C maj 9,548** |
| | | | | 0.4% | | | 15.1% |

**PATRICK NICHOLLS,** b Nov 14, 1948. Solicitor. Elected 1983. Environment Under Sec July-Oct 1990; Employment Under Sec 1987-90. Sec, former joint vice-chair, C backbench legal cttee. Vice-chair of C Party 1993-94. East Devon district cllr 1980-84. Parly rep, Nat Ex-Prisoner of War Assoc. Parly consultant to Hill and Smith Holdings; parly adviser to Wells tailors; and to British Shops and Stores Assoc. Consultant to Dunn & Baker, solicitors; vice-chair, Soc of C Lawyers 1986-87. Steward, British Boxing Board of Control, 1985- . Ed Redrice Coll, Andover; Coll of Law, Guildford.

**RICHARD YOUNGER-ROSS,** b Jan 29, 1953. Design consultant. Contested this seat 1992; Chislehurst 1987. Organising vice-chair (1979-80), Nat League Young Libs; member, Lib Party council, 1979-84. Exec member, British Kurdish Friendship Soc. Member, Howard League; Anti-Slavery International. Ed Walton-on-Thames Sec Mod; Ewell Tech Coll; Oxford Poly.
**SUE DANN,** b Jan 7, 1958. Part-time lecturer. Teignbridge district cllr. Member, NATFHE; Co-op Party. Ed Lordswood GS, Birmingham; South Devon Coll.

| TELFORD | | 37.1% change | | | | | Lab win |
|---|---|---|---|---|---|---|---|
| Electorate % Turnout | | 56,558 | 65.6% | 1997 | 57,194 | 71.2% | 1992 |
| +Grocott, B | Lab | 21,456 | 57.8% | +5.1% | 21,473 | 52.8% | Lab |
| Gentry, B A R | C | 10,166 | 27.4% | -5.9% | 13,546 | 33.3% | C |
| Green, N | LD | 4,371 | 11.8% | -0.6% | 5,049 | 12.4% | LD |
| Morris, C | Ref | 1,119 | 3.0% | | 634 | 1.6% | Other |
| C to Lab notional swing 5.5% | | 37,112 | Lab maj 11,290 | | 40,702 | Lab maj 7,927 | |
| | | | 30.4% | | | 19.5% | |

**BRUCE GROCOTT,** b Nov 1, 1940. Former lecturer and TV presenter. MP for The Wrekin 1987-97; for Lichfield & Tamworth, Oct 1974-79. PPS to Tony Blair 1994- . Lab spokesman on foreign and Commonwealth affairs 1992-93; dep Shadow Leader of the House and dep Lab campaigns co-ordinator 1987-92. Member, select cttees on nat heritage, 1994-95; on broadcasting 1988-97; on overseas development 1978-79. Bromsgrove district cllr 1971-74. Lecturer in politics, Manchester Univ, Birmingham Poly and N Staffordshire Poly, 1964-74; television presenter and producer

1979-87. Member, NUJ. Ed Hemel Hempstead GS; Leicester and Manchester Univs.
**BERNARD GENTRY,** b Dec 6, 1959. London Underground booking clerk. Contested Vauxhall 1992. Lambeth cllr 1994- (dep leader, C group, 1996- ); Lambeth rep to London ecology cttee and London boroughs transport scheme. Chair, Vauxhall C assoc. Ed Clapham Coll.
**NATHANIEL GREEN,** b Oct 6, 1966. Journalist working in field of international business, industry and development. Ed Priory GS for Boys; Bradford Univ.

| TEWKESBURY | | 92.5% change | | | | | C win |
|---|---|---|---|---|---|---|---|
| Electorate % Turnout | | 68,208 | 76.5% | 1997 | 64,159 | 82.0% | 1992 |
| Robertson, L | C | 23,859 | 45.8% | -8.1% | 28,300 | 53.8% | C |
| Sewell, J | LD | 14,625 | 28.0% | -7.1% | 18,503 | 35.2% | LD |
| Tustin, K | Lab | 13,665 | 26.2% | +16.1% | 5,297 | 10.1% | Lab |
| | | | | | 488 | 0.9% | Other |
| C to LD notional swing 0.5% | | 52,149 | C maj 9,234 | | 52,588 | C maj 9,797 | |
| | | | 17.7% | | | 18.6% | |

**LAURENCE ROBERTSON,** b March 29, 1958. PR consultant, charity fundraiser. Contested Ashfield 1992, and Makerfield 1987. Chair, Grindleford C Assoc, 1991-93. Director, L.A. Robertson (PR company); Philip Gore (Bolton) Ltd, general trading. Consultant to Church Army charity, Portman House Trust, Royal Acad of Music, Silverwood Forestry. Co-ordinator of £2.2 million appeal for homeless women in London 1994. Ed Farnworth GS.

**JOHN SEWELL,** b Jan 23, 1944. Engineer. Contested Gloucester 1992. Gloucs county cllr 1985- (group leader 1986- ). Dep leader of LDs, Assoc of County Councils. Member, Local Gvt Management Board. Member, Amnesty. Ed Chipping Campden GS; Bristol Coll of Commerce.
**KELVIN TUSTIN,** b Oct 2, 1953. Manager in aerospace industry. Tewkesbury borough cllr. Member, MSF. Ed Cheltenham HS; North Gloucs Tech Coll.

| THANET NORTH | | | | | | | C hold |
|---|---|---|---|---|---|---|---|
| Electorate % Turnout | | 71,112 | 68.8% | 1997 | 70,978 | 76.0% | 1992 |
| *Gale, R | C | 21,586 | 44.1% | -13.1% | 30,867 | 57.2% | C |
| Johnston, Ms I | Lab | 18,820 | 38.4% | +15.0% | 12,657 | 23.5% | Lab |
| Kendrick, P | LD | 5,576 | 11.4% | -6.3% | 9,563 | 17.7% | LD |
| Chambers, M | Ref | 2,535 | 5.2% | | 873 | 1.6% | Grn |
| Haines, Ms J E | UK Ind | 438 | 0.9% | | | | |
| C to Lab swing 14.0% | | 48,955 | C maj 2,766 | | 53,960 | C maj 18,210 | |
| | | | 5.7% | | | 33.7% | |

**ROGER GALE,** b Aug 20, 1943. Elected 1983; contested Birmingham Northfield 1982. Member, select cttees on home affairs, 1990-92; on broadcasting 1988-91. PPS to Armed Forces Min 1992-97. Chair, 1990- , vice-chair 1987-90, and sec 1985-87, C backbench media cttee. Chair, all-party animal welfare parly group. Member, nat cttee C trade unionists 1979- . Consultant in media and presentation to Scottish and Newcastle Breweries; Rhone Poulenc Rorer; and Organon UK Ltd, pharmaceutical companies. Ex-

producer Thames TV; director of BBC children's TV; producer, BBC radio current affairs. Member, Equity; NUJ; ACTT. Ed Hardye's School, Dorchester; Guildhall School of Music and Drama.
**IRIS JOHNSTON,** b Oct 23, 1948. Ex-NHS cardiographer. Volunteer organiser for Labour Helpline. Thanet district cllr 1993- . Ed in Ireland; OU.
**PAUL KENDRICK,** b Jan 10, 1959. Credit controller. Kent county cllr. Ed Kingsbury HS.

| THANET SOUTH | | 0.1% change | | | | | Lab win |
|---|---|---|---|---|---|---|---|
| Electorate % Turnout | | 62,792 | 71.6% | **1997** | 63,317 | 77.0% | **1992** |
| **Ladyman, Dr S** | **Lab** | **20,777** | **46.2%** | **+18.0%** | **25,222** | **51.7%** | **C** |
| +Aitken, J | C | 17,899 | 39.8% | -12.0% | 13,723 | 28.1% | Lab |
| Hewett-Silk, Ms B | LD | 5,263 | 11.7% | -6.6% | 8,936 | 18.3% | LD |
| Crook, C P | UK Ind | 631 | 1.4% | | 870 | 1.8% | Grn |
| Wheatley, D | Green | 418 | 0.9% | | | | |
| **C to Lab notional swing 15.0%** | | **44,988** | | **Lab maj 2,878** | **48,751** | | **C maj 11,499** |
| | | | | 6.4% | | | 23.6% |

**STEPHEN LADYMAN,** b Nov 6, 1952. Computer scientist; computing manager, Pfizer central research. Contested Wantage 1987. Chair, Thanet district LP. Thanet district cllr, 1995- . Member, Fabian Soc. Ed Liverpool Poly; Strathclyde Univ.
**JONATHAN AITKEN,** b Aug 30, 1942. Author and journalist. Elected for this seat 1983; MP for Thanet E Feb 1974-83; contested Meriden 1966. Treasury Chief Sec 1994-95; Min for Defence Procurement 1992-94.Member, employment select cttee, 1979-82.

Dep chair 1990-92, chair 1981-90, and co-founder AitkenHume International. Foreign correspondent for *Evening Standard* 1966-71; director, TV-am, 1981-88. Managing dir, Slater Walker (Middle East) 1973-75. Ed Eton; Christ Church, Oxford.
**BARBARA HEWETT-SILK,** b Sept 2, 1948. Nurse/NHS manager. Sandwich town cllr 1995-. Member, Royal Coll of Nursing. Ed Medway Tech HS; University Coll Hospital, London; Kent Univ.

| THURROCK | | | | | | | Lab hold |
|---|---|---|---|---|---|---|---|
| Electorate % Turnout | | 71,600 | 65.9% | **1997** | 69,171 | 78.2% | **1992** |
| **\*Mackinlay, A** | **Lab** | **29,896** | **63.3%** | **+17.5%** | **24,791** | **45.9%** | **Lab** |
| Rosindell, A R | C | 12,640 | 26.8% | -16.9% | 23,619 | 43.7% | C |
| White, J | LD | 3,843 | 8.1% | -1.4% | 5,145 | 9.5% | LD |
| Compobassi, P | UK Ind | 833 | 1.8% | | 391 | 0.7% | Pensioners |
| | | | | | 117 | 0.2% | Anti-Fed |
| **C to Lab swing 17.2%** | | **47,212** | | **Lab maj 17,256** | **54,063** | | **Lab maj 1,172** |
| | | | | 36.6% | | | 2.2% |

**ANDREW MACKINLAY,** b April 24, 1949. Regained this seat for Lab 1992; contested Peterborough 1987, Croydon Central 1983, Surbiton twice 1974; and London South and Surrey East in 1984 Euro elections. Member, transport select cttee, 1992-97; joint select cttee on consolidation Bills 1993-96, unopposed Bills panel 1992-97. Joint vice-chair, all-party Scout Assoc parly group; treas, Friends of European Movement group. Nalgo official 1972-92. Clerk, Surrey County Council, 1965-75. Member, Chartered Inst of Secretaries and Administrators. Ed Salesian Coll, Chertsey.
**ANDREW ROSINDELL,** b March 17, 1966. Freelance journalist.

Contested Glasgow Provan 1992. Researcher to Vivian Bendall, former MP. Chair, nat YCs 1993-94; chair 1987-88, and exec member 1983-89, Greater London YCs; chair, Euro YCs 1993- . Ex-member, C Party exec and gen purposes cttees. Havering borough cllr 1990- . Member, RAF Assoc; C Christian Fellowship; Anglo-Swiss Soc; C Way Forward; Monday Club; IoJ. Ed Marshalls Park Secondary, Romford.
**JOE WHITE,** b March 10, 1938. Havering Careers Service officer. Basildon district cllr 1987- (chair, LD group). Member, community health council, 1988-92. Ed Tottenham County School.

| TIVERTON & HONITON | | 30.6% change | | | | | C win |
|---|---|---|---|---|---|---|---|
| Electorate % Turnout | | 75,744 | 78.1% | **1997** | 71,796 | 82.9% | **1992** |
| **+Browning, Mrs A F** | **C** | **24,438** | **41.3%** | **-9.9%** | **30,536** | **51.3%** | **C** |
| Barnard, Dr J | LD | 22,785 | 38.5% | +6.8% | 18,872 | 31.7% | LD |
| King, J | Lab | 7,598 | 12.8% | +1.9% | 6,524 | 11.0% | Lab |
| Lowings, S | Ref | 2,952 | 5.0% | | 3,622 | 6.1% | Other |
| Roach, Mrs J | Lib | 635 | 1.1% | | | | |
| McIvor, Ms E | Green | 485 | 0.8% | | | | |
| Charles, D | Nat Dem | 236 | 0.4% | | | | |
| **C to LD notional swing 8.4%** | | **59,129** | | **C maj 1,653** | **59,554** | | **C maj 11,664** |
| | | | | 2.8% | | | 19.6% |

**ANGELA BROWNING,** b Dec 4, 1946. MP for Tiverton 1992-97; contested Crewe and Nantwich 1987. Parly Sec, Min of Agric, Fish and Food, 1994-97; PPS to Employment Min 1993-94. Member, Dept of Employment advisory cttee on women's employment, 1989-92. National chair, Women into Business; Western area C Political Centre; member, nat advisory cttee of CPC. Former self-employed management consultant and director of Small Business Bureau. Member, Nat Autistic Soc; Thomas Hardy Soc. Ed Westwood Girls' GS; Reading and Bournemouth Colls of Tech.

**JIM BARNARD,** b Jan 6, 1947. Dairy business owner, agricultural consultant. Contested Bristol in 1994 Euro elections. Adviser to UK and EU on food legislation. Member, NFU; Nat Governors Council; Amnesty; Friends of the Earth. Ed Wells Cathedral School; Leeds Univ.
**JOHN KING,** b April 25, 1951. Business manager for car dealership. Teignbridge district cllr (chair, Lab group). Member, TGWU. Ed Southampton Glen Eyre Sec Mod.

| TONBRIDGE & MALLING | | 45.8% change | | 1997 | | | C win |
|---|---|---|---|---|---|---|---|
| Electorate % Turnout | | 64,798 | 76.0% | 1997 | 64,102 | 80.7% | 1992 |
| +Stanley, Sir John | C | 23,640 | 48.0% | -12.8% | 31,462 | 60.8% | C |
| Withstandley, Mrs B | Lab | 13,410 | 27.2% | +10.2% | 10,721 | 20.7% | LD |
| Brown, K | LD | 9,467 | 19.2% | -1.5% | 8,841 | 17.1% | Lab |
| Scrivenor, J | Ref | 2,005 | 4.1% | | 522 | 1.0% | Grn |
| Bullen, Mrs B | UK Ind | 502 | 1.0% | | 189 | 0.4% | NLP |
| Valente, G | NLP | 205 | 0.4% | +0.1% | | | |
| C to Lab notional swing 11.5% | | 49,229 | | C maj 10,230 | 51,735 | | C maj 20,741 |
| | | | | 20.8% | | | 40.1% |

**SIR JOHN STANLEY,** b Jan 19, 1942. Elected Feb 1974; contested Newton-le-Willows 1970. N Ireland Min 1987-88; Armed Forces Min 1983-87; Housing Min 1979-83. PPS to Margaret Thatcher 1976-79. Joint vice-chair, all-party group on child abduction, 1994- . Unpaid trustee, Action Aid 1989-. Dir, Henderson Highland Trust, 1990- ; Fidelity Japanese Values (both investment trusts). Ed Repton; Lincoln Coll, Oxford.

**BARBARA WITHSTANDLEY,** b Oct 28, 1943. Medical secretary/OU student. Dartford district and borough cllr 1972-78. Ed Bexley Tech HS for Girls; OU.
**KEITH BROWN,** b June 21, 1949. Optician. Tonbridge and Malling borough cllr 1994- . Freeman of City of London; Worshipful Co of Spectacle Makers. Member, Stonewall. Ed Forest Hill Comp; City and East London FE Coll.

| TOOTING | | | | 1997 | | | Lab hold |
|---|---|---|---|---|---|---|---|
| Electorate % Turnout | | 66,653 | 69.2% | 1997 | 68,306 | 74.8% | 1992 |
| *Cox, T | Lab | 27,516 | 59.7% | +11.5% | 24,601 | 48.2% | Lab |
| Hutchings, J | C | 12,505 | 27.1% | -13.0% | 20,494 | 40.1% | C |
| James, S | LD | 4,320 | 9.4% | +2.0% | 3,776 | 7.4% | LD |
| Husband, Mrs A | Ref | 829 | 1.8% | | 1,340 | 2.6% | Lib |
| Rattray, J | Green | 527 | 1.1% | | 694 | 1.4% | Grn |
| Boddington, P | BFAIR | 161 | 0.3% | | 119 | 0.2% | NLP |
| Koene, J | Rights | 94 | 0.2% | | 64 | 0.1% | CD |
| Bailey-Bond, D | Dream | 83 | 0.2% | | | | |
| Miller, P | NLP | 70 | 0.2% | -0.1% | | | |
| C to Lab swing 12.3% | | 46,105 | | Lab maj 15,011 | 51,088 | | Lab maj 4,107 |
| | | | | 32.6% | | | 8.0% |

**THOMAS COX,** b Dec 9, 1930. Elected for this seat 1983; MP for Wandsworth Tooting Feb 1974-83; for Wandsworth Central 1970-Feb 1974; contested Stroud 1966. Asst gvt whip 1974-77; gvt whip 1977-79. Chair, all-party built environment group, member and ex-officer, British IPU group exec; joint vice-chair, Commonwealth Parly Assoc UK branch exec. Delegate to Council of Europe and WEU 1985-97. Electrician. Ed state schools and LSE.

**JAMES HUTCHINGS,** b Nov 5, 1962. Research asst to David Tredinnick, MP, 1990-92; nat chair, Youth for Peace through Nato, 1985-86. Lambeth cllr 1986-90. Director of business agency, East Europe and Ukraine; Future of Europe Trust director 1990-92. Manager, Kleinwort Benson, 1986-90; Barclays Bank 1984-86. Ed Canford School, Dorset; Exeter Univ.
**SIMON JAMES,** b April 1, 1967. Secretarial assistant. Member, Electoral Reform Soc. Ed Stamford School; South Bank Univ.

| TORBAY | | | | 1997 | | | LD gain |
|---|---|---|---|---|---|---|---|
| Electorate % Turnout | | 72,258 | 73.8% | 1997 | 71,171 | 80.6% | 1992 |
| Sanders, A | LD | 21,094 | 39.6% | -0.2% | 28,624 | 49.9% | C |
| *Allason, R | C | 21,082 | 39.5% | -10.3% | 22,837 | 39.8% | LD |
| Morey, M | Lab | 7,923 | 14.9% | +5.3% | 5,503 | 9.6% | Lab |
| Booth, G H | UK Ind | 1,962 | 3.7% | | 268 | 0.5% | NF |
| Cowling, B | Lib | 1,161 | 2.2% | | 157 | 0.3% | NLP |
| Wild, P | Dream | 100 | 0.2% | | | | |
| C to LD swing 5.1% | | 53,322 | | LD maj 12 | 57,389 | | C maj 5,787 |
| | | | | 0.0% | | | 10.1% |

**ADRIAN SANDERS,** b April 25, 1959. Funding adviser. Contested this seat 1992; Devon in 1994 Euro elections. Parly officer for LD whips' office 1989-90. Worked in Paddy Ashdown's office 1992-93. Political sec, Devon and Cornwall regional Lib Party, 1983-84; Nat League of YLs vice-pres 1987. Torbay borough cllr 1984-86. Policy officer, Nat Council for Voluntary Organisations, 1993-94. Member, British Diabetic Assoc. Ed Torquay Boys' GS.

**RUPERT ALLASON,** b Nov 8, 1951. Author (writing as Nigel West). Elected 1987; contested Battersea 1983 and Kettering 1979. Chair, all-party Bermuda group, 1996-97. European editor, *Intelligence Quarterly.* Lloyd's underwriter. Ed Downside School, Bath; Grenoble, Lille and London Univs.
**MICHAEL MOREY,** b Dec 13, 1946. Decorator/signwriter. Torbay borough cllr (leader, Lab group, 1990- ). Member, TGWU. Ed Homelands Tech HS; South Devon Tech Coll.

| TORFAEN | | | | | **Lab hold** | | | |
|---|---|---|---|---|---|---|---|---|
| Electorate % Turnout | | 60,343 | 71.7% | **1997** | 61,104 | 77.5% | **1992** |
| *Murphy, P | Lab | 29,863 | 69.1% | +4.9% | 30,352 | 64.1% | Lab |
| Parish, N | C | 5,327 | 12.3% | -8.0% | 9,598 | 20.3% | C |
| Gray, Ms J | LD | 5,249 | 12.1% | -0.9% | 6,178 | 13.1% | LD |
| Holler, Ms D | Ref | 1,245 | 2.9% | | 1,210 | 2.6% | Green/PC |
| Gough, R | PC | 1,042 | 2.4% | | | | |
| Coghill, R | Green | 519 | 1.2% | | | | |
| C to Lab swing 6.4% | | 43,245 | Lab maj 24,536 | | 47,338 | Lab maj 20,754 | |
| | | | 56.7% | | | 43.8% | |

PAUL MURPHY, b Nov 25, 1948. Became Minister of State, Northern Ireland Office, May 5, 1997. Elected 1987; contested Wells 1979. Member, Welsh affairs select cttee, 1987-89; Lab spokesman on defence 1995-97; on N Ireland 1994-95; on Wales 1988-94. Parly consultant to NATFHE. Torfaen borough cllr 1973-87. Lecturer in history and gvt at Ebbw Vale Coll of FE 1971-87. Ed West Monmouth School, Pontypool; Oriel Coll, Oxford.

NEIL PARISH, b May 26, 1956. Farmer. Somerset County cllr 1984-93; Sedgemoor district cllr 1983-95 (dep leader 1990-95). Vice-chair, Bridgwater C assoc, 1987- . Ed Brymore School; Taunton Tech Coll.
JEAN GRAY, b Nov 10, 1941. Registered nurse/midwife. Ex-Torfaen borough cllr. Member, Royal Coll of Midwives. Ed Stowhill Sec Mod, Newport.

| TOTNES | 38.4% change | | | | | | **C win** | |
|---|---|---|---|---|---|---|---|---|
| Electorate % Turnout | | 70,473 | 76.3% | **1997** | 68,071 | 83.1% | **1992** |
| +Steen, Sir Anthony | C | 19,637 | 36.5% | -14.3% | 28,736 | 50.8% | C |
| Chave, R F | LD | 18,760 | 34.9% | -0.7% | 20,110 | 35.6% | LD |
| Ellery, V | Lab | 8,796 | 16.4% | +4.3% | 6,842 | 12.1% | Lab |
| Cook, Ms P | Ref | 2,552 | 4.7% | | 853 | 1.5% | Other |
| Venmore, C | Loc C | 2,369 | 4.4% | | | | |
| Thomas, H W | UK Ind | 999 | 1.9% | | | | |
| Pratt, A | Green | 548 | 1.0% | | | | |
| Golding, J | Dream | 108 | 0.2% | | | | |
| C to LD notional swing 6.8% | | 53,769 | C maj 877 | | 56,541 | C maj 8,626 | |
| | | | 1.6% | | | 15.3% | |

SIR ANTHONY STEEN, b July 22, 1939. Barrister, youth leader, social worker, author, Lloyd's underwriter. MP for South Hams 1983-97 and for Liverpool Wavertree 1974-83. PPS to Nat Heritage Sec 1992-94. Chair, C backbench urban and inner cities cttee, 1987-94 and 1979-80; C trade and industry deregulation sub-cttee. Member, exec council of Nat Playing Fields Assoc; vice-chair, Task Force Trust; vice-pres, International Centre of Child Studies.

Adviser to board of Airlines of Great Britain; English Vineyards Assoc. Ed Westminster; Gray's Inn.
ROB CHAVE, b Jan 22, 1952. Accountant. Contested South Hams 1987. Teignbridge district cllr 1981- (group leader). Ed Exeter School; Portsmouth Poly.
VICTOR ELLERY, b Feb 11, 1952. Postman. Torbay borough cllr 1991- ; Devon county cllr 1993- . Ed Bristol Tech Coll.

| TOTTENHAM | | | | | **Lab hold** | | | |
|---|---|---|---|---|---|---|---|---|
| Electorate % Turnout | | 66,173 | 57.0% | **1997** | 68,319 | 65.6% | **1992** |
| *Grant, B | Lab | 26,121 | 69.3% | +12.8% | 25,309 | 56.5% | Lab |
| Scantlebury, A | C | 5,921 | 15.7% | -14.1% | 13,341 | 29.8% | C |
| Hughes, N | LD | 4,064 | 10.8% | -0.6% | 5,120 | 11.4% | LD |
| Budge, P | Green | 1,059 | 2.8% | | 903 | 2.0% | Grn |
| Tay, Ms E | ProLife | 210 | 0.6% | | 150 | 0.3% | NLP |
| Anglin, C | WRP | 181 | 0.5% | | | | |
| Kent, Ms T | SEP | 148 | 0.4% | | | | |
| C to Lab swing 13.4% | | 37,704 | Lab maj 20,200 | | 44,823 | Lab maj 11,968 | |
| | | | 53.6% | | | 26.7% | |

BERNIE GRANT, b Feb 17, 1944. Elected for this seat 1987. Joint vice-chair, all-party British-Caribbean parly group 1989- ; former joint vice-chair, PLP home affairs cttee. Chair, Campaign Group of Lab MPs, 1990-92; standing conference on race equality in Europe 1990- ; African Reparations Movement (UK) 1993- ; chair and founder member, parly Black Caucus, 1988- . Haringey cllr 1978-88, (leader 1985-87; dep leader 1982-83). Development worker, black trade unionists solidarity movement, 1983-84; member, exec cttee Anti-Apartheid Movement 1989-91. Former analyst,

British Rail clerk, telephonist and Nupe area officer. Newham senior district housing officer (community relations) 1985-87. Born Guyana, emigrated to UK 1963. Ed St Stanislaus Coll, Georgetown; Tottenham Tech Coll; Heriot-Watt Univ.
ANDREW SCANTLEBURY, b Dec 22, 1958. Manager, mental health community trust. Member, Board of Visitors, Brixton Prison, 1996-97. Ed William Blake School, Battersea; South Thames Coll.
NEIL HUGHES, b Dec 14, 1956. Voluntary worker. Hackney cllr 1996- . Member, Liberty; Charter 88. Ed Caldy Orange GS; OU.

## TRURO & ST AUSTELL | | | | | | LD hold

| Electorate % Turnout | | 76,824 | 73.9% | **1997** | 75,101 | 82.4% | **1992** |
|---|---|---|---|---|---|---|---|
| *Taylor, M | LD | **27,502** | 48.5% | -2.0% | 31,230 | 50.5% | LD |
| Badcock, N | C | 15,001 | 26.4% | -11.8% | 23,660 | 38.3% | C |
| Dooley, M | Lab | 8,697 | 15.3% | +5.5% | 6,078 | 9.8% | Lab |
| Hearn, C | Ref | 3,682 | 6.5% | | 569 | 0.9% | Grn |
| Haithwaite, A T | UK Ind | 576 | 1.0% | | 208 | 0.3% | Lib |
| Robinson, Mrs D | Green | 482 | 0.8% | | 108 | 0.2% | NLP |
| Hicks, D | Meb Ker | 450 | 0.8% | | | | |
| Yelland, Mrs L | PP | 240 | 0.4% | | | | |
| Boland, P | NLP | 117 | 0.2% | +0.0% | | | |
| C to LD swing 4.9% | | **56,747** | **LD maj 12,501** | | **61,853** | **LD maj 7,570** | |
| | | | 22.0% | | | 12.2% | |

**MATTHEW TAYLOR,** b Jan 3, 1963. MP for Truro since 1987 by-election. Member, environment select cttee, 1995-97. LD spokesman on environment 1994- ; on Citizen's Charter, and chair of campaigns and communications, 1992-94; on education 1990-92; on trade and industry 1989-90; on England, covering local gvt, housing and transport, 1988-89. From 1986-87, economic policy researcher for parly Lib Party and research assistant to the late David Penhaligon, MP for Truro 1974-86. Ed St Paul's, Truro; Treliske School, Truro; University Coll School, London; Lady Margaret Hall, Oxford (pres, students' union, 1985-86).
**NEIL BADCOCK,** b Sept 11, 1961. Farmer. Penwith district cllr 1987- . Member, exec cttee, St Ives C assoc; Western region agric and countryside forum; NFU. Ed Humphry Davy GS; Dorset Agric Coll.
**MICHAEL DOOLEY,** b June 20, 1961. Schoolteacher. Ed Dover GS; Queen Mary Coll, London; Hughes Hall, Cambridge.

## TUNBRIDGE WELLS | 14.0% change | | | | | | C win

| Electorate % Turnout | | 65,259 | 74.1% | **1997** | 66,280 | 77.6% | **1992** |
|---|---|---|---|---|---|---|---|
| Norman, A | C | **21,853** | 45.2% | -9.8% | 28,297 | 55.0% | C |
| Clayton, T | LD | 14,347 | 29.7% | +0.2% | 15,151 | 29.5% | LD |
| Warner, P | Lab | 9,879 | 20.4% | +5.7% | 7,563 | 14.7% | Lab |
| Macpherson, T | Ref | 1,858 | 3.8% | | 230 | 0.4% | NLP |
| Anderson Smart, M | UK Ind | 264 | 0.5% | | 203 | 0.4% | ISS |
| Levy, P | NLP | 153 | 0.3% | -0.1% | | | |
| C to LD notional swing 5.0% | | **48,354** | **C maj 7,506** | | **51,444** | **C maj 13,146** | |
| | | | 15.5% | | | 25.6% | |

**ARCHIE NORMAN,** b May 1, 1954. Chairman, Asda supermarkets since 1996; chief exec 1991-96. Member, British Rail Board, 1992-94; Railtrack board 1994- ; DTI deregulation task force; Anglo-German deregulation task force. Consultative cttee, Dulwich Picture Gallery, 1990- . Variously with Citibank, McKinsey, Woolworths, Kingfisher, Chartwell Land, and Geest. Ed Minnesota Univ; Emmanuel Coll, Cambridge; Harvard Business School.
**TONY CLAYTON,** b Feb 4, 1949. Industrial economist. Contested this seat 1992. Sevenoaks district cllr 1987- ; Sevenoaks town cllr 1987- (former Mayor). Ed Rugby; Sussex Univ.
**PETER WARNER,** b May 1, 1961. IT systems support. Tunbridge Wells borough cllr 1995- . Ed Edgebury School for Boys, Kent; Kemnal Manor School, Kent; Ruskin Coll, Oxford.

## TWEEDDALE, ETTRICK & LAUDERDALE | 41.2% change | | | | | LD win

| Electorate % Turnout | | 50,891 | 76.6% | **1997** | 50,228 | 79.3% | **1992** |
|---|---|---|---|---|---|---|---|
| Moore, M | LD | **12,178** | 31.2% | -3.8% | 13,953 | 35.0% | LD |
| Geddes, K | Lab | 10,689 | 27.4% | +11.0% | 12,218 | 30.7% | C |
| Jack, A | C | 8,623 | 22.1% | -8.6% | 6,835 | 17.2% | SNP |
| Goldie, I | SNP | 6,671 | 17.1% | -0.1% | 6,538 | 16.4% | Lab |
| Mowbray, C | Ref | 406 | 1.0% | | 276 | 0.7% | Lib |
| Hein, J | Lib | 387 | 1.0% | +0.3% | | | |
| Paterson, D | NLP | 47 | 0.1% | | | | |
| LD to Lab notional swing 7.4% | | **39,001** | **LD maj 1,489** | | **39,820** | **LD maj 1,735** | |
| | | | 3.8% | | | 4.4% | |

**MICHAEL MOORE,** b June 3, 1965. Chartered accountant. Scottish LD spokesman on small business and employment; research asst to Archy Kirkwood, MP, 1987-88. Member, Amnesty. Ed Strathallan School; Jedburgh GS; Edinburgh Univ.
**KEITH GEDDES,** b Aug 8, 1952. Full-time Edinburgh city cllr (leader, Lab group). Ex-Shelter advice worker. Pres, Cosla. Member, Friends of the Earth. Ed Galashiels Acad; Edinburgh and Heriot-Watt Univs; Moray House Coll of Ed.
**ALISTER JACK,** b July 7, 1963. Company director. Member, Scottish C econ affairs policy cttee. Ed Glenalmond.
**IAIN GOLDIE,** b Feb 8, 1941. Ex-teacher. Contested Ayr 1983, Falkirk W 1987, South of Scotland in 1984 Euro elections. Ed Glasgow, Paris, Tubingen Univs; Jordanhill Coll.

| TWICKENHAM | | 14.0% change | | | | | LD win |
|---|---|---|---|---|---|---|---|
| Electorate % Turnout | | 73,281 | 79.3% | **1997** | 71,805 | 83.3% | **1992** |
| **Cable, Dr V** | LD | **26,237** | 45.1% | +5.8% | **29,652** | 49.6% | **C** |
| +Jessel, T | C | 21,956 | 37.8% | -11.8% | 23,531 | 39.3% | LD |
| Tutchell, Ms E | Lab | 9,065 | 15.6% | +5.2% | 6,194 | 10.4% | Lab |
| Harrison, Miss J | Ind ECR | 589 | 1.0% | | 194 | 0.3% | NLP |
| Haggar, T | Dream | 155 | 0.3% | | 131 | 0.2% | DLC |
| Hardy, A | NLP | 142 | 0.2% | -0.1% | 109 | 0.2% | Lib |
| **C to LD notional swing 8.8%** | | **58,144** | LD maj **4,281** 7.4% | | **59,811** | C maj **6,121** 10.2% | |

**VINCENT CABLE,** b May 9, 1943. Chief economist, Shell International. Contested Westminster 1992, this seat 1987, 1983, Glasgow Hillhead for Lab 1970. Previously adviser to Commonwealth Sec-Gen; dep dir, Overseas Development Inst, special adviser to John Smith when Trade Sec. Glasgow city cllr 1971-74. Former qualified pilot. Member, HACAN (Aircraft Noise); Hospital Alert. Ed Nunthorpe GS, York; Trinity Coll, Cambridge (pres of Union); Glasgow Univ.
**TOBY JESSEL,** b July 11, 1934. Elected 1970; contested Hull N at by-election and general election, 1966, and Peckham 1964. Member, national heritage select cttee 1992-97; Commons art advisory cttee; Council of Europe and WEU 1976- . Chair, 1983-92, and joint vice-chair 1979-82, C backbench arts and heritage cttee. Greater London cllr 1967-73. Member, British Orchestras Assoc council, 1991- . Liveryman, Worshipful Co of Musicians. Unpaid dir, Warship Preservation Trust Ltd, 1994- . Ed Amesbury School, Hindhead; Royal Naval Coll, Dartmouth; Balliol Coll, Oxford.
**EVA TUTCHELL,** b April 18, 1941. Teacher. Member, advisory group on equal opportunities; NUT. Ed Godolphin and Latymer School, London; University Coll, London; London Univ Inst of Ed.

| TYNE BRIDGE | | 24.3% change | | | | | Lab win |
|---|---|---|---|---|---|---|---|
| Electorate % Turnout | | 61,058 | 57.1% | **1997** | 67,085 | 63.7% | **1992** |
| **+Clelland, D** | Lab | **26,767** | 76.8% | +10.0% | **28,520** | 66.8% | **Lab** |
| Lee, A | C | 3,861 | 11.1% | -11.0% | 9,443 | 22.1% | C |
| Wallace, Mrs M | LD | 2,785 | 8.0% | -3.1% | 4,755 | 11.1% | LD |
| Oswald, G | Ref | 919 | 2.6% | | | | |
| Brunskill, Ms E | Soc | 518 | 1.5% | | | | |
| **C to Lab notional swing 10.5%** | | **34,850** | Lab maj **22,906** 65.7% | | **42,718** | Lab maj **19,077** 44.7% | |

**DAVID CLELLAND,** b June 27, 1943. Became gvt asst whip, May 7, 1997. Elected 1985 by-election. Lab whip 1995-97. Member, select cttees on energy, 1989-90; home affairs 1985-88; Parliamentary Commissioner for Administration 1985-87. Chair, 1990-97, and joint vice-chair 1988-90, PLP environment cttee; chair, PLP regional gvt group 1992-93; sec and hon treas, Northern group of Lab MPs, 1990- . Joint vice-chair, tertiary ed parly group. Gateshead borough cllr 1972-86; nat sec, Assoc of Cllrs, 1981-86. Electrical tester 1964-81. Member, AEU. Ed Kelvin Grove Boys' School, Gateshead; Gateshead and Hebburn Tech Colls.
**ADRIAN LEE,** b 1966. Parliamentary researcher to Christopher Gill, MP. Chair, nat YCs, 1994-95; vice-chair, Ealing Southall C assoc 1983-85. Ed Ealing Coll Upper School; Thames Poly.
**MARY WALLACE,** b April 11, 1938. Retired teacher. Gateshead borough cllr 1996- . Ed Merchant Taylors Girls' School, Crosby; Newcastle Coll of Ed.

| TYNEMOUTH | | 9.2% change | | | | | Lab win |
|---|---|---|---|---|---|---|---|
| Electorate % Turnout | | 66,341 | 77.1% | **1997** | 68,616 | 81.1% | **1992** |
| **Campbell, A** | Lab | **28,318** | 55.4% | +13.1% | **27,056** | 48.6% | **C** |
| Callanan, J M | C | 17,045 | 33.3% | -15.3% | 23,527 | 42.3% | Lab |
| Duffield, A | LD | 4,509 | 8.8% | +0.7% | 4,507 | 8.1% | LD |
| Rook, C | Ref | 819 | 1.6% | | 543 | 1.0% | Grn |
| Rogers, Dr F W | UK Ind | 462 | 0.9% | | | | |
| **C to Lab notional swing 14.2%** | | **51,153** | Lab maj **11,273** 22.0% | | **55,633** | C maj **3,529** 6.3% | |

**ALAN CAMPBELL,** b July 8, 1957. Head of sixth form and of history at Hurst HS, Ashington. Tynemouth CLP sec and campaign co-ordinator. Ed Hirst HS, Ashington; Lancaster, Leeds and Northumbria Univs.
**MARTIN CALLANAN,** b Aug 8, 1961. Engineering projects manager with Scottish and Newcastle Breweries. Contested Gateshead E 1992; Houghton and Washington 1987. Gateshead metropolitan borough cllr 1987- (leader, C group); Tyne and Wear county cllr 1983-86. Nat chair, YC Initiative, 1989- ; member, nat union exec cttee, 1984-88; vice-chair, Northern area exec cttee, 1987-89. Ed Heathfield HS, Gateshead; Newcastle Poly.
**ANDREW DUFFIELD,** b Jan 12, 1963. Brewery area manager; ex-RN officer. Ed Plymouth Coll; St Chad's Coll, Durham.

| TYNESIDE NORTH | | 30.6% change | | | | | Lab win |
|---|---|---|---|---|---|---|---|
| Electorate % Turnout | | 66,449 | 67.9% | **1997** | 68,368 | 73.8% | **1992** |
| +Byers, S J | Lab | **32,810** | 72.7% | +11.8% | 30,764 | 61.0% | Lab |
| McIntyre, M | C | 6,167 | 13.7% | -12.3% | 13,130 | 26.0% | C |
| Mulvenna, T | LD | 4,762 | 10.6% | -2.5% | 6,580 | 13.0% | LD |
| Rollings, M | Ref | 1,382 | 3.1% | | | | |
| C to Lab notional swing 12.1% | | 45,121 | Lab maj 26,643 59.0% | | | 50,474 | Lab maj 17,634 34.9% |

**STEPHEN BYERS**, b April 13, 1953. Became Minister of State for Education with responsibility for school standards, May 5, 1997. MP for Wallsend 1992-97, contested Hexham 1983. Lab spokesman on education and employment, responsible for industrial relations and social chapter, 1996-97; Lab whip 1994-95. Member, home affairs select cttee, 1994; joint chair, all-party police party group. Chair, PLP home affairs cttee, 1992-94. North Tyneside cllr 1980-92 (dep leader 1985-92). Chair of ed cttee, Assoc of Metropolitan Authorities, 1990-92; leader, council of local ed authorities, 1990-92. Senior lecturer in law, Newcastle Poly, 1977-92. Ed Chester City GS; Chester Coll of FE; Liverpool Poly.

**MICHAEL McINTYRE**, b Nov 23, 1957. Partner in building firm. School governor. North Tyneside borough cllr 1992- .

**TOMMY MULVENNA**, b April 9, 1947. Probation officer. North Tyneside borough cllr (dep group leader). Ed St Columba's, Wallsend; Newcastle Coll.

| TYRONE WEST | | 56.0% change | | | | | UUP win |
|---|---|---|---|---|---|---|---|
| Electorate % Turnout | | 58,168 | 79.6% | **1997** | 56,970 | 71.3% | **1992** |
| Thompson, W | UUP | **16,003** | 34.6% | | 15,738 | 38.8% | DUP |
| Byrne, J | SDLP | 14,842 | 32.1% | +1.1% | 12,590 | 31.0% | SDLP |
| Doherty, P | SF | 14,280 | 30.9% | +10.9% | 8,102 | 19.9% | SF |
| Gormley, Ms A | Alliance | 829 | 1.8% | -2.9% | 2,282 | 5.6% | Other |
| Owens, T | WP | 230 | 0.5% | | 1,900 | 4.7% | Alliance |
| Johnstone, R | NLP | 91 | 0.2% | | | | |
| No swing calculation | | 46,275 | UUP maj 1,161 2.5% | | | 40,612 | DUP maj 3,148 7.8% |

**WILLIAM THOMPSON**, b Oct 26, 1939. Businessman. Won this seat 1997. Member of UU party exec and ex-chair of former Mid-Ulster constituency party. Elected to N Ireland Assembly 1973 and 1982, and to NI Convention 1975. Omagh district cllr for 12 years. Methodist lay preacher. Ed Omagh Acad.

**JOE BYRNE**. Economics lecturer. Omagh district cllr 1993- (vice-chair, 1994- ). Member, party exec cttee; party vice-chair; chair of party policy cttee; ex-asst treas. Ed Queen's Univ, Belfast.

**PAT DOHERTY**. Vice-pres, Sinn Fein.

**ANN GORMLEY**. Dental hygienist. Ex-chair, Omagh District Council. Alliance spokeswoman on women's issues.

| ULSTER MID | | 105.6% change | | | | | SF win |
|---|---|---|---|---|---|---|---|
| Electorate % Turnout | | 58,836 | 86.1% | **1997** | 56,935 | 82.5% | **1992** |
| McGuinness, M | SF | **20,294** | 40.1% | +15.9% | 19,274 | 41.0% | DUP |
| +McCrea, Rev W | DUP | 18,411 | 36.3% | -4.7% | 14,360 | 30.6% | SDLP |
| Haughey, D | SDLP | 11,205 | 22.1% | -8.5% | 11,340 | 24.1% | SF |
| Bogues, E | Alliance | 460 | 0.9% | -1.7% | 1,229 | 2.6% | Alliance |
| Donnelly, Mrs M | WP | 238 | 0.5% | +0.3% | 549 | 1.2% | Ind |
| Murray, Ms M | NLP | 61 | 0.1% | +0.0% | 107 | 0.2% | LTU |
| | | | | | 78 | 0.2% | WP |
| | | | | | 45 | 0.1% | NLP |
| DUP to SF notional swing 10.3% | | 50,669 | SF maj 1,883 3.7% | | | 46,982 | DUP maj 4,914 10.5% |

**MARTIN McGUINNESS**, b May 23, 1950. Chief negotiator of Sinn Fein. Contested Foyle 1983, 1987 and 1992 general elections. Ed Christian Brothers Tech Coll.

**THE REV WILLIAM McCREA**, b Aug 6, 1948. Gospel recording artist, Ulster Free Presbyterian minister. Elected 1983, resigned 1985 in protest at Anglo-Irish agreement, re-elected at 1986 by-election. Mid Ulster member, N Ireland Assembly, 1982-86. Magherafelt district cllr since 1973 (chair 1977-81); vice-pres, Assoc of NI Local Authorities, 1980-81. Ed Cookstown GS; Theological Coll.

**DENIS HAUGHEY**, b Oct 3, 1944. Founding member, SDLP, 1970; one of party's main strategists throughout the Troubles. Unsuccessfully contested Mid-Ulster 1983, 1987 and 1992. One of N Ireland's two representatives to European Union Cttee of the Regions. Ed Queen's Univ, Belfast.

| UPMINSTER | | 9.9% change | | | | | | Lab win |
|---|---|---|---|---|---|---|---|---|
| Electorate % Turnout | | 57,149 | 72.3% | **1997** | 58,553 | 79.2% | **1992** | |
| **Darvill, K** | **Lab** | **19,085** | **46.2%** | **+16.1%** | **25,121** | **54.2%** | **C** | |
| +Bonsor, Sir Nicholas | C | 16,315 | 39.5% | -14.7% | 13,964 | 30.1% | Lab | |
| Peskett, Mrs P | LD | 3,919 | 9.5% | -6.3% | 7,300 | 15.7% | LD | |
| Murray, T | Ref | 2,000 | 4.8% | | | | | |
| **C to Lab notional swing 15.4%** | | **41,319** | | **Lab maj 2,770** | **46,385** | | **C maj 11,157** | |
| | | | | 6.7% | | | 24.1% | |

**KEITH DARVILL,** b May 28, 1948. Solicitor. Chair, Upminster CLP. Member, TGWU; Fabian Soc; Co-op Party. Ed Norlingon Sec Mod; East Ham Tech Coll; Thurrock Coll of FE; Central London Poly; Coll of Law, Chester.
**SIR NICHOLAS BONSOR,** b Dec 9, 1942. Farmer, member of Lloyd's. MP for this seat 1983-97; for Nantwich 1979-83. Min of State for Foreign and Commonwealth Affairs 1995-97; chair, defence select cttee, 1992-95; vice-chair, C backbench constitutional affairs cttee 1994-95. Chair, Cyclotron Trust for Cancer Treatment 1984-92;

British Field Sports Soc 1988-94. Member, Country Landowners Assoc legal and parly sub-cttee 1978-82; Royal Yacht Squadron. FRSA. Ed Eton; Keble Coll, Oxford.
**PAMELA PESKETT,** b July 26, 1932. Genealogist/researcher. Winchester district cllr; Hampshire county cllr. Member, World Development Movement; CPRE; Age Concern; CPAG; Preservation Trust; European Movement. Ed Henrietta Barnett School; Willesden School of Art.

| UPPER BANN | | | | | | | | UUP hold |
|---|---|---|---|---|---|---|---|---|
| Electorate % Turnout | | 70,398 | 67.9% | **1997** | 69,079 | 65.8% | **1992** | |
| ***Trimble, D** | **UUP** | **20,836** | **43.6%** | **-15.4%** | **26,824** | **59.0%** | **UUP** | |
| Rodgers, Ms B | SDLP | 11,584 | 24.2% | +0.8% | 10,661 | 23.4% | SDLP | |
| O'Hagan, Ms B | SF | 5,773 | 12.1% | +6.0% | 2,777 | 6.1% | SF | |
| Carrick, M | DUP | 5,482 | 11.5% | | 2,541 | 5.6% | Alliance | |
| Ramsay, Dr W | Alliance | 3,017 | 6.3% | +0.7% | 1,556 | 3.4% | C | |
| French, T | WP | 554 | 1.2% | -1.3% | 1,120 | 2.5% | WP | |
| Price, B | C | 433 | 0.9% | -2.5% | | | | |
| Lyons, J | NLP | 108 | 0.2% | | | | | |
| **No swing calculation** | | **47,787** | | **UUP maj 9,252** | **45,479** | | **UUP maj 16,163** | |
| | | | | 19.4% | | | 35.5% | |

**DAVID TRIMBLE,** b Oct 15, 1944. UUP leader 1995- . Elected for this seat at 1990 by-election. Ex-UU spokesman on legal affairs. Member, N Ireland Constitutional Convention, 1975-76. Non-practising barrister. Lecturer from 1968, senior lecturer from 1977, Queen's Univ, Belfast, Faculty of Law. Ed Bangor GS; Queen's Univ, Belfast.

**BRID RODGERS.** SDLP spokeswoman on women's issues and Irish language. Craigavon cllr 1985-93 (leader, SDLP group). Former party gen sec. Ex-member, exec cttee, N Ireland Civil Rights Assoc. Ed St Louis Convent, Monaghan; Univ Coll, Dublin.
**BERNADETTE O'HAGAN,** b Dec 6, 1927. Founding member, Civil Rights Assoc in Lurgan, 1968. Campaigned on behalf of IRA prisoners during 1981 hunger strikes.

| UXBRIDGE | | 8.0% change | | | | | | C win |
|---|---|---|---|---|---|---|---|---|
| Electorate % Turnout | | 57,497 | 72.3% | **1997** | 59,528 | 75.9% | **1992** | |
| **+Shersby, Sir Michael** | **C** | **18,095** | **43.6%** | **-12.8%** | **25,467** | **56.4%** | **C** | |
| Williams, D | Lab | 17,371 | 41.8% | +12.8% | 13,099 | 29.0% | Lab | |
| Malyan, Dr A | LD | 4,528 | 10.9% | -1.6% | 5,663 | 12.5% | LD | |
| Aird, G | Ref | 1,153 | 2.8% | | 495 | 1.1% | Grn | |
| Leonard, Ms J | Soc | 398 | 1.0% | | 322 | 0.7% | BNP | |
| | | | | | 111 | 0.2% | NLP | |
| **C to Lab notional swing 12.8%** | | **41,545** | | **C maj 724** | **45,157** | | **C maj 12,368** | |
| | | | | 1.7% | | | 27.4% | |

**SIR MICHAEL SHERSBY,** b Feb 17, 1933. Died May 8, 1997, his death precipitating first by-election of new Parliament. MP for Hillingdon Uxbridge, 1972-83 and for Uxbridge since 1983. Joint chair, all-party police parly group; member, PAC; Chairmen's panel, since 1983-97. Chair, C backbench food and drinks sub-cttee, 1979-89. Member, exec cttee, UK Commonwealth Parly Assoc, 1988-97; chair, all-party British-Falkland Islands parly group, 1982-97. Parly adviser to Police Fed of England and Wales 1989-97. Paddington cllr 1959-64; Westminster cllr 1964-71 (dep lord mayor 1967-68). Unpaid dir, World Sugar Research

Organisation. Pres, London Green Belt Council, 1989-97; trustee, Harefield heart transplant trust, 1989-97. Member, Royal Over-Seas League; Court of Brunel Univ 1975-97. Ed John Lyon School, Harrow-on-the-Hill.
**DAVID WILLIAMS,** b Oct 30, 1955. Consultant, non-cash trading and credit unions. Hillingdon cllr. Member, TGWU. Ed St Philip's GS, Birmingham; Kent Univ.
**ANDREW MALYAN,** b Aug 13, 1965. Management consultant. Ed Sandbach HS; Cardiff and Aston Univs; Univ of British Columbia.

| VALE OF CLWYD | | 91.1% change | | | Lab win |
|---|---|---|---|---|---|
| Electorate % Turnout | | 52,418 | 74.7% | **1997** | 53,013 | 82.5% | **1992** |
| **Ruane, C** | **Lab** | **20,617** | **52.7%** | **+13.9%** | **19,118** | **43.7%** | **C** |
| Edwards, D G | C | 11,662 | 29.8% | -13.9% | 16,941 | 38.8% | Lab |
| Munford, D | LD | 3,425 | 8.8% | -3.7% | 5,435 | 12.4% | LD |
| Kensler, Ms G | PC | 2,301 | 5.9% | +1.1% | 2,095 | 4.8% | PC |
| Vickers, S | Ref | 834 | 2.1% | | 123 | 0.3% | Other |
| Cooke, S A | UK Ind | 293 | 0.7% | | | | |
| **C to Lab notional swing 13.9%** | | **39,132** | | **Lab maj 8,955** | **43,712** | | **C maj 2,177** |
| | | | | 22.9% | | | 5.0% |

**CHRIS RUANE,** b July 8, 1958. Dep head at local primary school. Contested Clwyd NW 1992. Rhyl town cllr 1988- . Founder, Rhyl Environmental Assoc; member, Vale of Clwyd Trades Council; welfare benefits advice shop management cttee. Chair, Clwyd West NUT, 1989-90; chair and founder member of Rhyl Anti-Apartheid Movement and Rhyl Environmental Assoc. Ed Blessed Edward Jones Comp, Rhyl; Univ Coll of Wales, Aberystwyth; Liverpool Univ.
**DAVID EDWARDS,** b Nov 12, 1965. Managing dir of publishing and PR company. Contested Ogmore 1992. Montgomeryshire district cllr 1990- . Member, C local gvt nat advisory cttee; chair, Welsh C agricultural and environmental policy forum. Ed Newtown HS; Harper Adams Agric Coll.
**DANIEL MUNFORD,** b Sept 28, 1968. Market researcher. Former part-time political researcher to ex-MP, Alex Carlile. Ed Fitzalan Comp; Oswestry School; University Coll, London.
**GWYNETH KENSLER,** b May 16, 1942. Language teacher. Clwyd county cllr. Ed Univ Coll of N Wales, Bangor.

| VALE OF GLAMORGAN | | 0.7% change | | | Lab win |
|---|---|---|---|---|---|
| Electorate % Turnout | | 67,213 | 80.2% | **1997** | 67,152 | 81.3% | **1992** |
| **Smith, J** | **Lab** | **29,054** | **53.9%** | **+9.6%** | **24,207** | **44.3%** | **C** |
| +Sweeney, W | C | 18,522 | 34.4% | -10.0% | 24,188 | 44.3% | Lab |
| Campbell, Mrs S | LD | 4,945 | 9.2% | -0.1% | 5,042 | 9.2% | LD |
| Corp, Ms M | PC | 1,393 | 2.6% | +0.5% | 1,159 | 2.1% | PC |
| **C to Lab notional swing 9.8%** | | **53,914** | | **Lab maj 10,532** | **54,596** | | **C maj 19** |
| | | | | 19.5% | | | 0.0% |

**JOHN SMITH,** b March 17, 1951. Chief exec, Gwent Image Partnership, since 1992. Gained this seat for Lab at 1989 by-election, defeated 1992; contested it 1987. Member, select cttees on broadcasting, 1991-92; on Welsh affairs 1990-92. Vale of Glamorgan borough cllr (ex-leader, Lab group). Building worker 1966-68; RAF 1968-71; joiner 1971-76; mature student 1976-83; univ tutor and lecturer 1983-89. Ed Penarth GS; Gwent Coll of Higher Ed; Univ of Wales Coll, Cardiff.
**WALTER SWEENEY,** b April 23, 1949. Solicitor. Regained this seat 1992; contested Stretford 1983. Member, select cttees on Welsh affairs, 1992-97; on home affairs 1995-97; on Channel Tunnel rail link 1995-96; joint cttee on statutory instruments 1996-97. Sec, C backbench home affairs cttee, 1994-97; joint vice-chair, 1995-97, and sec 1994-95, C legal cttee; vice-chair, all-party penal affairs parly group, 1993-97. Rugby borough cllr 1974-77; Bedfordshire county cllr 1981-89. Ed Lawrence Sheriff School, Rugby; Univ of Aix-Marseilles; Hull Univ; Darwin Coll, Cambridge.
**SUZANNE CAMPBELL,** b March 27, 1945. Financial adviser. Member, League Against Cruel Sports; Greenpeace; Amnesty. Ed Pembroke GS; Haverford West Tech Coll.

| VALE OF YORK | | 108.9% change | | | C win |
|---|---|---|---|---|---|
| Electorate % Turnout | | 70,077 | 76.0% | **1997** | 65,009 | 80.9% | **1992** |
| **McIntosh, Miss A** | **C** | **23,815** | **44.7%** | **-15.9%** | **31,854** | **60.6%** | **C** |
| Carter, M | Lab | 14,094 | 26.5% | +15.4% | 14,626 | 27.8% | LD |
| Hall, A C | LD | 12,656 | 23.8% | -4.1% | 5,837 | 11.1% | Lab |
| Fairclough, C | Ref | 2,503 | 4.7% | | 247 | 0.5% | Other |
| Pelton, T | Soc Dem | 197 | 0.4% | | | | |
| **C to Lab notional swing 15.6%** | | **53,265** | | **C maj 9,721** | **52,564** | | **C maj 17,228** |
| | | | | 18.3% | | | 32.8% |

**ANNE McINTOSH,** b Sept 20, 1954. Contested Workington 1987. MEP for Essex North and Suffolk South since 1994, for Essex North East 1989-94. Member, European People's Party bureau, 1994- ; Euro Parliament transport and tourism cttee 1994- . Spokeswoman on Euro Parliament rules cttee 1989-95; co-chair, European Transport Safety Council. Political adviser with European Democratic (C) Group in Euro Parliament 1983-89. Admitted to Faculty of Advocates, 1982; practised European law in Community Law Office, Brussels, 1982-83. Ed Harrogate Coll; Edinburgh Univ; Aarhus Univ, Denmark.
**MATTHEW CARTER,** b March 22, 1972. University tutor. Member, Nat Policy Forum, 1995- . Worked for David Blunkett. Ed Sheffield and York Univs.
**CHARLES HALL,** b Dec 18, 1943. Schoolmaster. Ryedale district cllr 1979-96 (chair of council, 1995-96); City of York unitary cllr 1995- . Member NASUWT (school rep). Ed Carlton-le-Willows GS, Nottingham; St John's Coll, York; Leeds Univ; Hull Coll of Tech.

| VAUXHALL | | 12.6% change | | | | | Lab win |
|---|---|---|---|---|---|---|---|
| Electorate % Turnout | | 70,402 | 55.5% | **1997** | 67,961 | 63.7% | **1992** |
| +Hoey, Ms K | **Lab** | **24,920** | **63.8%** | **+7.7%** | **24,278** | **56.1%** | **Lab** |
| Kerr, K | LD | 6,260 | 16.0% | +1.6% | 11,517 | 26.6% | C |
| Bacon, R | C | 5,942 | 15.2% | -11.4% | 6,247 | 14.4% | LD |
| Driver, I | Soc Lab | 983 | 2.5% | | 893 | 2.1% | Grn |
| Collins, S | Green | 864 | 2.2% | | 174 | 0.4% | DOS |
| Headicar, R | SPGB | 97 | 0.2% | | 169 | 0.4% | Rev Comm |
| LD to Lab notional swing 3.1% | | **39,066** | | Lab maj **18,660** | **43,278** | | Lab maj **12,761** |
| | | | | 47.8% | | | 29.5% |

**KATE HOEY**, b June 21, 1946. MP for this seat since 1989 by-election; contested Dulwich 1987. Lab spokeswoman on Citizen's Charter and women 1992-93. Member, select cttees on broadcasting, 1991-97; social security 1992-97; sec, all-party child abduction parly group, 1991-97; Bosnia group; Croatia group. Member, exec cttee UK branch, CPA. Former N Ireland athlete, educational adviser to London first division football clubs 1985-89. Lecturer, Southwark Coll, 1972-76; senior lecturer, Kingsway

Coll, 1976-85. Ed Belfast Royal Acad; Ulster Coll of Physical Ed; City of London Coll.
**KEITH KERR,** b July 17, 1955. General manager with British Airways. Wokingham district cllr. Ed Lanfranc, Mitcham; Thames Valley Univ.
**RICHARD BACON,** b Sept 3, 1962. Dep director of Management Consultancies Assoc. Chair, Hammersmith C assoc, 1995- . Member, education and training cttee, British Council. Ed King's, Worcester; LSE; Goethe Institut, Berlin.

| WAKEFIELD | | 69.1% change | | | | | Lab win |
|---|---|---|---|---|---|---|---|
| Electorate % Turnout | | 73,210 | 69.0% | **1997** | 71,951 | 75.5% | **1992** |
| +Hinchliffe, D | **Lab** | **28,977** | **57.4%** | **+9.1%** | **26,207** | **48.2%** | **Lab** |
| Peacock, J | C | 14,373 | 28.5% | -12.0% | 21,983 | 40.5% | C |
| Dale, D | LD | 5,656 | 11.2% | -0.1% | 6,128 | 11.3% | LD |
| Shires, S | Ref | 1,480 | 2.9% | | | | |
| C to Lab notional swing 10.6% | | **50,486** | | Lab maj **14,604** | **54,318** | | Lab maj **4,224** |
| | | | | 28.9% | | | 7.8% |

**DAVID HINCHLIFFE**, b Oct 14, 1948. Elected 1987. Lab spokesman on social services and community care 1992-95; member, health select cttee 1991-92; joint vice-chair, PLP social security cttee, 1990-91; vice-chair, PLP health and personal social services cttee, 1990-92. Joint sec, all-party rugby league parly group, 1987-92. Social work tutor, Kirklees, 1980-87. Social worker, Leeds, 1968-79. Ed Cathedral C of E Sec Mod, Wakefield; Leeds Poly; Bradford Univ; Huddersfield Poly.

**JONATHAN PEACOCK,** b April 21, 1964. Barrister. Business adviser, Prince's Youth Business Trust. Election campaign manager 1983, 1987 and 1992. Member, Tibet Support Group; Friends of Settle-Carlisle Railway. Ed King's, Macclesfield; Nunthorpe GS, York; Corpus Christi Coll, Oxford; Council of Legal Education.
**DOUGLAS DALE,** b Nov 28, 1930. Retired NHS catering manager. Contested Pontefract & Castleford for L/All 1983. Member, Wakefield community health council; ex-member Nalgo. National Union of Seamen. Ed Thomas Danby Coll, Leeds; Leeds Tech Coll; Sheffield Univ; New College, Durham.

| WALLASEY | | | | | | | Lab hold |
|---|---|---|---|---|---|---|---|
| Electorate % Turnout | | 63,714 | 73.5% | **1997** | 65,676 | 82.5% | **1992** |
| *Eagle, Ms A | **Lab** | **30,264** | **64.6%** | **+15.6%** | **26,531** | **49.0%** | **Lab** |
| Wilcock, Mrs P | C | 11,190 | 23.9% | -18.0% | 22,722 | 41.9% | C |
| Reisdorf, P | LD | 3,899 | 8.3% | +0.6% | 4,177 | 7.7% | LD |
| Hayes, R | Ref | 1,490 | 3.2% | | 650 | 1.2% | Grn |
| | | | | | 105 | 0.2% | NLP |
| C to Lab swing 16.8% | | **46,843** | | Lab maj **19,074** | **54,185** | | Lab maj **3,809** |
| | | | | 40.7% | | | 7.0% |

**ANGELA EAGLE**, b Feb 17, 1961. Became Under Secretary for Environment and Transport, May 5, 1997. Won this seat for Lab 1992. Member, PAC 1995-96; select cttees on employment, 1992-96; members' interests 1992-95. Lab whip 1996-97. Joint sec, all-party film industry parly group; chair, PLP employment cttee; Tribune group; former joint vice-chair, PLP Treasury cttee. Unpaid dir, Tribune Publications. Parly liaison officer to Cohse (now Unison) 1987-92; employed by union as researcher 1984; nat press officer 1986. Chaired Nat Conference of Lab Women, 1991.

Ed Formby HS; St John's Coll, Oxford. Her twin sister Maria won Liverpool Garston for Lab at 1997 general election.
**PATRICIA WILCOCK,** b Nov 30, 1949. Fenestration specialist. Treas, NW area C women's cttee, 1994. Technical manager for Chelsea Artisans plc in UK and Middle East 1989-91; worked for Pilkington plc 1967-88. Member, Merseyside E and Wigan Euro council, 1994. Ed Notre Dame Convent GS; St Helens Coll of Tech.
**PETER REISDORF,** b June 26, 1962. Insurance broker (retraining in computing). Ed Calday Grange GS, West Kirby.

## WALSALL NORTH

| | | | | | | | | | |
|---|---|---|---|---|---|---|---|---|---|
| | | | | | | **Lab hold** | | | |
| Electorate % Turnout | | 67,587 | 64.1% | **1997** | 69,604 | 75.0% | **1992** |
| *Winnick, D | Lab | 24,517 | 56.6% | +9.9% | 24,387 | 46.7% | Lab |
| Bird, M | C | 11,929 | 27.5% | -11.8% | 20,563 | 39.4% | C |
| O'Brien, Ms T | LD | 4,050 | 9.4% | -3.3% | 6,629 | 12.7% | LD |
| Bennett, D | Ref | 1,430 | 3.3% | | 614 | 1.2% | NF |
| Pitt, M | Ind | 911 | 2.1% | | | | |
| Humphries, A | NF | 465 | 1.1% | -0.1% | | | |
| C to Lab swing 10.9% | | 43,302 | | Lab maj 12,588 | 52,193 | | Lab maj 3,824 |
| | | | | 29.1% | | | 7.3% |

**DAVID WINNICK,** b June 26, 1933. Elected for this seat 1979; MP for Croydon S 1966-70; contested Harwich 1964; Croydon Central Oct 1974; Walsall 1976 by-election. Member, select cttees on procedure, 1989-92; Treasury and Civil Service 1987-89; home affairs 1983-87; environment 1979-83; race relations and immigration 1969-70. Joint vice-chair, PLP foreign affairs cttee, 1985-87 and 1991-97; vice-chair, British-Irish inter-parly body, 1993-97. Chair, Tribune Group, 1984-85; UK Immigrants advisory

service 1984-90. Ed state sec schools; LSE.

**MICHAEL BIRD,** b Jan 22, 1949. Credit manager, consultant with firm of insolvency practitioners. Dir, financial consultancy. Walsall cllr 1980- (council leader 1992-95; then principal opposition leader). Fellow, Inst of Credit Management. Ed Handsworth GS, Birmingham.

**TRACEY O'BRIEN,** b June 11, 1963. Advice worker/trainer. Member, GMB. Ed St Ambrose Barlow RC Sec Mod; Wolverhampton Univ.

## WALSALL SOUTH

| | | | | | | | | | |
|---|---|---|---|---|---|---|---|---|---|
| | | | | | | **Lab hold** | | | |
| Electorate % Turnout | | 64,221 | 67.3% | **1997** | 65,642 | 76.3% | **1992** |
| *George, B | Lab | 25,024 | 57.9% | +9.7% | 24,133 | 48.2% | Lab |
| Leek, L | C | 13,712 | 31.7% | -10.1% | 20,955 | 41.9% | C |
| Harris, H | LD | 2,698 | 6.2% | -2.0% | 4,132 | 8.3% | LD |
| Dent, Dr T | Ref | 1,662 | 3.8% | | 673 | 1.3% | Grn |
| Meads, Mrs L | NLP | 144 | 0.3% | -0.0% | 167 | 0.3% | NLP |
| C to Lab swing 9.9% | | 43,240 | | Lab maj 11,312 | 50,060 | | Lab maj 3,178 |
| | | | | 26.2% | | | 6.3% |

**BRUCE GEORGE,** b June 1, 1942. Elected Feb 1974, contested Southport 1970. Member, select cttee on defence since 1979. Joint sec, all-party social science and policy parly group; chair, British-Azerbaijan group. Member, N Atlantic Assembly, 1982- , rapporteur general of political cttee. Editor, *Jane's Nato Handbook.* Visiting lecturer Essex Univ 1985-86, senior lecturer in politics Birmingham Poly 1970-74. Patron, Nat Assoc of Widows; vice-pres, Psoriasis Assoc; co-founder, sec and captain House of Commons Football Club. Pres, Walsall and District

Gilbert and Sullivan Soc. Ed Mountain Ash GS; Univ Coll of Wales, Swansea; Warwick Univ.

**LESLIE LEEK,** b Jan 8, 1946. Company director; previously chief inspector with West Midlands Police. Awarded police exemplary service medal and RUC medal. Ed Boldmere HS, Sutton Coldfield; Handsworth Tech School, Birmingham.

**HARRY HARRIS,** b May 20, 1948. Teacher. Member, British Inst of Management. Ed OU; Keele Univ. Interests include writing poetry.

## WALTHAMSTOW — 33.3% change

| | | | | | | | | | |
|---|---|---|---|---|---|---|---|---|---|
| | | | | | | **Lab win** | | | |
| Electorate % Turnout | | 63,818 | 62.8% | **1997** | 66,412 | 71.4% | **1992** |
| +Gerrard, N | Lab | 25,287 | 63.1% | +18.8% | 21,001 | 44.3% | Lab |
| Andrew, Mrs J | C | 8,138 | 20.3% | -16.9% | 17,650 | 37.2% | C |
| Jackson, Dr J | LD | 5,491 | 13.7% | -2.1% | 7,489 | 15.8% | LD |
| Hargreaves, Rev G | Ref | 1,139 | 2.8% | | 822 | 1.7% | Grn |
| | | | | | 333 | 0.7% | Lib |
| | | | | | 130 | 0.3% | NLP |
| C to Lab notional swing 17.9% | | 40,055 | | Lab maj 17,149 | 47,425 | | Lab maj 3,351 |
| | | | | 42.8% | | | 7.1% |

**NEIL GERRARD,** b July 3, 1942. Elected for this seat 1992, contested Chingford 1979. Member, select cttees on environment, 1995-97; deregulation 1995-97. Sec, PLP environment cttee, 1995-97; joint vice-chair, all-party Aids parly group; home safety group; joint treas, greyhound group. Board member, Theatre Royal Stratford E; political advisory cttee, Inst of Data Processing Management (both unpaid). Waltham Forest cllr 1973-90 (leader, Lab group, 1983-90; council leader 1986-90). Hackney Coll lecturer in computing 1968-92. Member, NATFHE. Ed Manchester Grammar; Wadham Coll, Oxford; Chelsea Coll, London.

**JILL ANDREW,** b March 8, 1956. Solicitor running own practice in City. Bromley cllr. First woman board director, London Chamber of Commerce; dir, London S Business Link. Member, Bromley Enterprise Trust board; Bromley Business Partnership. Ed Chislehurst and Sidcup Girls' GS; Bromley Coll of Tech; Exeter Univ; LSE; Coll of Law, Guildford.

**JANE JACKSON,** b Feb 15, 1933. Retired public health physician. Contested Luton N 1992. Ed Wroxall Abbey, Warwicks; Trinity Coll, Dublin; Linacre Coll, Oxford; London School of Hygiene and Tropical Medicine.

| WANSBECK | | | | | Lab hold | |
|---|---|---|---|---|---|---|
| Electorate % Turnout | | 62,998 | 71.7% | **1997** | 63,457 | 79.3% | **1992** |
| **Murphy, D** | **Lab** | **29,569** | **65.5%** | **+5.7%** | 30,046 | 59.7% | Lab |
| Thompson, J A | LD | 7,202 | 15.9% | +0.7% | 11,872 | 23.6% | C |
| Green, P | C | 6,299 | 13.9% | -9.6% | 7,691 | 15.3% | LD |
| Gompertz, P | Ref | 1,146 | 2.5% | | 710 | 1.4% | Grn |
| Best, Dr N | Green | 956 | 2.1% | | | | |
| **LD to Lab swing 2.5%** | | **45,172** | **Lab maj 22,367** | | 50,319 | Lab maj 18,174 | |
| | | | 49.5% | | | 36.1% | |

**DENIS MURPHY,** b Nov 2, 1948. Underground electrician, Ellington colliery, Northumberland; director Wansbeck Energy Co. Ex-cllr and union official. Ed St Cuthbert's GS; Northumberland Coll.
**ALAN THOMPSON,** b May 8, 1936. Chartered engineer. ContestedNewcastle upon Tyne E 1992, this seat 1983, Morpeth 1979 and Dunbartonshire E Oct 1974. Wansbeck district cllr (opposition leader). Ed Dicksons Coll.
**PAUL GREEN,** b Feb 24, 1965. Assistant to Sir Paul Beresford, MP. Wandsworth cllr 1986- (chief whip 1996- ). Ed Nene Coll, Northampton; Kent Univ.

| WANSDYKE | | 58.6% change | | | | Lab win | |
|---|---|---|---|---|---|---|---|
| Electorate % Turnout | | 69,032 | 79.3% | **1997** | 68,742 | 85.8% | **1992** |
| **Norris, D** | **Lab** | **24,117** | **44.1%** | **+16.8%** | 27,852 | 47.2% | C |
| Prisk, M | C | 19,318 | 35.3% | -11.9% | 16,082 | 27.3% | Lab |
| Manning, J | LD | 9,205 | 16.8% | -6.8% | 13,921 | 23.6% | LD |
| Clinton, K | Ref | 1,327 | 2.4% | | 1,150 | 1.9% | Grn |
| Hunt, T | UK Ind | 438 | 0.8% | | | | |
| House, P | Loony | 225 | 0.4% | | | | |
| Lincoln, Ms S | NLP | 92 | 0.2% | | | | |
| **C to Lab notional swing 14.4%** | | **54,722** | **Lab maj 4,799** | | 59,005 | C maj 11,770 | |
| | | | 8.8% | | | 19.9% | |

**DAN NORRIS,** b Jan 28, 1960. Child protection social worker and lecturer. Contested this seat 1992, Northavon 1987. Bristol city cllr 1989- . Member, Nupe. Ed Avon Comp; Sussex Univ (Fellow).
**MARK PRISK,** b June 12, 1962. Self-employed business consultant, chartered surveyor. Contested Newham NW 1992. Campaign vice-chair, Westminster North C assoc 1986-91; chair, Cornwall YCs, 1978-80. Sec, Bow Group environment cttee 1984-86; member British Urban Regeneration Assoc. Member, nat cttee Peace through Nato, 1983-87. Director of surveyors, architects and engineers practice 1987-91, previously with Knight Frank & Rutley. Ed Truro School; Reading Univ.
**JEFF MANNING,** b May 23, 1944. Self-employed business consultant. Bath city cllr 1985-88, 1990-96 (ex-chair of council and Mayor 1995-96); Bristol and NE Somerset unitary authority cllr. Dir, Bath Festival Trust; Bath Archaeological Trust. Member, Electoral Reform Soc; Transport 2000. Ed Acton GS; Bristol Aeroplane Tech Coll.

| WANTAGE | | | | | C hold | |
|---|---|---|---|---|---|---|
| Electorate % Turnout | | 71,657 | 78.2% | **1997** | 68,328 | 82.7% | **1992** |
| *****Jackson, R** | **C** | **22,311** | **39.8%** | **-14.3%** | 30,575 | 54.1% | C |
| Wilson, Ms C | Lab | 16,272 | 29.0% | +9.6% | 14,102 | 25.0% | LD |
| Riley, Ms J G A | LD | 14,822 | 26.4% | +1.5% | 10,955 | 19.4% | Lab |
| Rising, S | Ref | 1,549 | 2.8% | | 867 | 1.5% | Grn |
| Kennet, Ms M | Green | 640 | 1.1% | | | | |
| Tolstoy-Miloslausky, N | UK Ind | 465 | 0.8% | | | | |
| **C to Lab swing 12.0%** | | **56,059** | **C maj 6,039** | | 56,499 | C maj 16,473 | |
| | | | 10.8% | | | 29.2% | |

**ROBERT JACKSON,** b Sept 24, 1946. Elected 1983, contested Manchester Central 1974. Civil Service Min 1992-93; Under Sec for Employment 1990-92 and for Education and Science 1987-90. Member, Commons art advisory cttee. Euro MP for Upper Thames 1979-84. Oxford city cllr 1969-71. Chair, Swaythling Assured Homes, Exeter Residences, Acton Assured Homes, Leicester Student Accommodation, Nottingham Trent Residences, Martin Engineering Systems. Trustee, Elderly Accommodation Council. Member, British Konigswinter steering cttee. Political adviser to Lord Soames, Governor of Rhodesia 1980 (served in his private office when he was Euro Commission vice-pres 1974-76). Ed Falcon Coll, Bulawayo; St Edmund Hall (pres of Union 1967) and All Souls Coll, Oxford (Fellow 1968-86).
**CELIA WILSON,** b March 22, 1947. NHS information manager, formerly Atomic Energy Authority physicist. Member, Greenpeace; Scientists for Labour; Computing for Labour. Ed London and Reading Univs.
**JENNY RILEY,** b April 7, 1946. Partner in exec recruitment consultancy. Contested Newcastle upon Tyne E 1987 and Wood Green 1979, both as C candidate. Greater London cllr 1977-81. Chair of Purley LDs and vice-chair LD London Region. Ed St Mary's Hall, Brighton; Girton Coll, Cambridge.

| WARLEY | | 18.6% change | | | | | | Lab win |
|---|---|---|---|---|---|---|---|---|
| Electorate % Turnout | | 59,758 | 65.1% | **1997** | 62,589 | 71.5% | | **1992** |
| +Spellar, J F | Lab | 24,813 | 63.8% | +10.7% | 23,743 | 53.1% | | Lab |
| Pincher, C | C | 9,362 | 24.1% | -10.2% | 15,334 | 34.3% | | C |
| Pursehouse, J | LD | 3,777 | 9.7% | -1.7% | 5,112 | 11.4% | | LD |
| Gamre, K | Ref | 941 | 2.4% | | 561 | 1.3% | | Other |
| C to Lab notional swing 10.5% | | 38,893 | | Lab maj 15,451 | 44,750 | | Lab maj 8,409 | |
| | | | | 39.7% | | | 18.8% | |

**JOHN SPELLAR,** b Aug 5, 1947. Became Under Secretary for Defence, May 5, 1997. MP for Warley W 1992-97, for Birmingham Northfield 1982-83; contested Birmingham Northfield 1987 and Bromley 1970. Lab spokesman on defence 1995-97. Sec, all-party construction group; joint treas, British-Finland group. Bromley cllr 1970-74. Political officer EETPU. Ed Dulwich Coll; St Edmund Hall, Oxford.

**CHRISTOPHER PINCHER,** b Sept 24, 1969. Management consultant. Dep nat chair, C Students, 1990-91; chair, Greater London Area C assoc, 1989-91. Ed Ounsdale Comp, Staffs; LSE.
**JEREMY PURSEHOUSE,** b May 30, 1957. PR/journalist. Tandridge district cllr. Member, Brit Assoc of Journalists. Dir, Enterprise Public Relations Ltd, Edge to Edge Publishing Ltd. Ed Ounsdale Comp, Staffs; Wolverhampton Poly; Middlesex Poly.

| WARRINGTON NORTH | | 9.5% change | | | | | | Lab win |
|---|---|---|---|---|---|---|---|---|
| Electorate % Turnout | | 72,694 | 70.5% | **1997** | 72,455 | 76.9% | | **1992** |
| Jones, Ms H | Lab | 31,827 | 62.1% | +8.9% | 29,626 | 53.2% | | Lab |
| Lacey, Ms R | C | 12,300 | 24.0% | -10.9% | 19,420 | 34.9% | | C |
| Greenhalgh, I | LD | 5,308 | 10.4% | -1.0% | 6,307 | 11.3% | | LD |
| Smith, Dr A | Ref | 1,816 | 3.5% | | 366 | 0.7% | | NLP |
| C to Lab notional swing 9.9% | | 51,251 | | Lab maj 19,527 | 55,719 | | Lab maj 10,206 | |
| | | | | 38.1% | | | 18.3% | |

**HELEN JONES,** b Dec 24, 1954. Solicitor. Contested Shropshire N 1983; Ellesmere Port and Neston 1987; Lancashire Central in 1984 Euro elections. Ex-Chester city cllr. Ed Chester Coll; University Coll, London; Liverpool Univ.
**RAY LACEY,** b Feb 20, 1945. Partner in family motor factors business. Crewe and Nantwich borough cllr 1993- (C group dep

leader since 1995). Member, CAB management board. Ed Wigton Sec Mod; Guildhall School of Music and Drama.
**IAN GREENHALGH,** b July 9, 1946. Professional fundraiser. Contested this seat 1992, and Heywood and Middleton for L/All 1987. Founder member of SDP. Member, Amnesty; MSF. Ed Smithills Secondary.

| WARRINGTON SOUTH | | 30.0% change | | | | | | Lab win |
|---|---|---|---|---|---|---|---|---|
| Electorate % Turnout | | 72,262 | 76.2% | **1997** | 69,324 | 81.1% | | **1992** |
| Southworth, Ms H | Lab | 28,721 | 52.1% | +11.4% | 25,698 | 45.7% | | C |
| Grayling, C | C | 17,914 | 32.5% | -13.2% | 22,945 | 40.8% | | Lab |
| Walker, P | LD | 7,199 | 13.1% | +0.1% | 7,316 | 13.0% | | LD |
| Kelly, G | Ref | 1,082 | 2.0% | | 290 | 0.5% | | NLP |
| Ross, S | NLP | 166 | 0.3% | -0.2% | | | | |
| C to Lab notional swing 12.3% | | 55,082 | | Lab maj 10,807 | 56,249 | | C maj 2,753 | |
| | | | | 19.6% | | | 4.9% | |

**HELEN SOUTHWORTH,** b Nov 13, 1956. Contested Wirral S 1992. St Helens borough cllr 1994- . Dir, Age Concern St Helens; governor, Age Concern England. Dir, Grosvenor Housing Assoc; non-exec dir, St Helens and Knowsley HA. Member, MSF; Co-op Party; Fabian Soc. Ed Larkhill Convent School; Lancaster Univ.
**CHRISTOPHER GRAYLING,** b April 1, 1962. TV producer, company exec and author. Member, Greater London area C political centre

gen purposes cttee; Bow Group council 1991-93. Ed RGS, High Wycombe; Sidney Sussex Coll, Cambridge.
**PETER WALKER,** b Oct 7, 1936. Retired marketing operations manager. Contested this seat 1992. Cheshire county cllr 1989- (dep group leader). Member, Salford Univ council. Ed Maidenhead County Boys GS; John Dalton School.

| WARWICK & LEAMINGTON | | 7.5% change | | | | | Lab win |
|---|---|---|---|---|---|---|---|
| Electorate % Turnout | | 79,374 | 75.7% | **1997** | 77,853 | 80.4% | **1992** |
| **Plaskitt, J** | Lab | **26,747** | **44.5%** | **+13.3%** | **31,028** | **49.5%** | **C** |
| +Smith, Sir Dudley | C | 23,349 | 38.9% | -10.7% | 19,564 | 31.2% | Lab |
| Hicks, N | LD | 7,133 | 11.9% | -5.3% | 10,729 | 17.1% | LD |
| Davis, Mrs V | Ref | 1,484 | 2.5% | | 865 | 1.4% | Grn |
| Baptie, P | Green | 764 | 1.3% | | 270 | 0.4% | Ind |
| Warwick, G | UK Ind | 306 | 0.5% | | 168 | 0.3% | NLP |
| Gibbs, M | EDP | 183 | 0.3% | | | | |
| McCarthy, R | NLP | 125 | 0.2% | -0.1% | | | |
| **C to Lab notional swing 12.0%** | | **60,091** | | Lab maj 3,398 | **62,624** | | C maj 11,464 |
| | | | | 5.7% | | | 18.3% |

**JAMES PLASKITT,** b June 23, 1954. Business consultant. Contested Witney 1992. Oxfordshire county cllr 1985- (leader Lab group 1990-96). Member, MSF; Co-op Party; Charter 88. Ed Pilgrim School, Bedford; University Coll, Oxford.
**SIR DUDLEY SMITH**, b Nov 14, 1926. Elected at 1968 by-election; MP for Brentford and Chiswick 1959-66. Under Sec for Army 1974; for Employment 1970-74; C spokesman on employment and productivity 1969-70; C whip 1964-66. Joint vice-chair, all-party British-Chilean parly group. Pres of WEU assembly 1993-97,

delegate since 1979; sec gen, Euro democratic group 1983-97; chair, WEU defence cttee, 1989-93. Member, Council of Europe, 1979-97. Middlesex county cllr 1958-63. Partner in Dudley Smith Management Consultancy. Journalist and senior exec with nat and regional newspapers 1943-66. Divisional dir, Beecham Group, 1966-70. Freeman, City of London; Liveryman, Horners' Co. Ed Chichester HS.
**NIGEL HICKS,** b June 11, 1955. Chartered quantity surveyor. Ed Falmouth GS; Trent Poly.

| WARWICKSHIRE NORTH | | 0.1% change | | | | | Lab win |
|---|---|---|---|---|---|---|---|
| Electorate % Turnout | | 72,602 | 74.7% | **1997** | 72,314 | 82.8% | **1992** |
| **+O'Brien, M** | Lab | **31,669** | **58.4%** | **+12.3%** | **27,577** | **46.1%** | **Lab** |
| Hammond, S | C | 16,902 | 31.2% | -12.5% | 26,124 | 43.6% | C |
| Powell, W | LD | 4,040 | 7.4% | -2.8% | 6,161 | 10.3% | LD |
| Mole, R | Ref | 917 | 1.7% | | | | |
| Cooke, C | UK Ind | 533 | 1.0% | | | | |
| Moorecroft, I | Bert | 178 | 0.3% | | | | |
| **C to Lab notional swing 12.4%** | | **54,239** | | Lab maj 14,767 | **59,862** | | Lab maj 1,453 |
| | | | | 27.2% | | | 2.4% |

**MIKE O'BRIEN,** b June 19, 1954. Became Home Office Under Secretary responsible for immigration, May 5, 1997. Solicitor. Elected for this seat 1992, contested it 1987. Member, Treasury select cttee, 1993-95; joint sec, all-party police parly group. Lab spokesman on Treasury matters 1995-97. Chair, PLP home affairs cttee. Ex-chair, Worcester CLP. Lecturer in law, Colchester Inst, 1981-87. Member, GMB/Apex. Ed Worcester Tech Coll; North Staffs Poly.

**STEPHEN HAMMOND,** b Feb 4, 1962. Asst director at Kleinwort Benson Securities. Chair, Stevenage and rural districts C assoc, 1991- . Ed King Edward VI GS, Southampton; Queen Mary Coll, London.
**BILL POWELL,** b Dec 14, 1938. Chartered engineer. Member, Assoc of LD Engineers and Scientists; CAB; Electoral Reform Soc. Ed Diocesan Coll, Cape Town; Univ of Cape Town; Imperial Coll, London.

| WATFORD | 24.7% change | | | | | | Lab win |
|---|---|---|---|---|---|---|---|
| Electorate % Turnout | | 74,015 | 74.6% | **1997** | 72,192 | 81.1% | **1992** |
| **Ward, Ms C** | Lab | **25,019** | **45.3%** | **+11.3%** | **28,159** | **48.1%** | **C** |
| Gordon, R | C | 19,227 | 34.8% | -13.3% | 19,896 | 34.0% | Lab |
| Canning, A | LD | 9,272 | 16.8% | +0.0% | 9,807 | 16.8% | LD |
| Roe, Dr P | Ref | 1,484 | 2.7% | | 514 | 0.9% | Grn |
| Davis, L | NLP | 234 | 0.4% | +0.2% | 159 | 0.3% | NLP |
| **C to Lab notional swing 12.3%** | | **55,236** | | Lab maj 5,792 | **58,535** | | C maj 8,263 |
| | | | | 10.5% | | | 14.1% |

**CLAIRE WARD,** b May 9, 1972. Trainee solicitor. Elstree and Boreham Wood town cllr 1994- (Mayor 1996-97). Member London Regional Co-operative Retail Soc cttee, 1993- ; Fabian Soc; Soc of Labour Lawyers; TGWU; Co-op Party. Ed Loretto Coll, St Albans; Hertfordshire and Brunel Univs; Coll of Law, London.
**ROBERT GORDON,** b March 29, 1952. Solicitor. Contested Torfaen 1987. Watford borough cllr 1982-90, Hertfordshire county cllr 1989- . Ed Watford GS.

**ANDREW CANNING,** b Dec 10, 1962. Investment manager. Southwark cllr 1986-90. Chair, Bermondsey LDs. Dir, BZW Investment Management. Member, Friends of the Earth; Greenpeace; Amnesty. Ed Sir Roger Manwood's School, Sandwich; LSE.

| WAVENEY | | 12.3% change | | | | | | Lab win |
|---|---|---|---|---|---|---|---|---|
| Electorate % Turnout | | 75,266 | 75.2% | **1997** | 74,320 | 81.2% | **1992** | |
| **Blizzard, R** | **Lab** | **31,846** | **56.3%** | **+16.5%** | **28,352** | **47.0%** | **C** | |
| +Porter, D | C | 19,393 | 34.3% | -12.7% | 23,976 | 39.7% | Lab | |
| Thomas, C | LD | 5,054 | 8.9% | -3.9% | 7,728 | 12.8% | LD | |
| Clark, N | Ind | 318 | 0.6% | | 265 | 0.4% | NLP | |
| **C to Lab notional swing 14.6%** | | **56,611** | | Lab maj 12,453 | **60,321** | | C maj 4,376 | |
| | | | | 22.0% | | | 7.3% | |

**ROBERT BLIZZARD**, b May 31, 1950. Teacher. Waveney district cllr 1987- (council leader since 1991). Head of English at local high school. Set up Lowestoft 2000 promotional partnership with town businesses to increase investment and tourism. Member, NUT. Ed Culford School, Bury St Edmunds; Birmingham Univ.

**DAVID PORTER,** b April 16, 1948. Ex-teacher. Elected 1987. Member, select cttees on education and employment 1996-97; on social security 1991-92; British-Irish inter-parly body. Sec, C backbench fisheries sub-cttee, 1987-97. Waveney district cllr

1974-87. Taught in East End of London 1970-72; dir and co-founder, Vivid Children's Theatre, 1972-78; head of drama, Benjamin Britten HS Lowestoft 1978-81. C Party agent in Eltham 1982-88, Norwich N 1983-84, Waveney 1985-87. Ed Lowestoft GS; New Coll of Speech and Drama, London.

**CHRISTOPHER THOMAS,** b April 20, 1948. Teacher. Contested Norwich S in 1992. Member, NASUWT. Ed Wolverhampton Poly; East Anglia Univ.

| WEALDEN | | 0.2% change | | | | | | C win |
|---|---|---|---|---|---|---|---|---|
| Electorate % Turnout | | 79,519 | 74.3% | **1997** | 74,245 | 81.3% | **1992** | |
| **+Johnson Smith, Sir Geoffrey C** | | **29,417** | **49.8%** | **-12.0%** | **37,256** | **61.7%** | **C** | |
| Skinner, M D | LD | 15,213 | 25.7% | -1.3% | 16,328 | 27.1% | LD | |
| Levine, N | Lab | 10,185 | 17.2% | +8.0% | 5,578 | 9.2% | Lab | |
| Taplin, B | Ref | 3,527 | 6.0% | | 1,002 | 1.7% | Grn | |
| English, Mrs M | UK Ind | 569 | 1.0% | | 182 | 0.3% | NLP | |
| Cragg, P | NLP | 188 | 0.3% | +0.0% | | | | |
| **C to LD notional swing 5.3%** | | **59,099** | | C maj 14,204 | **60,346** | | C maj 20,928 | |
| | | | | 24.0% | | | 34.7% | |

**SIR GEOFFREY JOHNSON SMITH**, b April 16, 1924. Won this seat 1983; MP for E Grinstead 1965-83 and for Holborn & St Pancras S 1959-64. Elected joint vice-chair, 1922 Cttee, May 21, 1997. Chair, select cttee on members' interests, 1980-95; member, select cttee on standards and privileges 1995-96. Parly Sec, Civil Service Dept, 1972-74; Army Under Sec 1971-72. Vice-chair, C Party, 1965-71; joint vice-chair, 1922 Cttee 1988- , member of exec 1979- . Chair, 1988-93. and joint vice-chair 1980-88, C backbench defence cttee. Joint treas, all-party British-American parly group; member, N Atlantic Assembly 1980- . London county cllr 1955-58. Non-exec

director, Taylor Alden;Glengate Holdings; and Monk Dunstone Associates (Benelux) SA. Ed Charterhouse; Lincoln Coll, Oxford.

**MICHAEL SKINNER,** b April 19, 1954. Banking systems officer. Contested this seat 1992. East Sussex county cllr; Wealden district cllr 1987-95 (ex-LD group leader). Member, Amnesty; Greenpeace, Wealden Line Campaign. Ed Bryanston School; Jesus Coll, Cambridge; Cambridge Dept of Ed; London Inst of Ed.

**NICHOLAS LEVINE,** b Dec 31, 1938. College principal. Crowborough town cllr 1995- . Member, Co-op Party. Ed Bryanston School; Jesus Coll, Cambridge; Cambridge Dept of Ed; London Inst of Ed.

| WEAVER VALE | | 121.6% change | | | | | | Lab win |
|---|---|---|---|---|---|---|---|---|
| Electorate % Turnout | | 66,011 | 73.2% | **1997** | 65,447 | 79.2% | **1992** | |
| **+Hall, M T** | **Lab** | **27,244** | **56.4%** | **+7.7%** | **25,265** | **48.8%** | **Lab** | |
| Byrne, J | C | 13,796 | 28.6% | -7.2% | 18,515 | 35.7% | C | |
| Griffiths, N | LD | 5,949 | 12.3% | -2.2% | 7,506 | 14.5% | LD | |
| Cockfield, R | Ref | 1,312 | 2.7% | | 537 | 1.0% | Other | |
| **C to Lab notional swing 7.4%** | | **48,301** | | Lab maj 13,448 | **51,823** | | Lab maj 6,750 | |
| | | | | 27.8% | | | 13.0% | |

**MIKE HALL,** b Sept 20, 1952. MP for Warrington S 1992-97. Member, PAC, 1992-97 (chair 1995-97). Ex-joint vice-chair, PLP education cttee; chair, Warrington N Lab Party 1983-85. Warrington cllr 1979-93 (leader 1985-92). Former non-paid dir, Warrington Borough Transport Ltd and Warrington Coachlines Ltd. Member, NUT. Ed St Damian's Sec Mod, Ashton-under-Lyne; Ashton-under-Lyne CFE; Stretford Tech Coll; Padgate Coll of HE; N Cheshire Coll; Manchester Univ.

**JAMES BYRNE,** b Jan 26, 1961. Barrister at Liverpool chambers. Frodsham town cllr 1995-. Ed Stonyhurst Coll; Liverpool Univ; Inns of Court School of Law.

**NIGEL GRIFFITHS,** b April 24, 1959. Area sales manager. Frodsham town cllr (chair 1990-91); Vale Royal borough cllr. Ed Helsby County GS.

| WELLINGBOROUGH | | | | | | | Lab gain |
|---|---|---|---|---|---|---|---|
| Electorate % Turnout | | 74,955 | 75.1% | **1997** | 73,875 | 81.9% | **1992** |
| Stinchcombe, P | Lab | **24,854** | **44.2%** | +10.3% | **32,302** | **53.4%** | C |
| *Fry, Sir Peter | C | 24,667 | 43.8% | -9.6% | 20,486 | 33.9% | Lab |
| Smith, P | LD | 5,279 | 9.4% | -3.4% | 7,714 | 12.7% | LD |
| Ellwood, A | UK Ind | 1,192 | 2.1% | | | | |
| Lowrys, Ms A | NLP | 297 | 0.5% | | | | |
| C to Lab swing 9.9% | | 56,289 | | Lab maj 187 | 60,502 | | C maj 11,816 |
| | | | | 0.3% | | | 19.5% |

**PAUL STINCHCOMBE,** b April 25, 1962. Barrister. Camden cllr 1990-94 (chair, Lab group). Member, MSF; Friends of the Earth; Christian Socialist Movement. Ed RGS, High Wycombe; Trinity Coll, Cambridge; Harvard Law School; Inns of Court School of Law.
**SIR PETER FRY,** b May 26, 1931. Won seat at 1969 by-election; contested Nottingham N 1964, Willesden E 1966. Former C spokesman on transport; member, transport select cttee, 1979-92;

unopposed Bills panel 1992-97. Joint vice-chair, C backbench aviation cttee, 1994-97. Ex-member, delegation to Council of Europe and WEU. Bucks county cllr 1961-66. Consultant to Parly Monitoring Services Ltd; Bingo Assoc of GB. Ed RGS, High Wycombe; Worcester Coll, Oxford.
**PETER SMITH,** b July 14, 1943. Supply teacher. Blaby district cllr. Member, Professional Assoc of Teachers. Ed Maidenhead County Boys GS; OU.

| WELLS | | | | | | | C hold |
|---|---|---|---|---|---|---|---|
| Electorate % Turnout | | 72,178 | 78.1% | **1997** | 69,833 | 82.7% | **1992** |
| *Heathcoat-Amory, D | C | **22,208** | **39.4%** | -10.2% | **28,620** | **49.6%** | C |
| Gold, Dr P J | LD | 21,680 | 38.5% | +0.4% | 21,971 | 38.0% | LD |
| Eavis, M | Lab | 10,204 | 18.1% | +7.5% | 6,126 | 10.6% | Lab |
| Phelps, Mrs P | Ref | 2,196 | 3.9% | | 1,042 | 1.8% | Grn |
| Royse, Ms L | NLP | 92 | 0.2% | | | | |
| C to LD swing 5.3% | | 56,380 | | C maj 528 | 57,759 | | C maj 6,649 |
| | | | | 0.9% | | | 11.5% |

**DAVID HEATHCOAT-AMORY,** b March 21, 1949. Chartered accountant. Elected 1983. Paymaster General 1994-96; Foreign Office Min of State 1993-94; dep gvt chief whip 1992-93; Energy Under Sec 1990-92; Environment Under Sec 1989-92; gvt whip 1989; asst gvt whip, 1988-89. Privy Counsellor 1995. PPS to Douglas Hurd when Home Sec, 1987-88, and to Financial Sec to Treasury 1985-87. Dir, Lowman Manufacturing Co; LDT Ltd, property management. Asst finance dir, British Technology Group, 1980-83. Ed Eton; Oxford Univ.

**PETER GOLD,** b June 20, 1944. Lecturer at West of England Univ, Bristol. Contested Sheffield Hallam 1992 and 1987. Chaired LD working group on higher ed policy. Former vice-chair, LD parly candidates' assoc. Treas, nat council for modern languages. Dir, Advanced Training Associates. Member, Amnesty; Friends of the Earth; Child Poverty Action Group; Assoc of Polytechnic and Coll Teachers. Ed Harrow County Boys' GS; Christ Church, Oxford.
**MICHAEL EAVIS,** b Oct 17, 1935. Farmer; chair, Somerset milk producers' group. Organiser of Glastonbury rock festival. Ed Wells Cathedral School; Thames Nautical Training Coll.

| WELWYN HATFIELD | | 6.5% change | | | | | Lab win |
|---|---|---|---|---|---|---|---|
| Electorate % Turnout | | 67,395 | 78.6% | **1997** | 68,502 | 83.3% | **1992** |
| Johnson, Ms M | Lab | **24,936** | **47.1%** | +11.1% | **27,139** | **47.5%** | C |
| +Evans, D | C | 19,341 | 36.5% | -11.0% | 20,556 | 36.0% | Lab |
| Schwartz, R | LD | 7,161 | 13.5% | -2.5% | 9,147 | 16.0% | LD |
| Cox, E | RA | 1,263 | 2.4% | | 247 | 0.4% | NLP |
| Harold, Ms H | ProLife | 267 | 0.5% | | | | |
| C to Lab notional swing 11.0% | | 52,968 | | Lab maj 5,595 | 57,089 | | C maj 6,583 |
| | | | | 10.6% | | | 11.5% |

**MELANIE JOHNSON,** b Feb 5, 1955. Schools inspector. Contested Cambridgeshire in 1994 Euro elections. Cambridge city cllr 1981- . JP. Former senior manager, Family Health Services Authority. Member, Unison; Greenpeace; CND. Ed Clifton HS, Bristol; University Coll, London; King's Coll, Cambridge.
**DAVID EVANS,** b April 23, 1935. Elected 1987. Member, deregulation select cttee 1995-97. PPS to John Redwood 1991-93; to Trade and Industry Min 1990-91. St Albans city cllr 1980-84. Chair, Luton Town Football & Athletic Co 1984-89, dir 1976-90;

chair, Broadreach Group 1990- , and dir of number of other companies. Master, Guild of Master Cleaners, 1981-82; Freeman of City of London; member, Worshipful Co of Horners. Chair, Lord's Taverners 1982-84; captained Club Cricket Conference 1968-74, and tour to Australia 1971; manager of 1975 tour. Ed Raglan Rd School; Tottenham Tech Coll.
**RODNEY SCHWARTZ,** b Oct 18, 1957. Investment banker. Member of LD business forum. Ed Benjamin Cardozo HS, New York; Rochester Univ, US.

261

| WENTWORTH | | | | | **Lab hold** | | |
|---|---|---|---|---|---|---|---|
| Electorate % Turnout | | 63,951 | 65.3% | **1997** | 64,914 | 74.1% | **1992** |
| **Healey, J** | **Lab** | **30,225** | **72.3%** | **+3.8%** | 32,989 | 68.6% | Lab |
| Hamer, K | C | 6,266 | 15.0% | -6.8% | 10,490 | 21.8% | C |
| Charters, J | LD | 3,867 | 9.3% | -0.4% | 4,629 | 9.6% | LD |
| Battley, A | Ref | 1,423 | 3.4% | | | | |
| **C to Lab swing 5.3%** | | **41,781** | Lab maj 23,959 | | 48,108 | Lab maj 22,499 | |
| | | | 57.3% | | | 46.8% | |

**JOHN HEALEY,** b Feb 13, 1960. TUC campaigns director. Former part-time tutor, OU business school. Member, Child Poverty Action Group; Liberty; Amnesty; World Development Movement. Ed Lady Lumley's Comp, Pickering; St Peter's School, York; Christ's Coll, Cambridge.

**KARL HAMER,** b Nov 26, 1968. Regional sales manager, pharmaceuticals. Ed Wath-upon-Dearne Comp; Portsmouth Univ (chair, C students, 1988-90).
**JAMES CHARTERS,** b May 9, 1949. Works in information technology. Chair, local branch of Camra. Ed Creighton School, Carlisle; Leeds, Liverpool and Cranfield Univs.

| WEST BROMWICH EAST | | **16.0% change** | | | | | **Lab win** |
|---|---|---|---|---|---|---|---|
| Electorate % Turnout | | 63,401 | 65.4% | **1997** | 67,232 | 73.8% | **1992** |
| **+Snape, P** | **Lab** | **23,710** | **57.2%** | **+9.2%** | 23,782 | 47.9% | Lab |
| Matsell, B | C | 10,126 | 24.4% | -13.5% | 18,797 | 37.9% | C |
| Smith, M | LD | 6,179 | 14.9% | +1.6% | 6,591 | 13.3% | LD |
| Mulley, G | Ref | 1,472 | 3.5% | | 477 | 1.0% | NF |
| **C to Lab notional swing 11.4%** | | **41,487** | Lab maj 13,584 | | 49,647 | Lab maj 4,985 | |
| | | | 32.7% | | | 10.0% | |

**PETER SNAPE,** b Feb 12, 1942. Ex-railwayman and soldier. Elected Feb 1974. Lab transport spokesman 1983-92, home affairs 1982-83, defence and disarmament 1979-82. Gvt whip 1977-79; asst gvt whip 1975-77. Served on Channel Tunnel Bill select cttee 1986-87. Chair, W Midlands group of Lab MPs 1985-97. Joint chair, all-party railways group; all-party Channel Tunnel group; joint vice-chair, aerospace group; chair, Thai group; joint sec, all-party Hungarian group, 1996-97. Bredbury and Romily urban district cllr 1971-74. Non-exec director, West Midlands Travel plc, subsidiary of National Express Group. British Rail clerical officer

1970-74, goods guard 1967-70, regular soldier 1961-67, rail signalman 1957-61. Ed St Joseph's School, Stockport.
**BRIAN MATSELL,** b Oct 18, 1936. Campaign manager for Angela Knight, MP, at 1992 general election. Chief exec, Derbyshire business chamber. Ed Nottingham Trent Univ.
**MARTYN SMITH,** b Feb 16, 1946. Chief officer of community health council. Contested this seat 1979, 1983, 1987 and 1992, and Stoke-on-Trent 1974. West Bromwich borough cllr 1980- (group leader 1980-95); Newcastle-under-Lyme borough cllr 1972-74. Member, Amnesty; CND; MSF. Ed Wyggeston Boys' School, Leicester; Jesus Coll, Cambridge.

| WEST BROMWICH WEST | | **47.9% change** | | | | | **Speaker** |
|---|---|---|---|---|---|---|---|
| Electorate % Turnout | | 67,496 | 54.4% | **1997** | 68,115 | 69.4% | **1992** |
| **+Boothroyd, Miss B Speaker** | | **23,969** | **65.3%** | | 23,937 | 50.6% | Lab |
| Silvester, R | Lab Change | 8,546 | 23.3% | | 17,763 | 37.6% | C |
| Edwards, S | Nat Dem | 4,181 | 11.4% | | 5,577 | 11.8% | LD |
| **No swing calculation** | | **36,696** | Speaker maj 15,423 | | 47,277 | Lab maj 6,174 | |
| | | | 42.0% | | | 13.1% | |

**BETTY BOOTHROYD,** b Oct 8, 1929. Unanimously re-elected by the House as Speaker on May 7, 1997. First elected Speaker on April 27, 1992, the first woman to occupy the chair. In July 1987 she was the first woman Labour MP to be a Deputy Speaker, being appointed second deputy chair of Ways and Means. Lab MP for this seat 1974-92, when elected Speaker. MP for West Bromwich, May 1973 to Feb 1974; contested Rossendale 1970, Nelson and Colne by-election 1968, Peterborough 1959, Leicester SE by-

election 1957. Privy Counsellor 1992. Member of Commons Chairmen's panel 1979-87, and House of Commons Commission 1983-87. Member, Lab NEC 1981-87; asst gvt whip 1974-76. MEP 1975-77. Member, BBC general advisory council 1987- . Chancellor, Open University, 1994- . Freeman, Boroughs of Sandwell and of Kirklees, and of City of London. Ed Dewsbury Coll of Commerce and Art.

| WEST HAM | | 38.6% change | | | | | Lab win |
|---|---|---|---|---|---|---|---|
| Electorate % Turnout | | 57,058 | 59.0% | **1997** | 64,245 | 58.4% | **1992** |
| +Banks, T L | Lab | **24,531** | **72.9%** | **+14.9%** | 21,717 | 57.9% | Lab |
| MacGregor, M | C | 5,037 | 15.0% | -15.0% | 11,229 | 30.0% | C |
| McDonough, Ms S | LD | 2,479 | 7.4% | -2.2% | 3,602 | 9.6% | LD |
| Francis, K | BNP | 1,198 | 3.6% | | 939 | 2.5% | Other |
| Jug, T | Loony | 300 | 0.9% | | | | |
| Rainbow, J | Dream | 116 | 0.3% | | | | |
| C to Lab notional swing 15.0% | | 33,661 | | Lab maj 19,494 | 37,487 | | Lab maj 10,488 |
| | | | | 57.9% | | | 28.0% |

**TONY BANKS**, b April 8, 1945. Became Minister for Sport with rank of Under Secretary, National Heritage Department, May 5, 1997. MP for Newham NW 1983-97; contested E Grinstead 1970, Newcastle N 1974, Watford 1979. Lab spokesman on London and on transport 1992-93, on social security 1990-91. Member, advisory cttee on works of art. Chair, PLP arts sub-cttee until 1990. Greater London cllr for Hammersmith 1970-77, Tooting 1981-86. Chair GLC 1985-86. Parly adviser to Bectu; Musicians' Union; London Beekeepers' Assoc (gets 12 jars of honey a year).

Member, London Marathon board. Board member, National Theatre, 1981-85, English Nat Opera 1981-83, London Festival Ballet 1981-83. Member, TGWU. Ed Archbishop Tenison's GS, Kennington; York Univ; LSE.
**MARK MacGREGOR**, b Feb 25, 1961. Chair, Nat Assoc of C Graduates 1990-91, Scottish Fed C Students 1985-86. Company director. Ed Emanuel School, Wandsworth; Heriot-Watt Univ.
**SAMANTHA McDONOUGH**, b Sept 28, 1962. Head of practice affairs at RIBA. Member, MSF. Ed Island School, Hong Kong; Hull Univ.

| WESTBURY | | 15.5% change | | | | | C win |
|---|---|---|---|---|---|---|---|
| Electorate % Turnout | | 74,301 | 76.4% | **1997** | 74,489 | 81.8% | **1992** |
| +Faber, D | C | **23,037** | **40.6%** | **-11.7%** | 31,821 | 52.2% | C |
| Miller, J | LD | 16,969 | 29.9% | -4.0% | 20,668 | 33.9% | LD |
| Small, K | Lab | 11,969 | 21.1% | +10.5% | 6,457 | 10.6% | Lab |
| Hawkins, G | Lib | 1,956 | 3.4% | +1.5% | 1,211 | 2.0% | Lib |
| Hawkings-Byass, N | Ref | 1,909 | 3.4% | | 746 | 1.2% | Grn |
| Westbury, R | UK Ind | 771 | 1.4% | | | | |
| Haysom, C | NLP | 140 | 0.2% | | | | |
| C to LD notional swing 3.8% | | 56,751 | | C maj 6,068 | 60,903 | | C maj 11,153 |
| | | | | 10.7% | | | 18.3% |

**DAVID FABER**, b July 7, 1961. Elected for this seat 1992; contested Stockton N 1987. PPS to Stephen Dorrell, Health Sec, 1995-97; PPS to Min of State, Foreign Office, 1994-95. Member, social security select cttee 1992-97; joint vice-chair, West Country group of C MPs; sec, C backbench education cttee, 1992-94. Parly adviser to Chartered Inst of Marketing. Campaigning dept, C Central Office, 1985-87; PA to Jeffrey Archer (dep chair, C Party) 1985-87. Co-founder and dir, Sterling Marketing Ltd (marketing consultancy) 1987- , chair 1994- . Underwriting member of

Lloyd's. Ed Summer Fields, Oxford; Eton; Balliol Coll, Oxford. Grandson of Harold Macmillan.
**JOHN MILLER**, b July 20, 1948. Publishing executive. S Somerset district cllr 1991- (currently leader). Member, Greenpeace. Ed Emanuel School; Middlesex Univ.
**KEVIN SMALL**, b Feb 1, 1966. Lab Party organiser. Wiltshire county cllr 1989- (joint leader 1993- ); Thamesdown cllr 1996- . Ed Westbourne Sec Lower School; Commonweal Sec Higher School; Swindon Coll.

| WESTERN ISLES | | | | | | | Lab hold |
|---|---|---|---|---|---|---|---|
| Electorate % Turnout | | 22,983 | 70.1% | **1997** | 22,784 | 70.4% | **1992** |
| *Macdonald, C A | Lab | **8,955** | **55.6%** | **+7.8%** | 7,664 | 47.8% | Lab |
| Gillies, Dr A | SNP | 5,379 | 33.4% | -3.8% | 5,961 | 37.2% | SNP |
| McGrigor, J | C | 1,071 | 6.6% | -1.8% | 1,362 | 8.5% | C |
| Mitchison, N | LD | 495 | 3.1% | -0.4% | 552 | 3.4% | LD |
| Lionel, R | Ref | 206 | 1.3% | | 491 | 3.1% | Ind |
| SNP to Lab swing 5.8% | | 16,106 | | Lab maj 3,576 | 16,030 | | Lab maj 1,703 |
| | | | | 22.2% | | | 10.6% |

**CALUM MACDONALD**, b May 7, 1956. Elected for this seat 1987. Former member, agriculture select cttee; joint vice-chair, PLP agric cttee, 1987-89; chair, PLP Treasury and Civil Service cttee, 1988-90. Joint chair, all-party future of Europe parly group; joint vice-chair, coastal group, Bosnian group, world govt group. Unpaid dir, Future of Europe Trust. Ex-teaching fellow in political philosophy. Member, TGWU; Crofters Union. Ed Bayble School; Nicholson Inst, Stornoway; Edinburgh Univ; Univ Coll of Los Angeles.

**ANNE LORNE GILLIES,** b Oct 21, 1944. Lecturer in Gaelic, writer, TV producer. Dir, Glasgow Highland Soc. Ed Oban HS; Edinburgh, London and Glasgow Univs; Royal Acad of Music; Jordanhill Coll of Ed.
**JAMES McGRIGOR**, b 1949. Farmer; ex-stockbroker and fish-farmer. Member, Scottish Landowners' Fed; Atlantic Salmon Trust Council; Queen's Bodyguard for Scotland. Ed Eton; Neuchâtel Univ, Switzerland.

| WESTMORLAND & LONSDALE | | 6.3% change | | | | C win |
|---|---|---|---|---|---|---|
| Electorate % Turnout | | 68,389 | 74.3% | **1997** | 67,523 | 77.5% | **1992** |
| **Collins, T** | **C** | **21,470** | **42.3%** | **-14.6%** | **29,775** | **56.9%** | **C** |
| Collins, S | LD | 16,949 | 33.4% | +5.9% | 14,381 | 27.5% | LD |
| Harding, J | Lab | 10,459 | 20.6% | +5.5% | 7,898 | 15.1% | Lab |
| Smith, M | Ref | 1,931 | 3.8% | | 273 | 0.5% | NLP |
| **C to LD notional swing 10.3%** | | **50,809** | | **C maj 4,521** | **52,327** | | **C maj 15,394** |
| | | | | 8.9% | | | 29.4% |

**TIM COLLINS,** b May 7, 1964. C party dir of communications, 1992-95. Appointed media consultant to party chair, Dr Brian Mawhinney, 1995; member of Downing St policy unit 1995. Was special adviser to David Hunt at Dept of Environment and to Michard Howard at Environment and Employment. Ed Chigwell School; LSE; King's Coll, London.

**STANLEY COLLINS,** b Aug 10, 1948. Business systems analyst. Contested this seat 1987 for L/All, and 1992. South Lakeland district cllr 1979- . Ed Roundhay School, Leeds; UMIST.
**JOHN HARDING,** b Jan 22, 1965. Tax consultant at Coopers & Lybrand. Member, Co-op Party; Fabian Soc; Chartered Inst of Taxation; GMB. Ed Bramhall HS; Salford Univ.

| WESTON-SUPER-MARE | | 10.6% change | | | | LD win |
|---|---|---|---|---|---|---|
| Electorate % Turnout | | 72,445 | 73.7% | **1997** | 70,851 | 79.5% | **1992** |
| **Cotter, B** | **LD** | **21,407** | **40.1%** | **+1.6%** | **27,063** | **48.1%** | **C** |
| Daly, Mrs M E | C | 20,133 | 37.7% | -10.3% | 21,691 | 38.5% | LD |
| Kraft, D | Lab | 9,557 | 17.9% | +6.5% | 6,420 | 11.4% | Lab |
| Sewell, T | Ref | 2,280 | 4.3% | | 1,131 | 2.0% | Grn |
| **C to LD notional swing 6.0%** | | **53,377** | | **LD maj 1,274** | **56,305** | | **C maj 5,372** |
| | | | | 2.4% | | | 9.6% |

**BRIAN COTTER,** b Aug 24, 1938. Managing director of plastics company. Contested this seat 1992. Woking district cllr 1986-90. Member, Charter 88; Amnesty; Green LDs. Ed St Benedict's, Ealing; Downside School, Somerset.
**MARGARET DALY,** b Jan 26, 1938. MEP for Somerset and Dorset West 1984-94; contested Somerset and Devon North in 1994 Euro elections. Member, Euro Parliament cttee on development and co-operation, 1984-94; vice-chair 1987-89, and C spokeswoman on it; vice-pres, joint EC/African, Caribbean and Pacific Assembly 1988-

94. Dir, JPB Public Affairs public relations co; Cophall Associates Ltd; board member, Traidcraft Exchange. Nat dir of C Trade Unionists 1979-84; consultant to trade union dept at C Central Office 1976-79. Official of insurance trade union which merged with ASTMS 1960-71; dep head, Phoenix Assurance, 1956-60. Ed Methodist Coll, Belfast.
**DEREK KRAFT,** b Nov 4, 1944. College lecturer in information technology. Ex-RAF elecronics fitter. Ed Bristol Poly.

| WIGAN | | 10.7% change | | | | Lab win |
|---|---|---|---|---|---|---|
| Electorate % Turnout | | 64,689 | 67.7% | **1997** | 65,629 | 75.5% | **1992** |
| **+Stott, R** | **Lab** | **30,043** | **68.6%** | **+7.9%** | **30,028** | **60.6%** | **Lab** |
| Loveday, M | C | 7,400 | 16.9% | -8.4% | 12,538 | 25.3% | C |
| Beswick, T | LD | 4,390 | 10.0% | -1.7% | 5,787 | 11.7% | LD |
| Bradborne, A | Ref | 1,450 | 3.3% | | 997 | 2.0% | Lib |
| Maile, C | Green | 442 | 1.0% | | 176 | 0.4% | NLP |
| Ayliffe, W | NLP | 94 | 0.2% | -0.1% | | | |
| **C to Lab notional swing 8.2%** | | **43,819** | | **Lab maj 22,643** | **49,526** | | **Lab maj 17,490** |
| | | | | 51.7% | | | 35.3% |

**ROGER STOTT,** b Aug 7, 1943. Elected for this seat 1983, MP for Westhoughton 1973-83; contested Cheadle 1970. Member, national heritage select cttee, 1995-97; Lab spokesman on N Ireland 1990-94; on trade and industry 1987-89; on transport 1980-83 and 1984-86. PPS to James Callaghan 1976-79. Sec, PLP N Ireland cttee. Vice-chair, all-party British-Egyptian parly group; joint sec, Mauritius and Turkish groups; treas, Lords and Commons cricket club. Rochdale cllr 1970-74. Pres. Bass Wingates brass band, since 1980. Telephone engineer 1964-73. Ed Greenbank Sec Mod; Rochdale Tech Coll; Ruskin Coll, Oxford.

**MARK LOVEDAY,** b June 17, 1960. Barrister. Hammersmith & Fulham cllr 1994- . Chair, Nat Assoc of C Graduates 1985-86. Aide to Morton C. Blackwell, President Reagan's special assistant, in White House 1982-83. Lawyer specialising in housing and law of landlord and tenant; member, legal panel of Associated Newspapers. Ed St Edmund's Coll, Ware; Kent Univ; Inns of Court School of Law.
**TREVOR BESWICK,** b March 17, 1935. Supply teacher. Contested Stoke-on-Trent N for L/All 1983. Ed Bradford GS; Leeds Univ.

| WILTSHIRE NORTH | | 16.4% change | | | | | C win |
|---|---|---|---|---|---|---|---|
| Electorate % Turnout | | 77,237 | 75.1% | **1997** | 71,312 | 83.9% | **1992** |
| **Gray, J** | **C** | **25,390** | **43.8%** | **-12.4%** | **33,626** | **56.2%** | **C** |
| Cordon, S | LD | 21,915 | 37.8% | +6.3% | 18,866 | 31.5% | LD |
| Knowles, N | Lab | 8,261 | 14.2% | +4.1% | 6,087 | 10.2% | Lab |
| Purves, Ms M | Ref | 1,774 | 3.1% | | 711 | 1.2% | Grn |
| Wood, A | UK Ind | 410 | 0.7% | | 521 | 0.9% | Lib |
| Forsyth, J | NLP | 263 | 0.5% | | 55 | 0.1% | Bastion |
| **C to LD notional swing 9.3%** | | **58,013** | | **C maj 3,475** | **59,866** | | **C maj 14,760** |
| | | | | 6.0% | | | 24.7% |

**JAMES GRAY,** b Nov 7, 1954. Writer, consultant. Contested Ross, Cromarty & Skye 1992. Special adviser to John Gummer and Michael Howard, Environment Secs, 1992-95. Dir, public affairs consultants, 1995- ; managing dir, GNI Freight Futures Ltd, 1985-92; senior manager, GNI Ltd (futures brokers), 1989-92; dir, Baltic Futures Exchange, 1989-91. Freeman, City of London, 1978. Ed Glasgow HS; Glasgow Univ; Christ Church, Oxford.

**SIMON CORDON,** b Aug 14, 1963. Management consultant. Contested Swindon 1992. Ex-Wilts county cllr; ex-Thamesdown borough cllr. Ed Goldsmith's Coll, London.
**NIGEL KNOWLES,** b Dec 5, 1946. Author. Contested Bodmin 1979, Hastings 1983, Wyre Forest 1987, Worcestershire S 1992. Hereford and Worcester county cllr 1989- . Ed King Charles I GS, Kidderminster; Birmingham Poly; Worcester Coll of HE.

| WIMBLEDON | | | | | | | Lab gain |
|---|---|---|---|---|---|---|---|
| Electorate % Turnout | | 64,070 | 75.5% | **1997** | 61,917 | 80.2% | **1992** |
| **Casale, R** | **Lab** | **20,674** | **42.8%** | **+19.5%** | **26,331** | **53.0%** | **C** |
| *Goodson-Wickes, Dr C | C | 17,694 | 36.6% | -16.4% | 11,570 | 23.3% | Lab |
| Willott, Ms A | LD | 8,014 | 16.6% | -4.7% | 10,569 | 21.3% | LD |
| Abid, H | Ref | 993 | 2.1% | | 860 | 1.7% | Grn |
| Thacker, R | Green | 474 | 1.0% | | 181 | 0.4% | NLP |
| Davies, Ms S | ProLife | 346 | 0.7% | | 170 | 0.3% | Ind |
| Kirby, M | Mongolian | 112 | 0.2% | | | | |
| Stacey, G | Dream | 47 | 0.1% | | | | |
| **C to Lab swing 17.9%** | | **48,354** | | **Lab maj 2,980** | **49,681** | | **C maj 14,761** |
| | | | | 6.2% | | | 29.7% |

**ROGER CASALE,** b May 22, 1960. University lecturer. Ex-policy adviser to John Prescott and Tony Blair. Member, Fabian Soc; Lab Movement in Europe. Ed Hurstpierpoint Coll; Brasenose Coll, Oxford; Ludwig Maximillian Univ, Munich; John Hopkins (Bologna); LSE.
**CHARLES GOODSON-WICKES,** b Nov 7, 1945. Occupational physician, non-practising barrister. MP for this seat 1987-97; contested

Islington Central 1979. PPS to Sir George Young, Transport Sec, 1995-97, and previously to three Treasury mins. Chair (unpaid), British Field Sports Soc, 1994- . Company director. Ed Charterhouse; St Bart's Hospital; Inner Temple.
**ALISON WILLOTT,** b Feb 21, 1946. Professional concert singer, teacher. Contested this seat 1992. Ed Wimbledon HS; Cheltenham Ladies' Coll; Durham Univ; King's Coll, London.

| WINCHESTER | | 44.3% change | | | | | LD win |
|---|---|---|---|---|---|---|---|
| Electorate % Turnout | | 78,884 | 78.7% | **1997** | 75,123 | 84.0% | **1992** |
| **Oaten, M** | **LD** | **26,100** | **42.1%** | **+5.2%** | **32,604** | **51.7%** | **C** |
| +Malone, G P | C | 26,098 | 42.1% | -9.6% | 23,286 | 36.9% | LD |
| Davies, P | Lab | 6,528 | 10.5% | +3.0% | 4,734 | 7.5% | Lab |
| Strand, P | Ref | 1,598 | 2.6% | | 2,468 | 3.9% | Ind C |
| Huggett, R | Top | 640 | 1.0% | | | | |
| Rumsey, D | UK Ind | 476 | 0.8% | | | | |
| Browne, J | Ind AFE | 307 | 0.5% | | | | |
| Stockton, P | Loony | 307 | 0.5% | | | | |
| **C to LD notional swing 7.4%** | | **62,054** | | **LD maj 2** | **63,092** | | **C maj 9,318** |
| | | | | 0.0% | | | 14.8% |

**MARK OATEN,** b March 8, 1964. Managing director of public relations consultancy. Contested Watford 1992. Elected first SDP cllr in Watford 1986 and became LD cllr when party was formed; then group leader (cllr 1986-94). Dir, Westminster Communications Ltd and Oasis Radio. Ed Greens Sec Mod, Watford; Hertfordshire Poly.
**GERALD MALONE,** b July 21, 1950. Solicitor, journalist. Elected for this seat 1992, MP for Aberdeen S 1986-87; contested Glasgow

Provan, Feb 1974; Glasgow Pollok, Oct 1974; Roxburgh, Selkirk and Peebles, 1979; Glasgow Hillhead 1982 by-election. Health Min 1994-97; asst gvt whip 1986-87. Dep chair, C Party, 1992-94. Editor, *The Sunday Times Scotland*, 1989-90; editorial consultant 1990-94; broadcaster, Radio Clyde, 1988-90. Ed St Aloysius' Coll, Glasgow; Glasgow Univ.
**PATRICK DAVIES,** b Oct 26, 1943. Solicitor. Ed Perse School, Cambridge; St Edmund Hall, Oxford.

| WINDSOR | | 106.1% change | | | | | C win |
|---|---|---|---|---|---|---|---|
| Electorate % Turnout | | 69,132 | 73.5% | **1997** | 67,545 | 75.4% | **1992** |
| +Trend, M | C | **24,476** | **48.2%** | **-4.5%** | **30,138** | **56.3%** | C |
| Fox, C | LD | 14,559 | 28.7% | +14.1% | 15,587 | 29.1% | LD |
| Williams, Mrs A | Lab | 9,287 | 18.3% | -12.7% | 6,645 | 12.4% | Lab |
| McDermott, J | Ref | 1,676 | 3.3% | | 1,184 | 2.2% | Other |
| Bradshaw, J | Lib | 388 | 0.8% | | | | |
| Bigg, Mrs E | UK Ind | 302 | 0.6% | | | | |
| Parr, R | Dynamic | 93 | 0.2% | | | | |
| C to LD notional swing 9.3% | | **50,781** | | **C maj 9,917** | **53,554** | | **C maj 14,551** |
| | | | | 19.5% | | | 27.2% |

**MICHAEL TREND**, b April 19, 1952. Journalist, editor and broadcaster. MP for Windsor and Maidenhead 1992-97, contested London NE in 1989 Euro elections. PPS to Brian Mawhinney when Transport Sec 1994-95 and Health Min 1993-94; member of Speaker's advisory cttee on works of art 1993-97. Dep chair (unpaid) of C Party, 1995. Chair, London NE Euro Council, 1985-88; former sec, C Foreign Affairs Forum. Consultant to International Distillers and Vintners Ltd, London. *Daily Telegraph* chief leader writer 1990-92; home editor of *The*

*Spectator* 1986-90. Ed Tormore School, Upper Deal, Kent; Westminster; Oriel Coll, Oxford.
**CHRIS FOX**, b Sept 27, 1957. Technical journalist, communications specialist. Aide to Robert Maclennan, LD pres. Hounslow cllr 1994- . Member, Charter 88; Amnesty; Assoc of LD Cllrs. Ed Minster School, Leominster; Imperial Coll, London.
**AMANDA WILLIAMS**, b Oct 6, 1954. Writer, freelance grants assessor. Berkshire county cllr. Member, Unison. Ed Croesycellog GS; Univ Coll of Wales, Cardiff.

| WIRRAL SOUTH | | 0.1% change | | | | | Lab win |
|---|---|---|---|---|---|---|---|
| Electorate % Turnout | | 59,372 | 81.0% | **1997** | 62,103 | 80.9% | **1992** |
| +Chapman, B | Lab | **24,499** | **50.9%** | **+16.4%** | **25,550** | **50.8%** | C |
| Byrom, L | C | 17,495 | 36.4% | -14.5% | 17,382 | 34.6% | Lab |
| Gilchrist, P | LD | 5,018 | 10.4% | -2.6% | 6,572 | 13.1% | LD |
| Wilcox, D | Ref | 768 | 1.6% | | 583 | 1.2% | Grn |
| Nielsen, Ms J | ProLife | 264 | 0.5% | | 182 | 0.4% | NLP |
| Mead, G | NLP | 51 | 0.1% | -0.3% | | | |
| C to Lab notional swing 15.4% | | **48,095** | | **Lab maj 7,004** | **50,269** | | **C maj 8,168** |
| | | | | 14.6% | | | 16.3% |

**BEN CHAPMAN**, b July 8, 1940. Won by-election Feb 1997. Consultant, director of own company, formerly regional dir of Dept of Trade and Industry, and commercial counsellor in Beijing Embassy. Fellow, Inst of Management. Member, board of Heswall Soc. Ex-pilot officer, RAFVR. Ed Appleby GS, Westmorland.
**LES BYROM**, b April 12, 1956. Chartered surveyor. Contested by-election Feb 1997, Knowsley S 1990 and 1992. Southport borough cllr 1985- (leader, C group, 1991- ); Sefton borough

cllr (C group leader 1991- ). Ed Crosby County School; Southport Tech Coll.
**PHILIP GILCHRIST**, b Nov 21, 1951. Education liaison officer. Contested Liverpool Derby Feb 1974, Bebington and Ellesmere Port 1979, this seat 1987. Merseyside county cllr 1977-86; Wirral borough cllr 1977- . Ed King's, Chester; York Univ; Edge Hill Teacher Training Coll.

*Details of 1997 by-election on page 278*

| WIRRAL WEST | | | | | | | Lab gain |
|---|---|---|---|---|---|---|---|
| Electorate % Turnout | | 60,908 | 77.0% | **1997** | 62,453 | 81.6% | **1992** |
| Hesford, S | Lab | **21,035** | **44.9%** | **+13.9%** | **26,852** | **52.7%** | C |
| *Hunt, D | C | 18,297 | 39.0% | -13.7% | 15,788 | 31.0% | Lab |
| Thornton, J | LD | 5,945 | 12.7% | -1.9% | 7,420 | 14.6% | LD |
| Wharton, D | Ref | 1,613 | 3.4% | | 700 | 1.4% | Grn |
| | | | | | 188 | 0.4% | NLP |
| C to Lab swing 13.8% | | **46,890** | | **Lab maj 2,738** | **50,948** | | **C maj 11,064** |
| | | | | 5.8% | | | 21.7% |

**STEPHEN HESFORD**, b May 27, 1957. Barrister. Contested Suffolk S 1992. Asst to Joan Lestor, MP, 1992-93. Member, Greenpeace; Fabian Soc; Liberty; Amnesty; Child Poverty Action Group; GMB/Apex. Ed Urmston GS; Bradford and Westminster Univs; Inns of Court School of Law.
**DAVID HUNT**, b May 21, 1942. Solicitor. Elected for this seat 1983, MP for Wirral 1976-83; contested Bristol S 1970; Kingswood 1974. Chancellor of Duchy of Lancaster and Public Service and Science Min 1994-95; Employment Sec 1993-94; joined Cabinet

1990 as Welsh Sec. Min for Local Gvt and Inner Cities, DoE, 1989-90; dep chief whip 1987-89; Under Sec for Energy 1984-87. Chair, inter-parly council against anti-Semitism, 1996. Member of select cttees on public service 1995-97; televising Commons 1988-89. Senior partner, Beachcroft Stanleys (solicitors). Ed Liverpool Coll; Montpellier and Bristol Univs; Guildford Coll of Law.
**JOHN THORNTON**, b July 13, 1930. Retired personnel manager. Contested Wirral W 1992. Wirral metropolitan borough cllr. Ed Sherborne School; Army Staff Coll.

| WITNEY | | 18.2% change | | | | | | C win |
|---|---|---|---|---|---|---|---|---|
| Electorate % Turnout | | 73,520 | 76.7% | **1997** | 69,746 | 83.7% | **1992** |
| **Woodward, S** | **C** | **24,282** | **43.1%** | **-14.8%** | **33,743** | **57.8%** | **C** |
| Hollingsworth, A | Lab | 17,254 | 30.6% | +12.5% | 13,150 | 22.5% | LD |
| Lawrence, Mrs A | LD | 11,202 | 19.9% | -2.7% | 10,582 | 18.1% | Lab |
| Brown, G | Ref | 2,262 | 4.0% | | 661 | 1.1% | Grn |
| Montgomery, M | UK Ind | 765 | 1.4% | | 124 | 0.2% | NLP |
| Chapple-Perrie, Ms S | Green | 636 | 1.1% | | 110 | 0.2% | FTA |
| **C to Lab notional swing 13.6%** | | **56,401** | | **C maj 7,028** | **58,370** | | **C maj 20,593** |
| | | | | 12.5% | | | 35.3% |

**SHAUN WOODWARD,** b Oct 26, 1958. Broadcaster and univ lecturer. Parly lobbyist, Nat Consumer Council, 1980-82; dir of communications, C Central Office, 1990-92. Chair, Understanding Industry. Professorial Fellow of Politics, Queen Mary and Westfield Coll, London. Ex-producer, *Panorama* and *Newsnight.* Ed Bristol GS; Jesus Coll, Cambridge; Kennedy School, Harvard.

**ALEXANDER HOLLINGSWORTH,** b April 1, 1969. Publisher. Oxford city cllr 1994- . Member, MSF. Ed King's, Ely; LSE; Univ of Texas. **ANGELA LAWRENCE,** b July 13, 1947. Primary teacher. Vale of White Horse district cllr 1991- . Member, Abingdon Peace Group. Serves on management boards, Oxford Housing Rights, Abingdon CAB. Ed North Kesteven GS; Kesteven Coll of Ed.

| WOKING | | 14.9% change | | | | | | C win |
|---|---|---|---|---|---|---|---|---|
| Electorate % Turnout | | 70,053 | 72.7% | **1997** | 69,318 | 79.9% | **1992** |
| **Malins, H** | **C** | **19,553** | **38.4%** | **-20.7%** | **32,718** | **59.1%** | **C** |
| Goldenberg, P | LD | 13,875 | 27.3% | +0.2% | 14,987 | 27.1% | LD |
| Hanson, Ms C | Lab | 10,695 | 21.0% | +7.6% | 7,398 | 13.4% | Lab |
| Bell, H | Ind C | 3,933 | 7.7% | | 257 | 0.5% | NLP |
| Skeate, C | Ref | 2,209 | 4.3% | | | | |
| Harvey, M | UK Ind | 512 | 1.0% | | | | |
| Sleeman, Miss D | NLP | 137 | 0.3% | -0.2% | | | |
| **C to LD notional swing 10.4%** | | **50,914** | | **C maj 5,678** | **55,360** | | **C maj 17,731** |
| | | | | 11.2% | | | 32.0% |

**HUMFREY MALINS,** b July 31, 1945. Lawyer and consultant. MP for Croydon NW 1983-92; contested that seat 1992, Liverpool Toxteth Feb 1974 and Oct 1974, and Lewisham E 1979. PPS to Virginia Bottomley when Min of State for Health, 1989-92, and to Timothy Renton, Home Office Min, and Douglas Hogg, Home Office Under Sec, 1987-89. Member, select cttees on broadcasting, 1991-92; statutory instruments 1991-92; consolidation Bills 1983-87. Joint vice-chair, C backbench legal cttee, 1986-87. Chair, Immigration Advisory Service, 1993- . Asst Recorder London

Crown Courts 1991-96, Recorder since 1996. Ed St John's, Leatherhead; Brasenose Coll, Oxford; Guildford Coll of Law. **PHILIP GOLDENBERG,** b April 26, 1946. Commercial solicitor. Contested Eton & Slough Feb 1974 and Oct 1974, 1979, and this seat 1983 and 1987; also Dorset and East Devon 1994 Euro elections. Woking borough cllr 1984-92. Member, CBI, Nature Council; Law Soc. Ed St Paul's; Pembroke Coll, Oxford. **CATHERINE (Katie) HANSON,** b Jan 2, 1966. Arts administrator. Ed Fulbrook School, Weybridge.

| WOKINGHAM | | 67.6% change | | | | | | C win |
|---|---|---|---|---|---|---|---|---|
| Electorate % Turnout | | 66,161 | 75.7% | **1997** | 66,150 | 80.0% | **1992** |
| **+Redwood, J** | **C** | **25,086** | **50.1%** | **-11.7%** | **32,692** | **61.7%** | **C** |
| Longton, Dr R E | LD | 15,721 | 31.4% | +5.7% | 13,575 | 25.6% | LD |
| Colling, Ms P | Lab | 8,424 | 16.8% | +5.5% | 5,987 | 11.3% | Lab |
| Owen, P | Loony | 877 | 1.8% | +0.7% | 548 | 1.0% | Loony |
| | | | | | 143 | 0.3% | WUWC |
| **C to LD notional swing 8.7%** | | **50,108** | | **C maj 9,365** | **52,945** | | **C maj 19,117** |
| | | | | 18.7% | | | 36.1% |

**JOHN REDWOOD,** b June 15, 1951. Elected for this seat 1987, contested Southwark Peckham 1982 by-election. Joined Cabinet 1993 as Welsh Sec, resigning 1995 to contest party leadership. Local Gvt Min 1992-93, Trade and Industry Min 1990-92, Min for Corporate Affairs, DTI, 1989-90. Head of Margaret Thatcher's policy unit 1984-85, adviser on nationalised industries to Treasury and Civil Service select cttee 1981. Oxfordshire county cllr 1973-77. Non-exec chair 1987-89, dep chair 1986-87 and dir 1985, Norcros plc; investment manager and dir, N.M. Rothschild

and Sons 1977-87, and non-exec dir 1987-89. Ed Kent Coll, Canterbury; Magdalen and St Antony's Colls, Oxford; Fellow of All Souls Coll, Oxford 1972. **ROYCE LONGTON,** b April 9, 1939. University lecturer. Berkshire county cllr 1993- (group chair 1996- ); Newbury district councillor 1995- . Ed King Edward VI, Macclesfield; Birmingham Univ. **PATRICIA COLLING,** b Oct 23, 1946. Teacher, market researcher. Member, Fawcett Soc; 300 Group; Charter 88; GMB. Ed Whitby GS; Kirkby Fields Coll of Ed; Birkbeck Coll, London.

| WOLVERHAMPTON NORTH EAST | | 1.7% change | | | | Lab win |
|---|---|---|---|---|---|---|
| Electorate % Turnout | | 61,642 | 67.2% | **1997** | 63,383 | 78.2% | **1992** |
| **Purchase, K** | **Lab Co-op** | **24,534** | **59.3%** | **+10.3%** | 24,275 | 49.0% | Lab Co-op |
| Harvey, D | C | 11,547 | 27.9% | -13.5% | 20,528 | 41.4% | C |
| Niblett, B | LD | 2,214 | 5.3% | -2.0% | 3,657 | 7.4% | LD |
| Hallmark, C | Lib | 1,560 | 3.8% | +1.6% | 1,087 | 2.2% | Lib |
| Muchall, A | Ref | 1,192 | 2.9% | | | | |
| Wingfield, M | Nat Dem | 356 | 0.9% | | | | |
| **C to Lab notional swing 11.9%** | | **41,403** | Lab Co-op maj 12,987 | | 49,547 | Lab Co-op maj 3,747 | |
| | | | 31.4% | | | 7.6% | |

**KENNETH PURCHASE**, b Jan 8, 1939. Regained this seat for Lab 1992, contested it 1987. Member, trade and industry select cttee, 1992-97; Commons administration cttee; chair, PLP trade and industry cttee, 1992- ; joint chair, all-party exports group. Wolverhampton borough cllr 1970-90, also served on Wolverhampton District HA, Wolverhampton and Dist Manpower Board, DHSS Benefits Tribunal. Business development adviser and company sec, Black Country CDA Ltd, 1982-92; previously toolmaker and housing manager. Member, TGWU (ex-shop steward, works convener); Co-op Party; Fabian Soc; SEA. Ed Springfield Sec Mod; Wolverhampton Poly.

**DAVID HARVEY**, b Oct 19, 1962. Chartered accountant, small business policy head for professional assoc, author and lecturer. Head of candidates information unit, C Central Office, 1992. Personnel manager, British Rail, 1985-86; defence lobbyist 1984-85. Ed Borden GS, Sittingbourne; Mansfield Coll, Oxford.

**BRIAN NIBLETT**, b June 5, 1957. Public affairs manager. Member, parly renewable & sustainable energy group. Ed Filton HS, Bristol; Salford and West of England Univs.

| WOLVERHAMPTON SOUTH EAST | | | | | | Lab hold |
|---|---|---|---|---|---|---|
| Electorate % Turnout | | 54,291 | 64.2% | **1997** | 56,158 | 72.9% | **1992** |
| **\*Turner, D** | **Lab Co-op** | **22,202** | **63.7%** | **+7.0%** | 23,215 | 56.7% | Lab Co-op |
| Hanbury, W | C | 7,020 | 20.2% | -11.6% | 12,975 | 31.7% | C |
| Whitehouse, R | LD | 3,292 | 9.5% | -0.0% | 3,881 | 9.5% | LD |
| Stevenson-Platt, T | Ref | 980 | 2.8% | | 850 | 2.1% | Lib |
| Worth, N | Soc Lab | 689 | 2.0% | | | | |
| Bullman, K | Lib | 647 | 1.9% | -0.2% | | | |
| **C to Lab Co-op swing 9.3%** | | **34,830** | Lab Co-op maj 15,182 | | 40,921 | Lab Co-op maj 10,240 | |
| | | | 43.6% | | | 25.0% | |

**DENNIS TURNER**, b Aug 26, 1942. Elected for this seat 1987; contested Halesowen and Stourbridge Feb and Oct 1974. Member, select cttee on ed, science and arts, 1989-94; unopposed Bills panel 1992-97. Lab whip 1993; chair all-party housing co-operatives parly group; joint vice-chair, non-profitmaking clubs group; personal social services group; adult education group. W Midlands county cllr 1974-86; Wolverhampton borough cllr 1966-86; member, Assoc of Metropolitan Authorities, 1980-86. Dir, Springvale Co-operative Ltd, sports and social club; Springvale Enterprise Ltd, sports, leisure and ed activities (both unpaid). Ed Stonefield Sec Mod, Bilston; Bilston CFE.

**WILLIAM HANBURY**, b Jan 2, 1962. Barrister, specialising in landlord and tenant and housing law. Member, Council for Protection of Rural England; Georgian Group; Leeds Community Mediation Service. Ed Broxbourne School; Downside School; E Herts CFE; Manchester Univ; Inns of Court School of Law.

**RICHARD WHITEHOUSE**, b Nov 27, 1951. Teacher. Wolverhampton borough cllr 1984- (group leader, ex-Mayor). Member, NUT (union rep); Amnesty. Ed Highfield School, Wolverhampton.

| WOLVERHAMPTON SOUTH WEST | | | | | | Lab gain |
|---|---|---|---|---|---|---|
| Electorate % Turnout | | 67,482 | 72.5% | **1997** | 67,288 | 78.3% | **1992** |
| Jones, Ms J | Lab | 24,657 | 50.4% | +10.5% | 25,969 | 49.3% | C |
| \*Budgen, N W | C | 19,539 | 39.9% | -9.4% | 21,003 | 39.9% | Lab |
| Green, M | LD | 4,012 | 8.2% | -0.3% | 4,470 | 8.5% | LD |
| Hyde, M | Lib | 713 | 1.5% | -0.9% | 1,237 | 2.3% | Lib |
| **C to Lab swing 9.9%** | | **48,921** | Lab maj 5,118 | | 52,679 | C maj 4,966 | |
| | | | 10.5% | | | 9.4% | |

**JENNY JONES**, b Feb 8, 1948. Director of management consultancy. Former Wolverhampton borough cllr; member, Wolverhampton police consultative cttee; ex-member, Wolverhampton community health council. Member, Co-op Party. Ed Tom Hood HS, Leytonstone; Bradford, Birmingham and Wolverhampton Univs.

**NICHOLAS BUDGEN**, b Nov 3, 1937. Barrister and farmer. MP for this seat 1974-97. Member, Treasury select cttee, 1983-97; PAC 1980-81. Asst gvt whip 1981-82; sec, C backbench finance cttee, 1979. Consultant to Barnett International, manufacturers of crossbow and archery equipment. Ed St Edward's School, Oxford; Corpus Christi Coll, Cambridge.

**MATTHEW GREEN**, b April 12, 1970. Managing director of own media consultancy. Member, LD West Midlands exec; treas of region's youth/student group. Ed Priory School, Shrewsbury; Birmingham Univ.

| WOODSPRING | | 33.9% change | | | | | C win |
|---|---|---|---|---|---|---|---|
| Electorate % Turnout | | 69,964 | 78.5% | **1997** | 68,755 | 80.5% | **1992** |
| +Fox, Dr L | C | **24,425** | 44.5% | -8.9% | 29,529 | 53.3% | C |
| Kirsen, Mrs N | LD | 16,691 | 30.4% | -1.3% | 17,523 | 31.7% | LD |
| Sander, Ms D | Lab | 11,377 | 20.7% | +8.3% | 6,863 | 12.4% | Lab |
| Hughes, R | Ref | 1,614 | 2.9% | | 696 | 1.3% | Lib |
| Lawson, Dr R | Green | 667 | 1.2% | | 666 | 1.2% | Grn |
| Glover, A | Ind | 101 | 0.2% | | 83 | 0.1% | NLP |
| Mears, M | NLP | 52 | 0.1% | -0.1% | | | |
| C to LD notional swing 3.8% | | 54,927 | | C maj 7,734 | 55,360 | | C maj 12,006 |
| | | | | 14.1% | | | 21.7% |

**LIAM FOX**, b Sept 22, 1961. Doctor. Retained seat for C 1992; contested Roxburgh and Berwickshire 1987. Under Sec, Foreign and Commonwealth Office, 1996-97; gvt whip 1995-96; asst gvt whip 1994-95; PPS to Home Sec 1993-94. Member, Scottish affairs select cttee, 1992; sec, C backbench health cttee, 1992-93; C West Country MPs 1992-93. Nat vice-chair, Scottish YCs, 1983-84. GP in Beaconsfield 1987-91; member, Royal Coll of General Practitioners, 1989. Member, central cttee, Families for Defence, 1987-89. Ed St Bride's HS, East Kilbride; Glasgow Univ (pres, univ C club, 1982-83).

**NAN KIRSEN**, b Aug 23, 1944. Contested this seat 1992. N Somerset unitary cllr (council leader); Woodspring district cllr 1986-96 (group leader). Former nurse. Ed Gordano Comp; night school.

**DEBBIE SANDER**, b March 20, 1952. Teacher. Contested Lewes 1983. Chair, N Somerset Lab Party. Member, Oxfam. Ed Somerville Coll, Oxford; Goldsmith's Coll, London; OU.

| WORCESTER | | 15.8% change | | | | | Lab win |
|---|---|---|---|---|---|---|---|
| Electorate % Turnout | | 69,234 | 74.6% | **1997** | 63,622 | 82.8% | **1992** |
| Foster, M | Lab | **25,848** | 50.1% | +10.2% | 23,960 | 45.5% | C |
| Bourne, N | C | 18,423 | 35.7% | -9.8% | 21,013 | 39.9% | Lab |
| Chandler, P J | LD | 6,462 | 12.5% | -0.6% | 6,890 | 13.1% | LD |
| Wood, Mrs P | UK Ind | 886 | 1.7% | | 521 | 1.0% | Grn |
| | | | | | 302 | 0.6% | Brewer |
| C to Lab notional swing 10.0% | | 51,619 | | Lab maj 7,425 | 52,686 | | C maj 2,947 |
| | | | | 14.4% | | | 5.6% |

**MICHAEL FOSTER**, b Jan 14, 1963. Lecturer in accountancy and finance; ex-management accountant at Jaguar Cars; trained head teachers in accountancy at Jaguar as part of industry-education compact. Member, Chartered Inst of Management Accountants. Campaigner against toxic waste depot in Worcester. Ed Great Wysley HS, Cannock; Wolverhampton Univ.

**NICHOLAS BOURNE**, b Jan 1, 1952. Law professor, barrister, author. Contested Chesterfield 1983, and 1984 by-election. Vice-chair, C party in Wales; chair, C political centre, Wales. Member, West Glamorgan regional HA. Ed King Edward VI School, Chelmsford; Univ Coll of Wales; Trinity Coll, Cambridge; Inns of Court School of Law; visiting scholar at Harvard Law School.

**PAUL CHANDLER**, b Nov 9, 1949. Tour operator. Contested Worcestershire S 1987 and 1992. Hereford & Worcs county cllr (dep leader); Malvern Hills cllr (leader). Dir, Travel Club of Upminster. Ed Felsted School; Essex and Birmingham Univs.

| WORCESTERSHIRE MID | | 107.8% change | | | | | C win |
|---|---|---|---|---|---|---|---|
| Electorate % Turnout | | 68,381 | 74.3% | **1997** | 63,596 | 78.8% | **1992** |
| +Luff, P J | C | **24,092** | 47.4% | -7.5% | 27,535 | 54.9% | C |
| Smith, Mrs D | Lab | 14,680 | 28.9% | +11.3% | 13,081 | 26.1% | LD |
| Barwick, D | LD | 9,458 | 18.6% | -7.5% | 8,832 | 17.6% | Lab |
| Watson, T | Ref | 1,780 | 3.5% | | 663 | 1.3% | NLP |
| Ingles, D | UK Ind | 646 | 1.3% | | | | |
| Dyer, A | NLP | 163 | 0.3% | -1.0% | | | |
| C to Lab notional swing 9.4% | | 50,819 | | C maj 9,412 | 50,111 | | C maj 14,454 |
| | | | | 18.5% | | | 28.8% |

**PETER LUFF**, b Feb 18, 1955. MP for Worcester 1992-97, contested Holborn & St Pancras 1987. PPS to Lord Mackay, Lord Chancellor 1996-97; and to Tim Eggar, Energy and Industry Min, 1993-96. Member, select cttees on public service 1996-97; Welsh affairs 1992-97; joint select cttee on consolidation Bills 1993-97. Joint sec, all-party overseas development group; sec, Asean-British group. Sec, Macleod group; patron, C students 1995- . Special adviser to Lord Young of Graffham 1987-89; head of Edward Heath's private office 1980-82. Consultant to Lowe Bell Communications 1989-90 and now adviser to Lowe Bell Political and Lowe Bell Consultants. Adviser to Visa International. Ed Windsor GS; Corpus Christi Coll, Cambridge.

**DIANE SMITH**, b Sept 26, 1959. Adult guidance adviser, audio-visual technician. Member, Inst of Biomedical Sciences. Ed Cowley Girls HS; Liverpool Poly.

**DAVID BARWICK**, b April 23, 1947. Adult education centre manager. Contested this seat 1992. Hereford & Worcs county cllr 1993- (dep leader); Wychavon district cllr 1995- ; Droitwich town cllr 1995- . LD regional exec. Member, NATFHE; Amnesty. Ed Caludon Castle School, Coventry; St Peter's Coll, Birmingham; OU.

| WORCESTERSHIRE WEST | | 49.5% change | | | | | C win |
|---|---|---|---|---|---|---|---|
| Electorate % Turnout | | 64,712 | 76.3% | **1997** | 63,144 | 80.0% | **1992** |
| +Spicer, Sir Michael | C | **22,223** | **45.0%** | **-9.7%** | 27,654 | 54.7% | C |
| Hadley, M | LD | 18,377 | 37.2% | +8.0% | 14,785 | 29.3% | LD |
| Stone, N | Lab | 7,738 | 15.7% | +1.9% | 6,967 | 13.8% | Lab |
| Cameron, Ms S | Green | 1,006 | 2.0% | | 1,104 | 2.2% | Other |
| C to LD notional swing 8.8% | | **49,344** | | **C maj 3,846** | **50,510** | | **C maj 12,869** |
| | | | | 7.8% | | | 25.5% |

**SIR MICHAEL SPICER**, b Jan 22, 1943. Author and journalist. MP for Worcestershire S from 1974; contested Easington 1966 and 1970. PPS to Min of Trade and Consumer Affairs 1979; PPS to Cecil Parkinson 1981; Under Sec for Transport 1984-87; Energy 1987-90. Min for Housing and Planning (DoE) 1990. All-party scientific cttee 1994, chair 1996- . Chair, European research group 1994- . Vice-chair C Party 1981-83, dep chair 1983-84. C research dept 1966-68. Has published six novels, and contributed to *The Sunday Times* Business News and *Daily Mail*. Ed Sacré Coeur, Vienna; Wellington Coll, Berks (governor, 1992- ); Emmanuel Coll, Cambridge.

**MICHAEL HADLEY**, b Feb 20, 1943. Pharmacist. Contested Dudley W by-election 1994. Wyre Forest and Shrewsbury district cllr (Mayor of Bewdley). Chair, Hadley Hutt Computing Ltd. Ed King Edward VI GS, Stourbridge; Aston Univ.

**NEIL STONE**, b Nov 21, 1958. Care manager. Ex-research assistant to Ken Coates, MEP. Formerly operating technician and RN communications officer. Member, Fabian Soc; Full Employment Forum; SERA. Ed Nottingham Univ.

| WORKINGTON | | 15.7% change | | | | | Lab win |
|---|---|---|---|---|---|---|---|
| Electorate % Turnout | | 65,766 | 75.1% | **1997** | 66,865 | 80.8% | **1992** |
| +Campbell-Savours, D | Lab | **31,717** | **64.2%** | **+10.0%** | 29,296 | 54.2% | Lab |
| Blunden, R | C | 12,061 | 24.4% | -12.0% | 19,696 | 36.4% | C |
| Roberts, P | LD | 3,967 | 8.0% | +0.6% | 4,028 | 7.5% | LD |
| Donnan, G | Ref | 1,412 | 2.9% | | 819 | 1.5% | Loony |
| Austin, C | UA | 217 | 0.4% | | 199 | 0.4% | NLP |
| C to Lab notional swing 11.0% | | **49,374** | | **Lab maj 19,656** | **54,038** | | **Lab maj 9,600** |
| | | | | 39.8% | | | 17.8% |

**DALE CAMPBELL-SAVOURS**, b Aug 23, 1943. MP for this constituency since 1979, when he regained it for Lab; contested seat in 1976 by-election, and Darwen in Feb and Oct 1974. Lab spokesman on agriculture, food and rural affairs 1992-94; on overseas development, co-operation and aid 1991-92. Member, select cttees on standards and privileges 1995-97; agric 1994-96; PAC 1982-91; procedure 1982-91; ex-member, cttee on MPs' interests. Vice-chair, Lab agric cttee 1994-95. Ramsbottom urban district cllr 1972-74. Dir, clock manufacturing company, 1971-76. Member, Lab Campaign for Electoral Reform; TGWU. Ed Keswick School; Sorbonne, Paris.

**ROBERT BLUNDEN**, b 1966. Solicitor; senior prosecutor, Crown Prosecution Service. Ed Eastbourne GS and HS; Eastbourne Coll of Arts and Tech; York Univ; Manchester Poly (chair, C assoc, 1987-89).

**PHILLIP ROBERTS**, b July 14, 1953. Social worker. Allendale borough cllr 1995- (group leader). Member, Unison. Ed McKenzie Sec Mod, Cheadle; Huddersfield Univ.

| WORSLEY | | 34.9% change | | | | | Lab win |
|---|---|---|---|---|---|---|---|
| Electorate % Turnout | | 68,978 | 67.8% | **1997** | 69,186 | 76.0% | **1992** |
| +Lewis, T | Lab | **29,083** | **62.2%** | **+8.4%** | 28,291 | 53.8% | Lab |
| Garrido, D | C | 11,342 | 24.2% | -7.9% | 16,888 | 32.1% | C |
| Bleakley, R | LD | 6,356 | 13.6% | +0.9% | 6,661 | 12.7% | LD |
| | | | | | 580 | 1.1% | Grn |
| | | | | | 151 | 0.3% | NLP |
| C to Lab notional swing 8.1% | | **46,781** | | **Lab maj 17,741** | **52,571** | | **Lab maj 11,403** |
| | | | | 37.9% | | | 21.7% |

**TERRY LEWIS**, b Dec 29, 1935. Personnel officer. MP for this constituency since 1983. Member, select cttee on consolidation Bills, 1993-97; members' interests 1992-95; environment 1991-92. Member, all-party animal welfare group. Kearsley urban district cllr 1971-74; Bolton borough cllr 1975-83; Kearsley urban district cllr 1971-74. Ed Mount Carmel School, Salford.

**DAMIAN GARRIDO**, b 1969. Barrister. Vice-chair 1995-96, exec cttee member 1993-95, of Tory Reform Group; political dir, Young Euro Democrats, 1988-90; information asst, Euro Democratic Group, 1988. Political asst to Sir Tim Sainsbury, ex-MP, 1989. Member, YC nat advisory cttee, 1986-90. Ed Manchester Grammar; Kent and London City Univs; Inns of Court School of Law.

**ROBERT BLEAKLEY**, b Sept 20, 1970. Administration assistant. Contested Leigh 1992. Chair, Worsley LDs, 1994- ; ex-member, LD northwest region exec. Ed Fred Longworth HS, Manchester; St John's Coll, Manchester.

| WORTHING EAST & SHOREHAM | | 71.1% change | | | C win | |
|---|---|---|---|---|---|---|
| Electorate % Turnout | | 70,771 | 72.9% | **1997** | 71,891 | 78.1% | **1992** |
| Loughton, T | C | 20,864 | 40.5% | -10.9% | 28,824 | 51.4% | C |
| King, M | LD | 15,766 | 30.6% | -3.1% | 18,919 | 33.7% | LD |
| Williams, M | Lab | 12,335 | 23.9% | +10.6% | 7,476 | 13.3% | Lab |
| McCulloch, J | Ref | 1,683 | 3.3% | | 909 | 1.6% | Other |
| Jarvis, Mrs R | UK Ind | 921 | 1.8% | | | | |
| C to LD notional swing 3.9% | | 51,569 | | C maj 5,098 9.9% | 56,128 | | C maj 9,905 17.6% |

**TIM LOUGHTON,** b May 30, 1962. Director, Fleming Private Asset Management. Contested Sheffield Brightside 1992. PA to Tim Eggar, ex-MP, 1987 election. Dep chair, Battersea C assoc, 1994- ; member, London area exec cttee, 1993- ; exec cttee, Selsdon Group, 1994- ; Carlton Club political cttee 1994- . Chair, Battersea business forum, 1994- . Member, Sussex Archaeological Soc and Soc of Sussex Downsmen; Securities and Futures Assoc working party on training. Ed Priory School, Lewes; Warwick Univ; Clare Coll, Cambridge.

**MARTIN KING,** b May 29, 1951. Management consultant. Contested Shoreham 1992. Adur district cllr 1980- (council leader 1986-95); leader, Assoc of District Councils LD group, 1989- ; member, Cllrs Assoc management cttee 1987. Member, Greenpeace;, Amnesty; Charter 88; Shelter. Ed Devizes School, Wilts; Filton Coll, Bristol; Harrow Coll.

**MARK WILLIAMS,** b June 7, 1960. Business lawyer. Member, Friends of the Earth; Soc of Lab Lawyers; Fabian Soc; Christian Socialist. Ed Pembroke Coll, Cambridge; City Univ; Inns of Court School of Law.

| WORTHING WEST | | 57.0% change | | | C win | |
|---|---|---|---|---|---|---|
| Electorate % Turnout | | 71,329 | 72.1% | **1997** | 71,764 | 78.5% | **1992** |
| +Bottomley, P J | C | 23,733 | 46.1% | -15.6% | 34,762 | 61.7% | C |
| Hare, C | LD | 16,020 | 31.1% | +3.6% | 15,483 | 27.5% | LD |
| Adams, J | Lab | 8,347 | 16.2% | +7.6% | 4,883 | 8.7% | Lab |
| John, N | Ref | 2,313 | 4.5% | | 1,175 | 2.1% | Other |
| Cross, T P | UK Ind | 1,029 | 2.0% | | | | |
| C to LD notional swing 9.6% | | 51,442 | | C maj 7,713 15.0% | 56,303 | | C maj 19,279 34.2% |

**PETER BOTTOMLEY,** b July 30, 1944. Economist. MP for Eltham 1983-97, for Woolwich 1975-83. Min for Agriculture and Environment in N Ireland 1989-90; Under Sec for Transport 1986-89; for Employment 1984-86. Member, transport select cttee 1992-97; unopposed Bills panel 1992-97; joint parly ecclesiastical cttee; C backbench media cttee; all-party film industry parly group; parenting matters group; race and community group. Unpaid adviser to International Fund for Animal Welfare; chair, C of E Children's Society, 1983-84; trustee, Christian Aid, 1978-84. Ed mixed comprehensive school in Washington DC; Westminster

School; Trinity Coll, Cambridge. His wife, Virginia, was Heritage Sec in the last Gvt and held Surrey SW for C 1997.
**CHRISTOPHER HARE,** b Jan 30, 1962. History lecturer. West Sussex county cllr. Runs his own business, Southern Heritage. Member, Stop Trunk Roads Over Protected Downs. Ed Durrington HS; Brighton Poly.
**JOHN ADAMS,** b Feb 17, 1969. Bank of England analyst. Member, exec cttee of Lab Finance and Industry Group; Young Fabian Soc; Bifu. Ed Cranford Comm School, Middlesex; Univ Coll of Wales, Swansea.

| WREKIN, THE | | 89.6% change | | | Lab win | |
|---|---|---|---|---|---|---|
| Electorate % Turnout | | 59,126 | 76.6% | **1997** | 58,103 | 83.8% | **1992** |
| Bradley, P | Lab | 21,243 | 46.9% | +15.0% | 23,259 | 47.8% | C |
| Bruinvels, P N E | C | 18,218 | 40.2% | -7.5% | 15,539 | 31.9% | Lab |
| Jenkins, I C | LD | 5,807 | 12.8% | -6.5% | 9,391 | 19.3% | LD |
| | | | | | 489 | 1.0% | Grn |
| C to Lab notional swing 11.3% | | 45,268 | | Lab maj 3,025 6.7% | 48,678 | | C maj 7,720 15.9% |

**PETER BRADLEY,** b April 12, 1953. Director of public affairs consultancy. Westminster city cllr 1986-96 (dep Lab group leader 1990-96). Member MSF; SERA. Ed Abingdon School; Sussex Univ; Occidental Coll, Los Angeles.
**PETER BRUINVELS,** b March 30, 1950. Broadcaster, journalist, barrister, managing director of news and media companies. MP for Leicester E 1983-87. Member, C backbench ed cttee, 1985-87; joint vice-chair, C urban and new towns affairs cttee, 1984-87. Dir, Radio Mercury and Allied Radio, 1994- . Member, General Synod of C of E 1985- ; social security appeals tribunal 1994- ; child

support appeals tribunal 1995- . Inspector, denominational church schools, Ofsted, 1994- ; Church Commissioner 1992- . Promoted Crossbows Act 1987. Freeman, City of London. Ed St John's School, Leatherhead; London Univ; Council of Legal Education.
**IAN JENKINS,** b Jan 10, 1951. Sales manager. Contested Dudley E 1992. Ex-chair, Wolverhampton NE LDs, and of Wrekin Libs. Member, MSF; Camra; Railway Development Soc. Ed King Henry VIII GS, Abergavenny; Wolverhampton Poly.

| WREXHAM | | 32.1% change | | | | Lab win |
|---|---|---|---|---|---|---|
| Electorate % Turnout | | 50,741 | 71.8% | **1997** | 51,318 | 78.8% | **1992** |
| Marek, Dr J | Lab | 20,450 | 56.1% | +6.2% | 20,191 | 50.0% | Lab |
| Andrew, S J | C | 8,688 | 23.9% | -8.6% | 13,101 | 32.4% | C |
| Thomas, A | LD | 4,833 | 13.3% | -1.7% | 6,054 | 15.0% | LD |
| Cronk, J | Ref | 1,195 | 3.3% | | 1,075 | 2.7% | PC |
| Plant, K | PC | 1,170 | 3.2% | +0.6% | | | |
| Low, N | NLP | 86 | 0.2% | | | | |
| C to Lab notional swing 7.4% | | 36,422 | Lab maj 11,762 | | 40,421 | Lab maj 7,090 | |
| | | | 32.3% | | | 17.5% | |

**JOHN MAREK**, b Dec 24, 1940. MP for this seat since 1983; contested Ludlow Oct 1974. Lab spokesman on economic affairs, Treasury and Civil Service 1987-92; frontbench DHSS team health spokesman 1985-87. Member, select cttee on Welsh affairs 1983-86; PAC 1985. Chair, all-party aviation group, 1989-90. Ceredigion district cllr 1979-83. Lecturer in applied maths, Univ Coll of Wales, Aberystwyth, 1966-83. Fellow, Industry and Parliament Trust. Ed Chatham House GS; King's Coll, London.

**STUART ANDREW**, b Nov 25, 1971. Organiser, British Heart Foundation, since 1994. DSS official 1992-94. Wrexham Maelor county borough cllr 1995- . Chair, Welsh YCs, 1991-93; N Wales Euro council 1993. Freeman, City of Chester.
**ANDREW THOMAS**, b Oct 18, 1965. Barrister. Contested this seat 1992. Ed Darland Comp; Yale Sixth-Form Coll, Wrexham; Peterhouse, Cambridge; Inns of Court. Son of Martin Thomas, QC, who contested this seat for L/All 1987.

| WYCOMBE | | 3.9% change | | | | C win |
|---|---|---|---|---|---|---|
| Electorate % Turnout | | 73,589 | 71.1% | **1997** | 72,794 | 77.5% | **1992** |
| +Whitney, Sir Ray | C | 20,890 | 39.9% | -13.3% | 30,040 | 53.2% | C |
| Bryant, C | Lab | 18,520 | 35.4% | +14.0% | 12,982 | 23.0% | LD |
| Bensilum, P | LD | 9,678 | 18.5% | -4.5% | 12,096 | 21.4% | Lab |
| Fulford, A | Ref | 2,394 | 4.6% | | 683 | 1.2% | Grn |
| Laker, J | Green | 716 | 1.4% | | 447 | 0.8% | Soc Dem |
| Heath, M | NLP | 121 | 0.2% | -0.1% | 167 | 0.3% | NLP |
| C to Lab notional swing 13.6% | | 52,319 | C maj 2,370 | | 56,415 | C maj 17,058 | |
| | | | 4.5% | | | 30.2% | |

**SIR RAY WHITNEY**, b Nov 28, 1930. Former diplomat. MP for Wycombe from 1978 by-election. Under Sec for Health, DHSS, 1985-86; for Social Security 1984-85; for Foreign and Commonwealth Affairs 1983-84. Member, PAC 1981-83; C foreign and Commonwealth affairs cttee, 1981-83; C backbench employment cttee, 1980-83. Chair, all-party British-Latin American parly group 1987- ; cable and satellite TV group; hospice group. Chair, Cable Corporation; Positive European Group 1993- ; Council for Defence Information 1987- ; Mountbatten Community Trust 1987- . Dep High Commissioner and Economic Counsellor,

Dacca, 1973-76; head of information research dept and overseas information dept, FCO, 1976-78. Ed Wellingborough School; Sandhurst; London Univ; Australian Nat Univ, Canberra.
**CHRIS BRYANT**, b Jan 11, 1962. C of E priest, writer, charity worker. Hackney cllr 1993- . Chair, Christian Socialist Movement. Member, Fabian Soc; Co-op Party; MSF. Ed Cheltenham Coll; Mansfield Coll, Oxford; Rippon Coll, Wimbledon.
**PAUL BENSILUM**, b Aug 19, 1971. Analytical chemist. LD party officer. Poet, and organiser of annual Dr Who conventions. Ed Clacton County HS.

| WYRE FOREST | | 2.7% change | | | | Lab win |
|---|---|---|---|---|---|---|
| Electorate % Turnout | | 73,063 | 75.4% | **1997** | 71,767 | 90.3% | **1992** |
| Lock, D | Lab | 26,843 | 48.8% | +20.4% | 27,999 | 47.5% | C |
| +Coombs, A | C | 19,897 | 36.1% | -7.1% | 18,414 | 31.2% | Lab |
| Cropp, D | LD | 4,377 | 8.0% | -20.5% | 12,551 | 21.3% | LD |
| Till, W | Ref | 1,956 | 3.6% | | | | |
| Harvey, C | Lib | 1,670 | 3.0% | | | | |
| Millington, J | UK Ind | 312 | 0.6% | | | | |
| C to Lab notional swing 13.7% | | 55,055 | Lab maj 6,946 | | 58,964 | C maj 9,585 | |
| | | | 12.6% | | | 16.3% | |

**DAVID LOCK**, b May 2, 1960. Barrister, legal adviser to Lab Party. Wyre Forest district cllr. Member Amnesty; Oxfam; Soc of Lab Lawyers. Ed Surbiton GS; St Peter's and Merrow Comp; Woking Sixth-Form Coll; Jesus Coll, Cambridge; Central London Poly; Inns of Court School of Law.
**ANTHONY COOMBS**, b Nov 18, 1952. MP for this seat 1987-97. Asst gvt whip 1996-97; PPS to David Mellor and then Gillian Shephard from 1989. Chair, all-party cable and satellite TV group; vice-chair,

human rights group, 1993-96; joint vice-chair, social science and policy group, 1994-96. Parly consultant, Nat Bed Federation, until 1996. Dir, Grevayne Properties Ltd, 1972-96; ex-dir of several Midlands-based companies, inc S&U Stores. Ed Bilton Grange School; Charterhouse; Worcester Coll, Oxford.
**DAVID CROPP**, b Aug 16, 1946. Head of special education unit. Contested Bromsgrove 1987, Birmingham Northfield 1992. Ed Reading School; Birmingham and Warwick Univs.

| WYTHENSHAWE & SALE EAST | | 47.8% change | | | | | Lab win |
|---|---|---|---|---|---|---|---|
| Electorate % Turnout | | 71,986 | 63.3% | **1997** | 75,738 | 71.8% | **1992** |
| **Goggins, P** | Lab | **26,448** | **58.1%** | +8.6% | **26,935** | **49.5%** | Lab |
| Fleming, P | C | 11,429 | 25.1% | -9.8% | 18,977 | 34.9% | C |
| Tucker, Ms V | LD | 5,639 | 12.4% | -2.1% | 7,869 | 14.5% | LD |
| Stanyer, B | Ref | 1,060 | 2.3% | | 600 | 1.1% | Other |
| Flannery, J | Soc Lab | 957 | 2.1% | | | | |
| C to Lab notional swing 9.2% | | 45,533 | Lab maj 15,019 33.0% | | 54,381 | Lab maj 7,958 14.6% | |

**PAUL GOGGINS,** b Oct 16, 1953. National director, Church Action on Poverty; ex-social worker. Salford district cllr 1990- . Chair, UK Poverty Coalition, 1996. Member, Oxfam; Greenpeace; TGWU; Ed St Bede's, Manchester; Manchester Poly.
**PAUL FLEMING,** b 1962. Aviation security officer at Manchester Airport; previously served as tank commander and communications specialist, 4th Royal Tank Regt. Vice-chair, new Wythenshawe and Sale East C assoc, 1995. Ed Bramhall HS; Salford Univ.
**VANESSA TUCKER,** b May 17, 1960. Secondary teacher. Member, Greenpeace; WWF; NUT. Ed Colston's, Bristol; Goffs Oak School, Herts; St John's Coll, York; Avery Hill Coll, London; OU.

| YEOVIL | | 1.0% change | | | | | LD win |
|---|---|---|---|---|---|---|---|
| Electorate % Turnout | | 74,165 | 72.9% | **1997** | 72,802 | 81.4% | **1992** |
| **+Ashdown, P** | LD | **26,349** | **48.7%** | -2.9% | **30,634** | **51.7%** | LD |
| Cambrook, N | C | 14,946 | 27.7% | -9.3% | 21,890 | 36.9% | C |
| Conway, P J | Lab | 8,053 | 14.9% | +5.3% | 5,702 | 9.6% | Lab |
| Beveridge, J | Ref | 3,574 | 6.6% | | 609 | 1.0% | Grn |
| Taylor, D | Green | 728 | 1.3% | | 370 | 0.6% | Loony |
| Archer, J | Musician | 306 | 0.6% | | 66 | 0.1% | APAKBI |
| Hudson, C | Dream | 97 | 0.2% | | | | |
| C to LD notional swing 3.2% | | 54,053 | LD maj 11,403 21.1% | | 59,271 | LD maj 8,744 14.8% | |

**PADDY ASHDOWN,** b Feb 27, 1941. Leader of the Liberal Democrats since 1988, former Royal Marine. Won this seat 1983, contested it 1979. LD spokesman on N Ireland 1988-90; Lib and then LD spokesman on educ and science 1987-88; Lib spokesman on trade and industry 1983-87. Capt in Royal Marines 1959-71, served with Commando units and Special Boat Service in Far East. Qualified as Chinese (Mandarin) interpreter at MoD Chinese Language School, Hong Kong. First Sec to UK mission to UN in Geneva 1971-76. Commercial manager's dept, Westland Helicopters, 1976-78; senior manager, Morlands, Yeovil, 1978-81. Local gvt officer, Dorset County Council, 1981-83. Ed Bedford School; MoD Chinese Language School, Hong Kong.
**NICHOLAS CAMBROOK,** b Jan 31, 1951. Financial adviser, associate with Allied Dunbar. South Somerset district cllr 1992-95. Worked for Plessey Electronic Systems and then in family business dealing with residential property rentals. Had short service commission in RN. Ed Pangbourne Coll; Britannia Royal Naval Coll, Dartmouth.
**JOE CONWAY,** b May 2, 1953. Engineer, Westland Helicopters. Yeovil town cllr; S Somerset district cllr. Senior TGWU shop steward. Ed Reckleford School, Yeovil; Grass Royal School, Yeovil.

| YNYS MON | | | | | | | PC hold |
|---|---|---|---|---|---|---|---|
| Electorate % Turnout | | 52,952 | 75.4% | **1997** | 53,412 | 80.6% | **1992** |
| ***Jones, I** | PC | **15,756** | **39.5%** | +2.3% | **15,984** | **37.1%** | PC |
| Edwards, O | Lab | 13,275 | 33.2% | +9.7% | 14,878 | 34.6% | C |
| Owen, G | C | 8,569 | 21.5% | -13.1% | 10,126 | 23.5% | Lab |
| Burnham, D | LD | 1,537 | 3.8% | -0.5% | 1,891 | 4.4% | LD |
| Gray Morris, H | Ref | 793 | 2.0% | | 182 | 0.4% | NLP |
| PC to Lab swing 3.7% | | 39,930 | PC maj 2,481 6.2% | | 43,061 | PC maj 1,106 2.6% | |

**IEUAN WYN JONES,** b May 22, 1949. Solicitor. Won this seat 1987; contested it 1983, W Denbigh in 1979 and Oct 1974, and North Wales in 1979 Euro elections. Member, select cttees on agriculture, 1992-97; Welsh affairs 1990-92. Joint vice-chair, all-party Friends of Croatia group, 1991-97. Nat chair, PC, 1990-92 and 1980-82; vice-chair 1975-79. Royal Coll of Nursing parly panel. Partner in solicitors' practice 1974-87. Ed Pontardawe GS, Glamorgan; Bala Comp; Liverpool Poly.
**OWEN EDWARDS,** b Aug 9, 1970. Barrister. Ed Yale Sixth-Form Coll; Univ of Wales Coll, Cardiff; Inns of Court School of Law. Son of Will Edwards, Lab MP for Merioneth 1966-74.
**GWILYM OWEN,** b Dec 13, 1938. Business consultant; divisional dir, Midland Bank Wales. Contested Clwyd SW 1992. Member, Welsh Language Board; Sec of State for Wales advisory group. Hon treas, Celtic film and TV assoc. Ed Tywyn GS.
**DEREK BURNHAM.** Business consultant. Ex-dir, NE Wales, Welsh Development Agency. Ed Oxford Univ (football Blue). Married to Eleanor Burnham, LD candidate for Alyn & Deeside.

| YORK, CITY OF | | | | | **Lab hold** | | |
|---|---|---|---|---|---|---|---|
| Electorate % Turnout | | 79,383 | 73.5% | **1997** | 79,242 | 81.0% | **1992** |
| *Bayley, H | Lab | 34,956 | 59.9% | +10.8% | 31,525 | 49.1% | Lab |
| Mallett, S | C | 14,433 | 24.7% | -14.5% | 25,183 | 39.2% | C |
| Waller, A | LD | 6,537 | 11.2% | +0.6% | 6,811 | 10.6% | LD |
| Sheppard, J | Ref | 1,083 | 1.9% | | 594 | 0.9% | Grn |
| Hill, M | Green | 880 | 1.5% | | 54 | 0.1% | NLP |
| Wegener, E G | UK Ind | 319 | 0.5% | | | | |
| Lightfoot, A | Ch Nat | 137 | 0.2% | | | | |
| C to Lab swing 12.6% | | 58,345 | | Lab maj 20,523 | 64,167 | | Lab maj 6,342 |
| | | | | 35.2% | | | 9.9% |

**HUGH BAYLEY**, b Jan 9, 1952. Won York for Labour 1992; contested it 1987. Member, health select cttee, 1992-97; vice-chair, PLP overseas development cttee; joint sec, all-party tourism cttee; campaign officer, Yorkshire group of Lab MPs. Camden cllr 1980-86. Research fellow in health economics, York Univ, 1987-92, and social policy lecturer, 1986-87. Nat officer, Nalgo, 1977-82. Founder and gen sec, International Broadcasting Trust, 1982-86. Former TV producer. Member, York HA, 1988-90; Friends of the Earth; Council for Voluntary Service; Anti-Apartheid Movement. Ed Haileybury; Bristol and York Univs.

**SIMON MALLETT,** b 1962. Barrister. Director, Ayre Mallett, family investment co. Member, Inner Temple Bar liaison cttee, 1992-94, and educ cttee 1993-94; Soc of C Lawyers; Tory Reform Group. Ed Shrewsbury School; Sheffield Univ; Inns of Court School of Law. **ANDREW WALLER,** b July 29, 1969. Trainee accountant with Intercity East Coast Ltd. York city cllr 1994-96 (group sec/whip). Chair, York LDs, 1993-96. Ex-scientist with Nestlé-Rowntree, specialising in Smarties. Member, Friends of the Earth; Voting Reform Group. Ed Hustler Comp, Middlesbrough; Acklam Sixth-Form Coll; Imperial Coll, London.

| YORKSHIRE EAST | | 70.9% change | | | | | **C win** |
|---|---|---|---|---|---|---|---|
| Electorate % Turnout | | 69,409 | 70.6% | **1997** | 67,185 | 75.7% | **1992** |
| +Townend, J E | C | 20,904 | 42.7% | -7.9% | 25,759 | 50.6% | C |
| Male, I | Lab | 17,567 | 35.9% | +9.4% | 13,487 | 26.5% | Lab |
| Leadley, D | LD | 9,070 | 18.5% | -4.3% | 11,629 | 22.9% | LD |
| Allerston, R | Soc Dem | 1,049 | 2.1% | | | | |
| Cooper, M | Nat Dem | 381 | 0.8% | | | | |
| C to Lab notional swing 8.7% | | 48,971 | | C maj 3,337 | 50,875 | | C maj 12,272 |
| | | | | 6.8% | | | 24.1% |

**JOHN TOWNEND**, b June 12, 1934. Wine merchant and chartered accountant. MP for Bridlington 1979-97; contested Hull N 1970. Member, Treasury and Civil Service select cttee, 1983-92; Commons catering cttee 1991- ; employment select cttee 1980-81. Chair, 92 Group of C MPs, 1996- . Member, C backbench finance cttee 1993- ; UK cttee, Euro Research Group. Hull city cllr 1966-74; Humberside county cllr 1973-79; chair, Humber Bridge Board

1969-71. Lloyd's underwriter. Vice-chair, Surrey Building Soc, 1984-93. Ed Hymers Coll, Hull.
**IAN MALE**, b Sept 26, 1944. Coach painter. Member of community health council. JP. Ed Hull Univ.
**DAVID LEADLEY**, b Oct 16, 1936. Farmer, partner in company marketing agric products. Ryedale district cllr 1995- . Previously farmed in New Zealand. Ed Scarcroft, York.

# ABBREVIATIONS

The following abbreviations have been used in the biographies of MPs and candidates:

| | |
|---|---|
| ABA | Amateur Boxing Association |
| Acad | Academy |
| ACC | Association of County Councils |
| ACTS | Administrative, Clerical & Technical Staff (section of TGWU) |
| ACTT | Association of Cinematograph, Television and Allied Technicians |
| AEEU | Amalgamated Engineering and Electrical Union |
| AEU | Amalgamated Engineering Union |
| AHA | Area Health Authority |
| ALC | Association of Liberal Councillors |
| ALDC | Association of LD Councillors |
| AMA | Association of Metropolitan Authorities |
| AMMA | Assistant Masters & Mistresses Association |
| Apex | Association of Professional Executive Clerical and Computer Staff |
| APCT | Association of Polytechnic and College Teachers |
| APT | Association of Polytechnic Teachers |
| ASH | Action on Smoking and Health |
| ASLDC | Association of Social and Liberal Democratic Councillors |
| Aslef | Associated Society of Locomotive Engineers and Firemen |
| Assoc | Association |
| Asst | Assistant |
| ASTMS | Association of Scientific, Technical and Managerial Staffs (now part of MSF) |
| ATL | Association of Teachers and Lecturers |
| ATTI | Association of Teachers in Technical Institutions |
| AUEW/TASS | Amalgamated Union of Engineering Workers (Technical Administrative and Supervisory Section) |
| AUT | Association of University Teachers |
| B | Born |
| BACM | British Association of Colliery Management |
| BEC | Building Employers' Confederation |
| Bifu | Banking Insurance and Finance Union |
| BMA | British Medical Association |
| BR | British Rail |
| C | Conservative |
| CAB | Citizens Advice Bureau |
| Camra | Campaign for Real Ale |
| CBI | Confederation of British Industry |
| CCC | County Cricket Club |
| CFE | College of Further Education |
| CHC | Community Health Council |
| CLA | Country Landowners' Association |
| Cllr | Councillor |
| CLP | Constituency Labour Party |
| CND | Campaign for Nuclear Disarmament |
| Co | Company |
| Cohse | Confederation of Health Service Employees |
| Coll | College |
| Coll of FE | College of Further Education |
| Comp | Comprehensive school |
| Confed | Confederation |
| Co-op | Co-operative Party |
| Corp | Corporation |
| Cosla | Convention of Scottish local authorities |
| CPA | Commonwealth Parliamentary Association |
| CPC | Conservative Political Centre |
| CPRE | Council for the Protection of Rural England |

| | |
|---|---|
| CPSA | Civil and Public Service Association |
| CSD | Council for Social Democracy |
| Cttee | Committee |
| CWU | Communication Workers Union |
| Dept | Department |
| DHA | District health authority |
| DHSS | Department of Health and Social Security |
| Dir | Director |
| Div | Division |
| DLP | Divisional Labour Party |
| DSS | Department of Social Security |
| DTI | Department of Trade and Industry |
| E | East |
| EC | European Community |
| Ed | Education/educated |
| EEC | European Economic Community |
| EETPU | Electrical, Electronic, Telecommunication and Plumbing Union |
| EIS | Educational Institute of Scotland |
| EPEA | Electrical Power Engineers Association |
| EU | European Union |
| Euro | European |
| Exec | Executive |
| FBU | Fire Brigades Union |
| FCO | Foreign and Commonwealth Office |
| FE | Further Education |
| Fed | Federation |
| FIMechE | Fellow, Institute of Mechanical Engineers |
| FoC | Father (chairman) of Chapel (branch), NUJ |
| FRS | Fellow of the Royal Society |
| FRSA | Fellow of the Royal Society of Arts |
| FRSC | Fellow, Royal Society of Chemistry |
| GLC | Greater London Council |
| GMB | General, Municipal, Boilermakers and Allied Trades Union |
| GMC | General management committee |
| Gvt | Government |
| GPMU | Graphical, Paper and Media Union |
| GS | Grammar school |
| HA | Health Authority |
| Hosp | Hospital |
| HS | High school |
| ILEA | Inner London Education Authority |
| Info | Information |
| Inst | Institute |
| IoD | Institute of Directors |
| IoJ | Institute of Journalists |
| IPCS | Institution of Professional Civil Servants |
| IPU | Interparliamentary Union |
| IRSF | Inland Revenue Staff Federation |
| ISTC | Iron and Steel Trades Confederation |
| IT | Information Technology |
| JP | Justice of the Peace |
| Lib | Liberal |
| L/All | Liberal Alliance |
| Lab | Labour |
| Lancs | Lancashire |
| LBC | London Broadcasting Company |
| Lincs | Lincolnshire |
| LD | Liberal Democrat |
| LSE | London School of Economics |
| MATSA | Managerial Administrative Technical Staff Association |
| MBC | Metropolitan Borough Council |
| MDC | Metropolitan District Council |
| Mencap | Royal Society for Mentally Handicapped Children & Adults |
| MEP | Member of the European Parliament |
| Min | Minister, ministry |
| MSF | Manufacturing, Science and Finance Union |
| N | North |
| Nacods | National Association of Colliery Overmen, Deputies and Shotfirers |
| NAHT | National Association of Head Teachers |

# ABBREVIATIONS

| | | | |
|---|---|---|---|
| **Nalgo** | National and Local Government Officers' Association | **SW** | South West |
| **NASUWT** | National Association of Schoolmasters and Union of Women Teachers | **TA** | Territorial Army |
| | | **Tech** | Technical or Technology |
| **Nat** | National | **TGWU** | Transport and General Workers' Union |
| **NATFHE** | National Association of Teachers in Further and Higher Education | **Treas** | Treasurer |
| | | **TSSA** | Transport Salaried Staffs Association |
| **NCB** | National Coal Board | **TV** | Television |
| **NCER** | National Council for Electoral Reform | **UA** | Unitary Authority |
| **NCU** | National Communications Union | **Ucatt** | Union of Construction, Allied Trades and Technicians |
| **NE** | North East | | |
| **NEC** | National Executive Committee | **UCW** | Union of Communication Workers |
| **NFBTE** | National Federation of Building Trades Employers | **UDC** | Urban District Council/Urban Development Corporation |
| **NFU** | National Farmers' Union | **UMIST** | University of Manchester Institute of Science and Technology |
| **NI** | Northern Ireland | | |
| **NLVA** | National Licensed Victuallers' Association | **UNA** | United Nations Association |
| | | **Univ** | University |
| **NLYL** | National League of Young Liberals | **Usdaw** | Union of Shop, Distributive and Allied Workers |
| **Notts** | Nottinghamshire | | |
| **NSPCC** | National Society for the Prevention of Cruelty to Children | **W** | West |
| | | **WEA** | Workers Educational Association |
| **NUJ** | National Union of Journalists | **WEU** | Western European Union |
| **NUM** | National Union of Mineworkers | **Worcs** | Worcestershire |
| **Numast** | National Union of Marine, Aviation and Shipping Transport Officers | **WRVS** | Women's Royal Voluntary Service |
| | | **WWF** | World Wide Fund for Nature |
| **Nupe** | National Union of Public Employees | **YCs** | Young Conservatives |
| **NUR** | National Union of Railwaymen (now RMT) | **YHA** | Youth Hostels Association |
| | | **YLs** | Young Liberals |
| **NUS** | National Union of Seamen/National Union of Students | **Yorks** | Yorkshire |
| **NUT** | National Union of Teachers | | |
| **NW** | North West | | |
| **OU** | Open University | | |
| **PAC** | Public Accounts Committee | | |
| **Parly** | Parliamentary | | |
| **PAT** | Professional Association of Teachers | | |
| **PLP** | Parliamentary Labour Party | | |
| **Poly** | Polytechnic | | |
| **PPS** | Parliamentary Private Secretary | | |
| **Pres** | President | | |
| **RCN** | Royal College of Nursing | | |
| **RCVS** | Royal College of Veterinary Surgeons | | |
| **RDC** | Rural District Council | | |
| **Reg** | Regional | | |
| **Rep** | Representative | | |
| **Res** | Reserve | | |
| **RHA** | Regional Health Authority | | |
| **RIBA** | Royal Institute of British Architects | | |
| **RMA** | Royal Military Academy | | |
| **RMT** | Rail, Maritime and Transport Union | | |
| **RNC** | Royal Naval College | | |
| **RNR** | Royal Naval Reserve | | |
| **RSPB** | Royal Society for the Protection of Birds | | |
| **RSPCA** | Royal Society for the Prevention of Cruelty to Animals | | |
| **S** | South | | |
| **SD** | Social Democrat | | |
| **SDLP** | Social Democratic and Labour Party | | |
| **SDP** | Social Democratic Party | | |
| **SE** | South East | | |
| **SEA** | Socialist Educational Association | | |
| **Sec** | Secretary/Secondary school | | |
| **Sec Mod** | Secondary modern school | | |
| **SERA** | Socialist Environment and Resources Association | | |
| **SFHEA** | Scottish Further and Higher Education Association | | |
| **SHA** | Secondary Heads Association/Special Health Authority | | |
| **SLDP** | Social and Liberal Democratic Party | | |
| **SLP** | Scottish Liberal Party | | |
| **Soc** | Society/Socialist | | |
| **SSAFA** | Soldiers', Sailors', and Airmen's Families Association | | |
| **SSTA** | Scottish Secondary Teachers Association | | |

# By-elections survey
# BLUE IS NOT THE COLOUR

### By Alan H. Wood

**T**ORY BY-ELECTION defeats during the 1992-97 Parliament and three defections to other parties steadily reduced, and then wiped out, the Government's majority. The situation for John Major was made worse when for a considerable time nine Conservative MPs were without the whip after disagreements over Europe, and when the Ulster Unionists withdrew direct support after publication of the Anglo-Irish framework document in 1995.

When Iain Mills, Tory MP for Meriden, died in January 1997 the Government went into a minority of one, but the death a few days later of Martin Redmond, Labour MP for Don Valley, left the Tories and the Opposition parties level. However, on February 27, 1997, Labour swept to victory in the Wirral South by-election on a Conservative to Labour swing of 17.2 per cent. And so the Tories went into the election as a minority Government, although they had regained the support of the Ulster Unionists, thus staving off the tabling of a no-confidence motion.

In Scotland in late June 1994, Helen Liddell scraped into the Monklands East seat, held formerly by the late John Smith, the Labour leader, with a near-16,000 majority in 1992. That was cut to only a 1,640 majority over the SNP, a 19.2 swing from Labour. The campaign was dominated by SNP allegations of nepotism, corruption and sectarianism within the local Labour-run council.

The by-elections were all a tale of woe for the Tories, who lost Newbury, Christchurch, Eastleigh and Littleborough & Saddleworth to the Liberal Democrats; Dudley West, Staffordshire South East and Wirral South to Labour; and Perth & Kinross to the SNP.

At the general election, Christopher Chope, former Roads and Traffic Minister, regained Christchurch for the Tories from the Liberal Democrat Diana Maddock, and Labour's Phil Woolas won Oldham East & Mexborough, defeating the Liberal Democrat Chris Davies, the Littleborough & Saddleworth by-election winner.

The following by-elections took place in the 1992-97 Parliament:

## 1993

### MAY 6: NEWBURY
Caused by death of Judith Chaplin:
**Total vote 57,773 (71.3%)**
**D Rendel (LD) 37,590 (65.1%)**
J Davidson (C) 15,535 (26.9%); S Billcliffe (Lab) 1,151 (2.0%); A Sked (Anti-Maastricht Anti-Fed League) 601; A Bannon (Con candidate) 561; S Martin (Commoners Party Movement) 435; Lord David Sutch (Loony) 432; J Wallis (Green) 341; R Marler (Ref) 338; J Browne (Con Party Rebel) 267; Ms L St Clair (Corrective Party) 170; W Board (Maastricht Referendum for Britain) 84; M Grenville (Natural Law Party) 60; J Day (People and Pensioners Party) 49; C Palmer (21st Century Party) 40; M Grbin (Defence of Children's Humanity Bosnia) 33; A Page (SDP) 33; Ms A Murphy (Communist) 33; M Stone (Give the Royal Billions to Schools) 21 (Others 6.1%). LD maj 22,055 (38.2%). LD gain from C. C to LD swing 28.4%.

### JULY 29: CHRISTCHURCH
Caused by death of Robert Adley:
**Total vote 53,370 (74.2%)**
**Mrs D Maddock (LD) 33,164 (62.2%)**
R Haywood (C) 16,737 (31.4%); N Linkley (Lab) 1,453 (2.7%); A Sked (Anti-Maastricht Anti-Fed League) 878; Lord David Sutch (Loony) 404; A Bannon (Con candidate) 357; P Newman (Sack Graham Taylor) 80; T B Jackson (Buy Daily Sport) 67; P Hollyman (Save NHS) 60; J Crockard (Highlander IV Wed Prom Night) 48; N Griffiths (NLP) 45; M Belcher (Ian for King) 23; K Fitzhugh (Alfred Chicken) 18; J Walley (Rainbow All Coalition) 16 (Others 3.7%). LD maj 16,427 (30.8%). LD gain from C. C to LD swing 35.4%.

## 1994

### MAY 5: ROTHERHAM
Caused by death of James Boyce:
**Total vote: 26,806 (43.7%)**
**D MacShane (Lab) 14,912 (55.6%)**
D Wildgoose (LD) 7,958 (29.7%); N Gibb (C) 2,649 (9.9%); Lord David Sutch (Loony) 1,114; K Laycock (NLP) 173 (Others 4.8%). Lab maj 6,954 (25.9%). No change. C to Lab swing 2.8%.

### JUNE 9: BARKING
Caused by death of Jo Richardson:
**Total vote: 19,017 (38.3%)**
**Mrs M Hodge (Lab) 13,704 (72.1%)**
G White (LD) 2,290 (12.0%); Ms T May (C) 1,976 (10.4%); G Needs (NF) 551; G Batten (UKI) 406; Ms H Butensky (NLP) 90 (Others 5.5%). Lab maj 11,414 (60.1%). No change. C to Lab swing 22.0%.

### JUNE 9: BRADFORD SOUTH
Caused by death of Robert Cryer:
**Total vote 30,753 (44.2%)**
**G Sutcliffe (Lab) 17,014 (55.3%)**
Helen Wright (LD) 7,350 (23.9%); R Farley (C) 5,475 (17.8%); Lord David Sutch (Loony) 727; K Laycock (NLP) 187 (Others 3.0%).

Lab maj 9,664 (31.4%). No change.
C to Lab swing 14.15%.

---

## JUNE 9: DAGENHAM
Caused by resignation of Bryan Gould:
**Total vote 21,492 (37.0%)**
**Mrs J Church (Lab) 15,474 (72.0%)**
J Fairre (C) 2,130 (9.9%); P Dunphy (LD) 1,804 (8.4%); J Tyndall (BNP) 1,511; P Compobassi (UKI) 457; M Leighton (NLP) 116 (Others 0.7%). Lab maj 13,344 (62.1%). No change. C to Lab swing 23.1%.

---

## JUNE 9: EASTLEIGH
Caused by death of Stephen Milligan:
**Total vote 55,262 (58.7%)**
**D Chidgey (LD) 24,473 (44.3%)**
Ms M Birks (Lab) 15,234 (27.6%); S Reid (C) 13,675 (24.7%); N Farage (UKI) 952; Lord David Sutch (Loony) 783; P Warburton (NLP) 145 (Others 3.4%). LD maj 9,239 (16.7%). LD gain from C. C to LD swing 21.4%.

---

## JUNE 9: NEWHAM NORTH EAST
Caused by death of Ronald Leighton:
**Total vote 19,573 (34.8%)**
**S Timms (Lab) 14,668 (74.9%)**
P Hammond (C) 2,850 (14.6%); A Kellaway (LD) 821 (4.2%); A Scholefield (UKI) 509; J Homeless (House Homeless) 342; R Archer (NLP) 228; V Garman (Daily Sport) 155 (Others 6.3%). Lab maj 11,818 (60.3%). No change. C to Lab swing 16.3%.

---

## JUNE 30: MONKLANDS EAST
Caused by death of John Smith:
**Total vote 34,084 (70.0%)**
**Mrs H Liddell (Lab) 16,960 (49.8%)**
Ms K Ullrich (SNP) 15,320 (44.9%); S Gallagher (LD) 878 (2.3%); Ms S Bell (C) 799 (2.3%); A Bremner (Network against Criminal Justice Bill) 69; D Paterson (NLP) 58 (Others 0.6%). Lab maj 1,640 (4.9%). No change. Lab to SNP swing 19.2%.

---

## DEC 15: DUDLEY WEST
Caused by death of John Blackburn:
**Total vote 41,307 (47.0%)**
**I Pearson (Lab) 28,400 (68.8%)**
G Postles (C) 7,706 (18.7%); M Hadley (LD) 3,154 (7.6%); M R Lloyd (UKI) 590; A Carmichael (NF) 561; M S Hyde (L) 548; M H Nattrass (New Br) 146; Ms M Nicholson (Forest) 77; D Oldbury (NLP) 70; C R Palmer, Lord of Manton (21st Century Pty) 55 (Others 4.9%). Lab maj 20,694 (50.1%). Lab gain from C. C to Lab swing 29.1%.

---

## 1995

### FEB 16: ISLWYN
Caused by appointment of Neil Kinnock as a European Commissioner:
**Total vote 23,166 (45.4%)**
**D Touhig (Lab) 16,030 (69.2%)**
Ms J Davies (PC) 2,933 (12.7%); J Bushell (LD) 2,448 (10.6%); R Buckland (C) 913 (3.9%); Lord David Sutch (Loony) 506; H Hughes (UKI) 289; T Rees (NLP) 47 (Others 3.6%). Lab maj 13,097 (56.5%). Lab to PC swing 7.0%. No change.

---

### MAY 25: PERTH & KINROSS
Caused by death of Sir Nicholas Fairbairn:
**Total vote 41,948 (61.7%)**
**Ms R Cunningham (SNP) 16,931 (40.4%)**
D Alexander (Lab) 9,620 (23.0%); J Godfrey (C) 8,990 (21.4%); Ms V Linklater (LD) 4,952 (11.8%); Lord David Sutch (Loony) 586; Ms V Linacare (UKI) 504; R Harper (Green) 223; M Halford (Scots C) 88; G Black (NLP) 54 (Others 3.4%). SNP maj 7,311 (17.4%). SNP gain from C. C to SNP swing 11.55%.

---

### JUNE 15: DOWN NORTH
Caused by death of Sir James Kilfedder:
**Total vote 27,388 (38.6%)**
**R McCartney (UK Unionist) 10,124 (37.0%)**
R A McFarland (UUP) 7,232 (26.4%); Sir O Napier (All) 6,970 (25.4%); A Chambers (Ind U) 2,170 (7.9%); S Sexton (C) 583; M Brooks (Free Para Lee Clegg Now) 108; C Carter (Ulster's Ind Voice) 101; J Anderson (NLP) 100 (Others 3.3%). UKU maj 2,892 (10.6%). UKU gain from UPUP.

---

### JULY 27: LITTLEBOROUGH & SADDLEWORTH
Caused by death of Geoffrey Dickens.
**Total vote 42,137 (63.6%)**
**C Davies (LD) 16,231 (38.5%)**
P Woolas (Lab) 14,238 (33.8%); J Hudson (C) 9,934 (23.6%); Lord David Sutch (Loony) 783; J Whitaker (UKI) 549; P Douglas (Con Party) 193; Mr Blobby (House Party) 105; A Pitts (Soc Party) 46; L McLaren (Old Lab: Probity of Imposed Candidates) 33; C Palmer (Lord of Manton 21st Century Party) 25 (Others 4.1%). LD maj 1,993 (4.7%). LD gain from C. C to LD swing 11.7%.

---

## 1996

### FEB 1: HEMSWORTH
Caused by death of Derek Enright:
**Total vote 21,993 (39.5%)**
**J Trickett (Lab) 15,817 (71.9%)**

---

N Hazell (C) 1,942 (8.8%); R Ridgway (LD) 1,516 (6.9%); Ms B Nixon (Soc Lab) 1,193 (5.4%); Lord David Sutch (Loony) 652; P Davies (UKI) 455; Ms P Alexander (Green) 157; M Thomas (Ind) 122; M Cooper (Nat Dem) 111; Ms D Leighton (NLP) 28 (Others 7.0%). Lab maj 13,875 (63.1%). No change. C to Lab swing 5.4%.

---

## APRIL 11: STAFFORDSHIRE SOUTH EAST
Caused by death of Sir David Lightbown:
**Total vote 43,497**
**B D Jenkins (Lab) 26,155 (60.1%)**
T D R James (C) 12,393 (28.5%); Ms J Davy (LD) 2,042 (4.7%); A L W Smith (UKI) 1,272; Lord David Sutch (Loony) 506; Ms S Edwards (Nat Dem) 358; S J Mountford (L) 332; L J Tucket (Churchill C) 123; News Bunny (Official News Bunny Party) 85; N A W Samuelson (Daily Loonylugs) 80; D J Lucas (NLP) 53; F J Sandy (Action against Crime) 53; A S Wood (Restoration of Death Penalty) 45 (Others 6.7%). Lab maj 13,762 (31.6%). Lab gain from C. C to Lab swing 22.1%.

---

## DEC 12: BARNSLEY EAST
Caused by death of Terry Patchett:
**Total vote 19,000 (35.6%)**
**J Ennis (Lab) 14,683 (77.3%)**
D Willis (LD) 1,602 (8.4%); Ms J Ellison (C) 1,299 (6.8%); K Capstick (Soc Lab) 949; N Tolstoy (UKI) 378; Ms J Hyland (Soc Equ) 89 (Others 7.5%). Lab maj 13,181 (68.9%). No change. C to Lab swing 9.2%.

---

## 1997

### FEB 27: WIRRAL SOUTH
Caused by death of Barry Porter:
**Total vote 43,293 (73.0%)**
**B Chapman (Lab) 22,767 (52.59%)**
L Byrom (C) 14,879 (34.37%); Ms F Clucas (LD) 4,357 (10.06%); R North (UKI) 410; H Bence (Company director) 184; M Cullen (Soc Lab) 156; P Gott (Disillusioned Cs - Campaign for Change) 148; R Taylor (Ind) 132; S Anthony (Stop Cs Poncing on Tobacco Companies) 124; G Mead (NLP) 52; C Palmer (21st Century Ind Foresters) 44; F Asbury (Thalidomide Action Group UK) 40 (Others 2.98%). Lab maj 7,888 (18.22%). Lab gain from C. C to Lab swing 17.2%.

---

Two seats were vacant when the general election was called:

### MERIDEN
Caused by the death of Iain Mills
### DON VALLEY
Caused by the death of
Martin Redmond

# STATISTICS

# HOW THE NATION VOTED

| MAY 1997 | | Lab | C | LD | Nat | Other | Total |
|---|---|---|---|---|---|---|---|
| **ENGLAND** | | | | | | | |
| Electorate 36,462,327 | Votes | 11,348,623 | 8,780,896 | 4,678,061 | 0 | 1,253,361 | 26,060,941 |
| C to Lab swing % -10.7 | % of vote/Turnout % | 43.5 | 33.7 | 18.0 | 0.0 | 4.8 | 71.5 |
| | MPs | 328 | 165 | 34 | 0 | 2* | 529 |
| | Candidates | 527 | 528 | 527 | 0 | 1,363 | 2,945 |
| **SCOTLAND** | | | | | | | |
| Electorate 3,946,113 | Votes | 1,283,353 | 493,059 | 365,359 | 622,260 | 53,408 | 2,817,439 |
| C to Lab swing % -7.4 | % of vote/turnout | 45.6 | 17.5 | 13.0 | 22.1 | 1.9 | 71.4 |
| | MPs | 56 | 0 | 10 | 6 | 0 | 72 |
| | Candidates | 72 | 72 | 72 | 72 | 143 | 431 |
| **WALES** | | | | | | | |
| Electorate 2,200,611 | Votes | 885,935 | 317,127 | 200,020 | 161,030 | 54,932 | 1,619,044 |
| C to Lab swing % -7.1 | % of vote/turnout | 54.7 | 19.6 | 12.4 | 9.9 | 3.4 | 73.6 |
| | MPs | 34 | 0 | 2 | 4 | 0 | 40 |
| | Candidates | 40 | 40 | 40 | 40 | 63 | 223 |
| **NORTHERN IRELAND** | | | | | | | |
| Electorate 1,175,508 | Votes | 0.0 | 9,858 | 0.0 | 0.0 | 780.920 | 790,778 |
| | % of vote/turnout | 0 | 1.2 | 0 | 0 | 98.8 | 67.3 |
| | MPs | 0 | 0 | 0 | 0 | 18 | 18 |
| | Candidates | 0 | 8 | 0 | 0 | 117 | 125 |
| **UNITED KINGDOM** | | | | | | | |
| Electorate 43,784,559 | Votes | 13,517,911 | 9,600,940 | 5,243,440 | 783,290 | 2,142,621 | 31,287,702 |
| C to Lab swing % -10.0 | % of vote/turnout | 43.2 | 30.7 | 16.8 | 2.5 | 6.8 | 71.5 |
| | MPs | 418 | 165 | 46 | 10 | 20* | 659 |
| | Candidates | 639 | 648 | 639 | 112 | 1,686 | 3,724 |

| APRIL 1992 | | Lab | C | LD | Nat | Other | Total |
|---|---|---|---|---|---|---|---|
| **ENGLAND** | | | | | | | |
| Electorate 36,853,746 | Votes | 9,559,190 | 12,793,487 | 5,426,242 | 0 | 374,232 | 28,153,151 |
| C to Lab swing % -2.6% | % of vote/turnout | 34,.0 | 45.4 | 19.3 | 0.0 | 1.3 | 76.4 |
| | MPs | 196 | 324 | 9 | 0 | 0 | 529 |
| | Candidates | 529 | 529 | 529 | 0 | 684 | 2,271 |
| **SCOTLAND** | | | | | | | |
| Electorate 3,928,996 | Votes | 1,142,911 | 751,950 | 383,856 | 629,564 | 23,417 | 2,931,698 |
| C to Lab swing % +2.5% | % of vote/turnout | 39.0 | 25.6 | 13.1 | 21.5 | 0.8 | 74.6 |
| | MPs | 50 | 11 | 8 | 3 | 0 | 72 |
| | Candidates | 72 | 72 | 72 | 72 | 48 | 336 |
| **WALES** | | | | | | | |
| Electorate 2,227,984 | Votes | 865,663 | 499,677 | 217,454 | 154,390 | 11,590 | 1,748,774 |
| C to Lab swing % -2.7% | % of vote/turnout | 49.5 | 28.6 | 12.4 | 8.8 | 0.7 | 78.5 |
| | MPs | 27 | 8 | 1 | 4 | 0 | 40 |
| | Candidates | 40 | 40 | 40 | 37 | 30 | 187 |
| **NORTHERN IRELAND** | | | | | | | |
| Electorate 1,153,477 | Votes | 0 | 44,608 | 0 | 0 | 740,859 | 785,467 |
| | % of vote/turnout | 0.0 | 5.7 | 0.0 | 0.0 | 94.3 | 68.1 |
| | MPs | 0 | 0 | 0 | 0 | 18 | 18 |
| | Candidates | 0 | 11 | 0 | 0 | 94 | 105 |
| **UNITED KINGDOM** | | | | | | | |
| Electorate 44,164,203 | Votes | 11,567,764 | 14,089,722 | 6,027,552 | 783,954 | 1,150,098 | 33,619,090 |
| C to Lab swing % -1.9% | % of vote/turnout | 34.4 | 41.9 | 17.9 | 2.3 | 3.4 | 76.1 |
| | MPs | 273 | 343 | 18 | 7 | 18 | 659 |
| | Candidates | 641 | 652 | 641 | 109 | 856 | 2,899 |

* includes the Speaker

# METROPOLITAN AND COUNTY VOTING

## By Alan H. Wood

**THE TIMES** has calculated the following analyses of voting in the 1997 general election on May 1, 1997, in which 659 seats were contested compared with 651 in 1992. There are 529 parliamentary seats in England (compared with 524 in 1992), 72 in Scotland (72), 40 in Wales (38) and 18 in Northern Ireland (17).

Statistics are set out for the metropolitan areas and non-metropolitan counties (including two former metropolitan counties, Avon and Cleveland, which now have unitary authorities). Scotland has been analysed on a regional basis and Wales by county because, when the Boundary Commissions for Scotland and for Wales undertook their tasks, the unitary authorities were not in place.

Although the Greater London Council and the six metropolitan county councils were abolished some years ago, the metropolitan county boundaries are still in place and thus these metropolitan counties continue to provide a good basis for comparison of voting between 1992 and 1997 in the areas of heaviest population in England.

The metropolis has been divided into two areas — Outer London and Inner London — and the two have also been combined to give a Greater London area table among the regional tables.

Seats making up metropolitan counties and the voting in them was as follows:

| GREATER MANCHESTER | | | Lab | C | LD | Other | Total |
|---|---|---|---|---|---|---|---|
| 1997 | Electorate | 1,891,138 | Votes | 724,905 | 310,635 | 206,469 | 44,461 | 1,286,470 |
| | Turnout % | 68.0 | Votes % | 56.3 | 24.1 | 16.0 | 3.5 | 100.0 |
| | Swing % | -10.2 | Seats | 25 | 2 | 1 | 0 | 28 |
| | C to Lab | | Candidates | 28 | 28 | 28 | 56 | 140 |
| 1992 | Electorate | 1,899,993 | Votes | 682,848 | 511,945 | 226,066 | 22,445 | 1,443,304 |
| | Turnout % | 76 | Votes % | 47.3 | 35.5 | 15.7 | 1.6 | 100.0 |
| | | | Seats | 20 | 9 | 1 | 0 | 30 |
| | | | Candidates | 30 | 30 | 30 | 49 | 139 |
| | | Change 92-97 | | 9.0 | -11.3 | 0.4 | 1.9 | |

Altrincham & Sale West, Ashton-under-Lyne, Bolton North East, Bolton South East, Bolton West, Bury North, Bury South, Cheadle, Denton & Reddish, Eccles, Hazel Grove, Heywood & Middleton, Leigh, Makerfield, Manchester Blackley, Manchester Central, Manchester Gorton, Manchester Withington, Oldham East & Saddleworth, Oldham West & Royton, Rochdale, Salford, Stalybridge & Hyde, Stockport, Stretford & Urmston, Wigan, Worsley, Wythenshawe & Sale East.

| INNER LONDON | | | Lab | C | LD | Other | Total |
|---|---|---|---|---|---|---|---|
| 1997 | Electorate | 1,609,932 | Votes | 568,648 | 253,157 | 132,735 | 56,584 | 1,011,124 |
| | Turnout % | 62.8 | Votes % | 56.2 | 25.0 | 13.1 | 5.6 | 100.0 |
| | Swing % | -11.0 | Seats | 22 | 2 | 1 | 0 | 25 |
| | C to Lab | | Candidates | 25 | 25 | 25 | 109 | 184 |
| 1992 | Electorate | 1,631,434 | Votes | 519,972 | 408,597 | 149,142 | 51,984 | 1,129,695 |
| | Turnout % | 69.3 | Votes % | 46.0 | 36.2 | 13.2 | 4.6 | 100.0 |
| | | | Seats | 20 | 8 | 1 | 0 | 29 |
| | | | Candidates | 29 | 29 | 27 | 72 | 157 |
| | | Change 92-97 | | 10.2 | -11.1 | -0.1 | 1.0 | |

Battersea, Bethnal Green & Bow, Camberwell & Peckham, Cities of London & Westminster, Dulwich and West Norwood, Eltham, Greenwich & Woolwich, Hackney North & Stoke Newington, Hackney South & Shoreditch, Hammersmith & Fulham, Hampstead and Highgate, Holborn & St Pancras, Islington North, Islington South & Finsbury, Kensington & Chelsea, Lewisham Deptford, Lewisham East, Lewisham West, Poplar & Canning Town, Putney, Regent's Park & Kensington North, Southwark North & Bermondsey, Streatham, Tooting, Vauxhall.

## METROPOLITAN TABLES

| MERSEYSIDE | | | Lab | C | LD | Other | Total |
|---|---|---|---|---|---|---|---|
| 1997 | Electorate | 1,057,256 | Votes | 442,362 | 141,120 | 103,152 | 28,157 | 714,791 |
| | Turnout % | 67.6 | Votes % | 61.9 | 19.7 | 14.4 | 3.9 | 100.0 |
| | Swing % | -9.9 | Seats | 15 | 0 | 1 | 0 | 16 |
| | C to Lab | | Candidates | 16 | 16 | 16 | 44 | 92 |
| 1992 | Electorate | 1,079,446 | Votes | 411,412 | 232,147 | 134,878 | 21,248 | 799,685 |
| | Turnout % | 74.1 | Votes % | 51.5 | 29.0 | 16.9 | 2.7 | 100.0 |
| | | | Seats | 12 | 4 | 1 | 0 | 17 |
| | | | Candidates | 17 | 17 | 17 | 33 | 84 |
| | | | Change 92-97 | 10.4 | -9.3 | -2.4 | 1.3 | |

Birkenhead, Bootle, Crosby, Knowsley North & Sefton East, Knowsley South, Liverpool Garston, Liverpool Riverside, Liverpool Walton, Liverpool Wavertree, Liverpool West Derby, St Helens North, St Helens South, Southport, Wallasey, Wirral South, Wirral West.

| OUTER LONDON | | | Lab | C | LD | Other | Total |
|---|---|---|---|---|---|---|---|
| 1997 | Electorate | 3,291,818 | Votes | 1,074,685 | 783,018 | 353,278 | 99,483 | 2,310,464 |
| | Turnout % | 70.2 | Votes % | 46.5 | 33.9 | 15.3 | 4.3 | 100.0 |
| | Swing % | -14.3 | Seats | 35 | 9 | 5 | 0 | 49 |
| | C to Lab | | Candidates | 49 | 49 | 49 | 156 | 303 |
| 1992 | Electorate | 3,245,170 | Votes | 812,452 | 1,221,736 | 394,602 | 37,360 | 2,466,150 |
| | Turnout % | 76.0 | Votes % | 32.9 | 49.5 | 16.0 | 1.5 | 100.0 |
| | | | Seats | 15 | 40 | 0 | 0 | 55 |
| | | | Candidates | 55 | 55 | 55 | 88 | 253 |
| | | | Change 92-97 | 13.6 | -15.7 | -0.7 | 2.8 | |

Barking, Beckenham, Bexleyheath & Crayford, Brent East, Brent North, Brent South, Brentford & Isleworth, Bromley & Chislehurst, Carshalton and Wallington, Chingford & Woodford Green, Chipping Barnet, Croydon Central, Croydon North, Croydon South, Dagenham, Ealing Acton & Shepherd's Bush, Ealing North, Ealing Southall, East Ham, Edmonton, Enfield North, Enfield Southgate, Erith & Thamesmead, Feltham & Heston, Finchley & Golders Green, Harrow East, Harrow West, Hayes & Harlington, Hendon, Hornchurch, Hornsey & Wood Green, Ilford North, Ilford South, Kingston & Surbiton, Leyton & Wanstead, Mitcham & Morden, Old Bexley & Sidcup, Orpington, Richmond Park, Romford, Ruislip Northwood, Sutton & Cheam, Tottenham, Twickenham, Upminster, Uxbridge, Walthamstow, West Ham, Wimbledon.

| SOUTH YORKSHIRE | | | Lab | C | LD | Other | Total |
|---|---|---|---|---|---|---|---|
| 1997 | Electorate | 983,182 | Votes | 392,835 | 105,209 | 104,842 | 27,989 | 630,875 |
| | Turnout % | 64.2 | Votes % | 62.3 | 16.7 | 16.6 | 4.4 | 100.0 |
| | Swing % | -6.7 | Seats | 14 | 0 | 1 | 0 | 15 |
| | C to Lab | | Candidates | 15 | 15 | 15 | 32 | 77 |
| 1992 | Electorate | 1,003,827 | Votes | 418,792 | 186,270 | 113,692 | 4,585 | 723,339 |
| | Turnout % | 72.1 | Votes % | 57.9 | 25.8 | 15.7 | 0.6 | 100.0 |
| | | | Seats | 14 | 1 | 0 | 0 | 15 |
| | | | Candidates | 15 | 15 | 15 | 11 | 56 |
| | | | Change 92-97 | 4.4 | -9.1 | 0.9 | 3.8 | |

Barnsley Central, Barnsley East & Mexborough, Barnsley West & Penistone, Don Valley, Doncaster Central, Doncaster North, Rother Valley, Rotherham, Sheffield Attercliffe, Sheffield Brightside, Sheffield Central, Sheffield Hallam, Sheffield Heeley, Sheffield Hillsborough, Wentworth.

| TYNE AND WEAR | | | | Lab | C | LD | Other | Total |
|---|---|---|---|---|---|---|---|---|
| 1997 | Electorate | 847,151 | Votes | 372,999 | 96,141 | 65,594 | 21,183 | 555,917 |
| | Turnout % | 65.6 | Votes % | 67.1 | 17.3 | 11.8 | 3.8 | 100.0 |
| | Swing % | -10.8 | Seats | 13 | 0 | 0 | 0 | 13 |
| | C to Lab | | Candidates | 13 | 13 | 13 | 21 | 60 |
| 1992 | Electorate | 866,508 | Votes | 359,060 | 181,296 | 86,122 | 2,724 | 629,202 |
| | Turnout % | 72.6 | Votes % | 57.1 | 28.8 | 13.7 | 0.4 | 100.0 |
| | | | Seats | 12 | 1 | 0 | 0 | 13 |
| | | | Candidates | 13 | 13 | 13 | 4 | 43 |
| | | | Change 92-97 | 10.0 | -11.5 | -1.9 | 3.4 | |

Blaydon, Gateshead East & Washington West, Houghton & Washington East, Jarrow, Newcastle upon Tyne Central, Newcastle upon Tyne East & Wallsend, Newcastle upon Tyne North, South Shields, Sunderland North, Sunderland South, Tyne Bridge, Tynemouth, Tyneside North.

| WEST MIDLANDS | | | | Lab | C | LD | Other | Total |
|---|---|---|---|---|---|---|---|---|
| 1997 | Electorate | 2,065,425 | Votes | 715,916 | 435,011 | 156,752 | 99,662 | 1,407,341 |
| | Turnout % | 68.1 | Votes % | 50.9 | 30.9 | 11.1 | 7.1 | 100.0 |
| | Swing % | -9.9 | Seats | 24 | 6 | 0 | 1 | 31 |
| | C to Lab | | Candidates | 30 | 30 | 30 | 74 | 164 |
| 1992 | Electorate | 1,957,966 | Votes | 650,483 | 622,505 | 177,828 | 28,082 | 1,478,898 |
| | Turnout % | 75.5 | Votes % | 44.0 | 42.1 | 12.0 | 1.9 | 100.0 |
| | | | Seats | 21 | 10 | 0 | 0 | 31 |
| | | | Candidates | 31 | 31 | 31 | 25 | 118 |
| | | | Change 92-97 | 6.9 | -11.2 | -0.9 | 5.2 | |

Aldridge-Brownhills, Birmingham Edgbaston, Birmingham Erdington, Birmingham Hall Green, Birmingham Hodge Hill, Birmingham Ladywood, Birmingham Northfield, Birmingham Perry Barr, Birmingham Selly Oak, Birmingham Sparkbrook & Small Heath, Birmingham Yardley, Coventry North East, Coventry North West, Coventry South, Dudley North, Dudley South, Halesowen & Rowley Regis, Lichfield, Meriden, Solihull, Stone, Sutton Coldfield, Tamworth, Walsall North, Walsall South, Warley, West Bromwich East, West Bromwich West, Wolverhampton North East, Wolverhampton South East, Wolverhampton South West.

| WEST YORKSHIRE | | | | Lab | C | LD | Other | Total |
|---|---|---|---|---|---|---|---|---|
| 1997 | Electorate | 1,551,571 | Votes | 581,256 | 310,247 | 139,007 | 45,382 | 1,075,892 |
| | Turnout % | 69.3 | Votes % | 54.0 | 28.8 | 12.9 | 4.2 | 100.0 |
| | Swing % | -8.9 | Seats | 23 | 0 | 0 | 0 | 23 |
| | C to Lab | | Candidates | 23 | 23 | 23 | 49 | 118 |
| 1992 | Electorate | 1,563,354 | Votes | 542,644 | 455,513 | 179,116 | 14,911 | 1,192,184 |
| | Turnout % | 76.3 | Votes % | 45.5 | 38.2 | 15.0 | 1.3 | 100.0 |
| | | | Seats | 14 | 9 | 0 | 0 | 23 |
| | | | Candidates | 23 | 23 | 23 | 27 | 96 |
| | | | Change 92-97 | 8.5 | -9.4 | -2.1 | 3.0 | |

Batley & Spen, Bradford North, Bradford South, Bradford West, Calder Valley, Colne Valley, Dewsbury, Elmet, Halifax, Hemsworth, Huddersfield, Keighley, Leeds Central, Leeds East, Leeds North East, Leeds North West, Leeds West, Morley & Rothwell, Normanton, Pontefract & Castleford, Pudsey, Shipley, Wakefield.

283

# NON-METROPOLITAN COUNTIES

**T**HERE ARE 37 non-Metropolitan counties containing 330 parliamentary constituencies (311 in 1992), none of which crosses county boundaries. The Isle of Wight is still one seat (its detailed analysis is in the election results). In some counties unitary authorities are now in place. The analysis in these counties in comparisons with 1992 is as follows:

| AVON | | | | Lab | C | LD | Other | Total |
|------|---|---|---|-----|---|-----|-------|-------|
| 1997 | Electorate | 739,487 | Votes | 202,778 | 181,606 | 146,270 | 24,724 | 555,378 |
| | Turnout % | 75.1 | Votes % | 36.5 | 32.7 | 26.3 | 4.5 | 100.0 |
| | Swing % | -10.4 | Seats | 6 | 1 | 3 | 0 | 10 |
| | C to Lab | | Candidates | 10 | 10 | 10 | 34 | 64 |
| 1992 | Electorate | 722,632 | Votes | 161,952 | 261,772 | 155,663 | 8,891 | 588,278 |
| | Turnout % | 81.4 | Votes % | 27.5 | 44.5 | 26.5 | 1.5 | 100.0 |
| | | | Seats | 3 | 6 | 1 | 0 | 10 |
| | | | Candidates | 10 | 10 | 10 | 20 | 50 |
| | | | Change 92-97 | 9.0 | -11.8 | -0.1 | 2.9 | |

Bath, Bristol East, Bristol North West, Bristol South, Bristol West, Kingswood, Northavon, Wansdyke, Weston-super-Mare, Woodspring.

| BEDFORDSHIRE | | | | Lab | C | LD | Other | Total |
|--------------|---|---|---|-----|---|-----|-------|-------|
| 1997 | Electorate | 401,076 | Votes | 131,978 | 115,838 | 38,514 | 13,898 | 300,228 |
| | Turnout % | 74.9 | Votes % | 44.0 | 38.6 | 12.8 | 4.6 | 100.0 |
| | Swing % | -14.1 | Seats | 3 | 3 | 0 | 0 | 6 |
| | C to Lab | | Candidates | 6 | 6 | 6 | 16 | 34 |
| 1992 | Electorate | 385,188 | Votes | 95,403 | 167,375 | 46,549 | 5,276 | 314,603 |
| | Turnout % | 81.7 | Votes % | 30.3 | 53.2 | 14.8 | 1.7 | 100.0 |
| | | | Seats | 0 | 5 | 0 | 0 | 5 |
| | | | Candidates | 5 | 5 | 5 | 10 | 25 |
| | | | Change 92-97 | 13.6 | -14.6 | -2.0 | 3.0 | |

Bedford, Bedfordshire Mid, Bedfordshire North East, Bedfordshire South West, Luton North, Luton South.

| BERKSHIRE | | | | Lab | C | LD | Other | Total |
|-----------|---|---|---|-----|---|-----|-------|-------|
| 1997 | Electorate | 566,509 | Votes | 117,950 | 174,727 | 101,621 | 19,388 | 413,686 |
| | Turnout % | 73.0 | Votes % | 28.5 | 42.2 | 24.6 | 4.7 | 100.0 |
| | Swing % | -9.6 | Seats | 3 | 4 | 1 | 0 | 8 |
| | C to Lab | | Candidates | 8 | 8 | 8 | 27 | 51 |
| 1992 | Electorate | 547,835 | Votes | 86,863 | 242,594 | 103,072 | 6,358 | 438,887 |
| | Turnout % | 80.1 | Votes % | 19.8 | 55.3 | 23.5 | 1.5 | 100.0 |
| | | | Seats | 0 | 7 | 0 | 0 | 7 |
| | | | Candidates | 7 | 7 | 7 | 14 | 35 |
| | | | Change 92-97 | 8.7 | -13.0 | 1.1 | 3.2 | |

Bracknell, Maidenhead, Newbury, Reading East, Reading West, Slough, Windsor, Wokingham.

| BUCKINGHAMSHIRE | | | Lab | C | LD | Other | Total |
|---|---|---|---|---|---|---|---|
| 1997 | Electorate | 495,249 | Votes | 111,289 | 158,884 | 76,993 | 16,497 | 363,663 |
| | Turnout % | 73.4 | Votes % | 30.6 | 43.7 | 21.2 | 4.5 | 100.0 |
| | Swing % | -12.3 | Seats | 2 | 5 | 0 | 0 | 7 |
| | C to Lab | | Candidates | 7 | 7 | 7 | 19 | 40 |
| 1992 | Electorate | 471,168 | Votes | 72,684 | 216,219 | 83,745 | 6,868 | 379,516 |
| | Turnout % | 80.5 | Votes % | 19.2 | 57.0 | 22.1 | 1.8 | 100.0 |
| | | | Seats | 0 | 7 | 0 | 0 | 7 |
| | | | Candidates | 7 | 7 | 7 | 16 | 37 |
| | | | Change 92-97 | 11.5 | -13.3 | -0.9 | 2.7 | |

Aylesbury, Beaconsfield, Buckingham, Chesham & Amersham, Milton Keynes North East, Milton Keynes South West, Wycombe.

| CAMBRIDGESHIRE | | | Lab | C | LD | Other | Total |
|---|---|---|---|---|---|---|---|
| 1997 | Electorate | 501,052 | Votes | 128,183 | 156,154 | 66,411 | 20,714 | 371,462 |
| | Turnout % | 74.1 | Votes % | 34.5 | 42.0 | 17.9 | 5.6 | 100.0 |
| | Swing % | -11.8 | Seats | 2 | 5 | 0 | 0 | 7 |
| | C to Lab | | Candidates | 7 | 7 | 7 | 24 | 45 |
| 1992 | Electorate | 492,526 | Votes | 89,734 | 209,831 | 75,972 | 9,622 | 385,159 |
| | Turnout % | 78.2 | Votes % | 23.3 | 54.5 | 19.7 | 2.5 | 100.0 |
| | | | Seats | 1 | 5 | 0 | 0 | 6 |
| | | | Candidates | 6 | 6 | 6 | 20 | 38 |
| | | | Change 92-97 | 11.2 | -12.4 | -1.9 | 3.1 | |

Cambridge, Cambridgeshire North East, Cambridgeshire North West, Cambridgeshire South, Cambridgeshire South East, Huntingdon, Peterborough.

| CHESHIRE | | | Lab | C | LD | Other | Total |
|---|---|---|---|---|---|---|---|
| 1997 | Electorate | 753,951 | Votes | 262,655 | 188,250 | 69,182 | 44,268 | 564,355 |
| | Turnout % | 74.9 | Votes % | 46.5 | 33.4 | 12.3 | 7.8 | 100.0 |
| | Swing % | -9.4 | Seats | 7 | 3 | 0 | 1 | 11 |
| | C to Lab | | Candidates | 10 | 11 | 10 | 23 | 54 |
| 1992 | Electorate | 734,282 | Votes | 234,333 | 268,313 | 91,956 | 5,315 | 599,917 |
| | Turnout % | 81.7 | Votes % | 39.1 | 44.7 | 15.3 | 0.9 | 100.0 |
| | | | Seats | 5 | 5 | 0 | 0 | 10 |
| | | | Candidates | 10 | 10 | 10 | 14 | 44 |
| | | | Change 92-97 | 7.5 | -11.4 | -3.1 | 7.0 | |

Chester City of, Congleton, Crewe & Nantwich, Eddisbury, Ellesmere Port & Neston, Halton, Macclesfield, Tatton, Warrington North, Warrington South, Weaver Vale.

| CLEVELAND | | | Lab | C | LD | Other | Total |
|---|---|---|---|---|---|---|---|
| 1997 | Electorate | 410,939 | Votes | 180,729 | 72,990 | 28,402 | 7,564 | 289,685 |
| | Turnout % | 70.5 | Votes % | 62.4 | 25.2 | 9.8 | 2.6 | 100.0 |
| | Swing % | -12.2 | Seats | 6 | 0 | 0 | 0 | 6 |
| | C to Lab | | Candidates | 6 | 6 | 6 | 5 | 23 |
| 1992 | Electorate | 414,282 | Votes | 161,764 | 120,080 | 41,329 | 550 | 323,723 |
| | Turnout % | 78.1 | Votes % | 50.0 | 37.1 | 12.8 | 0.2 | 100.0 |
| | | | Seats | 4 | 2 | 0 | 0 | 6 |
| | | | Candidates | 6 | 6 | 6 | 1 | 19 |
| | | | Change 92-97 | 12.4 | -11.9 | -3.0 | 2.4 | |

Hartlepool, Middlesbrough, Middlesbrough South & Cleveland East, Redcar, Stockton North, Stockton South.

| CORNWALL | | | Lab | C | LD | Other | Total |
|---|---|---|---|---|---|---|---|
| 1997 | Electorate | 375,788 | Votes | 47,913 | 85,077 | 123,210 | 24,093 | 280,293 |
| | Turnout % | 74.6 | Votes % | 17.1 | 30.4 | 44.0 | 8.6 | 100.0 |
| | Swing % | -7.8 | Seats | 1 | 0 | 4 | 0 | 5 |
| | C to Lab | | Candidates | 5 | 5 | 5 | 25 | 40 |
| 1992 | Electorate | 369,826 | Votes | 41,593 | 127,678 | 124,553 | 5,133 | 298,957 |
| | Turnout % | 81.5 | Votes % | 13.9 | 42.7 | 41.7 | 1.7 | 100.0 |
| | | | Seats | 0 | 3 | 2 | 0 | 5 |
| | | | Candidates | 5 | 5 | 5 | 14 | 29 |
| | | | Change 92-97 | 3.2 | -12.4 | 2.3 | 6.9 | |

Cornwall North, Cornwall South East, Falmouth & Camborne, St Ives, Truro & St Austell.

| CUMBRIA | | | Lab | C | LD | Other | Total |
|---|---|---|---|---|---|---|---|
| 1997 | Electorate | 381,791 | Votes | 129,438 | 94,686 | 46,637 | 11,565 | 282,326 |
| | Turnout % | 73.9 | Votes % | 45.8 | 33.5 | 16.5 | 4.1 | 100.0 |
| | Swing % | -10.8 | Seats | 4 | 2 | 0 | 0 | 6 |
| | C to Lab | | Candidates | 6 | 6 | 6 | 10 | 28 |
| 1992 | Electorate | 381,046 | Votes | 113,401 | 142,126 | 49,086 | 2,302 | 306,915 |
| | Turnout % | 80.6 | Votes % | 37.0 | 46.3 | 16.0 | 0.8 | 100.0 |
| | | | Seats | 4 | 2 | 0 | 0 | 6 |
| | | | Candidates | 6 | 6 | 6 | 7 | 25 |
| | | | Change 92-97 | 8.9 | -12.8 | 0.5 | 3.4 | |

Barrow & Furness, Carlisle, Copeland, Penrith & The Border, Westmorland & Lonsdale, Workington.

| DERBYSHIRE | | | Lab | C | LD | Other | Total |
|---|---|---|---|---|---|---|---|
| 1997 | Electorate | 734,213 | Votes | 293,561 | 161,396 | 75,862 | 17,041 | 547,860 |
| | Turnout % | 74.6 | Votes % | 53.6 | 29.5 | 13.8 | 3.1 | 100.0 |
| | Swing % | -11.1 | Seats | 9 | 1 | 0 | 0 | 10 |
| | C to Lab | | Candidates | 10 | 10 | 10 | 16 | 46 |
| 1992 | Electorate | 718,805 | Votes | 256,102 | 244,949 | 87,033 | 2,416 | 590,500 |
| | Turnout % | 82.2 | Votes % | 43.4 | 41.5 | 14.7 | 0.4 | 100.0 |
| | | | Seats | 4 | 6 | 0 | 0 | 10 |
| | | | Candidates | 10 | 10 | 10 | 6 | 36 |
| | | | Change 92-97 | 10.2 | -12.0 | -0.9 | 2.7 | |

Amber Valley, Bolsover, Chesterfield, Derby North, Derby South, Derbyshire North East, Derbyshire South, Derbyshire West, Erewash, High Peak.

| DEVON | | | Lab | C | LD | Other | Total |
|---|---|---|---|---|---|---|---|
| 1997 | Electorate | 809,101 | Votes | 157,776 | 224,454 | 190,786 | 36,974 | 609,990 |
| | Turnout % | 75.4 | Votes % | 25.9 | 36.8 | 31.3 | 6.1 | 100.0 |
| | Swing % | -8.7 | Seats | 3 | 5 | 3 | 0 | 11 |
| | C to Lab | | Candidates | 11 | 11 | 11 | 36 | 69 |
| 1992 | Electorate | 786,921 | Votes | 122,854 | 303,234 | 193,817 | 18,229 | 638,134 |
| | Turnout % | 81.1 | Votes % | 19.3 | 47.5 | 30.4 | 2.9 | 100.0 |
| | | | Seats | 1 | 9 | 1 | 0 | 11 |
| | | | Candidates | 11 | 11 | 11 | 26 | 59 |
| | | | Change 92-97 | 6.6 | -10.7 | 0.9 | 3.2 | |

Devon East, Devon North, Devon South West, Devon West & Torridge, Exeter, Plymouth Devonport, Plymouth Sutton, Teignbridge, Tiverton & Honiton, Torbay, Totnes.

| DORSET | | | Lab | C | LD | Other | Total |
|---|---|---|---|---|---|---|---|
| 1997 | Electorate | 534,115 | Votes | 73,821 | 164,650 | 134,045 | 21,047 | 393,563 |
| | Turnout % | 73.7 | Votes % | 18.8 | 41.8 | 34.1 | 5.3 | 100.0 |
| | Swing % | -9.0 | Seats | 0 | 8 | 0 | 0 | 8 |
| | C to Lab | | Candidates | 8 | 8 | 8 | 19 | 43 |
| 1992 | Electorate | 520,248 | Votes | 54,613 | 222,031 | 127,062 | 3,766 | 407,472 |
| | Turnout % | 78.3 | Votes % | 13.4 | 54.5 | 31.2 | 0.9 | 100.0 |
| | | | Seats | 0 | 7 | 0 | 0 | 7 |
| | | | Candidates | 7 | 7 | 7 | 8 | 29 |
| | | | Change 92-97 | 5.4 | -12.7 | 2.9 | 4.4 | |

Bournemouth East, Bournemouth West, Christchurch, Dorset Mid & Poole North, Dorset North, Dorset South, Dorset West, Poole.

| DURHAM | | | Lab | C | LD | Other | Total |
|---|---|---|---|---|---|---|---|
| 1997 | Electorate | 463,722 | Votes | 223,242 | 57,441 | 31,496 | 13,608 | 325,787 |
| | Turnout % | 70.3 | Votes % | 68.5 | 17.6 | 9.7 | 4.2 | 100.0 |
| | Swing % | -11.1 | Seats | 7 | 0 | 0 | 0 | 7 |
| | C to Lab | | Candidates | 7 | 7 | 7 | 10 | 31 |
| 1992 | Electorate | 467,749 | Votes | 204,437 | 101,620 | 50,883 | 1,167 | 358,107 |
| | Turnout % | 76.6 | Votes % | 57.1 | 28.4 | 14.2 | 0.3 | 100.0 |
| | | | Seats | 7 | 0 | 0 | 0 | 7 |
| | | | Candidates | 7 | 7 | 7 | 2 | 23 |
| | | | Change 92-97 | 11.4 | -10.8 | -4.5 | 3.9 | |

Bishop Auckland, Darlington, Durham North, Durham North West, Durham City of, Easington, Sedgefield.

| ESSEX | | | Lab | C | LD | Other | Total |
|---|---|---|---|---|---|---|---|
| 1997 | Electorate | 1,207,900 | Votes | 320,231 | 354,014 | 160,082 | 44,249 | 878,576 |
| | Turnout % | 72.7 | Votes % | 36.4 | 40.3 | 18.2 | 5.0 | 100.0 |
| | Swing % | -13.3 | Seats | 6 | 10 | 1 | 0 | 17 |
| | C to Lab | | Candidates | 17 | 17 | 17 | 36 | 87 |
| 1992 | Electorate | 1,173,526 | Votes | 222,675 | 510,710 | 205,214 | 9,147 | 947,746 |
| | Turnout % | 80.8 | Votes % | 23.5 | 53.9 | 21.7 | 1.0 | 100.0 |
| | | | Seats | 1 | 15 | 0 | 0 | 16 |
| | | | Candidates | 16 | 16 | 16 | 17 | 65 |
| | | | Change 92-97 | 13.0 | -13.6 | -3.4 | 4.1 | |

Basildon, Billericay, Braintree, Brentwood & Ongar, Castle Point, Chelmsford West, Colchester, Epping Forest, Essex North, Harlow, Harwich, Maldon & Chelmsford East, Rayleigh, Rochford & Southend East, Saffron Walden, Southend West, Thurrock.

| GLOUCESTERSHIRE | | | Lab | C | LD | Other | Total |
|---|---|---|---|---|---|---|---|
| **1997** | Electorate | **423,132** | Votes | 109,689 | 127,593 | 72,971 | 13,765 | 324,018 |
| | Turnout % | **76.6** | Votes % | 33.9 | 39.4 | 22.5 | 4.2 | 100.0 |
| | Swing % | **-9.4** | Seats | 3 | 2 | 1 | 0 | 6 |
| | C to Lab | | Candidates | 6 | 6 | 6 | 16 | 34 |
| **1992** | Electorate | **411,245** | Votes | 78,210 | 160,244 | 95,646 | 3,984 | 338,084 |
| | Turnout % | **82.2** | Votes % | 23.1 | 47.4 | 28.2 | 1.2 | 100.0 |
| | | | Seats | 0 | 4 | 1 | 0 | 5 |
| | | | Candidates | 5 | 5 | 5 | 8 | 23 |
| | | | **Change 92-97** | 10.7 | -8.0 | -5.8 | 3.1 | |

Cheltenham, Cotswold, Forest of Dean, Gloucester, Stroud, Tewkesbury.

| HAMPSHIRE | | | Lab | C | LD | Other | Total |
|---|---|---|---|---|---|---|---|
| **1997** | Electorate | **1,223,687** | Votes | 253,445 | 369,213 | 226,992 | 45,825 | 895,475 |
| | Turnout % | **73.2** | Votes % | 28.3 | 41.2 | 25.3 | 5.1 | 100.0 |
| | Swing % | **-11.3** | Seats | 3 | 11 | 3 | 0 | 17 |
| | C to Lab | | Candidates | 17 | 17 | 17 | 50 | 101 |
| **1992** | Electorate | **1,286,031** | Votes | 179,840 | 548,183 | 282,054 | 11,874 | 1,022,951 |
| | Turnout % | **79.5** | Votes % | 17.6 | 53.7 | 27.6 | 1.2 | 100.0 |
| | | | Seats | 1 | 15 | 0 | 0 | 16 |
| | | | Candidates | 16 | 16 | 16 | 17 | 65 |
| | | | **Change 92-97** | 10.7 | -12.5 | -2.2 | 4.0 | |

Aldershot, Basingstoke, Eastleigh, Fareham, Gosport, Hampshire East, Hampshire North East, Hampshire North West, Havant, New Forest East, New Forest West, Portsmouth North, Portsmouth South, Romsey, Southampton Itchen, Southampton Test, Winchester.

| HEREFORD AND WORCESTER | | | Lab | C | LD | Other | Total |
|---|---|---|---|---|---|---|---|
| **1997** | Electorate | **539,832** | Votes | 132,541 | 166,848 | 89,060 | 18,449 | 406,898 |
| | Turnout % | **75.4** | Votes % | 32.6 | 41.0 | 21.9 | 4.5 | 100.0 |
| | Swing % | **-8.7** | Seats | 3 | 4 | 1 | 0 | 8 |
| | C to Lab | | Candidates | 8 | 8 | 8 | 17 | 41 |
| **1992** | Electorate | **524,113** | Votes | 105,080 | 216,841 | 98,412 | 6,228 | 426,561 |
| | Turnout % | **81.4** | Votes % | 24.7 | 50.9 | 23.1 | 1.5 | 100.0 |
| | | | Seats | 0 | 7 | 0 | 0 | 7 |
| | | | Candidates | 7 | 7 | 7 | 8 | 29 |
| | | | **Change 92-97** | 7.9 | -9.8 | -1.2 | 3.1 | |

Bromsgrove, Hereford, Leominster, Redditch, Worcester, Worcestershire Mid, Worcestershire West, Wyre Forest.

| HERTFORDSHIRE | | | Lab | C | LD | Other | Total |
|---|---|---|---|---|---|---|---|
| **1997** | Electorate | **757,868** | Votes | 229,011 | 234,340 | 92,346 | 21,508 | 577,205 |
| | Turnout % | **76.2** | Votes % | 39.7 | 40.6 | 16.0 | 3.7 | 100.0 |
| | Swing % | **-13.2** | Seats | 5 | 6 | 0 | 0 | 11 |
| | C to Lab | | Candidates | 11 | 11 | 11 | 27 | 60 |
| **1992** | Electorate | **737,054** | Votes | 157,252 | 322,667 | 123,161 | 5,619 | 608,699 |
| | Turnout % | **82.6** | Votes % | 25.8 | 53.0 | 20.2 | 0.9 | 100.0 |
| | | | Seats | 0 | 10 | 0 | 0 | 10 |
| | | | Candidates | 10 | 10 | 10 | 14 | 44 |
| | | | **Change 92-97** | 13.8 | -12.4 | -4.2 | 2.8 | |

Broxbourne, Hemel Hempstead, Hertford & Stortford, Hertfordshire North East, Hertfordshire South West, Hertsmere, Hitchen & Harpenden, St Albans, Stevenage, Watford, Welwyn Hatfield.

| HUMBERSIDE | | | Lab | C | LD | Other | Total |
|---|---|---|---|---|---|---|---|
| 1997 | Electorate | 667,453 | Votes | 227,441 | 137,105 | 71,426 | 15,070 | 451,042 |
| | Turnout % | 67.6 | Votes % | 50.4 | 30.4 | 15.8 | 3.3 | 100.0 |
| | Swing % | -10.7 | Seats | 7 | 3 | 0 | 0 | 10 |
| | C to Lab | | Candidates | 10 | 10 | 10 | 18 | 48 |
| 1992 | Electorate | 666,567 | Votes | 202,202 | 208,825 | 87,076 | 2,869 | 500,972 |
| | Turnout % | 75.2 | Votes % | 40.4 | 41.7 | 17.4 | 0.6 | 100.0 |
| | | | Seats | 5 | 4 | 0 | 0 | 9 |
| | | | Candidates | 9 | 9 | 9 | 6 | 33 |
| | | | Change 92-97 | 10.1 | -11.3 | -1.6 | 2.8 | |

Beverley & Holderness, Brigg & Goole, Cleethorpes, Great Grimsby, Haltemprice & Howden, Hull East, Hull North, Hull West & Hessle, Scunthorpe, Yorkshire East.

| KENT | | | Lab | C | LD | Other | Total |
|---|---|---|---|---|---|---|---|
| 1997 | Electorate | 1,163,017 | Votes | 317,762 | 346,885 | 145,896 | 45,998 | 856,541 |
| | Turnout % | 73.6 | Votes % | 37.1 | 40.5 | 17.0 | 5.4 | 100.0 |
| | Swing % | -12.7 | Seats | 8 | 9 | 0 | 0 | 17 |
| | C to Lab | | Candidates | 17 | 17 | 17 | 57 | 108 |
| 1992 | Electorate | 1,146,298 | Votes | 223,225 | 488,399 | 195,859 | 12,029 | 919,512 |
| | Turnout % | 80.2 | Votes % | 24.3 | 53.1 | 21.3 | 1.3 | 100.0 |
| | | | Seats | 0 | 16 | 0 | 0 | 16 |
| | | | Candidates | 16 | 16 | 16 | 29 | 77 |
| | | | Change 92-97 | 12.8 | -12.6 | -4.3 | 4.1 | |

Ashford, Canterbury, Chatham & Aylesford, Dartford, Dover, Faversham & Kent Mid, Folkestone & Hythe, Gillingham, Gravesham, Maidstone & The Weald, Medway, Sevenoaks, Sittingbourne & Sheppey, Thanet North, Thanet South, Tonbridge & Malling, Tunbridge Wells.

| LANCASHIRE | | | Lab | C | LD | Other | Total |
|---|---|---|---|---|---|---|---|
| 1997 | Electorate | 1,073,348 | Votes | 382,476 | 265,819 | 98,744 | 30,445 | 777,484 |
| | Turnout % | 72.4 | Votes % | 49.2 | 34.2 | 12.7 | 3.9 | 100.0 |
| | Swing % | -10.5 | Seats | 13 | 2 | 0 | 0 | 15 |
| | C to Lab | | Candidates | 15 | 15 | 15 | 33 | 78 |
| 1992 | Electorate | 1,066,413 | Votes | 331,430 | 383,313 | 129,268 | 7,311 | 851,322 |
| | Turnout % | 79.8 | Votes % | 38.9 | 45.0 | 15.2 | 0.9 | 100.0 |
| | | | Seats | 7 | 9 | 0 | 0 | 16 |
| | | | Candidates | 16 | 16 | 16 | 23 | 71 |
| | | | Change 92-97 | 10.3 | -10.8 | -2.5 | 3.1 | |

Blackburn, Blackpool North & Fleetwood, Blackpool South, Burnley, Chorley, Fylde, Hyndburn, Lancashire West, Lancaster & Wyre, Morecambe & Lunesdale, Pendle, Preston, Ribble South, Ribble Valley, Rossendale & Darwen.

| LEICESTERSHIRE | | | Lab | C | LD | Other | Total |
|---|---|---|---|---|---|---|---|
| 1997 | Electorate | 686,196 | Votes | 221,422 | 185,787 | 76,500 | 21,667 | 505,376 |
| | Turnout % | 73.6 | Votes % | 43.8 | 36.8 | 15.1 | 4.3 | 100.0 |
| | Swing % | -11.3 | Seats | 5 | 5 | 0 | 0 | 10 |
| | C to Lab | | Candidates | 10 | 10 | 10 | 23 | 53 |
| 1992 | Electorate | 667,442 | Votes | 177,438 | 261,339 | 91,864 | 6,359 | 537,000 |
| | Turnout % | 80.5 | Votes % | 33.0 | 48.7 | 17.1 | 1.2 | 100.0 |
| | | | Seats | 3 | 6 | 0 | 0 | 9 |
| | | | Candidates | 9 | 9 | 9 | 15 | 42 |
| | | | Change 92-97 | 10.8 | -11.9 | -2.0 | 3.1 | |

Blaby, Bosworth, Charnwood, Harborough, Leicester East, Leicester South, Leicester West, Leicestershire North West, Loughborough, Rutland & Melton.

## NON-METROPOLITAN TABLES

| LINCOLNSHIRE | | | Lab | C | LD | Other | Total |
|---|---|---|---|---|---|---|---|
| 1997 | Electorate | 479,476 | Votes | 128,147 | 147,196 | 60,923 | 10,880 | 347,146 |
| | Turnout % | 72.4 | Votes % | 36.9 | 42.4 | 17.5 | 3.1 | 100.0 |
| | Swing % | -11.1 | Seats | 1 | 6 | 0 | 0 | 7 |
| | C to Lab | | Candidates | 7 | 7 | 7 | 10 | 31 |
| 1992 | Electorate | 457,485 | Votes | 93,869 | 194,470 | 71,840 | 3,121 | 363,300 |
| | Turnout % | 79.4 | Votes % | 25.9 | 53.5 | 19.8 | 0.9 | 100.0 |
| | | | Seats | 0 | 6 | 0 | 0 | 6 |
| | | | Candidates | 6 | 6 | 6 | 3 | 21 |
| | | | Change 92-97 | 11.1 | -11.1 | -2.2 | 2.3 | |

Boston & Skegness, Gainsborough, Grantham & Stamford, Lincoln, Louth & Horncastle, Sleaford & North Hykeham, South Holland & The Deepings.

| NORFOLK | | | Lab | C | LD | Other | Total |
|---|---|---|---|---|---|---|---|
| 1997 | Electorate | 600,137 | Votes | 179,504 | 165,055 | 81,817 | 23,123 | 449,499 |
| | Turnout % | 74.9 | Votes % | 39.9 | 36.7 | 18.2 | 5.1 | 100.0 |
| | Swing % | -10.6 | Seats | 4 | 4 | 0 | 0 | 8 |
| | C to Lab | | Candidates | 8 | 8 | 8 | 17 | 41 |
| 1992 | Electorate | 586,027 | Votes | 147,954 | 233,410 | 88,329 | 4,593 | 474,286 |
| | Turnout % | 80.9 | Votes % | 31.2 | 49.2 | 18.6 | 1.0 | 100.0 |
| | | | Seats | 1 | 7 | 0 | 0 | 8 |
| | | | Candidates | 8 | 8 | 8 | 13 | 37 |
| | | | Change 92-97 | 8.7 | -12.5 | -0.4 | 4.2 | |

Great Yarmouth, Norfolk Mid, Norfolk North, Norfolk North West, Norfolk South, Norfolk South West, Norwich North, Norwich South.

| NORTHAMPTONSHIRE | | | Lab | C | LD | Other | Total |
|---|---|---|---|---|---|---|---|
| 1997 | Electorate | 452,559 | Votes | 152,090 | 136,488 | 37,550 | 11,628 | 337,756 |
| | Turnout % | 74.6 | Votes % | 45.0 | 40.4 | 11.1 | 3.4 | 100.0 |
| | Swing % | -11.4 | Seats | 5 | 1 | 0 | 0 | 6 |
| | C to Lab | | Candidates | 6 | 6 | 6 | 15 | 33 |
| 1992 | Electorate | 434,501 | Votes | 118,634 | 183,101 | 50,436 | 1,438 | 353,609 |
| | Turnout % | 81.4 | Votes % | 33.6 | 51.8 | 14.3 | 0.4 | 100.0 |
| | | | Seats | 0 | 6 | 0 | 0 | 6 |
| | | | Candidates | 6 | 6 | 6 | 3 | 21 |
| | | | Change 92-97 | 11.5 | -11.4 | -3.2 | 3.0 | |

Corby, Daventry, Kettering, Northampton North, Northampton South, Wellingborough.

| NORTHUMBERLAND | | | C | Lab | LD | Other | Total |
|---|---|---|---|---|---|---|---|
| 1997 | Electorate | 240,101 | Votes | 85,289 | 39,722 | 43,708 | 6,409 | 175,128 |
| | Turnout % | 72.9 | Votes % | 48.7 | 22.7 | 25.0 | 3.7 | 100.0 |
| | Swing % | -8.5 | Seats | 2 | 1 | 1 | 0 | 4 |
| | C to Lab | | Candidates | 4 | 4 | 4 | 6 | 18 |
| 1992 | Electorate | 237,101 | Votes | 76,050 | 58,770 | 53,816 | 1,961 | 190,597 |
| | Turnout % | 80.4 | Votes % | 39.9 | 30.8 | 28.2 | 1.0 | 100.0 |
| | | | Seats | 2 | 1 | 1 | 0 | 4 |
| | | | Candidates | 4 | 4 | 4 | 3 | 15 |
| | | | Change 92-97 | 8.8 | -8.2 | -3.3 | 2.6 | |

Berwick-upon-Tweed, Blyth Valley, Hexham, Wansbeck.

| NOTTINGHAMSHIRE | | | Lab | C | LD | Other | Total |
|---|---|---|---|---|---|---|---|
| 1997 | Electorate | 777,374 | Votes | 302,419 | 169,979 | 60,464 | 23,673 | 556,535 |
| | Turnout % | 71.6 | Votes % | 54.3 | 30.5 | 10.9 | 4.3 | 100.0 |
| | Swing % | -11.0 | Seats | 10 | 1 | 0 | 0 | 11 |
| | C to Lab | | Candidates | 11 | 11 | 11 | 17 | 50 |
| 1992 | Electorate | 782,127 | Votes | 276,354 | 265,655 | 75,435 | 4,517 | 621,961 |
| | Turnout % | 79.5 | Votes % | 44.4 | 42.7 | 12.1 | 0.7 | 100.0 |
| | | | Seats | 7 | 4 | 0 | 0 | 11 |
| | | | Candidates | 11 | 11 | 11 | 11 | 44 |
| | | | Change 92-97 | 9.9 | -12.2 | -1.3 | 3.5 | |

Ashfield, Bassetlaw, Broxtowe, Gedling, Mansfield, Newark, Nottingham East, Nottingham North, Nottingham South, Rushcliffe, Sherwood.

| OXFORDSHIRE | | | Lab | C | LD | Other | Total |
|---|---|---|---|---|---|---|---|
| 1997 | Electorate | 437,725 | Votes | 105,131 | 126,100 | 81,832 | 18,459 | 331,522 |
| | Turnout % | 75.7 | Votes % | 31.7 | 38.0 | 24.7 | 5.6 | 100.0 |
| | Swing % | -10.6 | Seats | 1 | 4 | 1 | 0 | 6 |
| | C to Lab | | Candidates | 6 | 6 | 6 | 26 | 44 |
| 1992 | Electorate | 418,794 | Votes | 79,168 | 171,208 | 78,269 | 4,900 | 333,545 |
| | Turnout % | 79.6 | Votes % | 23.7 | 51.3 | 23.5 | 1.5 | 100.0 |
| | | | Seats | 1 | 5 | 0 | 0 | 6 |
| | | | Candidates | 6 | 6 | 6 | 14 | 32 |
| | | | Change 92-97 | 8.0 | -13.3 | 1.2 | 4.1 | |

Banbury, Henley, Oxford East, Oxford West & Abingdon, Wantage, Witney.

| SHROPSHIRE | | | Lab | C | LD | Other | Total |
|---|---|---|---|---|---|---|---|
| 1997 | Electorate | 321,345 | Votes | 93,463 | 87,561 | 48,229 | 6,274 | 235,527 |
| | Turnout % | 73.3 | Votes % | 39.7 | 37.2 | 20.5 | 2.7 | 100.0 |
| | Swing % | -9.4 | Seats | 3 | 2 | 0 | 0 | 5 |
| | C to Lab | | Candidates | 5 | 5 | 5 | 8 | 23 |
| 1992 | Electorate | 313,122 | Votes | 76,281 | 115,060 | 54,547 | 2,443 | 248,331 |
| | Turnout % | 79.3 | Votes % | 30.7 | 46.3 | 22.0 | 1.0 | 100.0 |
| | | | Seats | 1 | 3 | 0 | 0 | 4 |
| | | | Candidates | 4 | 4 | 4 | 3 | 15 |
| | | | Change 92-97 | 9.0 | -9.2 | -1.5 | 1.7 | |

Ludlow, Shrewsbury & Atcham, Shropshire North, Telford, Wrekin The.

| SOMERSET | | | Lab | C | LD | Other | Total |
|---|---|---|---|---|---|---|---|
| 1997 | Electorate | 373,152 | Votes | 49,409 | 103,503 | 115,155 | 15,402 | 283,469 |
| | Turnout % | 76.0 | Votes % | 17.4 | 36.5 | 40.6 | 5.4 | 100.0 |
| | Swing % | -6.6 | Seats | 0 | 2 | 3 | 0 | 5 |
| | C to Lab | | Candidates | 5 | 5 | 5 | 11 | 26 |
| 1992 | Electorate | 363,847 | Votes | 38,561 | 134,983 | 119,774 | 4,589 | 297,907 |
| | Turnout % | 81.9 | Votes % | 12.9 | 45.3 | 40.2 | 1.5 | 100.0 |
| | | | Seats | 0 | 4 | 1 | 0 | 5 |
| | | | Candidates | 5 | 5 | 5 | 10 | 25 |
| | | | Change 92-97 | 4.5 | -8.8 | 0.4 | 3.9 | |

Bridgwater, Somerton & Frome, Taunton, Wells, Yeovil.

## NON-METROPOLITAN TABLES

| STAFFORDSHIRE | | | Lab | C | LD | Other | Total |
|---|---|---|---|---|---|---|---|
| **1997** | Electorate | 805,473 | Votes | 301,258 | 197,643 | 63,030 | 24,746 | 586,677 |
| | Turnout % | 72.8 | Votes % | 51.3 | 33.7 | 10.7 | 4.2 | 100.0 |
| | Swing % | -9.9 | Seats | 9 | 3 | 0 | 0 | 12 |
| | C to Lab | | Candidates | 12 | 12 | 12 | 26 | 62 |
| **1992** | Electorate | 800,541 | Votes | 267,799 | 281,715 | 85,665 | 5,527 | 640,706 |
| | Turnout % | 80.0 | Votes % | 41.8 | 44.0 | 13.4 | 0.9 | 100.0 |
| | | | Seats | 5 | 6 | 0 | 0 | 11 |
| | | | Candidates | 11 | 11 | 11 | 11 | 44 |
| | | | **Change 92-97** | 9.6 | -10.3 | -2.6 | 3.4 | |

Burton, Cannock Chase, Lichfield, Newcastle-under-Lyme, Stafford, Staffordshire Moorlands, Staffordshire South,Stoke-on-Trent Central, Stoke-on-Trent North, Stoke-on-Trent South, Stone, Tamworth.

| SUFFOLK | | | Lab | C | LD | Other | Total |
|---|---|---|---|---|---|---|---|
| **1997** | Electorate | 496,632 | Votes | 149,090 | 139,400 | 65,246 | 16,898 | 370,634 |
| | Turnout % | 74.6 | Votes % | 40.2 | 37.6 | 17.6 | 4.6 | 100.0 |
| | Swing % | -11.9 | Seats | 2 | 5 | 0 | 0 | 7 |
| | C to Lab | | Candidates | 7 | 7 | 7 | 14 | 35 |
| **1992** | Electorate | 478,310 | Votes | 110,665 | 192,513 | 78,683 | 4,209 | 386,070 |
| | Turnout % | 80.7 | Votes % | 28.7 | 49.9 | 20.4 | 1.1 | 100.0 |
| | | | Seats | 1 | 5 | 0 | 0 | 6 |
| | | | Candidates | 6 | 6 | 6 | 9 | 27 |
| | | | **Change 92-97** | 11.6 | -12.3 | -2.8 | 3.5 | |

Bury St Edmunds, Ipswich, Suffolk Central & Ipswich North, Suffolk Coastal, Suffolk South, Suffolk West, Waveney.

| SURREY | | | Lab | C | LD | Other | Total |
|---|---|---|---|---|---|---|---|
| **1997** | Electorate | 786,842 | Votes | 130,916 | 271,690 | 144,132 | 40,996 | 587,734 |
| | Turnout % | 74.7 | Votes % | 22.3 | 46.2 | 24.5 | 7.0 | 100.0 |
| | Swing % | -11.1 | Seats | 0 | 11 | 0 | 0 | 11 |
| | C to Lab | | Candidates | 11 | 11 | 11 | 34 | 67 |
| **1992** | Electorate | 777,509 | Votes | 84,942 | 373,343 | 158,831 | 6,597 | 623,713 |
| | Turnout % | 80.2 | Votes % | 13.6 | 59.9 | 25.5 | 1.1 | 100.0 |
| | | | Seats | 0 | 11 | 0 | 0 | 11 |
| | | | Candidates | 11 | 11 | 11 | 14 | 47 |
| | | | **Change 92-97** | 8.7 | -13.6 | -0.9 | 5.9 | |

Epsom & Ewell, Esher & Walton, Guildford, Mole Valley, Reigate, Runneymede & Weybridge, Spelthorne, Surrey East, Surrey Heath, Surrey South West, Woking.

| SUSSEX EAST | | | Lab | C | LD | Other | Total |
|---|---|---|---|---|---|---|---|
| **1997** | Electorate | 552,772 | Votes | 117,400 | 158,427 | 96,606 | 29,769 | 402,202 |
| | Turnout % | 72.8 | Votes % | 29.2 | 39.4 | 24.0 | 7.4 | 100.0 |
| | Swing % | -12.5 | Seats | 4 | 3 | 1 | 0 | 8 |
| | C to Lab | | Candidates | 8 | 8 | 8 | 29 | 53 |
| **1992** | Electorate | 545,086 | Votes | 74,797 | 225,334 | 117,248 | 9,163 | 426,542 |
| | Turnout % | 78.3 | Votes % | 17.5 | 52.8 | 27.5 | 2.2 | 100.0 |
| | | | Seats | 0 | 8 | 0 | 0 | 8 |
| | | | Candidates | 8 | 8 | 8 | 16 | 40 |
| | | | **Change 92-97** | 11.7 | -13.4 | -3.5 | 5.3 | |

Bexhill & Battle, Brighton Kemptown, Brighton Pavilion, Eastbourne, Hastings & Rye, Hove, Lewes, Wealden.

| SUSSEX WEST | | | Lab | C | LD | Other | Total |
|---|---|---|---|---|---|---|---|
| 1997 | Electorate | 563,966 | Votes | 101,289 | 186,569 | 106,987 | 22,770 | 417,615 |
| | Turnout % | 74.0 | Votes % | 24.3 | 44.7 | 25.6 | 5.5 | 100.0 |
| | Swing % | -11.1 | Seats | 1 | 7 | 0 | 0 | 8 |
| | C to Lab | | Candidates | 8 | 8 | 8 | 17 | 41 |
| 1992 | Electorate | 553,419 | Votes | 64,450 | 252,117 | 113,302 | 10,267 | 440,136 |
| | Turnout % | 79.5 | Votes % | 14.6 | 57.3 | 25.7 | 2.3 | 100.0 |
| | | | Seats | 0 | 7 | 0 | 0 | 7 |
| | | | Candidates | 7 | 7 | 7 | 17 | 38 |
| | | | Change 92-97 | 9.6 | -12.6 | -0.1 | 3.1 | |

Arundel & South Downs, Bognor Regis & Littlehampton, Chichester, Crawley, Horsham, Sussex Mid, Worthing East & Shoreham, Worthing West.

| WARWICKSHIRE | | | Lab | C | LD | Other | Total |
|---|---|---|---|---|---|---|---|
| 1997 | Electorate | 384,826 | Votes | 127,606 | 112,619 | 40,503 | 10,419 | 291,147 |
| | Turnout % | 75.7 | Votes % | 43.8 | 38.7 | 13.9 | 3.6 | 100.0 |
| | Swing % | -10.7 | Seats | 4 | 1 | 0 | 0 | 5 |
| | C to Lab | | Candidates | 5 | 5 | 5 | 17 | 32 |
| 1992 | Electorate | 374,228 | Votes | 103,708 | 154,125 | 49,776 | 2,844 | 310,453 |
| | Turnout % | 83.0 | Votes % | 33.4 | 49.7 | 16.0 | 0.9 | 100.0 |
| | | | Seats | 2 | 3 | 0 | 0 | 5 |
| | | | Candidates | 5 | 5 | 5 | 7 | 22 |
| | | | Change 92-97 | 10.4 | -11.0 | -2.1 | 2.7 | |

Nuneaton, Rugby & Kenilworth, Stratford-on-Avon, Warwick & Leamington, Warwickshire North.

| WILTSHIRE | | | Lab | C | LD | Other | Total |
|---|---|---|---|---|---|---|---|
| 1997 | Electorate | 446,636 | Votes | 92,995 | 133,788 | 87,156 | 18,532 | 332,471 |
| | Turnout % | 74.4 | Votes % | 28.0 | 40.2 | 26.2 | 5.6 | 100.0 |
| | Swing % | -10.2 | Seats | 2 | 4 | 0 | 0 | 6 |
| | C to Lab | | Candidates | 6 | 6 | 6 | 19 | 37 |
| 1992 | Electorate | 428,935 | Votes | 64,053 | 177,987 | 100,218 | 7,649 | 349,907 |
| | Turnout % | 81.6 | Votes % | 18.3 | 50.9 | 28.6 | 2.2 | 100.0 |
| | | | Seats | 0 | 5 | 0 | 0 | 5 |
| | | | Candidates | 5 | 5 | 5 | 14 | 29 |
| | | | Change 92-97 | 9.7 | -10.6 | -2.4 | 3.4 | |

Devizes, Salisbury, Swindon North, Swindon South, Westbury, Wiltshire North.

| YORKSHIRE NORTH | | | Lab | C | LD | Other | Total |
|---|---|---|---|---|---|---|---|
| 1997 | Electorate | 567,933 | Votes | 138,046 | 168,210 | 96,941 | 17,578 | 420,775 |
| | Turnout % | 74.1 | Votes % | 32.8 | 40.0 | 23.0 | 4.2 | 100.0 |
| | Swing % | -11.1 | Seats | 3 | 4 | 1 | 0 | 8 |
| | C to Lab | | Candidates | 8 | 8 | 8 | 14 | 38 |
| 1992 | Electorate | 554,589 | Votes | 104,227 | 233,634 | 101,376 | 2,874 | 442,111 |
| | Turnout % | 79.7 | Votes % | 23.6 | 52.9 | 22.9 | 0.7 | 100.0 |
| | | | Seats | 1 | 6 | 0 | 0 | 7 |
| | | | Candidates | 7 | 7 | 7 | 5 | 26 |
| | | | Change 92-97 | 9.2 | -12.9 | 0.1 | 3.5 | |

Harrogate & Knaresborough, Richmond (Yorks), Ryedale, Scarborough & Whitby, Selby, Skipton & Ripon, Vale of York, York City of.

# SCOTLAND

**T**HERE ARE still 72 parliamentary constituencies in the nine regions of Scotland and the island constituencies of Orkney & Shetland and Western Isles. The Boundary Commission for Scotland in its review paired the Borders and Lothian regions and also Central and Tayside. Glasgow lost a seat. New unitary authorities have been set up but the Boundary Commission did not consider these simply because they were not known to them when they were reviewing the boundaries. The analysis of the voting has to be done on the basis of the seven regional areas. It is as follows (the voting in Orkney & Shetland and Western Isles is in the constituency details elsewhere):

| BORDERS AND LOTHIAN | | | | Lab | C | LD | Nat | Other | Total |
|---|---|---|---|---|---|---|---|---|---|
| 1997 | Electorate | 685,340 | Votes | 214,150 | 98,983 | 89,953 | 87,808 | 8,216 | 499,110 |
| | Turnout % | 72.8 | Votes % | 42.9 | 19.8 | 18.0 | 17.6 | 1.6 | 100.0 |
| | Swing % | 8.0 | Seats | 9 | 0 | 3 | 0 | 0 | 12 |
| | C to Lab | | Candidates | 12 | 12 | 12 | 12 | 26 | 74 |
| 1992 | Electorate | 666,760 | Votes | 179,714 | 143,865 | 89,452 | 90,723 | 7,507 | 511,261 |
| | Turnout % | 76.7 | Votes % | 35.2 | 28.1 | 17.5 | 17.7 | 1.5 | 100.0 |
| | | | Seats | 8 | 2 | 2 | 0 | 0 | 12 |
| | | | Candidates | 12 | 12 | 12 | 12 | 13 | 61 |
| | | Change 92-97 | | 7.8 | -8.3 | 0.5 | -0.2 | 0.2 | |

East Lothian, Edinburgh Central, Edinburgh East & Mussleburgh, Edinburgh North & Leith, Edinburgh Pentlands, Edinburgh South, Edinburgh West, Linlithgow, Livingston, Midlothian, Roxburgh & Berwickshire, Tweeddale Ettrick & Lauderdale.

| CENTRAL AND TAYSIDE | | | | Lab | C | LD | Nat | Other | Total |
|---|---|---|---|---|---|---|---|---|---|
| 1997 | Electorate | 515,858 | Votes | 150,708 | 82,266 | 25,073 | 116,976 | 4,239 | 379,262 |
| | Turnout % | 73.5 | Votes % | 39.7 | 21.7 | 6.6 | 30.8 | 1.1 | 100.0 |
| | Swing % | 7.2 | Seats | 6 | 0 | 0 | 3 | 0 | 9 |
| | C to Lab | | Candidates | 9 | 9 | 9 | 9 | 14 | 50 |
| 1992 | Electorate | 512,734 | Votes | 129,499 | 115,474 | 29,352 | 114,174 | 1,822 | 390,321 |
| | Turnout % | 76.1 | Votes % | 33.2 | 29.6 | 7.5 | 29.3 | 0.5 | 100.0 |
| | | | Seats | 5 | 3 | 0 | 1 | 0 | 9 |
| | | | Candidates | 9 | 9 | 9 | 9 | 7 | 43 |
| | | Change 92-97 | | 6.5 | -7.9 | -0.9 | 1.6 | 0.7 | |

Angus, Dundee East, Dundee West, Falkirk East, Falkirk West, Ochil, Perth, Stirling, Tayside North.

| DUMFRIES AND GALLOWAY | | | | Lab | C | LD | Nat | Other | Total |
|---|---|---|---|---|---|---|---|---|---|
| 1997 | Electorate | 115,510 | Votes | 30,389 | 26,710 | 8,187 | 24,426 | 1,833 | 91,545 |
| | Turnout % | 79.3 | Votes % | 33.2 | 29.2 | 8.9 | 26.7 | 2.0 | 100.0 |
| | Swing % | 12.4 | Seats | 1 | 0 | 0 | 1 | 0 | 2 |
| | C to Lab | | Candidates | 2 | 2 | 2 | 2 | 5 | 13 |
| 1992 | Electorate | 115,619 | Votes | 20,440 | 39,770 | 9,575 | 23,184 | 419 | 93,388 |
| | Turnout % | 80.8 | Votes % | 21.9 | 42.6 | 10.3 | 24.8 | 0.5 | 100.0 |
| | | | Seats | 0 | 2 | 0 | 0 | 0 | 2 |
| | | | Candidates | 2 | 2 | 2 | 2 | 2 | 10 |
| | | Change 92-97 | | 11.3 | -13.4 | -1.3 | 1.9 | 1.6 | |

Dumfries, Galloway & Upper Nithsdale.

| FIFE | | | Lab | C | LD | Nat | Other | Total |
|------|---|---|-----|---|----|-----|-------|-------|
| 1997 | Electorate | 273,834 | Votes | 90,722 | 27,786 | 34,200 | 35,438 | 2,448 | 190,594 |
|  | Turnout % | 69.6 | Votes % | 47.6 | 14.6 | 17.9 | 18.6 | 1.3 | 100.0 |
|  | Swing % | 7.9 | Seats | 4 | 0 | 1 | 0 | 0 | 5 |
|  | C to Lab |  | Candidates | 5 | 5 | 5 | 5 | 5 | 25 |
| 1992 | Electorate | 262,788 | Votes | 81,308 | 47,089 | 34,435 | 36,117 | 379 | 199,328 |
|  | Turnout % | 75.9 | Votes % | 40.8 | 23.6 | 17.3 | 18.1 | 0.2 | 100.0 |
|  |  |  | Seats | 4 | 0 | 1 | 0 | 0 | 5 |
|  |  |  | Candidates | 5 | 5 | 5 | 5 | 2 | 22 |
|  | Change 92-97 |  |  | 6.8 | -9.1 | 0.7 | 0.5 | 1.1 |  |

Dunfermline East, Dunfermline West, Fife Central, Fife North East, Kirkcaldy.

| GRAMPIAN | | | Lab | C | LD | Nat | Other | Total |
|----------|---|---|-----|---|----|-----|-------|-------|
| 1997 | Electorate | 403,734 | Votes | 72,581 | 70,937 | 63,998 | 71,457 | 4,498 | 283,471 |
|  | Turnout % | 70.2 | Votes % | 25.6 | 25.0 | 22.6 | 25.2 | 1.6 | 100.0 |
|  | Swing % | 8.9 | Seats | 3 | 0 | 2 | 2 | 0 | 7 |
|  | C to Lab |  | Candidates | 7 | 7 | 7 | 7 | 7 | 35 |
| 1992 | Electorate | 393,946 | Votes | 53,864 | 102,753 | 55,348 | 72,456 | 381 | 284,802 |
|  | Turnout % | 72.3 | Votes % | 18.9 | 36.1 | 19.4 | 25.4 | 0.1 | 100.0 |
|  |  |  | Seats | 1 | 2 | 1 | 2 | 0 | 6 |
|  |  |  | Candidates | 6 | 6 | 6 | 6 | 1 | 25 |
|  | Change 92-97 |  |  | 6.7 | -11.1 | 3.1 | -0.2 | 1.5 |  |

Aberdeen Central, Aberdeen North, Aberdeen South, Aberdeenshire West & Kincardine, Banff & Buchan, Gordon, Moray.

| HIGHLAND | | | Lab | C | LD | Nat | Other | Total |
|----------|---|---|-----|---|----|-----|-------|-------|
| 1997 | Electorate | 218,180 | Votes | 48,492 | 19,469 | 45,455 | 36,382 | 3,868 | 153,666 |
|  | Turnout % | 70.4 | Votes % | 31.6 | 12.7 | 29.6 | 23.7 | 2.5 | 100.0 |
|  | Swing % | 8.5 | Seats | 2 | 0 | 3 | 0 | 0 | 5 |
|  | C to Lab |  | Candidates | 5 | 5 | 5 | 5 | 12 | 32 |
| 1992 | Electorate | 210,153 | Votes | 34,315 | 31,524 | 50,483 | 32,491 | 2,014 | 150,827 |
|  | Turnout % | 71.8 | Votes % | 22.8 | 20.9 | 33.5 | 21.5 | 1.3 | 100.0 |
|  |  |  | Seats | 1 | 0 | 4 | 0 | 0 | 5 |
|  |  |  | Candidates | 5 | 5 | 5 | 5 | 4 | 24 |
|  | Change 92-97 |  |  | 8.8 | -8.2 | -3.9 | 2.1 | 1.2 |  |

Caithness Sunderland & Easter Ross, Inverness East Nairn & Lochaber, Orkney & Shetland, Ross Skye & Inverness West, Western Isles.

| STRATHCLYDE | | | Lab | C | LD | Nat | Other | Total |
|-------------|---|---|-----|---|----|-----|-------|-------|
| 1997 | Electorate | 1,733,657 | Votes | 676,311 | 166,908 | 98,493 | 249,773 | 28,306 | 1,219,791 |
|  | Turnout % | 70.4 | Votes % | 55.4 | 13.7 | 8.1 | 20.5 | 2.3 | 100.0 |
|  | Swing % | 6.6 | Seats | 31 | 0 | 1 | 0 | 0 | 32 |
|  | C to Lab |  | Candidates | 32 | 32 | 32 | 32 | 74 | 202 |
| 1992 | Electorate | 1,726,033 | Votes | 643,768 | 271,420 | 115,211 | 260,419 | 10,895 | 1,301,713 |
|  | Turnout % | 75.2 | Votes % | 49.5 | 20.9 | 8.9 | 20.0 | 0.8 | 100.0 |
|  |  |  | Seats | 30 | 2 | 1 | 0 | 0 | 33 |
|  |  |  | Candidates | 33 | 33 | 33 | 33 | 24 | 156 |
|  | Change 92-97 |  |  | 6.0 | -7.2 | -0.8 | 0.5 | 1.5 |  |

Airdrie and Shotts, Argyll & Bute, Ayr, Carrick Cumnock & Doon Valley, Clydebank & Milngavie, Clydesdale, Coatbridge & Chryston, Cumbernauld & Kilsyth, Cunninghame North, Cunninghame South, Dumbarton, East Kilbride, Eastwood, Glasgow Anniesland, Glasgow Bailliestown, Glasgow Cathcart, Glasgow Govan, Glasgow Kelvin, Glasgow Maryhill, Glasgow Pollok, Glasgow Rutherglen, Glasgow Shettleston, Glasgow Springburn, Greenock & Inverclyde, Hamilton North & Bellshill, Hamilton South, Kilmarnock & Loudoun, Motherwell & Wishaw, Paisley North, Paisley South, Renfrewshire West, Strathkelvin & Bearsden.

# WALES

**W**ALES HAS 40 parliamentary seats. The review by the Boundary Commission for Wales had regard, as required by the Boundary Commissions Act 1992, to the county boundaries as they existed on June 1, 1994, rather than to the boundaries defined in the Local Government (Wales) Act 1994 under which 22 new unitary authorities were set up, replacing district and county councils.

Although the county councils were abolished, the Act retained county boundaries as a relevant criterion for the work of the Boundary Commission. Four of the eight counties retained their existing boundaries: Dyfed, Gwent, Gwynedd and West Glamorgan. There were relatively small changes to the other four: Clwyd, Mid Glamorgan, Powys and South Glamorgan.

| CLWYD | | | | Lab | C | LD | Nat | Other | Total |
|---|---|---|---|---|---|---|---|---|---|
| 1997 | Electorate | 321,905 | Votes | 127,141 | 62,670 | 25,329 | 13,688 | 8,056 | 236,884 |
| | Turnout % | 73.6 | Votes % | 53.7 | 26.5 | 10.7 | 5.8 | 3.4 | 100.0 |
| | Swing % | 10.6 | Seats | 6 | 0 | 0 | 0 | 0 | 6 |
| | C to Lab | | Candidates | 6 | 6 | 6 | 6 | 9 | 33 |
| 1992 | Electorate | 318,746 | Votes | 114,943 | 99,446 | 31,995 | 10,103 | 1,297 | 257,784 |
| | Turnout % | 80.9 | Votes % | 44.6 | 38.6 | 12.4 | 3.9 | 0.5 | 100.0 |
| | | | Seats | 4 | 1 | 0 | 0 | 0 | 5 |
| | | | Candidates | 5 | 5 | 5 | 5 | 5 | 25 |
| | | Change 92-97 | | 9.1 | -12.1 | -1.7 | 1.9 | 2.9 | |

Alyn & Deeside, Clwyd South, Clwyd West, Delyn, Vale of Clwyd, Wrexham.

| DYFED | | | | Lab | C | LD | Nat | Other | Total |
|---|---|---|---|---|---|---|---|---|---|
| 1997 | Electorate | 275,592 | Votes | 92,958 | 39,084 | 22,597 | 47,082 | 6,452 | 208,173 |
| | Turnout % | 75.5 | Votes % | 44.7 | 18.8 | 10.9 | 22.6 | 3.1 | 100.0 |
| | Swing % | 7.2 | Seats | 4 | 0 | 0 | 1 | 0 | 5 |
| | C to Lab | | Candidates | 5 | 5 | 5 | 5 | 6 | 26 |
| 1992 | Electorate | 273,312 | Votes | 84,571 | 59,530 | 31,209 | 43,482 | 642 | 219,434 |
| | Turnout % | 80.3 | Votes % | 38.5 | 27.1 | 14.2 | 19.8 | 0.3 | 100.0 |
| | | | Seats | 3 | 0 | 0 | 1 | 0 | 4 |
| | | | Candidates | 4 | 4 | 4 | 4 | 2 | 18 |
| | | Change 92-97 | | 6.1 | -8.4 | -3.4 | 2.8 | 2.8 | |

Carmarthen East & Dinefwr, Carmarthen West & Pembrokeshire South, Ceredigion, Llanelli, Preseli Pembrokeshire.

| GLAMORGAN MID | | | | Lab | C | LD | Nat | Other | Total |
|---|---|---|---|---|---|---|---|---|---|
| 1997 | Electorate | 402,503 | Votes | 196,965 | 30,672 | 27,055 | 23,034 | 8,099 | 285,825 |
| | Turnout % | 71.0 | Votes % | 68.9 | 10.7 | 9.5 | 8.1 | 2.8 | 100.0 |
| | Swing % | 5.0 | Seats | 0 | 7 | 0 | 0 | 0 | 7 |
| | C to Lab | | Candidates | 7 | 7 | 7 | 7 | 12 | 40 |
| 1992 | Electorate | 405,020 | Votes | 207,971 | 55,524 | 26,217 | 25,554 | 860 | 316,126 |
| | Turnout % | 78.1 | Votes % | 65.8 | 17.6 | 8.3 | 8.1 | 0.3 | 100.0 |
| | | | Seats | 7 | 0 | 0 | 0 | 0 | 7 |
| | | | Candidates | 7 | 7 | 7 | 7 | 2 | 30 |
| | | Change 92-97 | | 3.1 | -6.8 | 1.2 | 0.0 | 2.6 | |

Bridgend, Caerphilly, Cynon Valley, Merthyr Tydfil & Rhymney, Ogmore, Pontypridd, Rhondda.

## GLAMORGAN SOUTH

| | | | Lab | C | LD | Nat | Other | Total |
|---|---|---|---|---|---|---|---|---|
| 1997 | Electorate | 308,033 | Votes | 118,922 | 60,761 | 29,110 | 7,403 | 11,136 | 227,332 |
| | Turnout % | 73.8 | Votes % | 52.3 | 26.7 | 12.8 | 3.3 | 4.9 | 100.0 |
| | Swing % | 8.6 | Seats | 5 | 0 | 0 | 0 | 0 | 5 |
| | C to Lab | | Candidates | 5 | 5 | 5 | 5 | 10 | 30 |
| 1992 | Electorate | 301,491 | Votes | 111,482 | 91,289 | 29,411 | 4,777 | 1,502 | 238,461 |
| | Turnout % | 79.1 | Votes % | 46.8 | 38.3 | 12.3 | 2.0 | 0.6 | 100.0 |
| | | | Seats | 3 | 2 | 0 | 0 | 0 | 5 |
| | | | Candidates | 5 | 5 | 5 | 5 | 6 | 26 |
| | Change 92-97 | | | 5.6 | -11.6 | 0.5 | 1.3 | 4.3 | |

Cardiff Central, Cardiff North, Cardiff South & Penarth, Cardiff West, Vale of Glamorgan.

## GLAMORGAN WEST

| | | | Lab | C | LD | Nat | Other | Total |
|---|---|---|---|---|---|---|---|---|
| 1997 | Electorate | 279,317 | Votes | 131,186 | 28,595 | 21,612 | 11,641 | 6,651 | 199,685 |
| | Turnout % | 71.5 | Votes % | 65.7 | 14.3 | 10.8 | 5.8 | 3.3 | 100.0 |
| | Swing % | 6.4 | Seats | 5 | 0 | 0 | 0 | 0 | 5 |
| | C to Lab | | Candidates | 5 | 5 | 5 | 5 | 9 | 29 |
| 1992 | Electorate | 284,254 | Votes | 135,682 | 50,389 | 20,989 | 11,978 | 1,907 | 220,945 |
| | Turnout % | 77.7 | Votes % | 61.4 | 22.8 | 9.5 | 5.4 | 0.9 | 100.0 |
| | | | Seats | 5 | 0 | 0 | 0 | 0 | 5 |
| | | | Candidates | 5 | 5 | 5 | 5 | 5 | 25 |
| | Change 92-97 | | | 4.3 | -8.5 | 1.3 | 0.4 | 2.5 | |

Aberavon, Gower, Neath, Swansea East, Swansea West.

## GWENT

| | | | Lab | C | LD | Nat | Other | Total |
|---|---|---|---|---|---|---|---|---|
| 1997 | Electorate | 331,297 | Votes | 157,567 | 47,776 | 24,247 | 7,271 | 8,903 | 245,764 |
| | Turnout % | 74.2 | Votes % | 64.1 | 19.4 | 9.9 | 3.0 | 3.6 | 100.0 |
| | Swing % | 5.7 | Seats | 6 | 0 | 0 | 0 | 0 | 6 |
| | C to Lab | | Candidates | 6 | 6 | 6 | 6 | 8 | 32 |
| 1992 | Electorate | 333,442 | Votes | 163,637 | 73,614 | 26,153 | 4,358 | 2,904 | 270,666 |
| | Turnout % | 81.2 | Votes % | 60.5 | 27.2 | 9.7 | 1.6 | 1.1 | 100.0 |
| | | | Seats | 5 | 1 | 0 | 0 | 0 | 6 |
| | | | Candidates | 6 | 6 | 6 | 3 | 4 | 25 |
| | Change 92-97 | | | 3.7 | -7.8 | 0.2 | 1.4 | 2.6 | |

Blaenau Gwent, Islwyn, Monmouth, Newport East, Newport West, Torfaen.

## WELSH TABLES

| GWYNEDD | | | | Lab | C | LD | Nat | Other | Total |
|---------|---|---|---|-----|---|----|----|-------|-------|
| 1997 | Electorate | 187,204 | Votes | 43,163 | 26,806 | 17,907 | 48,681 | 3,518 | 140,075 |
| | Turnout % | 74.8 | Votes % | 30.8 | 19.1 | 12.8 | 34.8 | 2.5 | 100.0 |
| | Swing % | 9.7 | Seats | 1 | 0 | 0 | 3 | 0 | 4 |
| | C to Lab | | Candidates | 4 | 4 | 4 | 4 | 6 | 22 |
| 1992 | Electorate | 185,869 | Votes | 31,628 | 43,086 | 19,605 | 52,139 | 1,577 | 148,035 |
| | Turnout % | 79.7 | Votes % | 21.4 | 29.1 | 13.2 | 35.2 | 1.1 | 100.0 |
| | | | Seats | 0 | 1 | 0 | 3 | 0 | 4 |
| | | | Candidates | 4 | 4 | 4 | 4 | 5 | 21 |
| | | Change 92-97 | | 9.7 | -10.0 | -0.5 | -0.6 | 1.4 | |

Caernarfon, Conwy, Meirionnydd Nant Conwy, Ynys Mon.

| POWYS | | | | Lab | C | LD | Nat | Other | Total |
|-------|---|---|---|-----|---|----|----|-------|-------|
| 1997 | Electorate | 94,760 | Votes | 17,533 | 20,763 | 32,163 | 2,230 | 2,117 | 74,806 |
| | Turnout % | 78.9 | Votes % | 23.4 | 27.8 | 43.0 | 3.0 | 2.8 | 100.0 |
| | Swing % | 5.0 | Seats | 0 | 0 | 2 | 0 | 0 | 2 |
| | C to Lab | | Candidates | 2 | 2 | 2 | 2 | 3 | 11 |
| 1992 | Electorate | 92,895 | Votes | 15,749 | 26,799 | 31,878 | 1,999 | 901 | 77,326 |
| | Turnout % | 83.2 | Votes % | 20.4 | 34.7 | 41.2 | 2.6 | 1.2 | 100.0 |
| | | | Seats | 0 | 1 | 1 | 0 | 0 | 2 |
| | | | Candidates | 2 | 2 | 2 | 2 | 2 | 10 |
| | | Change 92-97 | | 3.1 | -6.9 | 1.8 | 0.4 | 1.7 | |

Brecon & Radnorshire, Montgomeryshire.

# A TWO CLOSE MARGIN

**T**HE CLOSEST contest in the general election was at boundary changed Winchester, which the Liberal Democrats won after recounts by a mere two votes, defeating the Tory Health Minister, Gerald Malone. On May 16, Winchester Conservatives were given leave to have the matter referred to the courts.

Of the 659 MPs, 158 have majorities of less than 10 per cent, compared with 170 in 1992, when there were eight fewer Members. Of the 158, Labour have 64, the Conservatives 65 and the Liberal Democrats 21. The most marginal Labour seat is Wellingborough, which it won by 187 votes. The huge Labour contingent has 63 MPs with over 50 per cent majorities. The table shows the majority both as a percentage and number of votes over the runner-up.

## LABOUR

| Seat | % | Votes | Runner-up |
|---|---|---|---|
| Wellingborough | 0.33 | 187 | C |
| Kettering | 0.33 | 189 | C |
| Milton Keynes NE | 0.47 | 240 | C |
| Rugby & Kenilworth | 0.81 | 495 | C |
| Northampton South | 1.30 | 744 | C |
| Romford | 1.54 | 649 | C |
| Lancaster & Wyre | 2.20 | 1295 | C |
| Harwich | 2.27 | 1216 | C |
| Castle Point | 2.30 | 1116 | C |
| Norfolk North West | 2.32 | 1339 | C |
| Harrow West | 2.36 | 1240 | C |
| Bristol West | 2.38 | 1493 | C |
| Braintree | 2.61 | 1451 | C |
| Shrewsbury & Atcham | 3.02 | 1670 | C |
| Enfield Southgate | 3.08 | 1433 | C |
| Conwy | 3.84 | 1596 | LD |
| Gillingham | 3.91 | 1980 | C |
| Sittingbourne & Sheppey | 4.18 | 1929 | C |
| Colne Valley | 4.48 | 2530 | LD |
| Clwyd West | 4.59 | 1848 | C |
| Stroud | 4.67 | 2910 | C |
| Inverness East, Nairn & Lochaber | 4.90 | 2339 | SNP |
| Falmouth & Camborne | 5.01 | 2688 | C |
| Hastings & Rye | 5.22 | 2560 | C |
| Warwick & Leamington | 5.65 | 3398 | C |
| Shipley | 5.67 | 2996 | C |
| Chatham & Aylesford | 5.68 | 2790 | C |
| Newark | 5.80 | 3016 | C |
| Wirral West | 5.84 | 2738 | C |
| Wimbledon | 6.16 | 2980 | C |
| Reading West | 6.19 | 2997 | C |
| Eastwood | 6.20 | 3236 | C |
| Oldham East & Saddleworth | 6.26 | 3389 | LD |
| Finchley & Golders Green | 6.34 | 3189 | C |
| Thanet South | 6.40 | 2878 | C |
| Ilford North | 6.60 | 3224 | C |
| Hemel Hempstead | 6.60 | 3636 | C |
| Wrekin, The | 6.68 | 3025 | C |
| Upminster | 6.70 | 2770 | C |
| Putney | 6.76 | 2976 | C |
| Selby | 6.81 | 3836 | C |
| Croydon Central | 6.98 | 3897 | C |
| Bexleyheath & Crayford | 7.08 | 3415 | C |
| Hammersmith & Fulham | 7.11 | 3842 | C |
| Gedling | 7.29 | 3802 | C |
| Reading East | 7.56 | 3795 | C |
| Aberdeen South | 7.64 | 3365 | LD |
| Brighton Kemptown | 7.66 | 3534 | C |
| Leeds North West | 7.79 | 3844 | C |
| Hove | 8.23 | 3959 | C |
| Carmarthen East & Dinefwr | 8.27 | 3450 | PC |
| Dartford | 8.32 | 4328 | C |
| Stafford | 8.33 | 4314 | C |
| Bradford West | 8.51 | 3877 | C |
| Monmouth | 8.52 | 4178 | C |
| Wansdyke | 8.77 | 4799 | C |
| St Albans | 8.78 | 4459 | C |
| Glasgow Govan | 9.04 | 2914 | SNP |
| Ribble South | 9.20 | 5084 | C |
| Scarborough & Whitby | 9.43 | 5124 | C |
| Rochdale | 9.45 | 4545 | LD |
| Portsmouth North | 9.55 | 4323 | C |
| Broxtowe | 9.59 | 5575 | C |
| Birmingham Edgbaston | 9.99 | 4842 | C |

## CONSERVATIVE

| Seat | % | Votes | Runner-up |
|---|---|---|---|
| Dorset South | 0.16 | 77 | Lab |
| Bedfordshire SW | 0.25 | 132 | Lab |
| Teignbridge | 0.45 | 281 | LD |
| Hexham | 0.49 | 222 | Lab |
| Lichfield | 0.49 | 238 | Lab |
| Bury St Edmunds | 0.66 | 368 | Lab |
| Wells | 0.94 | 528 | LD |
| Meriden | 1.06 | 582 | Lab |
| Dorset Mid & Poole N | 1.34 | 681 | LD |
| Boston & Skegness | 1.39 | 647 | Lab |
| Beverley & Holderness | 1.53 | 811 | Lab |
| Totnes | 1.63 | 877 | LD |
| Uxbridge | 1.74 | 724 | Lab |
| Bosworth | 1.97 | 1027 | Lab |
| Chipping Barnet | 2.09 | 1035 | Lab |
| Norfolk North | 2.20 | 1293 | LD |
| Norfolk Mid | 2.33 | 1336 | Lab |
| Eddisbury | 2.40 | 1185 | Lab |
| Billericay | 2.45 | 1356 | Lab |
| Tiverton & Honiton | 2.80 | 1653 | LD |
| Altrincham & Sale West | 2.91 | 1505 | Lab |
| Bridgwater | 3.29 | 1796 | LD |
| Dorset West | 3.44 | 1840 | LD |
| Eastbourne | 3.79 | 1994 | LD |
| Suffolk West | 3.80 | 1867 | Lab |
| Christchurch | 3.85 | 2165 | LD |
| Norfolk South West | 4.19 | 2464 | Lab |
| Basingstoke | 4.20 | 2397 | Lab |
| Shropshire North | 4.26 | 2195 | Lab |
| Wycombe | 4.53 | 2370 | Lab |
| Surrey South West | 4.77 | 2694 | LD |
| Orpington | 4.91 | 2952 | LD |
| Grantham & Stamford | 5.08 | 2692 | Lab |
| Dorset North | 5.22 | 2746 | LD |
| Aldridge-Brownhills | 5.45 | 2526 | Lab |
| Southend West | 5.62 | 2615 | LD |
| Thanet North | 5.65 | 2766 | Lab |
| Suffolk Coastal | 5.78 | 3254 | Lab |
| Hertfordshire NE | 5.94 | 3088 | Lab |
| Wiltshire North | 5.99 | 3475 | LD |
| Cheadle | 6.08 | 3189 | LD |
| Hertsmere | 6.11 | 3075 | Lab |
| Spelthorne | 6.69 | 3473 | Lab |
| Suffolk Central & Ipswich North | 6.70 | 3538 | Lab |
| Yorkshire East | 6.81 | 3337 | Lab |
| Old Bexley & Sidcup | 6.94 | 3569 | Lab |
| Stone | 7.19 | 3818 | Lab |
| Canterbury | 7.33 | 3964 | Lab |
| Havant | 7.72 | 3729 | Lab |
| Worcestershire West | 7.79 | 3846 | LD |
| Suffolk South | 8.03 | 4175 | Lab |
| Banbury | 8.10 | 4737 | Lab |
| Rushcliffe | 8.14 | 5055 | Lab |
| Faversham & Kent Mid | 8.41 | 4173 | Lab |
| Guildford | 8.41 | 4791 | LD |
| Derbyshire West | 8.59 | 4885 | Lab |
| Westmorland & Lonsdale | 8.90 | 4521 | LD |
| Rochford & Southend E | 9.07 | 4225 | Lab |
| Beckenham | 9.11 | 4953 | Lab |
| Cambridgeshire NE | 9.20 | 5101 | Lab |
| Bromsgrove | 9.38 | 4895 | Lab |
| Sleaford & North Hykeham | 9.63 | 5123 | Lab |
| Ashford | 9.68 | 5355 | Lab |
| Worthing East & Shoreham | 9.89 | 5098 | LD |
| Epping Forest | 9.91 | 5252 | Lab |

## LIBERAL DEMOCRATS

| Seat | % | Votes | Runner-up |
|---|---|---|---|
| Winchester | 0.00 | 2 | C |
| Torbay | 0.02 | 12 | C |
| Kingston & Surbiton | 0.10 | 56 | C |
| Somerton & Frome | 0.23 | 130 | C |
| Eastleigh | 1.36 | 754 | C |
| Weston-super-Mare | 2.39 | 1274 | C |
| Lewes | 2.64 | 1300 | C |
| Colchester | 3.04 | 1581 | C |
| Devon West & Torridge | 3.31 | 1957 | C |
| Northavon | 3.42 | 2137 | C |
| Tweeddale, Ettrick & Lauderdale | 3.82 | 1489 | Lab |
| Taunton | 4.00 | 2443 | C |
| Sutton & Cheam | 4.45 | 2097 | C |
| Carshalton & Wallington | 4.68 | 2267 | C |
| Richmond Park | 5.19 | 2951 | C |
| Aberdeenshire West & Kincardine | 6.16 | 2662 | C |
| Twickenham | 7.36 | 4281 | C |
| Caithness, Sutherland & Easter Ross | 7.74 | 2259 | Lab |
| Southwark North & Bermondsey | 8.30 | 3387 | Lab |
| Portsmouth South | 8.37 | 4327 | C |
| Isle of Wight | 8.76 | 6406 | C |

## PLAID CYMRU

| Seat | % | Votes | Runner-up |
|---|---|---|---|
| Ynys Mon | 6.21 | 2481 | Lab |

## SDLP

| Seat | % | Votes | Runner-up |
|---|---|---|---|
| Newry & Armagh | 9.18 | 4889 | UUP |

## SF

| Seat | % | Votes | Runner-up |
|---|---|---|---|
| Ulster Mid | 3.72 | 1883 | DUP |

## SNP

| Seat | % | Votes | Runner-up |
|---|---|---|---|
| Perth | 7.05 | 3141 | C |
| Tayside North | 9.12 | 4160 | C |

## UKU

| Seat | % | Votes | Runner-up |
|---|---|---|---|
| Down North | 3.96 | 1449 | UUP |

## UUP

| Seat | % | Votes | Runner-up |
|---|---|---|---|
| Tyrone West | 2.51 | 1161 | SDLP |
| Londonderry East | 9.96 | 3794 | DUP |

# RECORD NUMBER OF WOMEN

**IN THE NEW** Parliament, there are a record 119 women MPs compared with 60 after the 1992 general election. The women MPs in this Parliament are:

## The Speaker

Betty Boothroyd (West Bromwich West)

## Labour (101)

Diane Abbott (Hackney North and Stoke Newington); Irene Adams (Paisley North); Janet Anderson (Rossendale and Darwen); Hilary Armstrong (Durham North West); Candy Atherton (Falmouth and Cambourne); Charlotte Atkins (Staffordshire Moorlands); Jackie Ballard (Taunton); Margaret Beckett (Derby South); Anne Begg (Aberdeen South); Elizabeth Blackman (Erewash); Hazel Blears (Salford); Helen Brinton (Peterborough); Karen Buck (Regent's Park and Kensington North); Christine Butler (Castle Point); Anne Campbell (Cambridge); Judith Church (Dagenham); Linda Clark (Edinburgh Pentlands); Ann Clwyd (Cynon Valley); Anne Coffey (Stockport); Yvette Cooper (Pontefract and Castleford); Jean Corston (Bristol East); Ann Cryer (Keighley); Clare Curtis-Tansley (Crosby); Valerie Davey (Bristol West); Janet Dean (Burton); Julia Drown (Swindon South); Gwyneth Dunwoody (Crewe and Nantwich); Angela Eagle (Wallasey); Maria Eagle (Liverpool Garston); Louise Ellman (Liverpool Riverside); Lorna Fitzsimons (Rochdale); Caroline Flint (Don Valley); Barbara Follett (Stevenage); Maria Fyfe (Glasgow Maryhill); Linda Gilroy (Plymouth Sutton); Llin Golding (Newcastle-under-Lyme); Eileen Gordon (Romford); Jane Griffiths (Reading East); Harriet Harman (Camberwell and Peckham); Sylvia Heal (Halesowen and Rowley Regis); Patricia Hewitt (Leicester West); Margaret Hodge (Barking); Kate Hoey (Vauxhall); Beverley Hughes (Stretford and Urmston); Joan Humble (Blackpool North and Fleetwood); Glenda Jackson (Hampstead and Highgate); Helen Jackson (Sheffield Hillsborough); Melanie Johnson (Welwyn Hatfield); Fiona Jones (Newark); Helen Jones (Warrington North); Jenny Jones (Wolverhampton South West); Lynne Jones (Birmingham Selly Oak); Tessa Jowell (Dulwich and West Norwood); Sally Keeble (Northampton North); Ann Keen (Brentford and Isleworth); Ruth Kelly (Bolton West); Jane Kennedy (Liverpool Wavertree); Oona King (Bethnal Green and Bow); Tessa Kingham (Gloucester); Jackie Lawrence (Preseli Pembrokeshire); Helen Liddell (Airdrie and Shotts); Fiona MacTaggart (Slough); Alice Mahon (Halifax); Judy Mallaber (Amber Valley); Christine McCafferty (Calder Valley); Siobhain McDonagh (Mitcham and Morden); Anne McGuire (Stirling); Shona McIsaac (Cleethorpes); Rosemary McKenna (Cumbernauld and Kilsyth); Gillian Merron (Lincoln); Laura Moffatt (Crawley); Margaret Moran (Luton South); Julie Morgan (Cardiff North); Estelle Morris (Birmingham Yardley); Kali Mountford (Colne Valley); Marjorie Mowlam (Redcar); Diana Organ (Forest of Dean); Sandra Osborne (Ayr); Linda Perham (Ilford North); Bridget Prentice (Lewisham East); Dawn Primarolo (Bristol South); Joyce Quin (Gateshead East and Washington West); Barbara Roche (Hornsey and Wood Green); Joan Ruddock (Lewisham Deptford); Christine Russell (Chester, City of); Joan Ryan (Enfield North); Debra Shipley (Stourbridge); Clare Short (Birmingham Ladywood); Angela Smith (Basildon); Geraldine Smith (Morecambe and Lunesdale); Jacqui Smith (Redditch); Helen Southworth (Warrington South); Rachel Squire (Dunfermline West); Phyllis Starkey (Milton Keynes South West); Gisela Stuart (Birmingham Edgbaston); Ann Taylor (Dewsbury); Dari Taylor (Stockton South); Joan Walley (Stoke-on-Trent North); Claire Ward (Watford); Betty Williams (Conwy); Rosie Winterton (Doncaster Central); Audrey Wise (Preston).

## Women candidates and MPs at general elections since 1945

| Year | No of women candidates | C | Lab | Lib and L/SDP All LD | Others | Total elected |
|---|---|---|---|---|---|---|
| | | | Number of women Members of Parliament | | | |
| 1945 | 87 | 1 | 21 | 1 | 1 | 24 |
| 1950 | 126 | 6 | 14 | 1 | - | 21 |
| 1951 | 74 | 6 | 11 | - | - | 17 |
| 1955 | 87 | 9 | 14 | - | 1 | 24 |
| 1959 | 75 | 12 | 13 | - | - | 25 |
| 1964 | 89 | 11 | 17 | - | - | 28 |
| 1966 | 80 | 7 | 19 | - | - | 26 |
| 1970 | 97 | 15 | 10 | - | 1 | 26 |
| 1974 (Feb) | 143 | 9 | 13 | - | 1 | 23 |
| 1974 (Oct) | 150 | 7 | 18 | - | 2 | 27 |
| 1979 | 206 | 8 | 11 | - | - | 19 |
| 1983 | 276 | 13 | 10 | - | - | 23 |
| 1987 | 327 | 17 | 21 | 2 | 1 | 41 |
| 1992 | 568 | 20 | 37 | 2 | 1 | 60 |

## Conservative (13)

Virginia Bottomley (Surrey South West); Angela Browning (Tiverton and Honiton); Cheryl Gillan (Chesham and Amersham); Teresa Gorman (Billericay); Julie Kirkbride (Bromsgrove); Eleanor Laing (Epping Forest); Teresa May (Maidenhead); Anne McIntosh (Vale of York); Marion Roe (Broxbourne); Gillian Shephard (Norfolk South West); Caroline Spelman (Meriden); Ann Widdecombe (Maidstone and the Weald); Ann Winterton (Congleton).

## Liberal Democrat (3)

Jackie Ballard (Taunton); Ray Michie (Argyll and Bute); Jenny Tonge (Richmond Park).

## Scottish National Party (2)

Roseanna Cunningham (Perth); Margaret Ewing (Moray).

# BOWING OUT AND VOTED OUT

**T**WO CONSERVATIVE Cabinet ministers — Sir Patrick Mayhew, the Northern Ireland Secretary, and Lord Mackay of Clashfern, the Lord Chancellor — retired at the general election, along with seven Tory and three Labour ex-Cabinet ministers. The ten were:
**Conservative:** Kenneth Baker (ex-Home Secretary, Education Secretary, and party chairman); John Biffen (ex-Leader of the House); Paul Channon (Transport); David Howell (Energy and Transport); Douglas Hurd (Foreign, Home and Northern Ireland Secretary); Michael Jopling (Agriculture and Chief Whip); John Patten (Education).
**Labour:** Roy Hattersley (ex-deputy leader); Peter Shore; Stanley Orme.

Richard Ryder and Tim Renton, ex-Government Chief Whips, decided to stand down. Tim Eggar, Energy Minister, and Steven Norris, a Transport Minister, and several other middle and junior ministers called it a day. Three Tory Dames — Janet Fookes (a Deputy Speaker), Elaine Kellett-Bowman and Jill Knight — retired. Sir David Steel, former Liberal leader, headed the Lib Dem departures. Sir Harold Walker, a former Deputy Speaker and Employment Minister, also went.

In the Lords, Baroness Chalker of Wallasey, Overseas Development Minister since 1989 and a Foreign Office Minister of State since 1986, announced that she was retiring from the front bench.

A total of 117 MPs retired, compared with 79 in 1992. Among the 56 Tories who retired then was Alan Clark, who became MP for Kensington and Chelsea at this election.

## FULL LIST OF RETIRING MPs

### Conservative (72)

Michael Alison (Selby); Sir Tom Arnold (Hazel Grove); David Ashby (Leicestershire North West); Jack Aspinwall (Wansdyke); Kenneth Baker (Mole Valley) — created life peer; Nicholas Baker (Dorset North) — died during election campaign; Robert Banks (Harrogate); John Biffen (Shropshire North) — created life peer; Hartley Booth (Finchley); John Butcher (Coventry South West); John Carlisle (Luton North); Sir Kenneth Carlisle (Lincoln); Paul Channon (Southend West) — created life peer; Winston Churchill (Davyhulme); Sir Julian Critchley (Aldershot); Terry Dicks (Hayes and Harlington); Sir Anthony Durant (Reading West); Tim Eggar (Enfield North); Barry Field (Isle of Wight); Dudley Fishburn (Kensington); Dame Janet Fookes (Plymouth Drake); Tristan Garel-Jones (Watford); Sir Anthony Grant (Cambridgeshire South West); Sir Michael Grylls (Surrey North West); Sir John Hannam (Exeter); David Harris (St Ives); Sir Robert Hicks (Cornwall South East); Sir Terence Higgins (Worthing); Sir Peter Hordern (Horsham); David Howell (Guildford) — created life peer; Sir Ralph Howell (Norfolk North); Sir John Hunt (Ravensbourne); Douglas Hurd (Witney) — created life peer; Michael Jopling (Westmorland and Lonsdale) — created life peer; Dame Elaine Kellett-Bowman (Lancaster); Dame Jill Knight (Birmingham Edgbaston); Sir David Knox (Staffordshire Moorlands); Sir Michael Marshall (Arundel); Sir Patrick Mayhew (Tunbridge Wells) — created life peer; Sir Patrick McNair-Wilson (New Forest); Sir David Mitchell (Hampshire North West); Sir Hector Monro (Dumfries); Sir Fergus Montgomery (Altrincham and Sale); Richard Needham (Wiltshire North); Anthony Nelson (Chichester); Steven Norris (Epping Forest); Sir Cranley Onslow (Woking); John Patten (Oxford West and Abingdon) — created life peer; Sir Geoffrey Pattie (Chertsey and Walton); Tim Renton (Sussex Mid) — created life peer; Sir Wyn Roberts (Conwy); Richard Ryder (Norfolk Mid) — created life peer; Sir Tim Sainsbury (Hove); Sir Nicholas Scott (Chelsea); Sir Giles Shaw (Pudsey); Sir Roger Sims (Chislehurst); Sir Trevor Skeet (Bedfordshire North); Tim Smith (Beaconsfield); Sir Keith Speed (Ashford); Sir James Spicer (Dorset West); Michael Stephen (Shoreham); Allan Stewart (Eastwood); Roy Thomason (Bromsgrove); Patrick Thompson (Norwich North); Cyril Townsend (Bexleyheath); Neville Trotter (Tynemouth); Sir Gerard Vaughan (Reading East); George Walden (Buckingham); John Ward (Poole); Sir John Wheeler (Westminster North); Sir Jerry Wiggin (Weston-super-Mare); Mark Wolfson (Sevenoaks).

### Labour (38)

Roland Boyes (Houghton and Washington); Jeremy Bray (Motherwell South); Jim Callaghan (Heywood and Middleton); Bryan Davies (Oldham Central and Royton); Don Dixon (Jarrow) — created life peer; Jimmy Dunnachie (Glasgow Pollok); Kenneth Eastham (Manchester Blackley); John Evans (St Helens North) — created life peer; Andrew Faulds (Warley East); John Fraser (Norwood); John Garrett (Norwich South); John Gilbert (Dudley East) — created life peer; Mildred Gordon (Bow and Poplar); Peter Hardy (Wentworth); Roy Hattersley (Birmingham Sparkbrook) — created life peer; Douglas Hoyle (Warrington North) — created life peer; Norman Hogg (Cumbernauld and Kilsyth); Robert Hughes (Aberdeen North); Roy Hughes (Newport East); Greville Janner (Leicester West); Joan Lestor (Eccles) — created life peer; Robert Litherland (Manchester Central); Sir Geoffrey Lofthouse (Pontefract and Castleford) — created life peer; Edward Loyden (Liverpool Garston); Max Madden (Bradford West); William McKelvey (Kilmarnock and Loudoun); Alfred Morris (Manchester Wythenshawe); Gordon Oakes (Halton); Stanley Orme (Salford East); Robert Parry (Liverpool Riverside); Stuart Randall (Hull West); Peter Shore (Bethnal Green and Stepney) — created life peer; Nigel Spearing (Newham South); Jack Thompson (Wansbeck); Sir Harold Walker (Doncaster Central); Gareth Wardell (Gower); Mike Watson (Glasgow Central); David Young (Bolton South East).

## Liberal Democrat (6)

David Alton (Liverpool Mossley Hill) – created life peer; Alex Carlile (Montgomery); Sir Russell Johnston (Inverness, Nairn and Lochaber) – created life peer; Emma Nicholson (Devon West and Torridge); Sir David Steel (Tweeddale, Ettrick and Lauderdale) – created life peer; Peter Thurnham (Bolton, North East).

## Ulster Unionist (1)

James Molyneaux (Lagan Valley) – created life peer.

**FULL LIST OF DEFEATED MPs**

## Conservative (126)

Jonathan Aitken (Thanet South); Richard Alexander (Newark); Rupert Allason (Torbay); Jacques Arnold (Gravesham); Robert Atkins (Ribble South); Matthew Banks (Southport); Michael Bates (Middlesbrough South and Cleveland East); Spencer Batiste (Elmet); Henry Bellingham (Norfolk North West); Vivian Bendall (Ilford North); Sir Nicholas Bonsor (Upminster); Sir Andrew Bowden (Brighton Kemptown); John Bowis (Battersea); Sir Rhodes Boyson (Brent North); Gyles Brandreth (Chester, City of); Sir Graham Bright (Luton South); Michael Brown (Cleethorpes); Nicholas Budgen (Wolverhampton South West); Alistair Burt (Bury North); Peter Butler (Milton Keynes North East); Matthew Carrington (Hammersmith and Fulham); Michael Carttiss (Great Yarmouth); Sebastian Coe (Falmouth and Camborne); David Congdon (Croydon Central); Derek Conway (Shrewsbury and Atcham); Anthony Coombs (Wyre Forest); Simon Coombs (Swindon South); Sir John Cope (Northavon); James Couchman (Gillingham); Edwina Currie (Derbyshire South); Nirj Deva (Brentford and Isleworth); Tim Devlin (Stockton South); Lord James Douglas-Hamilton (Edinburgh West); Den Dover (Chorley); Robert Dunn (Dartford); Hugh Dykes (Harrow East); Harold Elletson (Blackpool North and Fleetwood); David Evans (Welwyn Hatfield); Jonathan Evans (Brecon and Radnorshire); Roger Evans (Monmouth); David Evennett (Bexleyheath and Crayford); Dame Peggy Fenner (Medway); Nigel Forman (Carshalton and Wallington); Michael Forsyth (Stirling); Sir Marcus Fox (Shipley); Roger Freeman (Kettering); Douglas French (Gloucester); Sir Peter Fry (Wellingborough); Phil Gallie (Ayr); Dr Charles Goodson-Wickes (Wimbledon); Sir John Gorst (Hendon); Harry Greenway (Ealing North); Peter Griffiths (Portsmouth North); Neil Hamilton (Tatton); Keith Hampson (Leeds North West); Jeremy Hanley (Richmond Park); Andrew Hargreaves (Birmingham Hall Green); Warren Hawksley (Stourbridge); Jerry Hayes (Harlow); Charles Hendry (High Peak); Sir James Hill (Southampton Test); Robert G. Hughes (Harrow West); David Hunt (Wirral West); Toby Jessel (Twickenham); Gwilym Jones (Cardiff North); Robert Jones (Hemel Hempstead); Timothy Kirkhope (Leeds North East); Roger Knapman (Stroud); Angela Knight (Erewash); Gregory Knight (Derby North); George Kynoch (Aberdeenshire West and Kincardine); Jacqui Lait (Hastings and Rye); Norman Lamont (Harrogate and Knaresborough); Ian Lang (Galloway and Upper Nithsdale); Sir Ivan Lawrence (Burton); Barry Legg (Milton Keynes South West); Sir Mark Lennox-Boyd (Morecambe and Lunesdale); Sir James Lester (Broxtowe); Lady Olga Maitland (Sutton and Cheam); Gerald Malone (Winchester); Keith Mans (Lancaster and Wyre); Paul Marland (Forest of Dean); Antony Marlow (Northampton North); John Marshall (Finchley and Golders Green); David Martin (Portsmouth South); David Mellor (Putney); Andrew Mitchell (Gedling); Sir Roger Moate (Sittingbourne and Sheppey); Michael Morris (Northampton South); Sir Michael Neubert (Romford); Tony Newton (Braintree); David Nicholson (Taunton); Phillip Oppenheim (Amber Valley); Sir Irvine Patnick (Sheffield Hallam); James Pawsey (Rugby and Kenilworth); Elizabeth Peacock (Batley and Spen); David Porter (Waveney); Michael Portillo (Enfield Southgate); William Powell (Corby); Tim Rathbone (Lewes); Rod Richards (Clwyd West); Graham Riddick (Colne Valley); Malcolm Rifkind (Edinburgh Pentlands); Raymond Robertson (Aberdeen South); Mark Robinson (Somerton and Frome); Dame Angela Rumbold (Mitcham and Morden); Tom Sackville (Bolton West); David Shaw (Dover); Sir Colin Shepherd (Hereford); Sir Dudley Smith (Warwick and Leamington); Robert Spink (Castle Point); Iain Sproat (Harwich); Robin Squire (Hornchurch); Michael Stern (Bristol North West); David Sumberg (Bury South); Walter Sweeney (Vale of Glamorgan); John Sykes (Scarborough and Whitby); Sir Donald Thompson (Calder Valley); Sir Malcolm Thornton (Crosby); Richard Tracey (Kingston and Surbiton); Ian Twinn (Edmonton); William Waldegrave (Bristol West); William Walker (Tayside North); Gary Waller (Keighley); John Watts (Reading East); Timothy Wood (Stevenage).

## Liberal Democrat (3)

Chris Davies (Oldham East and Saddleworth); Liz Lynne (Rochdale); Diana Maddock (Christchurch).

## SDLP (1)

Joe Hendron (Belfast West).

## DUP (1)

The Rev William McCrea (Ulster Mid).

## Referendum Party (1)

Sir George Gardiner (Reigate).

# MANIFESTOS

# LABOUR MANIFESTO

## Britain will be better with new Labour

- Our case is simple: that Britain can and must be better.
- The vision is one of national renewal, a country with drive, purpose and energy.
- In each area of policy a new and distinctive approach has been mapped out, one that differs from the old Left and the Conservative Right. This is why new Labour is new.
- New Labour is a party of ideas and ideals but not of outdated ideology. What counts is what works. The objectives are radical. The means will be modern.
- This is our contract with the people.

**I** BELIEVE in Britain. It is a great country with a great history. The British people are a great people. But I believe Britain can and must be better: better schools, better hospitals, better ways of tackling crime, of building a modern welfare state, of equipping ourselves for a new world economy.

I want a Britain that is one nation, with shared values and purpose, where merit comes before privilege, run for the many not the few, strong and sure of itself at home and abroad.

I want a Britain that does not shuffle into the new millennium afraid of the future, but strides into it with confidence.

I want to renew our country's faith in the ability of its government and politics to deliver this new Britain.

I want to do it by making a limited set of important promises and achieving them. This is the purpose of the bond of trust I set out at the end of this introduction, in which ten specific commitments are put before you. Hold us to them. They are our covenant with you.

I want to renew faith in politics by being honest about the last 18 years. Some things the Conservatives got right. We will not change them. It is where they got things wrong that we will make change. We have no intention or desire to replace one set of dogmas by another.

I want to renew faith in politics through a government that will govern in the interest of the many, the broad majority of people who work hard, play by the rules, pay their dues and feel let down by a political system that gives the breaks to the few, to an elite at the top increasingly out of touch with the rest of us.

And I want, above all, to govern in a way that brings our country together, that unites our nation in facing the tough and dangerous challenges of the new economy and changed society in which we must live. I want a Britain which we all feel part of, in whose future we all have a stake, in which what I want for my own children I want for yours.

Rt Hon Tony Blair.

## A new politics

The reason for having created new Labour is to meet the challenges of a different world. The millennium symbolises a new era opening up for Britain. I am confident about our future prosperity, even optimistic, if we have the courage to change and use it to build a better Britain.

To accomplish this means more than just a change of government. Our aim is no less than to set British political life on a new course for the future.

People are cynical about politics and distrustful of political promises. That is hardly surprising. There have been few more gross breaches of faith than when the Conservatives under Mr Major promised, before the election of 1992, that they would not raise taxes, but would cut them every year; and then went on to raise them by the largest amount in peacetime history starting in the first Budget after the election. The Exchange Rate Mechanism as the cornerstone of economic policy, Europe, health, crime, schools, sleaze — the broken promises are strewn across the country's memory.

The Conservatives' broken promises taint all politics. That is why we have made it our guiding rule not to promise what we cannot deliver; and to deliver what we promise. What follows is not the politics of a 100 days that dazzles for a time, then fizzles out. It is not the politics of a revolution, but of a fresh start, the patient rebuilding and renewing of this country — renewal that can take root and build over time.

That is one way in which politics in Britain will gain a new lease of life. But there is another. We aim to put behind us the bitter political struggles of left and right that have torn our country apart for too many decades. Many of these conflicts have no relevance whatsoever to the modern world — public versus private, bosses versus workers, middle class versus working class. It is time for this country to move on and move forward. We are proud of our history, proud of what we have achieved — but we must learn from our history, not be chained to it.

## LABOUR MANIFESTO

### New Labour

The purpose of new Labour is to give Britain a different political choice: the choice between a failed Conservative government, exhausted and divided in everything other than its desire to cling on to power, and a new and revitalised Labour Party that has been resolute in transforming itself into a party of the future.

We have rewritten our constitution, the new Clause Four, to put a commitment to enterprise alongside the commitment to justice. We have changed the way we make policy, and put our relations with the trade unions on a modern footing where they accept they can get fairness but no favours from a Labour government. Our MPs are all now selected by ordinary party members, not small committees or pressure groups. The membership itself has doubled, to over 400,000, with half the members having joined since the last election.

We submitted our draft manifesto, *new Labour new life for Britain*, to a ballot of all our members, 95 per cent of whom gave it their express endorsement.

We are a national party, supported today by people from all walks of life, from the successful businessman or woman to the pensioner on a council estate. Young people have flooded in to join us in what is the fastest growing youth section of any political party in the western world.

### The vision

We are a broad-based movement for progress and justice. New Labour is the political arm of none other than the British people as a whole. Our values are the same: the equal worth of all, with no one cast aside; fairness and justice within strong communities.

But we have liberated these values from outdated dogma or doctrine, and we have applied these values to the modern world.

I want a country in which people get on, do well, make a success of their lives. I have no time for the politics of envy. We need more successful entrepreneurs, not fewer of them. But these life-chances should be for all the people. And I want a society in which ambition and compassion are seen as partners not opposites — where we value public service as well as material wealth.

New Labour believes in a society where we do not simply pursue our own individual aims but where we hold many aims in common and work together to achieve them. How we build the industry and employment opportunities of the future; how we tackle the division and inequality in our society; how we care for and enhance our environment and quality of life; how we develop modern education and health services; how we create communities that are safe, where mutual respect and tolerance are the order of the day. These are things we must achieve together as a country.

The vision is one of national renewal, a country with drive, purpose and energy. A Britain equipped to prosper in a global economy of technological change; with a modern welfare state; its politics more accountable; and confident of its place in the world.

### Programme: a new centre and centre-left politics

In each area of policy a new and distinctive approach has been mapped out, one that differs both from the solutions of the old Left and those of the Conservative Right. This is why new Labour is new. We believe in the strength of our values, but we recognise also that the policies of 1997 cannot be those of 1947 or 1967. More detailed policy has been produced by us than by any opposition in history. Our direction and destination are clear.

The old Left would have sought state control of industry. The Conservative right is content to leave all to the market. We reject both approaches. Government and industry must work together to achieve key objectives aimed at enhancing the dynamism of the market, not undermining it.

In industrial relations, we make it clear that there will be no return to flying pickets, secondary action, strikes with no ballots or the trade union law of the 1970s. There will instead be basic minimum rights for the individual at the workplace, where our aim is partnership not conflict between employers and employees.

In economic management, we accept the global economy as a reality and reject the isolationism and "go-it-alone" policies of the extremes of Right or Left.

In education, we reject both the idea of a return to the 11-plus and the monolithic comprehensive schools that take no account of children's differing abilities. Instead we favour all-in schooling which identifies the distinct abilities of individual pupils and organises them in classes to maximise their progress in individual subjects. In this way we modernise the comprehensive principle, learning from the experience of its 30 years of application.

In health policy, we will safeguard the basic principles of the NHS, which we founded, but will not return to the top-down management of the 1970s. So we will keep the planning and provision of healthcare separate, but put planning on a longer-term, decentralised and more co-operative basis. The key is to root out unnecessary administrative cost, and to spend money on the right things — frontline care.

On crime, we believe in personal responsibility and in punishing crime, but also tackling its underlying causes — so, tough on crime, tough on the causes of crime, different from the Labour approach of the past and the Tory policy of today.

Over-centralisation of government and lack of accountability was a problem in governments of both left and right. Labour is committed to the democratic renewal of our country through decentralisation and the elimination of excessive government secrecy.

In addition, we will face up to the new issues that confront us. We will be the party of welfare reform. In consultation and partnership with the people, we will design a modern welfare state based on rights and duties going together, fit for the modern world.

We will stand up for Britain's interests in Europe after the shambles of the last six years, but, more than that, we will lead a campaign for reform in Europe. Europe isn't working in the way this country and Europe need. But to lead means to be involved, to be constructive, to be capable of getting our own way.

We will put concern for the environment at the heart of policy-making, so that it is not an add-on extra, but informs the whole of government, from housing and energy policy through to global warming and international agreements.

We will search out at every turn new ways and new ideas to tackle the new issues: how to encourage more flexible working hours and practices to suit employees and employers alike; how to harness the huge potential of the new information technology; how to simplify the processes of the government machine; how to put public and private sector together in partnership to give us the infrastructure and transport system we need.

We will be a radical government. But the definition of radicalism will not be that of doctrine, whether of Left or Right, but of achievement. New Labour is a party of ideas and ideals but not of outdated ideology. What counts is what works. The objectives are radical. The means will be modern.

So the party is transformed. The vision is clear. And from that vision stems a modern programme of change and renewal for Britain. We understand that after 18 years of one-party rule, people want change, believe that it is necessary for the country and for democracy, but require faith to make the change.

We therefore set out in the manifesto that follows ten commitments, commitments that form our bond of trust with the people. They are specific. They are real. Judge us on them. Have trust in us and we will repay that trust.

Our mission in politics is to rebuild this bond of trust between government and the people. That is the only way democracy can flourish. I pledge to Britain a government which shares their hopes, which understands their fears, and which will work as partners with and for all our people, not just the privileged few. This is our contract with the people.

**Over the five years of a Labour government:**
1. Education will be our number one priority, and we will increase the share of national income spent on education as we decrease it on the bills of economic and social failure.
2. There will be no increase in the basic or top rates of income tax.
3. We will provide stable economic growth with low inflation, and promote dynamic and competitive business and industry at home and abroad.
4. We will get 250,000 young unemployed off benefit and into work.
5. We will rebuild the NHS, reducing spending on administration and increasing spending on patient care.
6. We will be tough on crime and tough on the causes of crime, and halve the time it takes persistent juvenile offenders to come to court.
7. We will help build strong families and strong communities, and lay the foundations of a modern welfare state in pensions and community care.
8. We will safeguard our environment, and develop an integrated transport policy to fight congestion and pollution.
9. We will clean up politics, decentralise political power throughout the United Kingdom and put the funding of political parties on a proper and accountable basis.
10. We will give Britain the leadership in Europe which Britain and Europe need.

We have modernised the Labour Party and we will modernise Britain. This means knowing where we want to go; being clear-headed about the country's future; telling the truth; making tough choices; insisting that all parts of the public sector live within their means; taking on vested interests that hold people back; standing up to unreasonable demands from any quarter; and being prepared to give a moral lead where government has responsibilities it should not avoid.

Britain does deserve better. And new Labour will be better for Britain.

## We will make education our number one priority

+ Cut class sizes to 30 or under for five, six and seven year-olds
+ Nursery places for all four year-olds
+ Attack low standards in schools
+ Access to computer technology
+ Lifelong learning through a new University for Industry
+ More spending on education as the cost of unemployment falls

Education has been the Tories' biggest failure. It is Labour's number one priority. It is not just good for the individual. It is an economic necessity for the nation. We will compete successfully on the basis of quality or not at all. And quality comes from developing the potential of all our people. It is the people who are our greatest natural asset. We will ensure they can fulfil their potential.

Nearly half of 11 year-olds in England and Wales fail to reach expected standards in English and maths. Britain has a smaller share of 17 and 18 year-olds in full-time education than any major industrial nation. Nearly two-thirds of the British workforce lack vocational qualifications.

There are excellent schools in Britain's state education system. But far too many children are denied the opportunity to succeed. Our task is to raise the standards of every school. We will put behind us the old arguments that have bedevilled education in this country. We reject the Tories' obsession with school structures: all parents should be offered real choice through good quality schools, each with its own strengths and individual ethos. There should be no return to the 11-plus. It divides children into successes and failures at far too early an age.

We must modernise comprehensive schools. Children are not all of the same ability, nor do they learn at the same speed. That means "setting" children in classes to maximise progress, for the benefit of high-fliers and slower learners alike. The focus must be on levelling up, not levelling down.

With Labour, the Department for Education and Employment will become a leading office of state. It will give a strong and consistent lead to help raise standards in every school. Standards, more than structures, are the key to success. Labour will never put dogma before children's education. Our approach will be to intervene where there are problems, not where schools are succeeding.

Labour will never force the abolition of good schools whether in the private or state sector. Any changes in the admissions policies of grammar schools will be decided by local parents. Church schools will retain their distinctive religious ethos.

We wish to build bridges wherever we can across education divides. The educational apartheid created by the public/private divide diminishes the whole education system.

## Zero tolerance of underperformance

Every school has the capacity to succeed. All Local Education Authorities (LEAs) must demonstrate that every school is improving. For those failing schools unable to improve, ministers will order a "fresh start" – close the school and start afresh on the same site. Where good schools and bad schools coexist side by side we will authorise LEAs to allow one school to take over the other to set the underperforming school on a new path.

## Quality nursery education guaranteed for all four-year-olds

Nursery vouchers have been proven not to work. They are costly and do not generate more quality nursery places. We will use the money saved by scrapping nursery vouchers to guarantee places for four-year-olds. We will invite selected local authorities to pilot early excellence centres combining education and care for the under-fives. We will set targets for universal provision for three-year-olds whose parents want it.

## New focus on standards in primary schools

Primary schools are the key to mastering the basics and developing in every child an eagerness to learn. Every school needs baseline assessment of pupils when they enter the school, and a year-on-year target for improvement.

We will reduce class sizes for five, six and seven year-olds to 30 or under, by phasing out the assisted places scheme, the cost of which is set to rise to £180 million per year.

We must recognise the three "r"s for what they are — building blocks of all learning that must be taught better. We will achieve this by improving the skills of the teaching force; ensuring a stronger focus on literacy in the curriculum; and piloting literacy summer schools to meet our new target that within a decade every child leaves primary school with a reading age of at least 11 (barely half do today).

Our numeracy taskforce will develop equally ambitious targets. We will encourage the use of the most effective teaching methods, including phonics for reading and whole class interactive teaching for maths.

## Attacking educational disadvantage

No matter where a school is, Labour will not tolerate under-achievement. Public/private partnerships will improve the condition of school buildings.

There will be education action zones to attack low standards by recruiting the best teachers and head teachers to under-achieving schools; by supporting voluntary mentoring schemes to provide one-to-one support for disadvantaged pupils; and by creating new opportunities for children, after the age of 14, to enhance their studies by acquiring knowledge and experience within industry and commerce.

To attack under-achievement in urban areas, we have developed a new scheme with the Premier League. In partnerships between central government, local government and football clubs, study support centres will be set up at Premier League grounds for the benefit of local children. The scheme will be launched on a pilot basis during the 1997-98 season.

We support the greatest possible integration into mainstream education of pupils with special educational needs, while recognising that specialist facilities are essential to meet particular needs.

## Realising the potential of new technology

Labour is the pioneer of new thinking. We have agreed with British Telecom and the cable companies that they will wire up schools, libraries, colleges and hospitals to the information superhighway free of charge. We have also secured agreement to make access charges as low as possible.

For the Internet we plan a National Grid for Learning, franchised as a public/private partnership, which will bring to teachers up-to-date materials to enhance their skills, and to children high-quality educational materials. We will use lottery money to improve the skills of existing teachers in information technology.

In opposition, Labour set up the independent Stevenson Commission to promote access for children to new technology. Its recent report is a challenging programme for the future. We are urgently examining how to implement its plans, in particular the development of educational software through a grading system which will provide schools with guarantees of product quality; and the provision for every child of an individual e-mail address. An independent standing committee will continue to advise us on the implementation of our plans in government.

## The role of parents

We will increase the powers and responsibilities of parents. There will be more parent governors and, for the first time, parent representatives on LEAs.

A major objective is to promote a culture of responsibility for learning within the family, through contracts between all schools and parents, defining the responsibilities of each. National guidelines will establish minimum periods for homework for primary and secondary school pupils.

Teachers will be entitled to positive support from parents to promote good attendance and sound discipline. Schools suffer from unruly and disruptive pupils. Exclusion or suspension may sometimes be necessary. We will, however, pilot new pupil referral units so that schools are protected but these pupils are not lost to education or the country.

## New job description for LEAs

The judge and jury of LEA performance will be their contribution to raising standards. LEAs are closer to schools than central government, and have the authority of being locally elected. But they will be required to devolve power, and more of their budgets, to heads and governors. LEA performance will be inspected by Ofsted and the Audit Commission. Where authorities are deemed to be failing, the secretary of state may suspend the relevant powers of the LEA and send in an improvement team.

## Grant-maintained schools
Schools that are now grant maintained will prosper with Labour's proposals, as will every school. Tory claims that Labour will close these schools are false. The system of funding will not discriminate unfairly either between schools or between pupils. LEAs will be represented on governing bodies, but will not control them. We support guidelines for open and fair admissions, along the lines of those introduced in 1993; but we will also provide a right of appeal to an independent panel in disputed cases.

## Teachers: pressure and support
Schools are critically dependent on the quality of all staff. The majority of teachers are skilful and dedicated, but some fall short. We will improve teacher training, and ensure that all teachers have an induction year when they first qualify, to ensure their suitability for teaching.

There will be a general teaching council to speak for and raise standards in the profession. We will create a new grade of teachers to recognise the best. There will, however, be speedy, but fair, procedures to remove teachers who cannot do the job. The strength of a school is critically dependent on the quality of its head. We will establish mandatory qualifications for the post. A head teacher will be appointed to a position only when fully trained to accept the responsibility.

## Higher education
The improvement and expansion needed cannot be funded out of general taxation. Our proposals for funding have been made to the Dearing Committee, in line with successful policies abroad.

The costs of student maintenance should be repaid by graduates on an income-related basis, from the career success to which higher education has contributed. The current system is badly administered and payback periods are too short. We will provide efficient administration, with fairness ensured by longer payback periods where required.

## Lifelong learning
We must learn throughout life, to retain employment through new and improved skills. We will promote adult learning both at work and in the critical sector of further education.

In schools and colleges, we support broader A levels and upgraded vocational qualifications, underpinned by rigorous standards and key skills.

Employers have the primary responsibility for training their workforces in job-related skills. But individuals should be given the power to invest in training. We will invest public money for training in Individual Learning Accounts which individuals — for example women returning to the labour force — can then use to gain the skills they want. We will kick-start the programme for up to a million people, using £150 million of TEC money which could be better used and which would provide a contribution of £150, alongside individuals making small investments of their own. Employers will be encouraged to make voluntary contributions to these funds. We will also promote the extension of the Investors in People initiative into many more small firms.

Our new University for Industry, collaborating with the Open University, will bring new opportunities to adults seeking to develop their potential. This will bring government, industry and education together to create a new resource whose remit will be to use new technology to enhance skills and education. The University for Industry will be a public/private partnership, commissioning software and developing the links to extend lifelong learning.

## Government spending on education
The Conservatives have cut government spending on education as a share of national income by the equivalent of more than £3 billion as spending on the bills of economic and social failure has risen. We are committed to reversing this trend of spending. Over the course of a five-year Parliament, as we cut the costs of economic and social failure we will raise the proportion of national income spent on education.

## We will promote personal prosperity for all
♦ Economic stability to promote investment
♦ Tough inflation target, mortgage rates as low as possible

♦ Stick for two years within existing spending limits
♦ Five-year pledge: no increase in income tax rates
♦ Long-term objective of ten pence starting rate of income tax
♦ Early Budget to get people off welfare and into work

The Conservatives have in 18 years created the two longest, deepest recessions this century. We have experienced the slowest average growth rate of any similar period since the Second World War. There has been a fundamental failure to tackle the underlying causes of inflation, of low growth and of unemployment. These are:

♦ too much economic instability, with wild swings from boom to bust
♦ too little investment in education and skills, and in the application of new technologies
♦ too few opportunities to find jobs, start new businesses or become self-employed
♦ too narrow an industrial base
♦ and too little sense of common purpose in the workplace or across the nation.

Britain can do better. We must build on the British qualities of inventiveness, creativity and adaptability. New Labour's objective is to improve living standards for the many, not just the few. Business can and must succeed in raising productivity. This requires a combination of a skilled and educated workforce with investment in the latest technological innovations, as the route to higher wages and employment.

An explicit objective of a Labour government will be to raise the trend rate of growth by strengthening our wealth-creating base. We will nurture investment in industry, skills, infrastructure and new technologies. And we will attack long-term unemployment, especially among young people. Our goal will be educational and employment opportunities for all.

Economic stability is the essential platform for sustained growth. In a global economy the route to growth is stability not inflation. The priority must be stable, low-inflation conditions for long-term growth. The root causes of inflation and low growth are the same — an economic and industrial base that remains weak. Government cannot solve all economic problems or end the economic cycle. But by spending wisely and taxing fairly, government can help tackle the problems. Our goals are low inflation, rising living standards and high and stable levels of employment.

## Spending and tax: new Labour's approach

The myth that the solution to every problem is increased spending has been comprehensively dispelled under the Conservatives. Spending has risen. But more spending has brought neither greater fairness nor less poverty. Quite the reverse — our society is more divided than it has been for generations. The level of public spending is no longer the best measure of the effectiveness of government action in the public interest. It is what money is actually spent on that counts more than how much money is spent.

The national debt has doubled under John Major. The public finances remain weak. A new Labour government will give immediate high priority to seeing how public money can be better used. New Labour will be wise spenders, not big spenders. We will work in partnership with the private sector to achieve our goals. We will ask about public spending the first question that a manager in any company would ask — can existing resources be used more effectively to meet our priorities? And because efficiency and value for money are central, ministers will be required to save before they spend. Save to invest is our approach, not tax and spend.

The increase in taxes under the Conservatives is the most dramatic evidence of economic failure. Since 1992 the typical family has paid more than £2,000 in extra taxes — the biggest tax hike in peacetime history, breaking every promise made by John Major at the last election. The tragedy is that those hardest hit are least able to pay. That is why we strongly opposed the imposition of VAT on fuel: it was Labour that stopped the government from increasing VAT on fuel to 17.5 per cent.

Taxation is not neutral in the way it raises revenue. How and what governments tax sends clear signals about the economic activities they believe should be encouraged or discouraged, and the values they wish to entrench in society. Just as, for example, work should be encouraged through the tax system, environmental pollution should be discouraged.

New Labour will establish a new trust on tax with the British people. The promises we make we will keep. The principles that will underpin our tax policy are clear:

♦ to encourage employment opportunities and work incentives for all
♦ to promote savings and investment
♦ and to be fair and be seen to be fair

New Labour is not about high taxes on ordinary families. It is about social justice and a fair deal.

New Labour therefore makes the following economic pledges.

## Fair taxes

There will be no return to the penal tax rates that existed under both Labour and Conservative governments in the 1970s. To encourage work and reward effort, we are pledged not to raise the basic or top rates of income tax throughout the next Parliament.

Our long-term objective is a lower starting rate of income tax of ten pence in the pound. Reducing the high marginal rates at the bottom end of the earning scale – often 70 or 80 per cent – is not only fair but desirable to encourage employment.

This goal will benefit the many, not the few. It is in sharp contrast to the Tory goal of abolishing capital gains and inheritance tax, at least half the benefit of which will go to the richest 5,000 families in the country.

We will cut VAT on fuel to five per cent, the lowest level allowed. We renew our pledge not to extend VAT to food, children's clothes, books and newspapers and public transport fares.

We will also examine the interaction of the tax and benefits systems so that they can be streamlined and modernised, so as to fulfil our objectives of promoting work incentives, reducing poverty and welfare dependency, and strengthening community and family life.

## No risks with inflation

We will match the current target for low and stable inflation of 2.5 per cent or less. We will reform the Bank of England to ensure that decision-making on monetary policy is more effective, open, accountable and free from short-term political manipulation.

## Strict rules for government borrowing

We will enforce the "golden rule" of public spending – over the economic cycle, we will only borrow to invest and not to fund current expenditure.

We will ensure that – over the economic cycle – public debt as a proportion of national income is at a stable and prudent level.

## Stick to planned public spending allocations for the first two years of office

Our decisions have not been taken lightly. They are a recognition of Conservative mismanagement of the public finances. For the next two years Labour will work within the departmental ceilings for spending already announced. We will resist unreasonable demands on the public purse, including any unreasonable public-sector pay demands.

## Switch spending from economic failure to investment

We will conduct a central spending review and departmental reviews to assess how to use resources better, while rooting out waste and inefficiency in public spending.

Labour priorities in public spending are different from Tory priorities.

## Tax reform to promote saving and investment

We will introduce a new individual savings account and extend the principle of Tessas and Peps to promote long-term saving. We will review the corporate and capital gains tax regimes to see how the tax system can promote greater long-term investment.

## Labour's welfare-to-work Budget

We will introduce a Budget within two months after the election to begin the task of equipping the British economy and reforming the welfare state to get young people and the long-term unemployed back to work. This welfare-to-work programme will be funded by a windfall levy on the excess profits of the privatised utilities, introduced in this Budget after we have consulted the regulators.

## We will help create successful and profitable businesses

♦ Backing business: skills, infrastructure, new markets
♦ Gains for consumers with tough competition law
♦ New measures to help small businesses
♦ National minimum wage to tackle low pay
♦ Boost local economic growth with Regional Development Agencies
♦ A strong and effective voice in Europe

New Labour offers business a new deal for the future. We will leave intact the main changes of the 1980s in industrial relations and enterprise. We see healthy profits as an essential motor of a dynamic market economy, and believe they depend on quality products, innovative entrepreneurs and skilled employees. We will build a new partnership with business to improve the competitiveness of British industry for the 21st century, leading to faster growth.

Many of the fundamentals of the British economy are still weak. Low pay and low skills go together: insecurity is the consequence of economic instability; the absence of quality jobs is a product of the weakness of our industrial base; we suffer from both high unemployment and skills shortages. There is no future for Britain as a low wage economy: we cannot compete on wages with countries paying a tenth or a hundredth of British wages.

We need to win on higher quality, skill, innovation and reliability. With Labour, British and inward investors will find this country an attractive and profitable place to do business.

New Labour believes in a flexible labour market that serves employers and employees alike. But flexibility alone is not enough. We need *"flexibility plus"*:

♦ *plus* higher skills and higher standards in our schools and colleges
♦ *plus* policies to ensure economic stability
♦ *plus* partnership with business to raise investment in infrastructure, science and research and to back small firms
♦ *plus* new leadership from Britain to reform Europe, in place of the current policy of drift and disengagement from our largest market
♦ *plus* guaranteeing Britain's membership of the single market — indeed opening up further markets inside and outside the EU — helping make Britain an attractive place to do business
♦ *plus* minimum standards of fair treatment, including a national minimum wage
♦ *plus* an imaginative welfare-to-work programme to put the long-term unemployed back to work and to cut social security costs.

## A reformed and tougher competition law

Competitiveness abroad must begin with competition at home. Effective competition can bring value and quality to consumers. As an early priority we will reform Britain's competition law. We will adopt a tough "prohibitive" approach to deter anti-competitive practices and abuses of market power.

In the utility industries we will promote competition wherever possible. Where competition is not an effective discipline, for example in the water industry, which has a poor environmental record and has in most cases been a tax-free zone, we will pursue tough, efficient regulation in the interests of customers, and, in the case of water, in the interests of the environment as well. We recognise the need for open and predictable regulation which is fair both to consumers and to shareholders and at the same time provides incentives for managers to innovate and improve efficiency.

## Reinvigorate the Private Finance Initiative

Britain's infrastructure is dangerously run down: parts of our road and rail network are seriously neglected, and all too often our urban environment has been allowed to deteriorate.

Labour pioneered the idea of public/private partnerships. It is Labour local authorities which have done most to create these partnerships at local level.

A Labour government will overcome the problems that have plagued the PFI at a national level. We will set priorities between projects, saving time and expense; we will seek a realistic allocation of risk between the partners to a project; and we will ensure that best practice is spread throughout government. We will aim to simplify and speed up the planning process for major infrastructure projects of vital national interest.

We will ensure that self-financing commercial organisations within the public sector — the Post Office is a prime example — are given greater commercial freedom to make the most of new opportunities.

## Backing small business

The number of small employers has declined by half a million since 1990. Support for small businesses will have a major role in our plans for economic growth. We will cut unnecessary red tape; provide for statutory interest on late payment of debts; improve support for high-tech start-ups; improve the quality and relevance of advice and training through a reformed Business Links network and the University for Industry; and assist firms to enter overseas markets more effectively.

## Local economic growth

Prosperity needs to be built from the bottom up. We will establish one-stop regional development agencies to co-ordinate regional economic development, help small business and encourage inward investment. Many regions are already taking informal steps to this end and they will be supported.

### Strengthen our capability in science, technology and design
The UK must be positively committed to the global pursuit of new knowledge, with a strong science base in our universities and centres of excellence leading the world. The Dearing Committee represents a significant opportunity to promote high-quality standards in science teaching and research throughout UK higher education. We support a collaborative approach between researchers and business, spreading the use of new technology and good design, and exploiting our own inventions to boost business in the UK.

### Promoting new green technologies and businesses
There is huge potential to develop Britain's environmental technology industries to create jobs, win exports and protect the environment.

Effective environmental management is an increasingly important component of modern business practice. We support a major push to promote energy conservation — particularly by the promotion of home energy efficiency schemes, linked to our environment taskforce for the under-25s. We are committed to an energy policy designed to promote cleaner, more efficient energy use and production, including a new and strong drive to develop renewable energy sources such as solar and wind energy, and combined heat and power. We see no economic case for the building of any new nuclear power stations.

### Key elements of the 1980s trade union reforms to stay
There must be minimum standards for the individual at work, including a minimum wage, within a flexible labour market. We need a sensible balance in industrial relations law — rights and duties go together.

The key elements of the trade union legislation of the 1980s will stay — on ballots, picketing and industrial action. People should be free to join or not to join a union. Where they do decide to join, and where a majority of the relevant workforce vote in a ballot for the union to represent them, the union should be recognised. This promotes stable and orderly industrial relations. There will be full consultation on the most effective means of implementing this proposal.

### Partnership at work
The best companies recognise their employees as partners in the enterprise. Employees whose conditions are good are more committed to their companies and are more productive. Many unions and employers are embracing partnership in place of conflict. Government should welcome this.

We are keen to encourage a variety of forms of partnership and enterprise, spreading ownership and encouraging more employees to become owners through Employee Share Ownership Plans and co-operatives. We support too the social chapter of the EU, but will deploy our influence in Europe to ensure that it develops so as to promote employability and competitiveness, not inflexibility.

### A sensibly-set national minimum wage
There should be a statutory level beneath which pay should not fall — with the minimum wage decided not on the basis of a rigid formula but according to the economic circumstances of the time and with the advice of an independent low pay commission, whose membership will include representatives of employers, including small business, and employees.

Every modern industrial country has a minimum wage, including the US and Japan. Britain used to have minimum wages through the Wages Councils. Introduced sensibly, the minimum wage will remove the worst excesses of low pay (and be of particular benefit to women), while cutting some of the massive £4 billion benefits bill by which the taxpayer subsidises companies that pay very low wages.

### We will get the unemployed from welfare to work
♦ Stop the growth of an "underclass" in Britain
♦ 250,000 young unemployed off benefit and into work
♦ Tax cuts for employers who create new jobs for the long-term unemployed
♦ Effective help for lone parents

There are over one million fewer jobs in Britain than in 1990. One in five families has no one working. One million single mothers are trapped on benefits. There is a wider gap between rich and poor than for generations.

We are determined not to continue down the road of a permanent have-not class, unemployed and disaffected from society. Our long-term objective is high and stable levels of employment. This is the true meaning of a stakeholder economy – where everyone has a stake in society and owes responsibilities to it.

The best way to tackle poverty is to help people into jobs – real jobs. The unemployed have a responsibility to take up the opportunity of training places or work, but these must be real opportunities. The Government's workfare proposals – with a success rate of one in ten – fail this test.

Labour's welfare-to-work programme will attack unemployment and break the spiral of escalating spending on social security. A one-off windfall levy on the excess profits of the privatised utilities will fund our ambitious programme.

## Every young person unemployed for more than six months in a job or training

We will give 250,000 under-25s opportunities for work, education and training. Four options will be on offer, each involving day-release education or training leading to a qualification:

♦ private-sector job: employers will be offered a £60-a-week rebate for six months
♦ work with a non-profit voluntary sector employer, paying a weekly wage, equivalent to benefit plus a fixed sum for six months
♦ full-time study for young people without qualifications on an approved course
♦ a job with the environment taskforce, linked to Labour's citizens' service programme
Rights and responsibilities must go hand in hand, without a fifth option of life on full benefit.

## Every 16 and 17-year-old on the road to a proper qualification by the year 2000

Nearly a third of young people do not achieve an NVQ level two qualification by age 19. All young people will be offered part-time or full-time education after the age of 16. Any under-18 year-old in a job will have the right to study on an approved course for qualifications at college. We will replace the failed Youth Training scheme with our new Target 2000 programme, offering young people high-quality education and training.

### Action on long-term unemployment

New partnerships between government and business, fully involving local authorities and the voluntary sector, will attack long-term joblessness. We will encourage employers to take on those who have suffered unemployment for more than two years with a £75-a-week tax rebate paid for six months, financed by the windfall levy. Our programme for the phased release of past receipts from council house sales will provide new jobs in the construction industry.

### Lone parents into work

Today the main connection between unemployed lone parents and the state is their benefits. Most lone parents want to work, but are given no help to find it. New Labour has a positive policy. Once the youngest child is in the second term of full-time school, lone parents will be offered advice by a proactive Employment Service to develop a package of job search, training and after-school care to help them off benefit.

### Customised, personalised services

We favour initiatives with new combinations of available benefits to suit individual circumstances. In new and innovative "Employment Zones", personal job accounts will combine money currently available for benefits and training, to offer the unemployed new options – leading to work and independence. We will co-ordinate benefits, employment and career services, and utilise new technology to improve their quality and efficiency.

### Fraud

Just as we owe it to the taxpayer to crack down on tax avoidance, so we must crack down on dishonesty in the benefit system. We will start with a clampdown on Housing Benefit fraud, estimated to cost £2 billion a year, and will maintain action against benefit fraud of all kinds.

### We will save the NHS

♦ 100,000 people off waiting lists
♦ End the Tory internal market

- End waiting for cancer surgery
- Tough quality targets for hospitals
- Independent food standards agency
- New public health drive
- Raise spending in real terms every year – and spend the money on patients not bureaucracy

Labour created the NHS 50 years ago. It is under threat from the Conservatives. We want to save and modernise the NHS.

But if the Conservatives are elected again there may well not be an NHS in five years' time – neither national nor comprehensive. Labour commits itself anew to the historic principle: that if you are ill or injured there will be a national health service there to help; and access to it will be based on need and need alone – not on your ability to pay, or on who your GP happens to be or on where you live.

In 1990 the Conservatives imposed on the NHS a complex internal market of hospitals competing to win contracts from health authorities and fundholding GPs. The result is an NHS strangled by costly red tape, with every individual transaction the subject of a separate invoice. After six years, bureaucracy swallows an extra £1.5 billion per year; there are 20,000 more managers and 50,000 fewer nurses on the wards; and more than one million people are on waiting lists. The Government has consistently failed to meet even its own health targets.

There can be no return to top-down management, but Labour will end the Conservatives' internal market in healthcare. The planning and provision of care are necessary and distinct functions, and will remain so. But under the Tories, the administrative costs of purchasing care have undermined provision and the market system has distorted clinical priorities. Labour will cut costs by removing the bureaucratic processes of the internal market.

The savings achieved will go on direct care for patients. As a start, the first £100 million saved will treat an extra 100,000 patients. We will end waiting for cancer surgery, thereby helping thousands of women waiting for breast cancer treatment.

**Primary care will play a lead role**
In recent years, GPs have gained power on behalf of their patients in a changed relationship with consultants, and we support this. But the development of GP fundholding has also brought disadvantages. Decision-making has been fragmented. Administrative costs have grown. And a two-tier service has resulted.

Labour will retain the lead role for primary care but remove the disadvantages that have come from the present system. GPs and nurses will take the lead in combining together locally to plan local health services more efficiently for all the patients in their area. This will enable all GPs in an area to bring their combined strength to bear upon individual hospitals to secure higher standards of patient provision. In making this change, we will build on the existing collaborative schemes which already serve 14 million people.

The current system of year-on-year contracts is costly and unstable. We will introduce three to five-year agreements between the local primary care teams and hospitals. Hospitals will then be better able to plan work at full capacity and co-operate to enhance patient services.

**Higher-quality services for patients**
Hospitals will retain their autonomy over day-to-day administrative functions, but, as part of the NHS, they will be required to meet high-quality standards in the provision of care. Management will be held to account for performance levels. Boards will become more representative of the local communities they serve.

A new patients' charter will concentrate on the quality and success of treatment. The Tories' so-called "Efficiency Index" counts the number of patient "episodes", not the quality or success of treatment.

With Labour, the measure will be quality of outcome, itself an incentive for effectiveness. As part of our concern to ensure quality, we will work towards the elimination of mixed-sex wards. Health authorities will become the guardians of high standards. They will monitor services, spread best practice and ensure rising standards of care.

The Tory attempt to use private money to build hospitals has failed to deliver. Labour will overcome the problems that have plagued the Private Finance Initiative, end the delays, sort out the confusion and develop new forms of public/private partnership that work better and protect the interests of the NHS. Labour is opposed to the privatisation of clinical services which is being actively promoted by the Conservatives.

Labour will promote new developments in telemedicine – bringing expert advice from regional centres of excellence to neighbourhood level using new technology.

## Good health
A new minister for public health will attack the root causes of ill health, and so improve lives and save the NHS money. Labour will set new goals for improving the overall health of the nation which recognise the impact that poverty, poor housing, unemployment and a polluted environment have on health.

Smoking is the greatest single cause of preventable illness and premature death in the UK. We will therefore ban tobacco advertising.

Labour will establish an independent food standards agency. The £3.5 billion BSE crisis and the *E. coli* outbreak which resulted in serious loss of life, have made unanswerable the case for the independent agency we have proposed.

## NHS spending
The Conservatives have wasted spending on the NHS. We will do better. We will raise spending on the NHS in real terms every year and put the money towards patient care. And a greater proportion of every pound spent will go on patient care not bureaucracy.

## An NHS for the future
The NHS requires continuity as well as change, or the system cannot cope. There must be pilots to ensure that change works. And there must be flexibility, not rigid prescription, if innovation is to flourish.

Our fundamental purpose is simple but hugely important: to restore the NHS as a public service working co-operatively for patients, not a commercial business driven by competition.

## We will be tough on crime and tough on the causes of crime
♦ Fast-track punishment for persistent young offenders
♦ Reform Crown Prosecution Service to convict more criminals
♦ Police on the beat not pushing paper
♦ Crackdown on petty crimes and neighbourhood disorder
♦ Fresh parliamentary vote to ban all handguns

Under the Conservatives, crime has doubled and many more criminals get away with their crimes: the number of people convicted has fallen by a third, with only one crime in 50 leading to a conviction. This is the worst record of any government since the Second World War – and for England and Wales the worst record of any major industrialised country. Last year alone violent crime rose 11 per cent.

We propose a new approach to law and order: tough on crime and tough on the causes of crime. We insist on individual responsibility for crime, and will attack the causes of crime by our measures to relieve social deprivation.

The police have our strong support. They are in the front line of the fight against crime and disorder. The Conservatives have broken their 1992 general election pledge to provide an extra 1,000 police officers. We will relieve the police of unnecessary bureaucratic burdens to get more officers back on the beat.

## Youth crime
Youth crime and disorder have risen sharply, but very few young offenders end up in court, and when they do half are let off with another warning. Young offenders account for seven million crimes a year.

Far too often young criminals offend again and again while waiting months for a court hearing. We will halve the time it takes to get persistent young offenders from arrest to sentencing; replace widespread repeat cautions with a single final warning; bring together Youth Offender Teams in every area; and streamline the system of youth courts to make it far more effective.

New parental responsibility orders will make parents face up to their responsibility for their children's misbehaviour.

## Conviction and sentencing
The job of the Crown Prosecution Service is to prosecute criminals effectively. There is strong evidence that the CPS is over-centralised, bureaucratic and inefficient, with cases too often dropped, delayed, or downgraded to lesser offences. Labour will decentralise the CPS, with local crown prosecutors co-operating more effectively with local police forces.

We will implement an effective sentencing system for all the main offences to ensure greater consistency and stricter punishment for serious repeat offenders. The courts will have to spell out what each sentence really means in practice. The Court of Appeal will have a duty to lay down sentencing guidelines for all the main offences. The Attorney-General's power to appeal against unduly lenient sentences will be extended.

The prison service now faces serious financial problems. We will audit the resources available, take proper ministerial responsibility for the service, and seek to ensure that prison regimes are constructive and require inmates to face up to their offending behaviour.

## Disorder

The Conservatives have forgotten the "order" part of "law and order". We will tackle the unacceptable level of anti-social behaviour and crime on our streets. Our "zero tolerance" approach will ensure that petty criminality among young offenders is seriously addressed.

Community safety orders will deal with threatening and disruptive criminal neighbours. Labour has taken the lead in proposing action to tackle the problems of stalking and domestic violence. Child protection orders will deal with young children suffering neglect by parents because they are left out on their own far too late at night.

Britain is a multiracial and multicultural society. All its members must have the protection of the law. We will create a new offence of racial harassment and a new crime of racially motivated violence to protect ethnic minorities from intimidation.

## Drugs

The vicious circle of drugs and crime wrecks lives and threatens communities. Labour will appoint an anti-drugs supremo to co-ordinate our battle against drugs across all government departments. The "drug czar" will be a symbol of our commitment to tackle the modern menace of drugs in our communities.

We will pilot the use of compulsory drug testing and treatment orders for offenders to ensure that the link between drug addiction and crime is broken. This will be paid for by bringing remand delays down to the national targets. We will attack the drug problem in prisons. In addition to random drug testing of all prisoners we will aim for a voluntary testing unit in every prison for prisoners ready to prove they are drug-free.

## Victims

Victims of crime are too often neglected by the criminal justice system. We will ensure that victims are kept fully informed of the progress of their case, and why charges may have been downgraded or dropped.

Greater protection will be provided for victims in rape and serious sexual offence trials and for those subject to intimidation, including witnesses.

## Prevention

We will place a new responsibility on local authorities to develop statutory partnerships to help prevent crime. Local councils will then be required to set targets for the reduction of crime and disorder in their area.

## Gun control

In the wake of Dunblane and Hungerford, it is clear that only the strictest firearms laws can provide maximum safety. The Conservatives failed to offer the protection required. Labour led the call for an outright ban on all handguns in general civilian use. There will be legislation to allow individual MPs a free vote for a complete ban on handguns.

Labour is the party of law and order in Britain today.

## We will strengthen family life
♦ Help parents balance work and family
♦ Security in housing and help for homeowners
♦ Tackle homelessness using receipts from council house sales
♦ Dignity and security in retirement
♦ Protect the basic state pension and promote secure second pensions

We will uphold family life as the most secure means of bringing up our children. Families are the core of our society. They should teach right from wrong. They should be the first defence against anti-social behaviour. The breakdown of family life damages the fabric of our society.

Labour does not see families and the state as rival providers for the needs of our citizens. Families should provide the day-to-day support for children to be brought up in a stable and loving environment. But families cannot flourish unless government plays its distinctive role: in education; where necessary, in caring for the young; in making adequate provision for illness and old age; in supporting good parenting; and in protecting families from lawlessness and abuse of power. Society, through government, must assist families to achieve collectively what no family can achieve alone.

Yet families in Britain today are under strain as never before. The security once offered by the health service has been undermined. Streets are not safe. Housing insecurity grows. One in five non-pensioner families has no one working; and British men work the longest hours in Europe.

The clock should not be turned back. As many women who want to work should be able to do so. More equal relationships between men and women have transformed our lives. Equally, our attitudes to race, sex and sexuality have changed fundamentally. Our task is to combine change and social stability.

## Work and family

Families without work are without independence. This is why we give so much emphasis to our welfare-to-work policies. Labour's national childcare strategy will plan provision to match the requirements of the modern labour market and help parents, especially women, to balance family and working life.

There must be a sound balance between support for family life and the protection of business from undue burdens — a balance which some of the most successful businesses already strike. The current government has shown itself wholly insensitive to the need to help develop family-friendly working practices. While recognising the need for flexibility in implementation and for certain exemptions, we support the right of employees not to be forced to work more than 48 hours a week; to an annual holiday entitlement; and to limited unpaid parental leave. These measures will provide a valuable underpinning to family life.

The rights of part-time workers have been clarified by recent court judgements which we welcome.

We will keep under continuous review all aspects of the tax and benefits systems to ensure that they are supportive of families and children. We are committed to retain universal Child Benefit where it is universal today — from birth to age 16 — and to uprate it at least in line with prices. We are reviewing educational finance and maintenance for those older than 16 to ensure higher staying-on rates at school and college, and that resources are used to support those in most need. This review will continue in government on the guidelines we have already laid down.

## Security in housing

Most families want to own their own homes. We will also support efficiently-run social and private rented sectors offering quality and choice.

The Conservatives' failure on housing has been twofold. The two-thirds of families who own their homes have suffered a massive increase in insecurity over the last decade, with record mortgage arrears, record negative equity and record repossessions. And the Conservatives' lack of a housing strategy has led to the virtual abandonment of social housing, the growth of homelessness, and a failure to address fully leaseholder reform. All these are the Tory legacy.

Labour's housing strategy will address the needs of homeowners and tenants alike. We will reject the boom and bust policies which caused the collapse of the housing market. We will work with mortgage providers to encourage greater provision of more flexible mortgages to protect families in a world of increased job insecurity. Mortgage buyers also require stronger consumer protection, for example by extension of the Financial Services Act, against the sale of disadvantageous mortgage packages.

The problems of gazumping have reappeared. Those who break their bargains should be liable to pay the costs inflicted on others, in particular legal and survey costs. We are consulting on the best way of tackling the problems of gazumping in the interests of responsible home buyers and sellers.

## The rented housing sector

We support a three-way partnership between the public, private and housing association sectors to promote good social housing. With Labour, capital receipts from the sale of council houses, received but not spent by local councils, will be re-invested in building new houses and rehabilitating old ones. This will be phased to match the capacity of the building industry and to meet the requirements of prudent economic management.

We also support effective schemes to deploy private finance to improve the public housing stock and to introduce greater diversity and choice. Such schemes should only go ahead with the support of the tenants concerned: we oppose the Government's threat to hand over council housing to private landlords without the consent of tenants and with no guarantees on rents or security of tenure.

We value a revived private rented sector. We will provide protection where most needed: for tenants in houses in multiple occupation. There will be a proper system of licensing by local authorities which will benefit tenants and responsible landlords alike.

We will introduce "commonhold", a new form of tenure enabling people living in flats to own their homes individually and to own the whole property collectively. We will simplify the current rules restricting the purchase of freeholds by leaseholders.

### Homelessness

Homelessness has more than doubled under the Conservatives. Today more than 40,000 families in England are in expensive temporary accommodation. The government, in the face of Labour opposition, has removed the duty on local authorities to find permanent housing for homeless families. We will impose a new duty on local authorities to protect those who are homeless through no fault of their own and are in priority need.

There is no more powerful symbol of Tory neglect in our society today than young people without homes living rough on the streets. Young people emerging from care without any family support are particularly vulnerable. We will attack the problem in two principal ways: the phased release of capital receipts from council house sales will increase the stock of housing for rent; and our welfare-to-work programme will lead the young unemployed into work and financial independence.

### Older citizens

We value the positive contribution that older people make to our society, through their families, voluntary activities and work. Their skills and experience should be utilised within their communities. That is why, for example, we support the proposal to involve older people as volunteers to help children learn in pre-school and after-school clubs. In work, they should not be discriminated against because of their age.

The provision of adequate pensions in old age is a major challenge for the future. For today's pensioners Conservative policies have created real poverty, growing inequality and widespread insecurity.

The Conservatives would abolish the state-financed basic retirement pension and replace it with a privatised scheme, with a vague promise of a means-tested state guarantee if pensions fall beneath a minimum level. Their proposals mean there will be no savings on welfare spending for half a century; and taxes will have to rise to make provision for new privately funded pensions. Their plans require an additional £312 billion between now and 2040 through increased taxes or borrowing, against the hope of savings later, with no certainty of security in retirement at the end.

We believe that all pensioners should share fairly in the increasing prosperity of the nation. Instead of privatisation, we propose a partnership between public and private provision, and a balance between income sourced from tax and invested savings. The basic state pension will be retained as the foundation of pension provision. It will be increased at least in line with prices. We will examine means of delivering more automatic help to the poorest pensioners – one million of whom do not even receive the Income Support which is their present entitlement.

We will encourage saving for retirement, with proper protection for savings. We will reform the Financial Services Act so that the scandal of pension mis-selling – 600,000 pensions mis-sold and only 7,000 people compensated to date – will not happen again.

Too many people in work, particularly those on low and modest incomes and with changing patterns of employment, cannot join good-value second pension schemes. Labour will create a new framework – stakeholder pensions – to meet this need. We will encourage new partnerships between financial service companies, employers and employees to develop these pension schemes. They will be approved to receive people's savings only if they meet high standards of value for money, flexibility and security.

Labour will promote choice in pension provision. We will support and strengthen the framework for occupational pensions. Personal pensions, appropriately regulated, will remain a good option for many. Labour will retain Serps as an option for those who wish to remain within it. We will also seek to develop the administrative structure of Serps so as to create a "citizenship pension" for those who assume responsibility as carers, as a result lose out on the pension entitlements they would otherwise acquire, and currently end up on means-tested benefits.

We overcame government opposition to pension splitting between women and men on divorce. We will implement this in government.

We aim to provide real security for families through a modern system of community care. As people grow older, their need for care increases. The Conservative approach is to promote private insurance and privatisation of care homes. But private insurance will be inaccessible to most people. And their policy for residential homes is dogmatic and will not work. We believe that local authorities should be free to develop a mix of public and private care.

We recognise the immense amount of care provision undertaken by family members, neighbours and friends. It was a Labour MP who piloted the 1995 Carers Act through Parliament. We will establish a Royal Commission to work out a fair system for funding long-term care for the elderly. We will introduce a "long-term care charter" defining the standard of services which people are entitled to expect from health, housing and social services. We are committed to an independent inspection and regulation service for residential homes, and domiciliary care.

Everyone is entitled to dignity in retirement. Under the Tories, the earnings link for state pensions has been ended, VAT on fuel has been imposed, Serps has been undermined and community care is in tatters. We will set up a review of the central areas of insecurity for elderly people: all aspects of the basic pension and its value, second pensions including Serps, and community care. The review will ensure that the views of pensioners are heard. Our watchword in developing policy for pensions and long-term care will be to build consensus among all interested parties.

### We will help you get more out of life
- Every government department a "green" department
- Efficient and clean transport for all
- New arts and science talent fund for young people
- Reform the lottery
- Improve life in rural areas
- Back World Cup bid

The millennium is the time to reaffirm our responsibility to protect and enhance our environment so that the country we hand on to our children and our grandchildren is a better place in which to live. It also provides a natural opportunity to celebrate and improve the contribution made by the arts, culture and sport to our nation. We need a new and dynamic approach to the "creative economy". The Department of National Heritage will develop a strategic vision that matches the real power and energy of British arts, media and cultural industries.

### Protecting the environment
Our generation, and generations yet to come, are dependent on the integrity of the environment. No one can escape unhealthy water, polluted air or adverse climate change. And just as these problems affect us all, so we must act together to tackle them. No responsible government can afford to take risks with the future: the cost is too high. So it is our duty to act now.

The foundation of Labour's environmental approach is that protection of the environment cannot be the sole responsibility of any one department of state. All departments must promote policies to sustain the environment. And Parliament should have an environmental audit committee to ensure high standards across government.

Throughout this manifesto, there are policies designed to combine environmental sustainability with economic and social progress. They extend from commitments at local level to give communities enhanced control over their environments, to initiatives at international level to ensure that all countries are contributing to the protection of the environment.

A sustainable environment requires above all an effective and integrated transport policy at national, regional and local level that will provide genuine choice to meet people's transport needs. That is what we will establish and develop.

### Railways
The process of rail privatisation is now largely complete. It has made fortunes for a few, but has been a poor deal for the taxpayer. It has fragmented the network and now threatens services. Our task will be to improve the situation as we find it, not as we wish it to be. Our overriding goal must be to win more passengers and freight on to rail. The system must be run in the public interest with higher levels of investment and effective enforcement of train operators'

service commitments. There must be convenient connections, through-ticketing and accurate travel information for the benefit of all passengers.

To achieve these aims, we will establish more effective and accountable regulation by the rail regulator; we will ensure that the public subsidy serves the public interest; and we will establish a new rail authority, combining functions currently carried out by the rail franchiser and the Department of Transport, to provide a clear, coherent and strategic programme for the development of the railways so that passenger expectations are met.

The Conservative plan for the wholesale privatisation of London Underground is not the answer. It would be a poor deal for the taxpayer and passenger alike. Yet again, public assets would be sold off at an under-valued rate. Much-needed investment would be delayed. The core public responsibilities of the Underground would be threatened.

Labour plans a new public/private partnership to improve the Underground, safeguard its commitment to the public interest and guarantee value for money to taxpayers and passengers.

### Road transport

A balanced transport system must cater for all the familiar modes of transport: cars – whether owned, leased or shared; taxis; buses; bicycles and motorcycles. All needs must be addressed in transport planning to ensure the best mix of all types of transport, offer quality public transport wherever possible and help to protect the environment.

The key to efficient bus services is proper regulation at local level, with partnerships between local councils and bus operators an essential component. There must be improved provision and enforcement of bus lanes. Better parking facilities for cars must be linked to convenient bus services to town centres.

Road safety is a high priority. Cycling and walking must be made safer, especially around schools. We remain unpersuaded by the case for heavier, 44-tonne lorries mooted by the Conservatives. Our concern is that they would prove dangerous and damaging to the environment.

Our plans to reduce pollution include working with the automotive industry to develop "smart", efficient and clean cars for the future, with substantially reduced emission levels. The review of vehicle excise duty to promote low-emission vehicles will be continued.

We will conduct an overall strategic review of the roads programme against the criteria of accessibility, safety, economy and environmental impact, using public/private partnerships to improve road maintenance and exploiting new technology to improve journey information.

### Shipping and aviation

The Tory years have seen the near-extinction of Britain's merchant fleet. Labour will work with all concerned in shipping and ports to help develop their economic potential to the full.

The guiding objectives of our aviation strategy will be fair competition, safety and environmental standards. We want all British carriers to be able to compete fairly in the interests of consumers.

### Life in our countryside

Labour recognises the special needs of people who live and work in rural areas. The Conservatives do not. Public services and transport services in rural areas must not be allowed to deteriorate. The Conservatives have tried to privatise the Post Office. We opposed that, in favour of a public Post Office providing a comprehensive service. Conservative plans would mean higher charges for letters and put rural post offices under threat.

We favour a moratorium on large-scale sales of Forestry Commission land. We recognise that the countryside is a great natural asset, a part of our heritage which calls for careful stewardship. This must be balanced, however, with the needs of people who live and work in rural areas.

The total failure of the Conservatives to manage the BSE crisis effectively and to secure any raising of the ban on British beef has wreaked havoc on the beef and dairy industries. The cost to the taxpayer so far is £3.5 billion.

Labour aims to reform the Common Agricultural Policy to save money, to support the rural economy and enhance the environment.

Our initiatives to link all schools to the information superhighway will ensure that children in rural areas have access to the best educational resources.

Our policies include greater freedom for people to explore our open countryside. We will not, however, permit any abuse of a right to greater access.

We will ensure greater protection for wildlife. We have advocated new measures to promote animal welfare, including a free vote in Parliament on whether hunting with hounds should be banned by legislation.

Angling is Britain's most popular sport. Labour's anglers' charter affirms our long-standing commitment to angling and to the objective of protecting the aquatic environment.

## Arts and culture

The arts, culture and sport are central to the task of recreating the sense of community, identity and civic pride that should define our country. Yet we consistently undervalue the role of the arts and culture in helping to create a civic society — from amateur theatre to our art galleries. Art, sport and leisure are vital to our quality of life and the renewal of our economy. They are significant earners for Britain. They employ hundreds of thousands of people. They bring millions of tourists to Britain every year, who will also be helped by Labour's plans for new quality assurance in hotel accommodation.

We propose to set up a National Endowment for Science and the Arts to sponsor young talent. NESTA will be a national trust — for talent rather than buildings — for the 21st century. NESTA will be partly funded by the lottery; and artists who have gained high rewards from their excellence in the arts and wish to support young talent will be encouraged to donate copyright and royalties to NESTA.

## Sport

A Labour government will take the lead in extending opportunities for participation in sports; and in identifying sporting excellence and supporting it. School sports must be the foundation. We will bring the Government's policy of forcing schools to sell off playing fields to an end. We will provide full backing to the bid to host the 2006 football World Cup in England. A Labour government will also work to bring the Olympics and other major international sporting events to Britain.

## A people's lottery

The lottery has been a financial success. But there has been no overall strategy for the allocation of monies; and no co-ordination among the five distributor bodies about the projects deserving to benefit from lottery funding. For example, the multi-million-pound expenditure on the Churchill papers caused national outrage. A Labour government will review the distribution of lottery proceeds to ensure that there is the widest possible access to the benefits of lottery revenues throughout the UK.

Labour has already proposed a new millennium commission to commence after the closure of the Millennium Exhibition, to provide direct support for a range of education, environment and public health projects, including those directed at children's play, a project currently excluded from lottery benefit. Because the lottery is a monopoly intended to serve the public interest, it must be administered efficiently and economically. When the current contract runs out, Labour will seek an efficient not-for-profit operator to ensure that the maximum sums go to good causes.

## Media and broadcasting

Labour aims for a thriving, diverse media industry, combining commercial success and public service. We will ensure that the BBC continues to be a flagship for British creativity and public service broadcasting, but we believe that the combination of public and private sectors in competition is a key spur to innovation and high standards. The regulatory framework for media and broadcasting should reflect the realities of a far more open and competitive economy, and enormous technological advance, for example with digital television. Labour will balance sensible rules, fair regulation and national and international competition, so maintaining quality and diversity for the benefit of viewers.

## Citizens' service for a new millennium

An independent and creative voluntary sector, committed to voluntary activity as an expression of citizenship, is central to our vision of a stakeholder society. We are committed to developing plans for a national citizens' service programme, to tap the enthusiasm and commitment of the many young people who want to make voluntary contributions in service of their communities. The millennium should harness the imagination of all those people who have so much to offer for the benefit of the community. We do not believe programmes should be imposed from the top down, but on the contrary wish to encourage a broad range of voluntary initiatives devised and developed by people within their own communities.

## LABOUR MANIFESTO

### We will clean up politics
+ End the hereditary principle in the House of Lords
+ Reform of party funding to end sleaze
+ Devolved power in Scotland and Wales
+ Elected mayors for London and other cities
+ More independent but accountable local government
+ Freedom of information and guaranteed human rights

The Conservatives seem opposed to the very idea of democracy. They support hereditary peers, unaccountable quangos and secretive government. They have debased democracy through their MPs who have taken cash for asking questions in the House of Commons. They are opposed to the development of decentralised government. The party which once opposed universal suffrage and votes for women now says our constitution is so perfect that it cannot be improved.

Our system of government is centralised, inefficient and bureaucratic. Our citizens cannot assert their basic rights in our own courts. The Conservatives are afflicted by sleaze and prosper from secret funds from foreign supporters. There is unquestionably a national crisis of confidence in our political system, to which Labour will respond in a measured and sensible way.

### A modern House of Lords
The House of Lords must be reformed. As an initial, self-contained reform, not dependent on further reform in the future, the right of hereditary peers to sit and vote in the House of Lords will be ended by statute. This will be the first stage in a process of reform to make the House of Lords more democratic and representative. The legislative powers of the House of Lords will remain unaltered.

The system of appointment of life peers to the House of Lords will be reviewed. Our objective will be to ensure that over time, party appointees as life peers more accurately reflect the proportion of votes cast at the previous general election. We are committed to maintaining an independent cross-bench presence of life peers. No one political party should seek a majority in the House of Lords.

A committee of both Houses of Parliament will be appointed to undertake a wide-ranging review of possible further change and then to bring forward proposals for reform. We have no plans to replace the monarchy.

### An effective House of Commons
We believe the House of Commons is in need of modernisation and we will ask the House to establish a special Select Committee to review its procedures. Prime Minister's Questions will be made more effective. Ministerial accountability will be reviewed so as to remove recent abuses. The process for scrutinising European legislation will be overhauled.

The Nolan recommendations will be fully implemented and extended to all public bodies. We will oblige parties to declare the source of all donations above a minimum figure: Labour does this voluntarily and all parties should do so. Foreign funding will be banned. We will ask the Nolan Committee to consider how the funding of political parties should be regulated and reformed.

We are committed to a referendum on the voting system for the House of Commons. An independent commission on voting systems will be appointed early to recommend a proportional alternative to the first-past-the-post system.

At this election, Labour is proud to be making major strides to rectify the under-representation of women in public life.

### Open government
Unnecessary secrecy in government leads to arrogance in government and defective policy decisions. The Scott Report on arms to Iraq revealed Conservative abuses of power. We are pledged to a Freedom of Information Act, leading to more open government, and an independent National Statistical Service.

### Devolution: strengthening the Union
The United Kingdom is a partnership enriched by distinct national identities and traditions. Scotland has its own systems of education, law and local government. Wales has its language and cultural traditions. We will meet the demand for decentralisation of power to Scotland and Wales, once established in referendums.

Subsidiarity is as sound a principle in Britain as it is in Europe. Our proposal is for devolution not federation. A sovereign Westminster Parliament will devolve power to Scotland and Wales. The Union will be strengthened and the threat of separatism removed.

As soon as possible after the election, we will enact legislation to allow the people of Scotland and Wales to vote in separate referendums on our proposals, which will be set out in White Papers. These referendums will take place not later than the autumn of 1997. A simple majority of those voting in each referendum will be the majority required. Popular endorsement will strengthen the legitimacy of our proposals and speed their passage through Parliament.

For Scotland we propose the creation of a parliament with law-making powers, firmly based on the agreement reached in the Scottish Constitutional Convention, including defined and limited financial powers to vary revenue and elected by an additional member system. In the Scottish referendum we will seek separate endorsement of the proposal to create a parliament, and of the proposal to give it defined and limited financial powers to vary revenue. The Scottish parliament will extend democratic control over the responsibilities currently exercised administratively by the Scottish Office. The responsibilities of the UK Parliament will remain unchanged over UK policy, for example economic, defence and foreign policy.

The Welsh assembly will provide democratic control of the existing Welsh Office functions. It will have secondary legislative powers and will be specifically empowered to reform and democratise the quango state. It will be elected by an additional member system. Following majorities in the referendums, we will introduce in the first year of the Parliament legislation on the substantive devolution proposals outlined in our white papers.

### Good local government

Local decision-making should be less constrained by central government, and also more accountable to local people. We will place on councils a new duty to promote the economic, social and environmental well-being of their area. They should work in partnership with local people, local business and local voluntary organisations. They will have the powers necessary to develop these partnerships. To ensure greater accountability, a proportion of councillors in each locality will be elected annually. We will encourage democratic innovations in local government, including pilots of the idea of elected mayors with executive powers in cities. Although crude and universal council tax capping should go, we will retain reserve powers to control excessive council tax rises.

Local business concerns are critical to good local government. There are sound democratic reasons why, in principle, the business rate should be set locally, not nationally. But we will make no change to the present system for determining the business rate without full consultation with business. The funnelling of government grant to Conservative-controlled Westminster speaks volumes about the unfairness of the current grant system. Labour is committed to a fair distribution of government grant.

The basic framework, not every detail, of local service provision must be for central government. Councils should not be forced to put their services out to tender, but will be required to obtain best value. We reject the dogmatic view that services must be privatised to be of high quality, but equally we see no reason why a service should be delivered directly if other more efficient means are available. Cost counts but so does quality.

Every council will be required to publish a local performance plan with targets for service improvement, and be expected to achieve them. The Audit Commission will be given additional powers to monitor performance and promote efficiency. On its advice, government will where necessary send in a management team with full powers to remedy failure.

Labour councils have been at the forefront of environmental initiatives under Local Agenda 21, the international framework for local action arising from the 1992 Earth Summit. A Labour government will encourage all local authorities to adopt plans to protect and enhance their local environment. Local government is at the sharp end of the fight against deprivation. Ten years after the Conservatives promised to improve the inner cities, poverty and social division afflict towns and outer estates alike. A Labour government will join with local government in a concerted attack against the multiple causes of social and economic decline – unemployment, bad housing, crime, poor health and a degraded environment.

### London

London is the only Western capital without an elected city government. Following a referendum to confirm popular demand, there will be a new deal for London, with a strategic authority and a mayor, each directly elected. Both will speak up for the needs of the city and plan its future. They will not duplicate the work of the boroughs, but take responsibility for London-wide issues – economic regeneration, planning, policing, transport and environmental protection. London-wide responsibility for its own government is urgently required. We will make it happen.

### The regions of England

The Conservatives have created a tier of regional government in England through quangos and government regional offices. Meanwhile local authorities have come together to create a more co-ordinated regional voice. Labour will build on these developments through the establishment of regional chambers to co-ordinate transport, planning, economic development, bids for European funding and land use planning.

Demand for directly-elected regional government so varies across England that it would be wrong to impose a uniform system. In time we will introduce legislation to allow the people, region by region, to decide in a referendum whether they want directly elected regional government. Only where clear popular consent is established will arrangements be made for elected regional assemblies. This would require a predominantly unitary system of local government, as presently exists in Scotland and Wales, and confirmation by independent auditors that no additional public expenditure overall would be involved. Our plans will not mean adding a new tier of government to the existing English system.

### Real rights for citizens

Citizens should have statutory rights to enforce their human rights in the UK courts. We will by statute incorporate the European Convention on Human Rights into UK law to bring these rights home and allow our people access to them in their national courts. The incorporation of the European Convention will establish a floor, not a ceiling, for human rights. Parliament will remain free to enhance these rights, for example by a Freedom of Information Act.

We will seek to end unjustifiable discrimination wherever it exists. For example, we support comprehensive, enforceable civil rights for disabled people against discrimination in society or at work, developed in partnership with all interested parties.

Labour will undertake a wide-ranging review both of the reform of the civil justice system and legal aid. We will achieve value for money for the taxpayer and the consumer. A community legal service will develop local, regional and national plans for the development of legal aid according to the needs and priorities of regions and areas. The key to success will be to promote a partnership between the voluntary sector, the legal profession and the Legal Aid Board.

Every country must have firm control over immigration and Britain is no exception. All applications, however, should be dealt with speedily and fairly. There are, rightly, criteria for those who want to enter this country to join husband or wife. We will ensure that these are properly enforced. We will, however, reform the system in current use to remove the arbitrary and unfair results that can follow from the existing "primary purpose" rule. There will be a streamlined system of appeals for visitors denied a visa.

The system for dealing with asylum seekers is expensive and slow – there are many undecided cases dating back beyond 1993. We will ensure swift and fair decisions on whether someone can stay or go, control unscrupulous immigration advisors and crack down on the fraudulent use of birth certificates.

### Northern Ireland

Labour's approach to the peace process has been bipartisan. We have supported the recent agreements between the two governments – the Anglo-Irish Agreement, the Downing Street Declaration and the Framework Document. The government has tabled proposals which include a new devolved legislative body, as well as cross-border co-operation and continued dialogue between the two governments.

There will be as great a priority attached to seeing that process through with Labour as under the Conservatives, in co-operation with the Irish government and the Northern Ireland parties. We will expect the same bipartisan approach from a Conservative opposition.

We will take effective measures to combat the terrorist threat.

There is now general acceptance that the future of Northern Ireland must be determined by the consent of the people as set out in the Downing Street Declaration. Labour recognises that the option of a united Ireland does not command the consent of the Unionist tradition, nor does the existing status of Northern Ireland command the consent of the nationalist tradition. We are therefore committed to reconciliation between the two traditions and to a new political settlement which can command the support of both. Labour will help build trust and confidence among both nationalist and Unionist traditions in Northern Ireland by acting to guarantee human rights, strengthen confidence in policing, combat discrimination at work and reduce tensions over parades. Labour will also foster economic progress and competitiveness in Northern Ireland, so as to reduce unemployment.

## We will give Britain leadership in Europe

- Referendum on single currency
- Lead reform of the EU
- Retain Trident: strong defence through Nato
- A reformed United Nations
- Helping to tackle global poverty

Britain, though an island nation with limited natural resources, has for centuries been a leader of nations. But under the Conservatives Britain's influence has waned. With a new Labour government, Britain will be strong in defence; resolute in standing up for its own interests; an advocate of human rights and democracy the world over; a reliable and powerful ally in the international institutions of which we are a member; and will be a leader in Europe.

Our vision of Europe is of an alliance of independent nations choosing to co-operate to achieve the goals they cannot achieve alone. We oppose a European federal superstate. There are only three options for Britain in Europe. The first is to come out. The second is to stay in, but on the sidelines. The third is to stay in, but in a leading role.

An increasing number of Conservatives, overtly or covertly, favour the first. But withdrawal would be disastrous for Britain. It would put millions of jobs at risk. It would dry up inward investment. It would destroy our clout in international trade negotiations. It would relegate Britain from the premier division of nations. The second is exactly where we are today under the Conservatives. The BSE fiasco symbolises their failures in Europe.

The third is the path a new Labour government will take. A fresh start in Europe, with the credibility to achieve reform. We have set out a detailed agenda for reform, leading from the front during the UK presidency in the first half of 1998:

- Rapid completion of the single market: a top priority for the British presidency. We will open up markets to competition; pursue tough action against unfair state aids; and ensure proper enforcement of single market rules. This will strengthen Europe's competitiveness and open up new opportunities for British firms.
- High priority for enlargement of the European Union to include the countries of central and eastern Europe and Cyprus, and the institutional reforms necessary to make an enlarged Europe work more efficiently.
- Urgent reform of the Common Agricultural Policy. It is costly, vulnerable to fraud and not geared to environmental protection. Enlargement and the World Trade talks in 1999 will make reform even more essential. We will seek a thorough overhaul of the Common Fisheries Policy to conserve our fish stocks in the long-term interests of the UK fishing industry.
- Greater openness and democracy in EU institutions with open voting in the Council of Ministers and more effective scrutiny of the Commission by the European Parliament. We have long supported a proportional voting system for election to the European Parliament.
- Retention of the national veto over key matters of national interest, such as taxation, defence and security, immigration, decisions over the budget and treaty changes, while considering the extension of Qualified Majority Voting in limited areas where that is in Britain's interests.
- Britain to sign the social chapter. An "empty chair" at the negotiating table is disastrous for Britain. The social chapter is a framework under which legislative measures can be agreed. Only two measures have been agreed − consultation for employees of large Europe-wide companies and entitlement to unpaid parental leave. Successful companies already work closely with their workforces. The social chapter cannot be used to force the harmonisation of social security or tax legislation and it does not cost jobs. We will use our participation to promote employability and flexibility, not high social costs.

## The single currency

Any decision about Britain joining the single currency must be determined by a hard-headed assessment of Britain's economic interests. Only Labour can be trusted to do this: the Tories are riven by faction. But there are formidable obstacles in the way of Britain being in the first wave of membership, if EMU takes place on January 1 1999. What is essential for the success of EMU is genuine convergence among the economies that take part, without any fudging of the rules. However, to exclude British membership of EMU forever would be to destroy any influence we have over a process which will affect us whether we are in or out. We must therefore play a full part in the debate to influence it in Britain's interests.

In any event, there are three pre-conditions which would have to be satisfied before Britain could join during the next Parliament: first, the Cabinet would have to agree; then Parliament; and finally the people would have to say "Yes" in a referendum.

### Strong defence through Nato

The post-Cold War world faces a range of new security challenges – proliferation of weapons of mass destruction, the growth of ethnic nationalism and extremism, international terrorism, and crime and drug trafficking. A new Labour government will build a strong defence against these threats. Our security will continue to be based on Nato.

Our armed forces are among the most effective in the world. The country takes pride in their professionalism and courage. We will ensure that they remain strong to defend Britain. But the security of Britain is best served in a secure world, so we should be willing to contribute to wider international peace and security both through the alliances to which we belong, in particular Nato and the Western European Union, and through other international organisations such as the UN and the Organisation for Security and Co-operation in Europe.

Labour will conduct a strategic defence and security review to reassess our essential security interests and defence needs. It will consider how the roles, missions and capabilities of our armed forces should be adjusted to meet the new strategic realities. The review we propose will be foreign policy-led, first assessing our likely overseas commitments and interests and then establishing how our forces should be deployed to meet them.

### Arms control

A new Labour government will retain Trident. We will press for multilateral negotiations towards mutual, balanced and verifiable reductions in nuclear weapons. When satisfied with verified progress towards our goal of the global elimination of nuclear weapons, we will ensure that British nuclear weapons are included in multilateral negotiations.

Labour will work for the effective implementation of the Chemical Weapons Convention and for a strengthening of the Biological Weapons Convention. Labour will ban the import, export, transfer and manufacture of all forms of anti-personnel landmines. We will introduce an immediate moratorium on their use. Labour will not permit the sale of arms to regimes that might use them for internal repression or international aggression. We will increase the transparency and accountability of decisions on export licences for arms. And we will support an EU code of conduct governing arms sales. We support a strong UK defence industry, which is a strategic part of our industrial base as well as our defence effort. We believe that part of its expertise can be extended to civilian use through a defence diversification agency.

### Leadership in the international community

A new Labour government will use Britain's permanent seat on the Security Council to press for substantial reform of the United Nations, including an early resolution of its funding crisis, and a more effective role in peacekeeping, conflict prevention, the protection of human rights and safeguarding the global environment.

The Commonwealth provides Britain with a unique network of contacts linked by history, language and legal systems. Labour is committed to giving renewed priority to the Commonwealth in our foreign relations. We will seize the opportunity to increase trade and economic co-operation and will also build alliances with our Commonwealth partners to promote reform at the UN and common action on the global environment. Britain has a real opportunity to provide leadership to the Commonwealth when we host the heads of government meeting in Britain at the end of 1997.

### Promoting economic and social development

Labour will also attach much higher priority to combating global poverty and underdevelopment. According to the World Bank, there are 1.3 billion people in the world who live in absolute poverty, subsisting on less than $1 a day, while 35,000 children die each day from readily-preventable diseases.

Labour believes that we have a clear moral responsibility to help combat global poverty. In government we will strengthen and restructure the British aid programme and bring development issues back into the mainstream of government decision-making. A Cabinet minister will lead a new department of international development.

We will shift aid resources towards programmes that help the poorest people in the poorest countries. We reaffirm the UK's commitment to the 0.7 per cent UN aid target and in government Labour will start to reverse the decline in UK aid spending.

We will work for greater consistency between the aid, trade, agriculture and economic reform policies of the EU. We will use our leadership position in the EU to maintain and enhance the position of the poorest countries during the renegotiation of the Lomé Convention.

We will support further measures to reduce the debt burden borne by the world's poorest countries and to ensure that developing countries are given a fair deal in international trade.

It is our aim to rejoin Unesco. We will consider how this can be done most effectively and will ensure that the cost is met from savings elsewhere.

## Human rights

Labour wants Britain to be respected in the world for the integrity with which it conducts its foreign relations. We will make the protection and promotion of human rights a central part of our foreign policy. We will work for the creation of a permanent international criminal court to investigate genocide, war crimes and crimes against humanity.

## A new environmental internationalism

Labour believes that the threats to the global climate should push environmental concerns higher up the international agenda. A Labour government will strengthen co-operation in the European Union on environmental issues, including climate change and ozone depletion. We will lead the fight against global warming, through our target of a 20 per cent reduction in carbon dioxide emissions by the year 2010.

Labour believes the international environment should be safeguarded in negotiations over international trade. We will also work for the successful negotiation of a new protocol on climate change to be completed in Japan in 1997.

## Leadership, not isolation

There is a sharp division between those who believe the way to cope with global change is for nations to retreat into isolationism and protectionism, and those who believe in internationalism and engagement. Labour has traditionally been the party of internationalism. Britain cannot be strong at home if it is weak abroad. The tragedy of the Conservative years has been the squandering of Britain's assets and the loss of Britain's influence.

A new Labour government will use those assets to the full to restore Britain's pride and influence as a leading force for good in the world. With effective leadership and clear vision, Britain could once again be at the centre of international decision-making instead of at its margins.

This manifesto contains the detail of our plans. We have promised only what we know we can deliver. Britain deserves better and the following five election pledges will be the first steps towards a better Britain.

♦ cut class sizes to 30 or under for five, six and seven-year-olds by using money from the assisted places scheme
♦ fast-track punishment for persistent young offenders by halving the time from arrest to sentencing
♦ cut NHS waiting lists by treating an extra 100,000 patients as a first step by releasing £100 million saved from NHS red tape
♦ get 250,000 under-25 year-olds off benefit and into work by using money from a windfall levy on the privatised utilities
♦ no rise in income tax rates, cut VAT on heating to 5 per cent and inflation and interest rates as low as possible

# CONSERVATIVE MANIFESTO

**T**HE CONSERVATIVE administrations elected since 1979 are among the most successful in British peacetime history. A country once the sick man of Europe has become its most successful economy. A country once brought to its knees by overmighty powerful trade unions, now has industrial peace. Abroad, the Cold War has been won; at home, the rule of law has been restored. The enterprising virtues of the British people have been liberated from the dead hand of the state. There can be no doubt that we have created a better Britain.

Why, then, do we still need a Conservative Government? Because resting on what we have achieved is not enough. To stand still is to fall back. Our goal must be for Britain to be the best place in the world to live.

We live in a tougher, more uncertain world. A fast-moving global free market is emerging. New economic powers are rising in the East. Family life and social attitudes are changing. Europe is adjusting to the end of communism. The European social model is failing. The nation state is under threat. We must respond to these challenges.

We have turned around our economic fortunes. We have fewer people out of work and more in work than any other major European economy. British people now have the opportunity of a prosperous future. But that prosperity cannot be taken for granted. We have to compete to win. That means a constant fight to keep tight control over public spending and enable Britain to remain the lowest-taxed major economy in Europe. It means a continuing fight to keep burdens off business, maintaining our opt-out of the European social chapter. If we relax for one moment, our hard-won success will slip away again.

We have strengthened choice and personal ownership for families, and rolled back the state from areas where it was interfering unnecessarily in our lives. But we now have the opportunity to achieve a massive expansion in wealth and ownership so that more families can enjoy the self-respect and independence that comes with being self-sufficient from the State. Our far-reaching proposals for personal pension funds are central to achieving this – so too are our plans to increase support for the family in our tax system. Our aim is to spread opportunity for all to succeed, whoever they are and wherever they come from, provided they are prepared to work hard. To turn the "have nots" into the "haves". To support the family in providing security and stability.

We have modernised and reformed many of the areas where the State still has a vital role. But we now have to build on these reforms to deliver even better services. We must continue providing the resources to invest in our modernised health service. We can now provide parents with a hard-edged guarantee of standards in schools. We need also to widen choice in areas where state bureaucracy has constrained it.

We have pioneered new ways of building partnerships that engage the private sector in areas previously dependent on the public purse. We now need to capture private-sector investment on a massive scale to regenerate our cities, transform our crumbling local authority housing estates and modernise other public assets.

The only way to secure this future of opportunity is to stick with the Conservative programme of continuing reform. Now would be the worst possible moment to abandon the pathway to prosperity on which we are set. We must keep up the momentum.

At the same time we must maintain the security that a stable nation provides in an uncertain, fast-changing world. We must protect our constitution and unity as a nation from those who threaten it with unnecessary and dangerous change. And we must stand up for our interests in shaping a free-market Europe of sovereign nation states.

There is, of course, an alternative on offer: to load costs on business while calling it "stakeholding"; to increase the role of the State, while calling it "the community"; to succumb to a centralised Europe while calling it "not being isolated"; to break up our country while calling it "devolution".

To risk this alternative would be a disaster for our country. We have come a very long way. We must be sure that we do not throw away what we have gained, or lose the opportunities we have earned.

You can only be sure with the Conservatives.

Rt Hon John Major.

## THE ENTERPRISE CENTRE OF EUROPE
### Our record

♦ The UK is on course to grow faster than both France and Germany for the sixth successive year in 1998 – a post-war record.

♦ Inflation has now been below 4 per cent for well over four years, the longest period of low inflation for over half a century.
♦ Mortgage rates are at their lowest levels for 30 years.
♦ Unemployment has fallen to its lowest level for six years. We now have a lower unemployment rate than any other major European economy. Youth unemployment in Britain has fallen to less than 15 per cent whereas by contrast, in France it has risen to 27 per cent and in Italy to 33 per cent.
♦ A higher proportion of our people are in work than in any other major European economy — 68 per cent against a Continental average of 57 per cent.
♦ The UK is the favourite location for inward investment into Europe, attracting around one-third of inward investment into the European Union.
♦ We have the lowest tax burden of any major European economy, with the government taking almost 8 per cent less of national income than the European average.
♦ Public borrowing has averaged 3.4 per cent of GDP since 1979 compared with 6.8 per cent (and a peak of 9.5 per cent) under the last Labour Government. Our level of public debt is now one of the lowest in the European Union — whereas it was one of the highest in 1979.
♦ In 1994 the UK lost 300,000 working days through strikes, the lowest figure ever recorded; in 1979 the figure was 29,500,000: nearly 100 times that figure.
♦ Britain ranks fifth in the world in international trade, and exports more per head than America or Japan. Exports account for 28 per cent of GDP as against 9 per cent for Japan, 11 per cent for the United States and 24 per cent for Germany and France. Britain's current account is broadly in balance, reflecting our increased competitiveness and improved trading.

### Doubling living standards

The free market is winning the battle of ideas the world over. From Russia to Vietnam, from China to Romania, people are realising that the socialist model has failed. This is not just an economic triumph. It is a triumph for human freedom. Britain helped to secure it. We should take pride in it.

The spread of the free market heralds a new age of global competition. That means new markets for British goods and services, but new competitors for British companies as well.

If we try to protect ourselves from these challenges with more regulations, public subsidies and a cosy dependence on government then Britain will fail. But if we boldly embrace these new opportunities by pushing forward the economic revolution we began in 1979, then we will enter the next millennium with boundless prospects for growth and prosperity.

That choice — between stagnation and dynamism — is the choice which faces Britain at this election. It is a stark choice between the British way — of trusting the people and unleashing enterprise — and the failing social model, practised on the continent, which the Labour Party wants to impose on us here under the guise of "stakeholding".

Hard economic evidence shows how great is the divide between these two strategies. Britain is now in its fifth year of growing faster than France or Germany. Unemployment in Britain has fallen to less than two million, while it rises across Europe. Britain attracts nearly forty per cent of all the American and Japanese investment in Europe. Our aim now is to safeguard these achievements and build on them, so Britain becomes the unrivalled enterprise centre of Europe.

### A low-tax economy

For enterprise to flourish, the state must get out of the way of the wealth creators. We are the only party that can cut taxes because we are the only party which is serious about controlling public spending. The choice between the two economic philosophies is clear. In the years before 1979, public spending in Britain kept pace with the average for Europe as a whole. Since then, it has continued rising on the Continent, while we have restrained public spending here. Now, public spending takes about 40 per cent of our national income as against an average of 50 per cent on the Continent. We have broken free from a trend in which the rest of Europe is still trapped.

Conservative government will keep public spending under tight control and ensure that it grows by less than the economy as a whole over the economic cycle. At the same time we will continue to spend more on the services which matter most to people — hospitals, schools and the police.

Over the next parliament, we will achieve our goal for the government to spend less than 40 per cent of our national income.

That means we can reduce the amount government borrows too, and meet our aim of moving towards a balanced budget in the medium-term. Our plans show how we can virtually eliminate public borrowing by the year 2000.

Thanks to our success in controlling public spending, Britain is now Europe's low tax economy. This is one of the reasons why we are becoming the enterprise centre of Europe.

Our aim is to ensure Britain keeps the lowest tax burden of any major European economy.

In the election manifesto of 1992, we promised that "We will make further progress towards a basic income tax rate of 20p". Since then, we have cut the basic rate of income tax from 25p to 23p, and extended the 20p band so that over a quarter of all taxpayers now only pay income tax at the 20p rate. Achieving our public expenditure goals will mean we can sustain permanently low tax levels.

Over the next parliament, our aim will be to achieve our target of a 20p basic rate of income tax, while maintaining a maximum tax rate of no more than 40p.

### Stable prices
Inflation has to be kept firmly under control for an economy to thrive. Britain is now enjoying the longest period of stable prices for almost 50 years. We are on target to reach our goal of 2½ per cent inflation this year.

Low inflation has delivered lower interest rates whilst preserving the value of people's savings. Homeowners are now enjoying mortgage rates at the lowest levels for 30 years.

It has taken tough decisions to break free from our reputation as a high-inflation economy. No Conservative government will jeopardise this achievement.

During the next parliament, we will maintain an inflation target of 2½ per cent or less.

### Rising living standards
The only secure base for rising living standards is a strongly growing economy, low levels of public spending and taxation, and stable prices. That is exactly what Britain is achieving. People are reaping the rewards of their hard work as their take-home pay increases. Between 1974 and 1979, the take-home pay for a family on average earnings rose, in real terms, by just £1 a week in today's prices. Since 1979 it has increased by £100 a week; this year alone it will increase by £7 a week. The goal which we set ourselves in 1995 is to double living standards over 25 years. We are on course to achieve our goal.

### JOBS AND BUSINESS
Our priority is to create jobs. This is not just an economic priority, but also a social and moral one. Jobs and enterprise are the best ways of tackling poverty and deprivation.

Britain is succeeding. 900,000 jobs have been created over the past four years. By contrast the European social model is stifling job creation on the continent by imposing regulations and burdens on business. In the United Kingdom, unemployment is much lower than in the rest of Europe and falling whereas in Germany, France, and Italy it has risen to its highest level for a generation. This is no accident. It is because we have pursued very different policies from those on the Continent.

Curbing the power of trade unions, opening up markets and cutting red tape, have given us a low-strike, low-cost economy: and as a result we are the number one location for foreign investment in Europe.

Never have such policies been so important. For the first time this century we face a world full of capitalist competition. The only way Britain will be able to compete and win in world markets is by sticking to the Conservative policies that are delivering success. We can earn prosperity as one of the world's most successful global trading nations. We should not risk this progress by adopting the very policies that have made the continent uncompetitive and have increased unemployment in Europe by 4.5 million over the past five years.

### Small businesses — Britain's risk-takers
Governments do not create jobs. Businesses do. The source of tomorrow's jobs will be small businesses, the seedcorn of Britain's prosperity. Over the last 15 years, small businesses have created over two million jobs. By the year 2000, over half the workforce should be working in companies which employ fewer than 50 people. Back in 1979, only a third of the workforce did.

Entrepreneurs often risk everything when they set up their own business. We have already helped them: raising the VAT threshold, cutting employers' National Insurance contributions, simplifying audit requirements and much more besides. Now we intend to go further, tackling the remaining problems they face.

High taxes and rates deter enterprise. Our low-tax structure has been crucial to our industrial revival. We already have the lowest corporation tax of any major industrialised country. As we want small businesses to flourish, we will go even further.

We will cut the small companies rate of corporation tax in line with personal taxation as we move towards a 20p basic rate.

Investment and enterprise are deterred if the tax man takes too much of the capital that is built up by a successful business. Capital is ever more mobile, flying around the world to places where the tax on it is low: Britain must be one of those places.

We will continue to reduce the burden of capital gains tax and inheritance tax as it is prudent to do so.

One of the heaviest burdens small businesses face is business rates. At the moment, this bears more heavily upon small businesses than large ones.

In the next parliament, we will reform business rates to reduce the cost that falls upon small businesses.

No businessman has time to fill out reams of forms. We will continue to simplify the administration of NICs and PAYE for small firms, allowing them to concentrate on satisfying customers not bureaucrats. We are also tackling a problem that hits small businesses particularly hard — the late payment of bills. On top of our programme to ensure government departments and local authorities pay on time, we have legislated to require companies to publish their payment policy and to report their record on how quickly they pay their bills to small businesses.

We have already abolished over a thousand regulations. New regulations must only be introduced if it is clear that their benefits exceed their costs and they do not place an undue burden on a small firm.

We will introduce "sunset" requirements into new regulations whenever it is suitable so that they are automatically reviewed or dropped after a specific period.

Many businessmen suffer regulatory burdens imposed by local government and quangos.

We will therefore insist that the whole of the public sector adopts the same stringent rules that we require of central government in justifying the benefits of new regulations against their costs.

## Reducing the burden on companies

Jobs depend on British firms winning orders: the difference between success or failure can be wafer thin. Any extra burden on business will destroy jobs.

Britain is enjoying more jobs and record investment, thanks to the competitive edge we have over other European countries. We are a low-cost economy. But that does not mean we are a low-pay economy. Our competitive advantage comes from the lower costs facing our businesses. It can be measured by the social costs an employer has to pay on top of every £100 of wages: in Germany it is £31, in France £41, but in Britain, it is only £15.

Many countries in Europe have tried to cocoon themselves from global competition behind layers of red tape and regulation — such as the social chapter and a national minimum wage. This provides a false sense of security, playing a cruel trick on working people. It also excludes the unemployed from work. As companies in the rest of Europe have grown more uncompetitive, employers have found it too expensive to employ new workers, investment has gone elsewhere, and the dole queues have lengthened. The European social model is not social and not a model for us to follow. But if Britain signed up to the social chapter it would be used to impose that model on us — destroying British jobs.

No Conservative government will sign up to the social chapter or introduce a national minimum wage. We will insist at the inter-governmental conference in Amsterdam that our opt-out is honoured and that Britain is exempted from the Working Time Directive: if old agreements are broken, we do not see how new ones can be made.

We will resist the imposition of other social burdens on the workplace through a new European employment chapter.

## Welfare into work

Although governments cannot create jobs, they can help people train and find work. We now have in place a battery of schemes working with Training and Enterprise Councils to provide targeted help and training, including remedial education in literacy and numeracy. We are also developing new incentives, alongside Family Credit, to help people move off benefit into work.

We will always help those in genuine need: in return, the unemployed have a responsibility to look for work and accept a reasonable offer. That belief underpins our new jobseeker's allowance which ensures that no one can refuse reasonable work opportunities and remain on benefit.

As unemployment falls, we want to focus on those who have been unemployed for some time. At present, Project Work is helping 100,000 people who have been unemployed for more than two years in cities around Britain. They are first given help in finding a job – which includes giving employers incentives to take them on.

Those who do not find jobs are then required to work for a specific period on a community project. This helps them regain work habits and ensures they are available for work.

As Project Work succeeds and demonstrates that its costs can be met by the savings from getting people into work, we will extend the programme to cover the long-term unemployed nationwide.

We will also develop an innovative "Britain Works" scheme which uses the experience and ingenuity of private and voluntary sectors to get people off welfare into work.

Britain has one of the most mobile economies in Europe. People move on and up, into better paid jobs more easily than on the Continent.

## The information society

Britain is at the forefront of creating tomorrow's information society. Already we have exposed domestic telecommunications to competition and stimulated investment in cable and satellite entertainment systems. And by opening up international telecommunications we will continue to encourage companies worldwide to base their global operations here. We will make sure that the digital revolution comes to Britain first.

We are launching an ambitious programme with industry to spread "IT for All", giving every adult the opportunity to try out and learn about new IT services. We will work with industry to ensure that all schools are connected to the information superhighway.

We will use the Millennium Lottery Fund to transform the computer facilities and information links available in schools, libraries, museums, voluntary organisations and other public places after the turn of the century.

This will give the public much wider access to information services in the years ahead. We will also take advantage of information technology to transform the way government provides services to the public.

We will keep Britain in the vanguard of new mobile service development – including mobile telephone and information services – by introducing a pricing system for the radio spectrum to achieve more efficient allocation of radio frequencies.

We will maintain a strong, free and competitive broadcasting and press environment at both national and local level, while continuing to be vigilant in monitoring whether action is needed to curb breaches of standards, and prevent unacceptable press intrusion.

## Science

British science enjoys a worldwide reputation for excellence and cost-effectiveness, which makes Britain an attractive base for many domestic and overseas companies. We will continue to invest in science and target funds at basic research, which would not otherwise be funded by industry. At the same time we will provide an enterprising environment which encourages firms to invest with confidence in applied science.

## 2020 vision

There is no part of the globe which has not been reached by British enterprise and British culture. We have always looked out beyond these shores, beyond this continent. Our language, our heritage of international trading links, our foreign investments – second only to America's – are historic strengths which mean we are ideally placed to seize the opportunities of the global economy.

Thanks to Conservative policies of liberalisation and privatisation we are strong in industries of the future such as telecommunications, financial services, and information technology. These are the industries that will benefit from opening up trade around the world. We will push for completion of the European single market and continue to pursue the objective of transatlantic free trade against the background of world trade liberalisation.

Our aim is nothing less than tariff free trade across the globe by the year 2020.

Free competition is important for free markets. Companies should not make agreements that restrict competition and hence result in poor value for consumers. We have set out proposals to give companies greater protection against price fixing, dumping, and other restrictive practices by larger competitors.

We will introduce a Competition Bill to take forward these proposals in the first session of the next parliament.

We are committed to pushing forward our competitiveness agenda which is making Britain the enterprise centre of Europe.

## OPPORTUNITY AND OWNERSHIP FOR INDIVIDUALS AND FAMILIES
### Our record
◆ The right to buy has allowed 1.5 million council tenants to become homeowners. There are over four million more homeowners today than in 1979.

◆ The Government has spent £6 billion through housing associations to provide homes for rent. Between 1992 and 1995 housing associations provided 178,000 new lettings – 25,000 more than promised in the 1992 manifesto.

◆ There are now around ten million private shareholders, up from about three million at the time of the last Labour government. 2.5 million people now have tax-free savings in Pep accounts, and 4.5 million in Tessas.

◆ Since 1979, the success of private pension provision has raised the average income of pensioners by 60 per cent more than inflation. Almost 90 per cent of recently retired pensioners now have incomes over and above state benefits.

◆ Savings in private pension funds have increased to £650 billion – more than four times the level in 1979. Their value is greater than the pension funds in all other EU countries added together.

◆ Over the period 1979 to 1995, education spending per pupil rose from £515 to £1,890 – an increase in real terms of 48 per cent. Real spending on books and equipment per pupil rose 56 per cent. Teachers' real pay rose 57 per cent: from £270 per week in 1979 to £420 in 1995.

◆ In 1979, 40 per cent of three and four-year-olds attended nursery school; in 1995 the figure was 59 per cent. Our nursery vouchers now give this opportunity to every child.

◆ The proportion of sixteen-year-olds staying on in full-time education rose from four out of ten in 1979 to seven out of ten in 1995.

◆ Almost one in three young people now go to university, compared with one in eight in 1979.

◆ The proportion of adults with no academic qualifications has halved since 1979 and the proportion of adults with a degree or equivalent has more than doubled rising from 5 per cent to 12 per cent.

## CHOICE AND SECURITY FOR FAMILIES
The family is the most important institution in our lives. It offers security and stability in a fast-changing world. But the family is undermined if governments take decisions which families ought to take for themselves. Self-reliance underpins freedom and choice.

Families are stronger if they have the money to look after themselves: that is why we are shifting power and wealth back to working families and away from the state. We have already achieved much – the average family's disposable income has gone up by 40 per cent since 1979. But we want to go further. The next Conservative government intends to reform the tax system so that it gives substantially more help to families.

We also want to encourage people to save so they have the security and self-respect that comes from being able to rely on their own resources rather than immediately turning to the state. We have already made much progress here too with widening ownership of homes, pensions, and the new Peps and Tessas. We now propose further radical measures for more saving for retirement.

### Families and tax
We believe families should be left with as much of their own money as possible. They know better than politicians how to spend it. We have already cut the basic rate of income tax from 33p to 23p, and our aim is to get it down to 20p, benefiting 18 million taxpayers. We intend to do even more to help families in particular.

At the moment, if one spouse does not take paid work in order to look after children or dependent relatives, they not only give up earnings but may also be unable to benefit from their personal tax allowance. Yet this is the time at which their income is often most stretched.

We believe our tax system should recognise and support the crucial role of families in their caring responsibilities. We will give them that support.

We will give priority to future reductions in personal taxation that help families looking after dependent children or relatives by allowing one partner's unused personal allowance to be transferred to a working spouse where they have these responsibilities.

This will provide a targeted reduction in the tax bill to those families who need it most. Around two million one-taxpayer couples with dependent children, or looking after elderly relatives and others needing care, would gain up to £17.50 a week — around £900 a year.

### Family savings

In the old days people just depended on the weekly pay packet or money from the state. But no job can be secure and the state cannot provide for every eventuality. It is ownership which brings true security and genuine independence from the state. That is why Conservatives have long dreamed of a property-owning democracy. Now we are delivering it in practice. Home ownership is up by 4.7 million. Ten million people own a direct personal stake in our economy. 16 million are gaining shares in their building societies thanks to our deregulation of them. We intend to carry forward our vision of a people's share. This is a significant increase in personal security. It is the Conservative vision of security through personal savings — not a socialist vision of security through the State.

We want people to enjoy Britain's success — especially by owning shares in the companies for which they work. We have already introduced a number of schemes to encourage employee share ownership. To encourage a further expansion of worker shares, our new Share Match Scheme will allow employees to be rewarded with additional free shares if they acquire a stake in their company.

Our goal is that by 2000, more than half of the employees of Britain's larger companies will own shares in those companies.

4.5 million people now benefit from tax free Tessas and 2.5 million from Pep schemes to encourage the accumulation of long-term saving. We will continue to build on this success by exploring ways in which existing tax exemptions for savings can be developed — allowing individuals to secure their futures and protect their families against unexpected contingencies.

We will continue to raise the threshold for inheritance tax as it is prudent to do so.

People are not just saving for themselves but for their children and grand-children. These savings should not be penalised by the tax system.

For many people their biggest asset is their pension. Thanks to the steps we have already taken to encourage occupational and personal pensions, we now have £650 billion invested in private pensions — more than the rest of the European Union put together. We now plan to build further on this achievement.

We will make it easier for small employers to set up personal pension plans for groups of employees.

We will create more flexibility for people who save in personal pension plans to continue investing in those schemes if they subsequently move to jobs with company pension schemes.

We will also create flexibility for employees with savings in Additional Voluntary Contributions (AVC) schemes to take part of that pension earlier or later than their main company pension.

But we believe the time has now come to plan for another important step in improving Britain's pension provision. Britain is already much better placed than many other countries to afford state pensions in the future, but we want even more people to be able to look forward to a properly-funded pension that grows with the economy and is free from dependence on taxes paid by future generations. We now propose a practical way of achieving a gradual transformation of the state pension scheme.

At the start of the next parliament we will set out proposals to provide all young people entering the workforce with a personal pension fund paid for through a rebate on their National Insurance contributions. At retirement they would be entitled to the full pension earned by this accumulated investment. This could give them a pension significantly higher than they would currently receive from the state. But they with be guaranteed a pension at least equal to the current basic state pension, increased in line with inflation.

This will be one of the most significant improvements in the state pension system since it was introduced.

Older people currently in the workforce would be unaffected — they will continue to contribute as now and receive the normal state pension when they retire.

This policy would come into effect early in the new millennium. Gradual phasing in of the new system over 40 years will make the impact on public finances affordable. Even at its peak, the net revenue forgone will be only a fraction of the savings from the recent Pensions Act. And eventually, the new policy will produce massive public expenditure savings.

This far-sighted idea is in the best Conservative tradition. The growing wealth of the nation will provide for the next generation through private funding, underpinned by a state guarantee. British people will be able to look forward to retirement with even greater confidence. And our young people will have a pensions opportunity unrivalled in the world.

### Support for families

Conservatives believe that a healthy society encourages people to accept responsibility for their own lives. A heavy-handed and intrusive state can do enormous damage.

Some families need help to cope with their responsibilities. For them, social services play a vital role. They help with children where parental care has failed. They deliver an ever-wider range of services to people with learning difficulties or who are mentally ill. Our community care reforms have given them a central role ensuring that elderly people get care of the highest quality: and in their own homes where possible. We need to ensure that role is properly fulfilled.

Early in the next Parliament we will introduce a Social Services Reform Bill which will create a new statutory framework for social services. The Bill will provide for greater openness and accountability in social services.

We will provide new guidance to ensure social workers properly reflect the values of the community — focusing their efforts on those families who most need support, and minimising unnecessary interference. Social workers working with children will receive special training to cope with the often heart-rending cases they face.

We will raise standards through a new regulatory framework which will apply the same standards in both the public and private sector.

We will also remove the power of local authorities to operate care homes where this is in the best interests of the people for whom they are responsible.

We believe that families who use social services should be able to exercise choice wherever practicable. We have given cash payments to disabled people to purchase the services they need directly.

We also want new ways of reinforcing individual choice where possible. We will therefore ensure no barriers stand in the way of local authorities wanting to issue their users with vouchers to buy certain services.

We will review the direct payment scheme, and provided it has been cost effective, we will extend it to other users of social services.

Above all, we want to help families to help themselves. Caring for older — or disabled — relatives is one of the most natural human instincts. We recognise the crucial — and often demanding — role carers play, and will help them more.

We will introduce a Respite Care Programme. This will enable family members with heavy responsibilities caring for a relative to take a much-needed break. We will also offer more practical advice for carers who want to go back to paid work.

But in some cases, elderly people need more care than their friends or relatives can provide. Financing long-term care worries many families. We will create an imaginative, fair partnership between individuals and the public sector to resolve this problem.

In the first session of the next Parliament we will implement our partnership scheme for long-term care, making it easier for people to afford the cost of care in old age without giving up their lifetime savings.

Good preparation for marriage can be an important aid to a successful family, while timely help in meeting difficulties can often avoid family breakdown. These are matters for voluntary effort, not the State, but we will continue to support such effort.

We need to make sure efforts to help struggling families does not turn into unnecessary meddling.

When the state goes too far, it is often the children who suffer. They become victims of the worst sort of political correctness.

We will introduce legislation to remove unnecessary barriers to adoption and introduce new rules to make adoption from abroad more straightforward.

We will also monitor the workings of the Children Act, and act if necessary to ensure it maintains a proper balance between the rights of children and the responsibilities of adults.

Social services departments are now the fourth arm of the welfare state. Most people will need them at some point in their lives. We will ensure that the Conservative revolution in public services now reaches social services.

### Disabled people

We have quadrupled real spending on long-term sick and disabled people since 1979, to £22 billion.

We have introduced the Disability Discrimination Act. This is the first legislation of its kind anywhere in Europe and it provides positive proof of our commitment to disabled people. We will monitor it to ensure it continues to meet its objectives.

We are also providing a continuing fund to support the most severely disabled people to stay in their homes.

### Security in retirement

Pensioners continue to make a positive contribution to society in retirement. They give more of their time in charitable work than any other age group. They lift some of the pressures on their own families. They help keep our nation's history and traditions alive.

They have paid their National Insurance contributions and taxes and rightly expect us to continue to protect the value of the basic state pension against price rises. We will do so. We will also ensure that less well-off pensioners continue to get extra help on top of the basic pension.

At the same time as protecting the state pension, our encouragement of private pensions is already transforming the living standards of pensioners. The average net income of pensioners has risen by 60 per cent since 1979. This has been achieved by our encouragement of saving for retirement.

The tax system must help pensioners who have saved. Our new lower 20p rate on income from savings directly helps 1.7 million pensioners and the special age allowances raise the point at which pensioners start to pay income tax.

### A better social security system

People in need can rely on our continuing support. And to ensure that taxpayers are willing to go on paying for that support, we have shaped a social security system we can afford, taking a steadily declining share of our national income. We are doing this by focusing benefits on those most in need, helping people off welfare and into work, and curbing welfare fraud. These policies are underpinned by our measures to help families help themselves.

Social security must be there to help families, pensioners and people in need. We will protect the value of child benefit and family credit which help with the cost of bringing up children. This is our Family Benefits Guarantee.

We will bring the structure of benefits for lone parents into line with that for two-parent families. We will continue to help lone parents obtain maintenance, and assist with childcare in work: both these measures help lone parents obtain work. We will pilot our "Parent Plus" Scheme that gives special help to lone parents who want to work, and extend it as it proves successful.

Social security fraud must be stamped out.

We will intensify our current initiatives of inspections and checks including more home visits, to crack down further on benefit cheats. We will introduce benefit cards across the country. We will establish a Benefit Fraud Inspectorate to monitor local authorities' performance. We will also improve the sharing of information between government departments to catch more fraudulent claims.

To ensure as much of the social security budget as possible goes into benefits, we will continue to improve the efficiency of administration, using the best mix of public and private sector operations.

### Housing

Owning one's own home is an aim shared by millions of people. Over the last 18 years, the number of homeowners has increased by 4.7 million – including 1.7 million who have brought their home under the right-to-buy scheme. Over the next ten years, we expect to see about 1½ million people buying their own homes – some 3,000 every week. To meet that demand, we will continue to allow local authority and housing association tenants to buy their homes or move to houses which they buy.

We will also carry through our draft Bill, creating the option for those buying flats to choose a new form of commonhold ownership.

For those who wish to rent their home, we are encouraging a thriving private rental market, building on the success of housing investment trusts and protecting assured tenancies.

Easier renting will help us meet our target of reducing the proportion of empty homes below 3 per cent. The number of empty houses has fallen in each of the last three years. But nothing is more frustrating for people who need social housing than the sight of a suitable property owned by the public sector lying boarded up and empty. We will stop that.

Public landlords will have to sell houses which are available for occupation yet have been left empty without a good reason for more than 12 months.

Housing associations and housing companies will continue to receive help in building new homes, and we will encourage more public-private partnerships. Together, these policies will help meet the demand for new public housing and make sure that there are decent homes for those in need.

### Opportunities for women

Women are succeeding in Britain. More women have jobs in Britain than in almost any other European country. Women have a better education, more financial independence and more opportunities than at any other time in Britain's history.

This success reflects the efforts and determination of many women. Government's role has been simpler – to level up the playing field, whether in education, where girls are now doing better than boys, or in the workplace, where opportunities for women are the best in Europe.

But we know our job is not yet done. Some women still face barriers to doing well. Some still do not have the financial security they deserve. And crime, and the fear of crime, often affect women more than men.

We will ensure women have equal opportunities in education and the workplace. This can best be achieved by keeping our economy buoyant and our labour markets flexible. And our proposals to bring crime rates down further will help women especially.

But many women – and some men – face a particular problem: how to juggle job and family. For those who need or want to work, we will seek further ways to minimise the barriers to affordable, high-quality childcare. For those who wish to be full-time parents, our proposals to enable them to transfer their unused personal allowance to their spouse will be worth up to an extra £17.50 a week.

We also want to give women more financial independence, particularly when they retire. We propose, as explained elsewhere, to improve flexibility in saving for retirement and to allow courts to split pensions on divorce.

### Looking outwards

The spread of share ownership, the transformation of pension provision, and the sale of council houses are revolutionising our nation. Personal prosperity and property ownership are not selfish or inward-looking.

People who are secure at home can look out for others in their community. Over two-thirds of adults engage in some form of voluntary activity. By the end of 1997 all young people aged between 15 and 25 who want to volunteer will be helped to find an opportunity to do so.

We will encourage voluntary work by others living on benefit while continuing to insist that those who are capable of work should actively seek employment. We will also develop accreditation for voluntary work to encourage employers to see it as preparation for a paid job.

We will make it easier for those receiving incapacity benefit to volunteer by removing the 16-hour weekly limit on their voluntary work.

It is wrong to imagine that compassion must be nationalised and that we can only help our fellow man through state action.

## EDUCATION AND OPPORTUNITY

All children dream of what they might do when they grow up. Our task is to help them turn those dreams into reality whatever their background may be. It is an exciting world, full of new opportunities for inquiring minds: it should be open to every child. Their future – and Britain's prosperity – depends on the quality of their education.

### Our Education guarantee

A good education is the birthright of every child. Literacy is the building block of all future learning: English is the global language of commerce and, much more, a thing of beauty. Without basic science and mathematics, the modern world is incomprehensible. Every child therefore must be taught to read, write and add up from an early age.

Years of mistaken, progressive education in the 1960s and 1970s denied these precious skills to too many children. We have worked ceaselessly since 1979 to put that right. Our decision to test children and publish the results has allowed standards to be measured and exposed. We have reformed the curriculum, toughened inspections, and given more information and power to parents. Our many excellent teachers now know what is expected of them, and already standards in schools are rising. But they are still not good enough. We must do more.

Building on what we have done, we can now offer a new pledge to parents – a guarantee of education standards.

First, we will set national targets for school performance that reflect our objective of ensuring that Britain is in the top league of international standards across the whole spectrum of education.

Second, we will require every school to plan how to improve its performance, and to set targets which relate to similar schools and national standards.

Third, we will give all parents full information on the performance of their child's school.

Fourth, to underwrite our pledge, we will ensure action is taken to bring any under-performing school up to the mark.

We will meet this pledge by using the full set of levers for improved standards that we have put in place. We are revising and simplifying the national curriculum in primary schools to emphasise high standards in the basic skills.

Parents and teachers must have an overview of not just how much a child has learnt while at school, but how the school performs against others. Poor schooling must not be protected by a veil of secrecy. Parent power is a vital force for higher standards.

Regular tests and exams are essential if teachers are to discover how much their pupils have learnt, and parents are to know how much progress their children are making against national standards. That is why children are already being tested at seven, 11 and 14. We will publish all school test results, including the results of tests of seven and 14-year-olds.

We propose also to assess every child at five. This will give teachers and parents a benchmark against which they can measure future progress. To give a better measure of pupils' performance, marks out of 100 will be made available to parents as well as the broad-brush levels.

We will also introduce a new test for 14-year-old children that covers the whole national curriculum – assessing progress before they choose subjects for GCSE.

Tests and exams need to be rigorous and demanding. We will insist that they establish children's command of spelling, punctuation, and grammar in English tests. Children will sit arithmetic tests without calculators. We will not allow such extensive use of open books in tests and in GCSE exams. We will establish an English Language GCSE. We will continue to uphold the gold standard of A-levels, and ensure that the great classics of our literature are studied at A-level. At the same time students should have the chance to study more subjects in the sixth form.

Rigorous tests show how individual children and schools are performing and expose schools that are not giving children the education they deserve. To underwrite our guarantee, we will then take action to improve standards. We cannot tolerate schools that fail their pupils.

By this summer every secondary school in the country will have been inspected by independent inspectors, and by summer 1998, every primary school will have been inspected as well. We have the power to take over failing schools directly and close them if necessary. We will now go further and require every school to set and publish regular targets and plans for improving their academic results. Independent inspectors will monitor the results of weaker schools and their plans for improvement at regular intervals.

Sometimes, though, schools are failing because the local education authority which runs them is failing. The authorities with the worst GCSE results and the worst results at Key Stage 2 (11-year-olds) are run by Labour. Those children need our help.

We will allow for an independent inspection of education authorities and intervene directly to raise standards where education authorities are letting children down.

Failing authorities will be required to set out their plans to raise standards, and work with education teams – directed by independent inspectors – to implement those plans.

The vast majority of teachers do an outstanding job. They have played a key part in implementing the reforms that we have introduced. A few though, fail their pupils.

We will establish a more rigorous and effective system of appraising teachers, which reflects how well their pupils perform in tests and exams: this will identify which teachers need more help and, where necessary, which teachers need to be replaced.

Many feel that the professional standing of teachers would be strengthened by the creation of a single body which could speak with authority on professional standards. We will consult with teachers and other interested parties about the possible role of such a body.

The school should be a place of stability and stimulation for children, especially if they come from a hostile or turbulent environment. To improve standards in future, our new teacher-training curriculum will stress traditional teaching methods – including whole-class teaching and learning to read by the sounds of letters. We will also encourage more teachers to enter the profession through practical training schemes focused on classroom experience such as the Graduate Teacher Scheme. A child is likely to learn more in a well-ordered school. Teachers must have the powers they need to maintain discipline. We will give teachers greater power to set detentions to exclude disruptive pupils and to use reasonable physical restraint where necessary.

Schools also have an important role to play in spiritual and moral education. We will take steps to ensure that every school fulfils its role of providing religious education and collective worship.

### Choice and diversity

When we came to power in 1979 the schools system was totally dominated by one type of school – the monolithic comprehensive. The system failed our children. It treated every child the same. It told parents where to send their children. It did not give schools the freedom to run their own affairs.

Since 1979 we have created a rich diversity of schools, to serve the varied talents of all children and give parents choice within that diversity, because we believe that parents know what is best for their children.

That is why we – and only we – are committed to giving the parent of every four year old child a voucher for nursery education so they can choose the pre-school education they want for their child, whether in a play-group, a reception class, or a nursery school in the private or state sector.

We will give more talented children, from less well-off backgrounds, the opportunity to go to fee-paying schools by expanding the Assisted Places Scheme to cover all ages of compulsory education, in line with our current spending plans. We propose to develop it further into a wider scholarship scheme covering additional educational opportunities. The freedoms and status of fee-paying schools will be protected.

Grant-maintained schools have been popular with parents across the country – whatever their politics. We will encourage more schools to become grant- maintained and will allow new grant-maintained schools to be set up where there is sufficient local demand. We will give all grant-maintained schools greater freedoms to expand and to select their pupils.

Grant-maintained schools are leading the way. Local authority schools are also benefitting from our policy of local management of schools. Our ultimate objective is that all schools should take full responsibility for the management of their own affairs. In the next parliament we will take another step towards giving them that freedom.

We will extend the benefits of greater self-governance to all LEA schools. We will require local authorities to delegate more of schools' budgets to the schools themselves. We will give them more freedom over the employment of their staff and over admissions. And, where they want it, we will allow them to take over ownership of their assets, so they can make best use of the resources.

Local authorities will continue to be responsible for their schools' standards. They will provide funds, and compete with other organisations to provide services to schools. We would expect the increased responsibility of head-teachers, and their role in achieving efficiency-savings, to be recognised by their pay review body.

Schools are stronger and more effective where head-teachers and governors can shape their own distinctive character. Sometimes that means developing a speciality in some subjects. Sometimes it means selecting children by their aptitudes: where parents want this we should not stand in their way. Special abilities should be recognised and encouraged.

We will continue to encourage the establishment of more specialist schools in technology, arts, languages and sport. We aim to help one in five schools become specialist schools by 2001.

We will allow all schools to select some of their pupils.

We will help schools to become grammar schools in every major town where parents want that choice.

The high standards, real choice and genuine diversity which we have introduced will produce the best results for all our children.

### Lifetime learning

Lifetime learning is a reality in Britain today. Over a half of all students in universities, and 70 per cent of those in further education colleges, are adults who have returned to education later in life. We will continue to create new opportunities for more people to participate.

There has been a revolution in further and higher education. Three and a half million people are in further education – up from just half a million in 1979. The number of young people going to university has risen from one in eight to one in three over the same period. We will ensure consistently high standards and will consult on the development of higher education when we receive the results of the Dearing Review. We have world-class research in British universities which we will continue to support.

Every young person should have the opportunity to continue in education or training. We will give students between 14 and 21 a learning credit which will enable them to choose suitable education or training leading to recognised qualifications up to A levels or their equivalents. We will also introduce National Traineeships and encourage employers to offer more work-based Modern Apprenticeships to young people. Objective external assessments of a proper syllabus will be made a part of all National Vocational Qualifications.

We will continue to support the network of Training and Enterprise Councils, which have created a valuable partnership between business and government. We will encourage more employers to become involved in "Investors in People", with the public sector matching the performance of the private sector.

Competitive markets demand high skills. If Britain is to win, we need to encourage learning and give people the opportunity to go where their interests and inquiring minds take them.

## WORLD-CLASS HEALTH AND PUBLIC SERVICES
### Our record
♦ Government spending has concentrated on priorities, not wasteful bureaucracy and overmanning. Despite tough overall spending plans, real spending on the NHS has risen nearly 75 per cent since 1979, on schools by 50 per cent and on the police by more than 100 per cent.
♦ The Health Service is treating over one million more patients each year than before our reforms.
♦ The number of people waiting over 12 months for hospital treatment has fallen from over 200,000 in 1990 to 22,000 last year. The average wait has fallen from nearly nine months to four months.
♦ The Government has set up the Citizen's Charter to provide first-class public services for all citizens. Nearly 650 organisations have received a Charter Mark for meeting demanding standards of performance, customer satisfaction and value for money.
♦ There are now 55,000 more nurses and midwives and 22,500 more doctors and dentists than in 1979. For every senior NHS manager, 77 people are providing direct patient care.
♦ Nurses' average earnings have grown 70 per cent in real terms: from £68 a week in 1979 to £325 in 1995. Doctors' pay has risen by a third. Under Labour both were cut.
♦ Infant mortality has fallen from 13.2 to 6.2 per thousand over the last 18 years.
♦ Deaths through road accidents are now the lowest since records began in 1926. Since 1979 road deaths have fallen by 43 per cent and serious casualties have fallen by 43 per cent despite an 85 per cent increase in motor traffic.
♦ The Government has invested record amounts on transport – more than £26 billion since 1979 in investment on motorways and trunk roads; £16 billion on railways; and over £8 billion on London Transport.
♦ Privatisation is delivering better services at lower costs. BT's main prices are down by more than 40 per cent in real terms. Average household bills for gas and electricity have also fallen in real terms since 1990.

### Security in health
We have been the guardians of the NHS for most of its life, improving its services and securing its funding. The benefits can be seen in our rising standards of health. 1993 was for example the first year in which no child in this country died of measles. Between 1979 and 1995 life expectancy at birth in England has increased from 70.4 years to 74.3 years for men and from 76.4 years to 79.6 years for women. We are getting healthier and we are better looked after when we are sick.

### Growing resources for a modern health service
This progress has been possible because we have increased spending since 1979 by 70 per cent more than inflation, to nearly £43 billion. And we are not stopping there. The next Conservative Government will honour a unique guarantee to the NHS.

We will continue, year by year, to increase the real resources committed to the NHS, so NHS spending will continue to share in a growing economy. Under Labour there have been years when resources for the NHS actually shrank – something that would be inconceivable with the Conservatives.

Money is only really a means to an end: better patient care. Now we are treating 9.2 million hospital in-patients and day cases as against 6.9 million in 1992 and 5.1 million in 1979.

### Investing in skilled staff

We are committed to expanding the medical staff of the NHS. We shall therefore increase medical school intakes to 5,000 a year by the year 2000 and are ahead of schedule in reaching the target.

Good nursing is the bedrock of the NHS. In particular we will increase the number of nurses with specialist qualifications in paediatric intensive care, emergency care, and cancer care. The number of nurses qualifying each year will increase in each of the next five years as we continue to expand Project 2000 training.

### Higher standards of service

We are tackling the problem of long waiting times which can cause so much worry, distress, and pain. We have set tough targets under the Patient's Charter and as a result average waiting times for inpatient hospital treatments have fallen from more than six months five years ago to four months last year.

Patients no longer put up with being kept in ignorance. They want to know more.

We will publish more information on how successfully hospitals are treating patients so that they and their GPs can make more informed choices between services in different hospitals and help stimulate better performance.

### Better primary care

Our vision of the NHS is one in which hospitals and family doctors gain greater power to run their own affairs. That is why we will continue to encourage the spread of fundholding among GPs. Labour by contrast would destroy the new freedoms that fundholding doctors enjoy by imposing a new layer of bureaucracy on top of them.

However, we do not want the benefits of better healthcare to be confined to patients of GP fundholders. Our proposals to shift more healthcare towards family doctors are open to all.

We shall implement the new Primary Care Act which will enable all family doctors to provide a broader range of patient services within their surgeries. This will include "super surgeries" and practice-based cottage hospitals that can offer faster and more local treatment.

We expect to see the number of nurses working in GP practices continue to grow, as will the number of GPs.

We will extend nationwide our plans to enable more nurses to prescribe a wider range of drugs for patients, recognising their contribution to primary care.

### Mental health

The last decade has also seen major changes to the care of mentally ill people. We will continue to develop a full range of services – including 24-hour nursed hostels and secure units – that can care for them in a way which is most appropriate to them and the interests of the wider community.

We will not close any long-stay mental hospitals unless it can be shown that adequate care services exist in the community.

We will strengthen co-operation between health and social services in the delivery of mental health services. Our recent Green Paper showed how this can be done. And we will monitor the progress of health authorities in developing proper mental health care plans.

### Health of the Nation

A modern health service is not just about treating illness, it is also about keeping people healthy. This is why we launched the Health of the Nation strategy in 1992 – the first time England has had a strategy for health. Its aim is to reduce illness and premature death by identifying common causes of ill health, like excessive smoking and obesity. Different groups in and outside the health service then work together to tackle the problems.

We are already seeing progress. Between 1990 and 1994, deaths from coronary heart disease among the over-65s, the suicide rate, and the number of teenage pregnancies fell substantially. And last year we announced that environmental targets would be added to Health of the Nation.

Improved general health means fewer people requiring attention in hospitals and GP surgeries – and more resources to be spent on helping patients. Our Health of the Nation strategy is a vital part of our vision of creating a health service fit for the 21st century.

## CONSERVATIVE MANIFESTO

### A modern health service

Healthcare is changing fast. Modern technology is constantly increasing the range of treatments which are available. Conservatives believe that the benefits of these advances should be made available to patients on the basis of their clinical need, without regard to their ability to pay.

Furthermore we also believe that the NHS must have access to sufficient resources to allow it to invest in the facilities required to deliver up-to-date healthcare. Since 1979 capital investment in the NHS has proceeded at an unprecedented rate. In the future we believe these requirements will be best met in a partnership with the private sector which allows the private sector to improve the facilities in which NHS healthcare is delivered.

We will promote the Private Finance Initiative which will unleash a new flow of investment funds into the modernisation of the NHS.

The NHS is a British success story. It commands universal support in Britain. It is widely admired all over the world. Conservatives are proud of the part we are playing in improving it still further.

### Better public services

The public sector is being transformed the world over. Britain is in the vanguard. Everyone else wants to learn from our vision of a smaller state doing fewer things and doing them better.

Old-style public services were centrally planned with little information or choice for the public who used the service. Our reforms have made these services more responsive to the public by breaking up cumbersome bureaucratic structures and shifting power to small responsive local institutions and the people who work in them. The schools, hospitals and police have all been transformed in this way. We support the people who do, not the people who plan.

In order to get better standards we are liberating services from centralised control over capital. We will push forward our Private Finance Initiative to break down these old barriers.

We have made public services genuinely accountable, with useful information and real choices for the people who use them. We set tough standards and they will get tougher. The Citizen's Charter has raised standards of customer service. When these high standards are reached we recognise and reward excellence through our Charter Mark initiative. There are now 647 Charter Marks and we will aim for more than 2,000 Charter Marks by the year 2000.

We will require all government agencies to apply for Charter Marks.

The days of the bureaucratic paper chase are behind us. The future is "government direct". We will harness the latest information technology to place the public sector directly at the service of the citizen. People will be able to use simple computer terminals to enter information directly. This will transform time-consuming transactions like completing a tax return or registering a new business.

### Privatisation and competition

In 20 years, privatisation has gone from the dream of a few Conservative visionaries to the big idea which is transforming decaying public sector industries in almost every country in the world. Britain has led the way with this new industrial revolution: we can be proud of what we have achieved.

In 1979 the Government inherited a range of businesses which had come into the public sector for different reasons. Many were known for their poor standards of service, and most were making large losses.

Over the past 18 years that situation has changed substantially. Privatisation has enhanced productivity, improved customer services, raised safety and environmental standards and substantially reduced prices.

Telephone, gas and electricity bills to the customer have fallen as never before. Telephone waiting lists are unknown, and water, gas and electricity disconnections have fallen dramatically. Nearly £40 billion in private sector funding has been committed to a major investment programme to meet higher-quality water standards. We can now look forward to water prices falling over the years ahead.

Service standards have improved substantially. Before privatisation published service standards did not exist. Now industry regulators monitor legal requirements to provide quality services in a competitive environment. Refunds may be made when performance standards are not met.

Privatisation has benefited — and will continue to benefit — consumers, shareholders, employees, and taxpayers. In 1979 the then-nationalised industries required a £50 million per week subsidy from the taxpayer. In 1996 those now-privatised companies paid taxes of £60 million per week.

We will ensure private ownership, competition and regulation continue to deliver lower prices and better services for consumers.

We will extend competition for domestic gas users, and introduce competition in the water industry, starting with large users.

The Post Office occupies an important part in national life. It comprises Counter Services, the Royal Mail and Parcelforce. The network of sub-post offices is vital and most are already run as private businesses. The Royal Mail provides a universal service at a standard price in every part of the United Kingdom. No one can imagine a stamp that does not bear the Queen's head. These characteristics must continue, but reforms are needed to allow the services to develop. The Royal Mail must face up to the challenges and opportunities that are arising from increasing competition and the international liberalisation of services.

We will guarantee to preserve the national identity, universal service and distinctive characteristics of the Royal Mail, while considering options — including different forms of privatisation — to introduce private capital and management skills into its operations.

We will transfer Parcelforce to the private sector whilst ensuring that every Post Office in the land continues to provide a full parcel service at an economical price.

Privatisation works. We will therefore continue to pass government activities into private ownership where this can bring benefits to consumers and taxpayers.

## Local government

We are developing a new vision for local government.

We believe local government should take a lead in the planning and development of their communities. To achieve that, we have encouraged them to work in partnership with central government, with private enterprise, and other organisations in their community. The impact of local government is multiplied when they work in this way.

To encourage this partnership, we have developed the new approach of Challenge Funding. We set up a fund to meet a particular objective and then invite competing bids for the money. Those who form effective partnerships are far more likely to win those bids. The Single Regeneration Budget Fund, for example, has stimulated many working partnerships that are bringing new life to their communities.

This innovation has the potential to transform the financing of the public sector.

We will push Challenge Funding further to reward effective local government.

In addition, we are encouraging higher standards and more cost-effective provision of local services. Local authorities can enable things to happen rather than necessarily running themselves. They must look after the interests of users of their services — and that is often best done by being a purchaser, not an employer.

Standards of service are rising in many local authorities. There are, however, still great disparities between the best and worst performers, as the Audit Commission shows in their thought-provoking reports.

We will keep up the pressure for higher standards and improved value for money by insisting on compulsory competitive tendering.

The development of Challenge Funding and the shift in the role of local authorities from direct employers to purchasers of services will transform local authorities over the coming years. In the meantime we will, for so long as is necessary, retain the power to cap local authorities to protect taxpayers.

## Strikes in essential services

Industrial relations in this country have been transformed. In so far as there is a still a problem it is concentrated in a few essential services where the public has no easy alternative and strikers are able to impose massive costs and inconvenience out of all proportion to the issues at stake. We will protect ordinary members of the public from this abuse of power.

We will legislate to remove legal immunity from industrial action which has disproportionate or excessive effect. Members of the public and employers will be able to seek injunctions to prevent industrial action in these circumstances. Any strike action will also have to be approved by a majority of all members eligible to vote and ballots will have to be repeated at regular intervals if negotiations are extended.

## Transport

Our railways are already improving now they have been liberated into the private sector.

Passenger numbers are up: more people are using the railways every day. Investment is up: Railtrack plans to spend £4 million each day on improving stations and maintaining and renewing the network. The new train operators are committed to investing £1.5 billion in new and refurbished rolling stock. And key fares are falling in real terms for the first time in a generation, with guaranteed price controls keeping fare increases below the level of inflation until at least 2003. We intend to build on this growing success story to create a thriving railway network for the new century.

We will complete the successful transfer of British Rail into the commercial sector.

We now want to draw in private investment to modernise London Underground and improve services to passengers.

We will bring forward plans to privatise London Underground. Proceeds from privatisation will be recycled in order to modernise the network within five years – creating an Underground system to serve the capital in the 21st century. We will regulate fares so they rise by no more than inflation for at least four years after privatisation. We will also protect services – including the Travel Card and concessionary fares.

After completing the modernisation of the network, the majority of the remaining surplus from privatisation will be channelled into additional support for transport investment in London and elsewhere in the country.

We will continue to encourage public transport. In particular, we will use the existing funding for local authorities to promote developments which make it easier to transfer from rail to bus.

We recognise the needs of road users, and will continue to work with the private sector to sustain our road building and maintenance programme. Already under the Private Finance Initiative the private sector is contributing some £1 billion to investment in roads and achieving significant savings in construction costs. We will also tackle road congestion by introducing new regional traffic control centres, by extending the use of variable speed limits, and by ensuring that local authorities have the necessary powers to act. We will promote a cleaner environment by supporting a Europe-wide reduction in vehicle emissions, and encouraging the manufacture of more fuel efficient vehicles.

We will continue to build on our record of improving safety on roll-on, roll-off ferries and cargo ships through higher standards of survivability and the measures in the Merchant Shipping Act.

We will continue to make it easier for people to travel by air. Already over the last five years opening up the market in Europe has led to more services and lower fares. We will build on that success in negotiations with the United States and other countries. We will also continue to encourage the development of regional airports offering new direct services to the rest of the world in the same way that we have already opened up new regional links with Europe and the United States. We will privatise the National Air Traffic System because it will be run better in the private sector.

Competition and enterprise are the best way to improve our transport system.

## A SAFE AND CIVIL SOCIETY
### Our record

♦ Spending on the police has doubled since 1979 after allowing for inflation. There are now about 16,000 more police officers than when we took office. 2,360 more constables have been recruited since the last election and the Government is giving Chief Officers the resources to recruit 5,000 extra police constables over the next three years.

♦ Recorded crime has dropped in each of the last four years. It is now over 10 per cent down on 1992 levels – more than half a million fewer offences – the biggest drop since records were first kept.

♦ There are now 153,000 neighbourhood watch schemes in England and Wales – 38,000 more than in 1992 – covering 5.5 million homes. We have helped fund over 4,000 closed circuit TV schemes over the last two years for additional security.

♦ Our national DNA database – the first in the world – now has over 112,000 samples on it. 3,300 matches have so far been made between suspects and crime stains.

♦ The Government has increased the maximum penalty for taking a gun to a crime and for attempted rape to life imprisonment. Since 1985 the average sentence for violence against the person has risen by a third and for sexual offences by nearly 40 per cent.

♦ The numer of cars stolen has fallen by nearly 20 per cent in the last four years – that is about 100,000 fewer cars stolen.

♦ We have built 22 new prisons since 1980. Slopping out has ended. No prisoners now sleep

three to a cell designed for one. Prison escapes have fallen by 80 per cent since the last election.
♦ Mandatory drug testing has been introduced throughout the Prison Service. Home leave has been cut back – down by half in two years.
♦ We have made witness intimidation a crime. 500 people were charged with that offence in 1995 alone.
♦ We have stepped up the fight against drugs and organised crime, giving the security services powers to support the police and Customs and Excise in tracking down the serious criminals.

## Law, order and security

People have a right to sleep safely in their homes and walk safely on the streets. Governments have a duty to maintain that security.

Our reforms are aimed at ensuring that crime does not pay. And they are working – the pessimists and the scoffers are wrong. Recorded crime has fallen every year for the last four years. It is now 10 per cent lower than it was in 1992. That is over half a million fewer crimes – the biggest drop since records were first kept in the middle of the 19th century.

But crime is still too high. We must do more. Our aim is to keep crime falling over the lifetime of the next parliament. This is what we will do.

## Safer communities

Anti-social behaviour and petty crime disrupt communities and spread human misery. The police are rightly now vigorously tackling problems such as graffiti, vandalism and drunkenness. Where such behaviour goes unchecked more serious crimes will follow.

We will support chief constables who develop local schemes to crack down on petty crime and improve public order.

Closed circuit television has proved enormously successful in increasing public safety.

We will fulfil the Prime Minister's pledge to support the installation of 10,000 CCTV cameras in town centres and public places in the three years to 1999. We will provide £75 million over the lifetime of the next parliament to continue extending CCTV to town centres, villages and housing estates up and down the country that want to bid for support.

We will also continue to take other steps to improve the safety of our streets and communities. In this parliament we have given the police power to seize alcohol from under-18s caught drinking in public. The police have been given the power to stop and search in a specified area for up to 48 hours if they reasonably believe people to be carrying knives.

Identity cards can also make a contribution to safer communities.

We will introduce a voluntary identity card scheme based on the new photographic driving licence. It will, for example, enable retailers to identify youngsters trying to buy alcohol and cigarettes or rent classified videos when they are under age.

## Tackling juvenile crime

A fifth of all crime is committed by under-18s. We are encouraging schools to reduce truancy through the publication of league tables and by supporting local projects to tackle the problem. We are developing a network of local teams to identify children who are at risk of turning to crime and to take early steps to address the factors which put them at risk.

We will encourage these local child crime teams to refer children from primary school age upwards who are at risk of, or actually, offending to programmes to tackle their behaviour and fully involve their parents.

The courts would be able to impose an order – a Parental Control Order – on the parents of children whom they believed could keep control of their children but were refusing to do so.

Courts will be given the power to attach conditions to Parental Control Orders. Conditions might include a requirement to keep their children in at night, taking their children to and from school, attending a drug rehabilitation clinic or going to sessions to improve their skills as parents. Parents who breached these conditions – in defiance of the court – would face a range of possible sanctions.

Appearing before a youth court should be a daunting experience for the juvenile concerned. All too often it is not. At the moment about a third of all juveniles appearing before the youth courts are discharged without any punishment at all. This sends all the wrong signals to youngsters – particularly first-time offenders – who then feel they can get away with crime.

We will give the courts the power to impose speedy sanctions on youngsters, involving wherever possible an element of reparation to the victim. The probation service – rather than social services – will be responsible for enforcing community punishments for under-16s.

Persistent juvenile offenders need to be properly punished. We are piloting a tough new regime, with a heavy emphasis on discipline, at a young offender institution and at the military prison in Colchester. In 1994 we doubled the maximum sentence for 15 to 17-year-olds to two years' detention in a young offenders' institution. We have given the courts the freedom to allow the publication of the names of convicted juveniles. We will give the courts the power to detain persistent 12 to 14-year-old offenders in secure training centres once the places become available.

We have given the courts the power to impose electronically-monitored curfews on 10 to 15-year-old offenders. We will introduce pilots to test their effectiveness. If successful we will consider extending them nationwide.

### Catching, convicting and punishing

We back the police every inch of the way. There are now about 16,000 more police officers – and over 18,000 more civilians helping them – than when we took office. We are providing chief constables with the resources to recruit 5,000 extra police constables in the three years to 1999.

We support police initiatives to target the hard core of persistent criminals. Intelligence is crucial for this. We will establish a national crime squad to provide an improved nationally co-ordinated approach to organised crime.

Once caught, criminals must be convicted and then properly punished. The public need to be protected. We have reformed the right to silence, despite opposition from Labour. The number of suspects refusing to answer police questions has nearly halved as a result.

We have piloted curfew orders for adult offenders. They have been shown to keep criminals indoors – curbing their freedom as a punishment – and keeping them out of trouble in the meantime.

We will extend electronically-monitored curfew orders nationwide for those aged 16 and over.

Persistent offenders account for a high proportion of all crime. Prison works – not only as a deterrent, but in keeping criminals off the street. Those sent to prison are less likely to re-offend on release than those given a community punishment. We will provide another 8,500 prison places by the year 2000.

We will introduce minimum sentences for violent and persistent criminals to help protect the public more effectively, reversing Labour's wrecking amendments to our tough Crime Bill.

Anyone convicted of a second serious sexual or violent crime, like rape or armed robbery, will get an automatic life sentence.

Persistent house burglars and dealers in hard drugs will receive mandatory minimum prison sentences of three and seven years respectively.

We will restore honesty in sentencing by ensuring that criminals serve the sentence intended without automatic early release.

### Support for victims

Concern for the victim must be at the heart of our entire approach to the criminal justice system. We will continue to give strong backing to Victim Support.

We will give courts in all cases the discretion to allow witnesses to give evidence anonymously if they believe them to be at risk from reprisal.

We will also take action to allow a judge to stop a defendant from personally questioning the victim in rape cases and other cases where the victim is particularly vulnerable.

Conservatives are on the side of the victims not the criminal.

### Strengthening the fight against city crime

Crime that takes place through manipulation of financial accounts and markets is as serious as crime on the street.

The City's unchallenged position as Europe's most dynamic and successful financial centre owes a great deal to its reputation for honesty and fair dealing. We will help ensure that this reputation is maintained.

We will bring forward in the next Parliament a package of measures designed to modernise the current systems for dealing with City fraud.

This will include legislation to allow the Inland Revenue to pass confidential information to the police, the Serious Fraud Office and the financial regulators to assist in the investigation of cases involving serious financial fraud. We will also remove the remaining legal obstacles to the controlled exchange of confidential information between the police and the regulators in this kind of case.

## Faster justice
Justice delayed is justice denied. It is wrong that people who are innocent should face an excessive wait before the start of their trial. The guilty need to be held to account for their actions promptly. And victims should be given the chance to draw a line under their experience as quickly as possible. We are determined to speed up justice without diminishing the genuine rights of every citizen to a fair trial.

Last October the Government set up a review of delays in the criminal justice system. It made a series of detailed recommendations. We see merit in those recommendations and will seek the views of interested parties. We believe that taken together they could dramatically speed up the prosecution process, bringing the guilty to justice and acquitting the innocent more quickly.

All defendants would appear in court the next working day after they were charged. At least half of them would be convicted the next day compared with just 3 per cent at the moment. And the time taken to bring juveniles to court would be cut from ten weeks to a matter of days.

## Civil justice
The civil justice system of this country is a vital part of its competitive economy and has a high international reputation. The commercial courts attract substantial litigation from all over the world, generating significant foreign earnings. We will seek to maintain the high standing of these courts.

We have greatly improved the service the civil courts provide for the aggrieved citizen. The simple procedure for small claims has been extended to claims up to £3,000. For large claims the county court now provides an efficient local service with specialised courts in many locations around the country, leaving the High Court to deal with the more complex and difficult issues. We will push ahead with the major reforms now under way which will greatly speed up the process and improve the delivery of justice without imposing additional burdens on the taxpayer.

## The legal profession
We will ensure that the framework in which the legal profession operates is responsive to the changing needs of our people and is one in which unjustified restrictions have no place. We have, for example, given most solicitors rights of audience in the higher courts under appropriate conditions.

## Legal aid
People are rightly concerned about the rising costs of legal aid. We have taken many steps to control the burden and to deny access to legal aid to the "apparently wealthy" – those who qualified technically, but whose lifestyles suggested they should not.

But more is required:

We will change the structure of legal aid to ensure that it, like other vital public services, functions within defined cash limits. This will enable us to identify priorities and serve them much more efficiently than the present system.

## Drugs
Drugs are a menace to the very fabric of our society. They ruin the life of addicts and their families. They can destroy whole neighbourhoods. The promising youth of today can too easily become the sad dropouts of tomorrow, turning to crime and violence.

The Conservative Government has a comprehensive strategy, launched in 1995, committed to fighting drugs in communities and in schools. It is tough on criminals and vigilant at our ports. It is respected throughout the world. We spend over £500 million every year in tackling all aspects of drug problems.

We will continue the fight against drugs through a co-ordinated approach: being tough on pushers; reducing demand by educating young people; tackling drug abuse at local level through Drug Action Teams; saying "No" to legalising drugs; and working with international agencies and foreign governments to resist the menace spreading.

This pernicious evil has to be fought by all of us.

## A CONFIDENT, UNITED AND SOVEREIGN NATION
### Our record
♦ Many of our old cities have been rejuvenated through a partnership of public and private investment.

## CONSERVATIVE MANIFESTO

♦ The area of green belt has doubled since 1979.
♦ Water and air quality in the UK have improved significantly.
♦ We are one of only a few nations on course to meet our commitment to return emissions of all greenhouse gases to 1990 levels by 2000.
♦ The Lottery has been established as the most successful in the world – raising £3 billion for good causes in a little over two years.
♦ More support is now given to arts and heritage than at any time in our nation's history. We now provide nearly 20 per cent more for the arts than the last Labour Government, over and above inflation.
♦ British talent was this year nominated for 30 Oscars. British music is again receiving international acclaim. The industry is worth £2.5 billion, more than shipbuilding or electric components: one in five CDs and records sold anywhere has a British connection.
♦ There is record investment in our sports facilities. Already the Lottery has provided £480 million for sport, including the planned British Academy of Sport, English National Stadium and for the first time direct funding for British athletes.
♦ We have continued to stand up for British interests in Europe, protecting our opt-out of the social chapter, maintaining our border controls, and preserving our budget rebate – worth £18 billion since it was introduced.
♦ We have the most professional armed forces in the world. We have modernised our nuclear deterrent by replacing Polaris with Trident.

### The best place in the world to live
Britain is admired the world over. Every year, millions of tourists travel here to enjoy our heritage and culture, our cities and countryside, our way of life. Our nation's history is an anchor in a sea of change. We need to protect, cherish and build upon what is great about our country, so our children grow up in a better Britain. We also must make sure that everyone, wherever they live, has the support of a strong, tolerant and civilised community.

Our aim is for this generation and future generations to take pride in Britain as the best place in the world to live.

### Britain's cities
London is one of the world's greatest cities. It is livelier than ever. Our vision of its future is set out in a separate manifesto.

Many of our cities have undergone a complete transformation over the last decade. We have promoted partnerships – through schemes such as the Urban Development Corporation, the Single Regeneration Budget and City Pride to attract private enterprise and investment back to inner-cities. These initiatives are bringing hope, opportunity, and prosperity to what were once wastelands of urban decline.

As the country thrives and becomes more prosperous, one of our central tasks is to apply the same approach to transform the legacy of soulless, decaying public housing estates. They are places that suffer from the very worst kind of poverty – poverty of aspiration.

We have already made a start – spending over £2 billion over the last ten years on improving 500 of the worst estates. And we have shown how it is possible to tackle the economic and social problems alongside new investment in buildings – where possible, bringing in a greater mix of public tenants and private housing to recreate a more balanced community. Now we will extend this approach, focusing the Single Regeneration Budget to launch a combined attack on crime, unemployment and under-achievement, and developing the government's partnership with the private sector to help fund the massive investment that will be required.

Over the next decade, we aim to raise some £25 billion of new private investment in housing estates by encouraging tenants in more than half of the remaining public sector housing stock to opt for transferring their homes to new landlords. These transfers will only occur where tenants choose this route to improve their estates.

We will use this approach to regenerate the worst housing estates and transform the lives of those who live on them – targeting support for programmes to improve education standards, employment and crime prevention alongside new private sector investment.

As well as this attack on poor housing, we will continue to help the homeless. We will carry through our planned extension of the Rough Sleeper Initiative from London to other big cities. We will provide sufficient hostel places to ensure that no one needs sleep out on the streets.

### Rural communities
Britain is blessed with some of the most beautiful countryside in Europe. We need to protect

the best of countryside whilst ensuring good jobs, and living conditions for people who live there.

We have to strike a balance: our rural communities must not become rural museums, but remain vibrant places to live and work. We will make sure government departments work together to ensure that balance is kept.

We will continue to protect the green belt from development making sure that derelict and under-used urban land is developed in preference to greenfield sites.

We will use the planning system to ensure that more new homes are built on reclaimed sites in our towns and cities. We will aim for more than 60 per cent of all new homes to be built on derelict sites. This will reduce the pressure to build in our countryside and expand choice where it is needed most.

We will support our rural communities, by giving special rate support to small village shops and post offices. The planning system can do more to help too.

We will introduce a new Rural Business Use Class to encourage job creation in the countryside.

We will increase support for schemes which promote care for the countryside – like Countryside Stewardship. We believe participation in traditional country pursuits, including fishing, is a matter for individuals. A Conservative Government will not introduce legislation that interferes with the rights of people to take part in these activities.

We will also encourage managed public access to private land – in agreement with farmers and landowners – but strongly resist a general right to roam, which would damage the countryside and violate the right to private property.

We aim to double Britain's forest cover over the next 50 years. We will continue to encourage tree planting by targeting grants, encouraging investment in wood processing, and using new freedoms with the reform of the Common Agricultural Policy.

### Agriculture and fisheries

We will continue to provide robust support to the British beef industry through the BSE crisis until its long-term strength is restored. We will vigorously pursue the eradication of BSE in the United Kingdom, as we have been doing successfully for the last eight years. We will spare no efforts in our fight against the unwarranted ban on British beef exports.

Public health and food safety have been the Government's top priorities throughout the BSE crisis. We will tighten up control over food safety by appointing a powerful and independent Chief Food Safety Adviser and Food Safety Council to advise government.

We will continue to push for fundamental reform of the Common Agricultural Policy, moving away from production support to measures that will give our farmers the opportunity to compete while safeguarding the rural environment. We will ensure that no change to the Common Agriculture Policy unfairly disadvantages British farmers.

Fishing is a vital industry in many parts of coastal Britain. We will continue our fight to secure a prosperous long-term future for the industry and sustainable management of our fish stocks.

We will insist at the IGC and elsewhere on measures to stop quota hopping and prevent the vessels of other countries from using UK fishing quotas.

The integrity of our six and 12-mile fishing limits is not negotiable. We reject any idea of a single European fishing fleet.

We believe that fishermen should have more say in decisions affecting their industry. We will press the European Commission to establish regional committees to give fishermen a direct influence in fishing policy. We will use these committees to develop new ways of managing quota and regulating fisheries which are more sensitive to the industry's needs.

### Animal welfare

A civilised society respects its animals. Britain will continue to take the lead in improving standards of animal welfare in Europe. In 1995 we secured a major breakthrough in the treatment of animals in transport; in 1996 we won victory in our campaign to ban veal crates throughout the EU. We are determined that standards should continue to rise and that all EU countries should have to meet them.

We will seek to ensure that all European countries have to raise animal welfare standards.

We are not going to take any risks with rabies. There may, however, be ways other than quarantine which maintain or increase protection for public health, while improving the welfare of pets and reducing the costs to travellers.

We will publish a Green Paper on rabies protection, setting out all the options including the existing controls, early in the new parliament.

## CONSERVATIVE MANIFESTO

### Britain's environment

Britain has an enviable track record in protecting our environment. Our rivers, beaches and water are cleaner and we are using our energy more efficiently. We are leading the world in reducing the level of the "greenhouse gases" that cause global warming and pressing for policies that will enable the world to sustain development without long-term damage to the environment. Our Green Manifesto is published separately.

We have clear objectives to build on this record. We will set tough, but affordable targets, with published environmental strategies to improve air quality and banish city smog — with tighter standards on vehicle emissions and pollution crackdowns around the country. We aim for sustained improvements in water quality, at a pace which industry and consumers can afford. We will develop labelling of products that gives consumers information to show the environmental impact of how they were made.

In addition, we will continue to use the tax system and other incentives to encourage the use of vehicles and fuel which do not pollute the environment. And, we will continue to explore policies based on the principle of polluter pays: those who contaminate land, pollute the environment or produce harmful waste should be made responsible for their actions and pay for the consequences.

### Britain — a tolerant country

Tolerance, civility and respect have always been hallmarks of our nation. It is thanks to them that we have an excellent record on race relations.

Everybody, regardless of colour or creed, has the right to go about his or her life free from the threat of intimidation. We are taking tough action to tackle harassment. Under proposals in the Protection from Harassment Act 1997, it will be a crime to behave in a way which causes someone else to be harassed. The maximum penalty will be six months in prison.

Firm, but fair, immigration controls underpin good race relations. We will ensure that, while genuine asylum seekers are treated sympathetically, people do not abuse these provisions to avoid normal immigration controls.

### A world leader of sports, arts and culture

Britain is enjoying a cultural renaissance. British music, films, television, fashion, art and food are winning plaudits the world over. They add excitement, fun and enjoyment to our lives. Our success brings pride to everyone.

The National Lottery, which John Major set up, will pump billions of pounds into Britain's good causes. Its proceeds will weave a new, rich thread of opportunity and charity into the tapestry of British life. In addition to benefiting major national institutions, about half of the awards are for amounts under £25,000 — benefiting local communities up and down the country. We will encourage new ways of distributing awards to support the performing arts — through support for amateur productions and community events, providing more musical instruments, and helping productions tour round the country.

The National Lottery will also help us train and promote British sporting talent. The English National Stadium and British Academy of Sport, funded by the Lottery, will be new focal points for sporting events and excellence. We will encourage more young people to play sport, by ensuring every school plays a minimum level of sport, including competitive sports, and developing a network of Sporting Ambassadors — sporting celebrities who will visit schools to inspire young people. We also encourage the Sports Council to use Lottery money to employ over 1,000 additional community sports coaches to assist in Primary Schools.

The development of young talent is important in all fields.

We will encourage the use of Lottery money to train young athletes and artists, with revenue funding for bursaries, concessionary tickets to professional performances and support for young people's organisations and productions.

The Lottery will also fund our Millennium celebrations. They will be inspirational as well as enjoyable. We want these be a showcase of British excellence. Britain will be able to look back on past achievements with pride, and look forward with confidence.

### Europe and the world

Britain is a world leader as well as a European nation. Our economic strength, our history and our language make us a global trading nation with links right around the world. Only the United Kingdom is a member of the European Union, the United Nations Security Council, the Commonwealth, Nato and the Group of Seven leading industrial nations. In the Gulf, Bosnia, Cyprus and Northern Iraq, John Major has shown how our nation can contribute to world peace.

We will continue to work with international partners to secure peace and stability in areas of tension such as former Yugoslavia; in Kashmir; in Cyprus; and in the Middle East. We will promote reform of the United Nations to make it a more effective organisation for securing international stability. Britain will continue to deploy our outstanding Armed Forces as peacekeepers under the United Nations. And we will support the aspirations of the Poles, Czechs, Hungarians and others to join the European Union and Nato.

After the transfer of Hong Kong, we will work under the terms of the Joint Declaration to help sustain the prosperity and way of life of the people of Hong Kong and build on the substantial British interests that will remain.

We will continue to support the Commonwealth, our unique global network, to encourage the spread of democracy, as set out in the Harare Declaration. We will focus our aid programme to encourage sustainable development in countries that are growing towards self-sufficiency under democratic government. We have taken the lead in alleviating the burden of debt for the world's poorest countries. We also have significant flows of private investment to developing economies. We are more than achieving the long term UN target of 1 per cent of GDP for the transfer of wealth to less developed countries. We will continue to maintain a significant bilateral and multilateral aid programme reflecting the aspiration of meeting the UN's target of 0.7 per cent of GDP for aid as a long-term objective.

We will also continue to provide leadership in Europe and internationally on environmental issues, building on the Rio Conference to encourage sustainable development – meeting our commitment to reduce carbon dioxide emissions by 10 per cent on 1990 levels by 2010 to prevent climate change. The Prime Minister has committed himself to attending the next UN Environmental Conference in June.

## Britain and the European Union

We believe that in an uncertain, competitive world, the nation state is a rock of security. A nation's common heritage, culture, values and outlook are a precious source of stability. Nationhood gives people a sense of belonging.

The Government has a positive vision for the European Union as a partnership of nations. We want to be in Europe but not run by Europe. We have much to gain from our membership of the European Union – in trade, in co-operation between governments, and in preserving European peace. We benefit from the huge trade opportunities that have opened up since Britain led the way in developing Europe's single market. We want to see the rest of Europe follow the same deregulated, enterprise policies that have transformed our economic prospects in Britain.

However, in June, the nations of the European Union will gather in Amsterdam to negotiate possible amendments to the Treaty of Rome. It is a moment of truth, setting the direction in which the European Union will go. It will also be crucial in ensuring that we have a relationship with the rest of Europe with which we can be comfortable.

A Conservative Government will seek a partnership of nation states. Some others would like to build a federal Europe. A British Conservative Government will not allow Britain to be part of a federal European state.

The diversity of Europe's nations is its strength. As more nations join the European Union, it needs to become flexible not more rigid. We must also ensure that any developments which only include some members do not work to the disadvantage of others.

Our priorities for Europe's development will be enlargement of the Community, completion of the single market, reform of the European Court of Justice, and further strengthening of the role of national parliaments. We will seek more co-operation between national governments on areas of common interest – defence, foreign policy and the fight against international crime and drugs. We also believe the European Union itself should do less, but do it better. So we have proposed incorporating the principle of subsidiarity – that the European Union should only do that which cannot be done by member states acting alone – into the Treaty. This is how we are approaching the inter-governmental conference.

We will argue for a flexible Europe which fully accommodates the interests and aspirations of all its member states and where any new proposals have to be open to all and agreed by all. We will not accept other changes to the Treaty that would further centralise decision-making, reduce national sovereignty, or remove our right to permanent opt-outs.

We will retain Britain's veto and oppose further extension of qualified majority voting in order to ensure we can prevent policies that would be harmful to the national interest. We will defend the rights of national parliaments and oppose more powers being given to the European Parliament at the expense of national parliaments.

We will take whatever steps are necessary to keep our frontier controls. We will resist attempts to change the inter-governmental nature of cooperation in justice and home affairs. We will not accept the development of new legal rights that extend the concept of European citizenship.

Britain's rebate has so far saved British taxpayers £18 billion and we will protect it.

One of the greatest challenges Europe faces is to cut unemployment and make its businesses competitive. Here Britain is leading the way. We will continue to argue for deregulation and lower costs on Europe's businesses, the policies that have helped give Britain one of the strongest economies in Europe. We will not put that achievement at risk by signing up to the social chapter, which would open the door to imposing the high costs of the European social model on British business. Once Britain accepted the social chapter we could not stop many of these damaging policies being imposed on us by qualified majority voting.

We will insist that any new Treaty recognises that our opt-out from the social chapter enables Britain to be exempt from the Working Time Directive, and prevents any abuse of our opt-out. And we will not accept a new employment chapter in any revised Treaty, which would expose British businesses to new costs.

We made it clear in the previous chapter that we will continue to work for further reform of the Common Agricultural Policy, and the lifting of the worldwide ban on British beef, and insist on measures to stop quota-hopping by foreign fishing vessels.

Protecting Britain's interests demands tough, experienced negotiation. John Major has proved he has these qualities – including the resolve to say no when necessary even if that means being isolated. Labour have said they would never want Britain to be isolated in Europe: they would damage Britain's success by undermining our veto, signing up to the social chapter and following in others' footsteps – even where they lead in the wrong direction. They support policies that would fragment the United Kingdom's influence within a Europe of regions. The Liberal Democrats welcome the end of the nation state. Only the Conservatives can be trusted to stand up for Britain in Europe: our national interest must be protected.

## A single currency: our referendum guarantee
The creation of a European single currency would be of enormous significance for all European states whether they are members or not. We must take account of all the consequences for Britain of such a major development of policy.

John Major secured for us at Maastricht an opt-out from the commitment to enter a single currency. It is only because of this opt-out that we have the right to negotiate and then decide whether it is in Britain's interest to join.

It is in our national interest to take part in the negotiations. Not to do so would be an abdication of responsibility. A single currency would affect us whether we were in or out. We need to participate in discussions in order to ensure the rules are not fixed against our interests. The national interest is not served by exercising our option – one way or the other – before we have to.

For a single currency to come into effect, European economies will have to meet crucial criteria. On the information currently available, we believe that it is very unlikely that there will be sufficient convergence of economic conditions across Europe for a single currency to proceed safely on the target date of January 1 1999. We will not include legislation on the single currency in the first Queen's Speech. If it cannot proceed safely, we believe it would be better for Europe to delay any introduction of a single currency rather than rush ahead to meet an artificial timetable. We will argue this case in the negotiations that lie ahead.

We believe it is in our national interest to keep our options open to take a decision on a single currency when all the facts are before us. If a single currency is created, without sustainable convergence, a British Conservative government will not be part of it.

If, during the course of the next Parliament, a Conservative government were to conclude that it was in our national interest to join a single currency, we have given a guarantee that no such decision would be implemented unless the British people gave their express approval in a referendum.

## Defence in an unstable world
The old rivalries of the Cold War have been replaced by new tensions. Britain must be able to react rapidly to protect our security and interests around the globe.

Our Armed Forces are the most professional in the world. We have cut unnecessary bureaucracy and increased efficiency, and directed money to support our services in the frontline. We have made the changes necessary to adapt our services to the threats which we might now face. We have set out defence plans based on stable levels of funding. There is no need for a defence review, which would raise fear and uncertainty about the future.

We will continue to ensure the Services have the modern weapons they need to guarantee their superiority against potential aggressors. We will make sure we can conduct military operations throughout the world, and develop our capability to deploy the three Services together and rapidly, including the ability to transport heavy equipment into an operational zone. We will take part in ballistic missile research so we can decide whether we should procure any such system for the United Kingdom.

We will continue to target our efforts on recruiting for the Armed Forces. We will set up an Army Foundation College, which will provide 1,300 places for 16 and 17-year-olds who want to join the Army.

We will also enable the reserve forces to play a more active role in operations. We appreciate the enormous value of cadet forces, and our current plans including resources to encourage their further development.

We will continue to support Britain's defence industry, and we will work with companies to identify the technologies of the future.

Nato will remain the cornerstone of our security. We will resist attempts to bring the Western European Union under the control of the European Union, and ensure that defence policy remains a matter for sovereign nations.

## The constitution

Alone in Europe, the history of the United Kingdom has been one of stability and security. We owe much of that to the strength and stability of our constitution – the institutions, laws and traditions that bind us together as a nation.

Our constitution has been stable, but not static. It has been woven over the centuries – the product of hundreds of years of knowledge, experience and history.

Radical changes that alter the whole character of our constitutional balance could unravel what generations of our predecessors have created. To preserve that stability in future – and the freedoms and rights of our citizens – we need to continue a process of evolution, not revolution.

Conservatives embrace evolutionary change that solves real problems and improves the way our constitution works. In recent years we have opened up government, devolved power and accountability, and introduced reforms to make Parliament work more effectively. It is that evolutionary process that we are committed to continue.

## Open, accountable government

In recent years we have taken significant steps to open up government to public scrutiny, and give individuals more information to hold government and public services to account.

We have introduced a code on access to government information, policed by the Ombudsman. We have published information on the workings of government previously held secret – including the composition of Cabinet Committees, and the structure of the security and intelligence services.

We have introduced a new Civil Service Code, and reformed the process for public appointments. We are pledged to legislate on the commitments in our 1993 White Paper on Open Government, including a statutory right of access by citizens to personal records held about them by the Government and other public authorities. And we have set up the Nolan Committee and have implemented its proposals to ensure that the highest standards are maintained in public life.

But our reforms go even wider than that. We have transferred power from central bureaucracies to local organisations such as school governors and hospital trusts. We have introduced the Citizen's Charter.

We have also required them to publish information on their performance – information which enables the local community to keep a check on standards and apply pressure where needed. Wherever possible, we are widening competition and choice in public services. We showed above how we wished to push this agenda forward.

Regional government would be a dangerously centralising measure – taking power away from elected local authorities. We wish to go in the opposite direction, shifting power to the local neighbourhood – for example by giving more power to parish councils.

## Parliament

Parliament – alongside the Crown and our legal system – is one of the three key institutions that uphold our constitution. The supremacy of Parliament is fundamental to our democracy, and the guarantee of our freedoms. The last 17 years have seen many changes to strengthen Parliament and make it more effective – the flourishing of select committees, new procedures to scrutinise European legislation, reform of Parliament's working day, and a budget that brings together tax and spending.

We have therefore already done much to improve the way Parliament works and will do more. We have accepted the proposal from the Public Service Select Committee and put before the House of Commons a clear new statement of the principles underlying ministerial accountability to Parliament.

All these developments have made Parliament open to the citizen, and the government more accountable. In the next session of Parliament we will continue this careful reform.

To give Parliament more time to consider legislation thoroughly we will extend the Queen's Speech to cover not only legislation for the immediate year but also provisional plans for legislation in the year after that.

This will mean that more draft bills will be subject to public scrutiny before they reach the floor of the House of Commons. It will give Select Committees more time to take evidence and report. And this should also mean better legislation.

We do not believe there is a case for more radical reform that would undermine the House of Commons. A new Bill of Rights, for example, would risk transferring power away from parliament to legal courts – undermining the democratic supremacy of Parliament as representatives of the people. Whilst this may be a necessary check in other countries which depend upon more formalised written constitutions, we do not believe it is appropriate to the UK.

Nor do we favour changes in the system of voting in parliamentary elections that would break the link between an individual member of parliament and his constituents. A system of proportional representation would be more likely to produce unstable, coalition governments that are unable to provide effective leadership – with crucial decisions being dependent on compromise deals hammered out behind closed doors. This is not the British way.

We have demonstrated we are not against change where it is practical and beneficial. But fundamental changes which have not been fully thought through – such as opposition proposals on the House of Lords – would be extremely damaging. We will oppose change for change's sake.

## The Union

The Union between Scotland, Wales, Northern Ireland and England underpins our nation's stability. The Conservative commitment to the United Kingdom does not mean ignoring the distinctive individuality of the different nations. On the contrary, we have gone further in recognising that diversity than any previous government. We are publishing separate manifestos for Wales and Scotland.

While preserving the role of parliament at the centre of the Union, we have given new powers to the Scottish Grand Committee and Welsh Grand Committee – enabling Scottish and Welsh MPs to call Ministers to account and debate legislation which affects those countries – something that would be impossible with separate Assemblies. For the first time, Welsh Members of Parliament can ask their questions to Ministers in Welsh in Wales. Most recently we have similarly extended the basic powers of the Northern Ireland Grand Committee.

We believe this is the right way to go. By contrast, the development of new assemblies in Scotland and Wales would create strains which could well pull apart the Union. That would create a new layer of government, which would be hungry for power. It would risk rivalry and conflict between these parliaments or assemblies and the parliament at Westminster. And it would raise serious questions about whether the representation of Scottish and Welsh MPs at Westminster – and their role in matters affecting English affairs – could remain unchanged.

Nor do we believe it would be in the interests of the Scottish or Welsh people. A Scottish tax-raising parliament, for example, could well affect the choice of where new investment locates in the United Kingdom.

In a world where people want security, nothing would be more dangerous than to unravel a constitution that binds our nation together and the institutions that bring us stability. We will continue to fight for the strength and diversity that benefits all of us as a proud union of nations.

## Northern Ireland

While we cherish the Union and Northern Ireland's place within it, we recognise that there exist within the province special circumstances which require further action to be taken.

After a quarter of a century we wish to see the unique and originally temporary system of direct rule ended and a successful restoration of local accountable democracy achieved. We want to see this brought about in a form which carries the broadest agreement possible. And we want to see the rights, traditions and interests of all parts of the community recognised within any such agreement.

We will accordingly continue to pursue a policy of dialogue and negotiation with and between the democratic Northern Ireland parties. We will continue to underpin such negotiations with the guarantee that the constitutional position of Northern Ireland cannot and will not be changed without the broad consent of the people of Northern Ireland. At the same time we will continue to take whatever security measures are required to protect the people of Northern Ireland from those who seek to achieve their political goals by violent means.

We seek peace. But we will never be swayed by terrorist violence nor will we ever compromise our principles with those who seek to overthrow the rule of law by force.

## A CHOICE OF TWO FUTURES
At this election the British people face a stark choice. A choice of two futures.

They can elect to continue down the road of success and achievement. An opportunity that has been hard-won by the efforts and sacrifices of the British people. An opportunity that has only come about because successive Conservative governments have been determined to face up to the long-term problems facing Britain, and take the tough steps needed to arrest our slow decline.

Or they can elect to take a huge risk with that future – the future of themselves, their children, their nation – by handing over the government of the country to politicians who have fought, opposed and denigrated every step that has been taken to restore Britain's economic health and standing in the world. Politicians whose own declared policies would burden the United Kingdom with new spending and taxation, new regulations, and new threats to the stability and sovereignty of the nation itself.

You can only be sure with the Conservatives.

## 25 PLEDGES FOR THE NATION
### The Enterprise Centre of Europe
**TAX AND SPENDING:** Keep tight control of public spending priorities, aiming for our target of a 20p basic rate of income tax over the next parliament.
**PRICES AND MORTGAGES:** Stick to the policies which have delivered the lowest inflation levels and mortgage rates for a generation, meeting our inflation target of 2.5 per cent or less.
**JOBS:** Protect jobs by keeping Britain out of the European social chapter; build on our record of falling unemployment; and help get the long-term unemployed back to work – including by requiring those on benefit for some time to undertake work experience on a community project.
**ENTERPRISE:** Support growth and investment by keeping Britain the lowest tax major economy in Europe, pursuing Britain's global trade opportunities and curbing unnecessary regulations.
**SMALL BUSINESS:** Reform business rates to help small businesses.
**THE FUTURE:** Keep Britain ahead in the technology of the future, encouraging new entertainment and information services, and using the Millennium Lottery Fund to give people access to new computers and information links in schools, libraries, and other public places.

### Opportunity and Ownership for individuals and families
**HELP FOR FAMILIES:** Give priority to reducing tax bills for families looking after dependent children or relatives by allowing one partner's unused personal allowance to be transferred to a working spouse where they have these responsibilities.
**HELP FOR CARERS:** Help family members with heavy responsibilities caring for a relative to take a much needed break through a new Respite Care Programme.
**OWNERSHIP:** Encourage schemes that help employees build a shareholding in the company they work for, alongside tax benefits for other savings schemes.
**PENSIONS:** Transform pensions by providing all young people entering the workforce with a personal pension fund paid for by a rebate on their National Insurance contributions, while maintaining a state pension guarantee.
**CARE IN OLD AGE:** Make it easier for people to afford the cost of care in old age without giving up their house and savings.

**SCHOOL STANDARDS:** Guarantee school standards by intervening directly to raise standards where schools or local education authorities are letting children down.

**SCHOOL CHOICE:** Widen choice and diversity in schools, with more freedom for schools to develop their own character, more specialist schools, and a grammar school in every town where parents want that choice. We will also maintain our nursery voucher scheme offering a choice of places for parents of all four-year-olds.

## World-class health and public services

**NHS FUNDING PLEDGE:** Continue, year by year, to increase the real resources committed to the NHS, so NHS spending will continue to share in a growing economy.

**FAMILY DOCTORS:** Enable all family doctors to provide a wider range of services in their surgeries and in practice-based cottage hospitals – offering faster and more local treatment.

**CITIZEN'S CHARTER:** Continue to improve the standards and value for money of Britain's public services, giving those who use them more information and, where possible, wider choice.

**ESSENTIAL SERVICES:** Introduce measures to protect the public against strikes that cause excessive disruption to essential services.

## A Safe and Civil Society

**PUBLIC SAFETY:** Support local police schemes to crack down on petty crime, and continue our funding for the installation of TV security cameras in town centres and public places that want them throughout the next parliament.

**JUVENILE CRIME:** Give the courts power to impose speedy sanctions on youngsters, including an element of reparation to the victim; and continue our war against drugs.

**PERSISTENT CRIMINALS:** Ensure persistent house burglars and dealers in hard drugs receive mandatory minimum prison sentences.

## A Confident, United and Sovereign Nation

**QUALITY OF LIFE:** Continue the renaissance of our towns and cities, in particular harnessing private capital to regenerate the worst public housing estates; continue to protect our countryside and heritage; and use the National Lottery to help promote British sports, arts and culture.

**THE ENVIRONMENT:** Maintain our international leadership role in protecting the environment, and continue improving air and water quality at home alongside effective conservation of our wildlife.

**THE NATION:** Maintain the unity of the United Kingdom and preserve the stability of the nation through an evolutionary – rather than revolutionary – approach to constitutional change.

**EUROPE:** Seek a partnership of nation states in Europe, and not allow Britain to be part of a federal European state.

**THE POUND:** Guarantee that Britain will not join a single currency in the next parliament unless the British people give their express approval in a referendum.

# LIBERAL DEMOCRAT MANIFESTO

**T**HIS WILL be the last election of this century. And one of its most important. We have ducked the challenges that confront our country for too long. It is time to face them. The choice you make will shape Britain's future for the next 50 years. There are no quick fixes, no instant solutions.

Eighteen years of Conservative government have left our society divided, our public services run down, our sense of community fractured and our economy under-performing. There is much to be done to prepare Britain for the next century and no time to waste in getting started.

Yet a terrible fatalism seems to grip politicians. Though the challenges are immense, the solutions we are offered are all too often puny. We are told we can't ask people to pay more for a better education. Or change the way we live to protect our environment. Or share more to give better opportunities to those who have less. Or modernise our politics to give people more say.

The Liberal Democrats reject this timidity. We are in politics not just to manage things better, but to make things happen. To build a more prosperous, fair and open society. We believe in the market economy as the best way to deliver prosperity and distribute economic benefits. But we recognise that market mechanisms on their own are not enough; that the private sector alone cannot ensure that there are good services for everyone, or promote employment opportunities, or tackle economic inequality, or protect the environment for future generations.

We believe in a society in which every citizen shares rights and responsibilities. But, we recognise that a strong country is built from the bottom, not the top; that conformity quickly becomes the enemy of diversity. And that the imposition of social blueprints leads to authoritarian centralised government. Liberal Democrats believe that power and opportunity, like wealth, should be widely spread.

Above all, Liberal Democracy is about liberty. That does not just mean freedom from oppressive government. It means providing all citizens with the opportunity to build worthwhile lives for themselves and their families and helping them to recognise their responsibilities to the wider community.

Liberal Democrats believe the role of democratic government is to protect and strengthen liberty, to redress the balance between the powerful and the weak, between rich and poor and between immediate gains and long-term environmental costs. That is the Liberal Democrat vision: of active government which invests in people, promotes their long-term prosperity and welfare, safeguards their security, and is answerable to them for its actions. Much of what we propose here requires no money — only political will. But where extra investment is required we say where it will come from.

This is a menu with prices. The purpose of this manifesto is to widen opportunities for all. And its aim is to build a nation of self-reliant individuals, living in strong communities, backed by an enabling government.

Rt Hon Paddy Ashdown.

## EDUCATION
**Our aim:** To make Britain the world's foremost learning society by 2010.
**The problem:** This country's education has been underfunded and undermined by repeated shifts in policy. Standards are too low, especially in core skills such as reading and maths. Britain is too low in the world league tables.
**Our commitment:** Liberal Democrats will make education the next government's top priority. We will invest an additional £2 billion per year in education, funded by an extra 1p in the pound on the basic rate of income tax.

### Our first priority is to:
♦ Give children the best start by providing high-quality early-years education for every three and four-year-old child whose parents want it.

### Key priorities are to:
♦ Increase funding for books and equipment in schools. In the first year, we will double spending on books and equipment to overcome the effect of recent cuts.
♦ Reduce primary school class sizes so that within five years no child between five and 11 will need to be in a class of more than 30.
♦ Tackle the backlog of repair and maintenance to buildings with £500 million additional investment over five years.

♦ Boost chances for all adults to improve their skills and get better qualifications.

## Making the best start
Early years education is the essential building block for higher standards and achievement later on. Every £1 spent on high-quality under-fives education raises standards in later life and adds up to £7 of value to the nation's economy.

### We will:
♦ Give children the best start by providing high-quality early years education for every three and four-year-old child whose parents want it. This will be the first call on our £2 billion annual programme of extra investment in education.
♦ Promote high standards in early years education. We will set minimum standards for care, curriculum and premises. We will ensure that those in early years education are supervised by qualified staff.
♦ Provide choice in early years education. We will scrap the bureaucratic voucher scheme. We will ensure a variety of provision from a wide range of public, private and voluntary providers.
♦ Raising standards in schools. We will raise standards in schools, especially in literacy and numeracy, which are still far too low.

### We will:
♦ Improve teaching standards. We will set up a General Teaching Council, charged with improving teaching standards and making teaching a profession to be proud of again. We will provide more opportunities for professional development and reward excellence in teaching. We will help poor teachers improve, but if they cannot, we will ensure they do not continue to teach.
♦ Encourage schools to succeed. We will strengthen the inspection system so that it helps schools and we will extend inspection to monitoring Local Education Authorities (LEAs).
♦ Strengthen discipline in schools. We will support teachers in maintaining discipline and provide them with the means to do so — for example, by providing better access to special referral units. We will require every school to develop a policy to tackle bullying and truancy. We will launch a national Truancy Watch scheme. We will oblige LEAs to fulfil their responsibilities to educate pupils excluded or suspended from school.
♦ Measure achievement in pupils and schools. We will give every pupil a Personal Record of Achievement which will enable them to build up a set of nationally-accredited qualifications and record their other achievements. We will require schools to publish meaningful information on their standards, achievements and plans for the future.
♦ Improve the national curriculum. We will replace the national curriculum with a more focused and flexible Minimum Curriculum Entitlement. We will ensure that religious education provides pupils with an understanding of the major traditions of belief in this country.
♦ Boost literacy. We will establish special literacy programmes involving parents with teachers in a drive to ensure that 90 per cent of all pupils reach their expected reading age by 2005.

## Investing in schools
Extra investment for well-equipped classrooms and better-maintained buildings is essential if standards are to improve.

### We will:
♦ Increase funding for books and equipment in schools. In the first year, we will double spending on books and equipment to overcome the effect of recent cuts. A typical primary school of 250 pupils will get an extra £16,000. A typical secondary school of 1,000 pupils will get an extra £110,000.
♦ Reduce primary school class sizes so that within five years no child between five and 11 will need to be in a class of more than 30.
♦ Tackle the backlog of repairs. We will invest an additional £500 million over five years in repairing crumbling and unsafe buildings.
♦ Support children with special needs. We will fully fund the implementation of the Code of Practice for Special Educational Needs.

## A new partnership for schools
Involving parents in the education of their children and ensuring schools are supported by

local communities are both essential to achieving higher standards and a better use of resources.

**We will:**

♦ Increase the role of parents in education. We will extend home/school/pupil links, develop home-school partnership arrangements and support parents with information and resources to help them help their child. We will require the schools inspection service to report on home-school partnerships as part of school inspections. We will promote school councils and guarantee automatic representation on governing bodies to staff and, where appropriate, students.

♦ Open up schools to the whole community. We will encourage schools to develop courses for parents, build links with local leisure organisations to open up school sports facilities to the community and work with local businesses to provide improved computer education.

♦ Give all schools more independence and allow them to develop their own styles and strengths. We will devolve as many powers as possible to schools and give them more control over their budgets. We will make new "light touch" LEAs responsible for those functions that cannot be undertaken by individual schools on their own, such as coordination, planning and monitoring standards. We will bring grant-maintained schools and City Technology Colleges into this new framework and scrap the Funding Agency for Schools. Liberal Democrats are opposed to selection, but believe that decisions on this should be made by local communities through their local Councils and not by politicians at Westminster.

♦ Recognise the valuable role of church schools in the maintained sector. We will initiate a dialogue with all the major faiths about the role they wish to play in education in the future. Where any of the major faiths wish to establish publicly-funded voluntary schools we will enable them to do so, provided that they enjoy substantial community support, offer acceptable programmes of study, provide equality of opportunity and are able to deliver the Minimum Curriculum Entitlement.

♦ Forge a new partnership with the independent sector. We will encourage independent schools to work with state schools. We will phase out the Assisted Places Scheme and use the money saved to enable LEAs, if they wish, to enter into local partnership schemes. These could include assisting the funding of pupils at independent schools. Pupils currently covered by the Assisted Places Scheme would, however, be protected until they finish their studies. We will require independent schools to offer the Minimum Curriculum Entitlement. We will extend charitable status to all schools without affecting total Council funding and maintain the VAT exemption on school fees.

### Extending lifelong learning

In the information age, education must be a lifelong activity from which people can benefit anywhere and at any time, rather than being something that only happens in school.

**We will:**

♦ Widen access to further education. We will give every person an Individual Learning Account as the basis for lifelong post-school education with contributions made by the state, individuals and employers. Our aim is that the state contribution will be at least equivalent to the cost of fees on approved courses. We will replace the Student Loans Scheme with a fair repayment scheme linked to salaries in later life. We oppose top-up fees for tuition. Our aim is to ensure that students on approved courses (including part-time courses) up to first degree level are treated equally.

♦ Promote flexible learning. We will create a higher standard credit-based system for all post-14 courses, including the current A levels and degree courses. We will work with the private sector to link all schools to the Information Super Highway and ensure that they have the equipment and skills to take advantage of this.

♦ Promote training in the workplace. To support companies that invest in education and training, and to encourage others to do so, we will introduce a 2 per cent remissible levy on company payrolls. This would be deductible against the cost of providing accredited training or making contributions to the Individual Learning Account. Small businesses will be exempt. We will give Training and Enterprise Councils the leading role in forging local partnerships to meet youth training and employment needs.

♦ Expand training opportunities for young people. Our aim is to ensure that 16-19 year-olds receive the equivalent of at least two days a week education or on-the-job training.

♦ Boost chances for all adults to improve their skills and get better qualifications. We will ensure that all adults on approved courses or training have access to financial support, either through their Individual Learning Accounts or from their employer using our new remissible training levy.

♦ Improve the quality of tertiary courses. We will create a new Quality Council to ensure high standards and value for money in all post-16 education and training courses.

♦ Secure academic freedom. We will ensure the funding of university teaching and research, safeguard academic freedom and standards.

## JOBS AND THE ECONOMY

**Our aim:** To end the cycle of boom and bust and equip Britain's economy to compete in the global marketplace.

**The problem:** Despite the current pre-election mini-boom, the fundamentals of Britain's economy remain weak. We continue to be held back by instability in economic management, an underskilled labour force and chronic under-investment. Britain continues to consume too much and invest too little.

**Our commitment:** Liberal Democrats will lock in economic stability, encourage saving and promote enterprise. We will raise the quality of Britain's workforce through additional investment in education and training. As part of our strategy to build a sustainable economy, we will shift the burden of taxation from employment to the depletion of natural resources.

### Our priorities are to:

♦ Provide stability in economic management to encourage long-term investment.

♦ Raise the quality of Britain's workforce and get people back to work.

♦ Promote enterprise and small businesses.

♦ Begin to shift taxation from jobs, wealth and goods to pollution and the depletion of natural resources.

### Investing in Britain's future

Long-term investment and economic stability are crucial to future economic success.

### We will:

♦ Secure stable prices and low interest rates. We will turn the Bank of England into a UK Reserve Bank, free from political interference. We will charge the Bank with keeping inflation low and make it accountable to Parliament for achieving this goal. Lower inflation and greater exchange rate stability can be better secured by working with Britain's European partners. The best framework for this is a single European currency and it is in Britain's interests to take part in this. However, three conditions must be met before this can happen. First, the single currency must be firmly founded on the Maastricht criteria. Second, Britain must meet those criteria. Third, the British people must have said "yes" in a referendum. If these conditions for a single currency are in place, Britain should join.

♦ Ensure responsible economic management. We will keep to the "golden rule" of public finance: over the economic cycle, total borrowing should not exceed total investment. We will make the government accountable to Parliament for keeping to this rule, and subject it to independent monitoring. We will cut wasteful spending and ensure new spending delivers value for money.

♦ Build up Britain's capital assets. We will distinguish between capital and current spending in the national accounting system. We will promote effective public/private investment partnerships at both national and local levels, with Councils' borrowing carefully controlled.

♦ Put Britain's people back to work. We will enable long-term unemployed people to turn their unemployment benefits into "working benefits" paid to an employer to recruit and train them. We will break open the poverty traps that stop unemployed people from working. Our plans for boosting investment in infrastructure, promoting small businesses and encouraging energy conservation will create hundreds of thousands of new jobs.

♦ Invest in a highly-skilled workforce. Our investment of an additional £2 billion a year in education and training will improve skills and increase the nation's knowledge base.

♦ Promote environmental sustainability. We will begin a long-term shift in taxation, reducing taxes on jobs, wealth and goods and shifting them to pollution and resource depletion. We will use new national indicators of progress which include measures of quality of life and environmental sustainability.

♦ Encourage people to save. Our aim is to extend the advantages of Tessas and Peps to a wider range of savers by developing a new save-as-you-earn scheme. We will encourage personal and portable pension plans.

## Investing in enterprise

Small business, enterprise and self-employment are the engine of a modern dynamic economy and a vital source of new jobs and growth.

**We will:**

♦ Support small and medium-sized businesses. We will encourage the banks to develop new sources of private finance, including grants, equity finance and mutual guarantee schemes. We will seek to expand the sources of "seed-corn" capital. We will legislate for a statutory right to interest on late debt payments. We will require the banks to develop new codes of banking practice for small businesses. We will cut red tape, for example by stopping European institutions interfering where they shouldn't and by preventing Whitehall departments "gold-plating" European regulations with extra rules. We will, in the long-term, abolish the Uniform Business Rate and bring in a new, fairer local rating system. We will ensure that government purchasing gives special emphasis and easier access to small and medium-sized firms.

♦ Boost regional and local economies. We will set up regionally-based Development Agencies to build new partnerships between small businesses, local Councils, Business Links, TECs and local Chambers of Commerce. We will encourage these bodies to come together to provide "one-stop shops". We will enable Councils to raise capital for local infrastructure investment, where they work in partnership with the private sector. We will encourage industrial development by promoting geographical centres of industrial excellence.

♦ Invest in research and innovation. We will expand support for science and research by shifting government funds away from military research and development and into civil science and research, and improve specialist research facilities for industry. We will encourage regional technology transfer centres to bring together the resources of industry, universities and government laboratories.

♦ Promote tourism. We will bring together the marketing and infrastructure work of government, local councils and tourist boards. We will ensure that local communities are involved in the planning of tourist developments from the earliest stages.

♦ Build new partnerships at work. We will give employees new rights to consultation and participation in decisions and give companies and their employees access to advice on the forms of partnership which best suit them. We will promote profit-sharing, mutual structures and employee share-ownership schemes. We will extend the benefits of the social chapter of the Maastricht Treaty to all UK employees, while resisting the adoption of new rules that unnecessarily harm job opportunities.

♦ Encourage a culture of long-term business investment. We will require companies to publish information on their long-term investment achievements, including environmental performance, research and development, and training. We will introduce greater shareholder control over directors' pay and appointments.

♦ Promote British exports. We will make export promotion and commercial activity a higher priority for British Embassies.

## Making Britain more competitive

A competitive domestic economy is essential if British companies are to succeed in the global market.

**We will:**

♦ Strengthen the law on competition. We will tighten the rules on monopolies and adopt a pro-competition stance on take-overs and mergers. We will combine the Monopolies and Mergers Commission and the Office of Fair Trading into a single powerful body, independent of government and charged with promoting competition.

♦ Give consumers more power. We will promote the establishment of industry-wide Ombudsmen schemes to improve complaints procedures and consumer redress. We will strengthen customer guarantees, improve product standards and labelling, especially for environmental purposes, and encourage products that are easier to repair, reuse and recycle. We will insist on clear labelling for food products which include genetically modified ingredients.

♦ Reform the privatised utilities. We will combine the existing regulators into a single Office of Utility Regulation, reporting to a Cabinet minister responsible for consumer affairs. This new office will contain a regulatory board for each industry and will be charged with protecting the consumer and ensuring that excess profits are used to reduce prices and increase investment in improved services. Starting with the water industry, we will encourage utilities to involve their consumers in ownership and control of their company, through mutual structures.

♦ Reinforce consumer and investor protection. We will introduce independent regulation of financial services and improve processes for redress (eg for mis-selling). We will protect pension and life assurance savings from fraud. We will work to maintain the City of London's pre-eminence as a financial centre and promote effective international banking standards.

## ENVIRONMENT

**Our aim:** To make clean air, pure water and a decent environment a central priority of Government.

**The problem:** For too long, the environment has been damaged by greed and indifference. This cannot go on. From global warming to polluted rivers and asthma in children, everyone is already paying the cost of environmental damage. The longer action is delayed, the higher the cost will be.

**Our commitment:** To save energy, cut traffic congestion, stop the unnecessary destruction of the countryside and stem the tide of pollution.

### Our priorities are to:

♦ Cut taxes on things we want to encourage, like jobs, by taxing pollution instead. This will not mean more tax, it will mean taxing differently.

♦ Build environmental objectives into every government policy.

♦ Set tough targets to cut energy waste, reduce traffic congestion and control pollution.

### A greener economy

Environmental protection must be built into every economic decision and every area of government policy.

### We will:

♦ Set tough new targets for the reduction of traffic pollution and waste. This will help reduce global warming, cut air pollution and prevent waste. Our targets include cutting carbon dioxide emissions (the main cause of climate change) by 30 per cent from the 1990 level over the next 15 years.

♦ Cut VAT and taxes on jobs, and make up the difference by taxing pollution instead. This will help create more jobs and a better standard of living.

♦ Adopt a Green Action Programme. We will set targets for sustainability and biodiversity, to be met by central and local government. We will measure these by using new indicators of quality of life, progress and wealth. The Prime Minister will report to Parliament each year on the country's success in meeting these environmental targets.

♦ Protect the local environment. We will pass stronger laws to conserve the countryside. We will cut road congestion and help local councils make Britain's towns and cities healthier and cleaner places to live.

♦ Improve the way environment policy is made. Environment policy is currently buried, with housing and local government, in a huge single government department. We will put environment and energy policy within a separate, new department and ensure that all government departments and agencies pursue environmentally-friendly policies. We will give the Environment Agency stronger powers to enforce compliance with environmental laws.

### Transporting people, tackling pollution

Travel delays and road congestion cost billions of pounds, and pollution damages the health of millions of people.

### We will:

♦ Invest in public transport by building new partnerships with the private sector. We will enable councils to introduce road pricing in the most congested urban areas and use the money to support clean and rapid public transport, and to improve cycle and pedestrian access. We will retain London Underground in public ownership and give it the right to seek private finance for new investment without an assured government guarantee.

♦ Treble the freight and double the number of passengers carried on Britain's railways by the year 2010. We will strengthen the powers of the rail regulators. We will require Railtrack to meet targets for greater investment and increased passenger and freight traffic. We will withhold public subsidies from Railtrack if the targets are not met and, in the case of persistent failure, use the funds to reacquire a controlling interest in Railtrack. We will provide for legislation enabling this.

♦ Encourage people to drive more fuel-efficient cars by cutting the annual car tax, from £145 to £10 for cars up to 1,600cc, over the period of the next Parliament, funded by gradually raising the duty on fuel by approximately four pence per litre. Under our proposals, a person with a typical family car could drive up to 23,000 miles per year and still be better off – even in rural areas, where the average motorist only drives 11,700 miles a year. We will reform tax relief on company cars to encourage smaller cars and give people new incentives to use public transport for getting to work.

♦ Reduce the need to travel. We will reform the planning system so that people have easier access to shops, offices and facilities, and promote the use of information technology to decentralise work.

## Warmer homes, saving energy

Official government figures show that half the energy used in Britain is wasted. This pushes up fuel bills, worsens pollution and speeds up global warming.

### We will:

♦ Cut fuel bills and make homes warmer. We will launch a National Homes Insulation programme to end fuel poverty starting with the two million lowest income households. Our proposals will be funded by the Energy Saving Trust and the energy supply companies. This will save these households an average £85 per year and reduce global warming emissions. By contrast, cutting VAT on fuel bills to 5 per cent would save the average household only £19 per year.

♦ Cut taxes on people by taxing pollution instead. To encourage energy saving, we will gradually introduce a "carbon tax" on fossil fuels, using the funds raised to cut VAT and employers' National Insurance Contributions (the tax on jobs). This is a tax switch, not a tax rise, and will be phased in gradually.

♦ Improve energy efficiency. We will bring in new minimum standards for the energy efficiency of products, buildings and vehicles. We will cut VAT on energy conservation materials to 8 per cent – the same as for energy supplies.

♦ Promote renewable sources of energy and combined heat and power schemes. We will shift funds from nuclear research into decommissioning and nuclear waste management, and support research for renewable energy sources. We will not provide any government subsidies for nuclear generation. We support on-site dry storage of nuclear waste, pending the long-term development of safe alternatives. Nuclear stations will not be replaced at the end of their design life.

## Protecting Britain's heritage

Britain's natural environment and heritage are being gradually destroyed.

### We will:

♦ Clean up Britain's rivers and beaches and ensure that the costs of investment are spread fairly. We will require water companies to contribute to the cost of national environmental projects. We will reduce the need for new water developments by setting targets to reduce leakage and by promoting efficiency in water use. We will introduce a fairer system of charging for water and require water companies to share excess profits with their customers through rebates or investments in environmental improvements. We will end, within ten years, discharges that cause unnecessary water pollution.

♦ Tackle marine oil pollution. We will implement tougher rules on shipping safety and bring forward the designation of marine high risk areas.

♦ Reform land use planning. We will make protection of the natural environment a major feature of the planning system through a new Wildlife Act. This will improve protection of National Parks, Heritage Coasts, sites of special scientific interest and areas of outstanding natural beauty.

♦ Green the countryside. Our proposed new Countryside Management Contracts will help farmers to protect vital habitats and convert to more environmentally-friendly farming methods. We will use tax and planning reforms to protect rural areas, encouraging development on derelict land sites rather than green fields.

## Thinking globally, acting locally

Most people understand the importance of thinking globally and acting locally. They want to play their part in protecting the environment. Government should help them do so.

**We will:**

♦ Encourage the manufacture of products that are easier to repair, reuse or recycle. We will introduce deposit refund schemes and back EU-wide standards for product design, energy efficiency and reuse.

♦ Help people to choose environmentally friendly products. We will press for comprehensive and understandable EU-wide ecologically friendly and energy-efficient labelling schemes.

### Promoting animal welfare
The way a society treats animals is a measure of its civilisation.

**We will:**

♦ Promote animal welfare. We will set up a compulsory national dog registration scheme. We will halt the trade in endangered species as pets. We will promote and extend training and qualification for those who work with livestock. We will insist on the enforcement of maximum time limits for transporting live animals in the EU, a stricter timetable for banning veal crates and improved rearing conditions for pigs and chickens across the EU. We will create an Animal Protection Commission to enforce animal welfare laws and improve animal welfare standards. We will ban animal testing for cosmetics, weapons and tobacco products. We will review the law in order to reduce the use of animals in scientific experiments and seek the development of alternatives.

♦ Protect wild animals. We believe that the issues of hunting with hounds and coursing should be decided by free votes in the House of Commons. We will ban snares and leg hold traps. We will press for stronger international laws to protect endangered species. We will ban the importation of products derived from threatened wild animals.

## SECURE COMMUNITIES
**Our aim:** To give every person in Britain the security of a decent home in a safe, strong community.

**The problem:** Crime, homelessness and insecurity now threaten the very fabric of British society. Many people feel too frightened to leave their homes. Many do not have a decent home. Our country is becoming more and more divided, our sense of community is being lost and our shared values are being undermined.

**Our commitment:** Liberal Democrats will pursue practical measures to rebuild Britain's communities, tackle the causes of crime, reduce homelessness and make people safer in their homes and on the streets.

### Our priorities are to:
♦ Put 3,000 more police officers on the beat.
♦ Build more affordable and secure housing.
♦ End, by the year 2000, the scandal of people being forced to sleep rough on the streets.
♦ Revive Britain's sense of community.

### Housing
Boom and bust house prices, a shortage of decent homes and poor housing have wrecked the lives of millions and damaged Britain's economy.

**We will:**

♦ Build more houses. We will encourage partnerships between the public sector, the private sector and housing associations to build high-quality homes to rent and buy. We will, within strict borrowing controls, give local authorities more powers to go directly to the market to raise finance for building new homes. We will begin the phased release of capital receipts from past sales of council houses and allow the money to be used to build new homes.

♦ Give financial security to all, whether they rent or own their homes. We will introduce a new Mortgage Benefit for first time buyers. They will receive this instead of Mortgage Interest Tax Relief. Those holding current mortgages will retain Mortgage Interest Tax Relief. Our aim is, over time, to merge the new Mortgage Benefit and the current Housing Benefit into one system of housing cost relief, available to those who buy or rent and focused on those most in need.

♦ End the scandal of people being forced to sleep rough on the streets. We will ensure that by the year 2000 no one is forced to sleep on the streets. We will require every council to set up self-funding rent deposit schemes to help homeless people take up private tenancies. We will fund more short-stay hostel places as the first rung on the ladder to permanent accommodation.

◆ Take action to tackle homelessness and raise housing standards. We will give councils greater power to act on unfit private housing, where the landlord has failed to do so. We will strengthen tenants' rights to repair and, in the public sector, give them rights to take part in the management and development of their homes and estates. Our Empty Homes Strategy will enable local authorities to work with, and as a last resort require, landlords to bring empty properties back into use. We will end discrimination against those under 25 by scrapping the "shared residency rule" when assessing housing benefit.
◆ Bring confidence back to the housing market by targeting low inflation and low interest rates.

## Crime and policing

Crime and the fear of crime affect almost every person and every community in the country.

**We will:**
◆ Put 3,000 more police officers on the beat. Within one year, we will give police authorities the resources to put an extra 3,000 police officers on the beat. We will increase the time the police spend on preventing and detecting crime by reducing unnecessary paperwork and making greater use of new technologies.
◆ Tackle youth crime. We will widen the use of schemes that require offenders to repay their debt to society and to confront the consequences of their actions. We will, where appropriate, require parents to participate in support projects where their children have been involved in juvenile crime. We will develop schemes that target disruptive children from an early age. We will reserve custodial sentences for more serious and persistent offenders. Our voluntary Citizens Service will enable young people to get directly involved in crime prevention schemes.
◆ Strengthen the criminal justice system. We will make the justice system work more quickly and effectively and review sentencing policy. We will overhaul the Crown Prosecution Service. We will encourage the use of community sentences, as an alternative to prison, where the result is likely to be less reoffending, and use prison sentences where they are essential to public protection or to make punishment effective. We will concentrate resources on crime prevention and on increasing conviction rates, rather than spending billions on building prisons.
◆ Focus on crime prevention. We will require councils to take the lead in establishing cross-community partnerships against crime, setting specific targets for crime prevention. We will give Councils powers and resources to support high-quality, targeted crime prevention initiatives.
◆ Wage war on drug abuse. We will give the police and Customs and Excise the support they need to stop drugs coming into Britain. We will set up a Royal Commission charged with developing policies to tackle the drugs problem at its roots.
◆ Give victims a new deal. We will promote restorative justice, under which offenders can be required to compensate victims for the damage they have caused. We will ensure that the Victim Support movement and the Witness Support schemes play a full role in the criminal justice system. We will provide victims with the practical support they need to prevent repeat attacks.
◆ Strengthen public confidence in the police. We will make police authorities more responsive to local communities by increasing their elected membership and creating an accountable police authority for London. We will improve co-operation between police forces and work more closely with Britain's European partners to combat international crime, terrorism, drug trafficking and fraud. We will ensure that the police take further steps to reduce the level of racial and homophobic violence.

## Rural communities

Britain's rural economy and communities have been transformed over the last fifty years. The challenge for the next fifty years is to protect and enhance the richness of rural life, while developing a thriving rural economy.

**We will:**
◆ Seek further reform of the Common Agricultural Policy (CAP). We will work to replace the CAP, which currently subsidises production, with Countryside Management Contracts – a targeted system of direct payments to support economic, social and environmental goals in rural communities. Countryside Management Contracts will enable farmers and landowners to choose from a wide range of options, for example, to improve the rural environment, maximise

food quality, protect natural habitats or move to less intensive or organic farming methods.

♦ Help rural economies through a period of change. We will, in partnership with the agriculture industry, draw up a national strategy for farming in order to provide a framework for public policy and private decision-making over the next ten years. We will promote agricultural research and development, and assist farmers wishing to diversify. We will promote local processing of agricultural products and expand support for small and medium-sized enterprises in rural areas.

♦ Tackle rural crime. We will put more police into rural areas, support Farm and Neighbourhood Watch schemes and give councils the duty to set up crime prevention schemes with the local police. We will enable rural police authorities to introduce mortgage incentive schemes to encourage rural beat officers to live in the areas they serve.

♦ Enhance rural services. We will support smaller village schools through greater use of information technology and specialist teaching teams. We will encourage schemes that enable local communities to make use of school buildings and equipment. We will promote community hospitals and use them for more out-patient consultations.

♦ Provide more affordable rural housing. We will encourage housing authorities, parish councils and housing associations to set up partnership schemes with the private sector in order to build low-cost homes for first-time home buyers and social needs.

♦ Improve rural transport. We will give local authorities the power to improve the co-ordination of local bus services and to reopen closed railway stations, in co-operation with Railtrack.

♦ Strengthen the network of rural sub-post offices and village shops. We will encourage the Post Office to invest in new point of sale technologies, in order to provide access, through sub-post offices, to a wide range of customer services. Where post offices and village shops which are vital to their local community are threatened, we will enable local Councils to support them with up to 100 per cent rate relief.

♦ Protect the countryside. We will help landowners meet the environmental costs of increased access to the countryside. We will take action to reduce the use of chemicals in farming.

♦ Protect rural areas from urbanisation. We will penalise the use of greenfield sites, set and enforce targets for greater use of brownland sites and encourage over-the-shop accommodation in market town centres. We will review the excessive housing totals in the current structure plans and scrap the "predict and provide" approach to housing development.

♦ Work to preserve fish stocks and protect the livelihoods of local fishing communities. Our aim is to scrap the Common Fisheries Policy and replace it with a new Europe-wide fisheries policy based on the regional management of fish stocks. We will take firm action to end quota-hopping, begin the phased abolition of industrial fishing and strengthen decommissioning incentives.

♦ Promote safe food. We will set up a Food Commission, independent from MAFF and accountable to Parliament, maintain strict controls on the use of bio-technology and press for higher common food standards across the European Union.

## Urban communities

Britain's towns and cities offer civic pride, accessible facilities and, potentially, a high quality of life. However, many suffer from alienation, joblessness, high crime rates, a run-down environment and loss of population. Urban areas should offer excitement, security and a strong sense of community.

## We will:

♦ Boost local economic development and job opportunities. We will support local development corporations. We will build new partnerships between local government and the private and voluntary sectors, to regenerate local economies and promote community enterprise. We will link local training to local jobs. We will encourage the establishment of community banks and credit unions.

♦ Tackle urban crime. We will expand community policing, ensure that all new planning takes account of the need to deter crime and focus on crime prevention.

♦ Encourage public transport. We will enable councils to co-ordinate bus and train services and give them powers to introduce urban road pricing schemes, using the revenue raised to invest in better public transport.

♦ Reform and strengthen elected local government. We will give local councils greater control over their own affairs. We will create a strategic authority for London. We will encourage the use of "planning for real" strategies, in which local people can make a direct input into major planning projects in their community.

## Arts and media

Flourishing arts and a diverse culture are essential for a lively and open society. They can be engines of innovation that bring life to the economy. At the same time, the world is experiencing an information revolution as important and far-reaching as the Industrial Revolution. Britain must maintain a free and effective media capable of being a check on the abuse of power, and of giving people the information they need to make informed decisions.

### We will:

♦ Tackle the concentration of media power. We will act to prevent media mergers or takeovers, except where these can be shown to advance quality, diversity and access. We will require the Independent Television Commission to protect the position of smaller regional ITV companies, within the network supply agreement.

♦ Maintain the role of the BBC as the benchmark of public service broadcasting, committed to quality, diversity and universal access. We will protect the independence and impartiality of the BBC through its Board of Governors and its licence fee.

♦ Improve access to information technology and the Internet. We will ensure that everyone in Britain can have access, either individually or through a wide range of public access points, to a nationwide interactive communications network by the year 2000.

♦ Increase access to the arts. We will use the National Lottery to endow, house and improve access to the arts. We aim to move towards the European average for public funding of the arts. We aim to restore the principle of free access to national museum and gallery collections, starting with the removal of charges for school parties.

♦ Promote Britain's culture. We will promote film production in Britain. We will actively support the British Council and rejoin Unesco. We will enhance the BBC World Service as a national asset.

## HEALTH AND COMMUNITY CARE

**Our aim:** To make year-on-year improvements in the health of Britain's people and the quality of the National Health Service.

**The problem:** The NHS has been squeezed between rising demand and government underfunding, and disrupted by repeated changes in government policy. Morale amongst NHS professionals is falling, and bureaucracy has grown at the expense of frontline patient care, while numbers of nurses and hospital beds have fallen.

**Our commitment:** Liberal Democrats will increase funding for the NHS and secure funding for the future. We will maintain the NHS as a comprehensive service, free at the point of need and funded primarily from general taxation. We will immediately tackle the crisis in the hospital sector, make the NHS more accountable and begin a long-term shift towards preventive medicine.

### Our priorities are to:

♦ Halt all finance-driven closures for six months, pending an independent audit of needs and facilities.

♦ Invest £200 million each year to recruit more staff for frontline patient care. This would be enough, for example, for 10,000 extra nurses or 5,000 extra doctors.

♦ Cut hospital waiting lists to a maximum of six months over three years.

♦ End the two-tier system in the NHS.

♦ Restore free eye and dental checks.

### Raising standards in the NHS

Whilst many of the recent reforms to the NHS have been beneficial, they have resulted in the creation of a two-tier health service. The standard of health care a person receives is increasingly becoming a lottery. The length of time people have to wait, the chance of treatment being postponed and the quality of health care vary enormously from one part of the UK to another.

### We will:

♦ Match NHS facilities to needs. We will place an immediate six-month halt on the finance-driven closure of beds and wards, and set up an independent audit of needs and facilities.

♦ End the built-in two-tier service in the NHS. We will end the present system where treatment depends on the type of GP people go to. We will treat all GPs equally, with a common basis for funding. We want all GPs to have the benefits of flexibility and access to services currently enjoyed by fundholders. Those who choose to manage their own affairs will be able to do so on their own or as part of a consortium. Those who do not will be able to leave management to the local health authority.

♦ Raise standards of care in all areas. We will set up a National Inspectorate for Health and Social Care to improve standards and promote patients' interests. This body will work with the Audit Commission to ensure that all spending is monitored and results in real improvements in patient care.

## Funding the Health Service
The NHS is underfunded. Too much goes into bureaucracy and not enough into patient care. There is a crisis in the NHS, especially in hospitals. Morale is dropping, standards of care are at risk from underfunding and highly-qualified doctors and nurses are leaving the profession.

## We will:
♦ Invest more in the NHS. We will invest at least an extra £540 million every year in the NHS to pay for our policy priorities. This will be paid for by closing the loophole that allows employers to avoid paying National Insurance contributions on certain benefits in kind and by putting 5p on the price of a packet of 20 cigarettes. We will use these extra funds to tackle the crisis in staffing, especially in the hospital sector, and begin a shift to preventive care. We will ensure that the NHS budget keeps pace with increasing cost pressures.

♦ Shift money from unnecessary bureaucracy into patient care. We will move from annual to at least three-yearly contracts between Health Authorities and Trusts, and shift the money saved into frontline patient care. We will replace time consuming local pay bargaining with a new national pay structure and a single NHS-wide Pay Review Body that covers all pay, from the cleaner to the chief executive.

## Building on the best of the NHS
The NHS needs to be strengthened and improved.

## We will:
♦ Cut waiting lists. We will cut waiting times between diagnosis and treatment to a maximum of six months over three years.

♦ Improve the quality of care and raise morale. We will recruit and train more professional staff. Our carefully costed plans would, for instance, pay for the equivalent of 10,000 more nurses or 5,000 more doctors. We will ban the use of "gagging clauses" in employment contracts which prevent professional staff from speaking out against unsafe standards.

♦ Tackle the crisis in NHS dental care. We will require local authorities to ensure that the public has access to NHS dentistry in all areas.

## Promoting good health
Britain has a health service that concentrates too much on curing illness rather than preventing it. A healthier nation and a more cost-effective NHS depend on shifting the emphasis towards prevention, tackling the root causes of ill health (eg poverty and homelessness) and making people more responsible for their own health.

## We will:
♦ Make prevention a priority. We will immediately abolish charges for eye and dental check-ups and freeze prescription charges as the first steps in a radical shift of policy that emphasises the prevention of illness rather than treatment.

♦ Encourage people to take more responsibility for their own health. We will improve health education and promote healthy living. We will ban tobacco advertising and promotion and increase the duty on tobacco products. We will make the Health Education Authority truly independent and free to criticise government policy.

♦ Ensure that food is healthy and safe. We will create an independent and powerful Food Commission, separate from MAFF, and responsible to Parliament for food quality and safety.

♦ Put health promotion at the heart of government policy. We will require all government departments to assess the impact of their policies on health. Each year there will be an independent report, to be published and debated in Parliament, on the state of the nation's health.

## Bringing health services closer to people

The local institutions of the NHS must become more accountable to those they serve and more responsive to patients' needs.

### We will:

♦ Enable citizens to play a part in setting health policies in their area. We will build on current pilot schemes to bring together Health Authorities and Social Services Departments, within the framework of elected local authorities.

♦ Give local people a stronger voice on NHS Trusts. We will end the right of the Secretary of State for Health to appoint members of NHS Trusts, Authorities and Boards. We will require at least half the membership of Trusts to be drawn from the population they serve. We will open up meetings of NHS Trust boards to the public and press, and give local people, staff and professionals speaking rights. We will guarantee direct representation from the staff of each Trust. We will give Community Health Councils improved rights to consultation and greater access to information and meetings.

♦ Give the public more say in setting priorities within the NHS. Difficult choices about priorities must be faced. They cannot be left to bureaucrats and health professionals alone. We will develop new ways of involving the public in setting health service priorities.

## Giving patients more choice

Patients should have more choice over their type of treatment, who delivers it and when.

### We will:

♦ Enhance the rights of patients. We will strengthen the Patient's Charter and include rights to treatment within a specified time, a choice of GP, information about the options for treatment, guaranteed access to health records and better redress.

♦ Ensure that action is taken to improve poor quality services. We will enable patients and staff to apply directly to our new National Inspectorate of Health and Social Care to carry out inspections and take action where deficiencies come to light.

## Community care

Our aim is to create a society in which people, whatever their needs, can live their lives with dignity.

### We will:

♦ Give people choice in the services they use and the way they are provided. We will require councils to extend to those over 65 the right to arrange their own care privately, if they wish. This will promote independence and enable them to find better value for money.

♦ Care for carers. We will introduce a new Carer's Benefit, in place of the Independent Living Allowance, in order to meet more of the financial cost of caring. We will extend the Carer's Benefit, as resources allow, to those over retirement age and work to improve advice, information, training and counselling for carers. We will seek to increase access to respite care and ensure that carers and users are involved in decisions about care. We will draw up a Charter that sets out carers' rights and responsibilities.

♦ Establish high national standards for all community care services. Our new independent Inspectorate of Health and Social Care will publish codes of practice for residential and nursing homes, and have the power to close any home that consistently falls short of national standards. We will introduce national charging and eligibility guidelines to ensure a "level playing field" of provision and charges.

♦ Protect people from the excessive cost of care. We will, as resources allow, raise the threshold at which older people are required to make a contribution to their long-term care. We are committed to working on a cross-party basis, to establish a national agreement on a system for funding care services that does not penalise thrift.

## REFORMING POLITICS

**Our aim:** To restore trust in British politics.

**The problem:** People know that British politics isn't working. Their politicians have lied to them, their Parliament has become tainted by sleaze and their government is out of touch and doesn't listen.

**Our commitment:** Liberal Democrats will modernise Britain's outdated institutions, rebuild trust, renew democracy and give Britain's nations, regions and local communities a greater say over their own affairs.

## Our priorities are to:
♦ Restore trust between people and government, by ending secrecy and guaranteeing people's rights and freedoms.
♦ Renew Britain's democracy, by creating a fair voting system, reforming Parliament and setting higher standards for politicians' conduct.
♦ Give government back to the people, by decentralising power to the nations, regions and communities of the United Kingdom.

## Restoring trust in politics
British politics remains far too secretive. We cannot rebuild trust in politics without making government more open and accountable.

## We will:
♦ Safeguard individual liberties, by establishing a Bill of Rights. As a first step, we will incorporate the European Convention on Human Rights into UK law so that it is enforceable by the courts in the UK. We will set up a Human Rights Commission to strengthen the protection of individual rights. We will create a Ministry for Justice responsible for protecting human rights and overseeing the administration of the legal system, the courts and legal aid. We oppose the introduction of Identity Cards.
♦ Break open the excessive secrecy of government, by passing a Freedom of Information Act establishing a citizens right-to-know.
♦ Cut back the quango state. We will scrap unnecessary quangos, handing their functions over to elected bodies. We will require those that remain to meet in public and to list their members' interests. We will establish a fair, open and more representative appointment process for all quangos.
♦ Give people more say in decision-making. We will make greater use of national referendums for constitutional issues, for example, changing the voting system or any further transfer of power to European institutions. We will enable referendums to be held on specific local issues where there is public demand.

## Renewing democracy
Britain's political institutions are outdated and unrepresentative.

## We will:
♦ Modernise the House of Commons. We will reduce the number of MPs by 200 (one-third) and introduce tougher rules for their conduct, behaviour and outside sources of income. We will improve drafting and consultation on legislation, and strengthen MPs' ability to hold the government to account.
♦ Create an effective and democratic upper house. We will, over two Parliaments, transform the House of Lords into a predominantly-elected second chamber capable of representing the nations and regions of the UK and of playing a key role in scrutinising European legislation.
♦ Introduce a fair system of voting. We will introduce proportional representation for all elections, to put more power in the hands of voters and make government more representative.
♦ Make politics more stable. We will establish a fixed parliamentary term of four years.
♦ Clean up party funding. We will reform the way political parties are funded and limit the amount they can spend on national election campaigns. We will make each party publish its accounts and list all large donors.

## Giving government back to the people
Far too much power has been concentrated in Westminster and Whitehall. Democratic government should be as close to ordinary people as possible.

## We will:
♦ Introduce Home Rule for Scotland, with the creation of a Scottish Parliament, elected by proportional representation, and able to raise and reduce income tax.
♦ Introduce Home Rule for Wales, with the creation of a Welsh Senedd, elected by proportional representation, and able to raise and reduce income tax.
♦ Create the framework to make existing regional decision-making in England democratically

accountable, and enable the establishment of elected regional assemblies, where there is demonstrated public demand. We will create a strategic authority for London.

♦ Strengthen local government. We will establish a "power of general competence", giving councils wider scope for action. We will allow local authorities to raise more of their funds locally, give them greater discretion over spending and allow them, within strict limits, to go directly to the markets to raise finance for capital projects. We will, in the long term, replace Council Tax with a Local Income Tax, and replace the Uniform Business Rate with a fairer system of business rates, raised through local councils and set in accordance with local priorities.

## Northern Ireland

Peace in Northern Ireland depends on containing and ultimately removing the entrenched hostility between the two main communities in Northern Ireland.

### We will:

♦ Establish a power-sharing executive for Northern Ireland, elected under a fair and proportional system of voting. We will press for a new constitutional settlement based on the protection of individual rights through a Bill of Rights, incorporating the European Convention.

♦ Give individuals more power and political responsibility. We will introduce a fair and proportional voting system for all elections, and reform and strengthen local government in the province.

♦ Ensure respect for civil liberties. We will introduce an independent procedure for investigating complaints against the security forces, and reform the Diplock system so that three judges instead of one preside over non-jury trials. We will urgently implement the North Report's recommendations for an independent commission to supervise parades and marches.

♦ Promote economic growth. We will strengthen the all-Ireland economy through the creation of effective cross-border agencies. We will invest in education and promote inward investment.

♦ Build on the Joint Declaration and the Framework Document, by working with the Irish Government to create agreement between as many of the constitutional parties as possible. Sinn Fein can only be admitted to this process if, in accordance with the Mitchell principles, they and the IRA turn their backs on terrorism. Meanwhile, we must remain vigilant and keep in place the present means for countering terrorism.

## OPPORTUNITIES

**Our aim:** To widen opportunities for everyone in Britain to make the most of their lives.

**The problem:** Poverty, lack of training, low pay and discrimination deny too many people the opportunity to make the most of their lives. Meanwhile, the welfare system no longer meets the needs of a modern society. It locks too many into dependency and, too often, penalises those who wish to work and save.

**Our commitment:** Liberal Democrats will promote individual self-reliance, strengthen equality for all before the law and in employment, and work for a society that cherishes diversity.

### Our priorities are to:

♦ Ensure that, by the millennium, every young person has had the opportunity to work, learn, train and make a positive contribution to society.

♦ Give women greater opportunities to play a full role in work and in society.

♦ Ensure dignity in retirement.

♦ Break open the poverty trap that makes people better off on the dole than in work.

♦ Modernise Britain's welfare state for the 21st century, building a new cross-party partnership for reform.

### Breaking the poverty trap

Unemployment wastes the talents and denies people the opportunity to contribute to the well-being of their families and increase Britain's wealth.

### We will:

♦ Help long-term unemployed people back to work. We will establish a self-financing Benefit Transfer Programme allowing those who have been unemployed for a year or more to turn their unemployment benefits into an incentive for employers to recruit and train them. The value of the benefit to employers will gradually be reduced.

♦ Break open the poverty trap. We will take nearly 500,000 low earners out of income tax altogether by raising tax thresholds. This will provide lower taxes and new incentives to work, while cutting the benefits bill and reducing tax for 99.5 per cent of all income taxpayers. This will be paid for by introducing a new top tax rate of 50p on taxable income of over £100,000 per year. We will replace income support and Family Credit with a simpler, more efficient Low Income Benefit that increases financial incentives for people going back to work.

♦ Modernise Britain's welfare system. We will initiate a comprehensive review of the welfare system to build a new framework for welfare and opportunity, on a cross-party basis. Our aim is to provide a more effective safety net for the disadvantaged, to encourage work, without compulsion, and to widen opportunities.

♦ Help parents to return to work. We will develop a national childcare strategy, drawing on public and private provision. We will, over time, extend tax relief on workplace nurseries to other forms of day nursery care.

♦ Establish a voluntary Citizens Service to give people, especially young people, up to two years' work on such projects as environmental conservation, crime prevention, housing renovation, social services and the Armed Services.

♦ Encourage a flexible labour market, while protecting the low paid with a regionally variable, minimum hourly rate.

♦ Crack down on social security fraud and tax evasion and shift the money saved into new policies to enhance opportunities. We will tackle the high levels of fraud and overpayment in the social security budget. We will stop tax evasion and close off tax avoidance loopholes.

## Older people
Everyone in Britain should be able to look forward to a retirement of security, opportunity and dignity. Old people feel that they are fast becoming Britain's forgotten generation.

### We will:
♦ Guarantee everyone an acceptable minimum standard of living in retirement. We will create an additional top-up pension for pensioners with incomes below the income support level. This will be indexed to earnings and tapered as outside income increases. The basic state pension will remain indexed to prices. We will start to phase out the expensive, unfair contributory system and base the right to a state pension on citizenship and residence.

♦ Enable people to choose when to start drawing a pension. We will bring in a flexible "decade of retirement", between the ages of 60 and 70.

♦ Protect the rights of older people. We will legislate against discrimination on the grounds of age.

♦ Expand private pensions and give people more control over their pensions. We wish to see more people making provision for their old age. We will replace the State Earnings Related Scheme (Serps) with a scheme under which all employees have personal or occupational pensions. Existing accrued Serps will, however, be preserved. We will expand occupational and personal pension schemes by giving all employees an entitlement to participate in a pension scheme of their choice, funded by contributions from employers and employees. Pension rights will be fully secured if people change jobs. We will treat pensions as deferred income over which pension-holders have full rights of security, control and portability.

♦ Abolish standing charges for water and create a fairer system of charging.

## Young people
We propose a new deal for young people, in which new rights and new responsibilities go hand in hand.

### We will:
♦ Expand opportunities. Our aim is that every young person between the ages of 16 and 19 will have the opportunity to either work, learn, train or take a place on our new Citizens Service.

♦ Restore security to excluded young people. The withdrawal of benefit rights has condemned thousands of young people to life out of work and on the streets, at great long-term public cost. We will restore access to benefits for 16 and 17 year-olds. In the longer term, we aim to scrap the lower rate of income support for those under 25.

♦ Ensure that young people can learn their rights and responsibilities, with citizenship classes in every school and parenting classes for young adults. We will give children and young people

access to information about their legal rights and obligations, review the age of majority and ensure that young people are represented on bodies that especially concern them.
♦ Expand local youth services. We will require local councils to provide a statutory youth service in partnership with the voluntary sector.

## Families
Families, in all their forms, are a basic building block of society. But the nature of families is changing. This has brought new stresses which must be addressed. But it has also brought new attitudes, such as the sharing of family responsibilities, which should be encouraged.

## We will:
♦ Give families more security. We will take nearly 500,000 low earners out of tax altogether, by raising tax thresholds. We will replace income support and Family Credit with a simpler, more efficient Low Income Benefit that helps people back to work. We aim to improve the support for those caring for older people and people with disabilities.
♦ Introduce fair and workable child support legislation. We will repeal the Child Support Act and abolish the Child Support Agency. We believe that parents should financially support their children at an appropriate level. Where there are disputes between the parents, these should be decided by the courts, not by an inflexible formula. We will create a new system of unified family courts to decide these questions, after they have heard all the evidence.
♦ Promote good parenting. We will encourage the provision of parenting classes for young adults. We will increase the role of parents in education by extending home/school/pupil links, and develop home-school partnership arrangements, to assist in addressing the needs of the child.
♦ Expand parental rights. We will introduce a statutory right to parental leave and develop Maternity Benefit into a new, flexible parental benefit to be shared between partners. We will ensure that fostering and adoption law is based on the suitability of prospective fosterers and the needs of the child.
♦ Help parents to return to work. We will, over time, extend tax relief on workplace nurseries to other forms of day nursery care. We will develop a national childcare strategy, drawing on public and private provision.
♦ Encourage flexible working patterns. We will encourage job sharing and family-friendly employment practices, especially in the public sector. We will give private sector employees approaching retirement age, or with responsibilities for young children, the right to negotiate reduced hours or a career break.

## Women
There is still a long way to go before women in Britain have equal opportunities.

## We will:
♦ Promote equality in the workplace. We will, over time, extend employment and pensions rights to part-time employees, on a pro-rata basis. We will bring in tougher obligations on employers to establish equal opportunities procedures and pursue the principle of equal pay for work of equal value.
♦ Make pensions fairer to women, by working to replace the contributory system with pension rights based on citizenship and residence in the UK. We will bring forward the introduction of pension splitting on divorce.
♦ Improve the services that women receive from the NHS. We will promote equal treatment of the sexes within the Health Service. We will set targets for the expansion of facilities which enable women to consult female health professionals.
♦ Make the legal system fairer to women. We will strengthen the civil law remedies for domestic violence and improve the treatment of rape victims by the court system. We will seek to improve the provision of refuge places for victims of domestic violence.
♦ Enhance the role of women in public life. We will tackle the under-representation of women on public bodies by setting a target that within a decade at least one-third of all those on all public bodies should be women. We will reform the procedures and facilities of the House of Commons to make them more accommodating to women and families.

## Disabled people
Progress in equal opportunities for disabled people remains patchy and unacceptably slow.

**We will:**
♦ Guarantee the rights of disabled people. We will ban discrimination on the grounds of disability and pass comprehensive legislation securing the civil rights of disabled people. We will draw up a Charter of Rights setting out what our new Bill of Rights means for disabled people.
♦ Give disabled people more independence. We will introduce a Partial Capacity Benefit, building on the Disability Working Allowance, to assist those in work who cannot fully support themselves financially. We aim to increase financial support for disabled people who cannot find work and to make provision for the real costs of disability.
♦ Improve access. We will publish a code of practice to improve access to buildings and transport. We will require government departments, local councils and public organisations to make their key public literature available in Braille or where appropriate tape.
♦ Make education inclusive. As part of our £2 billion investment in education, we will increase funding for, and enforce implementation of, the Code of Practice for Special Educational Needs.

## Ethnic minorities
Despite progress over recent years, members of ethnic minorities are too often denied equal opportunities and have to face racism and discrimination on a daily basis. Diversity, pluralism and a multicultural society are sources of strength for Britain.

**We will:**
♦ Strengthen action against discrimination. We will create a new Human Rights Commission, combining the Commission for Racial Equality and the Equal Opportunities Commission. We will give statutory force to the Commission for Racial Equality's Code of Practice in employment, and ensure that Britain plays a leading role in strengthening anti-discrimination legislation throughout the European Union.
♦ Ensure equal opportunities for all. We will require local authorities and housing associations to ensure equal opportunities in housing allocation. We will expand access to mother-tongue teaching, for both adults and children, where this takes place through self-help and community groups.
♦ Free immigration laws from racial discrimination. We will ensure that immigration policy is non-discriminatory in its application. We will reform current immigration laws so as to enable genuine family reunions. We will restore benefit rights to asylum seekers and ensure that asylum claims are dealt with swiftly.
♦ Increase ethnic minorities' confidence in the police. We will encourage the recruitment of ethnic minorities into the police force and require action to be taken against discrimination within the force. We will tackle any discriminatory use of police powers, such as stop and search, and enhance police action to deal with racial attacks. We will encourage the use of aggravated sentencing for racially motivated crimes.

## Lesbians and gay men
In a free and tolerant society, discrimination on any grounds is unacceptable. Diversity is a source of strength.

**We will:**
♦ Ensure equality before the law for lesbians and gay men through our new Human Rights Commission and the Bill of Rights. We will create a common age of consent regardless of gender or sexual orientation.
♦ Stop discrimination. We will outlaw incitement to hatred and discrimination in housing and employment, including the Armed Forces, on grounds of sexual orientation. We will repeal Section 28 of the 1988 Local Government Act. We will reform the law, ensure that the police and local authorities deal more effectively with homophobic attacks, and encourage police forces to be more representative of the communities they serve.

## BRITAIN IN THE WORLD
**Our aim:** To recast Britain's foreign policy and enable this country to play a leading role in shaping Europe and strengthening international institutions.
**The problem:** For too long British foreign policy has looked backwards to its imperial past. Britain's interests have been damaged by an attitude to Europe that has been, at best, ambivalent and, at worst, hostile. This attitude has also cost Britain opportunities for influence and advantage.

**Our commitment:** Liberal Democrats will ensure that Britain plays a leading role in shaping Europe, democratising its institutions and strengthening its role as a framework for prosperity, peace and security. Britain, with its world experience, expert armed forces and permanent membership of the UN Security Council, has a unique role to play in reforming international institutions for the next century.

### Our priorities are to:
♦ Make the European Union (EU) work more effectively and democratise its institutions.
♦ Widen Europe to include the new democracies of central and eastern Europe.
♦ Create a strong framework for Britain's defence and security through NATO and European co-operation.
♦ Give Britain a leading role in reforming and strengthening the UN and other international institutions.
♦ Promote an enforceable framework for international law, human rights and the protection of the environment.

### Positive leadership in Europe
Britain's interests can only best be pursued through constructive participation in an enlarged European Union. Our vision is of a European Union that is decentralised, democratic and diverse. A strong and united Europe, but one that respects cultural traditions and national and regional identities.

### In seeking to reform the EU, our priorities are to:
♦ Give the British people a say. Reform that fundamentally changes Britain's place in Europe should only proceed if it has the explicit support of Britain's people. If there is any substantial change in Britain's relationship with the EU, the British people must give their consent through a referendum.
♦ Make EU institutions more democratic and accountable. We will give the House of Commons a more effective role in scrutinising European policy. We also want the Council of Ministers and the EC Commission to be more accountable to the elected European Parliament. We will introduce a fair and proportional voting system for British MEPs in time for the 1999 European Parliament elections.
♦ Make EU decision-making more efficient and effective. Europe cannot effectively enlarge without improving its decision-making. We therefore favour the wider application of majority voting. But we will keep the veto on all issues relating to the constitution, budgetary matters and regulations on pay and social security. We support the use of the "double majority", especially on matters such as foreign and security policy. Each member state must retain the unfettered right to make its own decisions on the commitment of its national troops.

### Pursuing Britain's interests in Europe
Britain has much to gain from EU membership. This will take new leadership, a new approach and a renewed sense of national confidence.

### Our aims in Europe are to:
♦ Enhance economic prosperity, by promoting the freedom of movement of people, goods, services and money throughout the EU and by completing the European single market, particularly in areas of financial services, pensions and air travel.
♦ Participate in a successful single currency. Being part of a successful single currency will bring low inflation and low interest rates. Staying out will result in less investment and a loss of influence. However, three conditions must be met before Britain can join. First, the single currency must be firmly founded on the Maastricht criteria. Second, Britain must meet those criteria. Third, the British people must have agreed to it in a referendum.
♦ Strengthen the European framework for peace and security. Britain's security and national interests are best pursued in partnership with its European neighbours. We will work to strengthen European Common foreign and security policy to enable greater scope for united European action. Individual member states must be free to decide whether or not their national forces will take part in any particular action.
♦ Fight crime and protect citizens' rights through more effective co-operation between EU states' police and customs forces with greater democratic accountability. We will work to improve European co-operation against cross-border criminal activity and allow free movement for Britain's people throughout Europe. The administration of border controls

should remain with individual member nations until they can be confident that the EU's external borders are secure.
♦ Reform the Common Agricultural Policy, converting it into a system of direct payments to support economic, social and environmental goals in rural communities.
♦ Reform fisheries policies, scrapping the Common Fisheries Policy and replacing it with a new Europe-wide fisheries policy based on the regional management of fish stocks. We will take urgent action to end quota-hopping and begin the phased abolition of industrial fishing.

## Strong defence in an uncertain world
The first decades of the next century are likely to be turbulent and unstable everywhere, including within and around Europe. Britain must maintain an effective security capability. This will best be achieved through Nato and European co-operation, and this country must continue to play a full part in both.

## We will:
♦ Maintain a strong defence at home and enable the UK to play a leading role in keeping international peace. We will maintain Britain's overall defence capability at its current level, whilst ensuring UK forces meet current needs and are appropriate to potential threats.
♦ Retain Britain's basic nuclear capability through the Trident submarine force until such time as international multilateral nuclear disarmament can be achieved. We will restrict the number of nuclear warheads on Trident to the same number as previously deployed on Polaris.
♦ Resist the proliferation of weapons of mass destruction. We will press for the conclusion of a verifiable Comprehensive Test Ban Treaty. We will ensure that Britain plays an active part in talks to reduce the holdings of strategic nuclear weapons.
♦ Support the principle of common security. We support the extension of the security guarantees, from which western Europe has benefited, to the new democracies of central and eastern Europe. We support Nato and its enlargement.

## Working for peace, security and sustainability
In an increasingly inter-dependent world, the security of a medium sized nation like Britain is best preserved within a framework of international law that is effective and enforceable.

## Reforming the United Nations
Playing a leading role in strengthening and reforming the United Nations should be a central aspect of Britain's foreign policy over the next decade.

## We will work to:
♦ Strengthen the UN's peacekeeping capability so that it can take earlier and more effective action to prevent or suppress conflict. This should include establishing fast-track machinery for negotiations; permanent, on-call, peacekeeping forces made up from high-calibre troops provided by member states; the reinstatement of a Military Staff Committee; the establishment of a UN Staff College to train officers; and improvements to the UN's command control, communication and intelligence capabilities.
♦ Support the establishment of an International Criminal Court to deal with genocide and war crimes.

## Protecting the global environment
Pollution and environmental degradation do not respect national borders. Countries must work together if the world's environment is to be protected.

## We will:
♦ Take a lead in international environmental negotiations. We will press for tough and legally-binding international targets for greenhouse gas emissions and other pollutants.
♦ Develop a global system of environmental protection. We will work for the creation of a global environmental organisation. We will promote an environmental equivalent of the Geneva Convention, to outlaw gross acts of environmental destruction in times of war.

## Tackling world poverty
The elimination of global famine, pestilence and poverty is not only a moral challenge, it is also essential for the world's long-term stability and peace.

**We will:**

♦ Increase Britain's contribution to overseas aid. We will set out a timetable for sustained progress towards achieving the UN target for overseas development aid of 0.7 per cent of GNP within the next ten years.

♦ Promote a timetable for debt relief to the poorest states including a programme for cancelling debt and the creation of new and additional resources for debt relief.

♦ Target Britain's bilateral aid where it is most needed. We will focus Britain's bilateral aid on the least developed countries and end the practice of tying aid.

♦ Require states that receive UK development assistance to respect the fundamental human rights of their people and suspend UK programmes where these standards are breached.

### Controlling arms sales
The global arms trade fuels conflicts, hinders prosperity and robs the world's poor of resources. Its growth must be diminished.

**We will:**

♦ End the sale of British arms, war material, and "dual use" technologies to regimes which abuse human rights, and strictly control arms sales to regions of tension or potential conflict.

♦ Seek a new international regime to control the arms trade. We will support tighter EU-wide restrictions on transfers of military technology to non-democratic regimes and press for the establishment of a mandatory UN register, in which all arms sales and transfers must be listed.

♦ Ban landmines. We will place an immediate and total ban on the production, stockpiling and export of anti-personnel landmines and work towards a global ban on landmine production.

### Free and fair trade
Free and fair trade benefits all. The Gatt Uruguay Round has successfully lowered barriers to international trade, but further reforms are needed.

### We will seek action to:
♦ Enhance free trade by further reducing tariff and non-tariff barriers, especially against the poorest countries.

♦ Improve global labour standards by permitting countries to discriminate against goods produced by nations that maintain practices such as child, slave and forced labour. We will support the work of the International Labour Organisation in raising labour standards throughout the world.

♦ Advance environmental objectives. We support the addition of an environmental sustainability clause to the Gatt, setting out agreed principles of environmental policy against which trade measures can be judged.

♦ Reduce trans-national corporations' ability to abuse market power, through the development of a framework for global competition policy.

## ADDENDUM
### The Liberal Democrats and your tax
A copy of our Annual Tax Contract will be delivered to each UK household following the Budget each year. Some of the information which would be included is detailed below.

### This Annual Tax Contract will be in keeping with our four Tax Pledges:
1. No taxation without explanation. Central Government should inform taxpayers of the ways in which their money is raised and spent, just as local councils now do.

2. No promises unless the bill is attached. People have the right to know the Government's priorities and how much they will cost. When we make significant changes in our tax and spending priorities we will tell people where the money has come from. We will ask the National Audit Office to make sure that additional expenditure earmarked for specific projects is spent accordingly.

3. No more tax without tackling waste. Each year we will set out the measures which we plan to implement in order to reduce wasteful expenditure and deliver best value for money to taxpayers. We will never raise taxes without first scrutinising Government expenditure for waste.

4. Fair tax for all. Tax bands, rates and reliefs should ensure that everyone contributes according to their ability to pay and that the tax burden is fairly shared. We will aim to take more of those on low incomes out of tax completely. We will clamp down on tax avoidance and

evasion. We will provide a mechanism for people to give their views on tax and spending priorities.

## How the proposals in this manifesto would alter your tax and the Government's spending

### Costing our commitment
♦ We have issued alongside this manifesto a Costings Supplement to show in detail how our proposals will be financed.
♦ We will raise the basic rate of income tax by one penny in the pound – from 23p to 24p – to help finance our £2 billion per year programme of Education investment.
♦ We will increase the amount of income which people can receive before they start to pay income tax by £200 per year to £4,245. This tax cut will be paid for by introducing a new rate of income tax of 50 per cent, payable on taxable income of over £100,000 per year. Half a million people will be freed from income tax altogether. We will put 5p on a packet of cigarettes and use the money to restore free eye and dental checks for all and freeze prescription charges.

### How these proposals would change your income tax

### Main income tax changes:
♦ Around 70 per cent of adults will pay lower or unchanged income tax under our proposals.
♦ Around half of all income taxpayers would be better off or no worse off under our income tax proposals. Excluding those earning over £100,000 per year, the average income taxpayer will pay only around 45p extra per week in income tax under our plans.

In this manifesto, we have set out a practical, forward-looking programme to modernise Britain. Its central theme is the widening of opportunities. And its aim is to make Britain a nation of self-reliant individuals, living in strong communities, backed by an enabling government.

We do not duck the choices that have to be faced in this election. And we do not pretend that they are easy – or free. High-quality education has to be paid for. As do decent public services and a more secure society. You cannot, in the present climate, have these and tax cuts as well. You have to choose. We ask you to do so.

Your vote can make a real difference in turning our country away from short-term politics towards a more constructive long-term approach. And with your support we believe we can make a difference too. Every vote we receive is a vote for better education, the modernisation of our politics, a cleaner environment, a better health service and more crime- free communities.

Every vote we get and every seat we win will ensure that in the next Parliament, Britain can at last face up to the challenge, as we enter the next millennium.

# OTHER MANIFESTOS
## Summarised by Robert Morgan

### SCOTTISH NATIONAL PARTY

The party advocates the right of the people of Scotland to self-determination and to sovereignty over the territory and natural resources of Scotland, limited only by such agreements as may be freely entered into by it with other nations or states, or international organisations for the purposes of furthering international co-operation, trade and world peace.

These rights would be exercised in accordance with the Scottish constitution, but would recognise the rights and obligations of membership of the European Union.

The party states that EU membership should be the subject of confirmation or rejection by a referendum held within a reasonable period of Scottish independence.

Local government would be guaranteed genuine autonomy and freedom from interference by central government within the areas entrusted to local authorities.

Until such time as the people of Scotland decided otherwise, Scotland would retain a limited constitutional monarchy with the headship of state vested in the present Queen and her successors.

The party "recognises a strong anti-nuclear principle", but advocates participation in United Nations humanitarian peacekeeping and disaster relief operations. The Scottish defence force would be a flexible core of professionals able to expand rapidly to meet a crisis.

The party would seek to reintroduce wages councils and create new ones to cover areas of low pay and exploitation or workers.

Education would be put in the hands of local authorities. They would be expected to manage education in an open, democratic and decentralised manner, encouraging a supportive approach to the management of all staff.

The study and use of the Scots language would be encouraged and all universities would be urged to offer degrees in Celtic studies, Scottish history and Scottish literature.

The party supports the concept of a comprehensive health service of the highest standard, financed from general taxation and free to all at the time of need. The party would abolish charges for prescriptions, eye tests and for essential dental care.

### PLAID CYMRU — WELSH NATIONALISTS

The party aims to secure self-government for Wales and a democratic Welsh state. It wants to safeguard the culture, language, traditions, environment and economic life of Wales through decentralised socialist policies. It wants to secure a place for Wales in the United Nations.

Plaid Cymru MPs form a parliamentary grouping at Westminster with the Scottish National Party.

### ULSTER UNIONISTS

The party is committed to the maintenance of Northern Ireland's position as an integral part of the United Kingdom. It upholds the right of the province to self-determination based on the requirement for the consent of the majority to any constitutional change.

It demands the immediate unilateral withdrawal of the Irish Republic's claim over the Province as set out in the Republic's constitution.

The party supports the concept of a Bill of Rights for Northern Ireland. It stands firmly against the use of violence for political purposes and urges all terrorist organisations, including the IRA, to end all forms of violence, particularly savage punishment beatings, and further urges them to enter into the democratic process. It calls for a credible process of disarmament.

The party wishes to see the Anglo-Irish agreement replaced. Any new agreement would have to be based on the wishes of the people of Northern Ireland – the principle of consent. It would have to respect the wishes of by far the greatest number of the people of the Province to remain part of the United Kingdom.

The party wants to build a new and more accountable democratic system in Northern Ireland which will ensure that "faceless bureaucrats" and their unrepresentative quango nominees no longer rule from behind closed doors. The party advocates a Northern Ireland Assembly based on the principle of proportionality. Elected representatives would be able to participate at all levels and at all stages in proportion to their elected strength.

The party states that it is increasingly clear that Sinn Fein/IRA would only use political talks to consolidate its terrorist base and advance its objective of a United Socialist Ireland through violence. "In that knowledge, we will maintain our firm commitment to defend the democratic process against contamination and distortion from any source."

The party will continue to support the right of loyal orders to march lawfully on the public highway and the freedom of access to places of worship. "A solution will only be found when the police and the Government have the courage to prevent the manipulation of this issue by Sinn Fein/IRA to create tension in the community."

As cross-border trade with the Republic had been increasing, there is no need for any special measures. The party would actively facilitate business opportunites and develop them where they benefited the people of Northern Ireland, but would not invent bogus collaborative projects when the stimulus was political and the economic benefits not comensurate with the costs.

## SOCIAL DEMOCRATIC AND LABOUR PARTY

The party promotes the cause of Irish unity freely negotiated and agreed to by the people of the North and by the people of the South. It would abolish all forms of discrimination based upon religion, gender, disability, ethnic origin, class, political belief or sexual orientation, and the promotion of equality among all citizens.

It encourages the public ownership and democratic control of such essential industries and services as the common good requires.

The party will co-operate with other Labour and social democratic parties through the Party of European Socialists and the Socialist International.

## DEMOCRATIC UNIONIST PARTY

The party says that its task will continue to be to oppose Dublin rule and the processes designed to lead to it. It will continue to use its position at Westminster, as elsewhere, to defend Ulster and retain the union on terms that enjoy the consent of the people of Northern Ireland.

The DUP, its manifesto says, unlike other Ulster parties, is not in the pockets of either the Tories or Labour. It speaks and acts at all times in the interests of the people of Northern Ireland. It is a disgrace, it says, that the UUP had not used the parliamentary arithmetic in the last Parliament to better Northern Ireland's position.

The DUP would never negotiate Ulster's future with the murderers of the IRA or their representatives, nor would it be at any table where the Union was up for negotiation. While other Unionists have wavered, the DUP had led the battle to prevent Sinn Fein/IRA from coming to the table with their illegal weaponry intact and on the basis of another temporary and bogus ceasefire.

For many years, the border with the South had been used as a bolthole for terrorists. The Government of the Republic had shown sufficient resource to keep out "mad cows" during the BSE crisis. It would be relatively straightforward, if the will were evident, to take similar steps against the "mad dogs" of the IRA.

The British Government, it says, must radically change its approach to the United States authorities, pressing home the obscene nature of the Provo campaign and demanding action against supporters and sympathisers who illegally raised funds and assisted those who should be regarded as the equivalent of the Oklahoma bombers. Permission for Sinn Fein/IRA to open offices and raise funds in the United States must be revoked.

## SINN FEIN

The party seeks to end the partition of Ireland which is, the party says, the cause of conflict and injustice. Its objective is to end British rule in Northern Ireland. "We seek national self-determination, the unity and independence of Ireland as a sovereign state."

Peace, it says, is not just the absence of violence. A real and lasting peace is based on democracy, justice, freedom and equality. "We have sought with honesty and integrity to construct a peace process which reaches out and embraces everyone on the island on the basis of equality."

## ALLIANCE PARTY

The party believes that individual freedoms carry responsibilities to ensure that those freedoms are available for all citizens. It proposes the enactment of a Bill of Rights and the creation of a Department of Justice to be overseen by an elected Northern Ireland Assembly.

The fight against terrroism, it says, must continue unabated with the police supported by the Army and, most important, by the community as a whole.

The party advocates a power-sharing form of government. It says that it is essential to ensure that representatives of all sections of the people have an opportunity to work together at every level of government. Partnership in government, based on party strength, is the only proposal that has sustained substantial support across the divisions of Northern Ireland society.

North-South co-operation, it says, is important for practical and political reasons. However, there would be no change in the constitutional position of Northern Ireland without the consent of the people.

## ULSTER DEMOCRATIC PARTY

The party is dedicated, it says, to building a secure and better future for the people of Northern Ireland. It will work to cement Northern Ireland's position within the United Kingdom on the basis on equality of citizenship and sovereignty of the people.

## PROGRESSIVE UNIONIST PARTY

The party is committed to the proposition that there will be no diminution of Northern Ireland's position as an integral part of the United Kingdom whose paramount responsibility is the morale and physical wellbeing of all its citizens.

## NATURAL LAW PARTY

The party says that the best government is nature's government — Natural Law. Natural law, it says, governs all life, from the galaxies to the solar system to the Planet Earth. The party "has knowledge" to bring the support of natural law to every individual and the whole of the United Kingdom. National life would be in harmony with natural law and "everyone will enjoy peace, happiness and prosperity".

## REFERENDUM PARTY

The party proposes to hold a referendum on the future of the United Kingdom's relationship with the rest of the European Union.

The party has been established for no other purpose than "to obtain a fair referendum on Europe". Once the referendum has been held, the party will be dissolved.

## LIBERAL PARTY

The party was relaunched by those members of the old Liberal Party who rejected the merger with the Social Democrat Party. It stands for an open society and against all forms of prejudice and vested interest. The party does not seek merely to occupy the middle ground. Instead it wants to apply liberal principles. The party advocates co-operative ventures, employee participation and community involvement. The aim is to spread power and to give people influence over the decisions that affect them.

## GREEN PARTY

The party believes that the needs of the present can be met without compromising the ability of future generations to meet their needs. To do this, it says, resources must be used wisely to cut pollution to levels that nature can cope with. Greens believe that better results are achieved when those affected are involved in making those decisions.

## SOCIALIST LABOUR PARTY

The party, formed in 1996, believes that socialist policies for eliminating unemployment, poverty, homelessness, racism and all forms of discrimination must be put to the British people. Full employment, it says, must be the first aim of government. It wants the establishment of a minimum wage and the repeal of the "Tories' anti-trade union laws". It wants the privatised utilities returned to public ownership and their profits used to regenerate Britain.

## NEW COMMUNIST PARTY OF BRITAIN

The party wants to replace capitalism with socialism. It proposes to lower VAT, to control prices, to shift the tax burden to the wealthy, and to bring in a minimum wage. It wants controls on imports and the export of capital. It wants key sectors of the economy taken into public ownership.

## BRITISH NATIONAL PARTY

The party says that matters of British policy and law-making must be restored to the British government and Parliament.

It says that people of non-European origin cannot be absorbed into the British population.

The policy is not one of race hatred, it says. Every race has the right to self-preservation, including non-white races and "we respect those non-whites who wish to preserve their ethnic identities as we do ours".

## UK INDEPENDENCE PARTY

The party's main aim is the withdrawal of Britain from the European Union. The party is opposed to oppressive, unnecessary or confiscatory taxation of the kind, it says, the EU intends to introduce. It wants VAT on domestic fuel to be scrapped.

The billions of pounds that it says are now going to the EU should be used to help the sick, the aged and the infirm.

## PROLIFE

The party wants to confer the full protection of the law on all human life from fertilisation until natural death. It would repeal the 1967 Abortion Act and outlaw all abortions except where necessary to save the mother's life. It would also outlaw assisted conception techniques as well as voluntary, non-voluntary, and involuntary euthanasia.

## THE THIRD WAY

The party wants to encourage co-ownership as part of an overall strategy to increase property ownership and to spread decision-making throughout the community. It says that the people should be able to initiate legislation and there should be binding polls on changes in the law.

## ALBION PARTY

The party proposes a referendum on Britain's continuing membership of the European Union and would campaign for withdrawal. It proposes a "fair voting system" and a written constitution.

It says the people should know exactly where their taxes are spent. It favours energy-efficient forms of transport and a modern public transport system. It wants a ban on cosmetics testing on animals, a boost to organic farming, but says that country sports should be left alone.

## OFFICIAL MONSTER RAVING LOONY PARTY

The party wants to make Britain a tax haven for the rest of Europe. It would divert the Channel Tunnel to Jersey and use the "pound mountain" created by the National Lottery for improvements in the health service instead of using it for heritage and arts projects such as the Opera House.

It believes all defences should be creosoted.

# INDEX TO CANDIDATES

# INDEX TO CANDIDATES

# INDEX TO CANDIDATES

## INDEX TO CANDIDATES

# INDEX TO CANDIDATES